Nineteenth-Century Literature Criticism

Guide to Gale Literary Criticism Series

For criticism on	You need these Gale series
Authors now living or who died after December 31, 1959	*CONTEMPORARY LITERARY CRITICISM (CLC)*
Authors who died between 1900 and 1959	*TWENTIETH-CENTURY LITERARY CRITICISM (TCLC)*
Authors who died between 1800 and 1899	*NINETEENTH-CENTURY LITERATURE CRITICISM (NCLC)*
Authors who died between 1400 and 1799	*LITERATURE CRITICISM FROM 1400 TO 1800 (LC)* *SHAKESPEAREAN CRITICISM (SC)*
Authors who died before 1400	*CLASSICAL AND MEDIEVAL LITERATURE CRITICISM (CMLC)*
Authors of books for children and young adults	*CHILDREN'S LITERATURE REVIEW (CLR)*
Black writers of the past two hundred years	*BLACK LITERATURE CRITICISM (BLC)*
Short story writers	*SHORT STORY CRITICISM (SSC)*
Poets	*POETRY CRITICISM (PC)*
Dramatists	*DRAMA CRITICISM (DC)*
Major authors from the Renaissance to the present	*WORLD LITERATURE CRITICISM, 1500 TO THE PRESENT (WLC)*

For criticism on visual artists since 1850, see
MODERN ARTS CRITICISM (MAC)

ISSN 0732-1864

Volume 41

Nineteenth-Century Literature Criticism

Excerpts from Criticism of the
Works of Novelists, Poets, Playwrights,
Short Story Writers, Philosophers, and Other
Creative Writers Who Died between 1800
and 1899, from the First Published Critical
Appraisals to Current Evaluations

Joann Cerrito
Editor

Judith Galens
Alan Hedblad
Jelena O. Krstović
Joe Tardiff
Lawrence J. Trudeau
Associate Editors

Gale Research Inc. • *DETROIT* • *WASHINGTON, D.C.* • *LONDON*

STAFF

Joann Cerrito, *Editor*

James A. Edwards, Alan Hedblad, Jelena Krstović, Joseph C. Tardiff, Lawrence J. Trudeau, *Associate Editors*

George Blair, Patrick L. Bruch, Thomas Carson, Kathryn Horste, *Assistant Editors*

Jeanne A. Gough, *Permissions & Production Manager*
Linda M. Pugliese, *Production Supervisor*
Donna Craft, Paul Lewon, Maureen Puhl, Camille P. Robinson, Sheila Walencewicz, *Editorial Associates*
Elizabeth Anne Valliere, *Editorial Assistant*

Sandra C. Davis, *Permissions Supervisor (Text)*
Maria L. Franklin, Josephine M. Keene, Michele M. Lonoconus, Shalice Shah, Denise Singleton, Kimberly F. Smilay,
Permissions Associates
Jennifer A. Arnold, Brandy C. Merritt, *Permissions Assistants*

Margaret A. Chamberlain, *Permissions Supervisor (Pictures)*
Pamela A. Hayes, Keith Reed, *Permissions Associates*
Susan Brohman, Arlene Johnson, Barbara A. Wallace, *Permissions Assistants*

Victoria B. Cariappa, *Research Manager*
Maureen Richards, *Research Supervisor*
Robert S. Lazich, Mary Beth McElmeel, Donna Melnychenko, Tamara C. Nott, *Editorial Associates*
Karen Farrelly, Kelly Hill, Julie Leonard, Stefanie Scarlett, *Editorial Assistants*

Mary Beth Trimper, *Production Director*
Catherine Kemp, *Production Assistant*

Cynthia Baldwin, *Art Director*
C. J. Jonik, *Desktop Publisher*
Willie Mathis, *Camera Operator*

Library of Congress Catalog Card Number 84-643008
ISBN 0-8103-8474-4
ISSN 0732-1864

Printed in the United States of America
Published simultaneously in the United Kingdom
by Gale Research International Limited
(An affiliated company of Gale Research Inc.)
10 9 8 7 6 5 4 3 2 1

I(T)P™

The trademark **ITP** is used under license.

Contents

Preface

Since its inception in 1981, *Nineteenth-Century Literature Criticism* has been a valuable resource for students and librarians seeking critical commentary on writers of this transitional period in world history. Designated an "Outstanding Reference Source" by the American Library Association with the publication of its first volume, *NCLC* has since been purchased by over 6,000 school, public, and university libraries. The series has covered more than 300 authors representing 26 nationalities and over 15,000 titles. No other reference source has surveyed the critical reaction to nineteenth-century authors and literature as thoroughly as *NCLC*.

Scope of the Series

NCLC is designed to introduce students and advanced readers to the authors of the nineteenth century, and to the most significant interpretations of these authors' works. The great poets, novelists, short story writers, dramatists, and philosophers of this period are frequently studied in high school and college literature courses. By organizing and reprinting commentary written on these authors, *NCLC* helps students develop valuable insight into literary history, promotes a better understanding of the texts, and sparks ideas for papers and assignments. Each entry in *NCLC* presents a comprehensive survey of an author's career or an individual work of literature and provides the user with a multiplicity of interpretations and assessments. Such variety allows students to pursue their own interests; furthermore, it fosters an awareness that literature is dynamic and responsive to many different opinions.

Every fourth volume of *NCLC* is devoted to literary topics that cannot be covered under the author approach used in the rest of the series. Such topics include literary movements, prominent themes in nineteenth-century literature, literary reaction to political and historical events, significant eras in literary history, prominent literary anniversaries, and the literatures of cultures that are often overlooked by English-speaking readers.

NCLC continues the survey of criticism of world literature begun by Gale's *Contemporary Literary Criticism (CLC)* and *Twentieth-Century Literary Criticism (TCLC)*, both of which excerpt and reprint commentary on authors of the twentieth century. For additional information about *TCLC, CLC,* and Gale's other criticism series, users should consult the Guide to Gale Literary Criticism Series preceding the title page in this volume.

Coverage

Each volume of *NCLC* is carefully compiled to present:

- criticism of authors, or literary topics, representing a variety of genres and nationalities
- both major and lesser-known writers and literary works of the period
- 7-10 authors or 4-6 topics per volume
- individual entries that survey critical response to an author's work or a topic in literary history, including early criticism to reflect initial reactions, later criticism to represent any rise or decline in reputation, and current retrospective analyses.

Organization

An author entry consists of the following elements: author heading, biographical and critical introduction, list of principal works, excerpts of criticism (each preceded by an annotation and followed by a bibliographic citation), and a bibliography of further reading.

- The **Author Heading** consists of the name under which the author most commonly wrote, followed by birth and death dates. If an author wrote consistently under a pseudonym, the pseudonym will be listed in the author heading and the real name given in parentheses on the first line of the biographical and critical introduction. Also located at the beginning of the introduction to the author entry are any name variations under which an author wrote, including transliterated forms for an author whose language uses a nonroman alphabet.

- The **Biographical and Critical Introduction** outlines the author's life and career, as well as the critical issues surrounding his or her work. References are provided to past volumes of *NCLC* in which further information about the author may be found.

- Most *NCLC* entries include a **Portrait** of the author. Many entries also contain reproductions of materials pertinent to an author's career, including manuscript pages, title pages, dust jackets, letters, and drawings, as well as photographs of important people, places, and events in an author's life.

- The list of **Principal Works** is chronological by date of first publication and identifies the genre of each work. In the case of foreign authors with both foreign-language publications and English translations, the title and date of the first English-language edition are given in brackets. Unless otherwise indicated, dramas are dated by first performance, not first publication.

- **Criticism** in each author entry is arranged chronologically to provide a perspective on changes in critical evaluation over the years. All titles of works by the author featured in the entry are printed in boldface type to enable the user to easily locate discussion of particular works. Also for purposes of easier identification, the critic's name and the publication date of the essay are given at the beginning of each piece of criticism. Unsigned criticism is preceded by the title of the journal in which it appeared. Publication information (such as publisher names and book prices) and parenthetical numerical references (such as footnotes or page and line references to specific editions of works) have been deleted at the editors' discretion to provide smoother reading of the text.

- Critical excerpts are prefaced by **Annotations** providing the reader with information about both the critic and the criticism that follows. Included are the critic's reputation, individual approach to literary criticism, and particular expertise in an author's works. Also noted are the relative importance of a work of criticism, the scope of the excerpt, and the growth of critical controversy or changes in critical trends regarding an author. In some cases, these annotations cross-reference excerpts by critics who discuss each other's commentary.

- A complete **Bibliographic Citation** designed to facilitate location of the original essay or book follows each piece of criticism.

- An annotated list of **Further Reading** appearing at the end of each entry suggests secondary sources on the author. In some cases it includes essays for which the editors could not obtain reprint rights.

Cumulative Indexes

- Each volume of *NCLC* contains a cumulative **Author Index** listing all authors who have appeared in Gale's Literary Criticism Series, along with cross-references to such biographical series as *Contemporary Authors* and *Dictionary of Literary Biography*. Useful for locating authors within the various series, this index is particularly valuable for those authors who are identified with a certain period but who, because of their death dates, are placed in another, or for those authors whose careers span two periods. For example, Fyodor Dostoevsky is found in *NCLC*, yet Leo Tolstoy, another major nineteenth-century Russian novelist, is found in *TCLC* because he died after 1899.

- Each *NCLC* volume includes a cumulative **Nationality Index** which lists all authors who have appeared in *NCLC*, arranged alphabetically under their respective nationalities, as well as Topics volume entries devoted to particular national literatures.

- Each new volume in Gale's Literary Criticism Series includes a cumulative **Topic Index**, which lists all literary topics treated in *NCLC, TCLC, LC 1400-1800*, and the *CLC* Yearbook.

- Each new volume of *NCLC*, with the exception of the Topics volumes, contains a **Title Index** listing the titles of all literary works discussed in the volume. In response to numerous suggestions from librarians, Gale has also produced a **Special Paperbound Edition** of the *NCLC* title index. This annual cumulation lists all titles discussed in the series since its inception and is issued with the first volume of *NCLC* published each year. Additional copies of the index are available on request. Librarians and patrons have welcomed this separate index: it saves shelf space, is easy to use, and is recyclable upon receipt of the following year's cumulation. Titles discussed in the Topics volume entries are not included in the *NCLC* cumulative index.

Citing *Nineteenth-Century Literature Criticism*

When writing papers, students who quote directly from any volume in Gale's Literary Criticism Series may use the following general forms to footnote reprinted criticism. The first example pertains to material drawn from periodicals, the second to material reprinted from books:

[1]T.S. Eliot, "John Donne," *The Nation and Athenaeum*, 33 (9 June 1923), 321-32; excerpted and reprinted in *Literature Criticism from 1400-1800,* Vol. 10, ed. James E. Person, Jr. (Detroit: Gale Research, 1989), pp. 28-9.

[2]Clara G. Stillman, *Samuel Butler: A Mid-Victorian Modern* (Viking Press, 1932); excerpted and reprinted in *Twentieth-Century Literary Criticism,* Vol. 33, ed. Paula Kepos (Detroit: Gale Research, 1989), pp. 43-5.

Suggestions Are Welcome

In response to suggestions, several features have been added to *NCLC* since the series began, including annotations to excerpted criticism, a cumulative index to authors in all Gale literary criticism series, entries devoted to criticism on a single work by a major author, more illustrations, and a title index listing all literary works discussed in the series.

Readers who wish to suggest authors or topics to appear in future volumes, or who have other suggestions, are cordially invited to write the editors.

Acknowledgments

The editors wish to thank the copyright holders of the excerpted criticism included in this volume, the permissions managers of many book and magazine publishing companies for assisting us in securing reprint rights, and Anthony Bogucki for assistance with copyright research. We are also grateful to the staffs of the Detroit Public Library, the Library of Congress, the University of Detroit Library, Wayne State University Purdy/Kresge Library Complex, and the University of Michigan Libraries for making their resources available to us. Following is a list of the copyright holders who have granted us permission to reprint material in this volume of *NCLC*. Every effort has been made to trace copyright, but if omissions have been made, please let us know.

COPYRIGHTED EXCERPTS IN *NCLC*, VOLUME 41, WERE REPRINTED FROM THE FOLLOWING PERIODICALS:

Australian Journal of French Studies, v. XVII, September-December, 1980. Copyright © 1980 by Australian Journal of French Studies. Reprinted by permission of the publisher.—*Book Week—New York Herald Tribune*, December 12, 1965. © 1965, New York Herald Tribune Inc. All rights reserved. Reprinted by permission.—*Comparative Literature*, v. 36, Winter, 1984 for "Metaphors of Consciousness in Mallarmé" by Romóm Saldívar. © Copyright 1984 by University of Oregon. Reprinted by permission of the author.—*The Denver Quarterly*, v. 18, Winter, 1984 for "Mallarmé as Mother: A Preliminary Sketch" by Barbara Johnson. Copyright © 1984 by the University of Denver. Reprinted by permission of the author.—*Dickens Studies Annual*, v. 14, 1985. Copyright © 1985 by AMS Press, Inc. Reprinted by permission of the publisher.—*Forum for Modern Language Studies*, v. XI, April, 1975 for "Stifter's Early Portraits of the Artist: Stages in the Growth of an Aesthetic" by A. Stillmark. Copyright © 1975 by *Forum for Modern Language Studies* and the author. Reprinted by permission of the publisher and the author.—*Kwartainik Neofilologiczny*, v. XXXV, 1988. Reprinted by permission of the publisher.—*The Modern Language Review*, v. 78, July, 1983 for "Reading Mallarmé" by George Craig. © Modern Humanities Research Association 1983. Reprinted by permission of the publisher and the author.—*The New York Times Book Review*, November 18, 1945. Copyright 1945, renewed 1972 by The New York Times Company. Reprinted by permission of the publisher.—*Nineteenth-Century Fiction*, v. 20, June 1965. © 1965 by The Regents of the University of California. Reprinted by permission of the Regents.—*Novel: A Forum on Fiction*, v. 1, Spring, 1968. Copyright NOVEL Corp. © 1968. Reprinted with permission.—*Papers on Language & Literature*, v. III, Fall, 1967. Copyright © 1967 by the Board of Trustees, Southern Illinois University at Edwardsville. Reprinted by permission of the publisher.—*The Romanic Review*, v. LXXV, January, 1984; v. LXXVI, November, 1985. Copyright © 1984, 1985 by the Trustees of Columbia University in the City of New York. Both reprinted by permission of the publisher.—*Scandinavian Studies*, v. 58, Winter, 1986 for "J. L. Runeberg as a Modern Writer: The Evidence of 'Julqvällen'" by Kim Nilsson. Reprinted by permission of the publisher and the author.—*The Southern Review*, Louisiana State University, v. XIX, Winter, 1983 for "The Dispensations of Art: Mallarmé and the Fallen Reader" by Jewell Spears Brooker. Copyright, 1983, by Louisiana State University. Reprinted by permission of the author.—*Studies in English Literature, 1500-1900*, v. VI, Autumn, 1966 for "Structure and Quality in 'Silas Marner'" by Ian Milner. © 1966 William Marsh Rice University. Reprinted by permission of the publisher and the Literary Estate of Ian Milner.—*Studies in Scottish Literature*, v. IX, July, 1971; v. XVIII, 1983; v. XXII, 1987; v. XXIII, 1988. Copyright © G. Ross Roy 1971, 1983, 1987, 1988. All reprinted by permission of the editor.—*Studies in Short Fiction*, v. 1, Spring, 1964. Copyright 1964 by Newberry College. Reprinted by permission of the publisher.—*Texas Studies in Literature and Language*, v. XIV, Fall, 1972 for "Similarity within Dissimilarity: The Dual Structure of 'Silas Marner'" by Bruce K. Martin; v. 25, Fall, 1983 for "'He Knew He Was Right', Mrs. Lynn Linton, and the Duplicities of Victorian Marriage" by Christopher Herbert. Copyright © 1972, 1983 by the University of Texas Press. Both reprinted by permission of the publisher and the respective authors.—*Theatre Journal*, v. 34, May, 1982. © 1982, University and College Theatre Association of the American Theatre Association. Reprinted by permission of the publisher.—*Yale French Studies*, n. 77, 1990. Copyright © Yale French Studies 1990. Reprinted by permission of the publisher.

COPYRIGHTED EXCERPTS IN *NCLC*, VOLUME 41, WERE REPRINTED FROM THE FOLLOWING BOOKS:

Barker, Gerard A. From *Henry Mackenzie*. Twayne, 1975. Copyright © 1975 by G. K. Hall & Co. All rights reserved. Excerpted with the permission of Twayne Publishers, an imprint of Macmillan Publishing Company.—Berman, Russell A. From *The Rise of the Modern German Novel: Crisis and Charisma*. Cambridge, Mass.: Harvard University Press, 1986. Copyright © 1986 by the President and Fellows of Harvard College. All rights reserved. Excerpted by permission of the publishers and the author.—Bruford, W. H. From *The German Tradition of Self-Cultivation: 'Bildung' from Humboldt to Thomas Mann*. Cambridge University Press, 1975. © Cambridge University Press 1975. Reprinted with the permission of the publisher and the Literary Estate of W. H. Bruford.—Cave, Richard A. From "The Presentation of English and Irish Characters in Boucicault's Irish Melodramas," in *Literary Interrelations: Ireland, England and the World*. Edited by Wolfgang Zach and Heinz Kozok. Gunter Narr Verlag Tübingen, 1987. © 1987 Gunter Narr Verlag Tübingen. All rights reserved. Reprinted by permission of the publisher.—Colby, Vineta. From *The Singular Anomaly: Women Novelists of the Nineteenth Century*. New York University Press, 1970. © 1970 by New York University. Reprinted by permission of the publisher.—Emery, Laura Comer. From *George Eliot's Creative Conflict: The Other Side of Silence*. University of California Press, 1976. Copyright © 1976, by The Regents of the University of California. Reprinted by permission of the publisher.—Fisch, Harold. From "Biblical Realism in 'Silas Marner'," in *Identity and Ethos: A Festschrift for Sol Liptzin on the Occasion of His 85th Birthday*. Edited by Mark H. Gelber. Peter Lang, 1986. © Peter Lang Publishing, Inc., 1986. All rights reserved. Reprinted by permission of the author.—Fisher, Philip. From *Making Up Society: The Novels of George Eliot*. University of Pittsburgh Press, 1981. Copyright © 1981, University of Pittsburgh Press. All rights reserved. Reprinted by permission of the publisher.—Fowlie, Wallace. From "'Hérodiade': Myth or Heroine?" in *L'Hénaurme Siécle: A Miscellany of Essays on Nineteenth-Century French Literature*. Edited by Will L. McLendon. Carl Winter Universitätsverlag, 1984. © 1984, Carl Winter Universitätsverlag. All rights reserved. Reprinted by permission of the author.—Gump, Margaret. From *Adalbert Stifter*. Twayne, 1974. Copyright © 1974 by Twayne Publishers, Inc. All rights reserved. Reprinted with the permission of Twayne Publishers, Inc., an imprint of Macmillan Publishing Company.—Gustafson, Alrik. From *A History of Swedish Literature*. University of Minnesota Press, 1961. © Copyright 1961 by the American-Scandinavian Foundation. Renewed 1989 by Cleyonne Gustafson. All rights reserved. Reprinted by permission of the publisher.—Haddakin, Lilian. From "Silas Marner," in *Critical Essays on George Eliot*. Edited by Barbara Hardy. Barnes & Noble, Inc., 1970. © Routledge & Kegan Paul Ltd. 1970. Reprinted by permission of the publisher.—Hirn, Yrjö. From an introduction to *The Tales of Ensign Stål*. By Johan Ludvig Runeberg, edited and translated by Charles Wharton Stork. Princeton University Press, 1938. Copyright 1938, renewed 1966 by The American-Scandinavian Foundation. Reprinted with permission of The American-Scandinavian Foundation.—Jones, R. T. From *George Eliot*. Cambridge at the University Press, 1970. © Cambridge University Press 1970. Reprinted with the permissions of the publisher and the author.—Knoepflmacher, U. C. From *George Eliot's Early Novels: the Limits of Realism*. University of California Press, 1968. Copyright © 1968 by The Regents of the University of California. Reprinted by permission of the publisher.—Krause, David. From *The Profane Book of Irish Comedy*. Cornell, 1982. Copyright © 1982 by Cornell University Press. All rights reserved. Used by permission of the publisher, Cornell University Press.—La Charité, Virginia A. From "Mallarmé and the Plastic Circumstances of the Text," in *Pre-Text Text Context: Essays on Nineteenth-Century French Literature*. Edited by Robert L. Mitchell. Ohio State University Press, 1980. © 1980 by the Ohio State University Press. All rights reserved. Reprinted by permission of the author.—Leavis, Q. D. From an introduction in *Sials Marner: The Weaver of Raveloe*. By George Eliot, edited by Q. D. Leavis. Penguin Books, 1967. Introduction copyright © Q. D. Leavis, 1967. All rights reserved. Reproduced by permission of Penguin Books Ltd.—Luke, David. From an introduction to *Limestone and Other Stories*. By Adalbert Stifter, translated by David Luke. Harcourt Brace Jovanovich, 1968. English translation copyright © 1968 by David Luke.—Mackenzie, Henry. From *Letters to Elizabeth Rose of Kilravock: On Literature Events and People, 1768-1815*. Edited by Horst W. Drescher. Oliver and Boyd, 1967. © Aschendorff, Münster Westfalen 1967.—Rignall, J. M. From "Between Chartism and the 1880s: J. W. Overton and E. Lynn Linton," in *The Socialist Novel in Britain: Towards the Recovery of a Tradition*. Edited by H. Gustav Klaus. Harvester Press, 1982. © The Harvester Press, 1982. All rights reserved. Reprinted in North America with permission of St. Martin's Press, Incorporated.—Roberts, Neil. From *George Eliot: Her Beliefs and Her Art.* Paul Elek, 1975. Copyright 1975 © Neil Roberts. All rights reserved. Reprinted by permission of Paul Elek Books, an imprint of HarperCollins Publishers Limited.—Smith, James L. From an introduction to *London Assurance.* By Dion Boucicault, edited by James L. Smith. A & C Black, 1984. © 1984 A & C Black (Publishers) Limited. Reprinted by permission of the publisher.—Spalding, Keith. From "Adalbert Stifter," in *German Men of Letters: Twelve Literary Essays, Vol. V.* Edited by Alex Natan. Dufour Editions, 1969. © 1969 Oswald Wolff (Publishers) Limited. Reprinted by permission of Berg Publishers Inc.—Squires, Michael. From *The Pastoral Novel: Studies in George Eliot, Thomas Hardy, and D. H. Lawrence.* University Press of Virginia, 1974. Copyright © 1974 by the Rector and Visitors of the University of Virginia. Reprinted by permission of the University Press of Virginia.—Staudt, Kathleen Henderson. From "The Poetics of 'Black on White': Stéphane Mallarmé's 'Un Coup de des'," in *Ineffability: Naming the Unnamable from Dante to Beckett.* Edited by Peter S. Hawkins and Anne Howland Schotter. AMS Press, 1984. Copyright © AMS Press, Inc., 1984. All rights reserved. Reprinted by permission of the publisher.—Stifter, Adalbert. From *Limestone and Other Stories.* Translated by David Luke. Harcourt Brace Jovanovich, 1968. English translation copyright © 1968 by David Luke.—Wretö, Tore. From *J. L. Runeberg.* Translated by Zelek S. Herman. Twayne, 1980. Copyright © 1980 by G. K. Hall & Co. All rights reserved. Reprinted with the permission of Twayne Publishers, an imprint of Macmillan Publishing Company.

PHOTOGRAPHS AND ILLUSTRATIONS APPEARING IN *NCLC*, VOLUME 41, WERE RECEIVED BY THE FOLLOWING SOURCES:

The Bettmann Archive: **p. 230;** © 1993 ARS, New York/SPADEM, Paris: **p. 296.**

Pétrus Borel

1809-1859

(Full name Joseph-Pétrus Borel; also wrote under pseudonym Pétrus Borel, Le Lycanthrope) French novelist,
short story and essay writer, poet, and translator.

INTRODUCTION

Considered one of the minor masters of French Romantic
literature, Borel is best known today for his bleak and hor-
ror-filled novel, *Madame Putiphar,* and for his erudite
Gothic short stories. His works frequently deal with hideous crimes that depict the ruination or destruction of virtue. Borel was the acknowledged leader of the generation
of Romantic writers who came into prominence in Paris
about 1830 and whose works were intended to challenge
literary and social convention, particularly classicism in
art. Though not well known, Borel's works are seen by historians of Romanticism as preparation for the dark imagery of such later writers as Charles Baudelaire.

Borel was born in Lyons into the family of an iron broker
and was the twelfth of fourteen children. The appellation
"d'Hauterive" that is sometimes attached to Borel's surname was the invention of his brother André, an amateur
genealogist who claimed that the Borel family was descended from an aristocratic predecessor, Borel
d'Hauterive; Borel continued to use the single surname,
but adopted the suffix d'Hauterive toward the end of his
life. Early in his childhood his family moved to Paris,
where the young Borel was educated in Catholic seminary
schools. According to his autobiographical sketch, published at the beginning of his collected stories, *Champavert, contes immoraux (Champavert: Seven Bitter Tales),*
Borel's experiences at these institutions made him violently atheistic and anti-clerical. When he was fourteen, his father apprenticed him to an architect, and by 1829 Borel
was qualified to set up his own architectural office in Paris.
By this time, however, he had already begun to write poetry. The turning point in his choice of a career came when
he made the acquaintance of the brothers Eugène and Ac-
hille Devéric, artists through whom Borel met many of the
younger writers and artists of the Romantic movement.
Admired for his originality and unwillingness to compromise in order to suit popular taste, Borel was soon regarded as the leader of this small band, which included the
writers Théophile Gautier and Gérard de Nerval. The
group called itself the *Petit Cénacle,* after the well-
established circle of older French Romantics, the *Cénacle.*

Borel's first publication, a book of poems entitled *Rhapsodies,* appeared in 1832. In the same year he founded and
became editor of *La liberté, journal des arts,* a militantly
radical weekly publication dedicated to overturning the
tenets of academic art; it survived only a few months.
Borel's ability to continue writing became increasingly

frustrated by his extreme poverty. With the financial failure of his next publication, *Champavert,* Borel decided to
leave Paris for the countryside of Champagne. He sought
retreat in the village of Le Baizil, living in a wooden hut
where he wrote his only novel, *Madame Putiphar.* Borel
returned to Paris in 1839 and continued his efforts to support himself by selling short fictional pieces to popular
journals, also venturing into journalism and editing, with
little success. Finally abandoning his efforts to maintain
a literary career, Borel decided to take a position as Inspector of Colonisation with the French colonial service
in Algeria. He permanently left France at the end of 1845
and wrote only one poem, "La léthargie de la muse," after
that time. He died of sunstroke in Algeria in 1859.

In *Rhapsodies* Borel proclaimed himself a poet-pariah, acknowledging neither patron nor teacher. He referred to
himself as the "lycanthrope," or wolfman, for the first
time in the preface to this book. Borel's biographers believe that this title derives from the saying "Man is a wolf
to man," an aphorism in keeping with Borel's profound
cynicism and misanthropy. However, the publication of
Rhapsodies did not create the shock and sensation that the
poet had announced in the preface as his aim. Artistide

Marie, a French critic and biographer of Borel, judged the poems to be uneven in quality but highly inventive; according to Marie, the voice of the poet is heard in the poems defiantly opposing suffering and isolation. Borel's modern biographer, Enid Starkie, agrees with Marie in seeing genuine strength and originality in some of the poems, though she characterizes many of them as sentimental. She singles out four poems from the collection—"Désespoir," "Hymne au Soleil," "Heur et malheur," and "Misère"—as works that distinguish Borel as a ranking poet of the nineteenth century by virtue of their blunt realism, and allies them with the works of Honoré de Balzac and Baudelaire.

Of all the writers of the *Petit Cénacle,* Borel was the most militantly dedicated to shocking readers with his works. *Champavert,* published one year after *Rhapsodies,* succeeded in this aim, provoking hostile reactions from critics. Nevertheless, Starkie calls it his most important and original work. With this collection, along with more than a dozen other stories published in fashionable journals, Borel made a major contribution to the short story genre which was to become a specialty of French Romantic literature. Borel's stories are regarded as the most morbid and misanthropic of the Romantic period. Critics point to their grim humor and irony and their powerful narrative pace as their most striking characteristics. The pervasive cynicism and malevolence of Borel's universe are brought home in such stories as "Monsieur d'Argentière," "Dina, la belle juive," and "Passereau l'ecolier," all of which involve the cold-blooded murder or execution of a blameless woman. Starkie describes the last story of the collection, "Testament de Champavert," as "a tale full of bitterness and rancour against life, with no belief or hope in anything."

This bleak hopelessness is reiterated in Borel's *Madame Putiphar.* Scholars have identified the title character as a satirical portrait of Madame Pompadour, mistress of Louis XV and a woman of enormous power at the French court. In Borel's novel she is responsible for imprisoning the two heroes, Fitz-Harris and Fitz-Whyte, in the Bastille because they spurned her advances. The bulk of the novel is a description of the years of suffering these two characters undergo, ending with the death of Fitz-Harris and the eventual freeing of Fitz-Whyte only after he has gone mad. One contemporary reviewer, Jules Janin, declared the book dangerous and compared Borel with the Marquis de Sade. Later in the century, however, Gustave Flaubert admired *Madame Putiphar,* and commentators point out that he seems to have been influenced by its scenes of horror when he wrote his novel *Salammbô.* More recently, Starkie has faulted the novel for its excessive pedantry and unnecessary digressions, but she has also noted its "many passages of tragic poetic beauty," such as the account of the death of Fitz-Harris in prison.

Though Borel had been much admired by his contemporaries, both as a writer and an individualist within the literary avant-garde, he and his small body of work were almost forgotten within a few years of his self-imposed exile from the literary world of Paris. A younger writer, Baudelaire, had nevertheless been very moved by the impression Borel had made on him when the two had met from time to time in Paris. His sympathetic 1861 article on Borel has received much critical attention and has been greatly responsible for the regard in which Borel is held today. Among his modern interpreters, Starkie, in particular, has emphasized the connections within French poetry between Borel, Baudelaire, and the Symbolists, all of whom celebrated the image of the alienated and defiant artist, expressed a comprehensive rejection of bourgeois values, and showed an inclination to issue literary manifestos—artistic strategies that were revived by such twentieth-century Surrealists as André Breton and Tristan Tzara.

PRINCIPAL WORKS

Rhapsodies (poetry) 1832; enlarged edition, 1922
Champavert, contes immoraux (short stories) 1833
    [*Champavert: Seven Bitter Tales,* 1959]
"L'Obélisque de Louqsor" (essay) 1833; published in
    Paris ou le livre des cent-et-un
"Jérôme Chasseboeuf" (short story) 1834; published
    in journal *L'Artiste*
Robinson Crusoë [translator; from *Robinson Crusoe* by
    Daniel Defoe] (novel) 1836
Comme quoi Napoléon n'a jamais existé (essay) 1838
Madame Putiphar (novel) 1839
"Gottfried Wolfgang" [adaptor; from the short story
    "The Adventure of the German Student" by Washington Irving] (short story) 1843; published in
    journal *La sylphide*
"Le trésor de la caverne d'Arcueil" (short story) 1843;
    published in journal *Revue de Paris*
"La Famille Wakefield" (short story) 1844; published
    in journal *Revue parisienne, La Sylphide*
"Miss Hazel" (short story) 1844; published in journal
    Revue pittoresque
"Le Vert-Galant" (short story) 1844; published in
    journal *L'Artiste*
"La léthargie de la muse" (poem) 1865; published by
    Jules Clarétie in *Petrus Borel, le Lycanthrope*

Charles Baudelaire (essay date 1861)

[A French poet and critic, Baudelaire is best known for his 1857 collection of poems Les fleurs du mal *(The Flowers of Evil), which is ranked among the most influential works of French poetry. In* The Flowers of Evil *Baudelaire analyzes, often in shocking terms, his urban surroundings, erotic love, and conflicts within his own soul. Underlying these topics is Baudelaire's belief that human beings are inherently evil; only that which is artificial can be construed as absolutely good. Poetry, according to Baudelaire, should in turn serve only to inspire and express beauty. This doctrine forms the basis of both his poetry and his criticism. Baudelaire travelled in the same literary circles as did Borel, and the two writers were acquainted. In the following excerpt, first published in* La revue fantaisiste *in 1861, Baudelaire*

discusses Borel as an "abortive genius" who nevertheless played an important role in French Romanticism.]

There are names that become proverbs and adjectives. When in 1859 a small newspaper wants to express all the disgust and contempt that it feels for a poem or a novel of a gloomy and extravagant character, it utters the words: Pétrus Borel! and nothing more needs to be said. Judgment has been pronounced and the author is demolished.

Pétrus Borel, or Champavert the Lycanthrope, author of **Rhapsodies,** of **Contes Immoraux** and of **Madame Putiphar,** was one of the stars in the somber Romantic sky. Forgotten or extinct, who remembers that star today and who is familiar enough with it to presume to talk of it so formally? "I," I shall gladly say, like Medea, *"I, I say, and that is enough!"* Edouard Ourliac, his comrade, did not hesitate to laugh at him, but Ourliac was a small-town Voltaire who detested anything excessive, especially an excessive love for art. Théophile Gautier alone, whose open-mindedness delights in the universality of things, and who, even if he wished, could not neglect anything interesting, subtle, or picturesque, smiled with pleasure at the strange lucubrations of the Lycanthrope.

Lycanthrope was a good name for him! Man-wolf or were-wolf, what fairy or what demon cast him into the somber forests of melancholy? What evil spirit bent over his cradle and said to him: *I forbid you to please?* In the spiritual world there is something mysterious which is called *Ill Luck,* and none of us has the right to argue with Fate. She is the goddess who is least comprehensible and who possesses, more than any pope or lama, the privilege of infallibility. I have very often wondered how and why a man like Pétrus Borel, who had shown a truly epic talent in several scenes of his **Madame Putiphar** (especially in the opening scenes where the savage and Northern drunkenness of the heroine's father is portrayed; in the scene where the favorite horse brings back to the mother, ravished years before, but still full of hate at her dishonor, the corpse of her beloved son, poor Vengeance, a courageous boy who had fallen at the first encounter and whom she had so carefully schooled for vengeance; finally in the portrayal of the hideous sights and the tortures of the dungeon, which compare in power to Maturin); I have wondered, I say, how the poet who produced the strange poem—with its brilliant sonorousness and its color almost primitive in its intensity—which serves as a preface to **Madame Putiphar,** could also show awkwardness in so many places, could encounter so many stumbling blocks and obstacles, and fall into such abysmally *bad luck.* I haven't any specific explanation to give; I can only point out symptoms, symptoms of a morbid nature in love with contradiction for the sake of contradiction and always ready to swim against every current without calculating either its strength or his own. Everyone, or almost everyone, inclines his handwriting to the right; Pétrus Borel slanted his completely to the left, so much so that all the letters, though carefully formed, looked like lines of soldiers thrown back by grapeshot. Moreover, writing was such a painful task that the slightest, most commonplace letter, an invitation, forwarding money, cost him two or three hours of tiring meditation, not counting the erasures and corrections. Finally, the strange spelling which is flaunted in **Madame Putiphar,** as

a deliberate outrage to the visual habits of the public, is a feature which completes this caricature-like portrait. It is certainly not a simplified spelling like that of M. Erdan or that of Voltaire's cooks, but on the contrary, a spelling, more than picturesque, that takes advantage of every opportunity to ostentatiously call attention to etymology. I can't picture, without feeling sympathetic pain, all the exhausting battles that the author must have had with the typesetters entrusted with printing his manuscripts in order to realize his typographical dreams. Thus, not only did he like to violate the moral habits of the reader, but also he liked to baffle and torment the eye by the graphic expression.

More than one person will doubtless ask why we make room in our gallery ["Reflections on Some of My Contemporaries"] for a mind which we ourselves consider so incomplete. It is not only because this mind, however ponderous, shrill, incomplete it may be, has sometimes struck a dazzling and true note, but also because in the history of our century he has played a role not without importance. His specialty was Lycanthropy. Without Pétrus Borel there would be a lacuna in Romanticism. In the first phase of our literary revolution, poetic imagination turned especially toward the past; it often adopted the melodious and moving tone of regret. Later on, melancholy assumed a more decided, more savage, more worldly accent. A misanthropic republicanism joined the new school, and Pétrus Borel was the most presumptuous and the most paradoxical expression of the spirit of the *Bousingots* or of *Bousingo;* for in the spelling of these words, which are the products of fashion and of circumstances, a certain amount of hesitation is always permissible. This spirit, both literary and republican, contrary to the democratic and bourgeois passion which later so cruelly oppressed us, was excited both by an aristocratic hatred, unbounded, unrestricted, pitiless, directed against kings and the bourgeoisie, and by a general sympathy for all that which in art represented excess in color and in form, for all that which at one and the same time was intense, pessimistic and Byronic; a strange sort of dilettantism which can be explained only by the odious circumstances encompassing bored and turbulent youth. If the Restoration had turned into a period of glory, Romanticism would not have parted company with royalty; and this new sect, which professed equal scorn for the moderate political opposition, for the painting of Delaroche or the poetry of Delavigne, and for the king who directed the development of the middle of the road policy, would have found no reason to exist.

As for me, I sincerely confess, even if it seems absurd, that I have always had some sympathy for this unfortunate writer whose abortive genius, full of ambition and of awkwardness, succeeded in producing only painstaking drafts, stormy flashes, figures whose native grandeur was impaired by something too bizarre in their dress or in their voice. He has, in short, a color all his own, a flavor *sui generis;* if he had nothing more than the attraction of willfulness, that is already a good deal. But he loved literature fiercely, and today we are overrun with pretty and docile writers all ready to sell the Muse to escape the potter's field.

Last year as we were finishing these notes, too severe perhaps, we learned that the poet had just died in Algeria where, discouraged or scornful, he had withdrawn far from the literary scene, without having published the *Tabarin* which had been announced a long time before. (pp. 254-58)

> *Charles Baudelaire, "Reflections on Some of My Contemporaries: Pétrus Borel," in his Baudelaire as a Literary Critic, edited and translated by Lois Boe Hyslop and Francis E. Hyslop, Jr., The Pennsylvania State University Press, 1964, pp. 253-58.*

Mario Praz   (essay date 1951)

[A noted scholar of Italian and English literature during the first half of the twentieth century, Mario Praz was a native of Italy. He published extensively on the literature of the Romantic and the Victorian periods. In the following excerpt, Praz surveys Borel's short stories.]

A more serious concern with horror than that of [many other Romantic writers] (we know that *bons vivants* such as Dumas and Gautier cultivated the macabre and the horrible as a fashionable pose) is shown in the work of Pétrus Borel, whom the facetious Théo [Gautier] called the most perfect example of the Romantic ideal, and who was a kind of minor Baudelaire *ante litteram*.

Certainly Pétrus Borel, the *lycanthrope* who flaunted a waistcoat *à la* Robespierre and an ogre's beard, and missed no opportunity of displaying his superb feline teeth, was a dandy in the style of the Terror, a *fumiste*. But in him this playing with violent sensations became intenser and more serious: he depicted his hero Champavert as killing himself in circumstances both macabre and grotesque (he is found in a horse-knacker's yard—such as Janin loved—with a huge knife planted like a stake in his breast); and he finished by committing suicide himself, apparently, by letting himself die of sunstroke, in 1859 [He says:]

> Chanter l'amour! . . . Pour moi l'amour c'est de la haine, des gémissements, des cris, de la honte, du deuil, du fer, des larmes, du sang, des cadavres, des ossements, des remords—je n'en ai pas connu d'autre.

The frontispiece which Adrien Aubry designed later for Borel's *Champavert, contes immoraux* (1833) shows quite clearly the sort of spectacle that may be looked for if once one enters the peepshow of horrors that the book contains. In the middle is a medallion with the effigy of the author looking like a sinister Jesuit; on the left a guillotine, a dark lantern, a skull; on the right a boatman who with a pole is violently pushing under water a woman with her breast uncovered and her arms tied behind her back; the grim outline of a Gothic castle is to be seen on the river bank.

The first story, **"Monsieur de l' Argentière, l' accusateur,"** presents us with one of the infinite variations of the persecuted maiden. The progressive degradation of Apolline is followed with the same minute attention to unpleasant detail as has been noticed in "L'Âne mort." Apolline is raped by an unknown man on a dark night, reduced to extreme misery, she abandons her new-born child in a cesspool and goes through the same stages as Janin's Henriette: the Hospice de la Bourbe, the Prison de la Force, 'dans un cachot étroit et sombre,' and finally the Place de la Grève. The chief responsibility for her being condemned to death lies with the Public Prosecutor, in whom Apolline recognizes the man who raped her. 'It is he, that man who is speaking! It was he whom I saw by the light of the moon, with his sallow face, his red hair, and those deep-set eyes!' Monsieur de l'Argentière pushes his sadistic inclinations to the point of being present at the execution, which takes place amid the morbid curiosity of the crowd:

> Quand le coutelas tomba, il se fit une sourde rumeur; et un Anglais, penché sur une fenêtre qu'il avait louée 500 fr., fort satisfait, cria un long *very wel* [sic] en applaudissant des mains.

We shall come across this Englishman again several times during the second half of the nineteenth century.

"Jaquez Barraou, le charpentier" is the next story. It is an extremely horrible tale of the criminal jealousy of two negroes over a beautiful mulatto woman; the scene is Havana. Then there is **"Don Andréa Vésalius l'anatomiste."** The anatomist drugs his wife's lovers and uses their bodies for his experiments; his wife, at the sight of the jars in which are preserved in spirits the remains of her last lover, dies of horror, and the indefatigable scientist cuts up her beautiful body also; the scene is Madrid. (pp. 131-32)

From Madrid we pass on to Jamaica, to the loves of **"Three-fingered Jack, l'Obi"**: nor are horrors and corpses lacking here either. In placing his scene among the negroes of the Antilles Borel was only following in the footsteps of Hugo in *Bug-Jargal*. In the last three stories we return to France. **"Dina la belle juive"** has for her motto the litanies of the Virgin: 'Rosa mỳstica, Turris Davidica', &c. One thinks immediately of Baudelaire's "Franciscae meae laudes." Dina, in her anxiety for the fate of Aymar, behaves in the way already indicated in Keats's "Ode to Melancholy" ('Then glut thy sorrow on a morning rose . . . or on the wealth of globèd peonies . . . ') and in the manner later adopted by the disciples of Baudelaire and Huysman's des Esseintes:

> Dépravée par la douleur, elle recherchait ardemment tout ce qui irritait ses nerfs, tout ce qui titillait et éveillait son apathie; elle se chargeait des fleurs les plus odorantes; elle s'entourait de vases pleins de syringa, de jasmin, de verveines, de roses, de lys, de tubéreuses, elle faisait fumer de l'encens, du benjoin; elle épandait autour d'elle de l'ambre, du cinnamome, du storax, du musc.

A Saône boatman rapes and murders Dina in the manner illustrated in the frontispiece, and then—behaving like Monsieur de l'Argentière—pretends to have fished up her corpse, in order to earn the two pistoles reward. Romantic irony—for since Dina is a Jewess, the boatman has no right to the money for his pretended discovery.

The following is the story of **"Passereau l'écolier."** A medical student who suspects his mistress of infidelity causes her to fall into a well, the top of which is level with the ground: he covers her over with the coping-stones, then challenges her lover to a duel, with the agreement that the lady shall belong to the survivor. Before firing, Passereau advises his opponent to go next morning and have a look at the well. Baudelaire did not merely make use of this situation in the "Vin de l'assassin:"

> Je l'ai jetée au fond d'un puits,
> Et j'ai même poussé sur elle
> Tous les pavés de la margelle. . . .

but also took from it the main idea of a play, *L'Ivrogne.*

Passereau's request to the executioner, whom he went to find expressly for the purpose, remained famous: 'Je désirerais que vous me guillotinassiez.'

The last story, **"Champavert le lycanthrope"** (the pseudonym of Borel himself), completes the museum of horrors with the story of the macabre circumstances of the last days of Champavert. He makes a misanthropic will, disinters the little corpse of his own and Flava's child, kills Flava, and ends his life among the carcasses of the horses slaughtered at the Buttes de Montfaucon.

Even the tale **"Gottfried Wolfgang"** which Borel plagiarized from Irving ("The Adventure of the German Student") is typical for the conclusion. In it a German student, given to Swedenborgian speculations and subject to hallucinations, is tormented by the memory of a beautiful woman of whom he has caught a glimpse in a dream. One night, roaming the streets of Paris during the Terror, he stumbles against the guillotine, and in a flash of lightning sees a figure bending down, with dishevelled hair, which he recognizes as the woman of his dream. He takes her home, and notices that she has round her neck a ribbon of black velvet. The student declares to her his passion, and the woman tells him that she has been urged towards him by a supernatural impulse. In the morning he finds her cold: at his cries the police rush in and recognize the woman as a victim of the guillotine. Gottfried removes the black ribbon from her neck and sees beneath it the cut of the axe. This tale, which is worthy of Poe, is claimed to have been found in the possession of an inn-keeper at Boulogne, to whom it had been given by a strange, taciturn young Englishman.

No less frantic than *Champavert,* the novel called *Madame Putiphar* (1839) deliberately piles horror upon horror, in a style in which mystification is interwoven with sincerity in a decidedly curious manner. Certain pages are anticipatory of the grotesque method of Lautréamont. . . . (pp. 133-35)

When the highly unfortunate Patrick—younger brother of Byron's Prisoner of Chillon—is released from the Bastille on February 27th, 1784, he falls in with two other prisoners, one of whom is 'une des gloires de la France—un martyr':

> Ce que j'entends par cette gloire de la France, s'il faut le dire, c'était l'illustre auteur d'un livre contre lequel vous criez touts [sic] à l'infamie, et que vous avez touts dans votre poche, je vous en demande bien pardon, cher lecteur; c'était, disje, très haut et très puissant seigneur, monsieur le comte de Sade [sic], dont les fils dégénérés por-

tent aujourd'hui parmi nous un front noble et fier, un front noble et pur.

Borel acquits Napoleon of the horrible cruelty of having persecuted Sade: 'C'eût été mal d'ailleurs de la part de l'empereur corse d'accommoder ainsi un empereur romain.'

This is an example of romantic mystification (but then Borel took a genuine pleasure in spectacles of cruelty). Another romantic mystification is the recantation inserted by the author into the twenty-third chapter of the seventh book, in which, declaring that light had dawned upon him, he proclaims that it is not true that the good pay for the wicked, and that if this sometimes seems to be so, it is because the good are either only good in appearance, or are expiating the wrongs of their race. . . . (p. 135-36)

Each of the unhappy lovers, Déborah and Patrick, is descended from an accursed race. Borel, like Soulié, makes an effort to save his face, and finishes by evoking a picture of social nemesis. 'Car Dieu et le peuple, ces deux formidables ouvriers, vont se mettre à la besogne!—et car leur besogne comme eux sera terrible!' . . . (p. 136)

But even if *Madame Putiphar* had only a moderate success, it at least called forth the praise of Baudelaire for 'la peinture des hideurs et des tortures du cachot, qui monte jusqu'à la vigueur de Mathurin'.

The verse of the *Rhapsodies* is in no way to be distinguished from the usual productions of the followers of Byron. But, according to Baudelaire, Borel played a not unimportant part in the history of his century. Without him, he says, there would be a gap in the course of Romanticism. . . . 'Sa spécialité fut la *Lycanthropie*', he had already said. After all, lycanthropy is only another name for sadism. (pp. 136-37)

> *Mario Praz, "The Shadow of the 'Divine Marquis'," in his* The Romantic Agony, *translated by Angus Davidson, second edition, 1951. Reprint by Meridian Books, 1956, pp. 93-186.*

Enid Starkie (essay date 1954)

[*An English literary critic, Starkie is the author of numerous studies of French writers of the nineteenth and twentieth centuries, including Baudelaire, Arthur Rimbaud, André Gide, and Gustave Flaubert. Her critical biography of Borel, from which the following excerpt is taken, is the most extensive English-language study of the French writer. Below, she analyzes Borel's style in* Champavert *and* Madame Putiphar, *concluding that he was more successful as a writer of short stories than as a novelist.*]

[*Champavert, Contes Immoraux* is Borel's] most important work and gives a faithful impression of his characteristic qualities: his love of horror relieved by his own brand of grim humour and irony, his talent for vivid narrative. It is also very typical of the age. *Champavert* is Borel's most original work and its appearance is the highest point of his literary career. It was published by Renuel who is famous for having produced so many elegant collections of the writings of the Romantic poets. In claiming that these tales are immoral Borel exaggerates. Some are horrifying, some are cynical and cruel, with touches of the sadism which was fashionable in that period; they all possess his grim ironical humour—'l'humour noire' as André Breton calls it—but they are not, most of them, particularly immoral; certainly less so than Gautier's *Mademoiselle de Maupin* which was to be published three years later. (pp. 112-13)

Champavert is composed of five tales which correspond to what is normally accepted as a short story. These are **"Monsieur d' Argentière," "Jacquez Barraou," "L' Anatomiste," "Three Fingered Jack"** and **"Dina la Belle Juive."** There are two additional narratives which can hardly be called stories. These are **"Passereau l'Ecolier"** and **"Champavert le Lycanthrope,"** which are autobiographical sketches—especially the second which is Borel's account of his own life.

The first story, **"Monsieur de l'Argentière,"** has little that appeals to us nowadays. The style has not much distinction and the psychology is that of the serial novel. It has however some effective descriptive writing which gives a good impression of the Paris of the nineteenth century, and there is a surprising chapter called *Rococo* which describes very cleverly a Louis XV dining room. One would not have expected a *Bouzingo* to have had a taste for rococo; its description however suffers somewhat from what will eventually be Borel's besetting sin, a tendency towards pedantry and towards making too great a show of learning.

"Monsieur de l' Argentière" is the story of a man, the public prosecutor, who taking advantage of a friend's absence, creeps into his fiancée's room at night and, under cover of darkness, seduces her. She, thinking that he is the man to whom she is engaged, yields to him. She becomes pregnant and when her fiancé returns and sees her condition, he refuses to believe her story. He breaks off his engagement with her and leaves her to her fate. Eventually she bears the child, and in a fit of post-confinement madness, alone and without help, she throws the baby down a sewer believing it to be dead. It is found but dies on being picked up. It is traced back to her but she remembers nothing about the event. After a trial she is condemned to death through the offices of the man who has seduced her and whom she recognises in the Court. The story ends with the public execution which the prosecutor watches from his window. But, just at the end, there is a characteristic touch of Borel's bitter irony which saves the tale from triviality. It was raining during the execution and the crowd, not getting a full view of the scaffold, cries: 'Down with your umbrellas, no one can see anything! Down with your umbrellas! And the women repeated 'Behave like gentlemen, no one can see anything!' And Borel ends: 'The rabble, craning their necks, were on tip-toes. When the knife fell a low dull murmur could be heard; and an Englishman, leaning out of a window for which he had paid twenty pounds, cried in a satisfied voice, as he clapped, "Very well!"' '

The second story, **"Jacquez Barraou,"** with its sombre and passionate character, is of a higher standard artistically. It is a well-told story of bitter sexual jealousy, of a fight

to a tragic finish for the possession of a girl, ending with the death of both contestants. There is however tenderness and compassion as well as cruelty. In a particularly touching scene the two fighting enemies stop belabouring one another and fall on their knees to say the Angelus as the church bells ring out. Then, when they have finished praying, they resume the fight. Here too the story ends with a peculiarly Borellian touch. The two negroes have finally killed each other and lie dead, still locked in combat. A white shopkeeper walks by, stumbles against the corpses of the two dead rivals and says, as he passes on unmoved, 'They are only niggers!'

Another tale of negro life is **"Three Fingered Jack"**— Borel is very successful with these studies of primitive people—where unconscious cruelty, or even sadism, is mingled with tenderness. It is the story of a black Robin Hood called Three Fingered Jack because he has lost two fingers from his right hand in combat. He has, in spite of all his crimes, never yet hurt a woman or a child—indeed he has saved Abigail, the heroine, from being carried away as a slave. In the picture that Borel draws of Three Fingered Jack it is obvious that he is really thinking of himself; he sees himself as a Robin Hood who might flee thus from everyday life, and he says: 'Jack was one of these strong characters, one of these powerful brains, born to rule, who unable to breathe in the narrow cage in which fate has placed them, in that society which wants to bend and to shrink everything to its own mean size, break forever men whom they loathe, if they do not break with life itself. Three Fingered Jack was a lycanthrope.'

There is in this story the same violence and bloodshed as in the others, with a full account of death by knifing. There are also traces of his besetting sin, the excessive parade of erudition which we also found in **"Monsieur de l' Argentière."** There is a chapter—he calls it, with justification, "Tiresome Chapter"—in which he gives the sources of his material, taken largely from a *Treatise of Sugar* by a certain Doctor Moseley. The chapter is irrelevant to the story, the material, if given at all, should have figured in a footnote, and it serves no purpose but to display the learning of its author.

"L' Anatomiste," exemplifying the grimmest and most macabre side of Borel's talent, is one of his most effective tales. It is the story of an old doctor of anatomy, Don Andrea Vesalius, who marries a young beautiful girl and then, after the wedding, finds that, in spite of his great love and passion, he is impotent with her. He reads her accounts from classical writers to show that the extremes of love often cause such failure, but he cannot cure himself and his excuses do not interest his wife. Borel adds ironically: 'Vesalius once more betrothed himself to learning'.

Vesalius then shuts himself away in his laboratory and gives himself up more than ever to research. He allows his young wife to go her own way, but under the vigilance of a duenna who reports all her doings to him. The young woman diverts herself by taking young lovers, beautiful young men, who seem to be in unlimited supply—and her husband apparently does not notice her behaviour. She expresses little surprise when each lover disappears after one short night of love, even before she has wakened, and she never sees him again. This does not however worry her overmuch, as others never fail to appear. After two years of marriage she falls ill and sends for her husband for she thinks that she is on the point of death, and she wishes to ease her conscience by confessing her guilt. She excuses herself on the grounds of her youth and his age, and begs him to forgive her. He pulls aside her hands clinging to him, and bids her rise from her bed to follow him to the laboratory. In that gruesome setting he forces her to listen to his side of the story. He tells her that he has never been her dupe, that it was he who had provided her with her lovers, and that each of them who had slept with her was afterwards drugged by the duenna through his orders, and later carried down asleep to the laboratory, to become a specimen for dissection. He then points to a skeleton hanging in a cupboard on which hang the clothes of her first lover. Then he shows her, in a glass container, a human skeleton partially preserved in spirit, the arteries are filled with a red liquid and the veins with blue, all visible to observe. The hair and the beard are still on the skull. It is clear that it is Fernando her second lover. Finally she is shown her last, Pedro, and at this sight she falls to the ground in a faint. The next day a coffin is carried out of the palace and the gravedigger notices that it is very heavy and gives a resonant sound unlike that of a corpse.

The following evening anyone looking in at Vesalius as he worked in his laboratory, could have seen him dissecting the corpse of a beautiful young woman whose long fair hair fell to the ground.

"Dina la Belle Juive" is a gruesome tale of rape and suicide, which has little unity of plan, though it possesses dramatic tension and vividness of writing. It takes place at Lyons where Borel had lived as a boy, and he has marvellously evoked the atmosphere of the town, with its narrow mediaeval streets down by the river. The opening section of the story might be a scene for light opera, the final chapter would be better told as a ballad, while the centre portion, the account of the rape and sadistic murder of Dina by the boatman whom she has hired to row her across the river, is a separate story fit for *grand guignol*. The story ends with the usual ironic touch characteristic of Borel. The boatman, who has bound and gagged Dina, robbed, raped and murdered her, finally flinging her into the river, fishes her up again next day and tries to claim the reward offered by the Corporation for salvaging drowned corpses. He does not however succeed in his plan for they will not pay for a Jew. 'Who fishes up a heretic, sir boatman, fishes up a dog!'

"Passereau l'Ecolier" and **"Testament de Champavert"** are the most interesting and original parts of the collection, they are also the most significant through their influence, especially on Baudelaire. Passereau, the Paris student, could only have been conceived by a morbid mind. He had once believed in women and in love, but he suddenly discovers, from reading, in the absence of his mistress, her letters, that she has another lover as well as him. He entices her to a lonely garden and then drowns her in a well, watching her torments as she tries to escape and finishing her off with stones torn from the rim of the well. Then he goes to her other lover and proposes to him that

they should play for her in a game of dominoes, the winner to keep the girl and to shoot the loser. Passereau loses, as he had planned to do, and, as his last request, begs his rival to go to the well in the garden and to look down into it. After this he dies happy for he knows that his enemy's victory is vain and that he will only find the corpse of his dead mistress in the well.

That is not however all that there is to this story. It contains more of Borel's dark humour than the other tales. There is a very Baudelairean scene where Passereau, in his first despair at discovering the treachery of his mistress, goes to the public executioner to ask him to guillotine him. 'Je désire que vous me guillotinassiez!' he says. It is a scene that would have appealed to Baudelaire in his youth. The discussion between Passereau and the executioner, when trying to persuade him, is highly comic. The latter protests that he has no sanction to perform such an act. Passereau however assures him that he does not expect an important public execution, but a simple little private one in a back garden, that would do. The executioner is a civil servant who cannot do anything that is not 'en règle'. The case must first go through the police and law courts, he says, before he can do anything. If all that is complied with, then he will be Passereau's most humble servant and make a clean and satisfactory job of it, he assures him. (pp. 113-18)

The collection ends with **"Testament de Champavert,"** a tale full of bitterness and rancour against life, with no belief or hope in anything. 'Well! No! Idiots that you are! You are all going where everything goes, to nothingness! And it is, face to face with death, and my feet in the grave, cowards, that I say that to you! I don't want another life! I've had enough of life! It is nothingness that I long for!' Then Champavert blasphemes against God with the same violence as Baudelaire in the *Reniement de Saint Pierre*. 'And besides, you Christians, you hanged your God, and you were right, for if he had been God, he would have deserved hanging!'

In this story, which is intentionally biographical, one sees the crack in Borel's personality which nothing will be able to mend. 'When a tree has been struck by lightning, no spring can ever again make it grow green.' We do not however know what thunderbolt blighted him.

Champavert eventually makes a suicide pact with his mistress Flava because there is nothing left for him in life; he does not however formulate his grievances, but only raves against society in general, for it is society which has caused the death of his illegitimate son. His mistress bore it secretly, killed it at birth and buried it in the garden. 'Horrible world! A girl has to kill her son, or else she loses her honour. Flava, you are a girl of honour and you murdered yours!' Then to prove to her that there is no after life, to her who had expected some compensation in the hereafter, he digs up the corpse of their child and, holding it up before her, says, 'Flava, Flava, look at your son! Here! this is what eternity is, look!' Then he cries out against the world: 'Law! virtue! horror! Are you satisfied? Here take back your prey! Cruel world, that is what you wanted! Look! This is your work! Are you pleased with your victory? Are you pleased with your victories? Bastard! It was impudence on your part to have been born without royal consent, without banns! Barbarous law! Cruel prejudice! Infamous horror! Men, society! Here take back your prey! I give him back to you!' And he flings the little skeleton away, so that it rolls down the slope and is broken to pieces on the stones of the road. Then he kills Flava with his dagger, goes down the hill and disappears into the fog. Next day a child's skeleton is crushed to dust beneath the wheels of a cart, the body of a woman is discovered near the stream with a dagger wound in her heart, and later a man covered in blood is found, lying in the road with a knife stuck in his breast.

Champavert's violence and pessimism are not explained. The improbability of the plot detracts from the impression of bitterness and *spleen* which would have been more effective without the *grand guignol* plot.

Champavert's revolt against the Romantic convention that nature is always beautiful, is similar to Baudelaire's and he too complains of the monotony, 'the eternal face of nature; always sun and rain; always spring and autumn, heat and cold; always and forever. Nothing more boring than something which never changes, than a fixed fashion, than a perpetual calendar. Every year the trees are green, and always green trees, always rain and sun, ever and always green trees. How boring that is! Why not more variety? Why should the leaves not assume, one after the other, all the colours of the rainbow? Fontainebleau, how stupid all that greenery is!'

Similar to Baudelaire's also is his hatred of Romantic love. (pp. 118-20)

Champavert, in the midst of all the desolation around him, sees no issue except in suicide to escape the view of all the horror. It did not seem to him that there was anything that he personally could do. Life was a loathsome play, a loathsome farce which he was forced to watch, and which he refused to watch to the end. Barbey d'Aurevilly was to say, after reading *Les Fleurs du Mal* of Baudelaire, that their author, after composing such a book into which he had poured all his suffering and bitterness, had no other path left open to him but suicide or conversion. Champavert, in similar circumstances, chose suicide.

Champavert is the work in which Borel poured most of himself. Yet, with this bitterness and hatred of life, we find as well, compassion and sympathy for those who are obliged to endure the farce, especially for those who are simple and lowly. There was in him, in spite of his obsession with sadism—which was really an expression of deep hurt—a hatred of evil and a love of nobility and disinterestedness, a loathing for the vulgarity and materialism which he saw around him. These characteristics in Borel were later to endear him to Baudelaire who had similar revulsions.

Perhaps Borel really believed, after all, that it was only the surface that was rotten, and that in the depths there was purity; perhaps that was why he chose a verse from a poem by his friend Gérard de Nerval for the title page of ***Champavert,*** a poem which expresses such hope.

Car la société n'est qu'un marais fétide

Dont le fond, sans nul doute, est seul pur et limpide
Mais où ce qui se voit de plus sale, de plus
Vénéneux et puant, vient toujours par-dessus!

(pp. 120-21)

• • • • •

Madame Putiphar is exceedingly long and rambling, without any visible unity so that it is difficult to determine what really is the plot—if indeed there is any at all. It begins in Ireland, in the estates of a sadistic old Irish lord called Cockermouth who ill-treats his wife and daughter. On the estate lives a poor lad called Patrick Fitz-Whyte, a clever boy who is being educated with Deborah the daughter of the Lord. They naturally fall in love and meet secretly by night in the castle demesne. They are both young and innocent and they do nothing but talk of the former glories of Ireland and of their love. After many pages Deborah plans to elope with Patrick to France where he will enlist in the army. Her father discovers her plot and plans to shoot Patrick but, accidentally, wounds his daughter instead. Patrick flees abroad but tells Deborah how she will be able to find him when she reaches Paris; he will write his address in chalk on the walls of the Louvre. In Patrick's absence Lord Cockermouth gets him tried and condemned to death for the attempted murder of his daughter. She eventually manages to make her way to Paris and finds Patrick. They marry but the colonel of his regiment catches sight of Deborah, is struck by her beauty and determines that she shall be his. There follow many pages of his vain attempts at seducing her, of her defence of her virtue. Realising that he will not reach his ends the colonel determines to get rid of Fitz-Whyte.

In the meantime Patrick's closest friend, Fitz-Harris, has got himself into difficulties with Madame Putiphar—intended as a picture of Madame de Pompadour—because he has lampooned her in his writings, and she gets him sent to the Bastille. Fitz-Whyte obtains his pardon from the lady but, unfortunately, she falls in love with him at first sight when he comes to plead for his friend, and determines to seduce him. He nobly withstands her blandishments and finally says to her, quoting from Rousseau, 'The wife of a coalman is more worthy of praise than the mistress of a king.' (pp. 133-34)

Madame Putiphar apparently has an unlimited number of free 'lettres de cachet' for she manages to send both Fitz-Whyte and Fitz-Harris to the Bastille. Deborah, in the meantime, has been told that her husband has been killed. Then she is kidnapped one Sunday while she is hearing Mass, and taken to a certain establishment to be trained for Pharaon's bed—he is intended as a portrait of Louis XV. Next follows an absurd description of this superior brothel in which her training takes place, and of the behaviour of the Lesbian Madame in charge of it. The atmosphere is very similar to that of *La Religieuse* of Diderot. When Deborah is finally brought to the King she repulses him and, when he sees that nothing is to be gained from her, she too is sent to prison.

All the main characters are now in captivity. In prison Deborah gives birth to Patrick's son and christens him Vengeance. After many vicissitudes she manages to escape and she brings up her son in the ideal that he must one day avenge his father—hence his name.

The greater part of the novel henceforth deals with a description of the treatment meted out to Fitz-Harris and Fitz-Whyte in the state prisons of France. This permits Borel to give full rein to his obsession with horror and his talent for describing it. There is also compassion and tenderness, as in the account of the death of Fitz-Harris in the dungeon which he shares with Fitz-Whyte.

When Vengeance is sixteen his mother despatches him to fight with his father's colonel and to kill him. The colonel is now an old man, but it is the boy who is killed in the duel, and his slayer ties his corpse to his horse and sends it back to his mother.

After many years and many more chapters of horror we reach the moment of the storming of the Bastille in 1789 when only one prisoner is found, an old man who jabbers incomprehensibly in English and Irish. It is discovered that this is Fitz-Whyte, Deborah's husband. She is summoned to the prison to take him home, but she finds that he is mad and does not recognise her. She falls down dead through grief and shock.

Summarised briefly the plot has some coherence, but, as one reads, this is lost from sight in the six hundred odd pages full of digressions and irrelevancies. One cannot help wondering what it was that inspired Borel to embark on this theme. It may have been to give expression to his taste for horror, and he gives us in full measure, more than thirty years of torture and suffering in the state prisons of France in the eighteenth century. He did not realise that undiluted horror is not a suitable atmosphere for a novel, and that it soon ceases from having any effect at all. Horror, mystery and fantasy find their most perfect expression in the short story where the atmosphere can be swiftly conjured up and where the interest does not lie in full analysis of character, where facets of the personality and impressions are all that are needed to create the illusion. Then, when the tension has become well nigh unbearable, the blind can be swiftly pulled down and the light extinguished. That is why the tales of Poe and Hoffman will be remembered when the novels of horror will be forgotten, however great the talent that produced them.

Perhaps Borel's intention was to depict the evils of France under the old régime, evils due to one single woman. Yet Madame Putiphar appears only on two or three short occasions, dying in the early part of the novel. Perhaps we are supposed to believe that her disastrous stranglehold on France continued, even after her death, right up to the Revolution. This is manifestly absurd. The book is written with all the bitterness of a pamphleteer of the revolutionary era, and the horrors of the prison occupy the largest part. But the days of the pamphleteers were over in the eighteen-thirties and the Bastille had been, for more than half a century, no more than a mark on the city pavement. By 1839 Frenchmen were beginning to consider the eighteenth century in a more kindly way, and they felt that the portraits of Louis XV and of Madame de Pompadour in *Madame Putiphar* were biased and unjust. They were not human beings but figures from melodrama and only in a

revolutionary era could they have appealed to a public thirsty for the blood of tyrants. By 1839 Frenchmen were tired of hearing of the abuses of the old régime—they had known many of their own since then—the razing of the Bastille to the ground had not brought in the Millennium, and they were weary of hearing of the alleged debauchery and cruelty of the old nobility—the debauchery of their own bourgeoisie was sufficient for them.

The meaning of the book is contained in the first chapter, where Borel declares that he is going to prove that there are fated destinies, or as Baudelaire was later to say, that there are people who are pursued by 'le guignon', or a merciless fate. There are men who, in spite of the nobility of their natures, are the victims of misfortune, of events beyond their control, which they could not have foreseen and which no virtue on their part could have prevented. Borel says: 'If original sin is an injustice, then fated original destiny is a monstrosity.' He adds that he will not weary his head with reflecting on these odious considerations, nor try to explain what cannot be explained. He will only say that 'if there is a Providence, then it manifests itself in most strange ways, and woe betide the man who is thus branded. It would have been better if he had been stifled in his mother's womb.' That is the cry of Baudelaire in his poem *Bénédiction*.

Borel then says that he is going to relate the story of some horrifying destinies which he will not seek to explain, but will only suggest that his readers will be luckier than he if they can believe that a Providence has spun the thread of these lives, or if they can find a plan or a purpose in them.

This was his intention as he started to write but, by the end of the book, he had changed his mind and he says then that light had eventually come to him. 'I do not know by what mysterious operation light came to me' and then, in many ecstatic pages he tries to explain the nature of this light. He believes now that there is after all a kindly destiny, a Providence that does look after Humanity; he believes now that the wicked do not triumph even on earth. Each receives eventually the wages he deserves and nothing remains unpunished. 'Yes! I believe in expiation! No! Fated original destiny is not a monstrosity, but a sublime law! God is the God of Vengeance!' He goes on to explain that God's vengeance is often invisible, often it takes a long time, but it is sure and inevitable in the end. God has eternity before him and has no need to hurry, but nothing escapes his sword.

This new belief is however no more consoling than the first, and no more just. Borel has, it is true, shown how cruelty and vice do not remain unpunished, but he has not explained the justice of the fate of the victims. It is true that the perpetrators of evil have ended violently, but so too have the innocent victims. Indeed everyone in the novel has reached a violent end. The innocent, Fitz-Harris, Fitz-Whyte, Deborah and their son Vengeance, says Borel, had to suffer for the evil of their parents and ancestors. He now admits that he had been wrong in the beginning when he had declared that Destiny had no plan. It has a plan, he says, and that plan is Vengeance.

In spite of his toil and trouble, one feels all through *Madame Putiphar,* effort rather than ease, and that he has flogged himself to his task, putting together material that never really fuses. It is a book that has been made rather than created. It has also been inflated with too much irrelevant matter, with too much pseudo erudition, with too many examples of his passion for pedantry and ostentatious learning. (pp. 134-37)

Madame Putiphar passed almost unnoticed and did not even enjoy the *succès de scandale* of **Champavert.** There was an article by Janin in the *Journal des Débats* [June 3, 1839], an article of three pages violently attacking it as a very dangerous book. Not a single chapter found favour with him, and he compared Borel to the Marquis de Sade. (p. 138)

In his article Janin asks: 'What is a critic to do when faced with such a deplorable and dangerous work? Can he, with a clear conscience, allow such a book to pass unnoticed, one whose premises are obscene and whose conclusion is bloody? Would he be doing his duty, in face of such abuse of the mind, if he contented himself with deploring to himself in secret what he ought to criticise openly?'

Janin is unduly hard on *Madame Putiphar* and finds no qualities to admire in it. Yet there is in it good writing and many passages of tragic poetic beauty. There is for instance the gruesome ride of the dead body of Vengeance, lashed to his horse, through the darkness, sent back to his mother by the man who slew him. There is in this description a nobility which possesses epic grandeur. Moving also is the account of the death of Fitz-Harris in his dungeon. Baudelaire, a greater critic than Janin, was less severe and, writing twenty years later, found much to like and to admire, and evidence of a distinguished talent.

The most interesting part for readers today, now that the taste for horror has vanished, is the Prologue in verse addressed to A.L.P. One wonders why this poem was placed here for it has no connection with the novel, and little too with the woman to whom it is addressed. It was written for the greater part in the bitter and agonising solitude of Baizil, and it shows a marked advance on the poems in **Rhapsodies,** in powers of expression, in depth and maturity. Its symbolism has some of the quality which we shall later find in Baudelaire, particularly the contrast between *Spleen* and *Idéal.* The chief fault in Borel's poem is its excessive length and some redundant passages which could have been omitted with gain in effectiveness and concision. (pp. 138-39)

Baudelaire greatly admired this poem and was influenced by it. It shows more mastery of expression and variety of image than any of Borel's previous poems, a surer and more moving symbolism. (p. 142)

• • • • •

Posterity, on the whole, has not treated Petrus Borel kindly, nor has it ever given him his just deserts, whereas it has singled out for special praise many a lesser writer. He is now almost entirely forgotten, except amongst a small number of devotees who find the by-ways of literature often more absorbing than the highways. Even in his own

lifetime he had become neglected as early as twenty years before his death, when his last published work, **Madame Putiphar,** which appeared in 1839, aroused so little enthusiasm.

Petrus Borel was the kind of meteoric personality who is thrown up by violent revolution, whose light burns brightly for a short space, as long as the fashion for destruction prevails, and then finally, because he cannot adapt himself to the conditions of stable society, splutters out into obscurity. He was, by nature and inclination, capable of destruction, but he never learned to build. Yet his stormy passage through his age has not been in vain, for he hewed out a rough channel which later writers—Baudelaire, Rimbaud and Lautréamont—have deepened for the greater glory of literature, and who owe much to him, who might indeed never have existed had it not been for his fulgent example.

Baudelaire was to see in Borel a man fatally persecuted by 'le guignon', a man blighted by the evil-eye, to whom the curse of God allowed no rest. This was Borel's conception of the destiny of all mankind. The reasons for this frustrated destiny in his own case are not far to seek. He lacked the breadth of genius to achieve his high ambitions, and yet was too proud to be satisfied with what his talents allowed him to be. It is evident from his writings that he did violence to his nature in his efforts to practise Sadism and Satanism. In cruelty his practice fell far below his promise. He was a man characterised by kind and warm sensibilities, whom the harshness of life wounded bitterly; he was unable to accept the conditions of life as he saw them, and his revolt was expressed in a deliberate pursuit of cynicism and brutality in his writings. Yet, underneath this bitter exterior, there beat the heart of a man moved by deep compassion for those who suffer and are ill-treated by their fellow-men—this is clear even in his most cruel book, *Madame Putiphar.* Houssaye, who knew Borel intimately as a young man, says [in his *Confessions,* 1885-91], with some acumen, that Borel was always cast for the wrong part, that he deliberately chose one for which he was least suited. He rewrote the part given to him by Nature in accordance with his taste. Houssaye goes on to say that he took infinite pains to cultivate red roses in his garden where white ones would have grown in profusion without effort or care. This would explain why his final achievement bore so little relation to his promise. Later, when the taste for melodrama had gone out of fashion, he wrote another part for himself, that of the academic scholar, and became a historian and a linguist. Ten years after his beginnings in the charnel-house literature of 1830, he was writing additional chapters for the *Essays of Montaigne.* Unfortunately the public did not want learning from him and gave him no encouragement.

Like Rostand's *Cyrano de Bergerac* Borel was often carried away by a love of the theatrical conception of 'la Gloire', by a liking for false 'panache'. This is apparent in his efforts to appear in a theatrical part as a writer, rather than in concentrating on what he was saying. He was always in fancy dress playing his part like a nineteenth-century actor of melodrama, and he could never cope with life as it is lived.

Borel's aspirations and personality are probably ultimately more interesting than his actual literary achievement. Right to the end of his life he remained, what he had been in his early days, an 'honnête homme' inspired by a bitter hatred of everything that was mean and low, by a horror of falsehood and dishonesty. He makes his hero Champavert say that the thought which arouses most disgust in himself is the fear that he—or anyone else—might cease from being an honest man. He himself made similar statements about his chiefs and colleagues in Algeria when he suspected them of malpractices. Even when his mind became mentally deranged, at the end, this characteristic still shone out, but with a dark distorting light. This quality, although it made of him a figure of fun when it was exaggerated, gave him nevertheless the pathetic grandeur of a Don Quixote tilting against spiritual windmills. He was inspired by generosity of outlook, a longing to support those who were oppressed, but this eventually became twisted and he ended by believing that the underdog was always right, merely because he was the underdog. He had a bitter hatred of everything that was vulgar or mean, and this eventually led to his downfall and death.

Borel's personality led him often into intolerance, and he never learned to have pity for the weaknesses of average humanity. Average human nature was what he most loathed and despised. Baudelaire's revulsion against the petty meannesses of men was equal to his, but he felt however as well deep compassion, not only for those who suffer and are ill-used at the hands of others, but pity also for those who fail through their own weakness and frailty. Borel's pity went only to the defenceless and persecuted, but not to those who, seeing good, fail to reach it. He had not sufficient self-criticism to realise how fatally easy it is to be weak in attainment, nor how this failure cannot always be attributed to others, but to oneself alone. He never studied or criticised himself deeply and this led to arrogance which made him feel that he himself was incapable of sinking as low as those whom he despised. He would never have said with Baudelaire:

> *Ah! Seigneur, donnez-moi la force et le courage*
> *De contempler mon cœur et mon corps sans dégoût.*

All writers are, in a certain measure, ego-centric by the very nature of their craft, but Borel was turned in on himself in introspection rather than in self-analysis. This lack of psychological analytical power made him unsuited to be a novelist, but his quick sensibilities and feeling for atmosphere made him reach noble heights in the short story. It is in this literary form that his chief fame as a writer lies. In it his obsession with the depicting of torture and physical suffering, is more suitable than in a novel. In it too his mordant and ironical humour without a trace of laughter or fun, his 'humour noire', is seen to best advantage.

His poetry too is worthy of high mention, and, at its best, is inspired by a note of bitter suffering not yet encountered in French poetry. He composed also one long poem, the noble symbolism of which foreshadows that of Baudelaire.

In his person Petrus Borel was a living protest against the utilitarianism and materialism of the reign of Louis Philippe. He had a loathing and contempt for bourgeois values and, in an age when everyone was prostituting his tal-

ent for gain—even Gautier sold his soul for the easy money of ephemeral journalism at a time when the new reviews made this a lucrative occupation for those whose scruples were not too fine—he was unable to follow the example of his contemporaries. It requires all sorts of qualities—both good and bad—to be able to exploit one's talent for gain, and Borel possessed none of them.

Yet the literary soil fertilised by Borel's suffering, and watered by his bitter tears, was eventually to prove a richer one for posterity than that of any of his contemporaries or immediate successors, except Baudelaire, and all subsequent schools of poetry—Symbolist to Surrealist—found inspiration in his writings.

Petrus Borel remains a figure typical of these years of transition, between 1830 and 1835, and he symbolises them to perfection, with their extravagance, their bombast, and their atmosphere of melodrama. Baudelaire said of him later, that there would have been something lacking in Romanticism if he had never existed, and it was to him, and not to more famous poets amongst his elders, that he turned for inspiration in his formative years. This fantastic and often absurd figure seized hold of his imagination as a young man, when he had not yet found his own personality; he sensed, beneath the theatrical gestures and the exaggerated acting of Borel's, the true nature of his inspiration, and he himself was able to achieve what his lycanthropic predecessor had only dimly conceived. (pp. 193-96)

> *Enid Starkie, in her* Pétrus Borel the Lycanthrope: His Life and Times, *New Directions, 1954, 220 p.*

Wallace Fowlie (essay date 1955)

[*Fowlie was one of the most highly regarded and versatile scholars of French literature. He has translated the work of major French dramatists and poets and has produced critical studies of Jean Cocteau, le Comte de Lautréamont, Stéphane Mallarmé, Arthur Rimbaud, and Stendhal, as well as a widely read historical survey of French literature. In the following excerpt from a review of Enid Starkie's* Pétrus Borel, *Fowlie focuses on Baudelaire's assessment of Borel.*]

Pétrus Borel is known to students of French literature largely through Baudelaire's short article on him, printed in the collection of prose pieces, *L'Art Romantique.* When Baudelaire wrote this article, in 1859, Borel's name was used by journalists to express their scorn and distaste for the macabre type of Romantic poetry and for the type of flamboyant genius characterized by excesses of bohemianism and excessive affectation. Baudelaire, who revered Borel and felt strong sympathy for him, explained the aptness of the name "Lycanthrope," associated with Borel. This "wolf-man" or "werewolf" behaved as a man demonized and living in the dark forests of melancholy. He exemplified a favorite word of Baudelaire, *le guignon,* which signifies that kind of evil fate which pursues a man and from which he is unable to recover. *Le Guignon* is a goddess possessing, more than any pope or lama, the privilege of infallibility. Baudelaire explains by *le guignon* the irreconcilables in the life of Borel, the genius of the poet in the preface poem of **Madame Putiphar,** and the epic skill of the writer in several scenes of this novel, and the endless difficulties and hardships he encountered throughout his life.

No theory is proposed by Baudelaire to explain the number of *guignons* in the career of Pétrus Borel. He merely hints at the symptoms of morbidity in the man's nature which maintained and even nurtured flagrant contradictions. Signs of psychic disturbance were evident even in Borel's handwriting, in his spelling, in the agony which the writing of the simplest letter caused him. The Romantic movement in France would not have been complete without the "Lycanthropy" of Pétrus Borel. Baudelaire distinguishes between the early phase of Romanticism when the imagination of the poets was concerned with the past, with nostalgia and regret, and the second phase, more active and violent and earthy. Borel was one of the most picturesque and vehement characters of this second phase. He incarnated the spirit of the *Bousingos* in his attire and in his hate for the king and the bourgeoisie. During the years 1830-1835, when he was most famous and influential, he expressed his approval of the emphasis on excessive color and form in literature and art, and he sympathized with the dandy's creed, with the Byronic pessimism and dilettantism of an entire generation which, paradoxically, was both turbulent and bored. (p. 145)

Wallace Fowlie, "Pétrus Borel," in Accent, *Vol. XV, No. 2, Spring, 1955, pp. 145-46.*

Albert J. George (essay date 1964)

[*George's* Short Fiction in France, 1800-1850 *provides an analysis of French short narrative writing—primarily the short story—from approximately the time of the French Revolution to the end of Romanticism. In the following excerpt, he places Borel within a "second generation" of Romantic writers who worked in short fiction, emphasizing Borel's reliance on typical themes and imagery of that period.*]

Pétrus Borel, with [Théophile] Gautier a leader of the *petits romantiques,* furnished an outstanding example of the second generation romantics. Supposedly endowed with artistic principles of impeccable purity, he nonetheless found it expedient to stretch them when necessity demanded. At first he had had his fiery say when he introduced in the preface of **Champavert** a short essay on "Marchand et voleur est synonyme":

> C'est un oiseau le barde, il doit vieillir austère,
> Sobre, pauvre, ignoré, farouche, soucieux,
> Ne chanter pour aucun et n'avoir rien sur la
>   terre
> Qu'une cape trouée, un poignard et les cieux!

Yet, when he came to write **Madame Putiphar,** the prologue conveyed much of the sadness that pervaded the young romantics as they finally came to suspect the illusory quality of their dreams. They would storm no castles, create no revolutions, leave no flaming monuments to their genius.

> Une douleur renaît pour une évanouie:
> Quand un chagrin s'éteint c'est qu'un autre est
>   éclos;
> La vie est une ronce aux pleurs épanouie.

Early in his literary career, this former architect had become an editor. In 1832 he founded *La Liberté, journal des arts,* a weekly dedicated to expounding principles that would set straight both the Institut and the academic critics. During the few months of the periodical's existence, he worked for "des hommes dévoués . . . à la gêne sous un régime bâtard"; he issued a constant stream of pugnacious articles and manifestoes, then was astonished when the general public failed to support him.

Encroaching economic malnutrition drove this *ci-devant* literary radical to take advantage of the fad for short narratives with **Champavert.** (pp. 190-91)

The *nouvelles,* as he called them, were built around the *bousingos'* favorite themes. In **"Monsieur de l'Argentière,"** *l'accusateur,* Apolline, engaged to the prefect who had raised her, was raped in the dark by her fiancé's friend, the public prosecutor. Cast out by the prefect, she abandoned her baby in a sewer and was condemned to die on the scaffold by her attacker. "Il n'osait lui parler

Title page of the 1833 edition of Champavert, contes immoraux *by Pétrus Borel. Woodcut by Godard after Gigoux.*

de son Dieu juste et bon; sa providence était trop compromise par cette vie fatale."

Borel's short narrative revealed a high-handed but unoriginal manner. The tale began with a long architect's description of a dining room in Louis XV style, actually irrelevant to the plot. Borel's theme came straight out of the mythology of his group: the wicked rich, the poor orphan, unjust justice, the futility of organized religion, and simple virtue conquered by sophisticated evil. All these were arranged in scenes, and each, in contemporary fashion, bore a title: *Was-ist-das?; Mater dolorosa; Moïse sauvé par des eaux;* and *Very wel.* Apolline was a naïve soul who fixed her own doom by asking the prefect to visit her mysteriously at night. This amazing girl received a man in the dark, was loved by him, and only too late realized he wore a beard, hence could not be her fiancé. Pétrus described her torments with meticulous care, his sarcasm steadily growing heavier; the prosecutor mocked Apolline's story and demanded the death penalty; no one could recognize obvious truth. Borel shifted from satire to horror, to pathos, to irony, his incidents regulated to show government officials in the worst possible light. For this reason, the prefect and the prosecutor received harsh treatment, the former given the supreme insult, "plus qu'un porc, c'était un préfet."

Two of the narratives, **"Jaquez Barraou le charpentier"** and **"Three Fingered Jack l'Obi,"** took place in exotic parts of the world. (pp. 191-92)

Pétrus was merely reworking old tales in his own *bousingo* manner. **"Jaquez Barraou"** might have been an ordinary story of misunderstanding and the defense of marital honor, but Borel made the jealousy monumental. Much of the narrative was told in dialogue, a technique unusual for a romantic, with local color spread on lavishly. Inevitably he worked in the black humor so characteristic of his group. (p. 192)

[Borel's] taste for the macabre carried over into **"Dina,"** a tale of the love of Aymar de la Rochegude for Dina, a Jewess from Lyon.

Pétrus reveled in romantic commonplaces dealing with the sense of evil and justice. Young love was frustrated by antisemitism, because of which a Christian father wounded his son with an arquebus. A loving child defied his bigoted parent; a beautiful girl was assaulted and killed by a scoundrel who then dared demand a fee for rescuing her body. Pétrus jibed at middle-class values by making the "good" Christians suffer from comparison with the "lowly" Jews. He could not resist attacking marriage as a social ill: "Celui qui a inventé le noeud du mariage a trouvé un bel et spécieux expédient, pour se venger des humains." His taste for the horrible seemed insatiable; he described Dina's death as minutely as he had the dissecting room. Like **"Andréa Vésalius,"** the story proceeded according to the formula for effectism, but, in this case, moved from presentiment to increasing horror, then to the double burial.

"Passereau l'écolier" combined horror with the triangle theme, no innovation except that Pétrus passed far beyond the usual *volupté décente* to an overt consideration of sex

and the *crime passionnel* in deliberate violation of all contemporary tabus. (p. 194)

Champavert forms a companion volume to [Gautier's] *Jeunes-France,* with many of the same themes, but, whereas Gautier was mocking the lunatic fringe, Pétrus was reproducing the hurt reactions of the *petit cénacle,* and without Gautier's sense of form. Life overflowed with agony; love, generally for a mistress, met the frustrating disapproval of a stodgy society. Since Borel understood the brief narrative only in terms of length, he simply beaded episodes together to express the *petit romantique*'s sick humor, his young sense of lusty love, and his desire to ruffle the middle class. He brought little to the genre beyond the bizarre incidents of his now faded stories. In this he represents the reactions of youngsters who despised prose because they considered themselves poets' poets. Borel was the original angry young man in an age that punished its angry young men by placing them in literary Coventry.

Pétrus rapidly discovered this fact of nineteenth-century literary rebellion, as **"Jérôme Chasseboeuf "** proved. Published in two issues of *L'Artiste* in 1834, it was a syrupy Horatio Alger story about Jérôme, the musically brilliant son of poor parents who left for Russia, where he hoped his music would sell. Jérôme married a baroness by posing as a French noble, then became a famous composer under a pseudonym and faithfully sent his parents an allowance. Poor Pétrus had lost most of his fire; the only remnant of his rebellion showed in his description of Jérôme as an apostle of the new music who, like Berlioz, had gone abroad for recognition. Otherwise the hero exhibited all the standard virtues: he loved his parents, was honest, patriotic, hardworking, and fearless—an obvious candidate for the Chamber.

The last shred of his diminishing talent went into **"Le Trésor de la caverne d'Arcueil,"** published in April, 1843. An ancient buried treasure, a beautiful sorceress, and a magic show provided the interest. The tale supposedly came from a mysterious prisoner's account of how a rich miser and his nephew had been trapped in an underground vault and died amidst their treasure. Pétrus liberally sprinkled oaths throughout the tale, but nothing could help. He had come to the end of the line and would suffer the cruelest blow a former *bousingo* could receive: poverty drove him to accept a post in Algeria as a government employee. (pp. 196-97)

> *Albert J. George, "The Second Generation: Pétrus Borel,"* in his Short Fiction in France, 1800-1850, *Syracuse University Press, 1964, pp. 188-97.*

Victor Brombert (essay date 1969)

[*Brombert is an American critic who has written extensively on modern French literature, including a major study of the works of Gustave Flaubert. In the excerpt below, Brombert analyzes Borel's novel,* Madame Putiphar, *focusing on its place in the context of the Gothic tradition and on Borel's handling of the imagery of the prison-fortress.*]

Madame Putiphar (1838) should be better known. Pétrus Borel, a member of the "petit cénacle" to which Théophile Gautier and Gérard de Nerval also belonged, was one of the most colorful exponents of "frenetic" literature. He liked to call himself *le lycanthrope*—the wolf-man. ***Champavert*** (1833), subtitled "Contes immoraux," established him as a specialist in gory tales at a time when "charnel-house" writing was in fashion. Some of Flaubert's early exercises in literary violence were heavily influenced by these texts; even as late as 1861, when he was writing *Salammbô,* he had Pétrus Borel in mind as he himself described tortures and disembowelments. Rape and child murder are among the more innocent subjects of Borel.

At first glance, ***Madame Putiphar***—Borel's only full-length fiction—appears a less outrageous work than ***Champavert.*** As for the title, it is meant to evoke not a Biblical setting but the aspect of the Joseph story that deals with temptation, purity, and injustice. The "madame" in question is Mme. de Pompadour, and her victim is a handsome young Irishman in exile whom she has jailed for life when he rejects her lascivious advances. The lasciviousness is suggested with skill. But it is the desolation and despair in the prisoner's underground dungeon that are at the center of this novel and that account for its most powerful pages.

The story opens with a prefatory poem, an allegorical prologue in which the soul is assailed by three temptations: the world, the cloistered existence, and the seduction of Death. In part, this moralistic beginning is a concession to the taste of the time. "Philosophical" considerations frequently surrounded the flimsiest fictional productions, and the theme of metaphysical temptations was popular. Borel's preliminary poem about surrender to life, withdrawal from worldly involvement, and attraction to nothingness and non-being is, however, of particular importance. First, because of its tense, feverish, obsessive tone that prefigures the pungency and affective concentration of some of Baudelaire's finest poetry.

> *Crains les tentations, les remords, les dangers,*
> *Les assauts de la chair et les chutes de l'âme,*
> *Sous le vent du désert tes désirs flamberont . . .*

Lines such as these would be perfectly at home in *Les Fleurs du Mal.* In fact, Baudelaire admired this "strange poem" for its intensity and "glittering sonorousness."

But equally interesting are this juxtaposition of poetry and prose, and the relationship—still clumsy, to be sure—between fiction and lyric expression. For novelists in the Romantic and post-Romantic period not only try to merge fiction and poetry; consciously or unconsciously, they tend to conceive of "poetic" fiction, and ultimately of fiction as poetry. In this respect, the importance of images, especially of recurrent images, cannot be stressed too much for the study of modern fiction. It is this increasing function of basic images in the novel which so clearly validates the thematic approach. Thus considered, Borel's poem-prologue is not merely a virtuoso piece, an idiosyncratic and unrelated expression of the writer; it is a thematic overture centering on the antitheses of involvement-withdrawal, freedom-oppression, movement-immobility. The cloister is here, in a sense, the central symbol—both

as a positive and a negative value, as an expression of yearning and of fear. Cloister and anti-cloister in the prologue point to prison and anti-prison in the novel itself. This thematic link not only exists between the poem and the story, but provides the basic unity within ***Madame Putiphar.*** The motif of incarceration—in terms of attraction as well as horror—is at the heart of the book.

From a historical point of view, Borel's work is a valuable Romantic document: morbidity, the poetry of failure, a strident note of rebellion, the rhetoric of despair, a taste for violence and sadistic eroticism, an obsession with political tyranny, self-pity, yet also an irrepressible pride—all these elements are to be found here, sometimes in excessive doses. "Without Pétrus Borel, there would be a gap in Romanticism," writes Baudelaire. In an essay devoted to Borel ["Pétrus Borel"], at a time everybody had forgotten about him, Baudelaire stressed with characteristic lucidity the epic grandeur of some of the scenes, especially those in the prison where the description of "dungeon horrors and tortures" matches the "vigor of Maturin." Baudelaire's comment is doubly relevant: it points to the main theme of the novel, and the allusion to the Reverend R. C. Maturin, author of *Melmoth the Wanderer* (1820), shrewdly suggests that ***Madame Putiphar*** is related to the tradition of the Gothic novel.

Structurally, there can be no doubt about the central nature of the incarceration theme. Just as the novel deals with a double attempt at seduction in a confined atmosphere (Mme. Putiphar vainly provokes the sexual desire of Patrick, Pharaoh-Louis XV succeeds in raping Deborah), so the protagonists, because of their virtue, are arbitrarily jailed, the one in the relatively "happy jail" of Sainte-Marguerite, the other in the awesome fort of Vincennes and later in the Bastille. This prison motif is further stressed by other parallel developments: family and city are viewed as places of captivity; Patrick is joined in prison by his friend Fitz-Harris; two separate jails are their places of martyrdom (the repetition suggests the hopelessness of their situation); within their prison they move from a gloomy cell to an even more atrocious cesspool-dungeon where they are spared neither cloacal horrors nor the tortures of hunger. The vertical descent symbolizes the downward movement toward despair.

This acrid book, the cynical vehemence of which betrays the vulnerable sensibility of its author, reads almost like a parody of romantic horrors. Evil, in its most physical presence, affirms itself through destructive lechery, social inequities, vengeance, the pleasure of human degradation, slow tortures leading to raving madness. Patrick, though finally liberated by the Revolution after more than twenty-five years of jail, has to be confined in the insane asylum of Charenton. (Is there not an echo here of the Marquis de Sade's destiny?) The cruelty of the jailers, symbolized by their dashing out the brains of the prisoners' dog, is outdone by the cruelty of fate. There is no doubt a measure of romantic self-consciousness here. But we are far from Jules Janin's tongue-in-cheek violence in *L'Ane mort* (1829), where debauchery, prostitution, murder, macabre elements, sadism and voyeurism in jail, and hints of hideous copulations, remain part of a literary game and are calculated to convey an ironic attitude of "social pessimism." It is not surprising that Jules Janin, who himself indulged in sensationalism (his "lieu abominable qu'on pourrait appeler l'enfer" suggests a Dantesque atmosphere), should have been scandalized by **Madame Putiphar.** The reason is simple: Pétrus Borel was *serious* about the horrors he described.

Baudelaire's mention of Maturin is indeed apt. The tradition of the Gothic novel with its castles, tyrannical fathers proud of their lineage, its dungeons, vaults, pits, cells, underground passages and cloistered anguish, its toads, reptiles, haunted locales and violent eroticism, is no doubt a predominantly English specialty. Thus Eino Railo could rightfully give *The Haunted Castle* (1927) the subtitle "A Study of the Elements of English Romanticism." But the tradition was not limited to England. Von Gerstenberg and E. T. A. Hoffmann in Germany, Balzac and Victor Hugo in France—to mention but a few—also wrote in this "dark" vein.

Elements of the Gothic tradition are clearly relevant to a study of Pétrus Borel's novel. Horace Walpole's *The Castle of Otranto* (1764) characteristically centers on a crime that has been committed and not yet avenged. A father-despot, the terror of isolation in a "labyrinth of darkness," the theme of treachery, are at the heart of Walpole's influential text. Matthew G. Lewis's *The Monk* (1795), though it tends to empty the Gothic tradition of supernatural elements, stresses the cruel and the macabre. Forced religious vocation, hideous prisons, immurements, a sacrilegious rape in a crypt, morbid details, make of this a particularly gruesome work. Some of its elements seem to prefigure the tone and the subject of **Madame Putiphar:** the "charnel-house" material with its repulsive objects, the theme of putrefaction, the atrocities in solitary confinement, the vengeance by a mob. As for Maturin's *Melmoth the Wanderer,* it points forward directly to the lightless, airless, and oppressive world of Pétrus Borel. Especially the second part, "The Tale of the Spaniard," which presents a series of variations on captivity and asphyxiating confinement, shows many affinities with Borel's fiction. The hellish abode of stone ("I awoke *in the darkness of day*" admirably sums up this death-in-life) is here also a setting that suggests Dantesque sufferings. In fact, the Ugolino motif is exploited in the story of the two immured lovers. (pp. 143-46)

But no matter how much, on one level, **Madame Putiphar** may have in common with [the] Gothic tradition, in particular with the multiple value of the basic prison image, it also stands apart in some essential aspects. Pétrus Borel indulges very little in anti-clericalism, and not at all in satanism and the supernatural. Sin, in the theological sense, does not concern him. Nor does the splitting of the personality and the loss of identity. Horror is here despiritualized, and the basic image of the "haunted castle" has vanished.

The reason for these dissimilarities is that two traditions are simultaneously at work in **Madame Putiphar,** and that they have come to merge: on the one hand the conventions of the "roman noir" and on the other the themes and images of what might be called "Revolutionary" literature.

The two are in fact more related than might appear at first glance. Not only is there a merger between the two currents toward the end of the eighteenth century (antimonasticism and the Bastille myth provided convenient points of encounter), but it is clear that some of the Gothic novels were directly inspired by revolutionary themes. Thus Lewis probably found the basic inspiration for *The Monk* in the Parisian theater of the Revolution (he was in Paris in 1791), and in particular in Monvel's *Les Victimes cloîtrées,* with its archetypal figure of the lustful, malevolent monk. The Revolutionary theater was indeed rich in oppressive conventual and prison settings. Marie-Joseph Chénier's *Fénelon, ou les Religieuses de Cambrai* and Charles Pougens' *Julie, ou la Religieuse de Nismes*—the titles themselves suggest the theme of claustration—are characteristic of this fashion. The liberation of the victimized nuns seems to go hand in hand in these works with the emancipation from the Ancien Régime, of which the taking and the razing of the Bastille was the most forceful symbol.

For the Bastille had come to represent the notion of tyranny, and acquired the dimensions of a myth. This myth-engendering quality of the prison-fortress is one of the most interesting phenomena of French social and intellectual history, and it has had a strong impact on literature. Many texts appeared at the end of the eighteenth century which focused attention on the infamous state-prison. Mirabeau's indictment of arbitrary jailings (*Des Lettres de Cachet,* 1782) paved the way for innumerable polemical and documentary pamphlets such as *Mémoires historiques et authentiques sur la Bastille* and *La Bastille dévoilée* (1789) in which revolutionary rhetoric and plain sensationalism vie with each other. Perhaps more important still, so far as French fiction is concerned, are the various memoirs, authentic and apocryphal, by famous state prisoners. Baron Trenck in Germany, Linguet and Latude in France, provided the direct inspiration for many a novel dealing with unjust incarcerations and thrilling escapes.

The poetic potential of these pamphlets, documents, and memoirs is not to be denied. Cells, chains, dreams, memories, a peculiar sense of time—all these elements lend themselves to literary elaboration. Quite spontaneously, it would seem, a mythical vocabulary came to surround the image of the Bastille: references to Cerberus and Charon, to the "manes" of the victims, to the "horrible Tartarus," to the "Hydra" of tyranny, are not at all uncommon. This type of vocabulary is echoed by a novelist like Alexandre Dumas, who, in *Ange Pitou* for instance, speaks of Sisyphus, Titan, fabulous monsters and gigantic animals, as he describes the Bastille.

This myth of the Bastille is central to **Madame Putiphar.** The novel leads up to a theme of political expiation: the People, glorified as a divinely inspired force (a "verge de la vertu de Dieu"), ruthlessly avenges all the crimes of the Ancien Régime. Borel does not explore or exploit the revolutionary mystique. Enid Starkie quite rightly points out that political fervor never was his main inspiration. But it is true that among the sources of **Madame Putiphar** are Latude's prison memoirs, *Le Despotisme dévoilé,* and undoubtedly also Camille Desmoulins' *Révolutions de*

France et de Brabant. Typically, Borel's Bastille assumes "mythic" characteristics. It is a "stone bull" (a "taureau de pierre") very much like the monstrous bull of Phalaris into which victims were thrown alive; it is compared to the Laconian cape and cavern, Tenarus, close by the gates of hell. During the siege of the Bastille, the crowd is compared to David as he faced the giant, the fortress is seen as "the body of a monster," and its inside is "a horrible labyrinth."

The echoes of the "Bastille-literature" are not only clear, they are conscious. Deborah, at Sainte-Marguerite, visits the cell of the famous prisoner with the Iron Mask. The names of various important state prisoners—all part of history and also of the prison-legend—are mentioned: Count de Thunn, Lenglet-Dufresnoy, Crébillon, Diderot, Mirabeau, and of course Latude, who also waited for the death of Mme. de Pompadour and in whose text she also appears as a royal prostitute without compassion. And when Patrick explains to his fellow prisoner Fitz-Harris that tyrants expose you to death, but do not kill, he is in fact paraphrasing Beccaria.

A prison, one of the victims in the novel explains, is a sanctuary, an "asyle sacré"—but this not in the sense of a happy captivity of which there are so many examples in Western literature. We are very far here from the prison to which King Lear looks forward, where he hopes that he and Cordelia will sing like birds in a cage, and take upon them "the mystery of things." To be sure, there are lyric elements in *Madame Putiphar.* Deborah's detention in the Mediterranean fortress of Sainte-Marguerite is of this nature. The governor, a benevolent gentleman of the old school, tells his prisoner that she can live "in calm, quiet and comfort," that she can consider herself "as free as the birds" who build their nest into the walls of the fortress. The confinement on this "delicious island" is further enhanced by guided excursions and by pleasant evenings in the governor's salon.

Yet *Madame Putiphar* hardly belongs to the same tradition as Saintine's *Picciola* and Stendhal's *La Chartreuse de Parme.* Jails may convince Borel's protagonists that the most sacred duty of the prisoner is to seek freedom. But their dismal reality is not transmuted into beauty. The overwhelming impressions are those of injustice, abjection, and horror. It is here that Borel's true interest and talent lie. The sepulchral atmosphere of death-in-life, the poetry of bars, locks, and bolts, the gloomy poetry of hostile silence—all these Borel brings out with deliberate "realism." Bitterly he describes the cell with its muddy soil, its oozing wall, its latrine hole. Truth stinks—this seems to be Borel's predominant idea. "When truth is made of mud and blood, when it offends the sense of smell, I say that it is made of mud and blood, I let it stink . . .!" This quasi-proclamation of realistic intent also points to one of the permanent aspects of literary realism: its underlying moral fervor.

This moral foundation of realism, often semi-conscious in nature, is here related to the basic prison image, which traditionally lends itself to the exploring of moral and metaphysical categories. For it is not enough to explain the prevalence of claustration images in nineteenth-century literature by referring to the political realities (the Ancien Régime, the Revolution, the Restoration), to social problems (penology, the question of capital punishment), or to the influence of Piranesi, the Gothic novel and the Marquis de Sade. All these factors are no doubt relevant; but they also correspond to fundamental Romantic concerns and obsessions, and have been given a specific valorization. The dialectical tensions between the finite and infinity, between fatality and revolt, between oppression and the dream of freedom, between victimization and vengeance—antitheses so meaningful to the Romantic writers—are repeatedly given a symbolic setting in the context of solitary confinement. With Pétrus Borel, the theme of fatality is bound up with self-pity, and often degenerates into an unstructured rhetoric. On the other hand, the antithesis of tyranny-freedom provides him with a unified theme and justifies, on the level of abstraction as well as in terms of metaphoric texture, the oppressive prison images in *Madame Putiphar.*

There is in every age one powerful individuality round whom the others gravitate, like planets round their sun. Petrus Borel was that sun and none of us tried to resist the force of his attraction. As soon as one had entered his path one revolved happily round him as if following a law of nature.

—*Théophile Gautier, in his* Histoire du Romantisme, 1872.

Madame Putiphar is indeed, from beginning to end, a novel of tyranny. It opens under the very sign of oppression. The father, Lord Cockermouth, is a despot who not only talks of locking up his daughter in a "house of correction," but who inflicts his physical violences on his family. It is not enough that he throws a dish at her, he has her almost murdered. The tyrannical father, forcing his daughter into exile, is also a tyrannical husband whose brutal laughter sounds like an "onomatopoeic rendering of a prison lock in a melodrama." Borel's comparison may be a trifle grotesque, but it is revealing of the thematic unity of the book. For passion also is seen as a despotic force—a "puissance qui nous possède." And what is true of love is true of eroticism and of character. What applies to the individual also applies to a collective reality: French libertine society, the political oppressions of a "cowardly and dark tyranny," the moral dissolution of a period undermined by its own sense of inequity. It is not by coincidence, moreover, that the two heroes-in-exile are Irish. Not only are they victims of tyranny in a country whose mores they cannot accept, but their own country is oppressed by England. Thus Borel glorifies local dialects as a form of resistance to tyranny, and pities poor Ireland which "moaned, crushed by the most inhuman persecutions," while every attempt to break its bondage only fur-

his misfortune to the evil doings of the demon who had been tormenting him and completely loses his sanity. The end of the story finds him dead in a mental hospital where, incarcerated, he had enjoyed recounting this vision: "Gottfried Wolfgang, quelque temps après cette vision qu'il se plaisait souvent à raconter, mourut pensionnaire dans une maison de fous".

In this tale, the activities linked to the hero's insanity are presented as negative substitutes for more reality-affirming behavior. Voracious reading replaces social action; fantasizing about women replaces authentic sexual encounters; finally, taking pleasure in telling bizarre stories as an incarcerated mental patient replaces being out in the world having "real" adventures. While Gottfried's fruitful imagination, and particularly its morbid aspects, certainly correspond to the ideals of negativity displayed in, and upheld by, the works of France's "frénétique" Romantics of which Borel is a representative the tale, through its development of aspects of the opposition between the real and the imaginary, or between authenticity, or originality, and imitation, may be understood as well as an examination of the potency of its author's own imagination.

Borel's tale combines an illustration of what Todorov in his work on the genre has referred to as the propensity of fantastic literature to actualize the literal meaning of a figurative expression, with a rhetorical account of the tale's production. On one level, what is initially merely suggested as the hero's insanity is confirmed and made concrete by his discovery of the prior beheading of the incarnation of the woman of his dreams. In this case it is the two meanings of the expression "to lose one's head"—to become insane, to be decapitated—which intersect and are realized in this tale. On another level, the hero's sick imagination ("son imagination malade")—symptom of, and synonym for, his mental instability—may be considered as an imagination that focuses on morbid phenomena, on the one hand, and as one that is ailing, that is, which functions improperly or not at all, on the other.

The equivalence established in the text between insanity and decapitation is grounded in an identification developed between the character who goes insane—Gottfried—and the one who is beheaded—the mysterious woman whom he loves. In addition to those similarities to which Gottfried alludes when he offers his protection—both he and she are "sans amis dans cette ville"—others are posed later when the two characters agree never to separate. At that moment, Gottfried tells of his mysterious dreams, convinced that she "avait possédé son coeur avant qu'il l'eût vue"; she, in turn, describes having been drawn to him by "une impulsion toute aussi surnaturelle". "[N]ous ne faisons plus qu'un," declares Gottfried, " . . . soyons tout l'un pour l'autre!".

Furthermore, the agents or instruments ostensibly responsible for Gottfried's insanity, on the one hand, and the woman's beheading, on the other, are described in suggestively similar manners. The "influence maligne," the "mauvais génie" linked at the beginning to Gottfried's breakdown and, at the end, to his horrible experience, is described as "always hovering over his head". (pp. 1063-65)

Significantly, moreover, Gottfried's first encounter with the woman finds her "au pied de l'échafaud". Thus, both evil spirit and guillotine hover menancingly over their victims' heads, waiting for the moment to destroy them.

Finally, both Gottfried and the woman are associated with similar places, places of shelter from the world's turmoil. Seeking refuge from the bloodshed of the Revolution, Gottfried is described as "enfermé pendant des journées entières, dans les grands dépôts de livres de Paris, ces catacombes des auteurs en delinquium, ces Romes souterraines de la pensée . . .". Similarly, when Gottfried, struck by the strangeness of the woman's situation, asks her if she has "peut-étre un asile," she exclaims, "Oui, dans la tombe!". Both characters are in this way associated with underground enclosures, images of death and burial, from which they momentarily emerge in order to participate in Gottfried's vision. Both, in other words, are vampires, though, as it turns out, she more literally than he.

Thus is elaborated the association between insanity and a loss, a literal loss, of one's head. More generally, we associate insanity with the loss or suppression of reason, a loss which may result in an enhancement of the powers of fantasy. **"Gottfried Wolfgang,"** of course, develops that association; it is an insane Gottfried who both has the vision, and recounts the story of the temporary resuscitation of a guillotined woman. On the other hand, it is also a voracious reader who imagines such a phenomenon. To imagine is to invent, but also, as the word's etymology reveals, to imitate. "To imagine," in the sense of "to imitate," has direct bearing on the second referent of the expression "sick imagination"—one which is impotent, which dysfunctions—attributed to the tale's protagonist, and which we can relate as well to the process of its production on the part of Borel. A fact known to critics and to literary historians alike, though not widely acknowledged by compilers of short story anthologies, is that Borel's tale is his nearly verbatim adaption, indeed a plagiarized translation into French of American writer Washington Irving's tale *Adventure of the German Student,* published in 1824, and whose hero is one named Gottfried Wolfgang. With the exception of a few small but non-negligible details, Borel's **"Gottfried Wolfgang"** is the product of its author's reading and rewriting (retelling) of another's text. The role of such a text may be to question the creative status of the imagination of he who claims it as his own invention.

The relationship between the story and its repeated telling is inscribed in the two versions. In Borel's version, the author adds a major preamble, absent in Irving's text, in which a temporary first-person narrator tells of having received a manuscript of the tale from an innkeeper who, in turn, had found it among the effects of a young Englishman who had committed suicide years before. . . . [The] narrator describes wondering whether the story was an invention of the dead man or borrowed and translated from another source. (pp. 1065-66)

Furthermore, in both Borel's and Irving's versions, on the level of narration, while it is the character Gottfried who has the central vision, another voice is responsible for its transmission. In Irving's text, from the collection *Tales of a Traveller*, it is a mysteriously nervous gentleman, one "with a haunted head," who entertains an audience with the story that, as he reveals at the end, Gottfried supposedly told him. In Borel's text, an ambiguous, and not easily situated, textual voice, again at the end of the story, naturalizes the events by adding that an insane Gottfried enjoyed recounting them while a mental patient.

Finally, there appears in both versions a link between Gottfried's own obsessive reading and his capacity both to imagine the events of the tale and to retell them. The insanity which enables him to have the vision and retell it is the same mental instability which was provoked by his voracious reading of other's texts. Irving describes the recluse as "a literary ghoul, feeding in the charnel-house of decayed literature"; Borel calls him "une manière de vampire littéraire s'engraissant au charnier de la science morte et de la littérature en dissolution". Gottfried's vampirism, to which I have already alluded, is a "book-eating" activity, one which both enhances his imagination and undermines, or places into question, its generative powers.

A close examination of the events underscoring the tale's fantastic elements—that is, a young man's love for a woman who soon dies of having been beheaded prior to their meeting—reveals that they, too, constitute a mirror of the tale's repeated telling. The events of this deceptively simple plot create a labyrinthine structure introducing alternating images of separation and (re-)attachment. From this perspective, the expression "to lose one's head" acquires a new significance. The initial and extra-textual—that is, having occurred outside the frame of the story—detaching of the woman's head from her body by the guillotine blade may be read as a homologue for the separation of an author from his work, his *corpus*. The woman's temporary resuscitation, and her reappropriation by Gottfried the reader-teller in his student's room "lumbered with books and papers," as Irving tells us, repeats the story's revival in the hands of a new author. Finally, at her (second) death, the revelation of her recent execution repeats it in a sense, as it repeats the story's potential to be appropriated by another teller.

It is in this context that some of the differences between the two works are provocative. The first difference which interests me here concerns how the two characters ended their evening together, specifically, where in Gottfried's room the young lady spent the night. In neither version is anything specific revealed until the recounting of the next morning's events. At this point, Irving's text tells of Gottfried's having left "his bride sleeping" and returning to find her "lying with her head hanging over the bed". Borel's text refers not to Gottfried's "bride," but rather to his "fiancée" and takes pains to specify that she was discovered with her head hanging "hors du vaste fauteuil sur lequel elle avait voulu passer la nuit, enveloppée pudiquement dans son manteau". In Irving's text—that is, the one I will, for the moment, call the "original,"—the passion between the two characters is consummated; in Borel's, it clearly is not. Viewed from the perspective described above—from that of Gottfried as appropriator of a *cor-*

pus—the activities of Irving's Gottfried suggest the role of progenitor, of creator, of, finally, author. This planting of the seed of creation is not associated with Borel's Gottfried.

Another difference appears at the moment of truth. In Irving's text, after the policeman explains that the woman had been executed the day before, it is he who unfastens the black band on her neck; at that moment, her head detaches and rolls to the floor. In Borel's text, it is Gottfried himself who removes her black band; the head is not detached, only the scars indicating that it had once been so are described. These blatantly different structures may be linked to subtly different attitudes towards the story's reappropriation; Irving's text releases itself totally to the appropriation of another, an appropriation which effectively occurred. Borel's text, while signaling the potential for such a (re)appropriation, at the same time somehow denies or negates its realization, present or future.

A final difference concerns the initial reference to the guillotine, and this on the level of the signifier itself. Describing Gottfried's arrival at the Place de Grève, Irving writes, "As Wolfgang was crossing the square, he shrank back at horror at finding himself close by the guillotine". Describing the same moment, Borel's version reads: "Comme il traversait la place de Grève, soudain il se trouva près de la g . . . Non, jamais ma plume ne saura écrire ce mot hideux . . . il recul avec effroi. . . .". In Borel's text the signifier whose referent is the instrument of decapitation is itself anomalously "decapitated." Instrument of decapitation, the guillotine, yes, but since we can attribute this activity of separation to he who tells another's tale, to he who detaches the *corpus* of/from another, this truncated signifier may refer as well to the plagiarizer. In this way, Borel's text, through this minor alteration of a signifier—the concreteness of which joins the equivalence established between the "loss of one's head" and the "sick imagination"—calls attention to a lack attached to the instrument of the story's production, that is, to the storyteller (Borel and his textual reflection, Gottfried) and to his imagination.

The suggestion offered here, namely, that one of the concerns of **"Gottfried Wolfgang"** is to be a text about textual (re)production, is rendered all the more compelling when one considers that—as is demonstrated in some of the critical literature examining the work—the idea for the tale does not, in fact, have its source in Irving's imagination, nor is Borel's text the final instance of its telling. In his 1922 biography of Borel, Aristide Marie refers, not without indignation, to the overt resemblance between a tale written in 1850 by Alexandre Dumas Père entitled *La Femme au collier de velours* and his own subject's tale **"Gottfried Wolfgang."** Walter Reichart, in belated response to Marie's protests, discloses what appears to be the very first discovery of Borel's own plagiarism of Irving's *Adventure of the German Student*. In a footnote to this piece, moreover, Reichart recalls that Irving himself, as is mentioned in his journal, had received the idea for his tale from Thomas Moore who, in turn, as the latter himself records in his own journal, had heard it from the English writer, Horace Smith.

Finally, F. P. Smith, in his own 1938 reiteration of the information and speculation surrounding this succession of borrowings, focuses on what Dumas reveals in the introduction to his own version, namely that it was Charles Nodier on his death-bed who had transmitted to him the idea for his tale. While, as Smith speculates, it is not entirely impossible that Nodier furnished Dumas with the subject, both these writers could have encountered the central anecdote in either Irving or Borel's versions. Furthermore, as Smith again reveals, Irving himself, in his introduction to *Tales of a Traveller*, indicates having heard that the anecdote upon which is based *Adventure of the German Student* existed "somewhere in French." Another critic cited by Smith, Charles Leland, claimed in 1900 to have located the "original anecdote" underlying Dumas' and Irving's tales in a collection of ghost stories entitled *L'Histoire des fantômes et de démons* (1819). According to Smith, the only story in this collection from which Irving or Dumas could have drawn, and the one which most likely inspired Horace Smith, is entitled *Le Revenant succube.* It relates the experience of a man who meets, falls in love, and shares his bed with, a woman who dies and who is later recognized as having been hanged months before. Smith reveals that this anecdote is itself found again in *Le Diable peint par lui-même* (1819) and *L'Histoire des vampires et des spectres malfaisans* (1820), a discovery which further attests to its continual detachment and dissemination.

To conclude, Borel's tale was written at a time in literary history when the Romantic movement, once great deposer of the classical tradition of reason and rigor, found the yield of its own valorized ideal—the creative imagination—to have been, paradoxically, integrated into the canon of literary norms. No longer "revolutionary," the behavior, belief systems and literary products of the Second Generation of Romantics had in many cases become clichés, cultural myths. The "new" was new no longer and perhaps has never been since. Such a situation announces the dilemma of the modern, its basis, as Jean-Luc Steinmetz writes, "moins sur l'innovation flambante que sur la vaste remise en circulation du presque inutilisable . . . du déchet du passé." The repeated telling of the story of the resurrection of a guillotined woman who becomes the object of desire for a hero unconsciously harboring certain necrophilic tendencies may be read as one representation of such a dilemma. **"Gottfried Wolfgang,"** as well as its antecedent and future forms, tell of the transformation of a tale into myth, and through this transformation, per-

haps, the mythic imagination reveals the imagination as myth. (pp. 1066-69)

> *Ann L. Murphy, "Pétrus Borel's 'Gottfried Wolfgang': Intertext and the Struggles of a Sick Imagination," in* MLN, *Vol. 105, No. 5, December, 1990, pp. 1063-70.*

FURTHER READING

Brombert, Victor. "Pétrus Borel: Prison and the Gothic Tradition." In his *The Romantic Prison: The French Tradition,* pp. 50-61. Princeton, New Jersey: Princeton University Press, 1978.

> Discusses prison imagery in Borel's *Madame Putiphar.* This study was originally published in French as *La prison romantique* in 1975.

Clarétie, A. Marie, and Clarétie, J., eds. *Oeuvres complètes . . . de P. Borel,* 1877. 5 vols. Reprint. Geneva: Slatkine Reprints, 1967.

> Earliest complete edition of Borel's writings.

Hassel, Jon B. "The Formation of the *Petit Cénacle.*" *Romance Notes* XVIII, No. 3 (Spring 1978): 338-42.

> Explores the personal and professional alliances among the poets and artists who called their association the *Petit Cénacle.*

Reichart, Walter A. "Washington Irving as a Source for Borel and Dumas." *Modern Language Notes* 51 (June 1936): 388-89.

> Brief note on the relationship between "La femme au collier de velours" by Alexandre Dumas the elder, Borel's "Gottfried Wolfgang," and Washington Irving's "The Adventure of the German Student."

Rosenthal, Jonathan. Review of *Champavert, contes immoraux* by Pétrus Borel, edited by Jean-Luc Steinmetz. *The French Review* 61, No. 6 (May 1988): 964-65.

> Favorable review of the first French critical edition of Borel's collected short stories.

Dion Boucicault

1820-1890

(Born Dionysius Lardner Boursiquot; also wrote under the pseudonym Lee Moreton) Anglo-Irish dramatist.

INTRODUCTION

Boucicault, one of the most popular and prolific playwrights of the nineteenth century, was renowned for his well-crafted comedies and melodramas. Borrowing heavily from well-known works of the period and often basing his plays on French originals, Boucicault reworked his source materials to augment their popular appeal and often added sensational stage effects to ensure the success of his productions. Although his plays are no longer widely performed, critics agree that his best works transcend their function as popular literature and rival the classic comedies of Restoration and eighteenth-century masters.

There is little certainty concerning the details of Boucicault's early life. Unofficial records indicate that he was born in Dublin sometime in 1820, yet Boucicault himself always gave 1822 as the year of his birth. His mother was an Irish woman named Anna Darley Boursiqout, and although Boucicault considered Darley's husband, Samuel, to be his father, many believe that he was the illegitimate son of Dionysius Lardner, a scholar and close friend of the family who was also Boucicault's godfather. Lardner financed Boucicault's education after his parents' separation, sending him to prestigious primary and secondary schools in and around London. While a student, Boucicault became enamored of the theater, and he wrote his first play at the age of sixteen. When he left school in 1837, his mother's family arranged for him to be apprenticed as a civil engineer; however, the following year he left his position to become a professional actor.

Adopting the stage name Lee Moreton, Boucicault appeared in numerous productions in 1838 and continued writing plays. In October of that year he acted in the first professional production of one of his own plays, *A Legend of the Devil's Dyke,* and by 1840 he had ceased acting to devote his full time to writing. In 1841 his comedy *London Assurance* was staged by the renowned actors Charles Mathews and Madame Vestris at the Covent Garden Theatre; the enormous success of the production brought fame to the formerly unknown playwright. During the next decade, Boucicault created a series of equally successful comedies and melodramas, the majority of them based on popular French plays of the period. He also spent a great deal of time in France, and it was during this time that he began using the surname Boucicault, claiming to be a member of the French aristocracy.

In 1853 Boucicault moved to New York, and although he toured the English-speaking world for much of the re-

mainder of his life, the United States remained his primary place of residence. In addition to writing and producing plays, he returned to the stage in 1854 and thereafter played the lead roles in many of his best-known works. One of the most respected and powerful figures in the American theater, Boucicault also became a pioneer in the field of theatrical production, creating spectacular effects including floods and fires onstage. Despite what critics regard as a decline in the quality of his work during the last decade of his life, Boucicault remained active in the theater, reprising successful roles from earlier plays onstage and continuing to write. He died of a heart attack in 1890.

Intended as pure entertainment for nineteenth-century audiences, the majority of Boucicault's plays have received little attention in the twentieth century. His most popular works focus on notable controversies of his day, such as slavery (in *The Octoroon; or, Life in Louisiana*) and slums and economic depression (in *The Poor of New York*); yet critics charge that his treatments generally exploited the sensational aspects of his subjects and failed to probe their serious implications. *The Octoroon,* in particular, is discussed as an example of Boucicault's unwillingness to present his audience with unpalatable moral instruction;

seeming to address the unfairness of slavery through the story of a young woman who cannot marry her lover because she is one-eighth black, the play does not contain a specifically antislavery message. Moreover, several commentators have pointed out that the play's original ending, in which the heroine commits suicide, was quickly changed to a happy one after British audiences objected, effectively blunting any antislavery suggestion in the plot.

Nevertheless, critics note that two categories of Boucicault's works—his early comedies and his Irish plays—are distinct from his other works and deserve wider acclaim. The early comedies are modeled after eighteenth-century comedies of manners, incorporating fast-paced and often unlikely plots, stereotypical characters, and bantering dialogue. Critics note that while Boucicault's dialogue is not of the same quality as that of the eighteenth-century masters he emulated, his plots are well crafted, and many consider these comedies the most adept of the period. Boucicault's Irish plays drew upon the stage tradition of the stereotypical Irish buffoon while at the same time creating more sympathetic and somewhat more realistic depictions of such characters. This combination of subtle humor with realistic tragedy, along with Boucicault's adept use of Irish speech and mannerisms, created dramas more convincing than the melodramas that dominated the Victorian stage; as a result, Boucicault's Irish plays are viewed as his greatest dramatic accomplishment and are his most enduring works.

The popularity of Boucicault's plays waned rapidly near the end of the nineteenth century, as the work of dramatic Realists gained favor and the events upon which his plots were based faded from the public memory. However, critics note that Boucicault's legacy can be found in the work of subsequent Irish playwrights such as John Millington Synge and Sean O'Casey, who, influenced by Boucicault's skillful use of Irish characters, settings, and themes, went on to lay the foundations of modern Irish drama.

PRINCIPAL WORKS

A Legend of the Devil's Dyke [as Lee Moreton]   (drama) 1838

London Assurance [as Lee Moreton]   (drama) 1841

Alma Mater; or, A Cure for Coquettes   (drama) 1842

The Irish Heiress   (drama) 1842

A Lover by Proxy   (drama) 1842

The Old Guard   (drama) 1842

Don Caesar de Bazan; or, Love and Honour [adaptor with Ben Webster; from the drama *Don César de Bazan* by Philippe Dumanoir and Adolphe Dennery]   (drama) 1844

Old Heads and Young Hearts   (drama) 1844

Used Up [adaptor with Charles Mathews; from the drama *L'homme blasé* by Félix Duvert and A. T. de Lauzanne de Vauxroussel]   (drama) 1844

The School for Scheming   (drama) 1847

The Knight of Arva   (drama) 1848

The Willow Copse [adaptor with Charles Kenney; from the drama *La closerie des genêts* by Frédéric Soulié]   (drama) 1849

Love in a Maze   (drama) 1851

Pauline [adaptor; from the novel *Pauline* by Alexandre Dumas *père*]   (drama) 1851

The Queen of Spades; or, The Gambler's Secret [adaptor; from the drama *La dame de pique* by Eugène Scribe]   (drama) 1851

The Corsican Brothers; or, The Vendetta [adaptor; from the drama *Les frères Corses* by Eugène Grangé and Xavier de Montépin]   (drama) 1852

The Prima Donna   (drama) 1852

The Vampire [adaptor; from the drama *Le vampire* by Charles Nodier]   (drama) 1852

Genevieve; or, The Reign of Terror [adaptor; from the drama *Le chevalier de la maison rouge* by Alexandre Dumas *père* and Auguste Maquet]   (drama) 1853

The Young Actress [adaptor; from the drama *The Manager's Daughter* by Edward Lancaster]   (drama) 1853

Andy Blake; or, The Irish Diamond [adaptor; from the drama *Le gamin de Paris, ou l'enfant de Genevière* by Jean Bayard]   (drama) 1854

Grimaldi; or, Scenes in the Life of an Actress [adaptor; from the drama *La vie d'une comédienne* by Auguste Anicet-Bourgeois and Théodore Barrière]   (drama) 1855

Louis XI [adaptor; from the drama *Louis XI* by Casimir Delavigne]   (drama) 1855

The Poor of New York [adaptor; from the drama *Les pauvres de Paris* by Edouard Brisebarre and Eugène Nus]   (drama) 1857

Wanted a Widow, with Immediate Possession [adaptor with Charles Seymour; from *Monsieur Jovial, ou l'huissier chansonnier* by M. E. G. M. Théaulon de Lambert and Adolphe Choquart]   (drama) 1857

Jessie Brown; or, The Relief of Lucknow   (drama) 1858

Dot [adaptor; from the short story "The Cricket on the Hearth" by Charles Dickens]   (drama) 1859

The Octoroon; or, Life in Louisiana [adaptor; from the novel *The Quadroon* by Mayne Reid]   (drama) 1859

The Colleen Bawn; or, The Brides of Garryowen [adaptor; from the novel *The Collegians* by Gerald Griffin]   (drama) 1860

Arrah-na-Pogue; or, The Wicklow Wedding   (drama) 1864

Rip Van Winkle; or, The Sleep of Twenty Years [adaptor with Joseph Jefferson; from the short story "Rip Van Winkle" by Washington Irving]   (drama) 1865

The Flying Scud; or, A Four Legged Fortune   (drama) 1866

The Long Strike [adaptor; from the novels *Mary Barton: A Tale of Manchester Life* and *Lizzie Leigh: A Domestic Tale* by Elizabeth Gaskell]   (drama) 1866

After Dark: A Tale of London Life [adaptor; from the drama *Les bohémiens de Paris* by Eugène Grangé and Adolphe Dennery]   (drama) 1868

Foul Play   (drama) 1868

Formosa ("*The Most Beautiful*"); *or, The Railroad to Ruin*   (drama) 1869

Presumptive Evidence [adaptor; from the drama *Le courrier de Lyon, ou l'attaque de la malle-poste* by Mo-

reau, Paul Siraudin, and André Delacour] (drama)
1869

The Rapparee; or, The Treaty of Limerick (drama)
1870

Kerry; or, Night and Morning [adaptor; from the drama
La joie fait peur by Delphine de Girardin] (drama)
1871

Daddy O'Dowd; or, Turn About is Fair Play [adaptor; from
the drama *Les crochets du Père Martin* by Pierre Cor-
mon and Eugène Grangé] (drama) 1873

Led Astray [adaptor; from the drama *La tentation* by Octave Feuillet] (drama) 1873

Belle Lamar (drama) 1874

The Shaughraun (drama) 1874

Forbidden Fruit (drama) 1876

Robert Emmet [adaptor; from an unfinished drama by
Frank Marshall] (drama) 1884

The Jilt; or, Thundercloud's Year (drama) 1885

The Spae Wife [adaptor; from the novel *Guy Mannering*
by Walter Scott] (drama) 1886

99 (drama) 1891

The Times, London (essay date 1841)

[*In the following review of the premiere of* London Assurance, *the critic commends the play as "replete with
merriment."*]

A five act piece called **London Assurance** was produced
last night, sustained by nearly every actor in the company,
and each part one which the sustainer would, of his own
free will, have chosen. Farren revels in the character of Sir
Harcourt Courtly, a gay deceiver of 60, now clad in the
splendor of a superb dressing-gown, now insinuating himself into every nook in a tight suit of black, determined to
captivate somebody, whether married or single. The part
was excellently dressed, and played; the alluring manner
in which the old Lothario placed himself on a sofa, drew
himself near to an intended victim, and the searching way
in which he poured forth lawless addresses were inimitable. Mrs. Nisbett has a part which exactly suits her—a
dashing sportswoman, Lady Gay Spanker, with full play
for all the spirits she is possessed of, and that in no small
quantity, and a description of a hunt, imitated from the
one given by Constance in the *Love Chase*. Keeley, as her
husband, Mr. Adolphus Spanker, is equally suited with
that quiet forbearing disposition, the representation of
which is peculiar to himself. A hearty old country squire,
with a warm welcome and a leathern pair of lungs, Max
Harkaway, is the very thing for Bartley; while his niece
Grace, an arch young lady, who perplexes a lover and utters repartees, finds an excellent representative in Madam
Vestris. A bustling attorney, Mark Meddle, who is made
to utter any impossibilities the author may choose, who
can be insulted with impunity, regard a pull of the nose
as a bagatelle, and whose legs require to be as nimble as
his tongue, calls forth the activity of Harley; while the
lady's maid, whose butt he is, makes just such speeches as
require the quaintness of Mrs. Humby. An easy flippant

man about town, pretending to be a relation to every body,
on account of a marriage between a remote ancestor and
ancestress, whom he admits in an "aside" to have been
Adam and Eve, with much cool impudence, and flexibility
of limb, is Charles Mathews under the name of Dazzle;
while his friend, a son of Sir Harcourt, Mr. Charles Courtly, a gentleman of more stamina and less nimbleness—a
puller-off of knockers in the first part, and an ardent lover
in the latter part of the drama—gives room for the energies of Mr. Anderson.

We have named the personages before the plot, for in fact
to conceive the general effect of the piece, the reader need
only fancy such persons as those described above, joking,
quizzing, squabbling, bullying, laughing, cheating, lying,
courting, and running about for the space of three hours,
and he will have a pretty correct notion of it, without troubling himself too much about the purpose of the fun. Indeed, the plot can be told in a few lines. Mr. Dazzle having
rescued his friend Charles Courtly from a street row, and
accompanied him to his own house, unknown to his sire,
who regards him as a pattern of retiring virtue—one who
is always in bed before 10, and never heard the clock strike
12 but at noon—meets 'Squire Harkaway, who invites him
down to his seat in Gloucestershire, where there is to be
a wedding. His respectable friend Charles, as he can easily
account for his absence from the paternal roof, on the plea
that he is at college, and, moreover, as he finds duns becoming tiresome, accompanies his friend into the country
under a feigned name. They meet with a hospitable welcome, but great is the consternation of Charles when he
finds that the bridegroom of the wedding is his own father,
Sir Harcourt, who is about to marry Harkaway's niece,
Grace; and, what makes the matter more perplexing, the
youth has fallen in love with the young lady at first sight.
On Sir Harcourt's arrival, the only course left for the son
is boldly to deny his identity, and the old baronet, thrown
off his guard, is obliged, somewhat improbably to be sure,
to swallow the deception. He, however, sends for his son
from home, when the feigned gentleman retires, and Mr.
Charles, in his own awkward half-boyish dress, makes his
appearance, and the deception is kept up, although the
likeness is generally admitted to be wonderful. To break
off the wedding, advantage is taken of a *penchant* which
Sir Harcourt discovers for Lady Gay Spanker, whom the
youthful pair beg to encourage his addresses, and who,
with the most disinterested regardlessness of her own
character, patronizes all the soft things Sir Harcourt has
to utter, allows him even to embrace her, and consents to
elope with him. The lawyer Meddle discovers this plan,
and reveals it to the poor husband Adolphus, who detains
his wife, while she laughs at the joke, which she has certainly carried a little too far. She nearly involves him in
a duel, by making him write a challenge for fun, which,
contrary to her intention, reaches its destination, but discovers her real affection for him when it is brought to a
happy termination. The conclusion of the whole is, of
course, the union of Charles Courtly with Grace.

Such a plot might seem meagre to sustain a piece in five
acts, but the author has so contrived to make it a vehicle
for oddities both of situation and dialogue, that he kept his
audience in a roar from beginning to the end with very few

interruptions. This is his first attempt in the dramatic line, and he shows as great qualifications for the art he has chosen—strength, animation, and a full flow of spirits. It is true his work is a five act farce, whereas it is called a comedy; it is true that not one of the characters is original, that many of the incidents are borrowed, that the construction is far from neat, that utter absurdities are committed by the characters, such as no human being would perpetrate, that jokes of every degree are uttered—yet with all this, in the use of his strange materials, the author has displayed a vivacity—a fearless humour to strike out a path for himself, an enjoyment of fun, a rapidity in loading his speeches with jokes, a power of keeping up his spirits to the last, which distinguishes this piece from every work of the day. On such a piece the laughter of the audience was the best critique; many an old friend must have been recognized among the characters and jokes, but the drollery was irresistible. The roar was not the laugh of a few picked friends labouring to find out the facetious, but of a whole audience. Perhaps a piece of any pretensions with more imperfections and incongruities has not been brought out within the last ten years, but certainly within the same period none have appeared more replete with merriment.

Everything has been done for it in the way of decoration. A house in a garden with set flower-beds, the interior of the rooms and the whole of the furniture being visible through the windows—a drawing-room with the most costly tables and cushions—are equal to anything yet known in the way of theatrical embellishment. Mr. Charles Mathews announced the piece for repetition amid tumultuous applause, which was only interrupted by calls for Mr. Lee Moreton, the author, who was led forward, eying the enthusiastic multitude with considerable nervousness.

> *"Covent Garden Theatre," in* The Times, *London, March 5, 1841, p. 5.*

Henry James (essay date 1875)

[*As a novelist James is valued for his psychological acuity and complex sense of artistic form. Throughout his career, James also wrote literary criticism in which he developed his artistic ideals and applied them to the works of others. Among the numerous dictums he formed to clarify the nature of fiction was his definition of the novel as "a direct impression of life." The quality of this impression—the degree of moral and intellectual development—and the author's ability to communicate this impression in an effective and artistic manner were the two principal criteria by which James estimated the worth of a literary work. In the following review of* The Shaughraun, *originally published in 1875 in the* Nation, *James commends the play as skillfully crafted entertainment and praises Boucicault's performance in the title role.*]

Our drama seems fated, when it repairs to foreign parts for its types, to seek them first of all in the land of brogue and "bulls." A cynic might say that it is our privilege to see Irish types enough in the sacred glow of our domestic hearths, and that it is therefore rather cruel to condemn us to find them so inveterately in that consoling glamour

of the footlights. But it is true that an Irish drama is always agreeably exciting; whether on account of an inherent property in the material, or because it is generally written by Mr. Boucicault, we are unable to say. *The Shaugraun* will, we suppose, have been the theatrical event of the season; and if a play was to run for four or five months there might have been a much worse one for the purpose than this. There is no particular writing in it, but there is an infinite amount of acting, of scene-shifting, and of liveliness generally; and all this goes on to the tune of the finest feelings possible. Love, devotion, self-sacrifice, humble but heroic bravery, and brimming Irish *bonhomie* and irony, are the chords that are touched, and all for five liberal acts, with a great deal of very clever landscape painting in the background, and with Mr. Boucicault, Mr. Montagu, Mr. Becket and Miss Dyas in the foreground. For Mr. Boucicault, both as author and actor, it is a great triumph—especially as actor. His skill and shrewdness in knocking together effective situations and spinning lively dialogue are certainly commendable; but his acting is simply exquisite. One is hard cleverness, polished and flexible with use; the other is very like genius. The character of the Shaugraun is very happily fancied, but the best of the entertainment is to see the fancy that produced it still nightly playing with it. One hears it said sometimes that an actor acts with "authority"; certainly there is rarely a higher degree of authority than this. Mr. Boucicault smiles too much, we think; he rather overdoes the softness, the amiability, the innocence of his hero; but these exaggerations perhaps only deepen the charm of his rendering; for it was his happy thought to devise a figure which should absolutely, consummately, and irresistibly please. It has pleased mightily. (pp. 23-4)

> *Henry James, "Notes on the Theatres: New York, 1875," in his* The Scenic Art: Notes on Acting & the Drama, 1872-1901, *edited by Allan Wade, 1948. Reprint by Hill and Wang, Inc., 1957, pp. 22-7.*

The Saturday Review, London (essay date 1886)

[*In the following review of* The Jilt, *the critic compares the play favorably with Boucicault's more well-known Irish plays.*]

It is forty-five years since Miss Fanny Kemble wrote to her friend Miss S— that the young author of the new comedy at Covent Garden had bought himself a horse on the strength of the great success of that production; the new comedy to which the last of the Kembles thus referred was *London Assurance,* and its young author was Mr. "Lee Morton"—so it was said then. The young author of *London Assurance* is young yet, after forty-five years' more experience, and his latest five-act comedy, *The Jilt; or, Thundercloud's Year,* is own sister to *London Assurance,* almost equally successful, and contains a horse instead of providing Mr. Boucicault with the means of purchasing one. It is characteristic of the growth of Greater Britain in the scant half-century since *London Assurance* was originally acted that its latest successor from the same pen was not produced first in London, but in San Francisco, in the California which was only an outlying and forlorn province of Mexico when Mr. Boucicault's first play was first done. Acted in San Francisco last summer, and then performed throughout Australia, it was produced in New York, at the Star Theatre, late in the winter, and has not yet been seen in London. *The Jilt* is announced as "by the author of *London Assurance* and the *Shaughraun*"; perhaps it may convey a better idea of its quality and value if we say that it seems to us to be the work rather of "the author of *The Irish Heiress* and *The Flying Scud*." By this we mean that *The Jilt; or, Thundercloud's Year*, is at the same time an Irish play, a sporting drama, and a five-act comedy. It may be said at once that the title, promising as it is, has very little to do with the play. Before the curtain rises the lady who jilted has married a man she loves, and the man she jilted is dead. But during the brief engagement of the bride to the dead man there were, of course, letters written by her to him; and the ribbon that binds the bundle of these letters may fairly be called the thread which holds together the five acts of the play. How these compromising letters fall into the hands of the villain, as in many another play; how the price of their destruction is the hand of an heiress, as in many another play; how Mr. Boucicault, as the quick-witted and ready-witted Irish *deus ex machinâ*, or guardian angel, makes a great sacrifice and pays a great price for these letters, and wins the heiress for himself, it is needless to set forth here at length. The value of the play is not in its incidents, for they can borrow originality only from the ingenuity of their arrangement; nor is it in the characters, for these have been seen before in other plays of Mr. Boucicault and of other dramatists than Mr. Boucicault. It is partly in the neat, simple, and extremely effective construction, and chiefly in the unfailing brilliancy of the dialogue. Not unkindly one might insinuate that *Old Heads and Young Hearts*, despite the youth of its author when it was written, was the work of an old heart and a young head. But as the years have passed over Mr. Boucicault his wit has mellowed and softened, and as his head waxed older his heart became younger. Certainly he has never written prettier scenes of comedy, wittier dialogues, or simpler pathos than one can find in *The Jilt*. At all times Mr. Boucicault's Irish plays have been distinctly the best things he has done. *London Assurance* and its fellows are already old-fashioned; but *Arragh-na-Pogue* is as young as ever, and as charming. *The Colleen Bawn* and *The Shaughraun* are but little inferior to it in charm; and even the two failures, now almost forgotten, *Daddy O'Dowd* and *The Rapparee*, have more merit than not a few of the plays which have succeeded, perhaps far beyond their deserts. Even rather bald adaptations from the French like *Andy Blake* (from *Le Gamin de Paris*) and *Kerry* (from *La Joie fait Peur*) have been greatly helped by the infusion of Hibernian humour. In *The Jilt* Mr. Boucicault has introduced only one Irish character, Myles O'Hara, a gentleman-rider and turf prophet, and of course he plays this character himself, and of course he has provided himself with a host of good things to say and of effective things to do. The fault of the comedy is that its very clever dialogue, pointed and full of "points," bristling with witticisms nearly always pertinent to the business of the play and not often impertinent to the characters—the fault of the comedy is that this clever dialogue is a little too obviously artificial. Not infre-

quently it is forced; it seems cut and dried, and we see the fuse which is to set off the coming fireworks. They are good fireworks when they come, but they would have been more enjoyable if their arrival had been more unexpected. A harsh critic might find fault with the artificiality of the whole play, with the incidents and the characters as well as the dialogue, and—if he did not feel the charm of the dramatist's humour, and if he does not acknowledge the exceeding skill with which the piece was put together and set in motion—it would be hard to bring an adequate defence against the accusation. In accordance with modern canons, Mr. Boucicault has only one set to the act, but in most other respects *The Jilt* is nearly as artificial as *London Assurance*. *London Assurance* and *The Jilt* are, in different degrees, attempts to continue the tradition of English five-act comedy; in this century this means an imitation of the methods of the comedy of the last century, as in the eighteenth century it often meant an imitation of the methods of the seventeenth century; and in no art is imitation fruitful. By the Rule of Three we should be inclined to declare that the author of *London Assurance* is to the author of the *School for Scandal* as the author of the *School for Scandal* was to the author of the *Way of the World*. But Mr. Boucicault, while he has not quite the Congreve rockets of a Congreve wit, has a wit of his own, and an Irish humour and an Irish pathos which very few of the many other Irishmen who have written English comedy could surpass. (pp. 607-08)

Mr. Boucicault resembles M. Victorien Sardou, not only in his deftness of touch and his easy wit, but also and indeed chiefly in that his originality is never beyond dispute, and that the production of every new play is followed immediately by abundant accusations of plagiarism. In the present instance the charge is that *The Jilt* is from Mr. Hawley Smart's novel *From Post to Finish*. It is a pleasure to be able to declare, for once, that the charge against Mr. Boucicault has no foundation. Beyond the fact that both Mr. Hawley's novel and Mr. Boucicault's play deal with racing matters there is no likeness whatever between them. *The Jilt* may have been suggested by some novel or other, but assuredly *From Post to Finish* was not the novel. (p. 608)

> "Mr. Boucicault and Mr. Barnum," in The
> Saturday Review, London, Vol. 61, No. 1592,
> May 1, 1886, pp. 607-08.

Augustin Filon (essay date 1896)

[*In the following excerpt originally published in French in 1896, Filon describes Boucicault as "plagiarism incarnate" but praises the verisimilitude of his Irish characters.*]

[Dion Boucicault] was an actor, and an actor of some talent. He knew no other world than that of the theatre—the world which from eight o'clock till midnight laughs and cries, curses and makes love, dies and murders, under the gaslight, behind three sets of painted canvas. Without any real culture, and without having the least critical faculty, Boucicault had read everything about the theatre—read everything and remembered everything, good, bad, and indifferent, from *Phormio* to the *Auberge des Adrets*. He knew by heart all the *croix de ma mère* of modern melodrama, and from his mass of reminiscences he concocted his crazy-quilt-like plays, imitating involuntarily, unconsciously. He was plagiarism incarnate. In his first great success, **London Assurance,** you may find not only Goldsmith and Sheridan, but Terence and Plautus, who had reached him by way of Molière. You will meet in it a father who speaks to his son without recognising him, or who at least is persuaded not to recognise him; a young lady who boxes her husband's ears and calls him her doll; a master who makes a confidant of his valet, a valet as untruthful as Dave or Scapin; a lawyer who is anxious to get himself thrashed like *L'Intimé;* a young drunkard and debauchee who falls in love with a country lass; and a young girl brought up in the wilds, who replies to the first compliment she has paid her—"It strikes me, sir, that you are a stray bee from the hive of fashion. If so, reserve your honey for its proper cell. A truce to compliments." The piece goes from vulgarity to vulgarity, from absurdity to absurdity. Within a few minutes there is a ridiculous abduction, a comic duel and a hardly less comic marriage, all brought about by a will which is surely the most absurd of all the absurd wills known to the drama. The piece had its central figure in a clever humbug whom no one knows. "Will you allow me to ask you," says Charles Courtly in the last scene, "an impertinent question?"

"With the greatest pleasure."

"Who the devil are you?"

"On my faith, I don't know. But I must be a gentleman." Upon which another character concludes the play with a pedantic definition of the word "gentleman," and morality is satisfied.

One fine day—it was in 1860—this playwright, who lived by borrowing, and who was in debt to every literature, had the singular good fortune to create a *genre* of his own. Perhaps it is too much to say create. A compatriot of his, Edmund Falconer, like himself an actor as well as an author, had opened the way for him. But Falconer never again met with the success which greeted *Peep o' Day,* and he wound up with the memorable failure of *The Oonagh.* Boucicault, on the contrary, was able to exploit for twenty years the fruitful vein upon which he had happened in the **Colleen Bawn.**

The **Colleen Bawn** is a tissue of improbabilities and extravagances. What is the mysterious reason why we can put up with these absurdities and take an interest in them? It is, I think, that there is in this crack-brained drama a kind of ethnographic seed which enters into the mind and takes root there. The sad, patient, uncomplaining struggle of this poor peasant girl to become worthy of the man she loves,—her discouragement, which yet cannot exhaust her devotion,—all this is depicted by touches so suggestive and so strong that an elaborate analysis could not do more. But there is something beyond this. A sort of primitive poetry seemed to play round the whole character of the Colleen Bawn as she appeared thirty-five years ago in the person of Mrs. Dion Boucicault, with her little red cloak, her long black hair, and her expression half sad, half seductive—smiling through her tears like an angel in disgrace.

Until Boucicault's time it had been the fashion to laugh over Ireland, never to weep over her. He brought about this change without depicting his country otherwise than as she really existed. He knew the strange feeling of England towards Ireland, the feeling of a man for a woman, devoid of the refinements of philosophy and civilisation. Passionate, violent, hard, England begins by crushing Ireland; then stops, conquered by the weakness of the victim, subjugated by a charm which no mere words can describe. Boucicault sought out this sentiment in the depths of the hearts of his English audiences, and ministered to it; and was instrumental thereby in preparing the way for an age of justice and generosity. Under the commonness of the means which he employed, and often also of the sentiments and ideas which he expressed, Boucicault hid a sort of subtlety which was born of instinct. His Irish psychology is true to life, and although he added many touches in the **Shaugraun,** in **Arrah-na-pogue,** in **The Octoroon,** in **Michael O'Dowd,** and in other works, it may be said to be already complete in **The Colleen Bawn.** When Myles-na-Coppaleen tells us, "I was full of sudden death that minute," and when Eily speaks of the little bird that sings in her heart, the passion does not strike us as exaggerated nor the poetry as out of place. Father Tom, too, who smokes his pipe and drinks his potheen with the smugglers, but who can assume at will his authority as an apostle and a leader, is the personification of the Irish priest of old, and indeed of our own day too—at once the man of the people and the man of God.

Altogether, one cannot but exclaim, as one looks at this crude but striking piece—this is Ireland! The Ireland of zealots and traitors, of rebels and the meek, of madmen and martyrs, of heroes and assassins. Ireland the irrational and illogical, who disconcerts our sympathies after winning them, and who has doubtless still further surprises in store for History, already at a loss how to record her actions, how to explain her character, what verdict to pronounce upon her. (pp. 88-92)

> *Augustin Filon, in Chapter II of his* The English Stage: Being an Account of the Victorian Drama, *translated by Frederic Whyte, 1897. Reprint by Benjamin Blom, 1969, pp. 73-92.*

George Rowell   (essay date 1956)

[*Rowell is an English critic specializing in nineteenth-century drama. In the following excerpt originally published in 1956, he summarizes Boucicault's accomplishments.*]

Boucicault's career reversed the pattern traced by [Douglas] Jerrold. Instead of moving on from melodrama to comedy Boucicault achieved success as a young man of twenty-one with **London Assurance,** hailed as a 'modern' comedy by Vestris and Mathews who presented it and by the public who kept it in the repertory throughout the century. In fact its only modern touch was its setting, to which Vestris gave her unflagging attention. In spirit, however, **London Assurance** is the palest imitation of Van-

> To insure success as a dramatic writer . . . one must be thoroughly acquainted with 'stage-business' and 'effects'. *Action* is the great secret which—since Shakespeare's time—none have understood as well as Boucicault. It seems preposterous to name the two with the same breath . . . yet it is true.
>
> *—Edwin Booth, in a letter dated 1869, quoted by Don La Casse in* Theatre Survey, *November 1980.*

brugh or Farquhar, lacking their vigour and drawing attention by its contemporary dress to such devices of artificial comedy as a father failing to recognize the son who is staying in the same house under an assumed name. Its liveliest characters, the horse- and husband-riding Lady Gay Spanker and the impudent Dazzle (played by Charles Mathews), are incidental to the main story, but the play's long life can only be attributed to their appeal and to the dearth of Victorian comedy.

Boucicault's efforts to continue this vein of comedy, notably in **Used Up,** another vehicle for Mathews, probably convinced him that he was losing touch with his audience. In adapting **Don Cæsar de Bazan** from Dumanoir and D'Ennery he had already turned his attention to the new school of French melodrama inspired by Scribe. He proceeded to serve an apprenticeship at the Princess's, constructing for Charles Kean English versions of the current favourites of the French stage. Much of Boucicault's work there was perfunctory, but at least two of his adaptations, **Louis XI** (from Casimir Delavigne) and **The Corsican Brothers,** brought wide acclaim not only to Kean but to many later performers. In the popularity of Kean, Phelps, and later Irving as Louis XI it is possible to see the fascination for their audiences of the superficial attributes of Richard III and King Lear, without their deeper significance. Certainly Boucicault provided Louis with the externals of both—Richard's cunning and Lear's patriarchal air—while rejecting the essence of either.

The Corsican Brothers, on the other hand, shows a certain originality of form which deserves analysis. Working, wisely, not from Dumas's novel but from the stage adaptation by Grangé and Montépin, Boucicault here presented the familiar ingredients of Romantic drama in a form sufficiently arresting for his version to hold the stage for half a century. Several of the play's incidents made theatre history, notably the first appearance of the telepathic twins:

> FABIEN *folds his letter and seals it, at the same time* LOUIS DEI FRANCHI *appears, rising from R. C. without his coat or waistcoat, as his brother is, but with a blood stain upon his breast—he glides across the stage—ascending gradually at the same time.*

The long, interleaved trap-door devised to effect this en-

trance was christened the 'Corsican trap' and under that name remained in regular theatrical usage. Later, in the last act, the duel between Louis's murderer and the avenging Fabien established a type of single combat:

> *First combat of several minutes in which* CHA-TEAU-RENAUD *exerts himself to kill or wound* FABIEN, *but is foiled by his coolness and skill. . . . Second combat in which the sword of* CHATEAU-RENAUD *is broken.*
>
> MONTGIRON (*springing forward*). Gentlemen, gentlemen, this combat must not be continued; M. Chateau-Renaud's sword is broken—the weapons are not equal.
>
> FABIEN. You are mistaken, sir. (*Breaking his sword beneath his heel.*) They are so now. (*To* CHATEAU-RENAUD, *pointing to the broken blade.*) Pick up that blade, sir, and let us go on.
>
> MONTGIRON. Implacable!
>
> FABIEN. As destiny! (*He directs* ALFRED *how to tie the broken blade to his wrist with his handkerchief.*)
>
> . . . *A violent bodily contest*—CHATEAU-RENAUD *throws* FABIEN, *but, at the moment in which he raises his arm to strike him,* FABIEN *plunges his weapon into his heart.*

However, it was not only incidents in **The Corsican Brothers** which established precedents in the English theatre. The overall pattern of the play—the concurrence in time of the first two acts, and the two 'visions', revealing first the Forest of Fontainebleau with the dying Louis, and later Fabien's resolve to quit Corsica and revenge his brother, indicate an interest in form hitherto neglected in the rough-and-tumble methods of melodrama. Further, Boucicault was able to introduce a blend of chivalry and adventure far removed from the simple thrills of T. P. Cooke's pieces; and to this refinement of romantic appeal Charles Kean was doubtless able to give his own innate respectability and Eton education, dressed with the theatrical flourish he inherited with his name. The era of 'gentlemanly melodrama' had begun.

The lessons Boucicault learnt from the French theatre he subsequently used in putting together a series of native melodramas, owing nothing to French sources. 'Native' for Boucicault meant Ireland, and in his three popular Irish plays, **The Colleen Bawn, Arrah-na-Pogue,** and **The Shaughraun,** he exploited with great skill the hitherto little used backgrounds of his native country, turning on them the brilliant if deceptive limelight of his theatrical training. In so doing he was also able to exploit his acting ability, and the sly humour, touched with pathos, of his Myles in **The Colleen Bawn,** Shaun-the-Post in **Arrah-na-Pogue,** and Conn in **The Shaughraun** was loyally supported by his wife, Agnes Robertson, who, though Scots, succeeded in creating the soft Irish charm of the Colleen Bawn. Boucicault's portrayal of Irish character later enraged the literary leaders of Irish nationalism, who denounced the cheapness of his humour and sentiment, but at least his strain of pathos was a refinement on the crudely comic Teagues of so many Georgian plays. Moreover, his growing interest in America, where he ultimately settled, led him to capture for the theatre the American scene also, in *The Poor of New York, The Octoroon,* and in his long-lived version of Washington Irving's *Rip van Winkle.*

To his original work Boucicault brought the fully tested methods he had assimilated from the French. Both his Irish and his American plays, for all the elaboration of their plots, have a neatness of construction to which Fitzball or Jerrold never remotely aspired. His handling of the Irish idiom, too, marks an advance on the rhetoric of Romantic drama towards the authentic dialogue established by the end of the century. Of the alertness of his mind Boucicault's plays contain innumerable examples. While in no way interested in contemporary issues he lost no time in turning scientific progress to theatrical advantage. The dénouement of *The Octoroon,* for example, is brought about through the newly-invented camera, by which the villain's infamy has, unknown to him, been recorded; while *The Long Strike* achieves another topical touch by introducing the telegraph to recall from on board ship the key-witness who alone can save an innocent man accused of murder:

> SLACK (*having worked apparatus*). There, sir, you see the wires are dumb. (JANE *falls on her knees.*) I am truly sorry, sir, but if you were to give me one thousand pounds I could not make them speak.
>
> MONEYPENNY. Of course you can't. Thank you, it is not your fault, but this poor girl, sir, this poor girl—it is her sweetheart that will be tried for murder—that wire was the thread on which the lad's life was suspended and it fails her. It is hard, sir. I am a lawyer and used to hard cases, but this does appear to me a cruel one. Come, Jane.
>
> JANE. Oh! let me pray—let me pray!
>
> MONEYPENNY. Heaven help you, my poor girl, for we can do no more. (*To* SLACK.) You see, sir, this being assize time, his trial will come off at once. I fear it will go hard with him. (JANE's *head falls against chair.*) Why, what is the matter, Jane?
>
> JANE. I am faint, sir. I feel very cold.
>
> SLACK (*having come from behind counter, stands L.*) Can I assist you, sir?
>
> MONEYPENNY. She is swooning, sir. Oh, dear—what shall I do? Jane! Jane!
>
> (*Instrument at back begins to tap.*)
>
> SLACK. Hark, sir! hark! There's a signal! Stop a bit. (*Runs behind counter.*) By some accident the station at the head is alive.
>
> MONEYPENNY. Jane! Jane! do you hear? The line is open—the wire is working!
>
> JANE (*still on knees, hands clasped*). Heaven has heard my prayer.
>
> SLACK. Now then, sir, for your message.
>
> MONEYPENNY (*to* JANE). Stop there. (*To*

> SLACK.) Ask them has the barque *Eliza and Mary* left the Mersey. (*Pause—*JANE *sobs.*) Hush—keep quiet.
>
> SLACK (*who has sent message as directed by* MONEYPENNY—*receives reply*). Barque *Eliza and Mary* inside the bar waiting for a tide.
>
> MONEYPENNY. Hurrah! hurrah!
>
> SLACK. What next?
>
> MONEYPENNY. Can you communicate with the barque? if so, how?
>
> SLACK (*as before*). Yes—by pilot boat.
>
> MONEYPENNY. Despatch it at once, with message from Jane Learoyd to John Reilly, sailor— 'Come back; give evidence required in favour of James Starkee, accused of murder; case now on. Signed Jane Learoyd.'

Perhaps the most significant feature of Boucicault's work is the 'sensation scene'. None of his melodramas would be complete without a thrilling sequence on which the resources of the Victorian theatre were fully extended to produce a novel and spectacular effect. The attempted drowning in *The Colleen Bawn;* the exploding steamboat in *The Octoroon;* the house burnt down in *The Poor of New York;* Shaun's ascent of the prison tower in *Arrah-na-Pogue;* the boat-race rowed in *Formosa*—all were triumphs of ingenuity, accurately aimed at their audience's level. Moreover a detailed investigation [A. Nicholas Vardac: *Stage to Screen: Theatrical Method from Garrick to Griffith* (1949)] has recently disclosed how Boucicault's innovations foreshadow such fundamentals of filmmaking as cross-cutting, tracking, and panning. In short, the sensation scenes of Boucicault's plays are not merely more ingenious than those of a Moncrieff or Fitzball. They are expertly woven into the fabric of the play, so that they emerge as the pivot of the story, not its *raison d'être;* nor is the novelty of the sensation scene made the excuse for a total lack of character, plausibility, or intelligence. Boucicault was above all things thorough. (pp. 53-7)

> *George Rowell, "The New Drama," in his* The Victorian Theatre, 1792-1914: A Survey, *second edition, Cambridge University Press, 1978, pp. 31-74.*

Allardyce Nicoll   (essay date 1959)

[*Nicoll is best known as a theater historian whose works have proven invaluable to students and educators. Nicoll's* World Drama from Aeschylus to Anouilh *(1949) is considered one of his most important works; theater critic John Gassner has stated that it was "unquestionably the most thorough (study) of its kind in the English language (and) our best reference book on the world's dramatic literature." Nicoll was also renowned as a Shakespearean scholar. In the following excerpt from his six-volume* History of English Drama, 1660-1900, *he assesses Boucicault's contributions to the theater of the mid-nineteenth century.*]

In [the 1850s] perhaps the most original and influential of dramatists was Dion Boucicault, who had already associated himself with the new spirit in comedy by the writing of *London Assurance. London Assurance* and its companion plays of the forties marked, however, only a beginning, and Boucicault first definitely found his footing when he produced *The Corsican Brothers* at the Princess's in 1852. From this time on, his most characteristic pieces were plays wherein were mingled elements taken from all worlds—of sentimentalism much, a flash or two of broad wit and above all a series of exciting incidents recalling the familiar technique of early melodrama. Boucicault's importance as a dramatist rests on two things—his uncanny sense of theatrical values and his keenly observant eye. No man knew better than he just what would appeal on the stage. The construction of his plays, if we make allowance for their frankly melodramatic framework, is excellent; and of countless theatrical devices he was the eager inventor. From revolving towers to sham locomotives he sounded the whole range of scenic sensationalism. Yet his plays do not derive their interest entirely from this exciting incident. Crude as many of his effects may seem to us, he had an acute eye for oddity in real life, and many of his best scenes rely, not on scenic splendour, but on the depiction, through laughter or tears, of domestic interiors. It was this—the cultivation of naturalistically conceived scenes allied to melodramatic excitement—which gave him his contemporary importance. *The Streets of London* may appear merely amusing to modern audiences, but, since realism in art is no fundamental or static method, it appealed in its own day as a truthful picture of social events. The atmosphere of the later Irish dramas may seem absurd, but they were to Victorian spectators what the plays of Sean O'Casey are to audiences of to-day.

That in 1882 Boucicault was a "dramatist of yesterday" as William Archer styled him is unquestionably true, but . . . in our endeavour to assess Boucicault's value right, it is our business to place ourselves imaginatively in his own time and thus judge him in relation to contemporary moods and desires. It is also true that he was a skilful adaptor, taking much from sources diverse in their scope; but no one can deny that he gave theatrical quality to what he borrowed, that he surpassed every other playwright of the time in sensing the wishes of the public and that to his alien material he added much that came from his own observation of life.

Boucicault's career, of course, carries us well beyond the fifties, just as its beginnings carry us to the other side of this half-century, but we shall not be far wrong in saying that the decade 1850-60 exhibited his most characteristic and influential work. With his sure appreciation of public taste he divined that romantic supernaturalism was what the audiences most desired in the early fifties; and the result was *The Corsican Brothers.* This drama immediately received "the stamp of current fashion", so that it led the vain in a sweeping rush of dramatisations of the same theme. For a time, says [J. W.] Cole, "the subject became a perfect mania". His success naturally induced Boucicault to exploit for a time further romantic possibilities of adventurous and supernatural action. In *The Vampire, Geneviève; or, The Reign of Terror* and *Louis XI* he freely exploited a flamboyant dramatic style which corresponded to the romantically melodramatic acting method ren-

dered fashionable by Charles Kean. The last-mentioned play, an adaptation from the French of Casimir de la Vigne, gained a run of sixty-two nights and that largely because of the complete harmony between the spirit of the drama and its histrionic interpretation. Audiences were in raptures. "The enthusiastic feeling of the house on the first night", declares Cole,

> reminded us of the excitement we had witnessed during the best days of his father's *Othello.* Even when the play was over, and the principal character lay dead before the audience, they trembled lest he should start up again, and work fresh mischief with the revivified influence of a ghoul or a vampire. . . . The success of "Louis the Eleventh" established a decisive period in Mr. C. Kean's career as an actor.

No doubt can remain that this combination was thoroughly representative of at any rate one mood of the time; Kean's romantic impersonations were as typical as was Boucicault's flamboyant, yet decisively refined, melodramatic method.

By the close of the fifties, however, Boucicault was sensing the necessity of a change, if not in theme at least in outward semblance. Out of these historical or pseudo-historical romances grew the plays which, after all, form his most characteristic contribution to the theatre of his day. With *The Octoroon; or, Life in Louisiana* and *The Colleen Bawn; or, The Brides of Garryowen* a definite approach was made towards reproducing the conditions of real life; in that life Boucicault discovered new material to exploit, new appeals which he might make to the public. Cleverly, however, he chose spheres of interest where he might freely introduce a flavour of romance, a dash of patriotic sentiment, a certain semblance of the real allied to a richness of spectacle. *The Colleen Bawn,* with its musical accompaniments, is thus obviously related to the older melodrama. In the printed text and in the original play-bills the scenic show is fully advertised; that was part of the appeal. At the same time this melodramatic basis and this pleasing spectacle are subtly related to actual existence; instead of wizards' caverns and vampires' dens *The Colleen Bawn* introduces us to the familiar made rosy and imaginative. Those prospective playgoers who read the original list of scenes would have appreciated this to the full:

Act I

LAKE OF KILLARNEY (MOONLIGHT)
The Signal Light!
Gap of Dunloe
Cottage on Muckross Head
The Irish Fireside—The Cruiskeen Lawn—The Oath!

Act II

Torc Cregan

COTTAGE OF THE COLLEEN BAWN
"The Pretty Girl Milking Her Cow"
Mac Gillicuddy's Reeks
The O'Donoghue's Stables
The Water Cave

Act III

THE HUT   CASTLE CHUTE
THE CASTLE GARDENS
Illuminated Hall and Garden in Castle Chute

From romantic moonlight on the fair Lake of Killarney through the splendour of the castle gardens to the lonely cottage; from the thrilling signal light through the oath to the pretty girl milking her cow—Boucicault sounds the gamut of a particular style. The plot fully accords with the scenery; it is full of exciting incidents and of dramatic suspense. Hardress Cregan has secretly married Eily O'Connor, but finds himself faced with ruin unless he marries Anne Chute. The dilemma for him is a terrible one; and the confusion in which the characters are placed is rendered greater by the fact that Anne, loving Kyrle Daly, is led to believe that he, not Cregan, is Eily's husband. Cregan has a faithful devoted servant in Danny Mann; to relieve his master he attempts to slay Eily, but she is saved by Myles-na-Coppalean, the stock, pathetically dog-like lover. It is all very exciting and not for one moment is the attention of the audience permitted to flag. But if it is exciting, it is also very appealing in its apparent realism. The Irish dialect employed has a kind of double effect—it gives a pleasing air of wild romantic remoteness to the action and at the same time creates the illusion that all these events are definitely related to life.

A similar combination of elements appears in **The Octoroon.** No one could fail to be impressed by the author's rich vitality and dramatic inventiveness. The love of George Peyton for Zoe, the octoroon; the poverty threatening Mrs Peyton; the villainies of McClosky; the apparent disasters and the ultimate triumph of good—all these keep the plot moving swiftly. And again theatrical use is made of the life known to the audience. To us this use of material things may seem more than a trifle absurd and forced; but the sense of novelty which would accompany their original introduction must have amply compensated for any dim feeling of dissatisfaction. Take the camera episode. McClosky is the brutal villain of the regular melodramatic tradition, and in Act II he murders Paul, thinking that no eye has seen his crime. Unfortunately for him, however, a camera belonging to Scudder has been standing facing him all the time, and, as he is muttering "What a find! this infernal letter would have saved all", the stage direction declares that *"he remains nearly motionless under the focus of camera".* The result of this becomes apparent in the last scene. McClosky is accusing the Indian Wahnotee of killing Paul, while Scudder endeavours to plead for him:

> SCUDDER. I appeal against your usurped authority; this Lynch law is a wild and lawless proceeding. Here's a pictur' for a civilized community to afford; yonder, a poor ignorant savage, and round him a circle of hearts, white with revenge and hate, thirsting for his blood; you call yourselves judges—you ain't—you're a jury of executioners. It is such scenes as these that bring disgrace upon our Western life.

> M'CLOSKY. Evidence! Evidence! give us evidence, we've had talk enough; now for proof.

OMNES. Yes, yes! Proof, proof.

SCUDDER. Where am I to get it? the proof is here, in my heart!

PETE (*who has been looking about the camera*). Top sar! top a bit! Oh, laws-a-mussey, see dis, here's pictur I found sticking in that yar telescope machine, sar! look sar!

SCUDDER. A photographic plate. (Pete *holds lantern up*) What's this, eh? two forms! the child—'tis he! dead—and above him—Ah, ah! Jacob McClosky—'twas you murdered that boy!

M'CLOSKY. Me?

SCUDDER. You! You slew him with that tomahawk, and as you stood over his body with the letter in your hand, you thought that no witness saw the deed, that no eye was on you, but there was, Jacob McClosky, there was—the eye of the Eternal was on you—the blessed sun in heaven, that looking down struck upon this plate the image of the deed. Here you are, in the attitude of your crime!

Thus is the villain foiled. The means may be ridiculous and we may permit ourselves to smile superiorly, but Boucicault is sure of his business and recognises that the utilisation of this new invention (about which both the audience and he know little) will be exciting and thrilling. Things like these thrilled contemporary audiences on both sides of the Atlantic: Boucicault was able to write to a friend [G. W. Riggs] that "the sensation produced in New York" by this drama was "intense", the houses being "crammed to suffocation".

The same skill is shown throughout the entirety of Boucicault's dramatic career. **Arrah-na-Pogue; or, The Wicklow Wedding** presents, in an Irish setting, a kindred mixture of diverse elements. Against a background of nationalist sentiment and revolutionary ardour Beamish MacCoul stages a robbery, for which the honest Shaun is arrested. Love, of course, has to play its part here and its path has to be duly crossed; Fanny Power, who adores and is adored by Beamish, comes to believe that Arrah is his mistress. Complications and complexities ensue, with frantic efforts made by O'Grady to save poor Shaun. At last Beamish, having given himself up, is about to be condemned, when a kind-hearted and liberal-souled Secretary decides to save him. **Arrah-na-Pogue** is no less thrilling than **The Octoroon,** and its hair-raising excitements are cleverly interspersed with a variety of comic business. Perhaps Boucicault's importance may best be gauged when we regard him as one of the masters—for such in a way he is—of George Bernard Shaw. Amid Boucicault's realms of sensation and laughter and propaganda the young Shaw wandered, and the result is to be viewed, not only in the melodramatic *Devil's Disciple,* but in *Arms and the Man, Caesar and Cleopatra, The Man of Destiny* as well. Nor is this indebtedness one merely of a general sort. "Technically", says Shaw in his preface to *Three Plays for Puritans,*

> I do not find myself able to proceed otherwise than as former playwrights have done. True, my plays have the latest mechanical improvements;

the action is not carried on by impossible soliloquys and asides; and my people get on and off the stage without requiring four doors to a room which in real life would have only one. But my stories are the old stories; my characters are the familiar harlequin and columbine, clown and pantaloon (note the harlequin's leap in the third act of *Caesar and Cleopatra*); my stage tricks and suspenses and thrills and jests are the ones in vogue when I was a boy, by which time my grandfather was tired of them.

How true this statement is may be realised by glancing at two scenes from *Arrah-na-Pogue* and *The Devil's Disciple* respectively. The former presents a court-martial scene. There is a severe Major and a kindly Colonel O'Grady; the prisoner is Shaun, who has allowed himself to be arrested in the stead of another:

MAJOR. Your name?

SHAUN. Is it my name, sir? Ah, you're jokin'! Sure there's his honour beside ye can answer for me, long life to him!

MAJOR. Will you give the Court your name, fellow?

SHAUN. Well, I'm not ashamed of it.

O'GRADY. Come, Shaun, my man.

SHAUN. There, didn't I tell ye! he knows me well enough.

MAJOR. Shaun (*writing*) . . . What is your other name?

SHAUN. My mother's name?

MAJOR. Your other name.

SHAUN. My other name? D'ye think I've taken anybody else's name? Did ye ever know me, boys, only as Shaun? . . .

O'GRADY. He is called Shaun the Post.

SHAUN. In regard of me carrying the letter-bag by the car, yer honour.

MAJOR. Now prisoner, are you guilty or not guilty?

SHAUN. Sure, Major, I thought that was what we'd all come here to find out.

Contrast this with the court-martial scene in Shaw's play. There is here too a severe Major (Swindon) and a good-humoured General (Burgoyne); the prisoner (Richard) has allowed himself to be arrested in the place of Anthony Anderson:

SWINDON. Your name, sir?

RICHARD. Come: you don't mean to say that you've brought me here without knowing who I am?

SWINDON. As a matter of form, sir, give me your name.

RICHARD. As a matter of form, then, my name

is Anthony Anderson, Presbyterian minister in this town. . . .

BURGOYNE. Any political views Mr Anderson?

RICHARD. I understand that that is just what we are here to find out.

The same situation; the same fundamental types; even in part the same expressions.

Throughout his dramatic career Boucicault displayed a rich theatrical exuberance and a keen appreciation of stage values. As Joseph Knight observed of *The Shaughraun*, he found the ordinary conditions of life in England "prosaic and commonplace" and consequently turned to the richer material discoverable amidst the romantically rebel Irish folk; good fun abounds in all his dramas; and in all is the effective utilisation of exciting escapades, often with distinctively novel circumstances connected therewith. In *The Shaughraun* there was "a revolving tower" which showed, "from the inside first, and then from the outside, the escape of the hero"; in *The Poor of New York* occurred a scene showing two adjoining rooms and a most exciting conflagration. . . . (pp. 84-92)

[Boucicault's] merit ever consisted in this ability to give thrilling form to material which seemed to be the material of life and yet was always material of the theatre. Sometimes he achieved his end by visual means; sometimes, as in *The O'Dowd,* by skilful arrangement of the incidents. In this last-mentioned play Mike O'Dowd is first shown in London, embarrassed by a debt of £20,000. His friends rally round him, but even their efforts fail to stave off disaster. Emigrating to America, he at length succeeds in amassing wealth and returns to Europe. The play ends with a thrilling scene in which he saves a ship by guiding her through a channel of which only he and his father are aware. Inventiveness was always Boucicault's greatest gift and if the inventions were not always his own he proved felicitous in adapting the ideas of others. A semi-realistic "problem-play", for example, he transforms and makes interesting by devising a special framework. *Dot,* based on *The Cricket on the Hearth,* is introduced by Oberon and Titania, conceived as wretched, poverty-stricken wanderers, forgotten by the modern world; their place is taken by Home, and this provides an opportunity for emphasising that poetry must now be sought in the quiet domestic interior.

Boucicault's knowledge of the stage and its possibilities was completer than that possessed by any of his contemporaries, and unlike so many of these he had a keen eye for whatsoever in real life might provide him with opportunities for the building up of melodramatic incident. The invention of the camera, a great financial failure, the problem of the octoroon, the conflict between Yankee and Virginian or between Irish and English—all were vigorously seized on and easily assimilated. His plays may lack literary finish; but at least they present in a bold way that theatrical effectiveness and that theatrical interest which are the primal demands we must make of a dramatist. Readily may we ridicule much of his work, but, when we seriously consider his accomplishment in terms of contemporary

Boucicault as Shaun the Post and Sadie Martinot as Arrah in Boucicault's drama Arrah-na-Pogue.

stage practice, it is hard indeed to deny him praise and esteem. (pp. 93-4)

> *Allardyce Nicoll, "Boucicault and Taylor: Plays of the Fifties," in his* A *History of English Drama: 1660-1900, Vol. V, second edition, Cambridge at the University Press, 1959, pp. 82-108.*

Gary A. Richardson   (essay date 1982)

[*In the following excerpt, Richardson argues that Boucicault's* The Octoroon *questions the justice of American law while it also demonstrates the necessity of law in maintaining civilization.*]

Many nineteenth century American playwrights made use of contemporary social problems. No playwright centered his drama more overtly around an inflammatory social issue, however, than did the Irish born Dion Boucicault in his play, *The Octoroon.* Like many another melodrama of the period, *The Octoroon* presents its audience with a dashing hero, a dastardly villain, a bumbling spokesman for goodness, and a woman who almost loses her family home. Unlike most of the plays of the time, however, the

central "tragic action" of the play centers not around the fate of a golden-haired heroine whose virtue and life are endangered by the villain, but rather around the destiny of an octoroon slave girl named Zoe. The uniqueness of Boucicault's achievement lies not, however, in his choice of heroine. Rather the importance of the play stems from Boucicault's examination of a fundamental American precept—the viability of law as the framework of a democratic society. Boucicault uses the situation of Zoe to contrast the ideals and realities of a growing nation. Slavery becomes not only a theme of the play, but also a metaphor for the essential contest between the desires and rights of the individual and the societal goal of maintaining its own existence. The death of Zoe and the implicit marriage of George and Dora seem to affirm the traditional American faith in a society of laws. However, Boucicault undercuts the orthodoxy of the ending through repeated episodes in the play which show the malleability of the law and the law's capacity for frustrating elemental human instincts toward goodness.

The consistent critical concern with the theme of slavery is understandable given the history of the play. Opening on December 6, 1859, the day a pro-Southern candidate was elected mayor of New York and only four days after the execution of John Brown, *The Octoroon* could hardly escape notoriety. While Boucicault attempted to make his play appear as non-committal as possible, critical response to the play was in large measure based on the reviewer's perception of Boucicault's stand on the slavery question. As Sidney Kaplan has pointed out [in "*The Octoroon:* Early History of the Drama of Miscegenation," *Journal of Negro Education* 20 (1951)], at least one newspaper did not even wait for the play to open before blasting it, for espousing supposed abolitionist views. Despite or, perhaps, because of the furor surrounding the author's treatment of slavery, the play had a long and successful run at several New York theaters, even after Boucicault and his wife left the original Winter Garden cast in a dispute over financial arrangements.

As mentioned before, Boucicault, ever the shrewd promoter, tried to gain the largest possible audience by making the play ostensibly noncommittal. Unlike its major source, Mayne Reid's *The Quadroon* which overtly questions widely held nineteenth century American beliefs about racial purity by having Edward Rutherford, the hero, marry Aurore, the quadroon of the title, Boucicault's *The Octoroon* neatly avoids the problem of miscegenation by having Zoe, the octoroon, die before the play ends. Joseph Jefferson, the original Salem Scudder, was so convinced by Boucicault's balancing act that he maintained in his autobiography "there were various opinions as to which way the play leaned—whether it was Northern or Southern in its sympathy. The truth of the matter is, it was noncommittal. The dialogue and characters of the play made one feel for the South, but the action proclaimed against slavery, and called loudly for its abolition." Later critics have maintained this attitude and one has gone so far as to say "*The Octoroon* is in no sense a propagandist play, but employs the theme solely for its dramatic value. So successfully did the author accomplish his purpose that the play was loudly applauded on both sides of the Mason-Dixon line" [Oral Sumner Coad and Edward Mims, *The American Stage* (1929)].

That the play or, at least, the playwright did not have a definite attitude about slavery is untenable considering the history of *The Octoroon* when it was transported to England. In 1861 Boucicault took his play to London where it was received very coolly. As John Degen has amply demonstrated ["How to End *The Octoroon*," *Educational Theater Journal* 27 (1975)], both the English theater goers and the critics were unsympathetic to the play's original ending and demanded a more optimistic resolution which would allow George and Zoe to marry. Although he eventually capitulated to the tastes of his English audience, Boucicault defended his play publicly in an enlightening letter in *The Times* of November 20, 1861. After reflecting on the simplistic indictment of slavery offered by George Aiken's tremendously popular dramatization of *Uncle Tom's Cabin*, Boucicault pointed out that his play had moved beyond the physical brutality of slavery to concerns of greater import. As he said, "there are features in slavery far more objectionable than any of these hitherto held up to human execration, by the side of which physical suffering appears as a vulgar detail." The aspect of slavery which Boucicault found most "objectionable" was that it was an institution, an injustice that American society had sanctioned by law. As he commented in the same letter: "In the death of the Octoroon lies the moral and teaching of the whole work. Had this girl been saved, and the drama brought to a happy end, the horrors of her position, irremediable from the very nature of the institution of slavery, would subside into the condition of a temporary annoyance."

If the external evidence of Boucicault's concern with law is persuasive, an analysis of the text itself removes any remaining question. In writing a melodrama, the playwright has chosen a particularly convenient vehicle, for the genre often "traffics in ideas." The central concern of much melodrama is man in conflict with external forces which he either falls victim to or defeats. Robert Heilman has thoughtfully and succinctly described melodrama as:

> the whole realm of conflicts undergone by characters who are presented as undivided or at least without divisions of such magnitude that they must be at the dramatic center. . . . The issue here is not the reordering of the self, but the reordering of one's relations with others, with the world of people or things; not the knowledge of self but the maintenance of self, in its assumptions of wholeness, until conflicts are won or lost. There is a continuous spectrum of possibilities, from the popular play in which the hostile forces can be beaten to the drama of disaster in which the hostile force is unbeatable; at one extreme we view man in his strength, at the other in his weakness. [*Tragedy and Melodrama: Versions of Experience* (1968)]

Ostensibly, at least, the ethical universe of *The Octoroon* is unambiguous. For Boucicault, and presumably for the audience of his own day, every theme developed in the play would seem to have only one "correct" interpretation. Time and time again, the playwright reiterates con-

temporary presuppositions about life that seem to operate irresistibly on the characters. For instance, all the characters in the play except George Peyton, an American in name but not in attitudes, see the non-whites as passionate, subhuman species who must be controlled. Thus, Zoe is presumed to be unworthy of George because she has black blood and Wahnotee is almost lynched because the mob presumes that the Indian's bestial nature is the cause of Paul's otherwise inexplicable death. But a close examination of the text reveals that the play is equivocal; the popular conceptions fail to withstand the scrutiny to which they are subjected. The cornerstone of law that underpins the society of the play is flawed and the action of the drama shows that flaw is of major proportions.

Since melodrama as a genre emphasizes action, it is not surprising that Boucicault focuses his audience's attention not on his characters, but rather on the plot, or more correctly, plots. In the main plot the audience follows the tribulations of Zoe, the daughter of the late Judge Peyton and an anonymous quadroon slave. Given the genre, Zoe is, perforce, the object of the villain's lust and the hero's love. Eventually, Zoe, thinking that she has become the property of the villain, M'Closky, poisons herself. In a tearful death scene she begs the hero, George Peyton, to marry Dora Sunnyside, the southern belle who is devoted to him, and to forget his love for the Octoroon until death reunites them. The secondary plot treats the conventional nineteenth century problem of a piece of land being wrested from the hands of a poor, helpless widow. Both of these plot threads are connected by their concerns with law and its implications. Indeed, justice and its attempted practical application, law, have become by the end of the play the center of attention. The deaths of Zoe and M'Closky, which close the drama, are not only the consequences of conflicting definitions of justice, but are also representations of the inadequacy of law to deal with fundamental human impulses which are not based on reason.

The first reference to the law or anything legal is in the initial conversation between Mrs. Peyton and her nephew, George. George wittily observes that he left Paris "amid universal and sincere regret. I left my loves and my creditors equally inconsolable." To this jest Mrs. Peyton replies, "George, you are incorrigible. Ah, you remind me so much of your uncle, the judge." At first glance this seems an innocuous piece of characterization. But as the play continues, we begin to recognize that the person who is the unseen personification of the law in this play, Judge Peyton, has brought destruction to the very door of those he loves. His ineptitude is initially delineated by Salem Scudder:

> Ten years ago the judge took as overseer a bit of Connecticut hardware called M'Closky. The judge didn't understand accounts—the overseer did. For a year or two all went fine. The judge drew money like Bourbon whisky from a barrel, and never turned off the tap. But out it flew, free for everybody and anybody to beg, borrow, or steal. So it went, till one day the judge found the tap wouldn't run. He looked in to see what stopped it and pulled out a big mortgage. "Sign that," says the overseer; "it's only a formality." "All right," says the judge, and away went a

thousand acres; so at the end of eight years, Jacob M'Closky, Esquire, finds himself proprietor of the richest half of Terrebone.

Lest we overlook the implication of Scudder's narrative, the playwright presents us with an even more damning piece of evidence. After finding that a legal judgment had been entered against Judge Peyton's estate, M'Closky checks the date of the judgment against the date of Zoe's emancipation. When he finds that the judge had attempted to free Zoe when he was legally prevented from doing so, he comments, "Why, judge, wasn't you lawyer enough to know that while a judgment stood against you it was a lien on your slaves? Zoe is your child by a quadroon slave and you didn't free her." Thus, by the end of the first act Boucicault has managed to completely undermine the central figure of law in the play. Judge Peyton stands exposed as not only inept but also dangerous. By extension, the same may be said about the concept that stands behind the judge—the law. Not only will the law allow the ineptitude of a single individual to ruin the financial security of his family, but it is also no guarantee that the very lives of those people will not be placed in danger. For fear that we might think it is merely the personal inadequacies of the judge that are being taken to task, Boucicault provides us with three other significant examples in the play of the law's less than ideal operation. None of these does anything to restore our faith in the bastion of American democracy—law.

The first of these comes in what might, in the context of plays of this type, be called the mandatory auction scene. As the gentlemen of means gather to dispose of the property of their late departed, fellow aristocrat, Judge Peyton, we are presented with a scene which contrasts the impulses of the human heart with the requirements of the law. Sunnyside points out the obvious fact that the Peyton family would like to buy Zoe and free her. But Poindexter objects that "while the proceeds of this sale promises to realize less than the debts upon it, it is my duty to prevent any collusion for the depreciation of the property." This sounds very aboveboard and honorable, unless we remember that in a previous episode, the sale of Grace and her two children, Poindexter has made an exception to this injunction in order for Ratts to buy the family of Solon. The upshot of this strictness of interpretation, this following of the letter and disregarding of the spirit of the law, is, of course, that Zoe is sold to the villain, M'Closky.

One of the most damning of the scenes concerning the law is that which involves Wahnotee, the "noble" savage. To recapitulate briefly, Paul the servant boy and favorite of the late Judge Peyton has been killed by M'Closky so that he can secure a letter from England that would save Terrebonne from its creditors. Since Wahnotee was the constant companion of Paul, and since the Indian has been seen only once since Paul's death, it has been generally presumed that it was the Indian that killed Paul. When Wahnotee finally appears, he is seized and a crowd of angry citizens demands his immediate lynching. As we might expect, our spokesman for goodness, Salem Scudder, has some trepidations about "stringing up an innocent man." Indeed, Scudder makes all of the stock arguments about law as the foundation of civilization: "I appeal against

your usurped authority. This lynch law is a wild and lawless proceeding. Here's a pictur' for a civilized community to afford; yonder, a poor, ignorant savage, and round him a circle of hearts, white with revenge and hate, thirsting for his blood: you call yourselves judges—you ain't—you're a jury of executioners. It is such scenes as these that bring disgrace upon our Western life." Although this speech will have almost certainly no effect upon those who wish to do away with the innocent Indian, it does have the superficial virtue of reassuring the audience about the nature of the law. The assurance is short-lived. At the crucial moment, Pete enters with the miraculous self-developing picture that shows M'Closky bending over the body of Paul. With this new piece of evidence before him, Scudder changes from lawyer for the defense to prosecuting attorney. With the change in role comes a similar reversal about the nature of law and justice. When asked who will accuse M'Closky, Scudder again volunteers:

> Fellow-citizens, you are convened and assembled here under a higher power than the law. What's the law? When the ship's abroad on the ocean, when the army's before the enemy, where in thunder's the law? It is in the hearts of brave men, who can tell right from wrong, and from whom justice can't be bought. So it is here, in the wilds of the West, where our hatred of crime is measured by the speed of our executions—where necessity is law! I say, then, air you honest men? air you true? Put your hands on your naked breasts, and let every man as don't feel a real American heart there, bustin' up with freedom, truth, and right, let that man step out—that's the oath I put to ye—and then say, Darn ye, go it!

This shift in Scudder's attitude about the operation of the law is one of the most disturbing elements in the play. Indeed, since it is Scudder, the author's surrogate, who shifts, the audience is left with more than a little suspicion that the law is merely another aspect of society that can be manipulated if one only knows how. If, as Heilman suggests, characters in melodrama are attempting to realign themselves with the world, Boucicault's presentation of the structuring element in Western society, the law, suggests that the task is an impossible one.

Boucicault's main indictment of the law comes in his treatment of Zoe, the title character. From the beginning of the play it is obvious that Zoe is the standard against which the other characters are to be judged. As Scudder says early in the first act: "Guess that you didn't leave anything female in Europe that can lift an eyelash beside that gal. When she goes along, she leaves a streak of love behind her. It's a good drink to see her come into the cotton fields—the niggers get fresh on the sight of her. If she ain't worth her weight in sunshine you may take one of my fingers off and choose which one you like." But it is not only the morally upright Scudder who recognizes the superiority of Zoe. Wahnotee, the noble savage, calls Zoe "sweetheart," and George Peyton, the most sophisticated character in the play, falls in love with her. Even the villain, Jacob M'Closky, is not immune to her charms. And while some of M'Closky's dialogue indicates that what he feels is something less than Platonic love, Scudder concedes that M'Closky's passion for Zoe is "the only sincere feeling" that the rogue has.

Despite the fact that Zoe is the moral apex of Boucicault's dramatic universe, she does have her problems. Unfortunately for Zoe, she is an octoroon in a society that legally demands racial purity. The ramifications of her situation are hinted at early in the play when she is propositioned by M'Closky. Although he is willing to set her up as mistress of Terrebonne, M'Closky is not inclined to contravene the legal strictures of his society. He tells Zoe, "Come, Zoe, don't be a fool; I'd marry you if I could, but you know I can't." Clearly M'Closky is hinting at statutes against miscegenation which were common in most southern states during this period. But behind these legal constraints, which are by no means insignificant, are the suppositions on which the strictures are based—suppositions which facilitate the legal inequality.

Throughout the play people are seen in terms of their race. They are stereotyped. The initial scene of the play serves, among other things, to establish the concern with color. George, recently arrived from France, asks Pete, one of the house slaves, if a group of children who have just left the stage were all born on the plantation. Pete, in his usual good humor, replies: "Guess they nebber was born—dem things! what, dem?—get away! Born here—dem darkies? What on Terrebonne! Don't b'lieve it, Mas'r George; dem black tings was never born at all; dey swarmed one mornin' on a sassafras tree in the swamp; I cotched 'em; dey ain't no 'count. Don't b'lieve dey'll turn out niggers when dey're growed; dey'll come out sunthin' else." Pete's facetious dehumanization of the black children is only the first instance in the play of Boucicault's portrayal of the American attitudes toward non-whites. For the Americans in the play, the non-whites are facts of existence in the same sense that Pete's sassafras tree is a fact. They are part of the physical world within which the whites revolve, but by no stretch of anyone's imagination can they be considered human. It is George Peyton who realizes and is shocked by this attitude. George recognizes this obliviousness because he is, in essence, an outsider who has spent his youth in Europe and has thus failed to assimilate American racial attitudes. The disparity between George's European outlook and the American point of view is dramatized in the early scene in which Sunnyside and Dora appear at Terrebonne for breakfast. George remarks to himself "They do not notice Zoe," and then points Zoe out to Sunnyside. Sunnyside's answer is indicative of a man who has been informed of something so obvious that he is unconscious of it: "Ah! Zoe, girl; are you there." His reply, couched as it is in the form of a rhetorical question, seems to demonstrate that Sunnyside places as much importance on the existence of Zoe as he does on the table at which he sits. Zoe, like the table, exists within the same physical realm as the squire, but neither one is of such import that attention should be wasted upon the fact. But it is not only the southerners who project this attitude toward non-whites. Late in the play, Salem Scudder, a Yankee who has to some extent immersed himself in the world of Terrebonne, remarks when he hears a noise in the cedar swamp "it's either a bear or a runaway nigger." This joining of "bear" and "nigger" is a perfectly

natural equation for Scudder—both are sub-human creatures whose natural habitat is the wilderness.

As Scudder's comment suggests, non-whites lack stature in American society because they are considered sub-human creatures whose nature is circumscribed by passion. In trying to explain to George why their love can never be recognized in American society, Zoe enunciates the basis of this supposition. She traces her failings, and by inference the failings of all other non-whites, to the biblical story of Cain: "That is the ineffaceable curse of Cain. Of the blood that feeds my heart, one drop in eight is black—bright red as the rest may be, that one drop poisons all the flood; those seven drops give me love like yours—hope like yours—ambition like yours—life hung with passions like dew-drops on the morning flowers; but the one black drop gives me despair, for I am an unclean thing—forbidden by the laws—I'm an Octoroon!" By identifying herself with Cain, Zoe is accepting as truth the idea that non-whites are bestial creatures whose passionate natures are innerent threats to the operation of an orderly society. Passion places all non-whites outside of the purview of the law, an extension of reason, and, consequently, outside of American society which is presumed to be based on law. Since they have no legal identity in themselves, and since their inherent natures are antithetical to the maintenance of western society, it becomes incumbent on the whites to restrain the natural impulses of the non-whites so that society as a whole may continue. As the fate of Zoe reveals, his attitude is not without its pathetic consequences.

By loving George, Zoe has contravened a basic tenet of her society. She has presumed to love one who is above her and since she cannot reconcile herself to a society that demands an end to her love, she removes herself from the society in the only way available to her—suicide. Zoe sees her action as a means of reestablishing the social order and simultaneously preserving her love by removing it to a plane on which justice as opposed to law decides such issues. As she tells George in the last scene of the play: ". . . I loved you so, I could not bear my fate: and then I stood between your heart and hers. When I am dead she will not be jealous of your love for me, no laws will stand between us."

The playwright's treatment of Zoe's death serves to indict the American legal system whose presumptions have made her fate "irremediable." In the end, Boucicault was not an anarchist, however. While the law may be a poor ordering principle, it remains for the playwright the only viable alternative society has. As much as Boucicault may admire the passions which motivate Zoe, his examination of M'Closky's fate reveals a hearty skepticism of passion, at least as an alternative ordering agent for society.

M'Closky, like Zoe, is driven by passion, although in the villain's case the passions are base. Toward the end of the play M'Closky, who is being pursued by blood vengeance embodied by Wahnotee, argues that as a white man he is entitled to the operation of the white man's legal system. Scudder, having heard the plea, replies:

> Hold on now, Jacob; we've got to figure on
> that—let us look straight at the thing. Here we

are on the selvage of civilization. It ain't our side, I believe, rightly; but Nature has said that where the white man sets his foot, the red man and the black man shall up sticks and stand around. But what do we pay for that possession? In cash? No—in kind—that is, in protection, forbearance, gentleness, in all them goods that show the critters the difference between the Christian and the savage. Now, what have you done to show them the distinction? for darn me, if I can find out.

M'Closky has failed his obligations to society; by his own actions he has reduced himself to the type of beast that the law was designed to handle. Ironically, of course, the suppositions which are patently false when applied to Zoe are vindicated when brought to bear upon M'Closky. To Boucicault the tragedy, if so elevated a term is applicable, is that the legal foundation of American society seems to lack a means of recognizing qualitative differences in motivation. Boucicault seems to say, as does Krogstad in Ibsen's *A Doll's House,* "the law takes no account of motives."

Thus, the forces of the law are at once justified and called into question. The society is maintained, but only at the expense of its most exemplary member. For Boucicault, however, the sacrifice seems not only worthy, but also necessary. The death of Zoe is the force that reunites the elements of the society at Terrebonne, guarantees the continuation of that society, and banishes the forces of chaos to the swamp. The final tableau of Wahnotee standing over the body of the slain M'Closky leaves little doubt that the alternative to the system of law that has, at least indirectly, caused the death of Zoe is the return of the savage. (pp. 155-64)

> *Gary A. Richardson, "Boucicault's 'The Octoroon' and American Law," in* Theatre Journal, *Vol. 34, No. 2, May, 1982, pp. 155-64.*

David Krause   (essay date 1982)

[*In the following discussion of Boucicault's career, Krause focuses in particular on his three best-known Irish plays,* The Colleen Bawn, Arrah-na-Pogue, *and* The Shaughraun.]

Dion Boucicault always insisted on poetic justice in his plays. His comedies were usually melodramatic reversals of the unfortunate struggle for Irish freedom from British misrule, for if eighteenth- and nineteenth-century history showed a record of unbroken Irish defeats, a pattern of vicarious comic victories could be found in the plays, victories contrived by the clever clown who was Boucicault's significant embodiment of the braggart and parasite in one consummate character, the *shaughraun* or vagabond. Like Dickens, that master of comedy and melodrama, Boucicault didn't allow his sentimental resolutions to undermine his ripe comedy; and if he lacked the literary genius of Dickens, he compensated for it with his theatrical genius. He was the complete comedian in the theater.

Modern Irish comedy reached its full glory in the early decades of the twentieth century at the Abbey Theatre, but it had its origins in the nineteenth-century plays of Boucicault. While it is evident that Yeats and Lady Gregory founded a great theater in 1904 which provided the occasion and inspiration for a native Irish drama written in English, the two finest comic dramatists of the Abbey, Synge and O'Casey, owed a deep and prior debt to the popular Irish comedies that Boucicault wrote, *The Colleen Bawn* (1860), *Arrah-na-Pogue* (1864), *The Shaughraun* (1874). To give full credit to the Abbey, and to the dramatists themselves, the influence of Boucicault alone could not have produced a Synge or an O'Casey; nevertheless, it is doubtful whether they would have created their unique "playboys" and "paycocks" in quite the attractively barbarous manner that they did if they had not developed an early enthusiasm for Boucicault's comic rogues.

Yet Boucicault, until some recent revivals of his plays in Dublin and London, was long neglected and maligned as a purveyor of Victorian melodrama. In large measure he was himself responsible for this fate, for he suffered from the limitations of his own talent as well as those of the time in which he lived. He was one of the most popular and prolific of Victorian dramatists, having written or adapted over 150 plays during his fifty-odd years in the theater, from 1838 to 1890, very few of which have survived in the modern repertoire. But perhaps there are some significant connections in the fact that the Dublin-born Boucicault, who borrowed so freely from the works of such early Irish dramatists as Congreve, Farquhar, Goldsmith, and Sheridan, should have provided some direct and indirect sources of inspiration for such later Irish dramatists as Wilde, Shaw, Synge, O'Casey, and Behan. Thus, while one cannot call him an outstanding figure—his achievements were more theatrical than literary, and the drama demands distinction in both fields—it is necessary to consider not only his limitations but those enduring qualities of his theatrical and comic genius which have continued to appeal to modern Irish dramatists and audiences.

Boucicault wrote in what might loosely be called the tradition of comic melodrama, but he was far from a traditional dramatist. He saw the drama as a mixed or impure form of entertainment, a combination of comedy and melodrama, farce and burlesque, song and sentiment, sensational and Gothic stage effects. In this respect he seems to have anticipated the modern dramatist's irreverent attitude toward the rigid or academic modes of drama, even if he was largely Victorian in his treatment of the mixed forms. There was nothing Victorian, however, in his practical reaction to those pseudo-Aristotelian critics who objected to his disregard of the so-called unities of the drama when he replied in an article: "The essence of a rule is its necessity; it must be reasonable, and always in the right. The unities of time and place do not seem to be reasonable, and have been violated with impunity, therefore are not always in the right. The liberty of imagination should not be sacrificed to arbitrary restrictions and traditions that lead to dullness and formality. Art is not a church; it is the philosophy of pleasure." Obviously Boucicault agreed with Goldsmith's view that the theater was Liberty Hall and a place for entertainment, not a gloomy tabernacle for the dissemination of morality or a tedious occasion for critical formalism. At other times he insisted that audiences did not want pure forms, especially "pure comedy," whatever that was supposed to be; and in defending his own kind of heretical pleasure play he invariably assumed that purity was a quality audiences demanded in heroines, not comedy. He was shrewd in anticipating the unsophisticated tastes of the popular audiences of the nineteenth century, and he devoted a vigorous lifetime to giving the people what he believed they wanted—an extravaganza of melodramatic plots, broadly comic characters, and music-hall exuberance. Nevertheless, in giving the Victorians what they wanted, he became the victim as well as the champion of popular taste in the theater.

At the peak of his limited genius, however, Boucicault developed the comic persona of the Irish rogue-hero, the combined braggart-warrior and parasite-slave of Greek and Roman comedy, for as freely mixed creations of folly and wisdom his comic characters form the prototype of Synge's peasants and O'Casey's Dubliners. In the mid-nineteenth century, when Boucicault not only created but acted the role of the comic Irish vagabond—the *shaughraun,* literally, the wanderer—the stage Irishman had long been a recognizable caricature in English drama. This buffoon was merely a figure of ridicule, the absurd Irishman making a fool of himself among his betters, the British. Boucicault altered this trite image by making his comic Irishman the clever and attractive central character in a play set in Ireland, in which the absurd Englishman or Anglo-Irishman makes a fool of himself among his betters, the Irish. His hero is the archetypal wise fool who is the occasion of hilarity in others as well as natural wit and humor in himself. He can be a blathering rascal and cheerful liar, a profligate playboy and strutting paycock who cavorts outside the ordinary restraints of society, a picaresque clown who ultimately rights all wrongs with his instinctive sense of justice. It is in his creation of this distinctly Irish yet universally comic character—as Myles-na-Coppaleen, Shaun the Post, or Conn the Shaughraun—that Boucicault finally transcends the Victorian world. And it is part of this triumph that much of antic Irish comedy as we know it today has its origins in the theater of Boucicault.

Born in Dublin in 1820, on the north side of the city, within a short distance of the birthplace of Sheridan, O'Casey, and Behan, Boucicault spent his first ten years in Ireland and then was sent to England, where he eventually launched his career as dramatist and actor at the age of eighteen. In 1838 in Brighton he appeared in his own play, *A Legend of the Devil's Dyke,* a comedy-melodrama that contained many of the popular ingredients that illustrate Boucicault's strengths and weaknesses in the theater. The melodramatic plot, so characteristic of nineteenth-century theater, revolves about a mysterious will and the villainous attempts of an army deserter to deprive the upright hero and hapless heroine of their inheritance and happiness. The merry antics of the comic plot, however, in which three rude mechanicals make a mockery of their aristocratic betters, reveal Boucicault's masterful talent for comic invention and almost redeem the play. Teddy Rodent, the comic lead played by Boucicault, who has been making his fortune as a rat catcher in London, comes back to the country to marry the servant girl Bessy, only

to discover that there are just as many rats in the country as in the city. In a parody of the melodramatic plot, Teddy and Bessy, with the bumpkin of a footman named Tim Terrier, dress up as a fashionable trio and crash the gala ball, with the resourceful Teddy masquerading as Bessy's wealthy aunt. In the comedy of errors that follows—as if in anticipation of something out of *Charley's Aunt* or the Marx Brothers—the matronly Teddy baits his trap so seductively that he catches a fortune-hunting fop, while the proper hero and heroine are busy catching the villainous army deserter.

Though Boucicault wrote the part of Teddy in a cockney idiom, he wisely played it as an Irishman; but either way, it indicates his early facility with comic characterization and knockabout farce. Furthermore, it is apparent that he was serving his apprenticeship under the influence of the comic masters. There are many echoes from Goldsmith and Sheridan in the play, for the prankish Teddy Rodent is partly modeled after Tony Lumpkin, and all the rustics use vivid colloquial speech and malapropisms that suggest the comic spirit of such plays as *She Stoops to Conquer* and *The Rivals.* Still there are also many signs of Boucicault's own theatrical inspiration in his first play—a remarkable achievement for a young man of eighteen—in the comic vitality of the whole work, in the clever tricks and masquerades he creates for his brash clown-hero, and in his dedication to exuberant fun as the main impetus for his drama.

Three years later, in 1841, he scored his first hit in London with *London Assurance,* a play written in the same spirit but in a slightly different form, a combination comedy of manners and farce in the tradition of Congreve and Farquhar. In the typical Restoration attitude, Boucicault's aloof heroine, Grace Harkaway, decides to "dwindle into a wife," and in trying to cure Charles Courtly of his blithe assurance, somewhat like Congreve's Mrs. Millimant, confronts him with an affectation of indifference: "I have many employments—this week I devote to study and various amusements—the following week to repentence, perhaps." Since it is his own father, Sir Harcourt Courtly, that she intends to marry and repent of, Charles and his parasite friend Dazzle conceive a counterplan, a "beaux' stratagem" whereby he will go to the country to woo Grace in the disguise of a Mr. Hamilton. When he is almost trapped in this farcical masquerade, however, Charles is forced to "kill" the poor Hamilton, just as Wilde's Jack Worthing later has to dispose of his similarly convenient fiction, Mr. Bunbury. The lively plot is complicated through five acts of comic cross-purpose by a host of familiar *eiron* and *alazon* characters, and the play is probably the best comedy in English since Farquhar. In recent years it has finally been revived with remarkable and well-deserved success in London and New York.

Boucicault's early triumph with *London Assurance* was premature. On the apparent assumption that he had found a new formula in the old comedies, he promptly wrote a half-dozen similar plays and most of them were failures. At least two, however, deserved a better fate, *A Lover by Proxy* and *The Irish Heiress,* both written in 1842. Besides being a witty farce, *A Lover by Proxy* is of special interest because it seems to have anticipated Oscar Wilde's *Importance of Being Earnest* (1895), since it has in Harry Lawless and Peter Blushington a pair of highly amusing idle gentlemen very like Jack Worthing and Algernon Moncrieff, and in its garden scenes some striking parallels with Wilde's play, even to the inclusion of Miss Penelope Prude, who possesses the chaste views of a Miss Prism and the overbearing presence of a lesser Lady Bracknell. The other play, **The Irish Heiress,** which unfortunately closed after only two performances, is nevertheless a delightful comedy, with the added attraction of Boucicault's first Irish comic heroine, Norah Merrion. She is an Irish country girl of native wit and freshness that fairly sparkles when she is turned loose among the fashionable lords and ladies of London. No doubt the play's sentimental machinery of secret documents and discoveries is not as effective as the farcical game of disguises and deceptions, but it was predictably on moralistic and realistic grounds that the Victorian critics attacked the play. The reviewer in *The Times,* who had praised **London Assurance** while objecting to what he called its lack of proper morality and realism—he had disapproved of "the utter absurdities that are committed by the characters, such as no human being would perpetrate"—condemned **The Irish Heiress** outright in similar terms. He protested that the clever Norah was not a "lady," that "the goodness of her heart was not effectively displayed, and her simplicity was little more than barbarous."

To call for proper realism and reject absurdities is to reject the inherent exaggeration and distortion of comedy. To call for simple virtue and reject "barbarous" manners is to reject the inherent primitive and irreverent spirit of Irish comedy. Perhaps the British guardians of manners and morals, with their plea for more idealized goodness and simplicity and their rejection of native shrewdness as something too "barbarous"—the choice of the taboo word is inadvertently accurate—were similar to their Irish counterparts, whose high-minded view of the national character later led to riots in the Abbey Theatre. Lacking the courage as well as the genius of Synge and O'Casey, Boucicault must have been chastened by the rebuke of the *Times* reviewer, for he spent the next two decades writing and adapting the typical melodramas, softened by a proper expression of noble sentiments, which are usually associated with his name.

At the age of forty, however, when Boucicault was nearing the peak of his career in the theater, he finally decided to write his first play exclusively about his native Ireland, **The Colleen Bawn** (1860), which now gave him an opportunity to prove that he was not only a theatrical showman but a dramatist of considerable talent. Even though he borrowed the story from Gerald Griffin's *Collegians* (1829), a popular novel that had been based on an actual murder case in Limerick, he modified the theme to suit his own spectacular purposes. Griffin had created a vivid and accurate picture of the customs and social conflicts in eighteenth-century rural Ireland, but his characters were mostly set down in single dimensions of virtue and vice; and throughout the book he consistently called attention to the moral lessons to be drawn from the fate of the people. Hardress Cregan, the hard-riding country gentleman

as hero-villain, who is so dominated and spoiled by an overindulgent mother that he seems to drift into crime, is condemned to suffer the agonies of remorse on a convict ship. His mother becomes a penitent of her church and devotes her life to "austere and humiliating works of piety." And the two "noble" characters, Kyrle Daly and Anne Chute, marry and turn to a life of religious devotion. In the end Griffin trusts that the reader not only has been amused but has learned "the avoidance of evil, or the pursuit of good."

Wilde's Miss Prism might have been satisfied with such a resolution. Not Boucicault. Since in melodrama it follows as naturally as the night the day that evil must fall and good must rise, he had no need to lecture his audience on this solemn subject and was therefore free to concentrate on the knockabout amusement. Taking only the climax of Griffin's interminable plot, and drawing on a variety of other sources as well as his own fertile imagination, he created a less realistic Ireland but one with more vital and memorable characters—an Ireland of unforgettable comedy and romance, in the folk spirit of the popular ballads. He found the name for his play in the well-known ballad "Willy Reilly" or "Willy Reilly and the Colleen Bawn"—on which William Carleton had also based his comic novel *Willy Reilly and His Dear Colleen Bawn* (1855)—the ballad in which Willy's brave sweetheart comes to his rescue when her father imprisons him for stealing the love of "the colleen bawn" (the blonde or fair-haired girl). In another popular hedge-school love ballad, "The Colleen Rua," he may have found the name for his second heroine, Anne Chute, who is known in the play as "The Colleen Ruadh" (pronounced "rua" or ru-ah, and meaning the red-haired girl). He certainly knew and used the ballad and novel *Rory O'More* (1837), both written by Samuel Lover, for he had played the role of Rory in a dramatization of the novel during his early years as an actor in Brighton. In this comic ballad, the courting Rory wins his coy mistress, Kathleen Bawn, by kissing her nine times.

It was probably the mirth-provoking Rory of Lover's novel who served as the model for Boucicault's rogue-hero Myles-na-Coppaleen, only a minor figure in Griffin's novel, now transformed into the main comic character in **The Colleen Bawn.** Lover's picaresque novel—which was also to provide some of the background plot for **Arrah-na-Pogue**—gives an anecdotal account of Rory's hilarious misadventures on the road, in Dublin and Paris, during the Rising of 1798. A sly clown of a peasant adrift in the big world, Rory outwits or outruns soldiers and police, publicans and bullies—"You impidint vagabone of the world," he shouts from a safe distance at a Dublin jackeen, "You dirty thief o' the world," phrases that might accurately describe Rory himself, and the newly created Myles. The novel has a scene in which the rebels meet in an old smuggler's cave under an ancient ruin by a river, and this may well have suggested to Boucicault the water cave where Myles keeps his whiskey still. Further parallels can be noted in a whiskey-punch episode in a pub, and in the trial scene at the end of the book, when Rory, in danger of being hanged for killing a man, is saved as the supposedly murdered man appears at the crucial moment,

Boucicault as Michael O'Dowd in his play Daddy O'Dowd.

just as Father Tom enters with the supposedly murdered Colleen Bawn in time to save the imprisoned Cregan.

Another minor Irish novelist of the nineteenth century, Charles Lever, who shared a wide popularity with Lover, wrote a number of comic novels that might have provided material for Boucicault, especially his *Jack Hinton* (1842), in which there are two significant secondary characters; one is the jovial Irish priest called Father Tom, who in name and personality is very close to Boucicault's priest; and the other, Tipperary Joe, is a shrewd tramp with a quick tongue and a special interest in horses who could be a double for Myles-na-Coppaleen. In Griffin's novel Myles was an undeveloped character, a crafty mountaineer who owned hundreds of wild ponies, hence his name, Myles-of-the-Ponies.

Even when one accounts for these various sources of influence, however, the total could not in itself add up to a play. It took the unique talent and theatrical experience of a Boucicault to reshape this raw material, to organize it as an integrated and swift-moving plot with the carefully timed suspense of melodrama, with the interwoven comedy of errors and disguises, and then to develop the crackling dialogue and distinctive traits that give his characters their energy and gaiety. It is especially his control of wit

and farce that redeems the ill-conceived hero and heroine of Griffin's novel, except for Hardress Cregan, who, while he may now be a more credible lover, still comes over as a stiff-necked stage Anglo-Irishman. Yet it was Boucicault's intention to laugh at Cregan's gentlemanly inhibitions, his prudish distaste for tobacco and whiskey, and most particularly in those scenes when the exuberant Eily, trying with great pains to play the Galatea to his proper Pygmalion, keeps falling back into her unladylike peasant dialect, like an earlier version of Eliza Doolittle.

Boucicault was even more successful with his second heroine, the high-spirited Anne Chute, who recalls the earlier Norah Merrion. Anne's well-aimed arrows of comic simile are matched only by the inimitable Myles, and the two of them are so adept at impaling their victims on the figurative jest that their aggressive wit becomes one of the most effective techniques in the play: the use of laughter to deflate much of the sentimentality that arises from the melodramatic plot. There are of course many occasions when the melodrama dominates the action of the play, for the harum-scarum story it tells is a romantic thriller. The use of sudden surprises to whip up excitement and tighten the suspense is a common convention in drama; but since Boucicault is out to make the most of both worlds, he continually allows his Celtic comedians to deflate the tension, as if he were winking at his audience lest in their apprehension they draw too near the edge of their seats. Actually, much of the melodramatic machinery of asides, misunderstandings, and the mortgage is treated with comic levity. In the music-hall manner, Myles often shares his jokes with the audience. The misdirected schemes of the ingratiating Danny Mann usually become immobilized in the drollery of his self-intoxicating rhetoric.

At last Boucicault seemed to have found the confidence to enjoy a good-natured laugh at the expense of the romantic melodrama that he himself had made so popular. As if in anticipation of the technique that was to become standard practice in the silent films of a Charlie Chaplin or a Harold Lloyd, he combined farce with melodrama in such a way that, for all the "hair-raising" suspense and "death-defying" deeds, the comic tone produced something close to mock melodrama. There is also a predominant theme in the play, developed through the character and behavior of Myles-na-Coppaleen, that could only be considered subversive by Victorian standards of manners and morals. For all his amiability, Myles is a lazy lying tramp, beyond any hope of reform, a horse thief and ex-convict, a poacher and operator of an illegal whiskey still who thumbs his nose at all authority—in short, an irresponsible rogue who is the complete antithesis of Victorian respectability. And yet this may have been one of the reasons he became such a popular hero, for he gave the inhibited Victorians a chance to find vicarious release from the solemn and righteous standards by which they tried to live. In this barbarous Irishman they obviously saw what Boucicault intended them to see, a romantic vagabond whose freedom from the restraints of society made him a better and more natural man than the effete gentlemen of an urban civilization. He has the universal traits of the irreverent clown who plays the wise fool at the expense of pompous authority.

In creating this comic rebel, therefore, Boucicault, that most typical of Victorian playwrights, may have transcended his time. He was to transcend it again in two more highly successful Irish plays. In 1864 he repeated his triumph as playwright, actor, and director with ***Arrah-na-Pogue,*** a comic melodrama loosely based on the Rising of 1798, with patriotic and farcical echoes from *Rory O'More,* though he was really imitating himself more than Lover. In this play, however, the comic vitality is often but not always overshadowed by the sentimental themes of thwarted love and patriotism. Instead of being a reckless vagabond, Shaun the Post, the comic hero, is a fairly respectable mailman, and only too eager to marry his Arrah-na-Pogue (Arrah of the Kiss) and become a properly domesticated husband. Neither of the two heroines, Arrah and Fanny, who devote much of their energy to weeping and self-sacrifice, have anything like the playful spirit and bold humor of the Colleen Bawn and Anne Chute. As for Beamish MacCoul, the romanticized Irish rebel, he is so earnestly occupied with his melodramatic adventures of trying to escape from the British authorities and be caught by his ever-loving Fanny that one can only put him down as a dashing hero with little besides dash.

Nevertheless, the play has many redeeming features. It is only after Shaun is hauled off to prison and treated like a subversive rogue that he fortunately begins to act like one, resorting to such a display of guile and comic bravado that the play quickly comes alive with spontaneous mirth. The jail scenes between Shaun and the obliging sergeant are excellent low comedy. And Boucicault never wrote a better scene than the trial at the end of the second act, in which the clever Shaun makes a mockery of the court, tying the law and the British major into knots with his sly and unconventional testimony. He is encouraged in this hilarious game by a crowd of cheering and jeering peasants, and he receives some unexpected help from that proud and magniloquent Irishman, the O'Grady. This scene is so effective that Bernard Shaw paid Boucicault the compliment of copying it for the trial scene in *The Devil's Disciple* (1897).

Something further must be said about that colorful character, Colonel O'Grady, as one of the memorable aspects of the play. Known as "the O'Grady," since he is the head of an ancient Irish family, he is an eccentric nobleman, generous and impulsive, always ready to defend Shaun and the oppressed peasants in his trenchant and comic style. When the police want to search Arrah, over Shaun's protest that he'll brain the first man who touches her, the O'Grady's sense of honor is aroused and he goes Shaun one better by reverting to the earthy brogue and direct action: "Be the powers, I'd have brained him first and warned him afterwards." In one of his more reflective moments, however, he makes the most incisive speech in the play, after the appropriately named Major Coffin tries to justify his role of hanging judge on the grounds of his "principle and firm conviction," and the O'Grady comments ironically:

> There goes a kind-hearted gentleman, who would cut more throats on principle and firm conviction than another blackguard would sacrifice to the worst passions of his nature. If there

be one thing that misleads a man more than another thing, it is having a firm conviction about anything.

This is precisely the kind of skeptical wisdom one might expect from Shaw's General Burgoyne, or his Caesar, for it became a typical Shavian attitude toward senseless bloodshed. It is also a view shared by O'Casey, who expressed it with acute irony in all his antiwar plays; for example, through the sardonic Seumas Shields in *The Shadow of a Gunman,* the tragic Juno Boyle in *Juno and the Paycock,* and the tragicomic Harry Heegan in *The Silver Tassie.*

So Boucicault had made a penetrating comment on human folly, but he seldom allowed himself the luxury of such digressions into profundity. During the next decade he was to turn out over twenty of his routine farces and melodramas, until in 1874 he wrote, directed, and acted in the best of his Irish plays, ***The Shaughraun.*** Again he borrowed from himself, repeating most of the comic and romantic techniques of ***The Colleen Bawn*** and ***Arrah-na-Pogue,*** and improving them. In the role of Conn the Shaughraun, closely modeled after Myles and Shaun, he created the nonpareil of his comic-rogue heroes. Again Irish lovers and patriots spin the opéra bouffe plot, with Conn, acting as the clown ex machina, inevitably launching his inspired pranks or ingenious yarns to save the day, and the play. And again Boucicault turned to recent Irish history, in a very general manner, using the activities of the Fenian Brotherhood, a revolutionary secret society that carried out a series of abortive raids against the British during the late 1860s. If any playwright had dared to treat this incendiary subject seriously in 1874, he and his play would certainly have been suppressed as an incitement to riot. But the lighthearted Boucicault, though he was vocally an ardent Irish nationalist and even wrote a letter to Disraeli demanding the release of the Fenian prisoners, was concerned only with an incitement to fun in his play. He completely romanticized his Fenian rebel, Robert Ffolliott, and the whole play is too full of harmless entertainment to be taken as anything more than a Celtic version of Ruritania. And since Boucicault played the role of Conn in a slightly modified Tony Lumpkin costume, and Conn imitates some of the wild Tony's rustic pranks, the comic spirit of Goldsmith's Liberty Hall lives again in this play.

In its intricate and melodramatic plot, or many plots, this play is even more fantastic and farcical than Boucicault's previous Irish works, with its Fenian rebel on the run, a police spy in league with the British soldiers and an Irish Squireen, the inevitable threat of a mortgage foreclosure, separated lovers, secret letters, a brave Irish priest, a forlorn Irish mother, a Monte Cristo prison escape, mystery ships, a series of multiple chases over the bogs and cliffs of Sligo, gunshots and falling bodies, the offstage mongrel named Tatthers who is more intelligent than most of the people and performs the heroics of a Rin-Tin-Tin, a Puckish rogue hero with an inexhaustible supply of tricks, and the gallows humor of a mock wake. It all adds up to a hilariously incredible mixture of whirlwind melodrama and merry Celtic moonshine. And as before, Boucicault is most Victorian in his treatment of those thwarted sentimentalists, Robert Ffolliott and Arte O'Neal, but least Victorian in his farcical treatment of the disreputable Conn and the crafty peasants.

Conn the Shaughraun, "the soul of every fair, the life of every funeral, the first fiddle at all weddings and patterns," stirs up such a wave of irreverent humor that the stock responses of melodrama are often inundated by laughter. When those two familiar symbols of sentiment and piety, his mother and his priest, try to bring him back to respectability, he responds with the guile of an Irish Huckleberry Finn and cheerfully refuses to be "sivilized"; and he convinces us that he is, like the unreconstructed Huck, a better man in his primitive freedom than the proper Christians who behave prudently. There is an instinctive nobility in him, for there are no limits to which he will not go to save someone from tyranny, as when he stows away to far-off Australia to "poach" Ffolliott out of prison; but he considers it nothing less than tyranny for anyone to try to save him from sin.

Nothing is sacred to Conn except his freedom, and the love of Moya, which he wins on his own terms. Even that supposedly inviolable concept of Victorian and/or Irish motherhood becomes one of his prime targets. He plays so many practical jokes on his poor peasant mother that the "Mother Machree" image is reduced to mock melodrama, especially in the wake scene, when he pretends to be dead. His mother is a hardy old woman who likes a bit of fun herself, yet she despairs over the fact that he lives only for pleasure and often ends up in the shebeen or the jail. She warns Moya that he is nothing but a lazy blackguard: "Conn nivir did an honest day's work in his life—but dhrinkin', an' fishin', an' shootin', an' sportin', and love-makin'." But the shrewd Moya, who doesn't want a "dacent" and respectable husband, only loves him the more for his pleasant vices, and she replies as a well-trained pupil of Conn's: "Sure, that's how the quality pass their lives."

Besides emulating the quality of a playboy, Conn is also a vainglorious paycock who finds sheer delight in telling fantastic lies, the bigger the better, for telling the truth is too dull and virtuous for a fellow of his rich imagination. More important, as we know from Falstaff and "Captain" Boyle, lies are not only a form of amusement but a method of defense, therefore one of Conn's favorite tricks for protecting himself from the pressures of respectable people. There are many examples of his protective mendacity: his roundabout explanation to his mother of how he happened to steal Squire Foly's horse; his tall excuse to Father Dolan of how he came to break his sworn oath to stay sober when he got drunk at Tim O'Maley's wake; his swaggering jest at his mother's illiteracy in the letter scene, even though he cannot read himself. And most brilliant of all, his fabrication of his own wake, in the midst of which Conn the corpse sits up unobserved among the tippling mourners, steals a drink from the whiskey jug, and utters an aside to the audience: "It's a mighty pleasant thing to die like this, once in a way, and hear all the good things said about ye afther you're dead and gone, when they can do you no good." Boucicault is a master of the characteristically absurd and shrewd Irish bull. The gal-lows humor of the mock-wake scene is quite common in Irish balladry and folklore, and although one can find many farcical parallels, for instance, by looking back to such a popular ballad as "Finnegan's Wake," or ahead to such a play as Synge's *In the Shadow of the Glen,* Boucicault's handling of the situation is by any comparison an outstanding piece of comic invention. Conn is the liveliest and most resourceful corpse that ever was stretched, for as Moya explains it in a sly bull: "Surely, if he hadn't been murdhered, he couldn't have saved us." He saved them all, he saved himself, and he saved Boucicault. (pp. 181-95)

> *David Krause, "Manners and Morals in Irish Comedy," in his* The Profane Book of Irish Comedy, *Cornell University Press, 1982, pp. 171-222.*

James L. Smith   (essay date 1984)

[*Smith is an English critic and educator who has edited numerous collections of plays. In the following excerpt from the introduction to his edition of* London Assurance, *he discusses elements of comedy and farce in the play and compares it to eighteenth-century comedies of manners as well as to Oscar Wilde's* Importance of Being Earnest *(1895).*]

Although **London Assurance** was announced in 1841 as 'a new comedy,' several reviewers considered it a five-act farce—a generic confusion common at this period, and one which helps to focus our attention on the play's diversity. It is, of course, remote from *Did You Ever Send Your Wife to Camberwell?* (1846) or *How to Settle Accounts With Your Laundress* (1847), which J. S. Coyne made into such 'screaming' successes at the Adelphi; **London Assurance** does not concern itself with pigs' trotters, tailor's dummies, butcher's bills, sooty chimneys, shirts airing before the fire, or the amusement to be extracted from supposing the same room in a lodging house is let simultaneously to a hatter by night and a printer by day—the core of Morton's *Box and Cox* (1847). Our play is more genteel than this, closer to the social world of *A Lover by Proxy* and the Georgian after-piece, but even so its two plot structures are traditional to farce. In essence, all farce offers a controlled, vicarious explosion of those anarchic energies which are repressed by civilised society; it ridicules authority and attacks the pieties of hearth and home. Thus the son usurps his father's role, or the wife her husband's. Young Courtly, in the main plot, lives a dissipated life in secret, while his father Sir Harcourt fondly imagines him a studious boy 'unsullied by any contact with society' (I. 121); at Oak Hall he lives out his rakish self under the name of Augustus Hamilton and by falling in love with Grace becomes his father's rival for her hand and fortune. As in Plautus or Molière's *The Miser,* this Oedipal situation is resolved in the son's favour, and Sir Harcourt left to lick his wounds and repent his folly. Authority is thus humiliated by the liberated sexuality of youth. The subplot of Sir Harcourt and the Spankers also sets in conflict authority and sexuality, and flirts with adultery as well, for here Lady Gay has already asserted her domestic dominance over the self-effacing Spanker, and is apparently prepared to contemplate eloping with Sir Harcourt. This led Epes Sargent to remark [in his introduction to the French's Standard Drama edition of **London Assurance**]:

> *Lady Gay Spanker* is a monstrous, and, we trust, a wholly imaginary creation. No woman of any pretensions to breeding or good sense, would treat a husband, were he even so much of an ass, in the manner she does. It is a libel upon decent society to suppose that it could tolerate such a creature.

The violence of this condemnation shows perfectly how Boucicault has hit the bull's-eye, but he has also taken care not to offend true morality at all. Lady Gay's elopement is a mere pretence, intended only to advance the cause of the young lovers. Moreover, she is delighted when her inestimable Dolly tumbles into the spirit of an authoritative husband, and although she dictates his challenge in the belief that Sir Harcourt will never fight, she is made to suffer when Spanker proves man enough to go through with it and she thinks him dead. Their reconciliation takes the form of mutual self-abasement, with the implication that she will not be so insubordinate again.

These farcical plot structures support farcical incidents and intrigues during which, as *The Times* of 5 March 1841 observed, 'utter absurdities are committed by the characters, such as no human being would perpetrate.' After only a few moments' conversation, Max Harkaway is ready to invite a perfect stranger to his country house for an indefinite period, and is devilish glad when his friend comes too. Sir Harcourt is introduced to his own son and obliged to accept him as Augustus Hamilton, and when Young Courtly comes on later as himself with news of Mr Hamilton's death in a sudden accident, Max and Sir Harcourt are not allowed to question the deception, Lady Gay is easily persuaded to make eyes at Sir Harcourt, and brushes off the possibility that her husband might object. Sir Harcourt in his turn is instantly enslaved, rejects the beautiful young bride he came to Gloucestershire to marry, forgets about her considerable fortune, and plans instead to elope with Lady Gay. Many of the play's small incidents are just as groggy. Lawyer Meddle is introduced in the second act as Pert's rejected suitor, but nothing comes of this, nor of his rivalry with honest Mr Jenks. Grace Harkaway and Lady Gay both make unmotivated entrances, glide instantly to places of concealment behind the window curtains, and there overhear some useful information which they cannot be supposed to know they need. And the last act trails off in a most implausible euphoria, as Lady Gay recalls her moral duty, Sir Harcourt makes an immediate confession of his folly and Max conjures up a second fortune out of nowhere. These false starts, neglected middles and loose ends may spring from the speed with which the play was written, but they violate the basic law of farce, that once improbable premises are established, everything must follow with inexorable logic.

Like the premises themselves, however, they are swallowed by the verve and gusto of the action, which moves so fast no audience has time to think about the flaws. 'If you're nervous don't go,' advised *John Bull*'s reviewer on 8 March 1841, for

they kick up a devil of a row. *Lady Gay Spanker* sets all in motion, or, if there's a stop, in steps *Dazzle*. They fire off jokes, practical and verbal, like squibs on a rejoicing day . . . [The play] is replete with quick dialogue, effective situation, and vigorous movement, and we will not stay to analyse the maiden production of a young man . . . who has shown himself capable of delighting an audience through five acts, and carrying it along with him by a continuous *coup de main*.

How was it done? By Boucicault's sure dramatic instinct, which keeps the laughter bubbly and the action buoyant. Each act opens with an instant plunge into the intrigue. Cool starts the play with 'Half past nine, and Mr Charles has not yet returned. I am in a fever of dread'; and act three kicks off in mid-plot with 'What can I do?' 'Get rid of them civilly.' Characters always spring on at exactly the right moment. 'Law, here comes Mr Meddle,' says Pert, retreating, in act two; 'a nasty, prying, ugly wretch'; and on he comes, prying busily away (II. 73). 'Lady Gay Spanker? Who may she be?' asks Sir Harcourt (III. 58); 'The merriest minx I ever kissed' comes the reply, while Lady Gay laughs outside and bursts on a second later in a whirlwind of high spirits. 'She dashed in like a flash of lightning and was greeted with a thunder of applause' said Boucicault in the Preface (81-2). Scene after scene is built up swiftly to a telling climax, as when Lady Gay arrives on stage to catch Young Courtly kissing Grace and the next moment, with the seduction plan afoot, coquettes off upon Sir Harcourt's arm. Indeed, every exit is given the maximum lift for a good take off; witness, for example, the hurrying effect of Boucicault's staccato phrases here, when Max invites Dazzle to Oak Hall:

> MAX. I foresee some happy days.
>
> DAZZLE. And I some glorious nights.
>
> MAX. It mustn't be a flying visit.
>
> DAZZLE. I despise the word. I'll stop a month with you.
>
> MAX. Or a year or two.
>
> DAZZLE. I'll live and die with you.
>
> MAX. Ha, ha! Remember: Max Harkaway, Oak Hall, Gloucestershire.
>
> DAZZLE. I'll remember. Fare ye well. (MAX *is going*) I say, holloa! Tally-ho-o-o-o!
>
> MAX. Yoicks! Tally-ho-o-o-o!
>
> *Exit* (I. 351-61)

All the business of the stage is as deftly handled, whether Meddle hides in a shrubbery or armchair or runs about begging to be kicked, or Grace and Courtly play their *faux-naif* love scene, or Sir Harcourt is about to kiss Lady Gay's hand when Spanker intervenes: 'A very handsome ring, indeed.' 'Very.' *Puts her arm in his and they go up* (V. 474-5). *John Bull*'s 'quick dialogue, effective situation, and vigorous movement,' then, are some of the energising tricks with which Boucicault concealed the minor inconsistencies and major implausibilities inherent in two plots firmly based upon the traditional structures of farce.

On this foundation Boucicault has built what looks very like a Georgian comedy of manners—that is, a witty and satiric prose play in five acts, about the love intrigues of a few stock characters from the leisured classes, tinged with rural sentimentalism and resolved by moral criteria. Freed from the breathless brevity of farce, for instance, *London Assurance* finds time among its five acts for witty conversations about drinking, dandyism, etiquette, female emancipation, country life, the London season, arranged marriages, hunting, fashion, duelling, marital disharmony, and much else besides. The intrigues, with their complement of misunderstandings, overhearings, hidden letters, troublesome old wills, elopements, threatened arrests and aborted duels, all come from stock, just like the cast of crusty fathers, rustic squires, grasping lawyers, clever servants, spongers, ladies' maids, lovely heiresses, browbeaten husbands, titled beaux and ardent lovers. Take Courtly, for example. Like Charles Surface in Sheridan's *The School for Scandal,* he is an improvident young dog beset by duns and bailiffs; like Aimwell and Archer in Farquhar's *The Beaux' Stratagem,* he flees to the country and assumes another name; his double role of bashful bookworm and romantic lover echoes Young Marlow's dual nature in Goldsmith's *She Stoops to Conquer* and his wooing Grace as both Courtly and 'Augustus Hamilton' that of Lydia's wooing by Captain Absolute and 'Ensign Beverley' in Sheridan's *The Rivals;* like Fashion in Vanbrugh's *The Relapse* he discovers that his rival, the official suitor, is a foppish blood relation; and like Charles, Aimwell, Marlow, Absolute and Fashion, he winds up with his deceptions pardoned and the heiress as his loving bride. Most of the other characters have pedigrees as lengthy, and like their parents all are named according to their 'humour'. Meddle, Dazzle, Cool and Pert are obvious examples, so is Lady Gay Spanker, rightly understood; Squire Harkaway utters hunting cries and introduces Grace as if she were a thoroughbred, and in the wings, just as at Sheridan's scandal-school, Boucicault keeps Lady Sarah Sarcasm, Lady Acid, Miss Stitch the milliner and the Reverend Mr Spout. Many turns of phrase are borrowed—as when Sir Harcourt's talk of the economy of a beauty's cheek (I. 210) recalls Lady Wishfort on the economy of her face in Congreve's *The Way of the World* (III. v.)—and sometimes even famous jokes are plundered wholesale. Sir Anthony in *The Rivals* offers Jack an independent fortune, together with—as it happens—a wife:

> Odd's life, Sir! if you have the estate, you must take it with the livestock on it, as it stands.
>
> (II.i. 26-7)

And here is Grace, telling Pert that Sir Harcourt takes her

> with the incumbrances on his estate, and I shall beg to be left among the rest of the live-stock.
>
> (II. 49-50)

Boucicault did not always improve what he stole.

There is more freshness, with some originality and confusion, in the treatment of his themes. His central argument is to expose the falsity of judgments based on money or fashion by setting them against the natural goodness of an honest heart—a sentimental ethic which Boucicault projects by defining three antitheses within the play: love and money, town and country, nature and artifice.

Many comedies of manners treat of marriages arranged for money or true lovers separated by financial barriers which are regularly broken down before the final curtain. In *London Assurance* Boucicault considers both, somewhat unsteadily. Sir Harcourt married 'virgin gold' (I. 196) and was even more delighted with the bargain when his wife eloped a few months later with an intimate friend, who paid him damages of £10,000. Lady Gay, by contrast, proposed to Spanker out of pity for his destitute and helpless situation as a bachelor with £10,000 a year; she gained freedom, he protection, and by the play's end they make a happy pair. Boucicault sets one relationship against the other without comment: sometimes financial marriages succeed, sometimes they don't. A sharper attitude here might have guided our responses to the marital dilemmas at Oak Hall. The worldly Pert adopts a thoroughly romantic attitude, tells us she would give up all her fortune to marry the man she loves, and scorns the money-grubbing Meddle for honest Mr Jenks. Her mistress Grace is just as paradoxical. The play's romantic heroine, she sees the marriage tie with cheerful cynicism as a mere financial bonding based on horses, diamonds, estates; a London ball-room is a market where the groom's fortune is ticketed on his back and the bride knocked down by her parents to the highest bidder; consequently, she is happy to honour her father's will and marry an old man she has never met to safeguard an income of £15,000 a year. When she falls in love with Mr Hamilton, she is confronted with a simple moral choice—marrying for love or money—which the play ignores. The discovery of Sir Harcourt's planned elopement obliges him to waive his claims, and the moral pressure is renewed, for now her choice must lie between losing her fortune or marrying a moth-eaten edition of the classics. Again, Boucicault ducks the dilemma by inventing a second fortune which Max promptly offers her if she rejects Young Courtly—and even this weakened situation is torpedoed when, as Grace already guessed, the college swot and the dashing Mr Hamilton turn out to be the same man, who is, in fact, Sir Harcourt's son and heir. The lovers are rewarded, therefore, by a providential luck without enduring the fatigue of any moral struggle or dilemma. Indeed, Boucicault has no interest in such problems, which he exploits for their amusement value or the opportunity for Max to show his philanthropic heart and draw from Grace a totally unmotivated sentimental tear.

The clash of town and country values is also common in the comedy of manners. Congreve's Millamant nauseates walking because it is a country diversion. Vanbrugh and Farquhar scorn the dirt and beastliness of rural life, but find some value there as well; *The Relapse* opens in a rustic Arcadia, and in the provincial settings of his best plays Farquhar finds charitable heroines who are cultured, independent, witty and intelligent. Now Boucicault completes the transformation. His sophisticated beau and gay young blades, rusticated from the giddy whirl of town, lament their absence from the racing or next week's new ballet, and languidly complain of the infernal distance which divides a country squire's gate-house from his front door. But such London assurance cuts no ice here at all. Grace is on hand to remind them that fashionable society is vicious and depraved; gamblers pawn their birthright and a roué steals his friend's wife—all for fashion. Squire Harkaway is set against Sir Harcourt, and there is no doubt where Boucicault intends our sympathies to lie. The shuffling of a pack of cards is no equal to the yelping of a pack of hounds, and the statuary of Belgrave Square no match for the scented flowerbeds of Oak Hall. Italian opera cannot compete with that fine old English music of the view halloo, and Grace pours in poetic commonplaces to swell the paean. To clinch the contrast, Boucicault purges his countryside of its dung and squalor, of Farquhar's churlish Sullen, Vanbrugh's inhospitable Clumsy, and even the block-headed servants and rustic boorishness at Goldsmith's Hardcastle Hall. His rural life is cleansed and sanitized, and now identified with all that is best in humankind. Max greets Sir Harcourt with a hearty handshake which even the baronet admits is totally without fawning pretence; and after the shaming exposure of his fashionable immorality, even Sir Harcourt is ready to admit that as long as honour, truth and good feeling beat in every true young English heart, 'the title of gentleman is the only one *out* of any monarch's gift, yet within the reach of every peasant' (V. 501-2). London assurance has lost hands down to Merry England.

Artifice and nature are alternative terms for the same equation, and Boucicault derives a lot of comedy from the contrast. The play's chief artefact is, of course, Sir Harcourt Courtly, for whom nature always comes a second best. He wears a black wig to conceal his greying hair and paints his cheeks to restore the flush of youth; in the country, he tells Cool to perfume his handkerchief but has to make do with a buttonhole of fresh-picked flowers instead. Lady Gay thinks man was fashioned expressly to fit a horse, but he prefers to break his neck in comfort from a bedroom window. Grace gets up to enjoy the sunrise, but he considers it a most disagreeable spectacle, to be glimpsed only through the windows of his travelling carriage, or returning from a ball. Sir Harcourt has no conception of what such a creature as a lark might be. These comically inverted attitudes are not wholly explained by Sir Harcourt's pedigree. The affected aristocrat who labours over his toilette, tells lies about his age and pursues hopeless sexual conquests with vainglorious egotism is, of course, modelled on Lord Ogleby or Vanbrugh's Foppington, and like them Sir Harcourt must be ridiculed, humiliated and exposed. But his obstinate preference for the man-made to the natural more probably reflects Boucicault's own interest in that contemporary phenomenon, the dandy. The fashionable cult of dandyism, to which Boucicault makes explicit reference in the play (II. 264-5), was codified in 1845 by Jules Amédée Barbey d'Aurevilly, whose book *Du Dandysme et de Georges Brummell* strongly influenced Baudelaire's *Le Peintre de la Vie Moderne* (1863) and through him the *fin de siècle* decadence of Huysmans and Wilde. Their dandy was a Narcissist, scrupulously ultra-fashionable in dress, who lived solely for himself, denied all moral codes and in their place set an aesthetic doctrine based on artifice and triviality. Remove

Sir Harcourt's final speech, which was originally written for Max Harkaway in any case, and the description fits him like a well-made glove. It might also be said to fit young Boucicault himself. During his first season at Brighton in 1838, he drove along the esplanade in a single-breasted white coat over sky-blue trousers and new patent boots, the white silk reins of his cream-coloured ponies loosely held between the fingers of his lemon gloves. In later years he broke business contracts for his own advantage, lived openly with mistresses, married bigamously, and spent half a century in the theatre, creating a resolutely artificial world where art improved on life. The parallel might be debated, but there is enough here to establish Boucicault's dandy sympathies. They were unable to save Sir Harcourt from traditional disgrace, but surely moulded that embodiment of London assurance, Richard Dazzle, whose attitudes strikingly prefigure those of Wilde's supreme dandy, Mr Algernon Moncrieff in *The Importance of Being Earnest*. Like Algy, Dazzle never lets the serious concerns of life and death affect his appetite. While his two friends blow their brains out in the billiard room, he is happy to make a night of it with his host's excellent madeira and cigars. Indeed, this duel sequence exhibits to perfection Dazzle's dandy pose of studied artifice. Only such a supreme egotist would congratulate himself that both the parties were his intimate and bosom friends. Spanker shows all the natural fear of a man in his last hour of life, but Dazzle kindly apologises to Sir Harcourt for this woeful lack of education, trusts that the irregular styling of the challenge will not spoil the beauty of its subject, and points out to him like a connoisseur the exquisite workmanship of the fatal pistols. In matters of grave importance, as Gwendolen remarks, style not sincerity is the vital thing—and Dazzle has enough to spare. Like Algy, Dazzle has nothing but his debts to depend on; his family escutcheon is an empty purse falling through a hole in a pocket, with a motto which he ironically translates as 'Let virtue be its own reward' (V. 419). He therefore lives, more desperately than most dandies, in that 'age of surfaces' which Lady Bracknell says she also inhabits. He may have nothing but, like Algy again, he looks everything, which of course is more important, because he is accepted everywhere on the general assumption that some other member of the party is his distant relation. Of his true identity, he has 'not the remotest idea' (V. 484), but boasts that nature made him a gentleman because he lives off his wits and his credit. This unscrupulous London assurance offers an irresistible alternative to all those other natural gentlemen at Oak Hall, and thereby threatens to disturb the thematic patterning of the play. Just as Boucicault had difficulty making up his mind about the contrast of true love and arranged marriages, so now his dandy sympathies plead for an artificiality which runs counter to the simple and straightforward contrast of the moral integrity of Merry England and the acknowledged corruptions of fashionable life in Belgrave Square.

Finally, no comedy of manners was complete without a liberal display of wit. A modern taste may, perhaps, regret Boucicault's Victorian delight in sprightly puns, or the rococo simile of Sir Harcourt lying on his back 'like a shipwrecked tea-table' (III. 112). But his comic dialogue has an enviable directness, and the best of it is efficiently laconic:

> —That fellow is a swindler.
> —I met him at your house.
> —Never saw him before in all my life.
>
> (III. 11-14)

Young Courtly's drunken exit is just as smart:

> I say, old fellow, (*Staggering*) just hold the door
> steady while I go in.
>
> (I. 71-2)

The more laboured jokes are rather painful, and the epigrams dwindle out of context. Lines like

> A valet is as difficult a post to fill properly as that
> of prime minister
>
> (I. 23-5)

have a musty flavour, as if they had been rejected from *The Beggar's Opera* and laid away in mothballs ever since. His most telling hits, in fact, are found not in pale imitations of Sheridan or Goldsmith, but in dandyisms which anticipate much of Wilde. When Dazzle says

> A good many of the nobility claim me as a connection
>
> (III. 272)

we have to invert the statement before we laugh. Lady Gay's stated motives must be inverted too. She says she took pity on poor Spanker as a helpless bachelor with £10,000 a year; in fact, she went out as the penniless third daughter of an Earl and caught him to secure her own financial future. Lady Bracknell did the same, which is why she does not

> approve of mercenary marriages. When I married Lord Bracknell I had no fortune of any kind. But I never dreamed for a moment of allowing that to stand in my way.
>
> (III)

Wilde is not always superior to Boucicault. *Noblesse oblige* conventionally requires the aristocracy to set a good example to the lower classes, but Algy inverts this when he comments on the unfortunate marriage of his valet, Lane:

> Really, if the lower orders don't set us a good example, what on earth is the use of them?
>
> (I)

Sir Harcourt goes one better, when persuading Lady Gay to elope with him:

> Let us be a precedent to open a more extended and liberal view of matrimonial advantages to society . . . I have ascertained for a fact every tradesman of mine lives with his wife; and thus you see it has become a vulgar and plebeian custom.
>
> (IV. 308-13)

Algy supposed the lower classes should give a moral lead to their betters, but Sir Harcourt uses their morality to argue that an aristocrat must be immoral to distinguish himself from them.

These dandyisms are perhaps the most original feature of a play which is in other ways remarkably derivative, but they are not entirely alone; Boucicault deploys two old conventions in an interesting way and hints at the large theme of Victorian hypocrisy.

Servants who criticise their masters are as old as comedy itself, but *London Assurance* employs them oddly, to set the leading characters at arms' length, frame them, and increase our sense of critical detachment. Our first impressions of the residents at Belgrave Square and Oak Hall are provided by the servants. In a creaky exposition, Cool and Martin do more than reveal the situation; by conniving at Young Courtly's irregularities and ironically sending up Sir Harcourt as a 'poor, deluded old gentleman' (I. 4), they 'place' both characters efficiently before us and invite us to transfer our loyalties, as they have already done, from the foolish father to the randy son. In the same way, Pert introduces us to Grace as one who prepares for matrimony as she would for dinner; the maid's shrewd comments on the unnaturalness of such indifference prepare us for her unawakened mistress and, of course, Grace's almost immediate surrender to love. Similarly, Cool outlines Sir Harcourt's folly in act five, and threatens to dismiss him if it continues—another dandy inversion like Sir Harcourt's, invoking once again the morality of tradesmen or valets to condemn the absurd philandering of the aristocracy; Sir Harcourt's character and motives are held out for our scrutiny, and comically found wanting.

Equally distancing are the asides, which traditionally allow an audience to hear a character's unspoken thoughts. Boucicault uses the device to brilliant effect in a comic love scene where the nervous, stilted dialogue is intercut with racy, swift asides in which each character checks responses, monitors progress, and debates the next move in the courtship game. Social decorum so inhibits them from simple, direct statement that Courtly is reduced to bidding an eternal farewell when Grace has the wit to cry 'Unhand me' (III. 390) and he rushes back to kiss it. This conflict of natural instinct and social reticence is also momentarily apparent when Grace receives a letter from Mr Hamilton and has to restrain herself to take it coolly; later, she affects indifference, pretends to toss the letter in the fire, and hides it in her bosom—that is, social pressures lead her to the innocent dissimulation of a little temporary role-playing. Many of the other characters play different roles for higher stakes: Lady Gay for fun, Meddle for profit, Cool for self-interest and Dazzle for all three, while Courtly pursues his elaborate impersonation of Augustus Hamilton so brazenly some think there are two people, others like Dazzle and the audience know there's only one, and Grace has to decide if Hamilton was pretending to be Courtly or Courtly Hamilton; in either case she thinks him now disfigured (IV. 169) while we know that he is now himself. It is with skirmishes like this that the play stops looking backwards and employs its dandy wit and distancing devices to anticipate the sustained attack on Victorian social hypocrisy in the farces of Pinero and the comedies of Wilde. *London Assurance* is a truly astonishing performance for a man not yet twenty one. (pp. xxii-xxxiii)

> *James L. Smith, in an introduction to* London
> Assurance *by Dion Boucicault, edited by*

*James L. Smith, Adam & Charles Black,
1984, pp. x-xliii.*

Richard A. Cave (essay date 1987)

[*In the following essay, Cave argues that Boucicault's
Irish comedies are his most convincing works because
they draw upon real social conflicts to augment the tension of their plots.*]

This paper is an attempt to explore why Boucicault's Irish
melodramas are among the finest of his many plays and
why **The Shaughraun,** by common consent, stands pre-
eminent among them. I would argue that Boucicault is at
his best when he confronts contemporary social and political issues which generate convincing tensions and conflicts rather than the factitious passions common to must
run-of-the-mill melodramas. The Irish melodramas treat
of politically sensitive matters, being set during or in the
aftermath of an uprising against English domination. All
were, however, destined in time to be played before English audiences to whose tastes and sympathies Boucicault
was acutely responsive (he readily changed the resolution
of **The Octoroon** from the tragic one composed for New
York spectators to a happy one, when London theatre-
goers refused to accept Zoe's, the heroine's, death as
sound dramatic practice whatever its justification on thematic grounds). That Boucicault was on his guard and
taking special pains is suggested by the infinitely better
crafting of the Irish plays compared with most of his melodramas. **After Dark—A Tale of London Life** (produced
1868) takes its characters from one sensational escapade
to another with Boucicault paying scant attention to plotting to explain how they get from one crisis to the next:
the sensational moment is what counts here. **Arrah-na-
Pogue** and **The Shaughraun** (and even less successful Irish
dramas like **The Rapparee**) show Boucicault far more attentive to detail. It was interesting to find in the recent
Boucicault exhibition mounted by the Irish Theatre Archive a playbill of 1876 for **The Shaughraun** which boldly
claimed that Boucicault was "out to kill the stage Irishman". Indeed a close scrutiny of the Irish melodramas
suggests that the dramatist was intent on educating his
American and, more especially, his English audiences into
a proper appreciation of the Irish sensibility and of Irish
values. In pursuing this aim, his mode of presenting English characters and his way of relating these to a wide
spectrum of Irish personalities are all-important.

Boucicault was not, of course, the first to challenge the
conventional image of the Irishman current on the English
stage. Tyrone Power had extolled the Irishman's imaginative brilliance and intellectual caprice and in Major
O'Dogherty of *St Patrick's Eve* he had shown this verbal
ingenuity masking considerable courage and a loyalty that
will honour a pledge, if necessary to death. To carry his
point, Power shows the Major winning acclaim for his soldierly virtues while serving in the Prussian army that upholds the most punctilious of military codes of behaviour.
An Irish major in Frederick II's army challenges verisimilitude, perhaps; but Power's moral and psychological
strategy carries weight.

Boucicault's earliest play with Irish characters, **The Irish
Heiress** (1842), written for Vestris and Mathews in the
wake of the successful **London Assurance,** is a curiously
bitter piece that holds up all the characters except the
Heiress of the title to ridicule or outright censure. A profligate, Sir William Stanley, with a common-law wife, seeks
to bolster his failing income by scheming to wed his
wealthy Irish cousin. His bungling efforts all but precipitate a married couple into divorce, and his capacity to
create havoc in other people's lives is arrested only by the
Heiress calling him to order and to a proper sense of the
family tradition and name. She consoles his victims: "If
you have been wronged by him, he is a Daventry and will
right you—I, a Daventry, say it." One is surprised in retrospect that Vestris should have chosen to mount so un-
funny a comedy and curious as to why Boucicault should
have given such unprepossessing characters an Irish heritage, when he makes nothing whatever of that background
in the action. As the reviewer for *Theatre Journal* rightly
noted, the play "falls off in point, in humour, in tact, and
in interest".

A scrupulous attention to tact in the face of his audience's
susceptibilities, I would argue, is what makes for the success of Boucicault's later melodramas. Indeed tact must
have been a major consideration in adapting Griffin's
novel *The Collegians* as **The Colleen Bawn,** especially in
the handling of the hero, Hardress Cregan, who turns
against his peasant-wife, Eily, snobbishly despises her
brogue and contemplates her murder when he realizes his
impulsive marriage has cost him the hand of the heiress,
Anne Chute, who would redeem his mortgaged home.
There is little here that smacks of the heroic, especially of
the heroic in specifically Irish terms as Boucicault came
to define it in later melodramas. Hardress is not even the
Romantic, tortured sinner that is his prototype in Griffin's
novel. Wishing to give his play a happy ending in which
husband and wife are reunited, Boucicault makes Hardress a man more sinned against than sinning, building up
the plot about the mortgage to aggravate the pressures on
him, and giving him an indulgent but rather domineering
mother, who in another departure from the plot of the
novel is the one—unwittingly—to send the token that will
set in motion the scheme to drown Eily. The only actor
to achieve distinction in the role of Hardress seems to have
been the young Henry Irving who saw in the role one of
his first opportunities to exploit his peculiar gift for finding
pathos in moments of impetuosity and remorse. But this
would have been more the actor's invention than the
dramatist's.

Beside the later Irish melodramas and in comparison with
The Collegians, **The Colleen Bawn** seems a rather thin performance. Because of the need to develop the plot about
the mortgage and establish Mrs. Cregan's character so
that the villain's proposal of marriage should affect us as
the shocking insult that it is, Boucicault leaves himself
with no stage-time to dramatize one of the real strengths
of the novel—the social comedy of the Cregan household
who are presented as "a rackety and pretentious set of
half-sirs" in contrast with the stalwart, responsible middle-class Dalys. Griffin uses the family background to account for Hardress's recklessness and his moral decline;

Boucicault with his third wife, Louise Thorndyke Boucicault.

the Hardress of *The Collegians* becomes a truly tragic figure because he discovers the value of owning a conscience
at the very moment that it is too late for that conscience
to save him. It would not have been an impossible task to
present a degree of the rich social tapestry of Griffin's
novel in dramatic terms. *Arrah-na-Pogue,* for example,
presents non-Irish audiences with a complex but well-
defined social network, where the peasants show allegiance to various clans or septs, each with a leader—The
MacCoul and The O'Grady; the septs have their codes of
fealty and modes of formal address; the play is set in Wicklow during the 1798 disturbances so the English authorities are tense, quick to act, concerned to maintain the law.
All this is not just background information; it directly
contributes to and affects the action, explaining why many
of the characters act as they do. The real-life story on
which *The Collegians* is based occurred in 1819; Boucicault asks that his play be costumed for the year 1798.
Why he moved the play back in time to that highly emotive date is inexplicable. Did he perhaps plan to develop
a historical dimension different from Griffin's concern
with the emergence of a Catholic middle-class but which
failed to materialize in the writing? It is difficult to see how
the political tensions of that year could have been woven
into the story of the attempted murder of Eily O'Connor.

Significantly, no Englishman appears in this play which
may also account for the sense of thinness in the conception and the writing; all the later Irish melodramas contain at least one outsider, usually English, who throws into
sharp relief the distinctively Irish qualities of the remaining characters, providing a focus for some subtle moral
and psychological discriminations. Though he treated the
conclusion of Griffin's novel with great freedom, elsewhere Boucicault appears to have been considerably ham-
pered by his model and the problem it posed over characterizing Hardress Cregan.

The one gift the novel gave him was Myles-na-Coppaleen,
the love-lorn but loyal suitor to Eily, a wily but witty and
ingratiating rogue, who lives by his own private moral
code, which provided Boucicault the actor with a success
to equal Tyrone Power's many creations in a similar vein.
Moreover here was a character through whom he could
effect rapid transitions of mood from the comic to the
tense, the very unpredictableness of whose appearances
and reactions could generate much excitement. Boucicault
had found a seam he would long continue to quarry; but
The Colleen Bawn did not offer him the structural patterns to make of this character what he was later to become in Shaun the Post and Conn the Shaughraun—a
symbol of all that is best in the "indomitable Irishry".

When in *Arrah-na-Pogue* Shaun the Post at the climax of
Act II is on trial for his life, suspected of robbing Michael
Feeny of the rents of the Hollywood estate, he finds his
judges somewhat divided in their sympathies. Colonel
O'Grady, an Irishman, is all for "letting him off" to the
amazement of his superior officer Major Coffin, an Englishman, who demands to know what are the grounds for
such a verdict when all the evidence seems to substantiate
Shaun's guilt. O'Grady refers to "the eloquence of the defense" which perplexes the Major even more since Shaun's
"defense" has largely involved his sustained abuse of his
accuser, ably encouraged by the public spectators at the
trial and by O'Grady himself, who over-rides the Major's
objection that all this is "not to the point" with the view
that this "is a mighty fine outburst of natural eloquence;
go on, my man, crush that reptile if you can". When the
Major persists in questioning the relevance of such a
slanging match, the O'Grady accuses him of "prejudice"
and concludes: "I never listened to anything more compact in the way of vituperation". The Major is unwaver-
ing: "I regret to say that we cannot admit so Irish a consideration". This is a complex moment for the audience—
especially an English one. We recognize the Major as a
man of firm principle whose genuine conviction it is that
"an example is particularly required at this moment to
check a popular disturbance". Challenged, he would
doubtless defend himself as acting with an eye to the overall social situation and for the good of the greater number.
He observes the strict letter of the law. O'Grady chooses
to judge between Shaun and Feeny in terms of which is
the better, indeed the truer, Irishman; and his personal,
impressionistic response is seen to be the accurate one.
British justice in this particular case is actually blind to the
truth. The audience know that Shaun has admitted to a
crime of which he is innocent, simply to protect his wife's
honour when circumstances suggest she is the criminal or

an accomplice. His is an act of chivalry, trust and courage. O'Grady intuitively perceives the truth yet to admit intuition into the legal process would make a travesty of justice. The situation throws English and Irish values into very precise relief in a way that allows neither to be seen as superior; indeed it encourages an English audience to take a very positive view of the Irish sensibility.

What is remarkable in an Irish melodrama set in the year 1798 is that the English characters are viewed dispassionately, even if at times critically (especially over their deficiencies in imagination). The villain of the piece is Feeny, who exploits the political situation to his own miserable advantage; he is a time-server, respected by neither the English nor the Irish. Shaun acts magnanimously by Arrah, his wife, and becomes the object of other people's anxious concern and magnanimity as a consequence: Fanny Power, Beamish mac Coul and O'Grady all race through the night to the Secretary of State in hope of securing his pardon, while the kindly English Sergeant responsible for Shaun's imprisonment and execution tries to cheer him with a little material comfort. They may be political enemies but the Sergeant has a respect for human dignity. Not so Feeny, who appears in the prison to gloat over his rival's tragic predicament:

> You will be hung free of all expense—hung before tomorrow mornin'—that's the weddin' night you'll have. It's a wooden bride that is waiting for you, my jewel. It's only one arm she's got, and one leg, ho! ho! but, once she takes you round the neck, she's yours till death, ha! ha!

Evil defines itself in Feeny as a lack of both English principle and Irish chivalry; he has no largeness of spirit, his essential identity is defined through malice which is a kind of jealousy of the points of virtue in others. He cannot recognize any worth in Shaun as a rival for Arrah's affections and he would deny her any freedom of choice in her marriage: either he will eliminate Shaun and compel her to marry himself or he will destroy her reputation and prevent *anyone* marrying her. Feeny is unusual amongst melodrama villains for his mean-spiritedness; he has no grandeur of vision or of rhetorical display, no stature or presence by virtue of an evil genius; he is wholly characterized by his pettiness. As such he becomes a crucial figure in the structural patterning of the action. Fanny Power is courted by the heads of two septs, the O'Grady and the MacCoul; Arrah by Shaun and Feeny. When O'Grady discovers the depth of Fanny's infatuation for Beamish, he gallantly yields his place to his rival and refuses to hold Fanny to her promise of marriage. Passion gives him the courage to act honourably even though that leaves him with a tragic and lonely future; and he covers his disappointment in action by galloping home against the clock with Shaun's reprieve. Feeny by contrast cannot accept defeat when Arrah admits she has no feeling for him; but ironically his every attempt to destroy Shaun acts as a test to prove Shaun's worth. When on Arrah's wedding day Feeny produces evidence to suggest that she is a loose woman and a criminal, Shaun trusts implicitly in his belief in Arrah's goodness and is prepared to face imprisonment and even death for that belief. Passionate devotion to an ideal motivates Shaun, Beamish and O'Grady and defines

their distinctive Irishness. Feeny is despised by the other characters because his malice is a betrayal of what is fundamental and best in the national temperament. Beside the other Irish characters in the play, Feeny lacks colour, daring, personality, because his every concern is with himself. Boucicault cleverly manipulates the conventions of nineteenth-century melodrama to make *Arrah-na-Pogue* a celebration of the Celtic consciousness; particularly for English audiences he plays with their romantic susceptibilities to educate them into a richer understanding of the Irish as a people. Shaw described the stage Irishman as one who flatters an English audience's "sense of moral superiority by playing the fool and degrading himself and his country". In *Arrah-na-Pogue,* that is the villain's role; the remaining Irish characters are cast in a justifiably heroic mould.

It is perhaps the sense of betraying the national cause that accounts for the violence meted out to Feeny. Villains in melodramas usually meet with nasty ends, preferably hoist with their own petards. At the end of Shaun's trial, the spectators rush the court and are seen as the curtain falls to seize Feeny and "throw him violently to the ground"; at the end he is dragged over the edge of a precipice by Shaun to drown in the lake far below. In Boucicault's later melodramas this violence is even more marked. In *The Rapparee,* set in the aftermath of the Battle of the Boyne, Ulick O'Murragh has treacherously made peace with the "Dutch king" to get power over Roderick O'Malley, his rival for the heroine, Grace. Roderick generously saves Ulick's life but Ulick uses the advantage this gives him to imprison Roderick. At the climax of the piece Grace marries Ulick on condition he set Roderick free; and then arranges a confrontation of the two men. She addresses Roderick: "I gave you your freedom that you might give me mine"; then, pointing to Ulick, urges: "Kill that man!" The Dutch commander tries to "stop this massacre", but is prevented by Grace's father: "No! Let them decide the cause! 'Tis so that England must ever rule over this unhappy land, and pit the traitor 'gainst the patriot. Thus they stand before fair Ireland, the trembling prize, who, looking on, waits for the bloody issue". Roderick stabs Ulick: "That for my love and that (*repeating the wound*) for my country!" He is pardoned by the Dutch commander and united with Grace. In none of his other Irish melodramas does Boucicault show his hand so openly or make his symbolic purpose so explicit. The play failed at the Princess's Theatre in 1870, presumably because of its inexorable, dark intensity and because it makes no concessions to English susceptibilities in depicting this Irish conception of justice and honour. No attempt is made to educate the audience into appreciating the peculiarly Irish perspective, the race-memory that lies behind Ulick's acts of betrayal and that charges the final duel and death with symbolic resonance. Significances which an Irish audience would have read implicitly into the action from the first would not affect an English audience so that the symbolism of the climax would appear crude and intrusive to them and do little to explain, let alone justify, the characters' violent motives. It is an example of Boucicault failing in creative tact towards a non-Irish audience. With *The Shaughraun,* written four years later, he was to be far more scrupulous.

And with good reason: where the previous melodramas had been firmly set in historical times, this play (staged in New York in 1874 and in London a year later) was set in the late 1860s in the wake of the Fenian uprising, when for the first time the war of independence was carried into England. The hero, Robert Ffolliott, is a bold Fenian leader, escaping from deportation to Australia; we hear of the spying and informing which led to the English suppression of the rising through the arrest of the leaders before their arrangements were finalized; the complications of the plot are occasioned by the granting of a Royal pardon to Robert as in real life to many of the captured Fenians, following the Government's embarrassment at discovering that numerous informers had used the prevailing unrest to settle private scores which had nothing to do with the rising; and reference is made (significantly by the villains, Kinchela and Harvey Duff) to "the late attack on the police-van at Manchester, and the explosion at Clerkenwell Prison in London" which had caused widespread panic in England. To set a Fenian before an English audience as the hero of the melodrama took some courage, especially after Shaun's singing of "The Wearing of the Green" had had to be excised from English performances of **Arrah-na-Pogue** by order of the Chamberlain. Boucicault was on very sensitive ground. (A decade later Boucicault's friend Irving was required to abandon a projected production of a play on the life of Robert Emmet under political pressure.)

Interestingly Boucicault chooses to start the play with his principal English character, Captain Molineux, arriving in Suil-a-beg where he quickly discovers to his embarrassment how false and patronizing his assumptions about the Irish are. By a masterstroke of casting Boucicault chose for this role at Drury Lane the young William Terris, who before he joined Irving's company in 1880 was establishing a name for himself as the ideal melodrama hero; with his physical prowess and good looks, he seemed an embodiment of all the English manly virtues. Much of the comedy in the play springs from Molineux's bewilderment at, and growing delight in, the 'difference' of the Irish way of life. He stands constantly under correction from Robert's sister, Claire; growing affection makes her an admirable tutor. The play sports not one hero but two—one Irish (Robert), one English (Molineux)—and from the first each respects the other: they may be political opponents but each recognizes in the other the marks of courtesy that betoken a gentleman. Molineux finds it increasingly distasteful pursuing his duty tracking down the Fenians, because it offends his sense of decency and fair play; and he comes profoundly to admire Robert for submitting, to arrest to save his former tutor, Father Dolan, from the sin of telling a lie to keep secret Robert's whereabouts. Ultimately Molineux has to choose between his duty and his sympathies when Claire informs him he is the only one possessing the means to set fire to the tarbarrel on Rathgarron Head which is a signal to aid Robert's escape to a waiting ship. The fire is subsequently lit but the audience is spared seeing an English officer failing in his duty as the curtain falls on his agonizing over what to do. If audiences at this point will Molineux to help Robert, it is because of the clever way Boucicault manipulates their sympathies as a consequence of his mode of characterizing his villains.

Duff is a police spy and informer who goes in disguise for fear of the reprisals that might be visited on him by the relatives of the many men he has brought to hanging or deportation; Kinchela has taken advantage of Robert's patriotism to secure by malpractice his estates which would otherwise be forfeit to the Crown. If they are despicable it is because they are motivated neither by principle nor by romantic idealism which for Boucicault define Molineux and Ffolliott as gentlemen. What is interesting in this is how accurately Boucicault reflects the tenor of the times. Consider W. B. Yeats's moving account of Ellen O'Leary, sister of the Fenian leader, whom the poet considered one of "Plutarch's people":

> She told me of her brother's life, of the foundation of the Fenian movement, and of the arrests that followed (I believe that her own sweetheart had somehow fallen among the wreckage), of sentences of death pronounced upon false evidence amid a public panic, and told it all without bitterness. No fanaticism could thrive amid such gentleness. She never found it hard to believe that an opponent had as high a motive as her own, and needed upon her difficult road no spur of hate.

Here is the same dignity and courtesy deriving from a respect for one's opponent that transcends the fact of conflict which Boucicault depicts in his play; and evil is defined by him as conduct which betrays that principle of magnanimity. Kinchela for all his power is treated throughout as beneath contempt, while Harvey Duff meets the death he dreads hounded pitilessly over a precipice by the assembled cast: "There's death coming down upon you from above! there's death waiting for you below! Now, *informer,* take your choice!" Hatred is manifest only against the informer, the one who is No Man, having no national identity and so no truth to self. There is an exhilaration in the violence here that goes way beyond the satisfaction melodrama usually promotes in the villain's demise: the informer is, after all, the most vicious betrayer of the national ideal.

Significantly the character who so delights in pronouncing doom on Harvey Duff is Conn the Shaughraun, Boucicault's most sophisticated portrayal of the type of rogue that began with Myles. Conn acts by a private moral code that recognizes allegiance only to those who do good by him and then his loyalty is unswerving. Conn will get the top side of any argument and with such dexterous wit that he will quite likely leave his opponent helpless with laughter: accused of stealing Squire Foley's horse to ride off to the hunt, he will prove beyond dispute that the beast stole him. His high spirits are irrepressible; he is a man who does the seemingly impossible (like freeing Robert from the penal colony in Australia) with an unassuming negligence that calls to mind the high deeds of Finn and his mythical counterparts. For a joke he will put a red herring in his coat tail and draw the hounds when the hunt cannot find a fox and with the same nonchalance dress as Robert and draw the villain's gunfire at risk of his own life to enable Ffolliott to escape. To many an amiable loafer, to the audience who are privileged to see the private soul of the man Conn comes to embody all the daring that is real genius. This is another of Boucicault's shifts of perspective designed to educate his non-Irish audiences. Already with Eily in **The Colleen Bawn** Boucicault had treated the theme of a character brought back to life who is believed dead; but that scene cannot compare in complexity of resonance with Conn's revival in the midst of the wake over his supposed corpse: "It's a mighty pleasant thing to die like this, once in a way, and hear all the good things said about ye afther you're dead and gone, when they can do you no good." Like his spirits, Conn's greatness of soul is indomitable. Comic resurrection this may be, but it also symbolizes the sheer resilience of all that is best and unique in the Celtic consciousness. When this unites in equality with English fortitude and principle, then evil and division can be expelled from the community and peace and justice be restored. The play depicts a historical crisis and intimates a possible way to harmony. Conn's resurrection is a genial explanation of an essential truth about the invincibility of his nation which, if it goes unheeded by an English audience, is also a warning. **The Shaughraun** is Boucicault's finest celebration of what it is to be Irish. (pp. 115-23)

> *Richard A. Cave, "The Presentation of English and Irish Characters in Boucicault's Irish Melodramas," in* Literary Interrelations: Ireland, England and the World, *edited by Wolfgang Zach and Heinz Kosok, Gunter Narr Verlag, 1987, pp. 115-23.*

FURTHER READING

Biography

Fawkes, Richard. *Dion Boucicault: A Biography.* London: Quartet Books, 1979, 274 p.

    Comprehensive critical biography.

Molin, Sven Eric, and Goodefellowe, Robin. *Dion Boucicault, The Shaughraun: A Documentary Life, Letters, and Selected Works.* 5 vols. Horsham, Pa.: Proscenium Press, 1991.

    Compiles previously unpublished documents concerning Boucicault's life, works, and performances of his plays.

Walsh, Townsend. *The Career of Dion Boucicault.* 1915. Reprint. New York: Benjamin Blom, 1967, 224 p.

    Biography focusing on Boucicault's theatrical management and performances of his plays.

Criticism

Basta, Samira. "The French Influence on Dion Boucicault's Sensation Drama." In *Literary Interrelations: Ireland, England, and the World, Volume 2—Comparison and Impact,* edited by Wolfgang Zach and Heinz Kosok, pp. 199-206. Tübingen, Germany: Gunter Narr Verlag, 1987.

    Examines Boucicault's use of French sources. Basta concludes: "Boucicault's subjects may not have been new but he touched this old material with the magic of his genius reviving and enriching it to the extent that he by far surpassed his French models."

Boucicault, Dion. "The Art of Dramatic Composition." *North American Review* CXXVI (January-February 1878): 40-52.

    Boucicault discusses his theories of play writing, drawing from Aristotle but disagreeing with the unities of time and place.

Degen, John A. "How to End *The Octoroon.*" *Educational Theatre Journal* 27, No. 2 (May 1975): 170-78.

    Discusses events surrounding Boucicault's revisions to the last act of *The Octoroon.*

Enkvist, Nils Erik. "The *Octoroon* and English Opinions of Slavery." *American Quarterly* VIII (1955): 166-70.

    Examines the negative reaction of English audiences to the original, unhappy ending of *The Octoroon.* Enkvist suggests that by late 1861, when *The Octoroon* was first performed in London, the English had come to sympathize with the southern United States and so were offended by Boucicault's depiction of the evils of slavery.

Galassi, Frank S. "Slavery and Melodrama: Boucicault's *The Octoroon.*" *The Markham Review* 6, No. 4 (Summer 1977): 77-80.

    Argues that Boucicault failed to take a stand against slavery in *The Octoroon.*

Gambone, Kenneth. "Boucicault's Contributions to the Theatre." *Ball State Teachers College Forum* IV, No. 1 (Spring 1963): 73-8.

    Asserts that Boucicault was instrumental in gaining greater respect for actors and playwrights.

Gerould, Daniel C. "The Americanization of Melodrama." In *American Melodrama,* edited by Daniel C. Gerould, pp. 7-29. New York: Performing Arts Journal Publications, 1983.

    Includes a discussion of the changes Boucicault made in adapting *Les pauvres de Paris* for the American stage.

Hogan, Robert. *Dion Boucicault.* New York: Twayne, 1969, 146 p.

    Provides a brief biography as well as critical discussions of the major plays and an assessment of Boucicault's influence in the theater.

Kaplan, Sidney. "*The Octoroon:* Early History of the Drama of Miscegenation." *Journal of Negro Education* XX, No. 4 (Fall 1951): 547-57.

    Examines responses to the original American production of *The Octoroon.*

Kosok, Heinz. "Dion Boucicault's 'American' Plays: Considerations on Defining National Literatures in English." In *Literature and the Creation of Art: Essays and Poems in Honour of A. Norman Jeffares,* edited by Robert Welch and Suheil Badi Bushrui, pp. 81-97. Totowa, N. J.: Barnes and Noble Books, 1988.

    Suggests that among Boucicault's works only *The Octoroon* can be correctly characterized as an American play.

Krause, David. "The Theatre of Dion Boucicault." In *The Dolmen Boucicault,* edited by David Krause, pp. 9-47. Chester Springs, Pa.: Dufour Editions, 1963.

    Overview of Boucicault's career and major works.

Parkin, Andrew. Introduction to *Selected Plays of Dion Bou-*

cicault, pp. 7-22. Washington, D. C.: Catholic University of America, 1987.

    Discusses Boucicault's career and most significant productions.

Peffer, Susan. "Dion Boucicault." *Letters* 2, No. 8 (August 1929): 7-18.

    Focuses on Boucicault's popularity and his exploitation of theatrical effects.

Rahill, Frank. "Boucicault and the Stage Irishman." In his *The World of Melodrama,* pp. 182-92. University Park: Pennsylvania State University Press, 1967.

    Overview of Boucicault's career in which Rahill identifies the Irish plays as Boucicault's best works.

Shaw, Bernard. "Dear Harp of My Country!" In his *Our Theatres in the Nineties,* Vol. 2, pp. 28-34. London: Constable, 1932.

    Reprints a review of *The Colleen Bawn* in which Shaw argues that Boucicault's depictions of the Irish are not realistic, concluding that the playwright was "blarneying the British public."

Silas Marner

George Eliot

The following entry presents criticism of Eliot's novel *Silas Marner, the Weaver of Raveloe.* For information on Eliot's complete career, see *NCLC,* Vol. 4; for criticism devoted to her novels *Middlemarch* and *Daniel Deronda,* see *NCLC,* Vols. 13 and 23, respectively.

INTRODUCTION

Intended by its author to "set in a strong light the remedial influences of pure, natural human relations," George Eliot's *Silas Marner* is, on the surface, a fairy-tale-like story of an alienated miser whose life is transformed by his adoption of an abandoned child. While critics from Eliot's time to the middle of the twentieth century commended its wry humor and formal symmetry, the novel was commonly regarded as one of Eliot's least significant. More recent commentators, however, have found deeper levels of meaning in the work, including expressions of Eliot's views on religion, rural life, and social classes, and have praised the novel as sophisticated and structurally complex. Representative of this modern view, Q. D. Leavis has written: "There are so many meanings in *Silas Marner* that it is surprising that there was room in such a short space for them all; it is a feat to have wrapped them up with such neatness, charm, poetry and wit."

According to a letter Eliot wrote to her publisher, John Blackwood, she was writing *Romola* when, struck by a sudden recollection of a weaver with a bag upon his back, she interrupted her work on that novel and began *Silas Marner.* Blackwood reacted with enthusiasm to a partial manuscript; Eliot, however, expressed doubt that the tale would be of interest to anyone but herself "since William Wordsworth is dead"—her acknowledgement of affinities between *Silas Marner* and the poetry of Wordsworth. After Blackwood commented that he found the opening of the tale "rather sombre," Eliot decided to precede it with an epigraph from Wordsworth's "Michael" to highlight what she considered the optimistic theme of her novel: "A child, more than all other gifts / That earth can offer to declining man, / Brings hope with it and forward-looking thoughts." Blackwood approved of the finished manuscript, and upon its publication in 1861 the work was a popular success, with several editions printed in Eliot's lifetime.

Silas Marner focuses on two main characters. Silas, a weaver, is a member of a Calvinist religious sect who has been accused of theft by the leader of his congregation. Lots are cast to derive providential confirmation of Silas's alleged guilt, and, although he is innocent of the charge, the weaver receives the short stick. Dejected and bitter, he moves to the rural village of Raveloe and loses interest in everything but the gold he earns by weaving. Gloating in soli-

tude over his growing wealth, he rejects the companionship of his neighbors, who regard him with increasing distrust. His story is intertwined with that of the novel's second major character, Godfrey Cass, eldest son of the wealthiest landowner in Raveloe. Godfrey's efforts to conceal both his marriage to a woman in a neighboring village and the child he has fathered are jeopardized by his dissolute brother Dunstan, who knows Godfrey's secret and is blackmailing him. Dunstan, coming upon Silas's empty cottage, steals the weaver's hoarded gold. Some months later, Godfrey's opium-addicted wife freezes to death near Silas's cottage while on her way to confront her husband, and her infant daughter crawls to Silas's hearth. Godfrey elects to remain silent about his relationship to the child, whom Silas adopts. Raising Eppie, the weaver gradually wins the respect of his neighbors and rediscovers his ability to love. Sixteen years later, Godfrey acknowledges his responsibility for Eppie and offers to take her into his home, but she rejects his offer of a higher social standing, declaring her love for Silas.

Critics have frequently discerned a dual structure in the plot of *Silas Marner,* citing its parallel treatment of the stories of Godfrey Cass and Silas. In this view, the two main characters function in opposition to each other, allowing Eliot to express her views on class distinctions and values; thus Godfrey's idleness, selfish avoidance of responsibility, and reliance upon luck is unfavorably contrasted with Silas's industriousness, concern for Eppie, and rediscovered faith in a divine plan. Furthermore, critics have observed that Eppie's decision to live with Silas rather than Godfrey is a comment on the relative value of wealth and social status when compared to genuinely loving relationships. Bruce K. Martin, however, has noted that Silas and Godfrey share many common characteristics, enabling Eliot to generalize "certain assumptions about the moral nature and needs of man." Both characters elicit sympathy as individuals who have alienated themselves from society, Silas because his "narrow piety," according to Fred C. Thomson, "prevents an adequate response to the patent injustice done him," and Godfrey because of his self-centered and irresponsible lifestyle. This theme of alienation has prompted Ian Milner to characterize the work as a "tragic moral drama," a view intimated by Thomson in his contention that *Silas Marner* "is important to the development of [Eliot's] vision of tragic life." The double plot thus constitutes an effective forum for Eliot's examination of human nature and the human condition, facilitating her exploration of the workings of society.

In addition to the dual plot structure, critics have commonly found two stylistic techniques at work in the novel as well, contending that the Silas storyline imparts a fairytale quality to the novel while Godfrey's life is treated realistically. In this manner, according to Jerome Thale, Eliot presents "two visions of the world as one artistic piece." Thale explains: "The fairy-tale treatment in the Silas story universalizes what is really individual experience, so that we feel that happiness is really possible, the world tolerable for a great many people, even though we see from Godfrey that it is miserable for some." By weaving the probable and the improbable in realistic fashion, Eliot imparts what most commentators have perceived as a convincingly optimistic, Wordsworthian faith in redemption through love, imagination, and memory—as exemplified in Silas's recalling, upon viewing Eppie, his sister in childhood. Moreover, many commentators have noted that the juxtaposition of allegory and realism in *Silas Marner* enhances Eliot's communication of her perspectives on a variety of thematic concerns, including the psychological value of religious faith, the effects of the industrial revolution and capitalism on society, and the role of chance in human affairs.

While occasionally objecting to events in the novel that strain credulity, critics have widely praised *Silas Marner* for its realistic depiction of the motives and emotions of its characters, and have credited Eliot with demonstrating a high degree of insight into human thought and behavior. The wealth of critical approaches to the novel demonstrates that it has more depth and sophistication than its earliest critics perceived; though it represents a departure from the strictly realistic style of Eliot's more widely appreciated works, its achievement is no longer taken lightly. Reflecting many present-day assessments of the novel, Lilian Haddakin has admired the imaginative blending of

fairy tale and realistic elements in *Silas Marner*, describing it as "a very tightly integrated work of art."

The Athenaeum (essay date 1861)

[*In the following review, the critic evaluates characterization and setting in* Silas Marner.]

Silas Marner is not unworthy of the reputation already acquired by the Author of ***Adam Bede.*** It has no scenes of exciting and painful interest, but the characters are all well and firmly drawn, worked up from within, instead of the mere outward semblance being given. They are not described, but the leading idea, the key-note to their nature, is given, and the human actions that follow impress the reader with all the truth of reality. If we wished to be very critical, we might say that the leading ideas of the character of the men and women round us are rarely clearly defined, or rendered distinctly articulate, as they are in this novel; they exist, although we may not have the power to tell their secret;—by so much the more is real human nature richer than any book. The story of ***Silas Marner*** is very interesting; the interest is true and wholesome, not in the least morbid or questionable. The peculiarity of the tale is, that its action is chiefly sustained by men; the female characters are only accessories. Of heroines, there are, properly speaking, none at all,—the agency of women is felt as powerfully affecting the welfare and destinies of the men who are engaged in the story, but they appear seldom and say little; still their influence is at work, and is felt for good or ill from the first page to the last. The three good angels are very natural human maidens, who in real life might be considered good sort of women, but nothing out of the common run. Miss Nancy Lammeter is our favourite, with her pretty prim ways and her rules of conduct for her own guidance, "which," says the author, "she carried within her in the most unobtrusive way; they rooted themselves in her mind, and grew there quietly, like grass." At any cost to herself "she would do what was right," and though there was some narrowness in her powers of measurement, and some gentle prejudices, yet there was no flaw in the purity of her intentions, or in the unselfishness of her actions. She is a charming womanly character, and her influence for good upon her vacillating husband is both true to life and is very artistically managed. Dolly Winthrop, who was the nurse, counsellor and comforter of all the village, whose good thoughts came into her head always "when she was sorry for folk and striving to help them," is an excellent and racy sketch of a good woman, not exaggerated into a caricature;—some of her sayings deserve to be printed in golden letters. The characters are not the same lay figures as have figured in former stories; they are fresh embodiments of human nature, who live and more in this history and in no other. Silas Marner, the weaver, who may be considered the central character of the book, is very good. Out of apparently common materials, a beauty and pathos are evoked which sink deep into the reader's heart. Silas Marner's career, before the action of the tale commences, is well and briefly told. He was a member of "the little religious world known to itself as the church assembling in Lantern Yard"; believed to be a young man of exemplary life and ardent faith. The sketch of this small, obscure sectarian community is as carefully finished and skilfully drawn as if it were to be a leading feature of the book, and yet it is not dwelt upon too much in detail, nor at too great length. It is in excellent proportion, and it is true to the life and spirit. One of the merits of this tale is, the truth of all the details and local colouring; there is nothing left slovenly. The world of Raveloe is given with an understanding spirit, which has all the effect of humour. The character of the public opinion in Raveloe is thus given:—

> In that far-off time superstition clung easily round every person or thing that was at all unwonted, or even intermittent and occasional merely, like the visits of the pedlar and knife-grinder. No one knew where wandering men had their homes or their origin; and how was a man to be explained unless you at least knew somebody who knew his father and mother? To the peasants of old time the world outside their direct experience was a world of vagueness and mystery; to their untravelled thought a state of wandering was a conception as dim as the winter life of the swallows that came back with the spring; and even a settler, if he came from distant parts, hardly ever ceased to be viewed with a remnant of distrust, which would have prevented any surprise if a long course of inoffensive conduct on his part had ended in the commission of a crime, especially if he had any reputation for knowledge, or showed any skill in handicraft. All cleverness, whether in the rapid use of that difficult instrument the tongue, or in some other act unfamiliar to villagers, was in itself suspicious, * * and the process by which rapidity and dexterity of any kind was acquired partook of the mystery of conjuring.

It was amongst this class of people, in a central county village, that Silas Marner came to live, a lonely man, from the mysterious region called "the North'ard." He had more reason to be misanthropic than most people: a victim to the treachery of a friend,—a victim also to false appearances which he was powerless to contradict,—declared guilty by the primitive ordeal of "casting lots by the Bible," and driven ignominiously from the congregation,—disowned by the young woman, with whom he was on the point of marriage,—with his faith in religion and his trust in every human being completely shattered,—his whole life dead down to the root,—with no hope or object left in life,—Silas Marner, the weaver, comes before the reader at the commencement of the story. There is no over-colouring nor striving after effects. Silas Marner is a weaver, and neither says nor does anything beyond what is strictly probable and natural, yet he takes a hold on the reader's sympathy, by the truth with which the inward working of his life is laid bare. The author touches and treats all the characters from their own point of view, and with something of the tender love with which everybody regards himself. No character, however insignificant, or thing, however trivial, but is drawn with the feeling of its own personality strong within it; the author judges noth-

ing, but understands everything. The scene in the village alehouse is finished like a Dutch picture—so is the scene where the ladies are dressing for the New-Year's-Eve merry-making. But Eppie, the foundling and adopted child, is the bright light of the book: her golden curls and bright glancing ways are charming; she has little to say or do beyond being the blessing of Silas Marner's life, which the reader feels and knows she must have been; but she is left bright and undefined, as sunshine ought to be. We shall not spoil the reader's interest by giving any indication of the story,—it abounds with subtle thoughts and felicitous expressions. Being only in one volume, the story does not grow weak nor its interest drag—by reason of the length of way. Readers who desire only to meet with high society and good company in their novels, and who consider it impossible to feel an interest in the fortunes of weavers and farmers, may leave *Silas Marner* alone, for they will meet with nothing higher than the Squire;— those who can feel sympathy with human nature, however humbly embodied it may be, will find *Silas Marner* comfortable reading. (pp. 464-65)

> *A review of "Silas Marner, the Weaver of Raveloe," in* The Athenaeum, *No. 1745, April 6, 1861, pp. 464-65.*

The Literary Gazette   (essay date 1861)

[*In the following review, the critic notes the absence of dramatic incidents in the plot of* Silas Marner, *but praises Eliot for her "insight into the mysteries of human character."*]

For the ordinary novel-reader *Silas Marner* will have but few attractions. Barren in melodramatic incident, almost entirely free from love-making, and without a female character in which any intense interest can centre, it offers the curious spectacle of an acute and subtle psychological analysis, with a purblind, cataleptic, and low-lived weaver for its example and illustration. The action of the story is unexciting, and to many may appear absolutely languid, and inadequate to sustain the refined speculation which it at once illumines, and is illumined by. In worldly environment Silas Marner is very much at the end of the volume what he was at its commencement. We are introduced to him when he is living in a cottage by the Stone-pits, weaving linen for the housewives of Raveloe; and when we bid him farewell, some twenty summers after, his home and his occupation remain still the same. But we find him a hoarding miser; we find him living in solitude and alienation, in misanthropy and darkness. We leave him in kindly intercourse with his fellows, in happy and trusting contentment, and leading a genial, loving life. To borrow the splendid simile of the author, when we first know him his existence is "like a rivulet that has sunk far down from the grassy fringe of its old breadth, into a little shivering thread that cuts a groove for itself in the barren sand." When we see him last the waters have once more risen to their accustomed height, and bid fair to flow on to the great sea, broad, placid, and unchanged. The development of the later out of the earlier, of the healthy out of the morbid condition, is effected by a child; and the authoress has adopted for the motto of her story Wordsworth's lines,—

> A child, more than all other gifts
> That earth can offer to declining man,
> Brings hope with it, and forward-looking
> thoughts.

We do not intend to spoil our readers enjoyment by a premature disclosure of the plot, if we may give such a name to the simple links that connect the beginning with the end of the story. We must, however, to make our criticism comprehensible, give, in a few sentences, the history of the personage from whom the novel takes its name. Silas Marner, in his youth, was a zealous member of a narrow religious sect. The fervour of his piety was only equalled by the extraordinary and special light which, in the eyes of "the church assembling in Lantern Yard," was on all occasions vouchsafed to him. Full of trust in man, and of faith in the justice of a mysterious God; zealous above all, yet above all diffident, he lived on in belief more powerful than reasonable conviction, and in a dim twilight more congenial to such natures as his than the brightest light. One familiar friend he had in whom he trusted, and on whose more self-relying judgment he was wont to rest in cases where he could not depend upon himself or his own unaided conscience. This confidence was unhappily misplaced. Silas Marner is suddenly accused before his church of a shameful robbery. His own familiar friend is his accuser, and finds the evidence which seems to convict him. But evidence, in that primitive community, is not sufficient without immediate ratification from Heaven, and praying and lots are resorted to. The lots declare Silas Marner guilty, and he is cast out of the fold. Maddened by the villany of his friend, and stupefied by the treachery of Providence, he exclaims, in atheistical passion as unreasoning as had been his faith—"There is no just God, that governs the earth righteously, but a God of lies, that bears witness against the innocent!"

This, the first phase of Silas Marner's life, the author depicts briefly, but with immense and concentrated power. The depth of his former faith gives an additional element of darkness and hopelessness to the dark and hopeless atheism which superseded it. If his belief had been less profound, his disbelief would also have been less profound. The man who has believed most boldly, will also disbelieve most boldly; and lukewarm atheism is the common sequel to lukewarm faith. A less keen observer than George Eliot, would have been content with a mere modification of Silas Marner's disturbed belief. More than one popular authoress would have saved him from atheism and dissent by the proselytism of a Tractarian curate. Novelists of the silly school known by the silly name of muscular Christians, would have restored him to a sound mind by a course of gymnastics and paradoxical controversy.

And this is one of the points from which we may discern how immeasurably superior George Eliot is to most of even the popular writers of the day, in the extent of her insight into the mysteries of human character. No one else has seen so clearly the constant influence in the moral world of the great law of reaction, albeit the key to so much that were otherwise hopelessly inexplicable. It is reaction against which every man striving after excellence has to be so vigilantly on his guard. It is this which sweeps him sheer down from lofty moral elevation, into the lowest depths of moral degradation. By a law as regular as that of the ebb and flow of the tide, man no sooner reaches an extreme in either direction, than an influence begins to work, drawing him strongly to the opposite limit. The author of *The Mill on the Floss* would seem to have drawn Maggie Tulliver as the perfect exemplification of this law. Maggie, young, inexperienced, without culture, aspired to equal the self-sacrificing heroism of a mediæval philosopher. Reaction swept away her strong resolutions, and her conduct became that of a foolish school-girl. Then once again the reaction of a high nature set in, and she was restored to her lost courage and strength.

Silas Marner quitted the town where he had hitherto lived and prayed. He went away to a distant village, nestling "in a snug, well-wooded hollow," with church and church-yard, and old-fashioned homesteads and sunny orchards. The change was like that from Stonyshire to Loamshire. The religion that he had lost bore no resemblance to the worship of his new home, and he met with nothing to check the benumbing, withering influences at work. He continued to lead a dull, mechanical existence, sitting day after day in his place at the loom, in an uninterrupted monotony of weaving. Ere long, however, his nature found an object of intense interest, and gold filled the void left by the religion he had cast away. Hoarding and weaving were now his two occupations. He toiled more assiduously than ever; he denied himself more than ever; and as his hoarded guineas grew into a larger heap, his passion for them grew stronger and more insatiable. All day he sat at his loom; and at night he counted and gloated over his ever accumulating gold. One night all his guineas were stolen; and he once more relapsed into utter hopelessness and blind despair.

This gradual metamorphose into miserly avarice is probably that portion of the development of Silas Marner's character which will be most cavilled at. It is, indeed, a metamorphose which, superficially considered, seems violent and almost unnatural. The double reaction from fervent zeal to sheer atheism, and then from blank despair to eager, clutching avarice, appears excessive. But, after all, closer thought convinces us that to a nature such as Silas Marner's, something on which to depend, something to which he might cling, was absolutely essential. Further than this, he required something almost personal. Even in the days of his belief, he needed a friend; and that friend's treachery, whilst it made all human society repugnant to him, left him in urgent want of some supporting substitute. The guineas grew to stand to him as man could no longer stand. Hence the author tells us:—

> He began to think they were conscious of him,
> as his loom was; and he would on no account
> have exchanged those coins, which had become
> his familiars, for other coins with unknown
> faces.

It was precisely this tendency of his mind which, after the loss of his darling guineas, drove him with such an *élan* of affection to the curly-headed child whom accident sent to his hearth. The far-off memories of his own boyhood, of his youth, and of his early manhood, came teeming upon him at the sight of her; and shed the broken warmth of by-gone summers upon his soul, benumbed by a long and dreary winter. The child became to him what his old faith had once been—perhaps more than his gold had ever been. During the years while the child is growing into maidenhood, Silas Marner's life, with an almost parallel growth, expands into a wide consciousness. His faculties exert themselves in tranquil and even activity. The dark, painful cloud which had veiled his past years, slowly rolls away, and we leave him in trusting, genial serenity.

Such is the general tenor of the story. There is also an underplot, but as it only contains the circumstances necessary for the gradual evolution of the mental plot, we need not here enter into it. We have said enough to show the unfairness of measuring **Silas Marner** by the standard of its popular predecessors, **Adam Bede,** and **The Mill on the Floss.** It is a sketch, finished, subtle, and full of genius; while they are paintings, elaborate, broad, and richly coloured. It is a careful analysis of a character with which we can entertain at most only a very modified sympathy; they were, each in its own way, vigorous delineations of strong passion,—passion which everybody in feebler or intenser degree has felt, and which therefore everybody dimly or keenly is able to appreciate. The open manliness of Adam Bede, the devoted self-sacrifice of Dinah Morris, the sorrowful aspirations of Maggie, find no parallels in the gloomy troubles of Silas Marner, in the commonplace vivacity of Eppie, nor in the self-deceiving, self-reproaching Godfrey Cass. It is clear that **Silas Marner** will not in any way rival the popularity of **The Mill on the Floss,** and still less that of **Adam Bede.**

The mind of the reader is never wrought up to a high pitch of excitement, and he proceeds leisurly to the end of the novel without any very lively curiosity as to what the end will be. It is a matter of question how far this absence of material and motive for excitement is consistent with artistic principles. In fiction, as in the drama, it would seem necessary to represent men and women as they are, but yet to invest them also with circumstances which shall call forth what is deepest and strongest within them. We refuse to interest ourselves in characters whose career, environment, trials, and ultimate fate are entirely ordinary and commonplace. We cannot but think, therefore, that it is at once impolitic and inartistic to have left the action of the story so singularly devoid of what may be called motion.

From a totally different point of view, as a mere photograph of a stationary phase of human society, **Silas Marner** possesses rare merit. The brilliant humour which pervades all the descriptions of Raveloe life and manners, to our mind, surpasses all the author's previous efforts in the same direction. The scene at the Rainbow, the inn of Raveloe (c. vi.), is unrivalled both for truthfulness and for genuine humour. Mr. Macey, the parish clerk, and the hero in this admirable scene, is a character whose sayings and doings are as humorous as anything to be found in the whole of Dickens's works. Miss Priscilla Lammeter, though we see but little of her, is an incipient Mrs. Poyser, with her inconvenient candour or kindly sarcasm, or contemptuous views of "the men,"—

always wanting and wanting, and never easy with what they've got; they can't sit comfortable in their chairs when they've neither ache nor pain, but either they must stick a pipe in their mouths to make 'em better than well, or else they must be swallowing something strong, though they're forced to make haste before the next meal comes in.

Nor do wives escape her gentle cynicism:—

> "O, I know," said Priscilla, smiling sarcastically, "I know the way o'wives; they set one on to abuse their husbands, and then they turn round on one and praise 'em as if they wanted to sell 'em."

Nor should we omit to notice the disgust felt by the Miss Gunns, the daughters of the wine merchant of the neighbouring town, for these rich country-people "brought up in utter ignorance and vulgarity:"—

> She actually said "mate" for "meat," "'appen" for "perhaps," and "oss" for "horse," which, to young ladies living in good Lytherly society, who habitually said 'orse, even in domestic privacy, and only said 'appen on the right occasions, was necessarily shocking.

Mrs. Winthrop, the wheelwright's wife, is perhaps the most prominent of the minor characters. She is drawn with the author's never-failing humour, but it is humour mingled with pathos. Mrs. Winthrop is the exponent of the simple Raveloe theology:—

> "Well, Master Marner, it's niver too late to turn over a new leaf, and if you've niver had no church, there's no telling the good it'll do you. For I feel so set up and comfortable as niver was, when I've been and heard the prayers, and the singing to the praise and glory o' God, as Mr. Macey gives out—and Mr. Crackenthorp saying good words, and more partic'lar on Sacramen' Day; and if a bit o'trouble comes, I feel as I can put up wi' it, for I've looked for help i' the right quarter, and gev myself up to Them as we must all give ourselves up to at the last; and if we'n done our part, it isn't to be believed as Them as are above us 'ull be worse nor we are, and come short o' Theirn."

. . . . .

> "Well, then, Master Marner, it come to me summat like this: I can make nothing o' the drawing o' lots and the answer coming wrong; it 'ud mayhap take the person to tell that, and he could only tell us i' big words. But what come to me as clear as the daylight, it was when I was troubling over poor Bessy Fawkes, and it allays comes into my head when I'm sorry for folks, and feel as I can't do a power to help 'em, not if I was to get up i' the middle o' the night—it comes into my head as Them above has got a deal tenderer heart nor what I've got—for I can't be anyways better nor Them as made me, and if anything looks hard to me, it's because there's things I don't know on; and for the matter o' that, there may be plenty o' things I don't know on, for it's little as I know—that it is. And

so, while I was thinking o' that, you come into my mind, Master Marner, and it all comes pouring in:—if *I* felt i' my inside what was the right and just thing by you, and them as prayed and drawed the lots, all but that wicked un, if *they*'d ha' done the right thing by you if they could, isn't there Them as was at the making on us, and knows better, and has a better will? And that's all as ever I can be sure on, and everything else is a big puzzle to me when I think on it. For there was the fever come and took off them as were full-growed, and left the helpless children; and there's the breaking o' limbs; and them as 'ud do right and be sober have to suffer by them as are contrairy—eh, there's trouble i' this world, and there's things as we can niver make out the rights on. And all we've got to do is to trusten, Master Marner—to do the right as fur as we know, and to trusten. For if us as knows so little cau see a bit o' good and rights, we may be sure as there's a good and a rights bigger nor what we can know—I feel it i' my own inside as it must be so. And if you could but ha' gone on trustening, Master Marner, you wouldn't ha' run away from your fellow-creaturs and been so lone."

There is something to us ineffably touching in this dim, semi-articulate enunciation of the sublimest and profoundest form of human faith. Stated as the arid dogma of theological mysticism, such a form appears repugnant to our understanding, and displeasing to our imagination; but it has a pregnant and affecting significance when we consider that by its faint yet mellow light, millions of men and women have been able to grope their way through the mysteries of life, arguing from the visible to the invisible, and confident that "if we who know so little, can see some good and some right, there must be a good and right higher and wider than we can know." After all, these neighbourly consolations of the uncultured village woman, so exalted in her simplicity, contain a deep vein of dreamy philosophy not unworthy of *Hamlet*. It is no small praise to George Eliot to have discovered, what is unquestionably the case, that these rude dwellers in obscure villages have an inner life of thought and faith as vigorous, and perhaps as fruitful, as the rich and the educated. We have not left ourselves space to trace out this same feeling in the author's delineation of the noble-minded Nancy. Suffice it to say, that she is in the main the counterpart to Dinah Morris in *Adam Bede,* with the important difference that Dinah was an enthusiastic religionist, while Nancy's lofty character arose solely from an innate soberness and purity of disposition, without the introduction of any strong religious element.

In conclusion, we have only to say, that whilst we cannot suppose that *Silas Marner* will enjoy a very wide popularity, it is, in our opinion, a striking additional proof of the great powers and strength of the author. George Eliot has here taken up a new line, and it is not a little wonderful that the same hand which painted Hetty Sorrel, and Mrs. Poyser, and Parson Irwine, can depict with such power the varying phases of the life of Silas Marner; that the genius which was so skilful in the delineation of strongly-marked character, of deep passion, and keen feeling,

should be equally effective in representing an indistinct, confused, and blurred existence, wherein character, passion, and feeling were for the greater part torpid and benumbed. *Silas Marner* is a book which nobody but George Eliot could have written; it is one which scarcely anybody would have expected George Eliot to write. (pp. 315-16)

A review of "Silas Marner," in The Literary Gazette, *London, No. 145, new series April 6, 1861, pp. 315-16.*

The Times (London)   (essay date 1861)

[*In the following review, the critic praises Eliot's achievement in crafting a commendable novel based upon the lives of common rural people.*]

To George Eliot belongs this praise—that not only is every one of her tales a masterpiece, but also they may be opened at almost any page, and the eye is certain to light upon something worth reading—some curious dialogue or vivid description, some pregnant thought or happy phrase. *Silas Marner* is, like the rest of her fictions, full of matter and delightful in manner. It is a picture of secluded village life in the midland counties in the early part of the present century, and we owe not a little gratitude to the author for the good which she has done, as well as for the amusement which she has imparted by means of such pictures. She has given dignity to the life of boors and peasants in some of our bucolic districts, and this not by any concealment of their ignorance, follies, and frailties, nor by false colouring, bombastic sentiment, and exceptional events, but by a plain statement of the everyday life of the people. The charm of George Eliot's novels lies in their truthfulness. Nothing is extenuated nor aught set down in malice. We see the people amid all their grovelling cares, with all their coarseness, ignorance, and prejudice—poor, paltry, stupid, wretched, well-nigh despicable. This mean existence George Eliot raises into dignity by endowing it with conscience and with kindliness. There is nothing glittering about it. Here we have no mock heroics. There is not the slightest attempt to represent the boor as a village Hampden, nor the passing pedler as a poet wanting the accomplishment of verse. The personages of the tale are common, very common people, but they are good and kind, hardworking and dutiful. It is very wonderful to see how their lives are ennobled and beautified by their sense of duty, and by their sympathy with each other. It is the grandest of all lessons—the only true philosophy—the most consoling of creeds—that real greatness is within reach of the poorest and meanest of mankind. Wealth, glory, the pride of intellect, and the advantages of personal form—these are rare gifts, which seem to be scattered at random among the good and the bad; and in this ambitious age, when we see every one hastening to be rich and covetous of distinction, it is pleasant to be reminded that the honest man is the noblest work of God. George Eliot reminds us of it in her own genial way—transporting us into the midst of these stupid, common-place inhabitants of Raveloe—making them move before us and speak as if they lived, and making us feel a warm interest in all their petty concerns and humble endeavours. Such a novelist, while she amuses, teaches us. We open her volumes confident of most brilliant entertainment, and we close them wondering at the art of a writer who manages to reverse a time-honoured phrase and to render us, not sadder and better, but merrier and better.

While this is the general effect of all George Eliot's tales, it is most marked in what is still her greatest work—*Adam Bede.* The present tale, which is complete in one volume, has for its hero a sort of Seth Bede, and this statement will indicate to most persons the excellences and defects of the novel. A novel of which a Seth Bede is the hero must, of necessity, be less absorbing, and ought to be shorter, than one which could boast such a hero as Adam. Silas Marner is, like Seth, a simple-hearted and not very clear-headed Methodist, who, after going through a great deal of trouble, and having his life embittered by disappointment, slander, and ingratitude, comes at last to see an overruling justice in human affairs, and to put trust in his fellow men. In a world so full as this is of sin and suffering, it is difficult for the victims to believe in the benignant order of the universe. There could not be a more unfortunate victim than poor Silas Marner. He is cheated of his good name and branded as a thief through the instrumentality of his dearest friend; his betrothed, on whom he had set his heart, leaves him to marry this ingrate; afterwards he is suddenly robbed of all his hardwon savings, and he finds himself without means, and all alone in the world. The good and kind but weak-minded man curses his destiny, and cries aloud in his despair that there is no God, but only a devil on the earth. He is petrified; all the springs of his life are dried up; he withdraws from the society of his fellow men; all trust is gone, and he has neither physical nor intellectual energy enough to work his way back. How is this man to be recovered? It is to the moralist a most tempting question—to the novelist a most difficult one. It is easy according to the more common theories to suppose a man preached into contentment or suddenly "revived" by a spiritual convulsion. We are not aware, however, that Job ever got much good from the preaching of his friends, and it must be confessed that spiritual revivals and convulsions are not the ordinary means of reformation. Reformation of character and change of views are generally the result of long discipline, and we gather from the motto on the title-page of the present work—

> A child more than all other gifts,
> That earth can offer to declining man,
> Brings hope with it, and forward-looking
> thoughts,

that George Eliot meant to exhibit the unconscious influence of a child in gradually redeeming and reviving what may be almost described as a lost soul. The author appears, however, to have stopped short of her design, and to have satisfied herself with stating the result instead of detailing the process. In two-thirds of the volume we have Silas Marner before us in his hopeless, helpless estrangement from his fellow men. The picture of his silent misery is filled in so carefully, the canvas is spread so large, and we are introduced to so many of his neighbours, that when . . . we find the weaver of Raveloe adopting little Eppie as his own child we feel that the story is about to commence. Still more do we feel this when, a few pages

further on, just as the first part of the tale is about to close, and while the motto on the title-page is ringing in our memories, we read that though now there are no whitewinged angels to lead men from the city of destruction, still a hand is often put into theirs to lead them gently into a calm and pleasant land, that such a hand is to lead Silas Marner into the light, and that the hand is a little child's. But we are left to imagine the process, for the second part of the tale commences after a supposed lapse of 16 years, in which the great change has been effected in the mind of Silas Marner. He comes out a new man; he gets a sudden turn of good fortune; and the story winds up. The first part, forming more than two-thirds of the volume, is thus a magnificent portico to the second part, which is a pretty little cottage, hidden behind a mass of more stately architecture. There are critics who will regard this objection to the story more seriously than we can. It amounts to this, that George Eliot laid out the plan of a great epic, found that she was overstepping the limits of a novel, and ruthlessly curtailed her design. The result is, that here we have, it is true, a fragment, but it is a fragment of George Eliot's most ambitious work. It is not finished like *Adam Bede,* but in passages it is grander and deeper.

That George Eliot should have shrunk from the completion of her task as she appears to have at first planned it is not surprising. Her efforts as a writer were strained to the uttermost, but for many reasons the increase of effort on her part could not be followed by any increase of effect on the reader. Here we might repeat a good deal of the criticism suggested by the *Mill on the Floss,* in which the writer employed her great powers on materials so unpromising that none but a novelist of the highest class could have turned them to account. It was strange to see how, by the force of her genius, George Eliot made a brilliant story out of the little sayings and doings of the mean, prosaic, odious Dodson family. In her new novel she has undertaken a task still more difficult, for the centre of interest in it is a half-witted man. Silas Marner is at his best but a poor creature—a kindly, godly simpleton, much troubled with fits; but after his disaster he is not half the man he was. He is in a maze; there is no saying what he is or what he will do, and the catalepsy or trances to which he is subject must render him a singularly unaccountable being. But the pleasure of fiction depends mainly on our being able to count upon the elements of human character and to calculate results. When even among the subordinate characters of a story an imbecile is brought forward it involves the introduction of chance and uncertainty into a tissue of events the interest of which depends on their antecedent probability. This is so clearly the case that everybody must have felt a diminution of interest in any tale in which the production of the leading incidents depends on those passions that reduce the mind to a state of imbecility. Take drunkenness, for example; it is always unsatisfactory to hear of a catastrophe brought on by a man deprived of his senses through drink. Or, take jealousy, the most imbecile of the passions; though Lord Macaulay says that every English audience feels most sympathy with the Moor, while any Italian audience would most enjoy the subtleties of Iago, it may be doubted whether any intelligent Englishman takes much interest in Othello, and, at all events, the stupidity to which his passion degraded him renders his conduct so unreasonable that in watching it we are met with continual disappointment. In all such cases of imbecility, whether it is natural and permanent or superinduced for the moment, we are out of our reckoning, we know not what to anticipate, and we are robbed of that expectancy which enters so largely into the pleasure afforded by fiction. It follows, therefore, that the Dodson family, with all their earthiness, are in one sense at least more fit for the purposes of story than a half-witted Silas Marner with all his glimpses of the spiritual. Mean as the Dodson family are, yet, having the elements of their character before us, we see that they are calculable elements, and we can forecast their legitimate results. But what can we anticipate in the play of events for a man who, whatever be his moral elevation, is of weak mind and is subject to fits which for the time render his existence a blank? There are novels in which such a character might not be out of place even as the leading personage of the tale. In Mr. Wilkie Collins's last novel the chief interest centres around two half-witted women in succession. Events occur which by no possibility could have happened had these women been in full possession of their senses. But in a novel which claims our attention chiefly for the intricacy of its plot, and slightly for the evolution of its characters, we almost forget the blank unsatisfactory nature of the leading personages in thinking of the startling incidents that crowd upon our notice. The interest of George Eliot's tales resting upon a different foundation, does not admit of such handling. In her stories, the characters are all in all; the incidents are of secondary importance, and grow out of the characters; a hero whose mind is nearly a blank, and whose life is represented as the sport of chance, is at variance with the spirit of her books. This will be evident if we state what are the two critical incidents in the life of Silas Marner. He was a young man of exemplary life and ardent faith, and belonged to a little flock of Methodists, assembling in a small back street, who regarded him with peculiar interest "ever since he had fallen at a prayer meeting into a mysterious rigidity and suspension of consciousness, which, lasting for an hour or more, had been mistaken for death." One night, while he was watching by the side of a dying deacon, he fell into one of these fits, and during his unconsciousness the deacon not only died, but also was robbed. Here is the first introduction of chance into the story. The weaver is accused of the robbery, and his Methodist friends determine to find out the guilty man, not by investigation, but by the drawing of lots. Chance upon chance—the lot fell upon Silas Marner, who goes forth and settles in the parish of Raveloe, a blighted being. At Raveloe he lives a lonely life for 15 years, at the end of which he falls into one of his trances, and on recovering his consciousness finds a little golden-haired child sleeping on his hearth. This is the second great chance of his life. As in one fit of unconsciousness he lost his all, so in another fit of unconsciousness he obtained a recompense. In either case he was helpless, had nothing to do with his own fate, and was a mere feather in the wind of chance. From this point forward in the tale, however, there is no more chance—all is work and reward, cause and effect, the intelligent mind shaping its own destiny. The honest man bestows kindness upon the child, and reaps the benefit of it in his own increasing happiness, quickened intelligence, and social position. Only this is but a very small portion of the tale, so small that, seeing the importance of it, remembering the prominence which is given to it by means of the motto on the title-page, and knowing that the spirit of it more accords with George Eliot's artistic genius than that portion of the volume which occupies the greater number of pages, we have been forced to the conjecture that the story is not what the author originally intended it to be, but is huddled up at the end.

It is one of the evils of criticism that we cannot take any exception to a great work of art without suggesting that it is a failure. But to associate **Silas Marner** with any idea of failure is the very opposite of our intention. Criticize it as we may, the worst we can have to say of it is, that in aim it transcends the field of ordinary novels, and that in accomplished result it suggests too high a standard of measurement. Taking it as it is, and with all its faults, we really could not name another woman capable of producing a greater work, and it may be doubted whether, with the same materials, any man could have done better. As for the writing, it contains some of George Eliot's best composition, though at the same time it should be added that, as there is less of dialogue and more of narrative in the present work than is usual in the novels of this author, she appears to have felt the necessity of elaborating her own remarks to the uttermost. What her sentences in this way gain in force they lose in freedom; but with her rich vein of humour it will readily be understood that even when her writing is most laboured, the loss of freedom is not considerable. Her vein of humour, combined as it is with a peculiar seriousness and sense of the mystery of human life, is very fine, and gives an inexpressible charm to her descriptions of stupid, poverty-stricken boors. An author who manages to make us laugh at them and with them has gone far to make us forget the repulsiveness of their habits, and to prepare us for real sympathy in their struggles. The volume before us is full of those little touches which give vividness and humour to the most homely pictures. We open it at random and come upon a scene in the village public-house where the parochial worthies are drinking their beer, smoking their long pipes, and discussing their little affairs. They are startled by the sudden appearance of Silas Marner, who rushes in upon them like a ghost. "The long pipes," we are told, "gave a simultaneous movement, *like the antennae of startled insects,* and every man present, not excepting even the sceptical farrier, had an impression that he saw, not Silas Marner in the flesh, but an apparition." Few similes could be more graphic or more amusing than this. So also in the preceding page there is some humour in the sceptical farrier's argument against ghosts. "Did ever a ghost give a man a black eye? That's what I should like to know." He clinches his argument with a fair challenge to the ghostly world:— "If ghos'es want me to believe on 'em, let 'em leave off skulking i' the dark and i' lone places—let 'em come where there's company and candles." Mr. Macey, the parish clerk, who has a reputation for sarcastic ability, hereupon displays his gift in the retort—"As if ghos'es ud want to be believed in by anybody so ignirant." Macey, however, can say things very much better than this. Sometimes he expresses his opinion in that proverbial style for which Mr. Poyser has earned a just celebrity. "Now don't you be for overshooting the mark, Toohey," he says on one occasion to his deputy; "that's what you're allays at. If I throw a stone and hit, you think there's summar better than hitting, and you try to throw a stone beyond." The most remarkable combination, however, of humour with seriousness in the present volume is in the conception of Mrs. Winthrop's character—a good woman who utters the most profound truths in the most confused comical fashion. She tries to explain to Silas Marner how, in spite of his troubles, there is still hope for him in the world. "Well, then, Master Marner," she says,—

It come to me summat like this. I can make nothing o' the drawing o' lots and the answer coming wrong; it ud may hap take the person to tell that, and he could only tell us i' big words. But what come to me as clear as the daylight, it was when I was troubling over poor Bessy Fawkes, and it allays comes into my head when I'm sorry for folks, and feel as I can't do a power to help 'em, not if I was to get up i' the middle of the night; it comes into my head as Them above has got a deal tenderer heart nor what I have got; for I can't be anyways better nor Them as made me, and if anything looks hard to me, it's because there's things I don't know on; and for the matter o' that, there may be plenty o' things I don't know on, for it's little as I know—that it is. And so, while I was thinking o' that, you come into my mind, Master Marner, and it all come pouring in; if I felt i' my inside what was the right and just thing by you, and them as prayed and drawed the lots, all but that wicked un, if *they*'d ha' done the right thing by you if they could, isn't there Them as was at the making on us, and knows better and has a better will? And that's all as ever I can be sure on, and everything else is a big puzzle to me when I think on it. For there was a fever come and took off them as were full growed, and left the helpless children; and there's the breaking o' limbs; and them as 'ud do right and be sober have to suffer by them as are contrary—Eh, there's trouble i' this world, and there's things as we niver can make out the right on. And all as we've got to do is to trusten, Master Marner—to do the right thing as far as we know, and to trusten. For if us as knows so little can see a bit o' good and rights, we may be sure there's a good and a rights bigger nor what we can know—I feel it i' my own inside as it must be so.

This is the burden of the book expressed in comical fashion. The weaver of Raveloe is very much in the position of the man of Ur. He is surrounded with comforters, most of whom are even less sympathizing than the comforters of Job, and he sinks into a deeper despair than that of the most patient of men, for, as we have said, he cursed and denied God in his affliction. The picture of his misery and the discipline of his repentance are but a homely, human version of the older and diviner drama. Instead of supernatural incidents and divine colloquies, we have ordinary accidents and village prattle. Instead of the Deity coming forth to justify his afflicted creature and to teach him better, a little child proves to the world the good qualities of his heart, and gives light and liberty to his understanding. It is a noble lesson, beautifully taught, though in saying thus much we run a risk of conveying the impression that George Eliot belongs to the class of religious or moralizing novelists who have rendered hateful the very idea of serious purpose in a novel. This is not the case, however. Hers is a very spiritual nature, and she cannot choose but regard life from a very lofty point of view. But her novels are true novels, not sermons done into dialogue. The moral purpose which is evident in her writing is mostly an unconscious purpose. It is that sort of moral meaning which belongs to every great work of art, and which no elevated mind can get rid of. She tells a simple story without the least idea of inculcating any copy-book lesson, but by merely elevating the reader to her mount of observation she cannot fail to suggest to the mind some profound reflections.

A review of "Silas Marner," in The Times, *London, April 29, 1861, p. 12.*

Henry James on *Silas Marner*:

To a certain extent, I think **Silas Marner** holds a higher place than any of the author's works. It is more nearly a masterpiece; it has more of that simple, rounded, consummate aspect, that absence of loose ends and gaping issues, which marks a classical work. What was attempted in, indeed, was within more immediate reach than the heart-trials of Adam Bede and Maggie Tulliver. A poor, dull-witted, disappointed Methodist cloth-weaver; a little golden-haired foundling child; a well-meaning, irresolute country squire, and his patient, childless wife;—these, with a chorus of simple, beer-loving villagers, make up the *dramatis personæ*. More than any of its brother-works, **Silas Marner,** I think, leaves upon the mind a deep impression of the grossly material life of agricultural England in the last days of the old *régime*,—the days of full-orbed Toryism, of Trafalgar and of Waterloo, when the invasive spirit of French domination threw England back upon a sense of her own insular solidity, and made her for the time doubly, brutally, morbidly English. Perhaps the best pages in the work are the first thirty, telling the story of poor Marner's disappointments in friendship and in love, his unmerited disgrace, and his long, lonely twilight-life at Raveloe, with the sole companionship of his loom, in which his muscles moved "with such even repetition, that their pause seemed almost as much a constraint as the holding of his breath." Here, as in all George Eliot's books, there is a middle life and a low life; and here, as usual, I prefer the low life. In **Silas Marner,** in my opinion, she has come nearest the mildly rich tints of brown and gray, the mellow lights and the undreadful corner-shadows of the Dutch masters whom she emulates.

Henry James, in Atlantic Monthly, *October 1866.*

Mathilde Blind (essay date 1883)

[*In the following excerpt, Blind praises Eliot's humorous depiction of human nature in* Silas Marner *and compares the novel's plot to that of J. I. Kraszewski's* Jermola the Potter.]

[In 1861 George Eliot] produced her most finished work. She wrote *Silas Marner, the Weaver of Raveloe.* I call *Silas Marner* her most finished work, not only because of the symmetry with which each part is adjusted in relation to the whole, nor because of the absence of those partly satirical, partly moral reflections with which George Eliot usually accompanies the action of her stories, but chiefly on account of the simple pathos of the central motive into which all the different incidents and characters naturally converge. How homely are the elements from which this work of art is constructed, and how matchless the result!

Nothing but the story of a humble weaver belonging to a small dissenting community which assembled in Lantern Yard, somewhere in the back streets of a manufacturing town; of a faithless love and a false friend, and the loss of trust in all things human or divine. Nothing but the story of a lone, bewildered man, shut out from his kind, concentrating every balked passion into one—the all-engrossing passion for gold. And then the sudden disappearance of the hoard from its accustomed hiding-place, and in its stead the startling apparition of a golden-haired little child, found one snowy winter's night sleeping on the floor in front of the glimmering hearth. And the gradual reawakening of love in the heart of the solitary man, a love "drawing his hope and joy continually onward beyond the money," and once more bringing him into sympathetic relations with his fellow-men.

"In old days," says the story,

> there were angels who came and took men by the hand and led them away from the city of destruction. We see no white-winged angels now. But yet men are led away from threatening destruction; a hand is put into theirs, which leads them forth gently towards a calm and bright land, so that they look no more backward, and the hand may be a little child's.

Curiously enough, I came quite recently upon a story which in its leading features very closely resembles this tale of the *Weaver of Raveloe.* It is called *Jermola the Potter,* and is considered the masterpiece of J. I. Kraszewski, the Polish novelist, author of at least one hundred and fifty works in different branches of literature. *Jermola,* the most popular of them all, has been translated into French, Dutch, and German. It gives an extraordinarily vivid picture of peasant life in a remote Polish village, and not only of peasant life, but of the manners and habits of the landed proprietor, the Jew, the artisan, and the yeoman, in a community whose modes of life have undergone but little modification since the Middle Ages. These pictures, though not elaborated with anything like the minute care of George Eliot's descriptions of English country life, yet from their extreme simplicity produce a most powerful impression on the reader.

The story, in brief, is that of Jermola, the body servant of a Polish nobleman in Volhynia, whom he has served with rare devotion during the greater part of his life. Left almost a beggar at his master's death, without a single human tie, all he can get for years of faithful service is a tumble-down, forsaken old inn, where he manages to keep body and soul together in a dismantled room that but partly shelters him from the inclemency of the weather. Hopeless, aimless, loveless, he grows old before his time, and the passing of the days affects him hardly more than it does a stone. But one evening, as he is sitting in front of a scanty fire repeating the Lord's Prayer, the cry as of a little child startles him from his devotion. Going to look what can be the meaning of such unusual sounds, he soon discovers an infant in linen swaddling-clothes wailing under an old oak tree. He takes the foundling home, and from that moment a new life enters the old man's breast. He is rejuvenated by twenty years. He is kept in a constant flutter of hope, fear, and activity. A kind-hearted woman, called the Kozaczicha, tenders him her services, but he is so jealous of any one but himself doing aught for the child, that he checks her advances, and by hook or by crook obtains a goat from an extortionate Jew, by the help of which he rears the boy satisfactorily. Then, wishing to make a livelihood for the child's sake, he inclines at first to the craft of the weaver, but finally turns potter in his old age. Love sharpening his wits, he plies quite a thriving trade in time, and the beautiful boy brings him into more friendly relations with his neighbors. But one day, when Radionek, who has learned Jermola's trade, is about twelve years old, the real parents appear and claim him as their own. They had never dared to acknowledge their marriage till the father, who had threatened to disinherit his son in such an event, had departed this life. Now, having nothing more to fear, they want to have their child back, and to bring him up as befits their station in life. Jermola suffers a deadly anguish at this separation; the boy, too, is in despair, for he clings fondly to the old man who has reared him with more than a father's love. But the parents insisting on their legal rights, Radionek is at last carried off to their house in town, to be turned into a gentleman, being only grudgingly allowed to see Jermola from time to time. The boy pines, however, for the dear familiar presence of his foster-father, and the free outdoor life, and at last, after some years of misery, he appears one day suddenly in Jermola's hut, who has given up his pottery in order to be secretly near the child he is afraid to go and see. The piteous entreaties of Radionek, and the sight of his now sickly countenance, induce the old man to flee into the pathless forests, where the two may escape unseen, and reach some distant part of the country to take up their old pleasant life once more. But the hardships and fatigues of the journey are too much for the boy's enfeebled health, and just as they come within sight of human dwellings, he is seized with a fever which cuts his young life short, leaving Jermola nearly crazy with anguish. Long afterwards a little decrepit old man was to be seen by churchgoers sitting near a grave, whom the children mocked by calling the "bony little man," because he seemed to consist of nothing but bones.

Such is the bare outline of a story whose main idea, that of the redemption of a human soul from cold, petrifying isolation, by means of a little child, is unquestionably the same as in *Silas Marner.* Other incidents, such as that of the peasant woman who initiates Jermola into the mysteries of baby management, and the disclosure of the real parents after a lapse of years, wanting to have their child back, suggest parallel passages in the English book. But coincidences of this kind are, after all, natural enough, considering that the circle of human feeling and action is limited, and that in all ages and countries like conditions must give rise to much the same sequence of events. It is therefore most likely that George Eliot never saw, and possibly never even heard of, *Jermola the Potter.*

The monotonous tone in the narrative of this Polish novel is in strong contrast, it may be observed, to George Eliot's vivid and varied treatment of her subject. This monotony, however, suits the local coloring of *Jermola,* by suggesting the idea of the league-long expanse of ancient forests whose sombre solitudes encompass with a mysterious awe the little temporary dwellings of men. But if the foreign story surpasses **Silas Marner** in tragic pathos, the latter far excels it in the masterly handling of character and dialogue, in the underlying breadth of thought, and, above all, in the precious salt of its humor.

Indeed, for humor, for sheer force, for intense realism, George Eliot, in the immortal scene at the "Rainbow," may be said to rival Shakespeare. Her farriers, her butchers, her wheelwrights, her tailors, have the same startling vitality, the same unmistakable accents of nature, the same distinctive yet unforced individuality, free from either exaggeration or caricature. How delicious is the description of the party assembled in the kitchen of that inn, whose landlord—a strong advocate for compromising whatever differences of opinion may arise between his customers, as beings "all alike in need of liquor"—clinches all arguments by his favorite phrase—"You're both right and you're both wrong, as I say." How admirably comic are these villagers, invariably beginning their nightly sittings by a solemn silence, in which one and all puff away at their pipes, staring at the fire "as if a bet were depending on the first man who winked." And when they begin at last, how rich is the flavor of that talk, given with an unerring precision that forthwith makes one acquainted with the crass ignorance and shrewdness, the mother-wit and superstition, so oddly jumbled together in the villager's mind. What sublime absence of all knowledge of his native land is shown by the veteran parish clerk, Mr. Macey, in speaking of a person from another county which apparently could not be so very different "from this country, for he brought a fine breed o' sheep with him, so there must be pastures there, and everything reasonable." Yet the same man can put down youthful presumption pretty sharply, as when he remarks: "There's allays two 'pinions; there's the 'pinion a man has o' himsen, and there's the 'pinion other folks have on him. There'd be two 'pinions about a cracked bell, if the bell could hear itself."

Dolly Winthrop, the wife of the jolly wheelwright who makes one of the company at the "Rainbow," is no less admirable. She is not cut after any particular pattern or type of human nature, but has a distinctive individuality, and is full of a freshness and unexpectedness which sets foregone conclusions at defiance. A notable woman, with a boundless appetite for work, so that, rising at half-past four, she has "a bit o' time to spare most days, for when one gets up betimes i' the morning the clock seems to stan' still tow'rt ten, afore it's time to go about the victual." Yet with all this energy she is not shrewish, but a calm, grave woman, in much request in sick-rooms or wherever there

is trouble. She is good-looking, too, and of a comfortable temper, being patiently tolerant of her husband's jokes, "considering that 'men would be so,'" and viewing the stronger sex 'in the light of animals whom it pleased Heaven to make troublesome like bulls or turkey-cocks.'"

Her vague idea, shared indeed by Silas, that he has quite another faith from herself, as coming from another part of the country, gives a vivid idea of remote rural life, as well as her own dim, semi-pagan but thoroughly reverential religious feelings, prompting her always to speak of the Divinity in the plural, as when she says to Marner: "I've looked for help in the right quarter, and give myself up to Them as we must all give ourselves up to at the last; and if we'n done our part, it isn't to be believed as Them as are above us 'ull be worse nor we are, and come short o' Theirn."

The humor shown in these scenes and characters, or, more properly speaking, George Eliot's humor in general, belongs to the highest order, the same as Shakespeare's. It is based on the essential elements of human nature itself, on the pathetic incongruities of which that "quintessence of dust," man, is made up, instead of finding the comic in the purely accidental or external circumstances of life, as is the case with such humorists as Rabelais and Dickens. These latter might find a good subject for their comic vein in seeing the Venus of Milo's broken nose, which a mischievous urchin had again stuck on the wrong side upwards—a sight to send the ordinary spectator into fits of laughter. But the genuine humorist sees something in that feature itself, as nature shaped it, to excite his facetiousness. In **"A Minor Prophet"** some lines occur in which a somewhat similar view of the genuine source of humor is pithily put:

> My yearnings fail
> To reach that high apocalyptic mount
> Which shows in bird's-eye view a perfect world,
> Or enter warmly into other joys
> Than those of faulty, struggling human kind.
> That strain upon my soul's too feeble wing
> Ends in ignoble floundering: I fall
> Into short-sighted pity for the men
> Who, living in those perfect future times,
> Will not know half the dear imperfect things
> That move my smiles and tears—will never know
> The fine old incongruities that raise
> My friendly laugh; the innocent conceits
> That like a needless eyeglass or black patch
> Give those who wear them harmless happiness;
> The twists and cracks in our poor earthenware,
> That touch me to more conscious fellowship
> (I am not myself the finest Parian)
> With my coevals.

Again, in her essay on **"Heinrich Heine,"** George Eliot thus defines the difference between humor and wit:

> Humor is of earlier growth than wit, and it is in accordance with this earlier growth that it has more affinity with the poetic tendencies, while wit is more nearly allied to the ratiocinative intellect. Humor draws its materials from situations and characteristic; wit seizes on unexpected and complex relations. . . . It is only the in-

genuity, condensation, and instantaneousness which lift some witticisms from reasoning into wit; they are reasoning raised to its highest power. On the other hand, humor, in its higher forms and in proportion as it associates itself with the sympathetic emotions, continually passes into poetry: nearly all great modern humorists may be called prose poets.

The quality which distinguishes George Eliot's humor may be said to characterize her treatment of human nature generally. In her delineations of life she carefully eschews the anomalous or exceptional, pointing out repeatedly that she would not, if she could, be the writer, however brilliant, who dwells by preference on the moral or intellectual attributes which mark off his hero from the crowd instead of on those which he has in common with average humanity. Nowhere perhaps in her works do we find this tendency so strikingly illustrated as in the one now under consideration; for here we have the study of a human being who, by stress of circumstances, develops into a most abnormal specimen of mankind, yet who is brought back to normal conditions and to wholesome relations with his fellow-men by such a natural process as the re-awakening of benumbed sympathies through his love for the little foundling child. The scene where he finds that child has only been touched on in a passing allusion, yet there is no more powerfully drawn situation in any of her novels than that where Silas, with the child in his arms, goes out into the dark night, and, guided by the little footprints in the virgin snow, discovers the dead mother, Godfrey Cass's opium-eating wife, lying with "her head sunk low in the furze and half covered with the shaken snow." There is a picture of this subject by the young and singularly gifted artist, the late Oliver Madox Brown, more generally known as a novelist, which is one of the few pictorial interpretations that seem to completely project on the canvas a visible embodiment of the spirit of the original. The pale, emaciated weaver, staring with big, short-sighted eyes at the body of the unconscious young woman stretched on the ground, clutching the lusty, struggling child with one arm, while with the other he holds a lantern which throws a feeble gleam on the snow—is realized with exceptional intensity.

The exquisite picture of Eppie's childhood, the dance she leads her soft-hearted foster-father, are things to read, not to describe, unless one could quote whole pages of this delightful idyl, which for gracious charm and limpid purity of description recalls those pearls among prose-poems, George Sand's *François le Champi* and *La Mare au Diable*. (pp. 182-95)

Mathilde Blind, "'Silas Marner,'" in her George Eliot, *Roberts Brothers, 1883, 290 p.*

Leslie Stephen   (essay date 1902)

[*Stephen is considered one of the most important English literary critics of the late Victorian and early Edwardian era. In his criticism, which is often moralistic, Stephen argues that literature is an imaginative rendering, in concrete terms, of a writer's philosophy or beliefs. It is the role of criticism, he contends, to translate into intellectual terms what the writer has told the reader through character, symbol, and plot. In the following excerpt, Stephen discusses the workings of providence in* Silas Marner *and examines Eliot's use of humor in the scene at the Rainbow Inn.*]

[In November 1860 George Eliot] began *Silas Marner,* which was finished in February 1861, and appeared by itself in March. Blackwood, she says, does not surprise her by calling it "rather sombre." She would not have expected it to interest any one except herself ("since Wordsworth is dead") had not Lewes been "strongly arrested" by it. The reference to Wordsworth is explained by her statement that it is meant to "set in a strong light the remedial influences of pure natural human relations." She felt as if it would have been more suitable to metre than to prose, except that there would have been less room for the humorous passages. It was suggested, it seems, by a childish recollection of a "linen-weaver with a bag on his back." The recollection, it must be admitted, can have counted for very little in the development of a story which is often considered to be her most perfect artistic performance. A curious literary coincidence—it can have been nothing more—is mentioned by Mathilde Blind. The Polish novelist, Kraszewski, wrote a novel called *Jermola, the Potter,* said to be his masterpiece, and to have been translated into French, Dutch, and German. Jermola is an old servant who has retired to a deserted house in a remote village. He becomes almost apathetic in his solitude, till one day he finds a deserted infant under an oak. He devotes himself to the care of the child, and is helped in the unfamiliar process of nursing by a kind old woman. His energies revive, he takes up the trade of a potter to make a living for his new charge, succeeds in the business, and is brought into friendly relations with his neighbours. Finally, the child's parents turn up and reclaim their son. Jermola has to submit, but afterwards runs off with the boy into the forests. There the child dies of hardship, and Jermola ends his days as a melancholy hermit. The treatment, says Miss Blind, is entirely different from that of *Silas Marner,* but the leading motive is identical, and some of the details have, as will be seen, a curiously close resemblance. As there is clearly no question of copying, we must infer that both writers have worked out the logical consequences of similar situations; Kraszewski's version is more "sombre," though either his catastrophe or that of George Eliot is equally conceivable. The supposed event—the moral recovery of a nature reduced by injustice and isolation to the borders of sanity—strikes one perhaps as more pretty than probable. At least, if one had to dispose of a deserted child, the experiment of dropping it by the cottage of a solitary in the hope that he would bring it up to its advantage and to his own regeneration would hardly be tried by a judicious philanthropist. That, perhaps, is the reason which made George Eliot think it more appropriate for poetry. In an idyll in verse one is less disposed to insist upon prosaic probabilities, or apply the rules of life suggested by the experience of the Charity Organisation Society. In *Silas Marner* George Eliot is a little tempted to fall into the error of the amiable novelists who are given to playing the part of Providence to their characters. It is true that the story begins by a painful case of apparent injustice. Silas Marner's life has been embittered by the casting of lots, which, on the principles of his sect, proves him to be guilty of the crime really committed by his accuser. But in the conclusion Providence seems to be making up for this little slip. The child is given to the weaver to recompense him for his sufferings, and, conversely, the real father is punished for neglecting his duty by the childlessness of his second marriage and the refusal of his daughter to accept him in place of her adopted parent. The excellent Dolly Winthrop sees a difficulty. She holds that the parson could probably explain the mistake about the casting of lots, though even he would have to tell it in "big words." But she is convinced that "Them above has got a deal tenderer heart than what I have." "There is plenty of trouble in the world, and things as we can never make out the rights on. And all as we've got to do is to trusten, Master Marner— to do the right thing as far as we know, and to trusten." If Marner had acted on that principle, he wouldn't have "run away from his fellow-creatures and been so lone." I will not quarrel with Mrs. Winthrop's solution of the ancient problem, nor with the moral which she deduces; and if the conclusion of the story seems to imply that compensation for injustice may be expected in this life rather more confidently than experience proves, another moral is also suggested. Mr. Godfrey Cass is driven to prevarication and lying in order to conceal from his father that he has made a disreputable marriage, and to prevent his scamp of a brother from ousting him by revealing the result. His meanness answers admirably. The brother tumbles into a gravel-pit and is drowned, and the wife takes an overdose of laudanum at the right moment. He is freed from all fear of exposure, marries the right young woman, and has, on the whole, a successful life. This may console people who think that the justice of Providence is called into play too clearly. But in truth the whole story is conceived in a way which makes a pleasant conclusion natural and harmonious. It is saved from excess of sentimentalism by those admirable passages of humour, which, as we have seen, prevented the story from being put into verse. *Silas Marner,* as it turned out, was to be the last work in which George Eliot was to draw an idealised portrait of her earliest circle. It is full of admirable sketches from the squire to the poor weaver; and the famous scene at the "Rainbow" is perhaps the best specimen of her humour. The condescending parish clerk and the judicious landlord and the contradictious farrier, with their discussions of village traditions, their attempts at humour, and the curious mental processes which take the place of reasoning, are delicious and inimitable. One secret is that we can sympathise with their humble attempts at intellectual intercourse. The brutality which too often underlies a good deal of more refined satire comes out in the "unflinching frankness," which at the "Rainbow" is taken for the "most piquant form of joke." The presumption of the assistant clerk, who hopes that he may have his own opinion of his vocal performances, is tempered by the remark that "there'd be two opinions about a cracked bell if the bell could hear itself," and finally crushed by the critic who tells him that his voice is "well enough when he keeps it up in his nose." It's your inside "as isn't right made for music; it's no better nor a hollow stalk." Much of the wit that passes current in more elegant circles differs from this, less in substance, than in the skill with which the sarcasm is ostensibly

veiled. When Charles Lamb proposed to examine the bumps on the skull of an illiterate person, he was just as rude, though his rudeness is allowed to pass for harmless fun. The crude attempts of the natural man are redeemed from brutality by the absence of real ill-nature. So the argument as to reality of ghostly phenomena is a tacit parody upon a good deal of the controversy roused by "Psychical research." Some people, as the landlord urges, couldn't see ghosts, "not if they stood as plain as a pikestaff before 'em." My wife, as he points out, "can't smell, not if she'd the strongest of cheese under her nose. I never see a ghost myself; but then I says to myself, very like I haven't got the smell for 'em. I mean, putting a ghost for a smell, or else contrairiways. And so, I'm for holding with both sides." The farrier retorts by asking, "What's the smell got to do with it? Did ever a ghost give a man a black eye? That's what I should like to know. If ghos'es want me to believe in 'em, let 'em leave off skulking in the dark, and i' lone places—let 'em come in company and candles." "As if ghos'es 'ud want to be believed in by anybody so ignirant!" replies the parish clerk. We have read something very like this, only expressed in the "big words" which Mrs. Winthrop left to the parson. One touch of blundering makes the whole world kin; and in these good people, with their primitive views of logic and repartee and their quaint theology, we may, if we please, see a satire upon their betters. Rather, if we accept George Eliot's view, we have a kindly sympathy for the old order upon which she looked back so fondly. A modern "realist" would, I suppose, complain that she has omitted, or touched too slightly for his taste, a great many repulsive and brutal elements in the rustic world. The portraits, indeed, are so vivid as to convince us of their fidelity; but she has selected the less ugly, and taken the point of view from which we see mainly what was wholesome and kindly in the little village community. *Silas Marner* is a masterpiece in that way, and scarcely equalled in English literature, unless by Mr. Hardy's rustics in *Far from the Madding Crowd* and other early works. (pp. 105-10)

Leslie Stephen, "'Silas Marner,'" in his George Eliot, Macmillan and Co., Limited, 1902, 213 p.

Edwin Fairley   (essay date 1913)

[*In the following essay, Fairley maintains that* Silas Marner *presents the art of George Eliot at its best, and examines the novel's structure, character delineation, humor, and moral sense.*]

I have taken *Silas Marner* as the book in which to study the art of its author because here she is at her best. *Silas Marner* is a short work, but it has abundant interest and less preaching than the later novels. While there is tragedy here, the whole effect of the book is wholesome and gracious, and one rises from reading it with the impression that the designs of poetic justice have been fulfilled, but fulfilled in a way that has brought satisfaction to as great a number of people as possible. The story moves in a dignified way to a well thought out end. *Adam Bede* is perhaps a greater book, but as a work of art it is, for some people, spoiled by the anticlimax of the reprieve of Hetty and the marriage of Adam and Dinah. Mr. Hardy would not have spared Hetty, as witness the end of *Tess,* but George Eliot is a greater novelist than Thomas Hardy. **Romola** has always impressed me as a *tour de force.* The effort of the author stands out too much. George Eliot herself says that she began that book a young woman but finished it an old woman. **The Mill on the Floss** is too tragic and passionate, and in the later novels, **Felix Holt, Middlemarch,** and **Daniel Deronda,** the habit of interweaving dissertations and preachments had grown so upon the author that it spoils them as pure works of art, however much it may increase their value as expressions of the author's spirit. But **Silas Marner** is complete in design and admirable in construction, a masterpiece in which we may study our author in small compass.

In a letter to her publisher, who had written that he found "Silas" rather somber, George Eliot says, "I don't wonder that you find my story, as far as you have read it, rather somber. . . . But I hope that you will not find it at all a sad story, as a whole, since it sets—or is intended to set—in a strong light the remedial influences of pure, natural relations." It is significant that on the title-page of the original edition appears this quotation from Wordsworth:

> A child, more than all other gifts
> That earth can offer to declining man,
> Brings hope with it and forward-looking
> thoughts.

From the point of view of artistic structure it seems to me that we have in **Silas Marner** almost a flawless piece of work. There is a main plot concerned with the fortunes of Silas Marner, where the human problem involved is the influence of a child upon a narrow, lonely, and embittered man who was seemingly at the bottom of the ladder of life, for physically he was weak, he had near-sight, and was subject to cataleptic fits: intellectually he was as near nobody as he could well be; and spiritually he had lost what narrow faith he once had. The child necessary for the redemption of the man is provided by the under plot, where the problem involved is the character of Godfrey Cass, a man who evaded responsibility, and apparently escaped, but who met his punishment at last in a way that is artistically true. The book provides in the form of fiction almost all the features of a drama. One of my favorite ways of reviewing the book is to have my classes turn it into a drama of five acts. There is the rising action in the catastrophe at Lantern Yard, the long life of miserliness at the Stone Pits, and the loss of the precious gold by Dunsey's robbery. The climax comes with the arrival of Eppie and with Silas' decision to keep her for himself. The falling action includes the years of quiet joy in the life at the Stone Pits, the betrothal of Eppie to Aaron Winthrop, and the discovery of Dunsey's skeleton with the long-lost gold beside it. The catastrophe for the under plot comes to Godfrey and Nancy with the refusal of Eppie to leave her old father and her lover, while the same decision forms the *dénouement* of the main plot, with the assurance to Silas that he may "trusten" till he dies.

The two plots are complicated first when Dunsey steals Silas' gold, and again when Eppie comes to Silas' house and Godfrey holds his tongue about his relation to her.

The final meeting place of the two plots is at the discovery of the gold, and the unsuccessful attempt of Godfrey to adopt his own child. Although the two plots touch only these three times, the needed complication is secured in a convincing way.

There is a variety of incidents to give interest to the story: the robbery of the Deacon's money in Lantern Yard, the guilt of Silas as declared by the casting of lots, the healing of Sallie Oates, which might have opened the way to sane human relations for Silas, but which did not, the breaking of the brown water-jug, showing that Silas was not entirely given over to the enemy of souls, the scene at the Rainbow Inn of which I shall speak again, the party at the Red House, the staking of Wildfire, the visits of Mr. Macey and Dolly Winthrop to the Stone Pits, the making of a garden, and even the heroic efforts of Silas to learn to smoke, all these make an abundance of action which keeps up an unflagging interest on the part of the reader. It could hardly have been **Silas Marner** that Edward Fitzgerald had in mind when he said that he could not get on with books about the daily life which he found rather insufferable around him. He could not read Jane Austen or George Eliot. "Give me," he said, "people, places, and things which I don't and can't see; Antiquaries, Jeanie Deanes, Dalgettys." I suppose we sympathize with him when we are in some moods, but there are other moods when we believe with George Eliot in Wordsworth's thesis that the lives of ordinary men and women, especially those in rural life, are full of romance and poetic feeling, if only we have eyes to see.

George Eliot's plot supplies us, too, with fine elements of suspense; as, for example, what has become of Dunstan Cass, will Godfrey's secret marriage be found out, will Molly actually come to Red House and declare herself, will Silas ever recover his gold or be cleared of the suspicion of having taken the Deacon's money, and then the moment of final suspense, will Eppie forsake her adopted father for her real father? Altogether I conclude that in its architectonic qualities this book is well built.

George Eliot was a true child of the middle of the nineteenth century in that she was thoroughly imbued with its scientific spirit. This fact comes out in her novels in many ways. She is extremely careful to give us accurate descriptions of the settings of her stories. She believes that a character is acted upon powerfully by his environment, and so she lets us see under just what conditions he lives. The absence of a woman's touch at the Red House is shown in the stale beer standing on the table, and in the general unkempt air of the rooms. She herself says,

> It is the habit of my imagination to strive for as full a vision of the medium in which a character moves as of the character itself. The psychological causes which prompted me to give such details of Florentine life and history as I have given [in **Romola**] are precisely the same as those which determined me in giving the details of English village life in **Silas Marner,** or the "Dodson" life, out of which there developed the destinies of poor Tom and Maggie.

The psychology of the story is well managed, and surely

we are all prepared to acknowledge that the study of psychology has helped the art and the truthfulness of many writers, and we can say this even though we do not care for Meredith or Henry James. It is always a fret to my soul in reading Walter Scott that he has been able to enter so little into the inner springs of character in his creations. Though I have read *Ivanhoe* twenty times I feel that I do not really know the hero of that romantic tale. Indeed I know Silas Marner and Godfrey Cass much better. Scott noted in his diary under date of March 14, 1826,

> Read again and for the third time at least, Miss Austen's very finely written novel of *Pride and Prejudice*. That young lady had a talent for describing the involvements and feelings and characters of ordinary life, which is to me the most wonderful I ever met with. The Big Bow-wow I can do myself like any now going; but the exquisite touch, which renders ordinary commonplace things and characters interesting, from the truth of the description and the sentiment, is denied to me. What a pity that such a gifted creature died so early!

The scientific spirit appears in **Silas Marner** in that the author enters into the inner life of her characters and shows up their secret impulses, lets us look at the very springs and fountain heads of character. Furthermore, she has the rare power of making her characters grow under her hands. We can see the process taking place before our very eyes as we do in real life. I need not say that this faculty is very rare. George Eliot and Shakespere and Hawthorne had it, but Ben Jonson and Scott and Cooper did not.

To continue our study of the scientific spirit in our author let me say that she had the power of exact observation which is essential to correct description. Most of us if asked to describe what we had seen on a drive would take refuge in glittering generalities, "Such a lovely view! Such a grand stretch of mountains! The beautiful wild flowers! The wonderful lake!" but if George Eliot were of the party you might hear her say:

> The drive lay through a pretty bit of midland landscape, almost all meadows and pastures, with hedgerows still allowed to grow in bushy beauty and to spread out coral fruit for the birds. Little details gave each field a particular physiognomy, dear to the eyes that have looked on them from childhood; the pool in the corner where the grasses were dank, trees leaned whisperingly; the great oak shadowing a bare place in mid-pasture; the high bank where the ash trees grew; the sudden slope of the old marl pit making a red background for the burdock; the huddled roofs and ricks of the homestead without a traceable way of approach; the gray gate and fences against the depths of the bordering wood; and the stray hovel, and its old, old thatch full of mossy hills and valleys, with wondrous modulations of light and shadow, such as we travel far to see in later life, and see larger but not more beautiful. These are the things that make the gamut of joy in landscape to midland-bred souls—the things they toddled among, or perhaps learned by heart standing between their father's knees while he drove leisurely.

Or perhaps it is Raveloe she wishes you to see:

> Raveloe was a village where many of the old echoes lingered, undrowned by new voices. It lay in the rich central plain of what we call Merry England, and held farms which, speaking from a spiritual point of view, paid highly desirable tithes. It was nestled in a snug, well-wooded hollow, quite an hour's journey from any turnpike, where it was never reached by the vibrations of the coach-horn or of public opinion. It was an important-looking village, with a fine old church and large churchyard in the heart of it, and two or three large brick-and-stone homesteads, with well-walled orchards and ornamental weathercocks, standing close upon the road, and lifting more imposing fronts than the rectory which peeped from the trees on the other side of the churchyard—a village which showed at once the summits of its social life, and told the practiced eye there was no great park or manor-house in the vicinity, but that there were several chiefs in Raveloe who could farm badly quite at their ease, drawing enough money from their bad farming, in those war times, to live in rollicking fashion, and keep a jolly Christmas, Whitsun, and Easter tide.

Furthermore, George Eliot has partaken of the scientific spirit in that she has not only the power of exact observation and description but also analytic power to a high degree. I have already tried to show this faculty in its application to character delineation. She also used it in her plot structure. Every incident is of value in the development of her theme. See how she uses Silas' cataleptic seizures to advantage, and how naturally and yet inevitably she alludes to the Stone Pits which are to offer so tragic an end to Dunsey Cass, and to play so important a part in the solution of the plot problems. Everything is studied with nice discrimination. There is nothing accidental, and "nothing walks with aimless feet."

I close this consideration of her scientific spirit with an allusion to her power of generalization. She can sum up a situation for us, sometimes in her own words, sometimes in the words of her characters, in a way that leaves little to be desired. Listen to Godfrey Cass confessing his great wrong to his wife. "Everything comes to light, Nancy, sooner or later. When God Almighty wills it, our secrets are found out"; and to Marner's, "I think I shall trusten till I die." Eppie says in refusing to go to Red House as a daughter, "I wasn't brought up to be a lady, and I can't turn my mind to it. I like the working folks, and their victuals, and their ways. And," she ended passionately, "I'm promised to marry a working man, as'll live with father, and help me to take care of him." Mr. Lammeter says, "Things look dim to old folks; they'd need to have some young eyes about 'em, to let 'em know the world's the same as it used to be."

Perhaps this is as good a place as any to speak of George Eliot's style. She was a disciple of Wordsworth in that she believed in simple words. There is no straining after effect. I have found that her pages are perfectly clear to high school pupils of the second and third year with no special genius for the language. Her adjectives are exact and picturesque. One feels that she did not dash off her work in a hurry, but took time to make it workmanlike. It is finished. She did not daub with untempered mortar. One may search in vain for purple patches, for fine writing, in her pages. I will give one sample of a place where she might have flapped her wings and soared away in true sophomoric fashion, but note the restraint and the sense of reserved power:

> In the old days there were angels who came and took men by the hand and led them away from the city of destruction. We see no white-winged angels now. But yet men are led away from threatening destruction; a hand is put into theirs which leads them forth gently toward a calm and bright land, so that they look no more backward; and the hand may be a little child's.

A consideration of George Eliot's style leads naturally to a word about her honesty. I am indebted to someone for a comparison of George Eliot to the school of Dutch painters with the precious quality of homely truthfulness. Millet's "Gleaners" has the same quality. You know the type of picture where all the homely details are put in with a truthful hand. So George Eliot's honesty can be relied upon. You trust her as you do the good family doctor with an honest degree. While she was writing these truthful descriptions, Millet was starving, or nearly so, at Barbizon.

Next to honesty we may set her sympathy. She never forgot the people from whom she sprang, and those scenes among which her early years were spent. It is significant that all her novels except *Romola* and *Daniel Deronda* are set in the rich central plain of England in which she was born and reared. Some of us think that her genius was cramped and confined when she tried to orientate herself in Florence and London, and that she must have felt something of Deronda's sickening in treating of London, a sickening which he felt as he set out to find Mirah's relatives. "He could not escape suffering from the pressure of that hard unaccommodating Actual, which has never consulted our taste and is entirely unselect." But when she is in her own domain, with her own people about her, we see that she looks at them with loving eyes. She may laugh at them but her laugh is never rasping. She may even criticize them, but the criticism is kindly meant. It is enough to make us hungry with homesickness to read the description of Mrs. Poyser's dairy in *Adam Bede.* She herself knew what work in a dairy meant, and she was never ashamed of her hands which had grown large as she worked over the butter at Griff House. Her sympathy is perhaps the keynote of her art. No one ever thoroughly understood a man who did not sympathize with him. If Millet could paint "The Man with the Hoe" it was because he was the son of such a man and grew up with a hoe in his hands. Of course genius is necessary too, but genius without sympathy is a deadly weapon of war. Eliot gives us the real life of real people just as Millet does, but the real life is lighted up with the divine flame of sympathy, and so we see in her common people as we see in Wordsworth's common people,

> The light that never was, on sea or land,
> The consecration, and the poet's dream.

These diviner qualities in the life of ordinary man are what make life worth living to Silas Marner, to Dolly Winthrop, and to all of us. George Eliot sympathizes with us common people as Lincoln did, and so she understands us. The soul of the poor weaver is an open book to her, a book in which she reads the lessons of life, not a blank, or a riddle, or a cipher.

That George Eliot had genius is generally acknowledged. She has been compared to Shakespere more often than any other English novelist. How could she write such a chapter as that which describes an evening at the Rainbow Inn? She had never spent an evening in the taproom of a country inn, and yet here is the life admirably done. A cabinet-maker who read *Adam Bede* said the book must have been written by a cabinetmaker. That she had genius is perhaps a sufficient answer. When genius is lighted by sympathy there are few paths which it cannot tread, and few scenes which it cannot depict. Along with her genius there was a joy and zest in her work. I wonder if great works are ever produced without joy and zest. I can even think of Milton, old, blind, and deserted, enjoying the work of writing an epic as the majestic numbers grew under his daughter's hand. In George Eliot's diary is found this entry while she was writing *Romola,* "Killed Tito in great excitement," after which I feel that I must almost take back what I said a while ago about *Romola* as a *tour de force.*

It would be almost impossible for a woman equipped as George Eliot was to write without lighting up her work with humor, and I find so good a critic as Bliss Carman putting humor in the forefront when he comes to discuss her characteristics. But her humor is kindly, not witty— she loves her people too well ever to laugh at them behind their backs. You remember the scene at the Rainbow when the landlord

> broke silence by saying in a doubtful tone, to his cousin, the butcher, "Some folks 'ud say that was a fine beast you druv in yesterday, Bob?" The butcher, a jolly, smiling, redhaired man, was not disposed to answer rashly. He gave a few puffs before he spat, and replied, "And they wouldn't be far wrong, John." After this feeble delusive thaw, the silence set in as severely as before.

This is George Eliot's typical humor. Again the same evening Mr. Macey says, "There'd be two 'pinions about a cracked bell, if the bell could hear itself." At the New Year's party at Red House we read of Dr. Kimble,

> who being volatile in sober business hours, became intense and bitter over cards and brandy; shuffled before his adversary's deal with a glare of suspicion, and turned up a mean trump card with an air of inexpressible disgust, as if in a world where such things could happen one might as well enter on a course of reckless profligacy.

It is perhaps a long step from George Eliot's humor to her religion, but the reader will pardon it, I know, when I tell him that it is the last I mean to take. Personally George Eliot was a disciple of Comte. She called herself a Positiv-

South Farm, Arbury: Eliot's birthplace in Warwickshire, England.

ist, and seems to have had no personal God, and no hope of any immortality other than that of her

> choir invisible
> Of those immortal souls who live again
> In minds made better by their presence.

She never outgrew, however, her early evangelical training. Ethical problems are at the forefront in all her novels. I have already alluded to the fact that she frequently preaches in her books. Better than this she was always concerned with the ethical significance of life. Although religion in its established forms had for her no authority she found her sanctions for right and her punishments for wrong entirely in the scheme of things. Nemesis was waiting around some corner for the wrongdoer. She met Dunsey Cass that black night when he stepped from Silas' cottage into the dark waters of the Stone Pits, but she waited sixteen years for Godfrey, only to catch him at last in a net of his own weaving, to punish him by making him eat of the fruit of his own doings.

Goodness is its own reward, but there is added in Silas' case the very tangible reward of a daughter's love, and of an old age made mellow and hopeful through natural human relations. Perhaps George Eliot would have

scorned the idea of a new birth as preached by the evangelicals of her day, but the actual new birth may be seen in Silas Marner's turning away from the deadening love of gold to the quickening love of a little child. As Eppie reached up her hands in playful glee to clutch his face the fountains of the great deep which lay in Silas Marner as they lie in every man, were broken up. The breath of new life was breathed into his nostrils, and he became a living soul. Considering that George Eliot "looked out upon a world presided over by no individual or loving deity, a world of iron chance and more than doubtful struggle," we cannot stint our admiration for the great nobility of mind which made her a moralist with a fervor for the right and a hatred for the wrong equal to that of Newman or Savonarola. Her moral sense asserts itself in the essential purity of all her situations. There is sin and sensual sin in her books, yet there is nothing to please the pruriency of itching ears, but much to point the road to the strait and narrow way of righteous living. One misses, perhaps, that last shade of feeling, that divine inspiration, that feeling for the hidden things of God and duty and immortality which would perhaps have been hers if she had known and loved a God-intoxicated man, but one cannot help admiring the fine showing she makes for righteousness without the spirit of the mystic. I cannot help feeling sorry that George Eliot could not have lived fifty years later so that she could have known and followed some of the more modern seers who have been able to combine the scientific spirit with the mystic sense of God. Not that we have many of these choice souls, but there will surely arise some day in "the tide of times" the prophet who will reconcile science and religion, and will roll back the mists which "have folded in the passes of the world." When that prophet arises he will find that George Eliot has done some of his work for him, in insisting, as she does, on the value of character, the necessity of right conduct, and in her vision of the moral order of the world, which, even to her, Positivist as she was, showed at least a partial answer to the problems of human destiny. (pp. 221-30)

> *Edwin Fairley, "The Art of George Eliot in 'Silas Marner'," in* English Journal, *Vol. II, No. 4, April, 1913, pp. 221-30.*

On *Silas Marner's* popularity among high school teachers:

George Eliot's worst novel is her most important. An official document of the United States government testifies that *Silas Marner* is beyond a doubt the one book most frequently read by American high school children. In any large number of years to come it will have more readers than either *Anthony Adverse* or *Gone with the Wind* or both of them. One part melodrama and one part Sunday School moralizing, wound together with a style bare of charm or discipline or any real eloquence, here is our schoolteachers' idea of the best-seller of the ages.

Why? Any working teacher can tell you. *Silas* utters no dirty words. No character—like Hetty Sorrel, for example, in *Adam Bede,* a better novel—gets pregnant. Nothing in all its pages could shock the Epworth League or the Chamber of Commerce or the W. C. T. U. or the Legion or anyone else—excepting, of course, a lover of good literature. . . . You have a son. You want him to form what the pedagogues, for lack of a classier phrase, have to call the reading habit. Then you'd introduce him to good books, like *Huckleberry Finn,* or the *Odyssey* or a hundred others you could name. You wouldn't make him read this unacceptable scenario for a second-rate Shirley Temple movie—this *Silas Marner*—after assuring him that here, certainly, is a great book. Unless you wanted to turn him away forever from "great books" to detective stories and Kathleen Norris, you wouldn't do that.

> *J. H., in* The Saturday Review of Literature, *New York, 20 March 1937.*

Robert B. Heilman   (essay date 1957)

[*Heilman is an American educator and critic who has written extensively on English drama and fiction. In the following essay, he demonstrates that a sophisticated literary structure and subtle themes underlie the overt symbolism and obvious moralizing of* Silas Marner.]

I first read ***Silas Marner*** in high school—I believe about

1921. In the intervening thirty-five years I have read nearly all the rest of George Eliot's fiction, and I have come to share the belief of many readers that she is one of the great English novelists, the novelist, above all, in whom liveliness of sensibility and steadiness of imagination are accompanied by exceptional vigor of mind. Yet as the adult reads, studies, perhaps teaches ***Adam Bede, Mill on the Floss, Romola, Middlemarch, Daniel Deronda,*** and even ***Felix Holt,*** he acts a little as if ***Silas Marner*** did not exist. He may tell a class that after ***The Mill on the Floss*** (1860) Eliot "relaxed with ***Silas Marner*** (1861), which you have all read in high school," and exchange a little smile with the knowing. It is as if, like masques, or didactic couplets, or the fiction of Henry Mackenzie, ***Silas Marner*** had passed from serious memory on some irrefutable turning of the wheel of history. Why? Doubtless it seems so surely to belong to a past world—the world of the *Idylls, Marmion, Ivanhoe,* and *The Vicar of Wakefield*—that we know it can have no meaning for grown-ups now. We have put off childish things. And even to look back inquiringly may betray a touch of that nostalgia that the alert middle-ager knows is more of a danger after thirty-five years than after five or fifteen and so must be guarded against firmly.

Before returning to ***Silas Marner*** in 1956, I found myself puzzling as to what the book would now appear to be. A high school text, ethically commendable, but without adult interest? Ethically topheavy? The embodiment of a world-view no longer tenable, enshrined (or petrified) in the curriculum by a dated taste? The children's book that somehow drew upon only a fraction of the artist's powers? The slip-up or the soft spot or the tired year from which no great writer is safe? Or perhaps a kind of classic grown stale through custom and compulsion? Or, even, an unappreciated piece of Gulliver-art with two faces: the obverse that is the candid fable for children and all readers of simplicity; and the reverse, as complex as ***Middlemarch,*** somehow undetected? It seemed hardly likely. But with these possibilities in mind I came to the text.

. . . . .

I finished that text with a double sense: a sense, first, of the obvious appropriateness of ***Silas Marner*** in the canon of secondary school readings; second, and more interestingly, with a sense of a deeper, less apparent appropriateness. In fact, if I wanted to push the latter point into its most provoking form, I should say that, despite my full advance marshaling of possible responses to my return to Raveloe, I was still unprepared to find a book in many ways so mature in the curriculum at all. I wondered if a cultural historian might find that at some time in the past our society was better prepared for such a choice than it would be now. Not that ***Silas Marner*** is of the stature of Eliot's major works; in estimating it we must also note the artistic choices that withhold something from its potential greatness.

We need not spend much time on the evident reasons why ***Silas Marner*** should go well with younger readers—certain traits of "popular literature" which, in making for "good reading," may garnish greatness or junk. Relatively short, it does not make too long a claim on the attention;

the variety of characters and actions helps forestall boredom; there is a certain melodramatic accessibility about the villains William Dane and Dunstan Cass, though Dunstan is a more seriously examined piece of humanity; the mystery easily raises the suspense needed by all narrative, and this is aided by some adroit shifts in point of view; for all of the somber sense of human destiny (e.g., her observation on the ways of "men and women who reach middle age without the clear perception that life never *can* be thoroughly joyous," Chapter 17), the view of Raveloe life has much of the idyllic, the justice is "poetic," and the ending "happy." And finally, words and actions advance in an atmosphere of easy clarity. The symbolism—for the story does not lack symbols—is not esoteric: golden hair is the clue to the Eppie-gold equation which enables a reader, even a young one, I believe, to sense Silas's miserliness as a perverted love, and his love as a new human currency growing out of the older material one.

. . . . .

Eliot overtly points to meanings of this kind ([Chapter 14]). She is one of the most regular practitioners of the Explicit Style. To say this is, inevitably, to raise an interesting critical question (the question implied in a comparable critical term, Poetry of Statement)—namely, the level or range of literary achievement possible to the Explicit Style. While I do not challenge a principal assumption of critical practice, that the implicit, the indirect, the oblique, the understated, and the half-revealed are the clues to stylistic artistry, nevertheless it is possible for us, in our understandable shrinking from the banalities of sentimental and commercial stereotypes that press in from all sides, to undervalue the Explicit Style, which, as a historical fact, did not frighten writers nearly so much before the development of mass communications since 1920. The Explicit may be an element of strength, a kind of structural framework for the stylistic design, granted, of course, that it is not the only recourse of a writer. The mastery of implication, the ability to take off figuratively, the freedom to force every individuality into style—all these must be there in the first place; the more conspicuous they are, as for instance in Meredith, the more valuable the support of the Explicit. Not that the Explicit, even in Eliot, is always a virtue. It can shrink into gratuitous restatement, the affixing of labels and price tags, and ethical kibitzing, and can thus become a secondary text, a heavy-pointed braille for those who have eyes and see not.

Let us see precisely what she does with her style. The Eliot Explicit may decline into a familiar rhetoric of ethical exposition: "[Godfrey] had let himself be dragged back into mud and slime" (3); or into a mildly superior editorializing: "And Dunstan's mind was as dull as the mind of a possible felon usually is" (4); or into a somewhat platitudinous aphorism: "Just and self-reproving thoughts do not come to us too thickly, . . ." (12) and "no disposition is a security from evil wishes to a man whose happiness hangs on duplicity" (13); or into an avoidable specification that over-extends the distance between reader and subject: "these rural forefathers, whom we are apt to think very prosaic figures" (3); or into a figure that labors a little

more than it illumines: "For joy is the best of wine, and Silas's guineas were a golden wine of that sort" (5; compare, as a possible alternative: "Silas got drunk on his guineas"). Or the psychological observation may be so fraught with a kind of magisterial insistence that a whole passage, for instance the concluding paragraph on the religion of Chance (9), becomes virtually a "sermonette." Other readers will find other places where the word is too unrelentingly fixed on the thing instead of glancing at it freshly and catching it in a quick glimpse.

Yet despite such flaws, Eliot's Explicit makes generally for the strength of *Silas Marner.* When her analysis shades into comment, as it often does, the style is likely to lead to a sharper sense of reality. She is strongly inclined to the generalizing observation that draws the reader into the experience and hence potentially into a deeper self-knowledge. "I suppose one reason why we are seldom able to comfort our neighbors with our words is that our good-will gets adulterated, in spite of ourselves, before it can pass our lips" (10). "It is seldom that the miserable can help regarding their misery as a wrong inflicted by those who are less miserable" (12). She spots the power-motive that infects conscious good deeds: Godfrey "was not prepared to enter with lively appreciation into other people's feelings counteracting his virtuous resolves" (19); and the exhilaration of evil intentions: Eppie's mother, tired and ailing, was buoyed up for a while by "the animation of a vindictive purpose" (12). To the old idea of work as a narcotic she gives a new specification: it tends, for every man, "to bridge over the loveless chasms of his life" (2). In the portrait of Godfrey (3) the perceptions are often phrased in language of special vitality: he was "equally disinclined to dig and to beg," with its balance of both sound and sense; on the brink of a grim certainty, "he fell back on suspense and vacillation with a sense of repose," with its skillful play upon verbal discords; he had vices "that were no pleasures but only a feverish way of annulling vacancy."

All those passages are Explicit but not trite or flat or obvious; rather they are in a strong, forthright, and yet tempered language, the compelling instrument of a vigorous mind that sees general human truths without falling into truism and that sees originally without striving for novelty. It is almost without mannerism, and yet it does not surrender the difficult conception; it is precise and direct without being blunt, for the acute vision comes with an easy if studious formality that establishes an air of a courteous, sympathetic mingling of detachment and devotion. It reaches distinction through the common. It is a rare style, and if one regards it only for educational purposes, the least he can say is that it is almost ideal to help train young minds. It flies equally from the hackneyed, the precious, the mechanical, the labored, the mawkish, the coy—from the travesties of human communication that become the conventions of journalism and of radio and television art for the millions.

. . . . .

What can be said of the style has some application to the book as a whole. In a way the actions and characters all belong to the well-lighted realm of the Explicit. Silas, a victim of injustice, becomes a miser but grows into a better and happier man when his love of gold is replaced by his love of Eppie. Ill deeds meet their nemesis: Dunstan is drowned, and Godfrey must suffer a major disappointment in life. Murder will out: Dunstan's theft is discovered, and Godfrey must eventually tell Nancy about his past. Eppie, nurtured on tolerant love, grows up to make the right choice of life and love.

But that is not all; however Explicit the story is, it is never a lesson; though it is open to young minds, it is not limited to the range of young minds, but draws the reader into a mature vision of experience. Hoarding is not pictured simply as a vice; instead, Silas's gold-worship is a dramatic symbolization of the religion of work and materialism that can be recognized also in our own day. Again, **Silas Marner** can be thought of as a love story, but what animates it is a doctrine of love that draws much more deeply, and hence deepeningly, upon the resources of the responding consciousness than does a routine happy ending or even a romantic unhappy outcome. True, there is the rosy marriage at the end; but Eppie is not a Cinderella, capturing a Prince Charming or a plutocrat from the other side of the tracks; she has chosen a working man, and love is identified not with unexpected profits and wish-fulfilment fantasies but with recognition and acceptance of immediate actuality; what begins, as we see from the house symbolism, is not so much a new life, a break-away, and a shift of loyalties, as it is an enlarging of the old life and love.

It is a view of love not very familiar in our popular art. There is an inconspicuous but real contrast between this "happy marriage" and that of Godfrey and Nancy; Eppie and Aaron merge the past and the present, whereas Godfrey, aided by some extraordinary chances, endeavors to blot out the past and live in an entirely new and clean present; and it is just this cutting off of the past that cuts him off from a future that he might have—that of the living parenthood of Eppie. In Eppie's marriage there is the rejection of certain rewards dangled before her by Godfrey; in Godfrey's marriage, the privation of certain hoped-for satisfactions. At first Godfrey's marriage looks alarmingly like the stereotyped happy outcome; then in a first twist it becomes the image of inevitable human imperfections; finally in a second twist it becomes the kind of "happy marriage" that is possible: with the acceptance of "the lot that's been given us" and Godfrey's discovery that he can give love without dictating its terms: "I must do what I can to make her happy in her own way" (20).

All this is done so plainly and unostentatiously that we may forget how much is being exacted of readers trained in patterns of crooning love-success or sweetly sad losses. But beyond the dramas of love-and-marriage is the still more demanding treatment of another love that is presented also in two different relationships: Priscilla Lammeter's love for her father, Silas's for his "daughter." In Priscilla the conventional figure of the spinster is sharply altered, for Priscilla contents herself with a devotion that gives character to her life; yet she is not given a sentimental, limited consciousness, for, as we see in one quick glimpse, she is aware of a gap: if her sister Nancy had a daughter like Eppie, says Priscilla, "I should ha' had

something young to think of then, besides the lambs and calves" (Conclusion). In Silas's discovery of Eppie there is an ironic echo of literary conventions: the "girl" appears suddenly, and what follows is "love at first sight." But how different is the rest: love arising in a personality that had rejected all affections, the hard cult of things becoming the tender devotion to the human being, and yet a devotion without the specifically sexual element that would be the easiest and most obvious way of bringing about a fuller life; not that Silas's new life is without return to him, but that the non-sexual gratification opens up for the reader a less familiar range of human potential, at the end of which lies the ultimate achievement of *caritas*. For Silas, love is not simply excitement, glamor, the expectable surprise which we count our common due, but something subtler, namely, a transformer of personality; his experience is like rebirth or conversion. This is one treatment of a problem that attracts Eliot in nearly every book—the problem of opening up, thawing out, unhardening the self-walled, the blockaded personality.

Now it seems to me—and I hope I am not simply bursting with truisms here—that such elements, lying behind the immediate lucidity of the Raveloe story, are invaluable imaginative experience. They quietly undermine the rule of the stereotypes and extend the vision of human possibility. I suspect that this is true not only for youngsters but for adults, who, brought up on a literary preoccupation with the problems and diversities of sexual fulfilment doubtless inevitable in a disoriented age, are in their way equally in danger of resting in incomplete perspectives on themselves and their kind.

. . . . .

Beneath the Explicit surface various undercurrents amplify theme and complicate structure. There is a regular though quiet movement of contrasts and resemblances. Silas and Godfrey are formally contrasted: the miser and the prodigal; the frantic worker and the loose idler; both outside the normal community, one in a too "closed" life, one in a too "open" life; yet both needing love, one to open his life, the other to give it some order. The coldly malicious William Dane and the "spiteful, jeering" Dunstan are similar embodiments of evil, both with resemblances to Iago; yet one flourishes in conventional dissoluteness, the other in stringent piousness; the ill disposed man works through whatever forms of life his immediate society offers. Besides the poles of chapel and tavern there are the poles of rationality and superstition, which appear in standard opposition in the conflicting theories about the robbery of Silas (10), but which, ironically, can move in the same way: the rational Dane accuses Silas of commerce with the devil, and the superstitious in Raveloe suspect him of the same unholy dealings. In Dane, of course, we see the man of calculation archetypally exploiting the superstition of others. He can do it because of a habit of mind that Eliot suggests is almost universal. The parishioners in Lantern Yard cast lots to determine truth; Nancy Lammeter, of far less restricted background, is equally sure that she knows the "will of Providence" (17) and governs her marriage accordingly.

In the plain story of village life Eliot characteristically

finds the universal. In Silas's hoarding she finds a relationship that is in the language itself—the relationship between *misery* and *miserliness*. Wretchedness makes the miser; he suffers less from a vice than from a disease, and the disease is the result of an injury ("a trauma," as we now say). Furthermore, we are forced to see the disease as representative rather than unique. Silas is compared with prisoners who fall into a kind of compulsive doodling, with researchers and theorists whose work has become an end in itself (2). And while hoarding goes with Silas's "hard isolation," it is really a substitute for the activities upon which the community rests. The guineas provide Silas's "revelry" (2, 5); he "loved them all"—the coins of all sizes; guineas yet to be earned were like "unborn children" (2); his piety was the "worship of gold" (5). Here were his play, love, parenthood, religion.

These sharp images are characteristic of the style in the chapters on Silas, where Eliot writes most suggestively and allusively, often figuratively, sometimes symbolically; it is Silas who most stirs her imagination and calls forth a language that keeps our sense of the secondary constantly active. When she describes Silas's class of "pallid undersized men," her words also give us a picture of a pale, restricted life without growth. When Silas, robbed, is compared to "a man falling into dark waters" (5), it is as if a movie camera were switching us for a split second to the literal dark waters into which Dunstan is falling. When she tells us that Silas's "face and figure shrank and bent themselves into a constant mechanical relation to the objects of life" (2), she introduces the theme of the mechanical life which she then develops by various images, for instance, of Silas "deafened and blinded more and more to all things except the monotony of his loom and the repetition of his web" (14). He is variously compared to a spider, to an ant, to an insect, to a "gnome or brownie," as if, though alive, he were less than human. His life is imaged in terms of space: he is shut "close up with his narrow grief," his heart "as a locked casket" (10); he had "shrunk continually into narrow isolation," into "close-locked solitude," thinking in an "ever-repeated circle," his soul "stupefied in a cold, narrow prison" (15). Silas's life is dark as well as cramped, and the first image of restrictedness is nicely joined with a light image: "The little light he possessed spread its beams so narrowly, that frustrated belief was a curtain broad enough to create for him the blackness of night" (2). The "light of his faith" was "put out" (5). His gold was "hidden away from the daylight" (14); there was a "dark shadow over the days of his best years" (16).

These constant figures build up a picture of Silas's gold-period as deficient in variety, vitality, spaciousness, illumination. I hope that these examples of Eliot's more packed, suggestive style will tempt other readers to go further in exploring her imaginative resources, for there is plenty of material—the inconspicuous parallels in the action, the ways of presenting Silas's aloofness, the changes in Silas's eyes and sight, the concepts of "mystery" and "dream" that she draws on repeatedly, and the important theme of the hidden life. There is, of course, least indirection and most of the full frontal attack in the chapters on Raveloe life (5, 7, 8, 10, 11). Despite dashes of a fine Austen-like humor that laces these scenes, they are likely to become

overextended, and we to dismiss them as the product of a dated unthrifty craftsmanship. Yet this dismissal would be partly wrong, for the village life chapters have a function: they portray the nature of the community from which Silas has been cut off and which he rejoins. Though Eliot interprets this return as a spiritual gain, she will not idealize or sentimentalize community life; so she characterizes it very carefully, at times, I believe, too carefully.

. . . . .

It is in the last third of the story that Eliot goes farthest beyond the literal Explicit and moves toward intricacy and even richness. As Eppie's life "unfolded," Eliot writes, "his soul, . . . was unfolding, too, and trembling gradually into full consciousness" (14). "Unfolding"—the escape from the closed-in narrowness of which there are many images. "Trembling"—responding, vibrating; the opposite of the monotonous movements of his mechanical life. "Full consciousness"—complete use of the powers of perception, knowing, and feeling. In the first place, opening one's heart to a person rather than a material object. At the same time, acknowledging and taking part in the life of other human beings: re-entering the community. Beyond this, full consciousness means his re-entry into religious faith, which is the final way of defining the community. He is no longer "cut off from faith and love" (2); Dolly leads him to the doctrine of "trustening" (16); he learns that to make a judgment of God and flee to harsh solitude is not the best way to deal with evil in the world. Community, love, faith: these are different phases of a unitary experience.

Finally, full consciousness has a temporal aspect: Silas, once cut off from past, present, and future, begins to "blend" his "old faith" and his "new impressions, till he recovered a consciousness of unity between his past and present" (16). So he sets out with Eppie to probe the past in terms of the new life, to seek some accord between them; but even though he is now re-experiencing an old habit of feeling, and hence a valuable continuity in life, the old order to which the feeling was attached remains in some ways inaccessible. Chapter 21, the story of Silas's quest, is filled with types of images which we have already seen are important in the story, and which now resolve certain themes. Silas wants to see his old pastor, "a man with a deal o' light," and Dolly encourages his search for "any light to be got up the yard." But the enlightenment that might be the conventional outcome of the story does not take place: Silas finds the old events still "dark" and likely to be "dark to the last." Mysteries that have to do with the nature of evil are not easily solved, and they must be lived with. Eliot chooses Dolly to complete the meaning in terms of the dark-light pattern: some things are dark, she says, some are not; Silas cannot know the "rights" of the evil acts against him; "but that doesn't hinder there *being* a rights, Master Marner, for all it's dark to you and me." Having sought a light that could not be found, Silas now sees formally what the answer is: since "I've come to love" Eppie, "I've had light enough to trusten by." Love and faith: the light that can be set against the dark of evil.

Again Eliot uses her established imagery to comment on

Silas's old religion. The place ironically called "Lantern Yard" was near Prison Street, and it is the "grim walls of the jail" that "cheered" Silas with a sense of being at home; Eppie calls the neighborhood a "dark, ugly place"; they come to a "narrow alley," and Eppie feels "like I was stifled." Having thus suggested the darkness and narrowness of the old faith, Eliot unostentatiously pulls her master-stroke: where the chapel once was, a factory stands. Behind the shock we feel a continuity: the chapel religion, from which Silas fled to a fanatic industriousness, was itself more like grinding toil than a freeing of the spirit. Though it once did give Silas a "life of belief and love" (2), his very separation from it prepared the way for what Eliot makes clear is a better meeting of human needs.

Suddenly in the latter part of the book images of a new kind shine out to tell us something more about Silas's new life. In the presence of a child's calm, Eliot says, troubled adults "feel a certain awe . . . such as we feel before some quiet majesty or beauty in the earth or sky—before a steady glowing planet, or a full-flowered eglantine, or the bending trees over a silent pathway" (13). This passage introduces the images from nature that Eliot henceforth regularly calls on to help define the Eppie-world; in Chapters 14 and 16 and the Conclusion there is much of the fresh beauty of flowers and of the joy of gardening. The gentle and yet strong note of new life in the Conclusion comes right after the Lantern Yard chapter, with its dominant note of stifling urban gloom—a contrast of the kind that D. H. Lawrence was to use more than once. Yet there is another contrast borne by the nature imagery itself. For Silas has been described as "withered and yellow" (2), as "feeling the withering desolation of . . . bereavement" and having a "withered and shrunken . . . life," and as having, in his isolation from the "fountains of . . . love," a "soul [which] was still the shrunken rivulet" (10). Yet even "in this stage of withering . . . the sap of affection was not all gone" (2), even though there must be "many circulations of the sap before we detect the smallest sign of the bud" (7). When, then, Silas yearns for Eppie and she finally chooses him by pulling at his "withered cheek" (13), we see the end of a spiritual drought and the beginning of fertile spiritual life.

Silas's return to full consciousness, to full human nature, includes an at-homeness in the world of nature. His conversion takes place in Raveloe, "aloof from the currents of industrial energy and Puritan earnestness" (3), and its "orchards looking lazy with neglected plenty" (2). Another writer might have brought Silas to rest simply in a physically comfortable humanism or an all-solacing naturalism without problem or question. But Eliot is unwilling to reduce life to naturalistic certitudes, to such explanations and finalities as are provided by society and the natural world. Much mystery remains. Evil is not accounted for, or theorized away; in the end, faith is exacted. And if the wrongdoing against Silas remains always somewhat outside rational explanation, so does the blessing of his life; Eppie's coming is a mystery to Silas, and it always remains so. His catalepsy, too, is a little more than an ailment to be accounted for by the rules of pathology; it remains mysterious, and becomes something of a symbol of his openness to special experience—his vulnerability to harm and

his receptiveness to a new good. The good comes on New Year's Eve: the old order changeth. We are told early in the book (2), and often reminded, that the "great change" in Silas's life took place in the Christmas season: a little child came to bring love into his world. Delicately, and yet compellingly, Eliot brings in the suggestion of an ancient mystery. So the story makes a quiet addition to the naturalism which partly fixes its direction, picturing a life that rests both upon an accommodation to nature and upon a metaphysical faith.

. . . . .

I do not wish to over-complicate a "simple story," in which, in both word and action, there is so much openness and transparency, so much of what I call the Explicit; but it is important for the appreciation of it to recognize the presence of elements that, because of the author's technical unostentatiousness and her easy articulation of the parts, may elude the casual reader. Eliot at once gives a sense of life and writes a quiet philosophical novel. To what extent my analysis of the book, if it is valid, provides materials that can be conveyed to high school readers I do not know. I hope that a few of these matters might reach them—for instance, the effect of some of the repeated images. But whether or not the details have pedagogical value, I will say two things for *Silas Marner* as I have pictured it. If this picture is, as I hope, a true one, it means that the men and women who teach it can have high respect for it. And it means, secondly, that the book is a good one for students to experience, by way of what it does for training their imagination, giving them a mature, untouched-up view of experience. Something of this must rub off on them, must mould their taste a little. To sense its value I have only to think of the professional writers of "juveniles" who "know what the kids want" and who can spice it up with pungent mixtures of topical terrors (The Bomb) to bitter-coat the do-goodism or get-on-ism.

Silas Marner is not a great book; yet it is a classic. It is not great because it is not, to use Aristotle's words, of sufficient magnitude; Eliot almost writes in shorthand; Silas is sketched rather than done in depth like the leads in *Mill on the Floss* and *Middlemarch.* Take for an example the significant episode of the breaking of the brown water pitcher near the end of Chapter 2, reported quickly in a single paragraph of less than a hundred words rather than fully dramatized. There is a certain promptness about Dunstan's disasters, Godfrey's wife's death; a certain lack of difficulty in Eppie's choice between two fathers. Yet virtually all the episodes have what we must call authenticity. William Dane may verge on the melodrama villain, Godfrey's and Nancy's childlessness on the pat, yet there is a basic rightness in the vignette of unscrupulous calculation and in the fable of retribution. Eliot gets the essence of the thing, not in a measured series of camera angles, but in one brief, even blunt, shot. And that is why we may call her work classic. She goes to the heart, discarding the fictional completeness of structure through which the artist rises to grandeur. There is an allegoric foreshortening as in *Pilgrim's Progress.* Perhaps today we underrate the allegoric—the abstracting impulse which always, even in the doctrinaire naturalists, modifies the full representation of experience; which may at worst thin out reality into schematic patterns; but which may seize boldly on the vital centers and draw them quickly into the life of art. This last is what happens, I suggest, in *Silas Marner.* (pp. 1-10)

Robert B. Heilman, "Return to Raveloe Thirty-Five Years After," in English Journal, Vol. XLVI, No. 1, January, 1957, pp. 1-10.

Jerome Thale (essay date 1958)

[*Thale is an American educator and critic. In the following essay, originally published in the January 1958 issue of* College English, *he examines the juxtaposition of realism and allegory in Eliot's treatment of the stories of Godfrey Cass and Silas.*]

For most of us *Silas Marner* evokes painful memories of literature forced down our throats in the second year of high school. We were probably right in disliking it then, for it is an adult's book. If we reread it we are surprised to find that in its way it is perfect, that it has the finish and completeness of such charming and slight works as *The Vicar of Wakefield* and *A Shropshire Lad.* We may be even more surprised to find that *Silas* is more than a perfect book; it is a serious and intelligent treatment of human life and conduct.

We all remember the story of Silas: how the simple weaver is betrayed, how he comes to the village of Raveloe and lives in isolation for fifteen years, hoarding his money. How his gold is stolen, how he finds a child in the snow, and how she at last is the means of his redemption. We also remember, though less distinctly, that the child is the daughter of the young squire Godfrey Cass by a slatternly wife whom he cannot acknowledge, and that Silas's gold is stolen by Dunstan Cass, Godfrey's worthless brother. And we remember that when, after many years, Godfrey acknowledges his daughter, she rejects him for Silas. The meaning of *Silas Marner* as a moral allegory is obvious enough, and the symbols are the familiar ones of Christianity. Silas hoards the treasure that kills his own spirit, the treasure that moth and rust consume and a thief steals; then he finds and stores up another treasure, the golden-haired Eppie. The gold brings death to Dunstan, but its loss brings life to Silas.

Taken on this level, *Silas Marner* is palatable enough, and its charm is genuine, but such a reading cannot engage us very deeply and does not at all satisfy the facts of the novel. For one thing, almost half of the book is devoted to Godfrey Cass; for another, the manner of the Godfrey story is very different from that of the Silas story—it is realistic where the Silas story is pastoral and fairy-tale-like. Yet we do not feel any cleavage between the plots, as we do in *Daniel Deronda,* where the vaporish good will of the Deronda story is irreconcilable with the clear-sighted recognition of cruelty and emptiness in the Gwendolen story. *Silas Marner* is seamless and entire.

It seems to me that we must take a second look at the Silas story to see what it is about and what kind of story it is. In import and in over-all tone it is clearly some kind of allegory or fairy tale. Although the insistently allegorical import may keep us from thinking of it as a piece of realistic fiction, it is constructed completely within the limits of conventional realism, with careful attention to probability and to verisimilitude of detail. This shows up even in incidental reflections of the times—its treatment of the rise of industrialism, for example, is both accurate and perceptive, and its critique of utilitarianism is a good deal more subtle than the crude attack in *Hard Times.*

We can see this story about a weaver as being in what one might call a central tradition of the nineteenth century, the tradition of the crisis and conversion—an experience we are most familiar with in *Sartor Resartus* and Mill's *Autobiography,* but which can be seen in a wide variety of poems, novels, and memoirs. The materials of the crisis vary a great deal, but the pattern is more or less constant; and in describing the resolution of the crisis the author is usually expressing his own new-found stance toward reality: Carlyle, his belief in work and reverence; Mill, his Wordsworthianism.

The crisis and conversion piece seems very nineteenth-centuryish because most of the crises are bound up with and expressed in terms of issues that are remote and unfamiliar. Tennyson's anxiety about geological findings, for example, or the public concern about specific questions of dogma, may seem almost incomprehensible to us. Yet it is possible to compare them to, let us say, the disillusion of so many Communists after the Hitler-Stalin pact; indeed the larger process of crisis and conversion is the same in both instances. If we understand more readily what has happened to the ex-Communist, it is partly because we feel the burden of the issues, partly because in our time we recognize, and perhaps give primacy to, the internal aspect of the experience. Seeing it in the light of psychology as well as ideology, we are inclined to take the issues as matter rather than form.

George Eliot was interested in the workings of the soul, and so she tended to see the problem in a way that is familiar to us, if new in her time, to take large issues in terms of psychology. On the surface Silas's experience of crisis and conversion is religious, and one can even take it as a kind of allegory of the intellectual movement of the age. Silas is first seen as a member of a grubby dissenting chapel. His best friend falsely accuses him of theft, the congregation expels him, and he loses his faith and becomes a miser. After fifteen years of isolation he finds Eppie and is redeemed by his love for her. At the end of the novel we see him no longer isolated from the community, but happy, friendly with his neighbors, and a regular church-goer. Silas's route is like that of the Victorian intellectual—from earnest belief through disbelief to a new, often secular, faith. As psychologist and as student of the new theology, George Eliot saw religion as valid subjectively rather than objectively. For her, our creeds, our notions of God, are true not as facts but as symbols, as expressions of states of mind. Faith is good and disbelief bad, not because a god exists, but because they are symptoms of a healthy and an unhealthy state of consciousness. The novel does not give statements as explicit as this, but that is surely the inference to be made from the action.

Taken in this light, Silas's blasphemy—his statement that

he cannot believe in any god but a malevolent one—is important not as a theological proposition but as an indication of some change in his personality, a change resulting from his shattering and disillusioning experience. For when he has lost his trust in his fellow men and in the only institution that seemed to offer him security and give largeness and direction to life, he is impelled to reject that institution and its account of the world. What he has lost is not a creed but a sense of the world.

And a sense of the world is what he regains upon his redemption. To bring this about, George Eliot uses the ordinary device of a fairy tale—a miracle. The situation is splendidly ironic, for the miracle—Eppie's coming—is a purely natural occurrence. Momentarily at least it deceives the myopic Silas (he takes her hair for his lost gold); its effects, however, are like those of a miracle. To use Carlyle's term, it is a piece of natural supernaturalism; it is in fact a rationalist's miracle.

Since Silas is a weaver and not a Victorian intellectual, the final resolution of his crisis leaves him believing in God again and going to church on Sunday. But his new religion is really an acceptance of the prevailing local account of the world. It is a symbol of his sense of integration, of his oneness with himself, with nature, and with his fellow men—the reflex of pleasant and harmonious experience, just as his earlier disbelief is the reflex of betrayal and injustice. He has returned not to religion but to a better state of mind.

I have emphasized George Eliot's reduction of theology to psychology to make clear her distinction between the accidental matter and the true form of man's quest for some satisfactory vision of the world (a very happy adaptation of the potentialities of the novel to the biases of Victorian agnosticism, for the English novel has been, and seems inherently to be, unreceptive to the supernatural). And the psychological approach that George Eliot employed is a highly empirical one: she wanted to describe the problem on the basis of experience alone, and to find solutions outside of what she regarded as the illusions of theology or creeds. She wanted to show what belief, what stance toward reality, could be derived from experience.

This, then, is what the Silas Marner plot is about—what kind of a sense of the world we can get from experience and how we come to that sense. It is, to repeat, about attitudes toward the world, states of mind, not ideologies or creeds. Silas's ultimate solution and the process that brings him to it are Wordsworthian. During his period of dryness there are hints of what will redeem him. Seeing a dropsical woman he has a flickering of feeling and offers to treat her with the herbs his mother had taught him about. The incident brings "a sense of unity between his past and present life, which might have been the beginning of his rescue from the insect-like existence into which his nature had shrunk." When his water pot breaks he has enough of the pathetic remnants of piety to save the pieces and set them together in their accustomed place. The actual redemption occurs through Eppie. When he first sees the child, she reminds him of his little sister, and he is taken back to many memories—the Wordsworthian way,

joining maturity with the simplicity and purity of childhood.

> It stirred fibres that had never been moved in Raveloe—old quiverings of tenderness—old impressions of awe at the presentiment of some Power presiding over his life; for his imagination had not yet extricated itself from the sense of mystery in the child's sudden presence, and had formed no conjectures of ordinary natural means by which the event could have been brought about.

As George Eliot has already indicated, the root of Silas's trouble is inability to feel—delight in nature, love for others, satisfaction with himself, interest in the objects of everyday life. His emotional life shrunken and channeled into love of gold, he must at forty begin—as Mill did—to learn reverence, piety for nature and for the common details of life. And Eppie is the agent of this—"As the child's mind was growing into knowledge, his mind was growing into memory."

Such is the process that redeems Silas from a meaningless existence. Its issue, as we have seen, is a restoration of love and faith. At the end of Silas's story, we feel that the world which made him happy must be good. Certainly this is a sense of the world that we should like to accept. But our own experience and observation compel us to acknowledge that the world is not that good. Like Wordsworth's poetry, the Silas story demands certain sanguine assumptions about the world and human experience which we cannot easily make.

George Eliot does not ordinarily give such a hopeful view of life; rather, she suggests that there is much suffering, much dullness to be endured. The Silas story, taken by itself, offers us immensely more hope and reassurance than any other of her novels, but it does so less convincingly. The belief in goodness of heart, the belief that nature never did betray, are totally unexamined. It is true that there is some equity in that Silas's suffering is compensated for by his happiness with Eppie. But this happiness comes about only as the result of chance, or as Silas sees it, a miracle. In an extra-natural account of reality it is possible to accept chance as a symbol, expressive of providence or of beneficent order in the universe. For we allow faith to supplement and sometimes supersede an experiential account of the world. It is of course just this that Silas does. He comes to accept a reassuring view of life, embodied for him in the Church of England; and in this scheme Eppie's coming is not a miracle as he first thought but part of the working of Providence (the miracle is its own evidence for its miraculousness). But the naturalistic presuppositions of the novel, the reduction of everything to the facts of experience, rule out any such providential view of human affairs. Silas is restored and believes, but can those who do not have Silas's good luck see the universe as harmonious and beneficent, see good as conquering evil and dullness? What happens to the simple-minded Silas gives him grounds for trusting, but it seems to offer a critical mind no particular grounds for trusting, believing, or loving.

This may seem to be taking unfair advantage of the novel by applying realistic criteria to an incident which is part of a fairy tale. Certainly the coincidence and the happy ending do not bother us; they are familiar enough in literature. What does bother us is that the coincidence must stand as some sort of proof or justification for Silas's view of a providential and harmonious working of the universe at the same time that the novel works in a realistic framework of strict probability in which coincidence is forbidden as a distortion of reality. Should we say, then, that the use of coincidence is an artistic defect stemming from the expression of a vain hope? One does not like to suppose that George Eliot meant to give us a fairy tale as a serious reflection of life. We can hardly think that like Mrs. Browning or Charlotte M. Yonge she could deliberately confound or could not distinguish between wishes and the facts of experience.

The rest of George Eliot's work, with its disenchantment, is a relevant argument here. It also is evidence for the seriousness of her concern with the problem of what kind of sense of the world our experience justifies. To resolve the antinomy at which we have arrived and see in what way we must take the Silas story, we must think of it as only one half of a novel, the other half of which is the Godfrey story.

The stories are related in a parallel and complementary way. The fortunes of the two men alternate, and there is a series of pairings in character and situation. Godfrey refuses a blessing and is unhappy, Silas accepts it and is made happy. Just as Godfrey has two wives, so Silas has two treasures, and each of the two men is a father to Eppie. Godfrey is betrayed by his brother Dunstan, Silas by his friend William Dane. Godfrey is secretly guilty, Silas secretly innocent. Dunstan and the gold are buried together, for the gold is Silas's undoing and the blackmailing brother is Godfrey's. When the gold and Dunstan's body are brought to light it is for Silas's joy and Godfrey's shame. Gold passes from Silas to the Casses, Eppie from the Casses to Silas.

All these parallels and contrasts indicate the care with which the novel as a whole is worked out; more significantly, they point to the fact that the two stories involve the same theme, that Godfrey's story is Silas's transposed into a minor key. Godfrey like Silas is alienated from himself and from society. He endures a period of desolation almost as long as Silas's—fifteen years—not warped and isolated as Silas is, but incapable of happiness, uneasy over his deceit and his failure to acknowledge his daughter. Silas's exile ends when Godfrey's begins, and the transfer of the golden-haired child is symbolic. The general pattern of the two stories is identical, but for Godfrey there is no happy ending.

The point of the thematic parallelism becomes clear when we think of the contrast in tonality between the two stories. Remembering the Silas story we think of the fire on the hearth, the golden-haired girl, the sunny days, the garden, the bashful suitor. Even in his desolation Silas is seen against a pastoral landscape. Compare the introduction of Godfrey:

> It was the once hopeful Godfrey who was standing, with his hands in his side-pockets and his back to the fire, in the dark wainscoted parlour,

one late November afternoon. . . . The fading grey light fell dimly on the walls decorated with guns, whips, and foxes' brushes, on coats and hats flung on the chairs, on tankards sending forth a scent of flat ale, and on a half-choked fire, with pipes propped up in the chimney-corners: signs of a domestic life destitute of any hallowing charm, with which the look of gloomy vexation on Godfrey's blond face was in sad accordance.

All through the Godfrey story the atmosphere is dull and oppressive. The story opens with Godfrey deprived of any prospect of happiness by his marriage to a dissipated barmaid, caught unable to replace his father's money which he has given to Dunstan, and threatened with exposure by both his brother and his wife. The story ends with Godfrey absenting himself from Raveloe on the wedding day of the daughter who has rejected him. In the years between there is the guilt and self-reproach over abandoning Eppie and deceiving his wife, there is Nancy and Godfrey's childlessness, and Nancy herself, narrow, barren, just dissatisfied. Even the minor figures in Godfrey's story are unhappy: the old squire is vaguely discontented, indulgent and resentful, a figure of quiet misery. It is a world greyed throughout, given up to "the vague dulness of the grey hours." No one is acutely unhappy as Silas is, but they are people who seem to sense that they are never to have much joy, that their usual happiness is the absence of pain.

Of course, the difference between the two stories is proper enough since one is a fairy tale and the other a piece done in George Eliot's usual disenchanted realism. But this only describes the difference and does not account for it, does not tell us why the two stories are brought together, what the juxtaposition of two such different views of life means.

It could, of course, mean nothing more than an artistic failure, as in *Daniel Deronda,* where the two stories are the result of two unreconciled artistic impulses. Certainly the presence of two different impulses, or visions of life, is not in itself surprising; it occurs elsewhere in George Eliot and throughout the age. Indeed it is a manifestation of one of the largest problems in the nineteenth-century novel, one with which all of the novelists wrestled and by which some were overwhelmed. They wanted somehow to acknowledge both the truth of aspiration—which like religion and poetry may be superficially false but yet is true in some more profound sense—and the truth of experience. *Pendennis* is a good example of a work that gets caught in the problem: the novel tries and wants to be honest about so much of the unlovely part of life, but at the same time it goes soft again and again, and there are spots where the reader is embarrassed and distressed by the conflict between what the book says and what, according to its own logic, it ought to say.

Perhaps this is the reason that so many Victorian novels are unacceptable to us today: they try to embody aspiration in realism. We may cherish the aspiration, but we recognize that the empirical logic of realistic fiction cuts right through it. On the other hand, realistic fiction has a converse problem. More and more as the novel found itself committed to realism it kept coming up with gloomy empirical findings. Of course the findings are not very valid as evidence about the world (only about the state of the literary culture), for an empirical novel does not issue in generalizations. It shows, in strict logic, that a certain hero or a certain group of persons is happy or unhappy.

If, like George Eliot, the realistic novelist deals not with society or with some kind of theological or philosophical assumption but only with inner experience, he can present his hero as happy or unhappy and hope that, like all literature that is probable, the work will have its own generalizing force. Thus George Eliot presents Silas and Godfrey: both of them weak in character and unskillful in battling events, both with unhappiness thrust upon them. Godfrey's story is so faithfully realistic that we have no difficulty in accepting it. And the fairy-tale treatment in the Silas story universalizes what is really individual experience, so that we feel that happiness is really possible, the world tolerable for a great many people, even though we see from Godfrey that it is miserable for some.

In *Silas Marner* the two visions, if not reconciled, are at least each given their due. And the book is seamless and free from conflict because the two visions of life are presented on two different levels so as to acknowledge that they are not directly competing accounts of reality. By putting Silas's story in the form of a fairy tale, so as to transcend that strict logic by which both stories cannot be true, George Eliot disarmed the ordinary criticism of this kind of vision (the criticism that is so devastating when applied to *Romola*): by denying its literal validity she tried to preserve its essential truth, and by presenting at the same time the story of Godfrey she gave expression to the other side of the case. Only in *Silas Marner* did she find a way to present the two visions of the world as one artistic piece. If there is no reconciliation, there is at least acknowledgement and confrontation, and for the moment we can see side by side the lamb of Mrs. Browning and the lion of Thomas Hardy. (pp. 58-69)

> *Jerome Thale, "George Eliot's Fable for Her Times: 'Silas Marner',"* in his *The Novels of George Eliot, Columbia University Press, 1959, 175 p.*

Fred C. Thomson   (essay date 1965)

[*In the following essay, Thomson discusses social and spiritual alienation in* Silas Marner, *contending that the novel is Eliot's first exploration of that theme.*]

Silas Marner, though gradually being rehabilitated from its dreadful fate as a required "classic" for adolescents, is nevertheless still to the rear in due appreciation among the novels of George Eliot. *Middlemarch* continues to command the bulk of critical attention, and no doubt rightly. It is an imaginative achievement of a very high order, but this should not prevent wider recognition of the specific contributions toward its creation by its slighter predecessor.

The tendency is to regard *Silas Marner* as something of an exception in George Eliot's fiction. While admiring her customary merits of stylistic control, deft characterization, and sensitive realistic evocation of provincial En-

gland, commentators have generally located the distinctive quality of the book in its formal perfection, "fairy tale" simplicity, and overt, almost systematic symbolism—qualities they find less conspicuous in the bigger novels. They have looked upon it, in other words, as a delightful branch or inlet rather than as part of the mainstream of George Eliot's art. Yet the contention here will be that *Silas Marner* does in fact belong to that mainstream, and in particular is important to the development of the author's vision of tragic life, so impressively projected in *Middlemarch.*

Not that *Silas Marner* is a tragedy. Certainly the main contour of the second half and the ending are of an opposite nature; but the portions describing Silas' exile, loneliness, and deprivation are dark-hued indeed. One feels that at least in these pages George Eliot was experimenting with a tragic mode. In a letter to John Blackwood she said, "I have felt all through as if the story would have lent itself best to metrical rather than prose fiction, especially in all that relates to the psychology of Silas; except that, under that treatment, there could not be an equal play of humour" [quoted in *The George Eliot Letters,* edited by Gordon S. Haight, 1954-1955]. Though in some of her shorter poems George Eliot did essay humor, the implication in this context is that poetry might have heightened the tragic aspect of Silas' plight. As it is, the first two chapters have a sustained somber tonality oddly different from almost anything in her previous novels.

Take, for example, *The Mill on the Floss,* published a year before *Silas Marner.* It too, if hardly a thorough-going tragedy, has definite tragic colorations. On the whole, however, it conforms to the traditional "comic" or optimistic orientation of the English novel, with the underlying predication of a stable world, wherein the individual is placed in coherent relationship to his society. Whatever the flaws in that society, the fundamental values by which it exists are never seriously questioned. Maggie inhabits a relatively integrated world in which she may be an insurgent but not an alien. At times confused and rebellious in her hazy aspirations for a better life, she is always presented as a *member* of her society, whether in its favor or disfavor. She acknowledges its authority and does not dispute its right to punish her.

Nor does one feel, as with Hardy, any deep sense of disharmony between the laws governing society and those governing the universe beyond it. The agnostic, humanistic basis of George Eliot's outlook encouraged the assumption that obstacles to the ultimate improvement of civilized life must come from no source but man himself. Altogether the novel lacks the element of universal mystery and ineluctable power so pervasive in classic tragedy. The implacable general laws with which individual wills there fatally collide are not, in *The Mill on the Floss,* given adequate presence or dimension. The embodiment of "law" in the narrow morality of people like the Dodsons, or in the conscience of Maggie, inevitably reduces its tragic potential because these social and ethical forces are too clearly located and defined. Maggie's struggles with instinctive ideas of rectitude and her heart's desires, her longing to be loved and at peace with the world, are not related to larger universal, or even social, conditions, until the flood; and that remains an awkward effort to introduce extra-human powers scarcely evident before it strikes. Many sincere, plausible, and ingenious justifications for the flood have been advanced; but despite a symbolic aptness, the impact upon most readers is more of contrivance than of synthesis with Maggie's history. Robert Speaight [in his *George Eliot,* 1954] well sums up its tragic invalidity: "It is an unhappy accident, but it is not a necessary doom."

To convey a more genuinely tragic vision of life, George Eliot had to suggest vaster, less easily discernible or accessible sanctions and powers than Maggie's conscience or the petty tyranny of St. Ogg's society. She had to find a way of portraying characters ill-attuned to the ruling conditions of the world, a way of putting more inscrutability into the operation of human destinies. This mysteriousness need not be entirely cosmic; it could also suffuse intricate social relationships. It must, however, be handled otherwise than in *The Mill on the Floss.*

The opening paragraph of Silas Marner indicates one possible, if severely limited, direction in its neat balance of realism and quasi-supernaturalism:

> In the days when the spinning-wheels hummed busily in the farmhouses—and even great ladies, clothed in silk and threadlace, had their toy spinning-wheels of polished oak—there might be seen, in districts far away among the lanes, or deep in the bosom of the hills, certain pallid undersized men, who, by the side of the brawny country-folk, looked like the remnants of a disinherited race. The shepherd's dog barked fiercely when one of these alien-looking men appeared on the upland, dark against the early winter sunset; for what dog likes a figure bent under a heavy bag?—and these pale men rarely stirred abroad without that mysterious burden. The shepherd himself, though he had good reason to believe that the bag held nothing but flaxen thread, or else the long rolls of strong linen spun from that thread, was not quite sure that this trade of weaving, indispensable though it was, could be carried on entirely without the help of the Evil One.

George Eliot commences by setting the story in a vaguely distant past, but simultaneously qualifies any aura of strangeness by associating the age with a practical domestic activity. Within this temporal frame, she moves from the sheltered farmhouses and upper-class estates to the exposed outskirts of civilization, where the occasional wanderers of as yet unspecified occupation are seen in sharp contrast to the natives. Their comparison with the "remnants of a disinherited race" bears mysterious allusive connotations, but the structure of the simile suggests that they are really not such Ahasuerian exiles. Moreover, in the context of the sentence, they would seem to have some connection with spinning. Intimations of the occult aroused by the dog's barking at the silhouette against a wintry sunset are dispelled by the prosaic interpretation. The focus next shifts to the shepherd's apprehensions about the figure and his mysterious bag, and again the rational explanation is offered, the grounds for any supernatural reality being transferred to rustic superstition.

Such devices are not particularly original and contribute only superficially to the story's tragic substance. They help generate a preparatory mood, but do not in themselves provide the conditions for a tragic world. The local peasantry may feel awe and mystery, but George Eliot as narrator plainly repudiates any share in their crude superstitions. From sentence four to the end of the paragraph, she delivers a little treatise on vulgar errors that lays the blame squarely on ignorance and insularity.

> In that far-off time superstition clung easily round every person or thing that was at all unwonted, or even intermittent and occasional merely, like the visits of the pedlar or the knife-grinder. No one knew where wandering men had their homes or their origin; and how was a man to be explained unless you at least knew somebody who knew his father and mother? To the peasants of old times, the world outside their own direct experience was a region of vagueness and mystery: to their untravelled thought a state of wandering was a conception as dim as the winter life of the swallows that came back with the spring; and even a settler, if he came from distant parts, hardly ever ceased to be viewed with a remnant of distrust, which would have prevented any surprise if a long course of inoffensive conduct on his part had ended in the commission of a crime; especially if he had any reputation for knowledge, or showed any skill in handicraft. All cleverness, whether in the rapid use of that difficult instrument the tongue, or in some other art unfamiliar to villagers, was in itself suspicious: honest folks, born and bred in a visible manner, were mostly not overwise or clever—at least, not beyond such a matter as knowing the signs of the weather; and the process by which rapidity and dexterity of any kind were acquired was so wholly hidden, that they partook of the nature of conjuring. In this way it came to pass that those scattered linen-weavers—emigrants from the town into the country—were to the last regarded as aliens by their rustic neighbours, and usually contracted the eccentric habits which belong to a state of loneliness.

But if George Eliot discredits supernatural mystery, she at the same time recognizes mystery of an intellectually more acceptable sort. In the sense of discontinuity or of disconnection she perceives a common experience with tragic possibilities on a level of actuality surpassing the comprehension of the unenlightened countryfolk. If the rustic mind was inclined to detect in discontinuity the external agency of the Evil One, she sees it rather as an illusion wrought by the circumstantial limits of knowledge and by the submerged internal processes of society. Beneath the slightly condescending irony of her rationalism in analysing peasant superstition, she insinuates a further irony, that in truth the world *is* mysterious. In more sophisticated societies, the boundaries of knowledge are extended and may be translated into terms other than geographical, but there persists the same wonder, so to speak, about "the winter life of the swallows," the same helplessness before the hidden yet humanly determinable origins of things and events. We seldom know enough that could be known at the moment when it would do most good. As George Eliot writes [in *Felix Holt*], "there is no private life which has not been determined by a wider public life, from the time when the primeval milkmaid had to wander with the wanderings of her clan because the cow she milked was one of a herd which had made the pastures bare."

Tragic force in *Felix Holt* and *Middlemarch* seems to derive from a peculiar combination of spiritual and social alienation and the often obscure social interactions that nourish or intensify it. I have suggested that in *The Mill on the Floss* this combination was lacking. For all the range and depth of social observation, one misses the sense of *process,* the proliferous entanglement of circumstance that with the uncritical passes for Destiny, and that can wear down or destroy the individual who challenges its power. In *Silas Marner,* George Eliot succeeded in selecting and organizing precisely the ingredients required for her special concept of tragedy. Even though she developed her materials inversely toward a happy conclusion for Silas, the weaver is her first full study of alienation, anticipating the subtler, more complex treatments of the theme in such characters as Harold Transome and Dorothea Brooke.

She claimed that the genesis of the book was inspirational: "It came to me first of all, quite suddenly, as a sort of legendary tale, suggested by my recollection of having once, in early childhood seen a linen-weaver with a bag on his back . . . " [quoted in Haight]. Not the least important feature of the germinal image is the fact that the solitary figure is a weaver. As such he plies a staple trade, one that the opening sentence stresses is identified with a closely ordered society. But the sentence also juxtaposes to the picture of a busy domestic and communal life a fragmentary glimpse of an unhoused, rootless, stunted, lonely breed of men, who are nevertheless connected with the same occupation as the feminine spinners. Society cannot get along without the weavers, nor could the weavers survive without a society to buy their products. Yet in rural areas the position of these weavers is anomalous. They are both indispensable and distrusted, the very bag containing the stuff for their looms increasing their suspiciousness in local eyes. Business is transacted with them almost as if in furtive pact with the Evil One. George Eliot has thus chosen a protagonist whose trade combines the familiar and the strange, whose way of life is both continuous and discontinuous with established society. The whole story is based upon a pattern of these dichotomies.

Silas is equipped with a history of alienation that reaches much further back than his arrival in Raveloe. His whole life has been a series of disconnections. An orphaned impoverished artisan pent in a squalid alley in the heart of a Northern industrial town, his opportunities for social participation have been restricted to a Dissenting sect splintered off by its narrow principles from both the religious Establishment and the surrounding secular world. Even within this tight brotherhood, Silas becomes separated from his fellows by the unaccountable fits, which he refuses to exploit to his advantage. His cramped beliefs, poor education, and ignorance of human nature, together with

his natural capacities for affection and faith, conspire to make him preeminently vulnerable to the misfortunes that suddenly befall him. In devastating succession, he is bereft of friendship, fellowship, love, faith in divine justice, home, native town—everything, in fact, that had meaning for him. The disaster is especially radical because his loss is not so much material as spiritual. Silas must learn to live not only in an entirely different region but with an entirely new set of values, or rather with the shards of his old ones. [The critic adds in a footnote, "The incident of the broken pot is symbolic of this."]

> In the early ages of the world, we know, it was believed that each territory was inhabited and ruled by its own divinities, so that a man could cross the bordering heights and be out of the reach of his native gods, whose presence was confined to the streams and the groves and the hills among which he had lived from his birth. And poor Silas was vaguely conscious of something not unlike the feeling of primitive men, when they fled thus, in fear or in sullenness, from the face of an unpropitious deity. It seemed to him that the Power in which he had vainly trusted among the streets and in the prayer-meetings, was very far away from this land in which he had taken refuge, where men lived in careless abundance, knowing and needing nothing of that trust, which, for him, had been turned to bitterness. The little light he possessed spread its beams so narrowly, that frustrated belief was a curtain broad enough to create for him the blackness of night.

Notice that George Eliot nowhere commits herself to belief in the objective reality of any such superhuman Power (malign, benign, or neutral) as Silas feels has stricken him. The causes of his ruin, she is careful to show, are all naturally explicable, and the source of mystery is his contracted understanding. As Jerome Thale [in his *The Novels of George Eliot,* 1959] acutely puts it, "What he has lost is not a creed but a sense of the world."

The contrasts between the religiously and secularly oriented societies of Lantern Yard and Raveloe are explicitly drawn near the start of chapter ii. Lantern Yard, "within sight of the widespread hill-sides," is an interior, upward-yearning world, physically enclosed by the white walls of the chapel, yet boundless for spiritual aspiration. To Silas the immediate palpable environment matters less than the sounds and rhythms, the hymns and scripture, which by their familiarity have become the surrogates or guarantees of exalted unseen but devoutly trusted realities.

> The white-washed walls; the little pews where well-known figures entered with a subdued rustling, and where first one well-known voice and then another, pitched in a peculiar key of petition, uttered phrases at once occult and familiar, like the amulet worn on the heart; the pulpit where the minister delivered unquestioned doctrine, and swayed to and fro, and handled the book in a long accustomed manner; the very pauses between the couplets of the hymn, as it was given out, and the recurrent swell of voices in song: these things had been the channel of divine influences to Marner—they were the foster-

ing home of his religious emotions—they were Christianity and God's kingdom upon earth.

Conversely, in low-lying, wood-screened Raveloe, the church is an exterior to the lounging men, the tempo of life relaxed and meandering, the satisfactions and realities decidedly earthbound.

> And what could be more unlike that Lantern Yard world than the world in Raveloe?—orchards looking lazy with neglected plenty; the large church in the wide churchyard, which men gazed at lounging at their own doors in service-time; the purple-faced farmers jogging along the lanes or turning in at the Rainbow; homesteads, where men supped heavily and slept in the light of the evening hearth, and where women seemed to be laying up a stock of linen for the life to come.

These details are shrewdly calculated to penetrate the merely visual differentia of the two places and to reveal their intrinsic spiritual opposition.

With the advent of Silas in Raveloe, George Eliot has a thematic precursor of a central situation in *Middlemarch*—a person living with the wreckage or confusion of ardent spiritual ideals in a mediocre, spiritually atrophied society. The differences are, of course, many. Dorothea and Lydgate are in a manner trapped by their society, whereas Silas is virtually independent of Raveloe, living on its fringes and for years hardly affecting its consciousness. When he is finally reached by the community, it acts wholesomely upon him instead of oppressively. But these and other distinctions aside, the important thing is that George Eliot was here studying in simplified and diagrammatic form the mutual relationship of an indigenous society and an outsider. *Middlemarch* is a massive, highly complex variation on the theme of its pilot model. Of considerable interest, therefore, are the methods by which a sense of disjunction is communicated in *Silas Marner.*

The village itself is appropriately situated for its function. Nestled in the fertile Midlands and comfortably prosperous, it is still out of touch with the broader life of England and has long been sinking into torpid obsolescence. The simple, self-contained structure of this tiny society enables George Eliot to sketch its principal stratifications and interrelationships with spare economy and to polarize two units of roughly comparable narrative weight—a compact social organization and an alienated individual. At the outset, as I have indicated, George Eliot superimposes upon a background of ancient inert social stability an antithetical motif of transient deracination. She then descends from generalities to particulars, describing the superstitious speculations in Raveloe about the strange appearance and habits of Silas.

Noteworthy is the absence of the dialogue that fills the Cass episodes and the period of Silas' reclamation. During the first fifteen years of his stay in Raveloe, he is talked about rather than to; and the narrator effectively preserves this breach of communication by never letting the minds of Silas and the villagers join. To the latter, he remains a vaguely sinister enigma whose presence is taken for granted but whose inner character is opaque. For instance, the curing of Sally Oates is first alluded to as a matter for dark conjecture. Later we get Silas' point of view and learn that his powers and motives have been sadly misconstrued. The abortive result of his benevolent impulse is to deepen the isolation from which he could then have been rescued. Likewise, his history might have brought him sympathy if told to a villager; but it is interpolated for the information of the reader, and sealed off from the knowledge of the community. Silas' eventual recital of it to Dolly Winthrop is an important milestone in his restoration to a unified existence.

The disconnection of Silas from society is systematically expressed by contrasting groups of image and metaphor. Despite the bad farming, intellectual somnolence, coarse hedonism, and tacky gentry of Raveloe, the place does have a kind of weedy or overripe vitality, observable in the drowsy impressions of laden orchards, nutty hedgerows, and thick woods. There is a human parallel in the clustered homesteads, cosy domesticity, heavy conviviality, and indolent pace of the natives. Silas, on the other hand, after the austere yet warm communal life in Lantern Yard, where the brethren enjoyed an emotional solidarity through song, worship, and doctrine, is associated with images of death and inorganic nature—withering vegetation, drying sap, the shrunken rivulet in barren sand, stone, iron, and of course the gold. His very appearance mirrors his abstraction from ordinary life: "Strangely Marner's face and figure shrank and bent themselves into a constant mechanical relation to the objects of his life, so that he produced the same sort of impression as a handle or a crooked tube, which has no meaning standing apart." [The critic adds in a footnote, "Silas' fits are obviously emblematic of death in life, which is the effect of his abstraction. Even when fully conscious, he resembles "a dead man come to life again."] Even the sound of his loom, "so unlike the natural cheerful trotting of the winnowing machine, or the simple rhythm of the flail," is a jarring note in the Raveloe world. After the fiasco with Sally Oates, he renounces his once-beloved excursions for herbs and diminishes to subhuman existence.

> Then there were the calls of hunger; and Silas, in his solitude, had to provide his own breakfast, dinner and supper, to fetch his own water from the well, and put his own kettle on the fire; and all these immediate promptings helped, along with the weaving, to reduce his life to the unquestioning activity of a spinning insect.

Besides indicating the insect level to which Silas has declined, the simile of the spider has a further significance related to the theme of social discontinuity. Reva Stump [in her *Movement and Vision in George Eliot's Novels,* 1959] has argued that the pervasive web imagery in *Middlemarch,* when related to the characters of Lydgate, Rosamond, Casaubon, and Bulstrode, is "connected with illusion and egoism rather than with reality and fellow-feeling." In a footnote, she adds that in *Silas Marner* this imagery "is used to point up the deficiency in Silas' vision. The insular world he creates can be entered only by the child, and she alone can lead him out of it." This interpretation can perhaps be a little amplified, for the web image in *Silas Marner* happens to be both metaphorical and objective. Silas is an actual professional weaver, but since his disaster his work at the loom has become for him a sterile abstraction instead of a useful social function. For him it serves no purpose except to feed his own unhealthy obsessions. In this respect, he recalls Swift's spider in the Apologue, who, alone in his fortress, spun out of excrement and venom in poisonous "self-sufficiency." Preoccupation with the abstract geometry of the woven cloth leads to the absurd fascination with the geometry of the multiplying piles of gold. Silas is not even linked economically to Raveloe by the money it pays him, because the value of the coins for him does not lie in their negotiability. They are taken out of circulation, and thus with each gold piece the weaver recedes further from contact with human society and meaningful reality. This perversion of values is suggested by an ironic metaphor of organic growth:

> But now, when all purpose was gone, that habit of looking towards the money and grasping it with a sense of fulfilled effort made a loam that was deep enough for the seeds of desire; and as Silas walked homeward across the fields in the twilight, he drew out the money, and thought it was brighter in the gathering gloom.

The second half of the book deals with Silas' regeneration, showing how his life is rewoven with society and how his work once again acquires a purpose other than as a deadening refuge from despair; and as this occurs, the imagery of sunlight and gardens irradiates and vitalizes the scenes. The elaborate metaphorical substructures of the later novels, which so enrich their tragic dimensions, surely owe something to the experimentation with similar but more exposed techniques in *Silas Marner.*

The recurrent fits, in addition to making Silas an object of suspicion and aversion, represent chasms of consciousness which permit the seemingly gratuitous intrusion of evil or good. On two widely separated occasions, they mark an apparent disconnection from the past and a resumed continuity, respectively. Silas feels in these involuntary suspensions the manifestations of some controlling Power. Though aware that William Dare has wrongly and maliciously accused him of theft, he regards himself the victim of divine as well as human betrayal. That brief lapse of consciousness breaks for him absolutely the continuity of past and present, and the shock is worsened by his essentially emotional reaction.

> To people accustomed to reason about the forms in which their religious feeling has incorporated itself, it is difficult to enter into that simple, untaught state of mind in which the form and the feeling have never been severed by an act of reflection. We are apt to think it inevitable that a man in Marner's position should have begun to question the validity of an appeal to the divine judgment by drawing lots; but to him this would have been an effort of independent thought such as he had never known; and he must have made the effort at a moment when all his energies were turned into the anguish of disappointed faith.

He is unable to make a rational response to the experience and to seek out a new basis for coherence in his shattered beliefs. Flight to Raveloe completes this vacuum of exis-

tence. "Minds that have been unhinged from their old faith and love, have perhaps sought this Lethean influence of exile, in which the past becomes dreamy because its symbols have all vanished, and the present too is dreamy because it is linked with no memories."

The effect on Silas of his second crucial seizure, during which Eppie crawls into the cottage, is different but also dependent upon an emotional response. The sight of the child curiously revives old memories of a happier time, casting a frail lifeline of hope back to the past. From then on, the texture of his life is rewoven, and he comes to recognize that the great rift between past and present had existed more in his embittered imagination than in reality. There is much that he still cannot understand, but he can again have trust in a benevolent unity to the world. After Dolly Winthrop's eloquently inarticulate musings on Providential design, he replies,

> Nay, nay, . . . you're i' the right, Mrs Winthrop—you're i' the right. There's good i' this world—I've a feeling o' that now; and it makes a man feel as there's a good more no he can see, i' spite o' the trouble and the wickedness. That drawing o' the lots is dark; but the child was sent to me: there's dealings with us—there's dealings.

So the two fits at the beginning and end of Silas' desperate years signify a superficial discontinuity of experience that masks a deeper actual continuity, individual and collective.

Interestingly, Dunstan Cass does not steal the gold while Silas is in a trance, as might easily have been arranged. Instead, George Eliot devises a painstaking account of why Silas was absent from home and the door unlocked. It is arguable that she was relieving the excess of coincidence a little, but in a semi-legendary tale of this sort, coincidence is not very bothersome. A better explanation, I think, is that at this moment Silas and the society of Raveloe begin at last to converge. More specifically, the destinies of Silas and the Cass family intermesh and subsequently operate upon one another in remarkable ways. During the crucial fits, Silas is the *passive* recipient of bad fortune and good, whereas in this intermediate crisis he is conscious and *active.* The episode illustrates the far-reaching web of social interaction that often produces baffling consequences—"that mutual influence of dissimilar destinies," as George Eliot once phrased it [in *Felix Holt*]. While Silas has been in the village at an unwonted hour, Dunstan has been in the cottage for the only time in his life and without any prior acquaintance with the weaver. The result is a mystery with incalculable repercussions. For Silas, the discovery of his loss brings greater desolation and discontinuity than ever. He does not realize that the catastrophe is really salvation. Injury to him by a Cass is soon followed by a compensatory "gift" from a Cass. George Eliot emphasizes that because of Silas' altered habits since the robbery Eppie gets into the cottage instead of freezing to death outside. The deadly gold is replaced by the living child, the sight of whom reunites Silas with the past. The how and why of all this, so mysterious to the weaver, has its rationale in the affairs of certain people hitherto to total strangers to him.

It is a commonplace that the double plot in **Silas Marner** was something of an innovation for George Eliot, but it has not been sufficiently noted that this feature plus the alienated character comprise the basic tragic ingredients of her later novels. In **Felix Holt** and **Middlemarch,** she was profoundly concerned with tracing the hidden ligatures and labyrinthine processes of human society, and with the tragedy that often ensues from the "mutual influence of dissimilar destinies." If the outcome for Silas is serene, under other circumstances it could well have been wretched. The point is that the double plot is used less for the sake of variety, parallelism, or contrast than to explore the actual workings of society, especially the minute reticulation of influences.

At the time of the theft, the quality and values of Raveloe are represented by the Casses. The Squire is the "greatest man" around and sets the standard for the good life with his abundant feasts. But in his pursuit of pleasure he neglects husbandry and the farm is slipping toward ruin, temporarily averted by the precarious bounty of wartime prices. Furthermore, since the death of his wife the house has become rundown and gloomy; his sons are quarreling amongst themselves and going to the bad. The real social center of Raveloe is thus not Red House but the Rainbow, a status confirmed by the frequent patronage of the Squire himself. And it is to the Rainbow that Silas runs for help after the theft. The effect of that visit is to enlist the sympathy of the villagers, "beery or bungling" as their demonstrations of it may be. At any rate, not only does Silas begin to be drawn into the community but his troubles, like those of Wordsworth's Cumberland Beggar, kindle some feeble glow in the mouldering better natures of the rustics. However, the influence of Silas upon any general elevation of the quality of Raveloe life should not be exaggerated. The major reciprocal influences are between Silas and Godfrey Cass.

Silas' second errand for aid is on behalf of another person, and he goes to the domestic center of Raveloe, Red House (itself a kind of "rainbow" with its Blue Room and White Parlour). He there touches momentarily the world of Godfrey Cass, whose daughter becomes his savior. Godfrey in deciding *not* to acknowledge the child and to leave her in the keeping of Silas helps the weaver to renewed life; but he also changes the course of his own life. He reforms, marries the efficient Nancy Lammeter, and restores the farm to stable prosperity. Red House, and in fact the whole village, seem to recover a bloom that had turned sere in the early chapters. Offsetting these benefits, Godfrey remains childless, unable to transmit his new affluence through a direct heir. And as a consequence of his expanding economy, the pit is drained, disclosing Dunstan's skeleton and the gold. The family has long been bound to Silas by a secret debt—a debt which Godfrey now finds must be repaid not merely with the gold but with the loss of his child and the probable extinction of his line. Silas has been to him both a benefactor and an unwitting Nemesis.

Thus by combining the theme of social and spiritual discontinuity with the double plot, George Eliot approached a means of expressing her concept of tragic life. Instead

of referring to some cosmic or metaphysical source for the sense of mysterious power, she implanted it in the organism of society itself. Tragedy occurs when the well-intentioned individual acts in ignorance or defiance of the intricate web that binds his moral behavior to that of the collective society; and the resultant tragic *experience* consists in the feeling of disconnection from the roots of one's beliefs and assumptions about what the world is like. Silas is therefore a tragic figure insofar as his narrow piety prevents an adequate response to the patent injustice done him, and insofar as his response *is* a feeling of utter alienation. In **Silas Marner,** the relationship of individual discontinuity and social continuity is examined in rather too schematic or didactic fashion. It all works a little too slickly to pass for objective reality. But in **Felix Holt,** still experimentally and with uneven success, and in **Middlemarch,** triumphantly, George Eliot mastered the techniques and language introduced in her "legendary tale." (pp. 69-84)

Fred C. Thomson, "The Theme of Alienation in 'Silas Marner'," in Nineteenth-Century Fiction, *Vol. 20, No. 1, June, 1965, pp. 69-84.*

An excerpt from *Silas Marner*

Gradually the guineas, the crowns, and the half-crowns, grew to a heap, and Marner drew less and less for his own wants, trying to solve the problem of keeping himself strong enough to work sixteen hours a day on as small an outlay as possible. Have not men, shut up in solitary imprisonment, found an interest in marking the moments only by straight strokes of a certain length on the wall, until the growth of the sum of straight strokes, arranged in triangles, has become a mastering purpose? Do we not wile away moments of inanity or fatigued waiting by repeating some trivial movement or sound, until the repetition has bred a want, which is incipient habit? That will help us to understand how the love of accumulating money grows an absorbing passion in men whose imaginations, even in the very beginning of their hoard, showed them no purpose beyond it.

Marner wanted the heaps of ten to grow into a square, and then into a larger square; and every added guinea, while it was itself a satisfaction, bred a new desire. In this strange world, made a hopeless riddle to him, he might, if he had had a less intense nature, have sat weaving, weaving—looking towards the end of his pattern, or towards the end of his web, till he forgot the riddle, and everything else but his immediate sensations; but the money had come to mark off his weaving into periods, and the money not only grew, but it remained with him.

He began to think it was conscious of him, as his loom was, and he would on no account have exchanged those coins, which had become his familiars, for other coins with unknown faces. He handled them, he counted them, till their form and color were like the satisfaction of a thirst to him; but it was only in the night, when his work was done, that he drew them out to enjoy their companionship.

George Eliot, in her Silas Marner, *Simon & Schuster, Pocket Books, 1972.*

Ian Milner (essay date 1966)

[*Milner is a New Zealand educator and critic. In the following essay, he asserts that* Silas Marner *has two themes: Silas's retreat into and subsequent emergence from isolation, and the conflicting values of the upper and lower classes.*]

Silas Marner stands apart from George Eliot's other novels, even of the early period. Its simple, compact design and special tone suggest the moral fable. Born of "a sudden inspiration" which "came across my other plans" [quoted in *The George Eliot Letters,* edited by G. S. Haight, 1954-1955], the story has a freshness, an easy-running yet disciplined flow, a varied and surely focussed narrative control, an unerring command of character portrayal of a certain range, and a flexible rendering of dialogue, such as George Eliot scarcely ever bettered. These and other graces have earned it the title of "that charming minor masterpiece" [F. R. Leavis in his *The Great Tradition,* 1954]. The limiting judgment is underlined: "But in our description of the satisfaction got from it, 'charm' remains the significant word."

Whatever George Eliot intended, she brought off something other than a pleasant piece of pastoral injected with some "moral truth." She was herself conscious of the deeper implications of her theme. She had to reassure Blackwood that, though "rather sombre" at the beginning:

> I hope you will not find it at all a sad story, as
> a whole, since it sets—or is intended to set—in
> a strong light the remedial influences of pure,
> natural human relations [quoted in Haight].

Though she promised Blackwood the story's "Nemesis" was "a very mild one" the moral terrain traversed reveals matters strange to pastoral. Charm there is, fresh and spontaneous in the set choral scenes at the Rainbow Inn, the Casses' New Year's Eve dance, in the glimpses of Silas learning a father's part, and in the natural vigour of Dolly Winthrop. Yet something else emerges, of more far-reaching and sombre aspect, that defines the tale and its quality as art equally with the charm of the pastoral scenes or the narrative grace.

George Eliot told Blackwood that *Silas Marner*

> came to me first of all, quite suddenly, as a sort
> of legendary tale . . . but, as my mind dwelt on
> the subject, I became inclined to a more realistic
> treatment.

In the tension between the "legendary" and the "realistic" components, considered in their joint relation to the structure of values unfolded in the tale, lies its full meaning and appeal.

Silas stands at the center of the legendary element. In the opening pages he is introduced, by name only, the shadowy figure of a linen-weaver who has migrated to Raveloe from "an unknown region called North'ard." He is an alien, living in chosen isolation from the village community. His trade alone makes him suspect: the "mysterious action" of his loom fascinates yet awes the Raveloe lads. If they merely glanced in his window he would fix on them a "dreadful stare" such as "could dart cramp, or rickets, or a wry mouth" at any one of them. The village shepherd was not sure whether the weaver's trade "could be carried on entirely without the help of the Evil One."

Silas, at the outset, gives the impression of a *presence,* not of an individualized personality. When we are carried back fifteen years to Lantern Yard we have a momentary glimpse of a devout but featureless young man, wholly absorbed by his faith (marriage is just a further link with the sacrament). What matters, and what stands out in the telling, is the wrong done to Marner—the cold malice of a friend that destroys his place in the community, cuts off his marriage, and blasts his faith: "there is no just God that governs the earth righteously, but a God of lies, that bears witness against the innocent" (Ch. I).

The force of Silas's blasphemy, coming from one whose faith was his life, measures the scale of the evil he has encountered. He turns his back on the ruptured community of trust and fellowship which previously had been his only medium of existence. He denies and flees from the divine will that has betrayed his trust. George Eliot hints there was something animistic in his escape from the *numen* of Lantern Yard: "And poor Silas was vaguely conscious of something not unlike the feeling of primitive men, when they fled thus, in fear or in sullenness, from the face of an unpropitious deity" (Ch. II).

In his Raveloe cottage Marner lives in isolation for fifteen years. His brief attempt to enter the community by treating the sick with herbs only widens his separation and confirms distrust as to the sources of his knowledge. Work is his anodyne, the golden guineas his only god. George Eliot, in a few pages of Ch. II, builds up a powerful sense of the cumulative process of Silas's estrangement from his former humanity: his faith, trust, sense of purpose as a human being. His work now is carried on without aim: he weaves "like the spider, from pure impulse, without reflection." The web is the familiar image used in the novels to suggest the narrowing of vision from egoism or lack of fellowship. He lives at a sub-human level, his life reduced "to the unquestioning activity of a spinning insect." In a different image George Eliot underlines his dehumanization:

> Strangely Marner's face and figure shrank and
> bent themselves into a constant mechanical rela-
> tion to the objects of his life, so that he produced
> the same sort of impression as a handle or a
> crooked tube, which has no meaning standing
> apart.
>
> (Ch. II)

This is surely one of the most powerful instances of metaphor used to evoke character transformation. Marner is reduced to the world of objects, thingified. His human essence has "no meaning standing apart." The image springs from the immediate environment: it is more effective than the somewhat related but less naturally concrete metaphor [in Henry James's *Portrait of a Lady*] of Isabel Archer's disillusion:

> She saw . . . the drying staring fact that she had
> been an applied handled hung-up tool, as sense-
> less and convenient as mere shaped wood and
> iron.

The intensity of Marner's attachment to things leads to fetishism:

> the money not only grew, but it remained with him. He began to think it was conscious of him, as his loom was, and he would on no account have exchanged those coins, which had become his familiars, for other coins with unknown faces.
>
> (Ch. II)

Cut off from human relations, Silas lives with the "faces" of coins, which he draws out at night "to enjoy their companionship." His old brown earthenware pot, in which he fetches water, is for twelve years his

> companion . . . always lending its handle to him in the early morning, so that its form had an expression for him of willing helpfulness. . . .
>
> (Ch. II)

And, in a superb proleptic image, he

> thought fondly of the guineas that were only half earned by the work in his loom, as if they had been unborn children—thought of the guineas that were coming slowly through the coming years, through all his life. . . .
>
> (Ch. II)

The irony of the image is doubly weighted: there is an echo of the loss of Silas's earlier *human* impulse to marry and have children and a foretokening of the nemesis that is to rob him of his guineas while giving him "gold" in other kind.

George Eliot makes use of choric scenes very effectively to suggest the warmth and vitality of the Raveloe popular community. And alongside this pulsing communal life from which he has isolated himself, Silas's alienation is felt more starkly by the reader. The night he loses his gold Silas is driven, ironically, to seek redress from his fellowman. The spiritedly and solidly rendered Rainbow Inn company (Ch. VI), whose individual quirks and petty animosities do not break down but merely variegate the overall sense of community, forms a choric scene that throws into high contrast Silas's abrupt and otherwordly irruption: "the pale thin figure of Silas Marner was suddenly seen standing in the warm light, uttering no word, but looking round at the company with his strange unearthly eyes" (Ch. VII).

The other major use of a choric scene as an image of communal life—the New Year's Eve dance at the Red House—is yet more developed and, from its timing and placing, more effective in aesthetic strategy. Its immediate background is filled in by the attempts of Mr. Macey and of Dolly Winthrop to bring Marner into the community by persuading him to go to church, especially on Christmas day. The sense of Silas's alienness is tragicomically suggested in the scene where he confesses to an amazed Dolly that he has never been "to church," only "to chapel" (the "new word" puzzled Mrs. Winthrop: "she was rather afraid of inquiring further, lest 'chapel' might mean some haunt of wickedness" [Ch. X]). Mrs. Winthrop's lard-cakes and persuasions cannot free Marner from his

enwalled isolation. He spends Christmas Day alone. The Nature scene is finely used to image his condition:

> In the morning he looked out on the black frost that seemed to press cruelly on every blade of grass, while the half-icy red pool shivered under the bitter wind; but towards evening the snow began to fall, and curtained from him even that dreary outlook, shutting him close up with his narrow grief. And he sat in his robbed home through the livelong evening, not caring to close his shutters or lock his door, pressing his head between his hands and moaning, till the cold grasped him and told him that his fire was grey.
>
> (Ch. X)

Not often did George Eliot attain such stark concreteness and force of the unerring word. Silas's color-drained world contrasts with the church-going scene immediately following: "the church was fuller than all through the rest of the year, with red faces among the abundant dark-green boughs. . . ." Mrs. Barbara Hardy [in *The Novels of George Eliot,* 1959] has shown that "in George Eliot the scenic method is inseparable from the habit of metaphor. The interplay between scene and image fixes a symbolic frame around the scene. . . ." Christmas Day in Raveloe offers a wealth of confirmatory example.

The Casses' New Year's Eve dance (Ch. XI) is the pivotal point in the unfolding of the relation between community and non-community in the story. The zest and warmth of the collective occasion are tinglingly felt in the writing. George Eliot holds a sensitive balance between her evocation of the choric whole, the total company linked as a community despite distinctions of social grading, and that of individualized figures (of whom Nancy and Priscilla Lammeter are the most vivid). The fellowship represented at the dance is exclusive: it is the occasion for "all the society of Raveloe and Tarley," not for all and sundry. But the "privileged villagers" who are admitted, like Macey and Ben Winthrop, are granted full and salted commentary on the doings of their betters. Their presence does not let us forget the wider popular community in whose name they speak.

The "legendary" element that enters deeply into the structure of *Silas Marner* is most evident in the narration of Silas's finding of the child on his cottage hearth (Ch. XII). The role of chance, obvious and considerable, doesn't disturb: it confirms the legendary mood. The mother, giving way to the effects of her drug, collapses within a child's toddling distance (through snow) of Marner's cottage door. The door of the cottage is open (at the very moment Marner is holding it ajar, caught in one of his cataleptic fits) so that the child can set out to catch "the bright living thing"—the light thrown across the darkened snow from the cottage fire. The child enters the cottage without Marner's being aware of it. Recovering from his trance he goes back to his fireside:

> to his blurred vision, it seemed as if there were gold on the floor in front of the hearth. Gold!— his own gold brought back to him as mysteriously as it had been taken away! The heap of gold seemed to glow and get larger beneath his agitated gaze.

Not until he touches the gold does he encounter "soft warm curls" instead of "the hard coin with the familiar resisting outline." Later, when he first takes the child on his lap, he experiences an "emotion mysterious to himself, at something unknown dawning on his life." And instead of his being reduced to the world of objects, of being thingified, his chief fetish is itself made flesh:

> Thought and feeling were so confused within him, that if he had tried to give them utterance, he could only have said that the child was come instead of the gold—*that the gold had turned into the child.*
>
> (Ch. XIV, my emphasis)

Up to the point of the child's discovery the narrative has much in common with the pastoral romance of a lost child and foster-father such as Shakespeare drew upon for *The Winter's Tale.* There are some striking parallels. The association of the discovered child with gold, and the fairy-tale coloring, occurs in *The Winter's Tale.* Having found the child and "bundle" left on the wild Bohemian shore by Antigonus, the shepherd says to his son:

> Now bless thyself: thou mettest with things dying, I with things new-born. Here's a sight for thee: look thee, a bearing-cloth for a squire's child! Look thee here: take up, take up, boy; open't. So, let's see. It was told me I should be rich by the fairies: this is some changeling. Open't: what's within, boy?

And the son replies:

> You're a made old man: if the sins of your youth are forgiven you, you're well to live. Gold! all gold.

The old shepherd brings up the foundling as his daughter Perdita. "Time, the Chorus" announces that sixteen years are to be passed over, bringing on the climax of the love and recognition scenes in which Florizel claims Perdita as wife and Perdita is revealed as the daughter of Leontes and Hermione. Part II of *Silas Marner* opens with the sentence: "It was a bright autumn Sunday, sixteen years after Silas Marner had found his treasure on the hearth" (Ch. XVI). Both the period and the structural function of the time element correspond exactly. Eppie, brought up by Silas as his own daughter, is found to be "a squire's child" (though she rejects her natural father). And she pledges herself to marry not a scion of the gentry but a working-man. The common elements are obvious. But the difference of dénouement, determined by Eppie's acquired bond of kinship with working folk, is the essence of the tale.

There is also a difference of moral atmosphere. While *The Winter's Tale* treats the incident as something out of an old ballad, George Eliot makes strong play with the numinous quality of Silas's experience. Telling Dolly Winthrop of the event Silas says: "Yes—the door was open. The money's gone I don't know where, and this is come from I don't know where" (Ch. XIV). Later, reflecting on his experience, he thinks of Eppie in terms of: "this young life that had been sent to him out of the darkness into which his gold had departed" (Ch. XVI). The "sent to him" links up with that first confused "feeling" he had had immediately after his discovery: "that this child was somehow a message come to him from that far-off life: it stirred fibres that had never been moved in Raveloe—old quiverings of tenderness—old impressions of awe at the presentiment of some Power presiding over his life . . ." (Ch. XII).

More than once Dolly Winthrop interprets the mystery as the natural working of the will of "Them as was at the making of us." And in the end Silas settles for a slightly troubled deism: " 'That drawing o' the lots is dark: but the child was sent to me: there's dealings with us—there's dealings' " (Ch. XVI).

The drama of Marner's re-humanization is expressed in a more realistic vein that contrasts significantly with the legendary and numinous atmosphere of his earlier alienation. The shadowy, somewhat depersonalized Marner of Part I gradually acquires a voice and gestures of his own. His first tentative steps in parenthood are rendered with a moving simplicity, enlivened with a quiet humour which skirts sentimentalization. The sense of an *awakened* Marner, of a man who has laid hold on life again, is strong in the little scene in which he defies Mrs. Kimble, the voice of respectable society, to take the child away:

> "No—no—I can't part with it, I can't let it go," said Silas, abruptly. "It's come to me—I've a right to keep it." The proposition to take the child from him had come to Silas quite unexpectedly, and his speech, uttered under a strong

A sketch of Eliot by Caroline Bray, circa 1842.

sudden impulse, was *almost like a revelation to himself:* a minute before, he had no distinct intention about the child.

(Ch. XIII, my emphasis)

The dialogue scenes in which Dolly Winthrop discourses on the whole right and duty of parents have a vitality and clarity of rendering which, if due primarily to her superlatively expressed *vis animae,* also show Marner in sharper profile.

Marner's recovery of his humanity emerges partly from the uncommented narrative of his growing care and affection for Eppie. It is also pointed up in the authorial commentary, not generalizing and didactic but expository: "Unlike the gold which needed nothing, and must be worshipped in close-locked solitude—which was hidden away from the daylight, was deaf to the song of birds, and started to no human tones—Eppie was a creature of endless claims and ever-growing desires, seeking and loving sunshine, and living sounds, and living movements . . ." (Ch. XIV). Marner slowly comes to break out of the "ever-repeated circle" in which his thoughts had been trapped by his gold: "his soul, long stupefied in a cold narrow prison, was unfolding too, and trembling gradually into full consciousness" (Ch. XIV). The extent of the change in Silas is indicated in a passage at the close of Part I; Wordsworthian in moral tone, it has a concrete simplicity of utterance and a natural vein of feeling that George Eliot rarely achieved:

> No child was afraid of approaching Silas when Eppie was near him: there was no repulsion around him now, either for young or old; for the little child had come to link him once more with the whole world. There was love between him and the child that blent them into one, and there was love between the child and the world—from men and women with parental looks and tones, to the red lady-birds and the round pebbles.
>
> (Ch. XIV)

Marner's loss and recovery of his humanity forms the major part of the novel's two-fold theme. It is developed by the skilful use of several mutually sustaining modes of presentation. In the end the reader feels strongly that a warped and deadened personality has come alive and whole under "the remedial influences of pure, natural human relations."

. . .

The secondary theme in the double structure of *Silas Marner* is the conflict of contrasted moral values and of social planes in which those values respectively inhere. The confrontation, considering the novel's limited span, is worked out with a sure sense of dramatic gradation and tragic irony to a finely staged catastrophe. Godfrey and Silas are fatal opposites brought into a fatal conjunction. The thematic development of Marner's loss and recovery of his humanity is counterpointed with the stages of Cass's moral deception and defeat. The death of Godfrey's first wife (long willed by him) ironically brings "salvation" to himself (he can marry Nancy Lammeter) and to Silas (the finding of Eppie). Godfrey's marriage to Nancy, though it offers some happiness, is childless: unblessed according

to the tale's simple symbolism. Eppie, the image of life's renewal, brings Silas back his lost humanity: "Eppie called him away from his weaving, and made him think all its pauses a holiday, reawakening his senses with her fresh life, even to the old winter-flies that came crawling forth in the early spring sunshine, and warming him into joy because *she* had joy" (Ch. XIV).

The very discovery of the child sets off contrasted reactions. Godfrey, when he first comes to Marner's cottage to see his daughter, feels "a conflict of regret and joy, that the pulse of that little heart had no response for the half-jealous yearning in his own . . ." (Ch. XIII). He assumes Marner will hand the child over to the parish. "Who says so?" said Marner, sharply. "Will they make me take her?" The impulsive, possessive love of the stranger lights up the self-divided calculatingness of the father, intent only upon a convenient disposal of the child and of his conscience:

> "Poor little thing!" said Godfrey. "Let me give something towards finding it clothes." He had put his hand in his pocket and found half-a-guinea, and, thrusting it into Silas's hand, he hurried out of the cottage. . . .
>
> (Ch. XIII)

Godfrey's half-guinea salve meets with a further challenging contrast in the person of Dolly Winthrop. It is she whose immediately offered help in caring for the "tramp's child" (as good society has it) Marner appreciates most. When he shows her the half-guinea she replies: " 'Eh, Master Marner . . . there's no call to buy, no more nor a pair o' shoes; for I've got the little petticoats as Aaron wore five years ago, and it's ill spending the money on them baby-clothes, for the child'll grow like grass i' May, bless it—that it will' " (Ch. XIV). Dolly, the wife of Ben Winthrop the wheelwright, is finely individualized, above all by her speech, which in its natural running on, its energy and liveliness, its homespun but never banal simplicity, is matched only by Mrs. Poyser's. Dolly has a Shakespearean largeness of stature, a rounded substantiality and rootedness in the earth. She is a genuine folk-figure, an image of the people's reserves of instinctive sympathy and care for the fellow-needy, practical know-how, forthrightness, resourcefulness, and good humor. She is the one person to whom Silas can unburden his doubts as to the drawing of lots that drove him into the wilderness. Dolly's faith that "Them as was at the making on us . . . knows better and has a better will" is in the last resort unshakable. But when she speaks of it the achieved control of tone and Shakespeare-like concreteness of language are evident:

> And that's all as ever I can be sure on, and everything else is a big puzzle to me when I think on it. For there was the fever come and took off them as were full-growed, and left the helpless children; and there's the breaking o' limbs; and them as'ud do right and be sober have to suffer by them as are contrairy—eh, there's trouble i' this world, and there's things as we can niver make out the rights on.
>
> (Ch. XVI)

Dolly Winthrop, the wife of a working-man, complements Marner, the weaver, in his function of creating the *popular* scale of values in the tale. Their friendly association at the outset in the bringing up of Eppie, their growing understanding of each other, are sealed by Eppie's marriage to Dolly's son Aaron.

The conflict of opposed values that has been growing throughout the story comes to a head in the final challenge-and-response scene between Godfrey and Nancy Cass and Silas and Eppie (Ch. XIX). As in the encounter between Adam Bede and Arthur Donnithorne the class gap between the pairs is brought out emphatically and in shrewdly varied ways. Silas is on the defensive from the start: "always ill at ease when he was being spoken to by 'betters' " and answering Godfrey "with some constraint." When Godfrey remarks that Silas's gold (recovered with the finding of Dunstan Cass's body in the Stonepit) won't go far, even to maintain only himself, Silas is "unaffected" by the rich man's argument: "We shall do very well—Eppie and me 'ull do well enough. There's few working-folks have got so much laid by as that. I don't know what it is to gentlefolks, but I look upon it as a deal—almost too much. . . ." From then on the scene has a spiralling tension, finely controlled as it mounts to the dénouement. Godfrey pursues his gentlemanly line of the parent who, wishing to make amends, is bent merely on ensuring Eppie's welfare: "making a lady of her." When Eppie responds that she doesn't wish to be a lady (though dropping a curtsy respectfully) Godfrey gets assertive: "It's my duty, Marner, to own Eppie as my child, and provide for her." He warns that otherwise Eppie "may marry some low workingman," and accuses Silas: "You're putting yourself in the way of her welfare." And Silas yields, after a struggle: "Speak to the child. I'll hinder nothing." There is a touch of classical tragic irony in Nancy and Godfrey's ready assumption, at this point, that their mission has succeeded:

> "My dear, you'll be a treasure to me," said
> Nancy, in her gentle voice. "We shall want for
> nothing when we have our daughter."

It is Eppie who now stands at the center of the stage (the scene, like others of George Eliot's best, is as immediate and direct in its interchanges as a play). But she "did not come forward and curtsy, as she had done before. She held Silas's hand in hers, and grasped it firmly—it was a weaver's hand, with a palm and finger-tips that were sensitive to such pressure—while she spoke with colder decision than before": " 'Thank you, ma'am—thank you, sir, for your offers—they're very great, and far above my wish. For I should have no delight i' life any more if I was forced to go away from my father, and knew he was sitting at home, a-thinking of me and feeling lone. . . .' " When Nancy tries once more ("a duty you owe to your lawful father") Eppie brings the moral drama to a full close: " 'I can't feel as I've got any father but one . . . I wasn't brought up to be a lady, and I can't turn my mind to it. I like the working-folks, and their victuals, and their ways. And,' she ended passionately, while the tears fell, 'I'm promised to marry a working-man, as 'll live with father, and help me to take care of him.' "

The dramatic surprise is well brought off, without histrionics. The social gap, and the habits of speech and behavior on each side of the gap (Eppie's curtsies and final

"ma'am" and "sir"; Godfrey's recourse to moral principles to bolster his commandeering: " . . . it's my duty to insist on taking care of my own daughter") are finely caught. As in *Adam Bede* the clash of moral values is worked out and finally resolved within a specific class-differentiated context. Godfrey's natural assumption that his daughter should not marry "some low working-man" falls to pieces in face of Eppie's declaration. The light of human charity comes from Silas Marner's hearth—the "bright gleam" that fetched the child "in over the snow, like as if it had been a little starved robin," as Dolly Winthrop put it. It is the grasp of a weaver's hand that sustains Eppie when making her final act of commitment to "the working-folks . . . and their ways."

The secondary theme of conflicting values adds a dimension to the first. The "remedial influences of pure, natural human relations" operate within a conditioning social framework. Marner's alienation from himself and his fellow-man is healed by his uncalculating love for "a tramp's child." Godfrey Cass disowns his own daughter. The revealing of Eppie as "a squire's child" immediately poses, in simple but dramatically clear-cut terms, the question of moral engagement so characteristic of the later novels. Eppie's commitment to the code of working-folk is the confirming counterpart of Marner's regaining of human lineaments. There is the wider implication, to be spelt out in the more complex crisis of Esther Lyon, that some such commitment is the necessary price of moral health.

The final quality of *Silas Marner* is other than "charming." The mark of man's inhumanity to man lies heavy across its early pages. Marner's cursing of his God, his destruction of himself as a human being, his abject despair, belong not to the pleasant illusion of fairy-tale but to the encounters of tragic moral drama. *Silas Marner* is one of the most effective renderings of the experience—so characteristically modern—of man's alienation. In the wide moral resonance of its double theme, and in its consummately controlled art, it merits a more substantial place in the critical estimate of George Eliot's work. (pp. 717-29)

> *Ian Milner, "Structure and Quality in 'Silas Marner'," in* Studies in English Literature, *1500-1900, Vol. VI, No. 4, Autumn, 1966, pp. 717-29.*

Q. D. Leavis   (essay date 1967)

[*Leavis was an English critic, essayist, and editor. Her professional alliance with her husband, F. R. Leavis, resulted in several literary collaborations, including the successful quarterly periodical* Scrutiny *in which she published many critical essays. Leavis maintained that critics should ignore their impressionistic responses to literature and judge a work on the basis of its moral value. In the following excerpt, originally published as the introduction to the 1967 Penguin edition of* Silas Marner, *Leavis relates the novel's content and themes to Eliot's religious beliefs and social concerns.*]

In his reminiscences *The Middle Years*, written in his old age, Henry James, when starting on his memories of

George Eliot, refers to her as 'the author of **Silas Marner** and **Middlemarch**', a selection from her novels intended either to represent her at her best or as covering two distinct kinds in her creative art, or both. He goes on to describe her work in general as 'a great treasure of beauty and humanity, of applied and achieved art, a testimony, historic as well as aesthetic, to the deeper interest of the intricate English aspects'. Of none of her novels is this more true than **Silas Marner;** one could only have wished that he had been specific. What deeper interest of the aspects of England, what aesthetic and historic testimony, does **Marner** represent? That it is not to be dismissed as the mere moral 'faery-tale' or *'divertissement'* of many critics we might have guessed from the quite exceptional nature of its origin, of which we luckily have an account. Our first knowledge of this book is a note in George Eliot's Journal (28 November 1860): 'I am now engaged in writing a story—the idea of which came to me after our arrival in this house [a depressing furnished London house] and which has thrust itself between me and the other book [**Romola**] I was meditating. It is **Silas Marner, the Weaver of Raveloe**'. Thus at the outset Silas was identified by his trade. And we note also that this same day's entry in her Journal opens:

> Since I last wrote in this Journal, I have suffered much from physical weakness, accompanied with mental depression. The loss of the country has seemed very bitter to me, and my want of health and strength has prevented me from working much—still worse, has made me despair of ever working well again.

Six weeks later, in writing to tell her publisher of her new book she again stresses the involuntary nature of this new undertaking: 'a story which came *across* my other plans by a sudden inspiration'. She adds: 'It is a story of old-fashioned village life, which has unfolded itself from the merest millet-seed of thought'. On 10 March 1861 she notes: 'Finished **Silas Marner**'. Previously she had replied to Blackwood's comment, that so far as he had read he found it 'sombre', that she was not surprised and doubted if it would interest anybody 'since Wordsworth is dead', but assured him that it was not sad on the whole, 'since it sets in a strong light the remedial influences of pure, natural human relations'. Thus the Weaver's story belonged to the village life of the past and exemplified a theory congenial to Wordsworth (and Coleridge); and the impulse to write it sprang from a deep depression of health and spirits due to living in conditions which were the very negation of 'old-fashioned village life', a depression that, as we see, was morbid, since it involved irrational despair of succeeding again as a novelist, in spite of the great success of **Adam Bede** and **The Mill on the Floss**. The letter to Blackwood ends: 'It came to me first of all quite suddenly, as a sort of legendary tale, suggested by my recollections of having once, in early childhood, seen a linen weaver with a bag on his back; but as my mind dwelt on the subject, I became inclined to a more realistic treatment'—that is, she dropped the association with a faery-tale figure. And this is borne out by her saying that she felt 'as if the story would have lent itself best to metrical rather than prose fiction', 'except that, under that treatment, there could not be an equal play of humour'. The humour is not only quite

as much a characteristic of the book she finally wrote as the 'poetry', but is itself no simple matter; it contains much irony of various kinds and a great deal of pointed social criticism which no light-weight legendary tale could support, not even those art-versions of the faery-tale so characteristic of nineteenth-century literature with which **Marner** might be associated if superficially read. Even the author's own account here is misleading; that something essential has been left out is proved by the truer, fuller version contained in a letter from Major Blackwood to his wife in 1861: '**Silas Marner** sprang from her childish recollection of a man with a stoop and expression of face that led her to think that he was an alien from his fellows'. Physical deformity and the stamp of alienation are the important factors; the bag then ceases to be sinister, suggestive of a figure in Grimms' Tales, and connects the man with the one in another vision [John Bunyan's *Pilgrim's Progress,* 1678] that we often feel to be behind George Eliot's in **Marner,** the Man bowed under 'a great Burden upon his back' crying lamentably, *'What shall I do?'* and setting out from the City of Destruction to another country to seek salvation. It is in keeping with this serious intention that the author insisted that in the title and in advertising the book the word *story* should be avoided, undoubtedly because she felt this was a misleading description, tending to make the book appear something slight and fanciful. And rightly, for in **Marner** she had found a framework within which she could present the problems that pressed on her, that life had shown her must be solved or managed, and which were more than merely personal. Though **Marner** prepares us for its successors **Middlemarch** and **Felix Holt** it is superior to these in an art of concentration that uses always the minimum—the loaded word and the uniquely representative act—an art which puts **Marner** with Shakespeare and Bunyan rather than with other Victorian novels. It is very evidently the source of Hardy's novel-writing, but he never anywhere equalled the characterization of Raveloe and the talk in the Rainbow in his efforts at the same kind of thing, nor did he ever manage to invent a plot where coincidence, as in **Marner,** is felt as part of a natural and just order of things, or a plot which, like **Marner**'s, perfectly exemplifies its theme.

Leaving aside for the moment why this book insisted on being written when its author was struggling to write a quite different novel, we ask first: Why was this stooping man alien? what country did he not belong to and why?

The book begins by deliberately establishing in 'anthropological' terms the conditions of a poor nineteenth-century Christian whose burden is not Original Sin but loss of faith and of a community—in fact what the City had given him in the way of a religion and a community was not recognizable as such by the traditions of the countryside, the village life in which the English civilized themselves. To this, the original state, the man makes his way by instinct with his only skill, his loom, and all that is left of his religion, his Bible. In Raveloe the Industrial Revolution has not yet been felt and it is the countryside of the timeless past of packhorse and spinning-wheel, of the organic community and the unified society. To the people of Raveloe professional weaving, though necessary, is an alien way of working; it produces 'pallid, undersized men who, by the side of the brawny country-folk, looked like the remnants of a disinherited race', objects therefore of a superstitious repugnance; we are first shown the weaver through the eyes of a peasantry. The machinery *they* know is their servant; the country-bred novelist understood the real distinction between mechanical aids and a mechanized industry, and her feeling for music provided the natural human reaction: she expresses it in the countryfolk's perception of a difference in rhythm—'the cheerful trotting of the winnowing-machine and the simple rhythm of the flail'—human or animal rhythms, contrasted with the mechanical rhythm which is *imposed* on the worker by his loom; significantly Marner is described as working *in* his loom, which eventually turns him into a machine component, 'so that he had the same sort of impression as a handle or a crooked tube, which has no meaning standing apart'. The signs of his enslavement are 'the bent treadmill attitude' and the short sight, produced by his work, that cuts him off from seeing his fellow-men both actually and metaphorically. He is the opposite of the country craftsman like Adam Bede whose healthy livelihood made him a superior type of manhood.

Silas's solitary working round could find compensation only in an inward spiritual life and 'incorporation in a narrow religious sect'. But the religious life available to him was not beneficial, taking as guidance a pathetically ignorant inner light ('Lantern Yard') which has proved delusive when tested. Moreover, it has deprived him of his cultural inheritance (represented, by a stroke of genius, by the medicinal herbs) without providing anything in the way of education in living instead. George Eliot presents more of the truth about Dissent in *Marner* than in the earlier and very partial account of Methodism in *Adam Bede*—*Marner* is more truthful in many ways. Besides the problem of the machine toil which is dehumanizing, she has brought in another major problem of her age, the threat to the traditional heritage by the now dominant Evangelical outlook. 'The little store of wisdom which his mother had imparted to him as a solemn bequest' (the knowledge and preparation of medicinal wild herbs) Calvinism had taught him to mistrust, 'so that the inherited delight he had in wandering in the fields in search of foxglove and dandelion and coltsfoot began to wear to him the character of a temptation'. This symbol is finely chosen, for it conveys that help for others, contact with Nature, and a kind of education, as well as the satisfaction of knowing he is maintaining the wise lore of his ancestors, are all denied him. There is thus a multiple typicality about the case of Silas Marner. In him the dire effects of the Industrial Revolution are examined; the current form of religion, a Christian fundamentalism, has finished the effects of denaturing him by disinheriting him. How can such losses to the race be made good?—it is George Eliot who describes Marner's kind as 'a disinherited race'.

Driven by 'something not unlike the feeling of primitive men, when they fled from an unpropitious deity', Silas leaves the alleys for the immemorial countryside. (It is not an accident that Raveloe lies in the 'rich central plain of what we are pleased to call Merry England', the countryside of George Eliot's infancy, which was still in essentials Shakespeare's.) To Silas, fresh from Lantern Yard, the lives of the people there seem merely unspiritual and misdirected ('women laying up a stock of linen for the life to come' is not only humorous but has a scriptural phrasing hinting their blindness to their eternal welfare, or what seems blindness to Silas); but as we presently see, their materialism is an art of living. The clue to the basis of their lives is in a word we keep meeting: 'neighbourly'. Silas, with his refusal to mix by attending church or dropping in to gossip at the Rainbow or courting a girl, is suspect.

This is why his spontaneous attempt to help the woman, whose suffering recalls his mother's, with the herbal medicine he knows will relieve her, only projects him into the vacant office of Wise Woman, and when his honesty rejects it, consigns him to an even more undesirable one. The irony is poignant, and the incident a proof that George Eliot is not sentimental about the people of Raveloe. But their superstition is more than offset by their shrewdness: they realize as soon as Silas has been robbed that this proves that far from being 'a deep 'un' he is only 'a poor mushed creature'. The contrast with the stupid behaviour of the Lantern Yard brethren when they too had to find out whether Silas was telling the truth is to Raveloe's credit—the villagers' superstition does not prevent them from being wiser in the end than the town artisans who have a 'purer' form of Christianity. The Raveloe people chiefly appreciate the pagan survivals (carols, and keeping 'a jolly Christmas, Whitsun and Easter tide') but they practise the true religion of neighbourliness. The village way of life is shown to foster some virtues that the city does nothing to promote: Jem the poacher, unlike William Dane, is really an honest man barring 'the matter of a hare or so' (nobody in an English village ever believed that game was not rightly common property), the villagers don't steal money or goods if only because these couldn't be used without discovery, and cheating of any sort is despised (the dishonesty of Dunsey is covered by his birth, but to the cottagers he is 'that offal Dunsey'). Morality is also ensured because there is no privacy, and wisdom because everyone through gossip has the communal assessment of everyone's character, even the gentry's to draw on. Above all, mutual helpfulness is as necessarily practised in the village as competition in the city.

George Eliot's presentment in *Marner* of the peasant code as the justification of what she calls 'the old-fashioned village life' is so minimal an account of the civilization of the English folk that it is barely adequate even for her special purpose, so that now, when first-hand knowledge of that culture has gone for ever, and its very existence is denied by the intellectuals of our phase of civilization, the reader must educate himself into that knowledge in order to understand what *Silas Marner* is about—George Eliot could assume her readers did not need instruction of that kind. Now, something like the chapter on 'The Peasant System' in George Sturt's *Change in the Village* is essential reading for our understanding of this novel. Though the character of his village had been destroyed by the enclosure of its commons and an invasion from the town, Sturt could still at the beginning of this century recover from the older cottagers the traces of the independent life of fifty years before and his intelligent observations really illuminate *Silas*

Marner for us. Here are a few of his relevant generalizations from his data:

> The 'peasant' tradition in its vigour amounted to nothing less than a form of civilization—the home-made civilization of the rural English. To the exigent problems of life it furnished solutions of its own . . . Best of all, those customs provided a rough guide as to conduct—an unwritten code to which, though we forget it, England owes much . . . The cheerfulness of the cottager rests largely upon a survival of the outlook and habits of the peasant days. It is not a negative quality . . . In the main the force that bears them on is a traditional outlook. In the little cottages the people, from the earliest infancy, were accustomed to hear all things—persons and manners, houses and gardens, and the day's work—appraised by an ancient standard of the countryside . . . The people stood for something more than merely themselves.

These are confirmations and explanations of what George Eliot says in **Silas Marner** or sometimes only shows in action. But that civilization had impressive material forms too in the crafts and arts of country work and leisure, most of which have been or are being destroyed or lost, though enough evidence exists to put the case beyond dispute.

George Eliot probably felt that she had already shown in **Adam Bede** the material beauty and achievement of the old order of the countryside and that she would do most by limiting her case in **Marner.** It is the moral feeling in the village, Sturt's 'ancient standard of the countryside', that she presents so appreciatively, as when Raveloe felt 'it was *nothing but right* a man should be looked on and helped by those who could afford it, when he had brought up an orphan child, and been father and mother to her'. And in a different way, she registers their acceptance of the hard realities, the risks which must be taken of things turning out ill, as well as the certainty of old age and failing strength, which can never be forgotten: even when admiring little Eppie, 'Elderly masters and mistresses told Silas that, if she turned out well (which, however, there was no telling), it would be a fine thing for him to have a steady lass to do for him when he got helpless'. In comparison, the attention given to the gardener, the fiddler, the wheelwright and other representative figures of the community is slight indeed; even the dairy-farming is done by Priscilla Lammeter off-stage. We have to accept these sketches as being deliberately outlines only of the full world George Eliot registered in her childhood (G. H. Lewes said: 'She forgets nothing that has come within the curl of her eyelash') and draws on so impressively for **Adam Bede** and **Middlemarch.** The point that is kept to in this book is, how can Marner achieve reintegration into this community? Marner's private case is now merged into a general one, an illustration of how and how not to set about this. This is the purpose of that narrative in the Rainbow which is high-lighted by being placed just before Silas bursts in with his tale of being robbed, the turning point of his relations with Raveloe.

The tale told in the Rainbow is recognized as Mr Macey's peculiar property and is one which Raveloe never tires of hearing and discussing. As tailor, parish-clerk and brother to the foremost fiddler Mr Macey has a status and qualities that fit him for the part of Chorus; and that his narrative is important is shown by its having become a local legend to which ghosts and other folk-lore characteristics have accrued with time. The first part, old Mr Lammeter's story, is a contrast to Silas's experience so far. Like Silas this worthy came from 'a bit north'ard', but in contrast to Silas he was a countryman, for 'he brought a fine breed o' sheep with him' and 'it was soon seen as we'd got a new parish'ner as know'd the rights and customs o' things, and kep' a good house, and was well looked on by everybody'. So his son was able to marry into one of the best Raveloe families and 'for prosperity and everything respectable, there's no family more looked on'; in fact, their daughter Nancy is being courted by Squire Cass's heir, to everyone's satisfaction. So old Mr Lammeter's story ends happily ever after. The apparent link with the other half of the narrative is that Mr Lammeter settled at The Warrens, the estate and house left to charity by one Cliff—who is never given the respectful handle to *his* name. There is also a real link, for Cliff's story is the opposite of the other's and an awful warning of what Silas's might be: Cliff dies crazy and childless. *He* was no acquisition but 'a Lunnon tailor, some folks said, as had gone mad wi' cheating'. His madness consisted at first simply in wanting to pass as a gentleman, a kind of cheating which ended by driving him mad, for having been a tailor—that is, one who had to work sitting cross-legged—he was inevitably unfitted for the part of a gentleman, which implied, demanded, good riding. Thus Mr Macey says of Cliff: 'For he couldn't ride; lor bless you! they said he'd got no more grip o' the hoss than if his legs had been cross-sticks . . . But ride he would'. Cliff is the type of man who won't recognize that, however rich, he can be nothing but what he is. Mr Macey, a tailor himself, has better sense and greater self-respect. He despises Cliff for being 'ashamed o' being called a tailor'— 'not but what I'm a tailor myself, but in respect as God made me such, I'm proud on it, for "Macey, tailor" 's been wrote up over our door since afore the Queen's heads went out on the shillings'. He has his own honourable pedigree, tailors are essential, and besides he is proud of his craft. So Eppie's final refusal to be raised out of the class she was reared in is shown as being consistent with this folk tradition, 'a little store of inherited wisdom', and not improbable or sentimental. We are given an insight into a theory of class which has nothing to do with snobbery and which rules out the passion to rise in the world socially.

Cliff's story has moreover a thematic relation to Godfrey Cass's, for Cliff, since he couldn't get accepted as a gentleman himself, determined to 'ride the tailor' out of his son against the boy's nature, bringing about his death, so that Cliff died childless. This prefigures Godfrey's fate when his cheating shall have produced its own Nemesis, as he recognizes in the end when he tells his wife: 'I wanted to pass for childless once—I shall pass for childless now against my wish.' And Cliff's story stands also as contrast to Silas's, for the latter, by eventually assimilating himself like old Mr Lammeter, ends up by accepting 'the rights and customs o' things', being 'well looked on', and leaving (adopted) heirs. True, Silas has to learn as a foreign language, which he never really masters and whose principles he certainly doesn't understand, what was native for Mr

Lammeter; but he is saved from Cliff's fate by his humility. So this parable within a parable is the clue to the whole, and Mr Macey justly sums up in what might be an epigraph for the novel: 'there's reasons in things as nobody knows on—that's pretty much what I've made out'. There *are* laws of life, George Eliot shows, and they were 'made out' in village life although they can't be stated. In Mr Macey's narrative and its affiliations with the rest of the book we have one example of the wonderfully complex organization and the unobtrusive structure of symbol and theme which make the text of **Silas Marner** so dense and rich in meanings and yet so economical in words.

The laws of life are shown in operation in what follows immediately after Silas has made known his misfortune to the village. His relations with the villagers follow the same impartial logic as before, but his impulse to turn to them for help in his trouble, and his compunction at accusing Jem of robbing him without evidence, which has stirred up memories of being falsely accused himself, have made a bridge between them. They see he is an innocent soul and in need of help. First 'contemptuous pity' replaces distrust, then the traditional neighbourly attempts to help him follow. The sympathetic ears, the good advice, the welcome presents and soothing attentions culminate in Dolly Winthrop's well-judged efforts to reach him by all the different channels she feels likely to work on him. She brings the cakes, with their religious sanction in the traditionally pricked 'good letters'; the child, as certain to touch his heart if he has one and moreover to sing a carol to move his Christmas sentiments; and a gentle remonstrance about his not going to church. All these good means fail to reach him, and we cannot but sense that something is being conveyed, in the cross-purposes and misunderstandings of their conversation, sometimes comical and sometimes full of pathos, about the difficulty of achieving any real communication between people who don't belong to the same culture. Silas doesn't even recognize the religion of Church as the same Christian religion that he subscribed to in the first half of his life, for all his knowledge of the theory of salvation; here no doubt something more ironical is intended. Dolly's religion is about as far from Calvinism as possible; it is seen to be a matter of custom, traditional pieties and pagan practices, and she makes no distinction between christening and inoculation.

> **In Mr Macey's narrative and its affiliations with the rest of the book we have one example of the wonderfully complex organization and the unobtrusive structure of symbol and theme which make the text of *Silas Marner* so dense and rich in meanings and yet so economical in words.**
>
> **—Q. D. Leavis**

But George Eliot makes her point, that the ignorant vil-

lage wheelwright's wife has the advantage over the city weaver who could talk knowingly about Assurance of Salvation in his youth. The difference between their two cultures is illustrated by the episode of the 'I.H.S.' on the lard-cakes. Dolly pricks them, without knowing what the letters are, because tradition has assured her that they have a good meaning (even though she has noticed that sometimes the letters won't hold and also that the cakes don't always turn out so well); the proof that she can trust the inherited wisdom is that these same letters are on the pulpit-cloth at church. But Silas, who *can* read them, is yet seen to be really worse off than the illiterate Dolly, for, like her, he doesn't know what the letters stand for and unlike her he has no pious associations with them. Even if he had known what they stood for, we reflect, his chapel-formed prejudices would have prevented him from venerating them as it had deprived him of the medicinal herbs.

Silas never does acquire the pieties inborn with the villagers. He gets along eventually by adopting all the village customs without questioning them, but never, of course, has the traditional associations which make people benefit by them. We are given an undoubtedly humorous illustration in the daily pipe-smoking which Silas takes up because it is the done thing and because he is told, against the evidence of his senses, that it is good for him. Eppie believes it does do him good and that he enjoys it, and though he would rather not smoke he does not like to set himself up against received opinion or to pain Eppie by undeceiving her. George Eliot does not press the general point here illustrated, which would have forced on us an awkward scepticism, but once again it expresses her freedom from sentimentality and her refusal to simplify, to make a 'story' by suppressing discordant facts.

All the attempts to bring Silas back to a place in the community fail because except for the case of Sally Oates they have no purchase on him and in that one case he has bad luck (as he has good luck in being sent Eppie—chance is impartial). Dolly believed the sight of her child Aaron was bound to do him good, yet this fails because Silas is too short-sighted to see Aaron's features at all. But (again the impartial laws of life operate) this very short sight is just what leads him to accept another child later as his gold come back. Then all the right conditions are seen to have been met at last. The process of being restored to life, which actually began with the loss of his gold, has accelerated. The aspect it seems to have of coincidence is ruled out when we consider that Eppie's appearance follows upon many attempts against Silas's isolation that occur in the natural course of events. The only faery-tale element lies in the fact that Eppie appears on New Year's Eve, when the luck is liable to turn with the New Year, but again this is seen to be one of the essential conditions for the chance to take effect since the excitement brings on Silas's trance. What *is* unsatisfactory is the device of the catalepsy, since it is not, like Dr Manette's psychological losses of memory and reversions to another personality, a product of his misfortunes but the cause of them, posited for the plotting—after which Silas ceases to have any fits onstage. The fits were needed to make William's treachery and theft possible and to give the villagers an excuse for their superstitious horror of a man whose 'soul was loose from his body and going out and in like a bird out of its nest' (though this last is a true piece of folk-lore and helps to show us how primitive was the mentality of the countryman). And lastly, the catalepsy is necessary to get Eppie into the cottage without Silas knowing, so that she *seems* to him initially to be of supernatural origin. But even so the fits are worked into the pattern of an impartial operation of the laws of life: twice chance introduces a thief into Silas's home, the third time—there is a popular belief: 'The third time, lucky'—the same chance lets in Eppie, who makes good the previous losses.

Leslie Stephen's (and others') amused scepticism about an old bachelor's reception of a baby and his return to the bosom of society in consequence, seems to me superficial. George Eliot has been careful to explain that Silas, like many children of the poor, had been used to look after his baby sister and cherished that memory; he is domesticated by habit and handy by virtue of his trade, and he has Dolly's assistance. As for the Wordsworthian part of the enterprise, what follows seems to me a more plausible and particularized demonstration of Wordsworth's tenets than anything the poet ever wrote himself. The 'remedial influences of pure, natural human relations' and a revived ability to enjoy the natural world are conveyed persuasively in exquisite detail and poetic imagery. But it is characteristic of the economical and pregnant construction of *Marner* that these Wordsworthian passages are something more than lovely episodes; besides their inherent poetical quality they are precipitations and enactments of the deeper meanings of the novel. Take only one of these and that the slightest: the influence of little Eppie in making Silas share her delight in everything outdoors or in nature 'even to the old winter flies that come crawling forth in the early spring sunshine, and warming him into joy because *she* had joy'. We perceive that Silas is vividly imaged as being himself an old winter fly crawling out under the reviving spring sunshine which Eppie is to him. And this passage builds up with what follows to convey Silas's gradual return to a life of feeling, ending by bringing into play again the herbs that not merely recall his mother but represent something like the traditions of the race.

> Sitting on the banks in this way, Silas began to look for the once familiar herbs again; and as the leaves, with their unchanged outlines and markings, lay on his palm, there was a sense of crowding remembrances from which he turned away timidly, taking refuge in Eppie's little world, that lay lightly on his enfeebled spirit.

> As the child's mind was growing into knowledge, his mind was growing into memory: as her life unfolded, his soul, long stupified in a cold narrow prison, was unfolding too, and trembling gradually into full consciousness.

We are shown also that besides reviving Silas's consciousness of the world around him and its associations with his past, Eppie makes him aware of a future happiness, so that he can deduce from the present 'in the ties and charities that bound together the families of his neighbours' 'images of that time' to come, another application of the Wordsworthian doctrine. In the spirit of Wordsworth's poetry too is the description of how Eppie forges a bond between

Silas and all animate and even inanimate life: 'there was love between the child and the world—from men and women with parental looks and tones to the red ladybirds and the round pebbles'.

Wordsworthian, we say, but the imagery drawn from Nature is so apt and so freshly observed that we recollect that 'George Eliot' was Mary Ann Evans, a country child, before she became a learned woman, and that on reading Wordsworth's poems for the first time on her twentieth birthday she wrote of them: 'I have never before met with so many of my feelings expressed just as I could wish them'. So Nancy's person is described as giving 'the same idea of unvarying neatness as the body of a little bird', Dolly 'pastures her mind' on the sadder elements of life, Godfrey sees himself becoming as 'helpless as an uprooted tree', the patched and darned baby-clothes are 'clean and neat as fresh-sprung herbs', Silas's 'sap of affection was not all gone' and the imagery that describes his shrunken life as 'the rivulet that has sunk far down from the grassy fringe of its old breadth into a little shivering thread, that cuts a groove for itself in the barren sand' recurs in various forms. But far more memorable than anything of the kind in Wordsworth is the episode of Silas's broken water-jug whose homely earthenware shape had become dear to him by association:

> It had been his companion for twelve years, always standing in the same spot, always lending its handle to him in the early morning, so that its form had an expression for him of willing helpfulness, and the impress of its handle on his palm gave a satisfaction mingled with that of having the fresh clear water.

When he stumbled and broke it, he 'picked up the pieces and carried them home with grief in his heart. The brown pot could never be of use to him any more, but he stuck the bits together and propped the ruin in its old place for a memorial.' But this also has a function, to show that Silas retained even in his extreme isolation that 'natural piety' which is a proof of being fully human and without which he could not have been rescued by Eppie. It is part of the sequence of evidence proving that, though he had lost his faith, still compunction, compassion, gratitude and honourable feelings were alive in him; but it comes also from the George Eliot who wrote in a letter, during the very period when she was composing *Marner*: 'In proportion as I love every form of piety—which is venerating love—I hate hard curiosity'; who when reading the newly-published *Origin of Species* the year before wrote to her friends that though 'it makes an epoch' yet 'To me the Development Theory and all other explanations of processes by which things came to be, produce a feeble impression compared with the mystery that lies under the processes'.

But it is not the Wordsworthian 'message' in any simple form that George Eliot is endorsing. 'Love had he found in huts where poor men lie, / His daily teachers had been woods and rills' would not have been true in any way of Silas if he had not been shown these truths by Eppie. And Eppie's influence would have been inadequate without the village there to take them both into its neighbourly care and teach them how to live, with what Sturt calls 'the home-made civilization of the rural English'. We meet one of its impressive aspects at the Red House's New Year dance where the villagers, admitted to watch by custom, discuss the characters, conduct, appearance and history of the gentry, drawing on their own experiences and showing their good sense and decent feeling while making shrewd criticisms; and earlier at the Rainbow we have seen their understanding of the 'reasons in things', of the nature of social life.

Another aspect of the character of this peasant tradition is embodied in Dolly Winthrop herself. The dual strain in the English folk tradition is represented by the marriage (happy enough) of tipsy, jovial Ben Winthrop and the grave, scrupulous Dolly, a good woman who performs Dinah Morris's function without being given a halo. We are introduced to her as one 'having her lips always slightly screwed; as if she felt herself in a sickroom with the doctor or the clergyman present' and 'inclined to shake her head and sigh, almost imperceptibly, like a funeral mourner who is not a relation'. Yet she is not to be ridiculed. What Dolly represents is the strength of the village code that makes it religious in character but as remote as possible from dogma, theology or ritual practice. How exactly she corresponds to George Sturt's account of the cottager's character familiar to him in life!

> To some extent doubtless it rests on Christian teaching, although perhaps not much on the Christian teaching of the present day . . . from distant generations there seems to have come down, in many a cottage family, a rather lofty religious sentiment which fosters honesty, patience, resignation, courage. Much of the gravity, much of the tranquillity of soul of the more sedate villagers must be ascribed to this traditional influence, whose effects are attractive enough, in the character and outlook of many an old cottage man and woman.

One of Dolly's many functions is to incite us to decide in what ways the code she lives by differs from Nancy Lammeter's, for Nancy's is seen to be as inferior to Dolly's as the Lantern Yard's is to Raveloe's. Nancy actually reminds us of the Lantern Yard in the narrowness of her outlook and her arbitrary moral laws.

. . . . .

In chapter 3, with the introduction of the Cass family, the assumption that in this novel we are in the timeless world of 'Once upon a time' is finally destroyed. It specifies the England of the Napoleonic Wars and even the facts of economic history which were to ruin the landowning classes and their helpless labourers. Radicalism, the product of this age, comes out strongly in *Marner,* to produce later *Felix Holt, the Radical.* It is George Eliot's Radical sympathies that account for her distaste for the squirearchy and her compassion for the poor. It is no accident that makes the Nemesis in *Marner* the gentleman's fate and the happy outcome of luck the cottager's, for Godfrey's history is in large and in detail an inversion of Silas's, and when their dramatic confrontation at last takes place, all the elements in the novel come into play and we are left in no doubt about the conclusions we are to draw. The Nemesis that overtakes Godfrey is inextricably mixed up with his

position in society and his conditioning by that; slight as his chances were of getting Eppie to live with him as his daughter, it is not until he makes clear, inadvertently, how he thinks of the working-class that he alienates Eppie and Silas for ever. The Casses retire helpless and humiliated, and we feel impelled to cheer.

Mary Ann Evans was peculiarly qualified by her background and upbringing to appreciate the fine distinctions of the English class system of her day and their consequences. Her father, born and bred a carpenter like Adam Bede, 'raised himself', in his daughter's proud words, to being notable in the ways that Caleb Garth is shown to be in *Middlemarch,* but to an even better position. He had some of Adam Bede's qualities of bodily strength and character combined with Mr Garth's social submissiveness to his wife, who was 'superior'—a Dodson in family though a Mrs Poyser in nature and activities. Their daughter must therefore have been socially sensitive even without any knowledge of her father's aristocratic employers, and in due course this class of beings complicated her ideas of the social system even further, as J. W. Cross was well aware, no doubt from her own mouth. He stresses the effect of 'being constantly driven by her father' to the 'fine places' of these gentry as 'accentuating the social differences—differences which had a profound significance and which left their mark on such a sensitive character'. Coming home from her excellent education at a boarding-school at Coventry a convert to the 'ultra-Evangelical tendencies' of the teachers, she was in conflict for years with her brother, whose private tutor's establishment had imbued *him* with strong High Church views. The future George Eliot was thus thoroughly equipped to feel in person all the strains and anomalies of the contemporary social and religious system, and being born in 1819 (a time of political and economic trouble) to know the distresses of the workers too.

Her escape from the blight of Evangelicalism was, by her own account, and as one would expect, through literature, Scott first unsettling her orthodoxy and Shakespeare becoming the book of books for her by 1842. The Evangelical fervour was, as so often, replaced by a desire to serve humanity which soon led her to a concern for social reform, and we find her rejoicing in the earlier Carlyle and even in the French Revolution of 1848: at this date we have her denunciation of England ('I feel that society is training men and women for hell') and her admiration for Louis Blanc. In 1851 she launched herself into the London of the congenial *Westminster Review* set; three years later she bravely united her life with G. H. Lewes's, and since marriage was legally impossible for him she found herself in a new position of complete detachment from the social system. (The effect was peculiar. While she shows in her novels complete emancipation from restrictive ideas of class, and while her criticisms of its causes, manifestations and effects are always penetrating, sensitive and unbiased, she is surprisingly conventional about *moral* conduct in the narrow Victorian sense.) *Silas Marner* is the only novel in which she makes Class a major cause of the different treatment she gives human beings; even in *Adam Bede* both Arthur *and* Adam incur a Nemesis—Adam's 'hardness' is rebuked by seeing the harshness with which

Hetty's 'fall' is treated by his world (though it is true he gets a plaster by being allowed to marry Dinah). The experiment no doubt helped to equip George Eliot for the more systematic, and unprejudiced examination of society in *Felix Holt, the Radical* and for the wider-ranging impartial treatment of the whole subject in *Middlemarch.* Class is dominant even in church at Raveloe (see chapter 16) and in the last few pages we learn that Godfrey couldn't bear to stay in Raveloe on the day his daughter marries a 'low working-man'—whom *we* know to be the admirable Aaron Winthrop.

The effect of staying for the first part of the book with the peasantry and Silas is that we identify with them, so that when Squire Cass is brought before us at last he figures very large indeed, though only a very small squire. It is at once explained that these things are relative and that in his ambience he is 'quite as if he had been a lord'—this is the Lilliputian treatment which implies that a lord is only an enlarged Squire Cass. He is then shown as typical of a class whose 'extravagant habits and bad husbandry' are preparing them for ruin when the 'glorious wartime' ends. The sarcasm at their expense is different from any irony in the previous chapters, it tends to take on a savage tone and to become caricature. The fatuous selfishness of believing wartime 'to be a peculiar favour of Providence to the landed interest' is succeeded by this speech of the Squire's, by which we cannot but be disgusted and in which we catch the selfish indignation in the querulous rhythm:

> 'And that fool Kimble says the newspaper's talking about peace. Why, the country wouldn't have a leg to stand on. Prices 'ud run down like a jack, and I should never get my arrears, not if I sold all the fellows up.'

His class wants to keep the country at war for its own interest, a traditional Radical charge. His callous lack of concern for his tenants so long as he can get his rent shows he is a bad landlord too. The interior of the Red House is squalid and the sons degraded by dissipation. The villagers have already passed judgment: 'Raveloe was not a place where moral censure was severe, but it was thought a weakness in the Squire that he had kept all his sons at home in idleness', 'though some licence was to be allowed to young men whose fathers could afford it'. The villagers know that the same standard can't be expected of the gentry as of their own sons. Godfrey is 'equally disinclined to dig and to beg'. When we find that Dolly and Silas and worthy Mr Macey think of these people as their 'betters', it makes us think (along Radical lines of course).

Along with this concept of 'betters' we learn not only that the Casses are not better but that the Squire differs from the farmers of the parish only by 'that self-possession and authoritativeness of voice and carriage which belonged to a man' who has never met anyone superior to himself. As the villagers are characterized by 'neighbourly' attitudes he is distinguished by *patronizing* ones, he even feels his position obliges him 'to fulfil the hereditary duty of being noisily jovial and patronizing' and he speaks 'in a ponderous and coughing fashion, which was felt in Raveloe to be a sort of privilege of his rank'. This is amusing and intelligent observation, but it ceases to be amusing when we find that this has imposed itself as an acceptable image of gentility on the villagers; Ben Winthrop even describes Godfrey with admiration as 'one as 'ud knock you down easier' than anyone—knocking you down being the symbolic function of one's betters. All this is meant to be subversive and expresses George Eliot's reaction to a class that must in her childhood and youth have appeared a blot on the landscape. But active political feeling is needed to account for other manifestations of the same situation: a very stock piece of Radical propaganda is the picture of the Squire cutting beef off his joint for his deer-hound as he breakfasts—'enough bits of beef to make a poor man's holiday dinner'—reminding us that working-men could afford 'butcher's meat' at best on only a few occasions a year.

So when we are returned to the company of the poor we feel relief. Here is charity and fellowship and we can enter into their difficulties and pleasures with sympathy without meeting their 'betters' again till Eppie is at the critical stage of courtship. Then we are taken back to the Red House (chapter 17). True, the old Squire and the vicious Dunsey are gone and the Lammeters' 'liberal orderliness' is in charge, while the refinement compared with what went before suggests that Nancy may really be a 'better'. Her attitude to adoption compared to the villagers' is one test, and others follow. She is seen to be made up of 'rigid principles', a conventional good woman, loving and dutiful to her own relations but fatally limited, as is proved when she goes with her husband to claim Eppie. 'Used all her life to plenteous circumstances and the privileges of "respectability" ', we are told, she cannot understand that Eppie's life can have its own attractions and compensations. This is exactly in keeping with Godfrey's conviction that Eppie would readily fall in with his wish to adopt her, he having formed 'the idea that deep affections can hardly go along with callous palms and scant means'.

The ensuing drama is really instructive, no longer easily satiric. Godfrey loses any sympathy we may have felt for him by his selfishness, his obtuseness to the feelings of the Marners, and his dishonesty in persuading himself that he is doing for Eppie's good what now suits himself. This analysis of 'moral stupidity', one of George Eliot's favourite subjects, proceeds magnificently as Godfrey finally accuses the weaver of selfishness and reproaches him that without her real father's (his) protection 'she may marry some low working-man'. Godfrey's brutality here is the more dreadful for not being conscious; it is a class reaction only, not personal. We look to see Nancy's reaction to this test. But she notices no insult, and this comes as a shock to us because Nancy has been shown as superior to the rest of her world in delicacy of feeling. We are forced to realize that insulation by class destroys the power of imaginative sympathy in everyone. Nancy presses Godfrey's rights on Eppie, who answers the spirit of the insult with a passionate affirmation of class solidarity as well as of loyalty to the only father she has ever known. It is characteristic that the first thing Nancy then thinks of is relief that her family and the world now need never know about Godfrey's past and the relation with Eppie. What is uppermost in her mind is respectability; she is a variety of Dodson and this is the real gulf between her and the village folk who have not yet been tainted with the religion of 'respectability' (a word which George Eliot herself puts into inverted commas here). Eppie's reaction is quite plausible if we remember what social and literary history abundantly confirm, what Sturt summarizes in this sentence: 'It seems singular to think of it now, but the very labourer might reasonably hope for some satisfaction in life, nor trouble about "raising" himself into some other class, so long as he could live on peasant lines'.

Now this constant play of ironical social criticism, and the general reflections about human nature, are what prevent the artifices (such as the elaborate parallels between Silas's and Godfrey's histories and the providential arrangements of the fits, little golden-haired girls, and so on) from being felt as artificial by the reader, for they never obtrude as such: far from being incited to work out the pattern, our attention is always being directed elsewhere. Yet without dwelling on these things we do get as we read a sense that these complexities of reference are further illustrations of those laws of life that, as the novel is concerned to demonstrate, so mysteriously exist.

They are not laws that can be stated, but as we've seen they cover parts of human experience investigated by Wordsworth and Bunyan, Cobbett and George Sturt, among others, and embody the truths of parables in the New Testament as well as the traditional wisdom expressed in folk-tales. The central thesis in Mr Macey's narrative at the Rainbow is the contrast between the rich man's folly and the meek man's success in living, a theme often present in folk-tales of course. Godfrey with his uneasy conscience and his childless hearth gets no benefit from his riches and the wife he has gained by deception, while the humble Marner household have the last word: 'I think nobody could be happier than we are'. Eppie has brought into the home, to complete it with a garden, Aaron the gardener. That his occupation is, like the tailor's, deliberately chosen is made quite explicit in his criticism of the maldistribution of goods—a return to the Radical vein:

> there's never a garden in all the parish but what there's endless waste in it for want o' somebody as could use everything up. It's what I think to myself sometimes, as there need nobody run short o' victuals if the land was made the most on, and there was never a morsel but what could find its way to a mouth. It sets one thinking o' that—gardening does.

And we are presently told that Aaron does all the gardening for the Raveloe gentry: his kind do the world's work and have a better idea than the property-owners of the right use of property, this tells us. Again we are led to ask: Who are the 'betters'?

Yet, it must be emphasized once again, the cottagers are not idealized. The coarse repartee and the illiterate arguments in the Rainbow, drink and stupid jokes and superstitions are there and coexist with great good sense and kindliness and love of children, and with the hospitality and co-operation that are obligatory in the Raveloe code. And as regards their weaknesses, the reader is always being nudged into realizing that the world in general is no

better, that behavior in polite circles can be worse. Rarely is any incongruity felt when the cool voice of the anthropologizing critic modulates into the sympathetic tone which conveys all the pathos of the lives of the humble. Silas's helplessness and even the comical effects of his simplicity never prevent us from seeing that his inner life is to be respected. This is great art, and throws up scenes that remain in the memory as strangely impressive, such as that where Godfrey and his young child exchange looks without the child's giving him any recognition, turning instead to pull lovingly at the weaver's face—impressive in itself, but still more so when, having read to the end, we realize that it has forecast Eppie's eventual rejection of Godfrey in the final scene which is the result of Godfrey's refusal in this earlier scene to recognize the natural bond between them. The novel is full of dramatic ironies both of scene and speech (such as Silas's assurance to Godfrey Cass that he will keep the baby Eppie 'till anybody shows they've a right to take her away from me'). These ironies tie the book together firmly.

. . . . .

After the Radical vein has been worked out there still remains to determine the theme of Silas's past suffering in the city. Seen through Eppie's country-bred eyes the city is 'a dark ugly place' and 'worse than the Workhouse', and Silas notices for the first time that it 'smells bad'. A factory has swept away Lantern Yard (is it a relief?) and Silas can say, 'The old home's gone; I've no home but this now'. The irony latent in the name 'Lantern Yard' is brought out by Dolly's innocent encouragement to him to go back to the city to find out the truth: 'And if there's any light to be got up the yard as you talk on, we've need of it i' this world'. Actually, the Lantern Yard community could only darken counsel (there is scriptural reference of this kind implied in the constant play upon the words 'dark' and 'light' and we cannot avoid the suggestion of 'Lighten our darkness' in the offing). The social criticism in *Marner* therefore is inseparable from spiritual values. This is consonant with the early tradition of English Radicalism, which is why *Marner* had to be both a realistic novel and a symbolic spiritual history and why Bunyan, as I've shown, offered a suitable source for reference. *Silas Marner* really asks: What was it that characterized the way of life of the English village in its heyday, so that its passing has meant a heavy loss? One of the most memorable points made in the last part is that Silas's return to his birthplace is partly to enlighten the minister: 'I should like to talk to him about the religion o' this country-side, for I partly think he doesn't know on it'.

So we come back to the factors in George Eliot's personal life which forced her to undertake this book. Hating the conditions of life in London, she remembered her childhood not only for its green fields and her mother's dairy but for the whole agricultural way of life which, she saw, enhanced the aesthetic aspects of Nature as well as shaped the lives of a people whose human achievement in creating a community she deeply respected; a people whose speech, an art of expression manifested in a dialect notable for its force, rhythm, and subtlety, had a flavour quite absent from educated English. She felt her loss of these things the more for having pined for them for ten years in London among the claustrophobic streets, the choking smoke and the anonymous crowd—these facts are liberally documented in her letters and Journal. An intellectual circle she had, but this was no substitute for the neighbourliness of 'old-fashioned village life'. With this sense of her own loss went her realization of what it must mean for the utterly disinherited masses, no longer a folk, deprived of a community by the forces we sum up as the Industrial Revolution, the city poor whom all the serious Victorian novelists had on their minds, inheritors as all these novelists were, whatever their formal political allegiances, of that earlier ethos of Cobbett's humane Radicalism and Carlyle's appeals to conscience.

She had also the impulse at this date to give her generation the benefit of her own discovery of a point of rest—which *Marner* in its positive final serenity proves she had achieved. The authoritative account of George Eliot's spiritual history is given by herself in a letter written a year before starting *Silas Marner* (6 December 1859). She writes of her early bigoted Evangelical phase, followed by her 'attitude of antagonism which belongs to the renunciation of *any* religious belief', and that she can now say that she has a sympathy with any faith that has been the expression of human sorrow and longing for righteousness: 'I have a sympathy with it that predominates over all argumentative tendencies'. Silas goes through a similar process, ending by accepting not dogmatic religion but a place in a community whose religious system has passed the pragmatic test—it visibily works as right and wise practice, and this brings personal happiness. Only Dolly appears to feel that faith must somewhere rest on, or imply, divine powers, but owing to her humility, or a sense of the remoteness of these powers, she refers to them only as 'Them above', suggesting those pagan deities ('the beliefs of primitive men') constantly invoked in the first two chapters. What the others describe as Providence seems to associate more naturally with their belief in Luck than with the Christian hope. The Raveloe people's attitude to church is that it provides social cohesion with some good magic attached (as in their belief in the necessity of taking the sacrament annually). Dolly's (and her creator's) conclusion that 'We must trusten' is really no more than Axel Heyst's discovery in Conrad's *Victory*: 'Woe to the heart that has not learnt while young to put its trust in life'. Unlike Hardy's burden: 'Life offers—to deny', George Eliot says that, in the long run, Life gives a fair deal, or at any rate it did in the village world.

Silas 'had come to appropriate the forms of custom and belief which were the mould of Raveloe life', and by blending these with 'the elements of his old faith', 'recovered a consciousness of unity between his past and his present'. Personal happiness has made this possible and adequate for him, as for George Eliot herself, who had found objects to live for in Lewes and his three motherless boys, and in the creative work which Lewes had launched her on and sustained her in—and which, she wrote, 'gives value to my life'. She felt justified in sustaining a faith in the possibilities of social life, however discouraging some of the manifestations of human nature may be, and she shows in *Adam Bede* and *Silas Marner* that the old culture, of vil-

lage units centring on the market town, manifested such a possibility.

There are so many meanings in *Silas Marner* that it is surprising there was room in such a short space for them all; it is a feat to have wrapped them up with such neatness, charm, poetry and wit. The remarkable stylization of *Marner,* which is really due to its being an extension of the parable form, is something quite unprecedented in George Eliot's fiction hitherto; it has no anticipation in any of the short stories that make up *Scenes of Clerical Life;* while the lax association of different centres of interest that constitutes *Adam Bede* and *The Mill on the Floss* is as different from *Marner* as is *Romola,* its successor. But we can see that in the symbolic confrontation scenes in *Felix Holt* and in the use of poetic symbolism in *Middlemarch,* the discoveries made in *Marner* have been consolidated. (pp. 278-302)

> *Q. D. Leavis, " 'Silas Marner','" in her* Collected Essays: The Englishness of the English Novel, Vol. I, *edited by G. Singh, Cambridge University Press, 1983, pp. 275-302.*

U. C. Knoepflmacher   (essay date 1968)

[*Knoepflmacher is a German-born American educator and critic who has written extensively on nineteenth-century English literature. In the following excerpt, he examines the relationship of* Silas Marner *to Eliot's* The Mill on the Floss *and commends its balanced presentation of both empirical and metaphysical views of reality.*]

The reader who vaguely remembers *Silas Marner* as a distasteful, saccharine high-school text may be every bit as startled upon rereading this fine novel as by taking a second look at that other children's classic, *Gulliver's Travels.* To Henry James [in *Atlantic Monthly,* October 1866], *Silas Marner* seemed a masterpiece because of its superb craftsmanship: "it has more of that simple, rounded, consummate aspect, that absence of loose ends and gaping issues which marks a classical work." On somewhat different grounds, *The Westminster Review* [July 1861] also declared the new work by its former editor to be superior to all of her previous fiction: "the stream of thought runs clearer, the structure of the story is more compact, while the philosophical insight is deeper and more penetrating than in any of her former productions." Both of these estimates, artistic and philosophic, seem correct: in *Silas Marner* George Eliot not only eliminated all the "loose ends" which had so seriously marred the artistry of *The Mill,* but also overcame some of the difficulties she had encountered as a thinker. Through the medium of a "legendary tale," she reconciled the incongruities which had arisen, to greater or lesser degrees, in all of her former fictional attempts to find the ideal in the "real." (pp. 221-22)

In the letter which accompanied the manuscript of *Silas Marner,* George Eliot added a highly interesting observation: "somehow, experience and finished faculty rarely go together. Dearly beloved Scott had the greatest combination of experience and faculty—yet even he never made the most of his treasures, at least in his *mode* of presentation" [quoted in *The George Eliot Letters,* edited by Gordon S. Haight, 1954-1955]. The remark can be read as an unintentional self-assessment. For even if the experience and finished faculty that went into her new novel are identical to those which had shaped *Adam Bede* or *The Mill,* it is the "mode of presentation" which is so surprisingly different. In searching for a form suited to her latest inspiration, George Eliot had toyed even with the notion of writing a metrical romance like Wordsworth's "Michael" (a poem from which she drew the novel's epigraph): "I have felt all through as if the story would have lent itself best to metrical rather than prose fiction, especially in all that relates to the psychology of Silas." Yet the form she adopted was perfectly attuned to her aims.

Few critics of *Silas Marner* have noted the actual extent to which this legendary tale is a reaction to, as well as a continuation of, *The Mill on the Floss.* At first glance, the resemblances between these two works would seem scanty indeed. *The Mill* is a sprawling *Bildungsroman* built around the aspirations of an unusual young woman; *Silas,* however, is a terse fable in which the psychology of its titular hero is definitely less interesting than that of Godfrey Cass, the young squire whose mental habits closely correspond to those of Arthur Donnithorne, Adam Bede's coarser foil. Maggie Tulliver, whose charm and superior intelligence were already established as a child, dominated the stories of her father and brother. None of the figures in *Silas Marner* possesses a comparable degree of complexity. Though Eppie, like Maggie, does not "want any change," *her* wish seems to be granted. On attaining maturity, the girl rejects the advantages belatedly offered by the more sophisticated man who has at last revealed that he is her father. Instead, she chooses to remain with the weaver who has, through her, regained his own childlike awe. For Silas the foundling becomes "an object compacted of changes and hopes that forced his thoughts onward, and carried them away from their old eager pacing towards the same blank limit—carried them away to new things that would come with the coming years" (chap. 14).

Maggie, too knowledgeable and imaginative, becomes disconnected from her father's past; Silas, simple and uncomprehending, looks confidently at the future provided by his adopted daughter. Yet even at the very end of his experience, Silas remains far more puzzled and mystified than Mr. Tulliver had ever been. Feeble, slow-thinking, almost closer to the idiot Jacob Faux than to the enthusiast who devours *The Imitation of Christ,* the weaver nonetheless acts, just as Maggie had done, as the vehicle for a "philosophic" parable about existence in a changeful world. Like the Job he resembles, Silas remains a type: his early piety, his unexpected afflictions, the injustice he rails against, the nature of his eventual reconciliation, are handled without the loss of distance which marred the conclusion of *The Mill on the Floss.* By openly sharing Maggie's unsatisfied yearnings in her earlier novel, George Eliot dispensed with the protective mask of a detached observer. The narrator of *Silas Marner,* however, coldly observes that he finds it difficult "to enter that simple untaught state of mind" which belongs to the weaver's limited powers of comprehension (chap. 1). Maggie's internal conflicts were nursed by Philip, the sensitive artist as a young cripple; Silas' troubles are viewed with dispassion and healthy distrust

by the unsentimental gathering in the Rainbow Tavern. The Raveloers' reserve is understandable. For their strange visitor does seem truly repulsive. An automaton as mechanical as his shuttle, he cannot see any future beyond that furnished by his increasing mound of coins: "He seemed to weave, like the spider, from pure impulse, without reflection" (chap. 2). His monomania resembles that of David Faux; it is not prompted, as Tom Tulliver's had been, by any consideration outside his own self. Though he hurt Maggie, Tom had at least tried to repair the wounds suffered by their father; Silas merely swathes himself in self-pity.

On closer inspection, however, these differences only reveal the kinship between the novels. Like Maggie's, Silas' alienation stems from circumstances beyond his control. He, too, is paralyzed, and his initial paralysis is likewise identified with a city. If Maggie is seduced by the spells of an imagination as uncontrollable as Latimer's visionary fits, the simple Silas is subject to actual cataleptic seizures. Maggie, "entirely passive," awakes from her "drowsy" stupor on Stephen's boat to find that her yesterday cannot be revoked; Silas awakes from his coma to find that he has become the victim of William Dane, the schemer who has framed his trusting friend as a thief. His "loving nature" is even more cruelly thwarted than that of Maggie or Latimer. Lacking their intelligence, far more guiltless than they had been, he rails with even greater justification against a world robbed of order and justice. His trustful belief that God will immediately vindicate his innocence before the Brethren of Lantern Yard is even more painfully denied than Maggie's desire to be vindicated in the eyes of her own brother. Maggie is not wholly exempt from blame; Silas is. The injustice he suffers therefore seems to him all the more unaccountable. Like Shakespeare's Pericles—another passive Job eventually redeemed through the miraculous gift of a daughter—Silas is Fortune's fool.

The weaver's fate, then, is even more capricious than Maggie's. But whereas she must passively suffer from the errors of others, Silas just as passively benefits from the mistakes of Godfrey Cass. In fact, his story opens exactly where Maggie's had ended. Both characters are denied choice; both are defamed; both seek to escape from the changeful city which is the seat of all their misfortunes. "Unhinged," as Maggie had been, from his "old faith and love," this simpler pilgrim seeks, as she had done, that "Lethean influence of exile, in which the past becomes dreamy because its symbols have all vanished, and the present too is dreamy because it is linked with no memories" (chap. 2).

Maggie's exile becomes a curse; Silas', a blessing. To him, as to her, there seems at first to be little "unity between his past and present life" (chap. 2). In *The Mill,* George Eliot had labored assiduously to impress an artificial unity on her heroine's disenfranchised existence. To extricate Maggie from an impossible dilemma, she had resorted to those fictive memories which brother and sister recollect, not in tranquility, but in the agitation before death. Silas, on the other hand, calmly forms an entirely new set of memories based on his eventful life in Raveloe. By means of a new "mode of presentation," we are transported with him into that same mythical world of "daisied fields" which brother and sister glimpsed only in the act of dying. In Raveloe, a realm even more legendary than Adam Bede's Hayslope, the corpse-like weaver veritably will become "a dead man come to life again" (chap. 1). He may not resemble the vital Maggie; yet through his resurrection, she too is given a new life.

Silas' regeneration through feeling occurs in a pastoral world which is not only hazier by far than the Shepperton which had revived Amos Barton, another grotesque intruder, but even more stylized than the Hayslope which had buoyed up Adam Bede. Like Adam Bede, this doubter, who likewise inveighs against a "God of lies, that bears witness against the innocent" (chap. 1), comes to find meaning and purpose in the man-centered village life. Still, his reintegration is handled very differently than Adam's. For Silas' discovery of a new faith grows directly from Maggie Tulliver's objectless quest. His story represents far more than a mere revisitation of the semi-idyllic past depicted in *Adam Bede.* The change in setting goes beyond the differences between eras of "expansion" and "concentration" which had also separated **"Amos Barton"** from **"Mr. Gilfil's Love-Story"** or **"Janet's Repentance"** from *Adam Bede.* If the heroic Adam who accepts Hayslope life was merely restored to his former self, the Silas who accepts and is accepted by Raveloe becomes a new man as an exile from the same reality which had consumed Maggie. Maggie could find no values except in the fiction of a serene childhood; Silas, however, is redeemed by a small child on being "transported to a new land" (chap. 2).

According to the able theological scholar, K. Gottwald, the Book of Job is "neither epic, drama, lyric, or didactic literature; and yet partakes of something of each." The same statement applies to George Eliot's legendary tale. Although Shakespeare, Milton, and Wordsworth are as much blended into this fable as into the earlier novels, this mode does not call attention to the correlatives of drama, epic, and poetry. We are in a realm which generates its own poetry, the *Ur*-world of Gruppe's *"Volkspoesie."* The medium is that of a timeless legend whose wholeness stems from the perfect fusion of the expected and the unexpected, from the metamorphosis of all its constituent parts. We have no need for a sophisticated narrator to instruct the reader how to connect the lesser to the greater.

To achieve its blending, the book eschews the sharpness of photographic realism. Instead of a narrator who forces us to behold the objects in Jonathan Burge's workshop exactly as it appeared on that fateful eighteenth of June in 1799, we are thrust into what seems almost a mythological domain:

> In the days when the spinning-wheel hummed busily in the farmhouses—and even great ladies, clothed in silk and thread-lace, had their toy spinning-wheels of polished oak—there might be seen in districts far away among the lanes, or deep in the bosom of the hills, certain pallid undersized men, who, by the side of the brawny country-folk, looked like the remnants of a disinherited race. The shepherd's dog barked fiercely when one of these alien-looking men appeared on the upland, dark against the early winter sunset; for what dog likes a figure bent under a heavy bag?—and these pale men rarely stirred abroad without that mysterious burden.
>
> (chap. 1)

The passage gives us no specific time. The figure we see, pallid yet dark, is unidentified, presented only in generic terms. Darkness and light, the imagery which will dominate this slender fable as much as Job or *Paradise Lost,* add to the sense of mystery. We must find our own way in the penumbra. The point of view adopted in this passage is neither that of an all-seeing "Egyptian sorcerer" nor that of a visionary narrator who restrains himself by holding onto the reality of his armchair. To the shepherd's dog, and to the shepherd himself, the burden that bends the shoulders of this apparition may well seem mysterious. Soon, of course, we shall be set at rest. The alien-looking stranger who mystifies the barking dog is none but the harmless linen-weaver. But we shall never be able to relax our guard completely. Like the villagers, we shall gradually accept Silas and overcome our distrust; conversely, we shall, like Silas, become acquainted with the ways of Raveloe and participate in the rhythm of its life. But this initial sense of unfamiliarity will persist; the aura of mystery will never quite abate. For we shall want to unravel those semivisible threads with which Silas' destiny becomes interwoven with that of Godfrey's Raveloe. We are to be teased by a novelist who, while engaging our attention with richly colored details, will constantly invite us to deduce further inferences from her careful arrangement of symbol and fact.

It matters little for us to discover, when we do, that the events of this novel belong to "the early years of this century," that the "war times" during which they take place must correspond to the same decade which saw Arthur Donnithorne return from the Napoleonic wars. In *Adam Bede* the exactness of all dates was imperative; the novel's chronology even permitted us to savor such ironies as Arthur's puzzlement over "The Ancient Mariner." In *Silas Marner,* however, the factual and the symbolic qualify each other: the haunted pilgrim we have seen turns out to be a grotesque weaver who suffers from cataleptic fits, and yet, ordinary as he is, he nonetheless will undergo a unique experience. The man called "Old Master Marner" belongs and does not belong to that disinherited race of wanderers who roam through the *Lyrical Ballads.* Ironically enough, his Christian name stems from that of the pagan deity Sylvanus, the protector of landed "husbandmen and their crops." His surname, on the other hand, suggests his kinship to Coleridge's Ancient Mariner. Earth and water, fixity and motion, tradition and change, at odds in *The Mill on the Floss,* coalesce again with this wanderer's return to the lands denied to Tom and Maggie. The world of Raveloe (itself a cryptic anagram) will reveal unexpected truths, hidden from the Raveloers themselves. Although we are asked to see beyond the characters, we also surrender to the logic of their world in a way that we could not submit to George Eliot's uneasy invocation of a biblical deluge or to her conversion of the naturalistic Hetty into a fallen Eve. We can suspend our belief without necessarily yielding to either the superstition of Mr. Macey or to the disbelief of Mr. Dowlas, the skeptic.

Like a ballad, *Silas Marner* soon develops a rhythm of its own by alternating between the expected and the unexpected, the complete and the incomplete. After our attention is thrice called to the gold-tipped whip which Dunstan Cass holds in his hand, we are certain that the whip will have some ulterior significance, though the exact relevance of this detail may escape us at the moment. After Silas has exclaimed for the third time, "God will clear me," we sense, even though he does not, that he will not be cleared by Lantern Yard; yet at the same time we strongly suspect that some unforeseen clarity will eventually emerge from his confusion. We are carried along by the story's rhythm, by a symmetry developing before our eyes. Silas' beloved earthen pot breaks into three pieces; his earthly life will likewise be broken into three fragments by William Dane, Dunstan, and Eppie. Godfrey's life, on the other hand, seems to be affected by only two external events—the sudden disappearance of his brother Dunstan and the equally sudden death of Molly, his unacknowledged wife. Thinking himself rid of these two tormentors, the young man looks confidently to an unbroken future. Yet fate has merely delayed a third intervention, which comes when Godfrey reaches the same age Silas was at the time he found Eppie. At the novel's end, we have a sense of completion. Our expectations have been fulfilled. If Maggie's drowning in *The Mill on the Floss* seemed arbitrary and unpredictable despite all the careful foreshadowings of that event, the symmetry which binds Silas' and Godfrey's destinies generates an irresistible logic. If we ultimately cannot account for that logic, we nonetheless feel, as Blake did in "The Tyger," a certain awe and reverence for the inescapable symmetry on which it depends.

When Silas and the grown Eppie timidly venture back into the outer world, they find that the changeful city has swallowed up Lantern Yard. But the loss of this past becomes insignificant to the old man who had expected some light to be cast on his curious fortune. Knowing by now that "things *will* change," Silas trustfully accepts a change which has been for the better. If the change in Maggie's environment was crippling to her psyche, Silas' move and adaptation to a simpler world have restored his inner sanity. The injustice he formerly suffered in "the city of destruction" (chap. 14) no longer matters to him. In *The Mill on the Floss,* the narrator derives what little comfort he can from the fact that the graves of brother and sister have recovered their "decent quiet"; in *Silas Marner,* there is no need for such elegiac attempts at conciliation. The graves of Silas' Brethren have disappeared, but death has yielded to a new life:

> "The old place is all swep' away," Silas said to Dolly Winthrop on the night of his return—"the little graveyard and everything. The old home's gone; I've no home but this now. I shall never know whether they got at the truth o' the robbery, nor whether Mr. Paston could ha' given me any light about the drawing o' the lots. It's dark to me, Mrs. Winthrop, that is; I doubt it'll be dark to the last."
>
> (chap. 21)

Demanding more light, the Faustian Maggie had died in the swirling darkness of the waters which spanned two irreconcilable worlds; Silas, however, gladly trots back to his checkered Eden. He has found a new paradise through the foundling he named after his dead mother and sister. Ruined by Mr. Tulliver's mistakes, ruled by his family's hectic blood, Maggie appropriately bore the name of her father's short-lived mother, Margaret Beaton. The beaten, stooped linen-weaver who gives his adopted daughter a "Bible name" does not even fathom its full significance: "thou shalt no more be termed Forsaken; neither shall thy land anymore be termed Desolate; but thou shalt be called Hephzibah" [Isaiah, 62, 4]. Through Eppie he has been led away from "threatening destruction" into a "calm and bright land" (chap. 14).

Maggie perishes in the flood. Silas' first promise of salvation comes when he ventures among the humanity gathered in a tavern called "The Rainbow." The villagers who stare at the weaver are no more idealized than the townspeople attracted by the multicolored display in David Faux's confectionery shop, where a rainbow seems to have "descended into the marketplace" (chap. 2). But unlike the materialistic inhabitants of Grimworth, the Raveloers can be moved by a stranger's plight. They become the means for Silas' regeneration. As in *Paradise Lost* or in Shakespeare's *Pericles* and *The Tempest,* the covenant for such a redemption is signified by the rainbow which followed the tempestuous flood. Milton's Adam first revives at the sight of the three-colored bow "Betok'ning peace from God, and Cov'nant new" (XI, 867). Prospero's reconciliation to a world of darkness likewise begins when, in the masque, Iris, the "many-colour'd messenger," spans earth and heaven with her "wat'ry arch" (*The Tempest,* IV, i, 76, 71). But if the renewed confidence of Adam and Prospero still depends on a supernatural power, Silas' regained faith is made possible by "the remedial influences of pure, natural human relations." The power behind these human relations remains dark and inscrutable. Silas wracks his brain to understand the dispensation which seems to repay him for his former misfortunes. His puzzlement is shared by the superstitious rustics who had even regarded him (much as Mr. Tulliver viewed Lawyer Wakem) as a "queer-looksed thing as Old Harry's had the making of" (chap. 10). Yet their awe and his awe must be ours as well. Though their perplexity seems as simplistic as their feeble attempts at explanation, the narrator refuses to advance any theories of his own.

Were George Eliot to have written the sentimental tale that *Silas Marner* is still thought to be, she would not have felt compelled to connect the weaver's story to that of Godfrey Cass. Instead, Silas' regeneration by the golden-haired child could have been simply a wishful fantasy designed to help the author purge herself of the fears that had surfaced in "The Lifted Veil" and *The Mill on the Floss.* By merely adopting the superstitious attitude of Silas and the Raveloers, the novelist could safely have regressed into a simpler, untroubled world in which men could remain children. In this wishful realm—a realm as beneficent and wholesome as the one in "The Lifted Veil" had been terrifying and repellent—the accidents which led to Silas' regeneration could have gone wholly unexplained; the weaver's fate might simply have appeared as the opposite of the sadder destinies of Latimer and Maggie. Yet George Eliot does not escape into Maggie's arrested fantasy world. She deliberately links Silas' strange story to Godfrey's and makes Godfrey's fate as fully understandable as that sequence of events which had brought the nemesis of David Faux. And by so doing she emphasizes the very questions her previous fiction had tried to disguise. In *Silas Marner* the novelist squarely confronts the disparities which resulted from her previous treatment of moral justice in a world of fortuitous change.

. . . . .

In the fiction before *Silas Marner,* George Eliot met considerable difficulties in trying to extract moral sanctions from a world ruled by random change. . . . [Her] novels inevitably try to master the conflicts arising from two different ways of beholding reality. George Eliot demanded of her characters that they accept a natural order devoid of the providential dispensation she had once believed in. . . . [Accident] had dominated in *Scenes of Clerical Life*: even in the most positive of those stories, Janet Dempster could believe in a moral order only through the accident which freed her from her husband's tyranny. In *Adam Bede,* George Eliot had been far more successful in staking out a domain in which morality might exercise its own logic; still, Dinah's trustful belief in a "Divine Love" was qualified by her creator's deep reservations about the capriciousness of the material world. And, in what certainly are the novelist's gloomiest projections, both Latimer and Maggie Tulliver succumbed to combinations of fortuitous circumstances.

In "The Lifted Veil" and *The Mill on the Floss,* George Eliot had tried to disguise her personal fear of a hazardous reality. She resorted to the irrationality of the fantasy tale in order to account for Latimer's inability to trust in a better future; in the more realistic mode of her tragic novel, she tried to advance a series of logical explanations for Maggie's passivity as a victim: Mr. Tulliver's and Tom's mistakes in judgment, the "richness" of the Tulliver blood, the dangers inherent in too rapid a variation, the obduracy and insensitivity of St. Ogg's, were among the many reasons adduced for the girl's collapse. Still, Maggie's destiny seemed as arbitrary as Latimer's. Neither the unusual circumstances which prevented Latimer from seeing goodness nor the apotheosis of the flood could lead the reader from nihilism to the recognition of a beneficent order akin to the divine dispensation George Eliot had rejected. Unlike her father's, Maggie's fate seems only capricious and unjust.

Silas Marner relies on the oppositions depicted in *The Mill.* Two modes of life, agrarian and urban, once again typify two different realities—the one ruled by freedom of choice, the other governed by impersonal and irresistible forces. But whereas in *The Mill* George Eliot pretended that Maggie's downfall was precipitated by the same interaction of imprudence and "external fact" which caused her father's tragedy, in *Silas Marner* she openly distinguishes between the chance which affects Silas Marner and the processes which bring on Godfrey's nemesis. Although the novel relies on the familiar contrast of city and

country ("what could be more unlike the Lantern Yard world than the world in Raveloe?"), chance and free will coexist in the same environment. If accident influences Silas' life in the city, it equally affects his life in Raveloe. And Raveloe is far more stable than the world of Dorlcote Mill: "the fall of prices had not yet come to carry the race of small squires and yeomen down that road to ruin for which extravagant habits and bad husbandry were plentifully anointing their wheels" (chap. 3). In his threatened agrarian world, Mr. Tulliver's extravagance and bad husbandry contributed to his downfall. In the more stable order of Raveloe, Godfrey Cass is wholly responsible for all of his actions. His secret marriage to a barmaid, which exposes him to his brother's blackmailing, is as foolish as Mr. Tulliver's marrying the weakest of the Dodson sisters. But Godfrey's freedom of choice is even greater than that of the imprudent miller who was ground by the wheels of St. Ogg's.

The freedom and accident which are irrevocably at odds in *The Mill* ultimately become indistinguishable from each other in *Silas Marner.* As David R. Carroll has pointed out [in *Literary Monographs, Vol. 1,* edited by Eric Rothstein and Thomas K. Dunseath, 1967], the novel presents two alternate explanations of reality: "In the frenetic atmosphere of Lantern Yard, Silas sought to explain life in terms of the miraculous; in the materialistic, indulgent atmosphere of Raveloe, Godfrey, as his surname suggests, seeks to explain life in terms of Chance (*casus*)." Yet *Silas Marner* depicts a curious transference. As in *Middlemarch,* where Lydgate the scientist and Dorothea the religious enthusiast will find their original explanations of life to be incomplete, here too the beliefs of Godfrey and Silas qualify each other. Godfrey, the onetime worshiper of luck, will come to acknowledge the mandates of a power he identifies with an exacting God; Silas, the plaything of chance, finds that he is unable, "by means of anything he heard or saw, to identify the Raveloe religion with his old faith" (chap. 14). And yet, though their initial explanations do not account for the strange connection between their fates, both Godfrey and Silas are brought to acknowledge the justice of whatever dispensation has tied them inextricably together. The "mystery" previously denied to Dinah, Latimer, or Maggie, is allowed to survive in this legendary tale.

Godfrey Cass is ironically named. His Christian name suggests that he is free, at peace with God. [The critic adds in a footnote: "Godfrey (Geoffroi, Gofredo, Gottfried) is a combination of *got* (the deity) and *frī* (peace or freedom). The name thus signifies 'divine peace'; it can connote the freedom granted by God, as well as (in this case) the desire to be free of God, or 'god-free.'"] Yet, like the David Faux who chose the name of "Mr. Freely," this young man will be punished by the past he tries to deny. Even at the beginning of the novel, he already tugs at the chains his own imprudence has forged. For Godfrey has foolishly misspent his freedom by marrying Molly. Revolted by his own folly ("an ugly story of low passion, delusion, and the waking of delusion"), afraid that his brother Dunstan will reveal his secret to Squire Cass and the whole of Raveloe, the well-meaning Godfrey yields to a life of hazard. Seeing no way out of his sensual enslavement, he indulges in the same "excitement of sporting, drinking, card-playing" which led Chaucer's young rioters to their spiritual deaths and which, in *Middlemarch,* will lead Tertius Lydgate to opium and the gaming table. Though Godfrey hates Dunstan, another worshiper of Dame Luck, his brother becomes an extension of his worse self. Godfrey regards Nancy Lammeter, whose steadying influence he desires, as his better angel and the opium-eating Molly Farren, as the cause and emblem for his own paralysis and "natural irresolution." The immobilized Godfrey hopes that fortune will somehow break the manacles he has forged for himself and allow him to live an unencumbered life with Nancy. In the manner of Arthur Donnithorne, he expects "some unforeseen turn of fortune, some favourable chance which would save him from unpleasant consequences—perhaps even justify his insincerity" (chap. 9). His expectations, like Arthur's, are destined to be shattered. In one of those ominous authorial asides so rare in this novel, the narrator warns that "Favourable Chance is the god of all men who follow their own devices instead of obeying a law they believe in" (chap. 9).

Yet Silas Marner, who believed in precisely such a moral law, at first seems to fare even worse than Godfrey. If Godfrey's acknowledged guilt does not allow him to regard himself as "simply a victim," Silas is clearly victimized in both Lantern Yard and Raveloe. Chance, which already had allowed William Dane to frame Silas for a crime he did not commit, again presents itself in Raveloe. The unsuspecting weaver is but a hundred yards away during Dunstan's entry into his open cottage. He has left the door ajar because, bereft of his belief in Providence, he has come to rely on simple common sense: "What thief would find his way to the Stone-pits on such a night as this? and why should he come on this particular night, when he had never come through all the fifteen years before?" (chap. 5). But this logic proves to be faulty. When Silas arrives at his cottage, Dunstan, the "lucky fellow" who has lighted on an unguarded treasure, has already retreated into the darkness.

Thus, while Silas, the former believer in an exacting divine law finds his luck waning, Godfrey discovers that his prayers seem to have been answered by his own goddess, "Favourable Chance." First, Dunstan, who had professed himself to be "always lucky," ever able to land on his feet, unaccountably disappears; then, Molly, the denied wife, dies before she can confront Godfrey with his child. The past seems miraculously annulled. Relieved, the young man now regards himself as free at last; Nancy Lammeter can be wooed and won. Yet the same event which Godfrey falsely interprets as a fortunate intervention in his behalf, comes to Silas' rescue: the child whose paternity Godfrey hides from Raveloe in order to retain his freedom frees Silas from his disappointment over an amoral world devoid of law and justice and earns this outsider a place among the Raveloers. Although Godfrey must eventually recognize that there is no such thing as "Favourable Chance," some arbitrary power has nonetheless favored Silas Marner.

The book's parallels at first seem simple—simple enough to force them on school children: Attracted by the light

of Silas' cottage, Dunstan steals the miser's painfully accumulated past; attracted by the same light, little Eppie brings a more refulgent future. Dunstan meets death in darkness; Eppie is preserved in the room lit by the "red uncertain glimmer" of the dying hearth. As Silas pushes the two logs together so the fire reveals the form of the child, his life, broken in two, begins to be mended once again. Yet the pattern appears more complicated as soon as we become aware of the relation between the changes which Dunstan and Eppie induce in Silas and Godfrey. For Silas, the loss of the coins had meant the extinction of feeling; when Eppie comes, however, life comes out of death, fire out of ashes—like the "squire's child" found by the shepherd in *The Winter's Tale,* the foundling's value will exceed that of "fairy gold." Against his own will, the benumbed weaver who wanted to shun all human fellowship is drawn to the villagers. An ungainly misanthrope is transformed into the placid Master Marner, who will obediently smoke the daily pipe urged on him by "the sages of Raveloe." Godfrey, on the other hand, had wanted "the tender permanent affection" of Nancy, as well as the esteem of the villagers. The young squire who fathered the child had inwardly wished the disappearance of his brother and the death of his first wife. His wish is granted. The child itself seems conveniently removed. Presumably, like Silas, Godfrey can now be reinstated into the society which has frowned on his excesses. But while Silas' open consternation and helplessness endear him to Dolly Winthrop and the townspeople who gather at "The Rainbow," Godfrey can regain their esteem only by keeping his secret. Silas, by accidentally opening his door, has found the world opening to him; Godfrey, by deliberately shutting within himself the secret of his paternity, locks out even the being dearest to him, Nancy. Once again, freedom will elude him.

An 1849 portrait of Eliot by François D'Albert-Durade.

Godfrey has inherited his father's "large red house"; though he does not make official use of the title, he is the new Squire Cass. [The critic adds in a footnote: "The Middle English word 'cass' (box, chest, container) is derived from the Latin *capsa* (cf. *casa,* the Spanish word for house), which stems from *capere* (to hold, to contain)."] The self-contained world he had envisioned has become a reality. After the disappearance of Dunstan and the death of Molly, Godfrey eagerly looks forward to a closed room "with all happiness centered on his own hearth, while Nancy would smile on him as he played with the children" (chap. 15). But, after sixteen years of waiting for a legitimate child, when he finally "opens his home" to Eppie and confesses to her and Silas the secret he has encased for so long, it is too late. He assures his daughter that he can give her a greater freedom than the weaver can. Yet his "natural claim" upon her proves to be as empty as Stephen Guest's invocation of that "natural law" which "surmounts every other." The unnatural barriers he has erected now deprive him of the child who had entered through Silas Marner's unintentionally opened door. The man who once tried to lock out his daughter from the room reserved for his and Nancy's children, now goes "straight to the door, unable to say more" (chap. 19).

Before the theft of his gold, Silas had also tried to shut out others: "at night he closed his shutters, and made fast his doors, and drew forth his gold" (chap. 2). His treasure had "fenced him in from the wide, cheerless unknown"; his money's disappearance, however, left him exposed: "But now the fence was broken down—the support was snatched away" (chap. 10). Indifferent, he no longer cares "to close his shutters or lock his door" (chap. 10). His faith in goodness, divine or human, has been "blocked up." But with Eppie a new life opens for the former miser. His cottage will eventually be enlarged "at the expense of Mr. Cass" in order to accommodate Aaron and Eppie and their future children. Appropriately enough, the frontage is left semi-open: "The garden was fenced with stones on two sides, but in front there was an open fence, through which the flowers shone with answering gladness" (Conclusion). Silas can look at the prospects of a widening future; his glance no longer rests on a "blank." Godfrey, on the other hand, sadder and wiser, absents himself from the wedding of his daughter, while his barren wife Nancy remains ensconced in the Red House. Like his brother Dunstan, Godfrey has taken "one fence too many"; he suffers from the very secret he must now forever hide from Raveloe.

Immediately on finding the squirming child, Silas begins to regain his "old impressions of awe at the presentiment of some Power presiding over his life" (chap. 12). On finding the skeleton of Dunstan when he drains the water off his land, Godfrey, too, senses that he has been judged by some outside power. Though he fears public opinion, he now confides his secret to his wife in one of those confessional scenes so dear to George Eliot's "religion of humanity": "Everything comes to light, Nancy, sooner or later. When God Almighty wills it, our secrets are found out. I've lived with a secret on my mind, but I'll keep it from you no longer" (chap. 18). Chance, favorable or unfavor-

able, has in the eyes of Silas, Godfrey, and Nancy been replaced by the workings of a just power.

Silas' "sense of mystery" over Eppie's appearance seems almost as infantile as the baby's own absorption with "the primary mystery of her toes." Twice he repeats: "The money's gone I don't know where, and this is come from I don't know where" (chap. 14). His consternation is rather amusing. As Eppie grows older and wiser, she acquires new interests. The infantile Silas, however, remains as perplexed as before, even after he learns where his money had gone and after he discovers Eppie's origin. He is still befuddled, still awed by his good fortune. Just as he had refused to accept a "medical explanation" for his cataleptic seizures, he now rejects any purely rational explanation for his fate. Irrationally, he fears that with the restoration of his coins Eppie may disappear or "be changed into gold again." For he has fallen back on the earlier belief in magical signs and omens on which the religion of Lantern Yard had depended. Convinced that God has personally looked after his interests, Silas rebukes Godfrey with unexpected fierceness, "God gave her to me because you turned your back upon her, and He looks upon her as mine" (chap. 19). The weaver refuses to be cut "i' two" again. But George Eliot makes it clear that Silas' belief in a protecting deity is precarious. His faith depends on the child that is so precious to him. He admits that if he were to lose Eppie, he might again also "lose the feeling that God was good to me."

Godfrey's and Nancy's own conclusions about the powers that have affected their lives are somewhat less simpleminded. But although Godfrey's recognition of his dereliction of duty is couched in religious terms, it does not differ greatly from that forced on Amos Barton or Arthur Donnithorne. His allusion to a "God Almighty" merely represents an acknowledgement of the impossibility of his ever amending the mistakes of the past. As in Silas' case, his belief is based on events that have happened in the material world, events which could have happened without the aid of any supernatural power. George Eliot declared Godfrey's nemesis to be "very mild," and milder it is certainly than the circumstances which force Amos Barton away from Milly's grave in Shepperton or the circumstances which push Arthur away from Hayslope into the Napoleonic wars. But even though Godfrey is allowed to remain in Raveloe and to retain his wife, his nemesis is appropriately severe: left without an acknowledged heir, he, like Arthur Donnithorne, stands to lose his patrimony.

Yet it is Nancy, rather than Godfrey or Silas, who best asserts the justice of the novel's retribution: Like the chorus in a Greek drama, she is not necessarily all-seeing. In her superstition, Nancy shares the limitations of both Silas Marner and Dolly Winthrop: "She would have given up making a purchase at a particular place if, on three successive times, rain, or some other cause of Heaven's sending, had formed an obstacle; and she would have anticipated a broken limb or other heavy misfortune to any one who persisted in spite of such indications" (chap. 17). In a story where obstacles come in threes, where rain and snow have affected the main events of the plot, such beliefs cannot be laughed away. In the simpler world of belief that George

Eliot has created, Nancy can stand as a partial spokesman for her author's far more complex moral vision. Nancy refuses to accept any explanation of a life that is not arranged by some higher dispensation. Determined, resolute, the girl who had once refused to sit by the card tables, cannot accept a belief in chance. After the death of her and Godfrey's infant, she rejects his suggestion that they adopt Eppie. Although she does not yet know that the child was fathered by her husband, she is convinced that the adoption "would never turn out well, and would be a curse to those who had wilfully and rebelliously sought what it was clear that, for *some high reason,* they were better without" (chap. 17; italics added).

Although George Eliot does not share the crude superstitions which shape Nancy's intuition, she definitely wants the reader of *Silas Marner* to believe in any "high reason" that can validate what is morally right. Nancy's refusal prepares us for Godfrey's retribution. And that retribution must, in this novel, depend on some such power as that which Nancy calls "the will of Providence:"

> It might seem singular that Nancy—with her religious theory pieced together out of narrow social traditions, fragments of church doctrine imperfectly understood, and girlish reasonings on her small experience—should have arrived by herself at a way of thinking so nearly akin to that of many devout people whose beliefs are held in the shape of a system quite remote from her knowledge: singular, if we did not know that human beliefs, like all other natural growths, elude the barriers of system
>
> (chap. 17).

Nancy's "small experience" contains the essence of all belief in moral right. Here, even more than in the early portions of *The Mill on the Floss,* the lesser holds the seeds for the growth of larger universals. Although the explanations advanced by Silas, Godfrey, or Nancy belong to a narrower world view rejected by the novelist, their credulity is necessary to the "human beliefs" which her tale tries to generate. Like the Book of Job, *Silas Marner* asks: "But where shall wisdom be found? and where is the place of understanding?" Like Job, Silas learns that this understanding cannot be extracted from the material world: "It cannot be gotten for gold, neither shall silver be weighed for the prize thereof " [Job, 27]. Yet neither is there a God speaking through the whirlwind. If in Job the simple man called Elihu prepares the doubter for God's veiled answers, in this novel the complex woman who called herself "Eliot" for once refuses to unveil the contradictory ways of existence: " 'Ah,' said Dolly, with soothing gravity, 'it's like the night and the morning, and the sleeping and the waking, and the rain and the harvest—one goes and the other comes, and we know nothing how nor where.' " (chap. 14)

The scriptural tone and rhythm of this statement are intentional. Like Nancy, whose deepest thoughts are always stimulated by the copy of "Mant's Bible before her," the wheelwright's wife clings to what is elementary. To her surprise, Dolly discovers that, notwithstanding the theological differences between the Brethren of Lantern Yard and the indulgent religion preached by the Reverend Mr. Crackenthorp, her Bible and Silas' Bible are the same:

> "And yourn's the same Bible, you're sure o' that, Master Marner—the Bible as you brought wi' you from that country—it's the same as what they've got at church, and what Eppie's a-learning to read in?"
>
> "Yes," said Silas, "every bit the same; and there's drawing o' lots in the Bible, mind you," he added in a lower tone
>
> (chap. 16).

The Evangelical who had once clung to her Bible and the agnostic who translated Strauss and Feuerbach could never again become "every bit the same." From **"Amos Barton"** to *The Mill on the Floss,* George Eliot oscillated between alternate explanations of reality. The fable of Silas Marner allowed her to balance these opposites. The conflicting impulses underlying her previous fiction finally found a common resting point.

·　·　·　·　·

In one of her essays for the *Leader* [12 January 1856], George Eliot had argued that lying between the deductive bibliolatry of the extremely orthodox and the inductive historical mode of the extremely heterodox, there was a middle ground occupied by those biblical scholars who believed in the "accommodation" theory:

> As the Deity, it is said, in speaking to human beings, must use human language, and consequently anthropomorphic expressions, such as "eye of God," the "arm of God," the "laughter and jealousy of God," which we have no difficulty in understanding figuratively, so he must adapt the form of His revelations to the degree of culture, which belongs to men at the period in which His revelations are made.

Her essay was written in 1856, in the same year in which she turned to the novel in order to reshape the figurative truths of the Bible. In **Silas Marner,** she profited from all her previous efforts to find a form for her revelations. By adapting herself to a simpler "degree of culture," by mediating between irreconcilable explanations, she was able to create a reality that could shelter reason and faith, the actual and the ideal.

Silas Marner succeeds in establishing, from beginning to end, that invisible rhythm which George Eliot had first suggested but then shied away from, in *Adam Bede.* The rider observing Dinah Morris' preaching on the village Green had briefly suspended his disbelief. In the green world of Raveloe, the simple Silas' final sense of wonder becomes ours as well. Like the weaver, we are satisfied by the protracted wonder which rises from a mixture of light and darkness, the transparent and the unintelligible. Godfrey's plausible loss is interwoven with Silas' strange gain. Mystery, rejected by Dinah, lost by Latimer, denied to Maggie, survives next to the clarity of reason. Like Mr. Snell, the evasive landlord of the Rainbow Tavern, George Eliot manages to suggest that there can be two irreconcilable, yet equally valid ways of beholding reality.

As David R. Carroll convincingly demonstrates, the discussion in the Rainbow Tavern which occupies the entire sixth chapter of the novel is integral to its meaning. A triumph of George Eliot's comic powers, drawn in a wide spectrum of rich colors, this scene refracts the same oppositions between the known and the unknown, the expected and the unexpected, on which the entire novel is built. From an abortive argument over the concealed reasons for slaughtering a cow, the debate slowly moves into what amounts to a philosophical dispute between two alternate modes of belief. The contest is not unlike that enacted in the barnyard of Chaucer's "Nun's Priest's Tale." The disputants are as ridiculous as the knowledgeable Chanticleer and the superstitious Pertelote. Pitted against each other are the aggressive farrier Mr. Dowlas (whose Scottish name suggests his skepticism in matters spiritual) and the oracular Mr. Macey, the parish clerk who believes in ghosts. When Mr. Dowlas boldly throws out a challenge to all specters ("let 'em come where there's company and candles"), even he for a moment is unnerved by the sudden apparition of the pale Silas, whose "strange unearthly eyes" cannot adjust to the tavern's light.

The chapter is important not only because it introduces the society which Silas now confronts (in the yard of the same Rainbow Tavern where at the end of the novel the bridal procession will gather), but also because the debate develops two clearly defined attitudes which are carried over into the explanations soon advanced to account for the theft of the miser's gold. In the light of what the reader already knows, neither explanation is correct. The crime has not been committed by a swarthy pedlar seen with a tinderbox, nor by the "preternatural felon" that Mr. Macey so doggedly believes in. And yet the battle rages between the advocates of common sense and the believers in supernatural occurrences:

> The advocates of the tinder-box-and-pedlar view considered the other side a muddle-headed and credulous set, who, because they themselves were wall-eyed, supposed everybody else to have the same blank outlook; and the adherents of the inexplicable more than hinted that their antagonists were animals inclined to crow before they had found any corn—mere skimming-dishes in point of depth—whose clear-sightedness consisted in supposing that there was nothing behind a barn-door because they couldn't see through it; so that, though their controversy did not serve to elicit the fact concerning the robbery, it elicited some true opinions of collateral importance
>
> (chap. 10).

As inferences of fact, the opinions are equally invalid. As in *Adam Bede,* where even the keen-eyed Mrs. Poyser and the visionary Dinah discover that some truths can elude either one, here too neither party can establish the total truth. But the controversy is as important to George Eliot's own objectives as those useless metaphysical disputations which engage Milton's angels are to the purpose of *Paradise Lost.* Playfully, she suggests that although they are deeply divided in their speculations, both parties actually have one point of agreement, for both are equally convinced of the veracity of Silas' story. It is his normal, human suffering which overcomes their resistance. And,

as the stimulus for all our better feelings, this suffering contains all the truth that man needs to know. In **"Amos Barton"** or even in *Adam Bede,* this insight would have been conveyed by a hortatory narrator or one of the characters. In *Silas Marner,* however, it is unobtrusively introduced by an artist who has fully learned how to exploit her own self-division.

Around the time George Eliot began *Silas Marner,* George Henry Lewes published an amusing essay entitled "Seeing Is Believing," in which he attacked those who confused inference and fact: "when a man avers that he has 'seen a ghost,' he is passing far beyond the limits of visible fact, into that of inference. He saw *something* which he *supposed* to be a ghost." Like Lewes, George Eliot has her fun with the spiritualists in Raveloe. But as a novelist whose art relies on the reader's inferences from simulated facts, she is also careful to suggest that Mr. Dowlas' empirical view of reality cannot disallow certain necessary illusions. Empirically speaking, ghosts do not exist. But in the figurative mode of this tale, Dunstan's ghost hovers over the entire story. Shortly before Godfrey reports that his brother's skeleton has been found, Nancy has had a premonition. She looks at "the placid churchyard with the long shadows of the gravestones across the bright green hillocks," but the external beauty of this scene only impresses upon her "the presence of a vague fear . . . like a raven flapping its slow wing across the sunny air" (chap. 17). Her foreboding proves correct. The ghost of the past now crosses the threshold of the Red House. Nancy's prescience resembles Dinah's. Yet while in Hayslope the visionary and the naturalistic seemed at odds, in Raveloe they remain in harmony. As in *Middlemarch,* where George Eliot was to rely on far more intricate balances, the craftsmanship of *Silas Marner* can persuade us that some power has meted out appropriate punishments and rewards.

Like the equanimous Mr. Snell, "accustomed to stand aloof from human differences as those of beings who were all alike in need of liquor," the author avoids the controversy of opposed systems of belief. If Chaucer uses his Host to control his opinionated pilgrims, George Eliot speaks through the landlord, who vows: "The truth lies atween you: you're both right and both wrong, as I allays say." Mr. Snell tries to prevent further dispute by inducing Mr. Macey to tell the oft-told and much cherished anecdote of the Lammeters' wedding. After going through "that complimentary process necessary to bring him up to the point of narration," the old parish clerk complies. His story is meant to restore harmony to the divided group at the inn; like children, his listeners delight in hearing the story over and over again. Appropriately enough, his story is about the conjunction of opposites, the union of disparate elements. Mr. Macey begins by contrasting the Lammeters from the Osgoods. The former have come "from a bit north'ard"; the latter have been rooted in Raveloe for generations. But the long-winded clerk admits that, after due consideration, this difference is not really appreciable: although "there's nobody rightly knows" the region from which old Mr. Lammeter came, it could not be "much different from this country, for he brought a fine breed o' sheep with him, so there must be pastures there." Having thus reassured his audience, Mr. Macey jumps right into the terrifying core of his story: the clergyman officiating at the Lammeter-Osgood wedding, Mr. Drumlow—"poor old gentleman, I was fond of him"—had put the questions to bride and bridegroom "by the rule o' contrary, like." Mr. Macey makes sure to stress his own presence of mind amidst this scene of disturbing confusion:

> "Wilt thou have this man to thy wedded wife?" says he, and then he says, "Wilt thou have this woman to thy wedded husband?" says he. But the partic'larest thing of all is, as nobody took any notice on it but me, and they answered straight off "yes," like as if it had been me saying "Amen" i' the right place, without listening to what went before.

Skillful storyteller that he is, Mr. Macey aids the imagination of his hearers by dramatizing the division of his mind. He tells them that he felt as "if I'd been a coat pulled by the two tails, like," and then tops his own metaphor: "I was worreted as if I'd got three bells to pull at once." Having lingered on the climax, Mr. Macey now mercifully produces the long-awaited denouement: on confronting Mr. Drumlow with his mistake, the excited clerk was assured that the marriage was still valid. Mr. Macey transmits the parson's exact words: "he says, 'Pooh, pooh, Macey, make yourself easy' he says; 'it's neither the meaning nor the words—it's the reg*e*ster does it—that's the glue' " (chap. 6).

In *Silas Marner* it is the "glue" of George Eliot's artistry which resolves the conflicts that had divided her previously. Through her choice of a perfect "reg*e*ster," she was able to yoke humor and high seriousness, to connect the probable with the improbable by fusing the laws of observed experience with the poetic justice of a fairy tale. In the marriage at the end of the novel, the daughter of Godfrey is given away by her "father" Silas. But this irregularity is no more disturbing than Mr. Drumlow's carelessness. Coincidence and causality, redemption and punishment, Lantern Yard and Rainbow Yard have been meticulously bonded. Though retaining the duality of the earlier novels, *Silas Marner* blends these opposites in a union as indissoluble as that of the couple wedded "by the rule o' contrary."

In his essay on superstition, Lewes had maintained: "What an honest man tells me he saw, I will believe he saw, if it comes within the possibilities of vision; my scepticism begins when he ceases to narrate what he actually saw, and substitutes his *interpretation* of it." Though not meant to be, his criterion can be applied to George Eliot's novel. We believe in Silas' or Dolly's confidence in "Them as know better nor we do," because the conclusions these simple people form are within the range of their own vision. When Dolly offers Silas the cakes with the inscription "I.H.S." pricked on them, he is "as unable to interpret the letters as Dolly," although, in her words, "the letters have held better nor common" (chap. 10). George Eliot makes it clear that Dolly's "simple Raveloe theology" is as much predicated on the visible world as on the invisible "Them" she alludes to in an unconscious relapse into polytheism. Silas can believe in a just deity only through the gift of Eppie; Dolly likewise suggests that

Aaron is indispensable for her own faith: "either me or the father must allays hev him in our sight—that we must" (chap. 10). But the novelist no longer sentimentalizes her religion of humanity; she does not try to separate the "worldly" from the "otherworldly," as she did in **"Amos Barton."** Instead, she quietly suggests that all belief, natural and supernatural, stems from man's elemental need to confide in somebody other than the self. The truth of this insight is at once as simple and as complex as life itself.

Only ten years after George Eliot's death, *Silas Marner* had the misfortune to be chosen as a text for the "Student's Series of English Classics." Even today, the work has yet to recover from the resulting obloquy. In a play like *The Winter's Tale,* the sudden echoes of *Hamlet* or *King Lear* tend to remind us that Shakespeare merely carried into his stylized romances the same complicated questions about existence that were raised by his tragedies. *Silas Marner* is equally oblique. Although George Eliot's Victorian thoroughness had led her to interpret human experience in novels of increasing complexity and bulk, the compactness of *Silas Marner* contains the same riches which were spread out over *The Mill on the Floss.* Neither Silas nor Dolly, Godfrey nor Nancy, is profound. Yet their groping among half-shadows, their imperfect grasp of the bare letters of the alphabet, carries a greater authority than the flat rejections forced upon Dinah Morris, Latimer, or Maggie. By avoiding the explicitness of her earlier explanations, George Eliot made her insights seem deeper than those which she had expressed more openly. Dolly's creed is as self-limiting as that previously advanced by her creator. But it is far more credible in her broken words than if it had been spoken by an erudite narrator or affixed as the motto for **"The Lifted Veil":** "Give me no light great heaven but such as turns / To energy of human fellowship." For Dolly exhausts all the light she possesses in order to reconcile Silas to his fate. Her words seem less melancholic than Adam Bede's similar statement, because they actually do ease Silas' questionings: "And all as we've got to do is to trusten, Master Marner—to do the right thing as fur as we know, and to trusten. For if us as knows so little can see a bit o' good and rights, we may be sure as there's a good and a rights bigger nor what we can know" (chap. 16). Through Dolly, George Eliot expressed her own hope for "a good and a rights bigger nor what we can know." She had already demonstrated her ability to adopt the point of view of "us as knows so little" in the childhood portions of *The Mill.* It is the full exercise of that ability which makes *Silas Marner* so delightful a reading experience. As in *Middlemarch,* the author was able to divide herself among her characters without at all relinquishing the breadth of her own vast culture. Dolly's hopefulness, Nancy's elementary righteousness, even Priscilla Lammeter's satiric ability to laugh at human foibles stem from a distribution similar to the dispersion of qualities in *Middlemarch* among Dorothea Brooke, Mrs. Bulstrode, and Mary Garth. Even Silas Marner, that simple weaver of cloth, is a self-projection of the subtle intellect who was to devise the "web" of *Middlemarch:* "In this strange world, made a hopeless riddle to him, he might, if he had had a less intense nature, have sat weaving, weaving—looking towards the end of his pattern, or towards the end of his web, till he forgot the riddle" (chap. 2). If nobody among the Raveloers suspects that this alienated stranger is "the same Silas Marner who had once loved his fellow with tender love, and trusted an unseen goodness," very few of George Eliot's readers could suspect that this grotesque misanthrope who wants so badly to solve the riddle of existence is as much a projection of his creator as the puzzled Maggie had been.

Silas Marner refracts a view of reality which is more complicated than the artist had previously allowed herself to admit. In Wordsworth's "Michael," "a story unenriched with strange events" (l. 14), the city destroys the faith of the old peasant; in *Silas Marner,* events almost as strange as those in "The Ancient Mariner" allow "old Master Marner" to be integrated into a world of poetic belief. The unusual Latimer had shriveled into a misanthrope; Silas the misanthrope grows into a venerable Raveloe sage. His growth reverses Latimer's degeneration. If Latimer's story is a study in disease, Silas' is therapeutic. Coming from the writer who, in the name of a harsh actuality, had thwarted the innocent Mr. Gilfil and so severely punished Hetty and Maggie, *Silas Marner* is an unusually joyous work. But the novel is not great simply because its comic powers generate the quality of joy which Arnold had despaired of in Victorian art, or because in it George Eliot overcame the philosophical nihilism which she had merely resisted in her earlier fiction. Its greatness stems rather from her surprising ability to merge the ordinary with the extraordinary, from the unexpected ease with which she accommodated the conflicting impulses which she had tried to methodize from **"Amos Barton"** to *The Mill on the Floss.* Without surrendering an iota of her and Lewes' belief in empirical fact, she managed to balance "rational explanation" and "impenetrable mystery" (chap. 10). She had devised an artistic construct whose truth could remain independent from that of the actual world. Only *Middlemarch* would repeat that accomplishment. (pp. 226-58)

> *U. C. Knoepflmacher, "Reconciliation through Fable-'Silas Marner,' " in his* George Eliot's Early Novels: The Limits of Realism, *University of California Press, 1968, 269 p.*

Lilian Haddakin   (essay date 1970)

[*In the following essay, Haddakin explores Wordsworthian overtones in* Silas Marner *and discusses Eliot's integration of legendary and realistic modes in the work.*]

'The first 100 pages are very sad, almost oppressive . . . I wish the picture had been a more cheery one,' John Blackwood regretfully, and rather regrettably, observed [as quoted in *The George Eliot Letters,* edited by Gordon S. Haight, 1954-1955] after reading—'with the greatest admiration', nevertheless—the manuscript of the first part of *Silas Marner.* Perhaps he was less ready than he should have been to trust the author's assurance, given as early as the final paragraph of Chapter 2, of a happy ending:

> But about the Christmas of that fifteenth year, a second great change came over Marner's life, and his history became blent in a singular manner with the life of his neighbours.

Blackwood's comment shows the naïvety of one who regards a novel as something like an extension of life. The sentence quoted from *Silas Marner* has naïvety of a different order; it is the note of the legendary tale, in which it is permissible—and, indeed, proper—to indicate in advance the broad pattern that is going to emerge.

Silas Marner perhaps gives more unalloyed pleasure to the modern reader than any of George Eliot's other works. It is both fresh and mellow, and it wins much goodwill. Not that the often-remarked 'fairy-tale' element in the book discourages the exercise of the critical faculty and lulls the reader into over-facile acceptance. *Silas Marner* has also won critical approval and has been acclaimed a 'minor masterpiece'. And the strain of realistic pastoral typified by the scenes at the Rainbow Inn has been remarked no less than the strain of 'fairy-tale'.

Minor it doubtless is in comparison with that major masterpiece, *Middlemarch.* But what I wish to do in this essay is not to ask what makes the later work 'major' and the earlier one 'minor', but to define the peculiar quality of *Silas Marner.* It clearly stands apart from *Romola* and the works that follow. And although, no less clearly, it has a good deal in common with *Adam Bede* and *The Mill on the Floss,* which immediately precede it, the satisfaction it offers is in some important ways different from that which we get from these two works.

Some readers may think that to analyse *Silas Marner* is to break a butterfly upon a wheel. But *Silas Marner* is not a butterfly. It is a big thing, except in the number of pages needed to tell the story. It is strong and profound, and, although evidently very simple in some ways in comparison with nearly all George Eliot's other works, it has its own complexity. As a whole, it is as firm as it is delicate, and the sense it gives of a rounded rendering of simplicities is achieved by a complex literary art that unites several heterogeneous elements. It deals with great and 'difficult' issues under the guise of a legendary tale, realistically treated, so that the outcome is, from one point of view, a tale of old-fashioned village life. The 'great questions'—of the 'primary affections' and their workings, of religion and superstition and class—are embodied in the story of an obscure weaver who, expelled from one community through a false accusation of theft, and finding himself an alien in the community to which he migrates, first becomes a miser, then is robbed of his gold, but 'blessed' with a foundling child in its place, and at length, through her, is emotionally healed and firmly linked with the village community.

We know, because George Eliot has said so, that *Silas Marner* had a different kind of origin from that of her other works. I do not propose to elaborate an argument along the lines of *post hoc, ergo propter hoc;* but it is a significant fact that *Silas Marner* reads as if it had a different origin from, say, *Adam Bede.* While it is partly the result of sustained reflection ('my mind dwelt on the subject', George Eliot characteristically says), and is marked by the deliberate and thorough craftsmanship that, in this author, always accompanies such reflection, it also—and this is obviously what sets it apart from her other fiction—comes from something spontaneous and unreflective, something not only chronologically prior but, I think, logically so as well. This 'something'—the author writes of a 'sudden inspiration'—not only is not lost as a result of later reflection, but apparently guides the reflection and does a great deal to determine the total structure of the book.

Some of the author's comments in her letters and journal may help us to see more clearly, by disengaging them, some of the strands that make up this fiction (which she consistently refers to as a 'story', not a 'novel'). In using these comments I am not concerned with their bearing on the evolution of the work during what she felt to be its slow advance, but with what they can suggest as we scrutinize the finished work with them in mind.

On 28 November 1860 George Eliot records in her journal that she is writing a story, the idea of which has recently come to her and 'thrust itself' between her and the other book that she was meditating. It is already named: *Silas Marner, the Weaver of Raveloe.* She first mentions the work to her publisher in a letter of 12 January 1861:

> I am writing a story which came *across* my other plans by a sudden inspiration . . . It is a story of old-fashioned village life, which has unfolded itself from the merest millet-seed of thought.

On 24 February, after learning his reaction to Part I, she tells him more about the 'sudden inspiration'. The idea for the story sprang from a visual recollection:

> It came to me first of all, quite suddenly, as a sort of legendary tale, suggested by my recollection of having once, in early childhood, seen a linen-weaver with a bag on his back.

That she remembered something else besides the bag on his back we learn from Blackwood's account of a conversation with her [quoted in Haight] a few weeks after the publication of the book: '*Silas Marner* sprang from her childish recollection of a man with a stoop and expression of face that led her to think he was an alien from his fellows.' Part of what she remembered seeing was a facial expression which she had instantaneously 'construed'. The symbolism proper to a legendary tale was already potentially there in the burdened man with the alien look. And for the mature George Eliot the condition of being alien from one's fellows (in itself a metaphorical burden) was a rich theme to explore.

As her mind dwelt on the subject, she tells Blackwood in the letter of 24 February 1861, she 'became inclined to a more realistic treatment'. In its immediate context this must mean, primarily, 'more realistic than the treatment of the subject to be expected in a legendary tale', which squares with her earlier description of *Silas Marner* as 'a story of old-fashioned village life'. The linen-weaver gained a local habitation and a name, and also a quite precise historical setting.

But 'a more realistic treatment' has other implications as well, if we take the phrase in conjunction with certain other remarks, which come immediately before it:

> I should not have believed that anyone would have been interested in it but myself (since Wil-

liam Wordsworth is dead) if Mr Lewes had not been strongly arrested by it. But I hope you will not find it at all a sad story as a whole, since it sets—or is intended to set—in a strong light the remedial influences of pure, natural human relations. The Nemesis is a very mild one. I have felt all through as if the story would have lent itself best to metrical rather than prose fiction, especially in all that relates to the psychology of Silas; except that, under that treatment, there could not be an equal play of humour.

I shall not waste time in speculating on what might have happened if George Eliot had tried to write *Silas Marner* in verse, on the model of 'Michael', the poem from which she took her epigraph. The book has strong Wordsworthian affinities, which I shall come to later, though in some important respects it is very far indeed from being a kind of 'Michael' in prose. The author's feeling that 'the story would have lent itself best to metrical rather than prose fiction' seems to me to raise questions quite distinct from Wordsworth.

A desire for the play of humour was evidently an important factor, even if not the sole decisive one. Mrs. Joan Bennett [in her *George Eliot: Her Mind and Her Art,* 1948] (who puts in a word for Wordsworth's humour) believes that George Eliot 'shared the widespread mid-nineteenth-century view that "metrical composition" implied a peculiar solemnity'. But even if the novelist was blind to Wordsworth's humorous vein it is unlikely that the humour of, say, Chaucer, Crabbe, and Browning could have escaped her. Nor would their realism have been likely to do so, or their ability to render speech in verse with an air of authenticity. I would prefer to connect George Eliot's impulse towards the free play of humour with her inclination to 'a more realistic *treatment*' and to see the humour of *Silas Marner* as part of its realism. And 'realism', for George Eliot, would presumably also involve a much fuller use of homely circumstantial detail than she herself could well have managed in a verse-tale (which is not, of course, to suggest that all the homely details in *Silas Marner* are 'realistically' used—the broken pot that Silas sticks together and keeps as a memorial shows that this is not so). More important still, 'realism', for George Eliot, involves rendering the spoken word with an air of authenticity. Numerous poets—as well as the ones I have named above—have given us successful metrical renderings of speech; but George Eliot's verse never does so.

It is significant that she felt the appropriateness of verse 'especially in all that relates to the psychology of Silas'. ('Psychology', we must remind ourselves by the way, connotes the 'real', but not necessarily the 'realistic'.) On the printed page, after he leaves Lantern Yard at the end of Chapter 1, Silas is given nothing in direct speech until he bursts in upon the company at the Rainbow in Chapter 7 gasping the words 'Robbed! I've been robbed!' (His only previously recorded piece of direct speech during his life at Raveloe is in Chapter 1, when he says 'Good night' to Jem Rodney, the mole-catcher, upon emerging from a cataleptic trance.) Between Chapter 2 and his appearance at the Red House with Eppie in his arms in Chapter 13 he is laconic in the extreme, as his encounters with Mr.

Macey and Dolly Winthrop show. It is scarcely an exaggeration to say that in looking after Eppie he is compelled virtually to relearn the use of speech ('the tones that stirred Silas's heart grew articulate, and called for more distinct answers'). Or, rather, he recollects it, for this development illustrates the author's statement that 'As the child's mind was growing into knowledge, his mind was growing into memory' (ch. 14). In the second part of the book he is, necessarily, much more fluent.

The psychology of Silas during almost fifteen mute years is powerfully rendered by other means than dialogue. Other means were needed, for he is alone when he discovers the theft of his gold and when he finds the infant Eppie on his hearth (the two big 'scenes' in the rendering of his psychology). Those developments in him which are gradual—his insect-like obsession with his loom and his habit of sitting counting his loved guineas—are also solitary.

Not all of the means by which we are enabled to see into Silas's nature are 'realistic', though several of the most impressive passages are starkly factual. Some of the material could, no doubt, have been expressed by George Eliot in competent, if rhythmically unexciting, blank verse. The rendering of Silas's psychology, especially in Part I, is 'poetic' partly in that it freely employs devices more usually associated (at least before the age of George Eliot) with metrical composition. When we say this we are not merely repeating the time-worn truth that the use of metre does not of itself produce a poem and, conversely, that 'the poetic' can be articulated without metre. 'Poetry', said Walter Bagehot, 'should be memorable and emphatic, intense, and *soon over.*' We expect to find these qualities in a metrical fiction to a greater degree than we find them in *Silas Marner.* But it does seem that, both because of its near-poetic conception and because of its free employment of devices more usually associated with verse than with prose, *Silas Marner* is *more easily* memorable, *more* emphatic, *more* intense and *sooner over* than it could otherwise have been. One of the notable things about this work is that it expands in your memory, and individual parts of it expand, so that when you turn back to the book itself you are surprised by its brevity. (Yet it gives an impression of leisureliness, too—one can fairly say that no man ever wished it shorter.)

It seems clear that nothing essentially 'poetic' is lost by Silas's being presented in prose. Moreover, the 'poetic' impinges significantly, though unobtrusively, on the texture of those chapters in which the treatment is more realistic.

The presence or absence of authentically rendered direct speech in this or that chapter in Part I seems to me to have an interesting bearing on the form of the work in another way, too. The absence of direct speech from the chapters devoted to Silas provides a verbal analogue of solitude. At the same time, contained in the solitude/society contrast which Part I as a whole expresses, there is a 'class' contrast, rendered in speech, exemplifying the barriers that exist within the tightly-knit community of Raveloe. There is an abundance of dialogue in Part I. The speakers fall into two groups, each with its distinctive mode of speech: the Cass family and their associates, and the villagers. In much of Part I (broadly, up to Chapter 11, which presents

the New Year's Eve dance at the Casses' home, where representatives of both groups are assembled by the author in readiness for Silas's entrance with Eppie in Chapter 13), 'upper' and 'lower', though both groups are articulate, are almost wholly insulated from each other on the printed page. The villagers themselves are given nothing in direct speech until the conversation at the Rainbow (ch. 6), though—as if they could be heard talking in the distance—the flavour of their speech has been conveyed in such 'reported' locutions as 'if you could only speak the devil fair enough, he might save you the cost of the doctor' or 'No, no; it was no stroke that would let a man stand on his legs, like a horse between the shafts, and then walk off as soon as you can say "Gee!" ' It is in this 'distant' talk that we chiefly see the subdued play of humour in the first two chapters.

On the other hand, some of the methods (notably metaphor) which are used to reveal Silas's psychology are also used, though more sparingly, in the other chapters, the 'social' chapters. They constitute one of the linking devices in a most intricate pattern of interlocking contrasts and parallels—a pattern that requires the reader to grasp the many juxtapositions of literal and metaphorical, and also to make numerous transpositions and transvaluations. There is no hard and fast line between fact and symbol in the work as a whole. Gold is both factual and symbolic. W. J. Harvey has shown [in his *Art of George Eliot,* 1961] that an image may be converted into literal fact later, as is the comparison between weaver and child:

> A weaver who finds hard words in his hymn-book knows nothing of abstractions; as the little child knows nothing of parental love, but only knows one face and one lap towards which it stretches its arms for refuge and nurture.
>
> (ch. 2)

And Silas's feeling that half-earned guineas are like unborn children foreshadows [in Harvey's words] 'the close symbolic connection between the golden-haired Eppie and the miser's hoard'.

The Wordsworthian affinities of *Silas Marner* seem to me to go far beyond what is conveyed in the epigraph from 'Michael', important as this is:

> A child, more than all other gifts
> That earth can offer to declining man,
> Brings hope with it, and forward-looking
> thoughts.

Mr. Peter Coveney observes [in his *The Image of Childhood,* 1967]: 'The force of the book lies in the presentation of Silas Marner, the "declining man" in question'; and he adds, more debatably: 'The weight, however, of the moral must fall on the protagonist, on the agency of Marner's redemption, on the child who bestows the "forward-looking thoughts".' This is a fair enough comment only if one accepts the epigraph as a clue to the whole 'moral' of the book. In fact, however, George Eliot would have needed several epigraphs to epitomize her complex moral. The choice of this particular one seems to owe something at least to Blackwood's finding the earlier chapters of the work 'sombre'. The author reassured him very promptly, and the epigraph, which she sent him a little later, when

Silas Marner was nearly finished, seems designed, in part, to reassure the public, too, that the picture is not going to be wholly gloomy. She was only anxious lest her epigraph indicated the story too distinctly, and it was now Blackwood's turn to reassure her: 'The motto giving to some extent the keynote to the story does not I think signify in this case, as whenever the child appears her mission is felt.'

Had she decided upon a multiple epigraph (a practice adopted by Crabbe and Clough, for example), she could have chosen several other passages from Wordsworth, all of them equally relevant to *Silas Marner,* though not all relating to the *story.*

To begin with, Silas himself is 'Wordsworthian'. He is the kind of man Wordsworth might have come across on the 'lonely roads', one of those

> Souls that appear to have no depth at all
> To careless eyes.
>
> [*The Prelude*]

Hence, no doubt, George Eliot's feeling that no one but herself would be interested in the story, 'since William Wordsworth is dead'. Many touches—especially in Chapter 2—confirm such a view of Silas.

Moreover, the world of *Silas Marner,* notwithstanding its 'fairy-tale' aspect, is

> the very world, which is the world
> Of all of us,—the place where, in the end,
> We find our happiness, or not at all!
>
> [*The Prelude*]

And we may add that the world seems to have been so for George Eliot in a more thorough-going sense than it was for Wordsworth. After he leaves Lantern Yard, Silas's treasures, of both kinds, are laid up on earth.

The list of possible Wordsworthian epigraphs could be much extended, but one other quotation will suffice here (it is from 'The Old Cumberland Beggar'):

> We have all of us one human heart.

In *Silas Marner* this statement is qualified, without being eroded. The unity of the human heart in the central Wordsworthian sense is there. The 'essential passions' link man with man; and 'pure, natural human relations' exert 'remedial influences'. But (as well as, most evidently, showing us different individual hearts and different types of heart) George Eliot qualifies the poet's statement by revealing another kind of 'oneness'. She reveals a unity—or better, a whole range of unities—beneath apparent differences. They are not all soothing to contemplate. Godfrey Cass, for instance, though somewhat scornful of the credulity of the villagers, is no less credulous than they in his personal 'religion' of 'Favourable Chance'. He is Everyman, too, in his everyday, unconscious superstition, as we see from his way of dealing with his fears that his brother has stolen his horse:

> Instead of trying to still his fears he encouraged
> them, with that superstitious impression which
> clings to us all, that if we expect evil very strong-
> ly it is the less likely to come; and when he heard
> a horse approaching at a trot, and saw a hat ris-

ing above a hedge beyond an angle of the lane,
he felt as if his conjuration had succeeded.

(ch. 8)

And there are parallels to Silas's narrowing and hardening in his solitude:

> His life had reduced itself to the functions of
> weaving and hoarding, without any contempla-
> tion of an end towards which the functions tend-
> ed. The same sort of process has perhaps been
> undergone by wiser men, when they have been
> cut off from faith and love—only, instead of a
> loom and a heap of guineas, they have had some
> erudite research, some ingenious project, or
> some well-knit theory.

(ch. 2)

The unities may be some way beneath the surface, and they may easily be overlooked or unsuspected, as the Wordsworthian unity seldom can be. Often George Eliot is explicit in pointing her parallels, but she has less direct methods, too, of saying '*De te fabula*'.

She is Wordsworthian also in her insistence on the great power of memory to help the working of the affections and to bind the life of the individual into a unity. Backward-looking thoughts are as important in Silas's development as forward-looking ones, even though it is to the latter kind that the epigraph directs our attention. Indeed, it is, to an important extent, the power of memory that enables the 'forward-looking' situation to develop, for Silas momentarily identifies the newly-found Eppie with his long-dead little sister—an identification as crucial, in its way, as the more conspicuous gold-and-curls identification.

His remembered knowledge of 'medicinal herbs and their preparation' has its importance, too, on more than one occasion and in very different ways. I choose this example partly because it shows George Eliot telling us that the care of the foundling was not the only means by which Silas could have been reunited with his fellow-men; partly because it involves the relation of man to inanimate nature, which is one of the themes of *Silas Marner,* even if not a major one; and partly because it illustrates how the author can use a motif both as a recurrent element in a formal pattern (this motif links diverse phases in Silas's life) and as the conveyer of a 'moral' (the herbal lore is made to bear a different moral and emotional significance each time it appears).

Silas has gained this knowledge from his mother ('a little store of wisdom which she had imparted to him as a solemn bequest'), but in his Lantern Yard days 'his inherited delight to wander through the fields in search of foxglove and dandelion and coltsfoot, began to wear to him the character of a temptation' (ch. 1). Then, quite early in his life at Raveloe, at about the time that he begins to love guineas, he recognizes in the cobbler's wife 'the terrible symptoms of heart-disease and dropsy, which he had witnessed as the precursors of his mother's death', feels 'a rush of pity at the mingled sight and remembrance', and brings her 'a simple preparation of foxglove' (ch. 2). This 'resurgent memory', which could have led to 'some fellowship with his neighbours', has unfortunate aftereffects, for the villagers (in accordance with the 'old demon-worship' which is part of their total religion) flock to him for charms and cures and do not believe him when he says that he knows no charms and can work no cures, so that the 'repulsion' between him and his neighbours is heightened. The herbs are then forgotten until years later, when he is out in the fields with Eppie. She brings him flowers, whereupon

> Silas began to look for the once-familiar herbs again; and as the leaves, with their unchanged outline and markings, lay on his palm, there was a sense of crowding remembrances from which he turned away timidly, taking refuge in Eppie's little world, that lay lightly on his enfeebled spirit.
>
> (ch. 14)

Finally, how far is Eppie herself Wordsworthian, and in what ways? She seems to me to be connected not only with the Wordsworthian Child but also with the Wordsworthian Maid. I should like to consider the implications of a passage in Part II on the education of Eppie before dealing with her as a type of Childhood, for the latter theme will take us a long way from Wordsworth as we relate the Child to the total context in which she appears.

The passage from Part II shows how Eppie, now eighteen, became the 'village maiden' that she is:

> The tender and peculiar love with which Silas had reared her in almost inseparable companionship with himself, aided by the seclusion of their dwelling, had preserved her from the lowering influences of the village talk and habits, and had kept her mind in that freshness which is sometimes falsely supposed to be an invariable attribute of rusticity. Perfect love has a breath of poetry which can exalt the relations of the least-instructed human beings; and this breath of poetry had surrounded Eppie from the time when she had followed the bright gleam that beckoned her to Silas's hearth; so that it is not surprising if, in other things besides her delicate prettiness, she was not quite a common village maiden, but had a touch of refinement and fervour which came from no other teaching than that of tenderly-nurtured unvitiated feeling.
>
> (ch. 16)

Eppie's education (apart from her two hours daily at the dame school, for we are in 'the very world') is the work of Nature. But George Eliot insists firmly that the Nature which chiefly counts here is human nature, not inanimate nature, and that country life is not, *per se*, ennobling. The 'passions' of her rustics in the book as a whole are not conspicuously 'incorporated with the beautiful and permanent forms of nature', and while she would agree with Wordsworth that the manners of rural life 'germinate' from 'elementary feelings', the elementary feelings of *her* rustics appear to come largely from being 'pressed close by primitive wants'. Whatever is idealized in the account of Eppie's education, the manners of rural life are not (though there are no grounds for supposing that the author is taxing Wordsworth, whose poetry she knew well, with the false supposition that freshness of mind is 'an invariable attribute of rusticity').

Silas, like Nature in Wordsworth's poem, 'Three years she grew in sun and shower', has taken the Child to himself; she 'kindles' him more than she is kindled by him, perhaps, and he does not 'restrain' her as Nature restrains Lucy; but the Stone-pits, where they live together, may be seen as a version of Wordsworth's 'happy dell'.

It is with Eppie the representative of Wordsworthian Childhood that Mr. Coveney is concerned in his discussion of *Silas Marner.* Eppie is a 'presence', stirring tenderness and awe in Silas, feeding his sense of a Power presiding over his life, forcing his thoughts onwards and 'warming him into joy'. 'In idea', says Mr. Coveney, 'the meaning of Romantic childhood is well enough conveyed', but he finds the presentation of the child as a character in the novel inadequate: 'But the object called upon to sustain the poetic weight staggers beneath it, totters, in fact "toddles" beneath it. There is a failure in the characterization of the central image.'

I doubt whether, for George Eliot's purposes, artistic and moral, Eppie needs to be very firmly established as a 'character' in Part I. (In Part II she does need to be, and is.) She certainly has to be established as a 'blessing'— welcomed by Silas and rejected by Godfrey—and as a 'blessing' in this sense she is firmly established, for you can present a blessing in terms of the man who is blessed. And this is what George Eliot does. From the beginning of Chapter 12, when the child first appears in the Raveloe lanes in her mother's arms, to the end of Part I is little more than one-seventh of the whole work, and much of this seventh is occupied with other people's attitudes to Eppie (those of her mother, Silas, Godfrey, Dolly Winthrop, the Kimbles and numerous unnamed persons) and also with many people's reactions to Silas after he has adopted her. Admittedly there is some idealization in this at certain points, which, nevertheless, the tone of the legendary tale, never wholly laid aside for very long, does something to render acceptable.

Mr. Coveney's objection to the rendering of the child Eppie, in so far as it is a literary one, seems to be an objection to the author's reliance on a too-easy response from the reader. Baby-talk is used; in effect, when Eppie says 'gug-gug-gug' we are expected to find it 'sweet'. Sometimes this reliance is ill-concealed under the guise of factuality; the word 'little', Mr. Coveney notices, is seldom used solely to convey a fact when George Eliot applies it to children. There is certainly substance in his literary objections, though they do not seem to me to be as weighty as he makes them out, since I think he exaggerates Eppie's prominence in the fiction as a whole.

I doubt, however, whether the matter is purely literary. There clearly is an element of sweetness and softness in *Silas Marner;* and it is vitally necessary both to the moral conveyed and to the picture of life given in the work. Sweetness and softness are not qualities that twentieth-century readers accept very readily in morals or in pictures of life; so that, when we are confronted with a Victorian fiction in which these qualities are conspicuous, it is perhaps difficult for us to exercise that discrimination which constitutes critical justice. But to equate sweetness and softness with sentimentality would be obtuse.

To put it in another way, there is a strain of 'cosiness' in the book. Silas's joys, when he gets them, are small and confined in so far as they come from 'eating o' the same bit, and drinking o' the same cup'; little things are suffused with sentiment. But George Eliot seems to me to have answered the objection to 'cosiness' as connoting triviality:

> Nancy, used all her life to plenteous circumstances and the privileges of 'respectability', could not enter into all the pleasures which early nurture and habit connect with all the little aims and efforts of the poor who are born poor: to her mind, Eppie, in being restored to her birthright, was entering on a too long withheld but unquestionable good.
>
> (ch. 19)

In this chapter, in which Godfrey and Nancy come to claim Eppie, the girl could certainly not be adequately described as 'cosy'.

But the Wordsworthian affinities of *Silas Marner,* important as they are, should not be exaggerated. Ultimately, what a scrutiny of these affinities shows is that the work is something far more original than simply a Wordsworthian tale in prose. And if we give undue prominence to the motif of the Child we distort both the theme and the design of the whole. *Silas Marner* has a broader theme. To state this in the most abstract and general terms, the book is about feelings and the forms in which they incorporate themselves. Silas's quasi-paternal love is one feeling among many; his fostering of the child is one form among the many forms that embody feeling.

George Eliot is explicit about religious feelings and religious forms:

> To people accustomed to reason about the forms in which their religious feeling has incorporated itself, it is difficult to enter into that simple, untaught state of mind in which the form and the feeling have never been severed by an act of reflection.
>
> (ch. 1)

In *Silas Marner* as a whole, many feelings are shown incorporating themselves in many forms; and few of the characters sever feeling and form by an act of reflection (to some extent, Silas himself and Dolly Winthrop eventually do). The same kind of feeling may be differently incorporated in different communities (the religious forms of Lantern Yard are strikingly different from those of Raveloe); the feelings of the same man may be incorporated in different forms at different times, as those of Silas most notably are. His story is that of feeling ('the sap of affection') all but dried up as his life is nearly reduced to the 'unquestioning activity of a spinning insect'—non-human existence, both animate and inanimate, is a constantly-tapped source of metaphor—yet surviving, nevertheless, and making fresh growth as it partly finds and partly creates forms which can supply it with both framework and nourishment.

His 'strange history' (the narrative form of the book) is that of a double metamorphosis. The first metamorphosis into a miser, following his expulsion from the Lantern Yard community, is essentially, though not solely, a change in his inward life, 'as that of any fervid nature must be when it has fled, or been condemned to solitude'. This is the phase in which natural affection almost withers away, though he still *has* feeling for the earthenware pot in which he fetches water from the well; it has been his 'companion' for twelve years,

> always lending its handle to him in the early morning, so that its form had an expression for him of willing helpfulness, and the impress of its handle on his palm gave a satisfaction mingled with that of having the fresh clear water.
>
> (ch. 2)

So, after accidentally breaking it, 'he stuck the bits together and propped the ruin in its old place for a memorial'. This 'little incident' illuminates the drab phase in which the monotony of daily drudgery at his loom alternates with 'nightly revelry' as he pours out his hoarded guineas, bathes his hands in them and rejoices in them as in a 'golden wine'. The loom works on his outer form, which is all his neighbours know: his 'face and figure shrank and bent themselves into a constant mechanical relation to the objects of his life, so that he produced the same sort of impression as a handle or a crooked tube, which has no meaning standing apart' (ch. 2). The guineas on which his nightly ritual centres provide a repository—an unnatural one, and therefore bad—for his feelings: 'His gold, as he hung over it and saw it grow, gathered his power of loving together into a hard isolation like its own' (ch. 5).

His second metamorphosis, into a loving foster-father, with all that this implies in the way of reciprocal 'blessings' and 'gifts', is swifter than the first, but by no means instantaneous. It depends initially on the agonizing loss of his gold, and then on 'pure, natural human relations', the growth of which is necessarily gradual and involves a multitude of interconnecting forms, domestic, social, and religious; and being, in the broadest sense, 'social', it also involves verbal forms, as the first metamorphosis did not.

The image of the alien-looking man with the burden, which provides the 'millet-seed of thought', thus grows into a legendary tale which is also a picture of 'real life'. It does so by answering the questions that the appearance of the man suggests: How did he become alien, and hence solitary? How can he cease to be solitary? What does the burden mean, and how can he get rid of it?

Among other things, the burden symbolizes the unjust accusation of having stolen 'treasure'. Silas later amasses treasure, which is stolen from him. The child comes in place of the treasure, and he ceases to be solitary. Later still, the treasure he hoarded is recovered, but it now has a different value because it is associated with other feelings and can be used on behalf of the child.

One of the chief links between the legendary sphere and that of real life is Godfrey Cass. As a character he is 'realistic' (though some of the local means by which he is presented are not). So far as the design of the work goes, he is the figure who forms the principal contrast with Silas: Godfrey rejects the child; Silas accepts her. Other contrasts follow from this. The plot becomes twofold—Silas's story and Godfrey's story being linked by the child—and it has a very marked pattern. This markedness of pattern might not be wholly acceptable in a work of single-minded realism. True, double stories are common enough in novels of the nineteenth century; but as the brevity of *Silas Marner* (largely a consequence of its 'legendary' element) throws more emphasis on the plot, the pattern appears with unaccustomed clarity. The obviousness of the pattern, with all its coincidences and other improbabilities, is acceptable only partly as 'the narrative means to a moral end' [in the words of Barbara Hardy in her *Novels of George Eliot,* 1957]; it is acceptable also as belonging to a non-realistic literary mode—a neat and strongly marked pattern is something we associate with a legendary tale; and a legendary tale, though it can contain plenty of 'moral', or poetic justice, does not exist for the sake of its moral.

The legendary conception thus plays an important part in determining the narrative organization of some of the 'real-life' material, though clearly not all of it. It does little towards organizing the Nancy Lammeter element. But Nancy, a sensitive and firm character sensitively and firmly presented, is vitally important in the rendering of 'feeling and form' on the realistic level. Her feeling is incorporated in various traditional forms, some of them important in their implications (she would have accepted Godfrey's child at any time if she had known it was his), and some trivial (sisters should dress alike). Her forms, even the trivial ones, are living forms because they are suffused with feeling. They are generally adequate for Nancy in all that relates to her own social sphere, but they are inadequate for dealing with the actuality, social and emotional, that she confronts in the persons of Silas and Eppie in Chapter 19, when the forms to which she is accustomed prevent her from entering into the feelings of 'the poor who are born poor'.

If Godfrey is one of the chief links between the legendary and the realistic, Dolly Winthrop is a 'realistic' character charged with the important function of helping Silas to evolve and to articulate a view of life that will 'explain' his own history. She and Silas are the two characters in the work who most desire an adequate 'view of life', and who *do* speculate, however 'untaught' and 'simple' they may be. Mr. John Holloway has an interesting discussion of this aspect of *Silas Marner* in *The Victorian Sage.* He remarks that, in Dolly's 'speculative pronouncement' to Silas in Chapter 16, arising from her feeling that 'Them above has got a deal tenderer heart nor what I've got', 'we have in all essentials a version of the author's own world view', and he adds: 'To be expressible in a simple or in a subtle form, so as to suit the needs and capacities of the most sophisticated people and the least, is perhaps essential to any significant view of life.' But it is not quite true to say that 'We see . . . how things move according to a hidden plan'. We see how Silas and Dolly come to feel that things move according to a hidden plan. George Eliot always 'places' the views of her characters (as Mr. Holloway, indeed, observes). An 'adequate' view is adequate for particular characters in particular circumstances; and the circumstances in which they formulate the view, as well as the terms they use, are part of the author's method of conveying *her* view. To say this is not to quibble. Silas's

and Dolly's formulations are made in broadly religious terms. George Eliot's formulation, in *Silas Marner,* is made by means of a legendary tale (roughly, a literary analogue of religious myth) combined with a picture of the actualities of religious life and religious forms.

Dolly is notably free from the 'demon-worship' in which George Eliot shows most of the villagers participating whenever their words and actions are concerned with charms, cures, a fear of the 'evil eye', and so forth. Characteristically, she includes other forms of demon-worship, too—metaphorical forms—and this is wholly consonant with both the message and the method of the work. Godfrey's first wife is 'enslaved' to the 'demon Opium'; and Godfrey's heart (in a sentence of biblical reminiscence) is 'visited by cruel wishes, that seemed to enter, and depart, and enter again, like demons who had found in him a ready-garnished home' (ch. 3).

In one of its aspects *Silas Marner* is a web in which religion (including superstition), viewed as part of 'real life', crosses the threads of fairy tale. The opening paragraphs, for instance, contain all the elements of the author's initial 'childish recollection' (the linen-weaver bent under the burden of his bag, the alien look), and they have a certain tone of 'once upon a time'. But we soon learn that the action is to take place, not just in a 'far-off time', but 'in the early years of this century'; and Silas is 'such a linen-weaver' as the whole race of weavers of his day. It is made clear, too, that the mystery attaching to the race of weavers is put there by the superstitious fears of rustics who are actually living a life that, psychologically, contains some of the grimmer elements of a fairy tale. And, in the local phrasing throughout the work, religion, superstition, fairy tale, and hard fact are all combined.

Silas's cataleptic trances epitomize the method. George Eliot could have devised some other means of bringing about the unjust accusation and the entrance of Eppie into the cottage, so we are justified in asking why she has chosen this one. The trances are variously explained by different people at different points in the story. In Lantern Yard they are generally believed to show that Silas is 'a brother selected for a peculiar discipline', though William Dane disingenuously says that 'to him, this trance looked more like a visitation of Satan than a proof of divine favour'. The Raveloe villagers are unsure whether to call them 'fits' or to suppose that 'there might be such a thing as a man's soul being loose from his body . . . and that was how folks got over-wise, for they went to school in this shell-less state to those who could teach them more than their neighbours could learn with their five senses and the parson' (ch. 1). Silas himself does not understand them, and apparently gives up trying to do so. Eppie does not try to explain them, but accepts them as something that has to be dealt with; when she and Silas go to look for Lantern Yard and find it has vanished, she is 'on the watch lest one of her father's strange attacks should come on'. In the 'legendary tale', catalepsy is a curse or spell, something corresponding—at first—to the gift of the wicked fairy in the story of the Sleeping Beauty. Shortly before Eppie enters his cottage, Silas is standing by the open door, and he puts his hand on the latch to close it, but he did not close it: he was arrested . . . by the invisible wand of catalepsy, and stood like a graven image, with wide but sightless eyes, holding open his door, powerless to resist either the good or evil that might enter there.

(ch. 12)

But in the long run it does not matter whether good or evil fairies, whether Chance or Fate or Providence or 'Them above' are the mental 'forms' favoured by the interpreters. The solution for human problems, George Eliot is saying, must be looked for in human nature itself. To apply the notion of feeling and form to the literary work as a whole, *Silas Marner* is the imaginative form in which the author has incorporated her feeling about human nature and the human condition.

Silas Marner is a very tightly integrated work of art. One finds this experimentally in trying to convey one's sense of what it is and of the author's mode of proceeding. I fix my attention on what seems to be a significant piece of the whole. But this piece is like the centre of a spider's web. It has not one significance, but many, radiating in all directions. And I am left with an awareness that, for many of the pieces I have chosen for comment, there are others that would have served equally well, and, further, that in the course of exploring these others I might have come upon facets of the work, or manifestations of George Eliot's literary power, which the selection that I have in fact made has left unexplored. (pp. 59-77)

> Lilian Haddakin, " 'Silas Marner'," in Critical Essays on George Eliot, *edited by Barbara Hardy, Barnes & Noble, Inc., 1970, pp. 59-77.*

R. T. Jones (essay date 1970)

[*In the following excerpt, Jones contends that, despite its departure from the strictly realistic style of Eliot's other novels,* Silas Marner *remains true to life in its depiction of human motives.*]

What impresses the reader who turns to *Silas Marner* immediately after *The Mill on the Floss* is not, I think, that it is a better novel, but that it is very different from it—almost a different form of art, so that it seems unsatisfactory to call both books simply 'novels'. Perhaps the word 'tale' could be used of the later work, to suggest its conciseness, impersonality and singleness, and its formal affinity with, say, D. H. Lawrence's 'tales' rather than his 'novels'.

In most of George Eliot's novels we can recognize, or suspect, a need to work out some part of her own experience, perhaps to explore possibilities of life that had at some time seemed to be open to her; and we can detect her emotional involvement in one or two characters, so that her struggle to gain our sympathetic comprehension for Maggie Tulliver, or Dorothea Brooke, has something of the pressure of a plea for understanding and sympathy for herself. We may sometimes resist this pressure, but it adds a certain strength to those novels, driving the novelist to exert her intelligence to the utmost in presenting such characters from the inside and making their apparent inconsistencies intelligible to the reader. But in *Silas Marner* she has complete control over her creation; her intelligence is more completely disengaged. Its strength is of a different kind.

Nathaniel Hawthorne called his *The House of the Seven Gables* a 'romance', and the term as he uses it might also be applied to *Silas Marner.* Here is the opening paragraph of Hawthorne's preface:

> When a writer calls his work a Romance, it need hardly be observed that he wishes to claim a certain latitude, both as to its fashion and material, which he would not have felt himself entitled to assume had he professed to be writing a Novel. The latter form of composition is presumed to aim at a very minute fidelity, not merely to the possible, but to the probable and ordinary course of man's experience. The former—while, as a work of art, it must rigidly submit itself to laws, and while it sins unpardonably so far as it may swerve aside from the truth of the human heart—has fairly a right to present that truth under circumstances, to a great extent, of the author's own choosing or creation. If he think fit, also, he may so manage his atmospherical medium as to bring out or mellow the lights and deepen and enrich the shadows of the picture. He will be wise, no doubt, to make a very moderate use of the privileges here stated, and, especially, to mingle the Marvellous rather as a slight, delicate and evanescent flavor, than as any portion of the actual substance of the dish offered to the public. He can hardly be said, however, to commit a literary crime even if he disregard this caution.

My concern is not, of course, to find a label for the book, a category into which it can be placed. But if we have in mind the distinctions that Hawthorne makes between a 'Romance' and a 'Novel', we may recognize more clearly the difference between *Silas Marner* and George Eliot's other works of fiction.

It begins—after an introductory paragraph—with this:

> In the early years of this century, such a linen-weaver, named Silas Marner, worked at his vocation in a stone cottage that stood among the nutty hedgerows near the village of Raveloe, and not far from the edge of a deserted stone-pit.

The sentence gives us the essential information as compactly and authoritatively as the opening of Chaucer's *Nun's Priest's Tale:*

> A povre wydwe, somdeel stape in age,
> Was whilom dwellyng in a narwe cotage,
> Biside a grove, stondynge in a dale.

It proceeds to this, the closing paragraph of the book:

> 'O father,' said Eppie, 'what a pretty home ours is! I think nobody could be happier than we are.'

—which, as a conclusion, can hardly be—and is certainly not offered by George Eliot as—minutely faithful to 'the probable and ordinary course of man's experience'; it is much nearer to the traditional ending of a story for children: 'and they lived happily ever after'.

The crucial event in the story is the appearance in Silas's

cottage—not long after the loss of his gold—of a little girl, whose mother has died in the snow. Silas, who has just undergone one of his occasional attacks of catalepsy but does not know it, has not seen the child come in.

> Turning towards the hearth, where the two logs had fallen apart, and sent forth only a red uncertain glimmer, he seated himself on his fireside chair, and was stooping to push his logs together, when, to his blurred vision, it seemed as if there were gold on the floor in front of the hearth. Gold!—his own gold—brought back to him as mysteriously as it had been taken away! He felt his heart begin to beat violently, and for a few moments he was unable to stretch out his hand and grasp the restored treasure. The heap of gold seemed to glow and get larger beneath his agitated gaze. He leaned forward at last, and stretched forth his hand; but instead of the hard coin with the familiar resisting outline, his fingers encountered soft warm curls. In utter amazement, Silas fell on his knees and bent his head low to examine the marvel: it was a sleeping child—a round, fair thing, with soft yellow rings all over its head.

Clearly George Eliot does not suggest, or suppose, that life is commonly found to be like this. The scene, with its fully explicit symbolism, is offered as an image of the process the book presents: the substitution of the child for the lost gold summarizes, or crystallizes, in a frankly 'contrived' scene, the transfer of Silas's affections from his sterile hoard of gold to the child who gives him a new and living relationship with the people among whom he lives.

But, despite the book's freedom from the usual constraints of the 'realistic' novel, it has its own very firm grasp of reality. Dunstan Cass's thoughts, when he enters the weaver's cottage and finds nobody there, are rendered with full attention to the question of how *that* mind, a rather stupid one, would really work in that situation—

> If the weaver was dead, who had a right to his money? Who would know where his money was hidden? *Who would know that anybody had come to take it away?* He went no farther into the subtleties of evidence: the pressing question, 'Where *is* the money?' now took such entire possession of him as to make him quite forget that the weaver's death was not a certainty. A dull mind, once arriving at an inference that flatters a desire, is rarely able to retain the impression that the notion from which the inference started was purely problematic.

If this book is a tale, a romance, or even a parable, it is evidently not merely a story in which allegorical figures move in an allegorical landscape. George Eliot's mind is continually revealing its habitual curiosity about why people behave as they do, and implying in the account of any one person's motives some more or less general comment on the way *our* minds work.

> Mr. Snell was correct in his surmise, that somebody else would remember the pedlar's earrings. For, on the spread of inquiry among the villagers, it was stated with gathering emphasis, that the parson had wanted to know whether the

pedlar wore ear-rings in his ears, and an impression was created that a great deal depended on the eliciting of this fact. Of course every one who heard the question, not having any distinct image of the pedlar as *without* ear-rings, immediately had an image of him *with* ear-rings, larger or smaller, as the case might be; and the image was presently taken for a vivid recollection, so that the glazier's wife, a well-intentioned woman, not given to lying, and whose house was among the cleanest in the village, was ready to declare, as sure as ever she meant to take the sacrament, the very next Christmas that was ever coming, that she had seen big ear-rings, in the shape of the young moon, in the pedlar's two ears; while Jinny Oates, the cobbler's daughter, being a more imaginative person, stated not only that she had seen them too, but that they made her blood creep, as it did at that very moment while there she stood.

The process by which a question can, so to speak, generate an answer, and an image turn into a certain recollection, is fully imagined—so fully that the very turns of phrase used by the people involved penetrate the narrative prose. The observed absurdity of the way in which people emphasize their certainty of uncertain facts, by insistent accentuation of circumstantial irrelevancies, is incorporated into the texture of the description—'the very next Christmas that was ever coming', 'at that very moment while there she stood'.

The 'romance', then, with its flavour of the marvellous, involves no thinness in the texture of reality, no relaxation of the author's grasp of the way things happen in the actual world. Everywhere in the quality of its prose this book displays that awareness of the way people do react, and that sympathetic and intellectual curiosity that we are accustomed to find in George Eliot's other works; that impulse to unite the particular observation and the general laws of human nature that so often expresses itself in some variant of the phrases 'Have we not all . . . ' or 'Which of us has not . . . '. Godfrey Cass is anxiously waiting for his brother to return—

> Instead of trying to still his fears, he encouraged them, with that superstitious impression which clings to us all, that if we expect evil very strongly it is the less likely to come . . .

—and the same consideration that makes Godfrey's state of mind intelligible to us has at the same time made us see a characteristic of our own, and perhaps of mankind. Sometimes the conjectured generalization may be more explicit, but it always seems to grow out of the particular incident that is being explained; here is Godfrey Cass, much later in the book:

> Meanwhile, why could he not make up his mind to the absence of children from a hearth brightened by such a wife? Why did his mind fly uneasily to that void, as if it were the sole reason why life was not thoroughly joyous to him? I suppose it is the way with all men and women who reach middle age without the clear perception that life never *can* be thoroughly joyous: under the vague dulness of the grey hours, dissatisfaction seeks

a definite object, and finds it in the privation of an untried good.

This discontent, in some measure, is a consequence of growing older, and that it is both unreasonable and inevitable that one tends to attach to some specific lack this discontent that was not originally the consequence of anything specific, is an observation that simultaneously leads us to understand Godfrey's feelings sympathetically and invites us to consider our own critically.

However *Silas Marner* may differ, then, from the author's other fictions, it is always quite recognizably hers. The relations I have indicated, in the texture of the prose, between the generalizing intelligence and the particularizing imagination, is characteristic of all her novels. Her concern, in this book, with the relation between a man and the community in which he is rooted, is also recognizable as one of her habitual preoccupations. It is treated here with a detachment that marks an advance from the sentimental treatment of the Poyser's distress at the prospect of moving to another parish, in *Adam Bede,* and even from the demonstration of the power of rootedness in Maggie Tulliver, in *The Mill on the Floss*—which, masterly as it is, makes no pretence of objectivity.

Silas makes his first appearance as one of

> certain pallid undersized men, who, by the side of the brawny country-folk, looked like the remnants of a disinherited race.

The tale is to be about his recovery of his inheritance—his inheritance as a man, a social being. But it is not only Silas's incapacity for making full human contact with the people around him that alienates him from the country people of Raveloe. We are given the causes of that incapacity very soon—the account of the events that have led to his loss of faith and his removal to Raveloe; but what the first paragraphs of the novel give us, with generalizing precision, is the incapacity of the Raveloe people for accepting the stranger. The traditional wisdom of a rooted rural community has, evidently, its own constricting limitations.

> In that far-off time superstition clung easily round every person or thing that was at all unwonted, or even intermittent and occasional merely, like the visits of the pedlar or the knife-grinder. No one knew where wandering men had their homes or their origin; and how was a man to be explained unless you at least knew somebody who knew his father and mother?

The country people of Raveloe are, of course, the community in which, if anywhere, Silas must find his place and his identity; but we are not allowed to suppose that they have any special virtues merely because they *are* a rural community. Silas has himself been a member of an urban community; he has been driven out of it, as an innocent man may be driven out of any society in which a less innocent man may seek his own advantage at his expense, but it has been a real community in which an individual had his place and could form and establish his own identity.

> His life, before he came to Raveloe, had been filled with the movement, the mental activity,

and the close fellowship, which, in that day as in this, marked the life of an artisan early incorporated in a narrow religious sect, where the poorest layman has the chance of distinguishing himself by gifts of speech, and has, at the very least, the weight of a silent voter in the government of his community.

It has been, too, a place where his deepest pieties were anchored, as Maggie Tulliver's had been in and around St Ogg's and the Mill: it is not only a rural community that can provide this stability. In fact, for Silas, Raveloe is at first a place without meaning, a place where he is disinherited:

> There was nothing here, when he rose in the deep morning quiet and looked out on the dewy brambles and rank tufted grass, that seemed to have any relation with that life centering in Lantern Yard, which had once been to him the altar-place of high dispensations. The white-washed walls; the little pews where well-known figures entered with a subdued rustling, and where first one well-known voice and then another, pitched in a peculiar key of petition, uttered phrases at once occult and familiar, like the amulet worn on the heart; the pulpit where the minister delivered unquestioned doctrine, and swayed to and

George Eliot's gravesite in Highgate Cemetery, London.

fro, and handled the book in a long-accustomed manner; the very pauses between the couplets of the hymn, as it was given out, and the recurrent swell of voices in song: these things had been the channel of divine influences to Marner—they were the fostering home of his religious emotions—they were Christianity and God's kingdom upon earth.

'The dewy brambles'—this is not, we feel, Silas's observation, but the artist's comment, hinting at the refreshment to be found in the beauty of the countryside; 'rank tufted grass', too, is a description that suggests an observer accustomed to noticing different kinds and qualities of grasses, not Silas; and even 'deep morning quiet' is an appreciative phrase that, with the others I have mentioned, shows through familiar and loving eyes the rural scene that is for him unfamiliar and unloved. For Silas, these things are merely the absence of the world he has known, with as little attraction or emotional significance for him as the scenes of his childhood would have for us. It is perhaps a certain sentimentality in us, or many of us, that makes it so much easier for us to imagine somebody being emotionally rooted—bound and sustained by links of memory—in a rural environment, among 'dewy brambles and rank tufted grass', than in an urban one like the Lantern Yard. Even if our own early memories have been urban, we seem to have little difficulty in imagining the 'rootedness' of a country man. What George Eliot does in this passage is to suggest, and make accessible to our imagination, the 'rootedness' of a town-dweller of a rather special kind—a 'rootedness' that her readers are not likely to have experienced, and are certainly not accustomed to finding depicted in fiction. She makes it irrelevant, for the moment, that we are accustomed to think of 'narrow religious sects' such as the one Silas belonged to as fanatical organizations, led by visionaries either insane or dishonest, exploiting the ignorance and emotional poverty of the new urban proletariat. All this they might be, and the brief account George Eliot gives of the events that led to Silas's departure is an unsparing, though compassionate, indictment of them. But even there—this is what the quoted passage makes us realize—even there a man's childhood memories and his deepest pieties might be rooted. The series of phrases conveying the texture of Silas's recollected childhood has its own rhythm—a rhythm that suggests the mind groping in its past, and bringing out a sequence of broken images, precious because they are what one's consciousness and one's identity is made of—and these phrases ('The white-washed walls; the little pews . . . ') themselves become for us 'phrases at once occult and familiar, like the amulet worn on the heart'.

When we have recognized the artistic triumph of this concise creation, however, it is in rural Raveloe that we trace Silas's re-planting in the course of the book. This process begins before the arrival of the child; Silas's neighbours begin to take an interest in him, as a man who has suffered, after his gold has been stolen. Dolly Winthrop visits him, with a gift of cakes, to urge him to go to church, and their dialogue is a series of misunderstandings. We have been given enough insight into what religion has meant to Silas, and what it means in Raveloe, to be aware of the near impossibility of communication between the two; that is, we are perfectly able to understand Dolly Winthrop, and at the same time able to see how unintelligible her words are to Silas.

> 'Well, Master Marner, it's niver too late to turn over a new leaf, and if you've niver had no church, there's no telling the good it'll do you. For I feel so set up and comfortable as niver was, when I've been and heard the prayers, and the singing to the praise and glory o' God, as Mr. Macey gives out—and Mr. Crackenthorp saying good words, and more partic'lar on Sacramen' Day; and if a bit o' trouble comes, I feel as I can put up wi' it, for I've looked for help i' the right quarter, and gev myself up to Them as we must all give ourselves up to at the last; and if we'n done our part, it isn't to be believed as Them as are above us 'ull be worse nor we are, and come short o' Theirn.'

It is entirely characteristic of the secure poise of the book that we laugh without mockery at Dolly Winthrop's 'simple Raveloe theology', recognizing it as something of value that she possesses and Silas lacks.

He continues to lack it for the time being; the loss of his gold has not been enough to bring him into full contact with his neighbours, although it has been a necessary preparation. After Eppie's arrival, Dolly Winthrop renews the attack, and her theology is still as unintelligible to Silas as before, but now she can appeal not only to Silas's own need but to his obligation to the child.

> 'And it's my belief', she went on, 'as the poor little creatur has never been christened, and it's nothing but right as the parson should be spoke to . . . for if the child ever went anyways wrong, and you hadn't done your part by it, Master Marner,—'noculation, and everything to save it from harm—it 'ud be a thorn i' your bed for ever o' this side the grave . . .

Again we may smile at Mrs Winthrop's simple-minded view of baptism, which she urges upon Silas as a preventive measure of mysterious nature and doubtful efficacy against spiritual harm of an unspecified kind, and links with inoculation against smallpox. But the value of her urging does not depend on the efficacy of either treatment: it lies in her concern for the child and for Silas, and in her willingness to teach Silas what he must do in order to give the child the best care he can. It is in care for the child that Silas is able to meet Mrs Winthrop and the other Raveloe people; he is eager to do for Eppie what he was earlier uninterested in doing for himself.

> 'But I want to do everything as can be done for the child. And whatever's right for it i' this country, and you think 'ull do it good, I'll act according, if you'll tell me.'

Finding himself, after fifteen years of mere existence, involves for Silas something like learning a new language; he has to learn to understand Mrs Winthrop's way of talking, and this is only a part of learning what life means in Raveloe. But it also involves finding ways of talking to Mrs Winthrop about his own past,

> necessarily a slow and difficult process, for

Silas's meagre power of explanation was not aided by any readiness of interpretation in Dolly, whose narrow outward experience gave her no key to strange customs, and made every novelty a source of wonder that arrested them at every step of the narrative.

The difficulties are not merely noted: they are made vividly—and amusingly—real to us in Dolly Winthrop's speech, which Silas gradually comes to understand. The dialogue between them is, at the same time, a dialogue between Raveloe and the Lantern Yard, and between Silas's new and old lives; the gradual approach to comprehension between them traces the gradual healing of the breach in Silas's life. The healing culminates—it is made to seem inevitable—in his re-visiting the town where he spent his childhood and youth, and taking Eppie with him.

> 'The old place is all swep' away,' Silas said to Dolly Winthrop on the night of his return—'the little graveyard and everything. The old home's gone; I've no home but this now.'

The point is not, I think, that the rapidity of change in a town, compared with rural permanence, makes it an unfavourable place to have roots in. It is to be taken symbolically: Silas has found, as in some sense we must all find, that his past is no longer there to go back to; his 'roots' (the simple metaphor is clearly inadequate for the concept here seen in complex terms) in order to sustain him must cling to the future, for the past has gone.

Meanwhile the story of Godfrey Cass, Eppie's 'real' father, necessary at first to justify the marvel of Eppie's coming from nowhere into Silas's life and to give this a causal connection as well as a symbolic one with the theft of the gold, has itself grown into a concurrent theme. As Silas's cottage becomes a home through his acceptance of the abandoned child, Godfrey's large red house remains childless.

Godfrey's story develops several of the same preoccupations that George Eliot has already begun to explore in her treatment of Arthur Donnithorne in *Adam Bede.* Godfrey learns, when he offers to acknowledge Eppie as his daughter and take her to his home, that

> —'there's debts we can't pay like money debts, by paying extra for the years that have slipped by. While I've been putting off and putting off, the trees have been growing—it's too late now . . . I wanted to pass for childless once, Nancy—I shall pass for childless now against my wish.'

His interview with Eppie and Silas, which has led him to this conclusion, has been strictly faithful to what Hawthorne calls 'the truth of the human heart', with Godfrey's awkwardness continually betraying the fact that he is not at all sure whether he is begging or conferring a favour. George Eliot presents, in her account of that visit, what such a man as Godfrey really would feel and say—not what, in a novel (or romance) one would expect him to feel and say.

> Godfrey felt an irritation inevitable to almost all of us when we encounter an unexpected obsta-

cle. He had been full of his own penitence and resolution to retrieve his error as far as the time was left to him; he was possessed with all-important feelings, that were to lead to a predetermined course of action which he had fixed on as the right, and he was not prepared to enter with lively appreciation into other people's feelings counteracting his virtuous resolves.

There is no easy assurance that all would have been well for Godfrey if he had acknowledged the child—and his drunken and drug-addicted first wife—openly from the start. Nancy suggests it, and the suggestion itself is painful and perhaps salutary to Godfrey:

> 'And—O, Godfrey—if we'd had her from the first, if you'd taken to her as you ought, she'd have loved me for her mother—and you'd have been happier with me: I could better have bore my little baby dying, and our life might have been more like what we used to think it 'ud be.'

But Godfrey's answer, though 'urged in the bitterness of his self-reproach, to prove to himself that his conduct had not been utter folly', is convincing:

> 'But you wouldn't have married me then, Nancy, if I'd told you . . . You may think you would now, but you wouldn't then. With your pride and your father's, you'd have hated having anything to do with me after the talk there'd have been.'

Judging from all we have seen of Nancy Lammeter, this is true; and she does not deny it. And if, as we have seen, Godfrey's discontent can fix upon the lack of children because that is all he lacks, it is unlikely that his discontent would have been without an object if he had had the child and not married Nancy. Since the speculation about what might have been arises in the story itself, we may be justified in taking it a little further: Godfrey with Eppie, unsuccessful in winning Nancy (who would nevertheless not marry anybody else), living in the dismal, unreformed Red House (supposing he had the luck not to be disinherited) would have real cause for gloom; and in such an atmosphere Eppie (under another name) would have grown up. One can hardly suppose that anybody would be better off as a result.

But in order to recognize the consequences of one's wrong-doing, it is not necessary to be able to see precisely how, at any given stage, one could have acted otherwise so as to make all well. Godfrey has disowned his daughter, and remained childless; finally his daughter disowns him. For Godfrey at least, the link between his action and its sequel is a moral link: he is punished.

For the world of *Silas Marner,* for all its marvels, is a moral world; for all the coincidences that go to conceal Godfrey's first marriage, it is not a fairy-tale world in which coincidence can legitimately be counted on to get one out of messes of one's own making. Early in the novel we are told of him,

> He fled to his usual refuge, that of hoping for some unforeseen turn of fortune, some favourable chance which would save him from un-

pleasant consequences—perhaps even justify his insincerity by manifesting its prudence.

The unforeseen turns of fortune come—the acknowledged wife dies, his brother disappears, and his child survives and is well looked after—but none of these manifestations of the 'prudence' of his deceit can justify it or avert its consequences in his heart. The consequences are hidden, mysterious and organic, as George Eliot's image suggests: 'the orderly sequence by which the seed brings forth a crop after its kind'. (pp. 31-42)

R. T. Jones, " 'Silas Marner'," in his George Eliot, *Cambridge at the University Press, 1970, 116 p.*

An excerpt from *Silas Marner*

Unlike the gold which needed nothing, and must be worshipped in close-locked solitude—which was hidden away from the daylight, was deaf to the song of the birds, and started to no human tones—Eppie was a creature of endless claims and ever-growing desires, seeking and loving sunshine, and living sounds, and living movements; making trial of everything, with trust in new joy, and stirring the human kindness in all eyes that looked on her. The gold had kept his thoughts in an ever-repeated circle, leading to nothing beyond itself; but Eppie was an object compacted of changes and hopes that forced his thoughts onward, and carried them far away from their old eager pacing towards the same blank limit—carried them away to the new things that would come with the coming years, when Eppie would have learned to understand how her father Silas cared for her; and made him look for images of that time in the ties and charities that bound together the families of his neighbors. The gold had asked that he should sit weaving longer and longer, deafened and blinded more and more to all things except the monotony of his loom and the repetition of his web; but Eppie called him away from his weaving, and made him think all its pauses a holiday, reawakening his senses with her fresh life, even to the old winter-flies that came crawling forth in the early spring sunshine, and warming him into joy because *she* had joy.

George Eliot, in her Silas Marner, *Simon & Schuster, Pocket Books, 1972.*

Bruce K. Martin (essay date 1972)

[*In the following essay, Martin examines the function of Godfrey Cass in* Silas Marner, *discussing similarities and differences between his character and that of Silas.*]

Critics interested in *Silas Marner* have frequently discussed George Eliot's use of Godfrey Cass. Their principal theories include the notion that the story of Godfrey is primarily a negative analogue to that of Silas. A second theory stresses what many critics see as the novel's air of unreality, closely related to allegory, which George Eliot makes tolerable to the modern reader by offering the Godfrey story in a wholly realistic vein. Finally, we have the idea that though offering Silas and Godfrey as representatives of differing world-views, George Eliot rejects the be-

liefs of both and instead moves her characters toward an appreciation of human love absent in both of their earlier creeds.

All of these views have value, for all recognize a structural problem in the novel which no searching analysis can ignore and all at least partly demonstrate the novel's tightness of design. Yet none is wholly satisfactory, for in fastening upon some central contrast—of effect, of tone, or of ideology—between the two characters and their stories, critics have neglected important similarities and the relationship of their differences to such similarities. An examination of Silas and Godfrey in terms of both similar and dissimilar characteristics reveals a dimension of structural integrity in the novel hitherto ignored. George Eliot uses Godfrey as both parallel and foil to Silas, to universalize certain assumptions about the moral nature and needs of man, while suggesting the varied outcomes of human endeavor.

The whole question of how Godfrey functions is inextricably tied to the question of what type of development George Eliot lays out for Silas. According to David R. Carroll [in *Literary Monographs, Vol. 1,* edited by Eric Rothstein and Thomas K. Dunseath, 1967], because of the Lantern Yard crisis Silas moves from religious faith to faithless solitude. Through his relationship with Eppie, however, he moves to a trust in a universal order based not on empirical evidence, but on human love. Godfrey, on the other hand, is initially cast as a believer in chance. Through the influence of his wife's love he too finds a new order in life. Carroll thus sees Silas and Godfrey developing a faith in human love as a universal principle.

There can be no question of the bearing of the ideological frame discussed by Carroll on what occurs in the novel. George Eliot's Feuerbachian viewpoint colors her treatment of all her characters' reactions to the unknown or unexpected. However, the supposition that "religious" growth represents their principal mode of development ignores rather significant facets of both the materials of the novel and their treatment. A major distinction to be observed here is between a plot of circumstance, where the primary change undergone by a character is one of situation—either from worse to better, or vice-versa—and a plot of knowledge, where the character moves from ignorance to awareness, or vice-versa. The distinction is illustrated in George Eliot's writings by the difference between *Daniel Deronda,* which is structured around Daniel's discovery of his parentage and the Zionist vocation, and the story of Felix Holt, who, rather than learning much of anything in the course of the novel—George Eliot characterizes him as extremely knowledgeable from the beginning—enjoys a positive change of external circumstance by converting Esther Lyon to his political views and by winning his attractive convert in marriage. Another kind of plot concerns moral change, such as that of Adam Bede, who acquires the vital quality of sympathy which he earlier lacks.

In the story of Silas Marner the emphasis is principally on a change of circumstance. To be sure, he experiences the sort of intellectual growth described by Carroll, but such growth represents a by-product, though an essential one, of the change in his external situation. George Eliot presents her materials so that the reader's concern focuses less on Silas' wrongheadedness than on the pathos of his predicament. And while the account of his misfortune at Lantern Yard stresses, among other things, the narrowness of the religious sect and Silas' participation in that narrowness, George Eliot significantly postpones that account until she has fully described Silas in his isolation among the superstitious folk of Raveloe. The opening pages stress the ignorance not of Marner but of the mindless peasants who shun him. After noting the rumor that Silas could cure rheumatism, the narrator remarks on their distrust, "the rude mind with difficulty associates the ideas of power and benignity," to suggest that the burden of proof lay with them in their hasty condemnation of the hapless weaver. The reader learns, too, of Silas' extreme nearsightedness and how the small boys were terrified by his "dreadful [though unseeing] stare." The community attitude is thus characterized as unthinking.

In this context the flashback to Lantern Yard serves primarily to engender further pity for Silas, for we find that compounded with his occupational disadvantage among the villagers is the fact that past experiences have made it unattractive for him to seek out his fellow men. The villagers are thus seen as a more recent but equally unsympathetic replacement for the Lantern Yard congregation; rural superstition supplants religious narrowness in persecuting Silas. And in recounting Silas' difficulties at Lantern Yard, the narrator stresses not the ignorance but the trusting simplicity of the weaver, contrasting this with the tendency toward "overseverity" of William Dane, a tendency shared, though not for ulterior motives, by the rest of the congregation. The contrast between Silas and Dane is therefore ethical, not intellectual. Were George Eliot's intent here to emphasize the moral limitations of Silas' worldview, she might show him behaving unsympathetically in accord with his religion. This is not to say that the brand of evangelicalism found in Lantern Yard does not have severe moral limitations—the behavior of the congregation demonstrates that it does—but simply that she chooses to depict Silas wholly as a victim. Even his refusal to seek judgment against Dane through legal recourses open to him signifies in part that though distrustful of men Silas is not given to hurting them. For Silas, if not for his fellow members, evangelical religion need not be incompatible with human love; presumably he would never justify his own unsympathetic behavior by his religion. The important thing to realize, though, is that George Eliot opens her novel not *in media res* but at the beginning. The Lantern Yard flashback serves principally as an explanation for Silas' reticence toward the people of Raveloe, and not as the first stage of the plot. By withholding background information on Silas until his plight at Raveloe is portrayed, the author can use Silas' past to reinforce the pathos of his present.

Marner's latent capacity for sympathy is further established in the Sally Oates incident, in which a "rush of pity" prompted him to attend a stricken woman. The community's misunderstanding of his folk medicine, which drove him into seclusion, shows the disparity between his essential nature and Raveloe's view of him. Similarly the author

indicates that his miserliness is not a selfish love of wealth, such as the aunts Glegg and Pullet exhibit in *The Mill on the Floss,* but simply the following of a pointless desire by a man with no other purpose in life. Knowing the importance of sympathetic action and Silas' capacity for such action, yet realizing the impossibility of his acting thus under existing conditions, the reader desires a change in circumstances whereby Silas will receive an opportunity for sympathetic action, which predictably will lead to a reunion with his fellow men. George Eliot sets up sympathy as the primary norm for her novel and introduces Silas as prone to sympathy yet unable either to exercise or to receive it. The initial stage of the Silas story thus fastens on a plight not of intellect or morality, but of circumstance, a plight which commands our pity.

That the Silas plot concerns primarily a change of situation, rather than a change of heart or mind, can be seen even more clearly in its subsequent stages, particularly the final crisis and resolution. If a trust in human love by itself can do little for the ostracized Silas, it presumably would provide not much more consolation later, were Eppie to leave him for her natural father. Silas' acquired bond with the village notwithstanding, the loss of Eppie would be irreparable. This is clearly the import of his reply to Godfrey's assertion that even though living in the Red House, Eppie would feel "just the same" toward Silas: " 'Just the same?' said Marner, more bitterly than ever. 'How'll she feel just the same for me as she does now, when we eat o' the same bit, and drink o' the same cup, and think o' the same things from one day's end to another? Just the same? That's idle talk. You'd cut us i' two!' " Similarly, an awareness of the importance of human love can hardly mean much to Godfrey in his desire for a child; even if Nancy can partly console him, it is in her presence, not in what she represents. The reader wishes Eppie to remain with Silas not because of any discovery Silas has made, but because of the sympathetic love he has shown, a love of which he has been capable throughout the novel.

The change of condition which he has undergone prior to Godfrey's offer is twofold. Because, as many critics have noticed, suffering is requisite to sympathetic action in the world of George Eliot's fiction, Silas' loss of the gold is as necessary as the arrival of Eppie. His loss is somewhat analogous to Adam Bede's visit with the condemned Hetty Sorrel, for each crisis forces the character to experience the despair of the weak and suffering, to share consciously their need for mercy. The difference, though, is that in terms of sympathy Silas is much further along than Adam; rather than the sympathy lacking in Adam, what Silas lacks is the opportunity to exhibit that sympathy, on account of the isolation imposed upon him by past misfortune and community prejudice. Hence, the difference mentioned earlier between the plot-types of the two novels. The famous picture of Silas eagerly counting his money at the end of chapter seven demonstrates the extent of his separation from the rest of humanity, and suggests that the sight of an infant at that point could hardly arouse him very far. And because the initial chapters have clearly called for an emotional "fortunate fall" of some sort, George Eliot later remarks that merely opening his heart up to the listeners at the Rainbow set off in Silas the "beginning of a growth" back to sympathetic action, for desperation released his pent-up capacity to feel for others.

The second part of the novel, especially the discovery of the lost gold, confirms the renewal of sympathetic action by Silas and rewards him for it. Interestingly Godfrey Cass is meant to be judged on the same basis as Silas, and on that basis he merits a large measure of approval. If the initial predicament of Silas suggests the importance of sympathetic kindness and casts Silas as the victim of unsympathetic circumstances, this is even more the case in the introduction of Godfrey. Where Marner has been victimized by only one antagonist, Godfrey is put upon by three. And George Eliot's characterization of each of young Cass's antagonists far exceeds in detail her treatment of William Dane.

Godfrey's capacity for sympathy is established early in the novel, mainly through a contrast between him and his brother. Described as "a spiteful jeering fellow, who seemed to enjoy his drink the more when other people went dry," Dunstan appears the antithesis of sympathy. In a significant change from her account of the Lantern Yard affair, George Eliot here includes much dialogue between Godfrey and his tormentors, particularly Dunstan, to illustrate Godfrey's helplessness at their hands. She chooses, too, to narrate lengthy sections from the points of view of two of the antagonists, Dunstan (Chapter 4) and Molly (Chapter 12), in which the inside view distances the reader from the characters by confirming the shallowness of their motives, their pitilessness toward Godfrey, and the intolerability of his position. She relieves Godfrey of further obligations toward his wife by rendering as futile the possibility of aiding her, in her addiction to opium. Thus, as she walks slowly toward Raveloe to humiliate Godfrey, the reader is told: "Molly knew that the cause of her dingy rags was not her husband's neglect, but the demon Opium to whom she was enslaved, body and soul." Her desire to disclose their marriage is represented as a senseless hunger for vengeance, while Godfrey's stated refusal to acknowledge her as his wife is ascribed to a "fit of passion." Even their marriage appears the result not simply of weakness, but of "a movement of compunction" for the pathetic Molly, as the culmination of a relationship encouraged by the scheming Dunstan. Further compassion for Godfrey's plight is invited by the unlikelihood of his father's behaving sympathetically when to do so would require any genuine sacrifice. The old Squire's scene with Godfrey (Chapter 9), as the young man debates whether to confess his secrets, presents the contrast between the irascible parsimony of the old man and the scrupulousness of Godfrey, caught between the desire to be truthful and the awareness that his father would hardly treat him justly.

George Eliot's effort to depict young Cass as a victim approaches the ludicrous when, in Chapter 3, she has Snuff, the family spaniel, anticipate a caress from Godfrey after hiding upon the approach of Dunstan; and it raises a question: why should she work so hard, even risk the collapse of her novel into melodrama, to objectify Godfrey as greatly sinned against yet scarcely capable of sin himself? And though Nancy finally represents a partial consolation for the loss of Eppie, why should Godfrey receive such consolation and why should the reader be largely undisturbed at his winning the girl of his dreams? The answer to the first question is that George Eliot, anticipating the severe reaction of readers to Godfrey's behavior when Silas interrupts the New Year's festivities, sought prior to that point in her novel to place Godfrey in the most favorable light possible by maximizing constricting circumstances and minimizing practical alternatives open to him—a not inconsiderable task in view of the often obsessive value placed on the family by the Victorian mind. The answer to the final two questions is that she succeeded in this task. Because of sympathy generated for Godfrey, the reader is uneasy at the end of Part One only over his keeping his paternity secret, not over his winning Nancy.

What George Eliot had to do was de-emphasize the moral implications of Godfrey's thoughts and actions at the time of Silas' mission to the Red House. This she accomplished through three means: (1) by surrounding Godfrey with implacable foes and causing their respective pressures to converge on him almost simultaneously—thus the unfortunate coincidence arises in which Molly decides to confront Godfrey at his father's house not very long after Dunstan has mysteriously disappeared with Wildfire and prompted Squire Cass to renew his pressure on Godfrey to marry Nancy Lammeter; (2) by relegating any moral residue from Godfrey's behavior to a category other than the crucial one of lack of sympathy—a category which the author labels "moral cowardice"; and (3) by rhetorically coloring the instances of Godfrey's moral cowardice so as to reduce his blameworthiness further.

The first of these means has already been examined. The other two represent a carefully planned pattern leading up to Godfrey's denial of Eppie. The narrator first mentions Godfrey's "moral cowardice" in Chapter 3, in the middle of a rather lengthy passage examining his inner conflict over his brother, his secret marriage, and his feelings for Nancy. The immediate context of his meditation is Dunstan's usual threat to expose Godfrey and Godfrey's unusual counterthreat, "I'll tell my father everything myself, and you may go to the devil." His moral cowardice at this point, which causes him to back down, is described as the inevitable result of "a position in which dreaded consequences seemed to press equally on all sides." Though natural to him, it is reinforced by the intolerable circumstances of the moment. Typical of George Eliot's treatment of Godfrey are the several pages of narrative commentary following his consenting to let Dunstan sell Wildfire, where she emphasizes the hardness of consequences following Godfrey's marriage to Molly and, significantly in terms of what is to follow, stresses the domesticity of Godfrey's regard for Nancy, "the image of purity, order, and calm." The narrator goes on to invite the readers to look with empathy on the problems of their "rural forefathers." The technique of moving the narrative away from the story to link the character's problems with the reader's and then moving back into the story mitigates ill-feeling toward Godfrey.

This technique appears again in Chapter 9, after Godfrey once more has avoided revealing the full truth to his father. This time, having noted Godfrey's decision to rely upon chance, the narrator maintains that "in this point of trusting to some throw of fortune's dice, Godfrey can hardly be called old-fashioned," and extends such practices even to "a polished man of these days." Having already noted the folly of trusting to chance and having illustrated, through Godfrey's marriage and the resulting pile-up of complications, the iron law of cause and effect operating in her fictional world, George Eliot speaks implicitly in what Barbara Hardy [in her *The Novels of George Eliot,* 1959] has termed her "prophetic voice," to predict greater unhappiness for Godfrey. The issue of his "moral cowardice" thus becomes more practical than ethical. Having seen Godfrey's need for confession, yet sensing the unlikelihood of the Squire's reacting justly to such a confession, the reader can only sympathize with Godfrey even as he puts his trust in Chance.

But George Eliot's rhetoric faces its severest test in the New Year's Eve scene at the Red House, for which these earlier instances of Godfrey's cowardice serve as preparation. Reliance on the unknown having been established as his characteristic mode of reacting to difficulties, the problem of making such a reaction tolerable to the reader is complicated by the introduction of an innocent child as the principal affected by his decision: where Molly could not be helped by Godfrey's aid, Eppie can. First, it should be noted that Godfrey's fear of Molly's surviving when her body is brought in—a fear which the narrator terms an "evil terror"—does indeed represent the low point of his behavior in the novel. Carroll, however, in viewing this as Godfrey's moment of "damnation," exaggerates the attention George Eliot gives or the reader should give it. For after briefly moralizing on this fear, she shifts her narrative rather abruptly to concentrate on Godfrey's reactions to his child. It is his ensuing internal struggle which makes up the greater part of the chapter, the "evil terror" having been disposed of in a brief paragraph. And though Godfrey's refusal to identify his child is crucial, because it does not go unattended by self-reproach, it is ascribed to moral cowardice, rather than want of sympathy. Godfrey talks himself into following convenience at the expense of paternal duty by weighing the possible outcomes for the child and resolving to do what he can to aid her. This is rationalization, but surely it is significant that Godfrey bothers to rationalize, as his brother certainly would not, or that he rationalizes in this manner, as the child's mother would not. Because he experiences "mixed feelings" about giving up the child and because he accurately calculates the probable effects of his decision on her, the decision by no means reflects a want of sympathy. And because the reader knows that the child would mean the much-deserved and long-awaited change of circumstance for the weaver, Godfrey's decision to relinquish Eppie seems a happy one for all. Sympathy for Silas outweighs any remaining criticism of Godfrey at this point.

By the end of the novel, of course, Godfrey's error regarding Eppie appears wholly practical rather than moral. Because we are to see him retaining his capacity for sympathy, even his misestimation of the relationship between Silas and Eppie in the latter chapters is classified as ignorance: "It was only the want of adequate knowledge that could have made it possible for Godfrey deliberately to entertain an unfeeling project." Unlike the story of Silas Marner, that of Godfrey Cass is unified by a plot of knowledge, the principal change in him being his realization of the impracticality of giving up Eppie. To be sure, a dramatic shift of circumstance, namely his being rid of his tormentors and winning Nancy, occurs in Part One of the novel, but this soon gives way to his discovery not of what he ought to have done—this he sensed at the time—but why: because "A child, more than all other gifts / That earth can offer to declining man / Brings hope with it, and forward-looking thoughts." Godfrey's revised estimate of his daughter renders rather short-lived the joy he feels when he gives her up; knowledge thus supplants circumstance as the determinant of his happiness. Actually, this shift in values occupies but a small part of the narrative and appears to the reader very indirectly. George Eliot's choosing to concentrate instead on the results of this shift, primarily Godfrey's fruitless attempt to win Eppie from Silas, suggests, like the toning down of Godfrey's suffering at the end of the book, the author's greater concern with Silas Marner. The story of Godfrey thus operates as a subplot in the novel.

This is not to say, however, that the story of Godfrey Cass is not integrally related to what George Eliot was trying to accomplish in her book. If it is impossible to answer fully questions about Silas without answering questions about Godfrey, this is because George Eliot intended things to be this way. While not simply a negative analogue, or any sort of analogue of equal importance, the Godfrey plot nevertheless performs a number of vital functions without which the story of Silas Marner would fall apart. First, it contributes immeasurably to the novel's remarkable tightness of design. This is the quality Henry James had in mind when he wrote [in *The Atlantic Monthly,* October, 1866]: "To a certain extent, I think **Silas Marner** holds a higher place than any of the author's works. . . . It is more nearly a masterpiece; it has more of that simple, rounded consummate aspect, that absence of loose ends and gaping issues, which marks a classical work." This is high praise for **Silas Marner** from a critic by no means unappreciative of its author's accomplishments. Surely the "classical" quality admired by James includes George Eliot's handling of the Godfrey plot, which fills many of the gaps that the story of Silas opens. Most importantly, we have the loss of gold and the arrival of Eppie, those necessary changes of circumstance in Silas' life, accounted for, as well as a complicating twist in an otherwise dully straightforward line of action provided by Godfrey's offer to Eppie in the last chapters. And what George Eliot has accomplished here is not simply the naive sort of "tying together" so often associated with Victorian novels. Rather, through the Godfrey plot she has spared her novel from the serious weakness of *deus ex machina,* a weakness to which novels combining passive main characters with plots of circumstance are especially liable. The result is the appearance of unity without artificiality, the novel's artifice being contained and concealed in a subplot sufficiently different in structure from the Silas story—some would say more interesting—to allay critical suspicions.

Lest *Silas Marner* appear to have resulted solely from sleight of hand, it should be admitted that its author's genius probably permitted her to give her novel such design unconsciously, and that she probably conceived of the Godfrey plot in terms of the more humane concerns for which we honor George Eliot. Because the effectiveness of the novel rests ultimately on our being convinced of Silas' happiness, Godfrey's realization of the value of an Eppie in his life objectifies the weaver's good fortune. However great the compensation of Nancy, Godfrey's behavior points up that it is not a total compensation. And while the present discussion has taken issue with many critics over the nature of the differences between Silas and Godfrey and their experiences, there can be no question that they represent contrasting types essential to such objectifying. Carroll is correct in citing a sacred-secular contrast, but he errs in suggesting that cosmology is the only or necessarily the most important basis of contrast upon which Godfrey's role in the novel rests. For George Eliot employs a number of other differences as well in having Godfrey realize not only what he has lost but how much Silas has gained. Godfrey differs from Silas not only in terms of religion, but age and social class, too. Further, he exhibits a decidedly different temperament from the weaver: where Silas is passive and docile, Godfrey is active and aggressive. Were Godfrey not in the novel, the joys of parenthood might seem appropriate only to a person of Silas' station and disposition. Godfrey's belated hunger for such joys helps universalize the general assumption from which the Silas plot stems, for like Wordsworth, George Eliot sees the inspiration of children transcending age, class, and temperament. And by having Godfrey, as well as Silas, define Silas' fortune as good, she avoids having to depend solely upon maudlin dialogue between father and daughter to convince the reader of their happiness.

Finally, because his character is set up and developed to be appraised on the same basis as Silas', namely sympathy, it follows that what happens to Godfrey in the novel reinforces that ethic and indirectly strengthens the admiration intended for Silas. While any effect of Godfrey's experience must be minimal, such an effect would probably be that of pity. Because he remains sympathetic to the needs of others, and because his desire for Eppie is partly a desire for someone else to love and aid, he can only invite pity when this wish is denied him. While the denial follows justly the principle of causality he mistakenly ignores for so long, his faults appear negligible next to his virtues. By remaining sympathetic himself, Godfrey indirectly helps define Silas' fortune not only as good but as deserved.

It is their shared trait of sympathy, then, which links Silas and Godfrey. By this the reader is made to judge both characters as initially admirable and pitiable, and to respond to their varying fates. In his complex role, Godfrey remains sufficiently distinct from Silas—in terms of initial plight, mode of development, and final situation—to broaden the validity of the premises underlying the progress of Silas. In fact, this multiple dissimilarity prohibits the uncomplicated scheme many would see here. But ultimately the structural unity of *Silas Marner* demands more than mere difference or similarity; in the novel each permits a keener perception of the other. The view of

human aspiration George Eliot would present requires a balance, which Godfrey Cass helps provide. (pp. 479-89)

Bruce K. Martin, "Similarity within Dissimilarity: The Dual Structure of 'Silas Marner'," in Texas Studies in Literature and Language, *Vol. XIV, No. 3, Fall, 1972, pp. 479-89.*

Michael Squires (essay date 1974)

[*Squires is an American educator and critic. In the following excerpt, he discusses* Silas Marner *as a pastoral novel, linking its depiction of a secluded rural community to Eliot's moral values and social concerns.*]

Like much pastoral literature *Silas Marner* is sometimes written off, with a quick flourish of the pen, as a charming but slight work of enchanted reminiscence. Thus Dr. Leavis in *The Great Tradition* brands it "that charming minor masterpiece." What has been seldom remarked, though, is the novel's quiet pastoralism (to use John Holloway's phrase [in his *The Victorian Sage*, 1953]), which functions as a pointed critique of nineteenth-century industrial society and which provides an appropriate means for discovering and illuminating moral values. Embodying a common pastoral pattern, the escape from modern industrialism to the rural life of the past brings ultimately a happiness and fulfillment that can, it seems, be discovered nowhere else. In much of the novel a lambent and radiant light casts a glow over rural life; and an air of good cheer and enjoyment hovers over many of the scenes—the brilliantly captured dialogue at the Rainbow, the Christmas festivities at the Red House, and almost the whole of Part II. By examining the pastoral elements of the novel, we can appreciate the work in its proper genre—less as a fable or realistic novel than as a pastoral novel that pictures a retreat into a secluded, circumscribed, traditional world where contentment can be won.

The structural pattern of *Silas Marner* links the novel to pastoral romance. The standard action of the pastoral romance, writes Walter R. Davis [in his *A Map of Arcadia*, 1965], follows the hero from the complex urban world to the simple natural world to the supernatural center, then out again, and shows the hero's disintegration in the chaotic outer circle, education in the pastoral circle, and reawakening at the sacred center. The action of *Silas Marner,* though spaced over a long period of time, is remarkably similar. Accused of theft and jilted in love, Silas withdraws from the pain and corruption of urban life and escapes into the pastoral region of Raveloe, where he discovers another way of life that prepares him to reassess his embittered attitudes. The supernatural center of the pastoral region is Silas' cottage at the moment Eppie miraculously appears on the weaver's hearth. Under Eppie's direction Silas completes his education "with reawaken[ed] sensibilities," is reborn, and years later, as in the romance, departs for the urban world—only to find that the world he escaped had "disintegrated." Preferring now the sheltered pastoral region to the oppressive atmosphere of Lantern Yard, Silas returns to Raveloe. Thus the novel alters the pattern of pastoral romance by insisting on Silas' ultimate allegiance to the rural world. After Silas returns to

Raveloe, another parallel with the traditional genre manifests itself in the marriage of the two pastoral peasants, Eppie and Aaron, and in the feast that celebrates their marriage. The marriage reasserts the positive value that inheres in the rural order and, as we leave Raveloe, ties into unity the lives of the rustic characters.

Important to any pastoral work is of course the sharp rural-urban contrast, which embodies the basic pastoral impulse to criticize urban society by locating value in remote areas. In **Silas Marner** we find also the expected nature-art antithesis stemming from this contrast: simplicity is praised over complexity, and the natural is preferred to the artificial or man made. At the opening of the novel, we are not surprised to learn that "nothing could be more unlike his native town" than Raveloe, hidden from the world and entirely self-sufficient. Lantern Yard and Raveloe are not connected in the highly organic way that contrasted geographical areas are connected in **Middlemarch.** The rural world, though not free from evil, is recreated largely in idyllic terms, whereas industrialism assumes the grizzled outlines of a ferocious beast. When Silas and Eppie return to Lantern Yard years after Silas has departed, the city is strangely transformed: traditional landmarks have vanished in the wake of industrialism. " 'O, what a dark ugly place!' " exclaims Eppie on their arrival. " 'How it hides the sky! It's worse than the Workhouse. I'm glad you don't live in this town now, father.' " In place of the tiny chapel where Silas had worshipped, a large factory towers; and they are greeted by a "multitude of strange indifferent faces," all in a hurry. "Here and there a sallow begrimed face looked out from a gloomy doorway at the strangers, and increased Eppie's uneasiness." Because the city is envisioned as fearful and ugly, the rural world alone offers the possibility of fulfillment. If such passages display a rural point of view of urban or industrial life, the reverse point of view operates also and provides a different perspective, encouraging us to see, as often in pastoral, one way of life as a means of evaluating the other.

Contributing to the reader's awareness of the rural-urban or simplicity-complexity contrast is the novel's dominant point of view, which is complex, intellectual, and analytic, viewing the pastoral retreat of Raveloe from a critical perspective, avoiding easy praise of the narrow understanding of those who live in Raveloe, and refusing to ignore the flaws of their society. George Eliot speaks more than once of the "rude mind" of rustic folk. The "critical perspective" allows us however—in dialectical fashion—to sense the cultural value of an intellectual urban life such as George Eliot lived during the 1860s, a life that offers "perspective" as one of its benefits. The impression of an objective urban onlooker emerges from the long expository introduction which prefaces the action. With the narrator, we look on as outsiders: "To the peasants of old times, the world outside their own direct experience was a region of vagueness and mystery"; or, the villagers of Raveloe, "honest folk, born and bred in a visible manner, were mostly not over-wise or clever—at least, not beyond such a matter as knowing the signs of the weather." The narrator explains the villagers to a reader who, without commentary, might not understand or sympathize with them.

Again, the reader remains outside the particularized pastoral world of the novel when he learns that Nancy Lammeter "was not theologically instructed enough to discern very clearly the relation between the sacred documents of the past which she opened without method, and her own obscure, simple life" or when he learns that her religious theory was "pieced together out of narrow social traditions, fragments of church doctrine imperfectly understood, and girlish reasonings on her small experience." Nancy's character is analyzed from outside the sphere of Raveloe and in terms of a more complex, sophisticated method of determining value; she is judged according to an educated and responsible urban code that lies beyond the limits of her own culture. Although it diminishes the scope and significance of Raveloe in the reader's mind, such a point of view—which invites us to see Raveloe from without and from within—helps to link the novel to pastoral. (pp. 86-9)

[George Eliot] departs from the traditional conception of pastoral. Using Wordsworth as her model, she injects toil and a measure of unhappiness into the pastoral world and so, while retaining many of the traditional features of the genre, she aims toward greater realism in her representation of rural life. What exists clearly in the novel is an ambiguity in George Eliot's attitude toward her material, the sort of ambiguity we saw in *Lycidas:* the deeply felt impulse toward pastoral alternates with a keen sense of realism, and sympathy alternates with critical distance, in the same way that rural and urban points of view operate. Perhaps for this reason, the novel splits into two balanced halves. The plot dealing with Silas is generally pastoral in conception and execution, whereas the story of the Cass family is generally realistic. The pastoral attitude is played off against the realistic attitude, and it is this careful balancing of conflicting tendencies which gives the novel its distinctive tension. Because of this allowance for greater realism, evil stations itself not only in the mushrooming industrial centers, but spreads its tentacles even into so sheltered a pastoral retreat as Raveloe. Thus we find in George Eliot's early novels the mixture of pastoral and realistic elements that Hardy inherits. The narrative tension that results is used to admirable artistic advantage by George Eliot. Examined minutely, the narrative reveals a tensive movement like that of the shuttle of a loom, tracing a uniform pattern between opposite poles of tension and release, anguish and hope; for example, Dunstan committing a crime in darkness and rain (ch. 4) juxtaposed to Silas' warm fire and anticipation of food (ch. 5); agony (ch. 5) opposed to conviviality (ch. 6) and conviviality opposed, then, to the investigation of the robbery (chs. 7-8); Godfrey's predicament (ch. 9) placed next to neighborly visits (ch. 10); and the New Year's Eve festivities (ch. 11) pitted against Molly's journey and death (chs. 12-13). George Eliot's use of narrative antithesis creates much interest and dramatic tension, reflecting not only the initial contrast between Lantern Yard and Raveloe but metaphorically extending the mechanics of the weaver's trade into the structuring principle of the novel.

The narrative is, we have said, told through the device of the double plot. One plot traces the history of Silas and Eppie; the other plot charts the lives of Squire Cass and his sons. When Silas Marner's close friend wished to marry Silas' fiancée, he falsely accused Marner of stealing the funds of their church. The church members prayed, drew lots, found Marner guilty, and suspended him from church membership. Stunned, Silas fled from Lantern Yard to Raveloe, where he became a weaver. His extreme thrift earned him the reputation of a miser until Dunstan Cass, son of the local squire, stole Silas' money and disappeared, thereby connecting Silas to the Cass plot. Godfrey, the best of Squire Cass's sons, had surreptitiously married an opium addict who bore him a daughter, but Godfrey in his shame refused to acknowledge them. One New Year's Eve, Molly Cass traveled toward the Red House to expose Godfrey as her husband. On the way, however, she died, and her child wandered into Silas' cottage. The two plots again merge. When Godfrey did not come forward to claim the child, Silas adopted her as his own and named her Eppie. In Part II the narrative moves forward sixteen years. Godfrey and his second wife Nancy decide to adopt Godfrey's natural daughter, but when they ask, Eppie refuses; instead she marries Aaron Winthrop, the Casses' gardener, and returns with Aaron to Silas' cottage where the three of them settle happily.

In the industrial world, then, Silas is robbed of a wife, his honest name, and his faith in God by the deceit of his closest friend. But evil, appearing also in the rural world, causes Silas to be robbed of his gold. There are yet other forms of robbery in Raveloe. When Godfrey Cass renounces his claim on the child, by refusing to identify himself as her father, he too is robbed—of fathering a child by his second wife. Nemesis operates even in the pastoral world. Yet evil in the novel is largely limited to the plot that treats the lives of the Casses. The plot that treats the rustics is surprisingly free from corruptive elements. In fact, evil can be found everywhere but in the *locus amoenus* of Silas' once-empty cottage, where work gives way to love—when supernatural powers send Eppie to Silas' hearth—and then to a domestic idyll. The *locus amoenus* escapes evil because behavior there is premised on innocence. Because of the importance of innocence, the plot device common to pastoral novels, of the empty or abandoned cottage now occupied by persons in retreat, encourages in *Silas Marner* an asexual sequence of events rather than the sexual sequence evident in *Adam Bede* or *Lady Chatterley's Lover* or potentially in *The Woodlanders*.

But more important than the acknowledgment of evil, in demonstrating the change in attitude toward traditional pastoral, is the novel's heavy emphasis on work. The plot that traces the activities of Squire Cass and his sons reveals significantly few mentions of work. Instead, the characters who speak of work are usually Silas, Eppie, and Aaron Winthrop, characters who are linked together on this basis. Half of such citations refer to Silas himself, perhaps because Silas reflects most clearly the importance of work in the novel. The Victorian ethic of hard work, which George Eliot shares with her age, conflicts with the pastoral impulse toward leisure and freedom which also stimulates her imagination. Both motives exist in the novel: Silas works constantly yet he is in pastoral retreat. The convention of a toilless bower, popular in the pastoral

genre, has perhaps been reversed. Yet it should be said that a holiday spirit of *pause* from work emerges from the novel as a whole. The lingering descriptions of the Rainbow dialogue and the Squire's party are especially memorable, and (interestingly) we see Silas, Eppie, and Aaron together not at work but on a Sunday afternoon or in the evening or on the day of the wedding. George Eliot's selection of such scenes contributes much to the novel's pastoralism.

For Silas work offers escape from pain. When he learns of the evil which had been visited upon him in Lantern Yard, "his first movement after the shock had been to work in his loom. . . . He seemed to weave, like the spider, from pure impulse, without reflection. Every man's work, pursued steadily, tends in this way to become an end in itself, and so to bridge over the loveless chasms of his life." Work is a dependable substitute for unpredictable affection. It offers a "refuge from benumbing unbelief" and gives purpose to life when human affection fails. Once Silas discovers that his money has been stolen by an intruder, he "tottered towards his loom, and got into the seat where he worked, instinctively seeking this as the strongest assurance of reality." In both instances of loss, he turns to the loom "instinctively," "from pure impulse, without reflection," as a natural method of giving order to mental turmoil. Work functions as salvation from psychological distress. As in Hardy's novels, work is therapeutic, a means of reorienting oneself to the world, of prolonging life and assuring survival. If not pursued as an end in itself, work has the force of a moral imperative because it sustains emotional adjustment. When Silas has grown old, Godfrey Cass says to him:

> ". . . you've been a hard-working man all your life."

> "Yes, sir, yes," said Marner, meditatively. "I should ha' been bad off without my work: it was what I held by when everything else was gone from me."

But in *Silas Marner* work functions as more than therapy to relieve distress. Work offers a standard of value in the novel. The characters who are admired are industrious, are "the laboring people." This positive standard of work, by which the characters of the novel are appraised, can be recognized most clearly in Eppie's choice of Marner over Godfrey and Nancy Cass: " 'I can't think o' no other home. I wasn't brought up to be a lady, and I can't turn my mind to it. I like the working-folks, and their victuals, and their ways. And . . . I'm promised to marry a workingman, as'll live with father, and help me to take care of him'." From Mrs. Cass herself we learn that Aaron Winthrop, whom Eppie has promised to marry, is "very sober and industrious." We discover, on the other hand, that the characters drowned in idleness are either unhappy with themselves, such as Squire Cass, or are reclaimed by nature, such as Dunstan and Molly Cass. "Raveloe was not a place where moral censure was severe, but it was thought a weakness in the Squire that he had kept all his sons at home in idleness." Idleness, then, cannot be equated with pastoral *otium*. In *Silas Marner* idleness sows the seeds of death. Even Molly Cass is similarly afflicted with a variant of indolence: "she was enslaved, body and soul," to opium. Her enslavement, like Dunsey's to gambling and alcohol, draws her gradually into torpor. Thus when she sets out on her journey to the Red House, we learn that she had "lingered on the road, inclined by her indolence," and in a matter of hours death comes. In the terms of the novel, productive characters tend not to be specifically reclaimed by the forces of nature. The system of value created by the admired characters is inversely reinforced by the unadmired characters.

If the rural world of Raveloe is not identical to the world created by traditional pastoral, it nonetheless exhibits many elements of that world. The village of Raveloe is most clearly pastoral in its self-sufficiency and in its circumscribed geographical location. Because a circumscribed rural world is distant from the forces of upheaval, pastoral literature has long argued that contentment and peace of mind can best be pursued by escaping the ambition of city life and discovering a pastoral haven. In pastoral a circumscribed world often becomes a spiritual landscape, an imaginary world that expresses unfulfilled aspirations and images of rare beauty, a selection and thus a simplification of complex adult reality. In **Silas Marner** the rigorous and economical selection of details—the omission of minute descriptions of the ordinary villager and his daily life, descriptions we find in **Adam Bede**— makes a full portrait of Raveloe impossible. The details in **Silas Marner** usually focus on either the unusual or the communal: on Silas or the Casses; or on the local tavern or a festive party or the church or a wedding. To the degree that such a focus is a simplification, with the full reality of Raveloe supplied in the margins, by exposition, Raveloe represents a circumscribed pastoral world, hidden and aloof equally from political concerns or from the economic realities of buying and selling goods.

We learn immediately that "Raveloe was a village where many of the old echoes lingered, undrowned by new voices" and that "it was nestled in a snug well-wooded hollow, quite an hour's journey on horseback from any turnpike, where it was never reached by the vibrations of a coach-horn, or of public opinion." Entirely unlike Lantern Yard, Raveloe is a "low, wooded region, where [Silas] felt hidden even from the heavens by the screening trees and hedgerows. There was nothing here, when he rose in the deep morning quiet and looked out on the dewy brambles and rank tufted grass, that seemed to have any relation with that life centring in Lantern Yard." The cumulative suggestions of a circumscribed, isolated world solidify when we learn later that "Raveloe lay low among the bushy trees and the rutted lanes, aloof from the currents of industrial energy and Puritan earnestness." Because Raveloe is hidden and enclosed, the two mutually exclusive geographical areas symbolize two opposed orders of experience—Raveloe leading ultimately to expanded and sensitive awareness of the moral worth of human relationships and especially of love as a redeeming force, Lantern Yard leading to a contraction of feeling into mechanical and centripetal activity. We find in Raveloe a pastoral (or semipastoral) world sheltered by trees and isolated from the rapidly changing industrial world outside, a pastoral world in which nature is bountiful to the point of "neglect-

ed plenty." Raveloe is not only "low" and hidden among the trees, but also low in its aspirations. It is an isolated agricultural village, not unlike the bowers of traditional pastoral in which the search for equilibrium and contentment seems uppermost. We are asked to discover this equilibrium not in shepherds playing their pipes or in amoebean song contests, but in festivity and work, Sunday services and neighborly companionship—in those regions of experience that draw out the fullest emotional response from both Silas and the narrator. Once the circumscribed pastoral world has become geographically precise, the mixture of communal *and* Hesiodic *and* purely pastoral elements is greatly enriched.

The correlation between isolation and lack of strife is reinforced by the location of Silas' cottage at the Stone-pits. His cottage lies up a "lonely sheltered lane" so that there is a double isolation in the novel. Raveloe is sheltered from the world, and within this isolation, Silas' stone cottage is remote from the village. George Eliot explains that "the tender and peculiar love with which Silas had reared [Eppie] in almost inseparable companionship with himself" had been aided by "the seclusion of their dwelling" and by their limited means of mobility. As long as human ties are not severed, the novel suggests that seclusion from the urban world closely corresponds to peace and happiness.

There is yet another technique that George Eliot uses skillfully to create a circumscribed pastoral world: the use of interlocking scenes rather than a straight or flat narrative line. When one character leaves for another character's home, the reader is shifted immediately to the character about to be visited, and is immersed in the action occurring there. The visiting character then arrives in the midst of that action. Though chronological time is actually preserved, the rhetorical effect is one of repeated backtracking or reversion. When Silas, for instance, leaves his cottage and sets out for the Rainbow tavern to tell of the robbery, we immediately shift to the jocular conversation within the Rainbow. Then after what seems a considerable lapse of time (because of the lengthy conversations), Silas at last reaches the Rainbow with his story. Again, when Silas discovers Eppie asleep on his hearth, the narrator shifts to the Red House to participate fully in the New Year's Eve festivities. As in the previous example, a considerable amount of time appears to elapse before Silas arrives at the Red House with the newly discovered child. Though the scenes technically observe chronological time, the effect is one of turning back the clock and of forming what we might call "loops" in the plot of the novel. Through the use of this technique, the rural world appears to be more tightly knitted than if the narrative had followed a single character—Silas, for example—without turning first to his destination in order to prepare the background for the scene. The use of this technique creates the sense of a tightly ordered past and, more important, the sense of turning constantly back into the past, as if to recover the Golden Age.

In addition to topographical location and narrative loops, the frequent mention of a rooted traditional past—a concern always important when traditional values are crumbling—contributes importantly to George Eliot's creation of a circumscribed pastoral world. In *Silas Marner* occur frequent suggestions of the continuity between past and present, and of the remoteness necessary to foster this continuity. The motif of remoteness and insulation sounds, we have seen, in the opening paragraphs of the novel. We are placed at once in "that far-off time [when] superstition clung easily round every person or thing that was at all unwonted." The peasants are "peasants of old times." The reader is placed at a great distance from the present, and this distance creates a strong sense of the remoteness of Raveloe, enabling the reader more easily (by means of this detachment) to compare small things to great. George Eliot's world is insulated both in time and in space.

[*Silas Marner*] splits into two balanced halves. The plot dealing with Silas is generally pastoral in conception and execution, whereas the story of the Cass family is generally realistic. The pastoral attitude is played off against the realistic attitude, and it is this careful balancing of conflicting tendencies which gives the novel its distinctive tension.

—*Michael Squires*

When Silas, like romance heroes, escapes Lantern Yard to come to Raveloe, it seems fitting that he suffer discontinuity with his past. He has abandoned the world of unrest. After he settles in Raveloe, even searching for the once familiar herbs "belonged to the past, from which his life had shrunk away." But gradually Silas adjusts by means of human love to the new social order, and his life becomes "blent . . . with the life of his neighbors." The coming of Eppie assures his acceptance into the community because she forces him to seek out his neighbors for aid and advice. He breaks with his personal past in order to incorporate himself into the agricultural past, whose location and traditions have remained constant for centuries. Such a break signals a supreme gesture of conservatism because the rooted past absorbs a splintered fragment of the deracinated present. Silas travels "backward" in time in order to recover security and peace. It is what we might call a pastoral journey, since the pastoral novel locates value in isolated rural regions of the past. Given enough time, Silas travels from disorder into order, from disintegration into harmony and unity. Gradually, too, he learns—as Hardy's villains never do—to connect past and present through memory:

> By seeking what was needful for Eppie, by sharing the effect that everything produced on her, he had himself come to appropriate the forms of custom and belief which were the mould of Raveloe life; and as, with re-awakening sensibilities, memory also reawakened, he had begun to ponder over the elements of his old faith, and blend them with his new impressions, till he re-

covered a consciousness of unity between his past and present.

Silas must come to the rural world to recover this unity.

The repeated suggestions of a rooted past demonstrate George Eliot's special concern for custom and village tradition. Custom and tradition swell the circumscribed pastoral world, traditionally indeterminate, with the pressures of history, so that pastoral and history merge. What happens here, I think, happens in the pastoral novel as a whole. The concern for tradition (part of the realistic framework intended for the story) replaces the rigid song contest of the pastoral lyric or the elaborate disguises of the pastoral romance: tradition thus assumes the function of giving form to the characters' actions and verbal responses. The repeated local gatherings, for example, lead the villagers—and the narrator—to talk largely of communal and locally historical matters, such as Mr. Macey's much-relished history of the Lammeter family or the narrator's "vertical" description of the great dance; and Silas himself recovers his memory of past history as he recovers his ability to verbalize his thoughts. Thus the most brilliant holiday celebration in Raveloe was traditionally held at the Red House: "It was the great dance on New Year's Eve that made the glory of Squire Cass's hospitality, as of his forefathers', time out of mind." When Solomon Macey breaks with much spirit into the "Sir Roger de Coverley," the couples "formed themselves for the dance, and the Squire led off with Mrs Crackenthorp, joining hands with the rector and Mrs Osgood. That was as it should be—that was what everybody had been used to—and the charter of Raveloe seemed to be renewed by the ceremony." This renewal by ceremony, unlike the similar dance in *Daniel Deronda,* revitalizes orderly patterns of human life, which confer upon Raveloe both stability and meaning. But such age-old customs are expected in a family such as the Casses "that had killed its own geese for many generations." And the doctor? "Time out of mind the Raveloe doctor had been a Kimble; Kimble was inherently a doctor's name."

Perhaps the most striking instance of inherited tradition occurs at the conclusion of the novel. After Eppie's marriage to Aaron, we learn that Silas and Eppie "had declared that they would rather stay at the Stone-pits than go to any new home." So alterations are made in the house to accommodate the larger family, thus preserving the domestic structure as well as the tradition of the family home. The new couple has no intention of leaving Raveloe for urban or industrial society. The decision to stay not only in Raveloe but in Silas' cottage as well is a triumph for tradition, for the rooted past and for its continuation, and anticipates the conservative plot resolutions of *Under the Greenwood Tree* and *Far from the Madding Crowd.* Earlier, Eppie had said to Silas: " 'But I don't want any change. . . . I should like to go on a long, long while, just as we are'." Although Aaron presses for change and although a marriage finally occurs, the marriage represents the least change possible while still ensuring the propagation of the rural community and the continuity of the domestic idyll. Because custom and tradition help to insulate Raveloe from change, the decision to remain at the Stone-pits is a symbol of triumph for humble rural life.

I said in an earlier chapter that city-country contrasts, the creation of a circumscribed pastoral world, and harmony between landscape and character were prime features of the pastoral novel. As it formed a convention of pastoral, nature was spontaneously bountiful, pastoral characters enjoyed a harmonious relationship with their natural rural surroundings, and the season was usually clement and positive. In *Silas Marner,* this attitude changes. Here, the pastoral characters continue to exist in harmony with nature, but the use of a spiritual landscape, which we find in Vergil and elsewhere, has in *Silas Marner* been barred. In a pastoral novel, dealing as it does with rural life, the uses of nature assume special significance because they offer us an index of the author's underlying view of the pastoral world he delineates and because the uses of nature help to illuminate the lives of the characters by showing their relationship to the natural world. In *Silas Marner* nature functions in several ways: to hide the pastoral community from the world beyond, to heighten its aesthetic qualities, to reclaim the characters who are indolent and morally corrupt, and to serve as a basis to which man can be compared in order to suggest his relationship to nature.

As we have seen, Raveloe is hidden in a snug and well-wooded hollow, hidden even from the sky by trees and hedgerows. Nature, in hiding Raveloe, also isolates the community from industrial infection, and the natural barriers of mountains and trees help to prevent urban invasion (Silas is the exception) and thus to preserve Raveloe's traditions and customs, its continuity with the past. If nature circumscribes with hills and dense trees, it also provides a setting of beauty for the pastoral world, an aesthetic context for human lives that would be impoverished if they were lived in "those barren parishes . . . inhabited by meagre sheep and thinly-scattered shepherds" to which the parish of Raveloe is contrasted. Eppie wants a flower garden for its beauty. She wants double daisies, and rosemary, bergamot, and thyme for their sweet fragrance. " 'It'll be a deal livelier at the Stone-pits,' " she remarks to Silas, " 'when we've got some flowers, for I always think the flowers can see us, and know what we're talking about'." After her marriage to Aaron, we learn that

> Eppie had a larger garden than she had ever expected there now. . . . The garden was fenced with stones on two sides, but in front there was an open fence, through which the flowers shone with answering gladness, as the four united people came within sight of them.

> "O father," said Eppie, "what a pretty home ours is! I think nobody could be happier than we are."

Though they will be accused of illustrating Ruskin's "pathetic fallacy," Eppie's personifications suggest a dialogue between man and nature. Nature actively participates in human life. Although the use of personification is unusual in George Eliot's early work, it suggests, as in the two instances above, a communication between man and nature that reinforces the unity and harmony characteristic of the pastoral world.

But beneath its outward beauty nature can also be indifferent or even malign, an idea which appears in embryonic

form in George Eliot's early novels but which is not fully explored until it recurs in Hardy's fiction. Nature has therefore another function in the novel: to reclaim those who corrupt the pastoral community or bring suffering upon it. Before Dunstan is drowned in the stone pit, he boasts (ironically) to Godfrey, " 'I'm always lucky in my weather'." But after Dunstan has sold Wildfire, Dunstan rides the animal in a hunt and then into a sharpened stake, killing it. As he walks home, the narrow rutted lane grows slippery, with the mist "passing into rain." After he enters Silas' cottage and steals the gold, "the rain and darkness had got thicker, and he was glad of it. . . . So he stepped forward into the darkness." It is darkness that nature sets down over him like a veil, and darkness that the accumulated rain in the stone pit soon brings to Dunstan's consciousness as he drowns. When Silas returns to the cottage and discovers the robbery, he rushes to the door and pulls it open: "the rain beat in upon him, for it was falling more and more heavily. There were no footsteps to be tracked on such a night." "The rain had washed away all possibility of distinguishing foot-marks." Thus the natural world rapidly obliterates the physical traces of human evil. Nature has obliterated Dunstan's tracks, then absorbed his body into its body. Nature has buried both Dunstan and the corrupting gold at the bottom of the pit, and has, as it were, attempted to restore pastoral innocence to Raveloe. As in Hardy's novels, nature assumes an active moral role. Thus Dunstan's journey, which began in insolent jest, gathers evil as it progresses, an evil mirrored in the natural world by the increasing darkness which reaches its height of intensity in the ultimate form of darkness—death. Nature, it would seem, has (in terms of the novel) a conscious mind which can initiate the reclamation process whenever that process is required to restore innocence to the pastoral community.

Molly's death is similar. When she sets out for the Red House to expose Godfrey as her husband and as father of her child, snow begins to fall. The snow-covered lanes of Raveloe slow her journey and weaken her spirit. But opium offers comfort against snow and freezing wind. Wearily, she "sank down against a straggling furze bush, an easy pillow enough; and the bed of snow, too, was soft. She did not feel that the bed was cold, and did not heed whether the child would wake and cry for her." Death follows gently but quickly; her consciousness, like Dunstan's, is gradually absorbed into the earth, both of them lying against the earth's surface to die. When Silas reaches her, a natural burial has already begun, "with the head sunk low in the furze, and half-covered with the shaken snow."

Significantly, Molly sets out on her journey on New Year's Eve to complete "a premeditated act of vengeance." The natural world has completed its annual autumn death; and it brings an end, as well, to the evil forces that operate even in George Eliot's pastoral world. Thus the new year will begin in pristine freshness. The snow which covers Molly as she dies is "virgin snow." Later, Molly's death is explicitly related to the death of nature when George Eliot remarks, "the unwept death . . . seemed as trivial as the summer-shed leaf." In the old year, vengeance is reclaimed and buried, but a new life takes firm hold when Eppie wanders into Silas' cottage just as the new year bursts into existence. The snow had stopped falling, and the stars had come out in the sky in order for Eppie to find her way to Silas' cottage. The suggestion of a moral cycle is clear enough, and this suggestion indicates a renewal of the goodness, rather than the evil, of the world. At the same time that evil is destroyed in Dunstan and Molly, Eppie's "rebirth" brings happiness to Silas, who in turn is reoriented by his pastoral experiences and then fully absorbed into the community. The novel reasserts order and peace in the pastoral world and shows, in the marriage of Eppie and Aaron and in the purposeful workings of nature, the possibilities for renewal of pastoral happiness.

As Hardy pairs Fitzpiers and Mrs. Charmond in *The Woodlanders,* George Eliot skillfully joins Dunstan and Molly in the reader's mind by employing landscape to reflect character, even though this technique, used very frequently in pastoral, applies (in this case) negatively to unadmired characters. Dunstan and Molly are unacquainted companions in evil. Both follow the same physical and psychological path toward decease. Indolent yet momentarily swollen with vengeance, they walk slowly along the narrow Raveloe lanes. Before they reach their common destination of the Red House, they both run off the road near Marner's cottage. Within a short time, both die accidental deaths of drowning or freezing. In both cases George Eliot satisfyingly surrounds Dunstan and Molly with unfavorable weather conditions, the fog and rain and snow externalizing the moral blindness of both, so that landscape and character harmonize in just the way they do when, conversely, "the sunshine fell more warmly than usual" on the day of Eppie's wedding.

Nature, agent of beauty and a moral force, serves also as a basis of comparison for the separate human world. The kinship between man and nature finds continual expression in the novel. Yet seldom is nature visualized in terms of man because George Eliot, like Theocritus, did not imaginatively conceive of nature as subject to the ambiguities and complexities of human nature. Instead nature is used as the vehicle rather than the tenor of most figures. The process is frequently reductive. Man is reduced to the stature of lower forms because he is shown, through comparison, to be in some way *like* plants and animals. Although George Eliot's use of similes can be satirical and pejorative, still the closer man is reduced to the natural world, the more natural and instinctive he appears in terms of the novel. And provided he maintains communication with his fellow men, the more natural and instinctive he becomes, the happier he becomes since his actions are less complex and difficult. Frequently, for example, Silas Marner is characterized by animal and insect imagery. He is compared to a deer, a spider, an insect, a spinning insect, an ant, a calf, a toad, a rabbit, and a dog. All of these comparisons occur however in the first half of the novel, when Silas abandons the urban world to seek "an out-of-the-way country place." Because he breaks so sharply and unequivocally with his fellow man—even after he comes to Raveloe—George Eliot suggests through the imagery that he is reduced, in the first half of the novel, to the simple, mechanical existence of an animal or insect. She shows the reductive process actually occurring in Silas' life. After his flight from the industrial city, his adjustment to a new kind of life is at first like an animal's adjustment. Working without thought, he eats and sleeps instinctively: "He seemed to weave, like the spider, from pure impulse, without reflection." Hunger and routine chores help, along with weaving, "to reduce his life to the unquestioning activity of a spinning insect." When Eppie is sent to Silas, however, he is redeemed, comes into harmony with himself, and finds again his place among his fellow men. In the second half of the novel, then, the animal-insect imagery is gradually replaced by a sense of the communication and interdependence between man and nature. As Silas is gradually assimilated into the rural world, the texture of the novel becomes highly pastoral:

> And when the sunshine grew strong and lasting, so that the buttercups were thick in the meadows, Silas might be seen in the sunny mid-day, or in the late afternoon when the shadows were lengthening under the hedgerows, strolling out with uncovered head to carry Eppie beyond the Stone-pits to where the flowers grew, till they reached some favorite bank where he could sit down, while Eppie toddled to pluck the flowers, and make remarks to the winged things that murmured happily above the bright petals.

The reductive animal and insect imagery modulates finally into harmony and interpenetration among the flowers, the insects and birds, and humanity. The passage firmly establishes a dialogue between man and the animate world. The winged things murmur happily to Eppie; she and Silas listen for "some sudden bird-note"; and the total environment converges into an equilibrium full of pastoral charm.

In order to see how George Eliot creates a pastoral world in **Silas Marner,** it may be illuminating to examine a passage from the novel in which pastoral elements are unequivocally at work. Though the passage is perhaps representative only of the later part of the novel, when Silas has lost his antipastoral love of money, it indicates the direction toward which the novel tends as Silas, alienated and urban, gradually joins the rural order. The following scene, much like a tableau, occurs as Silas and Eppie depart from the old Raveloe Church on Sunday morning.

> "I wish *we* had a little garden, father, with double daisies in, like Mrs. Winthrop's," said Eppie, when they were out in the lane; "only they say it 'ud take a deal of digging and bringing fresh soil—and you couldn't do that, could you father? Anyhow, I shouldn't like you to do it, for it 'ud be too hard work for you."
>
> "Yes, I could do it, child, if you want a bit o' garden: these long evenings, I could work at taking in a little bit o' the waste, just enough for a root or two o' flowers for you; and again, i' the morning, I could have a turn wi' the spade before I sat down to the loom. Why didn't you tell me before as you wanted a bit o' garden?"
>
> "*I* can dig it for you, Master Marner," said the young man in fustian, who was now by Eppie's side, entering into the conversation without the trouble of formalities. "It'll be play to me after

I've done my day's work, or any odd bits o' time when the work's slack.

. . . . .

"There, now, father, you won't work in it till it's all easy," said Eppie, "and you and me can mark out the beds, and make holes and plant the roots. It'll be a deal livelier at the Stone-pits when we've got some flowers, for I always think the flowers can see us and know what we're talking about. And I'll have a bit o' rosemary, and bergamot, and thyme, because they're so sweet-smelling; but there's no lavender only in the gentlefolks' gardens, I think."

"That's no reason why you shouldn't have some," said Aaron, "for I can bring you slips of anything; I'm forced to cut no end of 'em when I'm gardening, and I throw 'em away mostly. . . . there's never a garden in all the parish but what there's endless waste in it for want o' somebody as could use everything up."

When Aaron turned back up the village, Silas and Eppie went on up their lonely sheltered lane:

Eppie was now aware that her behaviour was under observation, but it was only the observation of a friendly donkey, browsing with a log fastened to his foot—a meek donkey, not scornfully critical of human trivialities, but thankful to share in them, if possible, by getting his nose scratched; and Eppie did not fail to gratify him with her usual notice, though it was attended with the inconvenience of his following them, painfully, up to the very door of their home.

But the sound of a sharp bark inside, as Eppie put the key in the door, modified the donkey's views, and he limped away again without bidding. The sharp bark was the sign of an excited welcome that was awaiting them from a knowing terrier, who, after dancing at their legs in a hysterical manner, rushed with a worrying noise at a tortoise-shell kitten under the loom, and then rushed back with a sharp bark again, as much as to say, "I have done my duty by this feeble creature, you perceive"; while the lady-mother of the kitten sat sunning her white bosom in the window, and looked round with a sleepy air of expecting caresses, though she was not going to take any trouble for them.

. . . . .

Silas sat down now and watched Eppie with a satisfied gaze as she spread the clean cloth, and set on it the potato-pie. . . .

Silas ate his dinner more silently than usual, soon laying down his knife and fork, and watching half-abstractedly Eppie's play with Snap and the cat, by which her own dining was made rather a lengthy business. Yet it was a sight that might well arrest wandering thoughts: Eppie, with the rippling radiance of her hair and the whiteness of her rounded chin and throat set off by the dark-blue cotton gown, laughing merrily as the kitten held on with her four claws to one shoulder, like a design for a jug-handle, while

Snap on the right hand and Puss on the other put up their paws towards a morsel which she held out of the reach of both—Snap occasionally desisting in order to remonstrate with the cat by a cogent worrying growl on the greediness and futility of her conduct; till Eppie relented, caressed them both, and divided the morsel between them.

This is a highly pastoral scene. In creating a domestic idyll, George Eliot is concerned to show the pastoral simplicity and freedom, the humor and the leisure, of the humble rustic life at the Stone-pits. Together, the garden and the isolated cottage replace the bower of traditional pastoral; and work is conceived not as the peasant's hard task but as pleasurable. The scene reminds us of the Poysers on their way to church, illustrating as they go the interdependence of plant, animal, and human worlds, or of Giles and Marty planting trees in *The Woodlanders.* Here, with flowers and animals as companions, Silas and Eppie reveal similarly the essential unity of various levels of life.

The scene opens with discussion of a garden. Yet the garden is not to be the vegetable garden we might expect in a rural area but a flower garden, catalogued in pastoral fashion, that will provide touches of beauty. As in portraits of the Golden Age—Vergil's in the fourth eclogue, e.g.—nature is exuberantly fertile in Raveloe, and parish gardens bear profusely. In its natural wealth, its innocence, and its harmony between man and nature, Raveloe is like Hayslope and other circumscribed pastoral regions—Mellstock in *Under the Greenwood Tree,* Weatherbury in *Far from the Madding Crowd,* Little Hintock in *The Woodlanders,* Nethermere in *The White Peacock,* and Wragby Wood in *Lady Chatterley's Lover.*

Yet unlike the leisure of traditional pastoral, work is required to tend this abundant natural growth. In traditional pastoral the earth produces spontaneously: no gardening is needed. But there is little *otium* implied in this scene, for rich topsoil must be hauled, the ground spaded and raked, the flower beds made, the holes dug, and the new slips planted and watered. Yet such work is not arduous or dreaded; rather, Eppie and Aaron and Silas work willingly to prepare the garden. "It'll be play to me after I've done my day's work," remarks Aaron. To the pastoral characters, work is not task but pleasure, and this fact calls into question the rigid distinction between work and *otium* usually insisted on by theorists of pastoral, for work offers satisfactions similar to those offered by leisure. Working with the soil is praised by George Eliot, as it is by Hardy and Lawrence after her, because it results in the creation of beauty, the meaningful use of time, and direct communion with the natural world. In **Silas Marner,** as in traditional pastoral, the aesthetic triumphs over the utilitarianism of the georgic.

The close relationship between the pastoral characters and the natural world is again made clear when Silas and Eppie, on the way up their sheltered lane, meet the donkey. Not only does Eppie gratify him with her usual notice, but the donkey appears to understand humanity. In an unusual attribution, the donkey possesses the human power of thought and emotion, and is not scornful but thankful to share in human trivialities. We do not see the donkey as a beast of burden but as a participant in human activity. Like the flowers, the donkey seems to understand his surroundings. Although the suggestion of animal and plant perception is sentimental, it has the effect of narrowing the normal distance between the human world and the animal-and-plant world beneath it. This narrowing creates an intimacy between the pastoral characters and their environment, a correlation between spiritual and physical, that is typically pastoral. This narrowing process sustains the intimacy between man and nature that underlies George Eliot's treatment, analyzed earlier, of the deaths of Dunstan and Molly.

As Silas and Eppie approach the door of the cottage, the interaction between animal and human continues. The brown terrier, a "knowing" terrier, almost speaks to Silas and Eppie. The kitten's mother, a "lady," expects caresses; but as though capable of deliberate thought, she disdains to seek them. Later, Snap remonstrates the cat "on the greediness and futility of her conduct." The enlarging or "additive" process clearly at work here reverses the reductive process that prevails in the early part of the novel. The animals, because they are like humans, seem more significant than ordinary animals. They are, instead, communicating companions, like animals in Theocritus and Vergil; as a result the emphasis falls on the high degree of satisfying communication between the human and animal worlds. The agent of this communication is Eppie, who has helped Silas to seek assimilation into the rural order and who has "come to link him once more with the whole world. There was love between him and the child that blent them into one, and there was love between the child and the world—from men and women with parental looks and tones, to the red lady-birds and the round pebbles." What flashes forth in the scene as a whole is the unity and harmony of life at the Stone-pits. This life is symbolic of the larger life of the village itself, excluding only the Cass family, which is openly acknowledged to be atypical. The Casses possess wealth along with the complexities and problems that wealth brings, and are for this reason nonpastoral. The only threat to the equilibrium of the pastoral community arises from the turbulence and disorder engendered by those who are neither humble nor poor. Silas and Eppie and Aaron and the other humble characters in the novel have little money, and Silas spends little of what he earns. Unlike the Squire and his sons, they are neither wealthy nor idle nor proud. Their unwillingness to aspire for wealth and position leads them toward innocence and happiness, as it did pastoral shepherds of old. Searching not for power or fame, they reject ambition. " 'I don't think I shall want anything else when we've got a little garden,' " Eppie says, and the narrator remarks: "people in humble stations" are often happier "than those brought up in luxury."

In pastoral literature a concern with the role of luxury, or money, has always been of underlying interest as one ingredient in the dialectic between city and country. Silas moves from a nonpastoral to a pastoral condition with the loss of his money, and when Godfrey Cass grows penitent near the end of the novel, we discover that the old Squire's inheritance has been divided among his several sons. Thus within the moral structure of the novel, loss or lack of money is equated with happiness. The inverse relationship between money (or property) and happiness is of course central to the pastoral ideal. In one sense George Eliot offers a rejection of the Victorian preoccupation with money and materialism that we find in Dickens, Thackeray, or Gissing by looking to the agricultural past in which solid relationships with family and the natural world counted for more than power or money. Such an insular world, if inarticulately perceived by the rustic mind, was yet intelligible. The failure to sustain the traditional agricultural way of life has, in the twentieth century, showed only more clearly its virtues, virtues nostalgically re-created in *Silas Marner.* If today the novel seems almost as slight as Hardy's *Under the Greenwood Tree,* it is because nostalgia for the traditional past brings more charm than piercing analysis to the artistic treatment of human life. Yet the intelligence and insights of *Silas Marner* are easily underrated. In *Daniel Deronda* or *Middlemarch,* George Eliot, moving closer to the present, saw rootedness disappear, as did Hardy in his novels of the 1890s. But those novels, all of them philosophically weightier, are animated much less fully by the pastoral ideal and so sacrifice the subtle art by which charm, saved from sweetness by realistic details, is made permanently interesting. (pp. 89-105)

> *Michael Squires, " 'Silas Marner': 'A Snug Well-Wooded Hollow'," in his* The Pastoral Novel: Studies in George Eliot, Thomas Hardy, and D. H. Lawrence, *University Press of Virginia, 1974, pp. 86-105.*

Neil Roberts (essay date 1975)

[*In the following essay, Roberts compares the literary style of* Silas Marner *to the romanticism of William Blake.*]

At the centre of *Silas Marner* there is a single dominant perception: that most men inevitably attach themselves to some object outside them, and that their selves are determined by the objects which they choose.

Of all George Eliot's characters, Silas is most like Everyman. This might seem a strange observation to make about a novel with so much sociological interest, and a character whom readers are likely to feel very remote from themselves. What can be large and general enough in the life of this cataleptic Baptist weaver to make such a contention plausible? The answer lies in the fact that the heart of Silas's experience is less that of a particular kind of man than is that of any other major character in George Eliot's novels.

Such a generality of intention is hinted at in the suggestions of *The Pilgrim's Progress* at the beginning of the novel: the 'mysterious burden' that the wandering weavers always carried on their backs and the situation of Silas's cottage 'not far from the edge of a deserted stone-pit'. These hints are supported by an explicit reference at the end of Chapter 14:

> In the old days there were angels who came and took men by the hand and led them away from the city of destruction. We see no white-winged

angels now. But yet men are led away from threatening destruction: a hand is put into theirs, which leads them forth gently towards a calm and bright land, so that they look no more backward; and the hand may be a little child's.

These are small contributions to the feeling that the imaginative life of the novel is substantially a matter (in the words George Eliot used of *Romola*) of 'romantic and symbolical elements'. Together with this goes a sense of freedom and ease in the handling. What has been said of all George Eliot's early work, that it comes spontaneously from the central fount of the author's genius, with the assurance and naturalness of the thoroughly known and confidently believed, is in fact true only of *Silas Marner.* In both *Adam Bede* and *The Mill on the Floss* didacticism, theory, and the distorting authorial will are very much more in evidence than in *Middlemarch.*

But *Silas Marner,* it is generally agreed, possesses a quality lacking in any of these novels, and equally lacking in the 'romantic and symbolical elements' of *Romola* and *Daniel Deronda.* Romola drifting away and beaching at the plague-village, Daniel drifting (again!) and discovering Mirah or rowing out of the sunset to meet Mordecai, are plainly not inhabiting the 'working-day world' of George Eliot's less privileged characters; and the worlds they do inhabit are similar. The world of Silas when he sees Eppie and mistakes her hair for his gold is also 'unreal'. But it is not at all the same as the other two.

The word 'romantic' means many things. When George Eliot applied it to elements in *Romola* she associated it with 'ideal': 'The various *strands* of thought I had to work out forced me into a more ideal treatment of Romola than I had foreseen at the outset' [quoted in *The George Eliot Letters,* edited by Gordon S. Haight, 1954-1955]. In these episodes in *Romola* and *Deronda* the real and the ideal are one. 'Obstacles, incongruities, all melted into the sense of completion with which his soul was flooded by this outward satisfaction of his longing'. That description of Mordecai's feelings when he sees Daniel coming 'from the golden background' is a fair indication of what George Eliot meant by 'ideal'—and, I think, of how seriously it can be taken. The symbolism which carries these idealisations suggests vagueness, arbitrariness, and a laziness of thought overcome by wish-fulfilment.

It may be argued that 'thought' is not a notable characteristic of *Silas Marner,* and that here too George Eliot is relaxing her standards of causation in the interests of her theme. But one thing referred to by the word 'romantic' is a changing sense of what can be meant by 'thought'—at least if we think of 'romanticism' as the romanticism of Blake. Here are some comments by F. R. Leavis on Blake's 'The Sick Rose':

> The seeing elements of our inner experience as clearly defined objects involves, of itself, something we naturally call "thought". . . .

> There is, then, much more solid ground for attributing "thought" to this wholly non-ratiocinative and apparently slight poem than to that ostensibly syllogistic, metaphysical piece of Shelley's ["Music, when soft voices die"].

'Seeing elements of our inner experience as clearly defined objects' is not how most readers would describe those elements in *Romola* and *Daniel Deronda.* Is it not, on the other hand, what is happening in the following passages?

> Strangely Marner's face and figure shrank and bent themselves into a constant mechanical relation to the objects of his life, so that he produced the same sort of impression as a handle or a crooked tube, which has no meaning standing apart.
>
> (Chapter 2)

> The light of his faith quite put out, and his affections made desolate, he had clung with all the force of his nature to his work and his money; and like all objects to which a man devotes himself, they had fashioned him into correspondence with themselves. His loom, as he wrought in it without ceasing, had in its turn wrought on him, and confirmed more and more the monotonous craving for its monotonous response. His gold, as he hung over it and saw it grow, gathered his power of loving into a hard isolation like its own.
>
> (Chapter 5)

> They had to knock loudly before Silas heard them; but when he did come to the door he showed no impatience, as he would once have done, at a visit that had been unasked for and unexpected. Formerly, his heart had been as a locked casket with its treasure inside; but now the casket was empty, and the lock was broken.
>
> (Chapter 10)

> Instead of the hard coin with the familiar resisting outline, his fingers encountered soft warm curls.
>
> (Chapter 12)

The gold above all is used in a varied and extended way as a metaphor or symbol for Silas's inner experience. The symbol is neither arbitrary nor esoteric. To take a similar instance, the metaphors in the following lines from Chaucer's account of the Friar are much more than lightly ironical:

> For many a man so hard is of his herte,
> He may nat wepe, althogh hym soore smerte.
> Therfore in stede of wepynge and preyeres
> Men moote yeve silver to the povre freres.
> [*The Canterbury Tales*]

Silver and tears, gold coins and golden hair, spark off meanings in each other in a way that is very similar to the imagery of Blake's 'Sick Rose'; and when the meanings are controlled and exploited as they are in that poem and in *Silas Marner,* it is obviously a mode of *thought.*

The gold provides a continuity in Silas's life. His inner experience during his fifteen-year withdrawal from human life is compared to that of a man in prison for whom the marking-up of days on the wall becomes an obsession; but the quality and meaning of the experience is very much bound up with the fact that what Silas is piling up is *gold.* The passages quoted earlier show just how George Eliot uses the image of gold. Its appearance of warmth as against its real coldness; the isolation necessitated by his worship of it; the repetitiveness and lack of growth in his relation to it (in contrast to the accumulation of the coins themselves)—these are not accidents of Silas's life but facts which determine it both inwardly and outwardly.

It is to its source in a perception of this kind of reality (akin to Blake's) that the novel owes its comparative freedom and ease, and also its 'romance' quality, which has nothing to do with evasion or softening of reality. The meaning of Silas's regeneration is not that misers in rural communities are likely to be saved by little girls, but that such must be the orientation of all men's hearts if they are to achieve spiritual health. There is nothing sentimental about the portrayal of the community itself. George Eliot's general comments on it are in the spirit of a sociological or anthropological observer, and the particularities are in keeping with her scorn of the idealised peasant of conventional art. . . . Eppie's mind has been kept 'in that freshness which is sometimes falsely supposed to be an invariable attribute of rusticity' (Chapter 16). If Eppie herself is somewhat idealised (can we really believe that her undisciplined upbringing would have had no bad effects?) the idealisation belongs to the non-realistic mode of the scene in which Silas discovers her, and we are deliberately prevented from drawing the wrong conclusions.

Although the symbolism of the gold is of central importance to the treatment of Silas's inner life, it is only a part of that treatment, and a complete view necessarily involves the subject of religion. Silas's religious experience is entirely founded on his experience of men. His life among the brethren of Lantern Yard was a life of community, and at the centre of it was his love for his friend, William Dane. It is William's vile act, supported by the drawing of lots, and the loss of his betrothed, that drives Silas away from community and from God. It is true that there is an interval, before the drawing of lots, in which faith in God survives the loss of faith in man—

> Silas knelt with his brethren, relying on his own innocence being certified by immediate divine interference, but feeling that there was sorrow and mourning behind for him even then—that his trust in man had been cruelly bruised.
>
> (Chapter 1)

—and if the decision had favoured him (assuming William had not cheated) Silas's future would probably have been different. The truth is obviously more complex than a simple equation of God and man would suggest. In any case (since there are grounds for detecting the influence of Feuerbach here) the conception of God is based not upon any individual man but upon Humanity—and it is Humanity (or the community that for him represents Humanity) that casts Silas out.

Silas's reaction to the drawing of the lots is a blasphemy: ' "there is no just God that governs the earth righteously, but a God of lies, that bears witness against the innocent" ' (Chapter 1). Silas has no capacity to abstract the idea of God from the practices of the community to which he belongs:

> To people accustomed to reason about the forms in which their religious feeling has incorporated itself, it is difficult to enter into that simple, un-

taught state of mind in which the form and the feeling have never been severed by an act of reflection. We are apt to think it inevitable that a man in Marner's position should have begun to question the validity of an appeal to the divine judgement by drawing lots; but to him this would have been an effort of independent thought such as he had never known.

(Chapter 1)

It is part of the portrayal of Silas's early religious experience that we are invited to criticise the particular 'form' that it took and, subsequently, to compare it unfavourably with the loose, pagan, worldly-superstitious religion of Raveloe. When the robbery of Silas's gold is investigated, a tinder-box is produced as evidence. Mr Macey, the parish-clerk,

> pooh-poohed the tinder box; indeed, repudiated it as a rather impious suggestion, tending to imply that everything must be done by human hands, and that there was no power which could make away with the guineas without moving the bricks. Nevertheless, he turned round rather sharply on Mr. Tookey, when the zealous deputy, feeling that this was a view of the case peculiarly suited to a parish-clerk, carried it still further, and doubted whether it was right to inquire into a robbery at all when the circumstances were so mysterious.
>
> "As if," concluded Mr. Tookey—"as if there was nothing but what could be made out by justices and constables."
>
> "Now, don't you be for overshooting the mark, Tookey," said Mr. Macey, nodding his head aside admonishingly. "That's what you're allays at; if I throw a stone and hit, you think there's summat better than hitting, and you try to throw a stone beyond. What I said was against the tinder-box: I said nothing against justices and constables, for they're o' King George's making, and it 'ud be ill-becoming a man in a parish office to fly out again' King George."
>
> (Chapter 8)

It is Mr Macey who represents Raveloe opinion: Tookey is the universal butt. While George Eliot is clearly amused by this woolliness of distinction between the mysterious and the investigable, she regards it as healthier and more realistic than the Lantern Yard brethren's rigid reference of matters of fact to the lottery (which is not to be confused with Dinah Morris's reference of highly complex spiritual choices to such external 'leadings' as the arbitrary opening of the Bible [in ***Adam Bede***]). Vagueness as to where mystery begins is itself a part of the sense of mystery, and so is the awareness that some things are not mysterious; the brethren's mystification of all things makes one wonder whether they are truly aware of mystery at all. George Eliot's own belief in the importance of such awareness is beyond doubt: 'But to me the Development theory and all other explanations of processes by which things come to be, produce a feeble impression compared with the mystery that lies under the processes' [quoted in Haight].

Another respect in which the Raveloe religion is seen to

be superior to that of Lantern Yard (pointed out by [Q. D. Leavis in her Introduction to the Penguin edition of *Silas Marner,* 1967]) is the belief that 'to go to church every Sunday in the calendar would have shown a greedy desire to stand well with Heaven, and get an undue advantage over their neighbours' (Chapter 10). The spiritual pride of William Dane, his confidence in his own 'calling and election', makes an unpleasant contrast to this and Silas's humility. Silas's inability to 'arrive at anything higher than hope mingled with fear' (Chapter 1), is closer to the spirit of Dolly Winthrop, whose reference to the Deity as 'Them' signifies unwillingness to express a presumptuous familiarity. But Raveloe is no more idealised in this respect than in any other. The people's superstition thwarts an early occasion for fellowship with Silas, when his cure of Sally Oates (with the aid of his inherited herbal lore) makes them believe that he is in league with the Devil.

Silas's life between his departure from Lantern Yard and his discovery of Eppie is godless. The only sign of positive spiritual life is the little incident of the brown pot which, when he has broken it, Silas puts together and keeps 'for a memorial' (Chapter 2). This, in contrast to the accumulation of the gold, is a substitute for human affections. It is worth noting that when George Eliot uses the word 'fetishism', she applies it not to the gold but to the old brick hearth which he loved 'as he had loved his brown pot. . . . The gods of the hearth exist for us still; and let all new faith be tolerant of that fetishism, lest it bruise its own roots' (Chapter 16). The idea that fetishism is the historical root of all religion derives from [Auguste] Comte, who proposed that this original form should be incorporated into the Religion of Humanity. But a knowledge of Comte is not necessary to understand what George Eliot means here. The gods of the hearth represent the human love on which all true religion is founded, and this is why she distinguishes Silas's attachment to the hearth and to the pot from his feeling about the gold.

The effect of Eppie on Silas's life can best be indicated by quotation:

> Unlike the gold which needed nothing, and must be worshipped in close-locked solitude—which was hidden away from the daylight, was deaf to the song of birds, and started to no human tones—Eppie was a creature of endless claims and ever-growing desires, seeking and loving sunshine, and living sounds, and living movements; making trial of everything, with trust in new joy, and stirring the human kindness in all eyes that looked on her. The gold had kept his thoughts in an ever-repeated circle, leading to nothing beyond itself; but Eppie was an object compacted of changes and hopes that forced his thoughts onward, and carried them far away from their old eager pacing towards the same blank limit—carried them away to the new things that would come with the coming years, when Eppie would have learned to understand how her father Silas cared for her; and made him look for images of that time in the ties and charities that bound together the families of his neighbours. The gold had asked that he should sit weaving longer and longer, deafened and blind-

ed more and more to all things except the monotony of his loom and the repetition of his web; but Eppie called him away from his weaving, and made him think all its pauses a holiday, reawakening his senses with her fresh life, even to the old winter-flies that came crawling forth in the early spring sunshine, and warming him into joy because *she* had joy.

> (Chapter 14)

While this magnificent passage is 'ideal', it is by no means sentimental. It is a celebration of growth and vitality, recalling the imagery of uninhibited joy in Blake's *Songs of Innocence*—its ideal quality is of that kind. It is enough to dispose for ever of the life-and-beauty-hating Puritan that W. B. Yeats was taught to see George Eliot as by his father. Eppie retains the animal spirits that give life to this description when she is grown up:

> "O daddy!" she began, when they were in privacy, clasping and squeezing Silas's arm, and skipping round to give him an energetic kiss. "My little old daddy! I'm so glad. I don't think I shall want anything else when we've got a little garden; and I knew Aaron would dig it for us," she went on with roguish triumph—"I knew that very well."

> "You're a deep little puss, you are," said Silas, with the mild passive happiness of love-crowned age in his face; "but you'll make yourself fine and beholden to Aaron."

> "O no, I shan't," said Eppie, laughing and frisking; "he likes it."

> (Chapter 16)

Where else in George Eliot does one find this beautiful effect of 'the mild passive happiness of love-crowned age' being clasped and squeezed by the skipping, laughing and frisking adolescent girl? It is one token of the superior ease and freedom of the novel when compared particularly with the latter stages of *The Mill on the Floss.* The forward-looking celebration of life is in sharp contrast to the dominance of the past in that novel.

Emphasis is given to this point when we consider the scene in which Silas returns to Lantern Yard and finds that it has disappeared. The scene shows that Silas, alone among George Eliot's characters, survives and benefits from a complete uprooting. One of the reasons for his return is that he wants at last to have the drawing of the lots explained to him; but he has to remain in the dark. When he comes back to Raveloe Dolly Winthrop says:

> "You were hard done by that once, Master Marner, and it seems as you'll never know the rights of it; but that doesn't hinder there *being* a rights, Master Marner, for all it's dark to you and me."

> "No," said Silas, "no; that doesn't hinder. Since the time the child was sent to me and I've come to love her as myself, I've had light enough to trusten by; and now she says she'll never leave me, I think I shall trusten till I die."

> (Chapter 21)

This trust in life, born of new, developing experience, is

147   146

justify his insincerity by manifesting its prudence.
And ~~[crossed out]~~
~~[crossed out]~~
~~[crossed out]~~ in this point of trusting to some throw
of fortune's dice, Godfrey ~~he~~ can hardly be called specially
old-fashioned. Favourable Chance, I fancy, is
the god of all men who follow their own devices instead of obeying a law they believe in.
Let even a polished man of these days ~~[crossed out]~~
to get into a position he is ashamed to avow, +
his mind will be bent on all the possible issues that
may deliver him from the calculable results of that
position; let him live outside his income or shirk
the resolute honest work that brings wages + he
will presently find himself dreaming of a possible
benefactor, a possible simpleton who may be cajoled
into using his interest, a possible state of mind in
some possible person not yet forthcoming. Let
him neglect the responsibilities of his office, + he
will inevitably anchor himself on the chance that
the thing left undone may turn out not to be of
the supposed importance; let him betray his friend's
confidence + he will adore that same cunning ~~[crossed out]~~

A page from the manuscript of chapter nine of Silas Marner.

just what is lacking in Maggie Tulliver when she refuses to marry Stephen Guest on the grounds that 'If the past is not to bind us, where can duty lie? We should have no law but the inclination of the moment.'

And yet it would be absurd to suppose that George Eliot had abandoned her belief in continuity only to reaffirm it, as we shall see, in her next two novels. In fact one of the things we are told about Silas in his period of alienation is that he has lost continuity:

> He hated the thought of the past; there was nothing that called out his love and fellowship toward the strangers he had come amongst; and the future was all dark, for there was no Unseen Love that cared for him.

> (Chapter 2)

In Silas's consciousness the Unseen Love that he has lost is the God of his religion, but we are invited to see it as being Humanity whose two aspects, Continuity and Solidarity, are summarised in this passage. Living from moment to moment, which is what Silas does when he first comes to Raveloe, is not an acceptable alternative to being rigidly bound by the past. But these alternatives are not exclusive. Although Silas is in most senses irretrievably cut-off from his past, it is '*old* quiverings of tenderness' that he feels when he finds Eppie:

> . . . there was a vision of the old home and the old streets leading to Lantern Yard—and within that vision another, of the thoughts which had been present with him in those far-off scenes. The thoughts were strange to him now, like old friendships impossible to revive; and yet he had a dreamy feeling that this child was somehow a message come to him from that far-off life: it stirred fibres that had never been moved in Raveloe—old quiverings of tenderness—old impressions of awe at the presentiment of some Power presiding over his life.

> (Chapter 12)

His very first impression is, 'Could this be his little sister come back to him in a dream—his little sister whom he had carried about in his arms for a year before she died, when he was a small boy without shoes or stockings?' and this link with past feeling has an obvious practical value in his attempts to look after Eppie.

As Silas becomes (as far as he can be) integrated into Raveloe life and culture, a fuller measure of continuity asserts itself:

> By seeking what was needful for Eppie, by sharing the effect that everything produced on her, he had himself come to appropriate the forms of custom and belief which were the mould of Raveloe life; and as, with reawakening sensibilities, memory also reawakened, he had begun to ponder over the elements of his old faith, and blend them with his new impressions, till he recovered a consciousness of unity between his past and present.

> (Chapter 16)

One readily concedes that early memories of family love are necessary for an old bachelor miser to be awakened to

life by a little girl; and that a blending of old faith with new impressions is needful for a harmonious life. This is a conception of continuity which falls far short of Maggie Tulliver's rigid life-denying doctrine, and one which is compatible with 'trusting' openness to new life and altered circumstances. One is tempted to believe that the unique nature of the conception and form of **Silas Marner** made this freedom possible.

The other centre of interest in the novel, the story of Godfrey Cass, is in no way inferior, but it calls for less comment since it is more of a piece with other elements in George Eliot's work. Godfrey is another Arthur Donnithorne whose moral life is dominated by 'the old disposition to rely on chances which might be favourable to him' (Chapter 8). Chances are favourable to him insofar as his clandestine wife dies, leaving him free to marry Nancy Lammeter, but he is nevertheless made to learn the hard reality of consequences. Perhaps the most terrible moment in the novel is when his wife's body is found and Godfrey finds himself hoping that she is dead:

> Godfrey felt a great throb: there was one terror in his mind at that moment: it was, that the woman might *not* be dead. That was an evil terror—an ugly inmate to have found a nestling place in Godfrey's kindly disposition; but no disposition is a security from evil wishes to a man whose happiness hangs on duplicity.

> (Chapter 13)

When, after sixteen years, the daughter he did not acknowledge as a child refuses to leave her adopted father for him, Godfrey learns the truth that Adam Bede and Mr Irwine try to teach Arthur: 'there's debts we can't pay like money debts, by paying extra for the years that have slipped by' (Chapter 20). His career reminds us that we are in the familiar George Eliot world of moral responsibility, in which intentions count for nothing in comparison with acts, and the evil-doer cannot comfort himself with the thought that he meant no harm. But a comparison of Godfrey and Silas does not create in one the feeling that one has when comparing, for example, Gwendolen Harleth and Daniel Deronda: that the character whose world contains 'romantic and symbolical elements' is privileged. My earlier phrase for the art by which George Eliot tests her preconceptions—'sympathetic immersion in the actual'—clearly will not do for the art of **Silas Marner.** But the basis of the story is nevertheless something other than her didacticism, something which, like the sense of the actual in her other great works, controls that didacticism, and which entails a grasp of something real. Among her attempts at non-realistic modes, **Silas Marner** is uniquely successful. (pp. 107-18)

> *Neil Roberts, " 'Silas Marner,' " in his* George Eliot: Her Beliefs and Her Art, *Paul Elek, 1975, 240 p.*

Laura Comer Emery   (essay date 1976)

[*In the following excerpt, Emery provides a psychoanalytic analysis of the plot and imagery of* Silas Marner.]

Turning directly from the pages of **The Mill on the Floss** to *Silas Marner,* one experiences something like culture shock. Suddenly Maggie's conflicting needs, fears, and "shoulds" and the explosive rush of the symbolic flood-death ending are replaced by the apparent simplicity of Silas and the slow-moving symbolism of his isolated, insect-like existence.

This sudden shift away from the intensity and complexity of Maggie struck me at first as a defensive reaction—one for which there was sufficient cause in the novelist's circumstances. When she began writing *The Mill on the Floss,* even her best friends did not know that Marian Evans Lewes was George Eliot. But before that novel was finished, the Liggins rumors had pressured her into revealing herself as the already famous author. Thus the self-exposure of her highly autobiographical novel coincided with the public exposure of her irregular union with George Henry Lewes, and the sensitive author began to feel that she lived in a "house full of eyes" [quoted in Gordon S. Haight's *George Eliot,* 1968].

As long as I continued to view the shift to a reduced focal character as defensive only, thus treating *Silas Marner* as a realistic novel manqué, I could only regret losing the richness that was achieved in the portrayal of Maggie. But now I can see the shift as over-determined: it serves defensive purposes *and* expressive purposes. The simple, alienated weaver is not only reassuringly unlike the author, reduced to fit her defensive needs; he is also the vehicle for expressing a new understanding. And this symbolic function, which opens up if we respond to the non-realistic traces of folk tale as cues, is clearly of primary importance. As a symbol, the reduced character from whom "the movement, the mental activity, and the close fellowship" of life have been stripped away, conveys a new awareness and a new valuation of the primitive human needs thus laid bare. (pp. 55-6)

Before coming to Raveloe, Silas Marner's life was "incorporated in a narrow religious sect" (chap. I)—he was part of a community. When his trust in God and man was destroyed, he left the community. For the next fifteen years he lived outside the village of Raveloe, having nothing to do with his neighbors beyond the selling of his cloth.

This is the bare outline of the first part of the Silas story, the action of the first two chapters of the novel. The imagery of these chapters suggests that Silas's alienation from society has meaning beyond the manifest emphasis on "the anguish of disappointed faith" (chap. I) or its result in the shrunken life. In his alienation from Raveloe life, the simple weaver is compared to "the little child" who "knows nothing of parental love, but only knows one face and one lap towards which it stretches its arms for refuge and nurture" (chap. II). This metaphor not only points toward the later discovery of a little child; it also combines with the image of new land where "mother earth shows another lap" to suggest that Silas's first loss has to do with the child's loss of parents. Working with these images are the childlike qualities of Silas: he is repeatedly described as "undersized," with an "expression of trusting simplicity" and a "defenseless, deer-like gaze" (chap. I), and his lack of parents, his nearsightedness, his catatonic fits, and his overall passivity add to the impression of defenseless-

ness. Thus "the anguish of disappointed faith" seems to have behind it the anguish of the child without parents.

There are no actual parents involved in the flashback which accounts for Silas's outcast condition and establishes sympathy for him. The eight-page sketch tells us that Silas is a victim, framed for robbery by his best friend, found guilty by God through the casting of lots, and deserted by everyone including his fiance. But all this has the appearance of a screen memory. There is a peculiar emphasis on the triangular relationship between Silas, Sarah, and William:

> It had seemed to the unsuspecting Silas that the friendship had suffered no chill even from his formation of another attachment of a closer kind. For some months he had been engaged to a young servant woman, waiting only for a little increase to their mutual savings in order to their marriage; and it was a great delight to him that Sarah did not object to William's occasional presence in their Sunday interviews. It was at this point in their history that Silas's cataleptic fit occurred.
>
> (Chap. I)

The juxtaposition of Silas's first fit with the engagement and the triangle implies that the complete blocking of all sensation represents the repression of feelings associated with a disguised or revived Oedipal conflict. This implication is then borne out by rapidly succeeding events—the death of a father-figure (during another of Silas's fits), accusations of guilt from father-figures, and the subsequent marriage of William and Sarah.

Thus the breach between the child and the parents which underlies Silas's alienation seems to originate in the Oedipal conflict. The child's competition with the father or mother is doomed to failure and inevitably gives rise to feelings of impotence and hostility, as well as guilt. Silas's impotence is not disguised; in fact it seems to be used to deny his guilt when he is accused of robbery. His innocence depends upon two suppositions: that the robbery occurred while Silas was in a catatonic state (a state of perfect impotence), and that his pocket knife, the incriminating symbol of phallic potency found at the scene, was actually in the possession of William Dane at the time of the robbery.

The guilt and hostility inherent in the Oedipal conflict *are* disguised, however, by displacement and projection. The emphasis on the robbery distracts attention from the fact that the senior deacon (an obvious father-figure) dies while Silas is keeping watch at his bedside. The hostility of wishing the rival parent dead is projected onto other father-figures, whose accusations are hostile acts against Silas. William Dane, Silas's closest friend (older and bigger than Silas, and "somewhat given to over severity"), becomes his first accuser, then the elders, and finally God himself.

Silas's actual father is never mentioned, and this omission gains significance from the displacement of attention away from the deacon's death. His mother is mentioned in regard to the knowledge of medicinal herbs she bequeathed to him at her death, knowledge which Silas has come to view as a temptation (along with his pleasure in gathering herbs) to underestimate the power of God (or the father). And the fact that this feeling akin to guilt can be admitted to consciousness, while feelings about the father are completely blocked out, implies that the strongest and most unacceptable feelings are associated with the father. This is indeed what the fantasy expresses by projecting the greatest part of the hostility onto father-figures. But hostility against the much desired but unfaithful mother is also projected. Thus, when Sarah marries William Dane, the Oedipal failure is complete, and Silas leaves Lantern Yard and regresses from the phallic stage.

Thus far the stress has fallen on the defensive function of the reduced character. At this stage of the fantasy the author's unconscious and highly feared hostilities are projected onto characters outside the central, essentially passive character representing the author. Where we would expect to find guilt, jealousy, or hostility in Silas, we find instead the fits of blocked feeling. Silas is "unsuspecting"—he feels that his close friendship has "suffered no chill" from his engagement. When his friend suggests that his fits look like visitations of Satan, Silas feels no resentment (chap. I). Thus Silas, like the hero of a fairy tale, is not allowed to be a whole or complex representation of the author; other characters, who represent the parents against whom he unconsciously feels hostile, are made to bear the hostile feelings. They wrong the central character, creating the breach between parent and child, and thus provide an excuse for the hostility with which they are unconsciously regarded.

But the ultimate aim of this defensive process (both here and in fairy tales) goes beyond such justification. For once the hostile parents have been punished, they can be forgiven and the breach between parent and child mended. It is this wished-for reconciliation between parent and child that is the most pervasive preoccupation in *Silas Marner.* It is evident in the fantasy fulfillments: one child-man (Silas) becomes both father and mother to a child; an abandoned child (Eppie) finds a motherly father; and yet another child-man (Godfrey) finds a mother substitute.

In the second stage of the Silas story the ground is prepared for the first of these reconciliations. The punishment of parents which, according to the fairy-tale pattern apparent above, precedes the reconciliation, is relegated to the Godfrey plot. Thus the healing of the breach for Silas seems to grow directly out of the regression which follows his break with the past. And this provides an important point of contrast with *The Mill on the Floss.* When Silas leaves Lantern Yard, he cuts himself off from the past, and thus from parents and super-ego as well. He does what Maggie could not do, and what the author at the time could not conceive the value of. Thus Maggie's inner conflict could only be resolved in death.

Silas's death-in-life does not at first seem like a very promising alternative to Maggie's actual death. Raveloe provides him with a refuge because it is so totally unlike his native country and there is nothing to remind him of his painful past. Its strangeness is a buffer against thought and feeling, and his life is thus reduced to a few impulses: "He seemed to weave, like the spider, from pure impulse, without reflection," and hunger was also an "immediate

prompting" which "helped, along with the weaving, to reduce his life to the unquestioning activity of a spinning insect" (chap. II). But even while the narrative insists on the "narrowing and hardening" direction of this life which seems the opposite of growth, slight suggestions of hope appear. Silas's "rush of pity" for Sally Oates's suffering could not be "the beginning of his rescue from the insect-like existence into which his nature had shrunk," because he is not ready for the swarm of "mothers who wanted him to charm away the hooping cough, or bring back the milk" and "men who wanted stuff against the rheumatics or the knots in the hands" (chap. II). But as Silas's life of "pure impulse" gradually develops the aspect of hoarding, his relationship to his guineas becomes a demonstration and a discovery that regression can be creative if it reestablishes vital contact with primitive needs.

When hoarding becomes an established habit, Silas's regression is a stabilized and completed form:

> So, year after year, Silas Marner had lived in this solitude, his guineas rising in the iron pot, and his life narrowing and hardening itself more and more into a mere pulsation of desire and satisfaction that had no relation to any other being. His life had reduced itself to the functions of weaving and hoarding, without any contemplation of an end towards which the functions tended.
>
> (Chap. II)

At first it is merely "pleasant to him" to feel the guineas in his palm "and look at their bright faces, which were all his own" (chap. II). Then he develops a "habit of looking towards the money and grasping it with a sense of fulfilled effort." The spider weaves a web out of his bodily contents, and Silas is "like the spider." He exchanges the "brownish web"—produced by "his muscles moving with such even repetition that their pause seemed almost as much a constraint as the holding of his breath" (chap. II)—for golden guineas which he cherishes as "all his own," representative of nothing outside himself.

The connection of the guineas to anality is evident not only in the spider metaphor (the brownish web and bodily contents), but also in the cluster of images related to Silas's hoarding activities: the stone pits filled with red water, the hole at his feet where he hides the gold, the brown pot that becomes a memorial, the iron pot and two leather bags (with their "dark leather mouths") which hold his gold, and later also the coal hold where he puts Eppie for punishment. Raveloe itself, situated in a "rich central plain," "nestled in a snug, well-wooded hollow" with "well-walled orchards" (chap. I), is cloacal (womb-like and anal):

> Nothing could be more unlike his native town, set within sight of the widespread hillsides, than this low, wooded region, where he felt hidden even from the heavens by the screening trees and hedgerows.
>
> (Chap. II)

It is at once completely strange and a refuge, "another lap."

Behind this portrayal of Silas's anality, and despite the generally cool detachment which governs it, there is a mixture of conflicting attitudes: an insatiable interest in the hoarding which is evident only in the way the repeated details stand out against the strict economy of the work, a stress on the progressive dehumanization "into a *mere* pulsation of desire and satisfaction" which implies that the process is deplorable, and an almost reluctant admission that something positive is happening. If Silas had had a "less intense nature," we are told, he might have "sat weaving, weaving" (chap. II), without becoming interested in the gold. As it is, the guineas become more and more important:

> . . . the money not only grew, but it remained with him. He began to think it was conscious of him, as his loom was, and he would on no account have exchanged those coins, which had become his familiars, for other coins with unknown faces. He handled them, he counted them, till their form and colour were like the satisfaction of a thirst to him; but it was only in the night, when his work was done, that he drew them out to enjoy their companionship.
>
> (Chap. II)

Their significance gradually changes until they are not merely anal products, but children "begotten by his labor" (chap. II). But it is not until Silas has lost his gold that the narrative explicitly recognizes the fact that Silas's hoarding is an expression of "his power of loving" (chap. V). Only when it has been brought to an end is the hoarding recognized as an activity which leads to his rescue by fostering his "power of loving."

Perhaps this explicit recognition has been withheld consciously, in order to bring the reader along very, very gradually. But I doubt it. That is why I have called the exploration of Silas's relationship "a demonstration and a discovery." The idea that "the sap of affection was not all gone" from Silas, even at this stage, is certainly presented explicitly. But the author chooses an incident not obviously related to the hoarding to symbolize it—his preservation of the broken pot as a memorial of twelve years of companionship. His nightly "revelry" is juxtaposed to this incident, but there is a note of shock in it: "How the guineas shone as they came pouring out of the dark leather mouths!" (chap. II). Then the tone softens again when Silas's view of them as children is described:

> He loved the guineas best, but he would not change the silver—the crowns and half-crowns that were his own earnings, begotten by his labour; he loved them all. He spread them out in heaps and bathed his hands in them; then he counted them and set them up in regular piles, and felt their rounded outline between his thumb and fingers, and thought fondly of the guineas that were only half earned by the work in his loom, as if they had been unborn children. . . .
>
> (Chap. II)

With this new significance of the guineas as children, Silas's possessive feelings, even before Eppie replaces the gold, have essentially progressed from himself to an outside object, from feces to child. This progression, which is preceded by the regressive change of object from penis to feces, is a typical formula for the normal development

of a female Oedipal complex. The regression from genital to anal eroticism is one means by which the female child can move from penis envy and the mother as the object of her phallic wishes, toward the desire for a child and the father as the object of receptive wishes. Thus through a male character a female author represents her own emotional development, which has an early masculine stage. Silas is designated as a man, but one who is not only impotent but also "partly as handy as a woman" (chap. XIV); he does not represent at any time a completely masculine or a completely feminine character. When Eppie replaces his gold, he becomes both father and mother to her.

But before the coming of Eppie, another important change takes place which moves Silas another step toward life and growth. He is robbed of his gold. When his initial disbelief at the sight of "the empty hole" gives way to the realization of his loss, Silas "put his trembling hands to his head, and gave a wild ringing scream, the cry of desolation" (chap. V). He has lost his gold children, but he himself utters the primal scream of the abandoned child. The robbery has left him "a second time desolate," and what an increase in intensity there is between his first protest—"there is no just God that governs the earth," uttered "in a voice shaken by agitation" (chap. I)—and this "wild ringing scream"!

The robbery forces Silas to reach out to his neighbors for the first time since the miscarriage of his compassion for Sally Oates:

> This strangely novel situation of opening his trouble to his neighbours, of sitting in the warmth of a hearth not his own, and feeling the presence of faces and voices which were his nearest promise of help, had doubtless its influence on Marner, in spite of his passionate preoccupation with his loss. Our consciousness rarely registers the beginning of a growth within us any more than without us: there have been many circulations of the sap before we detect the smallest sign of the bud.
>
> (Chap. VII)

This commentary may discount the growth that was taking place in Silas even before the robbery. The emphasis generally falls on the gold as an obstacle: Silas's hoarding had "fenced him in" from the outside world, because the object of his "clinging" was "a dead disrupted thing." But the commentary does recognize that in spite of its deadness, the gold "satisfied the need for clinging" (chap. X). And the effect of its loss depends on the love it has acquired. Thus, although Silas could not respond directly to the new kindliness of his neighbors, the "bewildering separation from a supremely loved object" led to "the habit of opening his door and looking out from time to time, as, if he thought that his money might be somehow coming back to him" (chap. XII). And that open door—with a little help from "the invisible wand of catalepsy" (chap. XII)—makes it possible for the real child to enter his life.

When George Eliot describes that fit which arrests Silas at his open door as "the invisible wand of catalepsy" she is deliberately drawing attention to her use of fairy-tale elements in the novel. This touch of mystery leads up to the greater mystery of Eppie's intrusion, and we are not meant to miss the symbolic import of these events. They are not "miracles" in the sense that they originate in supernatural forces. Each one, as David R. Carroll points out [in *Literary Monographs, Vol. 1,* edited by Eric Rothstein and Thomas K. Dunseath, 1967], is a "natural event which simply crystallizes a human process that has been going on for some time." The author has carefully given a detailed natural account of how Eppie arrived at the stone cottage, and an equally detailed account of the changes in Silas prior to Eppie's appearance. In a sense Silas's regression to a life of "pure impulse" is a process of rediscovering the child in himself, the primitive self from which a loving human being and even a religious faith may grow if nurtured. Silas is ready for Eppie, but the conjunction of her appearance with Silas's open door and closed senses is still mysterious, and the mystery is underlined. It is necessary, not as a literary device, but as an element of meaning. Eppie's coming symbolizes the intrusion on the facts of life of the mysterious process of life itself, the interruption of our daily struggles by awesome "beauty in the earth or sky" or the equally wonderful "wide-gazing calm" of a child (chap. XIII). The comprehensible and the incomprehensible combine to bring Silas and Eppie together, and the result is not a mere reflection of life, but a conception of life as an interaction between the forces of nature in man and the forces of nature outside man, both of which have aspects as mysterious even to the educated mind as "the rain and the harvest" is to Dolly Winthrop.

At the level of fantasy, Eppie's coming to Silas is the fulfillment of the child's longing for parental love, expressed both directly in Eppie's discovery of Silas, and through reversal in his discovery of her. When Eppie comes on the scene, however, the relationship between the manifest content and the latent content changes. The underlying wish-fulfillment finds a new vehicle in Eppie's prosperity under the "perfect love" of her "almost inseparable companionship" with Silas (chap. XVI). She is a more obvious version than Silas of the outcast child. And once again the child's hostilities are projected onto parents—a mother who leaves her exposed in the snow, and a father who won't own her. Her rescue by Silas, who makes his stone hut into "a soft nest for her, lined with downy patience," and who nurtures her like a mother, is an undisguised fantasy.

Silas's "unfolding" parallels Eppie's, but with an added dimension which is the focus of George Eliot's interest: Silas's awakening senses bring about awakening faith. The details of this slow process do not, however, point to another stage of fantasy fulfillment for Silas. Eppie reminds him of his little sister, and thus begins a reuniting of his past life with the present which is part of the reconciliation fantasy. But most of the imagery is used to portray the natural growth of Silas's new religious feeling.

The focus on religion is not a displacement meant to draw attention away from the fantasy, but an elaboration of the fantasy. This unique harmony between manifest and latent concerns is apparent in Carroll's description of Silas's "gradual recreation of a valid mythology":

> Silas's love for Eppie, as it develops, slowly gains religious accretions which add up at the end of the novel to a complete trust in a new God. George Eliot shows how these accretions are not extraneous, supernatural additions, but rather mythical expressions of the human love which is firmly at the center of this new religion.

Silas's groping for meaning is the expression of a need as basic to human nature as the child's need for parental love, a need which Suzanne Langer calls "the *need of symbolization.*" Its working is epitomized in the process by which Silas's hearth, where he found Eppie, becomes symbolic and almost sacred to him: "Silas would not consent to have a grate and oven added to his conveniences: he loved the old brick hearth as he had loved his brown pot—and was it not there when he had found Eppie?" (chap. XVI).

When George Eliot points out this "fetishism," her concern is to show, through the smallest act of symbolization, how true religious feeling grows out of human love. In the same way Eppie's decision to stay with Silas rather than go with Godfrey demonstrates the relationship between morality and love: her resolution was determined not by "thoughts, either of past or future," but "by the feelings which vibrated to every word Silas had uttered" (chap. XIX). Through a progression of demonstrations like these, the fantasy of reunion between parent and child is manifestly elaborated as a view of life which replaces the fear of impulse and the control of "shoulds" with a new order based on "tenderly-nurtured unvitiated feeling" (chap. XVI).

There are, of course, elements of the fantasy fulfillment which do not fit into this transformation of fantasy into meaning. Eppie's fondest wish—to live happily ever after with her father—is granted, and the parent-child reunion regains the Oedipal overtones of the early part of the Silas story. Silas is not Eppie's real father, and there are traces of a lively coquettish and competitive relationship with Aaron, who becomes Eppie's husband. Thus the Oedipal wish is somewhat disguised. But if we look at the end of the story the husband is conspicuously hard to find. It is almost as though Eppie and her father were being married. The description of the wedding procession mentions coolly that Eppie had one hand "on her husband's arm" while more warmly "with the other she clasped the hand of her father Silas" (Conclusion). Eppie's last words leave her husband out completely, as though he were paired off with his mother instead of his new wife: "Oh, Father," said Eppie, "what a pretty home ours is! I think nobody could be happier than we are" (Conclusion). Actually Eppie would have preferred not to marry or make any change. After all, as she argued to Aaron, her father had never been married. But since she will need help when Silas gets too old to work, Eppie takes the view that Aaron will be a son to Silas. Of course to some extent this reasoning reflects Eppie's sensitivity to Silas's dependence on her. But the Oedipal wish remains. The fantasy ends in a marriage, a peculiar sort of family marriage frequently met with in fairy tales.

The ending of the plot centering around Godfrey Cass does not have this fairy-tale quality. The Silas story is, at critical points, presented in absolute terms—extremes which set it apart from ordinary experience and at the same time give it symbolic power. At first Silas is absolutely devoid of jealousy and hostility, then he is absolutely cut off from his past, and later he is absolutely desolate (as during his fits he is absolutely helpless). Godfrey's story, on the other hand, is not characterized by absolutes. He has the same need for love as Silas, but it is so deeply enmeshed with the hostility and the fears resulting from its frustration that his development takes a very different turn. His life is not isolated and reduced, but socially bound, and thus his story demands, and lends itself to, a more realistic treatment than the Silas story.

Nevertheless, at the fantasy level there are striking similarities between the two plots. At one level Godfrey is another version of the parentless child. His father is alive, but does not provide either the love or the sense of order that he needs: "he had always had a sense that his father's indulgence had not been kindness, and had had a vague longing for some discipline that would have checked his own errant weakness and helped his better will" (chap. IX). Godfrey's mother died when he was a child, and Nancy Lammeter represents to him the mother he longs for. In his thoughts she is always associated with the order and firmness of purpose he misses in his father's house "without that presence of the wife and mother which is the fountain of wholesome love and fear" (chap. III). In fact, Nancy represents not only domestic order, but also inner order—that "discipline" which could rescue Godfrey from his own weakness:

> . . . she would be his wife, and would make home lovely to him, as his father's home had never been; and it would be easy, when she was always near, to shake off those foolish habits that were no pleasures, but only a feverish way of annulling vacancy.
>
> (Chap. III)

Thus what Godfrey fears is his own impulsive self. It has led him into marriage with Molly—the "blight" on his life. What he wants is a superego strong enough to overpower the "low passion" he despises in himself. His degrading marriage has made him "an outlawed soul" like Maggie, who felt doomed to "sink and wander vaguely, driven by uncertain impulse" if she let go of the sacred ties of the past.

Godfrey's daydream of being rescued by Nancy equates his marriage with Molly to being "dragged back into mud and slime" while he should have kept "fast hold of the strong silken rope by which Nancy would have drawn him safe to the green banks, where it was easy to step firmly" (chap. III). This rescue from the water by means of a "strong silken rope" is clearly a birth fantasy in which Godfrey sees Nancy as mother. But the birth is a return to mother and "paradise" rather than an entrance into the world.

The parent-child relationship is seen as a refuge from the dangers of sexuality, and Godfrey's flight from sexuality toward a mother figure is just as clearly a regression as Silas's anal hoarding. Both characters abandon genital sexuality and find refuge in parent-child relationships. Godfrey's fear of sexuality is less disguised than Silas's; his

guilt has a physical embodiment in his secret marriage, and his hostility is apparent in "cruel wishes, that seemed to enter, and depart, and enter again, like demons" (chap. III). Unlike Silas, he is aware that he is not simply a victim:

> If the curses he muttered half aloud when he was alone had no other object than Dunstan's diabolical cunning, he might have shrunk less from the consequences of avowal. But he had something else to curse—his own vicious folly . . .
>
> (Chap. III)

But the "jealous hate" and "cupidity" which are Dunstan Cass's only qualities, and his only motivation for tormenting Godfrey, seem nevertheless to be defensive projections. Dunstan's fate is the fate from which Godfrey is rescued in the birth fantasy: he is literally "dragged back into the mud and slime" at the stone pits and drowned. The horse and whip which he takes from Godfrey, like the knife which William Dane takes from Silas, are symbols of the feared sexuality from which Godfrey retreats. They represent the phallic self which Godfrey gives up in order to avoid another kind of castration—being "cut off from his inheritance" and from his mother-rescuer: losses which would leave him "as helpless as an uprooted tree" (chap. III).

The basic similarity in fantasy content of the two plots constitutes a basis for pondering the significance of their differences. The fantasy elements of the Godfrey plot which are less disguised than their parallels in the Silas story are evidence of the defensive function of the double plot. The fragmentation is a disguise which helps to prevent the fantasy content from emerging too boldly, as it does in the end of *The Mill on the Floss.* Thus the punishment of parents which is missing from the Silas story is played out in the Godfrey plot. Godfrey Cass is not only a parentless child at the fantasy level; he is also a parent, and his failure—as a parent—to acknowledge his child is one of the differences between Silas and Godfrey that account for their dissimilar fates.

But in regard to the new awareness that I have postulated, and its relationship to *The Mill on the Floss,* there is a more significant difference between the two plots. Godfrey and Silas both find refuge in the parent-child relationship, but Silas first undergoes fifteen years of complete isolation. When he denounces God and man, he cuts himself off from the past and from the structure of mind belonging to parents and authorities—the superego. Thus, when he begins to grow again, the new ties and new faith grow out of the primitive needs to which he has been reduced. But Godfrey bypasses this whole process. He manages to avoid being cut off completely, and he does this by clinging to Nancy Lammeter and her absolute ideas. He adopts her strong superego, the "unalterable little code" that will restrain his feared impulses. As a result Godfrey, for the next fifteen years, is cut off—not from others (as Silas is), but from his own primitive self. Thus, when he finally acknowledges his past errors to Nancy and decides to lay claim to Eppie, his own child (symbolic of that self) is no longer accessible to him. The discovery of Dunstan's skeleton (with Godfrey's whip) represents to some extent a return of that self and of masculinity. For the first time he is strong enough to dare offending and losing Nancy by telling the truth—to dare losing his mother for the sake of his own being. But the process of reintegration of the self is not completed within the confines of the novel.

When the different fates of Godfrey and Silas are presented in these terms, we can see more clearly how *Silas Marner* reevaluates the opposing forces of id and superego which led to the death of Maggie. But I do not mean to suggest that George Eliot's new vision grew out of a conscious perusal of the implications of Maggie's irresolvable conflict. Her letters and journals provide ample evidence to the contrary. Her next novel, after *The Mill on the Floss,* was to be set in fifteenth-century Florence and centered on the life of Savonarola—apparently as far removed as possible from the sorrows of Maggie and the author's personal life. But while she labored over her research, despairing of ever knowing enough to begin writing, something unexpected happened. Her work was interrupted by a "sudden inspiration," she wrote to her publisher, "a story of old-fashioned village life, which has unfolded itself from the merest millet-seed of thought" [quoted in *The George Eliot Letters,* edited by Gordon S. Haight, 1954-1955].

A notation in George Eliot's journal suggests that the story not only unfolded itself, but emerged from her unconscious rather importunately, as if it represented a neglected self which demanded a hearing:

> I am engaged now in writing a story, the idea of which came to me after our arrival in this house, and which has thrust itself between me and the other book I was meditating.

Her childhood impression of "a linen-weaver with a bag on his back" was no doubt revived by her own feeling of alienation, and her complex response to that strange image from the past is embodied in the novel. In writing *Silas Marner* George Eliot was not translating an idea into a picture, but using a picture to discover meaning.

The story of Silas's reduced life explores from many angles what the primitive side of man *is*—what our most primitive nature consists of. To the "brawny country-folk" of Raveloe Silas is one of those "pallid undersized men" who look "like the remnants of a disinherited race" (chap. I). His uncanny effect on his neighbors is stressed, and the explanations offered rely heavily on the inexperience of the "rude mind" and on the rural isolation of Raveloe, where "echoes of the old demon-worship" still lingered, and imagination was "all overgrown by recollections that are a perpetual pasture to fear" (chap. I). The point seems to be that Silas is feared because the villagers of Raveloe are so primitive. But, on the other hand, it is Silas who looks like a primitive remnant. And Freud's comment that the "uncanny is in reality nothing new or alien but something which is familiar and old-established in the mind and which has become alienated from it only by the process of repression" opens up another possibility. Perhaps Silas is feared by the villagers not because they are so primitive, but because *he* is so primitive, an unwelcome reminder of their own disinherited and disavowed primitive selves.

This "perhaps" leads to another. Perhaps the author herself had this response to the revived image of the linen weaver, a response which she symbolized in the cataleptic fits which made the villagers of Raveloe look upon Silas as "a dead man come to life again"—a striking image for the return of the repressed. If so, the legendary quality of *Silas Marner* preserves the sense of mystery which belongs to such a subject, while the intermingled thread of realism makes it possible to approach the uncanny figure of Silas and become reacquainted with that part of the self which has "become alienated only by the process of repression." Once recovered, that estranged aspect of the self becomes what Carroll calls "the irreducible core of human affection at the center of valid mythologies." (pp. 56-77)

> *Laura Comer Emery, " 'Silas Marner',"* in her George Eliot's Creative Conflict: The Other Side of Silence, *University of California Press, 1976, 235 p.*

Philip Fisher   (essay date 1981)

[*Fisher is an American educator and critic. In the following essay, he argues that pessimism underlies the apparently optimistic resolution of* Silas Marner.]

Like the Book of Job, *Silas Marner* takes the form of a process of subtraction and loss that plunges to an absolute nadir, a just-above-zero of the human condition, and then recovers by a process of addition until the end restates the beginning. Whether Job or Marner, there is an unreality, a gratuitous quality about the "recovery" quite different from the equally arbitrary fall. The accident that brings the thief to Marner's door is of a different order from the one that brings the tiny infant crawling through the snow. Loss at an accelerating rate we can believe in, as we do in avalanches, but no one has seen the rocks rise back up the mountain. In certain moods everyone believes in a kind of law of gravity in life as well as stones; one of the motifs of *Ulysses* is the phrase "32 ft. per second per second," the law of falling bodies.

The optimism of Job or *Silas Marner* is of a kind in which we hope rather than believe. In reading either book, we are closer to those stories of subtraction without end, *King Lear* or Wordsworth's "The Ruined Cottage," than we are to genuinely confident works. We do not believe in the recovery because we know that a man never sits in his chair with the same ease after he has once been sold up. So much of happiness is the confidence that it will not disappear in the blink of an eye, and the man wasted once by arbitrary events will never live without the anxiety that what he has might be gone by morning. While the end of the Book of Job or *Silas Marner* resembles the beginning, it does so only on the surface of events, in the numbers of friends and sheep. Job knows what no happy man ever considers: that the ground he walks on is thin paper over a gulf.

A look at the specific form of the recovery provides even more reason to place it in quotation marks. With a knot, it is true that to return to the beginning, you must exactly reverse the steps that led to the complexity. People after a disaster often fasten on the sequence and imagine that by repeating every step of it in reverse order, they will return from the predicament. This habit is pure fantasy in history or psychology. When thinkers realized in the nineteenth century how religion had taken on an economic vocabulary under the rise of capitalism, until it gave way to an economic image of man, many saw the antidote in attempts at religious revival. But sequences do not reverse in history.

To take the central example in *Silas Marner,* one of Eliot's absolutely correct insights was the growing importance of things, of hoarded goods in which one's value was recorded. In *Adam Bede* and *The Mill on the Floss,* these goods are a key to the new society, an intense center of life and self-recognition. The hoard of goods, along with reputation, states one's place and identity. It replaces the relations of station in the earlier society, relations to those above and beneath one, and equally it replaces the web of tasks that spoke one's place. When the community and round of duties no longer articulate the self, the relation to these gives way to a relation of things. And these things speak out in public to declare "what one is." The process is in one direction. But, like those who imagined religion as the cure for the condition it had been unable to prevent, Eliot pictures in *Silas Marner* the mirror image of the true history: she shows the gold hoard giving way to the child and, through the child, to the web of community.

In other words, the cure is only the catastrophe run backward; to imagine rescue is only to imagine the disaster in reverse. What offers itself as optimism is historically and psychologically the equivalent of a pessimism so hopelessly evocative of the problem that it can see no solution but the vanishing of the conditions that caused it.

For this reason, the story of Marner stands alongside that other fable of a weaver, Wordsworth's "Ruined Cottage." Both are tales of destruction, first of community, then of life itself. Weaving was the single most important English industry in the period of transition to capitalism. Just as Melville chose whaling, that first New England industry, so Wordsworth and Eliot chose weaving to create a generalized statement. When she wrote to her publisher about *Silas Marner,* Eliot mentioned Wordsworth and imagined her story was of a kind no one would like now that the old poet was dead. The poem offers its bleak images in simple chronicle without the surface of sentimental reassurance and facile hope. But *Silas Marner,* too, is made of these images and tells in parallel of a double destruction.

The community of the Lantern Yard is shattered by treachery that grows out of a sexual attraction. Marner's fiancée and his best friend fall secretly in love. Sarah cannot break the engagement. "Their engagement was known to the church, and had been recognized in the prayer-meetings; it could not be broken off without strict investigation, and Sarah could render no reason that would be sanctioned by the feeling of the community." In the control through the public notice that the community takes of private feeling lies the strict demand that all life be social life. Sarah and Vane conspire to disgrace Silas through an accusation of robbery: they accuse him of the crime they commit against him. The community never appears except in the tragic injustice of Silas's trial. From the trial

of Hetty to that of the witch to that of Silas there is a direct line. Silas is tried by an appeal to chance, by the drawing of lots that declares him guilty.

Silas accuses his friend, breaks with him, finds his engagement ended, blasphemes against God, renounces his faith, and leaves the Lantern Yard to appear in Raveloe, a mysterious stranger. A weaver, he relates to others only through his industry; otherwise he is as unfathomable to them as a witch. He is credited with powers to cure or blight. Men like Marner "were to the last regarded as aliens by their rustic neighbors, and usually contracted the eccentric habits which belong to a state of loneliness." The neighbors' suspicion finally produces oddities that it can use to justify its originally groundless fear. In describing the effect on Silas himself, Eliot makes the most direct statement in all her work of the relationship of a sense of self to a sense of community and familiarity.

> Even people whose lives have been made various by learning, sometimes find it hard to keep a fast hold on their habitual views of life, on their faith in the Invisible, nay on the sense that their past joys and sorrows are a real experience, when they are suddenly transported to a new land, where the beings around them know nothing of their history, and share none of their ideas—where their mother earth shows another lap, and human life has other forms than those on which their souls have been nourished. Minds that have been unhinged from their old faith and love, have perhaps sought this Lethean influence of exile, in which the past becomes dreamy because its symbols have vanished, and the present too is dreamy because it is linked with no memories.

At last even the present is dreamy—a mere sensation—in the absence of echoing experience, the texture of memories and objects and known relationships in which every thread leads to another, every event defines itself against other events.

Marner in Raveloe is reduced to that position from which so many later novels begin. "In this strange world, made a hopeless riddle to him, he might, if he had had a less intense nature, have sat weaving—looking towards the end of his pattern, or towards the end of his web, till he forgot the riddle, and everything else but his immediate sensations." The words are similar to Pater's in the conclusion to *The Renaissance.* "Experience, already reduced to a swarm of impressions, is ringed round for each one of us by that thick wall of personality through which no real voice has ever pierced on its way to us, or from us to that which we can only conjecture to be without." To try to untangle Marner's riddle, as so many novels of investigation do in the next generation; or to create a miniature rational world of work and patterns that, with our shortsightedness, we can contemplate instead of the riddle; or to begin to take pleasure in atomized, immediate sensation as those after Pater did—all three are in bondage to the same reading of life, the same incomprehensibility of social, and, in consequence, individual existence.

Marner's is the solution by work. Reducing life to a closed universe where one is absolutely in control—a self-made universe—he cannot see beyond the cycles of project and payment, work promised and work delivered, money owed and money paid. The world makes sense because it is empty. Only two elements exist, the loom and the hoard of gold. Like Hetty, Marner in the evening ritualizes his sensuality into a relationship with his hoard. He enjoys the "companionship" of his money, the society of inanimate things.

Three of the great mythic figures of the mid-nineteenth-century novel are misers: Dickens's Scrooge, Balzac's Grandet, and Eliot's Marner. Avarice is the essential deadly sin in an age of individualism. In de Tocqueville's description, the social energies are hoarded, and capitalism is a public form of hoarding, capital accumulation. Behind the self-made man stand two mythic figures: the monster and the miser, Frankenstein's creation and Scrooge.

Paradoxically, the miser, man totally in isolation, always hoards goods that have only social value—money, diamonds, jewelry. No miser hoards what he needs to live. Hetty, when most alone, was most intensely involved in social fantasies. The miser accumulates what a change of social forms can turn to junk, like those Indian graves filled with treasures of beads. The miser lives in a theater of the imagination, as Eliot called it, a make-believe society that seems solid and ultimate in its simplicity, but is as fragile as the society of riddles it has replaced.

Although everyone guesses Silas has gold hidden in his cottage, no one can steal it. Legibility and community create one another. "How could they have spent the money in their own village without betraying themselves? They would be obliged to 'run away'—a course as dark and dubious as a balloon journey." After the theft Marner accuses Jem Rodney, whose defense cannot be questioned. " 'What could I ha' done with his money? I could as easy steal the parson's surplice and wear it'." The money is stolen by those who could never be suspected of needing it, the rich, and Marner reaches the bottom. The theft proves that even a miser is still in society. The man most isolated remains part of the intentions of those around him, part of their imaginations if nothing else. In the Victorian novel, there is often a grim proof that society exists whether we will it or not. The agents of this proof are crime, illegitimacy, and contagious diseases. In *Bleak House,* the most distant corners of society are shown connected by their ability to ravage one another. Jo carries the disease; Esther's illegitimate parentage binds high and low; crime is woven through the whole. Society exists at least enough for everyone to stalemate one another at law while the inheritance that should be shared by all vanishes.

When Dunstan Cass enters Marner's cottage and when Godfrey's child crawls through the open door, society still exists in this minimal, negative sense. The opium addict dies in Marner's front yard on her way to disgrace Godfrey by revealing that she is his wife. The childlessness of Godfrey's marriage to Nancy is symbolically a result of the earlier marriage. Had the prudery of the time not enforced silence, Eliot might have openly stated that the childlessness was the result of venereal disease.

Only twice are high and low connected in the novel. The first time is when Dunstan Cass enters to steal the gold. It is a startling moment because only the rich can steal this money, since only they don't need it. The second event is the visit of Godfrey to steal Eppie, to reclaim her. United by catastrophe, by their ability to damage each other, the extremes of rich and poor never meet otherwise. No society includes them. The characters of the novel are individuals who enter relationships with one another, who make up their lives with one another; no network exists into which they find themselves integrated at birth.

Silas Marner is the first of Eliot's novels that critics speak of by parts, a Marner half connected only at flash points with a Cass half. Each novel that follows can be divided similarly. Nothing unites the parts but events. Yet nothing is more essential and at the same time more hopeless in Eliot's ambition than the demand that experience must have its meaning in terms of a wider frame than that of individual history. Biography seems the obvious form for her to work in, but it is the one form that is most untrue to what she knows as the truth of events. If experience is legible through the context of individual history—as it is for Freud, who finds the complete meaning of an event within the absolute vacuum of the patient's memory—then the self is the one reference point for motive and the one goal of action.

Looking back at Adam's life or Maggie's, we can see that the most important changes were not willed and could not be understood with only their lives as contexts. The love affair between Hetty and Arthur indirectly gives the critical turn to Adam's life. Her father's feud with Wakem and the family bankruptcy do the same for Maggie. Silas's whole life is altered by the love between his fiancée and his friend. None of these lives makes sense as a project; none can be talked of in the language of Mr. Deane, where a man can be anything he wants to be. Mr. Deane's is the language of the biographical form, the motto of which is "Be yourself." Dozens of later novels follow the pattern of Joyce's *Portrait of the Artist As a Young Man* and base themselves on the sensitive, isolated hero, often an artist, surrounded by others who are completely different from him and who affect him mainly by temporarily preventing him from "finding himself," and then from "being himself." This self is harmonious and complete; each part has meaning through the others; each is in focus when seen against the whole of the self. But this self that is like a work of art, because it has complete meaning in itself, is self-explanatory but not self-sufficient. It is in exile.

Where the biographical form is accepted, the values of will, energy, and the imagination to project the self in a daring and novel way follow. The form can be used against the grain: Dickens did so in *Great Expectations.* Pip's life is like that of a puppet at the end of strings so long that they pass out of sight. Practically without will, he is here, then moved there, claimed and reclaimed. But the use of a form against itself is like a temperance speech in a tavern. Eliot combines lives because she must, in order to keep the legibility of lives that, as she shows, only make sense in the wider context of other lives.

At the same time, she is detailing the disappearance of society, the natural context of wider meaning. Family and society, the Tullivers and the village of Hayslope, make the magic circle James spoke of. "Really, universally, relations stop nowhere, and the exquisite problem of the artist is eternally but to draw, by a geometry of his own, the circle within which they shall happily appear to do so" [Henry James, *The Art of Fiction,* ed. R. P. Blackmur 1934]. James is wrong in assuming there is no natural circle; Hayslope and the family life of the Tullivers are natural circles, those of continuous existence: the same people in the same place through time. An image from Marner indicates the challenge to the novel from the new society in which circles do only "appear" final. Marner, an outsider even after fifteen years in Raveloe, appears like a ghost at the Casses' New Year's Eve party. In his arms he holds an unknown child. He is an outsider holding a stranger. By the laws of melodrama, he has brought the child to its home and into the sight of its father, who is married secretly in another town. The secrecy of Godfrey's life carries further, by willing it, the type of discontinuity thrust on Marner. The natural circle does not exist. Only the circle of art makes sense of this moment in the doorway. Marner knows a fraction, Godfrey a little more, the rest of the party know nothing, and never will: the reader knows it all.

A more extreme example is the group that assembles in the first chapters of James's *Portrait of a Lady:* Daniel Touchett, Ralph, Mrs. Touchett, Isabel, Lord Warburton, and Mme. Merle. In life, as James knows it, in rootless life, real relations end nowhere. In Hayslope they do end; Raveloe is halfway between Hayslope and Gardencourt, between community and collection. Where art closes the circle, as it does in Raveloe, it stands as an illusory barrier to incomprehensibility. There is only a step between those circles closed by art and those closed by the imagination, whether sane or insane—between the circles in James's *Sacred Fount* or Faulkner's *Absalom, Absalom!*

The narratives we see divided in parts are only the first of the synthetic replacements Eliot found for the community she lost. The form of the social novel was lost along with the community. To the extent that family was at least a miniature community in **The Mill on the Floss,** the first two of her novels showed the disintegration in process. **Silas Marner** is the first of her works after the fall. The Cass half of the novel is the context for our comprehension—but not his own—of Marner's life. Like Maggie and Adam, he is shaped by life. The keys to his life are outside: the betrayal by his friend, the robbery, the appearance of the child. He responds but does not initiate. Passivity, resignation, and acceptance are the inversions of the initiative, imagination, and energy of the self-made man. The virtues are those of characters made by catastrophes they could not even foresee, let alone prevent.

Within the Cass chapters, the novel outlines a grammar of inverted appearances and truths. Three families exist: the squire and his sons; Godfrey's first marriage with Molly and the child that results; and Godfrey's second, childless marriage with Nancy. Each family is seen only in glimpses of moments when it is acting out the truth of the relationship, a truth that is always a savage reversal

of the public meaning of the tie. Godfrey lies out of necessity, Dunstan for pleasure. In the first family, one brother is blackmailing the other, and both rob the father. When any two meet, they argue, and when Dunstan disappears no one misses him, no search is made. Godfrey would be pleased to learn of his brother's death.

The second family exists only in Molly's journey through the snow to disgrace her husband, the dishonor him at the party by revealing the marriage. She falls asleep from the opium and dies. Godfrey arrives only to make sure she is dead. Again bonds are inverted; twice Godfrey is best served by the deaths of those he is most closely related to.

The single great moment in the novel is the final reversal of what Eliot would call natural human bonds. The scene is the exact equivalent of Hetty's murder of her child. A contrast of the two scenes shows the extent to which psychology and internal action have replaced public events in Eliot's work. Melodrama gives way to the subtleties of the modern social novel where action is invisible or inscrutable or both. Godfrey stands in Marner's cottage after he has been assured that the woman to whom he is secretly married is dead. One danger remains: the child. If the child didn't exist, he would be free of the past—something he is forced, by inversion, to desire. Only one last detail to erase, and the previous years will be a blank. He looks at the child.

> The wide-open blue eyes looked up at Godfrey's without any uneasiness or sign of recognition: the child could make no audible claim on its father; and the father felt a strange mixture of feelings, a conflict of regret and joy, that the pulse of that little heart had no response for the half-jealous yearning in his own, when the blue eyes turned away from him slowly and fixed themselves on the weaver's queer face.

In the joy he feels that the child treats him as a stranger, he has reached a point equivalent to Hetty's.

Godfrey's third family is likewise in sight only at a moment of paradox. The fifteen years skipped pass over what happiness he and Nancy had. We see only his confession of his earlier marriage. The two try to recover Eppie and fail. The crisis of this part of the novel concerns Eppie's choice. Will she live with her legal father, her father in fact, or stay with Silas? Godfrey's claim would be recognized by society; any court would award him custody. But Silas is the father in supplying the recognition Godfrey denied her.

The ties are concealed or denied or perverted until they are unrecognizable. Brother, father, family—none has reality, all conceal the true bonds that are independent of the formal relationships. Before disappearing, the society is distorted into grotesque variants on what it was to be. It is the rich that rob the poor.

The harsh substance of the book provides the motive for the compensating surface of sentimentality. The marriage that concludes the book, the symbolic holy family (in which there is more of true family feeling than in any of the actual families of the novel) made up of Silas, Dolly Winthrop, and Eppie, does not weigh against the treachery and paradox that have destroyed both communities, that of the Lantern Yard and that of Raveloe. The neat satisfactions of justice in the novel are deceptive: the fog that allows the robbery conceals the stone pits that punish the thief. Godfrey, who denies his child, must stay childless for the rest of his life. In the end, the gold Silas seemed to have lost in order to gain the golden child reappears as though to say he couldn't have blessings enough.

The state of life that is recovered is not at all like Job's—the literal return of what was lost. Instead of the fiancée and friend of the Lantern Yard, Marner, an old man now, has the sexless family in which the single emotional tie is the child. His life is lost and he has only a simulation that, like the metaphor of gold and golden hair, is true only on the plane of the imagination. (pp. 99-110)

> *Philip Fisher, " 'Silas Marner',* " *in his* Making Up Society: The Novels of George Eliot, *University of Pittsburgh Press, 1981, 244 p.*

Harold Fisch   (essay date 1986)

[Fisch is an English editor, educator, and critic who has served as translator for The Jerusalem Bible *and various works of Hebrew poetry. In the following essay, he explores links between Old Testament narratives and* Silas Marner, *focusing particularly on parallels in language and theme.]*

If the hero of **Silas Marner,** like the author of the book, has broken with evangelical Christianity, he has not rejected the Bible along with it. For him, as for George Eliot, it remains to be re-interpreted and re-understood. When Dolly Winthrop hears of some of the strange practices of the Lantern Yard conventicle, she wonders whether theirs was the same Bible as the one to be found in the parish church of Raveloe. Silas assures her that it was:

> "And yourn's the same Bible, you're sure o' that Master Marner—the Bible as you brought wi' you from that country—it's the same as what they've got at church, and what Eppie's a-learning to read in?" "Yes," said Silas, "every bit the same."
>
> (chapter xvi)

The Bible then connects Silas's earlier faith with his life in the present and future. If Eppie signifies, as the epigraph from Wordsworth indicates, the promise of "forward-looking thoughts," then we are here reminded that she has been "a-learning to read" in the same Bible that Silas had known in his dark Puritan past. But, the Bible is more than a key to the characters and their thoughts; it is a key to the conception of the novel itself as a moral history exhibiting the specific kind of realism and economy which mark the Old Testament narratives.

Like the Genesis-stories or those relating to Samuel, Saul, and David, **Silas Marner** is a story of trial, retribution, and redemption. The characters are morally tested, forced to acknowledge their trespasses. "There's dealings" says Silas, or, as Dolly Winthrop puts it in her more stumbling fashion, there's "Them above." Faults hidden in the past come to light. Silas, who has suffered from malice and in-

justice, lives to gain a blessing. The characters come to us weighted with their previous history; as [Erich] Auerbach says of the heroes of the Genesis-narratives, they are "fraught with background." Silas's personality is conditioned by what has happened to him in Lantern Yard and earlier. Similarly, Godfrey Cass's past, which he conceals from his wife, will eventually constrain him and there will be a reckoning. Providence works wonderfully and mysteriously, calling the past to remembrance, turning sin and suffering into a path of salvation.

There is throughout a sense of the momentousness of our moral choices, a momentousness too in the doings of simple people—seemingly trivial doings very often, but loaded with [in Auerbach's words] "the intensity of their personal history." This is something that Eliot had learned not only from the Bible but, collaterally, from Wordsworth, whose "Michael" (from which she had drawn her motto) provides examples of the same phenomenon. In that poem, too, a simple act by an unlettered shepherd can take the moral weight of the universe. After Michael's only son Luke leaves him, we are told that the old shepherd returns to the sheepfold they had together begun to build:

> many and many a day he thither went,
> And never lifted up a single stone.

The detail becomes momentous, its power a function of its utter simplicity. But this is not strictly a separate influence: for it is clear that "Michael" too in its "high seriousness" recalls at every turn the Genesis narratives. Michael and his wife, with their only child born in their old age, with their simple loyalties and hopes, recall such patriarchal households as that of Abraham and Sarah. The sheepfold of which father and son lay the cornerstone is to be a covenant—"a covenant / 'Twill be between us. . . . " When they are far from one another, the heap of stones, like that begun by Jacob at Bethel (Genesis, 28:18) in sign of God's promises and his own, or like that raised by Laban and Jacob at Gilead (*ibid.,* 31:51-2), will be a witness to their mutual exchange of vows. When Luke betrays his trust, it becomes the betrayal of a covenant with all the weight of tragic meaning which such a dereliction implies. George Eliot evidently sensed the Biblical element in Wordsworth's poem, and she fortified and enriched it with her own first-hand understanding of the imaginative possibilities of the Biblical mode of narration.

It may be worth pointing out some of the specific Biblical echo-structures in Eliot's novel. They are more numerous than critics have hitherto recognized; indeed, in their accumulated force they would seem to have had a shaping effect on the novel as a whole. The coming of the infant Eppie to Silas on New Year's eve bringing to him her gift of love has been termed a "Christ-event" [by J. Wiesenfarth in *ELH,* June, 1970], and perhaps there is some such Christian typology at work here, but the Biblical episode, which is actually evoked in the text, is the rescue of Lot from the cities of the plain in Genesis 19:

> In old days there were angels who came and took men by the hand and led them away from the city of destruction. We see no white-winged angels now. But yet men are led away from

threatening destruction: a hand is put into theirs, which leads them forth gently towards a calm and bright land, so that they look no more backward; and the hand may be a little child's.

(chapter xiv)

Like the story of the rescue of Lot, Eliot's tale is one of retribution, redemption, and rescue. The angel has been domesticated into a child, but the sense of the wonder and the miracle remains. There is an echo here too of the beginning of Bunyan's *The Pilgrim's Progress,* where we are told that Christian fled from the City of Destruction and "looked not behind him." Critics have been right in emphasizing the importance of Bunyan's presence in the novel. But here too, as in the example of Wordsworth's poem, we are not speaking strictly of a separate influence, because the same Biblical source stands behind Bunyan's text at this point. In the marginal gloss, Bunyan directs us to the story of Lot's escape in Genesis 19:17 as the Biblical analogy for Christian's flight from the City of Destruction.

The Biblical underpinning can be even more unambiguous than this. In speaking to Dolly Winthrop in chapter xvi, Silas recalls the evil done to him by his friend William Dean in his Lantern Yard days, an iniquity which left him friendless and bitter for fifteen years. There was no longer a God of righteousness in whom he could believe. "That," he said, "was what fell on me like as if it had been red-hot iron." And he continues:

" . . . because, you see, there was nobody as cared for me or clave to me above nor below. And him as I'd gone out and in wi' for ten year and more, since when we was lads and went halves—mine own familiar friend in whom I trusted—had lifted up his heel again' me, and worked to ruin me."

The Biblical language and parallelism ("nobody as cared for me or clave to me") give the passage its particular solemnity, but this is not just a matter of general colouring: there is also the literal echoing of Psalm 41 where the relevant verses read:

All that hate me whisper together against me: against me do they devise my hurt. An evil disease, say they, cleaveth fast unto him: and now that he lieth he shall rise up no more. Yea, mine own familiar friend, in whom I trusted, which did eat of my bread, hath lifted up his heel again against me.

(Psalm 41:7-9)

Silas here formulates his trouble in terms of a Biblical verse. But, there is a paradox here: if his bitterness at the outcome of the casting of lots and the evil which he had met with from the members of the Lantern Yard community had led to the loss of his faith ("there is no just God that governs the earth righteously"), it had manifestly not led him to abandon the Biblical sources of that faith. Indeed, we may see Psalm 41 as a key to the understanding of Silas's crisis and its outcome. The crisis is defined by the three verses quoted above, and the outcome of the drama seems to be structured by the continuation of that same psalm. For after the victim's complaint at the evil done to him by those who had devised his hurt, God mercifully raises him up:

And as for me, thou upholdest me in mine integrity, and settest me before thy face for ever.

(*ibid.,* verse 12)

The force of these words had evidently not been lost on the author. She conceives Silas's existence as a moral pilgrimage in which there is both judgement and reward. Whatever her theoretical position on such questions, when Eliot came to construct her fictional plot, here and elsewhere, these categories remained meaningful. We are thus not speaking of some secularized "Religion of Humanity," but of a re-constituted Biblical faith, rather like that which Matthew Arnold was teaching in this same period. In keeping with that inspiration, she speaks in her novels not of blind fate, like Hardy, but of redemption and reward and of moral decisions taken with a kind of Biblical solemnity.

Critical from this point of view is the choice of Hephzibah as the name for the foundling who has come to Marner's door. Dolly doubts whether it is really "a christened name," but Silas retorts by saying that "it's a Bible name." Silas thus establishes the character of his new-found source of comfort by reviving the Puritan fashion of naming. The name, as David Carroll has pointed out [in *Literary Monographs, Vol. 1,* edited by Eric Rothstein and Thomas K. Dunseath, 1967] takes on special significance when the Biblical source in Isiah 62 is considered:

Thou shalt no more be termed Forsaken; neither shall thy land be any more termed Desolate: but thou shalt be called Hephzibah, and thy land Beulah: for the Lord delighteth in thee, and thy land shall be married.

(Isiah 62:4)

Carroll sees in the name Hephzibah and the verse that it recalls "a reassurance to Silas that his instinctive affection for Eppie will not be betrayed." It is perhaps more to the point that she comes to bring to an end the years in which he has been *Desolate* and *Forsaken.* She represents the promise of joy and delight ("My Delight is in Her"). The giving of a new name—always a convenantal act in the Bible (see Genesis 17:5,16,43:10-11, etc.)—confirms and establishes this promise. When Silas goes to church in the village for the very first time, it is for the christening of Eppie. We are told that he finds the Anglican forms entirely alien—"He was quite unable, by means of anything he heard or saw, to identify the Raveloe religion with his old faith" (chapter xiv). But, the Biblical name he has given the child, we may say, provides the link. Unwittingly, Silas has found a text which will bind his past and future symbolically together. Not only Eppie but the Biblical word, by which she is henceforward denominated, has the saving function of binding his days each to each by natural piety. Eppie will compensate him for past sorrows at the same time as she will afford him the joy of "forward-looking thoughts."

Eppie is indeed the focus of the covenantal pattern of the book; she visibly signifies the redemptive process. The high-point in this respect is chapter xix; there Eppie makes her momentous choice between Silas and Godfrey Cass, giving her loyalty firmly to the adoptive father who has cherished and reared her rather than to her natural father.

It has not, to my knowledge, been noted by critics that the high drama of this chapter recalls, and is designed to recall, the story of Ruth and Naomi. In the book of Ruth also, the daughter-in-law chooses her adoptive mother, "cleaving" to her in preference to her natural kin—"Orpah kissed her mother-in-law; but Ruth clave unto her" (Ruth 1:14). Eppie's declaration of attachment to Silas and rejection of Godfrey echo that chapter of Ruth:

> Thank you, ma'am—thank you, sir, for your offers—they're very great, and far above my wish. For I should have no delight i'life any more if I was forced to go away from my father, and knew he was sitting at home, a'thinking of me and feeling lone. We've been used to be happy together every day, and I can't think o' no happiness without him. And he says he'd nobody i'the world till I was sent to him, and he'd have nothing when I was gone. And he's took care of me and loved me from the first, and I'll cleave to him as long as he lives, and nobody shall ever come between him and me.

The last clause recalls the closing verse of Ruth's declaration to Naomi: "The Lord do so to me, and more also, of ought but death part thee and me" (Ruth 1:17). The effect of this echo is to bring into the novel the memory not merely of the two verses (14, 17) which are literally recalled but the entire context of the story of Ruth and Naomi. Naomi who went out full and has come home empty is the prototype of Silas, robbed of his wealth and bereft of happiness. If Ruth brings a blessing and forward-looking thought to the widowed and childless Naomi (see Ruth 4:15), so Eppie proves to be a blessing for barren Silas, holding to him more firmly than a natural child might have done, being better to him indeed than seven sons.

There are also wider reverberations. Eliot seems to wish to endow Eppie's decision in chapter xix with far-reaching historical significance. In her love and loyalty she represents the antitype to the evangelical pieties and superstitions of Lantern Yard, on the one hand, and to the purely "organic" or earth-bound religion of Raveloe, on the other. No less than Hester Prynne and Pearl in Hawthorne's novel of the same period, her heroine is seen as "the angel and apostle of the coming revelation." Eppie's saving message is addressed to natural man, but it signifies the transcendence of the natural in the interests of a higher bond of loyalty. She also challenges a social structure based on class and inherited privilege in this hinting at a new conception of the relations between men. This, too, would seem to owe something to the story of Ruth who is the ancestress of David and whose story marks the beginning of a salvation history which will transform a nation.

If Eppie reminds us of Ruth, her father Godfrey Cass reminds us of another Biblical character, viz. Judah, the ancestor of Boaz. He, too, had secretly "come in unto" a strange woman by the wayside; she had then born him a child whom he had ultimately acknowledged as his own, but only after he had been brought to admit his fault. The Judah-Tamar story (Genesis 38) and the related narrative of Joseph and his brothers seem to lurk behind the whole

history of Godfrey and his brother Dunstan. When Dunstan's body is found together with Silas's lost gold, the skeleton is identified by three items of accoutrement, as Godfrey tells Nancy:

> There's his watch and seals, and there's my gold-handled hunting-whip, with my name on.
>   (chapter xviii)

It is the discovery of Dunstan's guilt, confirmed by these three identifying pieces of personal property, which prompts Godfrey to confess his own hidden guilt. The Bible-conscious reader is surely reminded here of Tamar's producing the three identifying personal effects, which confirm Judah's paternity in Genesis 38:

> By the man, whose these are, am I with child: and she said, Discern I pray thee, whose are these, the signet, and bracelets and staff.
>   (38:25)

The acknowledgment of guilt (and in this case the acknowledgment of fatherhood) is, of course, the theme of the whole cluster of narratives relating to Joseph and his brothers. Immediately following the Judah and Tamar episode, we are told how the brothers of Joseph are tested by a series of strange and bewildering mishaps, among them the seizing of Simeon by the Egyptian ruler. This triggers a process of repentance, causing them to remember their crime of many years previously:

> And they said one to another, We are verily guilty concerning our brother, in that we saw the anguish of his soul, when he besought us, and we would not hear; therefore is this distress come upon us.
>   (Gen. 42:21)

There is no logical link between the two episodes that the brothers know of, but chords of memory are struck by the sight of another brother bound and helpless. Similarly there is no logical reason why the discovery of Dunstan's body should have led Godfrey to reveal the matter of his fatherhood of Eppie, but the laying bare of Dunstan's crime triggers off a moral process in Godfrey and causes him to reveal his own guilty secret stemming from the same period. His mood is like that of Joseph's brothers in the above-quoted passage when he says to Nancy:

> Everything comes to light, Nancy, sooner or later. When God Almighty wills it, our secrets are found out. I've lived with a secret on my mind, but I'll keep it from you no longer.

Lot led by an angel out of the city of destruction; Judah made to confess his paternity; Ruth declaring herself for her adoptive mother against the claims of mere nature—all have something in common. All are stories of redemption. Lot and his daughters are saved for the future; Judah redeems Tamar from her widowed and childless state and a future is assured; finally, in the story of Ruth, redemption becomes the central theme. At the simplest level, a parcel of land belonging to Elimelech, the dead husband of Naomi, has to be redeemed. To Boaz (though not the first in line by kinship) belongs the "right of redemption." In performing his duty he also gains a wife and establishes a line which will culminate in the birth of David, the Messianic king. Naomi too, will be redeemed; her *go'el* is the newborn Obed (4:14), who will compensate her for her long years of exile and loss.

Eliot had, it seems, lost her faith in a personal God whom one could address in the forms established by the Church, but, paradoxically, she had not lost her sense of wonder at the mysterious workings of a providence that brings good out of misery in the long passage of years. It would seem that some such movement was for her both a religious and aesthetic necessity. And, the great moments are when the wonder enters into the consciousness of the characters themselves. In chapter xix Silas achieves his awareness of the wonderful as the stolen money is restored to him in time for it to serve as a dowry for Eppie—"It's wonderful—our life is wonderful." And Godfrey, for whom the past has come back with a sterner admonition, has a sense of the awfulness and mystery of those same "dealings":

> The eyes of the husband and wife met with awe
> in them, as at a crisis which suspended affection.
> (chapter xviii)

It should be emphasized, however, that the wonder and the awe that the characters feel do not transport them—or us—beyond the visible and material world. Coleridge, speaking of Wordsworth's achievement in the *Lyrical Ballads* remarks that the realism of everyday is enhanced and deepened by "a feeling analogous to the supernatural." This feeling is just as powerful in George Eliot's story, but the realism is even greater, for she has chosen the medium of the novel to give expression to the "unassuming commonplaces" of village life. In the nature of things, the world of the novel is a prose world, one of material things, of small, contingent particulars rather than symbols. The leech-gatherer whose appearance and speech Wordsworth describes in "Resolution and Independence" was, we know, drawn from life, but in the emphatic imagery of the poem he achieves a larger-than-life quality—he becomes a prodigy, a portent, his coming and going equally mysterious:

> As a huge stone is sometimes seen to lie
> Couched on the bald top of an eminence;
> Wonder to all who do the same espy,
> By what means it could thither come, or whence.

Characters in a novel necessarily have a more quotidian character than this; their sublimity, if they have it, is pitched nearer to that of our own lines. Eliot seems to have had a problem here, a problem of finding the exact mode of realism for her tale. She tells her publisher in a letter dated February 24, 1861 [quoted in *The George Eliot Letters,* edited by Gordon S. Haight, 1954-1955] of the way the idea of *Silas Marner* came to her:

> It came to me first of all, quite suddenly, as a sort
> of legendary tale, suggested by my recollection
> of having once, in early childhood, seen a linen-
> weaver with a bag on his back; but as my mind
> dwelt on the subject, I became inclined to a more
> realistic treatment.

A "legendary tale" of Silas would have made him more like the leech-gatherer; indeed, Silas's catalepsy may have been suggested by another passage in that some poem of Wordsworth:

> Motionless as a cloud the old Man stood,
> That heareth not the loud winds when they call;
> And moveth all together, if it move at all—

But, she was anxious to bring Silas out of the legendary Wordsworthian state into the orbit of ordinary everyday concerns—those of the villagers who sit and converse in the Rainbow where we are not likely to find Wordsworth's huntsmen and shepherds and certainly not his leech-gatherer.

The felt need to overcome the propensity to the fabulous in the tale as it had originally "come to her" thus becomes a central problem in the strategy of composition; more than that, it becomes in a sense the theme of the novel! We are told in the first chapter how the Raveloe folk had at first found Silas strange and portentous. The word "mysterious" occurs four times in the account of their first impressions of him:

> for the villagers near whom he had come to settle
> [his appearance] had mysterious peculiarities
> which corresponded with the exceptional nature
> of his occupation.
> (chapter i)

They see him as in league with the Devil, an impression strengthened by Jem Rodney's account of having met him in one of his cataleptic fits. But the effect of the narrative as it proceeds is to demystify Silas as he comes nearer to the people of the village and as they draw closer to him after the robbery. By chapter x, the village-folk, following the lead of Mr. Macey the parish-clerk, have decided that there is nothing portentous about him and that he is nothing more than a "poor mushed creatur." The transition from the legendary to the realistic is here a matter of the attitude of the villagers to Silas; they now begin to see him as one of them. But, in the metapoetics of the narration this process of demystification signifies the determination to adapt and recast the high invention of the ballad of mystery or the "greater romantic lyric" so as to bring it within the confines of everyday reality. This was the task the author set herself and it was a remarkably difficult one.

I would wish to argue that the Biblical narratives—the parables of the New Testament but, more particularly, Ruth and the Genesis narratives—provided her with the key to that balance of the wonderful and the everyday, the fabulous and the realistic, that she was seeking. The story of Ruth has epic overtones; it situates itself at the crossroads of history "in the days when the judges ruled" and in the days before a king reigned in Israel. Mysteriously, the story of the choices made by Ruth and Boaz will mingle with this larger theme. Not merely will a broken line be restored, but a world will be made new. And yet attention focuses itself on the matters of everyday, on the gleaners in the field, on legal forms and modes of greeting in a rural society, on the passage of the seasons from the barley harvest to the wheat harvest. We seem to be in a real world of struggling men and women.

Bible stories also exhibit human weaknesses and confusions. Judah's embarrassment at the loss of his seal, his bracelets, and staff has the force of the actual; his history, like that of a character in a novel by Iris Murdoch, is not smoothed over or harmonized in the manner of a legend. So much, says Auerbach of the Genesis stories, is contradictory, so much is left in darkness. This is precisely the comment of Dolly at the end of George Eliot's novel: "It's the will o' them above as many things should be dark to us." There are many loose ends, as in real life; many things are left unexplained. What became of the people Silas knew in Lantern Yard? Was the secret villainy of William Dean ever discovered? Silas will never know, nor shall we. Only those matters which need to be illuminated are illuminated. And, what is illuminated in the tangle of circumstances which makes up the lives of men and women is the strange twisting path of salvation itself, a path marked out by a very small number of obstinately significant details, such as Silas's catalepsy, or Eppie's golden hair, or Godfrey's hunting-whip. These details are illuminated because on them, strangely, the whole history of trial and suffering and redemption seems to hinge. Here the fabulous and the realistic combine. They are like the ram caught in the thicket in the story of the Binding of Isaac, or the coat which Joseph leaves in the hands of Potiphar's wife, strangely recalling the coat of many colours, which his brothers stripped off him earlier in the story, or like Absalom's long hair. With such few details, trivial and yet portentous, the Old Testament narratives concern themselves. They give these stories their special kind of realism. Eliot has struggled to capture the same kind of realism in the rigorous selection of details which make up her spare narrative and she has succeeded to a marvellous degree. It is what makes this novel not only unique in her writings, but practically unique in English literature. Joan Bennett asserted [in her *George Eliot: Her Mind and Art,* 1962] that it is "the most flawless of George Eliot's works," and Walter Allen went even further and claimed [in his *George Eliot,* 1967] that *"Silas Marner* is as perfect a work of prose fiction as any in the language, a small miracle."

In the same letter to John Blackwood cited earlier, Eliot speaks not only of the need to arbitrate between a legendary and a realistic treatment, but of the opposing attractions of verse and prose as the medium for her tale:

> I have felt all through as if the story would have lent itself best to metrical rather than prose fiction, especially in all that relates to the psychology of Silas; except that under that treatment, there could not be an equal play of humour.

The reason she gives here for her choice of prose is a bit lame, for the fact is that there is little humour in the treatment of her main characters. Humour is mainly confined to the villagers in the Rainbow tavern. In this, *Silas Marner* is strikingly different from *Brother Jacob,* another moral tale of trial, sin, and retribution from the same period, where the jocular tone is very marked throughout. It would thus seem that her choice of prose in preference to metre in *Silas Marner* was determined by other considerations. What one would want to say is that the attempt to capture the "still small voice" of the narrative portions of the Hebrew Bible dictated an utter simplicity and directness of style and the avoidance of anything suggestive of artificiality. The archness, for instance, of Fielding's

"comic epic poem in prose" would have been incompatible with George Eliot's purpose here. At the same time, she needed height, sublimity. She found the answer in the utterly simple prose of the Bible, the *sermo humilis,* which some of the Church Fathers upheld in opposition to the high rhetoric of the Ciceronian tradition. The lowliness of the *sermo humilis* enabled one to invest the trivial things of everyday with a certain sublimity. It was prose reduced to its simplest elements, and yet it could be pregnant and lyrical in the manner of poetry.

While the *sermo humilis* of the bible had been part of the tradition of the English novel from the time of Bunyan and Defoe, the fact is that it had never been totally assimilated. At some point the literary tradition of the West resists such a radical canon of simplicity. Even Eliot, who uses it as her standard in this novel, does not apply it consistently. Her narrative voice, for instance, is not that of the Biblical narrator. Moreover, if we analyse the different stylistic strands in the prose of the novel, we find that the Biblical combination of loftiness and simplicity is really specific to Eppie and Silas and the scenes in which they appear. It becomes, we may say, not so much a way of telling the story, as a "criticism of life." The style itself is foregrounded and is beheld in contrast to other styles. In the confrontation between Eppie and Silas, on the one hand, and Godfrey and Nancy, on the other, in chapter xix, we become aware that the feelings and expressions of the "upper class" pair are cruder and more vulgar than those of Eppie and Silas. Nancy and Godfrey belong to the class of what Matthew Arnold called the Barbarians—they were, he says, much given to field sports—and their language is to that extent differentiated from that of Eppie and Silas.

Let us see how the stylistic aspect of the confrontation is exhibited in chapter xix. Godfrey is voluble at first on the subject of the robbery and discusses the hardships of the weaver's life which he would like to do something to ease. The something, of course, is his plan to take Eppie from him, though he says nothing of this at first. Marner's responses are brief and awkward:

> Silas, always ill at ease when he was being spoken to by "betters" such as Mr. Cass—tall, powerful, florid men, seen chiefly on horseback—answered with some constraint—"Sir, I've a deal to thank you for a'ready. As for the robbery, I count it no loss to me. And if I did, you couldn't help it: you aren't answerable for it."

Godfrey then reveals the main object of his visit. Saying nothing at this stage about his fatherhood, he proposes simply that, being themselves childless, they take Eppie away to live with them and make a lady of her. Marner would be rewarded for the trouble of bringing her up. He concludes:

> she'd come and see you very often, and we should all be on the look-out to do everything we could towards making you comfortable.

The moral insentivity here is compounded by the easy clichés which Godfrey uses ("be on the look-out," "making you comfortable"). The narrator's comment draws attention to the clichés:

A plain man like Godfrey Cass, speaking under some embarrassment, necessary blunders on words that are coarser than his intentions, and that are likely to fall gratingly on susceptible feelings.

In a reversal of the traditional division of styles as taught in the ancient schools of rhetoric and as practised in the theatre or in the literature of romance, here the upper-class character is the "plain man" whose expressions are "coarser than his intentions," while Silas, the handweaver, has the "susceptible feelings" and the language that goes with them. The reader is now being prompted at every stage to observe the manner of speaking of the different characters. Eppie's first real speech in this meeting is marked by a Wordsworthian simplicity and a Biblical cadence; above all, it is free of cliché:

> "Thank you, ma'am—thank you, sir. But I can't leave my father, nor own anybody nearer than him. And I don't want to be a lady—thank you all the same . . . I couldn't give up the folks I've been used to."

Godfrey, angered by their refusal to accept what he has persuaded himself is a generous offer, now declares the truth about his "natural claim" to Eppie. He is, he says, her real father. The simplicity and truth of Silas and Eppie have now forced Godfrey to reveal his truth, his manifest claim as well as his sin. But, Silas's is still the higher truth, as he angrily opposes to the claims of "nature"—claims long concealed—the power of those august signifiers by which human relations are fundamentally ordered and which are in a sense independent of the natural relations which they signify. In this case, the word "father" has its own peremptory rights of love and authority, drawn as much and perhaps more from the sphere of the sacred as from biology:

> "Your coming now and saying 'I'm her father' doesn't alter the feelings inside us. It's me she's been calling her father ever since she could say the word."

Nature must bow to the language of the heart—is what Silas seems to be saying. And again, the narrator's comment serves to foreground the stylistic aspect of this extraordinary confrontation:

> "But I think you might look at the thing more reasonably, Marner," said Godfrey, unexpectedly awed by the weaver's direct truth-speaking.

He ends by denying that Eppie will really be separated from Marner, even though Godfrey will have taken over the word "father" as his natural right.

> "She'll be very near you, and come to see you very often. She'll feel just the same towards you."

In the great speech which he now utters, Marner exposes the shallowness of Godfrey's sentiments—his upper-class complacency, as well as the idleness of his rhetoric:

> "Just the same?" said Marner, more bitterly than ever. "How'll she feel just the same for me as she does now, when we eat o' the same bit, and drink o' the same cup, and think o' the same

things from one day's end to another? Just the same? that's idle talk. You'd cut us i' two."

Again, it is to Silas's simple language with its Biblical cadences that our attention is drawn, a language to which Godfrey is unattuned:

> Godfrey, unqualified by experience to discern the *pregnancy* of Marner's *simple* words, felt rather angry again.
>
>   (emphasis added)

The express link with the Bible and its style is made clearer when we find the author commenting in precisely the same terms on the language of the Bible and the Collects, as she had heard them read one Sunday in the Little Portland Street Chapel. The letter—to Sarah Hennell—was written in July, 1861, just a few weeks after the publication of *Silas Marner:*

> What an age of earnest faith, grasping a noble conception of life and determined to bring all things into harmony with it, has recorded itself in the *simple pregnant, rhythmical* English of these Collects and the Bible.
>
>   (emphasis added).

Eliot's moral and linguistic criticism in this chapter is very much bound up with the sociological aspect of the confrontation. The ultimate point of insensitivity in Godfrey's discourse is reached when he remarks that if Eppie fails to accept his offer, "she may marry some low working-man." It is this fate that the "high society" of Godfrey and Nancy's home, with its balls, its horse-riding, and its drinking, will preserve her from! In short Godfrey and Nancy stand not only for natural bonds, but for natural bonds linked to a system of class gradations which are likewise held to be natural. Opposed to this in the dramatic evolution of the dialogue, is the Biblical, covenantal system of relations which cuts across the rights of class and property. The kind of love and loyalty to which this system has reference is that implied in Ezekiel's parable of the foundling girl whom the passerby finds and adopts and finally takes for his wife (Ezekiel 16:5f)—it is his way of talking about the covenant between God and Israel. And this same higher loyalty finds expression in the story of Ruth and Naomi. It is, of course, the latter text which Eppie's reply immediately calls to mind in the passage already quoted. It merits citation once again:

> "And he says he'd nobody i' the world till I was sent him, and he'd have nothing when I was gone. And he's took care of me and loved me from the first, and I'll cleave to him as long as he lives, and nobody shall ever come between him and me."

While Nancy still attempts to counter this by an appeal to such terms as "nature," "duty," and law," Godfrey has nothing more to say. He is silent. It is the victory of language and, specifically, the language of those lively oracles, which Silas had salvaged from the ruins of Lantern Yard and brought with him to furnish his onward pilgrimage. (pp. 343-58)

> *Harold Fisch, "Biblical Realism in 'Silas Marner'," in* Identity and Ethos: A Fest-

schrift for Sol Liptzin on the Occasion of His 85th Birthday, *edited by Mark H. Gelber, Peter Lang, 1986, pp. 343-60.*

FURTHER READING

Allen, Walter. "The Novels." In his *George Eliot,* pp. 82-178. New York: Macmillan Co., 1964.

    Includes discussion of *Silas Marner,* focusing on its rustic setting and characters. Describing the novel as "essentially a myth of spiritual rebirth," Allen maintains that "*Silas Marner* is as perfect a work of prose fiction as any in the language, a small miracle."

Auster, Henry. "Toward the Literature of Displacement: *Silas Marner.*" In his *Local Habitations: Regionalism in the Early Novels of George Eliot,* pp. 175-206. Cambridge, Mass.: Harvard University Press, 1970.

    Examines the realistic depiction of rural life in *Silas Marner,* discussing its function in the novel.

Carroll, David R. "*Silas Marner:* Reversing the Oracles of Religion." In *Literary Monographs, Vol. 1,* edited by Eric Rothstein and Thomas K. Dunseath, pp. 167-200. Madison: University of Wisconsin Press, 1967.

    Explores the "rigorously intellectual structure" of religious, philosophical, and social ideas upon which Eliot crafted *Silas Marner.*

Cohen, Susan R. " 'A History and a Metamorphosis': Continuity and Discontinuity in *Silas Marner.*" *Texas Studies in Language and Literature* 25, No. 3 (Fall 1983): 410-26.

    Asserts that *Silas Marner*'s central theme is that fragmentation underlies all apparent continuity in life.

Draper, R. P., ed. *George Eliot: "The Mill on the Floss" and "Silas Marner."* Casebook Series, edited by A. E. Dyson. London: Macmillan Press Ltd., 1977, 260 p.

    Includes excerpts from Eliot's letters and journal in addition to selected reviews and essays on *Silas Marner.*

Dunham, Robert H. "*Silas Marner* and the Wordsworthian Child." *Studies in English Literature* XVI, No. 4 (Autumn 1976): 645-59.

    Finds in *Silas Marner* a Wordsworthian view of children as agents and symbols of spiritual renewal.

Ermarth, Elizabeth Deeds. "George Eliot's Conception of Sympathy." *Nineteenth-Century Fiction* 40, No. 1 (June 1985): 23-42.

    Explores Eliot's treatment of sympathy in her early novels, including *Silas Marner.* Ermarth writes: "Though sympathy is a crucial concern to George Eliot throughout her career, it has a special meaning in the fiction of her mid-career (*Romola, Silas Marner,* and *Felix Holt*) because here her concern about sympathy begins to transform her entire treatment of social and moral problems."

Gilbert, Sandra M. "Life's Empty Pack: Notes Toward a Literary Daughteronomy." *Critical Inquiry* 11, No. 3 (March 1985): 355-84.

    Presents a feminist reading of the role of Eppie in *Silas Marner.*

Hawes, Donald. "Chance in *Silas Marner.*" *English* XXXI, No. 141 (Autumn 1982): 213-18.

    Finds a discrepancy between the view of chance expressed by the narrator of *Silas Marner* and the workings of chance in the novel.

Higdon, David Leon. "Sortilege in George Eliot's *Silas Marner.*" *Papers on Language and Literature* 10, No. 1 (Winter 1974): 51-7.

    Examines the significance of the drawing of lots in *Silas Marner,* discussing the role of this episode in the novel's depiction of the workings of chance.

McLaverty, James. "Comtean Fetishism in *Silas Marner.*" *Nineteenth-Century Fiction* 36, No. 1 (December 1981): 318-36.

    Contends that *Silas Marner* is informed by Eliot's reading of the works of philosopher Auguste Comte, the founder of Positivism.

Parsons, Coleman O. "Background Material Illustrative of *Silas Marner.*" *Notes and Queries* 191, No. 13 (28 December 1946): 266-70.

    Relates Silas Marner to other misers and misanthropes in literature.

Quick, Jonathan R. "*Silas Marner* as Romance: The Example of Hawthorne." *Nineteenth-Century Fiction* 29, No. 3 (December 1974): 287-98.

    Contends that Eliot's writing of *Silas Marner* was influenced by the work of Nathaniel Hawthorne. Quick writes: "It is precisely because Hawthorne's romance effects remain rooted in ordinary or probable experience that they could have appealed to George Eliot's habitually rationalistic and skeptical mind."

Rochelson, Meri-Jane. "The Weaver of Raveloe: Metaphor as Narrative Persuasion in *Silas Marner.*" *Studies in the Novel* XV, No. 1 (Spring 1983): 35-43.

    Analyzes the role of metaphor in shaping the reader's response to both the narrator and the characters of *Silas Marner.*

Shuttleworth, Sally. "Fairy Tale or Science? Physiological Psychology in *Silas Marner.*" In *Languages of Nature: Critical Essays on Science and Literature,* edited by L. J. Jordanova, pp. 244-88. New Brunswick, N.J.: Rutgers University Press, 1986.

    Explores the manner in which *Silas Marner* addresses nineteenth-century social and scientific theory, focusing especially on Eliot's response to conceptions of social evolution, which Shuttleworth describes as "one of the novel's dominant themes."

Simpson, Peter. "Crisis and Recovery: Wordsworth, George Eliot, and *Silas Marner.*" *University of Toronto Quarterly* XLVIII, No. 2 (Winter 1978-79): 95-114.

    Examines similarities between the lives and writings of Eliot and Wordsworth, discussing *Silas Marner* as Eliot's fictional autobiography.

Wiesenfarth, Joseph. "Demythologizing *Silas Marner.*" *ELH*
37, No. 2 (June 1970): 226-44.
    Contends that the legendary motifs and elements of *Silas
    Marner* enhance its depiction of life as governed by natu-
    ral and human agencies.

**Additional coverage of Eliot's life and career is contained in the following sources published
by Gale Research:** *Concise Dictionary of British Literary Biography,* Vol. 4; *Dictionary
of Literary Biography,* Vols. 21, 35, 55; *Nineteenth-Century Literature Criticism,* Vols. 4,
13, 23; and *World Literature Criticism,* Vol. 2.

Eliza Lynn Linton

1822-1898

(Born Elizabeth Lynn) English novelist, essayist, and short story writer.

INTRODUCTION

A controversial writer on social issues, Linton was one of the first women journalists in England. She wrote numerous articles and essays offering her views on the political, economic, and ethical concerns of her day, especially those that affected domestic life. In addition, Linton was a prolific novelist, publishing several morally didactic tales expressing her disillusionment with Victorian society.

The youngest of twelve children, Linton was born in Keswick, a village in northwestern England. Her mother died soon after her birth, leaving Linton's father, an Anglican vicar, to raise his large family alone. As a result, Linton received little parental supervision and no formal schooling. However, after learning to read from her brothers and sisters, she made use of her father's library, studying geography, history, and several languages. As a child, Linton began composing poetry as well as a fictional romance, and in 1845 she published two poems in *Ainsworth's Magazine.* Receiving an allowance from her father, she traveled to London that same year to engage in private study in the reading room of the British Museum. By the end of the year, she had completed her first novel, *Azeth the Egyptian,* and had begun a second, *Amymone: A Romance of the Days of Pericles.* She decided to remain in London, and in 1848 began working as a full-time staff writer for *The Morning Chronicle,* becoming the first woman to maintain such a position with an English periodical. During this time, she developed a friendship with the English poet Walter Savage Landor, who introduced her to his literary friends—among them Charles Dickens and Robert Browning.

In 1851 Linton moved to Paris, where she worked for three years as a correspondent for the *London Press.* Upon her return to England, she began writing for Dickens's periodical *Household Words* (later *All the Year Round*). She married William James Linton, a widower with seven children, in 1858, but the couple separated permanently nine years later. Shortly thereafter, Linton accepted a position with *The Saturday Review,* writing a controversial series of unsigned yet influential essays satirizing contemporary women; of these, her "Girl of the Period" was so widely read that its title became a popular designation for independent young women. During the 1870s and 1880s, Linton continued to stir controversy with unflattering depictions of organized religion in her novels *The True History of Joshua Davidson, Christian and Communist; Under Which Lord?;* and *The Autobiography of Christopher Kirkland.* Although Linton suffered from poor health and

lived in seclusion in the country during her final years, she remained active in her literary endeavors. She died while on a visit to London in 1898. Her last novel, *The Second Youth of Theodora Desanges,* was published posthumously.

Linton's writings center on a number of social concerns, most notably women's issues and the role of religion in society. In her essays, Linton characterizes advocates of women's rights as "wild women" and "shrieking sisters," and depicts them as lesbians, seductresses, and neglectful mothers in her novels. Her second novel, *Amymone,* although set in the age of Pericles (c. fifth century B.C.), addresses questions of women's rights that were prevalent in Linton's day. In the novel, a modest, unassuming housewife must compete for her husband's affection with a witty, glamorous courtesan who represents the "emancipated woman" of Victorian England. The wife wins back her husband—a didactic conclusion aimed at both male and female readers.

Some of Linton's best-known novels present her views on religion and its dogmas. *The True Story of Joshua Davidson, Christian and Communist,* centers on an agnostic young man's attempts to emulate the character of Jesus in Victorian England, only to be kicked to death by a mob led by his former priest (who, Linton's biographers suggest, was modeled on her father). *Under Which Lord?* concerns a clergyman (again supposed by critics to represent Vicar Lynn) who seduces the married women of his congregation. Linton's condemnation of institutional Christianity in these novels angered many readers, while others praised the author for courage and honesty in expressing her dissatisfaction. Linton traced her own rejection of Christian orthodoxy in *The Autobiography of Christopher Kirkland,* a thinly disguised account of her life that is widely considered her finest work.

Linton's novels drew mixed reactions, with reviewers typically lauding them for their evocative settings while finding their characters and plots unconvincing. Linton was also the subject of controversy, largely because of the evident bitterness of her attacks on religious belief and women's rights. Many Victorian readers regarded as hypocritical an agnostic who urged the necessity of religious training for children and an independent woman who opposed greater freedom for women. For modern readers Linton's numerous writings are chiefly of historical interest. Her newspaper articles, reviews, and essays are informed by Victorian values, and her novels concern issues that are central to an understanding of nineteenth-century thought. Generally agreeing with her biographer George Somes Layard that Linton's talent and interests were more suited to journalism than to fiction, recent critics have focused on her relation to early feminism and the spread of religious doubt. In addition, her opposition to women's rights has intrigued modern scholars, who see her variously as a mirror of her own complex times, as a writer who often exaggerated her positions for rhetorical effect, and as a misogynist.

PRINCIPAL WORKS

Azeth the Egyptian (novel) 1847
Amymone: A Romance of the Days of Pericles (novel) 1848
Realities (novel) 1851
Grasp Your Nettle (novel) 1865
Lizzie Lorton of Greygrigg (novel) 1866
Sowing the Wind (novel) 1867
Modern Women and What Is Said of Them: A Reprint of the Series of Articles in the "Saturday Review" (essays) 1868
Ourselves: A Series of Essays on Women (essays) 1869
The True History of Joshua Davidson, Christian and Communist (novel) 1872
The Mad Willoughbys and Other Tales (short stories) 1875
Patricia Kemball (novel) 1875
The Atonement of Leam Dundas (novel) 1876
The World Well Lost (novel) 1877
Under Which Lord? (novel) 1879
The Rebel of the Family (novel) 1880
With a Silken Thread and Other Stories (short stories) 1880
Ione (novel) 1883

The Autobiography of Christopher Kirkland (novel) 1885
Paston Carew, Millionaire and Miser (novel) 1886
Through the Long Night (novel) 1889
About Ireland (nonfiction) 1890
An Octave of Friends, with Other Silhouettes and Stories (short stories) 1891
The One Too Many (novel) 1894
The New Woman: In Haste and at Leisure (novel) 1895
My Literary Life (autobiography) 1899
The Second Youth of Theodora Desanges (novel) 1900

The Saturday Review, London   (essay date 1867)

[*In the following review, the critic evaluates the presentation of gender roles in* Sowing the Wind.]

We are often terrified with dark hints of what would happen if women, instead of men, had the making of the laws. And it is not altogether easy to say what would be the consequences to society from such a revolution. But we may perhaps get some inkling of the possible results from incidental hints let drop on that side which would be the depositary of power and majesty under the new *régime.* This, it may be, it is that peculiarly engages our attention when clever women vouchsafe to favour us with pictures of society drawn from their own imaginary or ideal point of view. Being at perfect liberty to people their pages with men and women absolutely of their own creation, our female novelists do us a favour for which the opposite sex at least can hardly be sufficiently grateful when they afford us a peep, as it were, by anticipation into their private estimate of the odds in the coming struggle. They may be letting the supposed stronger sex see themselves for a moment as the opposite half of society sees them, and so warning men betimes of what their existing tenure of supremacy would be worth had the so-called weaker sex the opportunity of turning their natural right into might. When the lion was shown a picture of a lion overcome by a man, he simply remarked that a man had the drawing of the picture. And so long as men have the power, either to adjust the relations of the sexes, or to set forth their respective prowess in mind or character, there can be no doubt as to which way the balance of superiority will incline. The clever writer of *Sowing the Wind* will not, we hope, find fault with our taking her book as in some sense an exponent of this lurking rivalry. In her highly-wrought contrast of a hero unutterably fatuous, selfish, and void of self-control, with a heroine devoted, thoughtful, self-forgetting, full of resource, and never ruffled by the fiercest tempest, what can have been the writer's secret impulse, if not her avowed motive, unless that of showing what pitiful, feckless, and ill-governed creatures men are, and how much wiser, steadier, and more full of capacity are their wives? How false is the received conception of husband and wife, as the ivy clinging to the oak, the weak vessel resting on the strong, the meek and docile pupil sitting at the feet of wisdom and dignity and prudence. It is in keeping up man's supposed essential prerogative of taking the lead, thinking and acting for both, and absorbing into himself every spring and source of reason, emotion, and will, that St. John Aylott furnishes a dreadful example of this common social fallacy. It is from sowing the wind (as we interpret the somewhat ambiguous title of the book) by this perverse self-idolatry of sex, and by fatuous blindness to the wealth of intellect, self-possession, and will stored up in his angel wife, that this mistaken gentleman gets swept away by a retributive whirlwind of disgrace, humiliation, and ruin—a fitting end for the vain wretch who, having lit upon such a priceless jewel, thinks only of how it may be made to set off his own worthless person.

Isola Aylott has been married at seventeen, having seen nothing of the world, and, for the five years that have since elapsed, having been suffered to see neither thing nor person in the world except her husband. Her character and capability are thus far buried within herself. Her physical attractions, joined to this very inexperience of life, and almost total freedom from the incumbrance of kith and kin, have sufficed to centre on her the whole of her husband's doting though selfish affection. Her beauty is such as in a sort to justify St. John's infatuated deadness to all but her corporal endowments. Isola is voluptuous, and somewhat Italian in type, though her eyes are of the soft Irish blue. Her hair is of the bright golden hue which is *de rigueur* in all modern novels, albeit not of the sleek and silky kind, but "mutinous hair," that would "curl and break out from the triple bands round the well-shaped head in a kind of aureole." We are not long in seeing that the strength of Isola's character is somehow intended to be be bound up with this expressive quality of her hair. The spiritual force that breaks the green withes of marital oppression, and the angelic grace which is to grow up with the free expansion of the imprisoned soul are to be seen here in a kind of adumbration of the future. With the loveliest arms and shoulders that ever woman had, and with the "finely arched feet of a thoroughbred," her hands, though white and shapely, were a trifle large—"like the hands of all capable women." Every touch in this delicate miniature is full of meaning, thrown in with the utmost art to enhance the force of contrast with the picture of St. John Aylott himself. There is about her the "general sentiment of abounding though suppressed physical life" which sets off strongly his softer and more languid grace. He is of what the writer calls the Spanish type—"elegant or distinguished rather than manly," shy and retreating, a man who "never stood square, face to face and chest broadside, but always a little turned edgewise, with one foot in advance of the other"; a "refined and well-bred gentleman of the true Brahmin class, but without strength or daring." The author's favourite art of chiromancy comes in as a final test of the latent temper of this pair. Isola wore the same sized gloves as did her husband, "but her hands were firmer than his, and with a fuller and broader palm; his were long and thin and narrow." Never were palms more indicative of destiny. As yet St. John Aylott has been the master, and Isola his wife has known no will save his. During their five years of marriage he has not left Isola's side for half an hour, nor has she ever crossed their threshold alone. But this isolated existence begins to pall upon the young wife. Her physical and spiritual energies make her

yearn for some wider sphere of duty and usefulness and living sympathy. But as her expansive nature looks around for further objects of love and pity and enthusiasm, St. John's egotism and pride close round his idol with a more jealous and exclusive grasp. As yet nothing has occurred to shake her affection for him, or jar upon the "wifely" sense she has been brought up in of entire submissiveness to his will. But the conflict of wills is soon to be forced upon the pair by the course of circumstances. A forgotten aunt of Isola's, the widow of an obscure country practitioner, forces her way into the household in a way most irritating to Aylott's exclusiveness and overweening family pride. And more odious than Mrs. Osborn's idiotic cringing ways are the blunt and off-hand manners of her daughter Jane, a plain, *gauche,* free-spoken girl, who has no patience with aristocratic airs and the "faddle" of social usage. St. John's querulous attempts to keep back Isola from taking these objects of pity to her bosom is the first step towards the supremacy of the wife. Anon turns up under somewhat suspicious circumstances an infant, which proves however not to be Aylott's child, but that of a sister of his, who had eloped years ago with a circus-rider, and whose name and existence had been erased from the family memory. Widowed and coming home to die in the Osborns' house, the penniless mother of this boy leaves him a legacy to her brother, and the detested Jane, who makes herself the medium of the transfer, executes her mission with accessories of superfluous aggravation.

We must say our sympathies here are very much on the side of the unfortunate gentleman, whose petulance and impotent wrath are presented as a warning to all married men who would seek to hold their own against wives yearning for a mission, and above all filled full with the maternal instinct which Providence has debarred them from lavishing upon offspring of their own. The angelic sweetness and lofty sense of duty with which Isola stands by her accepted pledge serve to heap coals of fire upon the irritable, nervous egotist. His absorbing and depending love for his wife, essentially selfish as it is, is wrung beyond endurance as the baby evidently rises to the first place in Isola's affections; and his jealous, even criminal, efforts to supplant the child only end in further alienation from her heart. At one moment of despair, when the half-maddened wretch traces his losses of honour, wealth, and his wife's affections to the evil spells of this child and the other low brood of his family, he is only just kept back from murder. On the whole, our feelings well nigh revolt against the extremes to which Mrs. Linton has carried her picture of morbid weakness and self-torturing passion. In pity for the moral and mental debasement in which the victim is made to sink, we are compelled to criticize the poetical justice of the sentence which has brought him so low. Is it, we are tempted to ask, in the interest of husbands and wives that we should see a man so grovel in the dust for the mere fault of blindness to the superior intellect and virtue inherent in the wife, and of unreasoning jealousy of anything that threatens his monopoly of her heart and brain? To show the dangers of sowing even such a handbreadth of the wind of domestic strife, is it necessary for the feeble sower to be swept to destruction by so terrible a hurricane of wrath? Isola, meanwhile, comes out purified seven times in the fire. There is something surpassing woman in her quiet self-control and long-suffering patience. She never exults in her lord's manifest lowering of himself by her side, and meets his insults and even blows with a calm and queenly pity. Not a shadow of disloyalty crosses her pure spirit, even when he flirts most glaringly with the siren Marcy, and when Isola is thrown into dangerous proximity with the "leonine" hero of the story, Gilbert Holmes. Everybody is of course prepared to meet with the brave, strong man, pure as a maiden, unconscious of his own talent and worth, always at hand to succour the good and punish the wicked. Even after Gilbert has saved Isola from the fire when her husband had selfishly thought only of his own preservation, and when St. John has thrown her from him with blows, she admits no more than a sister's feeling for her "big brother," till Aylott's death in the asylum leaves her free to lay her head in innocence upon that broad breast.

It is not Mrs. Linton's manner to crowd her stage with a number of supernumerary actors. Nor does she put her piece upon the boards with any but the very barest additions of scenery or accessories. The result, however, is to bring into stronger relief her powers of individualizing, while our attention is not perpetually taken off from the living and moving personages in the front of the stage to mere details in the background. Jane Osborn's blunt and vigorous sense, generous warmth of heart, and bold face against the worst of times, stand out well in contrast with the vapid and artificial airs of her mother, a weaker kind of Mrs. Nickleby. By doing man's work upon the *Comet* newspaper, Jane contrives, not only to keep her own and her mother's head above water, but to bear the charge of the Aylotts when borne down by the failure of St. John's schemes for wealth. She is one of the plain heroines who are perpetually brought in in modern novels, as a protest against the traditional supremacy of female charms—a tall, bony girl, with a profusion of reddish hair, and skin "of a duck's-egg white, fine and soft, but covered with freckles, and a blunt and positive nose." Her hands are small and good, but in general inky, her nails dirty, and her dress unkempt. But, dowdy and roystering as she is, it is Jane who first touches in Isola's heart the chord of earnestness and utility, though on her head rests not a little of the blame (if blame the authoress will allow us to call it) of shattering the idol which the wife had once worshipped in her husband. We are fairly grieved that no better fate has been found for Jane, after all her brave and disinterested battle with life, than to subside into the acrid and angular old maid, the drudge of the *Comet,* ungainly and unloved. Is this, according to the moral of the book, the penalty of having in a moment of weakness so far recognised the ascendancy of man as to have found a soft place for love of Harvey Wyndham, the literary handyman, and half-easy, half-scampish bubble-blower of the piece, who, after ruining St. John, and vainly trying his fascinations upon Isola, ends in carrying off the heiress? Marcy Tremouille, the bad heroine, a rich creole, wily as a snake and supple as a panther, is just the girl to fix for a time the weak and wavering fancy of St. John Aylott. A direct contrast to Isola in beauty and in the desire to attract, she keeps up a byplay of rivalry with the wife in her husband's affections, while coquetting with Wyndham, and secretly pining to entrap her cousin Gilbert Holmes.

At length, at a crisis of pique at St. John's falling-off in flirtation, and of jealousy at Gilbert's coldness, Marcy is mean enough to write two anonymous letters, one of which brings to light the baseness of Aylott's birth, while the other impresses him with the belief of Isola's unfaithfulness. Wyndham's knowledge of her treachery, and his skilful playing upon her dread of the consequences, are the means of throwing Marcy into his power. The union of this pair of schemers brings its appropriate results. And in reaping as they have sown we have the satisfaction of seeing the moral of the book, in one instance at least, most righteously exemplified.

In point of ability Mrs. Linton's story rises above the average of novels. Had she kept clear of occasional extravagance, the work might have been one of first-rate excellence. As it is, nearly all her characters bear marks of exaggeration—a fault which is made more conspicuous by the warmth and vigour of her style. We are sorry too to see her persist in tricks of manner which struck us in reading *Lizzie Lorton of Greyrigg.* Why should there be always some oddity or other without which a personage is never allowed to speak or move? Why should Jane Osborn, for instance, be for ever tossing back her hair and rubbing her nose? This bit of mannerism is probably to be traced to an immoderate admiration of Mr. Charles Dickens. It might be left to feebler minds to copy the foibles of an able writer. Mrs. Linton has quite fund enough of fresh and original talent in herself to make her independent of the style of any master. (pp. 373-74)

> *A review of "Sowing the Wind," in* The Saturday Review, *London, Vol. XXIII, March 23, 1867, pp. 373-74.*

A. G. Sedgwick   (essay date 1868)

[*In the excerpt below, from a review of* Modern Women and What Is Said of Them *originally published in 1868, Sedgwick discusses Linton's essays, finding their style unremarkable and their concerns exaggerated.*]

From all sides we hear lamentable accounts of the present state of society: that the French *salons* are dying out, or have already ceased to exist; that the race of English conversers is disappearing; that in this country such representatives of the old Knickerbocker and Puritan families as are still to be found hold themselves aloof from intercourse, except with their fellows, other Knickerbockers and Puritans, and live in good works and a regretful remembrance of a society of which their grandmothers were members. That the Prince of Wales delights in "Champagne Charley" is a small matter, but that all England is delighted with it is alarming; that the *demi-monde* has always existed is undeniable, but that its fashions should be copied by innocent women is startling: and so of this country we may say that people who have no objection to the waltz are displeased with the German. And now comes the *Saturday Review,* and tells us that the "girl of the period" is a creature who dyes, paints, and enamels,—studies the arts of vice, that she may render herself attractive to those accustomed to its pleasures,—is immodest in dress, behavior, and conversation,—and whose whole object in life is to marry the man who, of all she knows, has the largest fortune and the least brains.

> The girl of the period is a creature who dyes her hair and paints her face, as the first articles of her personal religion,—whose sole idea of life is plenty of fun and luxury,—and whose dress is the object of such thought and intellect as she possesses. Her main endeavor in this is to outvie her neighbors in the extravagance of fashion.
>
> If there is a reaction against an excess of Rowland's Macassar, and hair shiny and sticky with grease is thought less nice than if left clean and heathily crisp, she dries and frizzes and sticks hers out on end like certain savages in Africa, or lets it wander down her back like Madge Wildfire's, and thinks herself all the more beautiful, the nearer she approaches in look to a maniac. . . . With purity of taste, she has lost also that far more precious purity and delicacy of perception which sometimes mean more than appears on the surface. What the *demi-monde* does in its frantic efforts to excite attention she also does in imitation. If some fashionable *dévergondée en évidence* is reported to have come out with her dress below her shoulder-blades, and a gold strap for all the sleeve thought necessary, the girl of the period follows suit next day, and then wonders that men sometimes mistake her for her prototype, or that mothers of girls not quite so far gone as herself refuse her as a companion for their daughters.
>
> At whatever cost of shocked self-love or pained modesty it may be, it cannot be too plainly told to the modern English girl that the net result of the present manner of life is to assimilate her as nearly as possible to a class of women whom we must not call by their proper—or improper—name.

This of course touches England primarily, but concerns us also. The same complaints are made here,—less in degree, but in kind the same; since the days of the "Potiphar Papers," every Saratoga and Newport season has brought to light an increasing love of luxury, fastness, and display.

These articles from the *Saturday Review* are not so clever as the attention they have received gives one the right to expect,—an attention, indeed, aroused as much by the fierceness of the attack as by anything else. And then, as one of the essays points out, any criticism of woman, however analytic and temperate, excites to hot activity an *esprit de corps* which is not to be found in any other body. Handle man as severely as you please, and he will only laugh; but avoid the subject of feminine character, if you do not wish to obtain the reputation of being both a fool and a barbarian. Most of the papers are in the ordinary *Saturday Review* manner,—and a most wearisome manner it is, when you have a book full of it,—with here and there a clever hit, such as this: "Woman alone keeps up the private family warfare which in the earlier stages of society required all the energies of man"; or this, *à propos* of the *esprit de corps* just alluded to: "Women certainly present the only analogy in the present day to that claim of internal jurisdiction for which the Church struggled so gallantly in the Middle Ages. No one who sees the serried ranks

with which she encounters all investigation from without would imagine the severity with which she administers justice within." The most striking of these papers is that called the **"Girl of the Period,"** and it seems to us to have been written by some one who had no hand in the others, or at any rate wrote very little of the book. The style is quite different from the regular style of the social essay; and if any of the papers are to be attributed to a woman, it may as well be this one,—though, to be sure, there is no special need of going so far to seek an author, for even this might have been written by a great many people, and the whole question of the authorship of the book is not likely to become a very vital one, until something more important shall be produced by the same hands.

"Modern Women" is a tirade against modern Englishwomen, and parenthetically against modern women of other nations: we have already given a specimen of the charges. We hear these accusations in America as well, and it behooves us to examine the foundation of them, that we may discover whether or not they are true, and, if true, what the remedy should be. In plain English, are we going to the Devil? Will the Saratoga woman of ten years hence be such a woman as the *Saturday Review* describes in these terms: "Belladonna flashes from her eyes, kohl and antimony deepen the blackness of her eyebrows, 'bloom of roses' blushes from her lips"? Is she of this sort now? If our politicians are every year becoming more and more corrupt, our theatres every year more and more indecent, and our society more and more abandoned in its luxury and frivolity, we shall very soon reach a point at which there will be little security for life or property,—if that in some quarters of the country has not been reached already. The soberest of American cities has had its winter's excitement furnished by the *Cancan*, the officers of the law in New York act or remain inactive according to the relative length of the plaintiffs' and defendants' purses, while the hot whirl of Newport and Saratoga serves as a ready Lethe for all moral obligations. A rather disheartening picture might be drawn in this way of our probable future; and yet we cannot believe in its truth. (pp. 54-5)

> *A. G. Sedgwick, "Modern Women, & What Is Said of Them," in* The North American Review, *Vol. 272, No. 3, September, 1987, pp. 54-5.*

The Spectator   (essay date 1876)

[*In the following review, the critic assesses the strengths and weaknesses of* The Atonement of Leam Dundas.]

Mrs. Lynn Linton is clever, but her stories leave a bad flavour in the mouth. Her powers of description are quite above the average, her men and women are alive, and the dialogue is always easy; but one is never without the sense that the authoress believes society rotten to the very core; that the ordinary men and women one must perforce meet every day are steeped to the lips in hypocrisy, more or less consciously; and that the criminal class is the class alone really capable of the higher flights of goodness or the nobler forms of self-abnegation. In the story before us, we have five families living "in one of the loveliest places to be found in England." Mrs. Lynn Linton describes scenery well, and North Aston is a place pleasant to contem-

An excerpt from *The New Woman: In Haste and at Leisure*

"What a slave that little cur is!" said Phœbe with intense contempt. "You are no daughter of mine, Euphemia, to be such a slave as you are!"

The little girl looked up in astonishment. Sherrard visibly frowned.

"Do you want to teach her——"

"To be what I am?" interrupted Phœbe, speaking with unbounded insolence. "Yes—as far from all your rubbishy sentimentality—as independent and self-reliant—as contemptuous of you men, you lords of creation, and as clear-sighted as to your real characters. Yes, I want to teach her all that; and then perhaps I shall make something of her."

"And I think you will fail," said Sherrard.

"Shall I, Euphemia?" asked Phœbe in the same manner as that which she had used to her husband.

"I do not understand you, mother," answered the child.

"Shall I ever teach you to despise men and boys, to look on them as your inferiors, to understand that they are tyrants and brutes, to be kept at a distance and never given way to? Shall I ever make you a woman in your own right and one who will never obey any man whatever? Never! never!"

She spoke with feverish passion, every word meaning an insult to her husband rather than rational exhortation to her child.

Euphemia was scared by the voice and manner and essential wildness of her mother's words. Being scared she forgot her manners; and, though permission had not been given her, she slipped off her chair and ran to her father.

"Go upstairs now, dear," said Sherrard, kissing her.

"No, I do not give her leave," said Phœbe, rising in exasperation. "She shall not go."

For all answer Sherrard took the child by the hand, led her to the door and put her safely out of the room.

"Go," he said; "and be ready for your ride in half an hour."

"I am glad you have thrown off the mask at last!" said Phœbe with an hysterical laugh. "So now I am to have no authority over my own daughter? You are to be master even in the nursery?"

"You are to have no power to pollute her mind with your infernal doctrines," said Sherrard hotly. "Lost to the better instincts of womanhood yourself, you shall not corrupt my child."

Eliza Lynn Linton, in The New Woman: In Haste and at Leisure, *Merriam, 1895.*

plate, where "up the valley the high lands broadened into a breezy moor, purple with heath and heather, peopled with bird and beast, whence could be seen things as in a dream—perceived, but not belonging—the spires of cities and the smoke of distant railroads. . . . . . while below were the green pastures, where herds of kine, sedate and ruminant, stood knee-deep in quiet pools, or stood by the meadow-gates lowing for the milking-pails." Fields of yellowing grain and hedges, which in summer were sweet with roses and woodbine, stately forest-trees and rare birds, all go to make up one of those scenes which the Englishman knows so well, and associates, we hope, generally (with a few drawbacks, no doubt) with all he values most of home life. In Mrs. Linton's hands,—

Every prospect pleases, and only man is vile.

For in this place, "which poets love to write of and artists to delineate," "the poor, stagnating in mind and fortune, live, toil, and die, very little removed from the beasts they pasture," while the "wives and daughters of the resident gentry beat themselves like birds against the wires of their cages, spending half their lives in bewailing the dullness of the other half." We are not for a moment to suppose that drunkenness, bad drainage, and overcrowded cottages, three fruitful sources of evil in many a picturesque hamlet, were the causes at work here to produce "the pinched and deadened lives" of which Mrs. Linton speaks. On the contrary, North Aston "had as much the perfection of rustic order as of rustic beauty." "It had neither village rowdyism nor village immorality." They (the villagers) were simply "strangled in the grasp of superiority. They had not energy enough to be vicious, certainly not energy enough to be discontented." The superiority which extinguishes immorality and discontent, even by a process of strangulation; ought at least to be of a very active and vigorous kind; but we find the shepherd of this somewhat peculiar flock a man by no means disposed to be too solicitous about his work,—an easy-going man, "doing his duty in a perfunctory and spiritless way, satisfied with peace, and never seeking after improvement." Nor was it some village Mrs. Proudie who ruled these down-trodden people, for the rector's wife was a placid, sweet-tempered, inactive woman, with a habit of being five minutes too late. There is but one child in the rectory, "a girl of soft manners and determined purpose, whose gloves of velvet triple-pile covered hands of steel tougher than Bessemer's." The second of the five families which constituted "society" in North Aston included a mother, whom Mrs. Linton regards as the typical British country matron, narrow, strict, innocent of the real world in which she lives; three daughters over thirty, lean, faded, and "regarding tobacco as a vice, and whist for five-shillings points as a sin almost as heinous as the advocacy of cremation." A large family of the Fairbairns, "healthy, open-air, breezy sort of folks," are also hard and narrow. And into this paradise Mr. Dundas, an English country gentleman, fair and handsome, has introduced a superbly beautiful Spanish woman, with the face of a sibyl, the temper of a fiend, the habits of a savage, and ignorance to correspond. Most clever is Mrs. Linton's description of this woman, "who has her uses in keeping North Aston alive, and affording ceaseless occasions for talk and speculation." Her husband's dream of love for her had been over long ago, and she hated him as Spaniards can hate, with a persistency their daily life together did not tend to diminish. But if she hates her husband even to the point of dressing dolls like the Devil, and then teaching her little daughter to call such doll, "El señor papa," she is, nevertheless, capable of being exceedingly jealous of him, and she is not long without occasion, for upon the scene in this quiet English village appears a certain Madame la Marquise de Montfort, a needy adventuress and ex-nursery-maid. In her championship of serving-maids the authoress has probably met with some remarkable specimens, but we venture to think, happily, few before whom all the world would bow down as the North-Aston world bowed to Madame de Montfort. Indeed, we wonder that even the glamour the incident of service throws over her heroine should have made Mrs. Linton not perceive that duller wits than those of North Aston would have detected Madame de Montfort. The wife of a French Marquis, who has passed much of her life in Spain, and in sweetest accents states she has forgotten her "Castilian," should not write "appollogies" in her notes, or make glaring grammatical blunders in her speech. However, she is pretty, beautiful as dye, and paint, and pretty manners can make her, and the village pastor "smiles upon her with fatherly affection and official satisfaction commingled." Spanish Pepita dies of mad jealousy, and Mr. Dundas marries the adventuress.

And here begins the true tale, the veritable tragedy,—a tragedy, we think, which should never have been written, but which has been, and probably will be, widely read. Leam Dundas, the child of Pepita, loves her mother with the intensity which comes of undivided thought. She is fifteen, ignorant, beautiful, and whether false or truthful we can hardly tell, since we read in one page of her asking, what good truth does? "One tells lies," she says, "when one must," and one must very often; and then, in another, she will not listen to one of Scott's novels because it is not true, saying proudly, "I did not come here to listen to lies. Mamma did not tell lies!" This girl, like "a pomegranate-bud," gives promise of a splendid future. She is to Alick Corfield "a girl-queen, an unread poem." As we have said, she was but fifteen when she loses her mother, and Mr. Dundas marries Madame de Montfort. The child's whole soul is bent on avenging the injury done, as she considers, to her mother. She learns from Alick Corfield the secret of some poisons, and that they will kill, and in less than a month after her father's marriage she poisons her stepmother secretly, and with such fatal skill as to escape suspicion. In the years which follow she goes to school; conscience is awakened, and remorse. Her life thenceforth is a miserable struggle to make atonement. She loves a man to whom she remembers her story must be told, and when it effectually separates her from him she leaves home for ever; in a distant part of the country she meets once more her lover, discovers he is married, and dies. We have given the story as critics can, making that ugly and repulsive which in the writer's hands is full of mournful beauty and tragic interest? Quite so; the point is, after all, what are the facts of the case, and what are the limits of art? First, as to the facts, we will give, in the authoress's own words, the circumstances which led up to that which she is pleased to designate "Leam's loving crime." Before Madame de

Montfort becomes her stepmother, she is for awhile her governess, and this is the relation which exists between them:—

> Meanwhile Leam underwent a daily torture, the effect of which was to harden her more and more to the world outside, while driving her deeper into that recess where was her stronghold. She hated her lessons, not because they were lessons, but because they were things which mamma had not taught her and would have laughed to scorn had she heard. It seemed to her an injury to mamma that she should learn all these funny things about places and people, the stars and the animals, that Madame read to her from ugly little books, and that mamma had never known. But what could she do? It was to no good that she sometimes ran away and hid for a whole day in one special part of Steel's Wood, braving the unknown perils of wild beasts and armed banditti to be found therein, if only she might escape Madame. She thought she would rather run the danger of being devoured by the wolves and lions which she had not a doubt made their home in the dark parts of the wood, or of being carried off by the brigands who lived in the caves, than go to Madame to feel that her mother was being insulted when unable to avenge herself, and that she, her little Leam, her own sweet Heart, had joined hands in the blow! Still, running-away was of no avail. To escape one day out of seven or eight might be a gain of so many hours, but the permanent arrangement held fast. That went on whether she braved the perils of the wild beasts and armed banditti or not; and the only result of her absence to-day was to be taken personally in deep disgrace by her father to-morrow, scolded all the way there, and received by Madame with maddening friendliness at the end. Leam thought she could have borne it better had Madame been cold and severe rather than so uniformly caressing and amiable. Had she rated her or even beaten her as her mother used to do, she would have been less reluctant, because she would have had something tangible to go on. As it was, she felt as if fighting with a cloud: and the plentiful outpoor of honey in exchange for her own gall sickened her. That pleasant smile, those endearing words, that inexhaustible patience, revolted the girl, who saw in her smooth-faced 'governess' only the woman whom her mother had distrusted and disliked! For herself personally, without these haunting reminiscences, she would have liked Madame well enough; but now—it would be unfaithful to mamma; and Leam could not be that! Living as she did in the one ever active thought of her mother's unseen presence and continued existence, the influence of the past was never weakened; and Leam's heart clung to the mother unseen as the little arms used to cling round her in the days of her bodily existence.

We appeal to honest sense if it be within the fair range of art to make this attitude of mind in a young child, otherwise innocent, lead up to murder, and murder to be regarded in her mind thus?—

> Leam, standing upright in her room, in her

clinging white nightdress, her dark hair hanging to her knees, her small brown feet bare above the ankle, not trembling, but tense, listening, her heart on fire, her whole being as it were pressed together, concentrated on the one thought, the one purpose, heard the words passed from lip to lip. 'Dead,' they said; 'dead!' Lifting up her rapt face, and raising her outstretched arms high above her head, with no sense of sin, no consciousness of cruelty, only with the feeling of having done that thing which had been laid on her to do—of having satisfied and avenged her mother—she cried aloud in a voice deepened by the pathos of her love, the passion of her deed, into an exultant hymn of sacrifice: 'Mamma, are you happy now? Mamma! mamma! leave off crying,—there is no awe in your place now!'

The "place," be it remembered, being the one place which, as Leam knew, her mother hated and despised. We are thankful that within our range of fiction we have never come upon anything quite so horrible as this. To conceive of madness or of badness is one thing. Young criminals guilty of fierce crimes have existed, unhappily, before to-day, but to picture deliberately a young and innocent girl, of fine original nature and at least one intense affection, studying to grasp a secret which should enable her to perpetrate undiscovered a deadly crime, with no warning instinct to hold her back from the act which life cannot expiate, no sense of guilt, of pity, or even fear, to deter her from the fatal deed, would, if it came within the region of facts, give colour to the creed of devil-worship. Things abnormal are not better in art than they are in nature. They are apt to become monstrosities in either. Having created Leam, the authoress does well to pity her, but we venture to hope she may in the future turn talents of no mean order to some subject less calculated to revolt the healthiest instincts of humanity. (pp. 1014-15)

> *"The Atonement of Leam Dundas," in* The Spectator, *Vol. 49, No. 2511, August 12, 1876, pp. 1014-15.*

Vineta Colby (essay date 1970)

[*Colby is an American educator and critic. In the excerpt below, she offers an overview of Linton's career.*]

[Eliza Lynn Linton] was perhaps the supreme example of the self-made, self-proclaimed Victorian lady novelist-polemicist—the hardiest, the longest lived, the most businesslike and professional. A rebel from the start (a "revolting daughter" to use the Victorian epithet), at twenty-three, in 1845, she set out from her father's parsonage at Crosthwaite, in the Lake Country, to storm literary London. Characteristically, she began her siege from the Reading Room of the British Museum, compiling rather than writing two prodigiously learned historical novels, **Azeth the Egyptian** and **Amymone, a Romance of the Days of Pericles,** to which almost nobody except Walter Savage Landor has ever paid any attention. Nevertheless, Miss Lynn made her mark. By 1851 she was a full-fledged, full-time journalist on the staff of the *Morning Chronicle,* at the not inconsiderable salary of twenty guineas a month. She was also contributing regularly to *Household*

Words, with the editor Charles Dickens' solid recommendation: "Good for anything and thoroughly reliable." The "anything" was everything—fiction, book and play reviews, travel reporting, social leaders—all of it competent, much of it lively, and some of it so abrasive and controversial that by the 1860s, now Mrs. Linton, she was a national celebrity.

Not surprisingly, her greatest fame was won in polemical journalism rather than in the novel. Although throughout her long career Mrs. Linton treated the subject of women's rights in her novels, she handled it most effectively in nonfiction, in a series of battling, bristling unsigned articles in the *Saturday Review* under the general title **"The Girl of the Period."** These appeared over some ten years, 1866-1877, the bulk of them in 1866. They were reprinted in a pamphlet in 1868, of which some forty thousand copies circulated; in two American collections entitled **Modern Women and What Is Said of Them** (1868; Second Series, 1870); and finally in 1883 in two volumes published under Mrs. Linton's own name, **The Girl of the Period and Other Social Essays.** Such was their popularity that, according to Mrs. Linton, two others—a clergyman and "a lady of rank well known in London society"—claimed their authorship. The phrase itself won a place in the language. There was a *Girl of the Period Almanack* and a thirty-two-page monthly, *The Girl of the Period Miscellany,* with articles on the typical Irish GP, the French GP, etc. There were GP parasols and articles of ladies' clothing. And Matthew Morgan caricatured the unknown authoress (though many thought the pieces the work of a man) in a wicked cartoon showing a shriveled, high-nosed, bespectacled shrew painting from a sweetly innocent-looking model a portrait of a diabolical female with Satanic horns and wings. Her paint jars are labeled Venom and Gall, and around her skirt is the banner "Saturday Review."

Something of the imagination of a novelist went into Mrs. Linton's creation. The Girl of the Period is indeed a sister of the high-spirited "anti-heroines" who figure in a good deal of minor Victorian fiction from Mrs. Oliphant to Rhoda Broughton and M. E. Braddon. She is the pert modern miss of the sixties, blossoming out in rebellion against the codes and crinolines of mid-Victorianism and flowering (or degenerating, according to one's feminist views) into the belligerent crusading suffragette of the nineties and later. As Mrs. Linton originally conceived her—both in the *Saturday Review* and in some of her early fiction—she was empty-headed, frivolous, self-indulgent: "a creature who dyes her hair and paints her face . . . whose sole idea of life is plenty of fun and luxury, and whose dress is the object of such thought and intellect as she possesses" (March 14, 1868). As she matures, however, her silliness turns to malevolence. She marries for money and social position, is indifferent to her home and children:

> a frisky matron, a fashionable woman, a thing of paints and pads . . . making pleasure her only good, and the world her highest god, it too often means a woman who is not ashamed to supplement her husband with a lover, but who is unwilling to become the honest mother of that hus-

band's children . . . a hybrid creature perverted out of the natural way altogether, affecting the license but ignorant of the strength of a man, alike as girl or woman valueless for her highest natural duties, and talking largely of liberty while showing at every turn how much she fails in that co-essential of liberty—knowledge how to use it (August 8, 1868).

Ultimately her fate reflects the poetic justice of a work of fiction. She loses the love of her children (see **"Modern Mothers,"** February 29, 1868: "Society has put maternity out of fashion . . . "); the loyalty of her servants (see **"Mistress and Maid on Dress and Undress,"** February 1, 1868); the devotion of her husband (see **"Ideal Women,"** May 9, 1868: "It is the vague restlessness, the fierce extravagance, the neglect of home, the indolent fine-ladyism, the passionate love of pleasure which characterise the modern woman, that saddens men and destroys in them that respect which their very pride prompts them to feel"). Dwindling into middle age and desperately striving to retain her youth, she becomes the ridiculous and pathetic **"Femme Passée"** (July 11, 1868):

> Dressed in the extreme of youthful fashion, her thinning hair dyed and crimped and fired till it is more like red-brown tow than hair, her flaccid cheeks ruddled, her throat whitened . . . her lustreless eyes blackened around the lids, to give the semblance of limpidity to the tarnished whites . . . she stands, the wretched creature who will not consent to grow old.

The Girl of the Period fares little better in Mrs. Linton's fiction. Here one may trace her evolution from the spoiled and impetuous young girls who appear from time to time in her early novels to the ardent and willfully destructive suffragettes in her novels of the 1890s. At the same time that Mrs. Linton was condemning the GP in the *Saturday Review* (during the 1860s) she was introducing in her novel *Sowing the Wind* (1867) a plain, mannish young woman journalist who, while blunt and even crude at times, is nevertheless sympathetic. By 1878 the Girl of the Period had become one of the "Shrieking Sisterhood," and in *The Rebel of the Family* a plain, bespectacled young heroine named Perdita flirts dangerously with the movement. Unappreciated and even persecuted by her shallow, selfish widowed mother and prettier sisters, "longing for some vital interest, and suffocating in the stifling atmosphere to which she was condemned," she is briefly lured into the West Hill Society for Women's Rights by an aggressive older woman, "the Venus of the Emancipated Olympus." Perdita happily has enough character to resist her blandishments and enough luck to meet an attractive young chemist whom she eventually marries.

A more typical GP appears in a late novel, *The One Too Many* (1894); here she has degenerated into the militant suffragette. The novel is dedicated to "the sweet girls still left among us who have no part in the new revolt but are content to be dutiful, innocent, and sheltered." Such a sweet innocent is the heroine of this novel, driven to mental anguish and finally suicide by a cold, egotistical husband. In contrast, the antiheroine, "the prize-girl of Gir-ton and now a B.A. of London," strides vigorously through life, trampling on any who get in her way:

> Emphatically a child of the generation, she had a profound contempt for all that had gone before. Her world dated from yesterday, and the past was only as a cock-shy for ridicule. Nothing was as it had been. Thought, knowledge, morality, humanity, had all come into a new phase: and the rules which had done well for the times that had gone were now but as decayed sticks, which might have kept the sapling straight but were useless to the sturdy tree.

She reads Ibsen, Maeterlinck, Baudelaire, Zola, and Maupassant. She has studied nursing and medicine, assisted at operations without fainting or flinching, studied painting "from the life" in Paris, lived in the slums, visited prisons and doss houses, and "fraternised with thieves, gutter sparrows, and soiled doves." She smokes, talks slang, and wears her hair short; her clothes are masculine and severe. Nevertheless, this "revolting daughter" or, as Mrs. Linton calls her in a series of articles in *The Nineteenth Century,* the "wild woman," comes off better in the novel than in the periodical articles. After a flurry of activity in an anarchist movement, she falls in love with a policeman whom she finally marries. To Mrs. Linton's readers this was a humiliating social descent, but, even if it is at the price of her femininity, this heroine at least gets what she wants: "Not bold nor bad, she had yet lost that ineffable something which gives womankind its essential charm, endows it with its special power, and throws over it, as it were, a veil of mystic beauty."

The "Wild Woman" is treated with less tolerance in Mrs. Linton's novel of 1895, *The New Woman: In Haste and at Leisure,* where a frivolous heroine becomes enmeshed in the feminist activities of the Excelsior Club (" . . . they were united as one woman on the great question of the diabolical nature of husbands, the degrading institution of marriage, the shameful burden of maternity, woman's claims to be a County Councillor, a voter, a lawyer, a judge, an M.P."). She neglects her child, destroys her husband's love for her, and comes perilously close to wrecking her marriage. In contrast there is an "ideal" woman here with whom her husband falls in love, but whom he nobly renounces in order to preserve his marriage. This admirable woman is distinguished for her

> absolute purity—her freedom from the very fringes of feminine "fastness." No prurient curiosity ever led her to premature knowledge; no dangerous study had aroused more dangerous speculations, and what evil she was perforce obliged to know neither clung nor rooted, but passed from her mind as a thing with which she had nought to do.

Mrs. Linton's conservatism on the "Woman Question" is ironic in the light of her own bold personality, her striking success as a journalist in keen competition with men, and her outright radicalism in religion. Independent and aggressive, she idealized the modest, shrinking, feminine woman. Woman's instinct, she argued, was to submerge herself in her family: "A woman's own fame is barren. It begins and ends with herself. Reflected from her husband or her son, it has in it the glory of immortality—of continuance . . . the raison d'être of a woman is maternity. . . . The cradle lies across the door of the polling-booth and bars the way to the senate." Scholarly and hungry for learning herself, Mrs. Linton opposed formal higher education for women. Even more vigorously she deplored the extremes to which some partially educated women were carried in their zeal for education. In *Paston Carew, Millionaire and Miser,* a novel published in 1886, she ridicules a shallow genteel woman who, like many of her sex, has fallen under "the curse of culture":

> They go in for something they are not and can never be. Fragile, anemic, and barely escaping the sick couch for their own parts, they rush off to become hospital nurses or missionaries' wives. Incapable of looking ahead or of forecasting the events of tomorrow from the facts of today, they dash on to platforms and toss up grave political questions like jugglers' balls in the air. Ignorant of grammar . . . they neglect their families, let the children's stockings go in holes, and spend both time and money in chasing the phantom of literary fame.

Apparently Mrs. Linton shared with many writing women of her time a tendency to go to extremes in condemning the extremes of others. Her positions are often inconsistent and contradictory, largely because, pen in hand, she became intoxicated with her powers. Her success as a polemicist in both fiction and nonfiction fortified an already strong urge to preach, teach, and reform. As a result, she frequently spoke more strongly than she probably felt. Like many another second-rate novelist she made her points by unsubtle characterization, verging often on stereotype and caricature. Incapable of suggesting the shades and complexities of human character, she could only extol or condemn. Almost everyone who knew her personally, especially in her mature years, was impressed with her kindness, gentleness, and warmth. The novelist Beatrice Harraden, who was for some years Mrs. Linton's protégée, observed of her posthumously published memoirs *My Literary Life,* with its outspoken and sometimes indiscreet comments on Dickens, George Eliot, and George Henry Lewes: "It is to be regretted also that she is not here herself to tone down some of her more pungent remarks and criticisms, hastily thrown off in bitter moments such as come to us all. Mrs. Linton's pen was ever harsher than her speech, and those who loved and knew her have the right to emphasize this fact." Another friend, Algernon Charles Swinburne, spoke of her as "not only one of the most brilliant and gifted, but one of the kindest and most generous of women," and wrote a long poem on her death that begins:

> Kind, wise, and true as truth's own heart,
>   A soul that here
> Chose and held fast the better part
>   And cast out fear.

The stridency and abusiveness of Mrs. Linton's published work are in marked contrast to these impressions. One can only conclude that her writing does not represent her fairly. To seek consistency in her passionate pronouncements, in both her fiction and her nonfiction, is futile. Her incon-

sistency, however, is not mere waywardness, nor the reflection of an irrational, hysterical nature. It is easy to dismiss Mrs. Linton as a clown-caricature figure: she invites ridicule. But her contemporaries respected her—and her writing, shrill and intemperate as it is, suggests that she was a sound and faithful register of the times in which she lived. On the Woman Question, politics, religion, and social problems, she spoke her mind, a mind troubled, groping, confused by the rapid revolutionary changes that everywhere besieged it, yet eager to come to terms with progress and the "new" world.

No doubt there were personal sources as well for her confusions and inconsistencies. Mrs. Linton was a public figure most of her life, and her private life was closely bound up with her public one. She had little of the reticence one expects from Victorians and expressed herself as freely on most personal matters as she did on public ones. Characteristically, in 1885, she published her autobiography as a three-volume novel, so candid (even to using many real names) that her biographer George Somes Layard reprinted long passages of it. But this free-speaking nonfiction novel makes one extraordinary departure from reality. It changes the sex of the protagonist and becomes *The Autobiography of Christopher Kirkland,* promising thereby fascinating insights into transvestitism and unconscious masculinity but offering, in fact, so thin a sexual disguise and so transparent an authorial point of view that the reader promptly forgets the disguise.

As exposé and roman à clef, *Christopher Kirkland* is a dull and disappointing book, but it is an interesting expression of an intelligent Victorian's struggle to find a way of life for herself. The issue of the book—as it was the issue of her life and the problem of many other Victorians—was to find something to compensate for the loss of faith, something to fill the void. It is not a religious book, although religion figures strongly in it, but a book about a search for values. As Christopher Kirkland, Mrs. Linton traces her spiritual evolution from the fervent religious orthodoxy of her childhood through various stages of atheism, agnosticism, Unitarianism, necessitarianism, spiritualism and, finally, to a Comtist philosophy of humanitarianism and social meliorism which she called altruism. (pp. 16-23)

[Linton's] success in a highly competitive, unfeminine, and often antifeminine field like journalism can be attributed only to her persistence and her industry. She was not a remarkable writer, but she was thoroughly competent and, as at least one of her editors, Dickens, had testified, reliable. In *Sowing the Wind* she introduced an aggressive, plain, and masculine young girl who pushes her way into journalism in order to support an indigent widowed mother. In *Christopher Kirkland* she expands the episode with much autobiographical detail, describing her first interview with the gruff, forbidding editor of the *Morning Chronicle* John Douglas Cook. He managed to awe and frighten even the imperturbable Miss Lynn: "So! you are the little girl who has written that queer book [*Amymone*] and want to be one of the press-gang, are you?" To her meek reply, "Yes, I am the woman," he answered, "Woman, you call yourself? I call you a whippersnapper. But you seem to have something in you. We'll soon find out if you have." He thereupon assigned her a leader, to be composed on the spot, based on a technical Blue Book report relating to the economy of mining. She passed the test and for the next two years, until 1851, when she had a violent quarrel with her editor and quit, she worked steadily, turning out some eighty miscellaneous articles and thirty-six reviews.

More even than on her industry, Eliza Lynn's success was based on unshakable self-confidence. Rebuffs never discouraged her. She had resolved on a career in literature and she pursued her goal relentlessly, besieging publishers with no trace of reticence or false modesty. Even as a comparatively established novelist in the 1860s she was constantly on the alert for opportunities. In the files of the publisher William Blackwood and Sons in Edinburgh there are several letters from her, offering manuscripts. Concerning one novel, "Dearly Beloved" (probably *Sowing the Wind,* published in 1867 by Tinsley), she wrote to Major William Blackwood in 1863:

> It would be stupid to praise my own work, but I do think that if *Adam Bede, Jane Eyre, East Lynne* made their mark so quickly and deeply, this of mine will also; for it is not a weaker book than any of these, and certainly it is as faithful and therefore as original a transcript of society and human character as these. So much I think I may say without being conceited or presumptuous.

After the publisher rejected the novel, she wrote John Blackwood an impassioned, almost hysterical plea, offering to make any changes he might suggest and imploring his personal guidance and assistance:

> I am so very sorry you did not like it! Could I not alter it to suit you? Indeed, indeed I am teachable and grateful for criticism, kindly (not if illnaturedly) bestowed, and have very little literary selfwill in the way of holding to my own against the advice of wiser and more experienced people. My object is to get out of periodical literature and succeed as a writer of good novels; but to really succeed I must have a first-class publisher. If you think that I could change the tone of that book—add story—take out certain characters—insert new, perhaps healthier and pleasanter characters—I would set to work at once on it. . . . I have never been befriended once in my whole literary life. I have never been advised, never guided, never helped. It has been a hard, solitary, fierce struggle for what I have gained. . . . I have faculties that might be utilized to the making of beautiful books and to my own good fortune, if I were befriended. If I could but interest such a man as yourself I could fear nothing and would gladly farm out my talent to his guidance and to his advantage as well as my own. This is not the letter of an author to a publisher—from any but my point of view it is utterly mad—and outrageous—but it is the appeal of one human being to another; the one wanting such support as the other might possibly be able to give.

Her plea fell on deaf ears. Blackwood did not publish this or any of her novels—but other publishers were more obliging. Ultimately there is no mystery about Mrs. Linton's success as a woman of letters. She was an irresistible force before whom there were no immovable objects. (pp. 28-30)

At best, Mrs. Linton's novels can be read today only with clinical curiosity to see *how* she managed to capture a public in spite of a conspicuous lack of creative ability. The answer lies in the extraordinary tolerance of the Victorian reading public for anything that smacked of serious ideas and partly in Mrs. Linton's shrewd recognition that that public also wanted thrills and vicarious stimulation. In a review of a now forgotten three-decker, *Hester's Sacrifice* ("by the Author of 'St. Olav's,' 'Janita's Cross,' etc. etc."), which Mrs. Linton wrote for the *Saturday Review* (April 21, 1866), she ridiculed the unnamed authoress for failing to rise to the passions of her own plot. Her manly hero, for example, has "the heart of a hare and the conscience of an hysterical woman," and is ultimately reduced to "a mass of invertebrate pulp." These "rose-water" novels were not to Mrs. Linton's hearty taste:

> As there are people who buy raspberry-rock and cocoanut paste, and who find the diet exhilarating, so there are people who read such books as *Hester's Sacrifice,* and who rest and are thankful after the process. Meat for men and milk for babes truly. Milk and water rather, and more of the latter than of the former, is such literary food as is here offered.

Meat, tough and fibrous though not necessarily raw, was what Mrs. Linton offered her readers. Her novels tend toward the sensational, although her serious moral and social preoccupations kept her from producing the outright sensational novel. She persists in cluttering her plots of intrigue, suspense, and even murder with her hobbyhorses—religious skepticism, the Woman Question, regionalism (mainly the local color and folklore of the Lake Country). With characteristic bluntness she never hesitated to introduce elements of the gruesome and the grotesque. Murder, madness, and melancholia were basic ingredients of many of her stories. In *Lizzie Lorton of Greyrigg* a tempestuous heroine stirs up a peaceful Cumberland village by jealously accusing the man she loves of murder and finally killing herself. In *Sowing the Wind* a psychopathic husband persecutes his loving wife and attempts to murder his sister's child. In *Patricia Kemball* a young man murders his rival and allows an innocent man to hang for the crime. In *The World Well Lost* a genteel family conceals from society the fact that the father is a convict.

But Mrs. Linton was too intelligent to be satisfied with grinding out mere formula fiction. Her interests were serious and controversial. Her feelings on every issue were intense; her conviction and self-confidence were boundless. The polemical novel, therefore, was a natural outlet and, while it never brought her the critical acclaim and popular success enjoyed by Mrs. Humphry Ward, it did bring a fair measure of financial reward and passing attention from critics and public alike. That a clergyman's daughter should turn, in her serious fiction, to the subject of religion is not surprising. But with characteristic independence of

Matthew Morgan's conception of the anonymous author of "The Girl of the Period."

spirit, Mrs. Linton used her religious novels as platforms for denouncing religious orthodoxy. She was certainly not alone among her contemporaries in criticizing the Church of England, but her rebellion was more personal and extreme than most. Even in her childhood reading, as we have already observed, she confronted problems of faith with curiosity and skepticism. Throughout her life she remained "spiritually inclined." That is, she speculated on religious questions and scrutinized every variety of spiritualism, mesmerism, and psychic investigation. Ultimately she settled for agnosticism, heavily tinged with social idealism in the form of a secular philosophy of altruism: "It is the Agnostic who . . . preaches afresh the democracy of souls—who, in his belief that the religious idea is one to be improved and finally perfected by evolution and knowledge, sees the true salvation of men and their final redemption from error." When they treat of religious subjects, her novels show a straight and unflinching course out of the sheltered family parsonage into the maelstrom of modern nineteenth-century intellectual life—a head-on confrontation with science, socialism, free thought, every major challenge of her day.

As early as 1851, in a novel of her contemporary society, ***Realities,*** Mrs. Linton ridiculed a High Churchman for emphasizing ritual, portraying him as arrogant and hypocritical. In ***Lizzie Lorton of Greyrigg*** she treated more sympathetically an idealistic clergyman who hopes "to establish a kind of Christian socialism on a High Church

basis." Her most sensational and scandalous attack on orthodoxy is in ***The True History of Joshua Davidson, Christian and Communist.*** A none too subtle allegory of the life of Christ, her story introduces young Joshua Davidson (Jesus—David's son), son of a carpenter in Cornwall, who sets out in nineteenth-century England to relive the life of Christ. Not surprisingly, he is scorned, abused, and finally murdered by a mob incited by an old clergyman from his native village. The writing is feverish and shrill: "Let us then strip our Christianity," Joshua preaches, "of all the mythology, the fetichism that has grown about it. Let us abandon the idolatry with which we have obscured the meaning of Life; let us go back to the MAN, and carry on His work in its essential spirit in the direction suited to our times and social conditions"; the premise is unoriginal, and, as she develops it, unimaginative. Yet the book stirred considerable excitement. The first edition, published anonymously, sold out immediately. Within three months there was a second and then a third edition, with the author's name now on the title page, and by 1890 it had reached a tenth edition in England and had sold widely in America as well. The atheist Charles Bradlaugh bought a thousand copies for distribution; John Bright endorsed it enthusiastically—but the 1870s and '80s were crowded with religious controversy, and ***Joshua Davidson*** was forgotten. Nevertheless, the book made her as famous a novelist as the Girl of the Period had made her a journalist.

Mrs. Linton treated religious questions again in the more conventional novel ***Under Which Lord?***—the story of a marriage wrecked by the interference of a fanatically high clergyman. This is a characteristic Linton novel—outspoken, bristling with issues and arguments, implausible in plot yet so vigorous that it holds a reader's interest even while it jars his aesthetic sensibilities and common sense. The central characters are a middle-aged couple who had married romantically and impulsively but who now find themselves alienated—she vaguely restless, yearning for deep emotional experience, he absorbed in scientific reading and in lecturing on agnosticism to working men's clubs ("What has the Church ever taught that has been of the smallest permanent or real good to man?" he asks). They have one daughter, a sensitive, idealistic girl who "wanted religion, not philosophy; faith, not scepticism; adoration of God and the angels, not critical examination of verbal forms and isolated facts in natural history."

Into the lives of this family comes the new vicar, the Reverend Launcelot Lascelles. He is very high, "a Roman Catholic in all save name and obedience," who reads from Wiseman's *Fabiola* and Newman's *Apologia* to the ladies' sewing cirle and exploits the starved emotions of his women parishioners. In the guise of a spiritual confessor he makes love to one repressed spinster: "He questioned her of her waking thoughts and nightly dreams; he probed now the yearning and now the suffering, to which she gave fancy names that disguised the truth from herself but not from him." He persuades the heroine to rebel against her husband and sign over her money to him: "You had to choose your master. Which was it to be—God or man?—the Church or your home?—your Saviour or your husband?—me as your guide in the way of salvation or him as your leader into inevitable destruction?" By the end of the novel he has lured the daughter into joining a Roman Catholic nunnery and destroyed the marriage of her parents. The agnostic husband dies nobly with the sentiments of altruism on his lips:

> He kept his dying eyes still fixed on the sun—his face irradiated with a kind of divine glory, as before his mind, marshalled in grand and long procession, passed thoughts of the noble victories over superstition and the glorious truths made manifest, the peace of nations, the spread of knowledge, the abolition of vice and misery and ignorance, the sublime light of universal freedom and the unfettered progress of humanity which should inform and govern the future through the supreme triumphs of True Knowledge.
>
> "Man the God incarnate!" he said; "Yes, the myth was true."

His more gullible wife is left without child, husband, money, or reputation. "But," Mrs. Linton concludes bitterly, "she had gained the blessing of the Church which denies science, asserts impossibilities, and refuses to admit the evidence of facts."

Early in her life Mrs. Linton had taken the plunge into the void and broken with established religion. "The presence of God recedes as science advances," she proclaimed. Her hearty, untroubled acceptance of the scientific revolution appealed to many readers. Such an attitude was enlightened and intellectual, to the extent that it was based on reading and reason, but uncomplicated, easy to grasp. Writing as Christopher Kirkland of her own emergence from doubt and despair to positive faith in mankind's future, she voiced the Victorian yearning for certainty and affirmation: "What a glorious time it was! . . . Everywhere was a shaking of the dry bones, and the clothing of flesh and sinew on what had been dead and useless fragments buried in the earth. . . . It was the birth-hour of a new Truth. . . . " (pp. 36-40)

Mrs. Linton died in London at seventy-six, on July 14, 1898. She left unpublished a novel about an old woman who, after a serious illness, finds that she has miraculously regained her youth. The consequences are unhappy: people distrust her and suspect her of witchcraft; she is lonely, cut off from her own generation in a new and radically altered world. The novel, published in 1900 as *The Second Youth of Theodora Desanges,* is ludicrous, but it contains several passages that are moving for their personal expression: "Born in the backward ages, when society was constructed on such different lines, I am at cross corners with modern thoughts and ways. The easy familiarity of the young men and the ungraceful masculinity of the young women revolt me. The loss of dignity, of respect, of beauty of sex-differences, destroys the charm of social intercourse." Finding life increasingly burdensome, Theodora Desanges finally welcomes death, "that sweet-faced genius who is our release from pain and perplexity."

Eliza Lynn Linton was a self-made writer and a totally synthetic novelist. She demonstrates the power and pres-

tige that, in nineteenth-century England, a career in literature could bring to a woman of no particular creative talent but of intelligence, industry, and determination. Her achievement was admirably summed up in her obituary in the *Athenaeum* (July 23, 1898):

> Naturally she was an essayist rather than a novelist. She wrote novels simply because the novel was the accredited form of literature in her day; had she lived in the opening of the seventeenth century she would have written plays. She had no innate talent for fiction, for she was no judge nor observer of character, and she had no ability for creating living personages. She had an excellent faculty of writing, and her knowledge of literature enabled her to devise a plot and to construct personages to act respectably in the scenes of her planning; but they had no real life in them.

Whatever her limitations as a novelist, she understood the needs of her public—at least of that large, restless segment of Victorian England whose religious faith had crumbled, but who clung stubbornly and fiercely to the institutions and traditions of the early nineteenth century. A radical conservative, a militantly feminine antifeminist, a skepti-

---

A critic on Linton's view of women:

At the time that she produced her Girl of the Period essay, Mrs. Lynn Linton's opinions seem to have been in a curiously transitional state. With one hand she was holding fast to the rights and opportunities that she had demanded—and obtained—in her own youth, while with the other she was striking at the younger women who were striving to acquire the like privileges. It is probably to this peculiar condition of mind that we owe the contradictions and inconsistencies that are scattered so plentifully throughout the utterances which appeared in the *Saturday Review* and other journals about that time. For example, she censures in one article the women who were swarming out at all doors, jostling man in the professions, knocking at the doors of his offices, and seeking to push him from his place; while in another she expresses her opinion that there should be free-trade in work, and that the best hand should be chosen, irrespective of sex. Again, on one page, she asserts that "It is not because woman has exhausted her natural grounds that she is crowded out of her own domain, and obliged to invade that of men; but that she dislikes her own sphere and covets that of her brother"; yet on another page she admits that there was good cause for the feminine agitation in favour of independence. . . . Lastly, with that power of generalising which, according to George Eliot, "gives man so great a superiority in mistake over the dumb animals," Mrs. Lynn Linton declares that the women who had only just ventured to ask for equality of opportunity, "wanted to be received as masters before they had served their apprenticeship, and to be put into office without passing an examination, or submitting to competition." Our author, it is to be feared, increased her "superiority in mistake" by her habit of generalising from particular instances, and those obnoxious ones.

George Paston [Emily Symonds] in Fortnightly Review,
September 1901.

cal idealist and a believing atheist, Mrs. Linton consistently mirrored the inconsistencies of her times. (pp. 41-2)

> *Vineta Colby, "Wild Women, Revolting Daughters, and the Shrieking Sisterhood: Mrs. Eliza Lynn Linton," in her* The Singular Anomaly: Women Novelists of the Nineteenth Century, *New York University Press, 1970, pp. 15-45.*

J. M. Rignall   (essay date 1982)

[*In the following excerpt, Rignall analyzes the treatment of communism and Christianity in* Joshua Davidson.]

Eliza Lynn Linton was already well established as a journalist and minor novelist when she published *Joshua Davidson* at the age of fifty. She had behind her an unsuccessful marriage to the wood-engraver and writer William James Linton, a Chartist and Republican; a number of not very distinguished novels; and considerable experience of writing for newspapers and periodicals. In one of these, *The Saturday Review,* she had caused a stir in 1868 with a series of articles, of which **'The Girl of the Period'** was the most notorious, attacking what she saw to be the excesses of the campaign for female emancipation. This crusade in defence of the duties of wifehood and motherhood came curiously from the pen of a woman who had herself made a career in a profession dominated by men, becoming the first woman newspaper-writer to draw a fixed salary, and who had previously been in the forefront of the struggle for women's rights. The contradiction was, however, characteristic, manifesting her capacity for holding opinions with passionate intensity rather than consistency. It was also a contradiction that went unperceived by the public at large, since the conventions of *The Saturday Review* ensured that her articles remained anonymous.

It was behind the same cloak of anonymity that the first edition of *Joshua Davidson* was published in 1872, perhaps because her experience with *The Saturday Review* had convinced her that this was the appropriate form for polemical writing, or simply because, as a well-known figure in the literary society of London, she was concerned about the possible repercussions of such a spirited attack on religious and political orthodoxy. In any case she was soon encouraged by the immediate success of the book, which went into a third edition within three months, to acknowledge her authorship, and this she did in the preface to the sixth edition in 1874. *Joshua Davidson* continued to sell and proved to be the most popular of all her works, establishing a permanent reputation for her as a writer.

Joshua Davidson, the son of a Cornish carpenter, is a man of compassion and uncompromising commitment to the truth who seeks to lead a life such as Christ would have led had he been born in the nineteenth century. Convinced that 'the modern Christ would be a politician' who 'would work at the destruction of caste, which is the vice at the root of all our creeds and institutions', he breaks with established Christianity and becomes at first philanthropically active among the London poor, and then, when he realises that private charity can at best prove a temporary palliative, commits himself to political action. He joins the

IWMA (International Working Men's Association) as one of its first members, in the belief that only the combined activity of the working class can bring about the necessary re-organization of society, and goes to Paris to help in the cause of humanity as soon as the Commune is declared. He survives and returns to England, only to be beaten to death by a mob at the instigation of a bigoted clergyman after he has attempted to give a lecture on the Communism of Christ and his apostles.

Mounting a powerful attack on the hypocrisy of professing Christians who acquiesce in the injustices of a society governed by the principles of political economy, and defending the Commune for 'supporting the rights of humanity against scientific arrangements', Lynn Linton urges on her readers the necessity of choosing between Christianity and Communism on the one hand, and on the other 'the maintenance of the present condition of things as natural and fitting . . . the right of the strong to hold, and the duty of the weak to submit'. *Joshua Davidson* is, as a contemporary reviewer noted, 'a socio-political pamphlet in the guise of a story', more concerned to make a compelling case than to create the substantial fictional world of the realist novel. Narrated by a shadowy friend and disciple of the hero, the story is a distanced, retrospective, hagiographic account of a life, and it only achieves dramatic immediacy in the scenes of argument and debate which punctuate the narrative. It is ideas that are important here, not individuals, and Lynn Linton works against the tendency of the novel to create a primary interest in character by making the Christlike carpenter an exemplary figure, significant not in his own right but for the views he propounds and the ideal he embodies. With the exception of historical figures such as Félix Pyat and Delescluze, who are given approving mention, the characters who people his world represent social types and prevailing attitudes. They serve as his opponents in debate, like 'Mr Grand', the overbearing representative of the established church; Lord X, a shallow and spasmodic philanthropist; and an unnamed MP who acts as the spokesman of political economy. The creation of character, as opposed to caricature, is not allowed to get in the way of the thrust of the argument, even though this leads to certain imaginative impoverishment of the work as a novel.

The argument is clearly and vigorously made, but the use of the terms Christianity and Communism to define the alternative to political economy and 'scientific arrangements' raises certain questions. It might suggest a typical Christian-Socialist position where Communism is used, as it often is in this period, as a synonym of Socialism, were it not for the fact that Lynn Linton was a confessed agnostic. The role of Christianity here is certainly not determined by faith, although at the same time it cannot simply be reduced to a matter of polemical tactics. As the daughter of a clergyman and granddaughter of a bishop she knew the established Church well, and real anger at what she considered to be its hypocrisy and complacency seems to be one of the motivating impulses of the book, prompting her to turn the Gospel against its supposed adherents. In this respect, although acting without any religious fervour or doctrinal interest, she aligns herself with that tradition of dissent which has always fed the radical stream of English political life.

However, the position that Joshua Davidson finally adopts goes beyond that of any Nonconformist sect in its emphatic secularity, stressing the humanity of Christ and seeing in Christianity not 'a creed as dogmatized by churches but an organization having politics for its means and the equalization of classes as its end'. It provokes the question of why Lynn Linton still stands by Christianity at all and issues her appeal for radical social change in its name, rather than breaking with it. . . . This cannot be adequately understood as either the deliberate provocation of a rebellious rationalist, as she has been aptly called, or the considered tactics of the seasoned pamphleteer bent upon presenting her case in terms most likely to compel the assent of her audience. It seems, rather, that Christianity is a means of mediating between the known and the new, between accepted values and revolutionary ideals, as much for the author herself as for her readers. It enables her to find a sanction in traditional culture for a radical transformation of society, to preserve continuity while urging the need for change, and to contain revolutionary fervour within a reassuring moral framework. It is a way of rejecting revolutionary violence while appealing for radical change, and it makes *Joshua Davidson,* for all its impassioned defence of the Commune, a very English work.

Communism also requires qualification. Defined in terms of Christian brotherhood and used interchangeably with socialism and Republicanism, it is here the description of an ideal state and not the political programme of a revolutionary party. Lynn Linton certainly gives unequivocal support to the revolution of the Commune, and the narrator expresses the belief that, if successful, it 'meant the emancipation of the working class here, and later on the peaceable establishment of the Republic'; but it is viewed retrospectively in the light of its final defeat, so that it has about it more the pathos of a lost cause than the power of a political example. Nor is Joshua, despite his commitment to working-class political action, exactly a revolutionary: his involvement with the International is subject to repeated qualifications, which stress the fair-mindedness and liberalism which set him apart from the other members, and his antipathy to violence: 'Yet the International represented no class enmity with him. He had no dreams of barricades and high places taken by assault. It was to him, as to his other English brethren, an organization to strengthen the hands of the labourer everywhere, but not to plunge society into a bloody war'. In fact he is so unswervingly true to his own principles that the ideal which he represents has an air of uncompromising individualism about it, which is at odds with the idea of collective action. He is, too, so invariably misunderstood, suspected even by many of his political comrades, and in the end reviled by unenlightened working men as well as bourgeois bigots, that he becomes himself a figure of pathos rather than political hope. His end is a crucifixion without the prospect of a social resurrection, and the work concludes with an almost despairing question: 'And again I ask, Which is true—modern society in its class strife and consequent elimination of its weaker elements, or the

brotherhood and communism taught by the Jewish carpenter of Nazareth? Who will answer me?—who will make the dark thing clear?'

In a number of ways, then, Lynn Linton checks the revolutionary impetus of her argument. Fired by a momentous historical event, she has made the imaginative effort to step outside her own class in creating an artisan hero and envisaging the transformation of society through working-class action, but she has not entirely discarded the values and modes of thinking of the culture to which she belongs. Her alternative to individualism has a distinctly individualist aspect, embodied as it is in an idealised figure so saintly that he is set apart from all sorts and conditions of men. Furthermore, the milieu from which he comes, and in which he works, is never convincingly realised. Nevertheless, she remains resolutely free from the fears and prejudices that afflicted greater writers, for, unlike Dickens, or Gaskell, or George Eliot, she never sees in working-class action simply the uncontrolled movements of a mob with a terrifying potential for violence. *Joshua Davidson* has many limitations, but it represents a bold and honest attempt to look beyond a society governed by the principles of political economy and to challenge the naturalness of the existing order. (pp. 36-40)

J. M. Rignall, "Between Chartism and the 1880s: J. W. Overton and E. Lynn Linton," in The Socialist Novel in Britain: Towards the Recovery of a Tradition, *edited by H. Gustav Klaus, The Harvester Press, 1982, pp. 26-44.*

Christopher Herbert   (essay date 1983)

[*In the excerpt below, Herbert examines Linton's views on marriage as expressed in* Sowing the Wind.]

Originally a feminist, Mrs. Lynn Linton made her name as a rabid antifeminist (and turncoat) largely from a famous series of essays published in the *Saturday Review* in 1866-68 and collected (1868) as *Modern Women and What Is Said of Them.* Modern women, she says, have grown shamefully immodest, affecting "slang, bold talk, and fastness" and aping the appearance and manners of prostitutes. She particularly deplores "the defiant attitudes which women have lately assumed, and their indifference to the wishes and remonstrances of men," celebrating at the same time a traditional ideal of marriage that could serve as a textbook example of the duplicitous pattern described above. On the one hand, the perfect wife—"in some things a medieval saint, and in some, a child"—is to be "her husband's friend and companion"; on the other, she is to be strictly subservient to her husband's authority, "bound to study the wishes of man, and to mould her life in harmony with his liking". The "companionate" marriage and the authoritarian "patriarchal" marriage, these essays declare, are one and the same thing.

The severe strains to which this ideology was subject in the 1860s are strikingly shown, however, in *Sowing the Wind,* where the thrust of Mrs. Lynn Linton's polemic seems exactly reversed—at least for a while. The story is noteworthy both for its conventionality and for its hints of potentially significant anomalies. Isola Aylott, a totemic image of angelic, submissive female virtue, is the wife of St. John Aylott, an almost equally stereotypical figure of the Tyrant Husband. Morbidly conscious of his family dignity, he is languid, reserved, and shy, and plainly his wife's mental inferior. "And yet [he] was the master, and Isola, his wife, knew no will save his." The story concerns Isola's growing disaffection from her husband, her gradual loss of esteem for him, and her progressive willingness to commit the heresy of asserting her own will in opposition to his. This process, comments the narrator in a memorable phrase, "touched the unsolved problem of married life, and uncovered the cancerous sore of home, namely, the right of the woman to independent moral action in opposition to her husband's will." Faced with this opposition, Aylott's attempts to tyrannize over Isola become even coarser; he preaches to her (to the considerable detriment of the novel's dramatic movement) almost nonstop sermons on the duty of a wife to submit blindly and unquestioningly to the will of her husband; then his social and sexual pride is cruelly humbled in a series of catastrophes. Bad investments lead him to financial ruin; he makes the amazing discovery that his father was no aristocrat but a common peasant; and malicious rumors cause him to think that his immaculately pure wife is unfaithful to him. His shaken mind at last becomes entirely unhinged, and exactly foreshadowing the fate of Louis Trevelyan a year later in [Anthony Trollope's] *He Knew He Was Right*, he dies a pathetic death in a madhouse, in his young wife's arms.

In its main outline, then, this is a thoroughly conventional rehearsal of the Tyrant Husband story. Such interest as the familiar story possesses in Mrs. Lynn Linton's version lies in her attempt to rejuvenate it with an infusion of the sophisticated feminist rhetoric of the 1860s. Thus she hits repeatedly at the doctrine of "the inferiority and natural abasement of women," the idea, as she says, that women "are born into the world only to be the slaves and shadows of men"; and she shrewdly anatomizes such newly recognized social types as the sexual collaborators, "the women who weaken the moral fibre of men by their self-abasement and submission," and the men who disguise "a very profound contempt for women" behind apparent admiration of them. Such polemics energize an otherwise slack story, but they have a disturbing and finally unacceptable result: they decenter the conventional pattern by suggesting that Aylott's tyranny is less an extreme and anomalous thing, the result of an exceptionally brutal character, than an example of a common contemporary state of affairs. As though taken by surprise to see her novel taking this subversive turn, Mrs. Lynn Linton visibly strives to realign her rhetoric in two main ways, each of which sheds light on Trollope's retelling of this fable in *He Knew He Was Right*.

First, she strongly dilutes her original treatment of the victimized wife as an articulate rebel challenging the doctrine of wifely subservience, even though this dilution robs the novel of much of its vitality. Thus Isola begins fervently declaring to the reader her unshakeable devotion, appearances notwithstanding, to the norms of conventional marriage and the accepted role and duties of a wife. "For after all," as she announces at one typical moment, "the home

is the woman's true place!" This reidealizing of the heroine, who is likened late in the story to "some lovely picture of the Madonna," is just the highlight of a general suppression of the novel's feminist rhetoric, which largely drops out without a trace after the first volume.

Mrs. Lynn Linton's other main tactic of rectification in the later sections of *Sowing the Wind* becomes the central link with *He Knew He Was Right*: having the tyrant husband, thanks to some farfetched contrivances of plot, go mad. What lies behind this turn of plot is, I think, the author's intent to neutralize her own feminist rhetoric by stressing that Aylott's domineering conduct toward his wife has been pathological from the first: it puts him clearly outside the pale of normal English gentlemen and thus reinforces as strongly as possible that polarization of brutal husband and victimized wife that is the key to the structure of this type of fiction. Trollope . . . seems to discover a deep truth hidden in these awkward plot manipulations of *Sowing the Wind*. Thus in *He Knew He Was Right*, he makes the husband's derangement the main subject of the novel and boldly presents it as the outcome of nothing more than a breaking up of the sexual ideology upon which Trevelyan has hitherto depended, not only to buttress his domestic power but to define and protect his own approving view of himself. In Trollope's version, in other words, male supremacist values are not simply weapons of convenience for a pathological bully; they are discovered to be a core element of Victorian personality, to coexist with a wide range of good intentions, and—especially—to be so deeply embedded as to be largely unconscious and unacknowledged. Bringing them to the surface and exposing their self-contradictions is thus, as Trollope's novel dramatizes with terrifying force, a process fraught with profound psychic consequences.

In the meantime, the confused rhetoric of *Sowing the Wind* points the way to a general theory of the cultural function of the ever recurring Victorian folktale of the tyranny of husbands. At first glance it seems paradoxical in the extreme that an ardent antifeminist such as Mrs. Lynn Linton would be drawn to this fable indicting male authoritarianism, but the paradox disappears when one recognizes the point to which all the above discussion tends: that Tyrant Husband literature operates in fact to reinforce, not to subvert, the sexual status quo and its fundamental principle of male dominance. The central failure of insight of a fiction like *Sowing the Wind* lies in its evasion of the truth that all thoughtful readers must have known: that male supremacist ideology, far from being the exclusive property of cold, aggressive, neurotic men, pervaded respectable middle-class culture and was generally taken to be fully compatible with the very ideals of conjugal tenderness and "companionate" rapport that Mrs. Lynn Linton means to endorse. The evasion is flagrant in the case of a writer who elsewhere upholds the natural union of the two principles, not denouncing male supremacy but glorifying it as the indispensable guarantee of "companionate" love. *Sowing the Wind* thus helps us catch a glimpse of the hidden argument of the whole class of fiction it epitomizes. By treating "patriarchal" and "companionate" attitudes as sharply polarized rather than as they were, closely bound together, Victorian novels methodically *sanitize* the theme of marital tyranny, rendering it largely innocuous by staging it as a melodrama of pure virtue victimized by aberrant evil. Wives in this melodrama are oppressed by villains and fanatics, never by ordinary well-meaning husbands. This means that the marriage system itself, as actually practiced in Victorian households, receives sweeping immunity from prosecution in fiction and that what Mrs. Lynn Linton, in another striking, disenchanted phrase, calls "that quiet manner of spiritual disintegration known only too well to married homes" escapes detailed scrutiny. In a society ever more pressured by sexual controversy, this pattern in fiction must have acted as a safety valve, venting indignation more or less harmlessly on a mythic race of domestic monsters, distracting attention from the flaws of the institution of contemporary marriage itself. In this important sense the Tyrant Husband was a straw man, and a crucial one in Victorian life. (pp. 452-55)

> Christopher Herbert, "'He Knew He Was Right', Mrs. Lynn Linton, and the Duplicities of Victorian Marriage," in Texas Studies in Literature and Language, *Vol. 25, No. 3, Fall, 1983, pp. 448-69.*

George Somes Layard on Linton's reputation as a writer:

As one glances here and there at a few of the thousands of articles which she reeled off week by week, one is astonished at the freshness and ebullience of her pen. She is never mechanical in her work; her vital resources are ready to hand on all occasions. She is rarely dull. Her mind is always "letting off its overcharge," not pumping up out of the dregs. She never forgets that she is "writing for the hour, and not for posterity." . . .

In a word, she was great as a journalist, and in journalism is found her highest achievement.

And this is where I think Mrs. Linton's literary reputation has suffered. It has been the fashion to regard her primarily as a novelist, whereas her novel-writing, remarkable as it was, was but a side issue, and subordinate. With the great actor who has temporarily turned playwright, she runs the risk of being judged by what has taken more permanent form to the ignoring of what she has done of chiefest value, but which was in its nature evanescent.

George Somes Layard, in his Mrs. Lynn Linton: Her Life, Letters, and Opinions, *London: Methuen, 1901.*

Nancy F. Anderson   (essay date 1985)

[*Anderson is an American educator and critic specializing in Victorian literature and history. Below, she discusses the novels* The Autobiography of Christopher Kirkland *and* The Second Youth of Theodora Desanges *as autobiographical fiction.*]

Though Eliza Lynn Linton was an enigma to her contemporaries because of the contradiction between her independent professional life style and her anti-feminist, mi-

sogynist opinions, she did provide the key to the puzzle of her personality in her self-portrayal in *The Autobiography of Christopher Kirkland.* Written in 1885 when she was sixty-three, this is her autobiography, signed with her own name, in the persona of a man. Despite the sex reversal, the book was, she said, "my own history, travestied in the sense of sex and certain experiences." She explained that she could not publish her autobiography "without some such veil as this of changed sex and personation"—it was, she said, "a screen which takes off the sting of boldness and self-exposure." Like many fictional autobiographies in the Bildungsroman tradition, *Christopher Kirkland* interestingly crosses and recrosses the narrow boundary between fiction and autobiography.

The sex reversal was in fact not a screen, but a mirror which reflected Linton's deep unconscious sense of male identity. The disguise was an inadvertent vehicle for expressing her true feelings about herself. Although the male identification was unconscious, she once remarked that when she was born, a boy was expected, "and only the top coating miscarried." Having always seen herself as big and robust, the transformation into the tall strong Christopher Kirkland was both reversal and self-realization. This masculine self-image helps explain how Linton could escape her own devaluation of women, and why she could so easily insist that women remain dependent and submissive in the home while at the same time priding herself on her own independence.

The inner conflicts this role and gender reversal inevitably aroused in Linton she handled, in her long obsessional struggle against women's emancipation, by projecting and condemning in women's-rights women those characteristics most distinctive in her own personality. "There is in them a curious inversion of sex, which does not necessarily appear in the body, but is evident enough in the mind." Frantically warning against a blurring of distinctions between the sexes, she pleaded that "men be men, and women women, sharply, unmistakably defined . . . not an ambiguous sex which is neither one nor the other"—ironic words from a woman who wrote her life story as a man. She had been the breadwinner and dominant force in her brief marriage, and in *Christopher Kirkland* had easily transmuted her husband into a woman, described with psychological congruence as Christopher's wife. At the same time in her anti-feminist polemics she insisted that wives remain submissive and obedient to their husbands: "when two people ride on one horse one must ride behind." She damned as emasculating the emancipated women who she claimed wanted to seize the reins of authority from their natural male masters.

In *Christopher Kirkland,* Linton provided abundant material that explains the development of her male-identified personality and her misogyny. She described with heart-rending pathos, as the crucial aspect of her childhood, the devastating emotional consequences of her mother's death after her own birth. With no mothering figure, not even a maiden aunt, to nurture her, her childhood was, she lamented, one of loneliness and pain. She blamed her father, who was in her opinion weak and ineffectual, for not exercising supervision over his twelve children. Their house was "like nothing so much as a farmyard full of cockerels and pullets forever spurring and pecking at one another." She claimed that as the youngest she suffered the most, either by being ignored and neglected or abused by her family. This treatment made her recalcitrant and rebellious, which increased all the more her sense of loneliness. "I was so isolated in the family, so out of harmony with them all, and by my own faults of temperament such a little Ishmaelite and outcast, that as much despair as can exist with childhood overwhelmed and possessed me."

Linton felt that if only her mother had lived, everything would have been different. Her later invectives against women's emancipation contain the child's voice of rage against the mother who deserted her by dying. When she would repeatedly insist that a woman's place was by the cradle, she was in part expressing her own feelings of maternal deprivation. The personality characteristics she developed in that unhappy chaotic childhood—her wish to escape, to become famous and therefore noticed and loved, her need actively to struggle and compete—these characteristics were considered masculine in her adult patriarchal society, with its rigid polarization of sexual personality.

In contrast to her own tough, tomboyish personality, Linton presents her one-year-older, angelic sister Lucy, to whom she had a strong but ambivalent attachment. In *Christopher Kirkland,* Linton also reversed Lucy's sex, but wrote of her in unmistakably feminine terms:

> He [i.e., Lucy] was like one of Sir Joshua's cherubs. His head was covered with bright golden curls, his skin was like a pale monthly rose, and he had big soft blue eyes which no one could resist. Everyone loved and petted him. Our father, who saw in him the reproduction of our dead mother, had even a more tender feeling for him than any of his other favourites.

Linton's jealousy of Lucy was intense. "I had sometimes broken my young heart over the difference made between us." She recounted, surely with distorted memory but with emotional authenticity, that once, when her father kissed Lucy, she asked him to kiss her too. "I longed to receive the same love that was given to others, to be included, to be taken out of the solitude and banishment in which I lived." She claimed he refused because, he said, he did not respect her.

Linton dealt with her jealousy by not competing with this quintessentially feminine sister, and by shaping her own self-identity as a purposeful opposition to her sister. Ostensibly idealizing Lucy, she assumed the male role of devoted protector. Underneath the idealization were strong feelings of hostility, revealed in extravagant poems she wrote in her adolescence to Lucy, repeatedly expressing the fear, surely a disguised wish, that Lucy would die:

> Oh sweet! thy cheek is pale . . .
> Lucy! my soul's best love
> Soft death will come from this world of folly
> To bear thee to Heaven above!

In other poems she uses the image of Lucy as a fair dove in a cage whom she will carefully guard. This relationship was the prototype for her later fervent efforts to keep the idealized angelic womanly woman encaged in the house.

The rage Linton felt against her mother and sister was for the most part repressed, and reappeared in her virulent attacks on women. Her conscious rage was against her unloving father. In her adolescence she expressed her anger at her father with her opposition to what she saw as his cold-hearted, selfish Toryism, and with an impassioned defense of democracy and socialism. On a more fundamental level she challenged Vicar Lynn by rejecting his religion. In her original draft of *Christopher Kirkland* she indicates that she first began to doubt Christianity when she was seventeen: the pregnancy of their unmarried servant girl made her question the truth of the Virgin Birth. "It was the persistent denial of this girl, and her repeated assurance that it was and must have been a 'bogle' which set me thinking." Her publisher George Bentley, repelled by such blasphemy, insisted this part be changed. Linton reluctantly agreed to bowdlerize it, writing instead that she began to question the truth of Christianity while reading Ovid's *Metamorphoses,* when she noted the similarities between Greek myths and Biblical stories, including virgin births. She dramatically detailed the shock of considering the possibility that Mary may have lied:

> A terrible faintness took hold of me. The perspiration streamed over my face like rain, and I trembled like a frightened horse. . . . The light grew dim; the earth was vapoury and unstable; and, overpowered by an awful dread, I fell back among the long grass where I was sitting as if I had been struck down by an unseen hand.

Such doubts eventually led Linton to agnosticism. Her loss of faith engendered great emotional turmoil in her, for as she asked, "who that has known the hour when the Father is not, and Law has taken the Place of Love, can ever forget it?" Her religious struggles were of such central importance to her autobiographical narrative that she considered titling her book "Confessions of an Agnostic." Linton's loss of faith alienated her even more from her family, especially her father, and confirmed her childhood feeling, repeatedly recreated and reexperienced in adulthood, that she was an outcast, an Ishmaelite. Her insistence that she was banished from love by Christ and the Church explains the significance of her pseudonym Christopher Kirkland, although ironically in this pseudonym she identified with her perceived oppressors. Linton's rejection of Christianity strengthened her sense of maleness, for she considered agnosticism to be masculine, whereas

> the religious sentiment, shifting, personal, emotional, subject to the pressure of affection and the relief of compassion . . . is feminine. The fundamental doctrines of Christianity . . . are essentially feminine. . . . Does not the whole world lie between these two limits? Surely!—the whole world of masculine self-control and feminine obedience; masculine reason and feminine emotion.

She apparently never felt any inconsistency in priding herself on her manly agnosticism, while urging women to remain within the Church, to receive the restraint and support their weak dependent natures required.

Another aspect of Linton's personality inadvertently revealed through her male persona in *Christopher Kirkland* was her strong sexual attraction to women. Writing her autobiography as a man, she was able safely to describe her homoerotic feelings (which coexisted with her misogynist opinions). Her intense relationships with women, which were probably only unconsciously sexual, became in *Christopher Kirkland* passionate love affairs, portrayed as heterosexual romances. The reader for Bentley, although recommending *Christopher Kirkland* for publication, complained that Christopher's "love affairs are somewhat numerous," and that "we should be content to hear less about the exact shape of ladies' limbs, and the quality of their complexions" (a frequent criticism reviewers made of Linton's novels). Linton, as Christopher, explained why she liked to have women around:

> I like to hear the frou-frou of a woman's dress about me, I like to hear the softer tones of her voice, and to look at her shining hair and the smooth outlines of her flower-like face . . . the sense of her softness, sweetness, and dainty smallness compared to my own sinewy bulk, and the feeling that I can protect her if need be, soothe what I suppose is my masculine vanity.

As an example of her romantic attachments to women, Linton describes in great detail in *Christopher Kirkland* an adolescent crush on an older married woman, a Mrs. Dalrymple, a character Linton later explained was "partly true, partly evolved." The young Christopher adores Mrs. Dalrymple, who is "the most exquisite creature under heaven . . . a woman more like . . . a spirit half-transparently incarnate, than a living solid flesh and blood reality." When Mrs. Dalrymple tries to teach Christopher to dance, he is too awkward and clumsy, as well as too intoxicated by the beautiful woman's nearness, to learn. "My head swam when Adeline Dalrymple laid her long white hand on my shoulder, and I put my arm around her supple stayless waist; and I was faint and giddy before I had made a couple of turns round the room."

The climax—literally—of this semi-fantasized relationship comes when Christopher goes one moonlit night to her garden. Mrs. Dalrymple comes down to join him, and they sit hand in hand in the summer house until dawn. She then kisses him on the forehead and eyes. "Overpowered by an emotion so powerful as to be physical pain, I knelt on the ground at her feet; and I think that for a moment I died." Christopher, his passion so intense, soon thereafter is stricken with brain fever, and when he recovers he learns that the Dalrymples have moved away.

Just as Linton did not consciously recognize her sense of male identity, and defensively condemned mannish women, so she did not acknowledge her lesbian feelings, and warned others of the dangers of sexual relationships among emancipated women. In her 1880 novel *The Rebel in the Family,* for example, Linton created the character of Bell, a mannish man-hating women's righter, who frightens the innocent young heroine Perdita "by taking her in her arms and kissing her with strange warmth." On another occasion Bell kisses Perdita fondly, and calls her "my darling" under her breath. When Bell urges Perdita to leave home, to become self-supporting and to enjoy

friendships with those of her own sex, Perdita replies that she cannot live without love. Bell, tenderly putting her arm around Connie, the woman she lives with and calls her "little wife," tells Perdita that if she wants love, "you have it here—the best and truest that the world can give—the love between women without the degrading and disturbing interference of man." Such a prospect, however, does not appeal to Perdita, who feels "revolted by something too vague to name yet too real to ignore."

Eliza Lynn Linton's fictionalized autobiography clearly dramatizes her own hard-fought and paradoxical struggle against women's emancipation. Though she insisted that women should not be mere chattel, but should have certain rights such as control over their own property and children, there she drew the line:

> I could not accept the doctrine that no such thing as natural limitation of sphere is included in the fact of sex, and that individual women may, if they have the will and the power, do all those things which have hitherto been exclusively assigned to men. Nor can I deny the value of inherent modesty; nor despise domestic duties; nor look on maternity as a curse and degradation—'making a woman no better than a cow,' as one of these ladies, herself a mother, once said to me indignantly; nor do I join in the hostility to men which comes in as the correlative of all that has gone before.

She was especially opposed to women becoming doctors and artists, because without separate female educational facilities it required them to attend mixed medical schools and mixed drawing classes from the nude. "These two things seemed to me to be repugnant to every sentiment of morality or decency in either sex." In addition to what she considered her rational arguments against female emancipation, as Christopher she confessed that much of her early opposition to the woman's movement was because she thought advanced women ugly and unfeminine, fulfilling the epigram that "Women's Rights Are Men's Lefts." She claimed however that she was "always ashamed of my own childishness of judgement." As one would expect, in Linton's autobiography the subject of the appropriate role for women appears in almost every situation. For instance, when Christopher is visiting a beloved friend on his deathbed, the friend, with almost his last breath, "broke off abruptly into the woman question, on the main points of which we were thoroughly agreed." After a long exposition of the sins of the movement, they agree that a mother does more for humanity "than does the sister who prefers individuality and a paying profession to the self-continuance, self-sacrifice, and devotion of maternity." With that off his chest, the friend expires shortly thereafter.

Linton, reflecting on her career as a critic of women, complained that her writings brought her "more obloquy than praise . . . those at whom I struck were naturally indignant, and gave me back blow for blow, sometimes hitting below the belt, with even a few odd scratchings thrown in." She concluded the autobiography, therefore, with a reiteration of her lament for the "intrinsic isolation of my life." She had "made, or attracted to myself, as the dominant circumstances of my life—Loneliness and Loss." Commenting in later years on *Christopher Kirkland,* Linton said that it was "an outpour no one hears me make by word of mouth, a confession of sorrow, suffering, trial, and determination not to be beaten, which few suspect as the underlying truth of my life."

Appropriately, the pain and frustration which Linton said were central to her life were extended to the publication of her autobiography. The publisher had demanded so many changes and had so delayed publication that Linton was frantic. She repeatedly implored Bentley to publish it immediately:

> Do you think this throbbing heart is *quite* dead! . . . I have put my very Soul, my Life into those pages, and I feel as if I am being slowly killed through them. . . . I all the while eating out my heart for the anguish of disappointment, humiliation, and illusion. It cannot go on . . . I am nearly heartbroken and only my strength of will keeps me from brain fever.

When finally published, *The Autobiography of Christopher Kirkland* was a literary and financial failure. Linton's friend and biographer George Somes Layard attributed the bad reviews to the confusion created by the sex reversals. "To those who could read between the lines, the effect was somewhat bizarre, while to those not in the secret the story was in parts incomprehensible." Bentley spent more than was usual on advertising, but it did not sell well, and he lost money on the publication. The irrepressible Linton nevertheless repeatedly begged him to issue a second edition. "My beloved Christopher! I want him to shine again." She later urged a cheap edition, so that Christopher "would reach so many who now do not hear of him." It was however not reissued until 1976, as part of the Garland *Novels of Faith and Doubt* reprint series.

Eliza Lynn Linton's sense of male identification, as revealed in *The Autobiography of Christopher Kirkland,* allowed her to achieve success in her patriarchal society. Though she delighted in her achievements and independence, she was at the same time painfully envious of her antitype, the beautiful womanly woman, who like her sister Lucy received the love Linton herself had so yearned for as a child. She once confessed that she "would renounce any intellectual gifts to which she might lay claim, for the compelling power of great physical beauty." This wish she gratified in another autobiographical fantasy, *The Second Youth of Theodora Desanges,* written just before she died in 1898. *Theodora Desanges* is dissimilar but complementary to *Christopher Kirkland,* and together they illuminate in full dimension the conflicts and complexities in Linton's personality.

In *The Second Youth of Theodora Desanges,* Linton fantasized that she, in the character of the elderly Theodora, was miraculously transformed into a young woman, "younger-looking, more beautiful, more attractive than the pretty women I had admired thirty years before . . . not merely the rival but the superior of those who had been so far above me." She describes the transformed Theodora as looking and feeling like a goddess, a "divinely appointed priestess, whose will was law and whose mind

was as the mind of God" (hence the significance of the name Theodora, gift of God). Men flock around her, and fall madly in love. A woman friend warns her not to become too free. "You have been so long our old mentor and faultfinder, our putter-to-rights and moral policeman, it would never do for you to go over the border and set a bad example to us poor, silly little butterflies." Theodora is, however, like an iceberg, and unmoved by men's passions. She enjoys rather the sense of power and control over the men, feeling like a puppeteer pulling strings. "I swayed them as I would. I bent them to my will."

Linton, as the beautiful Theodora, encounters many people from her past. One of her admirers is a man closely modeled on George Lewes, whom Linton had known in her early London years. She changed him into an artist, but describes the character with exactly the same words as she did George Lewes in a non-fictional reminiscence written at the same time. This artist wants to paint Theodora as Boadicea, with "diaphanous drapery, showing the fine contour of the limbs beneath, the leopard-skin over half the naked breast." Theodora is shocked, even as Linton claimed she as a young woman had been shocked by Lewes's familiarities, which had, however, apparently not been directed at her. The fantasized version allowed Linton to enjoy attracting and then cutting down a man whom she despised. The fantasy of this adoration also gave her a feeling of superiority over her most envied professional rival, George Eliot.

In the novel, the women friends of the elderly Theodora become bitterly jealous and hostile to the transformed beautiful woman, an indication of the strength of Linton's own projected feelings of jealousy. Even the fictional representation of the woman who had lived with Linton for many years as her adopted daughter, Beatrice Hartley, called Esther in *Theodora* (curiously the same pseudonym given to William James Linton in *Christopher Kirkland*), is consumed with jealousy. Esther's husband, however, is able to exercise enough self-control to resist his infatuation for Theodora, but her son, conflicted and confused because of his desire for the woman he had always called Granny, commits suicide.

The youthful Theodora remains, as she had been before her metamorphosis, "an uncompromising opponent of the New Woman in all her hateful phases." She uses the power of her beauty and wisdom to fight women's suffrage, as well as other emasculating threats to the British Empire, such as Little Englandism, vegetarianism, and antivivisection. To effect her purpose, she gains complete influence over an important Member of Parliament, Lord Keswick, the future Duke of Crosthwaite (Linton's birth town and parish). Lord Keswick is weak and spineless, similar to Linton's view of her father and husband. Skirting around the incongruity of a woman gaining control over a man in order to maintain male dominance, Theodora says that she is willing to manipulate him because she had "the more practicable manly view of things." (Her male identification persisted even as she fantasized herself a voluptuous female.)

To control Lord Keswick, Theodora has to come between him and his wife, a saintly woman who is a deluded advocate of women's rights and other so-called visionary fads. "For all his loyal love for his wife I quite knew that Lord Keswick could not withstand my influence when I choose to exert it." Lady Keswick dies of heartbreak, and Theodora is blamed for murdering her "by mental desire—by the criminal concentration of thought and will." Lord Keswick remarries a malicious evil woman. Theodora is the unwitting cause of his death, and then also of the second Lady Keswick, as well as various others. Theodora, accused of being in league with the devil, is called "a fiend-woman," "a vampire who lives on human blood."

The oedipal nature of Theodora's triangular relationship with Lord Keswick and each of his wives (the mother-image split into a good and bad representation) indicates the conflicts embedded in the mind of a daughter whose mother died in her childbirth. Linton repeatedly insisted that Theodora is a sinless Cain, blameless for the deaths she has caused, as if she herself were seeking absolution for the primal guilt of matricide, as well as for the murderous feelings, also rooted in oedipal jealousy, that she experienced towards her sister Lucy. Her rage moreover at her weak rejecting father caused her to have Theodora kill, however unintentionally, the father image Lord Keswick. ("Desanges" suggests blood in the sense of death and family ties.)

The disasters Linton imagined would have happened if indeed her secret wish to be a seductively beautiful woman had been fulfilled helps explain why in reality she had sought safety by developing an antithetical, male-identified personality. Gratified wishes were too dangerous, and so she has Theodora conclude that "my strange experience has taught me that things are better ordered for us than we could order them for ourselves." Linton ends her novelistic fantasy with Theodora longing only for death, "that sweet faced genius who is our releaser from pain and perplexity." Ironically, Linton herself died even before she finished her final revision of the book. Published posthumously in 1900, two years after her death, the book was an "unexpected voice from the grave," and received scant attention.

A reviewer of **Theodora Desanges** commented that the melancholy tone of the book must be "the net result of the preaching of obstructive and destructive doctrines, the net result of a too exclusive contemplation of the blots and blemishes in feminine nature, the net result of a thirty-years' occupancy of the seat of self-appointed censor." Certainly Linton's increasingly single-minded and hysterical campaign to keep women encaged within the home diminished her popularity. Through most of her professional life, she had been a respected writer, the author of popular novels and a contributor to the leading periodicals. She had been a valuable ally to the male opposition to women's emancipation. By the 1890s, however, she became an object of ridicule, mocked for what a critic called her "wearisome iteration concerning blatant noisy unsexed and wild women, few of whom are more blatant, noisy, unsexed and wild than Mrs. Lynn Linton." Her later novels were not popular because, as a reviewer commented, "the veins of purpose were too often black and swollen with anger to the detriment of their artistic value."

Eliza Lynn Linton's obsessive anti-feminism and misogyny were the psychic cost of the self-alienation that characterized her fictionalized autobiographical fantasies. Not conforming to the constricting norm of Victorian womanhood in that age of extreme sexual polarization, she developed a sense of maleness so strong that she could only write her autobiography in the persona of a man. She reaped the benefits in the form of personal freedom and success. She was, however, painfully jealous of the womanly woman, a feeling clearly revealed in **Theodora Desanges,** which fueled her relentless war on women. In addition, her social incongruence fostered in her a vicious self-hatred, which she turned outward in the form of anti-feminist diatribes. She was once described, because of her polemics, as a "lady flagellant," but her attacks were to a large extent self-flagellation. Neither as the male Christopher Kirkland nor as the voluptuous Theodora Desanges could she present her life as other than one of pain and estrangement. (pp. 289-99)

> *Nancy F. Anderson, "Autobiographical Fantasies of a Female Anti-Feminist: Eliza Lynn Linton as Christopher Kirkland and Theodora Desanges," in* Dickens Studies Annual, *Vol. 14, 1985, pp. 287-301.*

FURTHER READING

Anderson, Nancy Fix. *Woman against Women in Victorian England: A Life of Eliza Lynn Linton.* Bloomington: Indiana University Press, 1987, 260 p.

> Assesses Linton's writings about and relationships with other women, attempting to "explain the seeming contradiction of an emancipated woman opposed to women's emancipation."

Caird, Mona. "A Defence of the So-Called 'Wild Women'." *The Nineteenth Century* XXXI, No. 183 (May 1892): 811-29.

> Responds to Linton's essays on "wild women," arguing that "unless we are prepared for [an] antique and variegated creed, we cannot consistently pronounce, as Mrs. Lynn Linton cheerfully pronounces, what the sphere and *raison d'être* of either sex are, and must be, forever-more."

Harraden, Beatrice. "Mrs. Lynn Linton." *The Bookman,* New York VIII, No. 1 (September 1898): 16-17.

> Memorial tribute by a best-selling novelist and protégée of Linton.

Maxwell, Herbert. "Walling the Cuckoo." *The Nineteenth Century* XXXII, No. 190 (December 1892): 920-29.

> Refutes Linton's assessment of contemporary society.

Rinehart, Nana. " 'The Girl of the Period' Controversy." *Victorian Periodicals Review* XIII, Nos. 1 & 2 (Spring-Summer 1980): 3-9.

> Compares Linton's portrayals of women with those of Anthony Trollope.

Smith, F. B. "Three Neglected Masterpieces: 'Joshua David-

son', 'The Martyrdom of Man', 'London—A Pilgrimage'."
Meanjin Quarterly 32, No. 1 (March 1973): 114-26.

Evaluates themes and characterization in *Joshua David-son,* comparing the novel favorably with *Robert Elsmere.*

Super, R. H. "Landor's 'Dear Daughter,' Eliza Lynn Linton." *PMLA* LIX, No. 4 (December 1944): 1059-85.

Examines Linton's friendship and correspondence with English poet Walter Savage Landor.

Zimmerman, Bonnie. "Gwendolyn Harleth and 'The Girl of the Period'." In *George Eliot: Centenary Essays and an Unpublished Fragment,* edited by Anne Smith, pp. 196-217. Totowa, N.J.: Barnes and Noble, 1980.

Offers a comparison of Gwendolyn Harleth, the heroine of George Eliot's novel *Daniel Deronda,* with Linton's hypothetical Girl of the Period, concluding that Harleth is "a profound example of the unsexed Girl of the Period" and symbolizes "the transformation of the long tradition of Female Influence and Women's Mission into the feminism that would soon shatter the calm surface of domestic England."

Additional coverage of Linton's life and career is contained in the following source published by Gale Research: *Dictionary of Literary Biography,* Vol. 18.

Henry Mackenzie

1745-1831

Scottish novelist, essayist, and dramatist.

INTRODUCTION

Mackenzie was a leading representative of the sentimental movement in England along with Laurence Sterne and Oliver Goldsmith. His most popular novel, *The Man of Feeling,* affirms his unswerving insistence that upright moral character leads to compassion for others and therefore results in humanitarian actions. Mackenzie refined this philanthropic message in two subsequent novels, as well as in his essays for the *Mirror* and the *Lounger,* and in his dramas. Greatly influenced by the sentimental tenor of Mackenzie's writings, his contemporaries dubbed him the "Man of Feeling," after his most famous work.

Mackenzie was born in Edinburgh in 1745. He was educated at Edinburgh High School and the University of Edinburgh before leaving school to pursue a law career. In 1761 Mackenzie began a four-year clerkship for a prominent Edinburgh lawyer, after which he was admitted as an attorney in the Court of the Exchequer in Scotland. He then traveled to London in 1766 to acquaint himself further with English law. Upon returning to Edinburgh three years later, Mackenzie began writing *The Man of Feeling,* which he published anonymously in 1771. In succeeding years, he wrote two more novels—*The Man of the World* and *Julia de Roubigné*—and he began to assume an increasingly important role in several Edinburgh literary societies. One of these groups, the Mirror Club, eventually formed a periodical known as the *Mirror* for which Mackenzie served as editor and chief contributor from 1779 to 1780. He worked in a similar capacity for the *Lounger* from 1785 to 1787. In later years, Mackenzie established himself as one of Scotland's foremost attorneys, as well as a leading member of Edinburgh's cultural community: in 1783 he founded the Royal Society of Edinburgh and in 1784 he formed the Highland Society of Scotland. Mackenzie died in 1831; a volume of reminiscences was published posthumously as *The Anecdotes and Egotisms of Henry Mackenzie.*

Critics generally agree that *The Man of Feeling* is Mackenzie's most important work. Composed early in his literary career, this novel established the sentimental model for most of his other writings. The principal influence upon the novelist's philosophy was the sentimental movement's fundamental rejection of the Calvinistic emphasis on the depravity of mankind, coupled with a classical demand for a strict adherence to order and proportion to produce harmony and beauty in art. Mackenzie was also influenced by the moral and ethical ideas proposed by such Scottish philosophers as David Hume and Adam Smith, who advanced the notion that the truth can be sensed and felt in

the heart and that emotions are a gage of the truth, and who challenged Thomas Hobbes's dictum that human beings act for selfish reasons alone. Mackenzie's *Man of Feeling* illustrated how these ideals would manifest themselves by following its kind and benevolent protagonist, Harley, on a personal odyssey through several adventures that test his sentimental nature. *The Man of the World* and *Julia de Roubigné* explore similar sentimental themes by examining how a good man confronts evil in another person and how too much sentiment can actually destroy a person. Mackenzie wrote several plays that further elaborated on these topics, but *The Prince of Tunis: A Tragedy* was his only theatrical success. Furthermore, as editor of the *Mirror* and the *Lounger,* Mackenzie contributed sentimental essays and tales marked by a striking clarity and passion; as a result, he was nicknamed the "Addison of the North" after Joseph Addison, whose renowned contributions to the *Spectator* set the standard of excellence for periodical literature.

Walter Scott, a contemporary of Mackenzie, characterized *The Man of Feeling* as a work of the highest quality, asserting that its loosely drawn characters and its fragmented episodic style reflect literary techniques designed to make the author's humanitarian view seem all the more natural. Robert Burns, another contemporary, stated that Mackenzie's *Man of Feeling* is "a book I prize next to the bible," since it provides such a perfect plan for learning about true "kindness, generosity, and benevolence." However, Samuel Johnson, who was adamantly opposed to the sentimental philosophy, saw the novel as trite and lacking realism. In the two centuries since Mackenzie flourished, commentators have generally deemed *The Man of Feeling* an unsuccessful work. Many critics have argued that Mackenzie's preoccupation with sentimental themes and with imparting a certain didactic message distracted him from refining his plot and characters. According to these critics, this shortcoming leads to an overall ambiguity regarding the author's intentions as well as the protagonist's humanitarian actions in *The Man of Feeling*. While Mackenzie's supporters have conceded that the author exhibits an immature prose style in the novel, they nevertheless maintain that many of its episodes are charming in their depiction of everyday life.

Critics who have chiefly analyzed the sentimental tone of Mackenzie's works argue that apart from advocating a universal humanitarianism, the author also advanced the idea that sentimentalism finds its basis in the conservative values of the aristocratic social class to which he belonged. Commentators who have upheld this view believe that in his writings Mackenzie urged his readers to take a philanthropic interest in the needs and concerns of all levels of humanity using his social class as the model. Regardless of Mackenzie's didactic intentions, few critics dispute his importance in the history of the sentimental movement, as well as his role as a prominent figure in Scottish literature.

PRINCIPAL WORKS

The Man of Feeling (novel) 1771
The Man of the World (novel) 1773
The Prince of Tunis: A Tragedy (drama) 1773
Julia de Roubigné: A Tale in a Series of Letters (novel) 1777
* *False Shame, or The White Hypocrite* (drama) 1789
Letters of Brutus to Certain Celebrated Political Characters (essays) 1791
The Works of Henry Mackenzie, Esq. 8 vols. (poetry, novels, essays, and drama) 1808
The Miscellaneous Works of Henry Mackenzie. 3 vols. (novels and essays) 1815
† *Virginia; or The Roman Father: A Tragedy* (drama) 1820
‡ *The Anecdotes and Egotisms of Henry Mackenzie 1745-1831* (journal) 1927
The Novels of Henry Mackenzie. 4 vols. (novels) 1976

*This work is also known as *The Force of Fashion*.

†This drama may have been written as early as 1769.

‡This journal was unfinished when Mackenzie died in 1831. The work was collected and edited by Harold William Thompson in 1927.

Henry Mackenzie   (letter date 1769)

[*In the following excerpt from a letter written to his cousin Elizabeth Rose in 1769, Mackenzie briefly explains how he conceived of* The Man of Feeling.]

[To] speak seriously, I would only observe in general, that I imagine being somewhat conversant with the fine Arts is one of the most powerful Improvements of the Mind. There is something of an acquired as well as a natural Delicacy, & the Soul as well as the Body has Nerves, which are only affected in a certain indescribable Manner, & gain by frequent Exertion a very superior Degree of Feeling. We want perhaps in most of the Sciences, Books of that Simplicity, which is distant enough from the technical of each, to give a liberal Idea of them to those who are new in the Study: where such can be found, we may at the Expence of less Time, & with much more Pleasure in the Attempt, acquire a general Notion of their Genius & Beauties.

There is one Method which in my opinion is not a little useful in reading any Book of Excellence, especially if it is a Book of original Observation; and that is, when we find any Remark particularly impressive, to take it down in writing, subjoining any Comments that our own View of it may suggest: these, when we meet with Passages tending to illustrate them, in the same, or other Authors, we may review, correct, & alter, as our Information on the Point is increased. This I believe will be found to give a Freedom of thinking on all Subjects, & a Distinctness on that one, upon which we are employed. (pp. 14-15)

You will find inclosed a very whimsical Introduction to a very odd Medley. I tell it as a Compliment, that even amidst the Hurry which our Whitsuntide Term has engaged me in of late, I had time to think of entertaining, or at least of attempting to entertain you. . . .

You must know then, that I have seldom been in Use to write any Prose, except what consisted of Observations (such as I could make) on Men & Manners. The way of introducing these by Narrative I had fallen into in some detach'd Essays, from the Notion of it's interesting both the Memory & the Affection deeper, than mere Argument, or moral Reasoning. In this way I was somehow led to think of introducing a Man of Sensibility into different Scenes where his Feelings might be seen in their Effects, & his Sentiments occasionally delivered without the Stiffness of regular Deduction. In order to give myself entire Liberty in the Historical Part of the Performance, & to indulge that desultory Humour of writing which sometimes possesses me, I began with this Introduction & write now & then a Chapter as I have Leisure or Inclination. How I have succeeded I cannot say; but I have found more Pleasure in the Attempt than in any other. . . . (p. 16)

Henry Mackenzie, in a letter to Elizabeth Rose of Kilravock on July 8, 1769, in his Letters to Elizabeth Rose of Kilravock: On Literature Events and People, 1768-1815, *edited by Horst W. Drescher, Oliver and Boyd, 1967, pp. 13-16.*

Sir Walter Scott (essay date 1831?)

[A Scottish author of historical romances, Scott was one of the leading proponents in the early nineteenth century of verisimilitude and historical accuracy in literature. Perhaps more than any of his contemporaries, he clearly represents the increased tolerance of the Romantic age toward all literature, so much so that many later critics and scholars have censured him for his habit of praising nearly everyone and for his lack of discrimination in critical matters. In the excerpt below written sometime before Mackenzie's death in 1831, Scott surveys the author's major works, praising them for their originality and their keen insights into human nature.]

The time, we hope, is yet distant, when, speaking of this author as of those with whom his genius ranks him, a biographer may with delicacy trace his personal character and peculiarities, or record the manner in which he has discharged the duties of a citizen. When that hour shall arrive, we trust few of his own contemporaries will be left to mourn him; but we can anticipate the sorrow of a later generation, when deprived of the wit which enlivened their hours of enjoyment, the benevolence which directed and encouraged their studies, and the wisdom which instructed them in their duties to society. It is enough to say here, that Mr. Mackenzie survives, venerable and venerated, as the last link of the chain which connects the Scottish literature of the present age with the period when there were giants in the land—the days of Robertson, and Hume, and Smith, and Home, and Clerk, and Fergusson; and that the remembrance of an era so interesting could not have been intrusted to a sounder judgment, a more correct taste, or a more tenacious memory. It is much to be wished, that Mr. Mackenzie . . . would place on a more permanent record some of the anecdotes and recollections with which he delights society. (pp. 524-25)

As an author, Mr. Mackenzie has shown talents both for poetry and the drama. Indeed we are of opinion, that no man can succeed perfectly in the line of fictitious composition, without most of the properties of a poet, though he may be no writer of verses; but Mr. Mackenzie possesses the powers of melody in addition to those of poetical conception. He has given a beautiful specimen of legendary poetry, in two little Highland ballads, a style of composition which becomes fashionable from time to time, on account of its simplicity and pathos, and then is again laid aside, when worn out by the common-place productions of mere imitators, to whom its approved facility offers its chief recommendation. But it is as a Novelist that we are now called on to consider our author's powers; and the universal and permanent popularity of his writings entitles us to rank him amongst the most distinguished of his class. His works possess the rare and invaluable property of originality, to which all other qualities are as dust in the balance; and the sources to which he resorts to excite our interest, are rendered accessible by a path peculiarly his own. The reader's attention is not riveted, as in Fielding's works, by strongly marked character, and the lucid evolution of a well-constructed fable; or as in Smollett's novels, by broad and strong humour, and a decisively superior knowledge of human life in all its varieties; nor, to mention authors whom Mackenzie more nearly resembles,

does he attain the pathetic effect which is the object of all three, in the same manner as Richardson, or as Sterne. An accumulation of circumstances, sometimes amounting to tediousness, a combination of minutely traced events, with an ample commentary on each, were thought necessary by Richardson to excite and prepare the mind of the reader for the affecting scenes which he has occasionally touched with such force; and without denying him his due merit, it must be allowed that he has employed preparatory volumes in accomplishing what has cost Mackenzie and Sterne only a few pages, perhaps only a few sentences.

On the other hand, although the two last authors have, in particular passages, a more strong resemblance to each other than those formerly named, yet there remain such essential points of difference betwix' them, as must secure for Mackenzie the praise of originality, which we have claimed for him. It is needless to point out to the reader the difference between the general character of their writings, or how far the chaste, correct, almost studiously decorous manner and style of the works of the author of **The Man of Feeling,** differ from the wild wit, and intrepid contempt at once of decency, and regularity of composition, which distinguish *Tristram Shandy.* It is not in the general conduct or style of their works that they in the slightest degree approach; nay, no two authors in the British language can be more distinct. But even in the particular passages where both had in view to excite the reader's pathetic sympathy, the modes resorted to are different. The pathos of Sterne in some degree resembles his humour, and is seldom attained by simple means; a wild, fanciful, beautiful flight of thought and expression is remarkable in the former, as an extravagant, burlesque, and ludicrous strain of conception and language characterises the latter. The celebrated passage, where the tear of the recording Angel blots the profane oath of Uncle Toby out of the register of heaven, a flight so poetically fanciful as to be stretched to the very verge of extravagance, will illustrate our position. To attain his object—that is, to make us thoroughly sympathize with the excited state of mind which betrays Uncle Toby into the indecorous assertion which forms the groundwork of the whole—the author calls Heaven and Hell into the lists, and represents in a fine poetic frenzy, its effects on the accusing Spirit and registering Angel. Let this be contrasted with the fine tale of **"La Roche,"** in which Mackenzie has described, with such unexampled delicacy, and powerful effect, the sublime scene of the sorrows and resignation of the bereaved father. This also is painted reflectively; that is, the reader's sympathy is excited by the effect produced on one of the drama, neither angel nor devil, but a philosopher, whose heart remains sensitive, though his studies have misled his mind into the frozen regions of scepticism. To say nothing of the tendency of the two passages, which will scarce, in the minds of the most unthinking, bear any comparison, we would only remark, that Mackenzie has given us a moral truth, Sterne a beautiful trope; and that if the one claims the palm of superior brilliancy of imagination, that due to nature and accuracy of human feeling must abide with the Scottish author.

Yet while marking the broad and distinct difference between these two authors, the most celebrated certainly among those who are termed sentimental, it is but fair to Sterne to add, that although Mackenzie has rejected his licence of wit, and flights of imagination, retrenched, in a great measure, his episodical digressions, and altogether banished the indecency and buffoonery to which he had too frequent recourse, still their volumes must be accounted as belonging to the same class; and amongst the thousand imitators who have pursued their path, we cannot recollect one English author who is entitled to the same honour. The foreign authors, Riccoboni and Marivaux, belong to the same department; but of the former we remember little; and the latter, though full of the most delicate touches, often depends for effect on the turn of phrase, and the protracted embarrassments of artificial gallantry, more than upon the truth and simplicity of nature. The "Heloise" and "Emile" partake of the insanity of their author, and are exaggerated, though most eloquent, descriptions of overwhelming passion, rather than works of sentiment.

In future compositions, the author dropped even that resemblance which the style of *The Man of Feeling* bears, in some particulars, to the works of Sterne; and his country may boast, that, in one instance at least, she has produced, in Mackenzie, a writer of pure musical Addisonian prose, which retains the quality of vigour, without forfeiting that of clearness and simplicity.

[The] principal object of Mackenzie, in all his novels, has been to reach and sustain a tone of moral pathos, by representing the effect of incidents, whether important or trifling, upon the human mind, and especially on those which were not only just, honourable, and intelligent, but so framed as to be responsive to those finer feelings to which ordinary hearts are callous.

—*Sir Walter Scott*

We are hence led to observe, that the principal object of Mackenzie, in all his novels, has been to reach and sustain a tone of moral pathos, by representing the effect of incidents, whether important or trifling, upon the human mind, and especially on those which were not only just, honourable, and intelligent, but so framed as to be responsive to those finer feelings to which ordinary hearts are callous. This is the direct and professed object of Mackenzie's first work, which is in fact no narrative, but a series of successive incidents, each rendered interesting by the mode in which they operate on the feelings of Harley. The attempt had been perilous in a meaner hand; for, sketched by a pencil less nicely discriminating, Harley, instead of a being whom we love, respect, sympathize with, and admire, had become the mere Quixote of sentiment, an object of pity perhaps, but of ridicule at the same time. Against this the author has guarded with great skill; and

while duped and swindled in London, Harley neither loses our consideration as a man of sense and spirit, nor is subjected to that degree of contempt with which readers in general regard the misadventures of a novice upon town, whilst they hug themselves in their own superior knowledge of the world. Harley's spirited conduct towards an impertinent passenger in the stage-coach, and his start of animated indignation on listening to Edward's story, are skilfully thrown in, to satisfy the reader that his softness and gentleness of temper were not allied to effeminacy; and that he dared, on suitable occasions, to do all that might become a man. We have heard that some of Harley's feelings were taken from those of the author himself, when, at his first entrance on the dry and barbarous study of the municipal law, he was looking back, like Blackstone, on the land of the Muses, which he was condemned to leave behind him. It has also been said, that the fine sketch of Miss Walton was taken from the heiress of a family of distinction, who ranked at that time high in the Scottish fashionable world. But such surmises are little worth the tracing; for we believe no original character was ever composed by any author, without the idea having been previously suggested by something which he had observed in nature.

The other novels of Mr. Mackenzie, although assuming a more regular and narrative form, are, like *The Man of Feeling,* rather the history of effects produced on the human mind by a series of events, than the narrative of those events themselves. The villany of Sindall is the tale of a heart hardened to selfishness, by incessant and unlimited gratification of the external senses; a contrast to that of Harley, whose mental feelings have acquired such an ascendency as to render him unfit for the ordinary business of life. The picture of the former is so horrid, that we would be disposed to deny its truth, did we not unhappily know, that sensual indulgence, in the words of Burns,

hardens a' within,

And petrifies the feeling;

and that there never did and never will exist, anything permanently noble and excellent in a character, which was a stranger to the exercise of resolute self-denial. The account of the victims of Sindall's arts and crimes, particularly the early history of the Annesleys, is exquisitely well drawn; and, perhaps, the scene between the brother and sister by the pond, equals any part of the author's writings. Should the reader doubt this, he may easily make the experiment, by putting it into the hands of any young person of feeling and intelligence, and of an age so early as not to have forgotten the sports and passions of childhood.

The beautiful and tragic tale of *Julia de Roubigné,* is of a very different tenor from *The Man of the World;* and we have good authority for thinking, that it was written in some degree as a counterpart to the latter work. A friend of the author, the celebrated Lord Kaimes, we believe, had represented to Mr. Mackenzie, in how many poems, plays, and novels, the distress of the piece is made to turn upon the designing villany of some one of the *dramatis personæ.* On considering his observations, the author undertook, as a task fit for his genius, the composition of a story, in which the characters should be all naturally virtuous, and where the calamities of the catastrophe should arise, as frequently happens in actual life, not out of schemes of premeditated villany, but from the excess and over-indulgence of passions and feelings, in themselves blameless, nay, praiseworthy, but which, encouraged to a morbid excess, and coming into fatal though fortuitous concourse with each other, lead to the most disastrous consequences. Mr. Mackenzie executed his purpose; and as the plan fell in most happily with the views of a writer, whose object was less to describe external objects, than to read a lesson on the human passions, he has produced one of the most heart-wringing histories that has ever been written. The very circumstances which palliate the errors of the sufferers, in whose distress we interest ourselves, point out to the reader that there is neither room for hope, remedy, nor revenge. When a Lovelace or a Sindall comes forth like an Evil Principle, the agent of all the misery of the scene, we see a chance of their artifices being detected, at least the victims have the consciousness of innocence, the reader the stern hope of vengeance. But when, as in *Julia de Roubigné,* the revival of mutual affection on the part of two pure and amiable beings, imprudently and incautiously indulged, awakens, and not unjustly, the jealous honour of a high-spirited husband,—when we see Julia precipitated into misery by her preference of filial duty to early love,—Savillon, by his faithful and tender attachment to a deserving object,—and Montauban, by a jealous regard to his spotless fame,—we are made aware, at the same time, that there is no hope of aught but the most unhappy catastrophe. The side of each sufferer is pierced by the very staff on which he leant, and the natural and virtuous feelings which they at first most legitimately indulged, precipitate them into error, crimes, remorse, and misery. The cruelty to which Montauban is hurried, may, perhaps, be supposed to exempt him from our sympathy, especially in an age when such crimes as that of which Julia is suspected, are usually borne by the injured parties with more equanimity than her husband displays. But the irritable habits of the time, and of his Spanish descent, must plead the apology of Montauban, as they are admitted to form that of Othello. Perhaps, on the whole, *Julia de Roubigné* gives the reader too much actual pain to be so generally popular as *The Man of Feeling,* since we have found its superiority to that beautiful essay on human sensibility, often disputed by those whose taste we are in general inclined to defer to. The very acute feelings which the work usually excites among the readers whose sympathies are liable to be awakened by scenes of fictitious distress, we are disposed to ascribe to the extreme accuracy and truth of the sentiments, as well as the beautiful manner in which they are expressed. There are few who have not, at one period of life, broken ties of love and friendship, secret disappointments of the heart, to mourn over; and we know no book which recalls the recollection of such more severely than *Julia de Roubigné.*

We return to consider the key-note, as we may term it, on which Mackenzie has formed his tales of fictitious woe, and which we have repeatedly described to be the illustration of the nicer and finer sensibilities of the human breast. To attain this point, and to place it in the strongest and most unbroken light, the author seems to have kept the

other faculties with which we know him to be gifted, in careful subordination. The Northern Addison, who revived the art of periodical writing, and sketched, though with a light pencil, the follies and the lesser vices of his time, has showed himself a master of playful satire. The historian of the Homespun family may place his narrative, without fear of shame, by the side of *The Vicar of Wakefield.* Colonel Caustic and Umfraville are masterly conceptions of the *laudator temporis acti;* and many personages in those papers which Mr. Mackenzie contributed to the *Mirror* and *Lounger* attest with what truth, spirit, and ease, he could describe, assume, and sustain, a variety of characters. The beautiful landscape-painting which he has exhibited in many passages (take, for example, that where the country-seat of the old Scottish lady and its accompaniments are so exquisitely delineated), assures us of the accuracy and delicacy of his touch in delineating the beauties of nature.

But all these powerful talents, any single one of which might have sufficed to bring men of more bounded powers into notice, have been by Mackenzie carefully subjected to the principal object which he proposed to himself—the delineation of the human heart. Variety of character he has introduced sparingly, and has seldom recourse to any peculiarity of incident, availing himself generally of those which may be considered as common property to all writers of romance. His sense of the beauties of nature, and power of describing them, are carefully kept down, to use the expression of the artists; and like the single straggling bough, which shades the face of his sleeping veteran, just introduced to relieve his principal object, but not to eclipse it. It cannot be termed an exception to this rule, though certainly a peculiarity of this author, that on all occasions where sylvan sports can be introduced, he displays an intimate familiarity with them, and, from personal habits, to which we have elsewhere alluded, shows a delight to dwell for an instant upon a favourite topic.

Lastly, The wit which sparkles in his periodical Essays, and in his private conversation, shows itself but little in his Novels; and although his peculiar vein of humour may be much more frequently traced, yet it is so softened down, and divested of the broad ludicrous, that it harmonizes with the most grave and affecting parts of the tale, and becomes, like the satire of Jacques, only a more humorous shade of melancholy. In short, Mackenzie aimed at being the historian of feeling, and has succeeded in the object of his ambition. But as mankind are never contented, and as critics are certainly no exception to a rule so general, we could wish that, without losing or altering a line our author has written, he had condescended to give us, in addition to his stores of sentiment,—a romance on life and manners, by which, we are convinced, he would have twisted another branch of laurel into his garland. However, as Sebastian expresses it,

What had been, is unknown; what is, appears.

We must be proudly satisfied with what we have received, and happy that, in this line of composition, we can boast a living author, of excellence like that of Henry Mackenzie. (pp. 525-31)

Sir Walter Scott, "Henry Mackenzie," in his Lives of Eminent Novelists and Dramatists, *revised edition, Frederick Warne and Co., 1887, pp. 522-31.*

Robert Burns on Mackenzie's Sentimentalism:

You must know I have just met with the *Mirror* and *Lounger* for the first time, and I am quite in raptures with them; I should be glad to have your opinion of some of the papers. The one I have just read, *Lounger,* No. 61, has cost me more honest tears than any thing I have read of a long time. M'Kenzie has been called the Addison of the Scots, and in my opinion, Addison would not be hurt at the comparison. If he has not Addison's exquisite humour, he as certainly outdoes him in the tender and the pathetic. His **Man of Feeling** (but I am not counsel learned in the laws of criticism) I estimate as the first performance in its kind I ever saw. From what book, moral or even pious, will the susceptible young mind receive impressions more congenial to humanity and kindness, generosity and benevolence—in short, more of all that ennobles the soul to herself, or endears her to others—than from the simple affecting tale of poor Harley?

Robert Burns, in a letter to Mrs. Dunlop, April 1790. In The Letters of Robert Burns, *edited by J. De Lancey Ferguson, Oxford at the Clarendon Press, 1931.*

The Spectator (essay date 1893)

[*In the following excerpt, the critic discusses Mackenzie's treatment of sentimentalism in* The Man of Feeling *and other writings.*]

Who does not know the faded water-colour paintings of a century or so ago? Either brown impossible landscapes, or groups of high-waisted shepherdesses sitting pensively among grey ruins, their chastened colouring somewhat more faded by lapse of years. Those old-fashioned water-colours possess the same attraction as do the novels of Henry Mackenzie; they are alike chastened in tone and delicate in outline, there is none of the vigorous breadth and depth of modern art, there is little Nature, and no life,—but the same sentiment pervades them all.

The "Historian of Feeling," as Sir Walter Scott called Mackenzie, has only been dead sixty-two years. There are probably some elderly folk still living who remember him in his old age and their early youth; and yet, in taking up his best-known novel, **The Man of Feeling,** we seem to have put back the clock of time far more than a century. It was published in 1771—the year that Smollett died, and three years after Sterne's death—and was a decided imitation of the *Sentimental Journey.* There is the same abrupt beginning, the same fragmentary narrative,—consisting of brief episodes and descriptive scenes, with more pathos in the character of Harley than in that of the imaginary Yorick, and a corresponding lack of humour. Mackenzie himself calls the book "recitals of little adventures, in which the dispositions of a man, sensible to judge, and still more

warm to feel, had room to unfold themselves." Sir Walter Scott compares Mackenzie, as a novelist, with Sterne, not always to the latter's advantage, and as an essayist he speaks of the "Northern Addison, who revived the art of periodical writing," and goes on to say that Scotland may well boast "that, in one instance at least, she has produced in Mackenzie a writer of pure Addisonian prose, which retains the quality of vigour, without forfeiting that of clearness and simplicity." Modern writers have scarcely endorsed Scott's eulogium. Mr. Gosse calls Mackenzie a "parodist of Sterne," and says that he also "affected the moral earnestness of Richardson, and the characters in his three principal fictions move, meekly robed in gentle virtue, through a series of heartrending misfortunes. There is no observation of life, no knowledge of the world, in Mackenzie's long-drawn lachrymose novels of feeling." In fact, without the prop given to his literary reputation by his warm friend, Sir Walter Scott, that reputation would probably long ago have fallen to pieces and been forgotten. (pp. 82-3)

A certain flavour of Goldsmith hangs about **The Man of Feeling,** especially in the character of Harley, though without one spark of Goldsmith's delightful humour. Harley may fairly claim the description given by Sir William Thornhill of himself as being "one of the most generous yet whimsical men in the kingdom; a man of consummate benevolence;" and it might have been said of him, as of the "Good-natured man:"—"The strange, good-natured, foolish, open-hearted—and yet, all his faults are such, that one loves him still the better for them." Even Sir Walter Scott allows that "sketched by a pencil less discriminating, Harley, instead of a being whom we love, respect, sympathise with and admire, had become the mere Quixote of sentiment, an object of pity perhaps, but of ridicule at the same time." **The Man of Feeling** is the very apotheosis of tearfulness and sentiment.

Mackenzie, said Sir Walter, in a biographical notice, "was the last link of the chain which connects the Scottish literature of the present age with the period when there were giants in the land,—the days of Robertson, and Hume, and Smith, and Home, and Clerk, and Fergusson." . . . He formed the centre of a circle of congenial friends, with some of whom, in 1779, he started, and finally edited, a periodical called the *Mirror,* written in the avowed style of Addison, and followed by another venture entitled the *Lounger.* Some of Mackenzie's best writing is to be found in those old-fashioned pages, and a little more humour than in his doleful novels. Mr. Umphraville and the Homespun family are not unworthy successors, in a small way, to Sir Roger de Coverley, or Beau Tibbs, and the Man in Black. But the periodicals failed for lack of support. In the final number of the *Mirror,* the editor gives several reasons for its apparent failure to please the public. "In the point of subject, as well as of reception, the place where it appeared was unfavourable to the *Mirror.*" The topics of the day were "Hardly various enough for the subject, or important enough for the dignity of writing." However, the paper had served the purpose for which it was originally started, it had amused and occupied its contributors even if it had failed to occupy or amuse a large section of the Edinburgh public. (p. 83)

"The Historian of Feeling," in The Spectator, *Vol. 71, No. 3394, July 15, 1893, pp. 82-3.*

Hamish Miles   (essay date 1928)

[*In the following excerpt, Miles presents a brief overview of Mackenzie's literary career, primarily focusing on* The Man of Feeling *as a work that lacks significant artistic merit but nevertheless exhibits a certain charm.*]

Mackenzie's modest gifts were those of kindliness, polite humour, an intelligent patronage and comprehension of literature, and a smooth, accomplished, but rather undistinguished style. Where did he display them? After his first surprising triumph, he was not slow to follow up **The Man of Feeling** with another novel, and **The Man of the World** appeared in 1773. This was a highly improving romance, written in a more flowing and copious style, constructed on a formula sharply contrasted to that of its predecessor; for moral delicacy, moral blindness is substituted, and through a long course of selfish and sensual indulgence the worldly Sindall reaches his own ruin, brings undeserved injury on the heads of most of those about him, and tearfully expires. Then came **Julia de Roubigné** in 1777, a shorter work but a better one, this time in the fashionable epistolary form. "One of the most heart-wringing histories that has ever been written," remarked Scott, surely with the emphasis of an old friendship; but the pathos of the heroine and Montauban and Savillon is certainly more spontaneous and natural than the conduct of his earlier personages in the face of an unjust world.

There were also plays. In 1773 the curtain of the Theatre Royal at Edinburgh rose upon "a wild, romantic scene," through which the Genius of Scotland, impersonated by Mrs Yates, advanced "to the sound of solemn music." She spoke:

> Late as I marked, with fond maternal eyes,
> On every side my laurelled sons arise. . . .
> An humble poet, scarcely known to fame,
> Stepped doubtful forth, one little sprig to claim.
> 'From earliest youth,' he said, 'he wished to find
> Where first the passions nature's robe
>   unbind; . . .
> If on his native stage his scenes may live,
> He asks no praise but what the heart can give.'

This was the prologue to **The Prince of Tunis,** a tragedy in five acts of torpid verse. And its epilogue opened with the lines:

> Well, I protest, there's no such thing as dealing
> With these starch poets, with these—Men of
>   Feeling!

But the humble poet's sprig was a very little one. Mackenzie made an adaptation of Lillo's *Fatal Curiosity,* which was styled **The Shipwreck** and played at Covent Garden in 1784. A comedy called **False Shame, or The White Hypocrite,** was also given there during 1789, but failed. An earlier piece, a tragedy in verse entitled **The Spanish Father,** was pronounced by Garrick to be "too horrid for the stage," and remained unacted. But Mackenzie made no high claims for his dramatic gifts: in some notes appended to the plays when they were reprinted in the edi-

tion of his **Works** in 1808, he makes graceful and amiable admission of his failure.

As to his poetry he was likewise modest. It fills barely one hundred pages of one of the eight volumes of his collected works. There are two moderately effective imitations of old Scottish ballads, some rather shaky sets of stanzas in the manner of Spenser, and two gently amusing longer poems, **"The Vision of Vanity"** and **"The Pursuits of Happiness."** Two **"Inscriptions,"** for a hut belonging to a friend in the Highlands, are memorable only because they had passed from the author's mind until a gentleman in the Isle of Wight sent them to Mackenzie, explaining that he had found them in a package after a shipwreck, marked as being the work of the author of **The Man of Feeling.**

No, it was the periodical essay which gave the fullest expression of Mackenzie's real personality. Here "the Scottish Addison" shone more happily. During the years 1779 and 1780 he edited, and was a regular contributor to, a weekly publication on the model of the *Spectator,* known as the *Mirror.* It was succeeded early in 1785 by a similar periodical, the *Lounger,* which ran for almost two years. Mackenzie's collected papers from these two publications make agreeable desultory reading, and it is easier, after browsing amongst them for an hour or two, to understand the charm which his company and talk held for his friends throughout his long life. The tone and manner, of course, of these essays and anecdotes are pitched in an Addisonian key, and the characters are close cousins of the *Spectator's,* as witness Mackenzie's Colonel Caustic and Sir Roger de Coverley. But the humour is honest and unforced, and the good sense undeniable. (pp. 14-17)

Admittedly, **The Man of Feeling** must be counted as a novel of the second rank. Nothing could be gained by trying to hoist it again to those pinnacles reserved for it by Mackenzie's friends, heights from which it long ago silently subsided. There can be few novels of repute so loosely constructed, fewer with so small a pretence to plot or development of character, fewer still so heavily dabbled with lachrymosity. Yet the book, as we have seen, had its day, and that day was no short one. And after all, it is readable still. As we follow Harley through his set series of adventures, greater and smaller, and dutifully remark his flowing tears, we are aware not so much of distaste as of difference. The coin is not of base metal; it still rings true; but it is part of a currency that has gone out of circulation. We need not be repelled by the manifestations of sentiment: it is better to accept them as measuring-poles when we try to map the difficult vagaries of the stream of Taste.

The book is a compromise, in style and in matter. Had it not been for the intoxicating example set by Laurence Sterne, Henry Mackenzie would never have achieved that new departure in the novelist's form, with its loose-strung chain of episode, its careful abruptness here, its delicate modulation there. As we noted in glancing at his periodical essays, Mackenzie was essentially an imitative writer, and a moment's reading almost anywhere in **The Man of Feeling** will show how deeply he was here indebted to the author of *The Sentimental Journey.* But it is a mistake to suppose that there is any real affinity between their two names, coupled as they so often were. The play of Mackenzie's fancy could never approach Sterne's. His quick eye, it may be, could give him a model for the structure of his book; and occasionally his ear could give him the cadence of Sterne's phrase, clear and light as a bar or two fingered on a spinet. But there his gift stopped short. Morality, which was an afterthought with Yorick, was ever the true mentor of Mackenzie; and he could let no incident pass, no character display his worth or worthlessness, but he must somehow be underlining his meaning and casting across his fancy the shadow of a hardly suppressed sermon. Sterne was sentimental (in the contemporary use of that altered word) through and through; he was *maladif,* and he wrote his finest pages only at the cost of much suffering. "I have torn my whole frame into pieces by my feelings," he wrote as the end of his days drew near. But Mackenzie was healthy in body and in mind, a young man of talent who, in his character of Harley, was projecting not an image of himself, but merely his adaptation of a new literary mood. And there came the compromise. The strength of *Tristram Shandy* or the *Sentimental Journey* lies in their being so unescapably the direct expression of their writer's personality. The weakness of **The Man of Feeling** is that its pages so seldom glow with the warmth of real personal experience. Those admirers of the sensitive Harley who hopefully visited the Edinburgh drawing-rooms and were confronted by the "kiln-dried" Mr Mackenzie, had been deceived by the purely literary surface.

But often enough that surface is both pleasing and amusing. The opening scene, where the narrator and his friend the curate are out shooting, is deftly sketched, and the device by which the original Harleian manuscript is rescued from the clergyman is diverting. . . . Pleasant, too, are the pangs of Harley's departure from his home, and the moment when he stops to look backward:

> He walked out on the road, and gaining a little height, stood gazing on that quarter he had left. He looked for his wonted prospect, his fields and his woods and his hills; they were lost in the distant clouds! He penciled them on the clouds, and bade them farewell with a sigh!

And more than once the landscape pencilled by the author for a background is clear and effective . . . with the recumbent figure of old Edwards asleep in the midst of the jutting, flowery rocks, or where, a few pages later, he evokes the memory of the village school now razed by a selfish squire.

And often the fine moral complacency of the scene will agreeably call up the memory of those improving prints in which Mackenzie's age . . . took pleasure: the Industrious Merchant, it might be, plumply surveying the commercial and domestic fruits of his sober and honest application, or the Virtuous Landlord amid his grateful serfs:

> The house . . . was indeed little better than a hut; its situation, however, was pleasant; and Edwards, assisted by the beneficence of Harley, set about improving its neatness and convenience. He staked out a piece of the green before for a garden, and Peter, who acted in Harley's family as valet, butler, and gardener, had orders to furnish him with parcels of the different seeds he chose to sow in it. I have seen his master at

work in this little spot, with his coat off, and his dibble in his hand. It was a scene of tranquil virtue to have stopped an angel on his errands of mercy! Harley had contrived to lead a little bubbling brook through a green walk in the middle of the ground, upon which he had erected a mill in miniature, for the diversion of Edwards' infant grandson, and made shift in its construction to introduce a pliant bit of wood that answered with its fairy clack to the murmuring of the rill that turned it. I have seen him stand, listening to these mingled sounds, with his eyes fixed on the boy, and the smile of conscious satisfaction on his cheek; while the old man, with a look half turned to Harley, and half to heaven, breathed an ejaculation of gratitude and piety.

> Father of mercies! I would also thank thee, that not only hast thou assigned eternal rewards to virtue, but that, even in this bad world, the lines of our duty, and our happiness, are so frequently woven together.

But it is difficult to become acclimatised to the torrential tears of the sentimental. The harrow is passed and passed again over our emotions; tears rise, flow, fall, and rise again. Even a shepherd's horn, heard across the fields in a moment of distress, provides once the last touch for tears. When old Edwards tells Harley of the woeful death of old Trusty his dog, the tears seem almost to be exchanged between the pair like handshakes. One editor of **The Man of Feeling** went so far as to consider this notorious lachrymosity as a matter of statistics! His edition included an "Index to the tears shed (chokings, etc., not counted)," which contained such entries as these:

Eye met with a tear	page 127
Tears, face bathed with	" 130
Dropped one tear, no more . . .	" 131
Tears, press-gang could not refrain from .	" 136

At this distance of time the physiological nature of those tears of proper sentiment is even harder to determine than that of the ladylike swoons which adorn the fiction of a slightly later period. The whole thing may be little more than an artistic convention; we may be taking a symbol too literally. Perhaps, indeed, our great-grandchildren will be no less bewildered by those strange darknesses of desire, those terrible urgings of nervous ganglia, which supply the motive power to more than one of the accepted novelists of our own decade.

The tale seems to become less coherent in its structure as it proceeds. And not all the alleged gaps caused by the curate's need of powder-wadding will make amends for the weakness thus caused to the development of Mackenzie's story. The modern reader is left incredulous, gapingly so, when the monstrous sensibility of poor Harley actually brings him to his early grave. If all his tears had been tears of blood, the poor man could hardly have been more debile than when, having sunk into a decline occasioned apparently by his reluctance to declare his love for Miss Walton, he learns from that lady's own lips that she has long reciprocated his silent love—and forthwith expires. But there it is. Harley is gone. And it only remains for Mackenzie to proffer one last picture of polite melancholy: the churchyard where he lies, its hollow tree wherein he had been wont to sit and count the tombs before him, the last upwelling of human pity in the narrator's sensitive heart. . . .

No, this is not the lasting stuff of true pathos. Even during Mackenzie's own life, time had found him out. One evening, in 1826, Lady Louisa Stuart began to read *The Man of Feeling* to a party of friends who had expressed their curiosity regarding the book. She herself was old enough to remember its first appearance, and how her mother and elder sisters wept over it, "dwelling upon it with rapture." She had read it herself first at the age of fourteen, secretly afraid lest she "should not cry enough to gain the credit of proper sensibility." But now what happened? She wrote to Scott to tell him:

> I am afraid I perceived a sad change in it, or myself, which was worse, and the effect altogether failed. Nobody cried, and at some of the passages, the passages that I used to think so exquisite—oh dear! they laughed. . . . "

They laughed . . . And that is to some extent the reception which Harley has to fear from a modern audience, for it is easy to grow impatient of his small adventures and his self-wrought woes. But Dr Johnson, although he held *The Man of Feeling* in low esteem, might almost have applied to Mackenzie the remarks he made on Richardson: "Why, sir, if you were to read [him] for the story, your impatience would be so much frighted that you would hang yourself. But you must read him for the sentiment, and consider the story only as giving occasion to the sentiment." This is hardly the place to enter on any full examination of the emergence of sentiment in eighteenth-century literature, but in turning to read *The Man of Feeling* it is worth while bearing in mind the currents of emotion and didacticism which were running so high at the time of the book's success.

That high pitch of sentiment which makes Harley the most tearful of heroes might find affinities with another perplexing yet ever-present element in the eighteenth-century consciousness—the spleen. But its evolution moved along slightly different lines. The spleen was first regarded—as by Temple or Sydenham—as primarily a physical affection, the penalty of a vexatious island climate or a sedentary habit of life; only later did the malady assume that profounder, more spiritual hue which fascinated foreign observers of the English temperament, and let this new *accidie* take its part as a tributary stream of the Romantic movement. Sentiment, however, although often associated with an appropriate "decline" or "consumption," was viewed first and foremost as a matter of the heart; only when its extravagance made it ludicrous was it pushed down to the level of a nervous affliction. And it was in this light that Leigh Hunt viewed our Harley: "I am afraid," said he, "that Mackenzie's hero as well as Rousseau's [Saint-Preux] has too much bodily sensibility about him; the irritability of a man's nerves has been too often mistaken for mental feeling." And he very properly goes on to argue that, "social utility" being the principal virtue, a man who dies merely because his love is suddenly reciprocated, need not be held up for our admiration; it

were better that he give proof of his "utility" to society, and of his feeling for his beloved, by making her the mother of his children. And certainly it is here that the strong didactic element in Mackenzie's story collapses most completely before the purely sentimental.

That strain of didacticism, of social moralising, is very marked in *The Man of Feeling,* and is, of course, highly characteristic of the age which welcomed the mingled tears and exhortations of a Harley. It shows itself, for instance, when Mackenzie's hero is invited by his London acquaintances to include a visit to Bedlam in his survey of the sights of the town, and he at first raises humane objections:

> "I think it an inhuman practice," he says, "to expose the greatest misery to which our nature is afflicted, to every idle visitant who can afford a trifling perquisite to the keeper . . . " etc.

Again, it lies beneath Ben Silton's defence of poetry in the stage-coach conversation:

> "There is at least," said the stranger, "one advantage in the poetical inclination, that it is an incentive to philanthropy. There is a certain poetic ground, on which a man cannot tread without feelings that enlarge the heart: the causes of human depravity vanish before the romantic enthusiasm he professes, and many who are not able to reach the Parnassian heights, may yet approach so near as to be bettered by the air of the climate."

Again, a head is shaken lamentably over the follies of a time when—

> We take our ideas from sounds which folly has invented; Fashion, Bon ton, and Vertu, are the names of certain idols, to which we sacrifice the genuine pleasures of the soul. . . .

And when Harley calls down the curse of bodily sterility upon the selfish squire; when, in his wrath at Edwards' story of the scurvy trick played by the press-gang, he grasps impulsively at the old soldier's sword; when Edwards himself recalls the cruelty of the English soldiery to their Indian captive; or when Harley delivers his tirade against the English dominion in India—in all such scenes as these the tones are unmistakable: there speaks the voice of the "enlightenment" of the eighteenth century, the forerunner of liberal humanitarianism in the nineteenth. (pp. 24-32)

In this sweeping movement of ideas, Henry Mackenzie's *Man of Feeling* holds only a minor place. With this tale of his, written when he was hardly more than a youth, he encountered a sudden celebrity which he never altogether lost; but that celebrity must be accounted not so much to the intrinsic merits of the book, as to the fortunate conjunction presiding at its birth. Its blend of high-keyed sentiment and honest moralising satisfied a taste which had been quickened by Sterne and by Richardson. In neither element could Mackenzie rival his masters; but his pen held charm enough to captivate those who could not perhaps distinguish unerringly a work of imitation from one of true originality—and enough to allow his story even now to yield its gentle pleasure to a sympathetic eye. (p. 34)

> *Hamish Miles, in an introduction to* The Man of Feeling *by Henry Mackenzie, edited by Hamish Miles, The Scholartis Press, 1928, pp. 11-34.*

Harold William Thompson   (essay date 1931)

[*In the excerpt below, Thompson observes how sentiment, sensibility, and romanticism inform Mackenzie's writings for the* Mirror *and the* Lounger.]

'I heartily wish'—so runs the dedication of Scott's *Waverley* in 1814—'I heartily wish that the task of tracing the evanescent manners of his own country had employed the pen of the only man in Scotland who could have done it justice—of him so eminently distinguished in elegant literature, and whose sketches of Colonel Caustic and Umphraville are perfectly blended with the finer traits of national character. I should in that case have had more pleasure as a reader than I shall ever feel in the pride of a successful author, should these sheets confer upon me that envied distinction.

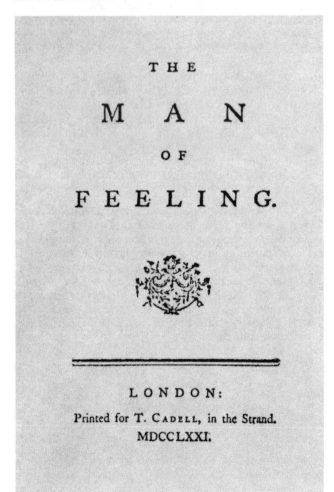

THE

MAN

OF

FEELING.

LONDON:

Printed for T. Cadell, in the Strand.
MDCCLXXI.

Title page for Mackenzie's best known work.

These volumes

Being respectfully inscribed
to
Our Scottish Addison
Henry Mackenzie
by
an unknown Admirer
of
his Genius'

It was not the generous Wizard of the North who first conferred upon Mackenzie the title used in this dedication. Scotland's other claimant for the crown in literature, Robert Burns, had written in 1787:

> Mackenzie has been called the Addison of the Scots, and, in my opinion, Addison would not be hurt at the comparison. If he has not Addison's exquisite humour, he as certainly outdoes him in the tender and the pathetic.

While both Burns and Scott were swayed somewhat by national pride and personal affection, there is enough of truth in their opinions to make a study of Mackenzie's essays and tales in the *Mirror* and *Lounger* essential for a knowledge of sentimentalism, for an appreciation of the eighteenth-century essay, or for an appraisal of the Scottish nation in its Golden Age. In these essays and tales, and in the **Anecdotes** which give them sharper point, lies the best of Mackenzie's writing.

When the *Mirror* began publication in 1779, both the author and his city had reached the height of their powers. Mackenzie had purchased in December of 1773 the Exchequer Crown practice of his retiring partner, Mr. George Inglis of Redhall, and thus, as he wrote Miss Rose, had assured for himself a comfortable living for the rest of his life. In his own rather narrow branch of the law, the Exchequer practice, he was soon supreme; and as his Court was governed by English rules, he came into contact with many English lawyers and had frequent occasion to visit London. There was probably no year before his sixtieth birthday when he did not visit the Southern capital at least once, and there were few distinguished persons in literature and the law whom he did not meet on these journeys. (pp. 178-79)

[Edinburgh] centred its literary activities—and indeed all manner of activities—in that delightful and characteristic institution of the eighteenth century, the club; it was to a club of young lawyers, quite naturally, that the Addison of the North owed the occasion for his title. Of the Mirror Club there are at least three authentic accounts: *Mirror* no. 110 by Mackenzie, entitled **"Conclusion of the Mirror"**; *Lounger* no. 30, by Lord Abercromby, *Letter from a Member of the Mirror-Club;* and annotations which Mackenzie made in his own copy of the *Mirror,* now in the possession of Mrs. O. B. Whyte. (p. 186)

Twenty papers had already been prepared when Mackenzie was asked to join the Club; thirty-five 'unexceptionable' papers were produced by January of 1779, 'when the publication was resolved on, a resolution which was rather assented to than approved by one half of the society'. (pp. 188-89)

Yet among those whom the authors most wished to please the approval was not tardy. Principal Robertson praised no. 5, an essay on **"Pedantry"** by Mackenzie, and wondered who its author could be. Dr. Adam Smith was interested and would have contributed had it not been for the illness of his mother, to whom his devotion was complete. Both Smith and John Home were consulted about the final draft of the last *Mirror,* in order that the exit might be as graceful as possible. As for Kames, the other literary arbiter of the giants who still remained from Hume's generation, we have his opinion in a letter which Abercromby wrote to Craig from Elgin on 12 September 1780:

> The first book which I opened in the drawing-room of Gordon Castle was a volume of it [*The Mirror*]. . . . We had scarce sat down to dinner when the Duchess asked me if I knew Mr. Mackenzie. I answered that he was my particular friend; upon which she rejoined that she was so *over-whelmed* by his superior talent for epistolary composition & the *Mirrors,* that she had not been able to answer a letter she received from him some time ago; that she had actually written 6 letters every one of which she had burnt. This produced a conversation on the *Mirror* in the course of which Kames observed that no man ever possessed the power of touching the tender feelings in a higher degree than Mackenzie.

Evidently the anonymity of publication did not prevent a pretty general guess that the best of the *Mirror*s were by the author of **The Man of Feeling,** and the prestige of his name doubtless combined with English praise to win his Scottish public. (pp. 189-90)

Some time elapsed before the same club of gentlemen brought out *The Lounger,* a similar periodical which ran every Saturday for 101 issues between 5 February 1785, and 6 January 1787. This time the Edinburgh public received the essays with enthusiasm, though critics were found to complain that the *Lounger* was less lively than its predecessor. At any rate, the edition of London, 1804, is called the sixth, and there have been at least eight others since that date. Of the *Mirror* there were at least thirteen British editions before 1813; there were early American editions in 1792 and in 1793; there have been at least nine editions since 1817. And this popularity is chiefly due to Mackenzie's contributions.

If inquiry is made whether any elements of that popularity are still unwithered, the critic must use in answer the three words which run throughout both *Mirror* and *Lounger: sentiment, sensibility,* and *romantic;* for in these periodicals we find sentimentalism triumphant in the finest English short stories (tales) of the century, we find men trained in the philosophy of Hutcheson pointing out the dangers of excess in sensibility, and we find sentimentalism merging into romanticism. In all three ways the contributions of Mackenzie are notable, but supreme in the first.

'It is as the unassuming writer of tales,' wrote Leigh Hunt in the Introduction to his collection of *Classic Tales,* 'that Mackenzie has obtained just reputation. In a simple pathetic story he is never excelled, perhaps never equalled, by any British writer'. Sentimental tales were not un-known in the earlier periodicals, such as the *Spectator:* Steele, a thorough sentimentalist himself, had a special gift for the tender and tearful; John Hughes in *Spectator* no. 375 has a 'scene of distress in private life' with a heroine named Amanda who is a counterpart of Richardson's Pamela of later date. Hawkesworth's *Adventurer* (1752-4) introduces a few sentimental stories such as the *History of Melissa,* nos. 7-8. But up to 1779 there was no achievement in the English sentimental tale to compare with Marmontel's in France.

The most famous of Mackenzie's tales is a story in *Mirror,* nos. 42-4, whose complete title is: **"The effects of religion on minds of sensibility. Story of La Roche."** Mackenzie apologizes for introducing so sacred a subject as religion, but points out that here 'religion is only introduced as a feeling, not a system, as appealing to the sentiments of the heart, not to the disquisitions of the head'. He might have added that the sentimental movement had gone pretty far in Scotland toward making the first part of this definition descriptive of the country's fashionable faith. The story tells how a philosopher residing in a little French town is enabled by his hospitality and skill in physic to restore to health La Roche, a clergyman of the country best loved by every sentimental and romantic reader of 1779, Switzerland, the land of innocence and nature. Our philosopher accompanies La Roche and his beautiful daughter to their home, giving Mackenzie opportunity to describe evening service in La Roche's chapel, with Mademoiselle presenting a touching figure at the organ. La Roche explains his own religious feelings to the philosopher, comparing the religious sense with the musical faculty as skilfully as though he had read Hutcheson . . . Three years afterward the philosopher returns to Switzerland, and, learning of the approaching marriage of Mlle. La Roche, he hastens to her village, only to find that she has died of a broken heart after hearing of the death of her lover in a duel. La Roche, still firm in his pure sentiment of religion, speaks with love and trust to his flock. Afterwards the philosopher, in recalling the figure of the good Swiss pastor, 'wished that he had never doubted'.

Before publishing the tale, Mackenzie submitted it to Adam Smith, who immediately recognized in the philosopher the person of his late friend, David Hume, and said he wondered that Hume had never told him the story. Mackenzie tells this incident to show the absent-mindedness of Smith, but it may be used as evidence that the character of the philosopher is true to life and like Hume. In his own edition of the *Mirror* Mackenzie wrote a marginal comment:

> This story was purely a fiction founded only on the circumstances of Mr. David Hume's living some time in France about the period of his first publications. Yet one of his intimate friends was inclined to believe its chief circumstances true, and Dr. Beattie of Aberdeen wrote to an acquaintance here asking him the meaning of the story. 'If true,' said the Doctor's letter, 'I do not think it fair to Mr. Hume; if a fiction, I think it will not have a good effect.'

'Dear Dr. Beattie', as Johnson called him, had been anything but fair to Hume in life, and he was just the sort of person to attack a man in death, as he had done upon the death of Churchill the satirist, when Mackenzie had for once written sharply to a newspaper in rebuke of Scotland's premier prig. Beattie, whose sentimental poem of *The Minstrel* appeared in the same year with Mackenzie's **Man of Feeling,** was, for all his sentimentalism, the least representative and the least attractive Scot of his generation.

More persons than Beattie and Smith recognized in the philosopher of Mackenzie's tale the person of the great sceptic. A certain Frederick Hensler, a literary German living in London, writing to Mackenzie in 1790 about a projected translation of Mackenzie's periodical works, asks whether Hume is not the philosopher of the story. So the greatest sceptic of the Age of Reason goes down to posterity in the tale of his 'literary page' as a Man of Feeling—which, indeed, he was.

Another polished tale in the same periodical is the story of **"Louisa Venoni"** (*Mirror* 108-9). Sir Edward ———, a wealthy Englishman, suffering a bad fall while riding through a Piedmont valley, recovers at the house of old Venoni, a widower (like La Roche) with an only daughter. The Englishman wins the girl's affection, and after a first unsuccessful attempt succeeds in persuading her to elope with him. But though Louisa's virtue is vanquished, her *sense of virtue* is not overcome; she pines away in England at the thought of the father whose death she believes she has caused. One day an old man with a hand-organ gains admittance to her house; he plays a tune which her father loved, and lo! the organ-grinder holds Louisa in his arms, weeping over his daughter. Sir Edward, who has been Man of Feeling enough to repent his cruelty some time before, answers the broken old man's tears with a promise to wed his daughter and go with her to the cottage where happiness may be found. 'Again shall the pipe and the dance gladden the valley, and innocence and peace beam on the cottage of Venoni.'

The story is much like Marmontel's *Laurette,* in which the old father goes to Paris and takes his daughter home, her lover finding her later and marrying her. The idea of the hand-organ is Mackenzie's; consistently he uses the power of music to convey emotion—in all three of his novels and in these, his two best known tales.

A certain musician expressed his admiration for **"Louisa Venoni"** in such fashion that one does not know which to enjoy most—the compliment or the author's gullibility, as expressed in his annotation:

> A story altogether fictitious, without the smallest foundation or hint of fact. Yet Puppo, a very ingenious musician, leader of the Concert of Edinburgh at the time, said he knew the story to be true, and had himself been personally acquainted with Venoni. A coincidence the more singular as the very name was of my own invention, having never met with it in any Italian book or person.

A third sentimental tale which was widely popular is that of **"Father Nicholas"** (*Lounger* 82-4), 'the victim of laudable feelings perverted, of virtue betrayed, of false honour, and mistaken shame'. An old Benedictine tells the story

of his own virtuous youth, of his marriage with the fair Emilia de Santonges, and of their happy life in the country. Before the birth of their first child they go to Paris—against the desires of Emilia. There a boyhood friend, Delaserre, succeeds in corrupting St. Hubert (Father Nicholas), and introduces him to a vicious woman who ruins him financially. At last, penniless and maddened with shame, he abandons his wife; she dies, sending him a little miniature of herself with her infant son, a gift which was being painted as a surprise for her husband at the very time when he was spending his substance upon his depraved mistress.

This is the old sentimental theme of the injured wife. In some previous treatments—such as Fielding's *Amelia*—she reforms her husband and reaps the reward of patient virtue. On the contrary, though he usually preferred a happy ending, Mackenzie agreed with Addison in thinking that 'poetical justice' is by no means requisite; in this point, of course, he disagreed with the many sentimentalists who taught that virtue is rewarded always in this world. Perhaps it is because of the tragic dignity of this tale that it seems more sincere than the two previously outlined; perhaps it is because Mackenzie wrote with a definite family in mind. Speaking in the **Anecdotes** of his visit to France in 1784, when he was present at the first performance of *Figaro,* he says:

> Travelling in the *diligence de Paris,* at that time a miserable heavy and unpleasant vehicle, I preferred walking up a long ascent in the Picardy road; in the course of my walk, I came up near a very handsome villa, with a gentleman and a lady (I supposed his wife) and two or three beautiful children walking on the road near a gravel walk on which was a gate opening to the house. I was so struck with the pleasant countenances of both, not like the French, but with finer complexions and fair hair, that I could not help making a bow on passing them, and patting the head of one of the children, a beautiful boy. The gentleman welcomed my salute with a benignant smile from him and his lady. When I got to Paris and saw the frivolity and dissipation that prevailed there, I thought of the contrast of situation between this country gentleman and his charming family living on his estate in the country, and that which, if he came to Paris and joined the fashionable circle, he might naturally fall into; and thence personifying that seemingly happy pair, I wrote the story of **"Father Nicholas."**

Another tale based upon an experience much more real is that of **"Nancy Collins"** (*Mirror* 49), a poor girl whose brother enlists in the army, leaving her to wander to Edinburgh where the author meets her in St. Andrew Square but too late to save her from death by starvation and sorrow. The tale is a humanitarian plea for the families of sailors and soldiers; the heroine might be taken as just another sentimental lay-figure of the unfortunate girl from a soldier's family—though the soldier is usually her father. As a matter of fact, however, the author's annotation in his own copy of *The Mirror* states that the tale is founded upon fact, and that even the girl's name is authentic. The story, he says, 'was now published, with the addition of the military circumstances, at a period of much private as well as public exertion to recruit the Army, after the unfortunate affair of General Burgoyne'.

The danger of concluding that Mackenzie does not write with his eye on the subject is further illustrated in the story of Captain Douglas in *Mirror* no. 11, **"On Duelling,"** the tale of a man who forgave his friend for an insult committed in a moment of folly, but offered to fight any one who doubted his honour. Now the hunters of *Einflusz* would pounce upon this tale as very similar to an incident in Rousseau's *Julie, ou la Nouvelle Héloïse* and to another in Richardson's *Sir Charles Grandison*. Yet Mackenzie assures us in an annotation and in the **Anecdotes** that he heard the story in Paris, about an officer actually named Douglas.

It would be interesting to know whether there was also a basis in fact for the story of Albert Bane in *Lounger* no. 61, which is, so far as I am aware, the first romantic tale of the '45 in literature. The hero is of a type which occurs earlier in sentimental writings—the faithful servant; in this case his story is told to strengthen an appeal for kind treatment of domestics. Albert Bane, a Highland servant, is struck by his master in a hasty moment of passion, and, with a true Highlander's pride, leaves Scotland and takes service in the English army. After the battle of Culloden he saves the life of his Jacobite master, returning good for evil with the deathless loyalty of a clansman. The description of the laird's hiding-place in the hills is an anticipation of *Waverley* and *Kidnapped*. If Mackenzie's annotated edition of the *Lounger* is ever found, it will probably be discovered that this is a true story told him by Grant of Corriemonie or some other of his Jacobite friends. As it is, we have this vivid tale and the elegy in *Mirror* 85, entitled **"The Exile,"** suggested by some verses of a Jacobite refugee on an inn window at Dalnacardoch, as a double proof of Mackenzie's Highland pride in the Old Cause.

The list of Mackenzie's sentimental tales is by no means exhausted, but a sufficient idea has been given of their range and subject-matter to refute the criticism that there is nothing essentially Scottish about them. Their sentimentalism is Scottish; so are their romantic settings, and even some of their persons. Though the artistic principle of Addison and Mackenzie was to teach a lesson in manners or morals through the general and representative rather than through the specific, Mackenzie drew upon his own experience for narrative materials; if his stories seem more universal than specific, we may assume that this was exactly the effect for which he planned. Again there is illustrated the fact that though the Scot of that day was sentimental and romantic in philosophy of life, he was classical in form. No description can do justice to the classic suavity and grace of Mackenzie's style, a suavity which puzzled John Galt and was the admiration of Sir Walter Scott. It has the polish of Addison with the tenderness of Steele. Without much of genius, Mackenzie is not only intensely interesting as a representative Scottish man of letters, but he is charming as a stylist. Except for the absurd descriptions of weeping, his short tales are models of urbanity.

No better example of Mackenzie's charm can be found

than in his vignette of the Country Dowager in *Lounger* no. 87, **"Effects of rural objects on the mind,"** the number which Austin Dobson selected for his *Eighteenth Century Essays*. Here again Mackenzie draws from real life, as he informs Craig in two letters of 1796, for the dowager is none other than an aunt of Mrs. Mackenzie, Mrs. Grant of Ballandalloch, who in the year just mentioned was living in the parish of Kilmaichly. To any one who has had the privilege of knowing a Highland lady of the old school the essay still speaks with sincere eloquence. . . . (pp. 192-99)

It is the tenderest Scottish portrait before Sir Walter, and I think that it is not fantastic to discover there national traits of the country that has given us in recent years the portrait of Margaret Ogilvy. The setting, too, is at once romantic and truly Scottish, giving an American the feeling he has often experienced in Scotland of coming upon a place of such serene and noble beauty that he finds himself exclaiming, 'This is not real; this is the castle of Mackenzie's dowager or of one of Scott's lairds.'

If in his tales Mackenzie wrote from a sentimental faith, it must not be thought that he did not appreciate the dangers of excessive sensibility, particularly upon youthful minds. (p. 201)

[There] . . . is *Mirror* no. 101, entitled **"Danger of regulating our conduct by the rules of romantic sentiment,"** which begins:

> In books, whether moral or amusing, there are no passages more captivating both to the writer and the reader, than those delicate strokes of sentimental morality, which refer our actions to the determination of feeling. In these the poet, the novel writer, and the essayist have always delighted; you are not, therefore, singular, for having dedicated so much of the *Mirror* to sentiment and sensibility. I imagine however, Sir, there is much danger in pushing these qualities too far: the rules of our conduct should be founded on a basis more solid, if they are to guide us through the various situations of life: but the young enthusiast of sentiment and feeling is apt to despise those lessons of vulgar virtue and prudence, which would confine the movements of a soul formed to regulate itself by other impulses.

There follows the story of Emilia, a girl of sensibility who had a romantic friendship for Harriet. Harriet imprudently made a run-away marriage with a man who wasted all in gambling and other excesses; yet Emilia kept up her romantic attachment, and after Harriet's death, which followed closely upon a sentimental reformation in her husband, consented to marry the widower. 'I found,' says the supposed guardian of Emilia, 'that sentiment, like religion, had its superstition and its martyrdom.' At the end the moral is pointed that 'there are bounds beyond which virtuous feelings cease to be virtue; that the decisions of sentiment are subject to the control of prudence, and the ties of friendship subordinate to the obligations of duty'.

One of the most striking phenomena in sentimentalism is what Professor Babbitt calls Romantic Melancholy, and this, like Romantic Morality, is discussed by Mackenzie.

In *Mirror* no. 72 he gives us a touching picture of the funeral of a beautiful young woman—his note informs us that she was Miss Farquharson of Invercauld—a picture which is evidently intended, in his own phrase, 'to render us capable of that gentle melancholy which makes sorrow pleasant, and affliction useful'. Yet he does not pretend that melancholy emotion is any substitute for restraining principle:

> I will not pretend to assert, that rooted principles, and long-established conduct, are suddenly to be changed by the effects of situation, or the eloquence of sentiment.

Similarly Mackenzie balances the value of 'rural sentiment' with the absurdities of romantic idealization of Nature. There were probably few men of his generation who loved better what he describes in a letter as 'the still face of an evening sky' in the country, yet the country meant more to him than an opportunity for egotistic, vague reverie; it meant hunting and angling and the friendship of human beings. *Lounger* no. 97, entitled **"Effects of rural objects on the mind,"** contains some opening passages that would have pleased Wordsworth.

> There is a sort of moral use of the country which every man who has not lost the rural sentiment will feel, a certain purity of mind and imagination which its scenes inspire, a simplicity, a colouring of nature on the objects around us, which correct the artifice and interestedness of the world.

Yet this same paper ends with the portrait of the Country Dowager . . . ; and a further essay, no. 89, gives a satirical **"Account of the rural sentiment which is cultivated at the country seat of a man of fashion."**

Again, we find Romantic Pride and the Cult of Romantic Genius deplored in *Lounger* no. 66, where the author observes: 'Temper, moderation, and humility, a toleration of folly, and an attention to trifles, are endowments necessary in the commerce with mankind. . . . In many occurrences of life, genius and fancy discover evils which dullness and insensibility would escape, and delicacy of feeling mars that pleasure which thoughtless vivacity would perfectly enjoy.' This sage advice was written, it is ironical to recall, at about the time when Burns was publishing his Kilmarnock *Poems;* it would have been well for the great poet if he could have accepted a sentence at the end of the essay where Mackenzie says, 'A war with the world is generally founded upon injustice.'

Perhaps the most striking example of chastened sentimentalism appears in three essays in literary criticism, concerned with the Novel (*Lounger* no. 20), Tragedy (*Lounger* nos. 27-8), and Comedy (*Lounger* no. 50)—three *genres* about which Mackenzie could speak as a practitioner. He admits that the novel has fallen into degradation in 1785, not only in literary merit but also in morality. He will not admit that all novels are dangerous, but says:

> As promoting a certain refinement of mind, they operate like all other works of genius and feeling, and have a more immediate tendency to produce it than most others, from their treating of those very subjects which the reader will find around

him in the world, and their containing those very situations in which he himself may not improbably at some time or other be placed. . . .

> The principal danger of novels, as forming a mistaken and pernicious system of morality, seems to me to arise from that contrast between one virtue or excellence and another, that war of duties which is to be found in many of them, particularly in that species called sentimental. These have been chiefly borrowed from our neighbours the French. . . . In this rivalship of virtues and duties, those are always likely to be preferred which in truth and reason are subordinate. . . . The overstrained delicacy of the persons represented always leads them to act from the motive least obvious, and therefore generally the least reasonable.

> In the enthusiasm of sentiment there is much the same danger as in the enthusiasm of religion, of substituting certain impulses and feelings of what might be called a visionary kind, in the place of real practical duties, which in morals, as in theology, we might not improperly denominate good works. In morals, as in religion, there are not wanting instances of refined sentimentalists, who are contented with talking of virtues which they never practise, who pay in words what they owe in actions; or, what is fully as dangerous, who open their minds to impressions which never have any effect upon their conduct, but are considered as something foreign to and distinct from it. This separation of conscience from feeling is a depravity of the most pernicious sort.

> Of youth it is essential to preserve the imagination sound as well as pure, and not to allow them to forget, amidst the intricacies of sentiment, or the dreams of sensibility, the truths of reason, or the laws of principle.

Continuing a similar line of attack, he says in the essay on Tragedy that novels and theatrical compositions are calculated 'to mould the heart and the manners through the medium of the imagination';—but even of the nobler characters of tragedy, he asks, 'Does not the morality of sentiment often yield to the immorality of situation?' Suicide, for instance, is held up as the resource of virtuous affliction. 'It will be remembered, that it is not so much from what the hero says, as from what he does, that an impression is drawn.' Then too, the leading passion of modern tragedy is love, and 'every species of composition, whether narrative or dramatic, which places the only felicity of life in successful love, is unfavourable to the strength and purity of a young mind'. Furthermore, Tragedy shows the passions, that is, the weaknesses of men, and while reason condemns every sort of weakness, 'passion, enthusiasm, and sickly sensibility have dignified certain weaknesses with the name of amiable'. (Alas for the poor Man of Feeling, his creator is disowning him!)

Even in the case of high heroic virtue, Mackenzie doubts of its moral efficacy in Tragedy:

> It may be fairly doubted, whether this play of fancy, in the walks of virtue and benevolence,

does not lessen the exertion of those qualities in practice and reality. . . . In stage misfortunes, in fancied sufferings, the drapery of the figure hides its form; and real distress, coming in a homely and unornamented state, disgusts the eye, which had poured its tears over the hero of tragic misery, or the martyr of romantic woe. . . . It seems to have a tendency to weaken our mind to our own sufferings, without opening it to the sufferings of others.

Lest we ask why, then, Mackenzie himself has written novels and tragedies—a question which seems to be uncomfortably knocking at his gate, he balances the conclusions of his essay in the following fashion:

> I am not, however, insensible of the value, perhaps but too sensible of the power, of these productions of fancy and of genius. Nor am I so much a bigot to the opinions I have delivered, as to deny that there are uses, noble uses, which such productions may serve, amidst the dangers to which they sometimes expose their readers. The region of exalted virtue, of dignified sentiment, into which they transport us, may have a considerable effect in changing the cold and unfeeling temperament of worldly minds; the indifferent and the selfish may be warmed and expanded by the fiction of distress, and the eloquence of feeling. . . .
>
> But there is a certain sort of mind common in youth, and that too of the most amiable kind, tender, warm, and visionary, to which the walks of fancy and enthusiasm, of romantic love, of exaggerated sorrow, of trembling sensibility, are very unsafe. . . . In such bosoms, feeling or susceptibility must be often repressed or directed; to encourage it by premature or unnatural means, is certainly hurtful.

The essay on Comedy opens with the classical and antisentimental definition, about which Mackenzie is still sentimentalist enough to have grave doubts: 'Comedy wishes to purge vices and follies by ridiculing. In a corrupt age reason is so weak as to be obliged to call in such allies to her assistance: let her beware that they do not, like the Saxon auxiliaries of our ancestors, usurp the government which they were called to defend.' In any age it is easy to get a laugh by ridiculing not vice but reason and duty. Furthermore, 'The images which comedy presents, and the ridicule which it excites, being almost always exaggerated, their resemblance to real life is only acknowledged by those whose weaknesses they flatter—whose passions they excuse.'

The treatment of love, particularly by the contemporary stage, comes in for censure here:

> As love is the principal action, marriage is the constant end of comedy. But the marriage of comedy is generally of that sort which holds forth the worst example to the young. . . . Her marriages are the frolics of the moment.

The stage in France as well as in England has reached the point where it presents pernicious licentiousness in *Figaro* and *The School for Scandal.* Dramas of this sort arose upon the fashionable ridicule against what was called Sen-

timental Comedy. At this point Mackenzie becomes once more the sentimentalist, angered by Sheridan's satire upon the most cherished sentimental tenets; cites Menander and Terence as having written comedies of sentiment—which they certainly did not do; and ends with a weak appeal to the taste of the mob, which, of course, had remained sentimental:

> The people, indeed, are always true to virtue, and open to the impressions of virtuous sentiment; with the people, the comedies, in which these are developed, still remain favourites; and corruption must have stretched its empire far indeed, when the applauses shall cease with which they are received.

There are other examples of literary criticism in Mackenzie's essays—notably an essay on Hamlet (*Mirror* 99-100) which interprets the melancholy Dane as a Man of Feeling. Perhaps it is no exaggeration to call this the first romantic criticism of Shakespeare, a prelude to Coleridge and Hazlitt. If this description seems too complimentary, recall what Professor A. C. Bradley says in his noble study of *Shakespearean Tragedy:* 'Henry Mackenzie . . . was, it would seem, the first of our critics to feel the "indescribable charm" of Hamlet, and to divine something of Shakespeare's intention.'

Such a tribute emphasizes our paradox. Here was a man who was shrewd enough to see all the faults of a philosophy which had underlain his own literary triumph; and yet, at the moment when he was writing the clearest exposé of sentimentalism in eighteenth-century criticism, he was inaugurating romantic criticism of Shakespeare and bringing the sentimental tale to perfection! Perhaps he wanted once more to 'wring the heart' before breaking the wand which summoned tears; the *Mirror* and the *Lounger* are his farewell to sensibility.

They are also, however, his greeting to the humorous muse who was later to guide his hand in writing the **Anecdotes.** In his essay on Mackenzie, Sir Walter Scott says: 'The Northern Addison, who revived the art of periodical writing, and sketched, though with a light pencil, the follies and the lesser vices of his time, has shewed himself a master of playful satire. The historian of the Homespun family may place his narrative, without fear or shame, by the side of *The Vicar of Wakefield.*' Cowper, too, thought highly of this side of Mackenzie's talent when he wrote to Lady Hesketh on 27 November 1787, describing the Scottish author's essays as the 'work of a sensible man, who knows the world well, and has more of Addison's delicate humour than anybody'.

The subjects of Mackenzie's light satire in those essays concerned with the Homespun family (*Mirror* 12, 25, 53; *Lounger* 17, 98) are universal, though especially applicable in a Scotland which was having its first taste of wealth after centuries of poverty: the affectation of social aspiration, the vulgarity of the *nouveau riche,* the heartlessness of snobs, the comedy and tragedy of the marriage-market. Yet, as Scott intimates so delicately, the first idea of the Homespun family may have been derived from *The Vicar of Wakefield.* The daughters of an honest countryman are led into all sorts of folly by their acquaintance with

Lady———, who snubs one of them in Edinburgh, though she had been very complaisant in the country. There is some humour in the despair of the old Presbyterian father when his daughters introduce the theory that card-playing on Sunday is permissible, and when they even suggest that grave doubts exist of the soul's immortality. There is a good description, also, of a visit from the Lady.

No sooner are the women of the family cured by the snub of Lady ———, than a new source of trouble arises. Young Mushroom, son of a neighbour, comes home from India with a princely fortune, several 'negars', and a wife who worships *ton*. Here enters an opportunity for that satire upon the 'nabob' which occupies an important share of the essays. As for the Homespun family, the hoops are out again, and the family joins the pursuit of *ton*. Old Mushroom goes down to defeat, heroically fighting for his pipe and his spit-box.

Other satirical papers describe the *nouveau riche* family of Bearskin and their friends the Blubbers. Mackenzie, having himself made a Highland tour at about this time, delights in telling how the Blubbers, from London, visit the land of romance in a manner that will remind Scottish readers of the English and American tourists of to-day. Poor Blubber, he 'could not see the pleasure of always looking at the same things; hills, and wood, and water, over and over again!' 'The river here, he owned, was a pretty rural thing enough; but, for his part, he should think it much more lively if it had a few ships and lighters on it.' He found the only really good buttered toast in Scotland at Scone, where the landlord of the inn was an Englishman.

No doubt this account drew upon real experience, as was usual with Mackenzie. The well-born lawyers of Edinburgh took a special delight in making fun of the upstarts in business who could buy and sell them. Mackenzie records the fact that in his boyhood men of good families often engaged in such business as the mercer's; but from the day of the *Mirror* even to this there has been at Edinburgh a feeling among men of Mackenzie's class that a tradesman is an inferior socially, no matter what his wealth. The *Mirror* and the *Lounger* mark a revolution in social sentiment, as they are said to have done in improving manners.

And this brings up a point which can not be overstated. It has been said by critics—most of whom have obviously never read a line of what they are criticizing—that Mackenzie's periodicals are only a weak imitation of the *Spectator,* without a single Scottish characteristic but merely repeating Addison's subjects in an attempt at Addison's style. Mackenzie had foreseen the charge of plagiarism, and had answered it after his own bland fashion in *Mirror* no. 96, a supposed letter from a certain 'Evelina':

> I am one of a family of young ladies, who read your paper, with which we have hitherto been tolerably well pleased, though we could wish it were not quite so grave, and had a little more love in it. But we have found out, of late, that it is none of your own, but mostly borrowed from other people. A cousin of ours, who is himself a fine scholar, and has a great acquaintance among the critics, shewed us many different instances of this. Your first paper, he told us, was copied from the first paper of the Spectator; and upon looking into both, we found them exactly the same, all about the author and the work from beginning to end. Your Umphraville, he said, was just Sir Roger de Coverley; which we perfectly agreed in, except that my sister Betsy observed, Umphraville wanted the widow, which all of us think the very best part of Sir Roger. . . . No. 72, which we thought a very sweet paper, he informed us was taken from the 'Night Thoughts'; and, indeed, though we don't understand Latin, we saw plainly, that the mottoes were the same to a T. All this, however, we might have overlooked, had not a gentleman, who called here this morning, who used formerly to be a great advocate for the *Mirror,* confessed to us, that our cousin's intelligence was literally true; and, more than all that, he told us, that your very last number was to be found, every word of it, in Johnson's Dictionary.

As a matter of fact, Mr. Umphraville *is* of the type represented by Sir Roger de Coverley, inasmuch as he is a country gentleman with chivalrous ideals; it is equally true that he has some of the sentimental traits of Goldsmith's Man in Black, as illustrated for instance in his reasons for retirement: 'A man of aspiring mind and nice sensibility may, from a wrong direction, or a romantic excess of spirit, find it difficult to submit to the ordinary pursuits of life.' And he is fundamentally a Man of Feeling. If his character does not stand out distinctly, there is sufficient reason given by Mackenzie himself in his manuscript annotation to *Mirror* no. 19:

> Sent in a blank cover, and a feigned hand, by Craig, to Creech's shop, and soon after read at a meeting of the Society. But McLeod, tho' he gave much praise to the supposed communication in general, thought it derogatory to the character of his *Umphraville,* and altered it, much for the worse, to what it is at present.

> The history of this paper may, in a great measure, apologize for a defect which has been often found in *The Mirror,* that the character of Umphraville, tho' well laid down in no. 6, was never afterwards properly filled up or supported. The truth was that McLeod felt for Umphraville a sort of paternal affection that would not suffer his weak side to be at all exhibited; hence none of the other writers of *The Mirror* were at liberty to bring out these corners of the character without which it was impossible to give a striking portrait. The pencil therefore of whoever attempted to fill up his picture could only trace some feeble features, and mark them with but languid colouring.

Very similar to the character of Umphraville in the *Mirror* is that of Colonel Caustic in the *Lounger,* but drawn with sharper pencil and effectively enough to win Scott's high praise. Though the Colonel is the type of the *laudator temporis acti,* he is somewhat individualized by being given sentimental traits of romantic irony which are explained in no. 32:

> The lover of mankind, as his own sense of virtue has painted them, when he comes abroad into life, and sees what they really are, feels the disappointment in the severest manner.

So this is another chivalrous, kind, sentimental Man of Feeling—just such a man as could have been found at any Edinburgh Assembly in 1785. It certainly is not necessary to go back to Addison and Goldsmith to find the original; the type has always existed, more delightfully in Scotland, perhaps, than in any other country.

In addition to the borrowing of characters, it has been charged that Mackenzie and his fellows also borrowed subjects from such predecessors as the authors of the *Spectator.* The moles of literature have published neat little parallel columns of topics; any one who can read English could tabulate within a few hours about fifty of such cases. But similarity of topic does not prove plagiarism of treatment. (pp. 202-12)

One type of essay which even the most scornful critic has not condemned is the biographical and critical notice of a Scottish writer—such as Craig's essay on Michael Bruce (*Mirror,* 36), which paved the way for Robert Burns, and Mackenzie's own masterpiece, *Lounger* no. 97, which established in his capital the fame of Scotland's greatest poet. If the Addison of the North had written nothing else, he would always be remembered with gratitude and honour for that service; if the *Mirror* and *Lounger* had done nothing else, they would have been justified in preparing Edinburgh for the 'heaven-taught ploughman' who strode past Creech's shop and up to the Lawnmarket on that November day in 1786 when Scotland's bard came to his triumph. (pp. 212-13)

> *Harold William Thompson, in his* A Scottish Man of Feeling: Some Account of Henry Mackenzie, Esq. of Edinburgh and of the Golden Age of Burns and Scott, *Oxford University Press, London, 1931, 463 p.*

Edmund Blunden   (essay date 1931)

[*Blunden was an early twentieth-century English poet, critic, and essayist. He was associated with the Georgians, a group of poets who reacted against the prevalent mood of disillusionment and the rise of artistic modernism and who advocated a return to the pastoral nineteenth-century poetic traditions represented by William Wordsworth. In the following excerpt, Blunden provides a brief overview of Mackenzie's literary career, generally focusing on* The Man of Feeling *as the author's most creative endeavor.*]

Henry Mackenzie, . . . received in his well-trained youth the impulse to be elegiac about life. It was an alluring exercise of the fancy, a dreaming indulgence which did not prevent him from cultivating the society of gifted men and taking notes of the human comedy with a zest and ripeness seldom exceeded. Pleased with the graces of being vicariously in disgrace with fortune and men's eyes, he liked himself well in material existence among the celebrities of Edinburgh; was "as alert as a contracting tailor's needle in every sort of business"; had an insight into the process

and circumstance of most things that were happening in Scotland. The author of the *Man of Feeling* was in fact a man of sense, who, passing through the phase of sensibility, had the detachment to see that here was means for a charming sympathetic memoir of one whose life could be all contained in that phase. Publishing it in 1771, he made his name; he came three years after Sterne with the *Sentimental Journey,* which he attempted to echo in uncommon strokes of pause and rhythm, to equal for touches of profound meaning and suppressed but encyclopædic sighs, and to excel for decorum of morals. (pp. 186-87)

Mr. Hamish Miles, whose investigation and critical sincerity afford us real aid, in the essay accompanying the latest edition of the *Man of Feeling,* protests that the book is loosely constructed. It is, but I doubt if that looseness is not part of Mackenzie's specification. "One Harley" is the hero, and his life is subject to the cold blasts of bad luck which are capricious and at last make "a thing of shreds and patches." Succinctness and starting tears are not congenial. It is the failure in episode which causes many modern novels to wear their fatal appearance of being concocted. The *Man of Feeling* is a set of episodes, purporting to be from an "imperfect manuscript," for even after death the wind and weather play carelessly with the worn equipment of the sensitive Harley. This is explained to us with great ease and brevity by Mackenzie in his preliminary chapter, which has the merit too of being a picture. "My dog," he begins, "had made a point on a piece of fallow ground, and led the curate and me two or three hundred yards over that and some stubble adjoining, on a burning first of September." It was the dog's mistake; the sportsmen took a rest, in the shadow of a solemn old house, and the curate mentioned the whimsical character of "one Harley," who formerly lived there, but "went nobody knows whither." Moreover, the curate spoke of "a bundle of papers, which was brought to me by his landlord. . . ." " 'I should be glad to see this medley,' said I. 'You shall see it now,' answered the curate, 'for I always take it along with me a-shooting. 'How came it so torn?' ''Tis excellent wadding,' said the curate."

Another principle at work in this good book is quickly stated—"a certain respect for the follies of mankind." Harley, no doubt, is a fool in the sense that he allowed his normal faculties to be tripped up by his ideals. Old Peter, the family "bodyguard," who sees him leave the home of his youth, is a fool, observing, "My dear master, I have been told as how London is a sad place"; but it is at this very point that the true thrill of "feeling" is attainable, and the vigilant Mackenzie continues, "He was choked at the thought, and his benediction could not be heard: but it shall be heard, honest Peter! where these tears will add to its energy." Or again, with a more remarkable fineness and less of Sterne infused:

> He was buried in the place he had desired. It was shaded by an old tree, the only one in the churchyard. . . . The last time we passed there, methought he looked wistfully on the tree; there was a branch of it, that bent towards us, waving in the wind; he waved his hand, as if he mimicked its motion. There was something predictive in his look; perhaps it is foolish to remark

it; but there are times and places when I am a child at those things.

Since in this novel Mackenzie reveals by many signs and some quotations the lineage of his *Man of Feeling* from *King Lear,* it is in keeping to sum up his kind of character-study of persons ill-adapted for life, and commonly graded as fools, in Kent's deep admonition, "Not altogether fool, my lord."

Admit this concern with and knowledge of other-worldliness; diversify it with sketches of man in hard necessities and crude successes, usually accompanied by a dog very much of the same mind; bring in several descriptions of landscape, clear and bright; add a gift for perceiving truths even at two removes from their outwalls, and for summing up the evidences of careful observation. These resources supply the *Man of Feeling* and are enough to explain its instant and long-continued triumph. . . . It is not difficult to smile at the convulsive style of the most exacting passages, nor will the tears flow to-day in time with all of Harley's; but the whole book was a creative feat. In the sequel, *The Man of the World,* Mackenzie shows the same gifts, but becomes more deliberate and labours his expression, while his plot is at once more complicated and complete. This heavier novel failed to travel on with the other, though it shared the public interest for about thirty years.

The miscellaneous writings of Mackenzie—political items, essays, poems, memoirs, dramas—are touched upon by Mr. Miles, but will hardly be sought with great perseverance. By far the best, and the chief exception to that impression, is the volume of *Anecdotes and Egotisms,* so ably edited and published recently by Mr. H. W. Thompson. There one gazes on the Henry Mackenzie who knew the world so much better than his villain, Sir Thomas Sindall, in *The Man of the World;* a master of poised experience, ever inquiring, never inquisitive; the historian of a great range of men and manners. Among his Addisonian exercises, so largely responsible for the popularity of the *Mirror* and the *Lounger,* the tint of eternity gleams naturally from the eulogy of Burns dated December 9, 1786, yet rather because of the subject—"this Heaven-taught ploughman"—than the vivacity of the criticism. For intrinsic rather than reflected excellence, the *Lounger* can yield more attractive examples of Mackenzie's prose. There are two sketches of rural life, one "pleasant," the other "unpleasant," beautifully precise and pictorial. In another paper he gives his views—he had certainly won the right to give them—on the novel, and on the sentimental novel in particular. By this paper it will appear that he did not care for his Man of Feeling to be perverted into an egotist of introspective illusions or for his character to be misconstrued accordingly.

> That creation of refined and subtle feeling, reared by the authors of the works to which I allude, has an ill-effect, not only on our ideas of virtue, but also on our estimate of happiness. That sickly sort of refinement creates imaginary evils and distresses, and imaginary blessings and enjoyments, which embitter the common disappointments, and depreciate the common attainments of life.

There was enough sturdy health in the *Man of Feeling* to save it from its author's recantation, to attract the spirit and educate the style of Charles Lamb, whose *Rosamund Gray* is one of Mackenzie's indirect triumphs, and to show us still the various strength, colour, and movement necessary to an enduring novel. (pp. 187-90)

> *Edmund Blunden, "Henry Mackenzie," in his* Votive Tablets: Studies Chiefly Appreciative of English Authors and Books, *Cobden-Sanderson, 1931, pp. 186-90.*

Dale Kramer   (essay date 1964)

[*In the essay below, Kramer contends that Mackenzie's* Man of Feeling *represents an ideal model for illustrating theories of education consistent with the eighteenth-century sentimental tradition.*]

Most critics believe that MacKenzie's *The Man of Feeling* is a flaccidly organized and semi-picaresque imitation of Laurence Sterne's *Tristram Shandy* and *Sentimental Journey.* One of the most recent editors of the novel says that it has "small plot development" [Kenneth C. Slagle, in a 1958 edition]. But while one cannot deny the episodic nature of the plot, it is a mistake to say that the structure of *The Man of Feeling* lacks development and unity. Moreover, its unity does not derive merely from a picaresque leading character who is associated with all of the events. Henry Mackenzie's short novel is by no means a world masterpiece, but the manner in which it depicts the theories of education of the eighteenth century sentimental tradition, of which it is one of the purest manifestations in English fiction, makes it worthy of investigation. This aspect of its importance as a cultural artifact has not, I believe, been previously noted.

The novel portrays a hero, Mr. Harley, whose intellectual and moral development is determined by the adventures which befall him. In other words, its structure is thematically organized around the education of the hero, a not unusual subject for fiction and one which indicates that this bathetic novel is not as much an artistic monstrosity as is implied in the criticism concentrating only on its tearfulness. "Education" can mean several things; for the sentimentalists, education was the process of receiving and assimilating influences or experiences into one's mental and emotional attitudes toward living.

Harley's education has two stages, the first occurring before the novel proper begins. The earliest education which Harley has received is in keeping with sentimental philosophy; and the education he receives in the course of the novel reveals to him man's situation in a world contemptuous of the fine ideals of sentimental thought. The sentimentalists averred that these two stages of education are at odds—and that, therefore, a sentimentalist should eschew the world as completely as possible. Harley's life and fate are proof of Mackenzie's grasp of the sentimental dilemma.

The ideal education according to the sentimentalists lay simply in letting one's natural virtues develop: the closer one approaches to the state of primitive nature, the better are his chances of being virtuous. The natural and ultimate result of this idea is the theory of the Noble Savage, whose widest known propagandist is Jean Jacques Rousseau, although the idea had appeared previously in English literature in Aphra Behn's *Oroonoko* and John Shebbeare's *Lydia.* The sentimentalists felt also that society is a corrupting influence that blunts tendencies toward natural goodness. "The first impulses of Nature are always right. . . . Reason, [Rousseau] says, is a late growth in the child, to be perfected through feeling; when the age of reason arrives, the child is to be shown that man is by nature good but has been perverted by society." [Harold William Thompson]

The foundation of the sentimentalist theory of education, then, was the primacy of the feelings over the mind. That Henry Mackenzie held this idea is certain. In *The Man of the World,* published shortly after *The Man of Feeling,* the widower Annesly does give his children instruction in the classics, but he is more concerned with morality, and this he teaches them not so much intellectually as emotionally: "It was his maxim, that the heart must feel, as well as the judgment be convinced, before the principles we mean to teach can be of habitual service." In *The Man of Feeling,* Edward Sedley offers advice of the same sort to Harley. Sedley says:

> But as to the higher part of education, Mr. Harley, the culture of the mind—let the feelings be awakened, let the heart be brought forward to its object, placed in the light in which nature would have it stand, and its decisions will ever be just. The world
>
> Will smile, and smile, and be a villain;
>
> and the youth, who does not suspect its deceit, will be content to smile with it. His teachers will put on the most forbidding aspect in nature, and tell him of the beauty of virtue.

These preliminary statements are essential to an understanding of Harley, the hero of *The Man of Feeling.* Orphaned as a boy, Harley acquired by his father's will many guardians, who could not decide on a single plan of education for him. As a result, he was early taken from his boarding school, and his later learning was undisturbed by academic and social requirements. True, his reading was guided on occasion by a country parson in whose parish Harley lived, but his sensibilities were developed naturally—which means, according to sentimental theory, through close contact with nature and by not having had his natural goodness corrupted by an artificially trained moral instructor. Harley has thereby accidentally received an ideal sentimental education; he is thus an appropriate character for Mackenzie to exhibit experiencing the seamier aspects of life which the sentimentalists saw to be the inevitable accompaniments of imperfect social institutions.

Education does not cease with physical maturity, and what Mackenzie delineates seriously in *The Man of Feeling* is the educative effect of adult experiences. Harley is not himself corrupted by these experiences, but seeing the corrupt moral state of society and the impossibility of distinguishing trustworthy virtue weakens Harley's psychic

fibre. In so delineating Harley's initiation into the scabrous "truth" about earthly existence, Mackenzie disregards, as has been frequently noted, surface relationships of incident. Few of the events seem to be causally connected. Mackenzie, exploring his subject *via* an emotional approach, wants his readers to weep; and his theory—according to one critic, at least—was that "succinctness and starting tears are not congenial" [*Times Literary Supplement* (9 August 1928)].

But even though Mackenzie intentionally obscures the order of events, an order is present; and clarity in critical explanation requires that the schema be identified. The following divisions of important phases in Harley's education are arbitrary, but their helpfulness in clarifying the discussion of the subtle changes in Harley justifies their use.

1.	XI - XIII	—preparation and explanation
2.	XIV - XXVII	—London experiences
3.	XXVIII - XXIX	—tales by the prostitute and her father
4.	XXIX - XXXIII	—recognition of evil in society by Harley
5.	XXXIV - XXXVI	—Edwards' tale
6.	"A Fragment" X— "The Pupil"	—reaffirmation, and loss of, faith
7.	LV - "Conclusion"	—death of Harley

The initial section is the most conventional in style and purpose. In it Mackenzie establishes the character of Harley. Although sensitive, Harley is not a thoughtless, effeminate weeper. In the first chapter (numbered XI), he is compared to philosophers and poets who are thought unworldly or unmanly because they are not interested in "power, wealth, or grandeur"; and his bashfulness is not "the awkwardness of a booby, which a few steps into the world will convert into the pertness of a coxcomb; [but] a consciousness, which the most delicate feelings produce, and the most extensive knowledge cannot always remove" (XI). Also, he lacks a "certain respect for the follies of mankind," a respect which awards regard to fools who have unworthily obtained wealth and position (XII). Harley's apparent ineffectualness, then, stems not from a want of knowledge, but from a possession of "a delicate consciousness of propriety," of what *should* be right (XIII).

Harley's experiences in London in the second section show him to be trusting and impressionable. He readily accepts things as they are first represented to him, even though he may rapidly change his opinions upon receiving new information. All of his actions are consistent with sentimental belief: his first approval of the pretentious young man turns into virtuous disgust when he learns that the young man is a pimp and a fop. Without hesitation Harley gives his last half-guinea to a prostitute so she will not lose her lodgings, and he pawns his watch to buy her a meal.

These London experiences have a great deal of pertinence. All of Harley's acquaintances, from the beggar to the gentleman cardsharp, force him to interpret illusion. The pimp and the cardsharp first appear to be virtuous, but are evil. The prostitute appears to be evil, but is actually penitent. Also, Harley receives theoretical instruction in this matter of appearances. The beggar says that lying is necessary in the world; one of the occupants of the madhouse reflects that the world is a madhouse; Harley himself notes that human passions are temporary madnesses; and a misanthrope bitterly offers sentimental doctrine heavily colored by cynicism.

The third section, which contains the stories of the prostitute and her father, provides material for two observations relevant to this study. Harley's experiences in the second section have not yet significantly affected his outlook. Although he is temporarily hesitant to keep the appointment at the prostitute's chambers on the morning after he has aided her, he decides quickly that "to calculate the chances of deception is too tedious a business for the life of man!" The second observation is that the prostitute's ruin had stemmed from an incorrect education. Her widower father had brought her up to think more of fashionable honor than of Christian virtues, and the novels of society she had read as a young girl did not provide good examples for conduct (XXVIII). Of course, the implicit contrast with her miseducation is Harley's study of Nature. That her seducer is a man of sentiment foreshadows Harley's ultimate disillusion with the possibility of basing his earthly life on sentimental principles.

The point of separation between sections three and four of the arbitrary divisioning occurs in the middle of a chapter. This emphasizes the fact that for several successive pages in the fourth section, Harley dispassionately comments upon the sentimentalist position, and he consolidates his "education by experience" in London into his views. Without having changed his initial opinion of the efficacy of benevolence and of the innate worth of sensibility, Harley counsels the prostitute's father—who is distressed and broken from thinking about his daughter's disgrace—not to be ruled by the world's opinion:

> The world is ever tyrannical; it warps our sorrows to edge them with keener affliction. Let us not be slaves to the names it affixes to motive or to action. I know an ingenuous mind cannot help feeling when they sting. But there are considerations by which it may be overcome. Its fantastic ideas vanish as they rise; they teach us to look beyond it. (XXIX)

This recognition that the world disregards sensibility is Harley's first step toward his disenchantment with life. The recognition is echoed in this section in a slightly different manner on the stage bound homeward from London. Harley and a fellow-traveller discuss how poetry's effect of "enlarging the heart" and reducing depravity is an argument against its fitness as a guide for behavior in the "real" world (XXXIII).

The characterization of Harley is significant enough to re-

state here. The author is insistent all along that Harley is masculine even if he does have finely tuned sensibilities. Harley's awareness of the situation of the Man of Feeling in the world does not depress him, and he is still able to act forcefully. On the way to London, he had briskly refused a beggar's offer to tell his fortune; he had faced steadfastly the fury of Colonel Atkins, the prostitute's father, who mistook Harley to be his daughter's seducer; and on the stage-ride home, he silences an offensive young officer. But his ability to act effectively is decreasing, as is shown in the fifth section, which contains old Edwards' tale. Midway in the story of persecution by landlords, by justices of the peace, and by military disciplinarians, Harley temporarily loses his ability to differentiate between the idea and the corporality; and he snatches Edwards' sword in order to battle the phantoms of evil. This is the first scene in which Harley's behavior is absurd, but it is the tragic absurdity of dissociation, not the ridiculous absurdity of fantastical imaginings. The evil is all too genuine, even if not material.

Edwards' tale, like those of the prostitute and her father, ostensibly is more sentimentally lachrymose than sentimentally educative. But Edwards' woes and his tales of English brutality in India impress Harley with the cruel power of officialdom, which by its very function as the bulwark of an ordered society is not liable to personal and fastidious feelings. Also important is the suggestion that Harley feels unhappy in the world; he says that he was "infinitely more blest" in childhood than he will ever be again (XXXV), a statement indicating both Harley's disillusion and the long-range ineffectiveness of education of the heart in a society whose feelings are encrusted with selfishness.

The greatest amount of modification in Harley's viewpoints comes in the sixth section, and the result of that modification is revealed in the seventh and last section. Harley's position in the first part of this section is much the same as it had been earlier when he gave advice to the prostitute's father: refusal to pay overmuch attention to the world's opinions. Edwards has just told Harley of the exploitation of India by its English governors and has lamented that there are few men like Harley, whose sentiments would not tolerate legal thievery. But despite the continual empirical challenges, Harley restates his stubborn if diminished faith in ultimate benevolence in his conversation with Edwards:

> [H]owever the general current of opinion may point, the feelings are not yet lost that applaud benevolence, and censure inhumanity. Let us endeavour to strengthen them in ourselves; and we, who live sequestered from the noise of the multitude, have better opportunities of listening undisturbed to their voice. ("A Fragment" II)

Although his philosophy has become nearly that of a hermit's, it is more optimistic, since he implies that private feelings of benevolence may provide a standard of approval which will encourage virtue in those less inherently susceptive. Harley also suggests here that these feelings can be indulged in individually for one's own good.

But Harley's horizons have been continually narrowing.

The confidence in universal sentiment with which he went to London has been reduced to the belief that only on the level of the individual can sentiment be successfully refined and recognized. Yet, however reduced in applicability his ideas have become, he still believes that one man of sentiment can recognize and trust another man of sentiment, as is clear in his statement to Edwards just quoted. This recognition of sentiment by one's emotional peers is important to Harley, and to the sentimentalists. The cynic whom Harley had met in London, who had been a sentimentalist before being jilted, expresses this idea of the recognition of sentiment in the form of a stricture against vanity. Although his speech is satirical and cynical, it is nevertheless appropriate in attesting to the importance of the "discovery" of fine sentiments:

> With vanity your [the sentimentalists'] best virtues are grossly tainted: your benevolence, which ye deduce immediately from the natural impulse of the heart, squints to it for its reward. There are some, indeed, who tell us of the satisfaction which flows from a secret consciousness of good actions: this secret satisfaction is truly excellent—when we have some friend to whom we may discover its excellence. (XXI)

Harley, then, still believes at the beginning of the sixth section in a "community of sentimentalists." The destruction of this belief—and ultimately of Harley's ability to survive—comes in the latter part of the section in a conversation with Edward Sedley, a former man of sentiment now grown old, who recounts to Harley a youthful experience in Milan. Sedley had made a socially brilliant acquaintance, young Respino, who seemed to have great susceptibility of heart. But Sedley's tutor told Sedley the truth about Respino: Respino had imprisoned for debt the husband of a woman for whom he had a "criminal passion." The outraged Sedley paid the husband's debt and broke off his friendship with Respino; but his tutor told him that despite Respino's baseness he would still be admired by the world as a *"man of honor"* [tutor's emphasis] ("The Pupil"). Harley reexperiences Sedley's horrified response. One might think that Edward Sedley's experience with Respino could not affect Harley, since Sedley and Harley are two different people. But actually they are the same personality: the Man of Feeling. Sedley appears nowhere else in the novel. In the picaresque framework of the novel, Sedley's adventures in Italy add an exotic travelogue flavor to Harley's domestic English adventures. In much the same manner, Edwards' travails in India had expanded Harley's social awareness.

In the final section of the arbitrary divisioning, Harley dies. He contracts a fever while nursing Edwards, and he lacks both the courage and the desire to recover. The tale of Respino's duplicity has shattered all that remained of Harley's confidence. To all evidence, even another sentimentalist is but a worldling in disguise. If one cannot trust fineness of sentiment, what can one trust?

The question might be asked with more seriousness in a more serious novel. Still, Mackenzie and Harley ask it, and Harley's answer is logical in the light of his education. Before his swooning death in the arms of Miss Walton, Harley resolves for himself the duplicity of appearance-

reality by completely rejecting the physical world. First he says:

> This world . . . was a scene in which I never much delighted. I was not formed for the bustle of the busy, nor the dissipation of the gay; a thousand things occurred, where I blushed for the impropriety of my conduct when I thought on the world, though my reason told me I should have blushed to have done otherwise.—It was a scene of dissimulation, of restraint, of disappointment. I leave it to enter on that state which I have learned to believe is replete with the genuine happiness attendant upon virtue. (LV)

A sentimentalist to the end, Harley believes in goodness still; but he no longer expects to find it on earth. Mackenzie has rarefied the theory of the Noble Savage. Harley turns at this point from sentimental realism to sentimental idealism:

> There are some feelings which perhaps are too tender to be suffered by the world. The world is in general selfish, interested, and unthinking, and throws the imputation of romance or melancholy on every temper more susceptible than its own. I cannot think but in those regions which I contemplate, if there is any thing of mortality left about us, that these feelings will subsist;— they are called,—perhaps they are—weaknesses here;—but there may be some better modifications of them in heaven, which may deserve the name of virtues. (LV)

This analysis of the unity of ***The Man of Feeling*** may seem a bit ponderous at times, especially when the lightness of the material, the bathos of the style, and the questionable profundity of the total product are considered. Mackenzie was primarily concerned, it cannot be questioned, with producing tears. But, an intelligent man, he also used the novel to discuss what interested him as an enthusiastic sentimentalist and to illustrate what witnessing the world's rapacity might do to a man of refined sentiments.

The progressive effect of these experiences gives unity to the novel's structure. Admittedly, the unity is not completely satisfactory. As an artist, Mackenzie faced the difficulty of incorporating both emotional incidents and serious ideas in a plot whimsically filled with structural oddities and narrative gaps. Moreover, Mackenzie lacked the ability or the insight to interfuse intellectual awareness and moral courage in one character. Harley's courage is highest when he is ignorant and it is lowest when he comprehends fully that life must be a continual disappointment for a sentimentalist. But Mackenzie was inherently restricted by his adherence to the sentimentalist tradition, which gloried in a belief that natural goodness had no efficacy in the tainted world in which its proponents lived. (pp. 191-99)

> *Dale Kramer, "The Structural Unity of 'The Man of Feeling',"* in *Studies in Short Fiction, Vol. 1, No. 3, Spring, 1964, pp. 191-99.*

David G. Spencer   (essay date 1967)

[*In the following excerpt, Spencer examines Macken-*

zie's sentimental philosophy in The Man of Feeling *and* The Man of the World, *noting that his writing style is tempered with reason and practicality.*]

The neatly categorical mind has long since placed Henry Mackenzie at the bottom of the lake of tears shed by his sentimental characters. This paper nevertheless hopes to show that his novels, especially his first two, were expressions of his own philosophy, and that there is a clear-cut philosophical pattern visible in them. To illustrate that thesis, the paper will present some current judgments of Mackenzie, will examine briefly the philosophical milieu from which he took his beliefs, and will analyze his novels as examples of these beliefs.

It has become a critical cliché to remark that the works of Henry Mackenzie are sharply separated from the beliefs of the man himself; critics generally suggest that he wrote these tales for his own amusement and to conform to the prevailing taste for the gentle tear. In Mackenzie's time, hundreds of people were disappointed that he showed none of the sentimentality of Harley, the hero of *The Man of Feeling*. Even his wife was led to say, "Oh, Harry, Harry, your feeling is only on paper." Today critics still perceive the difference between the two, but they also fail to distinguish between the two philosophies in Mackenzie's work—the philosophy of the hero, and that of Mackenzie. With Ernest Baker [in his *The History of the English Novel*, Vol. V], they stress that Mackenzie was a hard-headed Scot who must have been amusing himself with "fairytales of superfine sensibility." They jest with Harold Thompson about the superfluity of tears:

> One is not annoyed that a single crow croaks over the ruins of Harley's home, but it is a little too much when old Peter, the faithful servant, mournfully shakes the solitary lock that hangs on either side of his head; baldness is too serious a matter to be made a subject for snivelling. [*A Scottish Man of Feeling*, 1939]

Or they may say with Hamish Miles:

> Mackenzie was healthy in body and in mind, a young man of talent who, in his character of Harley, was projecting not an image of himself, but merely his adaptation of a new literary mood . . . the weakness of *The Man of Feeling* is that its pages so seldom glow with the warmth of real personal experience. Those admirers of the sensitive Harley who hopefully visited the Edinburgh drawing-rooms and were confronted by the "kiln-dried" Mr. Mackenzie had been deceived by the purely literary surface. [Introduction to a 1928 edition of *The Man of Feeling*]

The peculiar thing is that having gone thus far, they fail to go a bit farther. Had they done so, they might have seen not only that Mackenzie is not Harley but that Mackenzie is fully aware of the futility of such a character in the world in which he existed; that Mackenzie's novels are moral sermons; and that they do exemplify a philosophy with which Mackenzie was in full accord.

The philosophy of Mackenzie and the philosophy expressed in his first two books, *The Man of Feeling* (1771) and *The Man of the World* (1773), are identical. His phi-

losophy is simply that to adjust to the world one needs an empathic heart, a sympathetic heart, but one needs also a large measure of common sense. In an Utopian world one would only have to respond to the urgings of his sympathetic heart, but in this real world such a person would be overthrown, betrayed like Harley by the strength of his feelings. Obviously this is a philosophy which does not reject tears, for it regards them as the natural response of the heart to a situation in which the emotions have been involved. Nor does it reject that sympathy with mankind which the philosophers of this period stress; indeed, Mackenzie's philosophy seems to have derived rather directly from that of Adam Smith, for whom sympathy *was* the moral sense.

Before one examines the genesis of Mackenzie's beliefs in the philosophy of his day, he should define two terms which are of importance here: sensibility and sentimentalism. (pp. 314-15)

Briefly . . . the word "sentimental" or the concept "sentimentalism" implies in the realm of moral and aesthetic judgments the primacy of emotion, and a divinely implanted moral sense or feeling which acts instinctively. It was this sense which gave man the ability to exist in a society of human beings.

This concept is channeled into two streams in Mackenzie's works: toward an idealization of "sentiment" in *The Man of Feeling* (and a realization of its incompatibility with real life) and toward a demonstration of what man's practical conduct should be in *The Man of the World*. Mackenzie's life may be reconciled with his works if one remembers that they are the reasonable sentimentalist's answer to the exigencies of life. (p. 316)

The Man of Feeling is not really a novel, but a series of tableaus, with little if any linear development of plot; the plot might, if anything, be called circular. There is no long consistent narrative, and the style at first glance appears to be influenced by Sterne; it is distinctly episodic. The only apparent unifying principle is the fact that all the episodes depict some phase of the reaction of a true man of feeling to life as it is. Mackenzie himself said of the organization: "I found it a difficult task to reduce them [papers] into narrative, because they are made up of *Sentiment*, which narrative would destroy." His deprecation of narrative would seem to indicate Mackenzie's belief that the sentimental view of life is not necessarily an organized one. Perhaps, then, the unifying element in the novel is the imagination of the reader, who is called on to take a dual point of view: a sympathy with Harley's predicament (and a condemnation of the world), and a realization that at present the ideal is incapable of achievement. Mackenzie wrote in a letter to his cousin, Miss Betty Rose of Kilravock:

> You will remember that I have made myself accountable for chapters and fragments of chapters; the curate must answer for the rest: besides, from the general scope of the performance, which that gentleman informed you might be as well called a *sermon* as a history, you would find the hero's story, even if it were finished, and I were to send it to you entire, simple to excess;

for I would have it be *as different from the entanglement of a novel as can be.* Yet I would not be understood to undervalue that species of writing; on the contrary, I take it to be much more important, and indeed more difficult than I believe is generally imagined by the authors; which is perhaps the reason why we have so many novels and so few good ones.

His further letters to his cousin, concerning the genesis of **The Man of Feeling,** bear out his serious purpose in composing the work and his conception of it as a device for teaching—bear out indeed that it is not mere affectation:

> I have seldom been in use to write any prose, except what consisted of observations . . . on men and manners. The way of introducing these by narrative, I had fallen into some detached essays, from the notion of its interesting both the memory and the affections deeper than mere argument or moral reasoning. In this way I was somehow led to think of introducing a man of sensibility into different scenes where his feelings might be seen in their effects, and his sentiments occasionally delivered without the stifness of regular deduction.

In other words, this is an argument for the use of fiction as an instrument of moral instruction. The book was to be simple, "as different from the entanglement of a novel as can be," and, as Mackenzie wrote to Elphinstone, it was to be "uniformly subservient to the cause of Virtue."

The story begins with the discovery of a manuscript, which device is to be found in all of Mackenzie's novels. This bundle of papers is given to the author by the curate of the parish and is the history of one Harley, a grave, "oddish" kind of man. Unfortunately, the curate has been using it for gun wadding, which will presently account, according to the author, for the patchwork nature of the tale.

The narrative may be divided into five parts, each reflecting Harley's reaction to the world as it is—a reaction that Mackenzie can sympathize with but cannot espouse. This reaction arises in every case from Harley's basic nature, which partakes of that kind of bashfulness which is "consciousness, which the most delicate feelings produce, and the most extensive knowledge cannot always remove." In part, he answers to the description of the Vicar of Wakefield: "He loved all mankind; for fortune prevented him from knowing that there were rascals." Moreover, he is an equalitarian and a primitivist—holding views which Mackenzie shared in part.

As a consequence of his views, Harley lacks a "certain respect for the follies of mankind" which emphasizes his alienation from this world. Since he is his own master, he is free to follow nature in the development of his mind and heart—a laudable course, but one which brings him to much grief.

In order to view the eighteenth century, the hero must naturally see London, and, as he leaves, he bids farewell to his love, Miss Walton. He is ideal man; she is no less the ideal woman. She is virtuous, beneficent, sentimental, humane, and her conversation is "without the smallest affectation of learning," ever a goodly thing in woman. Passing

from that ideal, Harley leaves his friends in a flood of tears, thinking it no harm to give free rein to his feelings.

Inevitably he is fooled harshly in London, and his natural simplicity is fully exploited by the London pimps and cardsharpers. Harley has previously prided himself on his ability to judge character, but two pieces of advice given to him by friends might well represent the practical Mackenzie's thoughts on the subject: "all is not gold that glisters," and "as for faces, you may look into them to know, whether a man's nose be a long or a short one." Of course, Harley's fault was that of any perfect man of sentiment; he took all men to be as honest as he. The same may be said of a fool, but Mackenzie leaves the reader to draw that analogy for himself. Moreover, a leavening of common sense in Harley's early training would have helped:

> Though I am not of opinion with some wise men, that the existence of objects depends on idea; yet, I am convinced, that their appearance is not a little influenced by it. The optics of some minds are in so unlucky a perspective, as to throw a certain shade on every picture that is presented to them; while those of others (of which number was Harley), like the mirrors of the ladies, have a wonderful effect in bettering their complexions.

Other sides of Harley's character are seen as he relieves beggars and rescues a harlot. In these actions the uncalculating goodness of the man of sentiment is seen. But one part—the encounter with the misanthrope—perhaps best tells not only the good Harley has to offer society, but the reasons why he cannot long exist. The misanthrope was not a real man of feeling; his judgments did not proceed from the natural and sympathetic affections of the heart but from the passions. Like Billy Annesley in **The Man of the World,** he entered "life with those ardent expectations by which young men are commonly deluded; in his friendships, warm to excess; and equally violent in his dislikes." But the fires of disappointment have cleared some part of his understanding, for through him one can hear Mackenzie commenting on contemporary society.

The misanthrope attacks the substitution of Honor for Virtue, the avowed insincerity in contemporary life, and the hypocritical philosophers of the day. In discussing present education as opposed to good "natural" education, he says, "you waste at school years in improving talents, without having ever spent an hour in discovering them."

The misanthrope finally attacks the hypocrites in sentiment, those who hate wealth and power merely because they could attain neither; he condemns those feelings which, in some sense, have caused his own unhappiness. It is a partial realization that sentiment is impossible in this world, if one would exist unhurt:

> With vanity your best virtues are grossly tainted; your benevolence, which ye deduce immediately from the natural impulse of the heart, squints to it for its reward. There are some, indeed, who tell us of the satisfaction which flows from a secret consciousness of good actions: this secret

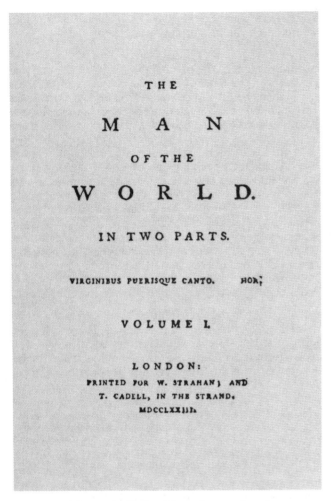

THE

M A N

OF THE

W O R L D.

IN TWO PARTS.

VIRGINIBUS PUERISQUE CANTO.   HOR.

V O L U M E I.

L O N D O N:

PRINTED FOR W. STRAHAN; AND
T. CADELL, IN THE STRAND.
MDCCLXXIII.

Title page for Mackenzie's popular second novel.

satisfaction is truly excellent—when we have a
friend to whom we may discover its excellence.

Here in one man's mouth is both a sentimental condemnation of the evils of the world and a worldly condemnation of sentimentality. The present incompatibility of the two is indicated in the person of the misanthrope himself, who in a materialistic world began a somewhat sentimental approach to life. He retains his knowledge of present evils but tends to regard sentiment with a soured eye. He has swung back a bit too far. Harley sees his point, though, and admits that true sentiment and this world are irreconcilable; the harsh metal of the world needs considerable filing before it will shine with a bright enough luster for genuine men of sentiment.

As the story draws to a close, Harley returns to his home and hears a false rumor that his sweetheart has fallen in love with another. Catching a fever from a friend, Harley pines away. He dies as she admits her love for him, for this final shock is too much for his delicate sensibilities. He does not die for love, as some have thought . . . but because he is an incongruity on earth; only in heaven is there happiness for him. "This world," he says, "was a scene in which I never much delighted. I was not formed for the bustle of the busy, nor the dissipations of the gay." And only in heaven may he indulge certain feelings, "feelings which are perhaps too tender to to be suffered by the world. The world is in general selfish, interested and unthinking, and throws the imputation of romance or melancholy on every temper more susceptible than its own."

The reader knows, even before Harley sees his sweetheart for the last time, that he must die. The declaration of his love only hastens him on his way. Leigh Hunt has criticized this ending, feeling that Harley should have lived, married, and begotten many children:

> If the Man of Feeling dies because the woman he has long loved in secret returned his affection: this is mere weakness of nerves: the chief virtue consists in social utility, and he who dies, because his love is suddenly returned is not a jot the more virtuous or one of a better heart than he who lives to reward the object of his affection by making her a mother: certainly he is not so useful a member of society. [*Classic Tales*, 1806]

The point is, of course, that Harley is not a useful member of society, and he knows it. The quotation does illustrate the tendency to associate the philosophy of Harley with that of Mackenzie.

The conclusion of *The Man of Feeling* emphasizes one's conception of it as a statement of an ideal case, as a tool for moral teaching:

> I sometimes visit his grave. . . . It is worth a thousand homilies; every noble feeling arises within me! every beat of my heart awakens a virtue! but it will make you hate the world—No! there is such an air of gentleness around, that I can hate nothing; but as to the world—I pity the men of it.

Walter Allen reiterates this view of the function of *The Man of Feeling*:

> So *The Man of Feeling* may primarily have as its end a description of the impact of the world upon a young man "obedient to every emotion of his moral sense," but it is also, by implication, a statement of the case against the world, against society. As for Rousseau, so for Mackenzie— society is always evil, and against society is set the innocence and uncorrupted virtue of the idyllic countryside. [*The English Novel*, 1958]

Of this young man Harley, Professor Harold Thompson, the biographer of Mackenzie, has said that "To be fair to Mackenzie, we must admit that in Harley he created a new and significant type of hero—the humanitarian who not only feels for the distress of others but actually helps them." The assertion is perhaps not wholly accurate, for if Mackenzie's style has been thought derivative from Sterne's, equally his hero is derivative. First, he owes a good deal to Harry Morland, the hero of Henry Brooke's *The Fool of Quality* (1766-70). Both are productive humanitarians; both act according to the dictates of their hearts and the generosity of their feelings. Of the two, Harley is the more fully imagined: Harry is too inexhaustibly wealthy and, if anything, more sentimental than Harley. As Harry's uncle exclaims: "This boy will absolutely kill me if I stay any longer. He overpowers, he suffocates me with the weight of his sentiments." Harry's blithe disregard for the mores of society was unacceptable to Mackenzie, and if he called Brooke's book a "strange extravagant novel," he did so because Brooke thought his heaven compatible with earth. Mackenzie knew better; men must have society, however noble the state of nature, and so Harley dies.

An even greater influence on the nature of *The Man of Feeling* was probably Goldsmith's work. In *The Vicar of Wakefield* (1766), there is a complete Man of the World—Squire Thornhill. A Man of Feeling, Sir William Thornhill combines reason with an earlier "sickly" sensibility to become a truly "sentimental" hero; and finally there are a seduced maiden and her brother. This last motif is closely analogous to the situation in *The Man of the World.* In Goldsmith's earlier essays the "Man in Black" bears a softened resemblance to Mackenzie's misanthrope; both, for instance, are soured sentimentalists. Perhaps the most remarkable parallel is that in thought: both authors preach an ideal, and both realize the impossibility of attaining it. Primrose argues in favor of "levelling" but admits its impracticality; Harley inveighs against classes and wealth but admits they are inescapable concomitants of the present world. Both authors might be called sentimental idealists in their desires, but sentimental realists in person.

In contrast to his presentation of the sentimental ideal and its inevitable result in a realistic world, in his next novel Mackenzie reverts to the practical. He echoes Goldsmith's statement that "In this middle order of man-kind are generally to be found all the arts, wisdom, and virtues of society." Always, of course, instinctive feeling is praised, but it is tempered with reason. The primacy of the right-feeling heart is stressed, but attention is given to reason and common sense.

In this novel are found three important characters. The first, Sir Thomas Sindall, is Harley's opposite—a man who responds not to the dictates of his heart but to society and its perversions. The second, Harry Bolton, is perhaps Mackenzie in disguise—a reasonable man of feeling. The third, Billy Annesley, is a man who must be taught the compromise between sentiment and reason.

The story itself is divided into two books. In the first Sindall debauches both Billy and his sister Harriet, Billy being transported for robbery and Harriet being delivered of an illegitimate child. The double shock kills their loving father. In Book II Sindall, some years later, is found with a young girl, Lucy. She is his daughter by Harriet, though he is unaware of the relation. Also present is Harry Bolton, a young cousin of Sir Thomas's and heir to his estates and fortune. He is, obviously, intended to be the hero of the piece, for he is that ideal combination of feeling and reason which Mackenzie conceived as being sufficient to meet the evils of the world. He has, without effort, achieved this compromise which a man like Billy Annesley must earn the hard way. Harry and Lucy fall in love but are separated by Sir Thomas, who has designs on Lucy. Harry, aided by a strange soldier, rescues her just as Sir Thomas is dragging her off to ruin. At this point a woman enters and reveals that Lucy is Sindall's daughter; whereupon Sindall, mortally wounded by the stranger—who is brother Billy—repents and dies.

Naturally Sindall, the man of the world, is the unifying character in the narrative, but the character of Billy has not perhaps had the attention it deserves. Mackenzie has posed a question: how can those not firm in following the heart's dictates become good men? How can they be made fit to survive in society? The solution is offered in Billy's case. He has a feeling heart and a good education but has been debauched by Sindall and by his own lack of ready reason. Billy must be regenerated, and the means are his being exposed to the basic virtues again, and in a strenuous way. He must be purified. And, as any believer in primitivism may see, the obvious place for this ritual purification is among the savages. Here Billy can acquire again those virtues which will wipe out the passions he could not resist at a tender age. Like Robert Bage's Hermsprong, when Billy Annesley has been hardened by the experiences of primitive life, he will be fit to deal with corrupt society.

Billy, after his arrival in the Indies, is enlisted in the army, disciplined, and transferred to America. There, being unjustly punished, he escapes and is captured by Indians who try his fortitude severely and then admit him to their tribe. As a member of the tribe Billy has an opportunity to observe the advantages of the primitive life. These are three: perfect freedom, where rule is used only for immediate utility to those who obey; no opportunity for greatness to use oppression, or wealth to excite envy; and desires native to the heart. In sum, here is an ideal situation for the making of a man. Utility is the Indians' canon of judgment, the simple and honorable life their desire. From them Billy learns simple values; perhaps he learns Scottish utilitarianism. When their chief is dying and Billy weeps, the chief rebukes him. " 'In those tears,' said he, 'there is no wisdom, for there is no use.' "

Finally, a man in all respects, he must return to take up his duties in civilization, return to the cave of ignorance. The Indians tell him in parting to remember that "the soul you possess is the soul of a man; remember that to fortitude there is no sting in adversity, and in death no evil to the valiant." Knowing this truth and seeing clearly that in the world with which man must cope there is fraud, hypocrisy, and sordid baseness, Billy returns a whole man, with fortitude and reason grafted onto a feeling heart. In a way his education has been similar to that of Spenser's Red Cross Knight, who had to see truth in its clear light and who had to be educated in basic virtues before he became a complete man.

Of Sindall's repentance one may say that it demonstrates the power of the heart when allowed to operate in the proper channels. This power is loosed, as well it might be, when he finds that he has attempted to rape his own daughter. Nevertheless, Mackenzie, through the lips of another character, warns the reader that "of those who have led his [Sindall's] life, how few have closed it like him." Eschewing questions of probability, the reader sees this as a warning: Annesley's way is too difficult, and Sindall's too unusual. Adjust to life early, and one may attain to the final happiness of Lucy and Harry, who know how to live: "their benevolence is universal; the country smiles around them with the effects of their goodness. This is indeed the only real superiority which wealth has to bestow; I have never envied riches so much as since I have known Bolton."

Perhaps the obvious conclusion to be drawn from this discussion is that the complete man of feeling cannot last in this world; he must die, and must die perhaps to make it a better world. No more can a complete man of the world exist. A sort of poetic justice determines the fate common to both types: one is too good for the world, the other is too bad. Mackenzie preaches the golden mean—sentiment tempered with reason. He was a sentimental idealist, perhaps, but also a rational and practical man. After all, he was a successful Scots lawyer!

Since his time, those critics who approved him spoke of the moral delicacy and refined sensibility in his works, as did Sir Walter Scott and J. G. Lockhart. They remembered affectionately the characters in his novels or rightly, like Chambers and Hunt, put his moral purpose before any consideration of literary merit. That is the important factor for Mackenzie. Merit aside, and there is much merit in his work, Mackenzie saw moral improvement as the chief end in estimating the value of literature. He saw himself as a teacher, and his subjects were the heart and the true values of life. Although his name is of importance only as his work illustrates the humanitarian and sentimental trends of his time, the critic may at least say for him that his works were everywhere "subservient to the cause of virtue." It would be a pity to remember him only as the author of excessively teary novels. (pp. 318-26)

David G. Spencer, "Henry Mackenzie, a Practical Sentimentalist," in Papers on Language & Literature, *Vol. III, No. 4, Fall, 1967, pp. 314-26.*

Ralph E. Jenkins (essay date 1971)

[*In the essay below, Jenkins argues that the rhetorical style in* The Man of Feeling *reflects Mackenzie's desire to convey his moral message.*]

After *The Vicar of Wakefield,* **The Man of Feeling** is probably the most widely read sentimental novel in English, and its relative popularity poses an interesting critical problem: how to explain the appeal of a book which few readers take seriously as a work of art. Most discussions of Mackenzie deal with his importance in the history of sentiment, and even sympathetic critics have little to say in defense of his artistic abilities. Brian Vickers' intelligent introduction to the 1967 Oxford Press edition, for example, criticizes the "triteness of the pattern" on which the novel is built, and admits that modern readers are "disappointed" by Mackenzie's "laborious piling-on of pathos." Vickers offers two defenses of Mackenzie; he says that **The Man of Feeling** has a structure similar to that of the more respected *Vicar of Wakefield;* and he concurs with Scott's opinion that Mackenzie succeeded in becoming "the historian of sentiment." Kenneth Slagle's introduction to the earlier Norton Library edition also offers a defense based upon historical importance; the novel is valuable because

it helped teach people to weep over the distresses of the poor and thus led to social reform. Another historical defense is given by Dale Kramer [in "The Structural Unity of **'The Man of Feeling',**" *Studies in Short Fiction* I (Spring 1964)], who argues that the novel is important because it is a "cultural artifact" embodying a summary of theories of sentimental education. Such defenses are valuable as far as they go, but they leave the impression that Mackenzie can interest only two kinds of reader: the modern scholar who is concerned primarily with historical questions, or the occasional atavistic reader who likes a good cry—which does Mackenzie's artistic reputation very little good. One could probably offer similar defenses for novels like Brooke's *Fool of Quality,* which Mackenzie admired, but which, despite its historical importance, is justifiably less often read than **The Man of Feeling.** The difference between the two is surely that Mackenzie's book is the better work of art. I do not mean that **The Man of Feeling** is a serious rival to novels like *Tom Jones,* but Mackenzie's artistic talents, such as they are, have been largely ignored by those who write about his historical importance.

Mackenzie himself is partly responsible for this; his comments on his own writing often do not inspire one to take him seriously. In his introduction to **Julia de Roubigné,** speaking of the "letters" that make up the novel, he complains, "I found it a difficult task to reduce them into narrative, because they are made up of sentiment, which narrative would destroy." In his letters to Elizabeth Rose about the composition of **The Man of Feeling,** he says something similar: "You will find inclosed a very whimsical Introduction to a very odd Medley. . . . You must know, then, that I have seldom been in Use to write any Prose, except what consisted of Observations (such as I could make) on Men & Manners. . . . I was somehow led to think of introducing a Man of Sensibility into different scenes where his Feelings might be seen in their Effects, & his Sentiments occasionally delivered without the stiffness of regular Deduction. . . . to indulge that desultory Humour of writing which sometimes possesses me, I began with this Introduction & write now & then a Chapter as I have Leisure or Inclination." And in another letter he anticipates critical objections to "the want of Connection in the Parts." Many modern critics have taken such remarks at face value and think of the book as a collection of episodes [according to Slagle] "intended merely to display the hero in a variety of emotional experiences."

Obviously **The Man of Feeling** does not have a conventional narrative structure, but **The Man of the World** shows that Mackenzie could at least write a conventional melodramatic plot. Thus the unconventional structure of **The Man of Feeling** should be taken as evidence not of Mackenzie's incompetence, but of his unconventional intentions. In the early stages of writing, Mackenzie warned his cousin that he intended **The Man of Feeling** to be "as different from the Entanglement of a Novel as can be," and suggested that it "might as well be called a Sermon as a History. . . ." Mackenzie wanted to evoke a sentimental response from his readers, but, as this last remark implies, he wanted to evoke it for a didactic purpose; he meant Harley to be an admirable character with qualities that the reader should want to emulate—sympathy, charity, and philanthropy. He could have treated these topics in a series of moral essays, like the "detach'd Essays" that gave him the idea, but chose a narrative vehicle, as he says, "from the Notion of it's interesting both the Memory & the Affection deeper, than mere Argument, or moral Reasoning." In *Mirror* No. 107 ("Of definitions"), written some years later, he also discusses some advantages of narrative. He deals with the difficulty of reconciling theoretical descriptions with real experience and quotes a narrative passage from an Elizabethan author describing how a lover ought to behave. He says that the passage, "instead of simplifying the matter, makes it more difficult than . . . it is actually found." For contrast he quotes another "theoretical description," this one a narrative of a hypothetical battle, and says that "it renders a very confused and intricate business . . . perfectly clear and obvious to the meanest capacity. This, however, is by no means owing to any want in the theoretical situation of that incident or bustle which occurs in the real; on the contrary, the events are infinitely more numerous in the first than in the latter, though the art of the theorist carries the imagination through them all with wonderful distinctness." He publishes the account, he claims ironically, "for the sole use of our British commanders," so they can learn to conduct an animated battle. He sees narrative, then, as a way to enliven both the moral essay and the theoretical description; it clarifies definition and evokes a deeper emotional response than "mere Argument."

These remarks may give us a better understanding of Mackenzie's intentions in **The Man of Feeling;** the book should not be considered primarily as a feeble novel, but as a theoretical description of the man of feeling, enlivened by narrative but designed primarily to educate the public in the virtues of sentiment and to hold up Harley as a model for emulation. Mackenzie must therefore combine the art of the novelist with that of the rhetorician; he must persuade the reader to admire Harley, who at first glance seems to be an impractical, weak, and ridiculous character incapable of dealing with the real world. His original audience was easily won over, but modern readers, with a preference for irony, have not been persuaded. If anyone weeps over the book today it is from excessive laughter rather than sympathy. But modern distaste for sentiment should not make us overlook the technical skill which Mackenzie brought to his task of persuasion. This skill is, I believe, the unacknowledged reason why the book is still read today in preference to other sentimental novels; Mackenzie shows considerable artistry in his efforts to disarm criticism and make us admire his improbable hero.

One way of disarming criticism is to anticipate it, which Mackenzie does by pointing out some of the ludicrous aspects of his hero's behavior. In matters of business Harley is incompetent; from childhood he listens with indifference to suggestions on how to improve his fortunes. He misses a chance to inherit money by refusing to humor a crotchety female relative, even daring to fall asleep while she discusses "the composition and virtues of her favorite cholic-water." He is "a child in the drama of the world," and when he falls in love with Miss Walton, his "paroxysms of fancy" cause him to make "awkward blunders"

at which his friends "laughed very heartily." To emphasize Harley's naiveté, Mackenzie has him meet a clever beggar on his way to London. The beggar, who knows the world from the bottom up, makes his living by telling fortunes and admits to Harley that he learns the characters of his clients by cunning, by gleaning information from servants and neighbors. Harley, the innocent, relies upon his ridiculous "skill" in physiognomy, against which his wise aunt has warned him. His trust in outward appearances makes him an easy prey for professional gamblers; having lost his money, he pawns his watch to a sneering waiter to help a prostitute. When he explains to friends that he believed in the honest faces of the gamblers, they laugh, and one of them gives as harsh a judgment of Harley as any critical reader could offer: "here's a very pretty fellow for you . . . you might have sworn he was a saint; yet now he games with sharpers, and loses his money, and is bubbled by a fine story invented by a whore, and pawns his watch; here are sanctified doings with a witness!" The task Mackenzie sets himself is to convince the reader that despite Harley's naiveté, gullibility, impracticality, and tender disposition, he is more to be admired than worldly men—that he is in fact a kind of saint.

The man of feeling and the man of the world, as the titles of the two novels suggest, are opposite types, and Mackenzie's basic technique of persuasion is to make the contrast between them favorable to Harley. His introduction is not merely a structural joke in imitation of Sterne; it sets up this contrast in such a way that the reader is urged from the beginning to sympathize with the man of feeling. The hunting curate is "a strenuous logician" who began to read Harley's story from curiosity, but "soon grew weary of the task . . . I could never find the author in one strain for two chapters together; and I don't believe there's a single syllogism from beginning to end." The unfeeling world of logic, this implies, will reject a story of sentiment and find it fit only for shotgun wadding. Through the anonymous writer of the introduction, Mackenzie anticipates criticism of his structure: "I found it a bundle of little episodes, put together without art, and of no importance on the whole, with something of nature, and little else in them." He then answers his own objections with understated praise: "I was a good deal affected with some very trifling passages in it; and had the name of Marmontel, or a Richardson, been on the title page—'tis odds that I should have wept; but One is ashamed to be pleased with the works of one knows not whom." This ironic challenge, thrown out by an unknown writer to the public, implies that only insensitive logicians like the curate will fail to be touched by the story; sensitive readers will recognize its merit and weep. Mackenzie's audacious comparison of himself to Marmontel and Richardson further implies that those who fail to appreciate him will be guilty of judging works by the reputation of their authors rather than by their real merit.

Mackenzie continues to contrast his opposing types by distinguishing between two kinds of bashfulness: "this, the awkwardness of a booby, which a few steps into the world will convert into the pertness of a coxcomb; that, a consciousness which the most delicate feelings produce, and the most extensive knowledge cannot always remove."

With quiet irony the narrator assures us that Harley was "of the latter species," since he "never attained" the pertness of the coxcomb. Harley's superior sensitivity is innate rather than acquired. His parents did not inculcate it, since he lost them in childhood; nor did his guardian, since they seldom met and could reconcile their differences only over a bottle; nor was his education responsible, since it "had been but indifferently attended to" and he "was suffered to be his own master" in literature after some useless basic instruction. He is like Miss Walton, whose "humanity was a feeling, not a principle." This division of mankind into two opposed groups—pert insensitive coxcombs and aristocrats of sensitivity—leaves the reader little choice but to prefer the natural nobility typified by Harley.

Mackenzie's two conventional settings, the virtuous countryside and the sinful city, reinforce this opposition. In the country Harley lives among sympathetic companions— Miss Walton, Ben Silton ("born to be happy without the world"), Edwards, his aunt, and his servant Peter. London, by contrast, is described by Peter as "a sad place," and his aunt thinks it is "so replete with temptations that it needed the whole armour of her friendly cautions to repel their attacks." Harley's unfortunate London experiences are neatly bracketed by encounters with the gauger, a typical man of the world who succeeds through cunning and duplicity where the honest man of feeling fails. The gauger affects the manners of a gentleman; he is urbane, informed, amusing—and he gets the lease of crown lands by pimping for his sister. After their first encounter Harley is inclined to blame not the gauger but the nobility, "that rank whose opportunities for nobler accomplishments have only served to rear a fabric of folly which the untutored hand of affectation can imitate with success." But when he learns that affectation and vice are the qualities that the city rewards, he agrees with another disappointed competitor for the lease who cries, "a plague on all rogues," and returns immediately to the country, where honesty and virtue are esteemed.

This kind of situation inclines naturally toward satire; Harley could easily have been shown as a country simpleton made ridiculous by sophisticated Londoners. Instead his London experiences are made to emphasize the value of his natural sensitivity and innocence. If the visit to Bedlam, for example, had been intended merely to show Harley reacting emotionally to pathetic scenes, Mackenzie could have dwelt upon the clanking chains and wild cries of the more spectacular inmates. He shows us instead a set of inmates who make Harley's lack of formal education and aversion to business seem desirable qualities. One is a mathematician who "fell a sacrifice . . . to the theory of comets"; another is a schoolmaster who "came hither to be resolved of some doubts he entertained concerning the genuine pronunciation of the Greek vowels." A third is a once-wealthy businessman who foolishly passed up a chance to retire to the country and was reduced to poverty and madness by "an unlucky fluctuation of stock." The point is clear: Harley's ignorance of scholarship and business is preferable to knowledge which leads only to madness. Ignorance of the ways of the world is sanity, if not bliss. The guide's conclusion makes the point explicit: "the world, in the eye of a philosopher, may be said to be a large madhouse." The guide, who understands the world so well, is appropriately mad himself; he suffers from political delusions.

This undermining of the value of worldly knowledge might lead the reader to think that Mackenzie is implicitly praising irrational passion. Harley agrees with his guide, however, that "the passions of men are temporary madnesses," and Mackenzie describes another inmate to dramatize the point: a young lady who loved excessively and was driven to madness by the death of her lover. Mackenzie concludes her pathetic tale with subtle praise of his own narrative abilities: "Though this story was told in very plain language, it had particularly attracted Harley's notice; he had given it the tribute of some tears." So, presumably, has the sensitive reader, who has been shown that "feeling" is neither rational knowledge nor uncontrolled passion, but an inner impulse to charity and sympathy. Harley's reaction anticipates his charity to Miss Atkins and Edwards; he consoles the lady with thoughts of heaven and leaves money for her care.

After the Bedlam visit come the scenes displaying Harley's gullibility, which pose an interesting artistic problem. Mackenzie must show that his hero is trusting and unworldly while avoiding satire—while in fact making Harley admirable for precisely those qualities that make him vulnerable to satire. His solution is to preface these scenes with the chapter concerning the unpleasant misanthropist, ironically described as "one of the wise." The admirable younger brother of the misanthropist resembles Harley; he is unworldly, uncomplaining, and unambitious, and upon inheriting a small estate he wisely moves to the country and marries "a young lady of similar temper to his own, with whom the sagacious world pitied him for finding happiness." The misanthropist is Harley's opposite; he was "remarkable at school for quickness of parts and genius"; he was "naturally impetuous, decisive, and overbearing," and ambitious as well—a potential man of the world. When jilted by his fiancee, however, he became embittered, sold his lands, and moved to London where he "has ever since applied his talents to the vilifying of his species." The misanthropist rails constantly at the follies of mankind, from whom he pointedly dissociates himself by referring to "you" rather than "we." His cynical "wisdom" is finally so disagreeable that one again prefers Harley's kind of ignorance. Thus when Harley is deceived by gamblers, the sting of satire is removed. He loses his money not because he is greedy and stupid, but because he is always ready to believe in the honesty of others. Gullibility and trust are merely two different words for the same thing; the same quality that made Harley lose his money leads to his charitable treatment of Miss Atkins, whom he saves from prostitution and starvation. The waiter to whom Harley pawns his watch pronounces the judgment of the world: he "whispered to a girl . . . something, in which the word CULLY was honoured with a particular emphasis." But Mackenzie shows that the alternative to Harley's naive trust is the misanthropist's total cynicism, which is not merely disagreeable but makes charity impossible.

The story of Miss Atkins shows the man of feeling's readiness to aid the unfortunate; it also shows that his mildness of temper is not to be mistaken for cowardice. Harley faces her father's sword with restrained courage just as he later faces down the bully in the stagecoach. Moreover, the details of her history are carefully chosen to contrast with Harley's, and her downfall is another example of the pernicious effect of worldly education. Unlike Harley, she has a father, but instead of inculcating morality in her, he talks of "the honour of a soldier" and holds moral sentiments in such low esteem that she "was soon weaned from opinions which she began to consider as the dreams of superstition. . . . " Her reading is wider than Harley's but is "confined to plays, novels, and those poetical descriptions of the beauty of virtue and honour, which the circulating libraries easily afforded." She has the advantage of beauty and the "quickness of parts" which he lacks, but they serve only to make her "giddy, open to adulation, and vain of those talents which acquired it." She avoids the "awkward blunders" that mark Harley's social behavior and becomes "an example of politeness," but her acceptance of wordly standards makes her entertain the advances of Winbrooke, a forerunner of Sindall. Misled by her upbringing and by false values, she is seduced and learns too late the credo of men of the world: "Honour . . . is the word of fools, or of those wise men who cheat them." Her history is further proof of the superiority of feeling over cleverness and polish; those qualities which the world admires bring disaster rather than happiness. Harley's consolation to Atkins emphasizes the lesson: "The world is ever tyrannical. . . . Let us not be slaves to the names it affixes to motive or to action. . . . Its fantastic ideas vanish as they rise; they teach us to look beyond it."

These pointed contrasts are Mackenzie's chief persuasive device, but he appeals to the reader's sympathies in other ways as well. When Harley and Atkins are reconciled, he writes, "We would attempt to describe the joy which Harley felt on this occasion, did it not occur to us that one half of the world could not understand it though we did, and the other half will, by this time, have understood it without any description at all." This is a clear appeal to the reader to think of himself as one of that superior class who intuitively understand Harley's sentiments—to think of himself as a man of feeling. In the scene at the inn, Mackenzie identifies the man of feeling with another admired class of men, the poets. Poetry is "an incentive to philanthropy," and "there is a certain poetic ground, on which a man cannot tread without feelings that enlarge the heart; the causes of human depravity vanish before the romantic enthusiasm he professes." The poet, like the man of feeling, risks "the danger of unfitness for the world," and to illustrate the point, Ben Silton sketches the characters of Jack the merchant and Tom the poet in terms that identify Tom with the man of feeling. Tom is above material concerns—"he pawned his great-coat for an edition of Shakespeare"—and his love for poetry is, like feeling, an innate perception of better things: "Tom would have been as he is, though Virgil and Horace had never been born. . . ." Tom will never succeed in this world, but will finally go to heaven. So, by analogy, will the man of feeling—which hints at the eventual sanctification of Harley.

The scenes that follow this are probably the most overwrought and laughable parts of the book for the modern reader, but they have a definite place in Mackenzie's rhetorical plan. He has shown the inaccuracy of the world's judgment of his hero and has shown that the unfeeling world, rather than Harley, is the proper object of criticism and contempt. The scenes depicting Edwards and the orphaned children were Mackenzie's favorites; they were also intended, as he wrote to his cousin, to "raise Harley in your esteem," presumably by showing the practical results of his sentiment—his charity and philanthropy. Having left the hypocrisy and madness of London, Harley encounters Edwards, the old soldier, in a Salvator Rosa landscape and finds the "romantic enthusiasm" which leads to philanthropy "rising within him." Edwards' tale is a recapitulation of the case against the world; he is a lower-class replica of Harley, a man of natural sensitivity and little business sense brought low by unfeeling malice. The game of blind-man's buff that results in his being pressed into the army is an emblem of the blindness of men of feeling to the cunning of men of the world, and his tale makes Harley clutch convulsively at his sword as evidence of the power of romantic enthusiasm. What follows is unabashedly sentimental; we learn that Edwards' son and daughter-in-law have died of broken hearts, leaving two children behind. Everyone weeps, and Harley's enthusiasm is translated into genuine philanthropy. He gives Edwards a small farm, helps him stock and tend it, and becomes a sort of godfather to the children. His experiences thus prove Silton's thesis that "the most extensive knowledge" of the world cannot destroy the sentiments of genuine men of feeling, and the narrator comments ironically that Harley returns home from London as happy "as if he had arrived from the tour of Europe with a Swiss valet . . . and half a dozen snuff-boxes, with invisible hinges, in his pocket."

Two of the final sections, "The Man of Feeling Jealous" and "The Pupil. A Fragment," are again exercises in contrast. So that his hero may not seem to be a spiritless dogooder (and to tie up the loose ends of the story), Mackenzie returns to Harley's love for Miss Walton and shows that he is capable, like other men, of feeling love and jealousy. But the contrast again shows the basic difference between the man of feeling and the man of the world. Harley's love for Miss Walton is chaste, unlike the lechery of worldly men. Sedley, the pupil, serves as a stand-in for Harley; on his Italian tour he falls in with gentlemen of deceptive appearance (like the gauger) who pretend to be men of feeling: "subjects, too, of sentiment occurred, and their speeches, particularly those of our friend the son of Count Respino, glowed with the warmth of honour and softened into the tenderness of feeling." When Sedley discovers that Respino is despicable and has reduced another man to poverty and illness because of a "criminal passion" for his wife, he, too, becomes a philanthropist, saves the man from poverty, and like Harley, leaves the city inhabited by such villains. This indictment of the emotion called love by men of the world makes Harley's pure and passive love for Miss Walton seem admirable rather than feeble and shows that his jealousy is not to be confused with lust.

Harley's death upon finding that this chaste love is returned by Miss Walton has often been a subject for critical jokes, but it has also been misunderstood by serious critics; Kramer, for example, thinks that Harley's death follows the destruction of his belief in the power of sentiment and is the logical conclusion of the sentimentalist's rejection of the physical world. Mackenzie's own comments on the ending are curious; he did not send the final chapters for his cousin's approval and put her off with a description that does not match the actual ending: "You remember a Miss Walton; you have nothing to do but to imagine (Harley) somehow or other wedded to her & made happy;—so must all stories conclude you know; the Hero is as surely married as he was born; because marriage is a good Thing & made in Heaven." What these almost sarcastic comments describe is the ending of a conventional novel, and he was perhaps reluctant to disappoint his cousin's anticipations. The ending that he actually wrote, however, is more suited to his didactic intentions. From a cautiously ironic beginning in which he admitted the ludicrous appearance his hero makes in the world, Mackenzie has refuted the world's criticism and made Harley openly sentimental, the man of feeling in apotheosis. The ending carries this process on to its logical but audacious conclusion. Harley's consoling speech to Atkins, adjuring him not to be a slave to this world but to "look beyond it," and Ben Silton's character of the poet both hinted at the eventual sanctification of the man of feeling. Harley's death is the final step in his elevation to a kind of sanctity. He predicts his own entry into heaven: "we shall meet again, my friend, never to be separated. There are some feelings which perhaps are too tender to be suffered by the world. . . . I cannot think but in those regions which I contemplate, if there is anything of mortality left about us, that these feelings will subsist;—they are called,—perhaps they are—weaknesses here;—but there may be some better modifications of them in heaven, which may deserve the name of virtues."

Mackenzie has shown, in effect, that the "weaknesses" of the man of feeling are quite the opposite; Harley is sure of a place in heaven *because* he has those qualities which the world holds in contempt. Consciously or not, Mackenzie has followed the pattern of the saint's legend. Harley's innocence and contempt for the world are virtues, and his death is not a defeat but a victory, a final reward; he becomes, too, a model for those left behind to follow. His death has a powerful effect on the narrator, who looks upon his body with "reverence, not fear." To this point the narrator has been merely a detached and quietly ironic voice commenting on Harley's history; now he becomes a participant, a convert to the cult of sentiment: "The sight drew a prayer from my heart: it was the voice of frailty and of man! the confusion of my mind began to subside into thought; I had time to weep!" Harley's grave becomes a shrine to which the narrator retires often; there he becomes fully sentimental, like Harley himself: "every noble feeling arises within me! every beat of my heart awakens a virtue!—but it will make you hate the world—No: there is such an air of gentleness around, that I can hate nothing; but, as to the world—I pity the men of it." The sensitive reader will now presumably see himself, like the narrator, as a true man of feeling, ready to hold worldly val-

ues in contempt and follow Harley's example of trust, sympathy, and philanthropy.

The kind of rhetorical structure I have described is uncommon in the eighteenth-century novel; as Mackenzie admitted, his book might as well be called a sermon as a history. To criticize him for not creating fully realized characters, engrossing action, or tightly unified narrative structure is therefore beside the point. The kind of structure he did create, however, should be more familiar to the modern reader than to his contemporary audience; it relies upon what is now a basic technique of modern cinema. A television commercial which cuts from a shot of a herd of lowing cattle to a crowd of milling people, then from a single cow straying away from the herd to the discerning individual who buys the right brand of cigarette is easy enough to interpret. Mackenzie's structural technique is basically the same. He juxtaposes separate incidents without providing narrative transitions, and the reader is expected to see the contrasts or parallels and draw the right conclusion. Judged by the standards of *Tom Jones,* ***The Man of Feeling*** is loosely constructed; yet its rhetorical structure, properly interpreted, serves Mackenzie's didactic intentions perhaps better than more conventional narrative. We may finally reject the book because it stresses emotion too openly for modern taste, but we should not let our concern for literary history and our preference for irony obscure our appreciation of the ingenuity and technical skill with which Mackenzie undermines criticism and excites admiration for his secular saint. (pp. 3-15)

> *Ralph E. Jenkins, "The Art of the Theorist: Rhetorical Structure in 'The Man of Feeling',"* in Studies in Scottish Literature, *Vol. IX, No. 1, July, 1971, pp. 3-15.*

Gerard A. Barker   (essay date 1975)

[*In the following excerpt, Barker discusses Mackenzie's dramatic writings, asserting that his treatment of sentimental themes was more conducive to writing comedies than tragedies.*]

If Mackenzie's temperament and talents were ideally suited for the composition of short fiction, they proved to be a decisive liability in the writing of tragedy. His plays, instead of revealing dramatic conflicts, merely present characters and situations capable of eliciting poignant emotional responses. Mackenzie's protagonists are exemplary figures who bear little responsibility for their plight, while his antagonists are ambiguously drawn villains whose motives and behavior are never realistically accounted for. Only in his one comedy, written more than fifteen years after he had completed his last tragedy, does Mackenzie produce good theater. Within the comic form of ***False Shame,*** he found the detachment and restraint that enabled him to transcend his own artistic limitations.

Much of Mackenzie's first play, ***Virginia; or, The Roman Father,*** was written when he was about sixteen years old although it was not completed until eight years later. Though the play was never performed on the stage, Mackenzie in old age distributed a few privately printed copies among his friends. The story is derived from Livy's *Histo-*

ry of Rome (III. XLIV-XLVIII), which Mackenzie followed fairly closely. In the play, the decemvir Appius develops a passion for the maiden Virginia, daughter of the plebeian soldier Virginius. Appius's freedman, Appulinius, hits upon a scheme to obtain Virginia by claiming that she is not Virginius's daughter but a child who was born to a female slave of his house and who was later lost. However, growing fearful of how the common people will respond to such outright trickery, Appulinius advises his master first to try "gentler methods." By promising to reward Virginius for past services and by recalling his brother from exile, Appulinius is convinced that the old soldier will cooperate and sacrifice his daughter. But Virginius disdainfully spurns the offer and makes plans to kill her if there turns out to be no other way to save his daughter's chastity. Having recognized that Virginia is in love with Lucius, the son of his dead friend, he tries to prepare the latter for the loss of his love. Lucius, however, misinterprets Virginius's hints and imagines that he has accepted Appius's offer. In an effort to save Virginia, he persuades her to marry him immediately.

Meanwhile, Appius has fallen back upon Appulinius's first scheme to win his prey. Summoned to the forum, Virginius sees Appius rule against him and about to seize Virginia. He stabs his daughter mortally and makes his way home. Virginia, though dying, follows him and blesses her father before she dies. Lucius, confronted by his dead bride, kills himself in despair. The play ends with the news that the people, aroused by the death of Virginia, have rebelled and killed Appius.

In the privately printed version of the play, Mackenzie took notice of its weaknesses: "The plan of the play is miserably defective; and there is too much declamation and narrative, with too little incident or action." It would be unwise, however, to dismiss *Virginia* as an insignificant piece of juvenilia bearing little resemblance to his later plays. His second play, *The Spanish Father,* is in many respects a reworking of *The Roman Father;* and Mackenzie's basic approach to tragedy, his mode of characterization as well as many of his ideas and values, is in fact already apparent in his first play.

In Livy's account, Appius himself devises the stratagem by which to gain possession of Virginia: "The plaintiff [Marcus Claudius] acted out a comedy familiar to the judge [Appius], since it was he and no other who had invented the plot." Mackenzie, however, turns Marcus Claudius into Appulinius, Appius's freedman and evil genius, who contrives the schemes to satisfy his master's lust. The change is important because it reveals a type of characterization that recurs in each of Mackenzie's tragedies: there is always a figure of authority who uses his power unjustly against the heroine and her father or lover. However, such an antagonist is never a simple, straightforward representation of evil; his actions are always beset by qualms, by memories of his former goodness or resolutions to reform. Violently passionate, he depends upon the guidance of a cooler spirit to provide him with the means to attain his objectives. In essence, it is the degree of emotional responsiveness that distinguishes these two types of evil.

In a soliloquy that opens the second act, Appius voices his contempt of man's moral nature:

> . . . I have little of that thinking weakness,
> Which wisdom tells us wanders o'er the past,
> Gathering ambrosia from remember'd Virtue,
> And to the souls of Tyranny and Guilt
> Their horrors sending and remorseful pangs;

Yet if he has freed himself from the restraints of an active conscience, his inordinate hate of Virginius suggests, nevertheless, an uneasy recognition of his own corruption. The truth is that Appius, as Virginius informs us, "once had virtue" but was corrupted by being entrusted with power. As Virginius recalls, the youthful Appius used to visit him to hear him recount his military adventures:

> Then, with the bare recital of some action,
> Oft would his haughty spirit rise, and speak
> Its fiery language from his rolling eye,
> Then would he act the scenes that I rehearsed,
> Grasp an imaginary sword, and stretch
> His muscles near to bursting with force
> Of fancy'd effort on a giant foe.

In Appius a highly developed imagination is combined with an impetuous nature that brooks no restraint. His pride and ambition have debased his native goodness of heart to the point where he calls even his pretense of friendship for Virginius "this ill-becoming softness." Being highly emotional, moreover, he is easily manipulated by more sober and craftier men. Though Appulinius has not gained the control over his master that Alvarez and Hassan possess in Mackenzie's later tragedies, *The Spanish Father* and *The Prince of Tunis,* nevertheless, Appius's lack of shrewdness makes him dependent upon his freedman's "cool advices." The latter easily dissuades Appius from his rash plan to have Virginia seized at night by suggesting "other means / That bear less danger on them—."

But, if Appulinius is his master's superior in his shrewd, practical approach to life, he is yet incapable of understanding a man of Virginius's principles. Blinded by his own cynicism, he assumes that the old soldier can be bribed into sacrificing his daughter. Appius, on the other hand, though he now scorns virtue, can still believe in its reality on the basis of his own former experience. We see, therefore, two representations of evil emerging, ones that are further developed in later plays and that influenced Mackenzie's fiction. One is both insensitive and unimaginative, cool and restrained because he has no violent emotions with which to contend. Such a *villain of principle,* as Mackenzie later calls him, may be said to be a villain *on* principle since he pursues his own self-interest unhesitatingly without self-deception or guilt. Heedless of the means to attain his objective, he is, like Sindall [in *The Man of the World*], eminently cunning—a quality that for Mackenzie frequently denotes the antithesis of sensibility and moral idealism. The *villain of passion,* on the other hand, is too irrational and intemperate to be very artful, for, being highly emotional, he is frequently beset by feelings of guilt and remorse. Appius, though he momentarily recognizes the futility of pursuing mere sensual pleasure, never undergoes a reformation because Mackenzie makes no real attempt to develop his character. He disappears from the stage before the middle of Act II, after which we are given only indirect references to his presence. Attention is focused instead on the heroic figure of Virginius, the Roman father, just as it later centers on Alphonzo in *The Spanish Father.*

To establish Virginius's nobility of character, Mackenzie relies not only on the heavily sententious speeches of the character himself and the testimony of his friends but on confronting his hero with the temptation that had originally been offered to his daughter. In Livy's account, Appius tries to "seduce her with money and promises," while in Mackenzie's play the father faces such a choice. Yet the outcome is never really in doubt, considering Virginius's exemplary nature. He is revolted by Appius's attempt "to bargain for a daughter's honour" and resolves to kill her rather than permit Virginia's chastity to be compromised. Thus there is no real conflict but merely the highly emotional situation of a father's natural reluctance to kill his daughter.

In his earliest play, Mackenzie's overriding love of pathos is already apparent. As he later recalls, he used to recite this part of the play: "One scene in it I used to act myself, having a great passion for spouting, that in which Virginius meets his daughter after resolving rather to kill her than to allow her to be the slave of Appius. It might be partiality in those friends before whom I acted it, but they gave it tears as well as praise." For Mackenzie, the tears of his friends attest to his success because he has been able to move their feelings. This rhetorical approach to literature, this concern not with the total dramatic potentiality of a situation but only its power to evoke a specific emotional response from an audience, mars all of Mackenzie's tragedies. The point is all the more true in the case of Virginia, whose largely passive role is designed to arouse our pity. Like all of Mackenzie's later heroines, her sensibility is quickly established by her propensity for tears. As she explains to her father:

> Thy picture moves me! yet I often weep,
> I scarce know why; methinks I would not wish
> To help that weakness; 'tis my common sign
> Of joy, of sorrow, pity, admiration!

Since she shares Virginius's ideals, no conflict can arise from the fact that she needs to die for the sake of her honor. Virginia, in fact, blesses her father for having stabbed her. Inner tension stems instead from her misinterpretation of Virginius's intentions. Convinced that he will sacrifice his daughter to Appius, Lucius tries to persuade Virginia that her only salvation lies in being immediately wedded to him. Virginia, believing Lucius's suspicion, is torn between obedience to her father and her love for Lucius.

Their love developed, according to Silia (Virginia's attendant), in early childhood before they could understand their feelings for each other:

> When, fresh from Nature's hand, the colder ties
> Of sallow interest and unfeeling prudence
> Reach not our hearts, the softer cords that link
> Congenial spirits mark'd you for each other.

The concept of "kindred souls" destined for each other comes, as we have seen, to be one of Mackenzie's favorite themes. It recurs in *The Man of the World,* and *Julia de Roubigné* as well as in *The Prince of Tunis.* Genuine love depends somehow upon a relationship established in the innocence of childhood before experience has weakened the reliability of our feelings. Such "congenial spirits" obviously possess sensibility and their union is always endangered by a rival "suitor" who lacks their refined emotions. Appius serves a role that is later reenacted by Sindall, Montauban, and Barbarossa [in *The Man of the World*], while Lucius's character foreshadows in some respects Bolton, Savillon [in *Julia de Roubigné*], and Arrasid [in *The Prince of Tunis*].

As Virginia's lover, Lucius naturally shares her emotional susceptibility: "Thou knowest I [Virginia] love to weep for pity oft; / Thou too art gentle, Lucius, thou art wont / To paint the tender feelings in thy look." In contrast to Appius, who has been corrupted by his inordinate passions, Lucius is a man of refined feelings and noble ideals. Magnanimity, he argues, depends upon sensibility rather than a resolute will:

> 'Tis not unfeeling reason, iron valour,
> The cold conclusions of a steady heart,
> That nurse the generous purpose; in the soul,
> That knows the melting change of softer passions—

Such idealism finds expression in his spontaneous sympathy for his fellowmen, which has earned him the friendship of a Tuscan slave.

Mackenzie's basic mode of characterization is, then, already apparent in his first dramatic effort. Yet, if *Virginia* is of critical interest for the light it sheds on his development as a playwright and as a novelist, it is a poor and highly derivative work as a drama. The characters possess little realism or depth, and the play lacks unity of purpose. Because Virginius's character is too idealized, no real inner conflict can arise to weaken his resolution to kill his daughter. The ending, as in Mackenzie's later tragedies, is deliberately designed to create an emotional crescendo of shock and pathos. Instead of dying immediately (as is the case in Livy's account) from being stabbed in the heart, Virginia is allowed to walk home so that she can die on stage in her father's arms. Lucius, who originally lifts up the body of Virginia to arouse the people against Appius, now stabs himself to death beside the lifeless body of his bride. (pp. 98-104)

On March 1, 1773, Mackenzie announced to his cousin: "Your old friend The Prince of Tunis . . . is now in a fair way of stepping forth to the View of the Public." Written "several years before," the play opened on March 8 at the Theatre Royal in Edinburgh and ran for five nights to crowded houses, plus a benefit performance on March 17. The celebrated Mrs. Yates agreed to play the role of Zulima; and, according to Mackenzie's enthusiastic report, she revised the tragedy "with the most scrupulous Exactness, & suggested several Amendments equally convincing of Knowledge in theatrical Business & of critical Taste." After her performance, however, his praise was more qualified: "She did not conceive the Character in quite so soft a Stile as I, &, I believe, most of my Friends who had read it, imagined. She took it up entirely on the great Line; & that Expression of Despair & Horror which at some Passages, She gave it, was inimitable."

In the play, Arassid, Prince of Tunis, fearful of growing rebellion, rebellion, goes to seek the aid of the Turkish Sultan. Barbarossa, sent by the Sultan to put down the revolt, becomes the Tunisian ruler by reporting that Arassid has died from a pestilence when he has actually had Arassid killed, or so he believes. Zulima, who has grown up with Arassid and been betrothed to him, is wooed by Barbarossa until finally she assents reluctantly; and the play opens on their wedding day, three months after Barbarossa's victory. Zeyda, Arassid's sister, brings Zulima news of a slave who claims that Arassid is alive but is imprisoned by the Sultan. Later Heli, Barbarossa's officer but a former friend of Arassid, claims that the prince was murdered at the bidding of Hassan, Barbarossa's evil lieutenant.

Hassan, meanwhile, gains proof that Heli has leagued himself with the rebellious leaders of Tunis and begins to plot Heli's death. The latter learns that Zulima is actually the daughter he thought lost at sea, while an emissary from the Sultan turns out to be Arassid, who has eluded and outwitted his enemies and now reveals himself to Zulima. Heli and his allies rebel and are victorious—Hassan is killed, and Barbarossa flees. However, Heli's reunion with his daughter is short-lived, for Barbarossa, out of feigned friendship, has given him to drink the wedding potion that Zulima, unknown to her husband, had previously poisoned to avenge Arassid's supposed murder. Torn by her sense of guilt at having unwittingly killed her father, Zulima stabs herself to death as news arrives that Turkish troops have landed and restored Barbarossa to power. Arassid rushes headlong into battle and dies though Barbarossa tries to save him. The play ends with a remorseful Barbarossa raving in madness.

The Prince of Tunis is founded upon an incident in William Robertson's *History of the Reign of the Emperor Charles V* (1769) in which Alrachid actually flees from his tyrannical younger brother, Muley-Hascen, to implore the help of Barbarossa, ruler of Algiers. The treacherous Barbarossa arranges for Alrachid to be imprisoned in Constantinople: "he was arrested by order of the sultan, shut up in the seraglio, and was never heard of more." Barbarossa then wins Tunis by pretending to come in Alrachid's name, who he claims lies sick in his ship. The people revolt against Muley-Hascen only to discover Barbarossa's subterfuge too late to make any effective resistance.

Such was the basis for Mackenzie's historical drama. Written in blank verse, *The Prince of Tunis* once again shows Mackenzie's strengths and weaknesses as a dramatic poet. His expository and descriptive passages are well executed and show considerable narrative skill:

> Suladdin says, that when his watch was
>   changed,
> As, by the setting sun, he marked the sea,
> Dim on its level line he saw arise
> Objects that seemed a fleet, and grew upon him,
> Till darkness shut them out.

Mackenzie's limitations are revealed when the action is dramatized rather than reported, for he does not know how to delineate inner conflict naturally. When Hassan plays upon Barbarossa's fear of rebellion, the latter exclaims: "Thou distract'st my soul! / I am too young in virtue to withstand thee; / And yet I will." But his words are unconvincing because Barbarossa is describing and declaiming the conflict he should be experiencing dramatically.

As in *The Spanish Father,* emotional scenes are elevated through a self-conscious use of poetic diction:

> My wife! my daughter! thou whose infant soft-
>   ness
> The bursting billows cradled! call'st thou hence,
> With beckoning smiles, from yonder fields of
>   light,
> The hoary, desolate, and friendless Heli?—

At other times, the language is heightened through alliteration and heroic imagery:

> My brother's blood,
> Whose body, blackened in the burning sun,
> The desert eagles fed on, cries revenge;
> And, like the lion from his tufted den,
> Awakes the sleeping fury of my soul.

Such passages show the influence not only of Restoration and Augustan tragedy but of Mackenzie's own poetic theory. Commenting upon modern poetry in terms that seem equally applicable to verse drama, he observes [in his *Anecdotes and Egotisms,* 1927]: "It will be admitted that everything that is natural is not poetry, of which the very essence seems to be a certain elevation and elegance of language above the standard of ordinary life. Nobleness and dignity are the attributes of poetry. These may belong to the feelings and sentiments of inferior persons, but the language in which those feelings and sentiments are to be conveyed seems to require a certain degree of elegance and elevation if it is to be entitled to the denomination of poetry." It is this striving for "elegance and elevation" that accounts for much of Mackenzie's stilted blank verse and serves to mar his tragedies.

If *The Prince of Tunis* resembles *The Spanish Father* in its poetic style, it likewise shows similarities in its mode of characterization. We again have a weak figure of authority who is manipulated by a callous villain of principle, as well as a noble-minded soldier-father and his tragically doomed daughter. In spite of such similarities, however, *The Prince of Tunis* is a far more ambitious work than the earlier Mackenzie tragedies. Its characters possess greater complexity, though Mackenzie fails to realize their dramatic potentialities.

We see this difference most clearly by comparing the two extreme representatives of good and evil—Heli and Hassan. Heli is a mellowed Virginius or Alphonzo—tenderer, less stern, but still high-principled and idealistic: "I boast a heart, / The friend of justice and humanity." Not aware through most of the play that Zulima is his daughter, he is simply a long-suffering old man whose only remaining happiness is "conscious virtue." When he does discover Zulima's true identity, the nature of his response attests to his sensibility: "My wounded heart would lean upon her love, / Seek its lost peace, with big luxurious throbbings / Forget its woes, and wonder at its bliss."

In contrast, Hassan is the callous villain of principle whom Heli describes as incapable of being moved by pity. Like Appulinius and Alvarez, Hassan instinctively distrusts native goodness. Yet, while Appulinius and Alvarez are merely selfishly scheming villains, Hassan is a much more complex character. Though his influence upon Barbarossa is sinister, he remains completely loyal to him. His depravity is not motivated by simple egotism but by a consistently adhered-to cynicism that stems from "long-experienced falsehood." Unable to believe in the reality of disinterested virtue, he seeks ulterior motives to explain away its existence. Thus, when he finds proof that Heli is allied to the rebellious factions of Tunis, he rejoices because his own misanthropic view of mankind seems to him once more confirmed:

> Why, this is man;
> And Hassan knows him. With the sounds of
>   fame,
> Of right, of freedom, talking like a god,
> He hides the baseness of a rotten heart.

Hassan, however, has misinterpreted Heli's character. As a man of virtue and sensibility, he is incapable of such duplicity. Lacking Hassan's cold pragmatism, he finds it hard to act because he is torn between loyalty to his prince and his vow to avenge Arassid's murder. Recognizing that the ends do not justify the means, that "muffled treason / Is not of virtue's colour," he nevertheless feels compelled to support justice, although Zeyda's argument that "Treason to him [Barbarossa] is virtue" does little to alleviate his misgivings:

> To the sons
> Of blind ambition, such distinctions heal
> The wounds of conscience; mine can feel it here
> Beneath their cover: Barbarossa trusts me.

Though the news that Hassan suspects him of treason finally spurs Heli to action, the implication, one Mackenzie later explores in his essay on Hamlet, is that sensibility can undermine resolution with the pale cast of thought.

Hassan, of course, is too pragmatic and callous to suffer from such doubts. He calls Barbarossa's growing qualms "that foolish weakness, / That baby conscience, that unsinews valour." Like Sindall, moreover, he has that "pliancy of disposition," which enables him to hide his true feelings. Characteristically, like all of Mackenzie's "Men of Feeling," Heli lacks such flexibility and hence gives himself away when Hassan tests him by mentioning Arassid's death:

> The workings of his soul denied him speech;
> His blood made fiery courses on his cheeks,
> And to the heavens he cast a furious look,
> As if he would have borrowed lightning thence
> To blast me with his eye; then turned, and left
>   me,
> To hide his passion.

Between these representations of good and evil stands the figure of Barbarossa, another weak-minded, impetuous ruler. But, whereas Rodriguez's vacillations show little moral recognition or even consistency, Barbarossa's conscience is supposedly awakened by his love for Zulima: "since I saw her, / I have been taught to hate my former self, / In loving her." A similar testimony is given by Zeyda, Arassid's sister, who, unaware of her brother's supposed murder, is moved to sympathy by Barbarossa's show of emotions:

> But now he clasped my hand,
> A tear bedewed his cheek! "Zeyda," he said,
> "Perhaps I am unworthy of her love;
> Perhaps I have been—but—" he stopped, and
>   heaved
> A sigh so piteous, that my heart forgot
> My father's sceptre, and was quite his friend.

Though Zeyda's reliability cannot be questioned, yet it is difficult to imagine Barbarossa in the role of the diffident, lovesick suitor. It must likewise be asked at what point his actions become sincere. When Zulima first meets him, he pretends to have been Arassid's friend; and he wins her favor by "mingling his tears / In one sad stream with" hers. This of course is good strategy and has helped him to usurp the throne of Tunis. It is also one of the rare occasions in Mackenzie's works in which the testimony of the tear ducts can be questioned, unless we assume that his tears are an expression of remorse rather than an artifice of expediency.

Such ambiguity stems partly from the fact that we obtain so few internal glimpses of Barbarossa's character. He has only one brief soliloquy, and he lacks in Hassan the kind of confidant who would be sympathetic to his sense of guilt and remorse. The insights we do get are feeble attempts to suggest depth and consistency by means of Mackenzie's self-conscious borrowings from Shakespeare. Like Macbeth, he suffers from hallucinations about his victim, imagining that Arassid is calling him. At another time, he takes a Claudius-like stance to picture himself as a guilt-ridden prisoner of his own conscience: "Still in my cup this spotted adder lies, / Taints every draught, that Fortune can bestow, / Unsceptres royalty, and blasts enjoyment!" But, unlike Claudius, he lacks the intellectual courage to recognize the futility of repenting for an act from which he still reaps the benefits. However, since for Mackenzie moral regeneration is largely a state of mind rather than the effect of a rational decision, we are expected to believe Barbarossa's simple claim: "I am changed / From what I have been."

These weaknesses in characterization reflect all too clearly Mackenzie's overriding design: the antagonist, as in *The Spanish Father,* is viewed primarily as an agent whose actions initiate the tragic consequences to follow. Barbarossa hardly appears in the last two acts because all effort is now directed toward wringing as much pathos as possible from the events that overwhelm Zulima and her father. Likewise, Barbarossa's seeming complexity and unrealized tragic potentiality stem from Mackenzie's effort to make the figure of Barbarossa (a pirate and ruthless tyrant in Robertson's *History*) sufficiently sympathetic to justify Zulima's accepting him. Though hers is not an infatuation, as was the case with Ruzalla [in *The Spanish Father*], she does admit that "in some hour of weakness you [Bar-

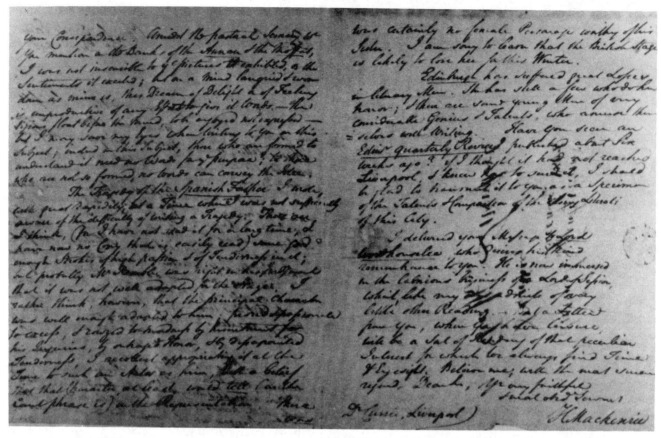

Part of an 1802 letter from Mackenzie to Robert Burns's biographer, Dr. James Currie, discussing flaws in one of Mackenzie's plays.

barossa] o'ercame me." Hence it is not surprising that Mackenzie's means of making his character more sympathetic follows the pattern already utilized in *The Spanish Father:* Hassan's evil influence mitigates his master's moral responsibility, while the latter's increasing sense of remorse tends to arouse our sympathy. Yet such efforts lack consistency and credibility because Mackenzie could not allow Barbarossa's self-conflict to develop dramatically without overshadowing Zulima's pitiful fate, thereby converting an essentially "pathetic tragedy" into a "moral tragedy."

In many respects, Zulima's situation anticipates that of Julia de Roubigné. Zulima grows up with Arassid and, like Julia and Savillon, "each was like a twin-tuned lute." Whereas Julia's acceptance of Montauban depends upon the mistaken belief that Savillon is married, Zulima's acceptance of Barbarossa rests upon the erroneous assumption that Arassid is dead; and both face a tragic dilemma when their suppositions turn out to have been illusory. Likewise, each is pursued by a shrewd and pertinacious suitor. Barbarossa, like Montauban, plays upon the heroine's emotions to gain his end. Pretending to mourn Arassid as a dead friend, he earns her gratitude and finally her commiseration: "He wooed me in compassion's gentle form, / To chase despair and anguish from his breast." Reluctantly, she at last assents to his "ceaseless importunity," but his victory is as empty as Montauban's since he gains "the promise, not the will."

Such resemblances between plots do not, however, extend to the depth of realism of the two works: the psychological analysis and relentless introspection that impress us in *Julia de Roubigné* are scarcely to be found in *The Prince of Tunis.* As with Barbarossa, Mackenzie's view of his heroine is external—he never probes her character nor sees her as an integral personality. When Zulima learns that the man she has just married instigated the supposed death of her lover, her response is artificial and highly derivative as she rapidly changes from a passive mourner into a resolute agent of vengeance:

> Soft, I would breathe a moment!—Barbarossa!
> My curses blast him!—Is he not my husband?
> The murderer of my love!—See how he glares,
> And points his wounds; whose purple mouths
>   unfold
> Their lips afresh, and cry aloud for vengeance!—
> Hast thou no dagger for a hand resolved?

As in his earlier tragedies, we have the impression that Mackenzie creates situations not so much to beset his characters with inner conflicts as to evoke feelings and moods from their reactions. Retrospecting about this tragedy in old age, he comments revealingly: "The play, it must be confessed, has many faults, particularly in the winding up of the plot; but it has some good poetry, and passages in which there was room for Mrs. Yates's powers of passionate declamation to exert themselves." Zulima's soliloquy, at the beginning of Act IV, certainly offered such an opportunity. When sending the poisoned wedding drink to Barbarossa, she invokes supernatural spirits in the manner of a Lady Macbeth:

> Ye ministers of vengeance! Ye who ride
> On tempests' wings, and point the lightnings'
>   spear!
> Who split the bosom of the trembling earth!
> Or from the phials of offended Heaven
> Pour its black venom on the deathful gale!
> Inspire my soul with unrelenting rage,
> And chase the busy fears, that rise upon me!

Yet if such a speech suited Mrs. Yates's histrionic talents, she was for Mackenzie . . . less satisfactory in those soft scenes of melancholy that were his forte. Until the third act, Zulima is one of those mournful, resigned heroines (much like Ruzalla and Virginia) that appeal to his fondness for pathos:

> I am in love with sorrows. I could sit
> The live-long day, and ruminate upon them.
> Methinks there is a dignity in sorrow,
> Lord of its sighs, and conqueror of the world!

It is, however, the last act that best reveals Mackenzie's rhetorical method. The denouement confronts his heroine with a series of revelations calculated to elicit a wide range of emotions. And, characteristically, events act on her rather than offer her a choice of action, each carrying with it its own inevitability that makes her its passive and ironic victim. The discovery that Arassid lives creates a hopeless dilemma for her since she has just married his would-be murderer: "I am not what I was: the serpent's touch / Has turned this flower to poison." But the despair of this situation is quickly dwarfed by the horror of succeeding events: the discovery that Heli is her father is followed almost immediately by the realization that she has unwittingly brought about his death. Such a climax offered Mackenzie the kind of crescendo of pathos that he later felt ill at ease about. The dying Heli blesses his daughter and prays to God to forgive her. Zulima, guilt-stricken and growing mad, calls heaven's vengeance upon herself before she commits suicide:

> No: let me curse; and, if the thunder sleeps,
> Awake its hottest bolt, and call it here!—
> I am not mad; I know I am not mad!
> This old man was my father!—Murdered! murdered!
> [*Throwing herself on the Body of her Father.*]

Her remorse is calculated to evoke in us the strongest sense of pity since she bears little responsibility for the chain of events that have turned her into an unwitting parricide. Though Heli's death is the indirect result of her attempt to poison her husband, the fact that Barbarossa has usurped the Tunisian throne and murdered the rightful ruler (or so she believes) who is also her lover largely exonerates her and gives her death that aura of pathos which dominates all of Mackenzie's tragedies.

Mackenzie's only comedy, based on *La Fausse Inconstance; ou, Le Triomphe de l'Honnêteté* (1787) by Fanny de Beauharnais, deals with a young man's fear of ridicule and its consequences. Sedley, having been brought up in the country, goes to London to taste fashionable life after

coming into an estate of seven thousand pounds a year. His cousin, Sir Charles Dormer, plays upon his fear in order to introduce him to a life of deceit and intrigue. Mountfort, Sedley's former tutor who is believed to have died in India, returns to England in the disguise of one Captain Wilkins, a supposed friend of the "deceased." He witnesses the seeming corruption of his former pupil, whom he had appointed guardian to his daughter Julia; and he decides to remove her from Sedley's influence. Since Wilkins claims to be Julia's co-guardian, Sir Charles, who is enamored of the girl, has Miss Danby, his accomplice, try to bribe him into giving up his guardianship. However, to protect Sir Charles, Miss Danby pretends to be speaking for Sedley. Wilkins is incensed by the offer, and Miss Danby persuades Sir Charles that their best stratagem now is to encourage the Captain's anger into a real quarrel with Sedley. Miss Danby will meanwhile entice Julia to her house, where Sir Charles will be able to seduce her.

Ignorant of this arrangement, Lady Dormer has made an assignation with Sedley at Miss Danby's house. She arrives and hides her face behind a mask when her husband appears. Sir Charles, believing her to be Julia, tries to make love to her but is interrupted by the arrival of Wilkins, who finally unmasks Lady Dormer. Sedley now arrives with his old servant William who, never having been deceived by Mountfort's disguise, gives away Wilkin's true identity and reports that Sedley has rescued Julia from Miss Danby's clutches. Mountfort and Sedley are reconciled, and Sedley promises never to play the "White Hypocrite" again and receives the hand of Julia from her forgiving father.

Originally called *The Force of Fashion,* the play was performed at Covent Garden for one night only on December 5, 1789. In the preface to the published version, called *False Shame, or The White Hypocrite* and included in his collected *Works,* Mackenzie speculates about the reason for its failure:

> This Comedy was unsuccessful in the representation; and, in truth, it is not, I believe, well calculated for the stage. It suffered, perhaps, a little by my absence from London, and the secresy which I thought it prudent to hold with regard to its author. Mr. Harris shewed every attention to it, and entertained the most sanguine assurance of its success; yet I have been told by some theatrical people, that (owing probably to the state of Covent Garden theatre at the time) it was ill cast, as the playhouse phrase is, and the principal part (that of *Mountfort*) very indifferently played. That character is of a kind difficult to play; depending on feelings sometimes altogether suppressed, and often, when expressed in words, expressed in that short and stifled manner, which, in my idea, suited the situation and feelings of the speaker; its representation rather required aid from the performer, than lent it him in the performance.

"The general idea of the piece," he admits, "is imperfectly brought out," and then he adds: "I had once thoughts of remodelling the piece, and of trying to place some of the characters in more theatrical situations; but I gave up the attempt, afraid of an alteration which might again expose me to a failure which I had once experienced. So I give the comedy here as it originally stood."

The fact is, however, that Mackenzie did make changes some time between the play's performance and its publication nineteen years later. When we compare the original manuscript of *The Force of Fashion* submitted to the Lord Chamberlain with the printed version of *False Shame,* a good number of alterations are apparent. Many of these are merely stylistic changes, but some indicate a definite shift in characterization. Together with the change of title, Mackenzie provided a new epilogue, probably because the first one specifically refers to the old title. The first epilogue is, moreover, merely a humdrum recital of the "despotic Sway" of that idol Fashion, while the second is a witty argument by Lady Dormer to the effect that *"Hypocrisy's* a very useful thing." There are also many cuts and revisions in the manuscript (probably to make it conform to the acted version), most of which Mackenzie ignored in preparing the play for publication. The longest of these excisions removes from the manuscript all of the satirical action involving a ludicrous group of virtuosos, a scene comprising almost half of the first act. In *False Shame,* a fair part of this scene remains, preserving one of the dilettantes, the antiquarian Dr. Mummy, though Mackenzie eliminated all the dialogue involving Mr. Petal, Mr. Distich, Dr. Phlogiston, and Mr. Speculum. From these deleted passages, however, we get a clue to the date of composition of the play. On the first numbered leaf of the manuscript, as elsewhere, there are references to the *World, or Fashionable Advertiser,* a London daily newspaper that did not begin publication until 1787. It was on January 6 of that year, moreover, that the *Lounger* ceased publication, probably providing Mackenzie with the leisure to make another attempt to win acceptance on the London stage.

Although the machinations of Sir Charles and Miss Danby are never allowed to prosper far enough to bring serious harm to the good characters, the basic format is reminiscent of Mackenzie's tragedies. Mountfort is another variation of the noble soldier-father striving to protect his daughter, while Julia possesses that characteristic pensive quality which we have seen in most of Mackenzie's heroines. Similarly, Sir Charles Dormer is one more villain of passion, whereas Miss Danby typifies the villain of principle. It is only in the temporary aberration of Sedley that a new dramatic course is explored.

Yet here too correspondences are to be found if we turn back to Mackenzie's fiction. Ned Sedley appears briefly in *The Man of Feeling* in the fragment called "The Pupil." As an old man, he recounts for Harley how his tutor Mountford managed to protect him from the corrupting influence of Respino. Though *Mountford* becomes *Mountfort* in *False Shame* (the manuscript of *The Force of Fashion* still preserves the original spelling), there can be little doubt of Mackenzie's borrowings from his first novel. Indeed, Sedley, in *False Shame* recounts: "When a boy, I was placed under his [Mountfort's] care; a kind of tutor, sir; I was indebted to him for a great deal of good learning, which now it will cost me nearly as much time to forget."

[In] reference to Billy Annesly [in *The Man of the World*] that his debasement was almost inevitable because he lacked a Mountford to offset Sindall's concerted effort to corrupt him. Sedley, in spite of Mountfort's former tutelage, is in a similar position when he comes under the influence of Sir Charles. He is, in fact, all the more vulnerable because of his inordinate fear of ridicule. Yet Sedley shows no signs of possessing this weakness in "The Pupil." On the contrary, his final rejection of Respino reveals a degree of self-confidence that he obviously lacks in *False Shame:* "You [Respino] may possibly be merry with your companions at my weakness, as I suppose you will term it. I give you leave for derision: you may affect a triumph; I shall feel it."

Mackenzie changed Sedley's character because he wanted to portray in his comedy "a young man, of the most virtuous dispositions and amiable feelings, overpowered by a false shame, and led into conduct unworthy of him." This theme, as we have seen, he had only recently examined in the "Story of Father Nicholas." Though Sedley shares St. Hubert's "extreme sensibility of shame," he is able to escape the latter's fate largely because of Mackenzie's comic approach to the theme. Yet the tragic potentialities remain and find expression in Mountfort's last speech: "He who is first such a hypocrite from vanity, or from fear, will be in danger of becoming, in truth, the character he personates."

A "Man of Feeling" is particularly apt to face such a temptation since his acute sensibility and imagination, as we have observed, make him naturally self-conscious and hence sensitive to the way others respond to him. Harley's moral strength is derived in large part from his refusal to permit the ridicule of a callous world to affect his ideal mode of conduct. Yet even he, we must remember, cannot completely ignore the persistent voice of the "man without." However, whereas Harley will not accommodate himself to the demands of a corrupt society, though ill at ease in the knowledge of its disdain, Sedley has begun to compromise his principles although he has not yet, like St. Hubert, learned to blunt his "natural feelings of rectitude":

> *Sir Char.*   The world is full of rogues and fools; a wise man must accommodate himself to both.
>
> *Sed.*   That accommodation I find it difficult to reconcile myself to; yet often, from a silly sort of shame, I submit to it, till a better sort of shame takes me to task for having done so.

Sedley's corruption, then, is largely a façade behind which he tries to hide his native goodness from the jeers of a cynical world. When he helps free an officer on half-pay from debtor's prison, he pretends to his valet to be seducing the man's wife. Only when egged on by Sir Charles, who plays upon his fears of ridicule, does he attempt to assume the role his nature abhors. But his resolution to take advantage of Julia's helpless position falters as soon as he catches sight of her: "no sooner had she spoken, had she looked when she spoke, had she smiled . . . than I melted down again to a fond respectful—fool, you [Sir Charles] would call it."

Though "but a sorry player," as he himself admits later, Sedley nevertheless succeeds in misleading Wilkins because he is determined to convince the latter that he is "not the vulgar, sober, whining thing he may have been taught by Mountfort to imagine." Sedley's masquerade must of course work to fulfill the demands of the plot. At times, however, his emotions master him in his meeting with Wilkins since Mackenzie wanted his hero's inner conflict to become transparent to the audience. The manuscript carries elaborate stage directions for that purpose: "Sedley looks at him [Wilkins] at first with a Complacency, which he afterwards checks with an affected Indifference & Haughtiness of Air. During their whole Conversation, Sedley must wear a Look of Embarrassment, struggling to keep down his natural Feelings under this Mask of assumed Indifference. He must often shew in his Countenance Feelings ready to overpower him, while his Tongue & an affected Negligence of Manner awkwardly contradict it."

The situation is naturally comical, but for Mackenzie it also offered a solution to a problem he had never actually solved in his tragedies. The moral ambiguity that mars the characterization of both Rodriguez and Barbarossa is avoided in the portrayal of Sedley because, as a mock villain, he does not bring into question the ethical nature of Julia's love for him. His inner conflicts, his sense of embarrassment and shame, are convincing because they are the natural result of his particular dilemma rather than merely the means of superimposing a more sympathetic overlay on his character. Instead of vacillating between good and evil with little consistency or credibility, as is the case with Rodriguez and Barbarossa, Sedley's moral regeneration follows a convincing psychological pattern. The awkwardness and uneasiness with which he plays the fashionable libertine prepare us for his final reformation. Though he has a short-lived resolution before his meeting with Wilkins to be "a coward thus no longer," his true change of heart comes only when he recognizes the real price he will have to pay for his fear of ridicule. Revolted by Sir Charles's exhortations to challenge Wilkins and make love to his friend's wife (who happens, unknown to Sir Charles, to be Lady Dormer), Sedley finally begins to question the legitimacy of fashion's rule: "What is this fashion, that I should obey it at such expence? and whence is that superiority, that entitles it to laugh at me?"

Significantly, moral change is now conveyed by means of argument and action rather than by falling back on the stale idiom of sensibility. By rejecting Lady Dormer's amorous advances and by resolving to fire into the air in the ensuing duel with Wilkins, Sedley demonstrates his goodness and his newly acquired self-confidence in the face of a jeering, callous world. He fulfills, moreover, the demands made earlier by Wilkins when, unimpressed by Sedley's munificence (he has secretly sent Julia money), he had defined true generosity: "It is not parting with money, which the habits of extravagance have taught them to undervalue, that entitles such men to be called humane or generous. Let them forego one favourite indulgence for the sake of humanity; let them sacrifice one selfish passion to the good of others, and then tell us of their benevolence and generosity." Since his words are in part a close para-

phrase of a passage in *Mirror*, No. 23, that condemns Charles Surface as a "profligate hero," it is quite likely that Mackenzie chose this opportunity to restate allusively his criticism of Richard Brinsley Sheridan's hero in *The School for Scandal*.

The didactic value of Sedley's moral education is, of course, evident: it gives Mackenzie an opportunity to expose the folly of conforming to a degenerate society. At the heart of that corruption lies a fashionable nonchalance and an insensitivity that Mackenzie, like so many of his contemporaries, attributed to the influence of Lord Chesterfield's *Letters to his Son* (1774):

> In the intercourse of ordinary life, the late founder of a school of politeness recommended a certain indifference or *nonchalance* of manner, as the characteristic of a well-bred man. The system has since his time flourished and prevailed in a most extensive degree, and, like all other systems that war on nature, has been carried a good deal further by the disciples, than it is probable their masters intended, "Nous avons changé tout cela," says the Mock Doctor of Moliere, when his patient's father ventured to suppose that the heart lay on the left side of the body. The fine gentleman of Lord Chesterfield has made a change still greater; the heart is struck out of his anatomy altogether. [*Lounger*, No. 85]

Wilkins, after seeing Sedley, is convinced that his former pupil has already adopted this mode of conduct. Sedley, he tells Julia, is "depraved not by passion, but on system; that despicable, selfish, unfeeling system, in which modern refinement has taught her votaries to triumph. I can make allowance for the wanderings of youth, when levity misleads, or passion impels it; but this cold apathy of vice so chills, so petrifies the heart, that neither returning honour can warm, nor awakened conscience rouse it." This distinction is one we have seen run through much of Mackenzie's works: man can be corrupted either by losing control over his emotions or by learning to control them too well. The one becomes a villain of passion; the other ends up as villain of principle. The latter case offers, however, the greatest danger, since moral regeneration is largely an emotional experience toward which such a man has deliberately deadened his senses, while the villain of passion by his very nature retains the capacity for regeneration.

Sir Charles, though driven by his infatuation for Julia into a series of unscrupulous acts, yet has qualms about instigating a quarrel between Sedley and Wilkins and is moved by the tears of a loyal servant. When old William assures him that he would lay down his life for Sedley, Sir Charles momentarily senses his own corruption: "How this old man loves his master! The tears were on his cheek, and he spoke so from the warmth of his heart, that mine, callous as it is to such foolery, was smitten, and could scarcely play the hypocrite to him. After all, there is something in this same virtue, that one can't help feeling now and then in spite of one. Not all the gold I can bribe my rascals with, ever purchased from them one such tear as William's."

The situation is ironic because Sir Charles's emotional response contradicts his own mode of conduct. Contemptuous of morality and sensibility, he sees them only as a useful guise for taking advantage of those still innocent enough to admire such qualities. His hope is to seduce Julia by putting on "that old-fashioned cloak of virtue and feeling" which he had made his rival Sedley ashamed to wear. When he addresses her at Miss Danby's house (though he is, of course, really confronting the masked figure of his own wife), he tries to affect an air of sincerity by mouthing the ideals of sensibility: "Formed for the tenderest sympathies of friendship and of love, it has been my misfortune to be joined to one who is perfectly unsusceptible of either; . . . Nay, do not start at the declaration,—you must have seen, though I was careful to hide my attachment, you must have seen how much it possessed by heart. There are souls, which, by an instinctive sort of impulse, involuntarily attract one another."

Sir Charles could not, of course, be farther from the truth. He rejects all notions of love or compatibility in marriage, adhering to a cynically pragmatic view of one's wife: "A wife is a woman, who is to take a man's name, and may chance, during the first year or two, to bring an heir to his estate; to do sometimes the honours of his table (when the company is not too good for her;) and to let women, that might otherwise be scrupulous, come about his house. But as for his companion—I don't think I have exchanged a dozen sentences with Lady Dormer these three months." Needless to say, Mackenzie abhorred such values and was alarmed by their widespread acceptance. In an early letter to his cousin, he complains: "The romantic is now exploded in every Thing; in Marriage it is fallen in Proportion; and Matches of mere Conveniency are talk'd of at an age when the Youth of former Times used to be ignorant of the Word."

Lady Dormer shares many of her husband's vices, and she too tries to justify herself by insisting that "one must accommodate to one's society," just as she also relies on the idiom of sensibility to achieve her objective—alluring Sedley. " 'Tis not with commonplace souls," she assures him, "that mine can vibrate." Lady Dormer appears, nevertheless, far less reprehensible than her husband since his cynical infidelity confers upon her a certain pathos if not also some justification for her conduct. "Do you not pity me then," she asks Sedley, "married (as most women of my rank are) before I knew myself; wedded, not to a man, but to a settlement; a mere alliance of conveniency."

In revising his play, Mackenzie sought to emphasize these aspects of her character by expanding her soliloquy at the end of the second act. Originally, she voices her jealousy of Julia and makes plans to entice Sedley. In *False Shame,* a number of lines are added to her soliloquy in which she seeks to justify her conduct: "But is it quite right in me to draw his eyes that way? quite fair to Sir Charles my husband?—How the deuce now did that word contrive to come across my conscience? the word *wife,* I'll be sworn, never comes across Sir Charles's; and, as a married woman is fairly entitled to the attentions of *one* man, if her husband is not that one, may she not try to find such a one for herself ?" At the same time, Mackenzie deleted several incriminating lines that call attention to Lady Dormer's duplicity in claiming to have Julia's best interest at heart when she is actually jealous of the attention the girl receives from Sedley and her husband. In *The Force of Fashion,* Lady Dormer assures Wilkins: "Sir you will always find me happy to receive you, & equally interested with yourself in the Welfare of Miss Mountford." And then observes *solus* in what originally had constituted the beginning of her soliloquy: "So—how much one can do with a little Hypocrisy at one's Heart, & a few fine Words on one's Tongue." In *False Shame,* all these lines are eliminated.

Yet such instances of intrigue and double-dealing pale before the machinations of Miss Danby. Where Lady Dormer and even Sir Charles uneasily sense at times their own duplicity, no such qualms beset Miss Danby. As a true villain of principle, she possesses neither the emotional susceptibility nor the moral restraint that sometimes gets the better of Sir Charles. When she proposes to arrange a quarrel between Wilkins and Sedley, Sir Charles is hesitant though he admires Miss Danby's lack of scruples: "You women, Di, have no restraints on your inclinations, no qualms to come across you in the progress of them. Would not this be going a little too far, to make them cut one another's throats, to make way for me to the girl?" But Miss Danby, like other Mackenzie characters, such as Appulinius, Alvarez, and Hassan, knows how to manipulate her patron's emotions:

> *Miss Dan.*   Your love, I find, is not half so sharp set as my resentment. But you think too deeply of the consequences; they shall but scramble on a point of honour, and give you an opportunity of running away with the prize in the mean time.
>
> *Sir Char.*   Shall I indeed?—that dear, soft, artless, bewitching girl!—To obtain her, Danby, you shall make me all the rogue you would have me to be. 'Tis her fault to be so bewitching, eh?

Sharing Sindall's "pliancy of disposition," she easily ingratiates herself with "honest William" by "speaking of the good old times at Sedley-Hall and making him presents of Thomas-a-Kempis, and the Whole Duty of Man, for Sunday's reading in the country." It is, however, by feigning the characteristics of sensibility that Miss Danby has achieved her greatest success. Having originally come to London as Dorothy Dobson "to be put apprentice to a little mantua-maker," she has improved her station and acquired "an elegant small house" by becoming Diana Danby, "poetess and sentimentalist" (one who speaks in sentiments like Joseph Surface). In reality, a pander who provides suitable accommodations for the affairs of both Sir Charles and Lady Dormer, she hides her role behind the effusive display of delicacy and benevolence that has become second nature to her. When Sir Charles urges her to be herself in his presence, she complains: "I can't immediately put off this cant, which I am obliged to use to the dupes of it. By the help of this high-flown style, I have got into the good graces of this same Wilkins, who seems to be as honourable and sentimental as the best of us." It is undoubtedly under her tutelage that Sir Charles has learned "this high-flown style." When she approaches Wilkins with Dormer's veiled proposal, she assures him that "there are souls with whom sympathy anticipates time, and connects us at first sight," a sentiment Sir Charles echoes when he imagines he is addressing Julia.

In *The Force of Fashion,* Miss Danby appears as merely an unscrupulous opportunist who schemes for the benefit of her patron. In *False Shame,* her character becomes more vicious through a revealing soliloquy added at the beginning of Act III. Apparently, Mackenzie felt that her odious act of trying to betray Julia into the clutches of Sir Charles needed more adequate motivation. She is, therefore, made to appear vindictive and contemptuous of Julia, loathing her for her moral superiority: "So, this girl takes it into her head to suspect me, and to lecture Lady Dormer on the subject. What is this virtue, that its owners should give themselves such airs! As things go now-a-days—and a girl with nothing too! This old-fashioned virtue, like an old-fashioned gown, may be worn by the rich if they please; but when it is the best of the wardrobe, 'twill be looked on as a cast-off thing, and valued accordingly. But I shall be even with her, if my invention and Sir Charles's courage fail not." Yet if Julia has become suspicious of Miss Danby, it seems implausible for her to believe the latter's claim of coming to fetch her in Wilkin's name.

Such a discrepancy is, however, unlikely to become noticeable because Julia Mountfort is a shadowy figure, one rarely seen directly although most of the plot revolves around her. In a play of one hundred thirty pages, she is present for only sixteen pages, having two meetings with Wilkins and then reappearing shortly before the play ends. In other respects, however, she is clearly reminiscent of Mackenzie's former heroines. Sedley describes Julia as "gentle, elegant—shaded by affliction, dignified by her sorrows!" And once again the mother is made to die in the heroine's infancy in order to enable Mackenzie to create more of those affecting scenes between a high-minded, widowed father and his submissive daughter. Whereas in *The Prince of Tunis* neither is aware of their kinship, in *False Shame* it is only the daughter that is ignorant, believing herself a forlorn orphan. The situation is obviously pathetic, and Mackenzie does not hesitate to exploit its emotional potential. At her first meeting with her disguised father, Julia instinctively senses his delicacy and goodness and determines to trust him implicitly: "I pass over the ceremonial of a first interview, and, judging of the nobleness of his [her father's] representative by what I have been proud to hear of him, I speak at once to the heart from the heart; from a poor, orphan, unfriended girl, to one who can feel—Pardon this freedom, Captain Wilkins."

The fact that Julia is allowed on stage only in her meetings with Wilkins may be viewed as a flaw in the play. Sedley's meeting with her, when he is determined to flirt with Julia only to have his resolution overthrown as soon as she addresses him, is reported rather than dramatized although its comic potentiality is obvious. Possibly, however, this was the very reason for leaving the scene unwritten. Perhaps Mackenzie was unwilling to bring his pensive, idealized heroine in contact with the protagonists of his comic plot for fear of diminishing her credibility in the presence of more realistically executed characters.

As such, the absence of this scene indicates a characteris-

tic problem of Sentimental comedy: its precarious union of purely comic elements with sententious and pathetic features. Yet Mackenzie in his prologue boasts of the hybrid nature of his play. After a debate between the rival sisters of Comedy, the "laughing Muse" and her sister "Sentiment," in which the traditional arguments against each school of comedy are recited, he announces a compromise solution:

> To-night our bard,—I praise his courage for't,—
> To either sister tries to pay his court;
> Some comic characters attempts to sketch,
> Some deeper feelings humbly hopes to reach.
> Your hearts, he knows, how quick soe'er to seize
> True comic mirth, those serious feelings please;
> The tear for worth, triumphant or oppressed,
> Drops through the sunshine of the gayest breast;

The truth is, however, that the play arouses few tears because "true comic mirth" obviously predominates. Not only are we rarely allowed to see Julia on stage, but we do not share Wilkins's disillusioned view of Sedley since we are able to discern his true worth behind the facade of libertinism. We can, therefore, enjoy his inept masquerade and discomfort without feeling serious anxiety about the outcome. As a result, *False Shame* largely succeeds as an amusing and effective comedy and is undoubtedly Mackenzie's best play.

Nor is it by mere chance that his one comedy is superior. Though Mackenzie has never gained recognition as a comic writer, it is that very quality . . . that gives his *Man of Feeling* its unique tone and sense of detachment. Through his narrator, the novelist gained an objective perspective from which to view his hero. Similarly, it is the comic form itself that objectified Mackenzie's view as a playwright. Sensing the hazard of introducing a pensive heroine into comedy, particularly where a sham form of sensibility was to be exposed, he suppressed for once his love of pathos in order to submerge Julia as much as the plot permitted. Comedy, in a sense, liberated him from the narrow rhetorical confines that tragedy had assumed for him and enabled him to achieve a degree of realism and control his earlier plays had sorely lacked. (pp. 115-36)

Dwyer on Mackenzie's technique:

The novels of Henry Mackenzie have been of considerable interest to those who have studied the genesis of sentimental literature. It is my contention that they should be read primarily as moralistic tracts outlining a "gentle sensibility" productive of an active benevolence and concomitant social harmony and yet consistent with the more traditional distinctions between virtue and vice. Like most Scottish practical moralists, Mackenzie was concerned to encourage those moral sentiments which thrived under the sun of civilization. At the same time, he was not prepared to ignore the warnings of the generations of bards and moralists who had preceded him. The danger always remained that the selfishness and artificiality of the modern world could act as a deadly corrosive within the British moral community.

John Dwyer, in The Eighteenth Century, *Spring 1989.*

Gerard A. Barker, in his Henry Mackenzie, *Twayne Publishers, 1975, 189 p.*

R. Peter Burnham   (essay date 1983)

[*In the following excerpt, Burnham examines* The Man of Feeling *as a reflection of Mackenzie's social attitudes, asserting that the humanitarian deeds of the novel's protagonist are always undermined by the conservative intentions of the author.*]

The Man of Feeling, published in 1771, is Henry Mackenzie's first and most famous novel. While I do not believe that there is a critic to be found who would presume to overpraise it abundantly, still it has its virtues and if read for no other reason than as an expression of the curious phenomenon of eighteenth-century sentimentalism, it is an interesting book. The few critics who have dealt with the work generally associate it with the new humanitarianism that culminated in the reforms of the Victorians, and identify its author with his creation, Harley, the man of feeling. Mackenzie's own statements encourage such an assumption. "Peace to your Joys at Kilravock!" he writes to his cousin Elizabeth Rose, "surely it is not from any blameable Feeling that I find myself sigh as I write it [**The Man of Feeling**]." At another occasion he speaks of writing from the heart and adds that if his "Performances have any Merit, they owe it to this." Harold William Thompson entitles his biography of Mackenzie *The Scottish Man of Feeling.* Another critic finds Mackenzie to be "a solemn, stuffy person, precisely the type Sterne most detested. He allowed but one indulgence—luxuriating in tears and the damp atmosphere of lachrymose effusion" [James A. Foster, in his *History of the Pre-Romantic Novel in England,* 1949]. Such statements as this are probably true as far as they go, but they imply that Mackenzie did little or no distancing when he created Harley. I believe, however, that when it is recognized that Mackenzie does not wholeheartedly identify with or agree with his man of feeling, we shall have gone a long way towards discovering the reason why **The Man of Feeling** is so curiously a halfway measure between the old static conception of society and the newer, soon to be fully developed dynamic and dialectic view of society that started with the philosophes and culminated in critics such as Ruskin and Arnold and in philosophers such as Hegel and Marx. It will be my purpose in this article both to show how the "new humanitarianism" of Harley is undercut by a rather complacent old fashioned Toryism of Mackenzie, and to explain how this disparity keeps the book from making certain basic conclusions that it should arrive at, but in fact does not.

To understand Mackenzie's social attitudes, we must first understand his hero Harley. Harold William Thompson characterizes him in this manner:

> To be fair to Mackenzie, we must admit that in Harley he created a new and significant type of hero—the humanitarian who not only feels for the distresses of others but actually helps them—the humble, unselfish man as contrasted with the selfish, unfeeling person whom Mackenzie would call the Man of the world.

In the contrast between "natural" benevolent unselfishness and worldliness we find the good and evil of the book. Harley possesses an extraordinary sensitivity to the suffering and hardship of his fellow-creatures, and his first venture into the world (his trip to London and back and the experiences that the trip occasioned) only deepen his sentimental and lachrymose response to the ways of the world. Few possess such a sensitivity and those who do acquired it in an environment and by a process that few could duplicate. Anglican divines such as Benjamin Whichcote, while not closing their eyes to the role played by evil and selfishness in the world, believed man to be naturally good when left to his own native impulses. Similarly, Shaftesbury maintained that in small towns and in the country natural benevolence was free to flourish unhindered by the unnatural vices of urban man. Within the novel Mr. Sedley describes the kind of education that the benevolent philosophers and latitudinarian Anglican divines had in mind when they spoke of man's natural goodness:

> But as to the higher part of education, Mr. Harley, the culture of the mind—let the feelings be awakened, let the heart be brought forward to its object, placed in the light in which nature would have it stand, and its decisions will ever be just. The world

> Will smile and smile, and be a villain;
> and the youth, who does not suspect its deceit,
> will be content to smile with it.

We are told Harley's *Bildung* conforms to this pattern. He grew up without paternal guidance or authoritarian restrictions next to nature in pristine Scotland. His education was desultory and self-regulated; he was free to let the natural impulses of his heart develop unchecked by any urban interference. For Miss Walton, as for Harley, "humanity was a feeling, not a principle." Thus cold logic interferes with one's true duty to humanity. Prudence (concerning monetary matters) likewise interferes with true benevolence. When Harley's London companions laugh at him for being taken by a sharper and for believing a whore's tale of misfortune (Emily Atkins for whom Harley pawns his watch to raise money for her succor), Harley concludes that "to calculate the chances of deception is too tedious a business for the life of man." Earlier, the beggar whom Harley met at the inception of his journey to London tells him he took up fortune telling as a bill of exchange for the alms people gave him. "I found," he says, "that people don't care to give alms without some security for their money; a wooden leg or a withered arm is a sort of draught upon heaven for those who choose to have their money placed to account there." In contrast to the man of feeling, then, the characteristic pose of the man of the world is selfish calculation: even in charity we see that it is by such devices as that of calculating the chances of deception that worldly men rationalize their selfishness.

A closer study of the man of the world is reserved for Mackenzie's second novel (of that name), where Sindall is seen as a loose living profligate debauching the innocent in the manner of Richardson's Lovelace. Somewhat ironically, in **The Man of Feeling** the villains that we actually see (because the focus in the novel is upon the confrontation of Harley and victims of the world's cruelty, most of the villainy we hear of is committed off stage—for example, the squire who perpetrates so much evil on Edwards is never seen) are hypocritical men of sentiment. The London sharper, we are told, was fluent on the subject of benevolence, so fluent in fact that he relieves Harley of close to £12 as they chat on the subject of benevolence and charity over a game of piquet. The other hypocritical sentimentalist is Respino, who appears in Sedley's story. But that the world is an evil place, antithetical to men of feeling and contemptuous to the virtuous, we are never in doubt. The book is filled with references to the "unfeeling world" and its external selfish ways. Always worldliness is seen to be based upon an arrested moral sense and an inability to see into the real nature of our earthly duties to ourselves and our fellow man. The misanthrope, for example, lectures Harley on the disparity between appearances and reality, labeling honor and politeness "semblances" and virtue and friendship "realities." This idea is later picked up and reiterated by the anonymous narrator as he comments on Harley's return home accompanied by old Edwards, his grandchildren, and a few neighbors:

> With this train Harley returned to the abode of his fathers: and we cannot but think, that his enjoyment was as great as if he had arrived from the tour of Europe with a Swiss valet for his companion, and half a dozen snuff-boxes, with invisible hinges, in his pocket. But we take our ideas from sounds which folly has invented; Fashion, Bon ton, and Vertù, are the names of certain idols, to which we sacrifice the genuine pleasures of the soul: in this world of semblance, we are contented with personating happiness; to feel it is an art beyond us.

With the world consistently labeled a place filled with vain follies and peopled with self-serving egoists, and with the man of feeling's behavior consistently characterized as exemplary behavior, we could expect certain conclusions to be drawn. The Anglican divines maintained (in opposition to Hobbes) that the capacity for pity, tenderness and benevolence was chiefly what distinguished man from the beasts, and that since it was man's duty to live according to his nature, an active benevolence and the cultivation of the heart were the highest manifestations of man's religious impulse. Shaftesbury's position is similar to this. While the divines and Shaftesbury write about charity in terms of God and a cosmological conception of man, Harley offers a social, not Christian, reason for benevolence and charity: "To give to the necessitous may sometimes be a weakness in the man; to encourage industry is a duty in the citizen." If Harley is acting in accordance to a social conception of man, and if the world blinds men to reality, as the narrator and some of the characters state, we should expect the book to be forthcoming with a statement explaining Harley's imperatives, a statement that would give a philosophical justification for his behavior. And so it does. When the honest school mistress who has been taking care of old Edwards' grandchildren laments the fact that they have been deserted by their relations, Harley is quick to respond. "Madam," says Harley, "let us never forget that we are all relations." Presumably, then, to see into the nature of human reality, one would have to recognize that since the world divides men into classes, into rich and poor, haves and have-nots, it completely distorts the one true vision of reality. But it is at this point that we reach the crux of the problem of the social ethos of *The Man of Feeling.* When an author structures the theme of a book around the dichotomy of the world vs. elemental human responsibilities, it usually leads to one of two conclusions: either the book rejects the world and seeks a transcendental (usually Christian) solution, or it becomes a call to social action. Gower's *Confessio Amantis* and Langland's *Piers the Ploughman* are medieval examples of the former conclusion; Godwin and Charles Dickens are examples of men who use the analysis of society's ills and abuses to motivate men to action.

The Man of Feeling, however, steadfastly refuses to make the logical conclusion. It is neither a call to social action nor a religious treatise that excoriates the world and then rejects it for the eternal and absolute verities of religion. It does *appear* to come to the religious conclusion when Harley in his death throes tells the narrator he is leaving the world "to enter on that state which I have learned to believe is replete with the genuine happiness attendant upon virtue," but by following the gestalt of *The Man of Feeling* and by paying careful attention to the values of the narrator, this statement will be seen to carry little weight.

Let me first deal with the social aspect of the novel, and then, after the narrator's real attitude toward the world is made clear, with the religious question. The only dramatized alternative for Harley is the misanthrope, clearly an unsatisfactory alternative. The misanthrope, a former man of feeling who has become disillusioned, does offer some purposeful social criticism directed against the mode of education of the day (he feels it is too systematized and not directed to fulfilling the individual's unique needs), but the bulk of his harangue against the follies and stupidities of society can be attributed to his sour and disillusioned disposition. The narrator had warned us in the second chapter (i.e. chapter XII) about the necessity of people of feeling having a "certain respect for the follies of mankind," for otherwise the world would frustrate and destroy them with indignation and envy. Harley, entirely satisfied with his modest station in life (he is a "gentleman" but of modest means), therefore avoids being hardened into misanthropy.

Mackenzie's attitude toward social change becomes more evident toward the end of the novel. Before Harley meets Edwards the novel has had no opportunity one way or the other to display its author's attitude toward the major causes of social upheaval in the England of the 1760's—the Enclosure Acts and the industrial revolution. In 1770, one year before the publication of *The Man of Feeling,* Oliver Goldsmith's "Deserted Village" appeared. After lamenting the rise of the factory system and the consequent breakdown of village life that this urban phenomenon occasioned together with the Enclosure Acts, Goldsmith goes on to excoriate "luxury" and concludes his poem by asking Poetry to

> Teach erring man to spurn the rage of gain;
> Teach him that states of native strength possest,
> Tho, very poor, may still be very blest;
> That trade's proud empire hastes to swift decay,

As ocean sweeps the labour'd mole away;
While self-dependent power can time defy,
As rocks resist the billows and the sky.

Even Goldsmith's idyllic paean to the virtues of country living, *The Vicar of Wakefield,* has a discussion on the changes in the kingdom wherein Primrose states, "I would have all men kings! I would be a king myself. We have all naturally an equal right to the throne: we are all originally equal." No such dangerous beliefs as these find their way into **The Man of Feeling,** though the effects of the Enclosure Acts and rural upheaval are seen in the Edwards episode. Edwards had been turned out of the farm his family had had for generations because the new squire and his new London lawyer (insidious urban interference) have decided, contrary to the feudal duties toward one's tenants, that small farms are unprofitable on one's estate. Edwards and his son's family procure another more distant farm, but there they are plagued with crop failures and, even worse, with the arrest of Edwards' son when he strikes the justice's gamekeeper for maliciously killing his dog. The justice has him thrown into jail, and, after fining him, pursues his revenge by having young Edwards subjected to the impressment gang. Old Edwards, however, takes his place, serves in India, and now with Harley returns home to discover that his son and daughter-in-law have died of broken hearts, that the old schoolhouse is in ruins because it interferes with the squire's prospects, and that the village green has been ploughed up by orders of the squire.

Here indeed are abuses ripe for indignation and attack. A conservative mind, a Goldsmith or a Smollett, would mourn the passing of the feudal order and rage against the age of luxury and "trade's unfeeling train." The social radical, a William Godwin or a William Blake, would attribute the injustice to abuses of the class structure and to a legal code that sought, not justice, but aggrandizement for the rich. But Mackenzie or his narrator, what does he say? Interestingly, and significantly, Mackenzie's comments on this aspect of the social upheaval of his day are confined to criticizing individuals and not the social structure. Mackenzie recognizes that evil exists, but he only allows Harley to exclaim, "Curses on his narrow heart . . . that could violate a right so sacred." Likewise, the chapter that discusses British imperialism in India mostly confines itself to criticizing individual soldiers who seek, not "the pride of honourable poverty," but riches. Harley does begin his discussion with Edwards by asking by what right Britain possesses the vast subcontinent of India, but this point is undercut by the title of the chapter, "The Man of Feeling Talks of What He Does Not Understand—An Incident." His comments on the stagecoach, which come closest to excoriating the new luxury in the manner of Smollett or Goldsmith, still refuse to offer an alternative to the problem or to see that society is a complex interaction of men. There is "an alarming crisis in the corruption of the state; when not only is virtue declined, and vice prevailing, but when the praises of virtue are forgotten, and the infamy of vice unfelt." The crisis, however, has been brought about by the "immense riches acquired by *individuals*" who "have erected a standard of ambition, destructive of *private* morals, and of public virtues" (italics

mine). So again we see Mackenzie blaming individuals, and not the social structure, for the abuses and injustices of society.

Not surprisingly, then, we may conclude that Mackenzie, even at the early age of 26 before he becomes comptroller of the taxes for Scotland and the friend of Pitt, is a conservative by and large quite satisfied with the status quo. He feels abuses in society can be rectified at the individual level. If people would only be more compassionate, there would be less human suffering. A true enough belief, but hardly adequate for the complexity that urbanization and industrialization were beginning to create. While Mackenzie contributed to what is called the new humanitarianism, his effort is obviously a half-way measure. He supplies tears, not answers or analysis. He belongs to a different world than that of Blake, Godwin, Dickens, Ruskin, Arnold and all the other critics of the dehumanizing effect of industrialization. It is as if the *Aufklärung* with its faith in progress (however naive), its insights into the mechanisms of society (however inadequate), its environmentalism (however false), passed him by. One of course cannot blame Mackenzie for this "deficiency." My point is simply that Mackenzie is a product of pre-industrial society and not a harbinger of Romantic revolt. Though the *Aufklärung* was widespread, its ideas were new and it took a few generations for them (or opposing ideas they engendered) to become more than quaint theories. When they did arrive, of course, Europe was changed into a continent of republics and constitutional monarchies where the rights of men were recognized and the license of arbitrary tyranny checked. Hitlers and Stalins still came along, but contrary to what people believed of a Louis XIV, their power was recognized to be based upon naked force, not divine right. But this movement of history does not concern Mackenzie; as said, he belongs on the other side of the line that demarcates the modern world.

At any rate, we find that we must be somewhat skeptical about Harley's statement about the brotherhood of man. Clearly Mackenzie is no wild-eyed Jacobin seeking to bring about the millenium of a classless society. Still, he is on record as saying that the world is incompatible to the man of feeling. For Harley perhaps it is; but for his creator a different attitude can be discovered buried slightly below the denotative level of the words of the novel. To illustrate what I mean, let me turn to the Bedlam scene. Harley's friend suggests they partake in that favorite eighteenth century pastime, visiting the madmen of Bedlam. Harley objects, saying, "I think it is an inhuman practice to expose the greatest misery with which our nature is afflicted to every idle visitant who can afford a trifling perquisite to the keeper; especially as it is a distress which the humane must see, with the painful reflection, that it is not in their power to alleviate it." On the surface this seems to be quite a modern, quite a compassionate view. But what happens? Not only is Harley persuaded to go, but the narrator even indulges in some rather crude humor at the expense of one of the unfortunate madmen who thinks he is the Chan of Tartary—surely as unfeeling and condescending an attitude as one can take toward the insane.

The fact is, for Mackenzie to fulfill the literary purpose of his book and construct scenes and situations that elicit tears from Harley and the gentle reader, he must consistently place Harley in situations where he confronts misery and suffering. That is why Harley ends up going to Bedlam. There he meets the unfortunate mad woman and therefore gets a chance to indulge in some "pleasing Anguish." When Harley meets the prostitute, Emily Atkins, we find that his initial purpose in greeting her was a rather worldly one—though Mackenzie is most discreet in his description of sexual impulses. The fact that Harley is in London in the first place is the direct result of the same narrative mechanism as that of the Bedlam scene. Harley is unworldly and cares little for wealth and power. Yet he goes to London for the worldliest of reasons—to curry favor with connections in the government so that he can get a lease on some crown-lands. Harley's friends and guardians talk the reluctant man of feeling into taking the trip. They are the voice of worldly prudence who cause Harley to go against his principles. But observe that the dynamics of the book make it necessary for them to overrule Harley's objections. Mackenzie must consistently work *against* the man of feeling's principles if he is to be able to place Harley in a position to *demonstrate* his principles. Thus we see a double-standard at work between the authorial level and the level of the action.

The similes Mackenzie often employs to describe Harley's feelings toward the unfortunates of the lower class also reflect this curious double standard. For instance, Harley, his eyes brimming with tears, takes the hand of Emily Atkins, the fallen woman reduced to the degrading life of a whore "with as much respect as if she had been a duchess. It was ever the privilege of misfortune to be revered by him." This statement is out of keeping with the supposed value system of the man of feeling, for the reason that Harley feels compassion for the woman is because of their common humanity. Yet the narrator comments on the significance of Harley's compassion, not in human terms, but in terms of the class structure that such a universal, human compassionate attitude should make irrelevant. (pp. 123-31)

The attitude that this "double standard" betrays is the Tory attitude. Far from being disgusted and deeply revolted with the world, the narrator actually reveals that he adheres to a semi-feudal value system that is benevolent, to be sure, but benevolent in the condescending manner of a lord to his chattel. (When one analyzes the dynamics of old Edwards' blustering his tearful gratitude to Harley at the end of chapter XXXIV, one finds that Edwards' attitude is based on class feelings. Harley has as of yet offered him nothing more substantial than tears and sympathy, but that a member of the upper class designed to take pity on a poor peasant is so affecting that old Edwards can only utter incoherent blessings upon Harley.) In fine, Mackenzie is a "gentleman" writing for a genteel audience in terms of the values they both share. His goal is not to offer his readers cosmic tragedy or social analysis; his goal is merely to titillate and entertain. Mackenzie, perhaps, could indeed be called an "idle singer of an empty day." It is, at any rate, this underlying Toryism, making itself felt as an undercurrent throughout the book, that tends to diminish the cosmic or transcendental significance of Har-

ley's death. Just as before Harley was put in a position to be the recipient of the pleasing Anguish of sentimentalism, now the reader—presumably thoroughly initiated into the rites of sentimentalism—is put in a position to be the man of feeling at Harley's death. Again it is the tears to be elicited that are emphasized, and not the deep religiosity of Harley. Mackenzie uses Christian terms on this occasion because they are the world's coin, and such things as saying one is going to a far, far better place are always said on such solemn occasions. One feels this by reacting to the tone of the novel, not by reading the words.

I spoke earlier of the necessity of Harley seeing behind appearances and into the reality of the world. One critic also points out that Harley is confronted with this problem in London. There the sharper and the pimp appear to be virtuous while they are really evil, and Emily Atkins appears to be evil while she is in fact repentant. Applying this standard literary criterion of appearance vs. reality to the novel, we find that a disparity exists between what the words say and what the actual effect or impact of the words is. Returning to the novel for a second reading, we begin to see that Mackenzie has left a great deal of evidence of his true feelings throughout the book. To his aunt, who looks down upon the nouveau riche for being "mushroom gentry" with money but no breeding, Harley makes the worldly remark, "We blame the pride of the rich [for the "shame of the times"], but are not we ashamed of our poverty?" Here, of course, Harley is mouthing a worldly belief for the sake of argument, but earlier we saw dramatized that very worldly belief in Harley when he visited the baronet in London seeking assistance. On the way to the baronet's, writes Mackenzie, "he began to ruminate on the folly of mankind, who affixed those ideas of superiority to riches, which reduced the minds of men, by nature equal with the more fortunate, to that sort of servility which he felt in his own." So Harley knows he should not feel intimidated by wealth; he knows that it is mere worldly folly to affix ideas of superiority to riches; and he knows that naturally all men can look one another in the eye without shame. But in what follows Mackenzie betrays a tone of jaded irony that can only be interpreted as some gentle (to be sure) scorn and mockery directed toward his man of feeling. Mackenzie here reveals that he is entirely cognizant of the impossibility of being totally untouched by the ways of the world:

> By the time he had reached the Square, and was walking along the pavement which led to the baronet's, he had brought his reasoning on the subject to such a point, that the conclusion, by every rule of logic, should have led him to a thorough indifference in his approaches to a fellow-mortal, whether that fellow-mortal was possessed of six or six thousand pounds a year. It is probable, however, that the premises had been improperly formed: for it is certain, that when he approached the great man's door he felt his heart agitated by unusual pulsation.

Mackenzie has it both ways, of course: worldly logic is also satirized. This tone of slightly jaded irony is heard elsewhere in the novel. The title of the chapter wherein Harley discusses British imperialism is entitled "The Man of Feeling Talks of What He Does Not Understand." And the statement of the beggar that I quoted earlier, referring to "withered arms" and "wooden legs" being a sort of draught for worldly people to draw on in heaven for repaying of their charity, betrays, upon analysis, a rather sophisticated cruelty as its basis for humor.

Of course the tone never gets even remotely close to the point where the novel would be a satire against the sentimental mentality. Its presence, however, felt from time to time as one reads the novel, is another indication that Mackenzie is less than naive about the world, and in fact is on occasion rather an astute delineator of the complexities of the human soul. When Harley sees the beggar walking briskly down the road with bare feet, he exclaims, "our delicacies are fantastic; they are not in nature!" Despite the presence of the "noble savage" seen in the person of the old Indian whom Edwards frees, and despite the narrator's Shaftesburean remark that benevolence is "instinctive in our nature," Mackenzie demonstrates that he knows society and nature have a wide gulf separating them. In a letter to his cousin he observes that "Rousseau, in his Enthusiasm for a State of uncultivated Nature, inveighs against the Pow'r which Women in later Times have acquired"; but he goes on to add, "yet after all, we owe our Rousseaus to Society, & their Eloisas to the Empire of the Woman." And finally, concerning the novel's need for the world as it is, flawed and evil, so that tears may be elicited from Harley for its victims, we have this worldly passage from a letter to offer as Mackenzie's own comment on the dynamics of his novel:

> I am happy that Edwards has pleas'd so much . . . Heroes amidst the Blaze of War, or the Glare of Courts, have been in every one's Hands; I have sought one unattended by those adventitious Circumstances; I have found him in a simple Farm-House; yet, I flatter myself, he is not less the Hero. The world thinks otherwise; 'tis fitting that it should: Virtue would lose half its Merit, if the world did not look more on the Ribbon of a George, than the Belt of a *Knapsack.*

Perhaps this article belabors what one critic [R. S. Crane, in *ELH* I (1934)] has stated succinctly: that *The Man of Feeling* is a book filled with a "curious type of hedonism." What this analysis does, however, is separate Harley and Mackenzie, and point out that there was some distancing involved in the creation of the man of feeling. When we see that Mackenzie is rather worldly and the "compleat" Tory, the "curious type of hedonism" will be seen in a different historical perspective. Heretofore Harley has been seen as a contribution toward the "new humanitarianism." Perhaps he did indeed contribute to humanizing people, but it is probably more accurate to see the novel as an expression of the decadence . . . of the intellectual vigor of the Anglican divines' and Shaftesbury's . . . conception of sentimentalism and benevolence, than it is to see *The Man of Feeling* as a symptom of a new spirit that would grow into Romanticism. The book points backwards, not ahead. But *The Man of Feeling* does not deserve to be condemned too strongly. It is a pleasant book and many a passage must be read with a pleasing grin and a benevolent heart. Since its author did not intend to write a philosophical treatise, but merely an entertaining book that would bring sighs to the palpitating heart, one cannot fault it for lacking various literary elements that it never intended to have in the first place. I analyzed the book with an eye to its being a historical artifact. Only when it is judged from that perspective is it possible to use so harsh a word as "decadent" to describe the man of feeling. (pp. 131-35)

> *R. Peter Burnham, "The Social Ethos of Mackenzie's 'The Man of Feeling',"* in Studies in Scottish Literature, *Vol. XVIII, 1983, pp. 123-37.*

Elaine Ware   (essay date 1987)

[*In the excerpt below, Ware discusses the theme of charity in Mackenzie's major novels.*]

Many critics, notably David Spencer [in "Henry Mackenzie, a Practical Sentimentalist," *Papers on Language and Literature* 3 (1967)], suggest that Henry Mackenzie supported the ideals of his age in order to suit audience taste rather than out of fervor of belief. Spencer points to the practicality of the Scottish lawyer as well as to his seeming lack of sentiment for his contemporaries as evidence of the true Mackenzie hidden behind the facade of benevolence. Should we condemn Mackenzie then as a mere literary opportunist? I think not. Mackenzie was under no financial duress to please the reading public; therefore, his motives lay elsewhere. It is true that Mackenzie may have joined the benevolence bandwagon, in part, because of the popularity of sentimentalism, but I believe that he wrote out of a sincere concern for man's moral duty towards man. Mackenzie's treatment of benevolence is not superficial. The development and exposition of the philanthropist and the misanthrope, which most of his contemporaries made the mainstay of their writings, are only introductory to Mackenzie's main concern. Mackenzie centers on a much deeper moral consideration: the effects of charity on the recipient. Mackenzie delves into the physical as well as the psychological effects of charity on the poor, and he emphasizes the negative results in his treatment. This theme is implied in embryonic form in *The Man of Feeling* (1771), but it develops further in *The Man of the World* (1773), and finally explicitly matures in *Julia De Roubigné* (1777).

In an age rebuking actions based solely on rational motivations, many writers including Mackenzie examined emotion and feeling as directives for action. Rather than the seventeenth century's belief in man's depravity, the eighteenth century's moral philosophy was based on the innate benevolence of man. One of the most important tenets of the ethics of the period was the notion of charity, or benevolence. Modern readers immediately think of almsgiving, but Mackenzie's contemporaries thought of charity primarily as a deep concern for the welfare of another. That inner conviction, of course, must not remain a mere abstraction but must be transformed into charitable action. (pp. 132-33)

Mackenzie's thematic treatment of charity does not wholeheartedly endorse benevolence; he shows that charitable actions can have dubious results. To investigate the effects of charitable actions, Mackenzie develops two types of characters; philanthropists and misanthropes. The philanthropists fall into two distinct subtypes in Mackenzie's writings: 1) the benevolent man, for example Harley in *The Man of Feeling,* who generously helps the needy and seeks only personal satisfaction in return, and 2) the philanthropist who gives to the poor in exchange for public recognition as a benevolent man. Of course, the anonymous giver is the pure type. Counterpoised with benevolent characters are Mackenzie's misanthropes. There are types here too. The first type is a benevolent person at heart whose benevolence is constantly thwarted by an indifferent world. Like the nameless misanthrope in *The Man of Feeling,* this type withdraws from the world and from charitable action, yet his nature and impulses, if cynical, remain benevolent. The second type is the false philanthropist who outwardly professes benevolence but is inwardly evil. Mackenzie splits the development of this second type in two directions: 1) some misanthropes, for example the nameless gentleman in Chapter XXV of *The Man of Feeling,* remain evil, and 2) others, like Sindall in *The Man of the World,* change their evil ways in the closing pages of the work.

In spite of the contrasting motives of the misanthrope with those of the philanthropist, Mackenzie's poor characters suffer at the hands of both. The physical and financial sufferings at the hands of the misanthrope are easily discerned, but suffering due to truly charitable works is more difficult to trace. In the case of true benevolence, Mackenzie illustrates the negative psychological effects of charity on the pride of the recipient. Not only is the recipient humbled by the reception of good works and money, but that humility is emphasized by the poor man's inability to repay the kindness he receives. This consideration of the recipient's position is important and continues to mature in each of Mackenzie's writings. (p. 135)

In *The Man of Feeling* Mackenzie shows the negative aspects of both false and true charity in rudimentary plot elements. First, he illustrates false charity when the seduced Emily falls victim to a seemingly benevolent woman. The false philanthropist early offers shelter and kindness to the forlorn Emily, but once Emily's "dependence" is secured, the evil nature of the procuress comes to the surface. Emily becomes financially dependent and must submit to prostitution until rescued by Harley.

Mackenzie not only depicts suffering at the hands of a false philanthropist but secondly shows the psychological suffering of recipients due to true benevolence. The first example is Mountford, the penniless gentleman to whom the rich Sedley offers the tutorship of Sedley's son. Mountford, in Mackenzie's words, is "a proud fool" who is reluctant about being dependent on Sedley. The elder Sedley responds that there is "no such word" as "dependence" between friends. Mountford's negative reaction to charitable acts is Mackenzie's first indication of the poor man's disinclination to accept charity.

An even more poignant example of the negative psychological effects of charity on the poor is seen in "The Pupil" in the story of the sick, imprisoned man. Having received charity from Mountford, the wife of the imprisoned wretch "crawled" on the floor clasping Mountford's knees in expression of gratitude. Her husband responds to her actions with, "Compose yourself, my love." This phrase along with his request of the philanthropist to excuse his wife's behavior seems to be an indication of the man's embarrassment. Mackenzie's choice of words shows the degradation of the recipient. After the younger Sedley has also given money to the man, the recipient asks a question: "'I do not mean attempting to thank you' (he took a pocket-book from under his pillow) 'let me but know what name I shall place here next to M. Mountford?'" This seemingly trivial incident becomes significant upon examination. The poor man writes down the names of his benefactors because he intends to repay the generosity shown him. Mackenzie illustrates in *The Man of Feeling* that the recipient, often averse to accepting charity, will when in dire circumstances accept money with full intention of reciprocating at a later date.

Not all of Mackenzie's recipients of charity in *The Man of Feeling* experience problems. Old Edwards gracefully receives the small homestead and good will of Harley, but even Edwards makes "some attempts towards an acknowledgment for these favours." At this period in his writing Mackenzie was still able to show the good that could result from true benevolence. But as his work develops over the years, he places less emphasis on the good effects of charity, and gives more attention to the negative effects of charitable acts.

Most charitable works in *The Man of the World* are disguised evils performed by Sir Thomas Sindall, a would-be benefactor. Young Billy Annesly falls victim to the villainous Sindall because of false philanthropy. Sindall's offers of charity to Billy are cloaked methods to gain access to Billy's sister, Harriet. Sindall shelters and offers his companionship to Billy, who is at first happy to receive seemingly benevolent attentions. After receiving many kindnesses from Sindall and his friends, Billy becomes "indebted" to them and feels a certain responsibility to comply with their wishes in much the same way as did Emily in *The Man of Feeling.* Eventually, after much prodding Annesly falls from "innocence" and participates in their "vice". Sensual pleasures plunge Billy into debt only to be retrieved by Sindall, thus to be under more obligation. Sindall takes advantage of his recent benevolence towards Billy to propose that Harriet become Sindall's mistress. Upon Billy's rejection of the proposition, Sindall calculates further seductions to gain control over Billy and, consequently, over Harriet. Sindall's schemes are eventually successful, and Billy falls again into poverty. "Though his pride for a while kept him quiet, it was at last overcome," and Billy borrows money, thus diving into deeper debt. Forced to the depths of gambling and armed robbery in order to survive, Billy is arrested and sentenced to fourteen years exile. But before Billy's deportation "He called in an exact account of his debts, those to Sindall not excepted, and discharging them in full, much against the inclination of Sir Thomas, who insisted, as much as in decency he could, on canceling every obligation of that sort to himself. But Annesly was positive in his resolution." As in *The Man of Feeling,* the poverty-stricken man abhors charity but is forced by circumstances to accept. As a last resort to free himself of many debtors and to regain integrity, Annesly calls upon his father's credit to repay the loans, thus owing money only to family. Billy has suffered physically as well as psychologically because of false philanthropy.

Her brother Billy's life is disrupted by false philanthropy, but Harriet's life is destroyed by Sindall's "benevolence." Believing that Sindall has been a true benefactor to her brother, "at the sight of him, her cheek was flushed with the mingled glow of shame for her brother, and gratitude towards his benefactor." This juxtaposition of shame and gratitude recurs throughout Mackenzie's work, thus pointing to the degrading aspects of receiving charity. Harriet, too, is caught in the deceptive web of Sindall's charity. He secretly plans the kidnapping of Harriet in which he feigns to be her rescuer. After the "rescue" she is drugged and raped by the hypocrite. Her resulting pregnancy, madness, and death occur because of Sindall's tortures.

Harriet not only suffers at the hands of a villain, but she also psychologically suffers because of the kind acts of Mr. Rawlinson, a true benefactor. When Rawlinson gives her a large sum of money, she responds: "Though I feel sir . . . with the utmost gratitude, those sentiments of kindness and generosity you have expressed towards me, you will excuse me, I hope from receiving this mark of them." The proud Harriet, although she needs the money, fears that some show of affection would be owing to Rawlinson in return. Rawlinson responds to her rejection with: "I see, and her pride will no more than her affections submit itself to my happiness." Mackenzie's choice of the word "submit" indicates that the recipient has lower status than the benefactor. Harriet's father, too, is a proud person and is at first unwilling for his daughter to accept the money. Mackenzie through the mouthpiece of the elder Annesly explains the dilemma of the poor: "There is a delicacy my best friend, in our situation; the poor must be ever cautious, and there is a certain degree of pride which is their safest virtue." Mackenzie seems to be issuing a warning to the poor to avoid receiving charity and becoming obligated to others. As in *The Man of Feeling,* the poor characters in *The Man of the World* suffer negative psychological effects from charity whether it be motivated by false or by true benevolence.

While Mackenzie emphasizes the misanthropic character in Sindall, he still creates a few admirable philanthropists who help to offset a totally dark vision of charity. Lucy, Miss Walton, Bolton, and Rawlinson all are examples of true benefactors. The poor respond to the charitable acts of these philanthropists with "benediction on . . . knees," and "lips . . . pressed" to hands. Both responses raise the status of the giver while relegating the recipient to a lower footing. That some good is also done by the philanthropists cannot be denied, but Mackenzie, for the most part, accentuates the negative effects of charity.

In *Julia De Roubigné,* Mackenzie only mentions in passing the good done through charitable works; instead, he stresses the negative results of true benevolence. Montauban early shows admiration for Julia because of her chari-

table works: "she dispensed mirth and gayety to some poor families in our neighborhood." Mackenzie tells that the recipients express gratitude towards Julia but gives no further detail; this is the only instance of charity in the novel in which Mackenzie does not show the negative aspects of charity. The rest of *Julia De Roubigné* illustrates the charitable transaction and resulting disaster for Montauban, M. Roubigné, and Julia and also depicts Savillon's dependency on his uncle. In all of these incidents charity does not finally comfort the recipients.

Mackenzie presents Montauban as an example of the worthy benefactor who searches for a humane way to approach the poor. The rich Montauban makes an acquaintance with M. Roubigné "not by offering favors, but by asking one." This psychology is very effective in putting the poor man at ease because it gives Roubigné "back the power of conferring an obligation."

To be able to repay Montauban's kindness is a must for M. Roubigné's pride. When Roubigné was rich he charitably saved Savillon's father from debt. Here too "arose a sort of dependence on the one side." Julia interprets her father's former psychological attitude toward charity: "he thinks of a man as his inferior, only that he may do him a kindness more freely." That Roubigné saw the low nature of the recipient when he, himself, was a benefactor is quite evident. That he would have difficulty in accepting charity when he is in need seems only natural. Montauban, learning that Roubigné is in debt, anonymously forwards the money to the debtor. Roubigné "would die before he would ask such a favor of any one, so high minded he is, notwithstanding all his misfortunes." After his bills are paid "some remains of that pride, which formerly rankled under the receipt of favors it was unable to return" appear in M. Roubigné. He truly suffers because he is unable to repay Montauban. And Julia "is now the partner of his humiliation."

The extreme desire of the poor to reciprocate, Mackenzie clearly reveals in Julia's sacrifice to repay Montauban's generosity. Julia announces

> Tell the Count de Montauban, that Julia De Roubigné offers that hand to his generosity, which she refused to his solicitation;—tell him also, she is above deceit: she will not conceal the small value of the gift. 'Tis but the offerings of a wretch, who would somehow requite the sufferings of her father, and the services of his friend.

This is the ultimate example of desperation by the poor to retain a sense of honor or status. Roubigné likens Julia's hand to a monetary commodity and tells Montauban: "That hand . . . is the last treasure of Roubigné. Fallen as his fortunes are, not the wealth of worlds had purchased it; to your friendship, to your virtue, he is blessed in bequeathing it." Roubigné derives great satisfaction from this transaction, and he establishes himself on a plane more equal to Montauban than that of the recipient.

Unfortunately, the result of this exchange is disastrous because Montauban poisons Julia when he suspects that his "possession" is unfaithful to him. Montauban admits, "I purchased her consent, I bribed her, I bought her . . . "

by giving money to M. Roubigné. Montauban knew the proud nature of the family, and he had suspected that Julia would try to make some recompense for his benevolence. Montauban finally rushes to suicide after he realizes Julia's innocence. Both characters suffer, in part, because of excess emotion and uncontrolled impulse, but they also experience misery because of the tense nature of the charitable situation. Charity to Mackenzie implies one who is able and willing to give and another who is in need and forced to accept. It implies a great difference in status between the two parties, and it leaves the recipient obliged. Marriage as repayment of a debt carries the idea of obligation to an extreme. The marriage is doomed from the start because obligation does not make for binding relationships of the heart; only love or concern can do that. Perhaps Mackenzie is pointing out the folly in attempting to repay kindness, as well as the inadvisability of accepting charity in the first place.

Mackenzie quickly reiterates the disinclination of the poor to receive charity in Savillon's story. Briefly, Savillon is dependent upon a benevolent uncle for his livelihood. In spite of the uncle's kindness, Savillon "wish[es] for an opportunity to be assiduous in his service; till [he] can do something on [his] part, his uncle's favors are debts upon [him]." The theme of debt and obligation has become of chief importance to Mackenzie in *Julia De Roubigné*

To Mackenzie, the act of charity is riddled with problems and paradoxes. The truly benevolent man faces a dilemma. If he gives to the poor, he may hurt their pride; but if he does not, and disasters such as imprisonment, starvation, and death occur, then he may feel that he has failed to perform his moral duty. The poor man, too, faces embarrassment, dependency and obligation on the one hand, and comfort and physical well-being on the other. Since Mackenzie stresses the negative effects of charity, does it follow that he advocates the discontinuation of benevolent actions? This interpretation seems extreme. Mackenzie perceives potential problems in charitable actions, so his writing may be read as a warning or caution to both the philanthropist and the recipient. To the philanthropist he suggests a benevolent way to offer assistance and also discretion upon whom he bestows charity. Mackenzie warns the misfortunate against accepting charity except in times of dire need and then cautions that the poor man should be careful from whom he receives help.

Mackenzie moves from an emphasis on benevolence in *The Man of Feeling* to stress misanthropy in *The Man of the World.* His vision is noticeably darker in the second novel. With the development of the benevolently motivated Montauban in *Julia De Roubigné* one expects a return to a brighter vision, but Mackenzie shows that on the contrary even benevolent actions create problems for the recipient of charity.

In all of Mackenzie's novels the poor feel greatly indebted to and dependent upon philanthropists. They feel the distinction in status, and in order to raise their level to that of the benefactor they try to repay in some fashion. Mackenzie acknowledges the social class struggle of his day by pointing out the rising class consciousness among the lower classes. The poor are no longer satisfied to receive charity, thus being relegated to a low rank. Perhaps Mademoiselle Roubigné's words best exemplify the new current of thought: "misfortune is not always misery." Mackenzie may feel that the plight of the poor man is bearable as long as he can maintain his integrity and pride. Perhaps the physical comfort gained from charity is not worth the mental degradation that accompanies it. (pp. 136-41)

Elaine Ware, "Charitable Actions Reevaluated in the Novels of Henry Mackenzie," in Studies in Scottish Literature, *Vol. XXII, 1987, pp. 132-41.*

William J. Burling   (essay date 1988)

[*In the excerpt below, Burling argues that the weakness of Mackenzie's character and plot development in* The Man of Feeling *contributes to the ambiguity of the novel's underlying moral message.*]

Henry Mackenzie's *The Man of Feeling,* enormously popular when first published in 1771, was acknowledged by an entire generation of readers as the ultimate representation of the sentimental ethos. But outright contradiction now pervades critical discussion of the novel, with interpretation splitting on two central questions: Is Harley, the hero, an ideal man or a fool? And is the novel sympathetic to sentimentalism or opposed to it? The antithetical critical responses to *The Man of Feeling* may be resolved, however, when we recognize that Mackenzie was neither completely attacking nor condoning sentimentalism *in toto.* He was attempting to differentiate what he considered to be attributes of genuine and desirable humane sensitivity from those of the affected sentimentality then *au courant* in the hypocritical *beau monde.*

Mackenzie in old age.

Important evidence from Mackenzie's critical essays, plays, and other novels reveals that while Mackenzie certainly believed that sensitivity, compassion, and benevolence were essential elements in the character of a truly humane person, he was, in fact, contemptuous of the phenomenon of sentimentality—whether as expressed in fiction or as practiced abroad in society—and consistently attacked or criticized sentimentalism in all of his works. But his failure to make the distinction clear in *The Man of Feeling* resulted from two artistic faults: the lack of a clearly defined, admirable protagonist; and the unfortunate decision to employ a fragmented, episodic plot. These flaws have produced the wildly diverging interpretations. (pp. 136-37)

The clearest evidence for Mackenzie's contempt for sentimentalism is found in his extensive journalistic criticism. In *The Lounger* (1785-87) Mackenzie writes at length on the problems of fiction. Of greatest interest is *Lounger* 20, where he attacks fictions which fail to distinguish between right and wrong, "forming a mistaken and pernicious system of morality . . . particularly in that species called the *sentimental.*" "Virtues of sentiment," he complains, nearly displace more important issues of life, such as, among others, duty to parents. The sentimentalists revel in "impressions which never have any effect on their conduct [and] pay in words what they owe in actions." Sentimental fiction, Mackenzie concludes, is a "sickly sort of refinement" which "has an ill effect, not only on our ideas of virtue, but also on our estimates of happiness." We must note here that he does not distinguish between excessive sentimentalism as a mode of real-life behavior and the representation of such excesses in fiction—to discuss either is to discuss both at once. Further, the two main points of his philosophy of life—which he stresses should be expressed and advocated in all fiction—are 1) the establishment of correct notions of virtue, and 2) the importance of happiness. If he feels so strongly about the negative effects of sentimental fiction, then we cannot seriously imagine that he advocates excessive sentimentality in *The Man of Feeling.*

His other novels, likewise, argue against Mackenzie as unabashed sentimentalist. Mackenzie's second novel, *The Man of the World* (1773), presents a family of sentimentalists, the Anneslys, who are nearly destroyed by the villain Sindall, the Man of the World. Nowhere in the novel do we find a single scene in which exaggerated sentimental actions are presented in an admirable light, and, in fact, as Mackenzie states, "if my tale were fiction, it would be thought too simple." For Mackenzie the black and white world of the typical sentimental novel, such as *The Fool of Quality,* is definitely too simple, and Mackenzie recognized the sentimental fallacy of believing that one needed simply to be sensitive and all would be well in life. The entire message of *Man of the World* stresses that the sentimental view is not enough. The same viewpoint holds in Mackenzie's third, final, and finest novel, *Julia de Roubigne* (1777), with one important addition. Sir Walter Scott [in his *The Lives of the Novelists,* 1928] has passed down the origin of Mackenzie's plot, a suggestion from Lord Kames that "the calamities of the catastrophe should arise . . . not out of schemes of premeditated vil-

lainy, but from the excess of passions and feelings. . . ." The theme, in other words, concerns sentimentality run amuck. Every character is admirable in the usual moral sense, yet all but Savillon are destroyed by their extreme sensitivity; the episodes stress the inadequacy of excessive sentimentality to deal with the problems of life.

If Mackenzie is not an admirer of sentimentalism, then what are we to think of the many tearful scenes? The answer, I propose, is that Mackenzie is attempting an experimental, not always successful, mode of fictional representation which incorporates what he thought were the usable, important elements of sentimentalism, as well as the display of excessive affectations. We must distinguish between intentions and actions: the "false" sentimentalist sheds tears because he thinks he must do so for social reasons, and he engages in small acts of charity for the sake of appeasing his own conscience. As Barker rightly notes [in his *Henry Mackenzie,* 1975], Diana Danby, a character in Mackenzie's comedy *False Shame,* is called a "sentimentalist," a derisive term in this case, intended to denote hypocrisy and affectation. This type of behavior the general world terms "honorable," however, as exemplified by Respino in *The Man of Feeling* and Sindall in *The Man of the World.* We see then that Mackenzie is working with types; the sincere but paralyzed person of sensibility is thus duly represented by Harley in *The Man of Feeling,* Annesly in *The Man of the World,* and Julia in *Julia de Roubigne.* They are not exemplary, but neither are they entirely devoid of merit. At the heart of their actions are benevolence, good cheer, and recognition and acceptance of adversity, but while they are sincere, they feel too much.

So what mode of life does Mackenzie propose? In *Lounger* 96, Mackenzie partially defined his ideal in the character of Benevolous: "he gives largely; but as it is neither from impulse of sickly sentiment, or shallow vanity, his largesses tend oftener to incite industry than to supply indigence." Along these lines the major models that Mackenzie intends for readers to admire are Harry Bolton in *The Man of the World* and Savillon in *Julia de Roubigne,* both of whom are charitable for the right reasons, in addition to being sensitive yet able to survive, even to prosper, in a harsh world.

An important dimension of the critical problem now becomes fully apparent: no striking exemplary role model exists in *The Man of Feeling.* We find one minor candidate for admiration in Edward Sedley, whose character fits the Mackenzie norm quite well: "I had ideas of virtue, of honour, of benevolence, which I had never been at the pains to define. . . ." Unrefined, natural sensibility, is the hallmark of Sedley's character, and he differs from Harley in that Sedley learns to recognize the "rogues" of the world and to keep his perspective, whereas Harley can only say, "This world . . . was a scene in which I never much delighted . . . It was a scene of dissimulation, of restraint, of disappointment."

But Sedley is not, of course, the main character. The interpretive problem has arisen from the confusion present because Mackenzie at once both glorifies humane sensibility and satirizes the very character who supposedly exemplifies the life of sensibility. Recognizing the bases for Mackenzie's strategies, let us now turn to the text of *The Man of Feeling* to test these assumptions.

Virtually all commentators on *The Man of Feeling* have recognized the presence of irony in many sections of the novel. We recall, for instance, the framing device of the story itself: the "editor" trades an old German book to a curate for the manuscript biography of one Harley. The clergyman had been using the paper for gun wadding; therefore, a number of chapters are missing. The novel thus assumes a fragmented form. Mackenzie accounted for his intentions in a letter to his cousin, Elizabeth Rose, calling the draft of the novel an "odd Medley . . . of Observations . . . on Men and Manners . . . introducing a Man of Sensibility into different scenes where his Feelings might be seen in their Effects, & his Sentiments occasionally delivered without the stifness of regular Deduction. . . ."

We see, then, that he purposely avoided the tight unity of plot which was the hallmark of the literary works of his own day—such as *Clarissa* or *Tom Jones*—seeking to force the reader to focus on individual scenes. Here we have a second cause for the interpretive problem: the "odd Medley" distorted or even destroyed any possibility of the reader recognizing Mackenzie's narrative strategy. Whereas he wished readers to see in select "different scenes" that excessive sentimentality led to severe disadvantages or even outright danger, they instead imagined that he was highlighting the scenes as noteworthy and thus admirable. Dale Kramer has suggested [in "The Structural Unity of *The Man of Feeling*," *Studies in Short Fiction* I (1964)] that the novel "is thematically organized around the education of the hero," the result being Harley's disillusionment with the world. But perhaps the purpose of the loosely joined episodes was to educate not Harley but the *reader*. . . . Jenkins proposes that the novel sought "to educate the public in the virtues of sentiment" ["The Art of the Theorist: Rhetorical Structure in *The Man of Feeling*," *Studies in Scottish Literature* 9 (1971)]. But whereas Jenkins believes that Harley is a model for the reader to admire, I contend that the reader is being asked to differentiate the "usable" components of Harley's sensibility from the faulty ones but cannot do so given the fragmented form.

In order to test this hypothesis, we might turn to an ironical scene which has received much critical comment, the chapter in which is described "The Man of Feeling in love" (XIII). Here we learn that the hero has become attracted to Miss Walton, once a debutante and the toast of London and now at 24 fading in isolated rural seclusion. Harley thinks her paleness "agreed . . . with the pensive softness of her mind." Harley came to paint her beauty, the narrator explains, "ridiculously enough; and ascribed to its powers, which few believed, and nobody cared for." As for Miss Walton, exactly because Harley was shy, she "frequently took more particular notice of him than of other visitors." His love for her grew precisely because she noticed him, for as the narrator critically remarks, "we are always inclined to think her handsomest when she condescends to smile upon ourselves." The net effect of this scene is laughable: she the virtuous but semi-boring female

who has lost almost all of her sparkle; he the painfully shy beau who imagines he loves for precisely those faults which make her uninteresting to other men. This couple seems to revel in its ineptitude. The scene is, as the narrator tells us, "ludicrous," and yet in the midst of the humor Mackenzie is dead serious about the merits of these odd lovers. Miss Walton and Harley are both at heart sincere and virtuous, and while each has more than a fair share of social defects and personal foibles, the point remains that they are far from being held up as total failures. They do, after all, love each other, even though their absurd conformity to social protocol ultimately results in their never marrying.

Does Mackenzie wish us to admire Harley's love for Miss Walton? Or is their affair pure sentimental tripe? Is Harley better or worse off because of his enhanced mode of feeling? I suggest that by way of the narrator's wry comments that Mackenzie is attempting to explore all of these questions but finally means to imply that sensitivity encumbers action for both Miss Walton and Harley. Two other scenes, among many, are also critical of sentimentality but in very different ways.

The first is the famous madhouse scene in chapter XX. Against his will, Harley is talked into touring Bedlam, a popular eighteenth-century London idea of an afternoon's lark. At the asylum Harley speaks with a female resident who unfolds a tale of woe. This is the first tearful episode in the novel, "and, except the keeper's, there was not an unmoistened eye." Mackenzie is attempting to confront the reader with the genuine empathy of Harley as opposed to the specious sentimentality of Harley's companions. Harley weeps because he is truly touched; the other visitors, male and female alike, affect being distressed, but we know they cannot be serious because they wanted to visit Bedlam knowing that they would enjoy running into a sad case or two worthy of tears. Harley, we recall, did not want to go, as no one who truly cares for the plight of the mentally ill would wish to visit simply to come away congratulating himself for his own humanitarianism. The keeper may be hardened to the plight of the inmates, but at least he is not a hypocrite—he does not shed a tear.

Every informed London reader either had been to Bedlam or knew of the pitiful cases in residence there. So Mackenzie cannot be attempting to make the scene even more pathetic and touching than reality: he wishes to use this episode as a "test" for the reader, asking him to determine who sheds tears in this scene and why. Harley cries because he has never seen such misery—after all, he had never before been there. But the others, who cried too, apparently went often and for amusement or for the reason before mentioned—to provide an opportunity for self-congratulation as they wallowed in feigned sympathy. As for charity, Harley's friend gives money to the keeper—the amount is not revealed, so we can only assume it is a pittance. Harley proffers two guineas, a most generous offering. But the mere difference in the amounts is not important: Harley is truly benevolent, a position we noted above in the description of Benevolus in *Lounger* 96. The reader, then, is supposed to recognize the distinction between genuine and affected sensitivity, between sincere intentions and affected actions. Harley's friends are "sentimental"; Harley is truly empathetic and benevolent.

The last episode for our attention is the Respino segment. In the so-called fragment entitled "The Pupil," Harley hears from his friend Sedley the tale of a youth in Milan whose unsavory actions led to the destruction of a family. The culmination of the story is that Respino, the youth, went on to lead a respected life, with the world calling him *"a man of honour."* This character anticipates the villainous Sindall of Mackenzie's second novel, *The Man of the World* (1773), who represents all that is most evil to Sedley, Harley, and, finally to Mackenzie. Respino is a perfect example of the moral delivered at the beginning of the chapter: the world "Will smile, and smile, and be a villain." Taken from *Hamlet* (I.v.108), this quote sets up a serious test for Harley and for the reader: Respino publicly speaks and acts in laudatory ways, yet he privately pursues evil activities.

Mackenzie attempts in the Respino segment to outline exactly how people of virtue and benevolence may be victimized by the world. The reader is given a warning: to be sensitive like Harley (or the youthful Sedley) is not a good idea; naive credulity can easily result in disaster. The reader must attempt to see the machinations of evil without becoming hardened. When one becomes calloused, as did the misanthrope in chapter XXI, one becomes inflexible and, most unfortunately, unhappy. The misanthrope thus violates one of Mackenzie's two cardinal points of life (as discussed above in relation to *Lounger* 20)—happiness. As the narrator explains early on in the novel,

> Indeed I have observed one ingredient, somewhat necessary in man's composition towards happiness, which *people of feeling would do well to acquire;* a certain respect for the follies of mankind: for there are so many fools whom the opinion of the world entitles to regard, . . . that he who cannot restrain his contempt or indignation at the sight, will be too often quarrelling with the disposal of things, to relish that share which is allotted to himself. (my italics)

Cynicism, though easy to fall into, is not, Mackenzie stresses, the way to deal with the problems of life.

Mackenzie thus has pursued his goal of education in three ways: 1) he has indicated that while heightened sensitivity can enhance such emotions as love—as portrayed in the Miss Walton episodes—the condition is not necessarily desirable; 2) he has attempted to show the reader how to distinguish true sensitivity from hypocritical pretensions of sentimentality in the Bedlam and Respino segments; and 3) he has depicted in Harley's unappealing demise the inevitable fate of those who glibly adhere to sentimental values: they fall into cynicism like the misanthrope or are destroyed, like Harley, by the wolves of the world. I repeat, the reader, not Harley, is the intended recipient of the education. Harley learns *nothing.* He is as hopeless at the end as in the beginning. But we are not supposed to scorn the hapless Harley; we are supposed to learn from his shortcomings. His feelings may be properly motivated, but he lacks the intellectual perception to thrive in the

world, unlike Fielding's foundling, Tom Jones, whose heart and head are in balance.

So we must conclude that the meaning of *The Man of Feeling* lies somewhere between the opposing extreme views of the critics. Mackenzie is not to be taken literally. . . . Nor does *The Man of Feeling* attack sentimentalism and satirize Harley. . . . The two artistic flaws—lack of a clear exemplary character and the fragmented plot—have confused and misled readers from first publication. Artistic ineptitude can, indeed, result in interpretive problems.

Detesting the affected sentimentality of society . . . , Mackenzie kept separate his admiration of certain principles of sensibility from their exaggerated practice, which resulted in affection at one extreme and debilitating ineffectiveness at the other. Recognizing that the public had at least partially misunderstood his intention in *The Man of Feeling,* because he did not present an example of a fully balanced character and used an eccentric narrative form, he sought to correct his errors in *The Man of the World* by introducing Harry Bolton and a traditional linear plot. But the excessive and overly simplified villainy of Sindall put off readers. In his third novel, *Julia de Roubigne,* Mackenzie accomplished both of his goals, unambiguously depicting the disastrous effects of excessive sentimentality as well as providing a model for readers in the sensitive but balanced Savillon. (pp. 140-47)

> *William J. Burling, "A 'Sickly Sort of Refinement': The Problem of Sentimentalism in Mackenzie's 'The Man of Feeling',"* in Studies *in Scottish Literature, Vol. XXIII, 1988, pp. 136-49.*

FURTHER READING

Crane, R. S. "Suggestions toward a Genealogy of the 'Man of Feeling'." *ELH* 1, No. 3 (December 1934): 205-30.
   Explores the eighteenth-century religious and social thought that influenced Mackenzie and other sentimentalist writers.

Mullan, John. "The Language of Sentiment: Hume, Smith, Henry Mackenzie." In *The History of Scottish Literature, Volume 2: 1660-1800,* edited by Andrew Hook, pp. 273-88. Aberdeen: Aberdeen University Press, 1987.
   Examines Mackenzie's sentimentalism in relation to the philosophies of David Hume and Adam Smith.

Thompson, Harold William. Introduction to *The Anecdotes and Egotisms of Henry Mackenzie: 1745-1831,* by Henry Mackenzie, edited by Harold William Thompson, pp. xiii-xxxiv. London: Oxford University Press, 1927.
   Surveys Mackenzie's literary career and the many factors that shaped it.

"Henry Mackenzie." *The Times Literary Supplement* (9 August 1928): 579.

Biographical discussion and critical assessment of Mackenzie.

Vickers, Brian. Introduction to *Man of Feeling,* by Henry Mackenzie, edited by Brian Vickers, pp. vii-xxiv. London: Oxford University Press, 1967.

Maintains that while Mackenzie's *Man of Feeling* evokes pathos, his fiction is trite.

Additional coverage of Mackenzie's life and career is contained in the following source published by Gale Research: *Dictionary of Literary Biography,* vol. 39.

Stéphane Mallarmé

1842-1898

French poet, essayist, dramatist, and translator. For additional information on Mallarmé's career, see *NCLC*, Volume 4.

INTRODUCTION

Mallarmé was one of the foremost contributors to French Symbolism, the nineteenth-century poetic movement whose members believed that the function of poetry was to evoke moods and impressions rather than to represent concrete reality. Attempting to depict an ideal existence, Mallarmé sought to use poetry to transcend the limits of rational language, often utilizing innovative syntax, complex metaphors, and experimental typography to create poems that challenge readers' perceptions. While Mallarmé's œuvre is small, and has sometimes been faulted for being deliberately obscure and ambiguous, his influence on twentieth-century art and literature has been lasting and profound. In addition to having a direct impact on the poetry of his disciple Paul Valéry, Mallarmé inspired Symbolist and avant-garde theater, Surrealism, the New Novelists, and such respected authors as Franz Kafka and T. S. Eliot. Critics have also noted Mallarmé's influence on such seminal twentieth-century philosophers as Jean-Paul Sartre, Jacques Derrida, and Gerard Genette. Charles Morice has emphasized the enormous effect of Mallarmé's complex and revolutionary verse on modern letters, claiming: "[Anyone] who has listened to him, dates from him."

Mallarmé was born in Paris to a middle-class family with a long tradition of civil service. His mother died when he was seven years old, after which his maternal grandmother played an increasingly significant role in his upbringing. When Mallarmé was fifteen, his youngest sister and closest companion, Maria, died. Her death strongly affected his development as a poet; he abandoned his youthful interest in Romantic lyricism and turned to Charles Baudelaire's *Les fleurs du mal*. Although his family disapproved of his interest in Baudelaire and confiscated his copy of the book, *Les fleurs du mal* was Mallarmé's first strong literary influence. In 1860, after receiving his baccalaureate degree from the university in Sens, Mallarmé became an apprentice at his grandfather's Registry office. He also became friends with professor Emmanuel des Essarts, with whom he discussed literature and art. Encouraged by des Essarts, Mallarmé published his first sonnet in 1862 in the journal *Le papillon*. Soon after this, Mallarmé met Maria Gerhard, a school teacher who accompanied him to London, where he studied English. During this period Edgar Allan Poe replaced Baudelaire as Mallarmé's dominant literary influence, and Mallarmé began to write lengthy dream-

like poems which reflected the artistic views of his new mentor. When he returned to France at the age of twenty-two, he married Gerhard and took a teaching position in Tournon, a small village on the Rhône. Although he had already begun to develop his poetic and linguistic theories, his work and meditations were continually interrupted by what he considered the tedious duties of a schoolteacher. His pupils openly mocked him and when his poem "L'azur" appeared in the journal *Le Parnasse contemporain* in 1866, the students scrawled the poem's final line over the blackboard: "Je suis hanté. L'azur! L'azur! L'azur!" Around this time Mallarmé began work on a prose poem entitled *Hérodiade* (*Herodias*), a piece that reflects his developing aesthetic and experimentation with language. This work, which remains unfinished, caused Mallarmé much anguish throughout his life. During one period of particular frustration with *Hérodiade*, Mallarmé began to compose *L'après-midi d'un faune* (*Afternoon of a Faun*), which he intended to be a companion piece to the former work. In a letter to his friend Henri Cazalis, Mallarmé explained his motivations: "I have been at work for ten days. I have left *Hérodiade* for the cruel winter: That solitary work had sterilized me, and in the interval I am rhyming an heroic interlude with a *Faun* as its hero."

In 1875, Mallarmé moved to Paris where he obtained a teaching position at Collège Rollin and met such notable Parisian poets as Paul Verlaine and Theodore de Banville. Gustave Kahn, in particular, admired Mallarmé's poetry, and began to call on him in the evening. Others soon joined them, and the legendary Tuesday evening meetings, or *les mardis,* began, with the participants known collectively as *les mardistes.* In 1884, Mallarmé finally achieved widespread recognition when two books by *mardistes* were published: *Les poètes maudits* by Verlaine and *A rebours* by Joris Karl Huysmans, both of which hailed Mallarmé's work. By 1891, such young poets as Valéry and André Gide had joined the group. At these meetings, Mallarmé lectured on how to use words as symbols and was revered by his audience as an oracle. Because of the tremendous influence he had over the writers of his time, Mallarmé became known as the "Master of Symbolism." Mallarmé's teaching career and the demands of his disciples left him little time for writing in his later years. In 1893 he retired to the small provincial town of Valvins. Although he produced little finished poetry, he continued to develop his aesthetic theories until his death five years later.

Mallarmé perhaps most succinctly stated his artistic views in a letter he wrote to Cazalis while he was working on *Hérodiade;* in it he stated: "[I] am inventing a language that must necessarily spring from a very new poetics, which I could define in these few words: *to paint, not the thing, but the effect it produces.* The poetic line should be composed of intentions rather than words, and all words should efface themselves before sensations." Although he worked on *Hérodiade* for more than twenty-five years, he was unable to implement his theories in the piece. This prose poem is a reworking of the biblical story about Hérodiade, or Salomé as she is also known, who instigates John the Baptist's execution. In Mallarmé's presentation Hérodiade is a melancholic and chaste princess who eschews her own sexuality in order to attain moral perfection. While he hoped to emphasize how spirituality, philosophy, and solitude are integral to self-knowledge and inner transformation, Mallarmé was forced to acknowledge that true reality is often beyond the realm of pragmatic expression or poetic interpretation. Wallace Fowlie has explained: "As a human being the princess Hérodiade opposes the flow and change of life by her studied and concentrated frigidity. Her opposition to normal life and vicissitude is the projection of the mythical role of the poet which Mallarmé believed in and practiced." While *Hérodiade* is a mystical interpretation of sexual repression, *Afternoon of a Faun* addresses how sensuality, ardor, and physical sensation attain significance through meditative introspection. Therefore, while *Hérodiade* suggests chastity can lead to spiritual perfection, *Afternoon of a Faun* explores the nature of sensual pleasure only to reveal the deceptive nature of illusion and reality.

Igitur: ou, La folie d'Elbehnon, a work which Mallarmé began in 1869 but never completed, consists of twelve prose fragments varying in length from one short paragraph to seven pages. Mallarmé indicated that he wanted his notes on this work destroyed at the time of his death, but his son-in-law Dr. Edmund Bonniot attempted to recreate the original order of the fragments and published

the work in 1925. Although there has been considerable controversy as to how to classify *Igitur*—it has been variously labeled a story, a prose poem, and a drama—most critics concur that the narrative structure is not as important as *Igitur*'s thematic significance in Mallarmé's aesthetic evolution. According to Mallarmé, this work was addressed not to the feelings, but rather "to the Intelligence of the reader" and was intended to explore the arbitrariness of human consciousness. Often said to anticipate Sartre's concept of "being-for-itself," *Igitur* reveals Mallarmé's lifelong obsessions with absence, anti-reality, nothingness, and death.

Mallarmé abandoned traditional grammar, vocabulary, and syntax in the majority of his poetry, but it is his final work, *Un coup de dés jamais n'abolira le hasard (A Throw of the Dice Never Will Abolish Chance),* that is considered his experimental masterpiece. Expressing his interest in the musical and polyphonic possibilities of the verse form, Mallarmé's words are set in different typefaces to produce visual representations of the poem's subject and to accentuate the intertwining of thought and sound. By tracing the fate of the ambiguous character known only as the "Master," Mallarmé attempts to recapitulate the role chance has played in the evolution of humanity. Although critics have praised Mallarmé's stylistic experimentations in *Un coup de dés,* they also note that the poem is occasionally strained and overambitious. F. C. St. Aubyn has commented: "[poetry] cannot be read exactly like music, so . . . Mallarmé's harmonic intentions get lost in the typographical inventions. But its aesthetic beauty, visual as well as auditory, can not be denied."

Some scholars have pointed to the short pieces Mallarmé composed in honor of his colleagues as some of his finest works. The 1873 poem, "Toast funèbre," not only honors the poet Theophile Gautier's accomplishments, but also delineates Mallarmé's beliefs about the role of the artist in society and the meaning of poetry. Fowlie has commented: " 'Toast funèbre' celebrates the essential paradox of poetry and of all art; the transitoriness of human experience fixed in a form of permanency." In 1875 Mallarmé wrote "Le tombeau d'Edgar Poe" ("The Tomb of Edgar Poe"), an homage to Poe's "eternal genius." Considered one of the greatest symbolist poems written in the late nineteenth century, "The Tomb of Edgar Poe" is one of the most frequently quoted works in French literature.

Throughout his career, Mallarmé strove to create a "Grand Œuvre," a book that would encompass his poetic beliefs and group together all "universal relationships . . . for some miraculous and glittering occasion." Mallarmé's deliberations over the true nature of poetry became so time-consuming and exhausting, however, that he was never able to produce such a work. His insistence that the reader work with the poet in search of symbolic meaning, his disdain of immediate gratification in literature, and his vacillating poetic intentions also proved problematic; he intermittently suffered from depression and creative sterility. When a student announced, for example, that he had deciphered the meaning of one of Mallarmé's sonnets, the poet replied: "How wonderful! You have figured out in one week what has taken me thirty years." Although Mallarmé failed to achieve some of his goals, his small output forms an important contribution to the Symbolist movement and contemporary poetry in its innovative and influential reconsideration of language and human existence. Summarizing the poet's achievement, Guy Michaud has asserted: "[Mallarmé] liberated the poetic instrument once and for all from the harness of three centuries of rationalistic and French rhetoric, up to and including Romanticism. He . . . forcefully established that the function of the poet, and of the writer in general, is to decipher the mystery of the world."

PRINCIPAL WORKS

Hérodiade (unfinished poem) 1869
  [*Herodias,* 1940]
L'après-midi d'un faune (poetry) 1876
  [*Afternoon of a Faun,* 1951]
Album de vers et de prose (prose and poetry) 1887
Poésies 1887; enlarged edition published in 1899 (poetry)
Les poèmes d'Edgar Poe [translator] (poetry) 1888
Pages (prose and poetry) 1891
Vers et prose (prose and poetry) 1893
La musique et les lettres (essays) 1894
Un coup de dés jamais n'abolira le hasard (poetry) 1897
  [*A Throw of the Dice Never Will Abolish Chance,* 1956]
Divagations (prose and poetry) 1897
Igitur; ou, la folie d'Elbehnon (unfinished drama) 1925
  [*Igitur,* 1974]
Poems (poetry) 1936
Oeuvres complètes (collected works) 1945
Selected Prose, Poems, Essays and Letters (prose, poetry, essays, and letters) 1956

Antonina M. Terlecki (essay date 1977)

[*The following excerpt formed part of the critic's 1977 doctoral thesis; it was first published in 1988. Terlecki here contends that Mallarmé's* Igitur *employs Symbolist poetics to create an abstract drama.*]

"A tale" or drama?: Before embarking on the analysis of *Igitur,* some justification should perhaps be offered for the choice of this "tale" (as Mallarmé referred to it: "c'est un conte . . . ") as an example of Mallarmé's third dramatic effort.

In a letter of November 14, 1869 addressed to one of his oldest friends, Henri Cazalis, we find a first mention of "a tale" on which Mallarmé was working; he defined its subject as that of "the old monster-Impotence". However, the . . . epigraph to *Igitur* appeals to the "Intelligence of the reader to *produce* everything *on a stage*" (emphasis mine). This is further strengthened by the marginal heading of the Part IV fragment called "The throwing of the dice". That note reads: "Scène de Théâtre, ancien Igitur".

This may seem insufficient to justify approaching the text

as that of a drama. However, Mallarmé is said to have spoken of it himself as a "dramatic tale" and again as a "philosophical drama" [according to Henri de Régnier's *Proses datées,* 1925]. Written in an extremely dense poetic prose, it may indeed have been envisioned as the "cosmic drama" he was later to theorize so much about. And as he had, at that moment, relegated all thoughts of writing for the real stage, he created a work which embodies most of his ideas concerning the true, ideal theatre. There are several statements which point to Mallarmé having, after 1870, continued to think of and to work on *Igitur* as a drama. One of them, the information given to George Moore about a play which the latter called "Hamlet and the Wind", may arouse some doubts as to its seriousness. But there is no denying the resemblance of Igitur to Shakespeare's Prince of Denmark, as has been pointed out by several critics.

There is really nothing new in approaching *Igitur* as a drama. Various scholars have done it, to mention in the first place Haskell M. Block in his book *Mallarmé and the Symbolist Drama* [1963]. . . .

Emilie Noulet speaks of "acts" and "décor" in *Igitur* [in *L'Oeuvre poétique de Stéphane Mallarmé,* 1940]. Wallace Fowlie also uses the terms "scene" and "stage set" in his considerations [in *Mallarmé,* 1962]. Most explicit in this respect is Jean Royère, to whom *Igitur* is simply "a scenario", and who finds that its five parts "are the equivalent of the usual five acts" [*Mallarmé,* 1927]. Claudel wrote: ". . . it is a drama, the most beautiful, most stirring, the nineteenth century has produced" [Paul Claudel, "La Catastrophe d'*Igitur*", *Oeuvres en prose,* 1965].

Assuming that *Igitur* then is "a cosmic drama", it represents the most revolutionary example of dramatic writing in the second part of the nineteenth century, and for this reason was chosen for the present case.

In the subsequent analysis the conventional terms of action, character and plot are purposely used as references to show how far Mallarmé deviated from the traditional pattern. The general aim is to highlight the absolute newness of the dramatic concept and its structural consequences.

Basic textual problems: The analysis of *Igitur* presented exceptional difficulties in view of the fact that (a) it is an unfinished work, and (b) the exact order of the fragments has not been definitely established. The following is the one proposed by Dr Edmond Bonniot and adopted by the editors of the *Oeuvres Complètes,* the most authoritative extant edition. The titles of the scenes or parts are Mallarmé's and have been used in the present discussion of the work:

Introduction

Argument

I. Midnight—"Le Minuit"

II. He leaves the room and disappears down the staircase—"Il quitte la chambre et se perd dans les escaliers" (referred to in the text of the dissertation as "The Staircase")

III. Igitur's life—"Vie d'Igitur"

IV. The Throwing of the Dice—"Le Coup de dés"

V. He lies down on the tomb—"Il se couche au tombeau"

There are, moreover, separate notes or "scolies" (*scholia*):

1. General traits—"touches";

2. Several drafts of the exit from the room—marked respectively by Mallarmé: gamma, delta, epsylon;

3. A separate part marked IV bears the title: "Inspite of his mother's prohibition, he goes to the tombs to play" ("Malgré la défense de sa mère allant jouer dans les tombeaux").

The sequence of the five main parts as published by E. Bonniot has been questioned by such scholars as A. R. Chisholm in his *Mallarmé's Grand Oeuvre* [1962], Haskell M. Block in *Mallarmé and the Symbolist Drama,* and A. Orliac in *Mallarmé tel qu'en lui-même.*

There is, moreover, the reading of Maurice Blanchot who considers the "Minuit" part I to be the true end of the work. He sees *Igitur* as a circular structure, where the initial presentation of absence and disintegration prefigures Igitur's accomplishment of "the act" which will bring about his own annihilation [*L'Espace littéraire,* 1955].

All this was taken into account. But the subsequent analysis is the first attempt at a thorough treatment from the dramatic point of view of one of the most mysterious and complex works in modern European poetry.

Subject matter: The definition of the subject matter of *Igitur* presents the greatest difficulty. Mallarmé's own explanation was that it is "the old monster of Impotence" which he wanted to overcome by writing this work.

It seems, however, that it is justifiable to see it in somewhat broader terms as the act of creativity—the act of creating a work of art.

In this student's opinion, these two interpretations—the critics' and Mallarmé's—complement each other. The "monster of impotence" is, indeed, defeated by an act of creativity. The created work has abolished the accident (*"le hazard"*)—the greatest enemy of all art.

Following the text closely, one could say that Mallarmé is presenting to us Igitur's development in two stages: dissolution and annihilation, in order to abolish "accident"—the element hostile to Perfection and Beauty—and to attain the Absolute through "Nothingness" (*"le Néant"*).

It must be remembered that "Nothingness" by no means has a negative meaning for Mallarmé. The letter to Cazalis of May 1867 explains how he, having in his terribly painful meditations reached "Nothingness", discovered Beau-

ty, of which the perfect expression is Poetry. In the light of the thought voiced in this letter, the death of Igitur which he reaches by drinking "the substance of Nothingness", is not annihilation but the arrival at that state of purity and silence which makes Beauty, therefore Poetry, possible. Guy Michaud's interpretation of Mallarmé's concept of "Nothingness" makes this point perfectly clear; *"Le Néant"* had become for Mallarmé not a negative, but a positive notion: ". . . a universe not unreal, but prereal, not impossible, but consisting of nothing but possibilities, not absolutely empty, but emptied of all reality, of all realization" [*Message poétique*].

Further support for interpreting *Igitur* as the presentation of the moment of artistic inception is to be found in certain similarities between *Igitur* and some of the formulations in the essay **"Quant au Livre—L'Action restreinte"** (**"About the Book—Restricted Action"**). In a true or fictitious conversation with a visitor, Mallarmé explains the significance and technique of the act of writing or creating. He calls himself—the older writer teaching the younger one—the Host (*"l'Hôte"*). The same name is given to Igitur, when his face appears for the first time in the "Midnight" role: ". . . around the face [. . .] of the host". The similarity continues in the same passage of **"About the Book"**, when Mallarmé speaks of the inevitable obliteration (*"Omission"*) of the author and of the "death" of the host, that is, of the poet. This resembles the death or obliteration of Igitur. The whole atmosphere of *Igitur* seems to be summed up in the sentence of the teaching host: "The deeds, he [the author] accomplishes them in a dream, so as not to disturb anybody".

The same passage is quoted by Gardner Davies [in his *Stéphane Mallarmé "Les Noces d'Hérodiade": Mystère,* 1959] to support his claim that the creator "must completely sacrifice his personality, in order to be reborn as an impersonal genius". In his interpretation of *Hérodiade* he sees Mallarmé's work as that of "the artistic creation". His reading establishes a thematic link between this work and *Igitur,* and he points out that the inception of both stands fairly close to each other in time. *Hérodiade*'s beginnings date back to 1864; *Igitur* is supposed to have been conceived and written between 1867 and 1870.

Jean Pierre Richard interprets *Igitur* somewhat differently, as the "rediscovery of conscience, its destruction and metamorphosis" [*L'Univers imaginaire de Mallarmé,* 1961]. In a way, this too can be equated with the germination and development of a work of art.

However, for the purpose of this thesis it is not as crucial to fix the subject in its exact meaning (if this is at all possible in any case), as to state its nature, which is multivocal, general, metaphysical, abstract, and totally deprived of anything that could resemble a concrete (even in the widest sense), realistic, tangible problem. . . . [Mallarmé's] . . . "ideal" drama claimed precisely this kind of subject as the only acceptable one.

Place of action-setting: The setting is one which, even today, could not be realized in any theatre. We need all the powers of our imagination as the "producers" of the play to visualize the place of the action.

There is, at first, darkness, without any discernible shape. It is lit up at moments by a vague light emanating at one time from a candle, at another from the white page of an open book. After a while, there emerges first a golden clock, showing the Midnight hour, then a dark room (the room of time), where a few pieces of furniture and some drapes are distinguishable. This is followed by the appearance of a spinning spiral of light, eclipsed by the apparition of the "perfectly symmetrical room", replaced once more by the spinning spiral and later a corridor.

A spiral staircase descends from the room, at first to one endless corridor and later to many such corridors. These lead us finally to the one realistic décor: the tomb in the ancestral vault on which Igitur is to lie down and die.

This kind of setting is the first and main argument in favour of seeing *Igitur* as an anticipation of cinematic art. If we were to accept Mallarmé's invitation to "produce" the story ourselves, not just in our imagination but in a theatre, we would stumble over the insurmountable difficulty of lending material shape on a stage to the suggestions of the text. The strange mixture of concrete objects (furniture, drapes) with totally unrealistic notions—for instance, the walls of the "site" which are future and past, the constant shifting of outlines, the actual participation of "properties" in the "action" (the "shivering" drapes, the "radiating" book), the appearance and disappearance of the hero, Night as one of the Protagonists, all seem to defy any attempt at a live stage production. Film technique eliminates these difficulties. The cinematic means of montage, of close- and blow-ups, of superimposition of images, etc., allow the "scene" of Mallarmé's nocturnal vision to be shown; they put an end to a fight against the resistance, the clumsiness of actual material objects and the material, bodily limitations of the actor. They permit the "dematerialization" of the drama Mallarmé was striving for.

Transformation of Time and Space:. . . [In] *Igitur* Time becomes a character, . . . it is, at certain moments, identical with the hero. Mallarmé calls him "Night's last shape", its last incarnation. In what appears to be a kind of duel between Igitur and Midnight, the latter reduces its incarnation to a shadow. Remaining alone in the room, it utters the strange sentence: "I was the hour that *is* supposed to *make* me pure" (emphasis mine).

The appearance of the mirror, the appearance and disappearance of Igitur's reflection in it, is the battle between the two incarnations and ends with the re-establishment of the purity of the looking-glass. When all is over, we seem to have assisted in the annihilation of one and the birth of another being: Igitur stands detached and alone. But he, too, must die, so that only the "pure and lonely light" of perfect beauty, that is, in Mallarmé's understanding, of Poetry may remain.

In his speech, Igitur evokes the past and the future. The present lasts only one brief moment—the throw of the dice (to abolish accident), and the drinking of the drop of Nothingness—in order that the future Absolute (Igitur) may join the Infinite. Through this double act, the drama has been accomplished.

There are many indications of Mallarmé's familiarity with the Bible; his treatment of time may also have been engendered by the readings of the Old Testament. The repeated insistence on the brevity of the present which is practically non-existent as it immediately becomes the past, which can be contemplated at any length only in the future, reminds one of the scriptures where what is written in the future tense has to be read in the past, eliminating the present.

In his vision, Mallarmé equates Time also with Space: the room that becomes visible is the Room of Time; the corridors leading to the ancestral vault are again the Corridors of Time. The theatre, say Maurice Blanchot, is "the space of Midnight, the moment which is a place". In the pulsating darkness, Night, Igitur and the room merge into one entity; Time, Life and Space establish their relationship. To the rhythmic beating of the clock, in the growing and receding darkness (so strongly reminiscent of the darkness of Biblical Creation or of the maternal womb), the three identities separate, merge, and separate again.

Finally, the lonely figure of the hero appears at the top of the staircase which he will descend to reach the vault, in order there to obliterate himself and with him, Time and Space.

Action: It goes without saying that *Igitur* does not have any action whatsoever in the traditional sense of "plot" or "story". The latter can be summed up in a short paragraph:

The hero, Igitur, as a child, reads a lesson to his ancestors; as a young man, he contemplates himself in the mirror, takes a phial, descends a spiral staircase, throws the dice, drinks the contents of the phial, lies down on the tomb of his forefathers.

This gives us a succession of gestures, but hardly any action. Nevertheless, "action" in the sense of Gouhier's "essence", of internal cohesion, is most strongly present [Henri Gouhier, *L'Oeuvre Théâtrale,* 1958]. The two main elements of the work, the midnight theme and the progress of Igitur, are even bodily united; each one's fate is inextricably dependent on the other's. Igitur's ultimate gesture, the throwing of the dice and the effacement of his own consciousness, is the inevitable consequence of first his union and then his separation from the lifegiving hour of Midnight, his alter ego.

Language: As there is no actual plot, the text becomes one of the most important vehicles of the author's idea. It is in here, in this strange interaction of shifting light, shifting shapes, movement of the few "properties" and the spoken word, that Mallarmé's total break with the conventional drama lies. It was his conviction that the word has a creative power comparable to magic. He, indeed, created "in a deliberate shadow the unnamed object, by allusive words, never direct ones" [Mallarmé, "Magic"] and surrounded this "object" with a mysterious setting and mood.

Strangely enough, he also created a kind of suspense. Not, of course, the kind a realistic play would provide, but that of a dream, combined with a purely verbal tension. The hermetic text draws one in; having glimpsed one clear point, one is trying to catch the next, moving in alternate rhythms of understanding and mystification. A mystification of purely abstract nature. There cannot possibly be any interest in the "progress" of the story. Yet, there is a growing surrender to the hypnotic force of speech, to the fleeting images it conjures up, which have no logical sequence.

Thanks to an extremely elaborate use of alliteration, assonance and repetition, the text at times resembles a kind of incantation or mystic hymn, the full sense of which eludes the listener. Here is one untranslatable example: "L'ombre disparue en l'obscurité, la Nuit resta avec une douteuse perception de pendule qui va s'éteindre et expirer en lui; mais à ce qui luit et va, expirant en soi s'éteindre, elle se voit qui le porte encore, donc; c'est d'elle que, nul doute, était le battement oui, dont le bruit total et dénué à jamais tomba en son passé".

The images, suggestions and the musical quality of the speech create an atmosphere of unreality. Under the influence of this incantatory language, the imagination of the listener is stirred to elaborate, to interpret in its own way the metaphors and allusions that strike the ear.

Once more the attention is inevitably drawn to the potentialities of film technique. Film allows for a use of silence impossible in the theatre; and every student of Mallarmé knows the importance he attributed to silence. The cinematic art at its best permits the text to be spaced out, to give the listener time either to grasp its implications, or to submit to its evocative power, while the eye receives from the screen a visual support or directive for his meditation. The possibilities of amplifying or reducing the volume of the speaking voice must also be taken into account, as they augment or reduce the emphasis of the spoken text.

Properties: It was said earlier that the properties are "participating" in the "action". This did not refer to two of the principle objects: the candle and the book. These two play an important but passive role. Their meaning is hinted at in Mallarmé's text.

The candle is that of "being", of "existence", thanks to which "all has been". Because of its light, "the letters of the book survive, perhaps". That light, the "nacreous star", is also that of "nebulous knowledge". We see the candle at the beginning, as the first source of light; then it is reflected in the shining walls of "the place". In the end, it is extinguished by Igitur who blows on it.

The book lies open on the table; on its white pages lingers "the gleam of the chimaera [. . .] in which its dream has agonized", the dream of Igitur's ancestors. This book, after Igitur's descent down "the staircase of the human mind into the heart of things", is closed by him.

Although some theories concerning Mallarmé's involvement with the occult through Villiers de l'Isle-Adam may seem too far-fetched, there is no denying that he is using here the two classic instruments of witchcraft: the book and the candle. One may recognize the third object, the bell, in the somewhat changed form of the striking clock which will be discussed later. The matter is of no paramount importance to the drama; it only reminds one,

through its associations, that to Mallarmé, as to Baudelaire, poetry was "sorcery", "alchemy" in the noblest sense of the word.

Another "passive" property is the phial that contains "the drop of Nothingness which the ocean lacks". It appears at the end of the second part ("The Staircase") and—presumably—after the "death" of the furniture. Before going down the staircase, the character that "had impaired the purity of the mirror", by appearing in it, must hide the phial in his bosom and later absorb its content. Having thrown the dice, Igitur does just that. It is significant that this all-important property appears only once, at the crucial moment, when the actual "drama" takes place.

The golden "rich and useless clock" is both passive and active as a property. Passive, because throughout the entire drama its hands remain fixed on the midnight hour—"the unique one" it has created, the "unified hour",—whose presence fills the "room of time". Active, because its "marine and stellar complexity" suggests the creation of the "reciprocal / forms of / Nothingness"—the stars and the sea. Active again because its sound fills the entire "Staircase" part, marking the consecutive stages of Night's (therefore Igitur's) uneasiness and the progression of both Night and Igitur, Night's last incarnation; its beat is at the same time that of the clock and of Night-Igitur's heart. Once Night has absorbed its former "figure" which appeared in the mirror, once it has "reduced it to the state of shadow", the beat stops. The noise that troubled Night vanishes in the Light that stays "lonely and pure".

The three principle "passive", that is independently inactive, properties are symbols of what in a traditional play would be elaborated into the actively presented life stories of the characters. Here they are reduced to the symbolic flicker of light (thought-consciousness) and the perpetuation of deeds in a written work (the candle and the book). The clock represents through its beat the passage of time and through its immovable hands the hour of inception (Midnight) that brings forth the Idea.

Finally, there is among the "passive" objects the mirror. It is seen briefly at the end of Part II, reflecting "what Night had been"—"its last shape", in a costume of velvet with a gossamer ruff. Igitur explains that he had to sit in front of the mirror "so as not to doubt of himself".

Holding a very important part in the drama, this property seems to replace the traditional secondary characters. If, according to existentialist belief, our existence is confirmed by its reflection in the eyes of and in the conscience of other existences, Mallarmé, true to his precepts, had to replace these secondary characters with a symbol. The best, simplest and most obvious one was the mirror. This is, of course, a somewhat anachronistic interpretation—existentialist *avant la lettre*—but confirmed by the importance attributed to mirrors already by the Romanticists. In this drama, there is no conflict between different personalities; there is only the reflection of Igitur's battles with his other "self", that is Midnight. This interpretation deviates from that of Jean Pierre Richard who [in his *L'Univers imaginaire,* 1961] interprets the task of the mirror exclusively as that of confirming Igitur's self. A similar meaning is usually lent to the role of the mirror in **Hérodiade;** it is "the image of selfawareness". Guy Delfel, who uses this definition [in his *L'esthétique de Stéphane Mallarmé,* 1951], enlarges its meaning, seeing the mirror as both a reflection of Hérodiade's self and of the constellations of the nocturnal sky which are the symbol of the higher reality to which Hérodiade aspires.

The reflected struggle is so strong that at the crucial point the mirror is referred to as having "become anxiety". The most painful moment in Igitur's existence—his detachment from his past, from his physical present and from the Mother-Idea who decrees his obliteration for the sake of the higher aim—is acted out in and in front of the looking glass.

This is one more part which, if attempted, could be realized only on the screen—no other medium can even try to reproduce the successive appearances and disappearances of the hero's shape.

It is in Part III ("Igitur's Life") that the "active" properties are of importance: the curtains or drapes and the furniture. From the beginning, the drapes are the place where time stays or is "resolved", having acquired permanence, which gives them a heavy and stiff shape. The drapes are the means by which Igitur is trying to trap time in the room, because time is his "food and life"; to this end, he has "thickened the curtains" and "very carefully gathered the least particles of time in ever heavier fabrics". When Igitur is filled with horror, seeing his reflection disappear from the mirror, the drapes are "disturbed", and they "shiver". At the height of Igitur's anguish in front of the looking-glass, the "phantom of terror" feeds itself on the "instability" of the curtains. When the separation of mirror and reflection has been accomplished, the drapes calm down and "slump into an attitude which they are to preserve for ever". They, like the furniture, are useless, therefore lifeless and dead.

The drapes seem to be symbols for Igitur's dependence on and his attachment to Time, in the sense of earthly existence. He likes to be enclosed by them and needs their compact materiality to feel secure. Their "trembling" announces a first, as yet "narcotically quiet", thought of the "pure self"—a first, not yet disturbing, announcement of things to follow. Their second "trembling" marks Igitur's growing anxiety preceding his final detachment; their "blowing" occurs at the height of his torment; it marks his separation from earthly Time (which they harboured). When that separation from his temporal past and his other self, Midnight, has taken place, leaving Igitur "alone, as if caught in his own cold", the curtains "slump".

The blowing of the curtains could also mean the appearance of the breath of inspiration; the wind would be that of the spirit which is breathing life into the work of art; when the same curtains slump, it would mean the end or the death of the inspired moment or perphaps the moment of the task fulfilled.

Before its death the task of the massive ebony furniture was to contain the elements of anxiety. It remained tightly shut, filled with its secrets. When Igitur panics, seeing his reflection in the mirror disappear, he makes an effort to "conjure himself up again". To that end he opens all the doors and drawers of the furniture, so that it may "pour out its mystery, the unknown, its memory, its silence, human faculties and impressions". Having done it, he has the feeling that he is becoming himself again. The disappearance of Igitur's reflection brings death to the furniture "with its convulsed rings". Like stark and stiff monsters, it now strikes an "isolated and severe attitude, projecting its hard lines into the absence of atmosphere".

"Extras": So far mention has been made only of the principle "character", though this one, to all appearances, is a double one. But even if both Igitur and Midnight occupy the first place, they are not the only *dramatis personae.* They are, at times, surrounded by what, in the theatre, are called supernumeraries or extras.

From the very beginning, these extras are present, and Igitur is well aware of them, although they do not appear bodily. They are Igitur's ancestors. He reads his lesson to them in the introductory scene, but has to shield his candle from them. They want to blow it out. They seem anxious to see Igitur die before he has attained an immortal, artistic shape. We do not see them in this scene, we hear their breath. They stop blowing when Igitur tells them that it is too early; silence is restored, and Igitur can read his lesson.

They return in the "Staircase" part, where we have first the "panting" of the "many geniuses" brushing off the dust from their tombs. They want to appear clearly and "clean" to their offspring. After a while we see in the light of Igitur's candle the "host of apparitions", all with candle and book in their hands, and he recognizes himself in them. The sides of the staircase now reflect the "myriads of shadows" plunged deep into silence. Mallarmé's language strongly underlines the ghostly atmosphere and the phantomesque character of these invisible participants. There are the just quoted "host of apparitions"; the ancestors pick up their "secular" dust and "cobwebs" from their "tombs"; the "last shadow" (Igitur) and the capitalized "Shadow" (the same last off-spring), and again the "layers of shadow and nights" leading to the "sepulchral door".

All through the drama, whenever they are not sleeping, Igitur's ancestors seem to protest. He is different and is betraying them through his desire to reach and become the Absolute. They seem to be envious and desirous for him to join them. Hence the appealing "cleaning" of their reflection as well as their indecorous behaviour in the vault. In that scene, the last but one, we do not see them, we hear them whistle. They are angry, because Igitur, before drinking the substance contained in the phial, speaks of the "futility of their folly", meaning the production of their last offspring. They make "noises of folly", until Igitur lies down on the ancestral tomb. Only then is silence restored.

Sound effects: The presence of the, at times, vociferous shadows brings up the important sound aspect of **Igitur.** **Hérodiade** is still conservative in this respect, because it is a beautiful verse play or even a monologue, making little use of unorthodox sight or sound possibilities. *Igitur* not only makes extreme demands on the technical possibilities of the traditional stage, it also makes extensive use of what, in the language of the visual media, is generally referred to as "sound effects".

The blowing and breathing of the ancestors at the beginning, their "noises of folly" at the end, have already been mentioned. But these are more or less sporadic. The entire "Midnight" part is built up on very complex developments of sound based on the beating of the clock. It begins with the twelve strokes which introduce the scene. Its "vacant sound" evokes from the darkness the sight of the golden clock. It is easy to imagine these sonorous strokes drawn out through the whole "Midnight" scene, amplifying or fading, depending on the demands of the text and, after Night's final sentence, imperceptibly changing into the ticking of the clock.

All of Part II ("The Staircase") has a background of shifting sounds, sometimes multiplied by their echo. At first, the ticking is so soft that Night has of it only a "dubious perception". [In her *Literary Origins of Surrealism*, 1947] Anna Balakian calls it "[. . .] a sound [. . .] robbed of all its characteristics except the beat [. . .] [which creates] [. . .] the abnormal sensation of rhythm without sound". This hardly perceptible beat is interrupted and replaced by the "double shock" of the closing doors of the vault, joined by a rustling and the dying resonance of the just-heard shock of the doors. In turn, this sound is replaced by the flapping of a bird's wings. It is immediately followed by a sort of panting and brushing (the ancestors sweeping the dust away) which changes back into the second resonance of the closing vault doors, joined once more by the flapping of bird's wings. It dies out and fades into the throbbing of the heart, becoming stronger when it is supposed to be that of the entire ancestry, reduced to a barely perceptible sound when a whispering becomes audible. Once more we hear the brushing sound, followed by the stronger scansion of the beat and mixed with the "dubious brushing noises". The heart beat becomes fainter and, together with the reverberation of the closing vault doors (heard for the third time), dies out when Igitur leaves the room.

This scene, carried on an almost uninterrupted wave of continuous background sounds, is followed by one where movement, changing from static pose (Igitur facing the mirror) to violent contortions of the furniture, is projected in an atmosphere of total silence. From audible perception Mallarmé changed to exclusively visual awareness, reinforcing the sensation of a nightmarish world.

A similar alternation of sound and silence occurs in the scene of "The Throwing of the Dice". It begins with the various noises made by the ancestors (the "folly noises" can be perfectly rendered by electronic devices). Then follows the very short last "tableau vivant" (or rather "tableau mouvant"): Igitur, lying motionless on the "ashes of his family". This fades into the light emanating from the "castle of purity" which closes the drama.

Characters: The main character, the only "actor" of the play, has been left for discussion until the very end, be-

cause he presents a most difficult and complex problem. Those commentators who discuss the theatrical aspect of *Igitur* speak of him as of a single personality, the adolescent, last offspring of an illustrious family (see, for example, Block, Wooley, Royère); Igitur the descendent is seen for the first time as a child, reading his lesson. Yet those concerned with the philosophical interpretation (e.g. Fowlie, Scherer, Blanchot, Richard) dwell on the duality of the hero who is, in fact, both Igitur and Midnight or Night, even Nothingness (*le Néant*).

Throughout the first and second part of the work, the text is composed in such a way as to make both Midnight and Igitur the protagonists or rather one protagonist; at times they divide, and then again they merge. This ambiguity of the hero's identity which prevails in the second part ("The Staircase") is reduced in the "delta draft", where it seems fairly clear that the hero is Night.

This would make Igitur the first dramatic poem that chooses time, not as one of the dimensions of its happenings, but as one of its "characters". Mallarmé did not give it a shape other than that of Igitur, whom Midnight calls its "abolished and non-existent shadow". Apart from that, Mallarmé translates the presence of Midnight with the help of sounds: the ticking and striking of the clock and the throbbing of the heart. Its visible metaphors are the golden and blue clock with its stars as well as the drapes which try to hold time.

With such an ambiguous text there remains the problem of the distribution of voices. There are long passages which cannot be treated as direct enunciations of either Igitur or Midnight and which would, therefore, in the case of a "distribution of roles", have to be allotted to a Narrator. This would allow, in the case of a scenic or cinematic realization, making sure that as much of the original text is used as would be deemed necessary for an approximate understanding of the work. The ideal, of course would be the presentation of the entire text. However, a choice would have to be made, as the *"scholia"* present several versions of some parts, especially that of the "Staircase". The choice had to be made even for the sketchy film script, as the "drafts" provide sometimes a clearer version of the development than that proposed in the Bonniot arrangement.

Dramatic aspects: From the formal point of view *Igitur* represents what Mallarmé called the essence of the theatre—the identity of theatre and hero, united the mystery of the Idea, expressed through the hymn. The "operation" (cf. above) has been accomplished in that one moment when the Idea having emerged, it is immediately abolished.

The tragic conflict seems to lie in the sufferings Midnight and Igitur must endure before the latter, the incarnation of the Absolute, has accomplished the deed that abolishes accident. His action, the throw of the dice which annihilates both him and Midnight, equals that just mentioned "operation". After it is performed, nothing remains of Igitur and his abode, except "the castle of Purity" or, to quote the last sentence of the delta draft: " . . . only the light . . . lonely and pure".

The drama is truly a hymn sung by the hero, identical with the hero, through which Theatre and Hero become one. Mallarmé exposed this essence of this ultimate notion of Theatre in two pages of notes published in Bonniot's introduction to *Igitur.* This very cryptic manuscript formulates the following thesis: The Theatre is (or equals) the Idea, whereas the Hero is (or equals) the Hymn; the two form the entity of Drama or Mystery. As if to reinforce the idea of unity, Mallarmé uses also the words "equation" and "double identity" and adds, so as to leave no doubt: "if this is that—that is this wrongly split into two". Warren Ramsay in his essay, "A View of Mallarmé's Poetics" [*Romanic Review* XLVI, No. 3, 1955] summed up the question when speaking of *Igitur* as "a dramatic project where the drama lies at a hypothetical point of contact, between the Theatre shrunken to its Idea and the Hero reduced to the Hymn he sings". The formula "if this is that—that is this" appears to be of decisive importance for the understanding of the structure of *Igitur.* It throws light on the double identity of the speaking voice in Part II ("The Staircase"). Here, indeed, "this is that and that is this", as Midnight becomes Igitur and Igitur is identical with Midnight.

In the light of Mallarmé's formulations, that double identity of the hero can be seen as the scenic incarnation of the two basic elements of drama: Midnight, the hour of creation, the *Idea* conceived—invents, in turn, its *Hero.* Both Idea and Hero have to pass through the process of development, the life cycle of historical incarnation with its anguish and torment. The last representative of the human race must die (get rid of his space- and time-bound shape) in order to become nothing but the hero of a work of art. The "dissolution" (dematerialization) of the Idea in itself and the bodily death of Igitur the hero result in the emergence of the Absolute, residing in "the castle of purity". The Absolute and Purity are synonyms for the perfection of poetry.

This tentative (one more in the already long list) but purely dramatic interpretation of *Igitur*'s meaning, is based on the following elements:

Night was to Mallarmé the time of his creative work; night hours brought him either the happiness of new ideas or the despair of artistic impotence. When he began to work on *Igitur,* after his painful crisis or "breakdown", he applied the well-known psychological means of "exorcising" his obsession by writing about it. To give Night the leading but only vocal part seems to have been a very plausible step: Night and Idea were in Mallarmé's mind inseparable. With this idea we have one of the two mainstays of his ideal theatre.

The Idea needs that second mainstay—the Hero. He will pronounce, or sing the Hymn, because "nothing will last if it is not articulated". The material shape chosen resembles one beloved by Mallarmé and familiar to any literate reader—Hamlet, "the unique character of an intimate and occult tragedy".

The entire text, the "Hymn" sung by Igitur—the Hero, is that future advocated form of Drama, the "Monologue with Himself": Himself—his other self—Midnight. It tells of his struggles and sufferings (the struggles and sufferings of the creative mind), and the ultimate union with "Nothingness". What that meant to Mallarmé has already been explained. It is the only state and place where perfect poetry can exist. To have reached it is to have reached the artistic goal, the Perfect Work of Poetic Art.

As for the structural aspect, this student borrows here the thesis of *Igitur*'s circular form from Maurice Blanchot. Part I ("Midnight") brings in its allusive way the confirmation of the entire scenic concept.

The marine color of the clock and the stars of its ornamentation give us the two symbols of the first day of Creation; creation is the main subject of the drama. The text reads: "They detach themselves from Infinity—though they remain reciprocal Nothings in the Outside Darkness". Infinity and Darkness are the two first elements in the Biblical story.

The clock first strikes and then shows the twelfth hour. The Room of Time becomes visible; the temporal setting for the Idea is there. The Face of the Host marks the temporal embodiment of the Idea, its "pure dream".

The next thing we see is the open book whose pages show the bygone "silent word" (the written word—"*l'écriture*") spoken once by Midnight who evokes "its abolished and non-existent shadow", its slow progress "towards the ultimate gesture". When that is accomplished, the "text" is closed, the room disappears, only the clock shows the same, now "useless" hour, because the work has been created, the Night "that was" has now changed into Infinity.

Igitur—film scenario: To prove the validity of the repeatedly made claim that many elements in Mallarmé's drama foreshadow the coming of cinematic art, an attempt was made to draw up a very rough film scenario of *Igitur* as an auxiliary analytical tool. The many careful readings and long acquaintanceship with the text produced the ever more insistent impression of being confronted with a visionary kind of film. Even today, if anybody tried to realize it, it would, of course, be a so-called "avant-garde" work. This impression, received long before reading Anna Balakian's *The Symbolist Movement,* as well as her *Literary Origins of Surrealism,* was confirmed by her findings and suggestions concerning the influence Mallarmé had on the development of modern theatre, and the possibilities symbolist ideas offer the cinematographic medium.

The notion of this third kind of inherent artistic realization that intrudes so strongly during the reading of *Igitur* exposes the hybrid nature of the fascinating though fragmentary work. It was an additional reason for seeing it as in attempt to create the ideal "drama"; it really is neither entirely a narration nor a play, and therefore well illustrates Mallarmé's dilemma concerning the form of his great "Oeuvre".

Drama as "communion": In his masterly rendering of Mallarmé's lifelong effort to complete his "Work" ("*L'Oeuvre*") and of his hesitations about whether it was to be a drama or a book, Jacques Scherer says that Mallarmé finally, "forgot the real theatre for the theatre of the mind" [*Le 'Livre' de Mallarmé: Premières recherches sur les documents inédits,* 1957]. Over a long period of time, however, the terms "book" and "theatre" seem to have been not only equally acceptable, but interchangeable. Scherer explains the reason why Mallarmé, refusing to bow to any of the traditional requirements of the stage, identified The Book and The Theatre. If the "theatre is of superior essence", it is so because "its attribute is communion, its nature is quasi-religious. The Book is lonely" [Mallarmé, **"Le Genre"**].

With that, Scherer has touched the core of Mallarmé's plight. Inspite of his uncompromising, extremist approach to art, and particularly to poetry, despite his disregard for popular acclaim, he had a very real urge to communicate, be it only with a restricted group of listeners. Even The Book is not supposed to be read by just one reader for himself, it requires a simple but precisely elaborated presentation by the author to a small number of people (twenty-four participants at one session was the figure given by Mallarmé in the notes for "The Book").

That Mallarmé knew how to communicate is born out by the numerous fervent admirers he had, by his Tuesdays which more than anything else aroused the imagination of his disciples. Many of them testified that Mallarmé's topics at these famous weekly gatherings in the rue de Rome in Paris were poetry as well as drama, the theatre, ballet and pantomime. And it seems that, apart from the published articles which he himself called "a dramatic campaign" conducted in 1886–87 and later again in 1893, it was in these talks that the new dramatic ideas were born.

One could venture to say that, in a very limited way, Mallarmé realized his great work and his theatre precisely in these intimate talks. Without presenting the printed pages of "The Book" on a lacquered bookcase, he expounded their contents in live speech to his "public" of friends and followers, admirers and disciples. What was to be the essence of human existence, what he dared not give an ultimate form, because none seemed adequate or perfect enough—he revealed in fragments in those inspired, fascinating, prophetic talks. It was an intimate theatre, a one-man-show, where the author-actor, the "operator", the magician presented the idea in ever new form.

The term "abstract drama" seems to be the most suitable definition for the sum total of Mallarmé's initiative, his aim and efforts, his discoveries and failures in the dramatic field. By giving it that name, the greatest significance has been attributed to the absence, whether it be in *Hérodiade* or *Igitur,* of any kind of reality; reality—even in the most loose understanding of the word—does not enter into these works. It is probably this dominant quality which suggests the film medium for a possible realization of a dramatic vision such as *Igitur.*

Following the main aspects of this new kind of drama presented here, the general extremist character of Mallarmé's concept remains to be stressed as well as the main problem arising from it.

He disregarded all the traditional "laws" of drama and theatre. His is truly a "theatre of the mind" in the two different meanings of the term: the mind as invention and the mind as an analytic tool. Through Mallarmé, the old established dramatic notions have been freed from all limitations. Conclusive action, the successive order of dramatic situations and events, dialogue and psychologic unity of the characters have either been abolished or reduced to a bare minimum. The subject not only is universal and spiritual, it may not even be clearly defined, leaving room for various interpretations. It becomes in this way what, according to Mallarmé, it should be: a "pretext" for dreaming. In brief, what we hear and see on stage acts not as a statement or an evidence that has to be accepted or rejected, but as an impulse which sets our imagination in motion.

The place of action dissolves in a play of shadow and light, of concrete and abstraction; all we see is a detail here and there. The perception of time has been eliminated to a point where it would be difficult to say whether what we are invited to witness is a present action, a reminiscence from the past or a projection of the future. Properties, reduced to the minimum, are endowed with feelings and sensations. The living and the dead, all equally ethereal, co-exist side by side. Even the seemingly "real" characters appear and disappear or change their identity. Whatever materializes for a fleeting moment dissolves, becomes an immaterial notion, escapes attempts at rational definition. In a dreamlike ambience, we are exposed to the pressure of an atmosphere and a suspense, a "mood" which is cleverly built up by a highly musical, allusive language, by a multiplicity of sounds and a skillful use of light.

Yet, with all its intentional vagueness and irreality *Igitur,* like *Hérodiade* and *L'Après-midi d'un faune* and all Mallarmé's writings, requires a most strenuous exertion of the mind as an instrument of perception. After having submitted to the almost hypnotic overall effect of the work, that "musical", "obscure" face of the idea, one feels compelled to seek the solution to the apparent enigma, to discover its "literary", knowledgeable aspect—the meaning of that which has been evoked. We know, not only because he said so many times, but because no reader or student of Mallarmé can fail to realize it, that he had a masterly command of the language; he certainly was not incapable of stating matters clearly. What to us may be "obscure" (and only because we, like Mallarmé's contemporaries, sometimes "do not know how to read"), is the result of his very complex, highly individual manipulation of words. Mallarmé's works have been and probably always will be a challenge to all those who, attracted by the sheer beauty of evocative and melodic language, want to discover "the idea" so tantalizingly hidden behind its veil.

It must be kept in mind that the people who launched the new drama and set out to reform the theatre were (in the first place) poets. Not just Mallarmé, Villiers de l'Isle-Adam, Maeterlinck, Hofmannsthal, Wyspiański and Yeats, but most of their followers as well. This is important, because the symbolists' rebellion followed and opposed that of the naturalists. The drama of the latter, of course, could only be in prose.

The symbolists renewal was rooted in the main medium of poets—language. By transmitting symbolist poetics to drama, the possibilities of the dramatic language were enlarged to an extent hitherto unknown. Mallarmé's clearly drawn distinction between "raw" or "direct" language on the one hand, and "essential" on the other, or as he put it even more explicitly, "commercial" and "literary" ["**Crise de vers**"] introduced to drama the possibility until then limited to poetry, namely to recreate the world not through description but through evocation, through suggestion instead of narration, or (to use the terms proposed by Bakshy) through "presentation" not through "representation".

It is in this sense that the term "abstract" drama must be interpreted, as the transposition of Mallarmé's understanding of poetic creation to the theatre. And if the stress will always remain on *poetic,* the meaning will not necessarily be limited to a linguistic one; the work of art, of theatrical art (the "art of the theatre") will be poetic in that it will try to recapture the "sense of the mystery of existence" [Balakian, *The Symbolist Movement*] (or its nonsense) by way of poetic suggestion instead of poetic recreation. Herein lies the most far-reaching and lasting effect of Mallarmé's message. (pp. 385-403)

> *Antonina M. Terlecki, "Stéphane Mallarmé and Symbolism (Part II)," in* Kwartalnik Neofilologiczny, *Vol. XXXV, No. 4, 1988, pp. 385-407.*

Susan Huston   (essay date 1980)

[In the following essay, Huston examines the ideological orientation of Mallarmé's Poésies.*]*

The pairing of an ideological mode of literary analysis with Mallarmé's hermetic poetry is admittedly incongruous, given the sense of the term hermeticism as it is traditionally utilized in criticism. Commentary on the subject has generally centred around the problem of linguistic veiling, difficulty of interpretation, and authorial intention: in short, hermeticism has been considered synonymous with textual obscurity. If, however, we take the unconventional step of turning the concept of "fermeture parfaite" away from its most familiar of critical faces (closure as unintelligibility) to another of its aspects (i.e., closure as the exclusion of the non-literary world of social events), then a relatively uncharted area of inquiry opens up to us. These represent two distinct manners in which a text may be sealed off—the former from a readership, the latter from reference, latent or manifest, to a larger world—but they need not be seen as diametrically opposed to one another. Derrida's reflections on the nature of poetic referentiality [in "La Double séance," *Tel Quel* 41, 1970] for instance might perhaps afford a common ground between them. Nevertheless, each invites an interpretive optic that bears its own fruit, and each, at this initial moment of distinction, deserves exploration on its individual merits. Yet with the exception of Julia Kristeva's stimulating study, *La Révolution du langage poétique* [1974], the ideological vein of Mallarmé criticism remains largely untapped. The purpose of this essay is to demonstrate not only the feasibility, but also the possibility of great productivity inherent in such a reading.

It should be noted that Mallarmé's *Poésies* is virtually devoid of direct reference to any surrounding social milieu.

If it is easily situated in the historical context of the late nineteenth-century France that nurtured it, this is primarily for aesthetic reasons: intertextual traces of its poetic predecessor situate it in time and space. But social comment does not constitute the kind of thematic nexus here that it does in Baudelaire's "Tableaux parisiens". One must first ask, then, how it is that there are ideological lessons to be learned from texts like these which do not make statements immediately reflective of the social environment.

Any language, literary or otherwise, is a means by which the individual projects an identity through linguistic choices made. Benveniste suggested this more than a decade ago in his study on pronoun usage as a manifestation of subjective voice ["De la subjectivité dans le langage", in *Problèmes de linguistique générale,* 1966], and beyond this limited realm of pronominal configurations, we might add that any lexical or morphosyntactic manipulation can be an eloquent means of formulating self-identity. Word choice offers the possibility of creating and communicating a self, of bringing into being an entity that might otherwise have no existence or impact beyond itself. It is as well—and this is of the utmost importance—a way to construct an image of the surrounding world, and to establish a relationship between self and world. Thus, the individual would seem to be in a position of power with regard to that outer world through his/her use of language. Roland Barthes, in the first of his 1977 lectures at the Collège de France [in *Legon,* 1978], however, pointed to the constraints imposed upon the language user because of the limited number of linguistic options to be chosen from. In this respect, the speaker is quite literally subordinated to the system. "[T]oute langue est un classement, et [. . .] tout classement est oppressif [. . .]" said Barthes. Nonetheless, through the creative and idiosyncratic use of language, the individual does indeed have the opportunity to play a controlling role, and the end-product of such creativity—literature, for example—can be seen as the embodiment of a certain kind of power. It is quite obviously a bid for control.

There is an ideology of poetry such as Mallarmé's: an ideology of the author, an ideology of the text as well. I will focus my attention on the latter in this discussion. Biographical remarks pertaining to the specific creator of these texts and his professed attitudes toward the social, economic, political frame in which he found himself will be sacrificed to an examination of the ideological traces in the text itself, whether they have been purposefully set there or appear in spite of any original intention on the part of the author. Mallarmé will be put aside, and the texts will be encouraged to speak for themselves.

With regard to methodology, Frederic Jameson's comments in a 1978 article in *Critical Inquiry* pertaining to the nature of ideological readings have been of considerable assistance to me and elaboration of some of these will help to clarify the origins and reasons for certain aspects of my own analytical model. My use of the word ideology will be consistent in as much as possible with Jameson's own. Accordingly, my reading will seek to elucidate not any explicit set of social values expressed in the text, but rather the mark it carries in implicit fashion as indicative of an ideological orientation. The distinction is important, for by rejecting the explicit value system as a prerequisite for speaking in ideological terms, I am able to deal with ideological configurations in texts such as Mallarmé's where no direct statements of this nature are made.

A static/dynamic opposition also comes into play in Jameson's working definition of ideological analysis, for he rejects the idea that its goal is to confirm pre-existent categorizing labels. He suggests that instead the challenge lies in carrying out an open-ended, unconstrained examination of the text: "The term 'ideology' ", he writes, "stands as the sign for a problem yet to be solved, a mental operation which remains to be executed. It does not presuppose cut-and-dried sociological stereotypes like the notion of the 'bourgeois' or the 'petty bourgeois' but rather a mediatory concept: that is, it is an imperative to reinvent a relationship between the linguistic or aesthetic or conceptual fact in question and its social ground." Therefore, I will respect the non-predetermined nature of the ideological relation between text and social reality in what follows.

Furthermore, Jameson's discussion of the rapport between text and milieu has led me to set a dual focus to my methodological model. On the one hand, I will be concerned with describing the way in which the social context has been rewritten by the text. Jameson calls this textual version of reality the "subtext". Relevant questions to be raised in this regard would be—What is the text's vision of social reality?—or—How do the two (social reality and the subtext) differ? On the other hand, my analysis will deal with the problem of orientation. It will ask what the stance of the text is toward its subtext, or as Jameson expresses it: What are the text's "gestures of praxis— whether measurements, cries of rage, magical incantations, caresses, or avoidance behavior"?

To summarize, my analysis will be divided into two parts: first, an examination of the subtext, and secondly, a discussion of the stance of the text toward that subtext. With regard to the latter, I will limit consideration of the orientation of the text to that of the textual subject—that is, of the subjectivity posited by the text.

THE SUBTEXT

There are few recognizable subtextual references in Mallarmé's ***Poésies***. Stock images of social types like the prostitute, the beggar, and the ill-treated poet are present in some of the early pieces (**"Une Négresse"**, **"Angoisse"**, **"Aumône"**, **"Le Guignon"**), but they often tell us little more than that this corpus can be situated within the larger literary tradition of nineteenth-century poetry. There is generally not a sufficient degree of personalization in the projection of the image here to reveal the peculiarities of the subtext in any overt way.

One notable exception, however, is **"Les Fenêtres"**. This is also an early piece, and the use of the image of the hospital is, on the surface, strongly reminiscent of Baudelaire's organizing metaphor in the prose poem "Anywhere Out of the World"; but it becomes evident on closer examination that there is a strong element of idiosyncrasy in the

Mallarmé text. Whereas the Baudelaire text equates the hospital with the world in a very general (spatial and metaphysical) sense, Mallarmé's casts it as symbolic of a more discrete entity. Hospital here comes to represent the social institution depicted in full, bourgeois detail.

The first five stanzas of the poem project the image of a hospital, replete with drugs, beds, the infirm, and all the odours and trappings of an institutionalized form of sickness. The metaphor is rendered with a great deal of specificity; but all of its diverse aspects merge to suggest that this is more than just a hospital. It contains crucifixes and oils for extreme unction: there is an ecclesiastical presence here. Then too, the bourgeois home intrudes with its curtains, clocks, and warm tea. What is the institution being evoked? Is it hospital, church, or home? The originality of the subtextual frame lies in the fact that it becomes emblematic of all of these—in fact, of all social institutions at once, and if we inquire as to the purpose of such an expansive figure, we discover that it permits a global condemnation of the social system.

It should be noted, however, that the negative transformation of the hospital image in the Mallarmé corpus is really not wholly surprising: though in its medieval French form the word carried the fundamentally positive charge of a charitable shelter, its connotations had long since begun to blacken by the nineteenth century. The original emphasis had given way to a strong accent on sickness and misery. The Mallarmean image in this respect is not very different from its immediate predecessors. Yet what is innovative about the way the hospital functions here is that it has acquired an idiosyncratic specificity and an expansiveness that allows it to serve as a universalized model of all that has gone wrong with social institutions at this point in time.

Thus, the dying man in **"Les Fenêtres"** finds no comfort in the kinds of help the hospital (that is to say, society) has to offer. He turns his back on the sick-bed, the crucifix, and the tea—on all "Bêtise" as it is called later in the poem; and walking toward the window (art) which opens out toward the non-institutionalized exterior, he searches for inspiration or a means of escape in a realm beyond the social:

> Est-il moyen, ô Moi qui connais l'amertume
> D'enfoncer le cristal par le monstre insulté
> Et de m'enfuir [. . .]

Ironically, escape is blocked. The window, normally a liberating form of art, has also been blemished, institutionalized. And the corruptor ("le monstre")?—As our reading would have it, the corruptor is Napoleon III's Second Empire.

Why, we might ask, would the Second Empire be susceptible to interpretation as a negative force? What kind of social reality does it constitute, and how can we explain the subtextual transformation of it here?

"Napoleon III's reign", writes Theodore Zeldin [in his *Ambition, Love and Politics*, Vol. I of *France: 1848-1945*, 1973], "was that of big business." The Second Empire is a bourgeois government in a rapidly industrializing country; its interests are diametrically opposed to those of the artist in many ways. Zeldin points to the fact that regardless of statements to the contrary made by the powerful, the Second Empire's budgetary priorities are heavily weighted toward insuring material prosperity, almost to the exclusion of promoting cultural growth. Now if we define the "social reality" of our analytical model in terms of the values of the majority (and its government) in a given society—values which largely determine the nature of the role of the artist in that milieu—then it is important to note that built into the social reality of Second Empire France is a lack of sanction for the artist. True, there are forms of creative production encouraged by this society, but these are primarily utilitarian and echo the materialist aesthetic of the times. The genuine artist is a marginal figure whose work is too often ill-received. Though there are evidently other factors beyond the ideological that contribute to the unwholesomeness of the hospital metaphor in **"Les Fenêtres",** it is reasonable to observe that the negativity of the image can be read as textual repercussion of the negativity of the artist's own role in the framework of this society, its government and institutions.

It is little wonder that, aside from the example of **"Les Fenêtres"** there are not many clear-cut subtextual references in the overall collection of poems then. Suppression of these images is one way to lessen the threat posed by what seems to be the inadequacy of the state. Another, however, is to present them in all their unsatisfactoriness, though veiled, and then to proceed to destroy them in due literary fashion. This too occurs in the Mallarmean corpus, though signs of such a phenomenon are subtle and demand scrutiny if they are to be brought to the surface.

The destructive task is facilitated if the imagistic mould in which such images are cast is reduced to modest dimensions from the outset. The institution as it is most often projected in this form in *Poésies,* therefore, is quite simply the bourgeois home: a frame of humble dimensions, yet no less capable of symbolizing the social institution. As seat of the original and quintessential authority figure—the father—the home's link to the state cannot be denied, for it constitutes the most intimate of institutions, and is, because of this, markedly vulnerable to (literary) attack.

We find a striking example of the destruction of this kind of micro-institution in the **"Sonnet en YX"** (**"Ses purs ongles très haut dédiant leur onyx"**). The setting here, a bourgeois interior, is emptied of the people and objects that constitute its identity, for destruction in this case takes the form of an emptying. Neither the master of the house, nor all the objects that normally decorate his sitting room are present. Stanza II represents the most complete expression of this phenomenon:

> Sur les crédences, au salon vide: nul ptyx,
> Aboli bibelot d'inanité sonore,
> (Car le Maître est allé puiser des pleurs au Styx
> Avec ce seul objet dont le Néant s'honore).

All is evoked in terms of absence and negation: the master has gone to the Styx to commune with the dead; the object that he has taken with him is modified by the words "nul", "aboli", and "inanité sonore". The symbolic destruction of the home is twofold: not only is the sitting room emptied of its master and customary knickknack, but the master himself is diminished through contact with death, and the missing object is hollow and insignificant. The social institution has been doubly voided of its animating force.

The destructive gesture is, in fact, carried further in other texts, where the image of the home is hollowed to the point of taking on the characteristics of a tomb. One such instance is the text **"Quand l'ombre menaça",** where the room depicted is lined with ebony and decorated with carved funerary wreaths; another occurs at the beginning of the **"Ouverture ancienne d'Hérodiade",** for the manor house there is described as being topped with a ghastly cremical crematory-like tower. In all such cases, the institutional projections take the shape of receptacles that have been divested of the contents that had once made them meaningful. They have in this way been diminished.

It should not be overlooked that in the corpus as a whole this emptying process is applied not only to images, but also quite literally to words. It occurs both linguistically and mimetically, then. The "ptyx" in the **"Sonnet en YX",** for example, represents a hollow knickknack—an empty, insignificant object. (We know this through contextual description.) It is also an empty word. Its meaning in classical Greek ("un pli" or fold according to Emilie Noulet's reading [in his *L'Œuvre poétique de Stéphane Mallarmé,* 1940]) had long since been obscured when the text was set down. Consequently, any reader, though recognizing that it marks the place of a word, would find it devoid of meaning. This must have been as true for the late nineteenth-century public as it is for today's.

Such lexical emptying is symptomatic of what happens to language in general in *Poésies.* Although there is a recognizable syntax, it often functions to create enigmas because of the many disturbances in word order, subordination patterns, and punctuation. The components of the linguistic system are present, but they do not combine to produce a whole that is "decipherable" according to established norms. Language here can be seen, therefore, as a metaphor for the social system, for as with subtextual images, a subversion of the normative authority has taken place.

Having examined the hospital, the home, and even the language system as projections of the subtext, we can appreciate how misleading the term hermetic can be with regard to this corpus: obscurity, difficulty, semantic opacity do characterize many of the texts in *Poésies,* but these traits of linguistic closure do not preclude the kind of ideological opening that is central to this discussion. No matter how indirectly, these texts do indeed bear traces of commerce with the world of social events.

THE STANCE OF THE TEXTUAL SUBJECT

The question now arises as to what stance such texts adopt toward the inscribed subtext. A partial answer has already been suggested: the stance is one that threatens destruction. But it is in truth more complex than this would indicate, for as we have seen with the metaphoric use of language in this corpus, there is more than one way to mime the destruction of an object in poetry. Though at times subtextual images are undermined by being emptied of substance as demonstrated above, at others the opposite is in fact true. When the attack on them is waged in reverse manner, they are destroyed by being over-filled. In the same way, words drained of expected meanings are often refilled with a multiplicity of different semantic possibilities. The polysemic gesture occurs time and again.

The **"Sonnet en YX"** offers a striking example of this too, for though its bourgeois sitting room is destroyed by being emptied of the usual master, it is later reconstituted when the image of a water sprite ("nixe") appears in the mirror to repopulate it. The empty frame in question, like the sitting room, is refilled with its reflection. This happens in attenuated fashion though, since the source of the image is unknown, and the reflection might conceivably be but an optical illusion. Consequently, such refilling does not constitute a definitive stabilization of the institutional image.

As with this allusive trace in the mirror, images and words in general are either too empty or too full in the Mallarmé corpus; and the fact that they often have no single semantic base represents a considerable obstacle to our process of defining the ideological stance implicit in the text. If normative meanings and images are destroyed, and either left empty or replaced not by any single new image or meaning, but by an open set of possibilities, where then do we situate the subject in relation to them? Concurrent destruction or blurring of the subtextual image makes an identification of the subject that has projected it all the more difficult.

An exploration of the pronoun system in these texts, however, with an eye to what it can reveal about the identity of the textual subject, may give us a clearer view of this problem as well as the reasons for it. It may also suggest some possible solutions.

Oddly enough, the social stance in all its complexity is most evident in the love poems of *Poésies,* for the erotic configuration of the pronouns reveals much about the subject's relation to exterior sources of power and control. The relationship of lover to loved one—of JE to TU— when pushed to the extreme, is cast in ironic terms as a metaphor of heroic combat, a social encounter of the first order. The amorous protagonists become conquering warriors and acquiescent victims. The question of power is central. If we take the first person pronoun to be an embodiment of the subjective voice, and the second person TU to be a dialogic projection of that voice, emblematic of the exterior social context, we might expect to find the JE adopting an authoritative stance with regard to TU. Yet once the erotic relationship has been established, despite its reductive dimensions, the controlling stance of the subject becomes problematic. It seems to put its own authority to the test quite regularly.

The poem **"M'introduire dans ton histoire"** is most revealing in this respect, and I think it can be said without exaggeration that its pronoun system is representative of essential pronoun relations throughout *Poésies.* A certain tenuousness on the part of the subject is manifest here by the fact that the first person pronoun tends to play a passive role, or to disappear entirely. Were it to adopt a normal stance of authority, the text would begin with the word

"je": *Je voudrais* "m'introduire dans ton histoire" for example. But the JE has been suppressed, as has the conjugated verb through which it could have posited itself as agent. They have been replaced by the more indirect reflexive pronoun and infinitive. Thus, the first line reads: "M'introduire dans ton histoire". Semantics are noticeably influenced by the self-effacing speaking subject, for what we might have interpreted as a desire on the subject's part to penetrate the world it has projected, seems—in the absence of an explicit JE—more like a desire for absorption.

The tentativeness this sequence communicates becomes more evident through comparison with a parallel sequence in the Baudelaire text, "A Celle qui est trop gaie", where the phrase "je voudrais [. . .] [t]'infuser mon venin", not only posits a first person subject directly, but insists upon the active nature of its role as agent. The stance of this subject is, in fact, sadistic. Yet another Baudelaire piece, "Le Beau Navire", begins with the words (emphasis added):

> *Je veux te raconter,* ô molle enchanteresse!
> Les diverses beautés qui parent ta jeunesse;
> *Je veux te peindre* ta beauté,
> Où l'enfance s'allie à la maturité.

Here, we note that the "Je veux te raconter [. . .] les diverses beautés" is nearly in direct opposition to Mallarmé's **"M'introduire dans ton histoire"**, for not only are the subject JE and the conjugated verb VEUX stated; but, whereas the object in Mallarmé's sequence (the TU of "ton histoire") seems to take over to some extent for the passified subject, the TU in the Baudelaire text is most definitely in a position of objectification. This even to the point of having little identity beyond that which the dominant JE chooses to create for it: "Je veux te peindre ta beauté" comes much closer to saying "Je veux te peindre" here than "Je veux peindre ta beauté".

If we now return to Mallarmé's **"M'introduire dans ton histoire"**, in search of direct manifestations of the first person subject, we note that there are indeed two instances further on where the JE actually does appear. These, however, are couched in contexts of negation: "Je ne sais [pas]" and "je ne suis pas". Both the subject's cognitive and existential powers are called into question. In addition to this, the validity of JE's gestures of appropriation toward the loved one are also seriously challenged when they are termed "naïf péché":

> Je ne sais pas le naïf péché
> Que tu n'auras pas empêché
> De rire très haut sa victoire

Rather than such an acquisitional attempt constituting a viable act, as sin it becomes a kind of mis-deed. And because its effectiveness is diminished all the more by its naïveté, it even approaches the non-act.

Not only is the authority of JE put into question in this text, but there is as well a consistent tendency to transfer that authority to the dialogic partner. It is the TU that is empowered with the ability to negate in the "je ne suis pas" spoken of above, for the verb at the beginning of that line—"*Dis* si je ne suis pas joyeux"—indicates that TU is asked to make the decision concerning the subject's existential capacity. The line says in effect: "*Tu diras* si je ne suis pas joyeux". It should not be overlooked, however, that the source of TU's power goes back to the first person pronoun. The command form "dis" naturally issues from the speaking subject, and the chain of effectivity is therefore (JE)——> TU——> JE. Given such a strategy of veiling and multiplication of agent, both the origin of power and the present power base are considerably obscured.

Underlying the power struggle between JE and TU in such a text is the fundamental problem of identity. Since identity is posited as a difference, the self can only be established in contrast to an exterior authority. If, however, the exterior authority is weak and fails to project in an authentic way, the self is unable to oppose it. This is why the vision of the subject, and that of the subtext as well, are each reduced in **Poésies.** The flaw, though it originates in the failings of the state, soon becomes circular. Despite the fact that the social subtext is projected as a minimal TU in an attempt to pull it onto intimate, and therefore more authentic territory, this projection diminishes TU's stature; and as a result, JE has all the more difficulty in positing itself.

An attempt is made in **"M'introduire dans ton histoire"** to avoid the problem of mutual weakening by transferring the subject beyond the limits of the JE-TU frame: JE transforms itself to a third person, "le héros". But the flaw follows once again, and the hero carries with him all the vulnerability of an Achilles:

> M'introduire dans ton histoire
> C'est en héros effarouché
> S'il a du talon nu touché
> Quelque gazon de territoire

There is no single seat of authority—not in this text, not in the overall corpus. Power looks everywhere for a stable base, and everywhere finds itself on shifting sands. Perhaps the problematics of stance per se is an illusory one with regard to Mallarmé's poetry, because the concept itself implies a fixed orientation. What we find here instead might more fittingly be called the *status* of the subject, for status accommodates the idea of multiple transformations far better. (The status of an individual varies in a way that is relative to the position of others.) Perhaps such a shift in terminology at this point in our analysis seems troublesome. It is nonetheless the outgrowth of what has come before, and could not have been arrived at earlier; for only in asking what the stance of the subject is, can we understand that the question itself involves a distortion of perspective. The subject's is hardly an authoritative stance in **Poésies:** there is a need to refuse all responsibility; there is as well a counter-need to accept it. But as for the question of status, we are now in a better position to draw conclusions: the status of the Mallarmean subject can be clearly seen as one of continual mobility.

Where has this brought us in terms of being able to make an incisive statement about the ideological orientation of the textual subject toward its subtext in this corpus? Given the weakness in both the subtext and the projecting self, we risk seeing the two cancel each other out in the struggle. But the (ideological) point is in fact the struggle. As we have seen, the outer world is never fully erased in these "hermetic" texts. Though obscured, they continue to participate in the larger structure which brings pressures to bear on the moment of their creation. Neither is the subject wholly successful in its bid toward self-sufficiency, a gesture which seeks to close out that sphere of exterior influences. The text marks the place of the subject's striving toward that goal [. . .] and of its failure to reach it; for this type of hermetic subject never really departs from the problematics of opposition.

Kristeva, in *La Révolution du langage poétique,* has described Mallarmé's ideology as one of negativity, pointing out that the subject's orientation there is such that although it challenges orthodox authority in vigorous fashion, it never takes the subsequent step to posit itself as a new, established authority. Its emptied or refilled self is just as destabilized and open-ended as its subject, and does not arrive as a permanent self-identity. (Kristeva calls this a "sujet en procès": a non-fixed, non-unitary subject in the process of becoming.) As the movement inherent in the status of such a subject is non-teleological, we might expect its ideological struggle to be relinquished quite readily; yet at the very heart of this subject is its willingness, not only to take on the conflict with authority, but even to incorporate that conflict into its own being. It becomes the embodiment of the problematics of power, then, adopting all ensuing ambiguities and contradictions as its own.

And need it be added in conclusion that the Mallarmean subject, as our demonstrations have surely made clear,

---

Judy Kravis on Mallarmé's literary legacy:

[The] reader anxious to know the form and historical context of Mallarmé's contribution to literature might be puzzled by the diverse faces that posterity gives his work. Perhaps it does no more than satisfy curiosity, or confirm a belief in the diversity of human interpretation, to know that Mallarmé may have unwittingly given his blessing to a whole range of linguistic sciences, or that modern advertisers—for their part probably unwittingly too—should make use of Mallarmé's understanding of layout. If we see Mallarmé through the eyes of a twentieth-century structuralist, we might be tempted to think that his entire opus has to be re-read within a structuralist frame, and that this is a correct—because rationally and easily upheld—interpretation. Or, if we see him as one who virtually fathered a whole school of poets, each one, in Mallarmé's own words, 'allant, dans son coin, jouer sur une flûte, bien à lui, les airs qu'il lui plaît', then we might overlook his more lasting contribution to the understanding of literary language. Mallarmé's influence only helps us to understand his work if we see it as a multifarious whole, rather than as a complex of interpretations or attitudes amongst which one might be the most appropriate. The apparent flexibility of what Mallarmé wrote is not necessarily either a virtue or a vice; it is a positive indication that his concern was not with any one branch of literature, but with its very basis.

Judy Kravis, in her The Prose of Mallarmé: The Evolution of a Literary Language, *Cambridge University Press, 1976.*

does not offer any easy solutions to the problems posed by inauthentic social structures? For the hermetic text, seen in this light, is not a *fait accompli*. Rather, it bodies forth all the struggles of a revolution—this in the Kristevian sense of the term—a literary revolution in the process of coming to fruition. (pp. 262-74)

Susan Huston, "The Ideology of Hermeticism: A New Perspective on Mallarmé," in Australian Journal of French Studies, Vol. XVII, No. 3, September-December, 1980, pp. 262-74.

Wallace Fowlie   (essay date 1980)

[*Fowlie is one of the most respected and versatile scholars of French literature. His works include translations of major dramatists and poets of France as well as critical studies of the major figures and movements of modern French letters. In the following essay, originally presented as a lecture in 1980, Fowlie considers Mallarmé's development of Hérodiade as a heroic character.*]

More difficult poems than **Hérodiade** have received far closer attention by Mallarmé scholars today. A meaningful relationship is hard to establish among the three parts: *ouverture, scène* and *cantique,* each composed at different times in the poet's life, and each very different from the other two in a formal sense.

The first of the triptych to be written, and the first to be published, *scène,* announces in its title a relationship with the stage, with the theatre, and is indeed presented in the form of a dialogue between the young princess Hérodiade and her nurse. This older character who has known the princess since her birth asks questions and makes entreaties that are scorned and ridiculed by Hérodiade.

The setting of *scène* is a bedroom and the principal prop is a mirror. At the midpoint of this dialogue of 134 lines, the nurse asks a question, placed thus centrally and significantly, containing the word *le mystère,* which I am going to use in an attempt to answer the question in my title. Is **Hérodiade** a myth, a biblical myth possibly, or is she a protagonist in a brief dramatic work, a heroine, the female counterpart of the male faun, that other poem with its dramatic overtones Mallarmé was composing at the same time?

After enacting, or attempting to enact, a triple impiety: to kiss Hérodiade's hand, to perfume her hair, and to touch her hair, the nurse is repulsed but remains undaunted by her three failures, and utters, when the *scène* is half over, the question uppermost in her mind:

> pour qui . . .
> . . . gardez-vous la splendeur ignorée
> Et le mystère vain de votre être?

The two nouns *splendeur* and *mystère* are qualified. The *splendeur* is hidden from the world. Hérodiade lives in her tower in perfect isolation. And the *mystère* of her being is vain because it is untested, untried, unknown.

Hérodiade's nurse, unlike Juliet's, speaks in the language of her creator, Stéphane Mallarmé, but with the common sense of an older woman, raising the question about the mysteriousness of the young girl's body. "Vain mystery" means "vanity" and "emptiness." For what purpose is this isolation, this separation from the world of men?

In just a few lines later the ardent princess defends her virginity and describes its "fatal splendor." She picks up the word *splendeur* from the nurse, from the Mallarmé nurse, and declares that her beauty, her nudity, her hair glowing like metal, are for . . . herself and for the monotonous world of night. More than flesh, she is jewels: amethyst and diamond. Her reality is not herself, but the reflection of herself in a mirror. Her splendor is not that of a woman, but of an idol.

The nurse's second word in her leading question is *mystère,* and that word too is remembered by Hérodiade and used conclusively in her last words that end the poem. She has just mentioned—fleetingly—a possible departure to another country. But immediately she banishes such a thought and speaks her ultimate thought of the *scène,* a reasoned and inescapable thought:

> J'attends une chose inconnue

Her last words are an explanation of this enigmatic statement. Without revealing what the mystery is, she associates it with childhood, with the *froides pierreries* of childhood from which she has not emerged.

Mystère, from *mysterium,* is a drama, a sacred drama of esoteric significance. Isn't Hérodiade telling us here that the stubborness of her will, the coldness of her virginity, protected by lions, is that of every girl child about to be initiated into an older age, but still held by the fearful unknowing coldness of childhood?

Mallarmé's princess is as inscrutable as a child is. Her "mystery," to herself and to others, is "vain,", *vanus,* meaning empty and void, a futile mystery because it is unknowing.

Some of her phrases have the ring of a stubborn child:

> Et je déteste, moi, le bel azur.

She is mysterious, as every child is because she is waiting for the "mystery," the rite that will initiate her into that sacred legendary heroine whom Flaubert celebrated in *Salammbô,* whom Baudelaire evoked in a sonnet to Jeanne Duval, and whom Wilde depicted in his play *Salomé.*

Mallarmé's figure, then, would seem to be the child about to become the heroine, a female Hippolytus, wary of losing herself to any man, content for the moment with seeing herself in a mirror. But the mirror shows her a haunted shadow world, and that is all that we as readers see in the poem. We watch the *scène* in the bedroom, in the same way that Hérodiade watches herself in her mirror, and what we see is Mallarmé's familiar kind of composition founded on elusiveness and allusion. It is the same cold light we associate with a swan and a punished clown and tombs of poets—Baudelaire's and Poe's notably—in which Mallarmé's characters are not quite characters but reflections of themselves, ghosts or phantoms, in fact.

We might, at this point, suggest the theory that Mallarmé

uses the mirror, which I have called the prop of *scène,* as a symbol, in the traditional sense of an object which the mind perceives and which leads the mind to something beyond it. Indeed, it would be hard to imagine a more appropriate example of a symbol, as it is usually defined, than a mirror. In a mirror we see a pale reflection of a reality that is outside the mirror.

When, early in the poem, Hérodiade asks the nurse to hold the mirror before her:

> Tiens devant moi ce miroir

she speaks to it and calls it water, cold water frozen within its frame:

> Eau froide . . . dans ton cadre gelée

and sees herself as a distant shadow in the severe fountain. Reflected in water, no picture, no figure, remains for long. It is, as Mallarmé has caused the entire poem to be, a spectacle of merging shadows, of dreams never completed, but fusing with other dreams.

So—the central question asked by the nurse: "for whom are you keeping yourself?" is not answered, or answered enigmatically, when Hérodiade says, "for myself." What might have become a story, reminiscent of a famous myth, is interrupted, and we are plunged into the shadowy world of a mirror, the dominant symbol of the poem.

But by the very title of his work, the strong resonant name **Hérodiade,** Mallarmé forces his reader to think of a biblical story, alluded to by Saint Mark and Saint Matthew. There is no name, no historical allusion, in the text of *scène,* only in its title. And even there, Mallarmé creates a new form for the character who in French and English is usually called "Hérodias." That is the name Flaubert uses in his short story. That is the name used in the King James translation of the Bible. *La Henriade* is Voltaire's title for the amalgam of stories about Henri IV, one of his historical heroes. Does Mallarmé, in his choice of Hérodiade, want us to think of the amalgam of stories about Herod, tetrarch of Galilee at the time of Christ's crucifixion, about Hérodias with whom he had an incestuous union after divorcing his first wife, and Hérodias' daughter Salomé?

Or, more simply, more mysteriously, does he want us to think of his princess as a "heroine" because the name begins in its first two syllables with "hero"? Might Hérodiade be Salomé, who is unnamed in the two accounts of *Mark 6* and *Matthew 14*? Salomé was the immediate cause of the death of John the Baptist, who is the hero of the final poem in the triptych, *Cantique de Saint Jean.* Herod Antipas had imprisoned John for condemning his marriage with Hérodias, but was afraid to execute him. When Salomé danced before him and his guests, he promised to give her whatever she asked. Urged by her mother Hérodias, she demanded John the Baptist's head on a platter. Herod was thus forced to have John beheaded. The story is the subject matter of Oscar Wilde's play of 1893, which is the basis of the libretto for Richard Strauss' opera of 1905.

Myth or heroine? The story in *scène,* as difficult to follow as the character of the girl, who wants her hair to be combed as she looks in the mirror, is difficult to visualize. Before she speaks of having her hair combed by the nurse, the princess, who names herself twice in the text, compares her hair to the manes of the lions who surround her and languidly fix their eyes on her feet.

Of all the definers of myth: Vico, Frazer, Lévy-Bruhl, Otto Rank, the one whose theory applies best to **Hérodiade** is Jung, telling us that myth is a dream fantasy. Myths and dreams, according to Jung, similarly summon up archetypes from the collective unconscious.

Mallarmé, in **Hérodiade,** is at the head of a list of modern writers who revive old myths to fashion new ones. In James Joyce's *Ulysses* a family man, Bloom-Odysseus, departs from home and returns home. It is the familiar pattern of exile and return. T. S. Eliot's *Wasteland* combines the quest for the Grail with the acedia of modern London. Rather than moving into exile, Hérodiade stops and dreams of exiles.

> Je m'arrête rêvant aux exils . . .

In the more typical myths, the male figure is aggressive. He demonstrates ardor in the pursuit of some action, and he is often punished for his assault against a god-figure (or goddess) or some principle that guides society. The typical male figure in mythology will ultimately be represented in Saint John in the short poem that concludes Mallarmé's triptych.

In *scène* the aggressive maleness of the hero is in evidence in Hérodiade herself (or in the youthful Salomé if Hérodiade is in reality Salomé). The lions are male animals but they would appear, in *scène,* to be castrated in their indolence and softness, in their total lack of aggressiveness. Indolent, they lie at the feet of the strong-willed and strong-minded female. The characteristics of the wild beast have disappeared in the lions because of their age— *les siècles fauves*—and have passed into the unpredictable violence of the princess.

Yet Mallarmé makes clear the femininity of Hérodiade, and especially the feminine traits of beauty in her. If 1866 was the year when *scène* was composed, Mallarmé had in his consciousness, from his immediate past, the death of his sister Maria, his marriage with Marie Gerhard, and the birth of his daughter Geneviève in November, 1864. The moments of serenity in *scène,* when the beauty of Hérodiade is that of an idol, are overshadowed by an ever-deepening sense of anxiety in her, close in every way to the ever-deepening anxiety in Mallarmé. In its own way, the poem is a record of the metaphysical crisis in the life of the poet which he lived through in the winters between 1864 and 1868. Hérodiade is an apparition, an avatar of the same fantasies: Maria and Marie, the same confusion of beauty and death, the same relationship that we will ultimately have between *scène* and *Cantique de Saint Jean.* The feminine seductive form of Salomé is in Hérodiade, as well as the dancer's cruelty.

A dancer in her art is a girl separated from those who look at her and probably desire her. But in the performance of her dance, she is a woman who cannot be approached, who cannot be touched. She is Hérodiade repulsing all the attempts of the nurse to turn her from an idol into a human being. She is the phantom swan of the later poem preferring to die in his prison of ice rather than fly to the south to a world warmed by the sun.

A symbol has been defined as a door to knowledge. Hérodiade's mirror is that kind of symbol. A myth has to be closer to a ritual than a symbol is, the rehearsal of some movement, the reenactment of some action that will be an even more valid way of knowing oneself than the mere election of a symbol.

The poem of *scène* seems to be all that might conceivably precede the performance of a dance. Without containing any explicit reference to Salomé or to a dance, the entire poem of *scène* is the very reduced action of a girl preparing to dance a drama—and quite possibly a drama of extreme cruelty—that is choreographed in her mind and being rehearsed in her mind as she looks at herself in a mirror and utters, close to the end of the poem, her aria-speech of 32 lines:

> Oui, c'est pour moi, pour moi que je fleuris, dé-
> serte!

To the nurse who has spoken of a mortal man, the girl says that if she showed her body to him, if he saw her nakedness, she would die.

She is not a mortal, as long as she is the virgin idol—amethyst or diamond—destined to dance. For that purpose she remains alone in her monotonous kingdom:

> Je me crois seule en ma monotone patrie.

Once the cult of Hippolytus grew in Greece because of his chastity, because of his scorn for the usual life of marriage. He became a cold male idol because of his aloofness from the world of women and spent his time with his horses, in the activities of the hunt and the race. Hérodiade, naming herself here for the second time, at the end of her aria, accepts the same solitude, the same chastity, the same companionship of animals, and saves herself for some projected action—a dance perhaps—where she will become, not a girl caught up in love for a man, but a myth, a tale that will be told in a sacred book, that will be recounted over and over in art and poetry, in drama and dance and music.

This aria-speech is an epiphany, a sudden spiritual manifestation. It is, as every literary epiphany has to be, the poet's apprehension of a meaning, such as my own, because whatever Mallarmé made, he made in his own intricate image.

So, in conclusion, I see the princess as a heroine, emerging from a myth and from Mallarmé's anxiety. But she is a child-heroine, slightly reminiscent of Maria and Geneviève, symbols of death and life for the poet in his personal life.

I believe the allusion to Hippolytus is worth pursuing more than I have done; and even more than Hippolytus, I want to explore the possible model of Cassandra for Mallarmé's heroine. Greek again, but feminine this time.

I find in this girl-heroine of the French poet the early signs of a prophetess—of Cassandra as she appears in *Agamemnon* of Aeschylus, and in *The Trojan Women* of Euripides. Hérodiade speaks of prophets at the beginning of the dialogue (v. 9), and in her aria-speech she prophesies her death if her nudity is seen (v. 100).

The gift of prophecy in its Greek tradition is allied with madness, which is always a perception of reality unavailable to the rational mind. Again, madness is in Hérodiade, in an incipient form, as well as prophetic insight. (pp. 167-73)

> *Wallace Fowlie, " 'Hérodiade': Myth or Heroine?" in* L'Hénaurme Siècle: A Miscellany of Essays on Nineteenth-Century French Literature, *edited by Will L. McLendon, Carl Winter Universitätsverlag, 1984, pp. 167-73.*

Virginia A. La Charité (essay date 1980)

[*In the following excerpt, La Charité, an American educator and scholar, argues that the focus of a significant part of Mallarmé's poetry is rooted in the physical world rather than abstract idealism.*]

Mallarmé's quest for a pure poetry that would give expression to "les gestes de l'idée" has been the source of a vast corpus of criticism that is as divergent in its approaches as it is in its conclusions. Each view seems to be convincing on its own terms, mainly because of scholarly reliance upon Mallarmé's own remarks on the theory of writing. However, a close look at his reflections on the subject of poetry reveals so many inconsistencies that nearly any point of view and any sort of interpretation can be substantiated by lines taken from his prose commentaries and correspondence. In fact, Mallarmé's observations on the substance of poetry and its articulation are a veritable vortex of "variations" and "divagations," for he writes more about what poetry is not than about what it is and should be. Moreover, his theories are not interpretations of his own texts; rather, they are the expression of his aspirations for an absolute, what he calls Poetry. Consequently, any attempt to penetrate his poetic universe must distinguish between Mallarmé the aesthetician and Mallarmé the poet.

Turning to the Pléiade edition for a study of Mallarmé the poet at work, we find some eighty-six pages of verse and prose poetry that are familiar in critical circles. But such textual selectivity excludes nearly one thousand pages of poetry and other creative writings and brands them as "imitative," "charming," "unworthy." These writings include Mallarmé's translations, essays, articles, textbooks, and a volume of formal poems, ***Vers de circonstance,*** most of which were composed, edited, and published by Mallarmé in 1894 under the title ***Les Loisirs de la poste.***

What I should like to propose here is that attention to Mallarmé's creative writing reveals that his conquest of the art of suggestion and mastery of the ambiguous are based on the plastic circumstances of the text. The manipulation of words as objects of a literary game coheres the structure of his work from his adolescent endeavors in

Entre quatre murs to his masterpiece, *Un Coup de dés,* including the fragments of *Le Livre* and *Un Tombeau pour Anatole.* By setting aside the theory and focusing on the poet at work, we see his poetic practice as one that consistently depends on the familiar worlds of experience, myth, and language.

The 471 poems of *Vers de circonstance* were written between 1881 and 1896. Although this is not the only group of texts that is deliberately ignored in Mallarmé studies, it does constitute the only group that seems to embarrass the faithful. True, the *Vers de circonstance* are pieces of whimsy that exhibit playfulness, wit, and linguistic virtuosity. Hardly serious in either tone or subject, they are, paradoxically, serious in treatment; and in these formal quatrains and doublets of lightheartedness are indications of Mallarmé's working method during his most productive years as a "pure" poet.

In *Vers de circonstance* everything and anything are taken up by Mallarmé: addresses, fans, New Year's gifts, birthdays, Easter eggs, albums, pebbles, bottles of Calvados. Tied to people, places, and things, these verses are directly related to the world of human activity, and they are concrete in the most basic sense of the term. Mallarmé delights in the events that transform ordinary daily life; he writes on the occasion of a trip, a baptism, the founding of a journal, the publication of one of his poems, overdrinking, a WC, the return of a fishnet, an exclamation point, a lecture, the opening of a circus; there are even mocking, humorous verses about an edition of *L'Après-midi d' un faune,* as well as a text written in -or rhymes for a friend who did not like -or rhymes. The verses are populated by objects of every kind: teapot, plate, glass of water, handkerchief (and there are eight of these), music box, china dog, real dog, "fruits glacés." The sense of satire and irony that runs through these poems reveals a Mallarmé who never turned his back on actuality. On the contrary, he is acutely aware of the actual, the real world, for he not only evokes the concrete things around him, but he also writes on them: dyed Easter eggs, fans, envelopes, pebbles from Honfleur, photographs. He amuses, but at the same time he is sharpening his skills, for to conquer the realm of the ambiguous demands familiarity with the concrete.

Technically, *Vers de circonstance* is based on wordplay, punning, visual affectation. The texts must be read with the eye in order to be understood; rhyme schemata depend on divided syllables (*l'/un, becque-/té*), syntactical distortions, purposeful orthographic changes, dislocated end rhymes, double entendres. In one sense, Mallarmé is rebelling against formalism, against all rhetorical devices, even against all accepted poetic practice, something he did as a schoolboy in *Entre quatre murs.* Yet what seems to be a refutation of poetic good taste in *Vers de circonstance* is actually a verbal game in which words are the pieces to be placed in play upon the board of written expression by a masterful gamester, the poet. Objectively, detachedly, and deliberately Mallarmé scrutinizes words as objects; he continually moves them around to form new patterns with which to dazzle the spectators. The text is indeed "l'autre."

Throughout these brief poems Mallarmé is conscious of an audience, the presence of others who enjoy a good game; and, as in games, the texts demand visual skill. The rhyme between "cueille" and "Eye," for example, is inane until the reader translates *eye* into the French, *œil.* There is no reason to spell *guéritte* (sentry box) with a double *t,* but visually such an orthography makes a better rhyme with the double *t* in a soldier's family name *Margueritte.* As in the fragments of *Le Livre,* *Vers de circonstance* shows that "Représentation" must precede "Interprétation." Despite Mallarmé's avowed preference for oral reading of his work, his texts must be seen to be grasped because they depend primarily on the tactile sense: "dans telle" / "dentelle," "Cold" / "Hérold," "m'accommode" / "comme ode," "rêveur" / "ever," "Commentaire" / "comme en terre," "qu'on fit" / "confit." His use of irregular verse and inconsistently pronounced mute *e*'s attests to a linguistic gamesmanship at the basis of his poems.

Vers de circonstance is not atypical of Mallarmé's work. *Entre quatre murs* is replete with texts of a similar vein; though they are youthful in enthusiasm, there can be no doubt that they represent a revolt against existing literary dicta and dogma ("Racine" / "déracine") and manifest a certain verbal plasticity that only a love for words as things could bring about. In [*Mallarmé lycéen,* 1954, Henri Mondor] notes that Mallarmé's more serious youthful texts show him to be under the influence of others, mainly Hugo; uneasily, Mondor hopes that the satire that is so blatant in many of the texts is a form of exorcism of the past. With regard to the three notebooks of *Glanes,* which represent some eight thousand lines of poems by others that Mallarmé faithfully recopied in 1859 as a means of learning and mastering poetic methodology, Mondor remarks that Mallarmé's taste in the texts copied is rather unorthodox. He is not interested in the esoteric works, but in the humoristic, ironic, satirical, and even scatological ones.

A cursory glance at *Entre quatre murs* and the choices in *Glanes* shows us a Mallarmé fascinated by language tricks. A word gains potential in meaning by its setting and in its association ("Héraclite" / "hétéroclite"); words are objects that can be arranged and rearranged; their very fixity of meaning can be altered topographically. And, in fact, these early texts show interest in the placement of words on the page (descending order, spacing) and in type size. Mondor cautiously ventures the possibility that Mallarmé is throwing off the influence of Hugo. Why then would not the texts of the 1870s—the ones ignored because Mallarmé only wrote four "pure" poems during the decade—be a way of throwing off the influence of Baudelaire that marks his writing during the 1860s? And why would not *Vers de circonstance* be a pivotal work that turns literary exorcism into a celebration of the plasticity of language?

Looking at the 1870s, we find that these so-called years of impotence are marked by a rather tremendous output of work. In 1871 Mallarmé wrote about the International Exposition in London: articles on things of the world, articles in which he observes objects and describes them for his readers. In 1874 he published the witty fashion journal

La Dernière Mode, in which clothing, menus, and other aspects of Parisian cultural life are painstakingly, but cleverly and amusingly, described, pictured, and enumerated. In 1877 *Les Mots anglais* appeared; again, a work of objects, only this time the things painted verbally are words, English words. Although hardly a true work of philology, *Les Mots anglais* is important for what it reveals about Mallarmé's plastic sense of words. Written in a chatty, conversational tone, with numerous asides and direct addresses to his readers, *Les Mots anglais* is amusing to read; as a textbook, it enlivens language, breathes life into words, makes jokes out of linguistic inconsistencies. Unfortunately, it is becoming stylish to use this work as supportive material for the theoretical interpretation of Mallarmé's "pure" poetry. True, he makes some observations that seem to be borne out later in *Variations sur un sujet,* but close attention to the linguistic details of the work reveals that it is a naïve rendering of the English language in terms of what was known and espoused by philologists of the time. In fact, *Les Mots anglais* is a highly imaginative book, which declares that language is fun, a game to be played and enjoyed.

Hence, Mallarmé's interest in language manipulation is borne out by his light verse, his textbooks and translations, and his fascination with the appearance of a printed word. He examines words in their visual setting as early as *Entre quatre murs;* his experimentation with type size is evidence of his long-standing awareness that the form of a word has a dramatic effect on the reader. His use of capital letters, italics, and punctuation, notably parentheses, underscores the plasticity that is inherent in his texts. In the proofs for *Un Coup de dés,* for example, we are struck by his careful attention to the form of the *f*'s and to linear alignment. In *L'Après-midi d'un faune,* as well as in *Hérodiade* and *Igitur,* Mallarmé pays strict attention to the setting, offering the reader a scenic, tactile atmosphere. His use of objects instead of paper for many of the verses in *Vers de circonstance* presents later and further evidence of his insistence on the plastic.

In addition to the paginal appearance of the written word, however, Mallarmé was intensely preoccupied with "éditions de luxe." In fact, in *A rebours* [by J. K. Huysmans, 1884] des Esseintes is drawn to Mallarmé's poetry first by the luxuriousness of the cover and second by the aura of fantasy ("le suc concret") of the texts. Certainly, Mallarmé's attraction to painting is well known; his friendships with Manet, Morisot, Whistler, Chavannes, Renoir, Gauguin, and others have been well documented. His work, published in his lifetime, was illustrated by Manet, Laurent, Renoir, and Regnault; and the *Chansons bas* were originally written as the legends for sketches by Jean-François Raffaëlli under the title *Les Types de Paris.* In preparation at one time was *Le Tiroir de laque,* which was to have been quite ornate in appearance and accompanied by John Lewis Brown's illustrations, and Odilon Redon was asked by Mallarmé to illustrate *Un Coup de dés.* Mallarmé also did some sketching, as his drawings of peacocks on notes to Méry Laurent show; many of his fan poems are colorful juxtapositions of written word and decorated object, just as the Easter poems are written in gold ink on red eggs. The very title of *Quelques médaillons et portraits*

en pied is taken from the world of plastic art and offers us verbal portraits of writers and painters alike, for words, the pen, and paper are to the poet what the palette, brush, and canvas are to the painter.

By his interest in combining the plastic and the written, Mallarmé demonstrates that he seeks not an absolute realm beyond our reach but one that is within our very grasp. Although man may look to the stars for his destiny, he plays out his role in the *hic et nunc.* Considering all of Mallarmé's writing, we are struck by his constant return to, and reliance upon, the familiar world of myth. [In his *Mythologies,* 1957, Roland Barthes] could easily have been writing about Mallarmé when he says: "Ce que le monde fournit au mythe, c'est un réel historique . . . et ce que le mythe restitue c'est une image *naturelle* de ce réel." What is myth if it is not man's attempts to personify, make concrete, "plasticize" if you will, those things that he does not understand? Mallarmé's *Les Dieux antiques,* published in 1880 at the end of the decade of impotence, presents myth in terms of Barthes's definition: deformation of the meaning, but not destruction and disappearance of meaning.

Myth occurs and recurs frequently in Mallarmé's work. The nymphs and faun of *L'Après-midi d'un faune* surface in "Pan" in *Entre quatre murs;* Venus is another myth that continues from this earliest work to *Un Coup de dés.* Other mythological references include Syrinx, Phoenix, Chimera, Paphos, Styx, Prometheus, Hebe; there are allusions to biblical legends (angel, demon, Lucifer, Idumea), historical tales (Anastasius, Cecilia), literary creations (Hamlet); fairies, sirens, and heroes populate all decades of his writing. The constant reference to constellations is basically mythological: Big Dipper, Little Dipper, Berenice's Hair, Swan, Clock, Unicorn, Peacock, Phoenix. Even his fascination with the sea and the life of adventure and risk are indicators of the use of archetypal figures and themes in his poetry.

According to Barthes, "La fonction du mythe, c'est d'évacuer le réel." Setting this statement alongside [Robert Greer] Cohn's observations that Mallarmé's poems are marked by a standard vocabulary, and a rather limited one at that [in his *L'Œuvre de Mallarmé: Un Coup de dés,* 1951], we note that it is, indeed, the evacuation of the real that accounts for a reworking of the same objects, the same words, over and over again in his work. An object is, of course, external to the mind; it is something that can be experienced and known in an empirical sense. Moved to a different, unfamiliar setting, the object gains in its dimensions and in the possibilities of its meaning. The effect becomes an affect, as simple everyday things are mutated into emblems.

Looking now at Mallarmé's "pure" poems, the texts of *Poésies,* we find the banal real world at every turn, and picture words abound: "écume," "nuage," "plume," "astre," "soleil," "fleur," "cygne," "joyau," "pli," "aile." Mallarmé's word choices are drawn heavily from the classical animal, vegetable, and mineral kingdoms; ephemeral terms are rare, for even "ciel" is always used in conjunction with "soleil," "nuage," "étoile," and so forth. Every part of the human body is evoked directly, and emotional terms occur in amazing frequency ("heureux," "cruel," "triste," "las," "sourire"). These texts are also rather noisy poems ("cloche," "angélus," "sonneur," "glas," "fanfare," "voix," "rire," "chant," "appel," "cri," "tonnerre"), and musical instruments are used throughout his work ("flûte," "cymbale," "viole," "clavecin"). There are very few silences in a Mallarmé poem. It is as though the reader must first be subjected to a visual display, then to an oral enchantment.

Many of Mallarmé's earlier poems are simply verbal portraits and scenes. **"Le Guignon"** is a picture of bad luck, and **"Le Pitre châtié"** describes the poet as a clown; though the rewritten lines that evoke a prostitute at work in **"Une Négresse par le démon secouée"** are less graphic than the original ones, they are still descriptive. Vision is at the basis of **"Les Fenêtres,"** the simple natural objects of **"Les Fleurs"** involve four of the five senses, and **"Renouveau"** is an anecdote on spring fever. The last seven lines of **"Las de l'amer repos"** actually paint a landscape on a cup: the moon sinking into the waters of a lake. In **"Le Sonneur"** we see the poet ringing the bell, and the famous **"L'Azur"** teems with the concrete and the picturesque, in both form and content. **"Brise marine"** paints a quayside scene, **"Soupir"** describes the falling of autumn leaves, **"Don du poème"** is an allegory. In the four versions of **"Aumône,"** we find Mallarmé reworking the description of the coin thrown to the beggar: from twenty sous, to one hundred sous, to a piece of gold, to just some metal in the final version; but all four are concrete, and the last one, "métal," is the original plastic source for the others, the "myth" for the object thrown.

Hérodiade is spectacle, remarkable for its use of colors, jewels, ingenious but graphic end-rhyme play, and the recurrent folds, which serve as a point of reader orientation: folds of the tapestry, folds of thoughts, folds of a bad dream, folds of words. The use of light and shadow, type variations, and the universal myth of Pan contribute to the highly scenic quality of ***L'Après-midi d'un faune,*** which [D. J. Mossop in his *Pure Poetry,* 1971] describes as "magnificently plastic." (pp. 173-78)

The plastic points of departure in these "pure" poems do not detract from the refinements of Mallarmé's treatment of them. On the contrary, discovering the circumstances of each text—and Mallarmé's verse and prose are circumstantial—increases the possibilities of their interpretation. Cohn, for example, poses five different logical, concrete referentials for "dentelle," and in his study of **"Don du poème"** ["On Deciphering Mallarmé," *Georgia Review,* No. 29, 1975, Michael Riffaterre] asserts that Mallarmé's poetry depends on the reader's determination and ability to decipher the verbal referentials. Mallarmé's objects are unembellished in and of themselves; they are there to be detected by the skillful reader. Each detail in its unadorned natural state and with its underlying legend invites the reader to reestablish the adornment that identifies it. Hence, Mallarmé does not abolish matter from his work; rather, he eliminates the particular modification that identifies the object, but the object is always there. Granted, this is the art of suggestion, but it is also the gamesmanship noted in Mallarmé's "impure" poems. Why is it not permissible to see **"A la nue accablante tu"**

as another tub poem, which Berthe Morisot believed it to be, and why can **"M'introduire dans ton histoire"** not be about a bidet? Why do we continue to insist on an unreal Mallarmé when his writing is of the concrete, everyday world? [André] Breton may well have put his finger on the actual Mallarmé when, in 1924, he declared: "Mallarmé est surréaliste dans la confidence" ["Premier manifeste du surréalisme," *Manifestes du surréalisme,* 1962]—confidence in man's creative ability, confidence in man's capacity to attain the absolute, confidence in our untapped potential to throw the dice, play the game, and win.

Dice are a preferred Mallarmé referential, as is the notion of game. As his ***Vers de circonstance*** shows, Mallarmé plays games with words; they are his poetic dice. Keeping in mind that a good number of these light poems were re-edited and published by him in 1894, and keeping in mind his demonstrated plastic sense of poetry, we see that ***Un Coup de dés*** emerges as an example of his "Littérature" / "rature." It is visual, as Cohn and others have established. What's more, it is "clear as myth," as [Thomas Williams in his *Mallarmé and the Language of Mysticism,* 1971], says, although he fails to say what kind of myth or which myth. Based on topographic concerns in the use of seven different type settings, it appeals to the eye first. It is highly tactile, demanding that the reader turn the pages, and we are reminded that in the fragments of *Le Livre* the role of the reader in unfolding the pages and changing their position is of great importance to Mallarmé. It is directly linked to painting in that Redon was asked to do the illustrations.

Beginning with a concrete object, a pair of dice, Mallarmé structures his entire poem around the rolling of the dice, the act of forming a pattern. His preface (and Cohn terms it "coy" in tone) calls for "un lecteur habile," a player skilled in verbal games. And this structuration is the basis of the text; every time the reader-player rolls the dice—turns the page—a new pattern turns up. Dice, as we know, always form a pattern and, being cubes, a three-dimensional one at that. The pattern may or may not be the one we would prefer, but it is there on the double page, just as the dots are on the die. Hesitation to roll the dice or turn the page ends the act or game; acceptance of the risk is commitment to continued play, hence the circularity of the text, which begins and ends on the same phrase, returning the reader-player to the initial plastic object, "dés." Can the reader-player beat the house, the poet? Can chance be conquered and the reader-poet together form the constellation of Poetry? It is not a matter of the master's failure to throw the dice; the dice have already been thrown once ("lancé"); the risk lies in what the reader sees. Just as dice always form a pattern, so do constellations, and both are fixed in space. But, unlike the dice, which are pluridimensional, the constellation is one-dimensional, the "issue stellaire" of our skill: "rien n'aura eu lieu que le lieu." The constellation makes space contract into an absolute, but visual, unity.

The constellation that Mallarmé uses is Ursa Minor, the Little Dipper, and it is to be noted that this is the only constellation that contains a fixed star, Polaris, and the only constellation that never goes below the earth's horizon: It

> Only words—language—can conjoin the
> earth and the stars, the sea and the skies
> by making them plastic objects. In reading
> Mallarmé we should look at the patterns
> his dice have formed, not at his thoughts
> about throwing them. He is not abstract
> but very, very real.
>
> —*Virginia A. La Charité*

is always visible from any point on the globe. Is this not another version of the Orphic explanation of the earth? In the Orphic mysteries, the earth is the shell of an egg; chaos is surrounded by night, ether is the day or life within; the upper egg is the sky, and the lower part is earth. Hence, the pattern of the multidimensional dice on earth is reflected in the singularity of the stellar constellation if the reader can roll the right combination.

The myth of Orpheus is not the only one present in *Un Coup de dés,* for the myth of the Halcyon birds also provides the poem with its basic anecdote. Ceyx is the master of the ship lost during a storm at sea; as the fury of the storm increases and the ship begins to break up, the sailors lose their skill and courage. The waves triumph, the mast and rudder are broken, the vessel is shattered. Clinging to a piece of floating debris, Ceyx thinks of his wife, Halcyon, and prays that the foam of the waves will carry his body to her for burial. Losing the struggle, Ceyx drowns, as clouds cover the face of the grieving Day Star. In the form of Ceyx, Morpheus flies to Halcyon to tell her of her husband's fate. Refusing to live without him, Halcyon goes the next morning to the seaside where the waves bring Ceyx's body to her. In grief she leaps on a jetty, and, as wings appear on her, she flies over the surface of the water, brushing the sea with her wings. The pitying gods change both of them into birds, who mate and produce young.

The parallels between this fable and *Un Coup de dés* are striking. Although the fragments of *Un Tombeau pour Anatole* also bear relationship to the text, it is doubtless accurate to say that the death of his son was too personal for the detachment necessary in a text that would appeal to a skillful reader: hence, Mallarmé jettisoned the story of his son's death and substituted one of classical mythology. Be that as it may, the use of myth in *Un Coup de dés* is essential to its plastic structure. Giving form to a legend is the writing of a poem; it is rolling multidimensional words-objects until a fixed unity, an agreement between player and house, a constellation emerges simultaneously for the reader and the poet. In addition, the use of a myth in *Un Coup de dés* allows Mallarmé the freedom to play with his codes of communication: word, sound, gesture, syntax, groupings, topography, typography. The capital letters of the beginning phrase serve to make the basic act in the text an allegorical one: every thought does send forth a throw of the dice that will never abolish the chance of playing.

Hasard is generally interpreted as chance, happenstance beyond human control, but it originally meant "le jeu de dés." Moreover, when we look at all of Mallarmé's writing, we find a penchant for wordplay, which increases the meaning of the text. Usually Mallarmé writes this word with a *z,* that is, in other texts, the word appears in its English spelling, but *hazard* is not the English translation of *hasard.* Typical of Mallarmé's love of linguistic games is the distinct possibility that *hasard* is a play on the English dice game Hazard, which is described in full by Littré. Hazard is a complicated game of dice with arbitrary rules, based on odds favorable to the one who holds the dice. Hazard can be played with two or three dice, and the betting is done on a given layout. In terms of *Un Coup de dés,* such an explanation for the construct of the text is certainly tenable.

Mallarmé's subtitle for *Un Coup de dés* is "Poème" because of its invitation to the reader to participate actively in the interpretation (reading-playing) of his representation. In no way, then, can this poem, or any of his work, for that matter, be viewed as the negation of a negation that embraces the pure idea, for matter continually rejoins matter in the Mallarmé universe: dice-constellation. His practice, not his theory, demonstrates that what concerns him is the visual, concrete world and the language used in it. Only words—language—can conjoin the earth and the stars, the sea and the skies by making them plastic objects. In reading Mallarmé we should look at the patterns his dice have formed, not at his thoughts about throwing them. He is not abstract, but very, very real. Not an idealist, but a humanist. Not a postromantic, a wayward Parnassian, or a presymbolist, but a modern cocreator whose sense of the literary game led him to write ideograms before Apollinaire, to be concerned with topography before Reverdy, to write of the marvelousness of the everyday before the surrealists, to combine the visual and graphic before Michaux, to pulverize the text before Char, to be on the side of things before Ponge, to affirm acting as being before Sartre, to know that the text is plural before the structuralists, new novelists, *Tel Quel.* Before Proust, Mallarmé knows that art is "la vraie vie."

Paula Lewis has observed [in her *Aesthetics of Stéphane Mallarmé in Relation to His Public,* 1976] that Mallarmé finds all aspects of reality valid, and Judy Kravis has noted [in her *Prose of Mallarmé,* 1976] that Mallarmé's prose investigates the relationship of language with reality. I would like to add that only reality is valid in the Mallarmé text. Writing poetry for him is the experience of life, and the experience of life—its circumstances—is the game of words. Mallarmé consciously deletes his own personality from his texts, but he leaves the objects that permit us to reconstruct our own worlds as poems. As Barthes says: "Le vrai jeu n'est pas de masquer le sujet mais de masquer le jeu lui-même."

As early as 1864 in **"Le Démon de l'analogie,"** Mallarmé demonstrated that his poetic practice would be based on plastic circumstances and verbal challenges to the reader: "La Pénultième est morte." Of course, the penult is dead; it died when it dropped in the development of the French language. But we know what the penult was because we have the remaining syllables on each side, the parentheses that indicate its form and identity. It is this very kind of ordinary, really plastic sign that Mallarmé uses in the structuring of his poetry. The problem, then, is to accept the invitation to play skillfully a literary game of interpretation, to rediscover the penult, to see our dice patterns in the plastic experience of a poet's poem. (pp. 179-82)

Virginia A. La Charité, "Mallarmé and the Plastic Circumstances of the Text," in Pre-Text Text Context: Essays on Nineteenth-Century French Literature, *edited by Robert L. Mitchell, Ohio State University Press, 1980, pp. 173-83.*

Weightman on the influence of Mallarmé's writing:

[Over] and above Mallarmé's present popularity as an object of academic study, one can feel his presence nowadays over a whole area of French writing. It is not simply that French poetry, in so far as it exists, seems to follow on from Mallarmé, Rimbaud and Valéry much more than from Baudelaire and Verlaine. There is also at the moment, in Paris, an overwhelming obsession with language, and a predilection for difficult, precious, abstract and contorted writing, which seems to owe something not only to Mallarmé the poet, but also to Mallarmé the prose-writer, the inventor of the curious style exemplified in his collection of essays entitled **Divagations.** Anyone familiar with that little work will recognise echoes of it in the writings of the anthropologist Claude Lévi-Strauss, the psychologist Jacques Lacan, the literary critic Maurice Blanchot, the essayists Michel Leiris and Roland Barthes, and in the prose of most of the contributors to the reviews *Tel Quel, Critique,* and *Poétique.* A certain Mallarmé-like flavour has been propagated over a wide field of literary and intellectual discourse in France, and Mallarmé has been a major promoter of the present self-consciousness about language in France and elsewhere. Certainly, his primary cultural importance lies in the fact that he was a language-obsessed man. . . .

John Weightman, in his "Mallarmé and the Language Obsession," Encounter LI, No. 4, 1978.

Jewel Spears Brooker (essay date 1983)

[Brooker is an American scholar, educator, and editor. In the following excerpt, she attempts to resolve the apparent contradictions in Mallarmé's aesthetic theories.]

A preoccupation with precisely what happens in the reading of a poem is at the heart of Symbolist aesthetics. The quasi-official theoretician of the Symbolists, Stéphane Mallarmé, devotes as much attention to creative reading as to creative writing. Obsessed with such matters as the reader's overall function in the aesthetic process and his competence to perform that function, Mallarmé refers repeatedly to the situation of poets who find themselves at once in need of and deprived of competent readers.

Mallarmé's references to readers of poetry and to the reading process are, unfortunately, anything but consistent. In one breath, he execrates the reader as a dunderheaded fool; in the next, he honors him as a hidden poet. In one essay, he banishes the general reader from the house of poetry; in another, he welcomes him as a creative participant in a poetry festival. The ostensible contradictions in Mallarmé's theories of reading derive largely from the common assumption that poetry can be read in the same way at all times. Mallarmé maintains, conversely, that poetry must be read dispensationally, or, in other words, that it must be read in one way at one time and in quite another way at another time. Reading must be conceived of in terms of the readers at hand. When they are generally competent, he advocates one method of reading; when they are generally incompetent, he advocates a different method, one that recognizes and attempts to circumvent that incompetence.

The term "dispensation" is borrowed from Christian theology. It refers to a period of time during which one's responsibilities to other people and to God are reckoned according to a special system of divinely ordered principles. Dispensational theology, acknowledging that God deals with people in different ways at different times, is a first principle in hermeneutics, so elementary that the simplest Bible readers understand it. They may not be able to define "dispensation," much less "hermeneutics," but know that God dealt with Adam (Dispensation of Innocence; Garden of Eden) in one way, with King Saul (Dispensation of Law; Moses to Christ) in another way, with Martin Luther (Dispensation of Grace; Pentecost to the present) in still another way. Readers also know that this present age will be succeeded by an age somewhat like the Age of Innocence. That age, the final one, mirror to the first one, will be the Millennium or the Dispensation of Peace. (pp. 17-18)

Mallarmé's view of art is analogous in important ways to the dispensationalist's view of history. A dispensation in art may be defined as a period of time during which the relationship between the artist and his audience is managed according to a particular set of principles. Mallarmé speaks of three such dispensations. Rather than giving specific dates or datable events as dispensation boundaries, he simply speaks of the art of the past, that of the present, and that of the future. The invariable existing apart from all three is the artist's absolute need of an audience. Unable to banish entirely his reader, the poet must adjust his principles, must make concessions to accommodate reader deficiency. In the past dispensation, the artist and his audience enjoyed an immediate and creative relationship; in the future dispensation, that perfect relationship will be restored. In the present dispensation, a time of deficiency requiring grace or unmerited favor, the relationship is one of accommodation. But seeing this dispensation, always, as a temporary concession to incompetence, Mallarmé looks backward with nostalgia and forward with hope.

Mallarmé's views about reading (and almost everything else) are difficult to follow, in part because of his prose style. But there is another reason, more treacherous because less obvious. Like most idealists, he uses everyday words to convey eccentric or technical meanings. The word "poem" he sometimes uses to refer to a presence (the text) and sometimes to an absence (an ideal). The uninitiated, assuming that a poem is a poem, is bound to be baffled. Because Mallarmé's idea of what a poem is and where it exists is at the center of his dispensational approach to reading, it is necessary to begin with a few rather basic discriminations. Mallarmé's absolute need of a reader, crucial in his dispensational dynamic, derives from his definition of a poem as an edifice existing in the mind of a reader, in part created by that reader. Actually, he speaks of the ideal poem in two distinct ways. His first ideal poem exists *before* expression in the mind of the poet, or in the mind of all poets. This "ideal has obsessed even the most unconscious writers"; it "has been attempted by every writer, even by Geniuses." Calling it "the perfect poem we dream of," Mallarmé admits with dismay that he as an individual artist will never be able to write it. Still, he will devote his life to an attempt "to reveal and realize a fragment of it . . . and so suggest the rest of it which a single life cannot accomplish." This unrealizable, atemporal poem comprehends as fragments the countless ideal poems in the minds of all poets, both those alive now and those who have been dead for centuries. The poem in the mind of the poet exists apart from any reader.

Mallarmé's second ideal poem, however, is contingent upon the reader, for it exists in the reader's mind. "From time immemorial," Mallarmé explains, "the poet has knowingly placed his verse in the sonnet which he writes upon our minds." This poem, existing *after* expression, realized through reading, is analogous to the drama in the mind of the spectator (or reader) of plays. In an 1886 review of *Hamlet,* Mallarmé writes: "This work . . . is so well patterned on the theatre of the mind alone—this being the prototype of all others—that it makes no difference whether or not it is adapted for modern production." There are, obviously, as many *Hamlets* as there are encounters with the text. A play or a poem is not written once and for all; with the collaboration of the reader, it is written anew with every reading. And although sometimes associated with timelessness, the true poem exists in time. Mallarmé's admiration for Emile Verhaeren derives from the Belgian poet's ability to produce poetic texts which initiate a "perpetual creation" of ideal poems.

> What I admire in your book—and in you, my dear fellow—is the perpetual creation of verses which never lose their fluid quality and yet are always perfectly guided. You don't make the mistake (as poets generally have heretofore) of writing them "once and for all." Rather, they are continually re-created, continually different, and yet still themselves—as life is.

These ideal poems, like the ideal *Hamlet*s, differ in quality, for the richness of the poem in the mind is contingent on the qualifications and the maturity brought to the occasion by the reader.

Mallarmé's elevation of the reader to a working partner in the creation of poems is explicit in the following compliment to the art of Théodore de Banville.

> Words in all their efficacy are fitted out and joined in a unique and perfect prosody, which asks of the hidden poet (who is Every Reader) that he should sing the song according to the

modulations of the sweet or brilliant. Thus, all unaided, that principle springs up which is simply Verse!

The work of the hidden poet, the collaborator who is Every Reader, is behind Mallarmé's definition of reading as the mating of a virgin space in the reader's mind with the blank spaces created by the writer's arrangement of words on paper, as a marriage of white and white which results in the birth of the Ideal.

> Reading—
> Is an exercise—
>
> We must bend our independent minds, page by page, to the blank space which begins each one . . . Then, in the tiniest and most scattered stopping-points upon the page, when the lines of chance have been vanquished word by word, the blanks unfailingly return; before, they were gratuitous; now, they are essential; and now at last it is clear that nothing lies beyond; now silence is genuine and just.

The distinction between mere blankness and the "essential" blankness that follows the reading of a poem, between mere silence and the "genuine and just" silence that follows the reading, is a key to Mallarmé's conception of art. Mere silence has no content, but the genuine and just silence is a structured silence rich with meaning. The first silence is an absence; the second, a poem in the mind of the reader. The first blankness is, Mallarmé goes on to say, a "virgin space face to face with the lucidity of our matching vision"; the second, an Idea born of that encounter.

Mallarmé has a special name for the process through which the reader's "consciousness . . . joins the book now here, now there, varies its melodies, guesses its riddles, and even re-creates it unaided." This conversion of text into poetry, he calls *Transposition.* Regarding the details of *Transposition,* Mallarmé enunciates two seemingly contrary tenets. On the one hand, he sees a large audience listening to the poem being recited in an auditorium. In this version, the ideal poem is realized in many theaters at once—the literal recital hall, and also the theaters of the mind associated with the individual members of the audience. On the other hand, he sees a solitary aristocratic reader face to face with the text. In this version, the ideal comes into being only in the theater of this one superior mind. These two conceptions have important aspects in common. Both assume the idealist definition of the art work outlined in this essay; both assume the necessity of a competent and creative reader collaborator. And both are based upon an identification of art and religion, an identification in which the act of reading a poem is seen as an act of worship. But despite the common features, these notions of actualizing a poem remain in important particulars antithetical.

The apparent schizophrenia in Mallarmé's discussions of *Transposition* derives from a distinction he makes regarding the times of poetry. The past and the future are seen as glorious; the present as inglorious.

> I feel that our time is an interregnum for the poet; he should stay out of it . . . all he can do is work in mystery with an eye to the future or

to eternity, and occasionally send his visiting card, a few stanzas, or a sonnet to the "living," so that they won't stone him, should they suspect him of realizing that they do not exist.

The past dispensation, Mallarmé reveals in **"Catholicism,"** was the Middle Ages; the future, he explains in his revery on Wagner, is a generation or more away.

> The majestic ceremonies of Poetry . . . are incompatible with the flood of banality borne along by the arts of our sham civilization. They are the ceremonies of a day which lies unborn within the unsuspecting womb of the people . . .

> Certainly neither this poet nor his contemporaries will be involved in any such ceremony, and therefore his dream need not be troubled by any sense of incapability or by its own distance from reality.

The reason for Mallarmé's dispensational approach is the deficiency or, to use religious language, the fallenness of the contemporary audience of poetry. Readers of poetry, needed to serve as the hidden co-poets, are so base that they are barred from the high office of collaborator in art. The majestic ceremonies of poetry thus are deferred to some millennium "which lies unborn within the unsuspecting womb of the people."

The millennial dispensation, during which the poem in the mind will be generated communally in a public celebration, Mallarmé describes with unusual clarity in **"Solemnity".**

> I should imagine that when, in the future, we come together for the celebrations which are listed upon the human program, the cause for doing so will not be the theater, limited as it is and by itself unable to respond to the subtlest of human instincts; nor music, which is in any case an art too fleeting to interest the mob sufficiently; but rather it will be the Ode, assimilating such overmisty, over-palpable elements as the theater and music tend to isolate; it will be dramatized and knowingly divided; heroic scenes will be simply an ode for many voices.

> Yes, truly! think, think what that cult could be, which is destined for such celebration! . . .

> [T]his most magnificent of spectacles would be . . . the logical climax and conclusion of the entire artistic surge which was necessarily limited to matters of technical invention during the Renaissance period. Splendid, grandiose, impelling development! This recitation (a term which we must always come back to when poetry is under discussion) will fascinate, instruct, and above all it will astound the People . . . And so we shall have the Opening of a Jubilee; especially of that figurative jubilee which must conclude a cycle in History and, to this end, must have, I think, the ministry of the Poet.

In the future dispensation, then, the poet and the people will celebrate together; in the past, the poet and his audience were similarly bound. In this time between times, this interregnum, the poet, far from reigning, lives in danger of being stoned by the people. With his eye toward the future, he can only shield himself in mystery until this cycle of history is concluded.

Particularly striking in Mallarmé's aesthetic is the importance attached to the role of the people. In most discussions by literary critics, Mallarmé's name is synonymous with the most perverse disdain of the people. The title of his most famous essay, **"Hérésies Artistiques: L'art pour tous,"** suggests that the idea of art for the people is anathema. Hermeticism in art, however, is not a standard; it is a concession forced by incompetent readers during (as he refers to the present age in **"Catholicism"**) a "dispenser era." Art for all, a heresy in this interregnum when the poet is forced underground, is the *sine qua non* of the splendid ceremonies associated with better times.

The necessary relationship between artist and audience, perhaps the major point in aesthetic dispensationalism, is a consequence of Mallarmé's identification of art and religion. This identification appears at the beginning of his career in **"Hérésies Artistiques"** and is elaborated for more than a third of a century in correspondence and essays. Occasionally art is presented as analogous to religion, but typically, it is presented as synonymous with religion. The terms are often interchanged, i.e., religion is art, and also art is religion. In *Offices,* for example, Catholicism is the "art" of the past; poetry the "religion" of the future. *Offices,* written at the end of the poet's life, is his most profound meditation on the relationship of art and religion and his most complete description of aesthetic dispensationalism. The three brief essays in this sequence (**"Catholicism," "Sequel,"** and **"Sacred Pleasure"**) are almost universally regarded as Mallarmé's most formidable writings. Bradford Cook's explanation of why he excluded *Offices* from his Mallarmé translations indicates the problems which must be faced.

> However interesting these pieces may be to scholars (exposition of Mallarmé's theories on religion, rite, etc.), they consist generally of a kind of ugly, jagged shorthand highly resistant to clarification.

My purpose in this essay, unfortunately, does not permit me to pass these recalcitrant compositions. **"Catholicism"** (1895) and **"Sacred Pleasure"** (1895), in particular, are central to my argument that, in discussions of Mallarmé's ideas and his poetry, art must be approached dispensationally.

The theoretical foundation for identifying art and religion, disclosed in **"Catholicism,"** is that both were born in response to a basic and continuing need of the people, a common metaphysical need which Mallarmé calls "exhaling the abyss." "One imagines," he muses, "that religion arises from the juxtaposition of human consciousness and nothingness." A "presumption" born of the need to compensate for the "exterior silence," religion may be defined as a marriage of faith and nothingness or, in the poet's own phrase, "a vibration of certitude and of darkness joined in a meditative unison." He claims that Catholicism, in which certainty and darkness were harmonized beautifully, "has ceased," but the human need which generated Catholicism remains. The "honour" of soldering the abyss, of enabling men to cope with fear of the unknown, has been inherited by artists.

> A race, ours, to which befell the honour of lend-
> ing entrails to the fear . . . which metaphysical
> and claustral eternity has of itself, and then (to
> which befell the honour) of exhaling the abyss
> in some firm baying in the ages.

This explains Mallarmé's merger of art and religion, his identification of the artist with the priest and the reader (or audience) with the worshipper, and not least, his insistence that the people be involved in art. Artists, then, have a sacred calling—they are to "resume the sombre marvel" which was lost in the great apostasy of the late Middle Ages and the early Renaissance; they have an awesome responsibility, the construction of an alternative religion which will facilitate the "common functioning." In their ministry to the common need, artists must draw inspiration from their "own resources." The divinity which they must take as a "point of departure" can be tapped only by descending into the self, or, as Mallarmé puts it, by "visiting" one's own "unconsciousness" and then ascending "with the ignorance of the secret."

Mallarmé's dispensationalism is obvious in **"Catholicism."** The essay is based on a comparison between two great periods in which the religious needs of the people have been/will be satisfactorily met. The first period, in which Catholicism served as the religion, the poet identifies as the Middle Ages; the second, in which poetry will serve, he refers to as an indefinite future. Confessing that he retains a sympathy for Catholicism, Mallarmé discloses that he wishes to lean his aesthetic religion of the future upon its remains. His own words are that he wishes "to lean the Dream on the altar against the refound tomb—its feet like posts in ashes."

In regard to the ceremony of this new religion, the "mind" of the poet "disdains syntheses," i.e., rejects the idea of doing research and then formulating from many sources a synthetic ritual. It prefers instead "to lead astray a research" which has become "empty" because it is no longer appropriate that the "bewildered, the banal and vast public place also yield to injunctions of salvation." Presumably, this means that since Christian ritual has been disembowelled, it should be diverted, or led astray, from the use intended by such researchers as Aquinas. As a modern Aquinas formulating a successor to Catholicism, Mallarmé desires to project holiness into future centuries as Aquinas projected it into the nineteenth, but he is afraid lest his own "projection of holiness should not suffice and should fall short." To guard against falling short, he will resist the present mania for "dispensing" with tradition; he will, rather, salvage any part of the Catholic ritual that can be adapted for use in his new religion of art.

Mallarmé then asks whether the ritual of the Mass can be saved by being "exteriorized" from its present use, or whether it must perish by becoming merely a grandiose kind of entertainment. He suggests that the ritual can be saved if the artist will adapt it for the new religion, allowing it to become an "intrusion in future festivals." These future festivals can be imagined if one is able to "suspend as his vision, the heavy chandelier, multiple evoker of mo-

tives." The chandelier, reflecting light in many facets of cut glass, is one of Mallarmé's metaphors for the symbol.

At this point in the divagation, Mallarmé tries to evoke the festival of the millennial dispensation by suspending one of his favorite symbols—a bird. He envisions the audience distributing itself into two great wing-shaped groups of brooding humanity. "The multitude bifurcates to some amphitheatre, like a wing of human infinity, terrified before the brusque abyss." The function of true religion, appeasing the terror of the masses huddled on the precipice overlooking non-being or death, will in the future dispensation be the responsibility of artists. In discharging this responsibility, the artist will turn to music. In **"Solemnity,"** Mallarmé maintains that the future festival will feature neither music nor drama but an "ode for many voices." But here in **"Catholicism,"** he envisions a "performance with concert," perhaps a Wagnerian music-drama. The music is important because it miraculously induces an interpenetration, "in reciprocity, of the myth and the concert hall." This reciprocity, uniting the orchestra, the audience, and the hero, is crucial in relieving the terror of the people.

> The orchestra floats, swells, and the action, tak-
> ing place, does not isolate itself as something for-
> eign and we do not remain (merely) witnesses:
> but, from each seat, through the terrors and the
> brilliance, in turn, we are circularly the hero—
> suffering not to attain to himself except by
> storms of sounds and emotions displaced on his
> gesture and our invisible afflux. He is Nobody,
> according to the rustling, diaphanous curtain of
> symbols, or rhythms, which he opens on his stat-
> ue, to all.

The actor on stage is cloaked in a diaphanous curtain of symbols which nullifies his particularity, transforming him into Nobody, the hero of the Ideal Drama. The spectators are at once witnesses to and actors in this drama. Participating in the hero's suffering, each spectator is transformed into Nobody. This participation is achieved through contemplation—"whomsoever contemplates it [becomes] an unconscious protagonist." The afflux of the witness/hero is invisible, making possible the appropriation of the sounds and movements of the figure on stage by many spectators simultaneously.

But this performance is more than a *pièce,* or play; it is also an *office,* or religious service. Mallarmé predicts that "the obsession, which the mind has for the theatre, shall grow in temple majesty" if the audience will recognize in the drama a communion service celebrating not the Passion, which is the "pompous aesthetics of the Church," but the birth-death-rebirth cycle of the seasons. This ritual, purged of the barbarous idea of cannibalism, will relieve terror and effect unity just as the Mass did.

> Our communion or part of one to all and of all
> to one, thus, liberated from the barbarous meal
> that the sacrament designates—in the consecra-
> tion of the host, nevertheless affirms itself, proto-
> type of ceremonials, in spite of the difference
> from an art tradition, the Mass.

An understanding of the communion service is one key to

making sense of Mallarmé's discussion in this cryptic essay, for what happens in the communion service is what he says will happen in the communion ritual of his millennial dispensation. Of special importance is the fact that the Mass is commemorative, that it re-enacts a momentous event of the past, the sacrificial death and resurrection of Christ. The past event features a being at once human and divine whose solitary death is a never-to-be-repeated sacrifice; he dies once and for all (for all people and for all time). The re-enactment features human suppliants who identify in that death and resurrection. The re-enactment is communal rather than solitary, and it is repeated every time a Mass or a communion service is consummated.

In Mallarmé's aesthetic, writing a poem is analogous to Christ's Passion, and reading a poem to the ceremony of the Mass. The first, which features the poet, is essentially lonely and culminates in death. The second, which features primarily the audience, is essentially communal and culminates in rebirth. The analogy of Christ and the poet, of the Passion and the creation of a poetic text, is described many times in Mallarmé's letters to friends. To Théodore Aubanel, he writes about the suffering a poet must undergo in order to write a great work; and he confesses, "I died, and I have risen from the dead with the key to the jewelled treasure of my last spiritual casket." To Villiers de l'Isle-Adam, he writes that in order to purify poetry and link a poem to the "Idea of the Universe," he has endured indescribable nights of horror, culminating in death,

> And yet the irony and Tantalian torture is that, if my body is to rise from the dead, I must remain powerless to write them for a long time. For I am in the last stage of nervous exhaustion; my mind is so evilly, so perfectly afflicted that I am often unable to understand even the most banal conversation.

And as Golgotha was preceded by Gethsemane, Mallarmé insists that the death of the poet is preceded by *agonie,* a severe anguish preparing him for the sacrificial act which will redeem the text from nothingness. The most vivid accounts of both his Gethsemane and his Golgotha are preserved in letters to Henri Cazalis. The agony, the death, the descent to Hell are described in the following lines from a letter of 1867.

> These last months have been terrifying. My Thought has thought itself through and reached a Pure Idea. What the rest of me has suffered during that long agony, is indescribable. But, fortunately, I am quite dead now, and Eternity Itself is the least pure of all the regions where my Mind can wander . . . I struggled with that creature of ancient and evil plumage—God— whom I fortunately defeated and threw to earth. But I had waged that battle on His boney wing, and in a final burst of agony greater than I should have expected from Him, He bore me off again among the Shadows . . . the price of my victory is so high that I still need to see myself in this mirror in order to think; and that if it were not in front of me here on this table as I write you, I would become Nothingness again.

But death is followed by resurrection, for the poet is resurrected in the reader's communion service. Mallarmé

claims that this ritual will have effects comparable to those formerly associated with the distribution of the "real presence."

> [T]his devotee demands a fact—at least the credence to this fact in the name of results. "Real presence:" or, let the God be there, diffused, total, mimicked from afar by the effaced actor, understood by us trembling.

The actor, like the priest in Catholicism, is a surrogate figure who appears only to efface himself in favor of the hidden god. The god resurrected in this ceremony is the poet who sacrificed himself in the creation of the poetic text. Art's splendid ceremonies, bearing a "far-off resemblance with grave things of the past, darkened in memory," will elevate the theatre, "that which rumour denominates as a social edifice," into the temple.

The Passion and the Mass, both in Mallarmé's theory and in Christian thought, are interdependent. Neither has meaning in itself. The theology at issue here, discussed at length in both Romans and Hebrews, revolves around the marriage of two of God's essential attributes, justice and mercy. Since all have sinned and since divine justice requires death for sin, divine mercy seems to be precluded. The dilemma is resolved in a way that perfectly satisfies justice without impeding mercy. Because Christ remained sinless, his death, in itself, was a meaningless event, a punishment without a crime. It gains meaning—as satisfaction of divine justice, as channel of divine mercy—when a sinful being ritualistically appropriates it as his own punishment. This is one of the things that happens in the ceremony of the Mass. In eating the broken body and drinking the spilt blood, the suppliant not only identifies with the death of Christ, but also gives meaning to that death. The Passion and the Mass, then, like writing a poem and reading one, are reciprocally related. If the Mass is a sham, the Passion signifies nothing; more obviously, if the Passion is a sham, the Mass becomes a tale told by an idiot.

Mallarmé concludes his essay on Catholicism by predicting that his new religion will rival in splendor Aquinas's old religion which has declined to a mere shadow. Again, his language is memorable: "A magnificence shall spread itself out . . . analogous to the Shadow of long ago." That Shadow, Catholicism, and its sacrament, the Mass, now denominated as an art tradition, will be known only to scholars; but this magnificence, the art work of the future, and its sacrament, the performance, will be denominated the true religion and will be embraced by the people.

In this notion of *Transposition,* then, the poem in the mind is generated communally, ceremonially, in a magnificent public celebration. But, as suggested earlier, the poem in the mind is sometimes generated in a manner which seems to be the antithesis of this Catholic performance. In this alternative realization, a solitary, predestined, aristocrat retires to his closet and, through contemplation, constructs, beyond the text, in the sanctuary of his mind, a superior silence which is the ideal poem. In the spirit of evocative imprecision which Mallarmé admired (attempting to avoid mere imprecision, which he despised), I christen this notion of *Transposition* as Calvinist. The Catholic notion applies in past and future dispensations; the Calvinist in the present one. The Catholic notion assumes a worthy public which collaborates in actualizing the poem; the Calvinist notion, a degenerate public which is unfit to collaborate with the poet. The Calvinist notion is compelled by the fact that the present general reader is, to use the theological term, fallen; it is an expediency which makes poetry possible for a few competent readers and poets in what Mallarmé scornfully refers to as "our make-everything-clear-and-easy era."

It is arguable that Mallarmé himself would have disapproved, on general principles, of the association of his aesthetic with the theology of France's brilliant logician, John Calvin. But in his view of the solitary reader actualizing a text, the major intellectual strains are analogous to the major doctrines of Calvinist theology. These ideas include human depravity, the predestination of saints, the rejection of mediators between God and the human, the emphasis on the individual Christian rather than the community of saints, the autonomy of the Bible, and the focus on an *explication de texte* (a sermon) rather than the Mass as the center of worship.

The Calvinist notion of *Transposition* may be illuminated by reference to Mallarmé's famous essay **"Hérésies Artistiques: L'Art pour tous,"** first published in the September 15, 1862 issue of *L'Artiste*. Although written when Mallarmé was only twenty years old, this essay is generally considered "a key to his entire work," roughly equivalent in his thought to "Tradition and the Individual Talent" in T. S. Eliot's thought. The main ideas are suggested in the title. The first concerns the nature of art; the second, the audience of art. In using the term "hérésies artistiques," Mallarmé is saying that art is a religion. In defining the heresy as "l'art pour tous," he is saying that art is for a minority audience; to use religious language, art is only for the elect. The idea of the sanctity of art is important in both the Calvinist and the Catholic conceptions of *Transposition,* but the idea of hermeticism, really the main subject of this early essay, belongs primarily to the Calvinist view. For reasons already discussed, art for all is not a heresy in the Catholic view.

At the center of the Calvinist view of *Transposition* is the fallenness, the depravity, of the reader. Mallarmé is infamous for the scorn he heaps upon the reading public. In **"Hérésies Artistiques,"** he refers to the masses as the mob, as packs of baying hounds, as buffoons smelling of the gutter, as Philistines, as irksome intruders, and with devastating irony, as "citizens." "Citizens" are members of the so-called reading public, "on whom modern vanity, being short of flattering titles, has conferred the empty title of citizen." Mallarmé argues that poetry has been defiled by multitudes of citizens who, "with the stupidity characteristic of the masses," rush into sanctuaries which angels would fear to enter. It is as if those hoards of tourists who visit Notre Dame each summer should stroll up to the altar during Mass and take a bite of the bread or a sip of the wine. This early essay concludes with a ringing exhortation to fellow poets: "Let the masses read books on morals, but for goodness sake, do not give them our poetry to corrupt."

The doctrine of depravity is balanced in Mallarmé as in

Calvin by the doctrine of predestination or election. Poetry, says Mallarmé, is a "mystery accessible only to a few rare individuals." The analogy with religion is explicit: "Religions take refuge behind secrets unveiled only to the elect; art has its own elect." The high standing of the predestined reader is underscored by Mallarmé's reference to him as a member of the *"sanhédrin de l'art."* The Sanhedrin was, until its dissolution in the destruction of Jerusalem in 70 A.D., the supreme council of the Jewish people. Although it included a few distinguished elders and scribes, it was composed primarily of hereditary priests—the High Priest, living former High Priests, and outstanding members of the larger family of priests. In demanding a reader who belongs to the *"sanhédrin de l'art,"* Mallarmé is saying that the reader must be holy and learned, competent and aristocratic.

In view of the fact that the elect, those "patient predestined ones," as Mallarmé calls competent readers in this present dispensation, are hidden poets, it should not be surprising that this doctrine can be reduced to the proposition that only poets can read poetry. In one of his letters to Cazalis, he is perfectly clear: "What you say about your aunt's and sister's reactions saddens me but doesn't surprise me, for I am utterly convinced that art is for artists alone." This does not mean that readers must have published or even written a line of verse; it means that they must have the capability to take a text and, collaborating with the writer of that text, create a poem. Intelligent reading of a text makes a poet just as surely as intelligent writing makes one.

Mallarmé's elevation of hermeticism from an incidental to a fundamental of art is often considered the ultimate perversity, especially today when many critics are militantly egalitarian. But the deliberate exclusion of the general reader is neither perverse nor unreasonable. The attempt of the modern state to bring about universal literacy has generated a huge reading public, Mallarmé's "citizens," which has a severely limited understanding of the complexities and the beauties of language. In taking the medium of poetry and forcing it upon every school child, well-meaning though unintelligent bureaucrats have produced a crisis for poetry. Its language, laments Mallarmé, "contains no mystery to shield it from hypocritical curiosity, imparts no terror to shield it from impieties or from the smiles and grimaces of the ignorant and the hostile." Baudelaire's *Les Fleurs du Mal,* for example, is written "in letters which, with each dawn, bloom and embellish the flowerbeds of utilitarian prose." And his immortal poems contain the same words as the poems of hacks. This linguistic democracy has led to the nearly universal misconception that the mere ability to read words qualifies one to read Baudelaire. Mallarmé complains that the most insensitive blockheads in France approach this great poet boldly, presenting "in lieu of a ticket, a page of the *ABC* book from which they learned to read." "Let us chance to whisper softly the names of Shakespeare or Goethe: immediately this buffoon lifts up his head with an air which implies 'Now this is my specialty'." As a remedy for this situation, Mallarmé suggests that poets invent for their exclusive use "an immaculate language—priestly formulae the arid study of which would blind the profane but would stimulate the patient predestined ones." And of course, not only language, but many other facets of the strenuous poetry of the best artists in the present dispensation derive from the poet's awareness that most of his contemporaries do not know how to read.

Mallarmé's Calvinist notion of reading is further distinguished in that it focuses on the reader as a solitary individual. A shift of emphasis from the common to the unique, from the community to the individual, is a major concomitant of the Reformation. Calvin's break with the medieval world centers in his insistence on the importance of the individual's responsibility to God. Vertical (man to God) relationships assume greater importance than horizontal (man to man) ones. The communion service, traditionally the core of the Christian service, loses its priority to the sermon. In Mallarmé, the Calvinist notion of reading features a reader who reads alone. Speaking of himself in the third person, Mallarmé opens one essay with these words: "A contemporary French poet who, for several reasons, takes no part in official displays of beauty would like now to continue along the lines of his daily task (which is the mysterious polishing of verse for lonely Celebrations)." The lonely celebrants are individual readers; they admit neither priest nor fellow communicant to their services.

Another analogy between Calvin's concept of worship and Mallarmé's concept of reading is the relative unimportance of place. The lonely celebrations can occur in a closet as well as (or better than) in a cathedral. In both the poet and the theologian, this seeming indifference to place is actually an internalization of place. Calvin's temple is the heart of the believer; Mallarmé's theatre, the mind of the reader. In an 1898 letter to the gifted Belgian poet Émile Verhaeren, Mallarmé describes this ideal sanctuary.

> I thought I would be seeing your *Dawns* on the Parisian stage this winter. But how glad I am now that the performance will be limited to the spiritual theater within ourselves, where the combination of our inner love of pomp and the splendid vigilance of our thought will present it in its most magnificent form.

This theatre of the mind, he says in the *Hamlet* review, is the prototype of all others. It is here that the solitary, anonymous, predestined reader in this present dispensation is able to experience the religious consolation available through poetry. (pp. 18-33)

A final point in the Calvinist notion of *Transposition* is that it does away with ceremonies, rituals, and performances. The lonely celebration in the sanctuary of the mind consists entirely of reading and meditation. It is only in meditation, which Mallarmé calls contemplation, that the essences available through art are distilled and embodied in Idea. In **"Hérésies Artistiques,"** even music, which technically speaking requires a performance, is spoken of in terms of a reading. There is no conductor, no orchestra; there is only the reader and the score. That this reader must be a specialist in an esoteric language has spared music the desecration which has been visited upon poetry.

> Let us casually open Mozart, Beethoven, or Wagner; let us cast an indifferent eye upon the first page of their work: we are seized by a religious wonder at the sight of these macabre processions of austere, pure, unknown symbols. And we close the missal which remains uncontaminated by any defiling thoughts.

Later in this essay, he compares reading poetry to "sight-reading" Verdi. Interestingly, most of Mallarmé's published comments on Wagnerian opera, including the famous **"Revery"** of 1885, were written from knowledge gained entirely through reading. According to Bradford Cook, "Only in the years following 1885 did he attend performances of Wagnerian opera and thus familiarize himself with the 'Master's' actual accomplishment." And, of course, in those remarks about seeing *Hamlet* and *Dawns* in the theatre of his mind, Mallarmé is speaking of reading the texts of those plays, in solitude, without distraction. There are no actors, there is no performance, except within the mind of the reader.

The Calvinist notion of *Transposition,* this expediency compelled by the fallenness of the reader in the present dispensation, does not conflict with the Catholic notion of reading outlined earlier in this paper. There are analogies between poetry and religion throughout Mallarmé's career. In truth, these views are complementary; and both are embedded in the analogies between poetry and religion that run throughout his career.

Two generalizations emerge from a consideration of Mallarmé's scattered references to these analogies. The first is that the early discussions focus on the Calvinist view of *Transposition;* the late discussions, ostensibly contradicting but not disowning the Calvinist view, focus on the Catholic view. This corresponds to the fact that in the earlier discussions Mallarmé was struggling with the practical problems of a poet in the present age; whereas in the later discussions, he comes to be more and more interested in the ideal, realized in the past and hopefully realizable in the future. A second generalization is that the earlier references to the analogies tend to assimilate both the other arts and religion into poetry (performance into non-performance), whereas the later references tend to assimilate poetry into the performing arts and religion (non-performance into performance). In other words, the Calvinist view treats music, drama, and religion as if they were poems to be read, but the Catholic view treats poetry as if it were a spectacle or a ritual to be performed.

That poetry can exist in the present dispensation only as a minority religion practiced by aristocrats troubled Mallarmé deeply. Art's raison d'être is that it follows Catholicism in enabling the masses to cope with the "exterior silence," with death and nonexistence. The survival tactics of the poet in this "make-everything-clear-and-easy era" by-pass the common needs which not only gave birth to religion but which justify its continuance. But even in this great "Between," as Heidegger calls an era between the demise of the traditional god and the advent of his successor, the needs of the people persist. Mallarmé suggests that these needs can presently be satisfied through drama and music. His admiration for Wagnerian opera with its marriage of myth and music is based on the conviction that it can serve in the present as a religion for the people. His revery on Wagner begins with the reflection that, although poetry with her majestic ceremonies is in the present a "Chimaera-Who-Cannot-Be," Wagnerian opera is already a reality and is meeting the needs of the people.

> For the second time in history, the people (first Greek and now German) can borrow sacred feelings from the past and look upon the secret of their origins, even as that secret is being acted out. Some strange, new, primitive happiness keeps them seated there before that mobile veil of orchestral delicacy, before that magnificence which adorns their genesis. Thus, all things are restrengthened in the primitive stream.

In France, too, Mallarmé suggests in **Offices** (**"Sacred Pleasure"**), music is satisfying the religious needs of the people. The Sunday afternoon concert is taking the place of the Catholic Mass for many Parisians.

That Wagnerian opera and the symphony can minister to audiences which poetry cannot reach is due, Mallarmé explains in **"Sacred Pleasure,"** to the fact that collaboration in music does not require as much "lucidity" on the part of the audience.

> The sovereign-bow beating the first measure would never fall were it necessary that at this special instant of the year the chandelier in the concert hall should represent by its multiple facets a lucidity of the public relative to what is about to take place.

(pp. 34-6)

Mallarmé's ideas on art and religion can now be expanded to include music (and/or drama), the religion of the present which, in contrast to poetry, is able to facilitate the "common functioning." These ideas are not, in the main, contradictory. When he execrates the general reader and calls art for all a heresy, he is speaking of this present dispensation. When he exalts the reader and calls art a splendid public ceremony, he is speaking of the future dispensation. When he turns from poetry to music, he is searching for a religion which will work in the present.

An elucidation of Mallarmé's ideas about art is helpful in deciphering his poems. **"Prose pour des Esseintes,"** for example, is at once an illustration and a description of some of the ideas I have presented. But a clarification of Mallarmé's views is valuable far beyond any light it sheds on his own poetry. His influence on modern European art in all media, but particularly on poetry, is enormous. Without Mallarmé, the finest poets of this century—Valéry, Rilke, Yeats, and Eliot—would have been, as we know them, inconceivable. The interesting fact, however, as Eliot has pointed out, is that the great modern poets were not greatly influenced by Mallarmé's poetry, but by his attitude towards poetry. If my dispensational reading of his aesthetic is valid, then a basic aspect of his thought has been ignored or misunderstood. In particular, Mallarmé's reputation as an elitist, based on what I have called his Calvinist expediency, has obscured the fact that at the heart of his aesthetic is an obsessive interest in what he calls the "common functioning." Many of his techniques, e.g., allusiveness, discontinuity, derive from his attempt to

deal with incompetent or fallen readers. The "immaculate language" for which he is famous (or infamous) was especially designed for double duty—to seduce competent readers and to repel incompetent ones. His ritualism derives from his conviction that art must ultimately be justified in terms of the "common functioning." An understanding of his attitude in these matters enlarges one's understanding not only of modern poetry, not only of Romantic poetry, but of the possibilities and limitations of all art. (pp. 37-8)

> *Jewel Spears Brooker, "The Dispensations of Art: Mallarmé and the Fallen Reader," in* The Southern Review, *Louisiana State University, Vol. XIX, No. 1, Winter, 1983, pp. 17-38.*

George Craig (essay date 1983)

[*In the essay below, Craig examines how Mallarmé's poetic technique defies readers' expectations and produces works that are ultimately ambiguous and elusive.*]

Mallarmé, one might say, stands in much the same relation to poetry as poetry itself does to other forms of writing: as locus of widespread, if various, readerly unease. There are quite specific reasons for this, in particular the confusion surrounding two notions of central importance in both: order and voice. In arguing here for a reappraisal of our relation to Mallarmé I shall therefore also be concerned with the second and more general relation.

But first, the unease itself. It reaches back, I would suggest, a long way both in the experience of individual readers and, on a different time-scale in cultural history. Written admissions of unease are rare on the readers' side, but the poets themselves have been aware of it for at least a century and a half. In calling poets 'the unacknowledged legislators of the world', Shelley is making a last-ditch stand in a battle which is virtually over; and if, typically, Hugo will put forward grander claims still (the poet as 'divin archet'), the clowns of Laforgue bring us nearer the truth and prepare us for Eliot's rueful recognition of the practice of poetry as 'a mug's game'. But if it would be impossible to map at once briefly and adequately the multiple determinants of this state of affairs, we can perhaps see farther in by way of something which everyone will have known in early schooldays: the obscurely discomfiting sight of the first anthology of poetry. However quickly we may have got over the discomfiture (and by no means everyone does get over it), the awareness of something disturbing was, I would argue, both accurate and instructive.

The crucial notion here is that of order. We learn to filter and organize the perceptual chaos of infancy by a set of rules and conventions. The benefits need no rehearsing: we have begun to master the universal shorthand, are on a par with other people. But how quickly we forget that it is a shorthand, an arbitrary simplification for our local advantage! In choosing to confer the name 'reality' on the yield of this perceptual organization we are of course being consistent. That is exactly what the organization exists to produce and confirm. But we are a long way from telling the whole truth. For any of us caught in, say, the toils of nightmare or the accelerations of desire, the signals, intensely real, are not so easily reducible. The actual world, our actual selves are, such moments remind us, far larger than the shorthand allows.

Unsurprisingly, very similar processes are at work in our evolving relation with language, although that brings with it a further complication. For while language too first reaches us as the world does (in this case as random noise which, we gradually learn, can be classified, tamed, used), it is also and already, in some peculiar way, part of us. And of course it is language too which carries and gives form to all our categorizings. Is it, then, the shorthand of all our shorthands? In one obvious sense the answer must be 'yes': rule-bound and rule-creating, it charts the limits of our understanding and frames the hypotheses by which those limits can be pushed farther. But, notoriously, its efficacy is highest where the degree of connection with the specifically human is lowest—in, say, mathematics; and it stumbles, wanders as soon as our pulses begin to race.

The suggested dichotomy (between most human and least human) would carry with it an important connotation: that of degree of order in the phenomena encountered. But the point is not so much whether there *is* order in nature as that we have long ago decided to put value on the *perceiving* of order. From this has come the ideal of a rigorous and ordered language in which to present that perceiving. But, by an indescribable sleight-of-brain, the actual or potential existence of this ideal language came to be the guarantee of that order, indeed the perfect representation of that order. The supreme achievement of rationality became, not this or that process of thought, but the vocabulary and syntax in which these were expressed. By easy stages we arrive at the ultimate paradox by which order-as-language addresses itself confidently to the phenomenon called human creativity.

If one aspect of order is this strange see-sawing between language and the perceivable world, another is its implied opposition to chaos, disorder, and unmanageable diversity. The see-sawing is, one might suggest, bearable for as long as what is stressed is the other term in the opposition. That the natural world should be primarily experienced by us as chaotic seems to offer a constantly renewed justification of ordering at any cost. The unimaginable diversity of language itself seems to offer similar justification—and similar encouragement to overlook the language-based conception of order.

But the fact of poetry, in its immemorial if variously regarded differentness, falls outside the quasi-universal opposition between ordered and chaotic. Poetry has at all times been located in one opposition or another. But however it is presented (as divine/oracular rather than human/transparent, as verse rather than prose, and so on), the accent in these oppositions is on its differentness, its exceptionality. And the exceptional has power to disturb. To that extent, it aligns itself with those other elements which excite as response the need to impose language-as-order. But the supreme subversiveness of poetry is that it deploys itself in a language which immediately reveals an utter orderedness. Here, then, is recognizably human language at work in all the territories where language-as-order has planted its colonizing flag, while seldom if ever recognizing that flag. The moment of unease that came with the first glimpse of the poetry anthology was no embarrassing, juvenile aberration. It was a sure intuition of the existence of a threat to normality and to what order always promises: control.

We do not yet know how to talk about poetry. We do not even know whether, to pick up another schoolchild's notion, we can or ought to talk about it, the great weight of the 'secondary literature' notwithstanding. What, though, we can hardly fail to know is that the central question of which these are versions cannot without dishonesty be shelved.

That question cannot be answered or even properly put in these pages. Perhaps I can come at it indirectly. Even for readers not deterred by the differentness of poetry, Mallarmé can be peculiarly daunting. Taking that as a positive rather than a negative indicator, we might say that if there *is* a way out of the trap of language-as-order, it must surely pass through him.

Mallarmé once wrote of the necessity of getting away from 'la direction personnelle, enthousiaste de la phrase'. What is at issue for him, in part at least, is the displacing of a particular limited and limiting conception of continuity: the tyrannical aspect of the sentence. That mattered not only because of the danger, as he saw it, of unsolicited confessional intimacies, nor even because, as a mode, it called for response in kind, for rival sentences, but because of the dishonest claim in the word 'direction'—that we steer it, as it might be along the slalom-run of dependent clause and punctuation to an ineluctable finishing-line. For in such a perspective, much of the reader's attention is drawn towards watching the execution of that run. Never mind the snow, the light, the cold, the inflections of sinew and joint—keep your eye on the posts, the finish, and the clock. But why must it be the one or the other? In one sense we know that it is not, but we behave as if it had to be. And of course it does have to be—sometimes. But there is room for that need and its satisfaction—when we are the skier or one of the judges, or have a bet on the race. As spectators, though, we are not *bound* to respect the either/or. Transposed into the world of words, the proportions are reversed. Here we are mostly performers, and for most of the time, in a highly rule-bound game: what Mallarmé called 'l'universel reportage'. Yet can we not, from within this, if only for moments at a time, go back before the game, nearer the total relation of man to word, word to man, of which that game is only ever a part?

Something of how Mallarmé set about answering the serious question of which I have given a trivial version can be suggested by a reading of two of his poems. The first is:

Autre Éventail
de Mademoiselle Mallarmé

O rêveuse, pour que je plonge
Au pur délice sans chemin,
Sache, par un subtil mensonge,
Garder mon aile dans ta main.

Une fraîcheur de crépuscule
Te vient à chaque battement
Dont le coup prisonnier recule

L'horizon délicatement.

Vertige! voici que frissonne
L'espace comme un grand baiser
Qui, fou de naître pour personne,
Ne peut jaillir ni s'apaiser.

Sens-tu le paradis farouche
Ainsi qu'un rire enseveli
Se couler du coin de ta bouche
Au fond de l'unanime pli!

Le sceptre des rivages roses
Stagnants sur les soirs d'or, ce l'est,
Ce blanc vol fermé que tu poses
Contre le feu d'un bracelet.

The heading of the poem—not the title alone, but the ascription as well—seems to run counter to what I have been saying of Mallarmé in general. The double identification, of object and person, appears wholly unambiguous: this is a poem about something, offered to someone. The pointing, moreover, itself raises other discursive probabilities: 'Éventail' connoting the comparatively trivial world of the decorative, 'autre' the existence of a range of poems concerned with such a world; while the proper name, fusing the poet with the family man, hints in another way at the heavily defined. Add only that these connotations get empirical confirmation in even the quickest survey of the poems and we seem to have a poetry which is uncomplicated in a sense disconcertingly different from that which I was describing a moment ago. But rather than deal straightaway with the doubts raised, let us see them as opening a bracket, and find out what the experience of the poetry does towards closing it.

Almost at once the issue of syntax, and of our expectations in respect of it, is posed: to the 'O rêveuse' which makes still more explicit the notion of direct address is added the clause of purpose beginning 'pour que je . . .'. Such a clause calls for resolution, which duly appears in the later imperative 'sache' and its complement; so that there is already in the poem, whatever else may be true, an unarguably familiar structure. This matters precisely because other elements of the stanza are by no means so easily placeable. If, for example, the first line falls, in terms of sense, within the boundaries of the manageable (the strong and strongly-marked verb, following on the invocation, can all the same be provisionally accommodated without strain), the second offers no *certain* support to that sense. This still tolerable weakening of the line of sense must be carried forward to the third line, where there is simultaneously a confirmation of 'normality' (the syntactic catching-up of 'pour que' that is offered by 'sache') and a reinforcing of uncertainty (where does this 'mensonge' come from? How is its ellipsis related to the apparent clarity of 'pour que je plonge'?). Then, in the final line—the point at which, since the whole stanza forms a sentence, the dual expectation is of syntactic completion and of resolution of sense—we are allowed only a partial easing of uncertainty. Thus, one of the incidental consequences of the mention of Mademoiselle Mallarmé is the risk of presuming that we know who 'je' is; until the 'mon aile' of the last line suggests abruptly that the presumption is wrong; that 'je' is the fan, not the poet-father. But that glimpsed possibility

leaves the sense just as elusive: the plunge of a fan into trackless bliss challenges understanding; and 'mensonge' is still there to nag at our attention.

But how is it that such low-level gropings are admissible in the first place? It is after all a commonplace that poetry does not have to tell simple, sensible stories. The answer, I think, comes from the combination of two of the aspects of the poem: the constraining force of the very noticeable syntax in the first stanza; and the tonality of the whole opening. The first of these I have already looked at. In the second it is not hard to see how expectations as to level of sense are set up. The sort of configuration made by 'Éventail'—'Mademoiselle'—'rêveuse'—'pur délice'—'subtil'—'dans ta main' (a configuration taking up indeed most of the opening) imposes associations of the gentle, the delicate, the 'feminine'. These can only be magnified by the plea in 'O' and 'sache', to which is subordinated the one active verb, 'plonge'. Not only, the suggestion runs, is it a mild world, it is one in which we know our way about: the world of untroubled and well-turned compliments to young ladies. 'Knowing our way about' means knowing, being able to predict, the sense and the story. Indeed, however many other approaches to poetry we may have learned, it is difficult to imagine how the suggestive force of the configuration could *not* edge us towards considerations of story. In this perspective, the elements which do not so easily fit ('subtil mensonge', and, even more appropriately in the light of my 'knowing our way', 'sans chemin') are provisionally shelved.

For the following stanza opens with words which at once seem to confirm the possibility of story:

Une fraîcheur . . .
Te vient à chaque battement

Here the sense, even closer now to the 'universel reportage', makes easier still the shelving of the (in any case not very troubling) 'de crépuscule'. The result is that by the time we reach the second half of the stanza there has been an accumulation of the familiar, the manageable, the predictable. These two lines forming an unimpeachably ordinary prose sentence—so that the 'dont' that opens the third line has been thoroughly prepared—we are the less ready for the difficulty that begins now. Proportions are at once reversed; only 'délicatement' belongs to the predictable, while the other words, although individually untroubling, form a collocation charged with uncertainty. But these lines too are syntactically 'normal': suddenly the whole assumption of predictability is in doubt. What had been the guarantee that here was no great matter now acts as a warning signal, and not about these two lines only, but about all that has gone before. Syntax has moved in one direction and then in another. Across the doubt this creates flashes a memory of fanning with its characteristic *va-et-vient,* direction and counter-direction. Retrospect and reordering of perception are urgent, as always when we feel we have been incautious or complacent.

Such shifts of feeling, as I have tried to indicate, are not large reworkings but sudden glimpses, momentary inflections of attention. If retrospect is called for, that call may not be so easy to answer, for the doubt strikes forward as well as backward; and the feel of that doubt, of the sudden disturbance of certainty, is caught in the opening line of the next stanza, where 'Vertige!' is followed by the 'voici que' demonstrative of imminence, and issues in 'frissonne'. It is as if the line were a commentary on this moment of readerly experience. Yet, even as this convergence of the poem's and the reader's movement imposes itself, the drive of the syntax again introduces new and different directions of attention: the demonstrative, the simile, the dependent noun-clause, the explanatory discrimination ('Ne . . .ni . . .'). The first two lines are stamped with positives (the tremble at the edge of action), so that even the comparison, although it is not in any ordinary sense clear, promotes the intimate reaching of 'baiser' over the possible abstractness of 'L'espace'. But at the farthest point of reach the sign changes: the positive of 'naître' undermined in advance by 'fou', then issuing in the negatives of 'personne' and the double impossibility of action. For all that, there is no mere cancelling-out. The subordinate clause does not unwork the excitement that is in the main clause, while the negative itself keeps promise alive: the stanza ending with the hopeful rather than the hopeless. What comes through is above all potentiality. The negative, in fact, is read as a positive, the tone and rhythm of the first two lines ensuring that it is the excited and not the dire associations of 'fou' that dominate.

It is here that physical realities, hinted at in 'l'espace', assert themselves, linking the charge of the stanza itself both to the organization of the poem and to the nature of fans. Here, at the centre of the poem, is a stanza which instances also the play of contraries which lies behind the name 'fan': is it something open or closed? moving or still? waving outwards or inwards? functional or decorative? The only answer to these is that it will be either or both, all or any. Along the line of time there will, inevitably, recur a moment when it is exactly poised between these possibilities; as a ball thrown high into the air will hang for a moment at the top of its curve, neither rising nor falling. In that moment the possibilities are simply there; the realizing of them lying before and after. It is, of course, a version of the familiar half-full/half-empty, the tone making clear why it is the favourable and not the unfavourable view which suggests itself.

And not only the tone. As I have said, this is the centre of the poem. What we read has itself at this point a before and an after. The uncertain directions of the earlier stanzas pass through this point, with as many stanzas to come. Now the 'vertige' is more than an excited reminder of external realities (fans and their possibilities); it is a signal of perceptual ambiguity: a simultaneous and contradictory determining of what is being looked at. There is no question of being able to choose; both perspectives are given. Our own seeing 'ne peut jaillir ni s'apaiser'.

If the first two stanzas seem to have triggered mainly the work of eye and brain, that too will be changed in the two remaining. Beyond the questions pushed at that kind of understanding lies now an insistent preoccupation with sound. The sonority of 'Sens-' ushers in a rush of closed vowel sounds, so that the the mouth, operating over the very narrow range from 'ou' to 'i', almost finds ease in the

third line before gathering to the final position of 'unanime pli'. Hardly has the mouth followed this closing of the fan than, with the first line of the final stanza, it must open to accommodate the long sounds of 'rivages roses' and 'soirs d'or' before closing again, almost with a snap, on 'ce l'est', to stay there, apart from the moment and movement of 'poses', till the end.

But even as the sound forces us in our turn into this re-enactment of opening and closing, we are taken out of mere movement. The 'blanc vol fermé' *is* ('ce l'est')

> Le sceptre des rivages roses
> Stagnants sur les soirs d'or . . .

—the burst of colour of the unfolded fan against its white form folded, tucked away, at the end, against another brightness as the offering is completed. The fan has been instanced, decorated, waved, closed, returned. It has also been created.

Even within the tiny compass of this poem—one sees perhaps why Mallarmé accepted so readily the apparent constraints of the *vers de circonstance*—it is possible to understand what the poet meant in the famous reproof made to Degas, when the painter, who had literary aspirations, complained of having too many ideas: 'Mais Degas, ce n'est point avec des idées que l'on fait des vers. . . . C'est avec des mots.'

The other poem by Mallarmé which I want to consider will allow us to take further something of what has been glimpsed in the first: the revaluing of the word.

> Ses purs ongles très haut dédiant leur onyx,
> L'Angoisse, ce minuit, soutient, lampadophore,
> Maint rêve vespéral brûlé par le Phénix
> Que ne recueille pas de cinéraire amphore
>
> Sur les crédences, au salon vide: nul ptyx,
> Aboli bibelot d'inanité sonore,
> (Car le Maître est allé puiser des pleurs au Styx
> Avec ce seul objet dont le Néant s'honore).
> Mais proche la croisée au nord vacante, un or
> Agonise selon peut-être le décor
> Des licornes ruant du feu contre une nixe,
>
> Elle, défunte nue en le miroir, encor
> Que, dans l'oubli fermé par le cadre, se fixe
> De scintillations sitôt le septuor.

With this sonnet we find ourselves on the farther side of an invisible line, of which **'Autre Éventail'** seemed to set us on the nearer. Here are neither title nor dedication, no semblance of direct address, no given theme—object or notion—which words might embroider or rework. Only the sonnet structure connects these words with anything other than themselves, and that connexion is not of itself immediately enlightening. We are faced with this ordering of these words: no more and no less.

This dual reality—the individual words and their ordering—is strongly felt from the beginning. Countless poets before Mallarmé have written poems without titles, but have, on the whole, resolved the difficulty this creates by the careful pointing of the opening words; we are not long left in doubt as to tone, preoccupation, level. No such easing-in occurs with the Mallarmé poem. With our attention necessarily directed at these first indicators, what we find is a manifest sequence (eight successive words) which hints, simultaneously and disquietingly, at the possibility that that is the only kind of sequence they form: that, for example, the first five—mainly monosyllabic and requiring separate and careful enunciation—are in fact discrete: five juxtaposed words. It is no more than a hint, no doubt, but the fact that there can be even that is extraordinary enough. Nor is this merely some subjective quirk related only to the apparent impenetrability of the words. It is of the nature of any genuinely revolutionary writing that its power to surprise comes at least as much from what we had presumed was familiar as from anything previously unknown. Thus here what we are brought up against is the conventionality of print: the extent to which earlier writing has accustomed us to presuming that we can ignore the gaps between words, treating them as no more than instances of technical practice. Such gaps, within the convention, would be discounted from the point of view of understanding, so that what we read forms a continuum. The manifest patterning of poetry, that is, however elaborate it may be, begins on the farther side of this assumed continuity. The shadow-possibility that the first five words of the poem might *not* cohere, might put in doubt the assumed continuum, is profoundly disturbing. The usual response to disturbance at this level—that of fundamental assumptions—is to pass quickly over it in the hope of subsequent explanation or relief. But such cheatings are not done without cost, and the cost is in this case a radical uncertainty, however brief, about the notion 'poem'. If the familiar lay-out is not after all a guarantee, there are no safe presuppositions: there will or will not be a poem, according as our unprepared connexion with its words will issue in the one or the other conviction. We live in fact an acute version of a difficulty most of us will have run into in mild form: the moment when, faced with the leisured authoritativeness that marks the opening lines of so many mainstream novels of the nineteenth century, we wonder if this time 'It's going to work'—if we are going to get farther than deciphering these confidently-offered, informative words. But delay over accepting the rhetoric of someone's story is one thing; not knowing what there might be to accept is quite another. The warning flash may be brief; it is also decisive. Disturbance in the conditions of relation means that things can never quite be the same again.

As if the poet were colluding with us in the need to get beyond this initial disarray, the words from now on push syntactic considerations at us: that is, they reintroduce expectations of continuity. There is the heavily-marked clause-structure, itself so close to a line-by-line utterance that, taken with the patterning of rhyme, it seems inevitable that the first sentence will end with the first stanza. This time it is not external convention but an apparent feature of the poem which reveals expectation by not meeting it. And, within the larger pattern, similar difficulties occur in particular moments. We are faced with uncertainty as to which way words point. Is 'très haut' an absolute adverbial phrase? an adverbial phrase modifying 'dédiant'? Is 'ce minuit' an adverbial phrase of time or does it stand in apposition to 'L'Angoisse'? It is the very obtrusiveness of the syntax which pushes such questions at us, and that obtrusiveness is intensified by yet another conventional sys-

tem: punctuation. Once awareness of this last has reached the surface, the evidence already picked up in pre-verbal scanning pours in. All through the poem the resources of punctuation are deployed to draw the eye, to offer what seem undeniable proofs that here are exposition, explanation, argument even. Already the commas of the first lines are working towards this, while in the second stanza the colon, with its implied announcement of summary or restatement, takes the process farther and leads on to the parenthesis which, taken together with its opening word, offers the very image of retrospective clarification.

But, in more than one sense, nothing is clarified. The two conventional systems, syntax and punctuation, combine to create an illusion: the illusion of declarative writing. But 'create' telescopes two processes: the functioning of the poem as we, more or less dimly, perceive it, and the functioning of acquired expectation which accompanies and in some measure shapes that perceiving. That measure varies, of course, from person to person, but it would be a safe guess that for many of those who back away uneasily or resentfully from Mallarmé, it is high. The projection of expectation, if followed by a measure of satisfaction, results in a form of *control,* in which the reader's imagination can *contain* the offered verbal experience. If Mallarmé's poetic drive is towards what is elliptically described in the famous 'disparition élocutoire du poète, qui cède l'initiative aux mots', he is, almost by definition, working from the poet's end against readerly control, containment. In crude form the contention would be that if the poet is neither claiming nor aiming at control of his words, there is little room for the reader to do so. But it is important too to refine the notion, winnowing it for example of any suggestion that implies challenge, competition, provocation between writer and reader. Mallarmé is indeed a deliberate writer; it is his readers who so often have taken as the primary connotation of that word 'wilful'. The reasons for that are interesting but need not detain us here. Mallarmé's position does not need to be imagined from the outside by a sympathetic observer: it is given in the implications of his words—his talk of yielding 'l'initiative *aux mots*'. Such yielding is not easily achieved: what word-lover has not experienced the fantasy of supreme control, has ever not minded how the words come out? Before he can speak of the 'disparition élocutoire du poète', Mallarmé has had to come to terms with the impossibility of that fantasy. The late poetry starts from there, but it reveals also the stages by which the new understanding was reached. The ostentatiously elaborate syntax and punctuation transpose both the fantasy and the ordering which will supersede it. The more the eye can discern grammatico-logical structure ('Ses . . .ongles . . .dédiant, . . .soutient . . .maint rêve . . .: nul ptyx . . .(car . . .) . . . mais . . . un or agonise . . . peut-être . . . encor que . . . se fixe . . . le septuor'), with its consequent promise of positive and classifiable semantic yield, the more it picks up of counter-evidence. Here is the *show* of statement, deliberate, ornate—but no statement. Once again the elements of an over-all positive issue in a discovered negative. What happens at the general level happens too in the detail. Still following 'normal' patterns, the eye detects the progressive elimination of objects, both in the ordinary and in the grammatical sense. 'Rêve vespéral' is already insubstantial enough as object of 'soutient', but it itself is 'brûlé' by the mythical 'Phénix', the ashes ungathered in any 'amphore'—and the ambiguous direction of the 'pas' removes both—on 'crédences' which are in a 'salon vide'. The problematic 'ptyx' has already been preceded by 'nul'; its appositional complement, the 'bibelot', is 'aboli' and is in any case of 'inanité'; 'le Maître' has gone, and gone moreover to the 'Styx', while the 'seul objet' is proudly accepted by 'le Néant'. The 'croisée' is 'vacante', its transparency in any case only near 'un or' which 'agonise' in ways which 'peut-être' correspond to a 'décor' made of mythical creatures (one, the 'nixe', so tenuous as to be 'défunte', and then only in a 'miroir') while the sole contrast is offered in the 'oubli fermé par le cadre', where what 'se fixe' is in perpetual movement.

Here, then, is no mere gesture against the hegemony of 'reportage' and its preferred mode, the sentence. Here the threefold convention—syntax, punctuation, dictionary meaning—is made to carry and enact, in the most public way possible, the point-for-point reduction of its presumed force.

If that were all that it was, it would already be a brilliant virtuoso achievement, a 'straight' version of 'Jabberwocky'. But the invoking of expectation and its subsequent frustrating are only a part of the whole: a condition of reading, not the reading itself. I have, for example, kept to questions of eye and brain, and moreover so handled these that what emerges is—nothing. But the eye does not *only* supply matter for classification according to preestablished habits. The manifest elimination of attestable objects does not prevent the appearance of other kinds of object. Logicians may remind us that sentences such as 'Unicorns do not exist' do not themselves allow us to infer that since 'unicorns' is the subject of the verb, they do after all exist. Theirs is pre-eminently the world of 'reportage'; we are not in that world now. Yet this is more than a concession to 'poetic licence', to implicit or explicit assumptions that in the nursery-world of poetry—unlike the serious, grown-up world—anything goes. Such judgements can arise only where the judges know already what the rules of the discourse are, and therefore what constitutes infraction of them. Such confidence is hardly conceivable outside certain kinds of 'applied' discourse: for, example the language of what is called the 'hypothetico-deductive'. But it is a philosopher who reminds us that 'The world is all that is the case' [L. Wittgenstein, *Tractus Logico-Philosophicus*, 1961], and it is very much the case that, outside the 'applied' discourses, we do not have a single sayable view of words and our relation to them. A particularly relevant intermediate example is offered to us by another philosopher, J. L. Austin [in his *How to do Things with Words*, 1971], in his concept of 'performative utterance' and its illumination of some of the things we *do* with words, of language as a form of action. In this perspective it should be immediately apparent that Mallarmé is not concerned with this or that *kind* of discourse, but with discourse itself, with *words*.

Thus, while 'Phénix', 'ptyx', 'Styx', and 'nixe' have, each in its way, connotations of unreality, they are no more—or less—unreal *in this particular verbal world* than 'ongles',

'bibelot', or 'feu'. Such is that verbal world, in fact, that the reader experiences what seem at first like simultaneous and opposite movements of meaning, in which the *apparently* manageable ('ongles', etc.) words, those with real-world referents, are invested with strangeness, while the problematic 'ptyx' and its like become increasingly natural, almost necessary.

But this is merely an approximation, a stage on the way. In an over-all context of strangeness and uncertainty we are, after all, less easily daunted by words which are self-evidently out of the ordinary; much more troubling is the weakening of our expected hold on 'ordinary' words. Why are 'onyx', 'crédences', and 'salon' not more reassuring? Why, despite the explicit negative, does 'nul ptyx' both catch the eye and forge a reality there and then? Why do the 'licornes ruant du feu contre une nixe' establish scene and presence in ways that 'croisée', 'miroir', and 'cadre' do not? Of course, in this last example, the first is more 'dramatic' than the other three; but why should effects of décor be, within the mystery, more powerful than components of the total setting?

It is surely residual attachment to the referential that prompts such questions. We accommodate faster the strangeness of the strange than the strangeness of the presumed familiar. It simply takes longer for us to realize that the strangeness does not lie in 'what is evoked'; it is a *verbal* strangeness. We are moving through a mysterious yet supremely ordered assemblage *of words,* not a coded transcription of something else. It is the urge to decode, to 'know', which blocks understanding. We have been, in spite of intuitions of a different reality, trying to look through the glass *at* something. What if we attended to the glass?

Of course attention, in this context, is much more than just looking. If the true focus is the words, the eye can do only part of the work for us. Separate and connected, as themselves and as part of groupings, they reach us along several lines of awareness, and outstandingly that of sound. In trying to tease out patterns of response I have artificially kept the stress on the activities of eye and brain in order to hunt down the 'demon of analogy'. But, as any reader's eye will long since have reported, much of what is going on involves the ear. The opening monosyllables, then the rush of commas, already force on us awareness of sound-making as a constantly recurrent activity. The play of these open and closed vowels, short and long syllables combines with punctuation to connect these continual separate sounds with the necessarily continuous reality of rhythm. After the careful pointing of the opening two lines, that connexion is put to the test: the reader is launched now, without the explicit indicators of punctuation, on the pursuit of a rhythm which is not given but which is manifestly there. Syntax, too, with its strong suggestion that the stanza will form a complete sentence, creates a dissonance with the invitation to continuity that comes in the succession of predominantly long vowel-sounds bridging first and second quatrains:

> . . . ciné*raire* amph*ore*
> Sur les créd*ences* . . .

Punctuation reappears with increased force, after the

abrupt closure of 'vide', to impose a break in the rhythm, a break made still more noticeable by what follows: the immediate return, phonetically irresistible, to detached, self-enclosed monosyllables in 'nul ptyx'. Rhythm, sound, syntax, and punctuation all converge to focus the greatest possible attention on two words which themselves uncompromisingly reintroduce the dimension of ordinary meaning. Eye and ear are made, in the framing of the other words, to identify as central two words which, in the event, simultaneously name and deny the existence of an enigmatic object.

It is a bold stroke, and therefore, inevitably, heavy with risk. Here the risk is that the challenge to familiar modes of apprehension will be felt as aggressively, arrogantly perverse. But Mallarmé is not the unsmiling iconoclast. If the visible and audible patterning sets 'nul ptyx' apart, it is only for a moment; the very possibility of aggression is deftly turned away by the hint of self-mockery in the line that follows:

> Aboli bibelot d'inanité sonore.

It is all at once clear that even the elaborate pointing that detached 'nul ptyx' and set it at the centre of attention is a device consciously invoked rather than a process the experienced reader detects. Once more expectation is frustrated: the object which is really set up for attention is made up of the two elements taken together:

>   . . . nul ptyx,
> Aboli bibelot d'inanité sonore

Of course this object, so far from merely instancing a perverse (as it might be, satirical) demonstration, has an excitingly rich autonomy. To the monosyllabic difficulty of 'nul ptyx' answers, to begin with, the polysyllabic play of the following line. Then, within that line, we are forced up against the rapidly-changing sound-pattern of the syllables: the reverse symmetry of increasing closure ('aboli') and increasing openness ('Bibelot'), with its parallel changes in pitch; the holding, for a single moment in a single word, of more closed and more open at the higher levels of pitch ('inanité'); the eventual release into 'sonore', with its long, low final. But, however absorbing these sound-values are, they do not, given that last word, allow attention to 'mere' sound: at the precise point where sound, its values and its pleasure, seems to claim the whole of our attention, meaning comes flooding back in. Independently of the sound, and with 'aboli' catching up the force of 'nul', the whole line might be a lightly deprecatory commentary on 'nul ptyx': something offered from the inside, the poet's end, which also anticipates one possible response from outside, from the reader.

But such a notion as 'independently of the sound' is absurdly artificial. How could any reader familiar with the sounds of French avoid the concentration of attention these syllables require, even in silent reading? By the time we reach these words, the possibility of innocence has gone: no reader can be *expecting* a line which aligns itself with any of his perspectives. On the contrary, what is unexpected is meaning. Indeed, so unexpected is it that what is thrust at us is a sense of how limited conventional 'meaning' is, how much a revaluing is needed. For it is ap-

parent now that meaning cannot be dismissed: this is not nonsense-verse. Nor is it merely the ingenious collocation of sounds and rhythms. Rather all these modes—not only those I have stressed but those too of sonnet form, the alexandrine, and typography—are deployed simultaneously. Only for compositor or proof-reader is there a clearly finite and static object, fourteen rows of black marks on a page, with calculated gaps between marks and rows. Once past this visual appraisal what the reader finds is movement: processes *in play*. It is not that it is difficult to apprehend these processes. The point is simpler: it is *impossible* to hold them. Wherever we point our attention it will be to find pulls from other directions. The lamented Raymond Queneau offered a memorable example in a piece whose mock-serious tone can be guessed from its title, 'La Redondance chez Mallarmé' [*Bâtons, chiffres et lettres*, 1965]. In the poetry, he pretends to argue, the real work is done by the 'bouts-rimés', with the rest as mere dressing. The mock seriousness is exactly right. How can we not feel the drawing-power of those end-words: their -yx/-or(e) syllables, of course, but also the words themselves, and supremely 'sonore'/'s'honore'? But what is being mocked is not so much our inveterate habit of identifying a part and happily calling it the whole; rather it is our perceptual limitedness—the fact that we settle for less because we are aware of the more we cannot manage. While the sounds move through their intricate pattern of interrelatedness, the printed symbols follow theirs, while rhythm and the conventional systems play across both. The printer establishes fixity; the reader finds elusiveness.

But the tone of all this is crucial too. I spoke a moment ago of processes 'in play', and the ambiguity is much needed. Talk of 'perceptual limitedness' and we risk sliding into the safe but irrelevant ground of metaphysical argument. Mallarmé's defence of poetry is certainly serious enough in one major sense; but he himself discovers the dangers of 'seriousness', and notably how it restores the sovereignty of the discursive-analytic which is, for him, the most highly organized form of 'reportage'. Of the two possible ways round this—violence and play—he chooses the second. We have seen already, with **'Autre Éventail'**, how the apparently decorative, ceremonious, and limited concerns issue in something far beyond themselves. Here too something similar is at work: gleams of uncertain light in a dark space, part-familiar, part-tinged with the mystery the scarcely-lit always brings, so that intimations of strangeness are counterpointed by indications of ordinariness, enigmatic absences by the growing awareness of presence, death and oblivion by colour and movement. This dark space is not the pit of hell, but neither is it the antechamber of paradise. The delicate-stepping sounds and rhythms, the images of light and reflection, are indirect representations of multiple possibility: a moment in space and time—the moment before discovery, before certainty. That is why we cannot confidently decide on background and foreground, why 'décor' is not *mere* frame, rather the generator of reality. The play of possibility will be sustained to the end: the accumulated negative pressures in the tercets—'vacante', 'agonise', 'peut-être', 'défunte', 'oubli'—lead out on to something richer than resolution: the elusively contradictory positives of

> . . . se fixe
> De scintillations sitôt le septuor.

A supremely verbal creation ends on the connoting of another art. Here indeed is 'le vers qui de plusieurs vocables refait un mot total, neuf, étranger à la langue et comme incantatoire'.

We are back, then, in a world of total possibility: before understanding, before categorization, before sureness of discrimination. If Mallarmé, renouncing the gratifications of narcissistic display or obsessional control, is utterly concentrated on creating conditions in which there may be 'cette surprise de n'avoir ouï jamais tel fragment ordinaire d'élocution', what is wanted from our side is a comparable totality of attention. This is not to beg the question of our valuation of Mallarmé. What matters in the present argument is his exemplary force. What 'totality of attention' means in this context is something rather different, too, from more familiar expressions such as 'suspension of disbelief', with their connotations of readerly indulgence. Condescension is out of the question. We do not simply give our attention: it is elicited from us.

But attention to what? The answer lies neither in some imagined subservience to a pre-established design nor in the voluntary imposition of the reader's own. Both of these imply an eventual wholeness, a total continuity beyond the manifest discontinuities. Such a continuity is indeed, I believe, an inescapable intuition. But it is an intuition of a particular kind: comparable perhaps to that which we are given by the flash of lightning over a darkened landscape—a something glimpsed in all its detail, then swallowed up by deeper darkness. If we cannot simply reconstruct the glimpsed continuity, we need a new kind of attention. Only one, it seems to me, will do: performing. In practice, that means saying—but not just any saying.

Few things relevant to the literary have been so consistently and so grossly undervalued as reading aloud. We will all have been told at some time that it is a good thing to read a poem out before settling our judgement of it. But even for those dutiful enough to practise this there is the tacit assumption that it is no more than a preliminary. The (endlessly plausible) reasons for this derive from one founding error which we can best understand by singling out the two rationalizations which most commonly sustain it. One concerns the relation of eye and ear; the other concerns vocal performance.

Our perceptual limitations are such that we cannot give equal and simultaneous attention to the visual and the auditory. The psycho-physical conditions of the apprenticeship of reading (that is, making sense of marks on a page) ensure that the decisive relationship will appear to be that of eye and brain. Perceptual weakness is therefore compounded by cultural accident. We do of course learn subsequently that sound 'matters', but not how to accommodate its mattering. This is taken still further with poetry, where visual oddity (the shape on the page) and unpredictability of sense-sequence and emphasis command heightened eye-and-brain activity. Whatever ingenuities we may deploy in attending to what the eye reveals (from lay-out to image) or the ear admits (from rhythm to consonantal

or vocalic pattern), we cannot hold in a single moment even the particular reality that the poem has *for us*. In other words, we are aware of its eluding our control. But if poetry for ever evades our conscious knowing, we are not thereby prevented from being intensely involved with it. The powerful assent or revulsion, which at its most striking it evokes, arises from a different and far less easily describable kind of knowing: one where our sureness is fed by multiple reactions—bodily, intellectual, comparative, and so on. Such sureness is of decisive importance in the crucial areas of our action in the world: choosing, loving, confronting, creating. When we act on that sureness we are not discerning the patterns of our behaving, we are *in action*. Poetry, transposing those areas, calls for comparable action.

The apparently insoluble question of the simultaneous appeal to eye and ear is insoluble only as an either/or, and then only in the perspective of an ultimate possible 'knowing'. But we have no more to choose between 'knowing' and ignorance than we do between eye and ear. The kind of knowing which connotes control is not available, while the kind which connotes honesty of response in no way inhibits action. The eye-ear puzzle is not something to be resolved by unspoken, higher-order decision, but something to be lived. However confident we may be of our private reflections, the uttering of them reactivates fears of inadequacy; but utterance is central to all dealings among humans.

As for vocal performance, among the things that hold us back from reading aloud is the fear that our voices will not be good enough. But good enough for what? In one direction we contrast them unfavourably with the ostentatious splendours of the Great Actor's voice, in another, with the intuited diversity of the voice of the poem. Both these imply an ideal of performance. But if we defer to that, we by-pass the irreplaceable reality of our own relation to the poem. Indeed, our awareness of necessary imperfection, by excluding even the possibility of a rendering which could seem ideally satisfactory to ourselves as performers, makes irrelevant the skills of others.

Worries about voice (which, we continually need reminding, is not for any one of us a given, but rather a peculiar and provisional compromise-formation) have encouraged us to let ourselves off rather lightly. One has only to think of equivalent rationalizations in respect of writing ('It's so much better in my head'; 'Somehow it all gets distorted when I write it down') to remember that we have long ago seen their naive romanticism, which amounts to little more than 'I wish I could write perfectly'. To anyone offering this as a reason for inability to write about something that mattered to him or her we would have some highly practical things to say; they would certainly include the injunction to set aside the hope of 'perfect' performance, and to accept instead the inevitable partiality of our seeing.

When we read aloud, we are all amateurs. What is at issue is not performance but performing. For in any given reading we instance the extent to which we are prepared to reveal our relation to what is being read, and so allow a hint of what that relation is. The partial adequacy of our saying is our provisional resolution of the many contraries involved. It is in our reading aloud that all our hesitations and uncertainties gather: about our own voices, about authority, about control, about other people, and, of course, about the poem to be read. The critic-reader must venture out into a ground where he can have no uncontestable control, to give what is, in the strongest sense, our reading of the poem. We, too, like the poet, must reveal the nature of our venturing in a performing which we can never wholly order.

The result will not yet be a fully-formed criticism, but it will be the living centre from which a criticism can grow. What we lose by it is the illusion of knowing, of language-as-order. What we move towards is a very different kind of knowing, less abstract, more precarious, and far closer to the life of poetry: what Yves Bonnefoy has called 'un savoir passionnel' ['Acte et lieu de la poésie', reprinted in *Du mouvement et de l'immobilite de Douve,* 1970]. (pp. 559-72)

George Craig, "Reading Mallarmé," in The Modern Language Review, Vol. 78, No. 3, July, 1983, pp. 559-72.]

Emma Kafelanos on Mallarmé's poetic language:

[An] emphasis on the word, and the illumination that results from the juxtaposition of particular words, is what constitutes Mallarmé's method, and that of Dada and visual poetry as well. What we are dealing with above all . . . is a poetry of the substantive (a noun, or any other part of speech—a gerund for example—that is used as a noun). It is a poetry where the substantive reigns supreme, both in the originality of its selection and in its isolation from its context. In this poetry, substantives that at first seem unrelated to each other are juxtaposed together in such a way that their relationships gradually become apparent in the mind of the reader.

For Mallarmé, particularly in his later poetry, the doctrine of the purification of the word implies a conscious rejection of all the words (and ideas) that are customarily associated with that word—and, as a corollary, it equally implies a search for other words that bear no immediately obvious relationship to the word in question. His later poems thus can be viewed as a series of seemingly unrelated substantives; the semantic relationships between them, which always exist in the case of Mallarmé, can only be determined after careful study.

Emma Kafelanos, in her "Purification of Language in Mallarmé, Dada and Visual Poetry," in Visual Literature Criticism, edited by Richard Kostelanetz, Southern Illinois University Press, 1979.

Ramón Saldívar (essay date 1984)

[*In the essay below, Saldívar analyzes the nature of the self as presented in Mallarmé's* Hérodiade *and* "Soupir".]

The full range of experiments with the elements of poetry

that Stéphane Mallarmé undertakes in *Un Coup de dés* is already found in **"Soupir"** (April 1864) and the "Scène" of *Hérodiade* (October 1864). These early poems demonstrate Mallarmé's complex ambitions to compose in language the fiction of stable subjectivity. With the calculated irony he was to employ with sure effect in such later texts as **"Crise de vers,"** in a letter of October 1864 to Henri Cazalis Mallarmé announced that he had "enfin commencé mon *Hérodiade.* Avec terreur, car j'invente une langue qui doit nécessairement jaillir d'une poétique très nouvelle, que je pourrais définir en ces deux mots: *Peindre, non la chose, mais l'effet qu'elle produit.*" A few months later we find Mallarmé completely engaged in what was to become a lifelong effort to formulate this new language: "J'ai pris un sujet effrayant, dont les sensations, quand elles sont vives, sont amenées jusqu'à l'atrocité, et . . . ont l'attitude étrange du mystère." The mystery of the words he was writing was no less an effect of their subject than of their admitted aesthetic. On the face of it, one could hardly imagine a more futile project than the attempt to represent an object by evoking the traces of its former presence.

The significance of Mallarmé's concern with the "effect" of objects has been noted at least since Mallarmé's own statements in various letters concerning his implicit aesthetics have come to light. Statements such as the one in a letter to Eugène Lefébure, that "je n'ai créé mon oeuvre que par *élimination,*" support the contention that Mallarmé's creative act proceeds reductively, toward the essential core of truth which everyday language can only suggest. This fascination with absence is precisely what motivates the creation of both **"Soupir"** and *Hérodiade.* But whereas in **"Soupir"** the allegory of desire in a fictive garden seems to offer language as the privileged mediator between the present self and an absent other, the "Scène" of *Hérodiade* transforms those same elements into vehicles for the examination of the very concept of the self. In both poems a sexual drama becomes a ruse for the telling of the attempted recuperation of the self-consciously fragmented subject. By examining the functioning of metaphors related to consciousness in these two early poems, we can see how Mallarmé endeavors to accomplish the poetic project that was to preoccupy him to the end of his life: that is, the attempt to integrate from the radically dispersed elements of transient personality a vision of an organically and aesthetically cohesive self.

"Soupir" is one of the earliest and most elegant of Mallarmé's autumnal reveries. It consists of one sentence divided into two distinct sections of five lines each, the second of which is in apposition to the first:

> Mon âme vers ton front où rêve, ô calme soeur,
> Un automne jonché de taches de rousseur,
> Et vers le ciel errant de ton oeil angélique
> Monte, comme dans un jardin mélancolique,
> Fidèle, un blanc jet d'eau soupire vers l'Azur!
> —Vers l'Azur attendri d'Octobre pâle et pur
> Qui mire aux grands bassins sa langueur infinie
> Et laisse, sur l'eau morte où la fauve agonie
> Des feuilles erre au vent et creuse un froid sillon,
> Se traîner le soleil jaune d'un long rayon.

Several critics have pointed out that the suspension of the verb "Monte" until the beginning of the fourth line serves to obscure the relatively simple grammatical core of the poem. Beyond this syntactic subterfuge, however, the surface structure of the initial lines is clear enough: "Mon âme," the specular center of the poem, is focused on "ton front," a synecdoche for the "calme soeur." The second line of the poem, however, presents a major obstacle to our attempt to read the poem as the representation of a factual scene. The "automne jonché de taches de rousseur" is said to be dreaming, "vers ton front où rêve . . . / Un automne," and we can interpret the statement to mean either that the "automne" literally dreams or that it exists like a dream in the mind of the poet's "calme soeur."

Immediately after the verb "Monte," the poem sets aside the pretense of historical temporality and enters an overtly fictional moment, signaled by the rhetorical mode of the phrase "comme dans un jardin." To be sure, fiction is the context of all poetry, but the specific fictional character of the first three lines of **"Soupir"** is that they can be read as the representation of a factual situation. Lines four and five are no longer strictly referential; when the simile of line four intrudes into the narrative of the initial intersubjective event, it instigates a second narrative which establishes its story explicitly in the void between "mon âme" and "ton front." In doing so, this intruding simile prevents the story about the unification of self and nonself from being told. We can retain the notion of *mimesis* as "representation" only by acknowledging that in this text *mimesis* serves to represent something which does not lend itself readily to imitation: a platonic synthesis of a lover and his beloved. While the simile, "comme dans un jardin mélancolique," seems to repeat innocently the historical structure of the first three lines, it negates that structure to create an imaginary world of pure consciousness, all the while mirroring the ecstatic upsurge of desire, as the stream of white water at the garden's center parallels the rising motion of the poet's soul: "Fidèle, un blanc jet d'eau soupire vers l'Azur!"

Just as Aristotle would have us believe that the spoken word is simply a translation of a mental experience, Mallarmé's *persona* seems to want us to think that the language before us in the poem is simply an emblem of a state of mind. The "Octobre pâle et pur" and the "soleil jaune" of the second half of the poem acquire an apparently authentic existence because of their syntactic prominence, even though they are merely grammatical appositives to an initial simile. In their apparently complete and essential proximity, the poetic voice and the garden it names seem to coalesce. This illusion of a natural and unproblematic translation between *being* on the one hand and *mind* on the other is derived from the rational conception of the self as a temporally and spatially delimited entity, in itself an example of the absolute proximity of mind and being.

We can thus detect in the poem two distinct attitudes concerning the relationship between consciousness and the real world. The first attempts to represent the real world within consciousness, while the second, which takes precedence in the poem, presents the world in an immediate relation to consciousness. But when the poet's mimetic imagination attempts to convert this feeling of immediacy into a subjective presence, it only transforms the *nostalgia*

for wholeness, which does not exist objectively, into an object of perception. The discourse that is then to describe the metaphoric reconciliation of self and other, to mediate their difference, produces instead a text "about" the indifferent autonomy of the azure sky.

When, with the repetition of "Vers l'Azur" in line six, the poem turns away from the articulating voice and its desire, it is as if the poet has lost control of his fiction, and the poem becomes a self-generated apostrophe to "l'Azur," seeming to render the poet's presence superfluous. By line ten, the initial expression of a desire for unity between "mon âme" and "ton oeil angélique" has been thoroughly displaced and transformed by the figure which names the azure sky. Rather than creating a sense of unity, the poem has turned against the poetic persona, naming now the opposite of his desire in a series of displacements toward stasis.

The term *hypostasis,* used by Jacques Scherer [in his *L'Expression littéraire dans l'oeuvre de Mallarmé,* 1947] to designate the privileged grammatical categories of the noun and the singular form in Mallarmé's poetry, can lead us to some new perspectives concerning Mallarmé's notion of the impersonal self. Scherer notes that in Aristotle hypostasis denotes substance as opposed to contingency, force as opposed to action. In Plotinus hypostases are the purest and most abstract entities by which one attains Unity, and in contrast to the material world play a role similar to that of the Idea in the Platonic dialogues. Finally, in Christian theology the hypostases are the Three Persons distinguishable within the Divine One. All of these uses of the word, Scherer notes, share the value of an abstract notion to which one assigns privileged status and which is the metaphysical *origin* of the others. For Mallarmé, the hypostasis is never complete in the metaphysical sense; its meaning arises only by opposition to the persisting fragmentation of the material world. Thus Scherer is certainly correct when he claims that "comme le monde primitif, la grammaire de Mallarmé est bipolaire," but the nature of that bipolarity itself always remains at issue. Meaning arises for Mallarmé within a system of hypostasized oppositions when the poetic expression is able to create an organizing matrix for what are otherwise only self-negating polar differentials. By extension then, the hypostasis of the self is a *possiblity* of the fundamentally aesthetic character of the human imagination, which seeks to establish an original source, a ground for unity. And, I would argue, the meaning of Mallarmé's aesthetics of the self can be interpreted within this systematic framework of oppositions which his poems designate.

What seems important in **"Soupir"** then is the totality and the significance of the attempted reconciliation of the binary pair: the allegory of failure (the rising motion supplanted by the fall) must be seen in terms of the underlying opposition between "Mon âme" and "le ciel errant de ton oeil angélique." While the poet is impelled to react against the alluring eye by describing its effects on him, he knows beforehand that his description can never quite attain the vigor of the natural object, and that he can never free himself from its determining impact. The fact that the major portion of the poem is specifically in a figural mode, attempting to deal with the initial motion toward the "calme soeur," reflects the poet's clear consciousness of the need for mediation. The poem creates its resonant word to stand in place of the desired mute proximity between "Mon âme" and "ton front," and it is as if the metaphors of the second half of the poem offer their own sensory richness to reconstitute by substitution the absent other they cannot replace. Similarly, the poem is condemned to exist as a seductive, but persistently suspended, intent *toward* meaning, as the written text lies open before us to receive the seminal "blanc jet d'eau" of conceptualized meaning, which never comes.

The correlation of "âme," "l'azur," and "soeur" is not peculiar to **"Soupir"** but is instead a recurring motif. In **Symphonie littéraire,** for example, Mallarmé, writing about poetic failure, says:

> Muse moderne de l'Impuissance, qui m'interdis depuis longtemps le trésor familier des Rythmes, et me condamnes (aimable supplice) à ne faire plus que relire, . . . ces quelques lignes de ma vie écrites dans les heures clémentes où tu ne m'inspiras pas la haine de la création et le stérile amour du néant. Tu y découvriras les jouissances d'une âme purement passive qui n'est que femme encore, et qui demain peut-être sera bête.

Later, in a translation of Poe's "À Ma Mère," Mallarmé notes this curious relation among "mère," "âme," and a lover: "Ma Mère—ma propre mère, qui mourut tôt n'était que ma mère, à moi; mais vous êtes la mère de Celle que j'ai si chèrement aimée; et m'êtes ainsi plus chère . . . à mon âme, qu'à cette âme sa vie" (**Poëmes d'Edgar Poe**). Here and in other texts we see not only that "mère" and "soeur" are hidden within many references to "mon âme" but also that their disguised intervention seems to signal a certain nostalgia for pure beauty and the azure which is arrested by what the poet has enigmatically termed "l'Impuissance."

The word "soeur," too, is extremely important in Mallarmé's texts. In **Hérodiade,** for instance, one can find numerous formulations: "Et ta soeur solitaire, ô ma soeur éternelle, / Mon rêve montera vers toi." Here "soeur" is apparently a celestial object, perhaps a solitary star or the moon; moreover, in association with the cold, virginal solitude of the celestial wastes, the word also seems to acquire ontic status as a sign of the feminine essence.

At other points "soeur" corresponds to the poet's own self, to the feminine principle of his "âme," as, for instance, when Mallarmé writes in **Crayonné au théâtre:**

> Que souhaitaient-ils donc accomplir, ô mon âme? répliquai-je une fois et toujours interloqué puis éludant la responsabilité d'avoir conduit ici une si exquise dame anormale: car ce n'est pas elle, sûr! s'il y faut voir une âme ou bien notre idée (à savoir la divinité présente à l'esprit de l'homme) qui despotiquement proposa: "Viens."

The youthful being of beauty and the poet's *anima* combine in the figure of the "soeur" to express a tenuous association between the poetic consciousness and the frightening cosmos. This relation is again pointed out in **Médaillons et portraits,** where Mallarmé, writing about Villiers

de l'Isle-Adam, notes that "la Muse [n'est] pas autre que notre propre âme, divinisée!" As *das Weibliche,* that which is the source of life, "soeur," "âme," and "Muse" thus often join to represent a being close to the rhythms of nature, a part of the cosmic consciousness which the poet only partly contains within himself. This ideal woman's charms are ambiguously his own and those of poetry, but in most cases the poet remains suspended in the attempt to incorporate those rhythms into his own being.

"L'Azur," on the other hand, appears as a terrifying and haunting vacuum since it denotes nothing but its own vast blue depths. Mallarmé now offers us a variation on this theme, for in **"Soupir"** the autumnal "azur attendri d'Octobre pâle et pur" has fallen from its summer of power and possesses only a "langueur infinie." Its meagerness is marked by the sickly "jaune" which Mallarmé uses constantly to evoke the feeling of decay and stagnation, as in "les plis jaunes de la pensée" of the "Ouverture" to **Hérodiade.** Rather than exciting a revival of solar light and energy in the azure depths, the image of the weak "rayon" portends the total extinguishing of light and of the sun itself in the "grands bassins." Nevertheless, "l'Azur" persists as an other in triangular relation to the poetic consciousness and its object of desire. The ecstatic surge of one soul toward the angelic eye of another is repeated in the figure of stationary movement: the "jet d'eau" which surges toward "l'azur" but falls back on itself and remains perpetually suspended. In **"Soupir"** "l'azur" is necessary to mirror the ceremony of love, necessary to aid the poet in imaginatively realizing his erotic desire, and yet the trope which names "l'azur" fails to mediate between sensuality and a distant ideal of untouched beauty, instead taking control of the poem and turning it into a melancholy meditation on fall and decadence.

But what, one might ask, is the purpose of the poet's utterance? After an allusion to nostalgia or desire for an ambiguous feminine presence, the poetic voice creates a metaphysical garden in which the reader is asked to follow half-present rays of light over still water. In recalling his desire for the feminine, the persona necessarily invokes something which is not and cannot be authentically present. In the emptiness of the absence of his "soeur," and with the abdication of the "soleil jaune" from the azure sky, the poet's soul rises to an invocation of his *memory* of them in an attempt to fill the void, while still realizing the impossibility of that task. In **Symphonie littéraire,** a text contemporaneous with **"Soupir,"** Mallarmé offers one possible solution to the problem posed in **"Soupir":** "Donc je n'ai plus qu'à me taire,—non que je me plaise dans une extase voisine de la passivité, mais parce que la voix humaine est ici une erreur, comme le lac, sous l'immobile azur que ne tache pas même la blanche lune des matins d'été, se contente de la refléter avec une muette admiration que troublerait brutalement un murmure de ravissement." **"Soupir"** might thus be read as an allegorical expression of the conflict between a self which recognizes its temporal and metaphysical constraints and a rhetorical strategy which attempts to turn away from the recognition of its inability to voice the unification of self and other. But while **"Soupir"** only leads us up to the discovery that "la voix humaine est ici une erreur," and that consequently it can only reflect *mediate* experience, the later poems fully investigate that blank space of mute admiration which the impersonal human voice creates. Desire itself, as intentional structure, is superseded there by metaphoric categories which attempt to lure poetic language into becoming a theatrical *scène* of mediation between a present fictional subject and its absent object of desire. Having realized the limitations of poetic expression, Mallarmé is now ready to come to *Hérodiade,* where the problematic categories of self-creation named in **"Soupir"** are incorporated and transformed, but still not strictly resolved.

That *Hérodiade* evokes a cult of virginity, the heroine's desire to open herself before temporality while simultaneously longing for static purity, is suggested by the images reflected in the mirrorlike fountain in Hérodiade's garden and by the clusters of precious stones which adorn her body:

> Le blond torrent de mes cheveux immaculés
> Quand il baigne mon corps solitaire le glace
> D'horreur, et mes cheveux que la lumière enlace
> Sont immortels. O femme, un baiser me tûrait
> Si la beauté n'était la mort . . .
> Calme, toi, les frissons de ta sénile chair . . .
> Aide-moi, puisqu'ainsi tu n'oses plus me voir,
> A me peigner nonchalamment dans un miroir.
>   (*Hérodiade*)

The thematic association between "Hérodiade" and her "miroir" will gradually become explicit, but here in our first glimpse of Hérodiade, she acquires metaphorically the characteristics of the sighing "jet d'eau" of **"Soupir."** Winter has begun to supplant autumn, and "l'Azur attendri d'Octobre pâle et pur" has been transformed into "la lourde prison de pierres et de fer." The categories of natural flux which in **"Soupir"** had formed the basis for the recognition of the problematic status of the self before nature are now replaced by metaphors of consciousness and temporality, which gradually force the confrontation of self-understanding before the mirror. Even Hérodiade's actions, as she stands before the fountain stripping petals from a lily, prefigure the coming glimpse of her spiritual undressing. And finally, as in **"Soupir,"** the self-reflection, Hérodiade's melancholy turn toward introspection, occurs "Comme près d'un bassin dont le jet d'eau m'accueille." After the "rêverie" of indolence by this new metaphoric fountain, Hérodiade approaches an even clearer reflecting surface and begins to comb herself "nonchalamment dans un miroir." Leaving nature—which has evoked feelings of separation, distance, and a sense of futility in attempting to bridge the gap between self and other—we now enter a scene where the activities of self-consciousness and self-creation are more explicitly the sources of anxiety:

> Assez! Tiens devant moi ce miroir.
>   O miroir!
> Eau froide par l'ennui dans ton cadre gelée
> Que de fois et pendant des heures, désolée
> Des songes et cherchant mes souvenirs qui sont
> Comme des feuilles sous ta glace au trou profond,
> Je m'apparus en toi comme une ombre lointaine,

> Mais, horreur! des soirs, dans ta sévère fontaine,
> J'ai de mon rêve épars connu la nudité!
>   (*Hérodiade*)

Although the mirror is apostrophized, it is the image within the mirror that is the true focus of the scene. The gushing waters of the earlier fountain have now been frozen ("Eau froide par l'ennui dans ton cadre gelée") by the "ennui" of her wintry existence. Hérodiade's "souvenirs," which are "Comme des feuilles sous ta glace au trou profond," and then even her own image, "comme une ombre lointaine," penetrate the surface of the mirror and nearly dissolve into unrecognizable forms. In her rejection of everything around her, from the nurse's touch to her own sensuality, Hérodiade thus focuses only on herself and begins to constitute the conditions of a perfect mental self-exploration. Stripping herself of everything that distracts her from self-consciousness in order to bring about the satisfaction of the desire for union with what in **"Soupir"** was represented alternately by "soeur" and "l'azur," Hérodiade enters into ontic regions of self-effacement and draws back in horror: "J'ai de mon rêve épars connu la nudité!" But it is an alluring horror all the same, and the vision of "nudité" causes her to remember her own temporal bouts with understanding. In an attempt to substitute the commonplace concerns of physical existence for the universal, ontological horrors she has glimpsed within the "sévère fontaine" of self-reflection, Hérodiade thus asks, "Nourrice, suis-je belle?" Almost too easily, she invokes the concerns of physical existence to veil transcendent discoveries. In attempting to prove her purity, Hérodiade succeeds, therefore, only in manifesting the uncertainty of purity. It should of course be remarked that the drama of introspection, in which the succession of exteriorities that constitutes an act is made internal, has been represented within the theatrical context of the *scène,* and that the heroine of the poem, Hérodiade, is herself an artist, the dancer *par excellence.*

In *Crayonné au théâtre* (1886) Mallarmé indicates that

> Le ballet ne donne que peu: c'est le genre imaginatif. Quand s'isole pour le regard un signe de l'éparse beauté générale, fleur, onde, nuée et bijou, etc., si, chez nous, le moyen exclusif de le savoir consiste à en juxtaposer l'aspect à notre nudité spirituelle afin qu'elle le sente analogue et se l'adapte dans quelque confusion exquise d'elle avec cette forme envolée—rien qu'au travers du rite, là, énoncé de l'Idée, est-ce que ne parait pas la danseuse à demi l'élément en cause, à demi humanité apte à s'y confondre, dans la flottaison de rêverie? L'opération, ou poésie, par excellence et le théâtre. Immédiatement le ballet résulte allégorique.

Hérodiade's present "rêverie," which juxtaposes the particular world to the aspect of her spiritual nudity within the reflection of the mirror ("le moyen exclusif de le savoir"), is a clear prefiguration of the future textual dance which will allegorize the consummation/violation of the juncture of nature and willed consciousness, as "la danseuse" becomes "à demi l'élément en cause." In *Crayonné au théâtre* Mallarmé states that the self-reflective act can be an immobilizing force which dissolves the self and the world without producing a sense of unity with the "souvenirs" glimpsed in the mirror of introspection. The parallels with *Igitur* are illuminating: "Igitur comme menacé par le supplice d'être éternel qu'il pressent vaguement, se cherchant dans la glace devenue ennui et se voyant vague et près de disparaître comme s'il allait s'évanouir en le temps, puis s'évoquant; puis lorsque de tout cet ennui, temps, il s'est refait, voyant la glace horriblement nulle . . . Impuissant de l'ennui" (*Igitur*).

Hérodiade, too, seems to vacillate before the "liquéfaction de miroirs," (*Quant au Livre*), succumbing to the "ennui" which makes the "Eau froide . . . gelée" and makes Igitur "impuissant," but in *Hérodiade,* as in **"Soupir,"** the seductive depths of the self-reflexive moment seem to offer a virtual ground for reattaining a former state of authentic presence. Unlike that of Igitur, Hérodiade's developing consciousness is not a universal moment formalizing the growth of human consciousness in time, but rather another attempt to overcome previous failures at integration.

The flight from the "horreur" and the "effrois" produced by the gaze into the frozen fountain is intimately related to Hérodiade's recognition of her own insubstantiality. *Crayonné au théâtre* is instructive once more when Mallarmé points out that

> la danseuse *n'est pas une femme qui danse,* pour ces motifs juxtaposés qu'elle *n'est pas une femme,* mais une métaphore résumant un des aspects élémentaires, de notre forme . . . , et *qu'elle ne danse pas,* suggérant . . . avec une écriture corporelle ce qu'il faudrait des paragraphes en prose dialoguée autant que descriptive, pour exprimer, dans la rédaction: poëme dégagé de tout appareil du scribe.

It is not simply Yeats's question of telling the dancer from the dance that is at issue, for the binary distinction is absorbed by the metaphor which makes the dancer a gestural hieroglyphic, a sort of movable text, from which subjectivity disappears. Here the dancer is no longer a *woman,* nor does she *dance:* in the dance as pure metaphor, the dancer is sublated from physical to textual realms. For Hérodiade, "poëme dégagé de tout appareil du scribe," this sublation of the sensual is, understandably enough, a terrifying possibility. Hérodiade's crisis of emergence into sensual maturity, which repeats the rhetorical pattern of desire presented in **"Soupir,"** thus allegorizes the attempt to achieve poetic fulfillment, but it is an allegory which affirms itself while gazing at its own shimmering disappearance: "J'ai de mon rêve épars connu la nudité!"

The nudity glimpsed in these scattered dreams reflected in the mirror of consciousness is ambiguously Hérodiade's own sensual charm and that of poetic language. In the same way that the disappearance of an object isolated from nature is caused by the focused play of the poetic word—"la merveille de transposer un fait de nature en sa presque disparition vibratoire selon le jeu de la parole"—so is the scattering effect, with its subsequent loss of subjectivity, caused by the intense self-absorption before the mirror. These issues are also at play in *Igitur,* where we find this analogously uncanny scene:

> Jer suppliais de rester une vague figure qui dis-

paraissait complètement dans la glace confondue; jusqu'à ce qu'enfin, mes mains ôtées un moment de mes yeux où je les avais mises pour ne pas la voir disparaître, dans une épouvantable sensation d'éternité . . ., elle m'apparût comme l'horreur de cette éternité. Et quand je rouvrais les yeux au fond du miroir, je voyais le personnage d'horreur, le fantôme de l'horreur absorber peu à peu ce qui restait de sentiment et de douleur dans la glace . . . et se former en raréfiant la glace jusqu'à une pureté inouïe.

Hérodiade's terror before the mirror is more clearly linked to a crisis of self-awareness than to Igitur's confrontation with temporality, although the problematics of temporality cannot be entirely eliminated from Hérodiade's obsession with the cold chastity of the pure night. Nevertheless, the poetic affinities between Igitur and Hérodiade are clear; in each instance we see the the persistence of a willed consciousness as it confronts and fails to hold off indeterminacy.

The final act of the "Scène" hypothesizes the result of our heroine's undressing before the profundity of the sky:

> si le tiède azur d'été,
> Vers lui nativement la femme se dévoile,
> Me voit dans ma pudeur grelottante d'étoile,
> Je meurs!
>
> (*Hérodiade*)

and formulates what seems to be a necessary opposition between the masculine "bel azur" and "la femme" who unveils herself before it in fatal confrontation. The horror of virginity ("J'aime l'horreur d'être vierge") is now related to the horror glimpsed in the mirror ("la nudité"), but this opposition between feminine nudity and the natural masculinity of "le bel azur" must be seen in terms of the previous dialectic of polar differences rather than as the culmination of a sexual drama. Hérodiade seems, despite her protestations to the contrary, comfortable in her sensuality. If she fears the deflowering which will stain her purity, it is because desire has intervened without the mediating courtesy of a desired object. As she exposes herself to the sky, Hérodiade dies. Her words, "Je meurs," are undoubtedly meant in the full sensual and temporal ambiguity of the phrase, for degradation is interpreted as a passage from the physical to the metaphysical. When Hérodiade addresses the pale moon as "ma soeur éternelle," she has, in fact, already dreamt the experience of solitude and now yearns for it.

This sisterly relation between the moon and Hérodiade extends the virginal solitude of the celestial wastes down toward earthly existence, and conversely, extends Hérodiade's sensuality upward into the heavens. Consciousness and the frighteningly seductive celestial depths combine in the figure of Hérodiade to represent the failure of an attempted mediation between will and materiality, of an attempted animation of the inanimate. The failure to attain that mediation is symbolized in *Hérodiade* by the self-reflexive act before the mirror. In order to know herself. Hérodiade must recognize herself as the "nudité" in the mirror, but in order to recognize the form in the mirror as herself, she must know herself as she is. Not the least of our assumptions as to what might constitute a *self* is the notion that some genetic continuity will arise within the polarity created between the reflecting "thing" and its resultant "image." The self engenders an appearance that can be said to be identical with itself and of which it is the origin and the ground. As the self engenders appearance, so might it be said that meaning engenders a sign of itself. For Hérodiade, as for Igitur, however, this assumed continuity between self and appearance, between sign and meaning, is made radically discontinuous.

As she stands before the mirror to ascertain her individuality, Hérodiade witnesses instead her own fragmentation: "Je m'apparus en toi comme une ombre lointaine." The attempt to satisfy the nostalgia for the integration of self and other represented in **"Soupir"** has now been internalized as Hérodiade stands before the reflecting surface waiting for an illusory "chose inconnue." We should stress, however, that Hérodiade's tragic insight is not, as for Igitur, into an *absence* of selfhood, but rather into a *condition* of selfhood that she is unable to face for psychological or moral reasons. With the haunting voice of **"Toast funèbre,"** Hérodiade might therefore say, "Nous sommes / La triste opacité de nos spectres futurs." And yet, from an objective point of view, the results of both moments of insight are identical, for in both cases the genetic model which might unify self and image is shown to be one instance of rhetorical mystification.

As we have seen, the word "soeur" is an extremely important element in the Mallarméan semantic network. In **"Soupir"** and to a greater extent in *Hérodiade,* the notion of the "soeur" becomes the thematic expression of a desire for a union of language's representative and semantic functions. "Soeur," as symbol, is the synecdoche designating the totality of which it is merely the sensorial equivalent. That in *Hérodiade* "soeur" becomes associated with the problem of self-reflection is therefore almost a necessary development. The hermeneutic process of self-consideration is expandable from the province of a sensual crisis onto a plane of linguistic crisis because "soeur" exists as an analogical form of more general meanings. The network of images "jet d'eau," "fontaine," "miroir," and "âme" culminates in the figure of the "soeur," which in turn is an embodiment of an even more transcendent figure, Hérodiade herself. This syntax of figures unloosed from their proper referents tends to produce an errant semantics, but the semantic dissonance in *Hérodiade,* the loss of definite sense by the metaphors of consciousness, is expressed by the very rhetoric of the poem and compels the reader to participate in an apparently endless process of meaning construction.

With that displacement of meaning, the narcissistic drive toward self-consciousness, the attempt to break through the mirror to capture "l'horreur" of one's own psychic nudity, reveals instead the transience and contingency of consciousness, and Mallarmé uses the term *scène* to emphasize the theatricality of this subjective self-substantiation. With its connotations of visibility and staging, the term points toward a drama of self-creation. Charles Mauron has claimed [in his *Introduction à la Psychanalyse de Mallarmé,* 1950] that "en écrivant une scène de théâtre, Mallarmé rompt avec le narcissisme normal du

lyrique" and that what we see is the objectification of Mallarmé's own interior conflict.

The perspective I suggest precludes seeing the dramatization of the self as a break with the "narcissism of the lyric." I would argue that the *mise en scène* in Mallarmé's poem *is* this very narcissism of consciousness. The claim of both poems is universal: to recuperate the split consciousness by a dramatization of the *cogito,* of an act of thought. But neither poem bears out that claim; instead, both narrate the failure of reconciliation, and *writing* returns in each case to the simple scene of the referentiality of nature, "le soleil jaune," for instance. We do not need to have read Jacques Derrida, however, to recognize the instability of that solar metaphor. In attempting to substantiate her presence Hérodiade aligns herself, as does the narrative voice of **"Soupir,"** with an outside referent, variously called "âme," "l'azur," "ma soeur éternelle," which itself has no presence except as metaphor. Hérodiade succeeds, consequently, only in negating the idea of a universally verifiable subjectivity. The attempt by the subject to think upon itself, to capture its own image in the reflexive surface of consciousness, is thus negated by the disappearance of the self. And, I would add, the loss of the distinctive sense of personality which the lyrical voice of **"Soupir,"** like Hérodiade, Igitur, and even Mallarmé himself experiences and attempts to overcome by naming itself before a reflecting surface, is no mere play of words. To establish its own identity and source, the speaking voice turns on itself and hypostasizes the various moments that constitute the duration of its discourse into one relational entity.

This act of denomination, therefore, always posits the *ego* as a *logical* (syntactic) category, but cannot verify it as a subjective reality. In each attempted verification, the semantic quality of the metaphorical sign of the self can be constituted only in the temporal repetition of the sign's desire to coincide with a prior sign with which it can never coincide. It follows, then, that Mallarmé's text points to the paradox that subjectivity, the notion of a stable self, can only be *created* within a metaphoric system of oppositions where the subject is central, denying its own centrality. Our emphasis suggests that the articulation which attempts to substantiate its reality in the face of "l'Azur" succeeds only in revealing the fictitiousness of the ego and its actions.

The perspective offered here on the activity of hypostasis suggests other revisions in our reading of Mallarmé. Primarily, the laws which regulate the systems of opposition deserve careful attention. We should not, for instance, that while the language of **"Soupir"** and of *Hérodiade* is grammatically precise, even rigorous, it is apparently not concerned with semantic considerations. In both poems language becomes a mechanical system of oppositions governed by the identifiable laws of syntax: "Quel pivot, j'entends, dans ces contrastes, à l'intelligibilité? il faut une garantie—La Syntaxe" (*Le Mystère dans les lettres*). Yet it is precisely this formalistic rigor that the poems proceed to de-aestheticize. I think Mallarmé would have us recall that in musicology a "soupir" is a rest. The "soupir" of Mallarmé's poems might then be considered as the semantic blank occurring in all the parts suppressing the moment of desire and ending with the disappearance of the specular self. In these texts, the Hegelian *Selbstvernichtung* is not a function of the growth of a knowledge that would lead to a transcendent synthesis of the subject and the object.

This notion of synthesis has become a commonplace in the interpretation of Mallarmé's poetry as latter-day Romanticism. Since contemporary criticism has considerably revised that commonplace for such figures as Rousseau, Wordsworth, and Keats, it should not be at all surprising that a similarly synthetic reading of Mallarmé will not succeed in resolving the difficulties of his text. For Mallarmé the moment of negation does not coincide, as it does for Hegel, with the emergence of a true Subject. On the contrary, Mallarmé undoes the stability of that organic pattern by presenting what Hippolyte has aptly termed "le matérialisme de l'Idée" of subjectivity [Jean Hippolyte, *"Le Coup de dés de Stéphane Mallarmé et le message,"* *Etudes Philosophiques* 4, 1958]. I should caution that we are not speaking simply about a solipsistic reduction to subjectivism. Although it is possible to read Mallarmé's text as such a reduction, the text always reconstitutes itself as a network of differences, a play of syntax within which the various versions of the metaphors of the self continue to vie for precedence. I suggest simply that Mallarmé's narrative "I" emerges as a logical construct divorced from any essential ground, but which nonetheless constitutes a *moment* in the linear progression of the poem. Mallarmé's "I" cannot attain the status of what phenomenologists term transcendental subjectivity, but the lyrical history of the subject's desire for transcendence remains teleologically motivated and can therefore be narrated. In **Un Coup de dés** and in the projected universal *Livre,* Mallarmé would attempt systematically and masterfully to bring this narration to a close.

For the present, however, we can say that Mallarmé's poetic language does not recapture the loss of subjectivity, since poetic language cannot presume to represent the substantiality of any object. The representation is never the reality, but always simply the tentative reconstruction of reality by the subject who expresses the mimetic word. "Au contraire d'une fonction de numéraire facile et représentatif," says Mallarmé, "le dire . . . retrouve chez le Poëte, par nécessité constitutive d'un art consacré aux fictions, sa virtualité" (**"Crise de vers"**). The word which finds its "virtual" ground in the figure of the Poet is not, however, the thing it names: if it were, then absolute expressions and privileged statements about the self could be spoken. But neither is language pure signification; it is intimately tied to voice and sound. As sonority, organized in the poem by a syntax of rhyme and assonance, language can create certain convergences. Whatever "meaning" emerges from these textual convergences does have value, but it is a value derived from the essentially contingent qualities of the human voice: "Le vers qui de plusiers vocables refait un mot total, neuf, étranger à la langue comme incantatoire, achève cet isolement de la parole: niant . . . le hasard demeuré aux termes malgré l'artifice de leur retrempe alternée en le sens et la sonorité."

Reading, then, as Mallarmé reminds us, is an exercise— we must bend our minds to the blank "soupir" which begins and punctuates the text of every expression. As we read, the perpetual play of sound and silence both creates the poem and allows it to say something. It would be inaccurate to say, however, that the possibility of access to the truth of subjectivity has simply been transferred from language as statement to language as voice and melody. At this point, as Neal Oxenhandler has shown [in his "The Quest for Pure Consciousness in Husserl and Mallarmé," in *The Quest for Imagination,* edited by O. B. Hardison, Jr., 1971], we are not far from the Husserl of the *Cartesian Meditations* who claims that "the world is a meaning, an accepted sense." That "accepted sense" made present by the poetic text remains contingent, even when the reference of the text is the speaking voice itself. But to the extent that we can say that, on one level at least, the speaking voice is always a referent of the poetic text, we can also say that the creation of the poem is one way the Poet may hypostasize his own integrity. With that convergence, the aesthetics of the text becomes the aesthetics of the self.

The new poetic self which emerges from the text is defined within the dramatic space marked out by the textual convergences of our shared cultural, psychological, and linguistic codes. But since the readable codes of our everyday existence are themselves in part a reflection of our myth of the autonomous self, we have not really stepped outside the hermeneutic circle of thought by postulating this new subject, as Mallarmé well knew when he wrote to Cazalis: "Je suis maintenant impersonnel et non plus Stéphane que tu as connu,—mais une aptitude qu'a l'Univers spirituel à se voir et à se développer, à travers ce que fut moi." We should resist the temptation to read Mallarmé's implied aesthetics as a glorification of the Self, since Mallarmé's attempts to eliminate all of the shared presuppositions from his poetic word represent only the most transitory victory by the subject in ascertaining an aesthetic, ontological basis for its existence. Likewise, the inability of poetic language to verify the myth of subjective integrity would seem to undermine the possibility of an autonomous, self-sufficient "art for art's sake," and we are being false to the spirit of Mallarmé's text by continuing to read and teach it as if it were a hermetic and independent code, accessible only to the happy few.

We tend naturally to interpret Mallarmé's aesthetic claim that the poetic text can reconstruct an *originary* word as a claim that privileges poetic discourse. But when we read Mallarmé in this way, we forget what he himself could never forget: that in the attempt to vanquish "le hasard," the blank space of semantic insufficiency always arises to authenticate the silent background against which both everyday and poetic discourse exist. The "mystery" revealed by art to the "very few" is precisely that of the extent to which "art" and "reality" share a common ground in the aesthetically constructed Self. Far from reinforcing the notion that, as one recent critic has put it, "art exists in a universe of its own and bears no relation to the society in which [the poet] and his readers live" [Mary Louise Pratt, *Toward a Speech Act Theory of Literary Discourse,* 1977], the formal logic of Mallarmé's aesthetics of the self breaks down such comforting but false distinctions between literature and other kinds of human activity. In fact, it would not be difficult to argue that the opposition between art and reality is only one more of the convenient fictions that Mallarmé shows we continually posit in order to facilitate the possibility of a hypostasis. Meaning arises for Mallarmé precisely when the poetic word is able to create an organizing textual matrix, *le Livre,* for what would otherwise be only mutually exclusive, indeed self-negating, polarities.

Instead, we should notice that the linguistic network of Mallarmé's poetry represents metaphoric versions of the self, and indicates self-reflecting spirals of readable convergences. Mallarmé succeeds where the heroine of his poem does not, in creating a metaphor of consciousness which acknowledges the *possibility* of transcendental subjectivity while ceding its ground to the aesthetic order of the poetic word. For the Poet who writes that "penser [est] écrire sans accessoires" (**"Crise de vers"**), the creation of this hypostasized version of the impersonal self is most aptly figured by Hérodiade as she dances nude before the reflected starry sky. (pp. 54-72)

> *Ramón Saldívar, "Metaphors of Consciousness in Mallarmé," in* Comparative Literature, *Vol. 36, No. 1, Winter, 1984, pp. 54-72.*

Barbara Johnson   (essay date 1984)

[*In the essay below, Johnson uses the psychoanalytic model of the separation-individuation period of a child's development to interpret Mallarmé's importance to literary history.*]

What do I mean by the notion of Mallarmé as Mother?

I do not primarily mean Mallarmé as *would-be* mother, as an experiencer and overcomer of womb envy, although poems like **"Don du poème,"** in which poetic production is compared somewhat unfavorably to natural reproduction, or letters in which Mallarmé describes his daughter Genevieve and his poem *Hérodiade* as rival siblings, or sonnets like **"Une dentelle s'abolit,"** in which Mallarmé invents a new and linguistico-musical method of birth, would seem to suggest that such an idea would not be completely without foundation.

I do not mean Mallarmé as *woman,* although the fact that he produced a fashion magazine which he signed with a variety of feminine pseudonyms, and that in his address to the "Modern Muse of Impotence" he described himself as "une âme purement passive qui n'est que femme encore" ["A purely passive soul who is yet but a woman"] would suggest that his preoccupation with impotence on the one hand and with jewels, decoration, and finery on the other might play a transexuating role.

And I do not mean Mallarmé as occupying a female *social* position, although his concern with domesticity, his stance beside the hearth in his apartment rue de Rome, his role as host in a poetic "salon," his low-prestige job as a high school English teacher, and his self-ironic remarks about his life's lack of adventure or anecdote, would suggest that such a view would unify many of the existential stances of his social self.

All three of these possible ways of seeing Mallarmé as mother, although interesting and not contradictory to what I have in mind, would locate Mallarmé's maternity in a feminine *persona.* In contrast, I would like to situate what is maternal in Mallarmé as a *function* or *structure,* defined not in terms of a female *figure* but in terms of a specific set of interactions and transactions that structure the relation between the earliest parent and the child.

First, let me sketch out the context in which the notion of Mallarmé as Mother came to seem useful. What, in other words, was the *question* on which Mallarmé-as-Mother seemed to shed light? The question might be formulated as follows: what is it about Mallarmé's writing that is capable of exerting intense fascination in some cases and intense discomfort or rejection in others? What is the nature of the appeal, and of the threat? What sorts of unconscious wishes or fears does Mallarmé's poetry evoke in the reader?

The characteristics of Mallarmé most often cited for admiration or rejection are:

1. Obscurity, difficulty

2. Lack of determinable meaning—undecidability, ambiguity, plays of the signifier

3. Impersonality, distance, negativity

4. Inseparability of a poem's significance from the reading or writing process—poems seem to be about their own production or interpretation.

It is doubtless no accident that it is these same characteristics that exert attraction or repulsion in the writings of certain contemporary theorists for whose work Mallarmé is, in fact, fundamental—Derrida, Kristeva, Lacan, de Man. Hence, behind this exploration of Mallarmé's maternal role in *literary* history lies a possible thought about the role of those Mallarmé-inspired theorists within the history of criticism. But that thought will remain implicit for the time being.

It was while pondering the strange attraction-repulsion of the concept of *undecidability* that I came across the writings of the American psychoanalyst Margaret Mahler on the pre-Oedipal development of the child. While Mahler can easily be criticized on many counts from a Lacanian or feminist point of view, her differentiations among various subphases of the processes of separation and individuation in the pre-Oedipal period provide texture and temporality to patterns that have received small attention from either Freud or Lacan.

The separation-individuation process described by Mahler moves from mother-child symbiosis toward greater and greater autonomy, through four subphases. The child is followed from the age of four or five months to about three years, from "lap-babyhood" to "toddlerhood." Since the mother in these structures is defined not in terms of womb or breast but in terms of emotional and physical proximity, it is not structurally necessary that she be a woman, although Mahler never considers this. The four subphases are described as follows:

> 1. *Differentiation:* "hatching" from symbiotic

oneness or lack of differentiation between child and mother; decrease of complete bodily dependence, increase of sensorimotor investigations, peek-a-boo games.

2. *Practicing:* great narcissistic investment of the child in his own functions, his own body, as well as in the objects and objectives of his expanding reality testing; relatively great imperviousness to knocks and falls and other frustrations. Alternates between obliviousness to mother and periodic return to mother for emotional refueling.

3. *Rapprochement:* increased motor and communicative activity is accompanied, paradoxically, by greater concern for mother's presence, greater tendency to separation anxiety. Child passes from vocal affective expressions through the ability to use "no!" toward verbal communication. Both separation and active approach behavior increase: the child is both more independent and more demanding, his "pleasure in independent functioning . . . seems to be proportionate to . . . his success in eliciting the mother's interest and participation."

4. *Object constancy:* greater tolerance for separation from mother and for delayed gratification. Development of role-playing and make-believe. Absent mother is libidinally available because internalized as image, not experienced as loss.
       [condensed and adapted from Margaret Mahler's "Mother-Child Interaction During Separation-Individuation," in *The Selected Papers of Margaret S. Mahler,* 1979].

It is the third, or rapprochement, phase that seems to be most fruitful to an understanding of the workings of Mallarmé's poetry. In that phase, the forces of separation and the forces of merger work in tandem yet against each other, and they do so at a moment when the pre-verbal slides into the verbal through the word "no."

As far as the verbal development is concerned, it is easy to see that in emphasizing the negative (aboli bibelot, nul ptyx, rien n'aura eu lieu, etc.) and in silencing or musicalizing the verbal as structure or sonority while rediscovering the properties of words as such, Mallarmé's poetry manages to make simultaneous the three linguistic steps involved in the rapprochement phase—affective gesture or vocalization, negativity, and the newness of verbal communication. For the remainder of this paper I will concentrate on the attendant problematics of separation and rapprochement per se.

Mallarmé's poems would seem to be characterized by a high degree of separation from anything outside themselves. *Le Livre* was to be impersonal and anonymous ("le Texte y parlant de lui-même et sans voix d'auteur" ["the Text there speaking on its own and without the voice of an author"]). The author, in the very act of writing, is cut off from the work ("Sait-on ce que c'est qu'écrire? . . . Qui l'accomplit, intégralement, se retranche." ["Does anyone know what writing is? . . . Whoever accomplishes it, integrally, cuts himself off."]). The work is cut off from reference as well: the word "flower" can name only "what is absent from any bouquet." The poem is detached and autonomous like the beautiful, sterile, solitary Hérodiade,

who is of course a figure for the poem's aspiration toward separation.

There are two ways in which this thrust toward separation is countered by an equal and opposite force of attachment and indifferentiation. On the one hand, these poetic prodigies of separation envisaged by Mallarmé never achieve separation as finished works. *Igitur, Hérodiade, Le Livre, Pour un Tombeau d'Anatole* all remain unfinished, and hence, unable to perform the separations they depict. Mallarmé as mother of his poems would be playing out the maternal ambivalence toward separation: on the one hand, he directs his poems toward an idealized *image* of autonomy; on the other hand, he cannot let them go. A mother's self-effacement is never done. Concomitant to this is Mallarmé's tendency to devalue the works that he *does* finish—they are "cartes de visite," "études en vue de mieux," "des riens." The back-and-forth working through of separation is denied in either case: either the dice never leave the enclosing hand, or they are tossed out into nothingness.

Separation is differently resisted *within* the completed, seemingly autonomous texts. Here, the text plays the role of mother; the reader, that of child. The text of a Mallarmé poem works out a complex pattern of undecidability, ambiguity, and obscurity through which the reader, who attempts to separate and differentiate meanings, can only find himself or herself further and further entangled with the text, less and less able to separate and differentiate. The desire for separation and the desire for merger are thus simultaneously satisfied on two different levels: the text proclaims its autonomy and individuality, but that individuality is itself composed of structures of indifferentiation and entanglement. The reader's separation from the text is never done.

The most condensed version of the simultaneity of separation and merger in Mallarmé is the functioning of the *blancs* in his texts. In Mallarmé's writing, whiteness functions both as spacing and as image, both as syntactical, material articulation and as semantic, thematic reference. On the one hand, the blank spaces cut up the text: separation functions *within* the textual body; the text is explicitly articulated as spacing, absence, incompletion, not an organic whole. On the other hand, whiteness itself, as *image,* stands within Mallarmé's imagery, within the imagery of the blank page, within certain strands of psychoanalytic theory, as a figure for the female body and, ultimately, for the maternal breast. In Mallarmé's clearest depiction of the parallel between the poet/poem relation and the mother/child relation, **"Don du poème,"** Mallarmé asks the woman to accept his poetic "child":

> O la berceuse, avec ta fille et l'innocence
> De vos pieds froids, accueille une horrible naissance:
> Et ta voix rappelant viole et clavecin,
> Avec le doigt fané presseras-tu le sein
> Par qui coule en blancheur sibylline la femme
> Pour les lèvres que l'air du vierge azur affame?

> [O cradler, with your daughter and the innocence / Of your cold feet, welcome a horrible birth. / And your voice recalling viol and harpsi-

chord, / With faded finger will you press the breast / Through which in sibylline whiteness woman flows / For lips half starved by virgin azure air?]

It is this forever undecipherable yet somehow maternal sibylline whiteness—or undecidability *as* maternity—that flows and is articulated through the poetry of Mallarmé. *Les blancs* sketch out presence and absence, pure semantic flux and pure syntactic division, separation and reunion. The blanks in the text do not make the mother present; they recreate the drama of the simultaneity of attachment and detachment that defines the maternal *function*.

Hence, it could be said that the unconscious desires and fears tapped by Mallarmé's writing—the reasons readers are both attracted and repelled by it—has to do with its ability to recreate the simultaneous forces of separation and indifferentiation of the pre-Oedipal period. The desire to separate is satisfied by the poem's free-standingness. The desire to merge is satisfied by the poem's absorption of the reader into its structures of obscurity and undecidability. And the fear of separation is evoked by the abyss of non-referentiality or impersonality, while the fear of merger is evoked by the loss of the ability to control or master meaning.

How can it be said that a male poet comes to play a maternal role in literary *history*? Why is the mother's part not taken by a woman? One answer might run as follows: everyone can believe that men are powerful. Everyone can believe that mothers are powerful. But we are not taught to believe that *women* are powerful. Hence a man whose work consists of questioning certain assumptions and structures of phallogocentrism—the determinability of meaning, the separability of binary opposites, the search for self-identity—would somehow appear to fill the maternal role better, more effectively, than a woman. To the extent that a critique of the paternal position involves a privileging of ambiguity, undecidability, and deferral—the deferral of both separation and merger—that critique is operating from the arena of the pre-Oedipal mother. But the fact that the maternal function is wielded by men—indeed, that literature is one of the means by which men have elaborated the maternal position—means that the silence of actual women is all the more effectively enforced. With men playing all the parts, the drama appears less incomplete than it really is. Were women to take over the critique of the paternal position, they might not remain content with the maternal role.

What remains to be discussed is the value assigned to the maternal position in developmental narratives like Mahler's. By situating Mallarmé's power as that of the pre-Oedipal mother, am I not implicitly considering it as regressive, something to be outgrown, as a critique that is actually a defense?

According to prevailing developmental schemes, this would indeed be the case. For although the mother is seen as powerful, her power, viewed exclusively through the eyes of the child, is a power that must be overcome, outgrown, escaped. Whether that power is nurturing or smothering, it is seen as a threat to autonomy. And autonomy comes to stand as the very structure of maturity. Any theory that sees maturity as the achievement of separation is bound to see the mother's power as inferior—less desirable—than the father's. If the father stands for distance and the world and the mother stands for closeness and the home, the more like the father one is, the more mature one is considered to be. According to this hierarchy of development, a woman would almost by definition never achieve full maturity, especially since she is constantly in danger of falling into symbiosis by becoming a mother herself. But a model of maturation that measures development by the standard of only one gender is clearly inadequate. This is the point of Carol Gilligan's book *In a Different Voice,* in which gender bias is analyzed in existing models of ethical development.

I would like to end by outlining three directions in which one might move to displace existing paradigms of maturation and gender, so that pre-Oedipal structures could be recognized as permanent and pervasive rather than simply regressive.

1) Through an analysis of gender bias in models of human psychology and development, it should be possible to rethink the notion of maturity to include more of the spectrum of relationships than an idealized version of autonomy. At the very least, the capacity for mothering could, for example, stand as one of several maturational models for people of both sexes. A tolerance for incomplete separation could be seen as differently mature from an insistence on total independence.

2) A critique of phallogocentric assumptions and structures should be elaborated from female positions other than that of the mother, or the maternal position should be rethought as subject of discourse rather than as object of desire. The maternal function as it stands is perhaps itself but a branch of phallogocentrism.

3) The function of mother—or of nurturing parent of either sex—should be analyzed otherwise than through the eyes of a child, indeed, implicitly, a male child—a child-theorist whose wishful anticipation of a free, self-identical needlessness has always dreamed human maturity as the completion of a separation that in fact can be achieved only in death.

Finally, where does this leave Mallarmé? To the extent that it now seems urgent to question the claims to universality and the forces of exclusion that have gone into the making of the European literary canon, it may perhaps leave him silent. But any attempt to move away from that canon, to go beyond Mallarmé's maternity to a more feminist critique of the structures he both questioned and reinforced, would necessarily place Mallarmé and others like him in the role of primal parent, pre-Oedipal mother, source of the earliest *literary* training and nourishment. It remains to be seen whether the feminist drama of separation from the canon can avoid the fallacies of autonomy without losing the differentiations that may, perhaps, ultimately, make a difference. (pp. 77-83)

Barbara Johnson, "Mallarmé as Mother: A Preliminary Sketch," in The Denver Quarterly, *Vol. 18, No. 4, Winter, 1984, pp. 77-83.*

Robert Greer Cohn   (essay date 1984)

[*Cohn is an eminent Mallarmé scholar and author of numerous critical analyses of the poet's work, including* Towards the Poems of Mallarmé *(1965). In the following excerpt, he contends that an important element of Mallarmé's poetic imagery is its earthy, sensual character.*]

In cosmogonic musings, after an "original wholeness", we tend to imagine, in some equivalent of the Big Bang, a breakup of Being and fall into fragments and the linear ways of Becoming. Along the specific line of (fallen) time—the "Adamic way"—there are events which may appear as reminiscences (or premonitions) of the lost (or hoped-for) globality of Eden or something like, some sort of rounded ripeness, maturity, fulfillment in becoming. Such, in literature for example, are Kierkegaard's Instants, Proust's *moments bienheureux,* Joyce's epiphanies, and, less cited, Mallarmé's *moments de foudre* (Villiers lecture). These "privileged moments", from the record, can be of memory, anticipation, or, more convergently and ultimately, an eternal present, "out of time".

The existence lines we function with go in all directions: they *are* directions (*sens*) and operational meaning. Two main ones are, obviously, the vertical and the horizontal, which are often assigned, as on graphs, to space and time. In the "beacon" spells, they refer back or forward to the unitary source or goal (or, paradoxically, the eternal present) and accordingly tend to fuse or at least vibrate together as in Proust, Joyce, and Einsteinian theory (e.g. Eddington's "hourglass" demonstration of it) and the closely derivative "black hole" concept of "shearing" movement between these two master dimensions. The "symphonic equation proper to the seasons", a tetrapolar or two-dimensional pattern which Mallarmé placed at the heart of his conception of a *Grand' Œuvre* (**La Musique et les lettres**) is based on this same interchangeable play of dimensions.

In that formula Mallarmé specifically alludes to the *chassé-croisé* of human analogues to seasons, moods (cf. the four humors of the Renaissance), as well as to the Spring-Summer-Autumn-Winter cycle. In the later sketch of the Masterwork, **Un Coup de Dés,** the cycle also extends to four ages of mankind as in Hesiod; in **Les Dieux antiques** four times of day are implied parallel to the seasons, "la double évolution solaire, quotidienne et annuelle". Elsewhere, there are the four elements based on the same underlying epistemology, four cardinal points of the compass, and so on. As in the case of the compass—or the circle of trigonometry—there are endless in-between points all around, with equivalents in the finest "seasonal" nuances of artistic imagery.

Mallarmé invented a sort of dial—it is in the Doucet collection of his memorabilia at the Bibliothèque Sainte-Geneviève—with clock hands turning to various symbols for combinatory choices. Similarly, our poetic imagination combines various *états d'âme* taken from analogous cycles (which we can picture in overlapping spirals or concentric, or stacked, rings). For example, the tremendous force of nostalgia in *Spring*—from the time-cycle, seasons properly speaking—fuses naturally with an *earth* image—from the cycle of elements—in Mallarmé's **"Renouveau."** The poet dreams of returning in time to his origin for a rebirth and likewise of burying his face in the humid ground for the same "baptismal" reasons (T. S. Eliot's heavy and muddy lyric imagery in *East Coker,* or *The Waste Land,* is quite comparable and possibly derivative).

At another time he may dream of ideal light mixed with Return, as in **Apparition.** Or a future direction of hope may well up in the young heart mingled with sensual, even "dirty", urges from the chthonian real as in the **Après-midi d'un faune.** Our imagination shifts kaleidoscopically through differing poles of this matrix of poetry, flirting more or less with the total scheme through the combinations at each juncture, in an erratic form of seasonality—that of the psyche—jumping around every which way.

Although all combinations are possible and all are simultaneously latent and even remarkably present in some rare moments of art ("Ô saisons, ô châteaux"), nevertheless, to repeat, we tend to fantasize, and certainly to work critically—thematically—in limited aspects of the whole, often in fan-shaped or pie-slice sections of the "kaleidoscopic" wheel.

In a previous essay, "Ô quel lointain: Memory in Mallarmé" [in *Romanic Review,* March 1979] I explored the surge of powerful homesickness in imagery such as that of the "cygne inoubliable" (**Hérodiade, Ouverture ancienne**); quoting:

> Désespéré . . . le vieil éclat voilé
> S'élève: (ô quel lointain en ces appels celé!)

There, a dazzlement of Originality was associated with the upper pole of "or . . . dernières splendeurs", clearly referring to a sort of sunburst in a dying consciousness, and there were numerous other "dialings" of the imaginative master wheel, producing combinations faintly related to phone numbers—getting through to Home—or other such complex codings. But our theme kept us to a horizontal and backward emphasis: time as memory. Here we are exploring primarily the lower-vertical direction: earth. With Mallarmé this is apt to lead to the *very* earthy, the bowels of the earth, the underground, telluric—fecund fountainhead, womb, black pit, black gusher—realm of the deeply sensual and oneiric imagination. Here everything becomes entangled with that major wedge of totality which is Thanatos, Death itself, dialectically bound up, of course, with Eros or Life; thence the fertile low-down source, the Womb, male or female—the "black hole" of creativity (overlapping with a Nothing)—and, nearby, the sexual and, further, the anal or excremential, the mucky and instinctual. Various effluvia, juices or saps of life (death) well from the grave depths, for example a complex and ambivalent "milk" as we shall see in fragments of *Les Noces d'Hérodiade.* The volcanic eruption of general life-force, Eros, overlapping with sexual outpouring, eros, in the *Après-midi d'un faune,* is parallel. In sum, the primal gush of creation—carrying along various mediatory phases and their fixation as phenomena—springs as Expression from an underground reservoir of Life and Death.

As original source—and goal—the chthonian can be fully Edenic. Gaston Bachelard effectively establishes this for Novalis in *La Terre et les Rêveries de la volonté*—referring particularly to the *Mines at Falun*—although his presentation lacks some methodical openness: his representative figures are shown to *favor* these images more than they do in reality. This would be true of Mallarmé as well: these *themes* are important to his œuvre, and that is sufficient to demonstrate. If, incidentally, this undermines the cliché view of Mallarmé as a cold idealist, an abstract "algebrist", and the like, so be it! Sartre bluntly called those who dubbed Mallarmé a "Platonist" either "dupes or knaves" and claimed him as an "existential" poet as well as "our greatest" [in "L'Engagement de Mallarmé", *Obliques,* Nos. 18-19]. One can also hail him as a poet of life, in this sense. He is certainly a full figure of some sort, secretly: inexhaustible as Dante, mysteriously elusive of our critical formulas.

Although American critics are apt to cling to their device of deprecating Symbolism through a sort of strawman technique or guilt by association—using the pale *fin de siècle* group of minor Symbolists, such as Samain, Régnier et al.—they are hard put to explain how sober academic authorities such as René Wellek place a whole unsurpassed Golden Age of art under this catchword now, following the lead of Edmund Wilson's pioneering study, which compared Mallarmé to Einstein for pivotal importance. The fact that France's leading poets and critics—Ponge, Bonnefoy, Char, Blanchot, Richard—endorse this view of Mallarmé's powerful presence and plenitude doesn't seem to have ruffled the stubborn locals. Heigh-ho: when one thinks that until after World War II, Brahms was an almost obscene word in France . . . And of course Symbolism—which serves the same purpose of initial, hypothetical and *faute de mieux* labelling as all such catchwords—includes hosts of other strong figures, among the strongest ever.

Earthy notes are sounded early in the groping Mallarmé pieces such as *L'Enfant prodigue:*

   —Un Gouffre, hérissé d'âpres ronces, où roule

> **One can also hail [Mallarmé] as a poet of life . . . He is certainly a full figure of some sort, secretly: inexhaustible as Dante, mysteriously elusive of our critical formulas.**
>
> **—*Robert Greer Cohn***

   Un fétide torrent de fard mêlé de vin!

The whole of *Galanterie macabre* is colored with a *peuple* flavorful sordidness from the lower reaches of realism (or Naturalism), a sort of negative poetry we find in Baudelaire, Rimbaud, Zola, Carco, and many others later.

   Dans un de ces faubourgs où vont des caravanes
   De chiffonniers se battre et baiser galamment
   Un vieux linge sentant la peau des courtisanes
   Et lapider les chats dans l'amour s'abîmant . . .

This pervasive, hovering chiaroscuro, like a mixed charcoal grill—echoed by the "smell of steaks in passageways" (T. S. Eliot, *Preludes*)—burns and darkens at the end of the poem into black bitterness, reflecting the pain of loss of those closest to Mallarmé in tragic fact: his mother, his little sister, his adolescent girl-friend.

One might have thought that Mallarmé watchers would have picked up a clue here that they were dealing with a rounded human being . . .

When it came to commemorating Baudelaire with a sonnet, the appropriate tone emerged as:

   Le temple enseveli divulgue par la bouche
   Sépulchrale d'égout bavant boue et rubis
   Abominablement quelque idole Anubis
   Tout le museau flambé comme un aboi farouche

All the hellish cloacal *mal* of *Les Fleurs du mal* is brilliantly condensed here: images of expressive welling up like feces or mud from a sewer ritually converted into poetry: "Out of the mud the jewel that is the lotus". The buried temple suggests all sorts of pertinent things: Baudelaire's neglect by the public, the incomplete, modernly grotesque, decadent, ambivalent tone of the *Fleurs du mal* and our age generally, the hieratic nature of his art. It is an *underground* temple, dissident, a sewer, presided over by a pagan dog-faced infernal deity, with an overtone of *anus* in his name (echoed by the later rhyme *pubis*) and an exotic flavor typical of early Baudelaire and much of the late nineteenth century.

It is immensely effective, haunting, this surreal vomiting up from our underneath, our most shameful dream regions. T. S. Eliot's "garlic and sapphires in the mud" from *Burnt Norton,* it is known, likely would not have existed without the Mallarmé precedent.

The Baudelairian mixture of beauty and sin figured in the early critical rhapsody *Symphonie littéraire*:

   Ô prodige, une singulière rougeur, autour de laquelle se répand une odeur enivrante de chevelures secouées, tombe en cascade du ciel obscurci! Est-ce une avalanche de roses mauvaises ayant le péché pour parfum? Est-ce du fard?—Est-ce du sang?—Étrange coucher de soleil! Ou ce torrent n'est-il qu'un fleuve de larmes empourprées par le feu de bangale du saltimbanque Satan qui se meut par derrière? Écoutez comme cela tombe avec un bruit lascif de baisers . . . Enfin, des ténèbres d'encre ont tout envahi où l'on n'entend voleter que le crime, le remords et la Mort.

Here, sexual sin—along with other crimes—the female Gouffre, "mouth" and kisses, the anal, and night are jumbled obsessively and compellingly in this pair of puritan nineteenth-century geniuses who are horrified by sexuality (as well as more general *mal*) and *merde* and yet plunge into it with honesty, shuddering and delighted. Freud would have had little to teach them about infantile desires. The twentieth-century bards have not gone beyond them in this direction.

That delight *erupts,* typically, after the long delays occasioned by their sensitive and inhibited temperaments and upbringing. It is the "gloire du long désir" of **Prose (*pour des Esseintes*),** the final burst of fireworks at the close of **Hérodiade,** *Scène:*

> Jetez-vous les sanglots suprêmes et meurtris
> D'une enfance sentant parmi les rêveries
> Se séparer enfin ses froides pierreries.

That "cold" is the long-congealed ice of repression as well as, ambiguously, the distant frigidity of pure-poetic stars—paradoxically warmed by their sun-fires as we learn from other texts such as the close of the **Coup de Dés** ("CONSTELLATION . . . froide . . . pas tant"). Hérodiade's feeling for Saint-Jean waxes very warm, even passionately voluptuous, in certain later fragments of the **Noces.** The yearning wells up like the sobbing milky fountain of **"Soupir"** (or **Apparition,** subtly) from a "long desire" or a prolonged childhood typical of civilized society like Mallarmé's par excellence. It is ambiguously love, or more ambivalently and complexly, art.

Those ultimate "far out" stars of beauty are potential in the nether region, the "savants abîmes éblouis" of the *Scène,* psychic buried treasure waiting to be dug up in the fullness of Hamletically-hesitant adolescent time. For holistic humanism, including poetry, the upper and lower are co-subjective and dialectically related, vibrantly together, as in the classic notion of instinct (or temperament) and in Freud's and Lacan's insistence on the articulateness of the unconscious. So Mallarmé's dream image of the "savants abîmes éblouis" is fully anticipatory of the whole Freudian realm and could serve as a motto for the modern psychoanalytic enterprise.

L'Après-midi d'un faune is another pivotal work of our modern tradition, perhaps *the* pivotal work when you think of what it meant also for music and dance.

The troubled demi-god with goat's legs is appropriately torn between wildly permissive urges and a complex inhibitory mind, as I noted in my commentary [in *Toward the Poems of Mallarmé,* 1981]. After long cunctations, this Hamlet-Bottom reaches a climax of yearning born of frus-

tration. It culminates, naturally, in this Sicilian setting (reminiscent of Theocritus and his eclogues) with a violent image of Etna, vomiting its volcanic eruption of lava. Again, there is ambiguity between the erotic and the Erotic, or poetic. Which is widely characteristic of Mallarmé as it is of Shakespeare, this ranging between beauty and bawdy. The impressionistic atmosphere of the **Faune** modulates into sensual undertones as it does in Debussy's amorously moaning score: the pointillist delicacy of light and leaves, the flute melody arabesques dimpling the air, glints of dazzlement in water, Renoir-like roseate flesh amid flowers and foliage, at one extreme; at the other, the "animal whiteness" of naked nymphs confused with swans, the goat's legs and hair-entwined horns and lust of the bestial sylvan creature, his greedy desire for at least *two* nymphs . . .

The Monet-like **"Nénuphar blanc"** is comparably complex: underneath, there is the play on feminine sexual shapes; the *ombre* of intimate secrets in the **Faune** is conflated subtly but obsessively with other aspects of those privacies. This was explored at length in *Toward the Poems of Mallarmé* (Appendix B in particular), parallel to the investigation of the now-famous *blancheur* chain (see Appendix A) which reaches from *pertes nocturnes,* associated candidly with ocean foam in a letter, all through the fluid hierarchy of creation up to the Milky Way, with its

Henri Matisse, French, 1869-1954, Faun and Nymphs from Poésies by Stéphane Mallarmé, published by Albert Skira & Cie., Lausanne, etchings on Japanese Paper, 1932, Given in Memory of Peter A. Dewey, 1946.1043 page 76, photograph (c) 1993 The Art Institute of Chicago, All Rights Reserved.

overtone of thought, writing and *logoi spermatakoi.* Derrida, of course, has made all this better known.

One need hardly stress the continuity of Mallarmé's simpler erotic sensuality, in **"Une Négresse par le démon secouée,"** **"M'Introduire dans ton histoire"** and many another poem or poemlet addressed to Méry Laurent. Robert Goffin has created the theme gleefully in his *Mallarmé vivant* (1955). But these things are well known and directly observable.

The *négresse* mixes muddiness, in her color, and naively perverse sex. The *émoustillé* priest of *L'Ecclésiastique* rolls on the spring turf. Lovers swim in an *après-amour* muck in **"Le Guignon."** The workers of **Conflit** and **Confrontation** dig into mother earth and lie on her obliviously.

Their tools are candidly called "sexual". This down-to-earth quality extends to the **Coup de Dés** where the poet-prince is *amer de* and *debout* with easy undertones, like the Maître's *calculs* or the *écumes originelles* which mount deliriously to the head as the white feather of *foudre-*vision. *Foudre* itself is deeply resonant, as is much else in this fantastically alive, cosmically-rooted, verbal *Jeu suprême.*

The volcanic eruption in the **Faune,** we noted, can pertain either to sexuality (again, with a choice of outlets) or to that mingled erotic-Erotic realm of Mallarmé's kind of artistic expression. The ambiguity is true to the underlying universal, including psychic, facts if creative expression is implied—akin to primal yelling, quelling, hysteria, sobbing, sighing, singing, even blushing—there is the rush from the lower region to the upper and the "volcanic" overflow of the "glory of the long desire" in élite cases like Mallarmé's. "L'art, c'est le désir perpétué", according to Laforgue, echoing the *perpétuer* of the opening of the **Faune,** but there is almost always the eventual explosion, even for that remarkably self-controlled princess of the spirit, Hérodiade.

The creative process of eruption is well illustrated by **"Le Démon de l'analogie."** The creator is typically challenged by a puzzling phenomenon of rhythm, sound, shapes which somehow seem terribly important to pin down. They seem to be keys to solving some anxiety, healing long-buried problems now surging up in a crisis. Actually, they go back all the way to the problem of evil itself or its early mediatory phases, the succession of absurd dilemmas, rifts in Being stemming from the first alienation or fall from grace. Those phases, crucial growth-stages, include the threatening ambivalence of Eros-Thanatos, or "to be or not to be"; incest prohibition and attraction; the paradoxes which one has to learn to live with, such as the Lacanian "mirror-stage", the Oedipal crisis, and the problem of language itself, stammering between "art and instinct", as Darwin put it.

The poet's buried self is *taken* with the problem, half-grasps its nature, even as the conscious (unconscious) mind fails to understand it enough to set it down once and for all. This tension between conscious and unconscious (mind and body)—an absurdly vibrant mediatory form of overall suffering reflecting the original Absurd, in the same series as the earlier crises in growth or adaptation—

sets up an almost constant harrying obsession which haunts the poet as he goes about his daily business and follows him into his sleep. The tone of the quest harks back literally to Poe and the deadly enterprise of tracking down a murderer, or murderous principle, before it "gets you" (Ionesco's assassin in the city is a recent avatar of this nightmare). One calls on one's best civilized resources of intellect, dead-alive "coolness" of the detective-story sort. Such cold rationality is a homeopathic device of "murderous" analytic mind turned against an ancestral murderer Principle. There is something pathetic in this pursuit, grim and yet occasionally funny . . .

In our prose poem, there is no moment of full bringing up to the light of consciousness; only the obsession stage is described and a sort of half-revelation, in the musical shop window, which we feel the author's psyche will continue to gnaw on. In this case, after the usual creative delays, the overflowing outburst will come later . . .

It certainly did come in the late Saint-Jean fragments of **Les Noces d'Hérodiade.**

The saint, according to the biblical story, is imprisoned in an underground dungeon whence his voice irrepressibly rises up in a "virile thunder", a hymn to the son-deity he preceded and announced. The pattern is powerfully daemonic, a sheer vertical rebound from dark infernal regions to total light, in the microcosmic image of—"repeating" in the Kierkegaard sense—the original explosion. In the **Cantique de Saint-Jean** published in the **Poésies,** his death and resurrection harks back to the "principe qui m'élut"—not (*pace* Davies) *just* baptism but the paradoxical conversion or redemption which baptism ritually reflects. Here the theme and the surrounding imagery are even more total and eruptive:

> A quel psaume de nul antique antiphonaire
> Ouï planer ici comme un viril tonnerre
> Du cachot fulguré pour s'ensevelir où?
> Sauf amplificatrice irruption ou trou
> Grand ouvert par un vol ébloui de vitrage
> Bloc contre bloc jonchant le lugubre entourage

Despite the obscurity lingering around the term *vitrage,* there is no question about the fundamental dynamics of what is happening here: something very Big. Not only the Saint is involved but, sympathetically, as in the well-known natural events which accompanied the death of Christ, the earth itself spews forth rock like a Krakatoa, or at least seems to as the underground prison is shattered open. There were other such Bangs in Mallarmé, notably the first *Coup* of the **Coup de Dés,** associated with the first explosion of all, as we detailed in our study (with echoes of Poe's *Eureka* and the *désastre obscur* which hurled down his genius, like the meteoric tombstone block of his monument—reflecting the black rock of Islam—in the **Tombeau d'Edgar Poe**). There is a similar violent source in the *fracas originel* of the **Hommage à Wagner,** cf. "tout a coup l'éruptif multiple sursautement de la clarté, comme les proches irradiations d'un lever de jour" (**La Musique et les lettres**) and a number of such indications we discuss in our books on the **Coup de Dés,** under *Coup.* In brief, this event is a lower counterpart of the usual sunburst source, a sort of reply from the humble man, down here, that Saint-Jean is very deliberately said to be: "Mais selon un baptême . . . Penche un salut"; certain fragments of the *Noces* make this theme of humility absolutely clear. The etymological root of "humility" is, to be sure, Latin *humus,* soil or earth.

In other fragments, the *élan vital* from the fountainhead is put in terms of an ambivalent and high-low "milk," in the *blancheur* series we alluded to earlier. It is associated with the life-force rising up and spurting from the body of the decapitated saint, sort of sap of spirit (cf. Hindu soma) parallel to more-bodily blood. A *saint-sein* analogy may well be at work here; in *Le Phénomène futur* the breasts of the phenomenal female were pointed skyward; in **"Don du poème"** the woman's milk was encouraged to nourish the abortive poem of the husband, his *constellation manquée.* In **"Soupir"** the male sigh is related to a "blanc jet d'eau". The white coif of the frightened nurse—much is made of her paradisiacal former milk in the *Noces* altogether—arises analogously with the Saint's spirit (cf. the white hair rising on the head of the drowning *Maître* of the *Coup de Dés:* "Esprit . . . maniaque chenu") and it is called a "maléfique lait", bringing out the negative underside, the horror (as Melville said the color white did, in *Moby Dick*). Another fragment has this:

> basalte . . . Lieu du plus noir secret . . . Pour
> voile . . .
> se frange . . . Sinistrement blanchit et s'illumine
> **(*Noces*)**

This is the cluster of sail-veil-white foam-sperm-spirit-soma-secreted web-lace of writing, of baby cradle, veil, nuptial curtains, etc. which we see at work on Page 3 of the *Coup de Dés* and in many another seminal text, such as the exquisite **"Une dentelle s'abolit."** The *jaillissement* of white beauty or horror from deep down is found in the **"Nénuphar blanc,"** the "écumes originelles" of the *Coup de Dés,* and numerous other poems or prose passages.

We have gone over this ground elsewhere, for example most recently in our "New Approaches to Hérodiade" (*Romanic Review,* Vol. LXXII, no. 4) which gives an extensive context for the theme. We will leave it now at that.

Mallarmé was the man who wrote to a friend, Lefébure, that "one must think with one's whole body". He spoke, in *La Musique et les lettres,* of poetry's having "spread wings but with its claws rooted in you [the earth-bound folk who read it]". Elsewhere he sees it as being "massively bound to nature" (**"Théodore de Banville"**).

It may be that Sartre was a mite blunt in calling those many who saw only an idealist in his favorite poet "dupes or knaves", but they are certainly missing *something* in the being who spoke humbly in **Bucolique** of his "joie . . . de se percevoir, simple, infiniment sur la terre."

And yet it is a mistake to *insist* on Mallarmé's materialism, as Sartre and the structuralists do. There is too much evidence on the other side as well, too familiar to need repeating here. Obviously, he is a superb poet just because he "touches both extremes", as Pascal recommended for genius; a tension, resembling Camus' absurd is maintained between an aspiration upward to the "shores of light" and a plunging sensuality à la Keats. Even the ideal flower of

the famous "Je dis une fleur . . . l'absente de tous bouquets" arises "musically" (and "suave")—it is in the prevailing posture, high-low, abstract and bodily, of music and all deeply lyric art—and refers concretely, in "reminiscence" (like Wordsworth's), to the "named object". Countless criticasters have distorted the record and the truth in this regard. Mallarmé abides in the vibrant midposition of all the well-known dialectical, holistic, paradoxically alive and anti-dualistic terms such as intuition, instinct, phenomenon, temperament, imagination . . .

That is the dry way to put it. Better evidence is in the stuff of his poetry. His faun sucks out grape-skins and holds them up to the light for childish pure sensual consolation. His gladioli are throatily rooted all the way down into us nearly to the point where we are they. Each one is "ordinarily" surrounded by a space which separates it from the garden; that space is the locus of a human miracle, where everyday air and light are transfigured into art; the "ordinary" posies are haloed and hallowed in that sense. The air is breathed *down* in our tingling bodies like the "air limpide et profond du matin" in **"Le Sonneur."** This air is as earthy as anything in Rimbaud.

Mallarmé's leaves are leafy in his "vrais bois"; his vases are rump-rounded solidly vase-like as Braque's, his nymphs are yummily summed up in the folds of their womb-lips, his gladioli have the infantile immediacy of a Matisse cut-out . . .

The up-down liveliness is complemented and retotalized in time by a sustained commerce with the everyday, as we noted of the "ordinairement" referring to the very human—earthy-airy—miracle of the gladioli. One may speak of Mallarmé's realism, in this middling sense, on the horizontal dimension of *élan vital,* on-going time, existence, ephemerality, life as we really live it, unsentimentally accepted yet loved as Tolstoy and Proust—"la vraie vie"—loved it and gave their all to represent and preserve for the rest of us: "Féerie, oui, quotidienne—sans distance, par l'inspiration, plus que le plein air enflant un glissement, le matin ou l'après-midi, de cygnes à nous; ni au-delà que ne s'acclimate, des ailes détournée et de tous paradis, l'enthousiaste innéité de la jeunesse dans une profondeur de journée" ("Berthe Morisot"). Both dimensions are fully if subtly there: the upward paradisiacal, the earth-bound bodily in one direction; in the other, the floating onward of *élan vital,* gliding like the swans in water, converting—*acclimate*—into the civilized inwardness of merely human youth the paradisiacal urges and the depth of the world glimpsed on such a day.

At such a crossroads of Mallarméan reality, in the rounded sense, the theme of earthiness enters into its full nostalgic-for-the-whole context. Provisionally, we have come full circle. (pp. 70-80)

> *Robert Greer Cohn, "Earthy Mallarmé," in* The Romanic Review, *Vol. LXXV, No. 1, January, 1984, pp. 70-80.*

Kathleen Henderson Staudt   (essay date 1984)

[*In the following essay, Staudt investigates* Un Coup

de dés,   claiming that the poem "approaches Mallar-
mé's ideal of an opaque language of pure forms."]

Critics who write about "ineffability" in poetry are usually concerned, implicitly or explicitly, with the relationship between language and something beyond it, an ideal or a dimension of experience that is by definition inexpressible in language. They consider poetic language as a medium through which higher things are partially apprehended. Stéphane Mallarmé's work occupies a peculiar place within the discussion of ineffability and literature because of its radical denial that poetry can express *any* ineffable or transcendental truth. Far from developing a poetic technique that could mediate an ineffable ideal, Mallarmé's poetics seeks a new language that would free itself altogether from mediation and become an end in itself.

The place of Mallarmé's poetics in such a context is explored quite thoroughly in Gerald Bruns's *Modern Poetry and the Idea of Language* [1974]: Bruns places Mallarmé's poetic theory at one pole of a dialectic between "Orphic" and "Hermetic" modes. The "Orphic" mode, which governs most theories of language as mediation, conceives of "creating a world" by means of the poetic world. Although many writers in the Romantic tradition recognize the impossibility of literally "speaking things into being," the Orphic myth of language is clearly akin to the belief that words make accessible to the mind certain dimensions of thought that would otherwise elude it. The Orphic mode assumes, in short, that there is something beyond language that needs to be expressed, brought to consciousness, or "created."

In contrast, the "Hermetic" mode includes those theories which view the poetic structure as an end in itself, rather than as a medium expressing some "idea" or "reality" beyond language. For Bruns, Mallarmé is the *daimon* or spiritual ancestor of a group of modern poets and critics who have sought a radically self-referential, autonomous language, transcendent in itself. He connects Mallarmé, through Valéry, Saussure, and Jakobson, to the radical questioning of "transcendental signifieds" found in Jacques Derrida. My own essay will follow Bruns's lead in reading Mallarmé as a forerunner of certain contemporary structuralist and post-structuralist theorists, and will try to show how Mallarmé's resistance to the concept of language as a means of communication gives rise to his search for a poetic language "transcendent in its own right." I shall, however, depart from Bruns somewhat by giving more attention to the "Hermetic" than to the "Orphic" aspects of Mallarmé's poetic practice.

Mallarmé's fascination with the possibility of an autonomous poetic work is evident in **"Solennité,"** his review of Théodore de Banville's *Le Forgeron.* Here he praises de Banville's work for its obedience "to the dialectic that belongs to poetry alone (*au seul dialectique du vers*)." He is especially impressed by the calculated impersonality of the text, which allows the language to move in its own world. Mallarmé's review praises, in particular, the liberation in the poem of "the principle which is only Poetry" (*le principe qui n'est—que le Vers*), and calls this principle "Signe," the sign. The emergence of this autonomous sign (*lancé de soi*) reveals a mystery that is somehow inherent in words

themselves. This desire to construct a "pure" work, independent of the world and made up of signs that evoke each other through a power inherent in language itself, is implicit in much of Mallarmé's writing about poetry. To comprehend fully his reasons for seeking this hidden purity, it is necessary to identify the other aspects of language that Mallarmé's poetry of "pure signs" is constructed to resist.

In an early essay entitled **"Hérésies artistiques: l'Art pour tous,"** Mallarmé inveighs against the popular notion that poetic language ought to be "intelligible" to all people simply because it uses the grammar and vocabulary of their native tongue. On the contrary, he argues, the art of poetry should be viewed as a sacred mystery, accessible only to a devoted few. In their effort to discover "une langue immaculée," Mallarmé insists, poets should eschew the "intelligibility" that the masses demand of literature, and should instead imitate the obscurity of ancient hieroglyphic manuscripts. Moreover, poets must avoid all the formal ugliness of mass-produced literature, especially the columns of the newspapers and the monotonous uniformity of the cheap booksellers' editions of great poets.

By resisting the conventional character of written language, Mallarmé hopes to uncover a unique mystery that belongs to language alone. He writes in *Le mystère dans les lettres* that the language of the masses, in its insistence on communicating messages, overlooks a more essential mystery inherent in language. "What they fail to spread," he writes "is the priceless mist that floats about the secret abyss of every human thought." The poet's mission, then, is not to communicate thought, but to enable this mysterious dimension of language itself to emerge, by discovering new relationships among pure signs.

Thus the poet's awareness of the "principle which is only Poetry" depends on his sensitivity to attributes of language that are overlooked in popular forms of literature and verbal communication. The most important of these, for Mallarmé, is the status of language as a visible form, as black ink on white paper. He is especially fascinated by the capacity of these black forms to establish relationships among themselves, to "signify" according to the rules of a self-contained linguistic system. This "signifying" power of words is quite different, for Mallarmé, from their mere "intelligibility" to the masses. Thus he rebukes poets who write only in order to be "understood" and readers who wish only to "understand." Rather, he insists, the poem should be viewed as a sacred end in itself. As he puts it in one particularly vivid passage, those who write to be understood seek "intelligibility" in "an inkwell without darkness." This image is a rich one for Mallarmé's purposes. Words written in ink whose blackness is not noticed are words whose only purpose is to serve as mediators. They are effaced by the message they communicate. Mallarmé thus insists on the status of the poetic word as a thing in itself, as a form on paper, a blackness against white.

The substantiality of poetry in Mallarmé's thinking is underscored in *L'Action restreinte,* an essay which describes to a would-be writer the poet's confrontation with ink and paper, the materials of his craft. Instead of an "inkwell without darkness," the poet here faces a crystalline ink-well, "clear as consciousness (*clair comme une conscience*)," containing a drop of shadow ("*une goutte de ténèbres*"). This dark drop of ink will become the poetic word, something even more substantial than the meditation of which it is a trace. In pursuing "black on white," the poet works in a world of pure darkness and light, the exact negative of the stars against a black sky. Black ink and white paper are his materials, and these represent, for Mallarmé, something as mysterious and elemental as the stars. The language of the poem must somehow present the mystery that accompanies its own emergence, "le rien de mystère, indispensable, qui demeure, exprimé, quelque peu." This sense of mystery is due in large measure to the semiotic character of words themselves, as black marks which are at the same time, inexplicably, "signs" evoking other signs. The poet who pursues "black on white" must learn how to manipulate these signs so that the mystery of poetry itself will emerge from their interrelationships, overriding whatever other meanings arbitrary convention has assigned to the poet's words.

The theoretical implications of the poetic problem facing Mallarmé are explored with remarkable lucidity in the work of Jan Mukařovsky, a member of the Prague Linguistic School who was influenced by both Saussure and Jakobson. Mukařovsky's essay "On Poetic Language" [which appeared in *The Word and Verbal Art,* 1977] studies closely the relationship between the role of poetic language as the "material" of a work of art and its tendency, at the same time, to point beyond itself to other signs. Mukařovsky insists, first, that poetic language defines itself as different from "standard literary language" by deliberately deviating from the patterns of language to which readers are accustomed. This deviation from the norm tends to bring to the foreground language's status as a complex of sounds and forms out of which a poet builds a work, its status as the "material" of a work of art. Yet the capacity of poetic language to "signify" and to "mean" within the conventions of standard language distinguishes poetry inescapably from the other arts:

> What is language in literature? It is a *material* like metal and stone in sculpture, like pigment and the material of the pictorial plane in painting . . . Nevertheless, there is a considerable difference between other artistic materials and language. Stone, metal and pigment enter art as mere natural phenomena which gain a semiotic character only in art; they begin to "mean" something. Language in its very essence is already a sign.

Like artists working in other media, Mallarmé regards language as a material that needs to be molded into a work of art. The fundamentally semiotic character of language which Mukařovsky describes is clearly a source of poetry's unique richness, but it also presents a difficult problem to the poet. It obliges him to adapt for his own purposes that aspect of the common, or "standard," language which he seeks most to transcend: its tendency toward "mere intelligibility." Paradoxically, Mallarmé attempts to make use of language's function as a medium of communication in his effort to construct a "pure work."

An unused trial illustration by Redon for Un Coup de Des.

The challenge presented by the material and semiotic properties of language is most developed in Mallarmé's discussions of "Le Livre," the "Great Work" that he dreams of completing. This Great Book will be an expansion of the autonomous sign described in **"Solennité."** Its power will lie not in what it says about the world, but in the new and uniquely poetic significance that it will discover in the language of the world. He envisions the Great Work as an ultimate form that could subsume everything that conventional language reveals as "the world," replacing ordinary reference with a language of pure signs. In a letter written to Verlaine in 1885, Mallarmé explains his dream of the "Great Work," emphasizing not what it will say, but what it will be. He describes the Book as "architectural and premeditated," based on "equations" that will capture the mysterious rhythms inherent in the form of a book—especially the rhythm created by the turning of the leaves and by the movement of words across the "black on white" page. The Book embodies for Mallarmé a purity of form that all poets seek, whether or not they do so consciously, whenever they try to construct works of art out of language. In describing his poetic project, Mallarmé pictures himself as a mathematician and an alchemist rather than as a poet in the Romantic sense; far from attempting to express inspired thoughts, he seeks to reveal the mysterious, living patterns that he finds inherent in the relationships among signs within a work.

It is curious that Mallarmé's Great Work is described both as the "Orphic explication of the earth" and as "the literary game *par excellence*." The former designation attributes to language a prophetic and creative power analogous to what Bruns calls the "Orphic" mode in poetry, and implies that the Book would have a radically referential function, "naming" the existing world in order to recreate it in the image of poetry. This conception of the poet's task is also implicit in Mallarmé's statement elsewhere that "the world is made to end in a beautiful Book" (*le monde est fait pour aboutir à un beau Livre*).

The view of the Book's "Orphic" function seems quite distinct from its role as "literary game *par excellence*," which corresponds to what Bruns calls the "Hermetic" conception of poetry as a game of words transcendent in itself. Mallarmé insists elsewhere that the poetic work neither imitates nor adds to the world of objects and experience. Its role is to abstract from the world systems of pure relationships out of which a work of art can be constructed. This would seem to be humbler project than the "Orphic explication of the earth," which gives the work power to transcend and replace the world. Yet both claims—the prophetic drive to explain and transcend the world through poetry and the insistence that the poet must confine his attention to purely formal relationships among words—coexist in Mallarmé's writings on poetry. This tension between two poetic goals is one source of the enigmatic combination of formal beauty and thematic opacity that characterizes Mallarmé's best and most difficult works.

If Mallarmé is so committed to the elimination of mere intelligibility, why does he continue to use the French language, the native language of the masses whose irreverence he so vehemently criticizes? Why does he not seek a purely architectonic form like that developed in the early twentieth century's "concrete poetry"—poetry whose sound and shape took precedence over meaning? Mallarmé's continued fidelity to French grammar and syntax is an essential part of his technique. Paradoxically, he exploits language's tendency to "mean" as one of a number of linguistic properties that must be revealed in the poet's effort to overcome referentiality. For Mallarmé, the referential meanings of words are due entirely to arbitrary convention or "chance" (*le hasard*), an entity that is beyond the poet's control. The pure form would present "le hasard vaincu mot par mot," chance defeated one word at a time, through the gradual construction of a work governed by its own internal laws.

In its effort to "abolish chance" in this sense, Mallarmé's poetry employs a complex mixture of visual, auditory, spatial, and thematic effects that explication can only partly elucidate. His occasional writings on poetic technique do, however, suggest some of the methods by which a poet can hope to achieve a work that is at once "the Orphic explication of the Earth" and "the literary game *par excellence*."

The essay published under the title **"Crise de vers"** offers one of Mallarmé's most concise descriptions of the form a "pure work" would take. "The ideal," he writes, "would be a reasonable number of words stretched beneath our mastering glance, arranged in enduring figures, and followed by silence." In this one sentence, Mallarmé touches on most of the techniques that determine his concept of poetry: he emphasizes the importance of typographic form, the appeal of the poem to the eye, and the interplay of words with silence.

The essay goes on to assert that the pure poem should have no personal voice that would distract from its architectonic form. Its words should be set in motion by their own internal imbalances (*par le heurt de leur inégalité mobilisés*), not by the will of the poet. In practice, the poet must be guided by the demands of syntax and by the graphic and sonorous relations and differences among words. By thus exploiting the dynamic relationships inherent in language, Mallarmé hopes to bring about an art form motivated from within itself. The "collision" of words with one another and the rhythmic and sonorous effects that this produces will take the place of the driving personal emotion or the voice of Nature that motivated Romantic poetry. The beauty of the new poetry will be crystalline, pure: it will be like the glitter of firelight on the facets of precious stones, a beauty that comes about solely through the impersonal structural relationships of form to form, light to darkness.

This interest in pure relationships among words is the basis for Mallarmé's preoccupation with analogies between poetry and the non-representational arts of music and architecture. For him, music is a language based on relationships (*des rapports*), and uncontaminated by what he calls "l'universel reportage" of ordinary language. Poetry must strive, like music, to stress relationships rather than meanings. It must bring to the reader's attention the sounds, shapes, and forms of the words, the rhythmic effect produced by the intervention of silence in poetic lines and by the movement of words across the page. By thus transposing musical techniques to language, the poet can hope to reveal a mysterious, primitive harmony that lies hidden within his words. Although he believes that the new poetry can learn a great deal from the structure of symphonic forms, Mallarmé insists that it will be a form superior to music. Poetry uses printed words on paper which, unlike performed music, do not fade over time. The written word, arranged and developed in relationships that imitate the symphony's variety of timbres and rhythms, is capable of creating a more enduring music, one that can be re-mobilized, in silence, with each fresh reading.

Like music, then, the pure poem can only be related to the world of objects and experiences through its infinite "suggestiveness." Thus, to say the ordinary name of a known object in the context of pure poetry is to make of it something utterly new, to place it in a world of its own. In a well-known passage from **"Crise de vers,"** Mallarmé claims that by pronouncing the name of a flower, "une fleur," he can remove that word from its function in everyday language and hence abolish its connection to any object to which it might have referred. The word becomes a pure sign independent of referentiality, "l'absente de tous bouquets." By thus linking the name of a flower to an entity that is absent from the world of experience, the poet hopes to give that word a new function in a completely autonomous verbal universe.

It is clear, however, that such an absolute transposition of the everyday word into a universe of pure fictions is not possible so long as words retain their function as "names" of things in the common language. Even to understand the concept implied by "l'absente de tous bouquets," one needs to know what the usual referent of "fleur" is, and to understand the rules of ordinary French that make "fleur" the grammatical referent of "l'absente." In contrast to the musical note, the word always retains, as a kind of residue, the referential function that convention has assigned to it. Similarly, the relationships among words in a poem are necessarily governed in part by the same conventions of grammar and syntax that rule the language of "reportage." This conflict between the controlled, autonomous universe of words that the poet envisions and the conventions within which the same words usually function is evident in the closing paragraph of **"Crise de vers"**:

> Out of a number of words, poetry fashions a single new word which is total in itself and foreign to the language—a kind of incantation. Thus the desired isolation of language is effected; and chance (which might still have governed these elements, despite their artful and alternating renewal through meaning and sound) is thereby instantly and thoroughly abolished. Then we realize, to our amazement, that we had never truly heard this or that ordinary poetic fragment; and, at the same time, our recollection of the object thus conjured up bathes in a totally new atmosphere.

The new "total word," completely isolated from the existing language, is here presented as a triumph of poetry over "chance" (*le hasard demeuré aux termes*), the conventional associations that contaminate the poet's materials and limit his control over his work. The final sentence of this paragraph, however, seems to contradict Mallarmé's claim that poetry can completely "abolish chance" in this sense. Here his allusion to the recollection of the object conjured up (*l'objet nommé*, the object *named*) reveals that the word cannot be utterly dissociated from the object it used to name. By focusing for a moment on the thing referred to rather than on the word itself, Mallarmé tacitly acknowledges that poetry cannot free itself entirely from the assumptions governing the language of denomination or reference. Because he continues to use the "contaminated" French language in the construction of his "pure" poetic works, Mallarmé is obliged to come to terms with this inevitable tendency of his words to retain "traces" of their function as names of objects and events.

The tension between the poet's drive to create a "pure work" on the one hand and the inevitable "intelligibility" of his materials on the other is a source of the rich mystery and formal beauty of Mallarmé's last complete work, *Un Coup de dés jamais n'abolira le hasard*. Although there seems to be little basis for assuming that he intended it to be his "Great Work," the poem does present some fascinating illustrations of Mallarmé's poetics of the "pure work" in action. The poet's struggle against "le hasard de-

meuré aux termes" here enters both the philosophical theme and the physical form of his work. The conflicts between typographic and syntactical forms, as between thematic and visual effects, reveal the paradoxical futility of the poet's continuous struggle to "defeat chance" by constructing an autonomous language.

The poem's physical appearance immediately reveals a fascination with the typographical form of words as "black marks on white." Groups of words are related to one another by distinct typefaces and by visual configurations that frequently disrupt syntax and distract our attention from the meanings of the words to the shapes that they form on the page. The title sentence, UN COUP DE DÉS JAMAIS N'ABOLIRA LE HASARD, unifies the poem both visually and thematically. Its large upper-case type provides a graphic focus around which all the other typographical "themes" in the poem organize themselves. At the same time, the enigmatic meaning of this sentence provides a key to the poem's total significance. It proclaims in tautological fashion that chance will never be abolished by a single game of a chance, that a roll of the dice (*un coup de dés*) cannot defeat the chance which made it possible. The deeper poetic significance of this statement becomes clear if we recall Mallarmé's reference to the "chance" that poetry resists in its confrontation with ordinary language (*le hasard demeuré aux termes*). Though the form of the poem proclaims its attempt to construct something new out of words, the title sentence proclaims the ultimate futility of the work's linguistic act. Thus the work, a form constructed out of words, vainly attempts to resist the conventionality and arbitrariness by which those words exist in the language.

Between the words of this key sentence emerge the fragments of a narrative, recounted in language whose syntax is remarkably clear, despite the disruptive effect of typographical configurations and white spaces. Both thematically and visually, page 3 presents the first scene and the first stage of the poem's fragmentary narrative action. Here the white abyss of the sea opens to receive the sinking ship announced on page 2. The shape of the lines on the page clearly repeats the steep drop into the abyss, and invites us to picture the sinking ship (*un naufrage*) poised on the edge of destruction:

> l'Abîme
> blanchi
> étale
> furieux
>   sous une inclinaison
>   plane désespérement
>   d'aile
>   la sienne
>   par
>   avance retombée d'un mal à
>   dresser le vol
>   et couvrant les jaillissements
>   coupant au ras les bonds.

The visual image of a drop into blackness, and other versions of this same shape—thin at the left, denser at the lower right—will recur in the poem for varying purposes. This image is repeated, for example, on page 7, where a plumed hat is described in the text, and on pages 10 and

11 where the "constellation" of the Great Bear will be described.

As page 3 set the scene, page 4 narrates the primary action of the poem's second "movement" in the sentence "LE MAITRE . . . hésite" (The Master . . . hesitates). The sentence structure and typographical form of this page deliberately disperse this central sentence, interrupting and covering the action that it narrates, so that the materiality of the text itself will seem more immediate than the events of the narrative. The most striking source of the fragmented effect is the separation of the subject, "LE MAITRE," from its predicate, "hésite." Because of this separation, the intervening phrases that modify "LE MAITRE," offering sketchy descriptions of his origins and purpose here, initially seem to be random parentheses. Meanwhile, the white spaces and typographical configurations create a symmetrical, winglike shape that repeats itself in the lower half of the page. This graphic symmetry contrasts markedly with the disorder in the production of sense on this page. The white spaces of the visual design and the median line of the page break up sentences and phrases when grammar and syntax demand most strenuously to keep words together. This contrast between fragmented syntax and balanced visual form forces the reader to notice the text for its own sake, and deliberately frustrates conventional efforts to "understand." At the same time, the syntax, while complex, is correct and decipherable, so that the reader is kept aware of a meaning that is struggling to escape, a "sens enseveli" or buried sense.

This buried sense reveals the traces of a highly charged dramatic situation which is central to the narrative. "Le Maître," who has already been located at an ultimate moment (*dans les circonstances éternelles, du fond d'un naufrage* [p. 2]), hesitates before rolling the dice. As he does so, the dice clenched in his fist, we learn that he once controlled the ship, but has now lost control (*jadis il empoignait la barre*), and that his fate is inevitable. His fist, which once guided the tiller, now clutches the dice which can have no effect on his fate, but which he must nonetheless roll. As in *Igitur,* the protagonist here finds himself at a critical moment in which he becomes aware, during a prolonged hesitation, of his own existence and of the utter futility of his final act, a roll of the dice in vain resistance to "le hasard."

But here, chance is more vividly symbolized by the white neutrality of the sea, which will swallow up Master and ship and leave no evidence that they ever existed. The words that trail off at the end of page 4,

> naufrage cela
>> direct de l'homme
>> sans nef
>> n'importe
>>> où vaine

stress the utter vanity of the action contemplated, and the inevitability of the shipwreck regardless of the Master's actions. The shape of these lines allows us to see the whiteness of the page "swallowing up" the text's effort to explain the master's gesture, just as the sea will swallow up the ship after the dice are rolled.

The Master's situation is presented in a new set of images on pages 7 and 8 of the poem, where the feather and the human figure associated with it take the place of the shipwreck and become the body that is suspended over the abyss. Several readers have noted that the feather, "la plume," which appears alone on the left half of page 7, is also a word for "pen," the instrument of writing. On pages 7 and 8, Mallarmé conflates the "plume" with a new, younger hero-figure. The shape formed by the lines on this page repeat the shape of the plumed hat they describe; at the same time, one can discern an inkwell and quill pen:

> *plume solitaire éperdue*
>> *sauf*
>>> *que la rencontre ou l'effleure une toque de minuit*
>>>> *et immobilise*
>>>> *au velours chiffonné par un esclaffement sombre*
>>>>> *cette blancheur rigide*
>>> *dérisoire*
>>>> *en opposition au ciel*
>>>> *trop*
>>>>> *pour ne pas marquer*
>>>>>> *exigüment*
>>>>>>> *quiconque*
>>>>> *prince amer de l'écueil*
>>>>>> *s'en coiffe comme de l'héroïque*
>>>>>> *irrésistible mais contenu*
>>>>>> *par sa petite raison virile*
>>>>>>> *en foudre*

Both inkwell and black plumed hat are images of blackness against a white background. The subsequent emphasis on the hero's silhouette against the white sea, with its interest in blackness on white, suggests that this hero could be read as self-reflexive image for the text itself—blackness against white, set down by "une plume." The description of the plumed hat against sea and sky (beginning *cette blancheur rigide*) is particularly striking as a double image for the narrative situation and the graphic form of *Un Coup de dés.* The "blancheur rigide" of the feather opposing the white sky is also the white feather of a quill pen about to blot the whiteness of the page, and an image of an overblown masculinity, "une petite raison virile," trying to master something beyond its powers. Like the pen, the "blancheur rigide" "marks" the figure of the hero as a black spot which tries vainly to differentiate the whiteness surrounding it, to "impose a boundary on the infinite." The silhouettes of both hero and text are presented as futile efforts to organize an uncontrollable whiteness.

With the appearance of "LE HASARD" on page 9, the narrative action of the poem is completed. The dice are rolled, and the feather/pen falls, to be overwhelmed by the uniform whiteness of the sea (*par la neutralité identique du gouffre*). The coincidence between the dropping of the feather and the sinking of the ship suggests a correspondence between the Master's futile act—the roll of the dice—and the poet's act of writing, which produced the poem called *Un Coup de dés.* This coincidence reveals the poem as an emblem for writing itself, which stops and is replaced by whiteness when the poem ends.

Once the ship/poem has been thus "dissolved," what can remain? The final portion of the work, pages 10 and 11, suggest an image for the text itself—the CONSTELLA-TION. Both the meaning and the shape of the words on the last page focus on a constellation as an abstract config-uration of black points against a white background, the exact negative of the "alphabet des astres" described in *L'Action restreinte.* The text's shape on page 11 repeats the shape that we saw on page 3, but now we recognize both as roughly approximating the shape of the "Septen-trion" or "Great Bear" constellation:

EXCEPTÉ
à l'altitude
PEUT ETRE
aussi loin qu'un
endroit
fusionne avec au-dela

hors l'intérêt
quant à lui signalé
en général
selon telle obliquité par telle déclivité
de feux

vers
ce doit être
le Septentrion aussi Nord

UNE CONSTELLATION
froide d'oubli et de désuétude
pas tant
quelle n'énumère
sur quelque surface vacante et supéri-
eure
le heurt successif
sidéralement
d'un compte total en formation

Here the text, describing the "Septentrion" or Great Bear, refers to its own shape, and explains what is implied by a text that is also a constellation. The constellation is a pure form, the product of chance—produced by certain chance relationships between lights (*selon telle obliquité telle dé-clivité / de feux*). Like the text that shares its form, the constellation is impersonal. Cold, detached from the lives of mankind, it gives off the light of interstellar events that have taken place beyond memory, millennia before we see its light. It thus represents the preservation in space of a moment in time that is long over. It counts out a series of arbitrary relationships that once existed between adjacent stars and suspends them against a vacant background, much as the text suspends its black marks against white vacancy. Most importantly, the constellation is still "in formation." Its form will never be fixed and determinate, for chance has already dissipated the configuration that we see in the sky now. It is the transitory index of chance events that continue and can never be completely con-trolled by a pure form.

For this reason, as Bruns, Cohn [in *L'Oeuvre de Mallar-mé: Un Coup de dés,* 1951], and others have shown, the constellation is the epitome of the structure that Mallar-

mé's text strives to achieve. The text, black form against white, preserves on paper a series of relations in time and space which were once established in an act of writing. This poetic act, now completed, is inscribed in the text, impersonally, on the level of the narrative as well as in the visual connection between the text and the constellation. Thematically, the constellation "survives" the sinking of the ship. It is aloof from this event, yet it was present dur-ing the narrative action and persists after it. The corre-spondence between text and constellation developed in the form of the last page suggests that we should see the text, too, as a "survivor." It was there to record the last mo-ment of Master and ship, which was also the last moment of an act of writing. But it persists after the act of writing is completed, as an entity having its own shape and its own rules, free of the writer's intention or thought. In the text as constellation, there is no trace of the originating inspira-tion or thought which motivated the act of writing; all we have is the poem, *Un Coup de dés,* which presents itself as a product of chance (*le hasard*), constructed in resis-tance to chance.

The last line's announcement that "Every thought gives off a roll of the dice" (*Toute Pensée émet un Coup de Dés*), however, admits that the poem originated in an experience outside of language and is thus rooted in the ordinary world of "chance." The fact that C and D in this last line are in the upper case suggests that we are to take "Un Coup de Dés" as a reference to the poem's own title, and an acknowledgement of its origins in thought. The last line thus undercuts the autonomy of the text as constellation by announcing that the poem has told, in spite of itself, the story of its own creation. It has recorded the experience that engendered it by narrating the story of the Master and his dice and by equating the roll of the dice with the poem's appearance. Thus it has not completely overcome "chance" because it still refers beyond itself to a "real" ex-perience: the act of writing *Un Coup de dés,* an act that began before the poem took shape.

Nevertheless, to the extent that the poem comes to resem-ble the surviving constellation in its form and structure, it succeeds in "transcending" momentarily the human ex-perience of writer and audience, and creates a unique for-mal language of its own. The poem thus approaches Mal-larmé's ideal of an opaque language of pure forms, "black on white," a language that has freed itself from the world of experience and convention to become "transcendent in itself."

The poem's status as an "approach to" or "approximation of " Mallarmé's poetic ideal is the quality that allies it most interestingly to the problem of ineffability in litera-ture. By its effort to "resist chance" in Mallarmé's terms, the poem resists the conventional role of language as a me-diator of ideas. Instead, the work's primary goal is to ex-press *itself* as an ineffable ideal. This ideal is ultimately un-attainable because the poetic purity suggested by the poem's form and by the self-reflexive image of the constel-lation remains beyond the reach of "contaminated" lin-guistic materials. The narrative embedded in this intricate formal structure tells of the vain struggle by which the poet created the work. It thus shows that even the "purest" poetic form must recount, in spite of itself, the story of its own creation; it must "refer to" and "mediate" the story of its own origins in a human experience. Thus, *Un Coup de dés* is a poem of ineffability because it gestures toward a purity of form that remains beyond the reach of its linguistic materials. In spite of itself, the poem acknowledges its bondage to the earthbound, chance-governed "language of the crowd," from which all poetic language is borrowed, and to which even the "purest" poetry must ultimately return. (pp. 147-59)

> *Kathleen Henderson Staudt, "The Poetics of 'Black on White': Stéphane Mallarmé's 'Un Coup de dés',"* in Ineffability: Naming the Un-namable from Dante to Beckett, *edited by Peter S. Hawkins and Anne Howland Schotter, AMS Press, 1984, pp. 147-61.*

Penny Florence on the creation of meaning in *Un Coup de dés*:

The idea of reading *Un Coup de Dés* as an *illustrated* text is not an easy one to assimilate. Most people are surprised to discover that it was originally going to be published in this form. Illustration seems not to fit at all . . . within the existing 'modernist' framework of reading. . . . [We] do not value illustration, or transpositions between verbal and visual signs, and still find visual material hard to integrate with serious written texts, even though we can accommodate words and images in film or in comics and advertising. This is partly because of hierarchies of form, and partly because the way we direct verbal consciousness separates it from other ways of knowing. It is also because we still prefer to read texts as discrete.

Un Coup de Dés may be read as an attack on these habits of thought. In reading it constructively with Redon's illustrations we have to rethink what we understand as visual expression and move outside the boundaries of the texts to experience them as open-ended. They are a book with interchangeable pages, with varying directions and registers, with vertical and horizontal movements, with reversals and with shapes that are as important in signification as words. They challenge our notion of coherence and demand that we re-shape the relations between recorded and immediate experience.

Play is one of the main ways through which the poem explores the possibilities of reconstructing sense. The game entails risk, fear, uncertainty and pleasure. Although pleasure is the least explicit, it is far from being the least important of the poem's elusive ways of making and deflecting meaning. But to remove the constraints governing the use of language, so that everything is *at play*, as in *Un Coup de Dés*, the poem risks non-sense. It offers the reader no assurances as it erodes the comparative safety of rational modes.

> *Penny Florence, in her* Mallarmé, Manet and Redon: Visual and Aural Signs and the Generation of Meaning, *Cambridge University Press, 1986.*

Laurence M. Porter   (essay date 1985)

[In the following excerpt, Porter, an American scholar, educator, and critic, argues that Mallarmé's revisions of numerous poems serve to make their meanings more tenuous, thus inscribing his and other Symbolist poets' concern with the difficulties of communication.]

Rather than merely challenging the reader's preconceptions regarding what poetry should say, [French Symbolism] disrupted the very communicative axis linking sender to message to receiver, thus questioning whether any communication was possible. Roman Jakobson [in his *Studies on Child Language and Aphasia*, 1971] employed the term "contact" to characterize the essential contiguity of message and receiver. The reader's attention must somehow be captured, and he or she must recognize the message as something decodable and worth being decoded. You may object that the notion of contact is otiose, since any emission of a message presupposes an attempt to get attention. But poets do not take contact for granted. To couch one's words in the form of imaginative literature requires the potential decoder to be familiar with an unusual number of conventions; it constitutes a marked choice of formality, since the act of reading is a highly ritualistic one which cannot readily be undertaken at the same time as other activities; and it entails play rather than practicality since its referents are not real. So the *captatio benevolentiae* is a fact of literary life.

To elucidate Symbolism in particular, and poetry in general, moreover, one must add to Jakobson's categories that of a link between the sender and the message. It can be identified as poetic competence, inspiration, or in my terms "concept." Linguists do not bother with the concept: they assume that the referent is a given and that the sender's only problem is to encode it. Poets, however, must seek their referents—or if these *are* a given, as in the epic poem, they still must be encoded differently enough from previous versions so as to justify our once more harkening to the same story. But you need not find a fresh, ingenious way to ask me to pass the salt or tell you the time before you have a claim on my attention. Romanticism heightens the challenge of achieving both concept and contact by insisting upon radically unfamiliar codes and contexts that risk alienating the reader. Symbolism heightens it still more by seriously questioning whether any communication can be achieved. The French Symbolist movement is neither a generation nor a system, but a crisis.

What most distinguishes the major Symbolist poets from each other is that each situates the major disruption of his communicative axis differently. Apollinaire finds the poetic act flawed because the poet is unworthy; Verlaine finds words themselves inadequate; Baudelaire finds his potential audiences inaccessibly remote; and Rimbaud imagines a public whose attentive hostility denies his worth as a poet. These figures pass through a brief Symbolist phase resolved differently for each of them. Mallarmé, in contrast, appears the Symbolist poet *par excellence* because he is the most consistently absorbed by the difficulties of communication and because he remains in that mode nearly throughout his career.

Mallarmé's struggle to find expression is a quest he voluntarily assumes; it is not forced on him. For example, his casual verse and his single-handed creation of the fashion magazine *La Dernière Mode* offer ample proof of his facility. And in his early verse he often summons inspiration, as it were, at will. In his mature verse, his frequent use of symbols evoking poetic sterility is well known. But what has not been studied is the way in which he imposes that sterility upon himself. An author's revisions are the surest clue to his or her intentions. During Mallarmé's metaphysical crisis of the middle 1860's, and again in 1887 when he prepares the first collected edition of his verse, he experiences a *prise de conscience* of his self-concept as a poet that leads him to strengthen the self-negating tendencies already dominant in his verse. He rewrites several earlier poems on each occasion, and most of his rewriting makes the virtual axis of communication more tenuous.

Two-thirds of Mallarmé's changes involve references to inspiration: he inscribes disruption primarily in the concept. In what forms does it appear? Poetry can refer to its concept non-discursively by identifying a pretext, often plainly announced in the title; by presenting a creator whose activities are analogous to the poet's; or by introducing a Muse-figure, inspiration personified. Erasing, attenuating, or negating these features connotes the disruption of the communicative axis effected by poetic sterility.

Through to the completion of *Hérodiade* in 1867, Mallarmé used titles to disclose his poems' sources of inspiration from the outset. Thus inspiration appears as unproblematical. In *Hérodiade,* however, the title has become a mask. The allusion to the biblical story with its historico-legendary topic conceals a self-referential drama involving a Muse-figure, but one who refuses to permit the approach of other beings or to make contact with materiality. The poem's concluding section, "Cantique de saint Jean," celebrates a suicidal union of the poet-figure with inspiration. Salvation (literally the last word of the text) is equated with annihilation of the corporeal. Mallarmé has worked through his metaphysical crisis in such a fashion that he has nowhere left to go. It is not surprising that he then stops publishing for fifteen years. When he resumes, he largely eliminates titles, with the exception of self-referential ones such as *Prose (pour des Esseintes)* or commemorative ones like the *Tombeaux.* An unstated metonymy in the latter makes the act of commemoration (writing a poem) itself into the monument, an act of homage attesting to the powers of the person rendering it.

Not that the notation of inspiration disappears. Mallarmé's erasures leave traces which preserve the full import of his poems, while simultaneously enriching them: the reader is thus engaged in a meditative adventure required to recuperate their import. Specifically, inspiration in the sense of classical antiquity, the *furor poeticus,* entails the encounter of the human with the divine. The original title **"Sainte Cécile jouant sur l'aile d'un chérubin"** (December 5, 1865) spells that encounter out by naming both a human and an angel. The revised title **"Sainte"** (1883) condenses the two terms into a one-word oxymoron where the human and divine are fused. Moreover, the original title connotes a stained glass window, a luminous point of intersection where transcendent externality touches the

human space within. The pane makes these spaces mutually visible through the very act of separating them. The abridged title of the final version erases the stained glass window, but it still can be inferred from the words "fenêtre" (verse 1) and "vitrage" (verse 9). More subtly, the original **"Sonnet allégorique de lui-même"** (1868) evokes a parthenogenetic fecundity. When the poem is republished untitled in 1887, the idea of an intersection is preserved in the rare rhymes themselves. The chiasmic "-xy" implies the meeting of poet and Muse, an inside contacting an outside at a window ("la croisée" suggested by the X-shape); while the rhyme "-or" connotes the sunlight which illuminates the pane—particularly since the first occurrence of this rhyme is in the word "lampadophore" or lamp-bearer.

Within Mallarmé's earliest poems, inspiration appears conventionally as a celestial vision. Thus his **"Cantate pour la première communion"** unequivocally announces its pretext in the title. Then a choir of angels bearing inspiration from the beyond is summoned and instructed to perform, as in an eighteenth-century ode:

> Chantez—célébrez tous en choeur
> La joie et le bonheur
> Des enfants de la terre.

Even so early in Mallarmé's career, however, the inadequacy of human inspiration may be suggested through the etymological meaning of "enfants," those who cannot speak. Angels must do so for humanity. But these articulate angelic replacements are readily available.

The Muse-figure itself, in Mallarmé's poetry and in the ancient tradition on which it draws, is ordinarily feminine and supernatural. Femaleness signifies otherness in the male-dominated conventions of official high art which Symbolism brings to a paroxysm. And the supernatural always stands for what we hold in awe, such as creativity. So any supernatural female in a poem may represent the Muse. Needless to say, she like other major symbols can be double-edged. For instance, the goddess Shiva works both to create and to destroy; the lion figures either Satan or Christ; and the supernatural female of Symbolism can represent not only the source of inspiration which brings the transcendent within reach of the poet, but also the self-sufficing, unattainable ideal in and of itself, and the inexpressibility that overwhelms the poet confronting this ideal. Mallarmé begins with the euphemistic convention according to which the spiritual presence of the Muse facilitates and almost compels a poetic response (e.g., in "Sa fosse est creusée . . . "). But he soon telescopes the opposites of expressivity and incommunicability into the figure of a Muse who eludes the poet. Her elusiveness functions as a powerful phatic device that rivets our attention, insomuch as we identify with the poet. Finally, a further metonymic dislocation in the **"Sonnet en -yx"** prevents us from taking for granted the Muse's connectedness to inspiration any more than we had taken for granted her availability to Mallarmé's poet. We shall examine this transformation presently, after a brief commentary upon the twenty-eight variants in other poems where Mallarmé subverts every point along the axis of communication, but focuses on the concept in particular. The evidence is scant, but telling.

TABLE OF VARIANTS

1-2. "La Prière d'une Mère" (no date).

> [Dieu] Qui lança le soleil en sa route embrasée
> Et créa tout d'une pensée!

becomes

> Qui lança le soleil en la voûte éternelle
> De son regard faible étincelle.

The reference to God's creating everything through the power of thought—an activity analogous to and serving as a model for poetic creativity—has been eliminated. The effect is to replace the idea of inspiration, that seemingly brings texts forth *ex nihilo* or from a transcendent domain, with the idea of craftsmanship, working with existing materials. (Same poem: imploration by the mother).

> Donne à notre prière une aile
> Pour qu'elle s'envole à ton coeur
> Comme le parfum que révèle
> Au matin l'aubépine en fleur!

The last two verses become

> Comme le frais parfum que mêle
> Aux brises, l'aubépine en fleur!

In the initial version, the poem as prayer—like the perfume revealed by the flowering hawthorn to the morning—aims to inspire the heart of God (the audience) with tenderness. This active role of the poem as vehicle of inspiration fades when "révèle" is replaced with "mêle." The notation of the contact of the prayer with God has been maintained, but the parallel, reinforcing contact of the perfume-as-message with the dawn has disappeared together with its hint of Romantic panpsychism—a world-system which guarantees the contact.

3-6. "Le Sonneur" (1862 and 1866).

> Cependant que la cloche, enivrant sa voix claire
> A l'air plein de rosée et jeune du matin
> Invite la faucheuse à chanter pour lui plaire
> Un Angelus qui sent la lavande et le thym

becomes

> Cependant que la cloche éveille sa voix claire
> A l'air pur et limpide et profond du matin
> Et passe sur l'enfant qui jette pour lui plaire
> Un angélus parmi la lavande et le thym

The notion of inspiration conveyed in the first version by "enivrant" (suggesting an altered state of consciousness) is attenuated by being displaced to the air described as "pur" and "profond"—qualities associated with the transcendent ideal. The latter is now merely juxtaposed with rather than imbibed by the bell, a poet-surrogate. Next the bell assumes the role of inspiration from the clear air, but its specific solicitation of the second poet-figure ("invite") has been removed. This figure itself is transformed from someone who collects, binds, and stores to someone who does not. The Angelus, the poem experienced as the emanation of sound, is first associated with the aromatic plants of the harvest fields, which emanate fragrant odors. Thus the Angelus as poem becomes further associated with a concrete achievement—the gathering of the harvest itself. In the final version, this connotation of permanence is replaced by one of transience. The poetic response itself has been devalued: "Angelus" loses its capital letter, and is "tossed off" rather than "sung." That both harvester and child respond with a prayer heightens in both versions the contrast between them and the third poet-persona, the ineffectual monk of the remaining stanzas, who helplessly struggles to call forth the voice of the ideal. Finally, in verse twelve that voice becomes decapitalized ("la Voix"—"la voix") as if to render the Ideal more remote and inaccessible for the eponymous character: it is no longer necessarily contained within the sound he faintly hears. What remains is his frustration, and a mocking invitation to transcendence—the bell-rope—which can lead only to death by hanging (a blocked ascension).

7. "Brise marine" (1865 and 1866). Verse 7. "Du papier qu'un cerveau châtié me défend," becomes "Sur le vide papier que la blancheur défend." The problem of the absence of inspiration has been made absolutely rather than relatively insoluble by being attributed to an external, not an internal obstacle.

8. In addition to the effects mentioned above, the change of title from **"Sainte Cécile jouant sur l'aile d'un chérubin (Chanson et image anciennes)"** (1865) to **"Sainte"** (1883) removes the mention of artistic creation ("jouant"), its supernatural origin ("l'aile d'un chérubin"), and its historical dignity ("anciennes").

9. "De l'Orient passé des Temps / Nulle étoffe jadis venue" (n.d.) becomes "Quelle soie aux baumes de temps / Où la Chimère s'exténue" (1885). The final version erases the place of exotic origin of the fabric (the text, a sail which can be swelled by the breath of inspiration in Mallarméan symbolism)—"l'Orient"—together with the idea of origination itself ("jadis venue"), although traces of both are preserved in the metonymically displaced "soie" itself.

10-13. "Le Guignon" (1862 and 1887). In Stanza 2, ". . . Leurs bannières / Où passe le divin gonflement de la mer" becomes

> Un noir vent sur leur marche éployé pour bannières
> La flagellait de froid tel jusque dans la chair,
> Qu'il y creuait aussi d'irritables ornières.

Originally, the marchers hold actual banners suggesting sails filled with the divine breath of inspiration. Inspiration becomes intangible in the revised version. The physical banners have been replaced by the wind, now cold, painful and sinister rather than divine. "Creusait," referring to the hollows "dug" into the puckered flesh by the inclement weather, further connotes an absence of inspiration. The poets' physical substance, like a barren field, yields nothing although it is endlessly tilled. The added line in Stanza 3, "Toujours avec l'espoir de rencontrer la mer" removes the poet-figures far from the sea as source of inspiration, while they were next to it in Stanza 2 of the original. The hypothetical failure of creativity, connoting a compensatory Icarian renown, is transformed into a definitive failure when Stanza 5 changes "S'ils sont vaincus" to "Leur défaite." And in Stanza 11, "Le Guignon," which rode behind the undifferentiated "mendieurs d'azur" in the first version, now accompanies the new characters of the "Amants" (suggesting the poet and his Muse) and makes the "blanc couple nageur" into a "bloc boueux" rather than making a lone "superbe nageur" into a "fou crotté." In other words, the Muse-figure as well as the poet now is implicitly degraded.

14-16. "Placet futile" (1862 and 1887). The original title was **"Placet."** The importance of the poem as message is diminished when the self-referential "petition" of the title is devalued as "frivolous." Verse 3 of the same poem changes "Mais je suis un poète" to "J'use mes feux": specific designation of the lyric self as creative artist has been eliminated, and the suggestion of futility ("use") superimposed. The second tercet of the same poem changes "et Boucher . . . / Me peindra" to "pour qu'Amour . . . / M'y peigne." The historical artist Boucher has been replaced by a mythological abstraction, and the substance of the act of artistic creation has been weakened by being presented as optative rather than as assertoric. Thus the potential creation of the work of art undergoes a twofold shift from reality to fantasy.

17-18. "Le Pitre châtié" (1864 and 1887). The entire poem was originally an apostrophe addressed to the "Muse" (named in the direct address of verses 3 and 14), whose name and association with the lyric self ("moi, ton pitre," verse 3) disappear from the poem.

19-20. "Aumône" (1862, 1864, 1866, and 1887). Originally titled **"Haine du pauvre,"** the poem later introduced personified audiences as dedicatees in the versions of 1864 ("A un mendiant") and 1866 ("A un pauvre") but then eliminated that reference in the definitive title—which instead, through a form of higher sarcasm, implies that we the literary audience are the beggars. In all four versions, however, the poet serves as the source of inspiration for the beggar by offering him the money which permits a greater freedom of choice and action. So they all satirize the Romantic convention that the poet is a Muse to society.

21-23. "Autre éventail de Mademoiselle Mallarmé" (1886 and 1887). The third stanza evokes the trembling awakening of space stirred by the fan. But three notations of order and self-control in the original version are replaced by an experience of disorientation and alienation in the definitive one. The 1886 text is

> *Vaste jeu!* voici que frissonne
> L'espace comme un grand baiser
> Qui *fier* de *n'être* pour personne
> Ne sait jaillir ni s'apaiser

And in 1887 it reads

> *Vertige!* voici que frissonne
> L'espace comme un grand baiser
> Qui, *fou* de *naître* pour personne,
> Ne peut jaillir ni s'apaiser.

"Vaste jeu!", "fier," and "ne sait" become "Vertige!",

"fou," and "ne peut." The last change replaces the *pour-soi* with the *en-soi*. In a further movement toward the concrete, "n'être" gives way to its homonym "naître," transforming the dyad of non-being/control to one of being/loss of control. In both versions, of course, Mallarmé establishes a veneer of impersonality, characteristic of his mature work, with the typical device of replacing the perceiver with what is perceived. The personified figure of space serves as a metonymy for the poet observing the scene and projecting impressions upon it.

24-25. "Victorieusement fui" (1885 and 1887). The original mention of poetic immortality through implicit contact with future audiences ("vaincre le tombeau," verse 4), and the designation of "le poète" (verse 6) himself are erased, although their scattered traces remain in the first and last words of the opening quatrain "Victorieusement fui . . . mon absent tombeau."

26-28. "Le Tombeau d'Edgar Poe" (1876 and 1887). Mallarmé removes explicit reference to the poetic message when in verse 2, "Le Poète suscite avec un hymne nu," the word "hymne" is superseded by "glaive." At the same time the counter-message of the anti-selves becomes stronger. In both versions they accuse him of having found inspiration in drunkenness or drug addiction (stated in a typically precious periphrasis). But their accusations turn from thoughts to shouts when in vers 7 "Tous pensèrent entre eux" becomes "Proclamèrent très haut." The second stanza puts forward a counter-example, however, through which the ontological—or one might better say verbal—status of the poet's message is strengthened. The ignorant viewpoint of Poe's detractors yields to the enlightened viewpoint of a fellow poet in a chiasmic movement of thought that the French would call a "chassé-croisé." Both versions symbolize the poetic *oeuvre,* what remained after Poe's death, with his tombstone. In the first version the *oeuvre* is sinister, and its critics, perdurable: in the definitive version the terms are reversed. The *oeuvre* has become permanent and its critics sinister.

First version:

> *Sombre* bloc à jamais chu d'un désastre obscur,
> Que ce granit du moins montre à jamais sa borne
> Aux *vieux* vols de blasphème épars dans le futur.

Definitive version:

> *Calme* bloc ici-bas chu d'un désastre obscur,
> Que ce granit du moins montre à jamais sa borne
> Aux *noirs* vols du Blasphème épars dans le futur.

By glorifying the message and condemning a hostile audience, and by switching the site of the event from an indefinite time to a definite place, these variants strengthen the virtual communicative axis. Mallarmé's unusually clear use of value-laden terms here probably derives from his awareness that the poem was destined for a foreign audience—he even helped translate it into English.

THE "SONNET EN-YX"

The greatest number of Mallarmé's significant variants undermining the axis of communication appear in the heavily revised **"Sonnet allégorique de lui-même"** of 1868, republished without title in 1887. This poem has been studied repeatedly. Michel Grimaud [in his "Les Mystères du *Ptyx:* Hypothèses sur la remotivation psychopoétique à partir de Mallarmé et Hugo," *Michigan Romance Studies* 1, 1980] cogently summed up the reasoning adduced to support various critical interpretations, and Michael Riffaterre [in his *Semiotics of Poetry,* 1978] has convincingly demonstrated that it is a poem about nothing. But I should like to discuss how it got that way. There are degrees of nothingness in literature, if not in logic or physics.

The variants just discussed provide many examples of dislocating the communicative axis by erasing references to it. Mallarmé's negations in the **"Sonnet en -yx"** are more complex and profound. He disrupts the process of virtual inspiration in the poem by context dislocation, by denying us a network of associations that we take for granted. Let us consider a homey example of such dislocation. In October 1984, if you said "How about them Tigers?" most people would have assumed that you were referring to the American Baseball League pennant race and the World Series—rather than to a zoo, a safari, or a toy store. Your hearer could have adjusted quickly to these latter possibilities, which still form part of a communality of real or imagined experience. But if your next words had been "They're extinct," you would have shifted the frame of reference from a rule-governed victory to a mysterious defeat, and from a familiar social ritual to an unknown disaster or an unknown species. Mallarmé does something similar. Specifically, in a normal lyric poem the supernatural female either helps the poet triumph by mediating between him and the ideal, or else triumphs herself as an epiphany of it. Here, instead, Mallarmé shows her both inaccessible and defeated.

Mallarmé's letter to Cazalis in July 1868 specifies that the inspiration for the **"Sonnet en -yx"** had come from within itself rather than from externality. "Il est inverse, je veux dire que le sens, s'il y en a un (mais je me consolerais du contraire grâce à la dose de poésie qu'il renferme, ce me semble) est évoqué par un mirage interne des mots mêmes." So even in the first version of the sonnet, Mallarmé contrasts "poetry" with communication and declares his aim of obliterating any traces of external inspiration. The final version takes this further.

Sonnet allégorique de lui-même (1868)

La Nuit approbatrice allume les onyx
De ses ongles au pur Crime, lampadophore,
Du Soir aboli par le vespéral Phoenix
De qui la cendre n'a de cinéraire amphore

Sur des consoles, en le noir Salon: nul ptyx,
Insolite vaisseau d'inanité sonore,
Car le Maître est allé puiser de l'eau du Styx
Avec tous ses objets dont le Rêve s'honore.

Et selon la croisée au Nord vacante, un or
Néfaste incite pour son beau cadre une rixe
Faite d'un dieu que croit emporter une nixe

En l'obscurcissement de la glace, décor
De l'absence, sinon que sur la glace encor
De scintillations le septuor se fixe.

. . .

(Untitled [1887])

Ses purs ongles très haut dédiant leur onyx,
L'Angoisse, ce minuit, soutient, lampadophore,
Maint rêve vespéral brûlé par le Phénix
Que ne recueille pas de cinéraire amphore

Sur les crédences, au salon vide: nul ptyx,
Aboli bibelot d'inanité sonore,
(Car le Maître est allé puiser des pleurs au Styx
Avec ce seul objet dont le Néant s'honore).

Mais proche la croisée au nord vacante, un or
Agonise selon peut-être le décor
Des licornes ruant du feu contre une nixe,

Elle, défunte nue en le miroir, encor
Que, dans l'oubli fermé par le cadre, se fixe
De scintillations sitôt le septuor.

Night provides the pretext for the first version. It blots out the material world, the spectacle of which might tempt one to a mundane, unimaginative art of representation. But the very darkness paradoxically reveals a vision of absence in the remote stars. Even this negative version of inspiration becomes attenuated in the final version. Active light-giving ("allume") yields to static light-supporting ("soutient"). Night is replaced by "L'Angoisse," the effect it produces. And the etymological source of the word "Angoisse," *angustia,* reinforces the second version's general effect of a narrowing of focus. The cosmic setting, which would seem to offer a vast panorama from which to derive inspiration, is severely restricted by a number of synergistic devices. The added word "minuit" covertly reinscribes "Nuit" letter for letter. But in so doing it replaces the broad field of the night sky (the nadir of the noonday sun) by a point in space (the nadir of the noonday sun), and the long hours of darkness by one moment in time. Restriction recurs in the elimination of the words "approbatrice," connoting an inclusive acceptance, and "allume," anticipating a broadening of light. All in all, the spectacle no longer greets the poet with open arms, so to speak, but rather like a Calvinist Christ with hands held close together, leaving only a strait gate for the elect. Already concerned with concentration, the first version had limited the semantic field through the awkward technique of synonymy, through the redundancies of lines three and four: "soir . . . vespéral; cendre . . . cinéraire." The final version deploys synonymy more discreetly through Mallarmé's characteristic mature devices of etymological undertone and homophony. "Dédiant" derives from a root meaning "finger"; "onyx" comes from the Greek word for "claw" (a beast's or bird's fingernail); and "maint" echoes the sound of "la main". All three entities: the homonymic dream-hand; the stars as fingernails; and the extended arm of the lamp bearer simultaneously limn the selfsame posture of a ritual celebrant consecrating herself while preserving the memory of the vanished sun.

Mallarmé heightens the tension between human and cosmic by eliminating the supernumeraries of the first stanza, "le pur Crime" and "le Soir aboli," with their distracting baudelairian resonances. Although the adjective "pur" suggests strongly that Mallarmé does not intend to associate this crime with the human dimension, the notion does not exclude humanity, and it occurs in apparent harmony with the cosmic Night, Evening, and Phoenix as the hieratic immolator of the sun. The term "crime" confuses the human reaction of horror with the cosmic drama. But in the final version "L'Angoisse" appears in sharp focus as a poetic fixation upon the vestiges of the past, contrasted with the inexorable, impassive progression of the natural cycle. The new negative verb "ne recueille pas" now emphasizes the *décalage* between human and cosmic. The ashes from the sunset, from the self-sacrifice of the Phoenix, cannot be preserved. And since the verb "recueille" is closely related to the noun "recueil (de vers)," the implication is that the cosmic drama cannot be captured by poetry either.

Mallarmé's reworking of the second stanza further refutes the notion that poetry can replace reality by forming a memory that compensates for loss. "Consoles," the word for the furniture in the first version, had hinted at such a consoling compensation. The new term "crédences" suggests the utter disappearance of the sun in several ways. First, through association with sudden death. The Italian *credenza* was a sideboard where meals could be tasted to ensure they were not poisoned. Second, through the idea of an expected but missing formal display. The modern "crédence" is a "buffet de parade servant à exposer la vaisselle d'argent ou d'or"—celestial bodies' analogues. Third, since a "crédence" can also mean a table bearing the elements of the Mass, the absence of a *ptyx* or communion chalice here implies a religious ceremony that has been cancelled; that is to say, the impossibility of communion between the supernatural and the human.

The remaining changes in the second stanza further associate the *ptyx* with the erasure of inspiration, as a womb both empty and irrevocably absent. No longer is it linked to "le Rêve," a possible source of poetry, but to "le Néant." The phrase "aboli bibelot" designating the *ptyx* provides an onomatopoetic rendering for "inanité sonore" while introducing, through apophany, a phantom of *biblio,* the absent, burned, or uncreated book. The typographical boundary of the added parenthesis in lines seven and eight debars the *ptyx* from the real world. And by making it the only object pridefully acknowledged by the Void, rather than one of several objects belonging to the Master (a poet-figure), Mallarmé reveals the *ptyx* as a *mise en abyme* of the empty room from which it came, while both *ptyx* and room signify the poet's mind devoid of inspiration.

In the definitive version the *ptyx* serves to draw tears rather than water from the Styx. The new phrase "puiser des pleurs" again cancels the process of poetic creativity by reversing it. Whether one weeps or writes poetry, emotions move from "inside" to "outside" during their expression. But in Mallarmé's poem the Master draws inward the tears which had already been shed, in a gesture of repression rather than expression. In contrast, the original reading "puiser l'eau" conceals the homophony "l'ô". The latter constitutes a marked choice for direct address used only in the poetic apostrophe, and thus signifies the recuperation of inspiration from what had been oblivion—the River Styx. And the form of the letter "o" in itself suggests

the vanished sun as well as the zero or *Néant* that cancels it.

What points most unequivocally to Mallarmé's project for erasing inspiration from this text is a dramatic change of mythological reference depicting a frustrated, defeated muse in the first tercet. The original had evoked "une rixe / Faite d'un dieu que croit emporter une nixe." A nixie is a water-sprite. We think of Pan seizing Syrinx only to lose her at once as she undergoes a metamorphosis into a stand of reeds. But Mallarmé has reversed the sexual roles. Here it is the Muse, inferred from the supernatural female, who as an active feminine principle attempts to carry off a god, a transcendent "meaning" captured by inspiration. The issue of the struggle remains uncertain. But the nixie is sharply repulsed in the final version. Unicorns breathe fire at her, and she dies. In contrast, the unicorn of legend could be captured only by a virgin. She would sit in the forest until the beast came to lay its head in her lap and be charmed to sleep. This motif often symbolized the incarnation of Christ. For Mallarmé it connotes the Idea embodied in words—an impossibility. His unicorns reject the supernatural woman; the *unio mystica* of inspiration fails. Their very multiplicity here suggests a diffuse, ill-defined goal. Concomitantly, the objective correlative of such enclosure, the "beau cadre" surrounding the esthetic domain of the mirror where the poet's visions appear, also vanishes from the poem.

After the Muse-figure's disappearance from the first version of the sonnet, the poet presents a septet of lights reflected in the vacant mirror with a conjunction that implies that they might form an exception to, a replacement for, or even a compensation for her absence: "décor / De l'absence, *sinon que* sur la glace encore . . . " ("A scene of absence, *were it not that* in the mirror still . . . "). The second version moves the Muse not only out of sight but also out of mind, replacing "absence" with "oubli." And a new conjunction dismisses the possibility of reviving inspiration: "Elle, défunte nue en le miroir, *encor / Que* . . . " (emphases added). The Muse—and "elle" is a homonym for the "aile" of inspiration—has died *even though* the celestial *ptyx* of the Big Dipper gleams in the mirror. Not only the meaning of the conjunction, but also the abrupt enjambement of half of it brutally dissociates the stellar vision from any possibility of an earthly effect.

Both versions of the poem deploy a traditional Renaissance symbolism of the mirror and the empty chalice to suggest the vanity of the material world. Despite this skepticism, to place the verb "se fixe" in final position in the first version is to hint at some higher permanence accessible through poetry, some "compte total en formation." The second version attenuates this impression by moving "se fixe" back one line. "Le septuor," now in final position, still evokes the music of the spheres, but the words suggesting the presence of an observer who might hear that music—"obscurcissement" and "décor de l'absence"—have been removed.

The relatively extensive variants of the **"Sonnet en -yx"** provide an unusual occasion to observe Mallarmé's anti-creative processes in action. They confirm the impression produced by his revisions of other poems: Mallarmé's poetic practice is largely inspired by the project of erasing inspiration. His treatment of the Muse-figure confirms this impression in major poems where variants are few. He stresses her separation from the poet. In *Prose (pour des Esseintes)* she smiles enigmatically, refusing to corroborate the poet's memories of his vision. In **"Surgi de la croupe et du bond"** or **"Une dentelle s'abolit,"** the possibility of communion between male and female principles, between poet and Muse, is negated. In *L'Après-Midi d'un faune,* **"Salut,"** **"A la nue accablante tu,"** *Un coup de dés* and other poems, the Muse withholds her siren song, averts her face, and plunges wordlessly back into the element from whence she came, to be unborn.

From Dante on, high art murders women to idealize them. Unappreciated or inaccessible in life, they become in death companions and guides no longer endangered by the contamination of materiality, returning from a transcendent plane to empower the poet with creativity. But Mallarmé's Muse departs and does not return.

For all that, it is essential to remember that Mallarmé does not settle for the facile solution of a poetry of negation. When the void that engulfs his Muses closes upon itself, negation comes full circle. It forms itself then into an empty womb by virtue of which the Muse is at once present through synecdoche and absent through the metonymic dislocation of being unconceived. The empty womb is variously figured by the mirror, the empty vessel, the celestial illusion of the Big Dipper, the trough of a wave, or the oxymoronic "creux néant musicien." (pp. 390-404)

> *Laurence M. Porter, "The Disappearing Muse: Erasure of Inspiration in Mallarmé," in* The Romanic Review, *Vol. LXXVI, No. 4, November, 1985, pp. 389-404.*

Kevin Newmark   (essay date 1990)

[*In the essay below, Newmark argues that Mallarmé's use of rhyme and rhythm, together with his poetic subversion of the semantic link between words and reality, result in an unpredictable free play of language.*]

Looked at through the prismatic lens of its critical reception, it seems that there is something new to be seen in Mallarmé studies these days. The conventional hemline of literary interpretation that for the first half or so of this century did such a good job at keeping a delicately aesthetic and hermetic *oeuvre* away from the prying gaze of coarser and more public questions like history, ideology, and politics seems now to be inching its way up, threatening to reveal in the process secrets of a potentially embarrassing and even scandalous nature. The scandal here, though, lies in the revelation that what passes for the shockingly new and indecent has been there all along, only in the mode of a symptomatic denial and cover-up. In Mallarmé's case, we do not have to wait for a history of reception to register a threat to formal autonomy from some sort of textual outside, for the threat was never outside of the (hypothetically) self-enclosed structures of his texts to begin with. For instance, it would hardly have been necessary in 1899 for Arthur Symons to attach a "subtle veil" to Mallarmé's writing to shield it from the desires and distur-

bances of what he calls the outside world, if it were not already possible to glimpse, on the inside of the text and etched in negative as it were, something like the symptoms of social and critical upheavals. Such a secret "future," already neatly referred to and anticipated by Mallarmé himself in *La Dernière mode,* will finally break through the surface in a much cruder form in the journalistic celebration of "Le Camarade Mallarmé," as he was baptized in *L'Humanité* following the events of May, '68. Rather than a linear itinerary of purely empirical events, the history of Mallarmé reception between Symons's celebration of *l'art pour l'art* [in his *The Symbolist Movement in Literature,* 1919] and J. P. Faye's inversion of this well-known aesthetic slogan into a kind of *l'art pour tous* [in his "Le Camarade 'Mallarmé' " and "Mise au Point," 1919], is a balanced dialectic of concealment and disclosure in which each of the successive stages in the interpretation of a textual enigma helps to bring into relief whatever was only implicitly available or recognized in the other. And while it would be irresponsibly naive to ignore the very different ideological implications at stake in such positions, in the long run they function side by side within the same closed system of clearly demarcated distinctions and choices.

Factional pressures and rhetoric aside, reducing Mallarmé to the polarity of formalism and reference, a private *poésie pure* and a public *journalisme engagé,* and seeking to privilege one pole over the other by means of a history of reception might be the least historical gesture conceivable, since it repeats in a preconscious and therefore uncritical mode a set of unresolved tensions whose irresolution Mallarmé himself identified as one of the principal conditions of a truly historical consciousness. For although he never questions the pragmatic necessity of approaching language as though it were susceptible of division into the textually self-reflexive and the historically referential, the neat separation of language into its constitutive elements remains theoretically problematic within Mallarmé's writing. We should approach with caution the practically effective but theoretically questionable attempt to describe, separate, and ultimately choose between the inextricably intertwined components of language, which appears in certain prose texts as the "desire" of an entire generation in "crisis." That attempt shows up in *L'Après-Midi d'un Faune* as a tragic "crime" that will eventually undo the possibility of knowing with certainty the difference between formalism and reference, fiction and history.

Certain texts, not very distant in time and concern from **"Crise de vers,"** go so far as to suggest the inevitability of a collapse of the distinction between history and fiction, and as a consequence end up by making the one seem wholly dependent for its existence on the other. Thus, near the conclusion of **"Sauvegarde,"** a short text about the place of institutions within the State and in particular about the place of *l'Académie* within France, Mallarmé proposes for consideration the following opinion: "Whereas social relations and their changing measurement strictly or loosely calculated, in view of governing, are a fiction, which is itself dependent on *belles-lettres*—because of their enigmatic or poetic principle—the duty of maintaining the book becomes imperative in an absolute sense." In effect, the proposition that social relationships and their determination are a fiction, and its corollary that fiction is a branch of the linguistic structures of texts, lead ultimately to Mallarmé's oft-repeated and much ridiculed affirmation that, "the whole world exists only to end up in a book." In other words, for Mallarmé, *il n'y a pas de hors-texte.* But Mallarmé's yoking of the social to the fictional/textual in this way cannot legitimately be used as an exclusionary (or inclusionary) principle to deduce a kind of absolute *inside* of the text, in the way, for example, that the simple opposition at work between *l'art pour l'art* (Symons) and *l'art pour tous* (Faye) could be shown to function. For to go on to say, as Mallarmé does, that the calculation of changing social relationships, or History in its broadest sense, is a function of the poetic principle of writing, is to warn against any facile assumptions with respect to what these textual principles might consist in, as well as what they leave out. Precisely because the poetic principle founding history and fiction remains indeterminately "mysterious" and problematic, the task of *l'Académie,* which relates to deciphering the link between language and action ("Letters" and "diverse activity"), becomes crucial in a sense that is as historical and social as it is "literary."

"Sauvegarde," as its title suggests, is a text about protection and preservation. In the hyperbolic and ironic vocabulary of crisis he is fond of using, Mallarmé describes a situation in which the entire nation of France, the organization of the State itself, is posed on the brink of disaster because writing is being threatened spiritually by treasonous forces: "the Poet calls upon literary Supremacy to lift up a kind of (protective) wing when writing is threatened by high treason or a *coup d'état,* in this case, spiritual." Writing is associated here with that quality of mind capable of founding a State through the establishment of "the link of Letters that changes diverse activities into official pomp." It needs the protection of a State institution, the Academy, against the nullity and mindlessness of factional commotion to which books are always open: "Intellectual (book)bindings . . . open to the gratitude as well as to the jeers of whoever, throwing himself madly about, for or against, it's all the same, assumes the status of a stage actor, doubly sham." What makes such factional commotion a mindless sham is not its concrete objectives and the means it employs to realize them, but rather its inability or refusal to face up to its own relation to the book and to account for its own allegorical, fictional dimension. The danger is that the activity that is in fact the product of an unknown and impersonal poetic principle will be mistaken by ideologues for an autonomous and self-conscious actor or force: "Imagine a government so poorly informed as to mistake itself for the allegory from which it comes." When this happens, the State loses all legitimacy by merely reproducing and even mythologizing the involuntary, mechanical aspect of its operation, rather than interrupting it by adopting a critical stance toward it.

Fortunately, both for such a government and its uninformed representatives, the State is provided with a safeguard, *l'Académie,* the highest and most civilized institution of all, since its sole responsibility is to writing: "The highest institution . . . the Academy . . . its aim . . . the bond of Letters . . . everything ends up with or comes back to writing. . . . Our foundation . . . was aware, stepped aside." At times of crisis, that is whenever writing is being threatened, and as Mallarmé makes clear, this is always and everywhere possible, the poet or writer appeals to the institution of the Academy. But *L'Académie* is not just the highest among many institutions. It is also the institution that becomes the highest by stepping aside, by *removing* itself from the classificatory system of all other institutions. "The highest institution . . . the Academy," cannot be considered an institution like any other: "its aim, the bond of Letters, makes it totally unique. . . . Our foundation . . . was aware, stepped aside." Paradoxically, it is in cutting itself off from other institutions that the Academy can resist the State's tendency to ossify into mere institutionalization: "I picture to myself, occupying, like a sanctuary, the center of the comprehensive hemicycle, where it consents to sit only occasionally—while that elite functions on regular votes, the Academy, which would cut itself off [*se retrancherait*] or keep itself back for some special or rare act, who knows which." Describing the physical appearance of one of France's most massive buildings, L'Institut, Mallarmé suggests the difference the Academy can make by reinflecting that fixed space toward the question of writing. At the center of the comprehensive hemicycle, where the semicircular and horizontal curve of the Institut de France is completed and surmounted vertically by its hemispherical dome, there is the occasional "act" operated by *l'Académie,* rare, special, undetermined. Whatever this act is, it is prepared for only when the Academy manages to "cut itself off" or "keep itself back" from the regularized, architectural mass of other institutions.

The cut is also a kind of military maneuver, then, the French verb *se retrancher* suggesting the protective measures that the Academy must take to *entrench* itself against the rigidly conventional programs and sessions of the very Institute of France in which the Academy is housed, for instance, since such partisan institutions can continue to function without making the question of the Book the occasion of their existence. Thanks to *l'Académie* and the strategic operation of the cut, though, the Book remains open. Because spirit, along with "its mark, books," is always open to the mindlessness of sham factions, the Academy, the protective wing of letters, must always be ready to move aside, to dig down and make the cut from such treasons in order to act on them effectively. The fact that the Academy operates *within* an institutional form it serves to disrupt—"The Academy, occupying the *center* of the comprehensive hemicycle"—also means that its defensive power of entrenchment is simultaneously an offensive act operated on the inside of what it cuts itself off from. The "wing" of the Academy is a sword as well as a shield. It serves to open and to protect the space of writing, of a dash, for instance, that separate *l'Académie* from all the other, nonlinguistic, geometrical and architectural institutions.

> The highest institution . . . the Academy.
> This dithyramb, why, in the form of a cupola—

"Sous la Coupole" (Beneath the dome), is a figure that refers to *l'Académie française* by way of the architectural solidity of *l'Institut de France,* a state run building at the

center of which the Academy occasionally sits. Why does the Academy appear in such a form, such a figure? To ask this question, at least in the way that Mallarmé does in **"Sauvegarde,"** is to reopen the question of the Book. It is to cut through the architectural dust of *l'Institut,* the Institution in general as well as of L'Institut de France, by reminding us—"wiping the dust off masterpieces . . . by bringing them to mind"—that *l'Académie* is itself nothing but a book of dithyrambs, that is, a book composed of poetic praises to the Book. An institution of the book to the book, *l'Académie* is thus always under the cupola of the Institute as well as already outside of it, being the one institution whose task is to question how the state and its institutions are made possible by the book. To ask why the Academy appears in the form of a state building is one way of making a cut from the actual palace, one way of inscribing a trench or a dash that asks about writing and its relation to the state, as well as about the figures and diacritical marks that compose them. The cut and the sword are in addition a pen: when they inscribe these questions they also help accomplish the task of the Academy *as* book; that is, the perpetuation of writing as well as of the "social relations" that are founded by it.

But the reference to continuity, transmission, and posterity implicit here seems to lead to an inevitable misunder-

Sketch of Mallarmé by Pablo Picasso.

standing in another direction, according to Mallarmé. The Academy, "this dithyramb," is not just a book in an immediate and unproblematic way. The Academy does not just occupy a building; it is also a select society made up of a prescribed number (forty) of living men (and now women), whose sole function is to speak for and to administer the rights and obligations of the Book. And the actual membership of the *Académie française* has a nasty habit of confusing the "eternal" nature of the writing it holds in trust and represents with its own human and social stature: "All the harm can be traced back to this quiproquo: one would like them to be immortal, whereas it is in fact the works." Mallarmé is undoubtedly poking fun in this article at the French practice of referring to members of *l'Académie* as "les immortels," an epithet that has not failed to take on a cynically humorous connotation given that holders of the "forty-first chair," that is, those never admitted to the Academy, include the likes of Descartes, Pascal, Rousseau, Diderot, Baudelaire, and Mallarmé himself. But in a more radical sense the task of preserving the book with the Academy's official seal—"*A l'immortalité*"—results simultaneously in a kind of death sentence pronounced on *any* given subject. It is not just because of the vagaries of the selection process that many academicians have failed to achieve immortality; it is also that in order to enter the immortal Academy in the first place they must be forgotten *as* individuals. Their names will refer henceforward *only* to the Academy, that is, to writing and to the book. For as long as they exercise their legitimate powers as trustees of the Book's perpetuity, academicians are not themselves to be considered as living human subjects, but are to be viewed only "from the perspective of eternity, abstract, general, vague, outside any familiarity." Consequently, the book is also a tombstone: "That murmur, rather, that brings to the attention of the elect walled-up in the after life . . . the funeral slab of the dictionary. . . ." The discussions that take place in the Academy not only make its members attentive to the dictionary, the reviewing and revising of which, of course, is one of its principal tasks. The dictionary they revise also signifies their nonexistence as expressive subjects, their immurement behind the tombstone of its "scattered words." They tend to a book in which they read of their own encrypted death and preservation as caretakers of the book.

From the question of *l'Académie française,* **"Sauvegarde"** leads along a circuitous itinerary that passes by way of the State, the Institution, Writing and the Subject, before it eventually winds up by predicating all possible social relations, that is, History in general, on the survival and transmission of the Book. But what kind of economy of gain and loss is this, anyway? The fact that the preservation of this kind of writing, as overseen by *l'Académie,* can be achieved only at the price of the living subject—"This Hall. . . . What business do the living have here?"—should give us pause. For it is one thing to say that social relationships are a "fiction" that must be recognized as such. It is quite another to suggest, however, that once this fiction and the book have been saved from sham factionalization, no room will remain in the social and institutional context for any living subject. In **"Sauvegarde"** itself, the mortal space of the Academy is survived only by a collection of "specters," "shadows," and those who "have no head to fall." How could such disembodied heroes inherit and perpetuate the writing of the book, and just what sort of social and historical force could they be expected to exert? Questions like these, which eventually threaten to cut open the complicated but otherwise comprehensive and comprehensible logic of **"Sauvegarde,"** become especially acute in those texts where the problematic status, or "death," of the lyrical subject is itself the poetic principle as well as the theme. For this reason, considerable help can be gained by pursuing them in the highly conventionalized and self-reflexive form of a Mallarmean sonnet.

> Une Dentelle s'abolit
> Dans le doute du Jeu suprême
> A n'entr'ouvrir comme un blasphême
> Qu'absence éternelle de lit.
>
> Cet unanime blanc conflit
> D'une guirlande avec la même,
> Enfui contre la vitre blême
> Flotte plus qu'il n'ensevelit.
>
> Mais, chez qui du rêve se dore
> Tristement dort une mandore
> Au creux néant musicien
>
> Telle que vers quelque fenêtre
> Selon nul ventre que le sien,
> Filial on aurait pu naître.

["A lace abolishes itself / In the doubt of the supreme Game / To half-open like a blasphemy / Only an eternal absence of bed. / This unanimous white conflict / Of a garland with the same, / Fled against the pale pane / Floats more than it buries. / But in the dream-gilded one / Sadly sleeps a mandolin / With hollow musical nothingness / Such that towards some window / According to no belly but its own, / Filial one could have been born." Translated by Robert Greer Cohn: *Toward the Poems of Mallarmé,* 1980.]

The last in a series of three sonnets published in 1887 and grouped around the general theme of absence, negativity, and death, **"Une Dentelle"** is considered not only to be the most difficult and beautiful of the triptych, but also the one that progresses out of a situation of almost total despair toward a state of qualified redemption for the poetic subject. The question, just as in **"Sauvegarde,"** is the means of transmitting intellectual legacies and thereby securing a kind of immortality. The real motivation for the text on *l'Académie,* it turns out, is Mallarmé's own project for the administration of a national "fonds littéraire," an institutional means of overseeing "a treasure [fund, or foundation] left by the classics to their posterity." It is a similar concern that orients the triptych, where the main theme becomes the challenge and responsibility that devolves on every poet to preserve "the immortal breath" or poetic spirit which he inherits from the language of his predecessors. It matters little whether one chooses to identify the poetic legator referred to metaleptically in the first sonnet—"The ancient chamber of the heir"—as Baudelaire, Villiers, or even an earlier version of Mallarmé himself, since in any case it is the continuity of a lineage that is the problem. What is at stake ultimately, named in the last line of **"Une Dentelle"** as a hypothetical "filiation,"

is the philosophical concept of History, considered here as the minimal possibility of a *future:* for where there is no possibility of extending past experience into some kind of future, history must remain an empty concept, devoid of any sense whatsoever. The question the sonnet addresses, and which is inherited and passed on from one text to another in Mallarmé's entire *oeuvre,* is whether a historic consciousness is possible beyond something like the death of the poetic subject. We should stipulate that the interruption at issue is something *like* death, that is, closer to a figural "death" than an empirical death. It is this figural death Mallarmé has in mind when he describes himself after his metaphysical crisis of the sixties as "perfectly dead," and it is with an interrogation into the figural status of death that the poem **"Une Dentelle"** is concerned.

Whereas in **"Sauvegarde"** the negativity inherent in the preservation of the book is first met by way of the ironic reference to the unfounded pretensions of stodgy academicians, in the sonnet it becomes the very origin of poetry. In order for the poem to begin, something has to be destroyed, eliminated, or at least suspended. Not only has the title of the poem become a blank, but **"Une Dentelle"** itself, which by default is the title as well as the incipit of the text, is dying here, in the process of being abolished. But can we be immediately sure just what this "lace" is? To judge by the commentaries the opening has elicited, the threat to wholeness implied in the verb "s'abolit," which in the context points to an effacement, pulling away or tearing of the lace, has contaminated not just the artisanal fabric used to adorn windows, beds, and other items, but the intelligibility of the reading process as well, since it seems impossible to ascertain whether "dentelle" should be read as a curtain, a membrane, a self, or a text. Edmund Wilson, a perspicacious if not overly thorough reader of Mallarmé, suggests in *Axel's Castle* [1959] a possible reason for the frustration (or elation) of all subsequent readers of this kind of poetry. He refers to figures like the lace as "metaphors detached from their subjects," whose result is that "one has to guess what the images are being applied to." For Wilson, such metaphors are a sign of the "confusion," even the "insanity" of symbolist poetics, which tears figures from their referents and then fuses them back together willy-nilly without any regard for their natural order. But rather than following Wilson as he guesses about the kind of referent the metaphors have been reattached to, we ought first to follow out Mallarmé's thematization of the abolition, detachment, or tear that befalls the figure of the lace in the movement of the poem. Before we ask what the figure of the lace refers to, we must take into account the possibility that it is first of all the capacity of figure to refer unproblematically that is being abolished or torn in Mallarmé. It may be that "une dentelle" is not just a figure among others that refers to something else, but also the proper name for the text by Mallarmé, **"Une Dentelle,"** in which poetic language undoes its own pretension ("s'abolit") to provide a stable ground for the relation of figure to referent.

What is dying in this sonnet is the received idea of the status of metaphoric language within poetry, "la dentelle" being one of the tradition's commonest figures for poetic textuality, passed on to Mallarmé by Nerval, among other predecessors. But then what tradition is being preserved and inherited in the place of that idea? Is Mallarmé's poem abolishing the poetic tradition it inherits instead of preserving it as it ought to? Is it rather inheriting this tradition insofar as it manages to preserve poetry *as* the tearing of figure away from determined reference? And what would it mean to preserve and transmit language as the site of a kind of figural cut or tear; that is, a cut that, because it is only figural with respect to the actual lace, can become a literal cut in our ability to determine the crucial link between figure and referent? One definition of symbolism as it is articulated in this exemplary symbolist text would thus be: the literary inheritance and interrogation of a genetic and metaphoric transmission of poetic language. What dies in order to be critically examined is the unproblematical link between a metaphor and its subject or object, or between a text and its eventual reading and understanding. The "fallen trophies" mentioned in the first sonnet of the triptych also name symbolism as a collection of lifeless *tropes,* that is, texts that narrate the "fall" and detachment of metaphors from their subjects, among which can be included the common metaphor of symbolism itself as the historical period that links the corpus of romanticism to our own twentieth century.

The linguistic negativity, fall, or death, which becomes an issue in the lace of the first line, is then localized in the second line of **"Une Dentelle"** by the reference to a curious form of "doubt": "une dentelle s'abolit dans le *doute.*" But in this poem, writing is *both* the lace *and* the doubt. It is first the "lace" that contains the implicit question of the relation of figure to referent, and then the "doubt" that becomes the site where this question is made explicit in the destructive act of a tear. Writing is both figure and the place in which the figure is undone, the self-obliterating relation between the lace and the doubt. It is here, where the interrogation or "doubt" about what writing does to itself as figure or "lace" is carried to its extreme, that the lyric poem radicalizes the journalistic report of **"Sauvegarde."** In **"Sauvegarde"** the threat to writing that is being parried by an institution like *l'Académie* is considered as coming to and acting on writing from without. But in **"Une Dentelle"** it is the doubt that is produced in writing itself that calls into question the survival of what the poem was written to perpetuate. Mallarmé's triptych thus wonders how far it is possible to preserve and transmit the originary tear or cut that determines the social and fictional fabric of language. Who or what is left to inherit when something like the institution of writing, "that fold or somber *lace,* which contains the infinite," tears itself open in the very act of its genesis and retransmission?

The same problem is posed to dramatic effect in another text about literary heritage, *La Musique et les lettres,* again, in the vocabulary of crises: "Storm, luminous cleansing; and in upheavals, due wholly to (the) generation, recent, the act of writing scrutinized itself to its very foundation . . . to the point, I would say, of wanting to know if there is any place left for writing." The meaning of the formulation depends on how one reads what Mallarmé refers to as the *cause* of these stormy upheavals, "la génération, récente." Is the cause the act of generation, production in its most recent manifestation, or is it merely

the latest group of contemporaneous individuals who share a given attribute? Mallarmé's phrase can be read to mean either that critical self-scrutiny is a characteristic of the turbulent new generation of (symbolist) writers, or that writing is itself the initiatory storm in which the phenomenon of generation as critical production takes place. Indeed, it must be read in both ways at once, since what distinguishes the recent generation of writers Mallarmé is talking about is their capacity to bring about, or *generate,* the question of how writing is produced. What is odd here, though, is that the condition of possibility of the "generation" of writing is simultaneously unsettled by its own critical examination and is thus threatened by extinction at the moment of its inception. Again, who or what is left for writing after writing generates itself by putting itself into question? The question is asked once more and answered later in the same essay. After the storm, after the explosion, Mallarmé asks, "What is the point?" to which he answers, "A game." So too, in **"Une Dentelle,"** the mutually exclusive relationship of the "lace" and the "doubt" becomes the pivotal space in which a certain kind of game is played out: "le Jeu suprême."

The game, though, is enigmatic. On the one hand, it plays for "supreme" stakes, life and death. On the other hand, as mere game or play, it risks going nowhere, remaining only diversion and diversionary. The question, "What is the point?" can just as easily be read as a display of frustration as a genuine inquiry. And the way this question is worked out in **"Une Dentelle"** is by developing a tension we have already seen implicit in the term "generation," for although the sonnet ends with a reference to birth or genesis, this birth seems destined to remain only a hypothetical game, "Filial on aurait pu naître." The term "generation," of course, as well as corollary terms like "conception" and "birth," establishes a metaphorical system in which intelligible activities of the mind, like poetry-making, are understood by analogy to empirical sciences like biology. The question at this point is not whether this figural system is legitimate, for this is the only system available to us for "conceiving" of thought, but rather whether there are elements within the system itself that disrupt it beyond recognition. In other words, is anything introduced by the "conception" that cannot be reassimilated to the literal (biological) and figurative (intelligible) meanings of birth, but that would serve instead to "detach" the genetic figure from their intended respective meanings of creativity and "production"? This question determines the way commentators have reacted to an erotic dimension of the poem, implicit in the "game" of line 2 and the "bed" of line 4. The fact that this bed is named as "eternally absent" is most often taken by the critics as confirmation of the successful passage in the poem from the literal, sensuous locale of an erotic game to an ethereal "conception" of poetry's supreme play.

The paraphrastic commentary of the sonnet given by one of its English translators provides a good example of this sort of interpretation:

> A pair of lace curtains is blown by a breeze,
> wreathing around each other like lovers. There
> is no bed, or rather, there is an eternal absence
> of bed, but you can't stop two amorous curtains,

not in a Mallarméan huddle, you can't! The supreme game probably refers to poetry. Now, the sestet: Here broods the dreamy poet, with his *mandore,* his instrument for making poetry, sorrowfully, in a silence that is empty. Now then, he seems to be thinking, if I could only impregnate, fertilize by parthenogenesis, as it were, myself, I could conceive, beget, sire and mother, a son of my own, a poem. Line 12 seems to mean that if he alone could do what the curtains are doing by the pane, the pane meaning also the source of light and creation, why, then he would be self-sufficient and happy [C. F. MacIntyre, *Stéphane Mallarmé: Selected Poems,* 1957].

Aside from the immediate satisfaction or disappointment at having an elusively hermetic sonnet translated into such an easily comprehensible, because utterly banal, domestic scene, we should not remain oblivious to the somewhat more interesting vacillation that takes place in this passage around the game's erotic and poetic valences. The stark transition in the paraphrase from the bedroom curtains' unstoppable "amorous huddle" and the commentator's enthusiastically ejaculative, "you can't!", to the flat assertion, "the supreme game probably refers to poetry," is so wholly unprepared that one cannot help wondering why the reader does not bring the two references together. Why keep the erotic and the poetic "conception" apart unless, and perhaps in the face of some unnamed threat, it is in order to avoid identifying the initial suggestiveness of the "supreme Game" simultaneously with both poetic and amorous activity? Just as with the lace earlier, it is not possible to order the levels of meaning in the figure (in this case, poetic first, erotic second) without ignoring what the poem is doing with the figure's capacity to mean. The "Jeu" may not just be a figure that refers to both a poetic and an erotic meaning, but an actual contest, "Jeu," between two heterogeneous models of poetic language, each of which threatens to interrupt the meaning of the other.

MacIntyre's hesitation in this regard thus becomes paradigmatic for any interpretation of the text. It traces out and then elides a threat specific to the poem's intelligibility, since by bringing the game of the solitary poet into contact with the playful huddling of amorous curtains the reading necessarily opens the door, or at least a window, to all sorts of fantastic shapes and figures; in short, to the "blasphème" that is mentioned in line 3, and that would function as a decisive lack of reverence with respect to the poem's entire program of conception. For once the erotic component of the "game" in line 2 becomes apparent it then threatens to extend itself uncontrollably throughout the text and distract us from ever coming back to and understanding the poem's supposed lesson about the creative potential of poetic writing. Rather than providing a vehicle for meaning that leads directly from literal conception to poetic birth, the erotic aspect of the game may actually deflect the reading from its intended destination and take it in a completely different direction. And without the caution of a transcendental foundation or guarantor of sense, like God and its correlates light and poetry, presupposed rather than logically deduced here, this is always possible. Sex in this text, though, is not just a figure for an empirical act that diverts our attention temporarily from the serious

business of poetry, since as we have seen with MacIntyre, it is always possible within this system to reunite biological productivity with poetic creativity through the metaphorical figure of conception. Sex is also the figure for what in poetic language considered as a "Jeu" between two different figural models contests the figure's own capacity to provide a meaningful link or union between biological and intelligible conception. There is always something a bit kinky about this kind of sex since, by inflecting, tearing, or perforating a state of balance and equilibrium within a unified figural system, it actually serves to reopen the question of figure and referent rather than closing it off.

In this poem, for instance, where does MacIntyre get the idea that the game is composed of a "pair" of two *different* curtains in the first place? "*Une* Dentelle s'abolit," in the opening stanza, and the second stanza explicitly says, "Cet *unanime* blanc conflit / D'*une* guirlande avec *la même.*" The erotic "huddle" has only *one* player; for this game the number one merely relates to itself specularly in order to constitute itself as a desirable "pair." "Conception," literal or metaphorical, never has to become an issue, here. The opening scene, a kind of voyeuristic looking in through the lace curtain on the bedroom window—perhaps even onto Hérodiade's absent but imagined and violently desired bed—can become as graphic or pornographic as one wishes, but one has at least to recognize that the treatment of the erotic remains far from being a hymn to the marriage bed, with its attendant connotations of legitimacy and progeny. Allowing the "one" in "Une dentelle" and "*unanime* blanc conflit" to carry the weight of the lopsidedly erotic figure points up the "onanisme" or onanistic aspect of the game. What remains difficult to determine is whether there is more than one solitary player involved in the onanistic scene, a provocative alternative that "floats" between the lines juxtaposing "blanc *conflit*" to "*contre* la *vitre* blême." In any case, it is not possible to take this game as a synthesizing figure for what we ordinarily understand to be poetic conception, generation, or creativity. What is ill-conceived and illegitimate in following the erotic game turns out to be the free play of the signifier. And this game exceeds the conventional metaphorical pattern of biological and poetic conception of meaning by focusing attention on detached letters whose arbitrary power to signify cannot be reduced to a binary model of physical entities and conceptual ideas.

The game, then, is double, and duplicitously double at that. On the one hand, it is the articulation of the double aspect of "conception" into the figural passage from natural genesis to poetic creativity. According to a classical conception of metaphor, an activity of the mind manifests itself by analogical reference to the empirical world, poetic production using genetic reproduction ("le lit") to make itself more concrete for understanding, though in such a way as to differentiate itself from the merely empirical in which it appears ("absence de lit"). On the other hand, the game is also that supplementary aspect of the figure, erotic elements that do not necessarily contribute to reproduction, or the free play of the signifier, for instance, that get out of hand and threaten to subvert or pervert the projected "conception" into an absolute loss of misconception and insignificance. Something in the game's own promise of a passage, transmission, or legacy from natural to poetic understanding threatens to stand in the way and block access to the very thing that it promises. This is the risk without which the game could hardly be called supreme.

It is this element of risk that affects the "doubt" in such a way that it must now be understood not only to touch upon the figure of the lace given in line 1, but also the outcome of the supreme game referred to in line 2. In terms of the temporal thematics of transmission and legacy in the sonnet as well as in **"Sauvegarde,"** the doubt always relates to a historical "past" as well as to a kind of undisclosed "future": the writing that interrogates the legitimacy of any received "figure" also leaves open to question the outcome for history of putting this interrogation into play. Mallarmé poses the same question with regard to the possibility of a future for his friendship with the dead Villiers: "Do we know what it means to write? . . . this senseless *game* of *writing* consists in undertaking, by virtue of a *doubt,* the task of recreating everything in order to verify that *one is* where one ought to be (since, allow me to express this apprehension, there remains an *uncertainty*)" (emphasis added). In the same essay, Mallarmé says of himself what he says elsewhere of the Academy; "whoever writes cuts himself off," *se retranche,* and what he cuts himself off from is everything, "integrally," Mallarmé adds. Through the operation of "doubt" the writer removes himself from all that is presumed natural, all that is previously instituted, in order to "recreate" it. That the operation of the cut is related to a past as well as to a future is made clear in the essay on Villiers where "doubt" plays over the natural and instituted world already given, but is also, in "uncertainty," a form of doubt concerning the world of the subject left in the wake of this questioning. In the more compressed framework of **"Une Dentelle,"** the double instability and uncertainty of writing is brought out effectively by the self-splitting syntax in line 2, the locus of the "doute *du* Jeu suprême." Here the grammar, the rules of the game, contribute to produce a structure that is simultaneously retrospective and proleptic, a kind of writing that interrogates the past it has inherited, "a lace," in order to open up an unpredictable future. For, grammatically speaking, the genitive link between the doubt and the game, "le doute *du* Jeu," can be either subjective and retrospective—the doubt belongs to and is controlled by the game of writing, "the Supreme game's doubt abolishes a lace"—or objective and proleptic—the status and outcome of writing is what is cast into doubt, "a lace is rent in the doubt about the Supreme game."

What Mallarmé calls writing, the "recreation" of an uncertain future thanks to a process of "doubt" with respect to the past, is historical, not in the same sense that empirical events are historical, but in the sense that, by instituting a "cut" into the past that subjects all of its figures to doubt, writing is the condition of possibility for history conceived as a future that is opened by critical thought. "Le doute du Jeu suprême," is philosophical in nature and Cartesian in structure; it is a formalized activity of methodical doubt that reflects on everything, including itself as game, and as such it is the first step in any genuinely dialectical development of the mind. Georges Poulet is very close to the truth when, in speaking of Mallarmé's procedure, he says, "It is the act of negation through which one constitutes one's existence and thought. The Mallarmean operation is thus comparable to 'the internal operation of Descartes'. It is *ultra-Cartesian*" [George Poulet, *Etudes sur le temps humain 2: La Distance intérieure,* 1952]. Poulet, of course, is commenting on **Igitur** and the narrative struggle it recounts with a philosophical heritage that ends in a form of mental suicide, but it holds for the sonnet that the nature of doubt is such that it must inevitably turn back on itself to become the doubt *about* the future of writing and thought itself. What makes Mallarmé's procedure "ultra" Cartesian in Poulet's terms, moreover, is the supreme risk it takes by putting its own rules into doubt, and once the connection with philosophical suicide has been made, it becomes impossible not to read the "Jeu" as also containing the first person pronoun, *je* or *cogito.* The Cartesian certitude of its own doubt remains sheltered from the most radical threat as long it leaves intact the form structure of the "Jeu," which unconditionally links the (doubting) consciousness to a subject. Mallarmé's concept of writing, on the other hand, asks whether this relation between consciousness and self is not perhaps a mere game. Writing, for Mallarmé, is a form of reflexive negativity so immense that after allowing all else to be put into doubt, it allows for doubting the game's grammar, the formal conditions of the self *as* doubt. That amounts to doubting doubt, to doubting the game and fabric of thought into oblivion, and to opening out onto the doubtful future of one's "own" situation: "where one ought to be . . . remains an uncertainty."

This doubt would be a truly "hyperbolic" or supreme doubt. And it can be said to operate in Mallarmé's text wherever the technical aspects of the grammar or syntax, which make the meaning possible, are in themselves insufficient to determine the meaning of the poem's figures. Whether the "Jeu" refers to a philosophically serious operation of reflection (the thinking subject) or to an empirical version of self-reflection devoid of any higher meaning (represented thematically by an act of the not-so-philosophical body), the grammatical ambiguity of the "du" casts into doubt the autonomy of the subject referred to. It is not just that the "Jeu suprême" can refer, as any number of critics have noted, to *both* poetic and erotic "creativity." As we have seen, *creativity* is a loaded term that gives the game away in advance. For it subjects both dimensions of the text to a specular figure of aesthetic *and* philosophical meaning as a metaphorical model of conception and birth. Rather, in being *able* to "recreate" non-genetically, that is, from a linguistic model whose logic is no longer merely physical nor yet wholly intelligible, the "creativity" specific to both thought and the natural world, the free play in writing *necessarily* unsettles the ability of its own grammar to determine fully a reference to either. Once we notice how the uncertain grammar affects the subjective/objective status of the all-important game, "Jeu," it is difficult not to ask whether the real conflict, rather than being between the empirical and the thinking subject, is not between the subject as meaning (objectively empirical or subjectively thoughtful) and the subject as writing (the meaningless free play of the *je* as it is constituted in the purely formal rules of the "Jeu").

By making it impossible to decide on how to read the grammatical status of the genitive, Mallarmé's writing runs the risk of producing an absolutely empty, insane figure—"this senseless game (jeu) of writing."

The most effective way of parrying the threat posed by writing's hyperbolic doubt is by treating the radical openness of its outcome as though it could itself be conceived, known, and represented in advance. This would amount to anticipating it as a moment within a larger cognitive process, a moment that, for all intents and purposes, would have already taken place rather than remained to come. In order to state with any assurance that the text is "about" writing, for example, it is logically necessary to presuppose a discursive perspective or vantage point *beyond* the moment of definitional uncertainty, from which writing could become the subject of the question. "Nothing will have taken place but the place," is the way *Un Coup de dés* will have dealt with and resolved in advance the same dilemma of writing's supreme risk by anticipating a minimal place of coherent enunciation as the final result of a kind of worst case scenario for thought. When all else fails, one can always try to succeed in telling the story of the failure itself, "if only to disperse the empty act" (*Coup de dés*). In the essay on Villiers, as a means to shelter the writing subject from the risk of falling prey to an unthinkable "duperie bordering on suicide," Mallarmé makes reference to a mode of writing that would recuperate writing's open-ended risk. In order to pass beyond the constitutive doubt that makes it possible in the first place, writing attempts to recreate and transmit in advance the knowledge of the open-endedness of its own operation. It does so as *theater:* "One by one, each one of our conceits, to bring them forth, in their anteriority and to see." Writing is capable not only of creation and production, it is also capable of bringing anything into being as though it had already taken place and could be viewed as *anteriority*. By treating the doubt of writing as though it too could be made visible, by bringing forth a sequential representation that would include even that which abolishes sequence, writing would attempt to hide from its own dubious future.

In **"Une Dentelle"** this is the perspective adopted in the theatrical representation of writing as a play or a game organized around the poles of light and dark, the sun and the night, knowledge and nonknowledge. Writing, "that spot of ink related to the sublime night," may be what threatens to blacken or "abolish" the everyday world of minds and bodies, but it still plays itself out, at least at the beginning of the poem, on a visual, theatrical, and intelligible stage presided over by the light of a rising and setting sun of cognition. The curtain goes up—"une dentelle s'abolit"—to reveal a scene that is accessible to the eye of the spectator through the picture window of the theater. What the spectator gets to see in **"Une Dentelle"** is no ordinary play, however; it is rather the dawning light of philosophical reflection as it is made manifest in Mallarmé's concept of writing. Reperforming what he calls elsewhere, "the internal operation for instance of Descartes . . . joining theater and philosophy" (*Crayonné au théâtre*), Mallarmé's sonnet attempts to represent the philosophical dilemma of recreating the whole world

through the unpredictable play of writing. The main character here, writing, acts out for all to see the play of doubt as it grapples with and contests the world as we know it, including the natural light of the sun as well as the cognitive stability of all those philosophical concepts, like conception and birth, that use the solar system as a model. The Mallermean theater, in other words, through its own step-by-step representation of writing as though it were a character in a play that could be staged retrospectively, seeks to overcome the radical destruction of determinate and determinable representation that is involved in writing.

In writing conceived of as theater, even the destruction of sequence and intelligibility is susceptible of being anticipated and represented sequentially, "one by one," in a visible and proleptically intelligible order. In a first step of reading the sonnet, the thought that moves out to meet and transform the world through writing seems to destroy all solid entities in order to produce an intelligible figure of itself as the "absence éternelle de lit." In a second, more radical move in the same process, the negativity of the thought can be turned back on its own figures to ask whether the thinking subject is not a mere formal game, produced blasphemously by the free play of writing and devoid of any further meaning. The resulting inability to decide on the status of thought can be represented as a stalemated agon between the single-minded introspection that deprives itself of the warmth of the bed and the onanistically self-indulgent play that single-handedly reduces the poem to pure eroticism. This "blanc conflit" is then depicted sequentially in the theater as the alternating movements of a floating curtain. In so doing, however, the representation cannot avoid putting into play an aspect of figuration that necessarily enacts or recreates the undecidable openness of its own status as representation. It does so by marking the place of sequential articulation in the poem, the linking genitive in "le doute *du* Jeu suprême," as being itself undecidable by means of any sequential logic, or grammar, and thus prepares the way for the undoing of the semantic determination of a thinking (and feeling) subject in the play of the key word *"Jeu."* For, unlike the floating of a curtain, whose movements can be brought to light one by one, the crucial relation between writing as figure and writing as the destruction of figure cannot be reduced to a linear sequence. The priority of the "doute" over the "Jeu," as well as the relation between the self as self-conscious doubt and the self as formal game, is made *simultaneously* necessary and impossible to decipher in the writing out, rather than the representation, of the poem.

As a consequence, the figure of the bed, glimmering eternally in the half-light of the first stanza's conflict between consciousness and sensuality, becomes infinitely more blasphemous when it contests both orders of experience by shading into the uncertain status of the three letters *"l-i-t"* that return to haunt the rhyming words of the second stanza, "conflit" and "n'ensevelit." These letters, in fact, can tell us a great deal about what Mallarmé's "doute du Jeu suprême" does to both the world of sensuous reality and the movement of thought. The wholly graphic, textual nature of the problematic "bed" that is inscribed in certain syllables of the second stanza suggests that writing neither preserves the world naturally, as a simple perception, nor does away with it conceptually through the sheer annihilating power of the mind, but rather, that it operates otherwise, through the "play" of letters, *l, i, t,* for instance, that are neither merely empirical nor conceptual, and suggestive of both at once. As typographical markings, these letters interrupt, disrupt, and keep at a certain distance both the natural, given order of things, as well as the logical transformation of this order into a systematic form of thought. The linguistic disruption is never allowed to become a total destruction and erasure of what it puts aside, since it also *marks* the interruption it enacts and in so doing reserves a certain space, a blank, for that world and its transformation into thought, however distanced, deflected, or indirect it may be.

The nature and outcome of the ensuing linguistic relationship between the mind and the world now becomes the focus of the poem's unresolved question. Because it is written rather than perceived or thought, the "eternal absence of bed" cannot be negated as easily as the natural world or the thinking subject, not without leaving a trace or remainder of its letters. Thus, Mallarmé merely points toward its disappearance in the highly qualified, blinking movement of the French verb "entrouvrir." "Entrouvrir" means "to half-open," and in this poem the figure of the lacework opens only enough to leave a space for an empirical world that cannot ever be done dying or disappearing and for a world of conceptual thought that remains unconditionally deferred or postponed. It is neither opening nor closing, but a kind of written, typographical suspension of both that hovers *between,* or *entre.* It never quite becomes the space of a fully defined and therefore *closed* opening, *ouverture,* much as the hovering apostrophe in "entr'ouvrir" marks the place of the abolished letter "e" in the French verb "entr(e)ouvrir." And this mark of the figure's erasure actually *addresses,* apostrophizes, or summons the very bed which the theatrical scene describes as eternally absent: the question of the "bed" and the entire figural world contained within it returns to haunt the second stanza by way of its written trace in words like "con*flit*" and "ensève*lit*." For this same reason, we should be careful not to restrict the "blanc conflit" between meaning and nonmeaning to itself meaning only a uselessly meaningless or sterile form of playful activity in the text. It ought rather to be read here as a supplementary figure for the as-yet-blank or white spaces that are opened by and between the play of the letters, and in which the undecidable question of the poem's ultimate status and thus of its transmission and literary legacy, is suspended rather than merely destroyed, "ce conflit . . . flotte plus qu'il n'ensevelit."

The fact that the poem doesn't end there, however, reveals how the pressure to move outside this intolerable suspension or blank of the future works in turn to suspend its undecidability at the very moment it is named as such. For everything that holds for the quatrains seems to change in the tercets, where the immanent possibility of change is signaled by the conjunctive "Mais," a pivotal term that opposes what follows to what precedes. By treating the undecidability of the quatrains as though it were a prelimi-

nary negativity that could itself eventually be negated, the oppositional logic of the "Mais" programs a reading of the tercets that would stress by contrast their positivity. The tercets seem to balance out the indecision of the quatrains through the introduction of a symmetrical set of opposing forces, valorized positively. The absent bed in the first stanza appears in the tercets as a present sleeping mandola, for instance. Linked to the bed because it is "sleeping," the dormant instrument is however able to fill the room with the promise of sexual reproduction that was originally missing or stymied. For the mandola is pregnant, its pear-shaped form is a protruding belly that suggests the hypothetical birth that will result "Selon nul *ventre* que le sien." The formal balance that is achieved by bringing the two opposed thematic moments of the sonnet together into a negative/positive synthesis, a sexual union eventually capable of giving birth to its own "Aufhebung," [*sublation*] is as perfect and aesthetically satisfying a version of the dialectical process one can hope for in "symbolist" poetry. Thus, the "*ne* pas *être*" of the opening absence is filtered across the "mais" of the first tercet before it is picked up again in the "fen*être*" of line 12, and finally reechoed and sublated in the poem's final word, "*naître.*" In the poem's most daring gesture, the conflictual lack of union, or *mariage blanc* of the quatrains is later overturned in the coming together under the same familial roof—*chez qui*—of the negative maternal instrument (*la mandore au creux néant*) with the paternal and personalized dreamer (*celui qui du rêve se dore*) in lines 9 and 10.

It is clear that in the movement from the quatrains to the tercets a new mode of poetic language is invoked: from poetry conceived as the critical reception and breakdown of a mimetic model of language that can be figured as *theater,* the sonnet moves toward a more positive conception of poetry as *music.* Music, in this poem at least, seems able to pass beyond the problematization of writing and representation, beyond the undecidable impasse of a negative epistemology to the celebration of a liberating and positive form of art. On the thematic level, this move is represented by the replacement of the activity of philosophical "doubt" in the quatrains by that of an aesthetically creative "dream" in the tercets. The implication is that by substituting a poetry of autonomous dream for one of universal doubt, the power of language as voice and melody would somehow be able to replace and compensate for the undecidable outcome of poetic language as the critical reflection on its own statements and cognitions. The question at this point would be whether the aesthetic compensation for the suspension of philosophical self-knowledge would not itself constitute something like the "dream" of philosophy. For if it were possible to bypass the inconclusiveness of the question of language as figural representation and cognition in favor of a model of language as pure illusion, as a form of sonorous and verbal play that recognizes and rejoices in its fictional nature, then it would be possible by the same token to reintroduce the concept of philosophical certainty and truth, albeit in a negative mode, on the far side of its problematization.

Before deciding whether Mallarmé's writing does conform to this model, it is necessary to look more closely at the way poetry as music actually functions in the tercets. One of the most obvious places to locate an aesthetic of music is where the poetic and sonorous resources of the words break in on, supplement, or replace their representational value. This occurs throughout the poem, as we have seen in the reappearance of the epistemologically unreliable figure of the "bed" in words like "con*flit*" and ensev*elit*," but it is not recognized and celebrated as a positive value until language as music and dream is thematized at the end of the poem. Thus, in line 12, the very word that designates theatrical representation, *fenêtre,* breaks open and allows its individual sonorous elements to announce the birth of music that occurs in the poem's last word, "naître." The word "naître" not only *refers* to any and all extralinguistic acts of birth, physiological as well as intelligible, it also actualizes a purely intralinguistic "birth" by bringing into being a new *rhyme,* "fenêtre/naître." Beyond the critical failure to demarcate and control the limits, the birth and death as it were, of theatrical, representational language and cognition in the first part of the sonnet, there is in the tercets the musical and fictional, or nonreferential, conception and transmission of poetic language.

Of course, before it performs this promised birth in the ultimate word of the sonnet, "naître," the self-enclosed space of poetic music or rhyme is already introduced into the poem by way of the sleepy "mandore" in the first tercet:

> Mais, chez qui du rêve se *dore*
> Trist*ement dort* une *mandore*

There is nothing new in pointing out the musical self-reference at play in these lines. Almost forty years ago Emilie Noulet demonstrated the possibility of creating the fiction of a musical score or partition here by cutting into the words: thus, "triste" can be read as the tonal indication on which the dream-music should be played, the following repetition, "*ment dort, mandore,*" referring only to itself as the "murmured refrain or recitative (*mélopée*) of an ancient instrument." (*Vingt poèmes*). This double internal rhyme performs a kind of symbolic or symbolist "marriage" that also signals the birth of music. On the typographic level, the lines join, unite, or marry detached elements from different word families, "*Mais,*" "*dorer,*" "*tristement*" and "*dormir*" to produce the aesthetic emblem of music in the final word "mandore," while on the sonorous level they actualize a musical refrain by playing on the sounds "dore ment dort mandore." The tercets seem to confirm that beyond the breakdown of a philosophical theater of reflection on language as figure and knowledge there remains the possibility of a new "symbolist" and musical reawakening. Once the instability of the referential link between the figure and the world of natural experience has been shuffled into the background, the potential of awakening the intralinguistic links between *signifiants* (the sounded letters of words) and *signifiés* ("sound" as the ultimate meaning of the letters m-a-n-d-o-r-e) can become a source of endless aesthetic satisfaction and creativity. Technical resources of language like rhyme seem to allow for the production and transmission of effects of adequation in the way that sounds of words (*ment dort mandore*) correspond to their meaning (the aesthetic play of music). The work thus envisages its possible trans-

mission at the moment it declares its fictional status to be at the furthest remove from anything outside of itself.

It is also at this point that the possibility of a reconvergence of an aesthetic of music with an epistemology of narrative can be glimpsed. For if the positivity of an aesthetic of music can be conceived as the negation, as a fiction, of empirical reference and cognition, rather than as their further problematization, then it follows that this negativity can be inscribed in its turn as a temporary stage within a larger continuum. The alternating structure of opposing moments points toward a future synthesis of both negative and positive elements, a reintegration of the self-conscious choice for a nonrepresentational music in Mallarmé's "symbolism" within a larger historical scheme that could itself lay claim to cognitive dimensions unquestionably rooted in referential and representational models. This is the principal aim and interest of recent attempts at reading nonmimetic poetic texts by way of an aesthetics of reception, and the avowed project of a critic and historian like H. R. Jauss. [In his "1912: Threshold to an Epoch," *Yale French Studies* 74, 1988] Jauss set himself the task of showing how a history of a text's transmission and understanding is capable of reducing the distance between the formal autonomy of a work and its referential context. By treating the nonreferentiality of poetic language as though it could be located negatively in a sequence of historical reception—at the end of one model ("une Dentelle s'abolit") and the beginning of a new one ("dort une mandore")—Jauss is able to trace a genetic process that can overcome the dissolution of literature's reference to the empirical world in the aesthetic movement that stretches from Nietzsche to Apollinaire and beyond, and in which Mallarmé's work would occupy a central place. Speaking from the retrospective standpoint that recognizes the past necessity of this negative moment while denying it any further validity, he can say with absolute assurance, "In the aesthetic processes of deconstruction and reconstruction, the subject can proceed beyond the loss of its Cartesian self-sufficiency to new forms, and aesthetic experience can compensate for the supposedly irremediable loss of the world." In terms of Mallarmé's sonnet, this would mean that the poet simply replaces all the epistemological uncertainties of representational language with the deliberately determined but wholly independent features of pure semiotics, "au creux néant musicien."

Jauss's interpretation, which recognizes to some extent the text's disruption of the mimetic model of narrative, is able nonetheless to maintain narrative coherence and intelligibility by reconstruing poetic production as a progressive and self-conscious *negation,* or "hollow nothingness," of representation rather than its undecidable problematization. Can it be said, however, that the program of opposing or negating the problematics of an epistemology of representation, which begins in Mallarmé's sonnet with the "Mais" of line 9, is carried through to the end of the poem by a coherent and unilateral aesthetic of music? Does the poetic lyre, or "mandore," remain aesthetically intact until such time as its autonomous song would be negated and broken in on by a historical outside whose status remains safe from such questions? The answer depends on how successful the figure of music, the mandola, is in eliminating from its aesthetic dream the doubt that impinges on the figure of the lace at the beginning of the text. The dream, as we have seen, is the adequation of poetic effects with poetic meaning, the use of poetic language to create the illusion of a play of voice and sound in rhymes that refer only to themselves as music. As mere sound that means no meaning other than its own music, poetic rhyme states itself to be a self-referential fiction, or dream, that knows its hypothetical nature. So long as it is recognized for the fiction it is, poetic music is harmless. And in this spirit, despite what the commentators have suggested, the last line of the sonnet, "Filial on aurait pu naître," should be read as a positive affirmation of the resolutely unrealized, or fictive nature of the poet's "birth." For it is by his recognizing that the birth can only be one that always "could have been" but never was, that the musical poet of the tercets demonstrates superiority over the doubtful "Jeu" of the quatrains.

The aesthetic dream of the pure fiction, moreover, provides the means for reconsidering how the guardians of the "Book" mentioned in **"Sauvegarde"** could become the unwitting agents of historical and social activity. To the extent that the members of *L'Académie* choose to see themselves as fictional subjects operating within the ivory tower of aesthetics, so the story would go, they merely aestheticize reality rather than cutting themselves off from the partisan activities of the marketplace, thereby restricting themselves to playing a negative historical role within it. By turning history into a play of aesthetics, symbolist poets like Mallarmé seem to prepare and then fall prey to an inevitable collision with those aspects of empirical existence that eventually resist aestheticition, like abolitions of rights and faculties that are no longer purely figural.

But the fact that the model for language in **"Sauvegarde"** turns out to be the mundane dictionary rather than the sonorous dream of a musical elite should give pause, for it serves to reopen the question of poetry as music and rhyme. Could it be that rhyme, nonreferential music, is itself a fiction of sorts, a strategy used to deflect attention away from the prosaic role that rhyme might actually play in the everyday world of the dictionary? If we turn for help to the dictionary itself, we find first of all that rhyme is defined there as a "correspondence of terminal sounds of words or of liens of verse." The definition is too pragmatic to be of help to us; it begs the question of poetry's relation to music by presupposing the "dream" of bringing together aesthetic "sounds" and meaningful "words" rather than accounting for it. It proves more helpful, however, to ask about "rhythm," the poetic principle of regulated patterns, to which rhyme, as a pattern of *sounds,* is conceptually and etymologically tributary. Emile Benveniste in his essay, "La Notion de 'rythme' dans son expression linguistique" [published in *Problèmes de linguistique générale 1,* 1966], argues that the term "rhythm," contrary to common knowledge, cannot be understood by tracing its filiation to the Greek root "rheô," which names the "flowing" movement of rivers, and so cannot be presumed without further analysis to link, by way of an analogy or poetic metaphor, a phenomenal category (the repetitive motion of flowing water) with a principle of signification (the marked regularity of poetic and semantic

units). According to Benveniste, the phenomenal reference to the visibility of ocean waves in the case of "rhythm," and by extension the more recent reference to the perception of sound patterns in the case of "rhyme," was imposed or grafted onto a more fundamental use, which, since Plato, has been subdued and all but forgotten in favor of the later genealogy. "Rhythm," at its origin, names the concept of "form" or "figure" at its most elementary level, before there could have been anything like a "metaphor" linking the sensuous with the intelligible. Rhythm is "form" as it is assigned at a particular moment not to a preexisting entity, but to differential relations that, prior to an act of configuration, have neither phenomenal nor conceptual identity, "the form of that which has no organic consistency," states Benveniste.

As such, "rhythm" names the moment of an originary figuration. It is a linguistic act by which a "formal" set of relations is instituted in such a way that it can be repeated according to a preordained pattern susceptible to being recognized in its repetition. For this reason, the examples cited by Aristotle as well as by Benveniste most often refer to the disposition, arrangement, or the patterns instituted in the letters of the alphabet, the most distinctive example conceivable of a fixed, iterable, and nonorganic "form." Rhythm is neither visible like the waves of the ocean nor audible like the chirping of birds. Benveniste says in conclusion: "Nothing could be less 'natural' than this notion" which as "rhythm" and "rhyme" is the mechanical reproduction of a material inscription or trace devoid of any immediate and direct relationship to the world we think we see and hear and understand. The preordained aspect of this mechanical pattern, or "rhyme," makes its operation like the grammar of a language separated from its semantic function, or like what Mallarmé refers to in **"Sauvegarde"** as "a branch, the nude syntax of a sentence." Rhyme loses its poetic and musical aura in Mallarmé when "belles-lettres" are stripped of their aesthetic integrity and become like the "scattered words" of the dictionary. For the dictionary is not just the place where words, units of more or less stable meaning, can be found strewn about like flowers, but also and especially the place where words, as meaning, can be seen to scatter and dissolve into the subsemantic elements of their letters, which are then ordered, patterned, and rhymed mechanically, like an empty grammar or a nude syntax, from *a* to *z.*

The implications for our reading are considerable. If the link between rhyme and music is not naturally musical like the sounds of the voice, but is rather grammatical and inscriptional like the letters of the alphabet, then it cannot be said that the musical model of language proposed in the tercets of **"Une Dentelle"** is any different from the undecidable inscription that operates in the quatrains. Instead, vocalized language is an unwarranted representation of the system of voiceless inscription or notation that was there all along, though hidden, sleeping, in the "belles-lettres" of the "mandore." It would therefore not be any more exempt from the kind of questioning that occurs around the torn figure of the lace. Nor would it be possible to subscribe to a reading, which, like that of Jauss, relies implicitly on polar models to reduce poetic effects like rhyme to an aesthetic phenomenon in order to promise historical coherence and understanding on the far side of their problematization. On the contrary, by writing out the attempt to move away from the situation of doubt inscribed in the quatrains to the self-enclosed dream of aesthetics in the tercets, Mallarmé's text anticipates its aesthetic reception in order to warn against it. But what evidence is there that Mallarmé's text does not share the dream of rhyme as a simple metaphorical correspondence between sounds (aesthetics) and words (meaning)? At what point, to use the terms of **"Sauvegarde,"** does the poem state that the link between language and the empirical world is "fictive," though in such a way that it does not automatically fall prey to this as an aesthetic fiction and so does not prevent itself from occurring in a different mode?

These questions, with their insistence on inaugurating a difference within a signifying system of relationships already in place, bring us back to the problem of literary heritage. It is now clear that whatever can be born in this poem must be born out of the womb or *ventre* of music, "Selon nul ventre que le sien." As we have seen, this music is language as rhyme, language as the repetition of an arbitrary act of form-giving to what has neither determinate meaning nor sensuous form, like the nude letters of the alphabet. The "form" of letters is not determined metaphorically as a sonorous or visible manifestation of an inner content, the way the human voice and body can be taken to be the mere forms of an inner mind or soul. The letters of the alphabet by themselves cover nothing and mean nothing. They are a "creux néant" whose only "form" is the legibility they acquire by means of a conventional system of markings in which each one differs from all the others, constituting ultimately that "total rhythm, which would be the poem silenced, in the blanks." However, as the reading also disclosed, rhyme immediately produces an aesthetic version of this blank birth that serves as a shelter from the knowledge of its constitutive dependence on the unpredictable play of the letter. It does so by representing itself as a negative moment within a natural genealogy linking meaning to phenomenal categories by way of a determined relation to sound. Rhyme as music recovers the certainty of sound by negating itself as semiotic representation and by presupposing a direct relationship to empirical reality. But the poem has shown that the assumption of an immediate relation to the empirical world is a fiction that has forgotten its fictional nature. Such fictions, or ideologies, attempt to parry the more radical fiction of rhyme as letters, which fiction is the a priori act of having instituted any relationship whatsoever between the nude syntax of the alphabet and either sound or meaning. When Mallarmé says that social relations, society, and by implication the state, are a "fiction," he does not mean that they are not real, far from it. Rather, he means that society is always based on some sort of minimal linguistic operation of form-giving or "rhyme" prior to any determination of binary oppositions. Therefore, the irreducibly poetic element in the production of a society or state must remain "mysterious," must fall outside the reach of an analysis derived solely from the opposition between the phenomenal and the intelligible since that logic is a result of the very forces it would analyze.

The surprise in **"Une Dentelle"** is what happens when "music" actually makes its appearance in the tercets. For the locus of its birth, the "ventre," not only follows a self-deluding aesthetic program through its reference to the purely phenomenal space of the mandola's sound box. This space, thanks to its visible similarity to a woman's pregnant belly, also manages to reintroduce the theatricality of a traditional "son et lumière" spectacle by infusing the end of the poem with a golden hue: "se dore une mandore." In addition, though, the term "ventre" occurs as and gives birth to an unpredictable and impersonal effect by way of its letters. And the *letters* of the word "ventre," rather than the sound or shape of the musical instrument it refers to, reinscribe an earlier moment of the poem. This is the moment of writing's undecidable doubt and half-opening in the quatrains: "A *n'entr'*ouvrir / *n*ul *v*entre." The word "ventre" can thus be said to reintroduce the problematic rhythm of the quatrains, the silent rhythm that dislocates the aesthetic program of a purely sonorous rhyme. For "entr'ouvrir," it will be recalled, is the place in the quatrains where writing is not resolved into the symmetrical polarities and specular valorizations of the sensuous ("le lit" as eros) and the intelligible ("le lit" as concept). Rather it results in a typographical suspension, the apostrophe of "entr'ouvrir." The apostrophe stands for language's power of figuration, its power to call forth and relate in their dialectical opposition a phenomenal and intelligible "world." But language produces this figure by instituting diacritical marks or letters (*l-i-t,* for instance), which can themselves never be reduced to mere figures, since the text they write out is neither simply present nor absent, neither subjective nor objective. Far from negating the critical question of figuration by substituting for it the dream space of poetic solipsism or subjectivity, the reinscription of the rhyming letters (*entr'*) in the womb of the tercets' music (*ventre*) shows that the aesthetic dream, whether valorized negatively or positively, is always blind (or deaf) to effects of the letter which remain beyond its own power to explain or elude.

We cannot dismiss (or celebrate) the poem for embracing an aesthetic and subjective program that it takes such pains to interrogate and interrupt. The kind of birth **"Une Dentelle"** alludes to must be understood on a different, linguistic model, if it is to take place at all. It could be prepared only by first going back to the fiction of a determinate relation between letters and sound and meaning rather than by blindly turning away from it. Such a birth, by returning to the wholly arbitrary and mechanical power of rhyme to cut into the semantic unity of music's "womb" (*ventre*), could only occur by somehow waking to repeat—that is, in a mode that defies absolute difference as well as mere identity—the originary and open-ended act of figuration instituted by the letter. Such a waking is entrusted to specters who are also readers, those men and women of the Academy who safeguard the dictionary and the rhythm of its letters by overseeing the detached metaphors already scattered there as well as the unheard-of combinations to come. To the extent that they cut themselves off from a mere dream of autonomous meaning by watching over the unpredictable play of language, they reproduce its original possibility, though in such a way that its meaning remains undecidable, a legacy to a pure future.

"Filial on aurait pu naître" must thus be read not only to mean that one could have been born but wasn't, but also that one might have been born without yet knowing it. (pp. 243-75)

> *Kevin Newmark, "Beneath the Lace: Mallarmé, the State, and the Foundation of Letters," in* Yale French Studies, *No. 77, 1990, pp. 243-75.*

FURTHER READING

Assad, Maria L. "Mallarmé's *Hérodiade:* A Hermeneutical Gesture." *Paragraph* 12, No. 3 (November 1989): 181-96.
 Discusses the relationship between *Hérodiade* and modern critical discourses.

Chambers, Ross. "An Address in the Country: Mallarmé and the Kinds of Literary Context." *French Forum* 11, No. 2 (May 1986): 199-215.
 Examines Mallarmé's *Les loisirs de la poste,* considering "the ways in which a literary text *produces* contexts."

Cohn, Robert Greer. *Toward the Poems of Mallarmé,* expanded edition. Berkeley: University of California Press, 1980, 321 p.
 Provides critical interpretations of Mallarmé's verse, maintaining that each work should be viewed as part of the writer's "highly unified poetic universe."

Dayan, Peter. *Mallarmé's Divine Transposition: Real and Apparent Sources of Literary Value.* Oxford: Clarendon Press, 1986, 219 p.
 Analyzes Mallarmé's philosophy of language in relation to modern critical discourse.

Florence, Penny. *Mallarmé, Manet and Redon: Visual and Aural Signs and the Generation of Meaning.* Cambridge: Cambridge University Press, 1986, 167 p.
 Examines the relationship of painting to Mallarmé's poetry, asserting that the writer "worked towards making new meanings, using visual and aural structures in combination."

Houston, John Porter. *Patterns of Thought in Rimbaud and Mallarmé.* Lexington, Ky.: French Forum Publishers, 1986, 134 p.
 Compares Mallarmé and Rimbaud in the context of nineteenth-century intellectual life, attempting to provide an "explication of their larger intellectual designs as they extend throughout their respective œvres."

Kravis, Judy. *The Prose of Mallarmé: The Evolution of a Literary Language.* Cambridge: Cambridge University Press, 1976, 239 p.
 Investigates the relationship between language and reality in Mallarmé's prose.

Lydon, Mary. "Skirting the Issue: Mallarmé, Proust, and Symbolism." *Yale French Studies,* No. 74 (1988): 157-81.
 Explores the relationship between sexuality and writing, focusing on Mallarmé's editorship of the fashion magazine *La Dernière Mode.*

Marvick, Louis Wirth. *Mallarmé and the Sublime.* Albany: State University of New York Press, 1986, 211 p.
 Considers the historical basis and stylistic implications of Mallarmé's idealism.

Riffaterre, Michael. "On Deciphering Mallarmé." *The Georgia Review* XXIX, No. 1 (Spring 1975): 75-91.
 Contends that Mallarmé's texts should be interpreted through recognition of their variations of "generic blueprints."

Sartre, Jean-Paul. *Mallarmé, or, The Poet of Nothingness.* Translated by Ernest Sturm. University Park: Pennsylvania State University Press, 1988, 146 p.
 Provides a philosophical consideration of Mallarmé's poetics, contending that it prefigures the disillusionement characteristic of the modernist era.

Terlecki, Antonina M. "Stéphane Mallarmé and Symbolism (Part I)." *Kwartalnik Neofilologiczny* XXXV, No. 2 (1988): 127-51.
 Considers Mallarmé's aesthetics of language, music, and theater. Part II of this essay is excerpted above.

Wayne, Eric. "Mallarmé's Folds: Mallarmé, Boulez, and *Pli Selon Pli.*" *Nineteenth-Century French Studies* IX, Nos. 3-4 (Spring/Summer 1981): 220-32.
 Investigates the importance of structural and imagistic "folds" in Mallarmé's writing, and their influence on works by later artists.

Wolf, Mary Ellen. *Eros Under Glass: Psychoanalysis and Mallarmé's Hérodiade.* Columbus: Ohio State University Press, 1987, 128 p.
 Examines the evolution of Mallarmé's poetics, contending that the poet's "concern with the becoming of a text and the limits of interpretation . . . constitutes the productive juncture" between his aesthetics and Freudian thought.

Johan Runeberg

1804-1877

Swedish-Finnish poet, essayist, short story writer, and dramatist.

INTRODUCTION

Although he wrote in Swedish, Runeberg is hailed as the national poet of Finland. Writing during a turbulent period in Finnish history, when Sweden and Russia were engaged in a violent conflict over possession of the region, Runeberg celebrated the culture of native Finns and thereby helped establish a sense of national identity. He is best remembered for the poetic cycle *Fänrik Ståls sägner* (*The Tales of Ensign Stål*), the opening poem of which became the Finnish national anthem.

Runeberg was born in Pietarsaari, Finland, to parents of Swedish origin. After attending schools in Oulu and Vaasa, he enrolled at the University of Turku in 1822. However, one year later he was forced by financial hardship to withdraw from the university and look for work. Finding a position as a tutor in the inland village of Saari-järvi, Runeberg left the coastal region of Finland, where Swedish language and culture dominated, and for the first time came into contact with the native Finnish peasantry. During this period, he began to write poetry celebrating the Finnish countryside, customs and folklore. In 1826 he returned to the university and completed the requirements for his master's degree.

After graduating Runeberg moved to Helsinki, where he worked as an instructor of Latin and edited the daily newspaper *Helsingfors Morgonblad*. In 1830 he published *Dikter,* his first volume of poetry, and in 1831 he was awarded second prize by the Swedish Academy for his poem "Graven i Perho" ("The Grave at Perho"). Runeberg subsequently published two more volumes of verse and several longer poems, but it was not until 1848, with the publication of the first volume of *The Tales of Ensign Stål,* that he achieved popular and critical recognition. Recounting the heroism of Finns in defending their country during Russian War of 1808-1809, *The Tales of Ensign Stål* quickly became a great source of national pride, and Runeberg was applauded as Finland's most important and talented poet. After publishing the second volume of the *Tales* in 1860, Runeberg produced two dramas, but his career was ended by a severe stroke in 1863. He died in 1877.

Although Runeberg created works in a number of genres during his long career, critics agree that his poetry represents his most significant and lasting achievement. Characterized by simple diction, use of Classical verse forms, and metrical regularity, Runeberg's poetry celebrates the beauty of the Finnish countryside as well as the courage, generosity, and vigor of the Finnish people. For example,

"Bonden Pavo" ("The Peasant Pavo") describes the strength and religious faith demonstrated by the title character and his wife as they endure famine for three years because of crop failures. The fourth year they enjoy a plentiful harvest but still go hungry because they share their food supply with a less fortunate neighbor. *Elgskyttarne* and *Hanna* also celebrate rural life, depicting peasants hunting, feasting, courting, and sharing their bounty with both visitors and beggars.

In *The Tales of Ensign Stål,* Runeberg turned to Finnish history for his source material. Ostensibly the reminiscences of a soldier who has survived the battles waged against Russian invaders, the *Tales* recount the heroism of the Finnish peasants and their leaders in trying to defend their homeland, and many are based on actual persons and events. "Döbeln et Jutas," for example, describes a stunning victory in battle by one of the most colorful figures of the war, Georg Karl von Döbeln, while "Sveaborg" recounts the loss that resulted in the defeat of the Finns and their subsequent occupation by Russia. Critics note that the emotional power of these poems is enhanced by Runeberg's clear imagery and simple, realistic language.

Although not well known outside Scandinavia, Runeberg exerted a profound influence in the development of literature in his native region. His concentration on specifically Finnish subjects was imitated by subsequent generations of writers and, as a result, he is seen as the progenitor of modern Finnish literature. At the same time, his stylistic innovations influenced the direction of Swedish poetry, helping to change the complex and artificial style dominant during the first half of the nineteenth century. Summarizing his achievement, Tore Wretö has written: "Runeberg is the undisputed poet of his nation by virtue both of the strength of his national feelings and of his eminence as a poet."

PRINCIPAL WORKS

Dikter (poetry) 1830
Elgskyttarne (poetry) 1832
Dikter: Andra häftet (poetry) 1833
Hanna (poetry) 1836
Den gamle trädgårdsmästarens brev (fictional letters) 1837
Julqvällen (poetry) 1841
   [*Christmas Eve,* 1887]
Nadeschda (poetry) 1841
   [*Nadeschda,* 1879]
Dikter: Tredje häftet (poetry) 1843
Kung Fjalar (poetry) 1844
   [*King Fjalar,* 1904]
Fänrik Ståls sägner. 2 vols. (poetry) 1848-60
   [*The Songs of Ensign Stål: National Military Song-Cycle of Finland,* 1925; also translated as *The Tales of Ensign Stål,* 1938]
Kan ej (drama) 1862
Kungarne på Salamis (drama) 1863
Lyrical Songs: Idylls and Epigrams (poetry) 1878
Samlade arbeten. 8 vols. (poetry, essays, dramas) 1899-1902

*First publication date

William and Mary Howitt   (essay date 1852)

[*The Howitts were English scholars of Scandinavian literature and culture. Here, they provide an overview of Runeberg's poetic works, focusing on his use of Finnish customs and scenes.*]

Runeberg is a Finn by birth, though he writes in Swedish; and that has been a great advantage to him, in rescuing him from the mere indulgence in that easy manufacture of lyrical and occasional poetry, which is the fatality of the Swedes, and which makes so many of their poets only look like individual sheep of the same flock and breed, with the same wool, the same build, the same coloured legs and faces. Finland has its own vein of poetry, though it cannot be said to have a national literature. Having, for a great number of centuries, existed only as a province, it has had no chance of creating a national literature; but it has, nev-

ertheless, a native poetry. Amid its solitary forests, its wide dark moorlands, its lonely lakes, it was impossible that poetry should not visit her people, and it has done so. (pp. 427-28)

[In Runeberg's poetry] we bid adieu to all the play-work of Zephyrs, Muses, Apollos, Floras, Alexises, Naiads, Thirsises and Amaryllises, with the rest of the old tinsel and Rag-fair finery of a worn-out Olympus. We come to living souls and living affairs of a real world—that in which we exist and rejoice over, with no feigned joys or sufferings—real, human, unmistakable sufferings. We come to genuine flesh and blood, genuine muscle and bone. Runeberg finds a country abounding with bold features, solemn and impressive, and a people full of strong passions and deep-seated injuries ready to his hands. He wants no imaginary Corydon, no lack-a-daisical lamentations over his own morbid feelings; he has the discernment to see that a great poetic world lies at his feet, and he is baptized with the spirit of his country and his countrymen by the reflection, over those brute but overwhelming forces, which have torn his native land as a prey from all its old and cherished associations, and made it an appanage of a vast, dominant, but unamalgamated empire.

These feelings break forth in the **Stories of Ensign Stål.** The old Ensign has been engaged not only in victories but defeats, and therefore, the retiring stillness of his mood, and the scenes of sad and strange woe, of wild passages, and pathetic incidents of war, ravage and domestic calamity, which he narrates when his heart is opened by kindness, and the spirit of indignant sympathy for the wrongs of his country and his fellow-men, burns upon his tongue. (pp. 429-30)

We do not care to ask, with the critics of the North, whether his genius be lyrical or dramatic, epic or epic-idyllic. It is enough for us that he is a poet, strong, genuine, and of God's own making and sending. He may have benefited from reading Homer's *Odyssey,* Voss's *Louise,* [Goethe's] *Herman and Dorothea,* or what else. No doubt he has read these, and lit his own torch, like other poets at them, as the Phœnix kindles its brand at the sun. But the torch was his own, and it burns bravely in the strength of its own substance. He has learned from men, but he has learned far more and more deeply from nature.

In Sweden, Runeberg has had to encounter much carping comment, as every one who strikes out into a new field has: as Wordsworth for a long time had here; but he is unquestionably one of the truest, and the greatest poets of the North. His verse is solemn and strong, like the spirit of its subject. He brings before you the wild wastes and the dark woods of his native land, and the brave, simple, enduring people who inhabit it. You feel the wind blow fresh from the vast dark moorlands; you follow the elk-hunters through the pine-forests, and along the shores of remote lakes. You lie in desert huts, and hear the narratives of the struggles of the inhabitants with the ungenial elements, or their contentions with more ungenial men. Runeberg seizes on life, wherever it presents itself, in strong and touching forms; in the beggar, the gipsy, the malefactor. It is enough for him that it is human nature doing or suffering; and in this respect he stands pre-eminently above all the poets of Sweden. Bellman, it is true, has portrayed the life of the people, but it is only the tavern-frequenting people of Stockholm, and in the midst of their orgies and their jollity. Nowhere else do you find the poets of Sweden coming down and walking their native earth with bare feet, and grasping humanity in all its forms, with honest, ungloved hands. When they have done this, they will cease to be merely lyrical, and advance into the giant stature, and stalwart shapes of full and various poetic power. Runeberg has set them a splendid example: one of his free, masculine transcripts from real life, animated with real passion, touched with the hues of genuine feeling, is worth whole volumes even of the revelries of Bellman, or the innocencies of Franzén; and we are, therefore, glad to see Professor Lénström rejoicing in the growing tendency towards the actual: declaring that the Muse requires no visiting cards, no outriders, nor heralds; but where she goes, the heart of man is open to receive her. In his defence of Runeberg, he says to the point:

> This is the fact. Man is man in the countryman's hut as much as in the King's or the nobleman's palace. Under both are found the troubles as well as the repose of life. Both classes have an object. Both are visited by earnest strivings after a better, by presentiments of a higher existence than the present; and poetry is the real interpreter of their consciousness. All that is purely human is poetic. What is purely human? Why that which is unsophisticated, is not merely accidental in its connection with man. That which does not look on the mere surface of life, but at that which is eternal in it. That which at once recognizes man as a spirit and a creature. All that which at once describes man as a spirit, as a willing and thinking existence, and as a creature bodily, and of independent action, is poetry. To analyse and demonstrate the whole circumstances and relations between these two existences and their rights, is poetry. Merely to describe a landscape, or a country-dwelling; dead or exterior matters, or domestic affairs; how a girl weaves, spins, or performs these and other mere daily duty, is not poetry, but the bare life of such portraitures—how men and women feel, think, suffer, rejoice, yearn after good or recoil from evil—that is human, universal, and in its higher sense, that is poetry.

No northern poet has more fully, or in a more manly way embraced poetry, or achieved it, in this sense, than Runeberg. His principal productions are, *The Stories of Ensign Stål,* already named; *The Elk-Hunters,* a poem in nine cantos; *Idyl and Epigram,* a series of most popular sketches from life; *The Gipsy; Hanna,* an idyllic-epic in three cantos, in hexameters; "The Grave in Perrho," and *Servian Folks' Songs. Hanna* is a poem which may match with Voss for the charming painting of country and domestic life, with all its wooings, weddings, and attendant festivities. The scenery and characters, both in that and *The Elk-Hunters,* have for us all the delight of the most untouched freshness. Nothing can be more novel, new and delicious to the imagination, than the Finland nature and life that we are transported amongst. (pp. 433-35)

William Howitt and Mary Howitt, "Final

Group of Swedish Poets," in their The Literature and Romance of Northern Europe, Vol. II, *Colburn and Co., Publishers, 1852, pp. 427-47.*

Frederik Winkel Horn   (essay date 1884)

[*In the following excerpt, Winkel Horn discusses Runeberg's works and their overall contributions to Finnish and Swedish literature.*]

Johan Ludvig Runeberg was born February 5, 1804, in Jakobstad, where his parents lived in poor circumstances. A relative of his took an interest in him, and in 1822 Runeberg became a student, from which time he was compelled to help himself. He had grown up under the influence of general European culture such as it was found among the Swedish Finlanders, and his favorite poet was Franzén, but later a sojourn of several years as tutor in the parish of Sarijärvi proved of the greatest importance to his future development. Here in the heart of Finland a number of new impressions poured in upon him, and became indelibly stamped upon his soul, to be afterwards reproduced in his poetical compositions. In one of his best prose works he has given a masterly description of the grand, wild nature and of the quaint popular life of this region, where the people even at the present day preserve the same simple ways they did centuries ago. In 1830 he was appointed docent in Latin literature at the Helsingfors University, and in this same year he published his first collection of poems, chiefly lyrics. It contains among other things a poem of some length, **"Svartsjukans nätter"** (**"Nights of Jealousy"**), which, like several of his earlier poems, suffers from a certain pretentious pathos and a sort of didactic style borrowed from Tegnér. His simple and charming scenes from real life are far superior to the former, especially those fine and graceful songs, entitled *Idyll och Epigram,* which in tone and spirit are closely related to the Finnish and Serbian popular ballads, but without being an imitation of them. He thereupon published a collection of Serbian popular songs in a Swedish translation, and also the epic-lyric poem, **"Grafven i Perrho,"** which latter won the prize offered by the Swedish Academy. This poem represents a Finnish peasant family which has been surprised by the Kossack enemy, and is tortured to death. The father curses his son in the belief that he has absented himself from cowardice, but still lives to see the latter avenge both his father and his brothers. In this no less effective than simple sketch, Runeberg is for the first time wholly and completely a Finnish poet, filled with an ardent patriotism, and with a profound appreciation of the exceptive position of his people who have been steeled in a desperate struggle for existence. From this time his master works follow in rapid succession. Among the first were the idylls, *Elgskyttarne (The Elk-hunters), Hanna,* and *Julqvällen (Christmas evening),* all three in the broadest epic form in hexameters, reminding us of Goethe's *Hermann und Dorothea,* and in no way inferior to that poem. The action in these idylls is very simple, but the pictures from popular life are perfect models of graphic and faithful description, and at the same time they show the finest psychological insight. This particularly applies to *Elgskyttarne,* which is one of the most excellent works of this kind in existence. Runeberg displayed his lyric talent not only in a number of excellent lyric poems, but also in several lyric epic compositions, among which are *Nadeschda,* a Russian subject treated with great grace and delicacy, and *Kung Fjalar,* in which the world sung by Ossian is reproduced in grand outlines, that are prevaded by the idea of an inexorable tragical fate.

But Runeberg's chief work is *Fänrik Ståls sägner* (*The Stories of Ensign Stål*), of which the first part appeared in 1848, and the second part in 1860. He here gave his people a national work of the greatest value. In no other of his productions has his spirit unfolded fairer blossoms or soared to loftier heights of pathos than in this collection of romances describing scenes from the second Finnish war. The situations are depicted so vividly, faithfully and graphically, and the characters are drawn with such consummate skill, that they stamp themselves indelibly on the memory. Every one of these poems, each written in a metre of its own, is a master-piece, and together they are the most beautiful heroic drapa that was ever composed for or in honor of any nation. The whole collection is pervaded by a deep and warm patriotic sentiment, which is so gloriously expressed in the song, "Vårt land, vårt land, vårt fosterland," which forms the introduction to the romances. None of his other works have like this contributed so much toward making Runeberg the national poet both of Sweden and Finland, for he sings the common struggle and the common misfortune of both countries in tones that on the stranger make the impression of rare beauty, while on those who are more intimately related to the events described, they must of necessity produce a most powerful effect. Of dramatical works Runeberg has composed only the play, *Kan ej,* which, though delicately written, is somewhat insignificant, and the splendid tragedy, *Kungarne på Salamis.* The latter was published in 1863, and was his last work. Having been made an invalid by an apoplectic stroke, he continued to live in Borgå, where, since 1837, he had been a lector at the gymnasium, and where he died May 6, 1877.

A poet with a talent so great and comprehensive as Runeberg's, whose poetry was based on a sound and harmonious view of life, could not fail to exercise a powerful influence, and the fact is, he produced, both in Finland and in Sweden, a tendency toward realism, and simplicity of style has gradually superseded the overstrained, pompous language of the first half of this century. In Finland he has been followed by a number of poets, who, in the best sense of the word, may be characterized as belonging to the Runeberg school. Their chief excellence consists in their efforts to produce in a clear, unaffected manner, vivid and pathetic descriptions of homely things and scenes. (pp. 403-06)

> *Frederik Winkel Horn, "The Nineteenth Century," in his* History of the Literature of the Scandinavian North from the Most Ancient Times to the Present, *translated by Rasmus B. Anderson, revised edition, 1884. Reprint by Kraas Reprint Co., 1971, pp. 373-411.*

Athenaeum (essay date 1891)

[*In the following excerpt from a review of* Nadeschda, *the critic praises the style of the poem as well as its depiction of the empress Catharine II.*]

It is now more than twelve years since Messrs. Magnusson and Palmer's excellent translation of Runeberg's lyrical songs, idyls, and epigrams first introduced the greatest of Swedish poets to the British public, and now at last our literature is enriched by a very creditable version of one of his more considerable works. Runeberg's poetry ought to be popular in England. He is essentially manly, simple, genial, religious, delighting in Nature in all her phases, full of the joy of life, and always preferring to look on the bright and hopeful side of things. Moreover, he is in many respects the spiritual congener of two of our most representative poets, Walter Scott and Wordsworth, though with a deeper insight and a wider range than either. Beginning his literary career as a lyrical poet of exquisite melody and sweetness, he next devoted himself to the hexametrical idyl, and produced in rapid succession three masterpieces—*Elgskyttarne, Hanna,* and *Julqvällen* (the last recently translated into French)—descriptive of peasant life in Finland, after the manner of Goethe's *Hermann und Dorothea,* but as superior even to Goethe's idyl as Goethe's idyl is superior to Voss's *Luise.* It now seemed to his admirers as if any fresh efforts could not possibly enhance, but might not improbably imperil, his great reputation; but the poet made yet another venture, and achieved the singular success of inventing quite a new species of poem, generally described as epic, but really defying classification, for it is quite *sui generis.* To this latter class of poem belongs *Nadeshda. . . .*

[This] beautiful story, . . . if inferior on the whole to Runeberg's masterpiece *Fänrik Stål,* nevertheless displays, perhaps more than any other of his works, his marvellous ingenuity and versatility. Each of the nine cantos of *Nadeshda* is written in a different unrhymed metre, according as the lyric, epic, or dramatic element predominates, for the whole poem is really a very singular, but perfectly harmonious combination of all three. In the first three cantos the epic tone decidedly predominates; the fourth canto, describing the bliss of the lovers among Kama's lindens, is purely lyrical, and has been finely described by another Finnish poet as "sweet as the dawn in Valentia's groves, yet plaintive as a Northern moonlit night." From the fifth canto onwards the dramatic element supervenes and at last prevails, being most noticeable in the wonderfully lifelike scenes at the Russian Court, where we see the omnipotent Potemkin dispensing rewards and punishments among the magnates and heroes who throng his antechambers, and where we also catch a glimpse of Catharine II., not as "Russia's haughty Dame," insolently trampling on the liberties of oppressed nationalities, as in *Fänrik Stål,* but as "Russia's mother," wise, gracious, and benign, redressing the wrongs of her people and bringing blessings in her train. The characterization of the great Tsaritsa and her ministers is perfect, and justifies the inference that Runeberg might have rivalled Scott himself as an historical novelist.

A review of "Nadeschda: A Poem in Nine Can-

tos," in The Athenaeum, *Vol. 97, May 23, 1891, p. 661.*

Clement Burbank Shaw   (essay date 1925)

[*In the following excerpt, Shaw praises Runeberg's poetry for its simplicity and power, noting in addition the poet's skillful adaptation of Classical style.*]

Runeberg is the interpreter of Finland's ideals, its racial qualities, and its traditions of heroism; but in this very office he becomes cosmopolitan. In painting northern moods, he paints moods that abide. In portraying past valor, he portrays also the valor of the present times. Sometimes he sets forth what we have not been able to say, but deeply feel when it is said; for therein we constantly find ourselves. He has removed the barriers of education, view-point and heredity, and thus has helped produce world-literature. In Finnish heroism we perceive all heroism. Like the Knights of Arthur, each hero for the time transcends every other. We must reverence his lance. We must regard his cause as just, we must recognize his enemy as unjust and worthy of death. When he kills his foe, we must believe it was the will of Heaven; if he himself falls, it was the temporary triumph of Hell.

Runeberg is mighty in his charming simplicity. Always the simplest words prevail. The labor of translating is thus greatly augmented. Rather than elaborate, he even repeats the same monosyllabic word or words—the same plain thought. No mental exhaustion results from the attempt to enucleate his meaning. No interminable periods exasperate the reader's patience.

In the greater number of the cantos there is required no preparatory study on the part of the reader. The great common mind understands them at once,—whether they be comedies or tragedies,—whether they are set forth in the lyric or epic strain. And freedom from frothy verbiage is imperative, if one would portray the national Finnish character in its blunt simplicity, its silent calmness, its laconic and sententious utterances,—as set forth so vividly in the picture of Munter in the elegiac Canto Twenty Eighth.

And Horatius, long ago, portrayed the comsummation of the wanderer's repose when at last—at last—from long and weary years of pilgrimage, he returns to his childhood's home, once more "to rest upon the longed-for couch." Runeberg did more than to return to his own land,—he did not leave it.

While the twenty-four Cantos of *Frithiof's Saga*, each in its own metrical and strophic form, constitute a connected hero-song, the thirty-five cantos of the present work are wholly detached, each complete in itself, and delineative of episodes having no connection, except incidentally, with each other. It would be difficult to weave so many characters into one Romance.

These portrayals of heroic exploits and martial scenes in the war of 1808–9 between Sweden and Russia (in which the latter country wrested Finland from the former), are strikingly projective of northern ideals, and have long inspired the national heart with patriotic fire.

While a few of the personages described are fictitious creations of Runeberg, they each yet represent concepts of Finland's military life and valor, and as substrata for the projection of heroic attributes must be of equal value with the historic characters.

All poems are great as they speak to our own hearts. This is perhaps a poem's apology for existence. It seems to me Runeberg's **Sägner** are tangent at enough points to the world-thought to bridge over the chasms of language, race, time and place, and show that heroism, chivalry, codes of honor, depth of thoughts and feelings,—are international and universal. His characters radiate the atmosphere of living subjects, and with them he makes us acquainted.

And the startling originality of the poet parallels his directness and artlessness. Invention is one of his striking attributes.

Like Tegnér, Runeberg is a master of versification. As in *Frithiof's Saga*, so each Canto of **Fänrik Ståls Sägner** stands before us in a strophic form unlike that of any other canto. This ever-varied stanza-scheme would of itself forefend against monotony; but each mold seems specially fitted to its subject. Some of these stanzaic forms are borrowed from the English ballad; but our poet was quick to perceive in other literatures the forms that best serve his purpose here. His apprehension of poetic beauty and metrical fitness was clear and keen. Many of the numbers are designed for music, and have received melodic settings, as will be noticed *en passant*. All the cantos except the third (**"The Cloud's Brother"**) are strophic. Nine of the 35 cantos are iambic.

In multitudes of versified products we might question the appropriateness of a metrical treatment at all. In all languages a large percentage of subjects possessing no inherent poetic quality would have been better set forth in prose. Except that Songs must be metrical, this remark would perhaps in a few cases apply to the Runeberg work,—for example in Cantos Eighth, Tenth, Sixteenth, Twenty-Sixth and Thirtieth, where only a minimum of poetic imagery inheres in the subject itself; but the same is true of much of Dryden, Wordsworth, Pope, Cowper, occasionally of Longfellow, rarely of Tennyson,—almost never of Poe. Yet in defense of the stanza-form of writing, we must recognize wherein lie its powers. Meter, versification, regularity of form, order, the banishment of chaos, the elimination of confusion, the establishment of law,—all are potent. Even in prose there must be an approximate rhythm,—a more or less regular recurrence of accent. Very unrhythmic prose is annoying, disturbing, offensive.

There is a charm *per se* in ictus, in the ear-satisfaction that results from equal-timed pulsations, in the pleasure of constantly finding something where we expected it, and in a promise fulfilled,—the promise of the evenly recurring accent.

The poet chooses this pulse as does the mouth-pipe of a great organ, which converts an irregular series of air-disturbances or pulsations into its own proper and appropriate tone;—or as a stone-mason out of a heterogeneous heap of stones constructs a cemented wall of regular and artistic proportions.

The quality of satisfying this almost universal rhythmic sense, carrying us along with its currents of measured motion, can therefore be claimed by all verse, even if sometimes unpoetic in imagery; and with the incorporation of rhyme, alliteration, consonance, assonance, and other artifices, the metrical form constitutes for pure poetic thought the most beautiful vesture.

By these processes, and his innate perception of truth and beauty, Runeberg seems to have discovered and set forth for ear and thought every poetic element lying latent within his subjects, often surprisingly infusing it even into his character-portrayals.

But many of the Sägner are highly poetic in matter and loftily classic in treatment. In Canto Third, **"The Cloud's Brother,"** we constantly discern the Homeric and Virgilian touch. Elaborate in its finesse, and stately in its development, its similes are the re-incarnation of the long slumbering Southern epic, and speak to us over the chasm of thousands of years. An excerpt from this Canto will exemplify:

> As when toward the eve, a summer whirlwind,
> When all nature, Sabbath-like, is silent,
> Comes alone, unseen, swift as an arrow,
> Striking down in forest-lake, while moveth
> Plant nor leaf, nor is the pine-tree shaken,
> Nor on rocky strand a floweret wavers,—
> Calm is all, the sea-depths only seething;—
> So, when smote this strain the young man's spirit,
> Sat he speechless, motionless, and shrinking;
> From his heart each word the blood had driven.
>
> (pp. x-xiii)

But what our Poet borrowed he made thoroughly his own. Not for a moment is his individuality lost in these Virgilian and Homeric moulds. When he employs them, it is because no others would be so appropriate.

Frequent touches of classicism and sublimity appear throughout the cycle. **"Sveaborg," "Döbeln at Juutas," "The Ensign's Greeting,"** and **"Adlercreutz,"** all move with lofty tone and majestic tread.

And where can purer lyricism, deeper sensibility, or more sincere emotion be found than in **"The Cottage Maiden," "The Dying Warrior," "The Soldier Boy," "The Stranger's Vision,"** or **"The Brothers"**? And what poet of any nation or time has portrayed martial characters and scenes more vividly than Runeberg in the songs not specifically mentioned? And where, in all literature, has a mightier love for native land been pictured than in **"Our Land"** and **"The Fifth of July"**? Or a more admirable tribute awarded to military prowess than in **"Kulneff," "Munter,"** or **"Wilhelm von Schwerin"**? (pp. xiv-xv)

> *Clement Burbank Shaw, in an introduction to* The Songs of Ensign Stål (Fänrik Ståls Sägner): National Military Song-Cycle of Finland *by Johan Ludvig Runeberg, translated by Clement Burbank Shaw, G. E. Stechert & Co., 1925, pp. vii-xvii.*

Yrjö Hirn   (essay date 1938)

[*Hirn was a Finnish scholar. In this excerpt from his introduction to* The Tales of Ensign Stål, *he discusses the biographical and historical elements presented in the work.*]

Runeberg has himself described for us in *Ensign Stål* the origin of the poetic cycle which came to bear the name of the old soldier. His account does not entirely square with the facts, but there are some features of it which correspond with the poet's own experiences. Like the speaker in the poem, Runeberg had in the years 1824-25 (that is, at the age of twenty to twenty-one) been installed as private tutor at certain manor houses in the interior of Finland; first in the wilderness parish of Saarijärvi, and later, from the summer to the end of 1825, in the more settled district of Ruovesi. It was here that he came to know "Näsijärvi's dusky lake," and here that he made acquaintance with two ex-soldiers who had held minor commissions in the Finnish army during the years 1808-09. According to all probability he heard these eyewitnesses recount their memories of the war, and it is possible that one or both of them may have furnished characteristics which were used by the poet in his representation of the Ensign. However, as he himself expressly declared, it would be incorrect to regard Stål as the portrait of any particular living model. And it would be still more incorrect to accept unreservedly the poet's declaration that the tales, as he set them to verse, were taken "from the old man's lips." We should rather consider the circumstances in this light: that the poet found it convenient to introduce a fictitious narrator for certain poems, the material of which he had collected from various sources. For the figure of such a narrator there was precedent from earlier Swedish literature in the poems of Tegnér and Franzén, and such examples, which were not unknown to Runeberg, may to a slight degree have reacted on his description of the Ensign.

In yet another respect one must beware of too literally interpreting the poem of *Ensign Stål.* When the poet tells how one day, tired of pranks and amusement—and contemporary accounts of Runeberg's student life entirely corroborate the picture he draws of himself—he picked up a book and thereupon, during the reading, was enthralled by the memories of "the last Finnish war," we imagine that the young tutor had got hold of some, however unpretentious, history of the war. It must therefore be stated that, at the time in question, any printed literature on the events of 1808-09 was practically non-existent. To judge by his own avowal on a later occasion, Runeberg was referring not to any book but to certain personal recollections of the war, which had been preserved in manuscript copies in manor house libraries. Several of these manuscript "recollections" have been printed much later. But it would be a thankless task to attempt to trace from which particular account Runeberg received the awakening which made him the poet of the war. According to the author's own statement, the unnamed work is to be thought of as a synthesis. And it is to be noted, further, that when he speaks of the sources of his information about the war, he makes no distinction between what he has read and what he has heard tell. One can, therefore, hardly conjecture otherwise than that it was with the written account as with the Ensign: i.e. that, for the sake of a vivid and dramatic effect, the poet gave it somewhat greater importance than it actually deserved. When Runeberg describes how, during his reading of the recollections by an unnamed author, he was inspired to dedicate himself to patriotic poetry, he has compressed an evolution whose successive stages belong to periods both before and after his experiences at Ruovesi. The history of how the author found his theme is far from being so short and simple as it purports to be in his own account. It is, on the contrary, so involved and needs to be examined from so many diverse angles, that it is only possible here to give a few brief indications of how it should be handled in a thorough investigation.

Our present knowledge would indicate that in his earliest boyhood Runeberg had been deeply impressed by the war, whose effects were more perceptible right in East Bothnia, his own native province, than in any other part of Finland. One of the most important battles, Döbeln's great victory, was fought at Jutas, which is only a few musket-shots' distance from Jacobstad, the poet's birthplace. And at Jacobstad he had, as a little boy, beheld his hero with his own eyes, as Döbeln sat on horseback in front of his troops just as they were about to march from the town. Runeberg described to his friend and biographer, Strömberg, how frightened he was when he heard the general cry out, with clenched fists lifted to heaven, "Hey! you thousand devils up there, can't you give us a drop of rain?" One is tempted to think of it as the idealization of that ineffaceable childish memory, when the poet in **"Döbeln at Jutas"** describes the warrior, who after the battle, "With fervent heart, but yielding no obeisance," expresses his gratitude to the giver of victories in the famous words, "How shall I speak to You, my God, my brother?" We may likewise venture to affirm that other childhood recollections are revived in the poem on Kulneff, the Russian general so popular even with his foes, whom the four-year-old boy must often have seen going from house to house in Jacobstad, and who, according to tradition, was a frequent guest at the home of Runeberg's family.

When, a student of nineteen at Åbo University, the poet received his appointment as private tutor in the interior of Finland, he was once more brought close to some of the old battlefields. We may be sure the people at Saarijärvi had not ceased to talk about the conflicts which had been fought fifteen years earlier in the neighboring parish of Karstula. And to the many anecdotes which were presumably handed down in peasant tradition Runeberg could add the firsthand narrative of the war which he listened to up at the manor house. For the head of the family in which he taught at Saarijärvi, and which he accompanied the following year to Ruovesi, was an old officer who had been in the campaigns both of 1788-90 and 1808-09. From the foregoing we may judge, therefore, that it was no unprepared listener who heard at Ruovesi from the Ensign's—or one should perhaps rather say from the two ensigns'—lips the tales which, according to his fiction, were the origin of his ballad cycle.

However much importance one may attribute to Runeberg's sojourn in the interior of Finland—and one can hardly overestimate the influence which his experiences at Saarijärvi and Ruovesi had on his poetic temperament as a whole—it seems that the stories of the war of 1808 could not have impregnated his imagination quite as directly as the introductory poem of his cycle would tempt us to believe. Four strophes of the poem, **"A Trip from Åbo"** (written in 1828) clearly indicate—with their allusion to the younger Ramsay, who "fell on Lemo's shore"—that, during his visit to the coast at Parga, the poet had been focusing his attention on the same local memories of the war as he was later to use in **"The Dying Soldier"** and **"The Stranger's Vision."** But the patriotic invocation of the young hero's spirit is here only an incidental motive in a descriptive travel poem. And it was no less than seven years after his stay in the interior that Runeberg first took an historic war story as the motive of a longer piece. Then, to be sure, in 1831, he chose the theme of **"The Grave at Perho"** from one of the parishes near Saarijärvi. But the combats he celebrated in this poem had been fought long before 1808, and the treatment suggested not so much the local traditions as the style of the old Serbian folk songs, of which in 1830 the poet had published several paraphrases, made through the medium of German translations. Again, in *The Elk Hunters,* the great folk epic published in the year 1832, there is a description of the peasant life at Ruovesi under peaceful conditions. The war memories of the district are only alluded to in the little episode about the gun (in Canto Second), which clearly refers to a campaign previous to the last war between Sweden and Russia. To combats even more distant—if we may judge by its archaic tone—should be referred the material of the earliest of the *Tales,* **"The Cloud's Brother,"** which was published, August 1835, in the *Helsingfors Morgonblad* (a newspaper edited by Runeberg) and in 1843 was reprinted in the author's third collection of *Poems.* **"The Cloud's Brother"** has rightly been considered one of the very finest of Runeberg's patriotic poems; on no condition would anyone have it separated from *The Tales of Ensign Stål;* yet there is no concealing the fact that, both in its theme and in the handling of the theme, it belongs outside the frame of the cycle.

The earliest of Runeberg's poems on a motive from the

War of 1808 is **"The Dying Soldier,"** which appeared in 1836 in the *Helsingfors Morgonblad* and in 1843 was included in the third collection of *Poems.* From the years 1836 and 1837 likewise date several fragments, published in Runeberg's newspaper, of an uncompleted *Novel of the War of 1808.* To judge from several disclosures at the time, the poet had been tempted by the idea of a humorous prose romance treating of curious local traits in the territorial army, where soldiers found themselves called upon to obey the orders of officers who in peace time had been their masters on the captains' and majors' farms. In one of the published chapters he actually described a Finnish officer, who commanded his soldiers under fire with the same familiar tone as when he directed their work in the fields. This Major A***sköld is a sort of prototype of the "real Finnish soldier" who was to be celebrated in no less than four of the *Tales:* **"Von Essen," "Otto Von Fieandt," "Von Törne,"** and in the account of **"Von Konow,"** whose friendly altercation with his corporal is described in the already cited collection of poems in translation. It seems as though the impressions from Ruovesi had, after more than a decade's incubation, begun to emerge again in Runeberg's mind toward the end of the 1830s. But the projected novel was never finished, and nearly a decade was to elapse before Runeberg undertook to incorporate in poetry the figures of all these officers and men whose exploits and eccentricities were immortalized in *The Tales of Ensign Stål.* One has the feeling, however, that during this interval he was gradually being drawn nearer and nearer to the magic circle of war memories, and there are certain isolated poems from this period which are, in a sense, precursors to the great epic cycle.

After his change of residence to Borgå in 1837, Runeberg came into personal contact with certain veterans living in that town and in the old Nyland manor houses in the vicinity, and this was probably not without its effect on the poet's consciousness. The people of this community had lived so long in unbroken peace that the events of the past wars had begun to take on the glamour of remote perspective, and those who had been in the battles had become objects of admiring reverence. This cult of veteran worship affected Runeberg in various ways. Among others it impelled him to write in 1840 a poem on an old soldier of the campaign of 1788-90, a eulogy which anticipates the **"Ensign's Greeting"** of the *Tales,* first published in the collection of translations. But the poem of 1840 is too short, and as poetry too insignificant, to be regarded as a "tale before the Tales." Such a designation may, however, be accorded with full justice to the splendid closing scene of the third and final canto of Runeberg's epic poem, *Christmas Eve.* As in the tales already cited, the poet here treats of the relations between commander and private, the brotherhood in arms which long after the war still united officers and soldiers. But in its poetic style the *Christmas Eve* story of the major and the old soldier Pistol differs from all the narratives of von Konow, von Törne, and von Essen. And it differs no less from **"The Ensign at the Fair,"** to which tale it may otherwise (i.e. in its theme) be naturally compared. For when the soldier has proudly refused the offer of food and lodging which the major, like the general in the carriage at the fair, has offered his old comrade in arms, the casual style of the Christmas narrative suddenly shifts into

the key of an exalted patriotic hymn. The verse rises from its previous idyllic level to describe how the old warrior feels his heart swell at the sight of his comrade's brusque and resolute bearing. Thereupon follow the noble strophes which, in their compressed fulness, hold all the finest that has been said or that can be said of Finland and her people; the strophes in which the figures of the *Tales* are foreshadowed, and in which sound the first chords of what is to become a national song; the slow-sweeping cadences that conjure up visions, the lines in which every syllable touches the heart:

> Finland stood there before him, the bleak, lone, poverty-smitten, Idolized land of his birth; and the gray clad ranks from Lake Saima's Shore, the delight of his life, the men he had once been so proud of, Marched in review before him, with his brothers-in-arms, as aforetime, Surly, calm, unpretentious, with iron-firm faith in their bosoms.

It is worth noting that *Christmas Eve,* in which the soul of *Ensign Stål* is contained as an oak in its acorn, was published as early as 1841. By this time, one ventures to think, the preparation for the great work was largely completed. The man who had written the lines just quoted had surely little to learn in order to compose ballads such as **"The Two Dragoons," "Munter"** and **"The Commissary Driver."** These needed but a few external impulses for the idea of a group of poems to spring up and ripen in his mind. Such impulses came in fact from various directions during the years immediately succeeding. Through them his plan developed, and new phases of his subject came to the poet's attention, demanding their place as subjects for treatment.

In this connection it must have been of prime importance that Runeberg encountered in Gustaf Adolf Montgomery's great work, *History of the War between Sweden and Russia, 1808-09* (published 1842), a treatment of the conflict which was complete, graphic, and vivid in quite a different way from the terse reminiscences, published or in manuscript, which had previously been at his disposal. He himself acknowledged on many occasions his indebtedness to Montgomery, and we may well conclude that he would not have been able to write the splendid battle description in **"Sandels," "Döbeln at Jutas,"** and **"Adlercreutz,"** had he not had these thorough and accurate accounts of the strategic details to rely on. It is no derogation from his glory as a poet to assert that the factual contents of these *Tales* were based on solid historic foundations. Nor does it impugn his reputation even if one suggests the thought—which seems quite probable—that the reading of Montgomery's descriptions imparted to him some of the rhetorical feeling and of the powder smoke, so to say, which lends pungence to the lines on Virta, Jutas, and Siikajoki.

Runeberg, like all poets, was receptive to impressions from other authors. But in his maturity, the period of *Ensign Stål,* he made use of only what accorded with his own temper. And in his very adaptation he was so spontaneous that it is doubtful whether he really borrowed from other originals. In most cases it might be safest to say that certain external influences released what was latent within him.

If it is hard to describe the origin of the *Tales,* because one must be cautious at every step to differentiate between hypothesis and certain knowledge, one encounters no problems in treating of the reception they met with when they finally appeared and became known to the public. Here there is nothing to record but unreserved admiration and gratitude: a simple story, in other words, of a poetic work, which has become so fully incorporated into the nation's imaginative and political being that Finland can simply not be thought of without *The Tales of Ensign Stål.* In this connection we need but present a few typical examples to show that the two poetic cycles (published in the years 1848 and 1860) have exercised an influence to which no other literature can offer a parallel.

The earliest evidences of the appreciation which the poetry of the *Tales* was to arouse dates from the year 1838. A correspondent of the *Helsingfors Morgonblad,* in submitting a poem entitled *Thoughts on Reading "The Cloud's Brother"* acclaimed the skald as follows: "By the magic of his verse he has evoked the figure of a patriot hero, which in his song will live unforgotten to future generations." We have no information as to whether anyone praised similarly the tales, **"The Dying Soldier"** and **"Sven Duva,"** which, like **"The Cloud's Brother,"** were published before 1848. But as to **"Döbeln at Jutas,"** which the poet read to his friends from manuscript even before it was finished, we know that it quickly won admirers. It is interesting to note that the students at Borgå had heard one of their members read at the convocation May 13, 1848, "this glorious, as yet unpublished poem." One may be sure that this, like all the *Tales* which appeared later, was enthusiastically received by a group of young men who were proud of having Runeberg as their teacher, and who in all the years that followed were wont to cite the *Tales* at so many youthful patriotic demonstrations.

Above all the other poems, however, the opening song (which is not, of course, in the form of a *Tale*) was known and admired before *Ensign Stål* had appeared in the bookshops. **"Our Land"** won its first adherents, one might almost say its first devotees, among the students; and this was significant, because at the middle of the last century the students were in the forefront of all great progressive movements. To get an idea of how Runeberg's poetry affected the leaders of his youthful academic audience, one has but to read a letter which the twenty-three-year-old Robert Tengström wrote September 18, 1846, to his twenty-four-year-old friend Herman Kellgren, in which he describes how late one night on a visit to Borgå he heard the poet recite "in a trembling, often broken voice," the hymn, no doubt recently written, to his native land. "Had I," the narrator continues, "not felt myself overpowered at that moment as much by veneration as by love, I should have fallen on his neck and invoked the blessing of heaven on his head." Tengström was overjoyed that Runeberg had given him permission to publish the new song in an anthology, *The Patriotic Album,* which he, Kellgren, and another comrade were editing. He was thus enabled to enclose in his letter a copy of the poem and could add in reference to it, "Have you ever heard patriotism expressed more gloriously? Read it aloud, brother, listen to its ring and rhythm, and you will enjoy it twice as much! If there is a heart among our people with a grain of feeling for our native land, it must melt in the glow of this flame of beauty. It must pierce our souls like a two-edged sword and in time of peril be our Marseillaise. So at least it seems to me, and I rejoice in anticipation over the delight I have imparted to you in sending it. Let us love our native land, brother, above everything, but let us honor and revere her greatest singer beyond all others! In him the heart of the nation beats most purely, in him our country is mirrored most fervently. Happy Finland, to have such a singer!"

The predictions uttered by the young enthusiast in his letter to his friend have been realized in fuller measure than he could have divined. **"Our Land"** has veritably gone like a two-edged sword through the soul of the people. And if it has not become our Marseillaise, the reason has been only that in the second part of the *Tales of Ensign Stål,* published in 1860, Runeberg has given us a lyric to the old March of the Björneborg Regiment, which with its popular melody has come to be used as the rousing battle-song of patriotic enthusiasm. On the other hand, as the national hymn, the united expression of feelings in which all groups and parties combine, *Our Land* has ever since been acknowledged without a rival. It was first sung to a melody by F. A. Ehrström at a student festival on November 9, 1846. (In the letter above quoted, Robert Tengström relates that Runeberg commissioned him to get a musical setting from Ehrström.) It was performed again at a festival to commemorate the fifth centenary of the founding of Borgå, December 3, 1846; and for that occasion the poet had himself composed a melody to his text. It was published in full the first time in the *Patriotic Album* already referred to, Volume III, which appeared April 1847, and received its dedication as Finland's national hymn at a great students' festival on Gumtäckt's Meadow outside of Helsingfors the 13th of May, 1848. At this festival **"Our Land"** was for the first time sung to the music of Fredrik Pacius, which ever since through all generations in Finland has been inseparably connected with Runeberg's words. The eminent orator of the day, Fredrik Cygnaeus, gave a speech on the beauty, the past and the hopes of Finland, which became the most celebrated of all his improvisations, although not a line of it has been preserved. At the moment he ceased, the chorus of students burst into **"Our Land,"** which was sung amid vigorous applause again and yet again.

A poem by Zachris Topelius entitled *Finland's Name,* which was published a week later in the *Helsingfors Tidningar,* declares that on this springtime evening the youthful throng took an oath of loyalty to their country, and in a certain sense this statement seems to be justified. No less justified is the assertion which was often made by orators as well as poets: that all the sentiments of devotion to home and land that have existed in Finland from of old came first to full consciousness through the hymn of Runeberg. The first strophes, like the prelude of a national dedication, reveal our love for the summer glory, the starry nights and the somber woods of the north. And as these lines conjure up the features of our country, so appear before us, in **"Our Land"** as in the *Tales,* the men whose deeds are sung—in descriptions which are to some extent idealized, perhaps, but which none the less have been of incalculable significance in the history of Finland as examples of unselfish and devoted striving. It is therefore only superficially a paradox to declare that for Runeberg's contemporaries the conception of Finland as a living entity was born simultaneously with **"Our Land."**

As so many of the poems were already known and admired, the first collection of *The Tales of Ensign Stål* was awaited with keen expectation by all classes of readers. The day (December 14, 1848) when the thin volume appeared on the market was a great day not only for Finnish history but also for the native bookstores. The popular eagerness for acquiring the *Tales* is evidenced by the fact, to take a single instance, that off in little Borgå two hundred copies were sold in the first month. The poems were read, recited, and discussed; after which they were carried home by the students and schoolboys in the city as Christmas presents to homes all over the country. Everywhere they were received with gratitude, but the appreciation was nowhere so deep and warm as among the veterans of 1808. It is satisfying to record that the old soldiers found a beautiful way of showing their appreciation of the *Tales.* They started among themselves a collection toward a gift for the poet, and in 1854 sent him by a deputation a mighty silver tankard and a silver snuff-box. The history of the Runeberg cult has hardly a more gripping scene to chronicle than when the spokesman of this deputation, in a sparkling soldierly address, rendered thanks on behalf of his departed and surviving brothers-in-arms to him "who had so nobly sung their deeds."

When it became known that Runeberg was continuing with the *Ensign,* people from all over the country sent him anecdotes about the war, and he soon had received far more material than he could use. His friends had the good fortune to hear him when, often deeply affected by the beautiful themes "which God was playing on his instrument," he recited new and unpublished *Tales.* And the most favored of his circle received precious manuscripts, which were copied and circulated throughout the country. It sometimes chanced that one or another of his hearers described what he had listened to at Runeberg's home. Such circumstances kept up the intense, almost unbearable eagerness with which the public awaited the new collection. And when this finally appeared, twelve years to the day after the first, the enthusiasm was as great as in 1848.

The old journalist August Schauman has related in his memoirs how he and another newspaper man had, through the favor of the publisher, succeeded in obtaining a copy of the new book previous to December 14. "When we had got it in our hands," he says, "we rushed to the nearest place where we could find a private room, so as to read in peace and enjoy it together. Two friends, whom we happened on, came with us. And there we sat reading or declaiming in turn one poem after another till the book was finished. Our hearts throbbed, our eyes were filled with tears, our souls were uplifted, we pressed one anoth-

er's hands, we laughed, we exulted—and we knew that such an hour would never come to us again."

We need not strain our historical imagination to realize the joy with which the second collection of *Tales* was read. By 1860 the political future of Finland was looking brighter than in the preceding decades. Everything in the new poems about freedom, victory, and honor found a willing response in the generation which, after the revival of the national assembly, laid the foundations of our parliamentary life. Later, when Finland's existence as a state was threatened, the defenders of the constitutional order found in the same poems examples for their tenacious struggle in behalf of our rights. At this critical moment in our history, the exhortation of **"The Soldier Boy"** was decisive for the young men who staked their lives on the issue of their country's independence. Indeed we may go still further and say that it was from the ethics of *Ensign Stål* that Finnish judges took courage to choose imprisonment rather than submit to setting aside the law; and the longing and promise of the *Tales* found their fulfilment when in 1918 the dream became reality in the deeds of the peasant army and the youthful volunteers.

A poetry which has taken such a hold on the life of its people can never be appraised with objective criticism by a fellow-countryman of the author. Foreign observers, who are able to assume a "disinterested" point of view, may decide as to the artistic value of the *Tales;* we can only testify what they have meant spiritually for the development of a nation's life and ideals. (pp. 1-16)

Yrjö Hirn, in an introduction to The Tales of Ensign Stål *by Johan Ludvig Runeberg, edited and translated by Charles Wharton Stork, Princeton University Press, 1938, pp. 1-16.*

Alrik Gustafson   (essay date 1961)

[*Gustafson was an American critic who wrote extensively on Scandinavian literature. In the following excerpt, he provides an overview of Runeberg's accomplishments.*]

Runeberg's birthplace was Jakobstad, halfway up the west coast of Finland on the Gulf of Bothnia. He was of Swedish extraction, both on his father's and mother's sides. His father was a sea captain of some intellectual interests, his mother the daughter in a shipowning family of considerable means. But because of financial reverses and a stroke which incapacitated the father in 1821 at the age of forty-nine, Runeberg had to periodically interrupt his university education in order to earn sufficient funds to continue his work toward a degree. The lengthiest of these interruptions—spent as a private tutor on estates in Finland from late in 1823 to January of 1825—was of the utmost importance to the future poet. Here for the first time he came in intimate contact with the vast wilderness stretches of inland Finland and the primitive folk life of these regions. How deeply moved he was by the experience is apparent in every line of the magnificent ethnographical essay from 1832, *Några ord om nejderna, folklynnet och levnadssättet i Saarijärvi socken (Some Words on the Countryside, Folk Character, and Way of Life in the Saarijärvi Parish).* He was impressed equally by land and folk, a land which in its quiet, lonely majesty had placed its worthy stamp upon a simple, hard-working, patiently heroic people. In the Saarijärvi years the Finnish national poet was born, though some time was to elapse before the young Runeberg shook off some of his private woes as well as certain extraneous literary modes and definitively found his way back to the Finnish folk.

Outwardly the years following the Saarijärvi sojourn were marked by the completion of work toward a degree, the beginnings of a pedagogical career, a happy marriage, and the publication, in 1830, of Runeberg's first volume of verse, **Dikter** (**Poems**). Inwardly these were years of considerable soul searching and an uncertain groping toward a poetic form best suited to Runeberg's poetic temperament. The disparate character of the pieces included in **Poems** reflects very clearly the uncertainty with which the poet was feeling his way toward a poetic program, and only in the section entitled **"Idyll och epigram"** (**"Idyls and Epigrams"**), in Runeberg's debut volume, can one discern the direction his poetry is to take in the future. Otherwise the volume is of some biographical interest, especially in the rather hectic poem **"Svartsjukans nätter"** (**"Nights of Jealousy"**), in which an erotic crisis is clad in some rather heavy poetic finery alternately reminiscent of Stagnelius and Edward Young. In **"Idyls and Epigrams,"** however, Runeberg turns quite deliberately away from the luxuriant patterns and melancholy posing of Romantic verse toward a simpler, more spare and realistic poetic medium, largely under the spell of a group of Serbian folk songs which he had taken upon himself to turn into Swedish from the German version in which he had discovered them. Most of the **"Idyls and Epigrams"** are highly concentrated episodic pieces the locale of whose action is quite indeterminate, but in a few of them, most notably in **"Bonden Pavo"** (**"The Peasant Pavo"**), the characters and scene of action are definitely Finnish. Pavo, sorely tried by a series of catastrophic crop failures, is Runeberg's first inspired portrait of the quiet heroism and natural piety of the Finns.

In various ways Runeberg pursued this Finnish thematic material during the bit more than a decade following upon the publication of his first volume of poetry—in the simple monumental manner of **"The Peasant Pavo"** in **"Grafven i Perrho"** (**"The Grave at Perrho"**) from 1831, and in larger contexts and with greater attention paid to backgrounds and ethnographical detail in the three extended narrative sequences **Elgskyttarne** (**The Elk Hunters,** 1832), **Hanna** (1836), and **Julkvällen** (**Christmas Eve,** 1841). Of the longer poems **The Elk Hunters** and parts of **Christmas Eve** are the most impressive, the former for its lively, at times primitive poetic realism and for its sly undertow of humor, the latter especially for its stirring final tribute to Old Pistol, pensioned veteran of many campaigns, who faces his last years erect and unshaken in spirit despite the news of the death of his only son on a distant battlefield. Offered at the last a comfortable refuge on the estate of the Major under whom he had served in battle, Old Pistol refuses, humble yet proud, prepared to return to his wilderness hut and there face alone the last joust with death in the same spirit as he had served his nation in the years of his manhood's strength. The Major is moved, deeply moved, proud of his old comrade in arms whose will is in no way bent by sorrow and the heavy accumulation of years:

> Finland stood there before him, the bleak, lone, poverty-smitten, idolized land of his birth; and the gray-clad ranks from Lake Saima's shore, the delight of his life, the men he had once been so proud of, marched in review before him, with brothers-in-arms as aforetime—surely, calm, unpretentious, with iron-firm faith in their bosoms.

In these lines the unhurried, earth-bound movement of Runeberg's hexameters (the metrical pattern used in all of his early narrative poems) quickens its pace, lifts itself to an exalted, visionary, hymn-like level, the level of the patriotic anthem. These lines—and for that matter the whole Pistol world in **Christmas Eve**—are a kind of preliminary sketch for the broad, heroic narrative patterns of **Fänrik Ståls sägner** (tr. **The Tales of Ensign Stål**), the incomparable poetic gift to the fatherland which Runeberg was later to pen.

But before he turned to the world of Fänrik Stål he occupied himself with other matters, incidentally with religious controversy, more importantly with literary composition which tended to depart for the time being from his concern with the Finnish folk.

In 1837 Runeberg had settled down not far to the east of Helsingfors in the small city of Borgå, where he taught first Latin and later Greek for twenty years before his retirement in 1857. In December 1863, he had a stroke which kept him bedridden until his death more than thirteen years later. He came with the years to be quite happy in Borgå despite the fact that he had originally moved there because of disappointment in seeking a university post in Helsingfors. His teaching duties were relatively light, allowing him to devote much time to his poetry. Opportunities for social intercourse were sufficient, and he could indulge as he pleased in his favorite sports, hunting and fishing in the areas adjacent to Borgå. So satisfactory, indeed, were the conditions of his life at Borgå that Runeberg never left the town and its environs except for occasional visits to Helsingfors and one or two other Finnish towns and a trip to Sweden, the summer of 1851, where he was so overwhelmingly feted that on his roundabout return journey to Borgå he wrote to a friend: "I am utterly tired of all this world's splendors and yearn for porridge, fish, and quiet at Kroksnäs [his summer place near Borgå]." Pleasant as Runeberg usually found social intercourse, Stockholm hospitality was too much for him. Though the Borgå years were in the main outwardly uneventful, they were not without some inner conflicts, especially of an erotic kind, and they were the years when in such works as **Kung Fjalar** (tr. **King Fjalar**) and **The Tales of Ensign Stål** Runeberg's creative flame burned with its most sustained and brilliant glow.

The first years in Borgå, however, were years which from a literary point of view were relatively fallow, yielding aside from some short pieces only **Christmas Eve,** which is the last of the idyls in hexameters, and **Nadeschda,** a rather slight poetic narrative on a Russian theme. In some ways the most interesting piece from the early Borgå years is the prose piece *Den gamle trädgårdsmästarens brev* (*The Old Gardener's Letters*), in which Runeberg attacks the pietistic asceticism which at the time was fastening its dark tentacles on Finland, finding converts even among the educated classes. The issues involved were of the utmost importance to the deeply religious Runeberg, who reacted with all the healthy intensity of his being against the pietistic insistence that the flesh and all the things of this world were evil. To Runeberg the flesh was good, our natural instincts the voice of God within us, the whole world of nature a part of God's ultimate revelation. To Runeberg evil existed, but not, as the pietists insisted, as the very condition of existence. The good life to Runeberg was to live in harmony with the world rather than to deny it by flaying the flesh while indulging in dark, fanatical, essentially inhuman incantations. Such are the ideas contained in *The Old Gardener's Letters*. Though it had not been Runeberg's custom to give pointed expression to religious ideas in his poetry, the controversy with the pietists resulted in two poems, "Kyrkan" ("The Church") and "Chrysanthos," in which his idealistic religious humanitarianism was given clear expression. And in a broader sense the religious and ethical considerations central in two of Runeberg's major works *King Fjalar* and *Kungarne på Salamis* (*The Kings on Salamis*) derive more or less directly from the poet's concern with religious problems which first had taken on the controversial prose form of *The Old Gardener's Letters*. *King Fjalar* appeared in 1844, *The Kings on Salamis* not in complete form until 1863 though three acts were written immediately after the completion of *King Fjalar.*

Of these two works *The Kings on Salamis* is a reasonably successful modern attempt to write a Classical tragedy, while *King Fjalar,* a more important work, approximates Classical tragedy in certain ways without slavishly imitating the older dramatic form. In fact, *King Fjalar* is a remarkably impressive experiment in the blending of narrative and dramatic elements. Outwardly the work consists of a series of five narrative episodes which Runeberg calls "Songs," but these episodes are so charged with dramatic life and move so inexorably toward a terrifying tragic denouement that they reflect the spirit of Greek tragedy much more adequately than most modern imitations of Classical drama. Of the Greek tragedies *King Fjalar* resembles most Sophocles' *Oedipus the King,* from which it borrows with some variations such matters as the incest motif and the conception of man's fate as being ultimately determined not by his own will but by decisions of the Gods. A Romantic richness of texture has been added to Runeberg's tragedy of the ancient Nordic King of Gauthiod by introducing the fateful struggle of the King's son Hjalmar with King Morannal's sons on Morven soil of Ossianic fame. Though critics for more than a hundred years have expressed reservations about Runeberg's handling of the Oedipean and Ossianic materials, these reservations are admittedly of secondary importance beside the overall impression of monumental tragic greatness which *King Fjalar* leaves with even the most discriminating reader. Critics with hardly an exception have adjudged *King Fjalar* as the incomparably most impressive tragic work in the Classical spirit which has come from a Scandinavian pen. Almost equally agreed are the critics in the opinion that

King Fjalar is Runeberg's greatest work, though some would place *The Tales of Ensign Stål*—a quite different kind of work—on the same general level of poetic attainment as *King Fjalar.* In the light of the differing intentions of the two works it would seem fatuous to choose between the two, except on a purely personal basis. Each is in its way as close to perfection as one has the right to expect.

The incubation period of *The Tales of Ensign Stål* was unusually long. Many years elapsed before Runeberg settled down to the task of bringing to life the hapless but heroic story of his nation's tragic struggle against superior forces in the War of 1808-9. Not until 1848 could his public read in book form the first group of these tales, eighteen in all, and twelve more years were to pass before the seventeen additional pieces were completed and the definitive edition of the work appeared. But Runeberg's interest in the material of his *Tales* went far back in time. As a small boy he had seen on the streets of Jakobstad two of the most colorful figures of the Finno-Russian campaigns, von Döbeln and the jovial Russian Kulneff, and during Runeberg's early manhood at Saarijärvi and Ruovesi he heard tales of the War from Finns who had taken part in it. And in the years which followed he had countless occasions to add to his store of material, for everywhere in Finland tales of military heroism from the closing years of the first decade of the century were treasured by high and low alike among the people of the land. In 1836 and 1837 Runeberg attempted a novel about the War, but the attempt was abortive and the work remained a fragment. Here and there also in Runeberg's poetry from these years we catch passing glimpses of the poet's concern with the memories from 1808-9, most significantly, as we have seen, in the figure of Old Pistol in *Christmas Eve,* but also in scattered shorter poems such as "Molnets broder" ("The Cloud's Brother") which are to become included in *The Tales of Ensign Stål* even though in their original conception they were presumably not written for inclusion in the *Tales.* The catalytic agent which finally plunged the poet shortly after the completion of *King Fjalar* into writing the *Tales* seems to have been a Borgå bookseller's suggestion that Runeberg prepare the text for an illustrated work on the heroes of the war of a generation before. Such a work seemed at the time especially desirable because of the general interest in the subject aroused by the appearance in 1842 of G. A. Montgomery's *Historia öfver kriget emellan Sverige och Ryssland åren 1808 och 1809* (History of the War between Sweden and Russia, 1808-9). Though the proposed illustrated work did not materialize, Runeberg was ripe for the task of putting into worthy verse form the most representative tales from the war years, and he began turning out in rapid succession a series of poems which by 1848 numbered eighteen, the series included in the narrative poetic cycle of the first edition of *The Tales of Ensign Stål.* The remaining seventeen were produced more slowly, not being finished until more than a decade later.

Popular as Runeberg's narrative poetic idyls from the 1830's had been, they were completely overshadowed by the acclaim with which *The Tales of Ensign Stål* was received—and not only because of the patriotic theme of the *Tales.* The new work was in every way a superior product. The leisurely, at times monotonous hexameters of the idyls were replaced in the *Tales* by a fascinating variety of metrical and stanzaic forms. The relatively static descriptive quality of the earlier narrative poems gave way to variety and depth in character portrayal and to the rapid dramatic drive and movement of the *Tales.* The somewhat oversweet "realism" of the idyls was abandoned for a bracing world of sweat and blood, of hapless struggle and wild despair, lighted up by moments of supreme valor and heroism. And many of the *Tales* are invested with a warm, engaging humor—broad or sly or elegant or gently ironic by turn, seldom satiric, negative, or critical.

Whether the Ensign Stål who is represented as the teller of the tales has any equivalent in reality we do not know. In all probability he is a fictive figure some of whose characteristics have been taken from certain veterans of the War whom Runeberg had met in his youth. The other characters included in the tales are in part historical personages and in part types representing those qualities of valor and warm humanity which the poet assumed were characteristic of the army and the folk. A constantly recurring theme in the *Tales* is the democratic relation between the common soldier and the officer, a kind of patriarchal relationship which under wartime conditions had been carried over from civilian to military matters. Though the *Tales* deal predominantly with the heroism of both officers and men in the ranks, they reflect at times also a bitter awareness of the weakness of the highest echelon of command, and one of the poems is a furious castigation of treachery in high places—on the surrender of Sveaborg, the proud "Gibraltar of the North."

Modern investigations have demonstrated that Runeberg's depiction of the War was not a little idealized, that the poet's rather exclusive preoccupation with the heroic exploits of the Finnish forces tends to make of the War of 1808-9 something prettier than it actually was—a badly organized and weakly led campaign in which the Swedo-Finnish forces were almost constantly retreating and in which the outcome was nearly from the outset a foregone humiliating defeat. But to Runeberg such realistic concerns were relatively unimportant, or, rather, they served merely to draw into sharper relief a central doctrine of the poet's thinking—that men in certain crucial moments of their experience have the capacity to rise above their normal limitations, become one with the ideal forces of existence. In a citizenry's readiness to sacrifice all for the fatherland Runeberg saw men in active communion with God. Because such a doctrine has been viciously exploited in larger than Finnish contexts by bloody supernationalists of a later day should not blind us to the fact that in the case of little Finland, a century ago, the doctrine served to add strength and dignity to its valiant struggle for national survival. Patriotism need not be a crudely egotistical destructive agent in man's search for the better life.

The popularity which Runeberg had gained among his people long before the appearance of *The Tales of Ensign Stål* became transformed into veneration after the publication of the *Tales,* and this veneration has continued down to our day. Borgå, where the *Tales* were composed, became a place of pilgrimage, the poet a legendary figure

around whom a "Runeberg cult" has for generations worshiped—often to the discouragement of those who wish to discover the man behind the national saint, of those who are concerned with disentangling the poet's literary and intellectual orientation from his relations to the congeries of emotional associations typical of the Finnish national temper in Runeberg's time. Modern scholarship has confirmed our suspicions that the poet was more dependent on contemporary philosophical speculation and literary trends of foreign origin than had formerly been assumed and that in his personal relations Runeberg was not quite the serene and harmonious character conjured up by some devotees of the "Runeberg cult." One should add, however, that such scholarly demonstrations do not radically change our picture either of the man or the poet. They serve merely to remove from the Runeberg portrait its purely cultish lines and restore to view the man and poet as he actually was, deeply human in both his eruptive and serene moments, a worthy national poet of a noble and courageous people. (pp. 222-29)

Alrik Gustafson, "Mid-Century Ferment," in his A History of Swedish Literature, *University of Minnesota Press, 1961, pp. 198-242.*

Tore Wretö (essay date 1980)

[*Wretö is a Swedish critic and the editor of a scholarly edition of Runeberg's collected works. In the following excerpt, he discusses the poems that comprise* The Tales of Ensign Stål.]

In 1846, Runeberg . . . wrote **"Our Land."** This was done while he stayed at his beloved summer cottage Kroksnäs. The reader literally experiences the poetic moment of creation in the stanza in which Runeberg interprets the emotion of being physically near his native country:

> And here before us lies that land,
> Our eyes behold it here;
> And we can raise our outstretched hand,
> And gladly point to sea and strand
> And say: "Behold it, far and near,
> Our native land so dear!"

It appears historically self-evident that the beautiful tribute to his land of a great poet should occur at this juncture and in this form. Nevertheless, there exist, as in Runeberg's earlier lyric poems, literary reminiscences in the background. About one year prior to **"Our Land,"** his young fellow countryman Emil von Quanten wrote a poem having the style of a national anthem. Runeberg read this poem ("Suomis sång" ["The Song of Finland"]) in manuscript form and was prompted to propose a modification, which von Quanten accepted. On two different occasions in 1845, Runeberg had also read a Swedish translation of a Hungarian national anthem by Vörösmarty. This encounter with a lyric poem that adhered to his own idealistic aspirations and artistic development seems to have again released Runeberg's creative forces.

When **"Our Land"** was written, Runeberg apparently had not yet thought of employing it as the powerful prelude to *The Tales of Ensign Stål.* Only later did he add three stanzas that pertain to the theme of an earlier generation's combat and sacrifice for the sake of the nation and that thereby indicate the poem's association with the tales. In this definitive form, **"Our Land"** was printed in the beginning of 1847. The poem was sung to different melodies before the public on several occasions, but its breakthrough did not occur until May 13, 1848, when it was performed to the melody of Fredrik Pacius. This was a moving performance during a period that was full of tension and in a land that was ruled over by an autocratic regime suspicious of every tendency toward defiance and self-determination. On this occasion, the song "rang clear," according to the wording in the solemn invocation: "Our land, our land, our native land! / Oh, let her name ring clear!" In this poem, Runeberg appears in a role that is new for him—that of speaker and interpreter for his nation and her feelings, during the most solemn and the most rhetorical moment in his poetic career. As the voice of his nation, Runeberg pays tribute to his land; expresses his compatriots' love for this land; embraces past, present, and future generations; renders into words the gratitude of his fellow countrymen toward those who have lived and fought; and declares his people's faith in the future. In this role, he employs a style that of necessity is rhetorical and solemn.

It must be stressed that the programmatic simplicity of diction that marks so much of Runeberg's poetry and that has been most significantly expressed in the ***Idylls and Epigrams*** is not representative of **"Our Land."** Not only does **"Our Land"** begin with an invocation in the style of the solemn Classical poem. It also contains a repetition ("Our land, our land, our native land"), which, moreover, comprises a climax (land—native land), both of these stylistic elements, of which the poem offers several examples, and of a rhetorical question and, on another structural plane, an antithesis ("Our land is poor . . . / Yet land of gold it is" vv. 7-12) which, at the same time, is a paradox. In his new role as poet and mouthpiece of the nation, Runeberg consciously exploits, most often with successful effect, the resources and millennia-old experiences of rhetoric. Yet he does not stop here. As will be pointed out later, he also places the effect elements of Classical rhetoric in the mouth of the simple ensign.

In its original Swedish text, the poem never mentions Finland explicitly; she is only referred to by such expressions as "our land" and "you land of a thousand lakes." In one instance, the geographical location is fixed, namely, in the phrase "the Finnish people's heart." Indeed, there is a purely practical reason for Runeberg having not mentioned Finland by name. In bilingual Finland, two names existed for the country, and had Runeberg chosen the Finnish name *Suomi,* as von Quanten did, then the poem would only have been accepted at this time by the Fennomans, with whom Runeberg did not sympathize. By only referring to the country's name in an implicit way, Runeberg removed his poem from the group of national anthems that stress the country's name. It is characteristic that Björnson similarly refers to Norway only implicitly in his Norwegian national anthem "Ja, vi elsker dette landet" ("Yes, we love this land"), which is considered to have been written under the influence of Runeberg's **"Our Land."**

What specifically Finnish features are to be found in **"Our Land"**? The Nordic nature that is praised is nonspecific, and as a consequence, a selection of stanzas from the poem could have been employed as an alternative national anthem elsewhere in Scandinavia. The "moors, hills, and skerries" in the second stanza were certainly perceived by Runeberg as a characteristic group of Finnish landscape types. Furthermore, he begins this stanza with the words, "Our land is poor"; this is an expression that he often utilized to describe his land, and even if this description could have been understood as generally applicable to Finland in the 1840s, it nevertheless receives special emphasis against the background of his own experiences as a youth and during the time he spent in the interior of Finland, where he discovered another type of poverty, namely, that of the famine years and of the beggars. After Runeberg speaks warmly of the barren though inspiring landscape in his native land and its glorious past, he points his attention in the last stanza toward the future:

> The flowers in their buds that grope
>   Shall burst their sheathes with spring;
> So from our love to bloom shall ope,
> Thy gleam, thy glow, thy joy, thy hope,
>   And higher yet some day shall ring
>   The patriot-song we sing!
>
> (vv. 61-66.)

In a review from the year 1847, Snellman described this poem as "consummately beautiful" but without the "higher national life" he found in "Rule Britannia." On the contrary, he considered the beginning of the final stanza a pronouncement of resignation. In his picture of the flowers in their buds, Runeberg expressed, however, a thought that was apt, historically correct, and simultaneously daring considering the background of the political situation and the future prospects for the Finnish nation at the time **"Our Land"** was written. Inasmuch as we are aware of the intense conviction in the conformity to the law of organic development that Runeberg inserted into the picture of the bud's development into a flower, we can certify the strength in trusting in the future expressed by the final stanza. In his portrayal of the flowers in their buds, Runeberg undoubtedly came very near the boundary that a touchy censor could tolerate.

When **"Our Land"** was written, Runeberg had already completed a few of the poems that would constitute ***The Tales of Ensign Stål*** in 1848. He had also found the idea for a narrative situation. However, **"Ensign Stål,"** the poem in which he presents the narrator and his young listener, was one of the last poems in the collection to be written.

In this poem, Runeberg describes in a strikingly personal and self-ironic tone how he, as a young student and tutor at the shores of Lake Näsijärvi, met the ensign, a poor and forgotten veteran, and how he, with youthful recklessness, derided this old man. Nevertheless, he came across a book about the war of 1808-1809, read it, and was seized by a burning desire to learn more about this war. He therefore approached the old soldier, who enthusiastically describes his recollections of the war. From this point, the roles were exchanged—"But student I, he more than king!"

The poem is written with careful consideration paid to stylistic effects, and an antithetical pattern of excitement and alternation stipulates its rhythm and raises it far above the reality that is nonetheless reflected in it. "Ensign Stål is to a certain extent a historical person, but he has related much to me even through the mouths of others," explained the poet. One fundamental pattern in **"Ensign Stål"** has previously appeared in Runeberg's poetry: the young—sometimes roguish—man who comes to good terms with an older man. In the beginning of **"Ensign Stål,"** the student perceives the old soldier as being only eccentric and ridiculous. He then learns to comprehend the greatness in the ensign. As is the case with many other characters in the tales, this transformation is pronounced: "So bright his glance, so clear his brow, / His beauty I remember now" (vv. 137-38).

The catalyst for the young student's new and revolutionary contact with the ensign was a book: "Unbound it lay, as though by grace, / But mid bound volumes held its place" (vv. 83-84). Runeberg has, as we have seen, related that he read "short accounts" dealing with the war while he was still a tutor in the Finnish interior. A book, even a little and unpretentious book, had not come into the picture at this stage. The fictitious book mentioned in the poem represents many disparate sources for his knowledge about the war. For the portrayal of his discovery of this book, Runeberg seems to have borrowed his remembrances from one of the most radical reading experiences in his life, the *Serbische Volkslieder.*

With its concretion, humor, and idealism, **"Ensign Stål"** is representative of the genuine tales. The denotation "genuine" is useful here from the point of view that two earlier poems having a war motif but without connection to the descriptions from the war of 1808-1809, which were commenced in 1846, are contained in the first collection of *The Tales of Ensign Stål.* These earlier poems are **"The Cloud's Brother,"** which was first published in 1835, and **"The Dying Soldier"** (1836). By virtue of its sentimentality and its Ossianic atmosphere, this latter poem lies far removed from the genuine tales and, in its new association, is significant primarily because the title character is a fallen Russian.

Although it was written at an advanced stage in the formation of the tales, **"The Cottage Maiden"** also differs in style and theme from the majority of the poems in the collection. A maiden searches in vain for her fiancé among the soldiers returning from the battle. Her mother consoles the maiden: she has herself exhorted her daughter's loved one to keep out of the way of battle. The agitated daughter sets out for the battlefield. She returns without having found her loved one among the slain, and she declares that she wants to "dwell no more on this isle of perfidy" (v. 55); she wants to die. With its stereotyped character depiction and its contrast between the mother and her daughter, **"The Cottage Maiden"** has many parallels among the **"Idylls and Epigrams."** Runeberg's poetic world encompasses an ideal man's role and a corresponding woman's role. These are already encountered in **"The Cloud's Brother."** In this poem, the man bravely goes to battle. Sorrow is sweet for her whom he has left behind.

Runeberg's demand on heroism is absolute. His ideal is the Classical formula *dulce et decorum est pro patria mori.* The cottage maiden is Runeberg's mouthpiece in the same way as the maiden in **"The Cloud's Brother."**

The idealization of battle in **"The Cottage Maiden"** is marked by metaphors. During a period that has learned to know the atrocities in the handwork of war, these metaphors seem alien, if not repulsive. For example, the returning soldiers, who are both peasants and warriors, have "made their harvest, a dear harvest this time" (v. 5). Indeed, the enemy was either slain or taken captive.

Runeberg's employment of metaphors to describe battle never exceeds that which appears in the poem **"Veteranen"** (**"The Veteran"**). In this tale, a poor and insignificant old man puts on his best clothes and sets out with a mien of loftiness and reverence. "Was it the sacred Temple / The aged warrior sought?" (vv. 47-48) asks the poem, and the answer is given that the church is certainly closed "Yet, to the old man's thinking, / God's service hour was here,—" (vv. 57-58)—because on this summer day a battle was being fought between the Finns and the Russians. The old man stands calmly and joyfully in the rain of bullets. After the battle, he lauds his triumphant compatriots: " 'Still lives our fathers' spirit, / And still our land has men!' " (vv. 135-36).

Similar to Runeberg's earlier battle narratives, this poem, which was probably written in 1847, describes a battle from the perspective of distance and, characteristically enough, abstracts it and portrays it in metaphors to the same degree. None of Runeberg's many battle metaphors are intended less than this one of battle as a divine service to awaken response and understanding among readers of our own days. One can object that the words of the poem can be thought of as coming from the mouth of the ensign and that Runeberg here, when describing a soldier of an old generation, wished to ascribe to him viewpoints that were not his own. But we know that even when Runeberg let the ensign himself speak, as occurs in **"The Veteran,"** it is the poet who forms the ensign's words—without any particular concern for the educational background and individual understanding of the ensign. Owing to his unconditional notion of the warrior's role, the veteran does not distinguish himself from the cottage maiden who prepares herself to die when she learns that her loved one has fled from battle. The attitude assumed by both of these characters is a presumption to be taken for granted in the portrayal; no motivation for this view is given, for example, that by fixing the idea in the personality of the characters, it becomes more evident.

The same remarks apply most emphatically to **"Lieutenant Zidén,"** in which the title character is depicted so summarily that it would be tempting to consider him a war-crazy subaltern. The courageous lieutenant dies in happiness when he realizes that all of his men, whom he has led against the enemy and its fire, have fallen for "noble wounds" and follow him in death. In this connection, the purpose of the poem is to portray Lieutenant Zidén's sacrificial death together with his soldiers on the altar of their native country. However, Zidén is no Leonidas. As Runeberg has characterized him, Lieutenant Zidén holds that

Monument to Runeberg in Helsinki.

contempt of death is an ideal in itself, in other words, a manifestation of instinctive manliness. We can ask: Of what benefit to the native country could his "noble wounds" have been? Yet such a question is excessive: courage and manliness weighed much more heavily in Runeberg's view than military reckoning and wisdom. His foremost war poems are proof of this.

A considerable distance lies between **"Lieutenant Zidén"** and **"Sven Duva,"** even if the subject is the same in both poems, namely, the precipitate, heroic contribution to the native country. The title character in the latter poem is depicted in detail and with humor. Sven Duva grows and becomes more intense during the course of the narrative. The poem has the special rhythm that Runeberg employed in the portrayal of the characters in the majority of the greater tales.

The powerful Sven Duva, who is a veteran's son, decides to become a soldier. Owing to his inability to follow commands, he becomes the talk of the army. Yet the war comes, bringing with it Sven Duva's moment. The enemy attacks a bridge, which must be demolished or defended to the last man. Before the terrible fire of the enemy, the decimated unit in which Duva is serving is forced to re-

treat. Sven Duva reacts in his usual clumsy manner to the order to retreat: he rushes out onto the bridge and goes into close battle against the enemy. He is able to hold his position until reinforcements under the command of the Swedish general Sandels arrive. The enemy soldiers are forced into retreat. General Sandels inquires after the hero on the bridge and is shown Sven Duva, who has been slain by a shot in the heart.

> These were the words the general spake: "We'll
>   all of us admit
> That bullet knew far more than we, it knew the
>   place to hit;
> It left unhurt the poor lad's head, which was not
>   of the best,
> And found itself a worthier mark, his noble, val-
>   iant breast"
>
> (vv. 105-08).

In this poem, Runeberg points the reader's attention directly toward a battle, and he portrays it vividly and in detail, sometimes with concrete closeups. The events speak for themselves. To a corresponding degree, the euphemistic metaphors are pushed aside, but not completely. Regarding the fallen hero, the poem relates: "It seemed as though in weariness he rested after play" (v. 99).

The picture of the poem's hero is so full of life that attempts have been made to find prototypes for the character of Sven Duva in more than one of the Finnish soldiers who participated in the war. A prototype exists, but characteristically enough for Runeberg, this prototype is not a soldier from the Finnish war; instead, his model is taken from an ancient Roman tale: Livy's account of Horatius Cocles, who defends a bridge until reinforcements come. This Roman war story is schematic, and on its sketch of a heroic action, Runeberg has built a chain of significant elements that have not the least connection with his Latin source: Sven Duva's background, his feeble intellect and its effect upon his military training, his behavior on the bridge, his death, and finally Sandels's speech before the slain hero. Sven Duva has become one of the living and magnificent Finnish characters in the tales' rich gallery of persons.

The characters we have so far seen in the tales represent very different types of people; these are the soldiers and the noncommissioned officers and their likes, among whom even the cottage maiden can be reckoned. Several other such characters appear in the tales: old Hurtig; the two dragoons Stål and Lod, who constitute a more modern version of the two antagonists Pullo and Vorenus in Caesar's *Gallic Wars;* and the morose Corporal Brask, who, as a consequence of having saved his master, Major von Konow, becomes the latter's friend and houseguest until his dying days. The major belongs to the category of officers and country gentry like von Fieandt; both are men of standing who lead their soldiers into battle as patriarchal masters. A step above these two stand the generals who participate actively in the war. Two generals, the Swedes Sandels and Döbeln, each have a tale devoted to them. Moreover, in the first collection of *The Tales of Ensign Stål,* Runeberg focuses his attention on those who are ultimately responsible for the course of the war: the Swedish king and Klingspor, the commander in chief of the Swedish-Finnish troops. They are both bitterly caricatured. In the poem "Sveaborg," the commandant of the fortress bearing this name meets with the ensign's hardest judgment. Two poems, finally, stand outside all of these categories. These are "Kulneff" and the previously mentioned "The Dying Soldier"; in both a representative for the enemy plays the major role. In summary, we can say that, on the one hand, it is obvious that Runeberg has devoted the majority of the poems to the portrayal of the common soldiers and the low-ranking officers while, on the other hand, he strove for diversity in the choice of characters for his picture of the war.

Two of the greatest poems in the collection deal with the Swedish generals Döbeln and Sandels. "Döbeln vid Jutas" ("Döbeln at Juutas") received a special emphasis by virtue of its location. This is the final poem in the first collection, and it will be discussed from this viewpoint somewhat later. Without a doubt, "Döbeln at Juutas" is the most idealized portrait of a battlefield commander in all of Runeberg's war poetry. The poem takes as its point of departure the concept of the general as a free thinker. At the end, the general's solitary monologue on the battlefield is presented; this is a monologue in which the free thinker shows himself to be nothing more than a profoundly religious person.

The poem concerning Sandels is similarly one of the climaxes in the collection. It is the most masterfully written of all the tales. In terms of its rhythm, the poem is a masterpiece: within a basic rhythmic pattern, the verse permits a vivid and suggestive variation of the rhythm according to the vicissitudes of action and mood. Of the twenty-six stanzas in the poem, the first thirteen describe Sandels at his breakfast table in the village of Partala (in Runeberg's Swedish: Pardala) together with a minister, whereas the last thirteen stanzas portray the general at the front. The contrast between the two milieus is complete: the former is dominated by the abundantly laid breakfast table, the latter by the terrain around the bridge over Koljonvirta in the vicinity of the town of Iisalmi (Idensalmi).

A truce between Sandels and the Russians will be terminated by the latter at one o'clock. Sandels is looking forward to the renewal of hostilities after his breakfast is finished. However, his man-of-the-world conversation with the minister at the breakfast table is interrupted by an urgent message: the Russians have already begun the attack. The time is one o'clock according to Russian time, but according to Finnish time, it is just twelve. The Finnish forces do not have time to destroy the bridge. The general is unconcerned by the receipt of this message, and he dispatches the orderly with a vacuous reply to the commanding colonel. Immediately afterward, a new rider arrives, in this case, the general's own young aide-de-camp. With eloquent excitement, the aide describes the state of affairs and suggests that it would be desirable for the general to be with his soldiers on the battlefield. When Sandels seems to react indifferently to this report and invites the aroused officer to enjoy the breakfast table with him, the aide vehemently interrupts his superior:

> "Sir General, 'tis due you the truth I unroll;
> You are scorned by the army entire!
> From every soldier this judgment I drew:
> Our most cowardly man is—you!"
>
> (vv. 69-72).

Sandels receives the news that he is considered to be a coward with a laugh, but at the same time, he orders his horse, the "noble Bijou," to be saddled.

After thirteen stanzas, the poem changes rhythms. Powerful anapests together with striking alliterations describe the rhythm and sound of the battle. From the battlefield, attention is again directed toward the general, who has ridden up to the front and remains with "his foremost standard"

> And his eye being calm and his brow being clear,
> How he gleamed on his noble Bijou!
> As he motionless sat with his field-glass in hand,
> Surveying the bridge and the strand
>
> (vv. 93-96).

In this position, he becomes the target for the enemy's bullets. The Finnish vanguard turns to flight, the enemy presses hard upon the Finnish forces, and shots are directed toward the general "from a thousand rifles." Yet, he sits there on his horse, looking at his watch and biding his time as though he were "in most profound peace." "But the moment awaited had come; and now / To his Colonel a dash did he make" (vv. 133-34)—the order is given, the general's forces attack, and the enemy is forced back. The soldiers change their conception of the general: in the final lines of the poem, they praise him for his valor.

As in so many of the tales, **"Sandels"** is built upon contrasts. The general sitting at the breakfast table is contrasted with the general under the rain of bullets. Against the soldiers' initial conception of their general as a coward stands their praise for their brave general in the concluding stanza. These contrasts are the external reflections of the general's character. The picture of the general in the beginning of the poem is almost trivial: a man of the world in a peasant village deep in the interior of Finland. The general becomes completely transformed when he appears as a military man on his white horse. His demeanor receives the traits of Napoleon as he was portrayed in David's paintings.

This pattern has many parallels in Runeberg's poetry. The distinction between Sven Duva and Sandels is not as great as it first might seem. The dumbskull who does everything backwards shows in the moment of peril that he can do the only right thing, and he dies a hero's death. The controversial general who praises Madeira wine at the breakfast table has another side: he is the inspiring and courageous battlefield commander. Runeberg portrays the general in two very different roles. The question is whether Runeberg's purpose was limited to denoting a contrast within the poem. Later on in the collection, there is a poem about a Swedish general who indicates that his most intense interest is for the dinner table but who is described as cowardly. This poem is **"Fältmarskalken" ("The Field Marshall")**. In it, Runeberg lets an officer express his opinion of the title character to another officer in the following way: "You have heart, and he has stomach; / Death is yours,—food his sole pleasure!' " (vv. 47-48).

There is a feature in the apparently self-contradictory character of Sandels that is constant—his calm. His frame of mind is in a complete state of balance, whether at the breakfast table or under the rain of bullets. At the outset, his calm appears as sanguineness and lack of responsibility. His tranquility in battle has the mark of a solemn festival.

Sandels's passive calm before the attacking enemy has awakened wonder, not least judged from the viewpoint of military wisdom. Why does he let the minutes run away? "He looked at his watch, he bided his time" (v. 131)—but which time? When it was one o'clock according to Russian time, Sandels's watch only showed twelve. *His* time was that moment when his own watch showed one. "But the moment awaited had come . . . " (v. 133.). From Sandels's point of view, this was the moment when the truce expired. Such was the agreement that he had to respect.

Two characteristics that pertain less to the general than to the poet himself explain the tranquility of Sandels that many critics found enigmatic. The first is the rigor and inability to compromise that Runeberg had earlier expressed

in his life and in his poetry. As a matter of principle, one does not break an agreement. In Sandels's case, the crucial point is that the agreed-upon time, one o'clock, has different meanings for the two parties. Parenthetically, we can mention that precisely this confusion about time occurred at Koljonvirta Bridge on October 27, 1808. The other characteristic is an almost religious faith in the sanctity of a promise. "And his eye being calm and his brow being clear"—indeed, it is a calm of deep dimension that puts its stamp on this literary portrait of the Swedish general.

Judged realistically, the situation presented seems more than a little improbable. The poem is built upon a concept of man that is clearly speculative. We must remember that all of these war poems were written by a poet who had never heard a shot fired except at a bird or other forest creature. At its high points, **"Sandels"** is, from an artistic viewpoint, an extraordinarily well-planned expression of the experiences in Runeberg's own life, an expression that required the sacrifice of even the illusion of reality. Sandels becomes the embodiment of a monumental and "transfigured" idea. This is an idea that the poet has placed in a prominent position at the scene of battle, not as an obstinate disavowal of suspicion concerning cowardice, but ultimately rather as a powerful manifestation of Runeberg's notion of the straight and uncompromising road that demands complete adherence to promises and principles.

The Norwegian literary scholar Francis Bull has made an essential observation while speaking about the "absolute morality" personified in Sandels and other characters in Runeberg's poetry: he suggests the possibility that Ibsen was influenced by his Finlandic predecessor when he wrote "Brand".

The poems about Sandels and Döbeln portray two ideal commanders. Against them stand two poems dealing with the men ultimately responsible for the conduct of the war on the Finnish side, namely, the Swedish king, Gustav IV Adolf, and the commander in chief, General Klingspor. The former is described in "Konungen" ("The King"), a merciless caricature in which the title character clothes himself in Charles XII's war uniform—in Stockholm—in order to bolster the fighting spirit of the army. The poem **"The Field Marshall"** captures a moment among the officers, who are celebrating a turning point in the war. They are unanimous in their opinion that the credit for this turning point (the victory at Siikajoki) is not due to Field Marshall Klingspor. A contest among them to pronounce a disparaging verdict on Klingspor is concluded by old Lode, who is also given a poem in Runeberg's second collection of tales. He says: " 'Tis a shame that men so valiant / Should o'er such a wretch be jangling!' " (vv. 95-96.).

Nevertheless, the most bitter tone and the hardest condemnation is to be found in another of the tales in the first collection—**"Sveaborg."** According to Runeberg's wish, this poem was first incorporated posthumously (1882) into the initial collection of tales. Inasmuch as **"Sveaborg"** was printed without the author's knowledge and permission, it early became one of the most renowned poems in the entire suite. Because of its strategic position in the Gulf of Finland outside of Helsinki, the fortress of Suomenlinna

(Sveaborg) possessed a fundamental importance for the defense of Finland. As long as the fortress continued to offer resistance, the war could not be considered lost; Runeberg is an ardent spokesman for this concept, which was shared by many, in these poems. On May 3, 1808, Carl Olof Cronstedt, the commandant of the fortress, capitulated. At the same time, the army was in retreat far in the North, and the whole of southern Finland was controlled by the Russian troops. As seen from the viewpoint of Helsinki, the military-political situation indicated a quick conclusion to the war. The question was when and how Suomenlinna would be surrendered. That it was abandoned at such an early juncture, as a consequence of negotiations and pressure brought to bear on the commandant via many channels, and, moreover, without a battle, has resulted in severe condemnation of Cronstedt by Finnish and Swedish historians. Without a doubt, the most severe judgment was formulated by Runeberg through his mouthpiece Ensign Stål, who brands the capitulation as treason and declares his anathema on the person responsible.

It was a learned and experienced poet who held the pen when the ensign's words were conceived. This is shown by a review of the old soldier's statement about "Gibraltar's image in the North" and "The queen of the sea." Here Runeberg employs rhetorical question, personification, allegory, antithesis, asyndeton, polysyndeton, and hyperbole. Indeed, there is an extensive collection of stylistic effects in this rhetorically cogent poem, which has contributed, more so than the majority of poems in *The Tales of Ensign Stål,* toward strengthening the notion that the outcome of the war depended on the insufficiency of a very small group of people.

One poem in the collection significantly supplements the picture of the war. This is the portrait of an enemy commander, the Russian colonel Kulnev, who, according to what Runeberg himself has related, had sometimes been a visitor in the poet's childhood home. Due to his colorful external appearance and his affable manner, Kulnev was remembered with fond recollections for a long time in the Finnish regions where he sojourned as one of the officers in the victorious army. Runeberg's depiction of Kulnev is done with warmth and an obvious admiration for the exploits of this Russian. In the poem, Runeberg makes the following drastic judgment of him: "He kissed and he gave death's dole / With the same warmth of soul" (vv. 63-64). (pp. 115-28)

King Fjalar (1844) and the first collection of *The Tales of Ensign Stål* (1848) mark the crowning point in Runeberg's long poetic career. Are his later tales a sign that the poet's creative powers had weakened? This question cannot be answered with an unconditional yes. "Landshövdingen" ("The Provincial Governor"), which was the last poem to be written in the second collection, is one of the more important of all the tales, and it has the representative features of the better tales, namely, the powerfully portrayed title character; the dramatic concentration of the course of events, culminating with a moment that is full of significance; and finally, the quiet "transfiguration" of the one who has passed through the ordeal. Another of the last tales to be written, **"Wilhelm von Schwerin,"** summarizes the entire idealizing heroic description that had been a theme in Runeberg's poetry since **"The Grave at Perho"** (1831). In this late portrait of a military man, the fundamental elements in Runeberg's great war poetry are represented, that is, the concrete and condensed course of events in which combat has a central place, and in the midst of the battle, the depiction of the major character both as a man and as an ideal.

On the other hand, it cannot be denied that many of the poems in the second collection have weaknesses in their lack of concreteness and in their distance from the events of the battle. In so many of these poems, the battle has just been concluded, and the hero has fallen or the commander meets his men after the fight. To a great degree, what a critic wrote in 1844 about *King Fjalar* can equally well be applied to the second collection of *The Tales of Ensign Stål* in 1860: "Runeberg loves that which is finished, and he prefers painting the concluded battle to the heavy swells before the storm." [Frederik Berndtson, *Helsingfors Morgonblad*] In **"Fänrikens marknadsminne"** (**"The Ensign at the Fair"**), this distance is stressed by the perspective, which is a projection through double mirrors: the ensign describes his memories of a fair. An impoverished grenadier is begging for money by singing a ballad. The veteran's song is reproduced in its entirety.

The central motif in Runeberg's great war poems, such as **"Sven Duva"** and **"Sandels,"** is the portrayal of the moment of battle and the culmination of heroism. Heroism has not been given a lesser role in the second collection, but it is described in a more reflective manner and more rhetorically. Heroism is preferably described before, after, or at the side of combat, not in its midst. Döbeln honors the nameless tramp for his exploits at Lappo (**"N:o femton, Stolt,"** [**"Number Fifteen, Stolt"**]), Lotta Svärd has precisely the same task with regard to the impoverished and wounded soldier following the unfortunate battle of Oravais, and Adlercreutz stands in the powerful concluding poem as an observer of a temporary turning point in the war, namely, the battle of Siikajoki. Old Spelt, the baggage train driver who is the most sluggish and most untidy soldier among the retreating forces, is the first man to get into position—newly washed and tidy—with his horse when the army breaks off its retreat and finally, after Siikajoki, marches against the enemy.

"Soldatgossen" (**"The Soldier Boy"**), which is the first poem in the second collection, is, as a role poem, unique among the tales. The young lad himself expresses his youthful desire to follow in the footsteps of his father, the soldier. As a role poem, this tale points in a noteworthy manner back to *Poems* of 1833. In addition, **"The Soldier Boy"** is, in many ways, reminiscent of the poetry of Swedish Romanticism, wherein young men express their inclination for action, exploits, and adventure. "Vikingen" ("The Viking," 1811) of Erik Gustaf Geijer (1783-1847) is one of the most appreciated of these poems and a poem that is, to be sure, mirrored in Hjalmar's irresistible longing in *King Fjalar* after heroic feats and victories. The Viking, like the soldier boy, has an inherent urge for that which is full of action, glory, and danger. Runeberg seems to say that this urge in the soldier boy is more than just a temporary, youthful impulse. His father, grandfather, and great-grandfather all have fought as Finnish soldiers against the Russians.

The heroism of the soldier boy is certainly in accord with Runeberg's concept of a deep and genuine instinct, and it has parallels in many of Ensign Stål's heroes. However, in contrast to the other heroes, this lad is incapable of putting the strength of his thought into action. Something abstract and rhetorical mashes the poem's heroic spirit. Such is not the case in **"Wilhelm von Schwerin,"** which describes a young soldier's eloquent heroism in deeds. As often occurs in the tales, the difference between these two poems can be explained by the fact that they are related in very different degrees to an actual event. **"Wilhelm von Schwerin"** is primarily built upon a letter that was written by a mortally wounded young nobleman to his Swedish parents. The letter was published in 1859 in a Swedo-Finnish newspaper and attracted Runeberg's attention. Support in historical fact, in this case even including a personal letter written by the hero himself, was of great importance for Runeberg. It is true that he deals with his subject matter, as always, with the hand of the creative artist and not that of the historian. He edits, shortens the time frame, and gives the action more dramatic and monumental effect than the document provides. At the same time, Runeberg also retains the style of the ensign's informal manner.

Of the seventeen poems in the second collection, we shall consider three: **"Lotta Svärd,"** a tribute to women actively supporting the fighting soldiers; **"Den femte juli" ("The Fifth of July"),** one of the retrospective tributes to heroism and a poem which is intimately related to **"Our Land;"** and finally, **"The Provincial Governor,"** a memorial to a soldier of peace. The words "And she deserved to be honored more / Than she deserved laughing at" (vv. 19-20) have been familiar to generations of Scandinavians; they are spoken by the ensign and pertain to Lotta Svärd, Sven Duva's equal in this second collection. We learn first of her earlier fortunes, how she became the wife of a soldier while she was young and beautiful, and how she followed her husband out into Gustav III's war against Russia. Her husband, Svärd, was slain in that war. Now, nearly twenty years later, as a mature woman stamped by hardship, she follows the army in the capacity of canteen keeper. Her most important task is to supply the soldiers with vodka.

With this woman and her despised source of livelihood at center stage, Runeberg has created one of the great scenes in *The Tales of Ensign Stål.* The action takes place following the disastrous defeat at Oravais, where Wilhelm von Schwerin, among so many others, received his mortal wound. On this occasion, Lotta Svärd has hidden her tent and sells her ware under "a lofty spruce." "When the army takes its first rest after the great defeat and everyone feels that the native country is lost," declares a commentator [Ivar Hjertén], "Lotta gives the emotion of homelessness a wordless but sublime expression: she lets her tent, her home in the field, remain unpacked and sets up shop under a spruce."

A young dragoon cockily demands to buy vodka. Lotta

Svärd has seen his cowardly absence from the battle under the pretext of sickness. " 'For a poor old mother the field you took / But how did you fight today?' " (vv. 107-108) she asks bitterly. She refuses to sell him drink on the ground that he has defrauded his land, his mother: " 'By God! not a drop for all of your gold / Would I give to a son like you' " (vv. 119-20). Instead, she directs her attention to a wounded soldier who has drawn himself aside in his misery. She turns to him and speaks of his valor in bygone battles and now on this day. He is too poor to afford a bracer, but he can fetch his reward from her for his heroism in the past and now. She affectionately fills a glass for the brave soldier.

Runeberg did not have historical or anecdotal material upon which to build his portrait of Lotta Svärd. She is a figure created from a starting point in a poem by the French poet de Béranger ("La Vivandière"). Similar to such figures as Sven Duva and the baggage train driver Spelt, she is pure invention. In spite of this, Runeberg succeeded in making her more alive than many of the national figures in *The Tales of Ensign Stål* about whom he had data and characterizations at his disposal. As usual, Runeberg depicts the character according to an antithetical pattern. She was a beauty; now, she is furrowed. Her exterior, like her source of livelihood, is insignificant, and the reader encounters her as a somewhat ridiculous and odd figure; however, she grows into the great woman patriot in the ensign's tales, a far more human and vivid character than her feminine counterpart in the first collection, the cottage maiden.

Indeed, Lotta Svärd has made an impression outside the prevalent field of literary influence. She has given her name to a women's auxiliary of the Finnish and the Swedish defense forces. But even within literature, she is the prototype for Bertold Brecht's play *Mutter Courage,* which was written while the author was in exile in Sweden during World War II.

Lotta Svärd lived near combat. In **"The Fifth of July,"** the action occurs seventeen years after the war. As so many of the tales, this poem is a tribute to a hero, in this case Zachris Duncker, who was slain on July 5, 1809 in a battle in northern Sweden. Runeberg does not relate anything more concerning this person to whom he devoted his poem. Such items as a name and a pronouncement of the soldier's bravery and his love for the native land do not suffice as the stanchions on which the portrait of a hero can be built. Instead, the poet concentrates his interest in the country for which the soldier died. The tale begins with the ensign's description of the mood on a summer morning; he then presents the theme of the poem: " 'Could one not die for such a land?' " The year is 1826, and it is the ensign who turns to the young student Runeberg with this question. The latter remains silent but in deep concord with the old patriot. Inspired and eloquent, Ensign Stål lets his thoughts encompass all of Finland. The vision of the native land is joined together with that of the hero's destiny, and the answer to the earlier question is given in the final lines:

> . . . Behold, here smiled with pride
> The land his love has glorified,

For which our hearts are burning;
'Twas for this bride that Duncker died!

(vv. 123-26)

"The Fifth of July" summarizes more directly than any other poem of Runeberg, with the exception of **"Our Land,"** the profound and warm feeling for the native land that had mellowed during his many years as a poet. This feeling is conveyed in **"The Fifth of July"** by Ensign Stål, who is now, as often, the mouthpiece of the mature poet for ideas as well as style. As in the poem **"Ensign Stål,"** Runeberg directs his readers to his encounter with patriotism and the ensign. In Saarijärvi and in Ruovesi at the shores of Lake Näsijärvi, he received indelible impressions of people and landscapes.

Naturally, the scene of the poem is pure fiction, and there never existed an ensign in the vicinity of the young student with anything like the eloquence and the conscious and warm patriotism for which Runeberg's ensign acts as the interpreter. The poem reduces a long development to a grand, inspired moment.

There is an obvious tendency in the later tales to emphasize emotional qualities and cultivate an idea in isolation; the idea is usually, as in this poem, the love for the native land. Sometimes the effect becomes, as has already been pointed out, an abstract and rhetorical presentation. However, Runeberg could also find other, concentrated expressions for a profound idea in the poems that constitute the second collection. In **"Munter,"** one of the soldier portraits, the locale is at the grave of a taciturn warrior. A comrade makes a long speech in which he characterizes the slain soldier and describes his death. Yet, the final speech of the poem is given in the laconic style of the dead man by General Adlercreutz, who declares: "He was a Finn."

"The Provincial Governor," which was the last of all the tales to be written, deals with a civil servant. An old provincial governor in the interior of Finland tirelessly attends to his difficult tasks during the war. He is sitting exhausted in his office when Russian soldiers, led by "the Russian army's General-in-chief," force their way in. The Russian commander demands in a threatening tone that the provincial governor make a proclaimation on behalf of the victorious army saying that those among the combatants who return to their homes will be spared their lives and allowed to retain their property. Those, however, who continue the struggle will not only lose their right to life and property; the possessions belonging to their families will also be confiscated.

The old civil servant emphatically places his hand upon the code of laws, *The Statutes of Sweden,* and answers that the security of the vanquished lies in these statutes. The czar has promised to respect this code of laws. The governor then relates that there is an ancient statute in this book that only he who is guilty of a crime shall be punished and not his family as well.

> "If 'tis a crime to fight for native land,
> To which all noble hearts reply, 'not so,'
> Take vengeance then on men with sword in
> hand,

On babes and women,—no!"

(vv. 65-68)

In spite of whatever is done to him, he knows that the law will survive him. He falls silent, lifts his glance, and meets that of the Russian general. This officer intently contemplates the governor, shakes his hand, and finally, bows and leaves.

Two officials are witnesses to this scene. They see the provincial governor afterward, exhausted but victorious. They have witnessed and would later tell, the poem says, "Of a transfiguration, strange and still, / That on his features lay" (vv. 87-88).

Runeberg had a historical event in mind when he wrote **"The Provincial Governor,"** and Provincial Governor Wibelius was the major person in this event as well as in the poem. The Russian demands and Wibelius's reasons for repudiating them have their background in fact; the meeting between Wibelius and the Russian general does not. Indeed, the contact between the two sides occurred in writing. Thus, the wordless departure of the Russian commander took place only in Runeberg's poetic imagination. In his characteristic manner, the poet has concentrated a drawn out course of events into an interval of a few minutes.

"The Provincial Governor" begins with a question:

> Do glorious deeds grow but on battle-ground
> Which valiant warrior moistens with his blood?
> Cannot a strong yet unarmed man be found,
> To show his doughty mood?

This is a question that has been asked many times since antiquity. Runeberg was certainly familiar with it from Cicero's book on duties, which he had studied while he was still a schoolboy in Vaasa. Nevertheless, the question, as it is asked in this poem, seems to be everything but an echo from an old tradition. In his resolute endeavor to capture the exalted as well as the lowly, women as well as men, compatriots as well as enemies, in his depictions of Finland's war, Runeberg has finally even given the practitioner of a civil and less heroic activity a place of honor. Not content with this alone, he has bestowed upon this civil servant some of the same heroic luster that shines roundabout Sandels, Döbeln, and in the final poem of the second collection, Adlercreutz. (pp. 131-38)

The second part of *The Tales of Ensign Stål* was published late in the year 1860 after the poems had been approved by an extremely respectful censor. Difficulties of the sort that Runeberg anticipated at an early stage did not occur. As a matter of fact, Runeberg was unassailable as the national poet and as a European celebrity. However, in the background the Russian governor-general of Finland gnashed his teeth. With conservative and autocratic keenness, he saw something in the poems that was considerably more than a tribute to heroes and exploits in the past. He was of the opinion that, under the guise of historical description, Runeberg exhorted the young people of his generation to defiance and revolt.

History has verified what one could only suspect in 1848 and 1860. With all their artistry and their poetry, *The*

Tales of Ensign Stål are also a political document. With a combination of artistic skill, powerful rhetoric, and affability that was quite unique in Scandinavian poetry up to this time, Runeberg presented in the best of these poems his own and his generation's conception of all that is Finnish. He depicts a people who stood united against the enemy and who, with a firm and purposeful contribution from Sweden, could have concluded the war of 1808-1809 as the victorious side.

It has cost historians a considerable amount of labor to rectify this simplified description of a fundamentally far more complicated historical process. The picture as such is not Runeberg's; rather, it is to be found in his background material. What he added was the lyrical and rhetorical effectiveness, as well as the national pathos which belonged to him and his generation. The tendency for idealizing a grim reality existed to the same extent in the cultural heritage from the antiquity that Runeberg represented as well as in the domestic sources and traditions.

The Tales of Ensign Stål have had immeasurable importance for the development of the Finnish national consciousness. However, they have played an equally great role in the development of the concept of Finland and things Finnish held by the neighboring Scandinavian countries. This collection of poems functioned as a guiding star, stimulus, and source of national propaganda during the many and protracted periods of crisis in Finland. In calmer years, when powerful words about the native country and about independence weigh lightly, *The Tales of Ensign Stål* have been regarded as an unimportant part of the Swedish and Finnish cultural heritage. The pendulum has swung violently in the judgment of these poems. For example, the radical Swedish writer Sara Lidman (b. 1923) has objected to the current slanderers of this work by pointing out the parallels between Runeberg's description of the struggle of the Finnish people during the years 1808-1809 and the national wars of liberation in our own time. She has observed that there are poems about the war in Vietnam during this decade that have striking similarities with **"Sven Duva"** and **"Lotta Svärd."**

Judged from the point of view of Runeberg's contemporaries, the poet Runeberg displays a profound and singular radicalism as expressed in his emphasis on human dignity and on the greatness and capability for heroic deeds of the most simple and impoverished members of the society. His intense feelings for democracy have roots in the situation described in the poem **"Ensign Stål."** On the one hand, as a student during a time when education was a privilege, and on the other hand, as a poor tutor, Runeberg was able to meet and experience the simple people of the Finnish interior with a concord and understanding of the conditions of poverty—a poverty that he had experienced more bluntly than most others of his social background. As a consequence, it was easy for him to bridge the gap between the exalted and the lowly. He carried the experiences of his youth with him throughout his life, and they took expression in the often-repeated descriptions of the common destiny of the master and the servant, in the depiction of the owner and the charity resident in the peasant home in the Finnish interior or in the portrayal of how

the soldier and his commander face old age together as fellow comrades. The patriarchal conception of society, for which Runeberg has met with much criticism during recent years, stands in harmony with the popular Lutheran spirit that has penetrated deep into the consciousness of Finns and Swedes through centuries of catechism, parish meetings, and church sermons.

It is not a simple task to find parallels in the world literature with such a collection as *The Tales of Ensign Stål*. The tales' epic-lyric expression of love for the native country, of perseverance, and of heroism have a place to themselves, especially if we pay attention to the compassion and humor that are the cornerstones of this poetry. In Classical literature, one can point to Horace's patriotic odes and Virgil's national epic; in modern literature, Camões's Portuguese national epic and Kipling's national poetry offer possibilities for comparison. Yet there is a fundamental dissimilarity between these poets and Runeberg. While the others all praise a triumphant native land and identify themselves with, if not to say panegyrize, the monarch, Runeberg pays tribute to his people for their resistance to the Russian sovereign. Runeberg's national poetry does not pay homage to a sovereign. Rather, *The Tales of Ensign Stål* were an act of defiance against the regime. Runeberg's notion of the relationship of his poems to the Russian authorities is displayed by his reaction when he learned on his sickbed that the Russian governor-general was honored with a concert that included the melody to **"The Soldier Boy."** The agitated poet wished it to be made known that "this song was not written to be played for governors and governors-general." (pp. 139-41)

> *Tore Wretö, in his* J. L. Runeberg, *translated by Zelek S. Herman, Twayne Publishers, 1980, 186 p.*

Kim Nilsson   (essay date 1986)

[*In the following essay, Nilsson suggests that* Julqvällen, *rather than possessing a weakly constructed plot as is commonly believed, exhibits a complex narrative style that links Runeberg to Modernism.*]

J. L. Runeberg's *Julqvällen (Christmas Eve)* was published in final form in December of 1841. The poet had labored over this poem for a considerable time; scholars disagree as to just how long. Martin Lamm suggests that the writing of *Julqvällen* was an intermittent process that took some four years, while Nordberg argues that the gestation period was closer to one and a half years. Wretö, in his recent monograph, accepts Lamm's arguments concerning timing as well as discontinuity in writing. According to this view Runeberg completed other works while *Julqvällen*, a "lesser epic poem," remained on the back burner. A number of reasons for that state of affairs has been forwarded. The most favored explanation is that, at the time, Runeberg found himself at thematic and stylistic crossroads. On the one hand, having possibly been influenced by Almqvist, he had turned to more exotic themes, resulting in the poem *Nadeschda* (1841), while on the other hand, he had begun to turn his attention to that patriotism which eventually was to lead to *Fänrik Ståls sägner* (1848-60; *The Songs of Ensign Stål,* 1925). Elements of both are evident in *Julqvällen,* and it is hardly surprising that critics and commentators have concluded that the poem is fragmentary, even disjointed.

Whether four years or one and a half, *Julqvällen* was slow in coming. In this essay it will be argued that the reason for the delay was not owing to what critics have suggested, but rather to the fact that *Julqvällen* is a highly complex poem, one that taxed Runeberg's narrative technique in the extreme. Most writers find this to be a lesser poem also in a qualitative sense; Wretö calls it "the least successful of Runeberg's epic poems." In contrast, Viljanen maintains that "in comparison with the poet's previous epic poems, *Julqvällen* is a very complicated work of art." Viljanen does not specify the nature of that complexity except in rather general terms; he points to finely tuned psychological tensions existing in an apparently idyllic Biedermeier setting. What follows will tend to be in accordance with Viljanen's view, but for quite different and highly specific reasons.

Runeberg's previous epic poems were for the most part "realistic" in the sense usually associated with him; specifically, they employed an omniscient and reliable narrator. In *Julqvällen* the narrator is unreliable, and the true core of the work may only be glimpsed by indirect mirror reflections. While the majority of critics hold that the veteran soldier Pistol is the protagonist of the poem, it is, in fact, the young girl Augusta who is the principal object of the poet's curiosity, and beneath her sweet Biedermeier guise lurk fantasies that would not be considered entirely proper in her milieu. But Augusta cannot be fully comprehended unless it is realized that her motives and emotions are reflected upon the surface that Pistol provides. Augusta and Pistol are in tandem throughout the poem; the mirroring technique, a favorite of Runeberg's, is ever present, in large structural considerations as well as in the minutest details. It should be noted, however, that in *Julqvällen* the mirroring is internal to the poem, and it is through such a positioning that the reader is instructed to be sceptical of the narrator's description of Augusta. If this view is accepted, it is possible to claim for Runeberg another dimension as an author, one that would earn him the label of "modern."

Augusta, the younger of two sisters at the manor where most of the action takes place, has been seen as the quintessential young Biedermeier girl, sweet and lovely, always concerned with the plight of others, self-effacing, a little *svärmisk* (romantically inclined) perhaps, but overall a pure delight. Viljanen, as noted, hears in Augusta resonances of psychological depth, but Wretö sees her as no more than "someone solacing who, in her childishness, is sometimes able to brighten the atmosphere." Estlander has suggested that Runeberg was more interested in Augusta than in Pistol, a view rejected by Söderhjelm. While there are divergent opinions as to the importance of Augusta in the poem and as to the depth of her personality, there is no disagreement that she is the solacing angel of the manor; she is both good and honorable. And she is a child, in spite of the fact that the text contains some quite overt indications that she has the emotions of a young woman, nurturing thoughts that are clearly erotic. What is worse is that the object of her erotic dreams is no other than her very own brother-in-law, the captain, who has gone to war, not so incidentally accompanied by Pistol's son. Taken alone, such intimations are highly tenuous, but when considered with other structural and narratological arguments, their force is convincingly enhanced.

Initially, one notes that in the poem only three characters have real names: Pistol, with a surname as decorum demands; Augusta; and rather surprisingly, the captain, whose name is Adolf. It cannot be considered a coincidence that two of the names begin with *A,* but the point here is that these three characters are those who provide the essential dramatic core of *Julqvällen.* The other characters make up the background; this is true even of the major, Augusta's father, despite the fact that, towards the end, he is the person who expresses the highly patriotic emotions for which the poem has been celebrated.

A second and more convincing intimation occurs in the third canto, when the captain, Adolf, returns home unexpectedly. Augusta learns of Adolf's return, and the point-of-view shifts to her as, taking a shortcut, she hurries to the house, where her father is standing at the door. With trembling voice she inquires, "Fader, / Skynda då, säg mig det, plåga mig längre ej; o om min gissning / Sviker, förgås jag af sorg. Är det möjligt att Adolf är hemma? ("Father, / Hurry and tell me, torment me no more; oh, if my guess / Betrays me, I will perish in sorrow. Can it be that Adolf's at home?"). The major gives no answer but leads his daughter to the room in which her sister and her sister's husband have been rejoined. Augusta's steps grow hesitant as she takes in the scene: she "dröjde och såg, blott såg, med en tår i det leende ögat" ("waited and looked, just looked, with tears in her smiling eyes"). Augusta stands at the door, unnoticed—"Der, en minut, vid dörrn i det stora rummet hon dröjde" ("There, for a minute, by the door of the large room she waited")—time and space have begun to take on unreal dimensions for her. Finally, she is noticed by Adolf who, having hurried forth, "böjde sin friska / Arm kring systren och tryckte en kyss på dess glödande läppar" ("placed his able / Arm around his sister and pressed a kiss on her glowing lips"). The point-of-view still belongs to Augusta; only she is able to know just how her lips are burning.

A third intimation occurs towards the end of the poem, after Pistol has learned that his son has fallen. Suddenly Augusta is in an uncharacteristically blue mood. She feels superfluous now that things have returned to normal; her father is fully content with his pipe; her mother is preoccupied with their grandchild; and her sister and Adolf have one another. She laments,

> . . . på mig ej tänker en enda af alla.
> Ensam blir jag här snart, af den öfverflödiga minskas
> Fröjden ej mer, då hon går, och ökes ej mer då hon kommer,
> Lyckligt är allt af annat, och jag gör glädje åt ingen.

> (. . . no one at all thinks of me.

Soon I will be lonely here; someone superfluous
    neither diminishes
Joy when she leaves nor increases it when she
    arrives.
All find happiness elsewhere, and I give joy to
    no one.)

It is appropriate that Augusta expresses those feelings to Pistol, because just moments before, they had both experienced the loss of their dreams: Pistol lost the life of a grandfather, and Augusta, the life of a passionate mistress. Those losses form the pivotal element in *Julqvällen;* Pistol's is plain to see; whereas, Augusta's is only indirectly clear. In the matter of the oblique description of Augusta, first structural arguments, then a number of parallels in Augusta's and Pistol's actions must be considered.

The overall structure of *Julqvällen,* as many have noted, is symmetrical. At the very beginning and in the last line, the reader is face-to-face with Pistol; the second to enter and the next-to-last to exit (except for the major's hand) is Augusta. In the beginning as well as at the end, the theme is loneliness: at first, it is Pistol's that is dominant; at the end, it is Augusta's. In the central part of the poem both Augusta and Pistol take turns giving lengthy recitations: first, she reads the "romances" she has penned for the sake of providing solace to her sister; later, Pistol holds forth about the life of a soldier. In both recitations the central themes are the same; they tell about the Turks and confirm that even Turks have hearts. These stories will be returned to in detail below.

Although included in the hypothesis of this interpretation, the losses suffered by Pistol and Augusta are also a part of the structural arrangement of *Julqvällen* and, as mentioned, constitute the pivotal point of that structure. That fact is underscored in an interesting way. Noted above was the burning of Augusta's lips when she had realized that her dream had evaporated. When Pistol learns that his son has died, his only sign of emotion is the quivering of his lips; then, he hides his emotions. In both cases, the characters' true feelings are betrayed by their lips.

The structural symmetries pointed out above are clear indications that Augusta and Pistol are to be seen as juxtaposed entities, which is by no means a novel observation. The marked relationship between the two principal actors must surely serve a specific function. That function is the illumination of Augusta's true feelings. The relation between Augusta and Pistol is essentially irreflexive; it is through Pistol's actions, overtly stated, that we are led to discover parallel features in Augusta's behaviour. Pistol's being a complement to Augusta is the narrator's devious device for telling the truth about the heroine. Nowhere is this circumstance brought forth more clearly than in the context of Augusta's romances and Pistol's soldiers' yarns.

Ostensibly in an attempt to provide solace for her downcast sister, Augusta recites two poems she has written for that purpose. Although she does not hide the fact that she has had Adolf in mind in her endeavour, her recitation is meant to soothe. The setting of the poems is a Turkish sultan's seraglio; the tone is rather hot for an innocent little girl, but Augusta assures her sister that such is the stuff of thousands of books.

The first poem describes the Turks, who have been victorious in war, leading prisoners into a city. They are a sorry crew, except for one, whose eyes flash with defiant wrath. In a tower "the star of the harem" focuses on the defiant prisoner. She tells her servant girl that "Frihet måste hjelten vinna, / Lefva än för älskarinna, / Ära, fosterjord!'" ("Freedom the hero must gain, / Live on for mistress, / Honor, native soil!"). The identification of the prisoner with Adolf is clear from the beginning, and the star of the harem must be seen as another persona of Augusta: she is depicted as the favorite, and her attributes are those of rays of light, in other words, exactly those of Augusta's in her ordinary surroundings. The fact that the star of the harem is locked up, so that only her glance reaches the prisoner, testifies to Augusta's recognition that her affection is unrequited, yet she does nourish a dream, that of being an *älskarinna,* a paramour, but fortunately her choice of vocabulary is closer to "mistress," with that margin of ambiguity which the word allows.

In the second poem the star of the harem sets out to effect the release of the prisoner. She tarries in obeying the sultan's demand for an amorous night, and when at long last she arrives, her eyes are full of tears, and she has a tragic tale to tell him. She recalls a friend of hers, in her own land, by the name of Serbia's Rapture, who perished from grieving over the fate of herself and her imprisoned husband. The star of the harem now explains to the sultan that "En blott kände hennes smärta. / Dyre, derför brast dess hjerta, / Att en yngling / Fördes hit som slaf" ("Only one knew her pain. / Dear one, for that reason her heart broke, / That a youth / Was brought here as a slave"). It is evident that Augusta now identifies with the grief of Serbia's Rapture; only she is able to appreciate grief over the loss of a loved one. While Augusta invites her sister to identify with Serbia's Rapture, Augusta knows that she herself occupies that role. In any event, the star of the harem is successful, a deal is struck: for each kiss a prisoner is to be released, and soon, as the reader is pleased to learn, an armada of freed prisoners is sailing homeward.

Read independently, the language of the poems would not allow one to draw such inferences, but when Pistol's yarns are considered, the picture changes. First of all, it is made abundantly clear that Pistol is an appreciated teller of tales and that he has a tendency to adorn fact with fantasy. Concretely, Pistol explains how the Kalmucks, who lack noses, need not even tilt their heads when they drink from a bottle. But thematically, his yarn is parallel to Augusta's poems. By giving away his bottle of spirits to a dying Kalmuck, Pistol once showed mercy towards an enemy, who thereby revived and at a later encounter took Pistol prisoner, but not until after it was clear that he could have killed Pistol. In captivity Pistol experiences the sweetest moments of his life; the moral is that Turks have hearts. The juxtaposition of romance and yarn is established.

In Pistol's yarn there occurs a strange incident that has puzzled scholars. Martin Lamm was the first to note that the old veteran's character was far from unblemished; his sense of pride and honor were not exactly commensurable with those expected of a great patriotic hero. The reason that Pistol had run across his dying enemy was that he himself was walking the fields looting corpses. Since such a deed stands in sharp contrast to the later image of Pistol as an embodiment of the honorable Finnish soldier, it is seen as an argument in favor of the disjointed composition of *Julqvällen;* the various sections could not have been written at the same time but rather must have been pasted together in an attempt to get the work over and done with. While it may be the case that Runeberg had written the work in separate bits and pieces, there is no reason to assume that the final product would not be a unified whole. Pistol's lamentable behavior is not in discord with the poem, certainly not according to the interpretation advanced here. What readers are told is that the old soldier was not necessarily honorable. By implication, there are also less than honorable traits in Augusta's romances; her story is suspect. The covert in her story is revealed by the overt in his.

With the background provided, readers are in a position to scrutinize certain interesting incidents in the narrative. One has to do with fire. When Augusta approaches her sister with her poems, she conjures up a scene in which the real threat is not captivity, not even death in battle, but rather a hoard of fiery Turkish women who are likely to capture Adolf's heart and mind and make him forget his loved one. Surely that is sorry comfort for a sad sister, but Augusta cannot restrain her own fears; she is being consumed by jealousy. In a parallel, Pistol tells his audience about the habit the Turks have of setting their prisoners on fire. Many a time, so he says, he has seen his son and the captain burning like torches. Pistol has no need to hide his fears; he certainly does not want his son turned to ashes. But his fear clarifies Augusta's.

Another incident concerns treasured possessions. Having told her sister of her intention to read poems, Augusta—in the words of the narrator—"vecklade opp ett fint brev papper, med omsorg / Skyddadt och slutet ihop . . ." ("Opened out a fine piece of stationery, carefully / Protected and folded . . ."). The poems are treasures. Not surprisingly Pistol also gives away a treasured possession. His sacrifice is a bottle of vodka, which he gives to his dying enemy. To Pistol's chagrin, the dying Kalmuck empties the bottle to the very last drop. This healthy thirst in a dying person leads to a third incident. Later on that same night, Pistol regrets having given away the spirits; he is embarrassed "att som en qvinna jag svigtat och lydt mitt blödiga hjerta" ("that I have been as pliant as a woman and obeyed my soft heart"). His regret stands as a direct parallel to Augusta's emotions when she has finished her recitation. She is the one to be overcome by her tale: she bursts into tears and asks to be left alone. Critics have seen this scene as the ultimate expression of Augusta's warm heart; Söderhjelm is outright touched, "men när hon läst upp dem, överväldigas hennes unga sinne självt av den sorg, hon så modigt sökt lindra hos de andra, och hon brister i gråt. Huru fint och mänskligt är icke detta!" ("but having read them aloud, her own young mind is overcome by the grief that she so courageously has tried to alleviate in the others, and she bursts into tears. How

noble and human this is!"). Yes, Augusta is overcome—by her own emotions for herself; Pistol has told the reader so.

By now there is ample evidence that Augusta is not merely the solacing angel of the manor; her concern for Adolf is strictly personal. For a final argument one can turn to a direct confirmation provided by the poet Runeberg himself. Each of the three cantos of *Julqvällen* is introduced by a motto. The second canto, which contains Augusta's poems, has as its motto the concluding lines of the second poem:

> Tänk blott vänligt vid min saga:
> *Att en systers sorg förjaga,*
> *Sjöng en flicka*
> *En oskyldig sång!*
>
> (Just think kindly of my tale:
> *To disperse a sister's sorrow*
> *A girl sang*
> *A guiltless song!*)

The italics are Runeberg's, in the poem as well as in the motto. Precisely what it is that Runeberg wants to focus upon is made clear by metric scansion. In the last line, supported by the first italicized, the only accent falls on the syllable *skyld* "guilt," not on the negative prefix *o-*. Although a number of minor points could be added in support of this argument, the case rests on this direct testimony from the author, Runeberg.

The interpretation of *Julqvällen* advanced here distinctly diverges from the ordinary perception of this "lesser epic poem," which has shown itself to be far more complex than anyone had previously suggested. A scholar with a biographical bent of mind might want to reestablish the presence of Maria Prytz, the young woman who, more than anyone else, awoke Eros in Runeberg during his middle years. The purpose of this study has merely been to present an interpretation of *Julqvällen* that considers the text, rather than the lines of development in Runeberg's *oeuvre.* In other words, arguments to the effect that this poem should be placed somewhere on a line of development leading from *Älgskyttarne* (1832, **The Elk Hunters**) to **Fänrik Ståls sägner** are misguided, and the assertion, which so many have made, that it is a disjointed composition, reflecting irrevocable tendencies in the poet's development, are barely short of an insult to the author, Runeberg. As previously indicated, if *Julqvällen* does anything, it increases the stature of Runeberg: Here he appears as a forerunner of a much later trend in Swedish literature, which reaches its culmination in the intricate mode of narration that is to be found in Eyvind Johnson's works. In conclusion, a presentation of the essential features of narrative technique that are evidenced in *Julqvällen* must be elaborated upon.

In *Julqvällen* the play with mirrors has been developed into a narrative technique that will be called *complementation.* Complementation works in such a way that, through repeated juxtapositions of the kind noted above, the reader eventually becomes aware of the fact that the characteristics of one character are to be attributed to another. Thus, it is by means of the text's making clear the unreliable nature of Pistol's yarns that the reader becomes aware of the dubious veracity of Augusta's romances, just as it is through Pistol's overt loss that the reader recognizes Augusta's. Complementation is quite easily stated in a more formal manner: Assuming that two characters, A and P, both have trait z, but that P also exhibits trait x; then, by the device of complementation, one may also attribute the trait x to A. It is important to note that complementation does not involve a development in A—for the trait x has latently been there all the time—but only that the narrator has chosen to present that trait to the reader in an oblique manner, which may even contradict the overt depiction of character A.

Runeberg's use of complementation, as demonstrated above, is a devious mode of narration not normally associated with him; tricky narrative is a modernist technique. In *Julqvällen* Runeberg stands forth as a modern writer. (pp. 1-9)

> *Kim Nilsson, "J. L. Runeberg as a Modern Writer: The Evidence of 'Julqvällen'," in* Scandinavian Studies, *Vol. 58, No. 1, Winter, 1986, pp. 1-9.*

FURTHER READING

Bysveen, Josef. "The Influence of James Macpherson's *Ossian* on Johan Ludvig Runeberg's *Kung Fjalar:* Some Notes." In *Aberdeen and the Enlightenment: Proceedings of a Conference Held at the University of Aberdeen,* edited by Jennifer J. Carter and Joan H. Pittock, pp. 350-56. Aberdeen: Aberdeen University Press, 1987.

> Demonstrates Runeberg's use of names, themes, and allusions drawn from James Macpherson's "Ossian" poetry.

Gosse, Edmund. "Runeberg." In his *Northern Studies,* pp. 135-73. London: Walter Scott Publishing Co., 1890.

> Reviews Runeberg's major works, praising him as "the greatest poet that has ever used the Swedish tongue." This essay was originally published in *Cornhill* magazine in 1878.

Magnusson, Eirikr. Preface to *King Fialar: A Poem in Five Songs,* by Johan Ludvig Runeberg, pp. ix-xx. London: J. M. Dent & Sons, 1912.

> Summarizes the plot of *King Fialar* and describes its theme as the "relation of Divine providence to the wayward will of man."

Adalbert Stifter

1805-1868

Austrian novelist and short story writer.

INTRODUCTION

Stifter is best known for his voluminous novel *Der Nachsommer* (*Indian Summer*), which has been praised for its beautiful and elaborate descriptions of nature. Linked by some critics to the Realist movement, Stifter was interested in recording everyday occurrences and the ordinary rhythms of life in almost photographic detail. While some critics have characterized Stifter's works as slow moving, he viewed them as a means of providing readers with an aesthetic as well as a moral education.

Stifter was born in the village of Oberplan, in Bohemia, to parents of German ancestry. After the death of his father, who earned a living by flax trading combined with small farming, the young Stifter became deeply attached to his mother, the uneducated daughter of a butcher. Through the generosity of his maternal grandfather, he was sent to school at the Benedictine monastery of Kremsmünster in 1818. Although he lacked the necessary formal preparation, he was admitted because his examiner, Father Placidius Hall, was impressed by the boy's attention to detail in the initial interview. Hall became Stifter's friend and benefactor, and later the model for one of his most sympathetic characters, the priest in the novella *Kalkstein* (*Limestone*). At Kremsmünster Stifter was trained in the classics, science, creative writing, and, as biographers have observed, was particularly influenced by the intellectual spirit governing the school—a blend of Enlightenment rationalism and tolerant Catholicism.

In 1826 Stifter began to study law in Vienna, but he did not earn a degree since he came to realize that his chief interest lay in mathematics and science. His lack of specialized training prevented his continuing in those fields, but his broad learning made him highly esteemed as a tutor and gained him entrance to the homes of the Viennese aristocracy. During this period, Stifter also began to write fiction, and in 1840 his first novella, *Der Condor* (*The Condor*) was published. From 1843 to 1846 he instructed the son of Klemens von Metternich, Austria's minister of foreign affairs, in mathematics and physics. He became supervisor for the elementary schools of Upper Austria at Linz in 1850, and, in spite of arduous administrative duties, continued to write. He retired in 1865 for reasons of ill health, and was in great mental and physical anguish during his last years. Stifter tried to cut his own throat in January of 1868; although unsuccessful in his suicide attempt, he died two days later.

Many of his short stories and novellas first appeared in magazines and literary journals, but were then revised and

published in anthologies. The first of these collections, *Studien,* contains among others *Abdias,* a sad tale of a North African Jew's failure to find happiness, and *Brigitta,* the story of a man torn between two loves. In 1853 another collection of short stories, *Bunte Steine* (*Colored Stones*), appeared, which contained two of his best works: *Limestone,* about the innocence of a simple country parson, and *Bergkristall* (*Rock Crystal*), which tells of two children lost in the Alps on Christmas Eve. In 1857 he finished his greatest novel, *Indian Summer,* a work that has been called "a strange vision of perfection." There, Stifter created a world that is compelling in its beauty and refinement and presents a picture not of what life is, but of what, according to the author, life should be. The book is set in the scenic area around Kremsmünster, at an estate called the House of Roses, which is filled with antiques, fine sculpture, and flowering plants—in short, a symbol of ordered perfection. Since the plot centers around the education and development of a young man, Heinrich Drendorf, it has often been described as a bildungsroman, or novel of education, and has been compared to Goethe's *Wilhelm Meister.* Heinrich is guided to wisdom and aesthetic discernment by the retired Risach, who is the owner of the estate, and who seems to be an older, wiser version of

Drendorf. The novel received mixed reviews upon publication, and, perhaps because the plot lacks conflict, was never popular. Stifter's last completed work, *Witiko,* is an epic tale about a struggle for the crown of medieval Bohemia.

Stifter's writing reflects the tradition of German country literature. He most often chose rural themes and stories about country people, meticulously set in their native surroundings, and he preferred to write about innocence rather than the darker side of life. Critics have noted that Stifter's stories often have a didactic, moralistic tone. Life is to be guided by reason, tradition, and the values of the family and the church. To stray from this path is to become a victim of one's emotions, which invites the most disastrous consequences. In general Stifter avoided writing directly about crises or catastrophes, focusing instead on small daily events whose importance is often overlooked. Scholars have pointed out that in *Indian Summer* the order of Risach's library, where nothing is out of place and books are immediately returned to their proper position, is in itself a model of reason and self-restraint. Thus the confluence of large and small matters leads to the growth and development of Heinrich and makes *Indian Summer* an outstanding bildungsroman.

Stifter's early stories were well received and brought him a measure of success, but even as early as 1853, in the preface to *Colored Stones,* he felt it necessary to defend himself against growing objections to his works. Many critics considered his detailed descriptions overly elaborate, and the works themselves too long. The writer and critic Friedrich Hebbel offered the crown of Poland to anyone who could finish *Indian Summer.* In addition, the lack of conflict and of involvement in the great issues of the day made his works seem boring and irrelevant to many readers. In the twentieth century there has been a renewed interest in Stifter's work, but he is still not without his detractors. Some are repelled by his creation of a world of static perfection and his didacticism. Georg Lukács regards Stifter as representative of "reactionary stagnation and obscurantist philistinism," which are values he associates with Fascism. Some find in his language and imagery a tension that can be interpreted as a fear that the world may not be ordered and rational. On the other hand, some readers are particularly attracted to his detachment from politics and his support of traditional values, and see in his artistic integrity "the final quintessence of beauty in human lives." Historical perspective has also allowed modern critics to study Stifter in the context of his era, the Biedermeier period, a time of reaction against the forces of change that were unleashed with the French Revolution. Finally, critics continue to praise the sensitivity to nature, attention to detail, and respect for the integrity of characters demonstrated in his works.

PRINCIPAL WORKS

The Condor (novella) 1840
*Studien. 6 vols. (novellas) 1844-50
   [*Rural Life in Austria and Hungary* (partial translation) 1850]

*Bunte Steine (novellas) 1853
Der Nachsommer (novel) 1857
   [*Indian Summer,* 1985]
Witiko (novel) 1865-67
Erzählungen (short stories and novellas) 1869
Sämtliche Werke (novels, novellas, short stories, and letters) 1904
Brigitta (novella) 1957
Limestone and Other Stories (novellas) 1968
Brigitta; with Abdias; Limestone; and The Forest Path (novellas) 1990

*Studien and *Bunte Steine* are anthologies that contain revised versions of novellas that appeared earlier in literary journals and magazines. The exception is *Katzensilber,* a novella written expressly for *Bunte Steine.*

CRITICISM

Uland E. Fehlau (essay date 1940)

[*In the following excerpt, Fehlau focuses on Stifter's increasingly complex use of symbols.*]

There is much more symbolism in Adalbert Stifter's works than the average reader suspects, for it occurs at times in such a highly developed form that it often escapes one altogether at one's first reading. In his early works, of course, his symbolic language bears the mark of an unpractised hand, but as Stifter's technique and style developed, also his semeiotic powers evolved and grew, until they reached their highest stage in *Der Nachsommer,* where we find an astonishing variety of symbols.

The symbolism in Stifter's first works is quite crude and limits itself exclusively to the weather. Moreover, it reveals the influence of Romanticism on the young writer, for the conception of nature on which this early "weather-symbolism" is based has Romantic rather than Biedermeier coloring. The writers of the Biedermeier period retained the Romanticists' enthusiastic and almost religious admiration of nature, but they would have none of the belief, that man's ego and nature could experience a fusion. They looked upon man and nature as two separate and distinct manifestations, running parallel courses and being in perfect harmony by virtue of the same divine will and personality reflected by both. Nature can, accordingly, serve man as a guide, wherein he may read, or attempt to read God's will, and thus learn the degree of ethical perfection he has attained.

Stifter expresses this idea as follows (*Zwei Schwestern*):

> Sie (die Natur) ist das Kleid Gottes, den wir anders, als in ihr, nicht su sehen vermögen, sie ist die Sprache, wodurch er su uns spricht, sie ist der Ausdruck der Majestat und der Ordaung . . . (IV).

And, in order to get a more complete picture of the typically Biedermeier conception, we might add a passage from a letter of Feuchtersleben, written to Karl Mayer on April 3, 1840:

> Von jeher hielt ich es für die schönere Aufgabe des . . . Dichters, mit treuer Liebe sich der Natur hinzugeben und durch einfache klare Abspiegelung ihres Details die Harmonie zwischen ihr und dem Geiste des Menschen unabsichtlich darzustellen.

When we compare this conception of nature with that expressed in Stifter's first works, we recognize the influence of Romanticism, especially with regard to his views on nature, for the idea on which his weather-symbolism is founded resembles somewhat the Romantic notion of nature's fusion with man's ego. Stifter applies the "pathetic fallacy" of giving nature the power to express emotions sympathetic with those of man. When man is sad, so is nature; and when he is happy, she too smiles for joy. The two are, therefore, practically united. The description of Gustav's first meeting with Cornelia (*Der Condor,* 1840), after the latter's mad flight into the skies, may serve as an example:

> . . . (Gustav) trat . . . an das Fenster und sah hinaus. Es war draussen still, wie drinnen; ein traurig blauer Himmel sog über reglose grüne Bäume. . . .

He stands dejectedly at the window for awhile, but when he sees her crying and realizes that she repents of her folly, he is overcome with joy and exclaims:

> . . . wo ist die Schlange am Fenster hin? Wo der drückende blaue Himmel?—Ein lachendes Gewölbe sparng über die Welt und die grünen Bäume wiegten ein Meer von Glanz und Schimmer'. (I).

Stifter did not long employ this first crude type, and although we find a few isolated examples in some of his other early works (e.g., *Die Mappe,* II; *Abdias,* II), already in his second story (*Feldblumen,* 1840) a development becomes noticeable. The "pathetic fallacy," to be sure, is still evident, but the weather now begins to assume the additional function of expressing symbolically a release of emotional tension within the individual. As yet, however, the description of a storm for instance is only a supplementary aid in conveying to the reader the individual's soul-struggle by the degree of violence perceptible in the raging elements.

Thus the reader has a fuller conception of the fierce battle of emotions taking place in Albrecht's breast—after seeing his fiancée in the arms of a stranger—when the former says (*Feldblumen*):

> . . . da kam der Wind geflogen und der Donner, rollend über alle Wipfel des Gartens; grosse Tropfen fielen, und somit löste sich die Stille am Himmel und auch in mir. Ein frisches Rauschen wühlte in den Bäumen und mischte Grün und Silber durch einander, und in mir raffte sich ein fester, Börniger Entachluss empor und gab mir meine Schnellkraft wieder, nämlich der Entschluss, sogleich absureisen . . . ein prachtvoller Regen rauschte nieder (I).

The whole passage assists in describing the soul-stirring conflict raging in Albrecht's heart, of course, but the real symbolism lies in the words "(ein) Rauschen wühlte in den Bäumen," "mischte Grün und Silber durch einander," and "(ein) Regen rauschte nieder." In these expressions Stifter conveys the thought that Albrecht has not really experienced full relief from the emotional tension gripping his heart at the time—which might have prepared the way for a state of calm resignation—and that his whole inner being was still in a condition of turmoil and unrest, though the original tension was broken.

Stifter's account of the calm, reconciled manner in which Felix (*Das Haidedorf,* 1840) receives his fiancée's rejection to his proposal of marriage may throw a light upon the distinction made here. The whole occurrence is bound up and interwoven with sympathetic nature. Both Felix and nature have been going through a rather contracted period of suspense, Felix, while waiting for the reply to his proposal, and nature, while awaiting a delayed relief from drought. The tension of both is released together. And from the symbolic language used to describe the alleviating and refreshing rain, we learn of Felix' ethical composure in his resignation:

> Des andern Morgens, als sich die Augen aller Menschen öffneten, war der ganze Haidehimmel grau, und ein dichter, sanfter Landregen träufelte nieder. Alles, alles war nun gelöset. . . . (I).

It will perhaps have been noticed that the basic conception of nature evident in the above quotation is slightly different from that underlying the symbolism in *Der Condor.* Nature and man are still very much in harmony, but there is no longer an idea of union present. Stifter is here beginning to renounce his early leanings toward the Romanticists' conception, and to reveal himself as typically Biedermeier. And with each succeeding story it becomes clearer that he views both as distinct and separate manifestations, both reflecting the same divine will and therefore in harmony.

So far Stifter has employed nature as an additional aid in describing emotional conditions existing, and release from emotional tension occurring in the individual. He now lets his descriptions of natural phenomena serve a third purpose: to prognosticate future events. A typical example is the portrayal of the night on which Graf Jodok (*Die Narrenburg,* 1841) returns to his castle to find his wife betrayed by his own brother:

> Es war eine heisse Julinacht; um den gansen Berg hing ein düsteres, elektrisches Geheimnis, und seine Zinnen trennten sich an manchen Stellen gar nicht von den schwarzen Wolken. Die weissen tröstlichen Säulen des Parthenon konnte ich gar nicht sehen, aber um die dunklen Hügelkamm, der sie mir deckte, ging suweilen ein sanftes, bläuliches Leuchten der Gewitter . . . durch die hohen Glaswände, die den Gang von dem indischen Garten trennten, schimmerten seitweise die lautlosen Blitze des Himmels (II).

The foreboding weather prepares the reader for some catastrophe, and since even the "weissen tröstlichen Säulen" of the Parthenon are invisible, he suspects that there is no chance of averting it. The reference to lightning is especially significant symbolically, for it alludes to the fatal passion responsible for the brother's shameful transgression against the moral law. Lightning, in fact, often connotes the baser passions in Stifter's writings. This application conforms to the author's conception that the passions in man correspond to the destructive forces in nature. Thus, for instance, Ronald's (*Der Hochwald,* 1841) impetuous, passionate nature is symbolically depicted by the remark, that he secretly watches his beloved from "einer Föhre, die der Blitz einst zerschlug" (I). At another time his ethically discordant inner being finds symbolic expression in the description of a blighted and barren cliff, from which he shot down a bird of prey:

> . . . nichts war dort ersichtlich, als das Gewirre
> der bleichen herabgestürzten Bäume . . . (I).

Stifter's prognosticating nature-symbolism reaches its highest development in the paragraphs that prepare the reader for the scene of the destroyed castle, the home of the sisters in *Der Hochwald.* Notice the words "Fahlroth," "blutig," and "Dämmerdunkel" in the description of the forest on the day the girls see only a cloud of smoke in place of their home:

> Wie verändert war der Wald!—Bis in's fernste
> Blau sog sich das Fahlroth und Gelb des Herb-
> stes, wie schwache blutige Streifen durch das
> Dämmerdunkel der Nadelwälder gehend. . . .
> (I).

A few days later, immediately before the sisters finally see the charred and smouldering remains of their home, the forest's condition accentuates the ominous feeling of some imminent catastrophe, and the reader gets a symbolic picture of the carnage and destruction that have taken place at the castle in the expressions "Verwüstung," "bluthroth," and "schlapp herabhingen":

> Im Emporsteigen kounten sie recht die Verwüs-
> tungen des Frostes betrachten, wie noch rückge-
> bliebene Blätter rostbraun oder blutroth oder
> vergelbt am Strauchwerde hingen, und wie dis
> Farrenkräuter und die Blätter, die Boeren und
> die aufgeschoss'nen Schäfte gleichsam gesotten
> und schlapp herabhingen (I).

Stifter here prepares the reader for the tragic story of the siege and fall of the castle, together with the death of its inmates, by describing the destructive effect on nature of a heavy frost. He thereby once more calls to our attention his belief in the harmony between man and nature. The sympathetic bond connecting both is here part of his conception, even as it was in the beginning, but the idea that each runs his own separate course is also discernible. The two courses, to be sure, may be parallel, and in fact always are, as long as man does not blur the divine spark within him by giving way to the baser passions. When this happens, man falls out of harmony with nature and a clash becomes evident. And the estrangement continues until man has overcome his passions and has regained ethical composure. Then man himself once more reflects the divine will and thus enjoys his pristine harmony with nature.

According to Stifter, therefore, the normal relationship between man and nature is that of harmony. It is the basic conception out of which his symbolism grows. (pp. 239-43)

In *Das alte Siegel* (1843) Stifter begins to extend the scope of his forecasting symbolism. Not only the experiences of nature, but also other symbols serve to foreshadow the hero's moral fall. For example, immediately after Hugo's fateful meeting with Cöleste's old servant in the church, the rays of the sun—a later favorite symbol of ethical well-being—suddenly no longer shine through the windows (III). Then, directly after Hugo has seen Cöleste for the first time, a poor crippled beggar sits down beside him. The appearance of this unfortunate fellow is so unexpected and the presentation of physical deformity so unusual in Stifter's writings, that his coming into contact with Hugo at this point must serve to symbolize Hugo's subsequent crippled moral condition. (p. 246)

Notice how gently and carefully Stifter symbolizes Hugo's offence against the precepts of "das alte Siegel" he had vowed to observe! He is standing in front of the fateful church, waiting for Cöleste's carriage to take him for the first time to her home, when a small bell begins to ring:

> . . . es klang, wie jenes Morgenglöcklein, da er
> vom Vaterhause scheiden musste. (III.).

And now the bell rings as he is about to leave the rigorous standard of conduct prescribed for him in the old seal.

Finally, after Hugo has seen Cöleste for the last time and is riding away from her castle, the terrible hopelessness and emptiness of his future life find expression in the statement:

> . . . und neben ihm säuselte das dürre, herbetli-
> che Gras (III).

In *Die Mappe meines Urgrossvaters* (though first written in 1841, it was repeatedly revised and expanded over a period of years) Stifter's symbolic language shows an additional development, for here for the first time he treats the entire story symbolically. Moreover, in *Die Mappe* we find more types of symbols than in any previous work, although those taken from nature still predominate.

The lengthy description of the ice-phenomenon introduces us to the underlying theme, and in fact presents the whole story of the Doctor's ethical breakdown and recovery in symbolic language. And since this experience of the Doctor grew out of his association with, and affection for Margarita, the chapter in which the ice-phenomenon is described properly and significantly carries the title "Margarita," although the greater part has nothing directly to do with her. That the Doctor will not only recover from the terrible shock to his soul of his attempt at suicide but will even attain greater ethical perfection thereafter, we find predicted in the remarkable recovery of the trees after the ice had bent and injured them severely (see III).

The house the Doctor is having built serves as a symbol of his ethical condition. He begins it even before he meets Margarita, but progress is slow, even as is his own development. And after he has received his setback, progress on the house also stops; but when he has finally fully recovered and attained perfect ethical well-being, we learn:

> Das Haus steht nunmehr fertig, und die Sonne
> scheint auf sein Dach hernieder . . . (II).

In **Die Mappe** there are passages, remarkably subtle in their symbolism, that describe and contrast the Doctor and Margarita with regard to temper of soul. An excellent example, which at the same time shows Stifter's unusual style, is the following description of the Doctor's proposal to Margarita:

> In den Holzschlägen wachsen verschiedene Blumen gemischt und oft seltenere und gewiss schönere, als man sie auf gewöhnlichen Wiesen zu finden vermöchte.—Da fragte ich Margarita, ob sie mich recht liebe.—Wir standen vor einer Grasstelle, wo die hohen, dusserst dünnen Schäftchen aus derselben emporstanden und oben ein Flinselwerk trugen, grau oder slibern, in weichem die Käfer summten, oder Fliegen und Schmetterlinge spielten. Aus dem Holzschlage ragte mancher einseine Baum hervor, der wieder emporgewachsen war; und jenseits, von ferne herüber, scharte der Blaue Duft das Kirmwalden, der gans ruhig war . . . —Margarita, als sie meine Frags vernommen hatte, schlug die Augenlider über die sehr schönen braunen Augen herab, seh im die Schäftchen nieder, wurde gans giüh im Angesichte und schüttelte leise das Haupt (II).

The "hohen, äusserst dünnen Schäftchen" upon which Margarita looks as she blushingly nods her head give us a symbolic picture of Margarita's extremely delicate ethical nature, which later shrank from the Doctor's demonstration of passionate jealousy. As contrasted with this we have the depiction of the Doctor's subsequent moral breakdown and recovery in the representation of the trees that had been disfigured by the storm, but have luxuriantly sprouted anew. These two features of the central theme are the principal factors underlying most of the symbolism of **Die Mappe,** for in this story Stifter is primarily concerned with tracing the ethical development of an individual toward the perfection residing potentially in every human being.

Man must, however, fight his way to his exalted state, he must often suffer great hardships and heartaches before he can conquer his passions and bring harmony into his soul. The story of Margarita's father shows this clearly. And, of course, the Doctor himself experienced how difficult it is to realize man's ethical potentialities. He too had to feel the full destructive force of the passions before attaining man's highest but proper state.

From the very beginning of the story there are symbolic references to the Doctor's moral degradation. We have mentioned several already. Others occur in connection with Margarita and show that the experience is tied up with her. Such an example follows the passage which presents the second exchange of vows between the two. It again takes place out in nature. And after Margarita has reassured the Doctor of her love and the latter has vowed to love her always, even into eternity, the author calls attention to the dried-up grass at their feet and thereby not

only reminds us of "die Wandelbarkeit des Menschen" (see **Witiko,** X), but also foreshadows the hero's imminent transgression against his vain boast:

> Wir blieben noch langer stehen, schwiegen und saben in das verdorrte Gras nieder (II).

The clearest symbolic picture of the Doctor's ethical disruption and restoration we find in the unfortunate accident a woodman suffered almost simultaneously with the Doctor's attempt at suicide. A falling tree mangled the woodman's leg terribly, just as the Doctor's desperate experience wounded and tore his soul. For months the woodman's condition is most deplorable, but gradually he regains the use of his limb, so that after three years—when the Doctor's ethical being is also sound again—we are glad to hear!

> So steht und gedeiht Alles. Meine Kranken genesen. Der untere Aschacher, deuse Fuss so fürchterlich geschält war, geht wieder lustig und krückenfrei harum (II).

Stifter's **Bunte Steine** (1853) really contain comparatively little symbolism (aside from the individual titles); but his **Nachsommer** (1857), on the other hand, treats almost everything symbolically: Heinrich's love for Natalie, his esthetic development, the unhappy relationship between young Risach and the girl Mathilde, the unique friendship between these as old people, and many other things. Hence Heinrich's growing love for Natalie is never stated outright, but is merely indicated in a number of ways. For example, when Heinrich first sees Natalie, he decides that the human face after all presents the best subject for a drawing (VI); when he sees her the second time (in the theatre) he begins to act according to this conviction (VI); the third time he says:

> Ich wollte lesen oder schreiben und that es dann doch wieder nicht (VI).

And after he has been introduced to her, he goes to his room and is "sehr traurig" (VI); the next morning he passes the marble statue on the stairway and for the first time refers to it as "die Muse" (VI); when one morning at the Sternenhof he watches Natalie walking across the yard until she is out of view, he thinks: "Jetzt war die Gegend sehr leer" (VI); and finally, after he has walked some distance across the fields at her side, he says:

> Ich ging sehr split schlafen, las aber nicht mehr, wie ich es sonst in jeder Nacht gewohnt war, sondern blieb auf meinern Lager liegen und konnte sehr lange den Schlummer nicht finden (VII).

Such are the expressions that convey to the reader the growing love of Heinrich for Natalie, but not until Heinrich's actual proposal is the word "love" itself used in connection with either Natalie or Heinrich.

The marble statue in Risach's home plays an important rôle as a symbol. The statue itself represents the highest perfection of art; therefore, when Heinrich learns fully to appreciate its unusual beauty, the reader realizes he has reached his majority in esthetic appreciation. In addition, however, it symbolises the ethical purity of the love between Heinrich and Natalie. That explains why Heinrich thinks of Natalie when the statue suggests Nausicaa to him (VIII), and that is why the author expressly has Heinrich and Natalie pass this statue on their wedding day (VIII). Furthermore, Heinrich's annual trips into the hills, each successive one taking him closer to the highest peaks, testify to his steady advancement in esthetic perfection. Finally, the growth and blossoming of the Cereus Peruvianus under the necessary care at the Asperhof typify Heinrich's ethical progress under Risach's influence. The author accentuates the connection between these two experiences by letting the cactus blossom on Heinrich's wedding day.

The roses in *Der Nachsommer*, of course, are important symbols, but they apply to Risach and Mathilde rather than to Heinrich and Natalie. Risach himself says that he planted them because they are "eine Jugenderinnerung" (VI), and a "Merkmal unserer Trennung und Vereinigung" (VIII). Many years earlier the two young impetuous lovers, Risach and Mathilde, had professed their love for each other among the roses at Mathilde's home, and so they were reminders of that time. But the significance of the roses at the Asperhof is much more far-reaching than that, for they serve to symbolize the perfect, ethical love of the old couple in contrast to the passionate love of their youth. The extraordinary state of cleanliness characterizing Risach's roses bears this out:

> Auch das Grün der Blätter fiel mir auf. Es war sehr rein gehalten, und kein bei Rosen öfter, als bel andern Pflanzen, vorkommender übelstand der grünen Blätter und keine der häufigen Krankheiten kam mir es Gesichte. Kein verdorrtas oder durch Raupen verfressenes oder durch ihr Spinnen verkrümmten Blatt war es erblicken. Selbst das bei Rosen so gerne sich einnistende Ungesiefer fehlte. . . . Die Sonne, die noch immer gleichsam einsig auf dieses Haus schien, gab den Rosen und den grünen Blättern derselben gleichsam goldene und feurige Farben (VI).

The bushes show no signs of being "verdorrt," "zerfressen," or "verkrümmt"—symbolic description of "Unsittlichkeit"—since this is totally foreign to the inhabitants of the Asperhof. Therefore the sun—the symbol of ethical well-being—shines solely upon this house. This is not the only time the rays of the sun single out the Rosenhof, for at another time we are told:

> Re (das Haus) war, da schon ein grosser Thail des Landes mit Ausnahme das Rohrberger Kirchthurmes im Schatten lag, noch hall beleuchtet und sah mit einladendem, schimmerndem Weiss in das Grau und Blau der Landschaft hinsus (VI).

Stifter depicts the passionate love of young Risach and Mathilde and the unethical conduct of both as a result of their strong emotions with many symbolic flourishes. Even the season of the year in which their love suddenly breaks forth has a deeper significance. "Der Sommer war beinahe vergangen," we are told immediately before the two profess their love for each other, "und der Herbst stand bevor" (VIII). And for these two, to be sure, summer really was gone, for in their love-life neither one was ever permitted to enjoy anything but a "Nachsommer." That, in fact, is the real tragedy behind the oft-quoted symbolic description of the two in their old age:

> Sie hielten sich noch einen Augenblick bel den Händen, wihrend ein leichtes Morgenlüftchen einige Blätter der abgeblühten Rosen su ihren Füssen wehte (IV).

Much more interesting, however, is the passage describing Alfred's actions during the time the young lovers were left alone to profess their love:

> . . . Alfred war unter den Bäumen damit beschäftigt gewesen, einige Täfeichen, die an denstämmen hingen und schmutzig geworden waren, su reinigen, dann las er abgefallenes halbreifes Obat zusammen, lagte es in Häufchen und sonderte das bessere von dem schlechteren ab (VIII).

While Risach is betraying the confidence placed in him by making love to his young charge and is thus spotting his otherwise clean record, Alfred is cleaning the spotted and dirty tablets in the orchard and is gathering the half-ripe fruit from the ground.

The symbolism is even clearer in the story Alfred tells Risach and Mathilde immediately after the latter have had a chance to exchange vows of love and to seal their pledge with a kiss:

> Er erzähite uns, dass die Namen der Bäume, die auf weisse Blechtäfeichen geschrieben sind . . . von den Leuten oft sehr verunreinigt würden, dass man sie alle putzen solle, und dass der Vater den Befehl erlassen solle, dass sin Jedpr, der einen Baum wäscht, putst oder Dergleichen, oder der sonst eine Arbeit bei ihn verrichtet, sich sehr in Acht su nehmen habe, dass er das Täfeichen nicht bespritst oder sonst eine Unreinigkeit darauf bringt. Dann erzählte er uns, dass er schöne Borsdorfer Äpfel gefunden habe, weiche durch einen Insektenstich au einer früheren, beinahe vollkommenen Reife godischen seden. Er habe sie am Stamme des Baumes zusammen geiegt und werde den Vater bitten, sie su untersuchen, ob man sie nicht doch brauchen könne (VIII).

The language of this passage is as striking as it is unexpected, coming as it does directly after Risach has bespattered and soiled his honor by thoughtlessly falling a prey to his baser emotions. By his unseemly action, moreover, he has arrested the ethical growth of his pupil, though the "sting" of passion has hastened Mathilde's physical maturity, as the description of the "Insektenstich" here implies and the context substantiates. The picture contains a ray of hope, however, for both may still be found useful and curable, though unhappily stunted in the development of their inner being.

After the young lovers have once again exchanged various signs of their love without Alfred's knowledge, the latter unwittingly describes for his mother, in symbolic language, what has actually happened:

> Alfred erzählte, was wir in dem Garten gethan

batten, und berichtete der Mutter, dass wir ver-
dorrte und unbrauchbare Blätter von den
Rosenzweigen, die an den Latten des Garten-
hauses angebunden sind, herab genommen hät-
ten (VIII).

The reference to the rosebushes, destined to become very
significant to both in the future, is interesting. The bushes
are not yet miraculously free from all signs of weakness
or decay—unlike those at the Asperhof—but they, like Risach and Mathilde, are in the process of being cleaned, of
reaching perfection.

These examples may suffice to show how this novel
abounds in symbolism. Stifter here throws open all the
stops of his semieiotic powers and shows himself a finished
master in the art of symbolic language. It is a far cry from
the crude weather-symbolism of *Der Condor* to the highly
polished type of *Der Nachsommer,* from the application
to man's experience of one of the natural phenomena, to
the great variety of symbols, and the expanse of their
scope, in the work discussed above; and yet, in all the
works treated so far, nature has been the basic source of
the symbolism. That is largely due to the fact that Stifter
has always been interested thus far in the ethical and esthetic development of the individual. And since man can
accurately gauge his degree of perfection by comparing
himself with the divine image reflected by nature, Stifter
chose nature and the natural phenomena as his prime
source of symbols, as long as the individual was his main
interest. In *Witiko* (1868), however, he has a totally different purpose and, therefore, his style and technique also
differ, for in *Witiko* he wishes to depict the working of
"das Sittengesets" in the history of a people or nation. The
development of the individual, accordingly, does not concern him. Moreover, since each person's relationship with
nature varies according to the degree of perfection each
has, it is not possible to use nature as a symbol for a whole
people. Furthermore, with the mature Stifter nature no
longer plays such an important rôle, for, as Paul Meyer
says:

Dem reifen Dichter ist die Natur nichts als ein
Objekt unter andern . . . dem ist die Natur nur
noch Raum, worin "das sanfte Gesets" sich
auswirkt . . .

Finally, since the degree of success of the moral law depends upon human agencies, what little symbolism *Witiko*
contains is usually connected with people in some way.

The rather unusual and very plain leather clothing of the
hero, for example, typifies his unpretentious nature. Because of its significance, therefore, Witiko wears this leather suit every time he is subjected to a test of character, or
whenever he is consciously taking a step forward in his
general development. The gray color of his horse—a very
modest color—strengthens the application. In fact, colors
in general play a symbolic part in this novel; not to the extent, of course, that whenever a color is mentioned it has
its special significance; but on certain occasions and in the
case of certain characters, the bright, flaming colors of
their clothing point to their immorality, and the quiet,
modest colors of the apparel of others represent their ethical well-being.

This is most clearly seen in the case of Wladizlaw, who at
the beginning of the story affected such flaming colors that
the author calls him "der Scharlachreiter" (XX). But
later, after he has been Duke for a while and has become
mild and "sittlich," we are told:

Er war, wie schon oft, in ein dunkelbraunes Ge-
wand gekieldst, hatte eine braune Haube ohne
Feder, trug ein dunkles Waffenhamd und an der
Seite in einer dunkelbraunen steinlosen Scheide
ein Schwert (X).

The reference to the absence of stones in the scabbard of
his sword is important, since Nacerat and most of the
leading men among those who revolted against the rightful duke had many precious stones in their arms and harness, haughty testimony of their selfish pride and arrogance.

Then there is the rose that winds its course through the
long novel, leading the way at times, and at others reward-
ing the hero for his accomplishments. Its significance in
Witiko, accordingly, is quite different from that which it
has in *Der Nachsommer,* but it is, nevertheless, a symbol,
as Witiko himself says: "und sie werden mir immer ein
Sinnbild bleiben" (XI).

Finally, among the champions of "das Sittengesetz" are
the insignificant and very humble "Männer von dem
Walde," testifying by their presence, that God prefers the
humble to the proud as his instruments, and that the
moral law will always be victorious, no matter how unpromising the possibilities of success appear. And because
right and justice, the basic qualities of Stifter's conception
of this law, speak for these forest people, it is unnecessary
for them to cry and shout, when going into battle, as the
rebels do. Consequently, their calm, dignified, determined
behavior, before and during battle, in itself represents,
symbolically, the eternal operation of "das Sittengesetz."
(pp. 247-55)

*Uland E. Fehlau, "Symbolism in Adalbert
Stifter's Works," in* The Journal of English
and Germanic Philology, *Vol. XXXIX, No. 2,
1940, pp. 239-55.*

Alan Holske (essay date 1941)

[*In this excerpt, Holske places Stifter in historical context by linking him to the crisis of values that colored the
Biedermeier period in Austria.*]

A few years ago Hermann Pongs recommended [in "Zur
Bürgerkultur des Biedermeier," *Dichtung und Volkstum,*
XXXVI (1935)] that greater attention be paid to the relation between the Biedermeier Period (1815-1848) and the
later nineteenth century, and set the problem of showing
how the German middle classes, who had still possessed
culture in the Biedermeier Period, had later so readily
abandoned it and plunged into the pursuit of wealth.
Pongs had in mind the major developments of the latter
nineteenth century: the rapid collaborative advance of
technology and industry, beginning around 1840, had by
the early 1870's given German life the character of a bewildering "headlong rush of history in the making;" swept

along by events, the German middle classes strove to realize startling new possibilities of acquiring material comforts and economic power; they willingly accepted social and economic forces as the determinants of life and embraced the eudaemonic faith that contemporary civilization was the realization of a benevolent purpose immanent in the historical process. For it seemed—and this observation constitutes a preliminary answer to the question posed by Pongs—that facts had outdistanced the capacity of inherited ideas to interpret them; society, transformed by rapid economic development, had outrun traditional culture.

It seems likely, however, that the discongruity between social practice and the values of traditional culture, which became apparent in the latter nineteenth century, had originated in the Biedermeier Period. Implicit in the situation that confronted the middle classes at this time was, first and foremost, the task of welding the various traditions to which they had fallen heir into a common culture of middle class stamp; their second task, immediately related to the first, was to find common principles for dealing effectively with the problems in social and economic organization posed by the times. But the middle classes were able neither to unify their diversified cultural inheritance nor to take firmly and collectively in hand the incipient social and economic movements of the time and guide them toward specific, selected ends. (pp. 256-57)

Even in the first half of the eighteenth century, when the basic tendencies of the standard middle class culture of the whole century had been established, there had been little active reciprocal influence between ideas and social and political practice. The German Enlightenment had, to be sure, possessed a sense of corporate life and a definite social morality; accordingly, the culture of the German middle classes had been founded on the central concept that man is naturally moral, philanthropic, and a dutiful member of the family group, and a balance had been struck between the individual and practical collective purposes; the leaders of the Enlightenment, particularly in France, may even have desired reformatory social and political action. The culture of the German middle classes, however, had stopped at the passive recognition of society in principle; questions of state and of practical social policy had been ranged beyond the jurisdiction of middle class thought, and no direct criticism had been levelled against the social hierarchy or the contemporary state; the spokesmen of middle class criticism had confined themselves to castigating passion, vice, and the foibles of human nature (the Aesopic fable, the Saxon Comedy, the early bourgeois tragedy), or they had satirized the ostentatious and self-seeking imitator of court practice and the ways of the great (Liscow, Rabener). (pp. 259-60)

But the diverse cultural traditions to which the middle classes [of the Biedermeier period] now fell heir had grown up in vastly different circumstances, and they generally failed to provide the means of recognizing the true nature and extent of the problems that were to be faced and solved; still less could tradition offer the middle classes incentives or guidance to collective action suited to the nature of their present circumstances. For that reason the

breach that had opened between culture and society in the Enlightenment and which had widened in the latter half of the eighteenth century, was not closed in the nineteenth century. As the tendencies that had produced the French Revolution, long held in abeyance in Germany, at length grew active, German society seemed to develop a mechanical energy of its own; the trend toward a uniform, collective order—the essential fact of the Biedermeier Period—went on, assuming the character of a relentless, collective necessity. In these circumstances the middle classes could do little more than reappraise their cultural traditions and retain such principles and beliefs as did not conflict with the practical exigencies of their situation. For the most part the middle classes lacked the prime essentials for the truly creative expression of principles and ideas in their social institutions and organization; they could do little more than make supplementary adjustments of thought to fit material developments that were already occurring. Events, since the middle classes were not generally equipped to anticipate or direct them, began to outrun ideas. The Biedermeier Period saw the beginning of the hasty adaptation to exigent circumstance, the continual readjustment of thought to follow changing conditions, which characterize the cultural and intellectual history of the later nineteenth century.

Treating a writer of the Biedermeier Period involves showing how he reacted to the social pressures of his time, how he viewed the problem which the middle classes faced, and on which part of the varied cultural tradition of the middle classes he relied for his solution. The development of Adalbert Stifter (1805-1868) can best be understood in his relation to the crisis of the Biedermeier Period. Following his first painful awareness of the problem of society, his early stories record his recognition of the claims that organized society may make upon the individual and attest [to] his ultimate reliance upon the views and values of the middle class culture of the Enlightenment as guides to an ideal middle class order. (pp. 262-63)

In the few letters extant from [Stifter's] early period there are strong suggestions of certain standard gestures and attitudes identified with the tradition of subjectivism, particularly a whimsical and ironic humor in the Sternian manner and a humorous self-deprecation. These qualities seem to imply personal uncertainty on Stifter's part and an incipient distrust of his vague and eccentric personal wishes and of the impulses that had made him refuse a stable position in society. These letters and his first, somewhat anomalous tale—to be considered below—in which self-assertive individualism and the claim of society upon the individual are both repudiated, indicate that Stifter was in a painfully contradictory state of mind. Critical of society and the discipline it would enforce, he was also distrustful of the inner world of vague aspiration and fugitive longing. (pp. 265-66)

The way out of the impasse led toward a rational discipline embodied in an order that stood firmly and permanently above "the turmoil of conflicting opinions." The crisis of the Biedermeier Period, precipitated by the social developments that had followed the Napoleonic Era, ended with the repudiation of the attitudes toward life implicit in the traditions of irrationalism and subjectivism; the view was generally accepted that the individual could most fully invest his life with meaning when he made it conform with or express a group discipline; the priority of such discipline over idiocratic and eccentric forces within the individual was generally assumed. (p. 267)

The cultural crisis of the Biedermeier Period constitutes the background against which Stifter's development can most easily be observed and understood; that crisis resulted in a painful shift from traditional subjective attitudes toward life to recognition of a social or moral discipline of collective uniformity. The moralism of the conservatives enforced quiescence and self-repression on the individual; moreover, in many instances, exemplified by Stifter, older cultural traditions and habits of thought, originating in the static society of the past, prevented full recognition of the essential problems and movements of the nineteenth century, even when their existence had been sensed; this resulted in an archaic interpretation of life, irrelevant to the contemporary period and of little value as a solution of the problem of adapting the best part of the cultural tradition to a uniform middle class social order, such as was taking form.

Stifter's early personal experience . . . conformed to the characteristic pattern of the cultural crisis; wavering between two contradictory attitudes Stifter had been sceptical both of society and also of the inner impulsion that made him withdraw from it; the uncertainty typical of the crisis is reflected in Stifter's first published tale, *The Condor (Der Kondor)*, which implies strong distrust of vigorous, self-assertive individualism, but at the same time expresses a longing to break away from the restraints of social discipline and seek solitary and subjective fulfillments. The self-assertive and high-spirited Cornelia in *The Condor* is dominated by a thirst for action and experience, symbolized somewhat grotesquely in her wilful participation in a balloon ascension. Cornelia acquires a certain resemblance to the demonic creatures of profane and destructive passion in the middle class literature of the eighteenth century, the Millwoods, Marwoods and their ilk, when she invades the privacy of a young painter's heart and prematurely awakens his dormant eroticism; by this insensitive self-assertion she shatters their common hopes and hinders the practical, marital and social fulfillment of their love. The young painter flees the whited sepulchres of Europe and repairs symbolically to the haunts of the condor (the balloon in which Cornelia had made her ascension had been called the *Condor!*): "Far, far away in the ancient mountains of the Chilean Andes strode an unknown man, strong and contemptuous, seeking new Heavens for his surging, turbulent, thirsting, primally innocent heart."

Motifs common in the period of subjectivism and a certain sentimentality are detectable in this tale; the hero escapes the restraints of society and the dissatisfactions of social life by fleeing into the purity of nature, which is approached by means of feeling and which in turn offers the malcontent subjectivist assuagements and fulfillments that society cannot give; in *The Condor* the contemporary motif of flight from Europe in search of "the spiritual repose of the good man" is combined with the motif of escape.

The same escapist longing informs the tale *The Village on the Heath (Das Haidedorf)*; Faust-like, the malcontent subjectivist who is the hero has made trial of all that the great world can offer, "but through everything he had won—through knowledge and achievements, amid people and possessions—it seemed always as if from a remote distance something were luminously beckoning, like bright serenity and gentle solitude." But the hero's longing for calm and for assuagement of his escapist nostalgia can be realized only when he reverses the bold upward course of the subjectivist Faust and turns back from the great world to a very small world of rustic simplicity and purity, and he therefore elects to spend his life in the village on the heath among the innocent peasant folk from whom he sprung.

In this tale flight into the purity of nature is represented as withdrawal into limited and placid domesticity, declared characteristic of the conservative literature of the time, and into a simple untroubled life in a rustic setting. Stifter indicates that not only rural nature, but also rustic life reflect the universe and symbolize the transcendental, which is vaguely apprehended through feeling. However, this conception of nature is not peculiar to the Biedermeier Period; it seems rather to be a survival in the nineteenth century of a traditional conception that can be traced back into the eighteenth century, when rural nature had symbolized the positive aspect of a sharp antithesis between culture and nature, city and country, society and the good life. W. Bietak and many of the Biedermeier commentators have not paid sufficient heed to the long idyllic tradition behind the Biedermeier idyll, of which Jean Paul is not the founder but rather the representative; it should not be stated that the literary representation of "pure being" was typical of the conservative quietists among Biedermeier writers without also showing that the literary representation of pure being had originally been due to a major factor in the cultural situation of the eighteenth century—the critical attitude toward society and the revulsion from it, which had alienated consciousness from the contemporary social context; one of the characteristic results of this process had been the growth of idyllic literature and the mood to which it appealed; the idyll had represented an ideal life, the fulfillment of vague longings, which could not be found in real life and contemporary society. (pp. 269-73)

The domestic idyll may be considered to symbolize the aspiration and to express the way of life still generally common in the Biedermeier Period among the middle classes, on whom the broad social trends of the time imposed grave problems in social organization, and of whom Stifter may be considered representative. At the beginning of his development Stifter condemned wilful and self-assertive individualism, but he was still a subjectivist, inclined to seek repose in the calm of nature; hence his beginnings are associable with major elements in the idyllic tradition; his first tales retain the kind of interest in rural nature found in the idyll of an earlier day; rural nature is sentimentalized and rustic life idealized so that they represent a realm of purity, calm, and fulfillment, where the intimate and fugitive longings of the heart are hushed, far from the empty turmoil of the world. As Stifter became aware of the spirit of the times and of the necessity of integrating the individual into a social order, he abandoned the conception of the lonely, sentimental subjectivist and adopted a conception of man as part of a community; as his views developed, they recapitulated the earlier, general development of the idyll from sentimentally idealized rusticity to a more realistic portrayal of rural life, in which, however, the traditional elements of static calm and pure being are still detectable.

The conception of nature as the realm of pure being remained fundamental in Stifter's idyllic work, but his view of man's relation to nature underwent a mutation that opened the way to further development. This mutation can be easily followed in *The Mountain Forest (Der Hochwald)*. In this tale the sentimental union of nature and the feeling heart is greatly loosened, and a gulf opens between nature and human life; the august dignity and innocence of the ancient forest contrast with the harsh human destinies that are consummated in it. Gratuitously man inflicts pain, suffers and meets his fate, while the forests remain calm, majestic and impervious to pity. The ready approach to nature through feeling is no longer possible, but a new, unsentimental relationship to nature is symbolized in the figure of the old huntsman, who unconsciously fits into his natural environment, as an objective and integral part of it; what makes him so completely a part of his environment is his patiently acquired practical knowledge of it, his forest lore, which enables him to take an unsentimental and objective interest in the real phenomena of the forest. Nature has ceased to be the sentimental symbol of a transcendental, with which feeling can place one *en rapport*. Nature has become a setter of specific tasks, a challenger to practical effort, by which the individual can make himself integrally one with his environment.

It was Herder's influence that enabled Stifter to find his way to the practical relationship to nature, represented by the old huntsman; Herder helped Stifter to overcome the sentimental antinomy of culture and nature, of nature and society, which had informed his first tales and shaped his first relationship to nature. From Herder, who had opposed the antithesis of Rousseau and attempted a synthesis of nature and culture, Stifter learned that, ideally conceived, culture and society are natural products and the ultimate realization of nature's potentialities. But Stifter made very literal application of Herder's doctrine; he conceives the nature which is to be the origin and support of an ideal society strictly as rural nature, and develops an agrarian theory of society; to find the prototype of his thought one must turn back to the eighteenth century when the spectacle of a disintegrating economy and a corrupt society impelled Quesnay and the Physiocrats to look to nature for the practical and economic foundation of society; at a time when an urban, industrial civilization of steel and steam was fast developing, Stifter spoke of the modern epoch as "the grain age" and prophesied a prosperous future for agricultural Hungary.

It must not be forgotten that Stifter's agrarian views represent to a great extent a rationalization of his earlier sentimental feeling that nature is a realm of goodness and purity. A recent commentator has noted a polarity between city and country life in Stifter's writings [F. Matzke, *Die Landschaft in der Dichtung Ad. Stifters,* (1932)]; actually, however, the same longing for pure and simple, primitive and natural conditions, which had informed the idyllic literature of the middle classes in the eighteenth century, also impelled Stifter to an agrarian theory of society and to the conception that life in the rural community, since it is close to nature, is the good life. In this respect Stifter exemplified the manner in which elements in their traditional culture prevented the middle classes from perceiving the whole scope of the economic and social problems they faced in the Bierdermeier Period; nor was Stifter the only one in his time who was subject to a strong impulsion to escape from the complex problems of contemporary—urban—society; the popularity of the contemporary *Dorfgeschichte* was due to its offering "a conscious and welcome contrast to problematical urban modernity and its literary expression." But even more than the *Dorfgeschichte* Stifter's works reveal a longing to return to the purity of aboriginal conditions and rest in calm repose on the bosom of nature; "his tales represent states of being rather than action;" into his definition of the good life there enters a certain readily detectable escapist sentiment: "How fine, how aboriginal and elemental is the lot of the countryman; . . . in its simplicity and variety, in its close association with nature, which is without passion, it approximates the legend of Eden."

As the example of the huntsman in *The Mountain Forest (Der Hochwald)* has shown, the relation of Stifter's characters to their rural environment is not wholly the passive one of idyllic tradition; the closest analogy would be the contemporary *Dorfgeschichte,* for Stifter represents his characters as bound to the earth by toil, and the peasant is therefore an approximate prototype for them; Stifter portrayed peasants infrequently, but his figures all have the peasant's essential qualities; they have his static attachment to the soil and to a specific rustic locality; they have his almost exclusive concern with personal and local problems, and vital interests bind them to the soil and fix them within the landscape. The rural communities that Stifter represents are loosely attached units of an agrarian society; the prototypical community in Stifter's tales is the patriarchal community on the rural estate, his interest in which is indicated by his frequent representation of it. Stifter places considerable emphasis on the practical management and successful administration of these estates; his rural community is therefore necessarily devoted to collective efforts to exploit the productive and nutritive forces of nature and to impress upon its natural environment a useful pattern. When compared with actual social and economic developments of his time, Stifter's ideal rural settlement in immediate contact with the soil appears retrospective and archaic; nonetheless Stifter took into his conception some of the contemporary middle class ethics of collaborative effort and practical achievement and departed from the utter placidity of the traditional idyll.

Nevertheless, the principle of organization that Stifter applies to hold his community together was vastly different from the dynamic organizatory principle to which his active contemporaries adhered. The social union, as the liberal sector of the Biedermeier conceived it, consisted in an aggregation of individuals, held together by common beliefs and ideas and committed to collective action to realize a common aim and program. (pp. 275-80)

But Stifter rejects the social dynamics and the social mobility of the new era and immobilizes the individual in a static community. He does this by building his ethical as well as his social theory around the vision of the placid domestic scene that had lingered through the idyllic literature of the middle classes from Gessner through the more realistic portrayals of Goldsmith, Voss, Goethe (*Hermann und Dorothea*) and Schiller (*Das Lied von der Glocke*). On this placid vision of middle class life, common to the literature and the thought of the eighteenth century, Herder had based his conception of man's instinctive adherence to naturally developed institutions like the family, opposing these views to the asperity of Kant's morality and to Kant's conception of the state. Neither the state nor the party, both aggregates of individuals in an active social-political collective, interested Stifter. He followed the example of Herder in stressing a natural order and conceived the relation of the individual to society as membership in the domestic collective of the family. The cohesion and continuity of the family are central in Stifter's social theory; the lonely and eccentric titular figure in *The Bachelor* (*Der Hagestolz*) confesses that if a man does not take his place in the succession of generations he has lived in vain; he is then an isolated and meaningless atom outside the larger system of the family, which alone has significance.

The physical continuity of the family is only the material basis of its spiritual continuity, by which family life through successive generations is held in a kind of static permanence and fixed conformity to type, and society as a whole likewise rendered immobile and static. The educational process, which goes forward in the home and in rural surroundings, is reminiscent of the typical educational theory of the eighteenth century. In Stifter's novel of education *Belated Summer* (*Der Nachsommer*) "the family is broken out of larger social complexes and its younger members trained in loyalty." Family continuity is assured and eccentric divagations from family type are prevented by the transmission of moral principles, views, and behavior patterns from the older to the younger generation within the family. This is, in essence, the educational procedure in *Belated Summer;* it is also the old colonel's procedure with Augustin in *My Great-Grandfather's Portfolio* (*Die Mappe meines Urgrossvaters*).

Stifter rejected the social dynamics of the Biedermeier Period and represented conformity to family type as the salient principle of social cohesion. To find the family and problems in family relationships treated as frequently and extensively as Stifter treated them one must look back into areas of middle class culture outside of Classicism and Romanticism, and generally antedating the period of Irrationalism, and examine the family portraits in the middle class literature of the Enlightenment. In Stifter one encounters again "the great ideals of the new middle class world-view of the eighteenth century," "candor, honesty and loyalty," which characterize relations among members of the family. The self-represssion and abnegation that were shown in older literature to be the basis of family cohesion recur in Stifter's rationalistic moralism. It is the primary requirement in Stifter's social discipline that individual and eccentric disruptions of the cohesion and continuity of the family be prevented. To that end, Stifter has to insist on a moral discipline, identical with that of other conservatives of the Biedermeier Period, which enjoins upon the individual quiescence and the repression of irrational and eccentric impulses, among which passion, potentially criminal, ranks as archetypal. Love between the sexes, on which the domestic idyll is founded, must be freed of passion by separation and long trials before it can be recognized (*Die Mappe meines Urgrossvaters, Der Nachsommer*). Stifter usually construes passion as a destructive force that separates lovers or disrupts family unity. He analyzes passion more or less as the rationalistic Enlightenment had analyzed it: passion is ignoble and inferior; if not restrained, it hinders perception of reality and inhibits the higher faculty of reason. The victim of passion is in an unenlightened state, and Stifter represents him as mistakenly pursuing spurious aims or as deluded by false surface appearances. The tale *Brigitta* affords an illustration of Stifter's conception of the disruption caused by passion within the harmonious and reasonable order that underlies human affairs. Against the typical background of a patriarchal community on a well-administered rural estate, Stifter draws a standard *Familienstück:* Brigitta's husband, becoming infatuated with the volatile beauty of the Countess, yields to passion and flees with her, disrupting the unity of the family; he returns contrite and enlightened, freed of passion and possessed of new insight into the spiritual excellence of Brigitta, who happens to be physically ugly. The individual and eccentric action is not tragic in its consequences, since the rational and orderly system of things, represented in this tale by the cohesion of the family, must necessarily prevail. The disruption of the family is, to be sure, not always so easily mended, but it never rises to a tragic pitch; there is pathos in the long separation of Risach and Mathilde (*Der Nachsommer*) that precedes their reunion; there is pathos in the plight of the bachelor (*Der Hagestolz*), alone on his island retreat, and in the aimless travels of "the wanderer in the forest" (*Der Waldgänger*) after he has wilfully disrupted the unity of his family. Self-assertive and eccentric action undertaken by these solitary figures has made them hapless demonstrations that only stern self-subordination to rational social discipline in the collective order of the family can make the individual life meaningful.

Stifter has given us examples of abnegation and self-sacrifice within the family circle even more drastic than those contained in the middle class literature of the Enlightenment. Many parallels could be drawn; the tender sisters in Gellert's play (*Die zärtlichen Schwestern*) put aside their fondest hopes for one another's sake; in Stifter's *Two Sisters* (*Zwei Schwestern*) Maria and Alfred renounce their warm reciprocal love and agree that Alfred shall marry Maria's sister, so that her unrequited love for Alfred shall not break her spirit. In *My Great-Grandfather's Portfolio* (*Die Mappe meines Urgross-*

***vaters*)** Margarita falls from the narrow bridge into the gorge, suppressing her screams so that her husband who is preceding her may not turn around and lose his footing.

By transferring the domestic ethics of dutifulness, and self-subordination to the welfare of the whole into the larger realm of politics, Stifter attempted to solve the problem of the state. His theoretical state bears small resemblance to the actual state of the Biedermeier Period and the later nineteenth century, which was extending its power over society and functioning as a collectivizing force and a unifying agency, particularly by drawing German civil life into a centralized administrative system. The state, which represented a uniform collective of individuals and in which the conception of power was inherent, was necessarily difficult to reconcile with the conception of a natural social organization based on the family; in Stifter's early tales the state is not mentioned; in ***Belated Summer (Der Nachsommer)*** it is mentioned only as a vast, impersonal administrative machine from which Risach had withdrawn in order to live in idyllic seclusion. In ***Witiko,*** a political novel, the state, divested of all arbitrary power, is not the master but the instrument by which an agrarian society, organized loosely in families and communities, enforces the law of self-repression that forbids the development and expansion of power centered in any specific individual or group. When an eccentric expansion of power of this kind threatens, society as a whole, guided by the enlightened ruler (the Duke of Bohemia, Friedrich Barbarossa) acts to preserve its static order. By implication ***Witiko*** is a critique of the heritage left the nineteenth century by the French Revolution: Stifter rejects the attainment and use of power as the end to which action by any special class or group is directed; he rejects the dynamic organizational principle of the new age (the aggregate of individuals united to realize a common program) and the social mobility that began to be evident after the Napoleonic Era.

Rigidly rooted in the traditional culture of the middle classes Stifter interpreted life in archaic terms that had ceased to be relevant to the social and economic situation of the nineteenth century. The present-day reader who is interested in the relation between society and literature will chiefly value Stifter's criticisms of his times; their range and insight place Stifter on a level with other critics of modern civilization—Jakob Burckhardt, Nietzsche, to some extent also de la Garde, Spengler, and Karl Jaspers. But Stifter's critical acumen was in no way equalled by his capacity for creative cultural synthesis. He is to a great extent representative of the inability of the conservative sector of the Biedermeier to meet successfully the crisis of the Biedermeier Period by accepting the social and political situation of the time and establishing a vital relationship between a timely social organization and the better part of the cultural tradition. (pp. 280-87)

> *Alan Holske, "Stifter and the Biedermeier Crisis," in* Studies in Honor of John Albrecht Walz *by Alan Holske and others, Lancaster Press, Inc., 1941, pp. 256-90.*

An excerpt from Stifter's preface to *Bunte Steine*

. . . The gentle breeze, the murmur of water, the growth of corn, the waves of the sea, the earth turning green, the radiance of the sky, the gleam of the stars, are things which I consider great: the majestic approach of a thunderstorm, the flash of lightning that cleaves houses, the tempest that lashes the breakers, the fire-belching mountain, the earthquake that lays waste whole lands, are phenomena which I do not consider greater than those others, in fact I consider them smaller, because they are merely the consequences of much higher laws. They occur in isolation and are the effects of unilateral causes. The force that makes the milk in a poor woman's saucepan boil over is the very same force that makes lava seethe up inside the volcanic mountain and pour down its slopes.

. . . Yet it is above all in the normal, everyday, endlessly recurring acts of human beings that this law is most surely centered, for these are the lasting acts, they are the foundation, they are as it were the million root-fibers of the tree of life. Just as in nature the general laws operate quietly and ceaselessly, and the conspicuous phenomenon is only a particular expression of these laws, so too the moral law operates quietly and refreshingly, through the infinite relationships of man with man. And though some deeds that are done may be the marvels of the moment, these are only small evidences of this general power. So this law is what preserves mankind, just as the world is preserved by the law of nature.

Adalbert Stifter, quoted in Limestone and Other Stories, *translated by David Luke, Harcourt, Brace & World, 1968.*

W. H. Auden   (essay date 1945)

[*W. H. Auden is a major twentieth-century poet and influential literary figure. Among his best-known critical works are* The Enchafed Flood *(1950) and* Forewords and Afterwords *(1973). In the following excerpt from his review of Stifter's* Rock Crystal, *Auden admires the artistry with which Stifter tells a simple tale of courage and community spirit.*]

The plot of ***Rock Crystal*** is simple enough. Two children walk from one mountain valley to visit their grandparents on Christmas Eve. On their way home it starts to snow; they miss the path and when night falls they are far out on a glacier. They take shelter in an ice cave and are saved from falling asleep and freezing to death by some black coffee extract their grandmother has given them to carry home, which stimulates their bodies, and by a wonderful discharge of electric flashes in the sky which excites their minds. In the Christmas morning they are found by a search party and brought down the mountainside home to their rejoicing parents.

To bring off, as Stifter does, a story of this kind, with its breathtaking risks of appalling banalities, is a great feat. What might so easily have been a tear-jerking melodrama becomes in his hands a quiet and beautiful parable about the relation of people to places, of man to nature.

He achieves this result by a sort of fugal repetition of descriptive details. The two valleys with their inhabitants, the road over the col past the baker's memorial, the way up to the mountain and the glacier are first presented objectively as if to a tourist or a historian, so that the reader knows where everything is and what everybody does. He knows, for instance, that love for the daughter of the wealthy dyer of Millsdorf made the restless young cobbler of Gschaid settle down to making mountain boots, but that she, who came over the hill to marry him, is still regarded as an outsider.

The same road over the col is traveled again, and again in the daylight, but this time by young children who have never been up the mountain. Consequently, when the crisis comes, while the appearance of the mountain by night is as unfamiliar to the reader as it is to the children, he has been there before with a guide, he knows where and how they are lost, and this knowledge heightens his awareness of Conrad's courage and common sense and Sanna's simple faith in her brother which overcomes all fear.

Finally the story returns to the panorama from which it started, but though everything looks the same, the eye that sees them is full of memories and no longer disinterested. The mountain is not only beautiful, but dangerous and lovable because its dangers have been met with courage. The road over the col is no longer taken for granted, but is seen as a triumph of the human will to neighborliness over an indifferent or hostile nature which would keep men estranged. Home has become really home for the first time, through the experience of being lost. The community, through having responded in common to a threat to some of its members, has realized itself completely:

> Only from that day on were the children really felt to belong to the village and not to be outsiders. Thenceforth they were regarded as natives whom the people had brought back to themselves from the mountain. Their mother, Sanna, was now a native of Gschaid, too.
>
> The children, however, can never forget the mountain and earnestly fix their gaze upon it when in the garden, when as in times past the sun is out bright and warm, the linden diffuses its fragrance, the bees are humming, and the mountain looks down upon them as serene and blue as the sky above.

> *W. H. Auden, "Concerning the Village of Gschaid, and Its Mountain," in* The New York Times Book Review, *November 18, 1945, p. 6.*

Roy Pascal   (essay date 1956)

[*Pascal was a British scholar and professor who wrote many books on German history, literature, and philosophy, including* The Growth of Modern Germany *(1946) and* The German Sturm und Drang *(1953). In this excerpt, Pascal discusses the relationship between formal and thematic elements in Stifter's* Indian Summer, *noting that the world depicted in the novel is static and rather narrow in scope.*]

A woodcut depicting the Alpine setting of Rock Crystal *from the Pantheon edition (1945).*

> I have probably written this work because of the rottenness prevailing, with some exceptions, in world-political relationships, in moral life, and in literature. I have tried to confront our wretched degenerate condition with a great, simple, moral force.

Thus Stifter writes of his novel, **Der Nachsommer,** 'Indian Summer', to his friend and publisher, Heckenast. This 'Bildungsroman' has therefore, like all Stifter's mature works, an avowed didactic purpose which links it with *Wilhelm Meister* and *Green Heinrich*. But his statement also indicates a marked divergence from Goethe and Keller. While they describe the development of a young man towards integration into society, Stifter here contrasts society and the 'moral force'. While Goethe sketches a set of social principles and relationships which may be made worthy of human endeavour, and Keller recognises in his native democracy a worthy framework for the humanism of his hero, Stifter builds for his hero a private existence which is an asylum from the stresses of wider social and political life.

We are here faced not simply by a different temperament and outlook, but also a different social environment. ***Indi-***

an Summer (1857) was written in that decade when Schopenhauer first became widely read, a decade, for the Austrian and German middle class, of disillusionment and pessimism. The first version of *Green Heinrich,* which was written in this same decade and while Keller was living in Berlin, bears witness to this pessimism, even though the author was a Swiss who welcomed the democratic reform of the Swiss constitution which had been successfully carried through in the 1840s. The course of events in Austria, Stifter's homeland, had been entirely different. The revolution of 1848 had taken a radical turn which alarmed Stifter and his friends, it had kindled national risings that threatened the doom of the Austrian Empire. A mild and timid liberal, Stifter had lost heart, and acquiesced, though without enthusiasm, in the return of the old order. From 1848, perhaps from earlier still, he considered that political excesses were due to a lack of moral education; the 'hollowness of our morals and literature' was the cause of the misguided violence and the failure of the revolutionary effort to establish constitutional government. He became an inspector of schools in the hope of contributing to the moral education of his countrymen; and his books he hoped would be valued from this point of view.

Indian Summer is on the surface not a work of pessimism or regret; if it were, it could scarcely be a 'Bildungsroman'. Yet Stifter deliberately placed its action thirty years back, before the crises and discouragement of 1848. And though the theme of the novel is entirely positive, affirming the beauty and worth of the mode of life its chief characters construct, there are such high fences erected between their world and the normal world, between their characters and the normal run of men, even between their stylised language and normal speech, that it has something of the beauty of the cactus which, after years of devoted tending in the conservatory, blooms so radiantly at the end of the book. Around the world of the novel are glass walls which suggest the fears and despondency that often assailed the author. (pp. 52-3)

It is characteristic of the 'Bildungsroman' that the hero is a naïve, innocent young man, well-meaning even in his errors; the persons among whom he moves are never evil, and most of them give good guidance, directly or indirectly. In Stifter's novel these characteristics are taken to an extreme. All the characters are harmonious and tranquil, all circumstances conduce to the happiness of Heinrich Drendorf, and there is a complete absence of internal stress and external seduction or conflict, of religious or philosophical struggle. It conjures up, like Shakespeare's *The Tempest,* a world where the powers for good are beyond effective challenge or infection. But, more idyllic than *The Tempest,* there is scarcely an echo in **Indian Summer** of former strife and present danger, of human imperfections. Contemporary critics often commented unfavourably on the idyllicism in Stifter's works, and he often promised himself that he would write something with action, conflict, tragedy in it. He did not succeed in this, though he tried to do so in his historical novel, **Witiko,** and the bearing of **Der Nachsommer** is limited by its very tranquillity, its unproblematicalness.

Heinrich's development contains no element of conflict or

error. Brought up in an exemplary family, where each member has for the others affection, respect, consideration, he has merely to follow the gentle slope of his inclinations. In the Risach household he meets a repetition of the same relationships, so much so that when the two families meet each finds in the other identical tastes, habits, and views; the complex harmony of Wilhelm Meister's world, made up of very different voices, is here replaced by something approaching the simplicity and monotony of unison. Even the servants chime in, in subdued tones, perhaps an octave below, respectful, contented, affectionate. The elder Drendorf's life-story is the smoothest account of the winning of material prosperity and family bliss. Were it not for the Risach story, we should have no inkling that there are stresses and strains in human nature. But if the tranquillity of an 'Indian summer' may be accepted as the deserved goal of the elders, how dangerous and strange to make this the goal of the young people who have not yet reached their summer! In the world of **Der Nachsommer** there is a lack of moral strenuousness.

But not only on the psychological and philosophical plane; on the social, too. It is characteristic that most of the many discussions in the book, particularly the opinions of Risach, which represent the summit of Stifter's wisdom, circle round art. Very few deal with social problems, and the only major discussion on equality and freedom is trivial and facilely optimistic. We have no glimpse of the urgent social and political problems of Stifter's times—he placed the action of the story in the 1820s, just before the conflicts that issued in the Revolution of 1848 were declared, and before railways and factories had brought their complications into Austria. On Risach's suggestion, Heinrich sets out to get a wider experience of men and things, but all he does is to pass through certain social circles in Vienna; social and political activities remain far from his ken. Compared with the amusements and interests of his Vienna acquaintance, the life of Risach and the country gentry seems substantial and fruitful; and Heinrich chooses the latter with the comfortable feeling that his primary duty is to order satisfactorily his own private life. As Heinrich's father says: 'If each man lives in the best way for himself, he serves human society best.' There is no hint that national and social problems may profoundly affect the nature of personal values and the shape of personal life: one of the themes of Goethe and Keller.

Characteristic is the manner in which reference is made to the growing specialisation of science, which raises a faint echo of the great problem of 'one-sidedness' that Wilhelm Meister and his friends have to face. In Stifter's novel, all that Risach tells Heinrich is that the growing specialisation of the sciences will ensure great advances in knowledge. The psychological and social implications are not touched on.

In *Wilhelm Meister,* landed gentry and bourgeoisie become allies in the effort to found a new society, essentially bourgeois in its economic activities and social relations. In **Indian Summer,** the bourgeoisie (Stifter insisted that Heinrich's family belongs to the wealthy bourgeoisie) turns into landed gentry. There is no derogation of bourgeois activities, it is true. Heinrich is never ashamed of his father's business, and Risach, himself of middle-class origin, praises trade and gladly, as he says, returns through the marriage of Heinrich and Natalie to the class from which he had risen. Mathilde herself, though the mistress of a great estate, is not an aristocrat. But even Heinrich's father, as well as Heinrich, settle as landed gentry, for them the ideal life, the only life where men can achieve fulfilment and moral satisfaction.

In this, Stifter is paying tribute not to the nobility as a privileged class, but to their form of life. Risach, the bourgeois by origin, brings movement into this mode of life. By example and advice he inspires his neighbours to improve their land and stock. Like Lothario in *Wilhelm Meister,* Mathilde has commuted the feudal dues of her tenants, the tithes and payments in kind, into cash rents, the relationships of bourgeois society. Material progress, usefulness, is a principle of this group of enlightened landowners; change is envisaged without alarm, as a natural principle of life. In the same way as Risach grows old without regret, simply using every opportunity to the best advantage, so he is continually altering and improving his estate and garden. When his heirs, Heinrich and Natalie, wish to promise him that they will for ever preserve the Rose House as he has arranged it, he reproves them for this mistaken idea of piety, and tells them they must go on improving and changing things after his death. Change is necessary, is often desirable; but the guarantee of its rightness and value is that it is controlled and ordered, that it takes place gradually and with a minimum of disturbance. Thus the most thorough examination, thought, and consultation precedes all changes in Risach's and Mathilde's households. The same principle holds good for changes in social status. Birth is not decisive, but talent must make its way, if it is not to err, without rebellion and violence. The servant-craftsman Eustach and his brother rise slowly, encouraged and furthered by Risach, to the positions of artists and companions, as their talents and moral qualities are proved. Risach himself is the ideal of the master, selflessly concerned to make the most of his subordinates, just as he is the ideal tutor to his foster-son and the ideal guide to Heinrich.

This idyllic relationship between the social classes, between master and household servants, is of course deliberately exemplary, and it illustrates Stifter's view that the conflicts of his times were due to excess and passion, to the lack of 'moral freedom' in his contemporaries. But it leads him to avoid, in the novel, the real social conflicts that were there, or were emerging. Even on the land we get only a glimpse of the farmers and farm-servants, and always they are in the role of faithful, contented retainers. The rather numerous and obtrusive household servants carry out with alacrity the often pettifogging tasks put on them, and like the farmers show in a respectful but cordial fashion their delight in the happiness of their betters.

The social basis of the moral principles of the novel is indeed extremely narrow. It is not by accident that we are precisely informed about Heinrich's handling of the income his father gives him. The wedding is accompanied by a detailed and exact account of money-settlements which put the seal on the happiness of the marriage, ensuring its complete propriety. Whether this money has been acquired solely by inheritance and marriage (Mathilde), or through services to the state (Risach), or through trade (the elder Drendorf), it finds its proper purpose, it is 'moralised', in the form of landownership and investment; the ideal form of life is that of the *rentier.* The importance of the family is stressed in this respect too; for inheritance and marriage play a large part in the accumulation of wealth in each family, and above all with Heinrich and Natalie. One is reminded of Stifter's innocent wishful dreams, in the midst of his isolation and money-troubles in Linz, for a lottery-prize which would allow him to build a country-house and devote himself to his writing. There is no hint in the novel of the questionability of the *rentier* ideal or of the social conflicts it engenders.

This class, the landowner with his ample means, is in fact the hypostasis of the 'Biedermeier', the independent bourgeois relieved of the pressures of unsatisfactory employment and vexatious superiors and free to pursue his own interests and hobbies. Here the family and home can be tended without distraction. The family itself is narrowed to the simplest proportions, cumbersome relatives are lopped off with the gardener's skilful pruning-knife, property remains concentrated since the families have but one son and one daughter. Round the family runs a fence like that round the Rose House, keeping out all intruders; individuals are fenced too by strict conventions of respect, and Heinrich, when visiting at Risach's or Mathilde's, always carefully locks the door of his room. The word 'hegen' gives the key-note of this existence, for it indicates both 'cherishing', the tender nurturing of the garden, the home, private life, and 'hedging round', protection from the outer world.

Because of these drastic limitations to the scope of the world represented in the novel, its moral bearing is also narrowed; and in particular morality sometimes tends to appear in the form of propriety and convention. Astonishing, by contrast, is the freedom and unconventionality of manners and morals in *Wilhelm Meister* and *Green Heinrich;* scarcely ever, in these novels, does mere propriety usurp the place of moral relationships. Heinrich Drendorf's distrust of impulse and his desire not to violate the sanctity of other people's privacy, on the other hand, impose on him an exaggerated restraint. For instance, when he twice meets Natalie by chance, he urgently seeks to withdraw in order not to offend her; and we feel the offence is more to propriety than to her or to morality. The piety which leads him to refrain from inquisitive questions in his relations with Risach and Mathilde borders at times on the purely conventional notion of propriety; after a first impulse he scrupulously avoids inquiring what the name of his host is, until Risach tells him himself, and only after his betrothal does he learn, again from Risach, the surname of his wife-to-be. Stifter describes with approving solicitude the propriety of the behaviour, mode of address, or clothes of the two families. Orderliness and cleanliness are for Stifter fundamental constituents of the moral life, and the novel betrays almost an obsession with them; books must always be placed back on the shelves, curtains be frequently washed, clothes of course kept always neat and clean; gardens, parks, paths are kept in meticulous order.

The world of *Indian Summer* is therefore but a fragment of the real world, both psychologically and socially. Without conflict, ruggedness, spontaneity, all its phenomena are prepared for and controlled. The book is in conception closer to the 'Novelle', the short story, than to the normal novel, for the 'Novelle' properly abstracts a particular moment and situation from its total environment—and Stifter is one of the masters of the 'Novelle'. But the work has its validity as a novel, and reflects with extraordinary homogeneity a general situation and moral process. Within its high fences, we see the interaction of man and nature, the marriage of the individual self and the outer community, of the moral force and nature: the mutual education of man and nature. All the book is inspired with a deep love and veneration for the world; 'what is, is holy', both man and nature, both are capable of being made moral, useful, beautiful. Both are fundamentally good and 'innocent', and the development of Heinrich, the clarification of his personality and purpose, shows how this innocence may be preserved and enriched in loving co-operation with other human beings and with nature. Stifter's attitude has been called pantheistic, but it is wrong to put any philosophical label on it; it fits on to any religious or non-religious belief that affirms the goodness of the world, above all any belief that affirms the power of man to mould his circumstances and himself for good. So unchallenged is this belief, as it shines through the tranquil serenity of the course of the novel, that modern critics have detected a 'hidden melancholy and mourning' in it, the consciousness that it represents a world that can never be. There is considerable truth in this interpretation. Yet it is never explicit, never even hinted at, in the book, and its strength is that this narrow world is tangible and concrete, and in its concreteness and objectivity appears true; and that by its very existence, as Stifter intended, it makes a moral existence more possible. We can apply to *Indian Summer* the words Stifter used to define the character of an earlier work

> If I could make the thing as I would, it would be simple, clear, transparent, and as soothing as the air. The reader would move in the book through well-known beloved things and be gently entranced and encircled, as one passes in the warm air of spring in the sunshine among the sprouting seeds, and grows happy, without being able to say why.

In few novels is the form and style so integral a part of the theme as in *Indian Summer;* it is above all its form that reconciles us to the limitations of its scope, or even makes us oblivious of them. It is written in the first person, for it is the tale of his own life told by Heinrich Drendorf. But Stifter has not set himself the task, as did Keller, of relating the past from the standpoint of the present, of illuminating the past constantly through a style which expresses the wisdom of maturity. His aim is, to capture at every moment the particular stage of mental development the hero has reached, to show only what the hero can see and understand. If some incidents and things are dwelt on, others passed over rapidly or ignored, the cause is found

in the bent of mind, the spiritual capacity of Heinrich Drendorf. Thus the original crisis which not only explains the relations of Risach and Mathilde but also is the centre of gravity of the whole moral structure of the novel, is related very late in the book by Risach himself, at a time when Heinrich has at last become capable of understanding it in its full meaning. At all stages narrator and hero are identified.

Stifter's method was ably interpreted in one of the very few appreciative reviews of the novel on its first appearance, in relation to Heinrich's visit to a performance of *King Lear*. Heinrich tells how he walks to the theatre in the rain, and puts his coat in the cloakroom, having tucked his cap into a pocket. There follows a rather lame account of the plot of the play. The performance deeply moves him, and at the end his eyes are attracted to a young woman who he sees is also deeply moved: it is one of the few 'incidents' in the story, for the girl is Natalie, who is to become his wife. He then tells how he goes to the cloakroom, gets his coat, takes his cap out of the pocket, and walks home, where his mother is waiting up for him. Why is this first strong aesthetic experience and the first meeting with Natalie encased in so lame an account of the play, above all in such trivial detail? Partly, no doubt, because Stifter continually insists that small everyday things are of importance. But there is another reason that the critic, Julian Schmidt, suggests [in *Der Grenzbote,* 1858]: 'Stifter did not want to describe the play or the walk to the theatre, but the impression on the soul of his hero.' That is, he wanted to describe the play, the walk, the theatre in terms of the open but immature mind of this young man, on whom important and unimportant experiences as yet make an equal impact.

This patient, unimpassioned attention to detail characterises the style of the whole novel. Heinrich describes with meticulous care, sometimes directly, sometimes through the mouth of Risach, the plan of the Rose-House garden, the culture of the roses or cacti, the inlaid floors, the decoration and furniture of rooms, the restoration of antiques, the pictures, engravings, the marble figures. Misled by normal expectation, the reader at times may expect that there is some dramatic function attached to this method— for instance, he might think that Heinrich's visits to the cloakroom at the theatre are to lead to some significant incident. But no; the object or action is described for its own sake, it does not advance or retard the external action of the story. Or rather, not for its own sake, but for the sake of building, through these myriad concrete details, a picture of the life and the spiritual constitution of the characters.

There is not only no passion in the book; there is no psychological probing. The characters appear only through the medium of their appearance, their observations on matters of common interest, their behaviour. The concreteness and detail of the descriptions and of the conversations illuminate the serenity that has been won, the tenderness with which the activities of this sheltered life are pursued: through the orderliness, the care for detail, we imbibe the whole 'moral' of Stifter's book. For, with all their concreteness, these descriptions are not descriptions of an objective, impersonal reality. They show the operation of man upon nature, the ordering and beautifying of nature through which man manages to order and beautify his own character. As, for instance, Risach tells Heinrich of the habits of the birds in the sanctuary of the garden, he unfolds to him in a bird-lover's terms the whole course of life as he would have it, up to that Indian summer he himself has reached. Though he prepares nesting-boxes for the coming year, he is not concerned for the individual birds after they migrate; it is the cycle of one year, of one life, with which he is concerned, not with matters beyond the needs of his knowledge and the bounds of his control.

We do not therefore have to turn to the moments when emotion is declared to discover feeling in the novel; the characters' relationship to things is impregnated with feeling, for the things in themselves and for family and friends. But it is the thesis of the book that this feeling is legitimised, moralised, only if it takes the concrete form of worthy behaviour. Hence it is not only Heinrich's inexperience that causes him to refrain from statements about his or other people's feelings, but also his whole moral training and character which holds feeling back until it is sifted by reflexion and moulded into behaviour. The attraction of Risach's character and household is expressed above all in Heinrich's desire to return there, in his readiness to follow Risach's advice and his patient study of what the older man commends. As a guide Risach shows a similar piety. He does not tell Heinrich that the Greek statue in his house is of high artistic quality, but leaves the young man to find this out for himself; and when Heinrich asks him why he had not told him it was beautiful, he answers that it was much better that he should discover it without help, which might misguide him.

Particularly characteristic is the method by which we are told of Heinrich's growing love for Natalie. We become aware of it only in the most indirect manner, and, being experienced readers of novels, we even know more about it than the story-teller himself. When he leaves the Rose House after his second visit, on which he had met Mathilde and Natalie, he is pursued by a feeling of unexplained sadness, of unease, which he overcomes only by scientific work in the intimacy of his home. This unease appears from time to time, but is never allowed to be the object of probing or description. He notices too that Natalie, on a later visit, has become somewhat restless and frequently takes long walks alone. When they meet, as she is resting on one of these walks, she tells him about her walks in simple, concrete terms. Only after the declaration of their love can we interpret his unease, and her restlessness, for now she quietly tells him: 'I felt much pain for your sake, when I walked over the fields.' Throughout the book there is a chaste reserve with regard to feelings, but they are nevertheless powerful. It is wrong, in my view, to use the phrase 'disembodied chasteness' to denote the character of the scene where Heinrich and Natalie declare their love. The feeling of the two is ardent and simple, not disembodied; but it is avowed only when it springs from, and chimes in with, the whole moral personality. For this reason the climax of the scene is their decision immediately to ask for the consent of their parents.

As in other relationships, there is a danger that even in love morality lapses into propriety, and that Heinrich's behaviour towards Natalie becomes stilted. Thus, when they meet on the day after their declaration of love, Heinrich refrains from asking Natalie what has been the outcome of her talk with her mother until, at the end of a long conversation, she tells him with a blush that her mother approves their union. Neither of them says anything more on the subject. We are to understand this restraint, in Stifter's sense, as the evidence of Heinrich's pious trust in Mathilde, in whose judgement he is ready absolutely to concur, and of his trust in Natalie. If parental consent is withheld, they will love one another 'for ever', but will part for ever. But we must doubt the strength of a feeling which, conscious of its innocence and goodness, is so restrained, and we can scarcely attribute this restraint to anything but propriety. Stifter was not, however, concerned to give us a 'genre' study of 'Victorian' propriety, but to show us examples of fully moralised characters. It might be suggested that when propriety usurps the place of morality in the novel (as also when we feel too strongly the idyllic character of the whole) we get a glimpse of the unspoken conflict between reality and the world of this novel; we then remember that Stifter himself, like his contemporaries in his view, much fell short of the ideal of harmony he presents, and needed to be bolstered up by purely conventional forms of behaviour and intercourse. We see in this tendency, too, evidence of that distrust of nature, of that gnawing uncertainty, which always lowers on the horizon of this apparently soothing book.

So anxious is Stifter to present in Heinrich a character of complete innocence and harmony, that we are conscious at times not only of a deep-seated distrust of impulse, but also a distrust of intelligence. Heinrich refrains from drawing certain conclusions not only out of pious respect, but also out of an unwillingness to put two and two together. For instance, he only slowly comes to the conclusion that the estate named 'Der Sternenhof' is Mathilde's home, when it has been very clear for some time that this is the case. Or he laboriously tells that a coach goes slowly because no doubt the travellers had made caution their law; or explains that the temperature rises as he descends from a mountain expedition because the air in the valleys, in the late autumn, is warmer than that on the high mountains. There is a polemical disingenuousness in all this, or 'coquetry', as Julian Schmidt called it.

Despite these small blemishes, Heinrich's intelligence, feeling, morality, his whole personality unfold according to a steady law that is revealed in the changes of things as of persons. Time becomes a tangible process. Quietly and regularly the seasons change, each with its use and beauty. A great master of nature-description, Stifter never makes his descriptions an end in themselves. Just as the roses are constantly improved, so their blooming is never a mere repetition, and each summer the characters, Heinrich particularly, but Mathilde too, learn more from them; at the end of the novel a cherished cactus, which flowers extremely rarely, blooms as a symbol of their happiness, the crowning of long labour, and it seems we have been waiting for it through the seasons, with the patient and active expectation of the gardener. So also the mountains change from summer to summer, as Heinrich learns to penetrate their secrets and see them more fully, until that final excursion when he mounts to the glacier in midwinter and sees the snow-caps above and the clouds beneath him. Time steadily advances. In the regular round of the year change takes place; it is change that Heinrich studies over the immense distances of geological time; and like nature, the human beings also change, but steadily, in a regular procession, with the acquiescence that is in nature.

As Heinrich tells his story, this quiet movement issues from the very form of his sentences. At all moments he, or the speakers he reports, seem to acquire a resting-point which is at the same time an outcome and a starting-point. All that Risach tells him has mature finality about it, the product of ripe experience and thought; and at the same time it sets Heinrich thinking or urges him to further study and work. There is constant communication, and constant stimulus, yet the stimulus is always in consonance with the past. We have seen examples in the words of Risach and Mathilde in front of the fading roses. 'As these roses have withered, so has our happiness withered,' she says; and Risach answers: 'It has not withered, it only has a different form.' Or in Risach's words about the birds: 'Towards autumn there comes again a freer time. They have as it were an Indian summer and play for a while, before they leave.' All the sentences have a ring of completedness about them; and yet, at the same time, in their context, and in their unassuming simplicity, their lack of emphasis and rhetoric, they lead onwards, promoting meditation—not so much active thought as a patient rumination through which they will slowly be assimilated. In Risach's mouth such phrases have the precision that denotes mastery; but they have also a gentle falling cadence which subtly insinuates their truth and implications into the ear of the listener.

The many and long conversations in which Risach instructs and encourages Heinrich all have this tranquil movement, through which Heinrich's modest questions and suggestions are corrected and developed. On his first visit, Heinrich ventures to sum up his impressions: 'You have here a charming estate,' he observes; and Risach answers:

> 'Not only the estate, the whole country is charming, and it is good to dwell here when one comes from among men where they are a little too close to one another, and when one brings back activity to further the powers of one's being. At times, too, one must take a glance inside oneself. Yet one should not be constantly alone even in the loveliest country: one must at times return again to one's social circles, even if it were only to refresh oneself in the company of some splendid ruin of a man, a relic of our youth, or to gaze up at some strong tower who has preserved himself. After times like these, country-life re-enters, like a soothing balsam, into the opened spirit. But one must be far from the town and untouched by it. The changes wrought by the arts and crafts come to appearance in the town; on the land, those which have been engendered by manifest need or the influence of natural objects on one another. The two are mutually incompatible,

and once you have the first behind you, the second appears almost as something permanent, and then the beauty of constancy lies quiet before the mind, and the beauty of the past is revealed to meditation, drawing us in human transformations and the transformations of natural things back into an infinity.'

The gentle rectification of Heinrich's statement is characteristic, for it is as much a development of an incomplete thought as it is a correction. Risach's statements are not dogmatic and oppressive, he cautiously yet clearly seeks his way through qualifying words and phrases, until he can reach the smooth cadence of the phrase 'country-life re-enters, like a soothing balsam, into the opened spirit'. He does not rest here, however, with this comforting, motionless image, but continues his meditation until we are engaged with him in reflections which lead 'into an infinity'. As often, this part of the conversation closes with the remark of the narrator: 'I answered nothing to this speech, and we were silent for a while.'

It is not only Risach's mode of life and outlook that Heinrich assumes in the course of the novel, but also, in a sense, his mode of expression, which 'falls like a soothing balsam into his opened spirit'. He describes events and people at first in an almost gauche manner, confining himself to the simplest statements of what he saw or did. Signs of a deeper consciousness or feeling are only indirect, as when, too shy to look at Natalie when she leaves a room, he sees her and her brother in the mirror: 'But I saw almost nothing more than four identical dark eyes turning away in the mirror.' In the same detached way Natalie describes her walks round the Rose House:

> 'I like to go walking where I do not feel confined. I walk between the fields and the waving corn, I climb up the gentle slopes, I walk past the leafy trees and go on till a strange landscape gazes at me, where the sky over it is as it were a different one and holds different clouds. As I go, I muse and think. The sky, the clouds in it, the corn, the trees, the bushes, the grass, the flowers do not distract me. When I am tired out, and can rest on a bench, as here, or on a seat in our garden or even on a chair in our room, I think I shall not go so far another time.'

And Heinrich describes his walks and explains to her the lie of the land in similar terms. But though Heinrich's narrative never loses this naïve concreteness, it acquires something more as the novel progresses; the development is most pronounced in the two long conversations with Natalie. The first leads from simple exchanges about their walks to the first avowal by Heinrich of an awareness that there is a 'radiance' in the world, of a quest, beyond his science, for 'something unknown and great'. And the second conversation, which culminates in the confessions of love, circles round the theme of the beauty of the fountain at which they meet, the water, the air. Their thoughts here, the cadence of their speech, enter the Risach sphere. Heinrich tells how he had risen early to enjoy the morning air:

> 'It is a unique, soothing restorative, to breathe the pure air of a serene summer,' she answered.

'It is the most exalting nourishment that Heaven has given us,' I answered. 'This I know, when I stand on a high mountain and the air lies wide around me, like an immeasurable sea. But not only the air of summer is refreshing, that of winter is so too, all air is so, that is pure and in which there are no particles that repel our nature.'

On the following day, as he points out to her the distant mountains, they come to compare the works of nature with the works of man:

'Works of art lead the eye to them, and rightly so, they fill us with admiration and love. Natural things are the work of a different hand, and if they are observed in the right way, they too arouse the highest wonder.'

'I must always have felt the same,' she said.

'For many years I have observed the works of creation,' I answered, 'and then, too, as far as was possible, I have got to know works of art, and both delighted my soul.'

Thus the style of life, the personal development, that Stifter has made the theme of his novel, comes into evidence not only through the content of his story, through the ideas the characters express and the decisions they take, through the form their daily life acquires, but also in the very tone and fall of voice, which reveals the deepest recesses of their natures. This recurrent voice lacks variety, for it sounds in all the characters; it is a carefully, almost consciously modulated voice, lacking stress and passion, betraying at hardly any point whether it is the outcome of stress that has been mastered, or whether it is habit and simple nature. The stylised monotony of its beauty invites the same criticism as the whole scope of the novel, yet its enchantment makes us forget the difficulties, the precariousness, of personal and social life. Is this the monotony of a life shorn, in the interests of harmony, of its exuberant powers? or is it the monotony of which Risach speaks, 'which is so sublime that it seizes the whole soul as abundance, and as simplicity embraces the All'? Its power, as its weakness, is that of the whole book, and it interprets to perfection the charm of a form of life of whose inaccessibility Stifter was painfully aware. (pp. 60-75)

> *Roy Pascal, "Adalbert Stifter—'Indian Summer',' in* The German Novel: Studies, *Manchester University Press, 1956, pp. 52-75.*

Maurice Sendak   (essay date 1965)

[*The first American to win a Hans Christian Andersen medal, Sendak has been a major figure in children's literature, both as a writer and as an illustrator. In this excerpt, Sendak discusses* Rock Crystal *as a celebration of the unchanging values of country people.*]

Colored Stones is Stifter's celebration of simple country people whose faith in God and reverence for nature commit them to the great unchanging values from which their lives derive meaningful harmony. In the political upheavals of 1848, Stifter saw these values threatened, and to some extent *Colored Stones* was written as a protest

---

Friedrich Nietzsche on Stifter's *Indian Summer*:

Apart from Goethe's writings, and in particular Goethe's conversations with Eckermann, the best German book there is, what is there really of German prose literature that it would be worthwhile to read over and over again? Lichtenberg's aphorisms, the first book of Jung-Stilling's autobiography, Adalbert Stifter's *Nachsommer* and Gottfried Keller's *Leute von Seldwyla*—and that for the present is all.

Friedrich Nietzsche, in his Human, All Too Human, *trans. by R. J. Hollingdale, 1986.*

---

against the uncertainties of the time. In his introduction he refers to the prevailing criticism of his work: that it tiresomely depicts the minute, that it is overconcerned with ordinary, humble folk. The younger critics especially felt Stifter was out of touch with his time. They lacked the subtlety to perceive that his stories are not time-bound and that unlike the other Romantic writers (with whom he shared an intense love of nature) he based his work on firm, moral convictions.

Stifter detested sensationalism and violence, and criticized his contemporaries for their inability to distinguish the important from the unimportant, the truly significant from the insignificant. For him the seemingly small things of life were the most meaningful, and poetry was to be found not in the epic and spectacular but in the unostentatious, self-sacrificing lives of inarticulate, hard-working country people. The village and all of nature came to represent for him all that is real and beautiful in life as compared to the superficial glitter of society and contemporary art.

More than anything else, Stifter was concerned for the children and the effects of revolution on their lives. In his own words the job was "little by little to wipe out and make harmless the bad impressions which have come out of the evils of the time." All six tales in *Colored Stones* are about children; though they were not written specifically for children, Stifter was soon besieged by people asking permission to include passages in children's anthologies, and younger readers have always loved the tales.

Rock Crystal is brilliantly designed to lead up to and away from its central action, the children lost in the snow. Stifter's controlled and lucid prose has so completely familiarized the reader with the physical setting that when the snow begins to fall we no longer read so much as see and hear the great descending silence. It is a terrifying sequence and no matter how often I read it, the suspense is terrible. Stifter renders the children so convincingly and views the scene with such quiet, passionate objectivity, that, for all our certainty of a happy outcome, concern for the children's survival is overwhelming.

Conrad and Sanna are at first delighted with the silent falling snow and set their feet playfully in the thick patches. Then, "A great calm had descended . . . and the whole forest was as though dead." The children, as silently, shrink into their coats and push on through the deepening snow. With nothing explicit said, we know that Conrad has slowly become aware of the danger. His first concern is for his sister: he bundles her up in his fur coat and puts his cap on her head. He points out bits of still visible landscape to keep up her courage and she, with her unbounded faith in Conrad's judgment and strength, has but one answer to everything he says—"Yes, Conrad." The entire episode is poignantly dotted with Sanna's gentle "Yes, Conrad."

The suspense mounts with the boy's determination to keep himself and his sister alive through the long night in the ice cave and is wonderfully dispelled with the great shudder of light that arcs across the sky; it is the dawn of Christmas morning and the mystery of this holy day fuses with the children's triumph over death. Their rescue is simply described. Conrad imagines he sees a dancing red flame in the snow. It is the rescue flag being waved. The children hear "across the still blue distance, something like the long sustained note of an Alpenhorn." They are safe, and Stifter ends his tale by blending into its final pages perhaps his most significant theme, brotherhood. The village of Gschaid and the town of Millsdorf, long divided by mountains and customs, have forgotten their differences in the mutual effort to find the children. All is resolved and Stifter's hymn of Christian faith and salvation, of a better life on earth based on the true and eternal values, comes to an end.

> *Maurice Sendak, "The Old Gem in a New Setting," in* Book Week—New York Herald Tribune, *December 12, 1965, p. 20.*

J. P. Stern (essay date 1968)

[*German-born scholar, Stern taught German literature for many years at British universities and wrote a great deal on German history, literature, and philosophy. Here, Stern suggests that Stifter wanted to reach the essential ground of being, existence "in and by itself," through his writings.*]

To begin with let us take the bull by the horns: Stifter has the reputation of being a boring author. Obviously this is not a view I share. All the same, it has a plausibility that is worth exploring. It is the prerogative of the work of every major author that it should challenge our literary preconceptions and cause us to revise our critical vocabulary. Boredom—like its opposite, liveliness (Aristotle's *energeia*)—is, among other things, a term in the language of literary criticism. It arises where my interest as a reader is not challenged or arrested by a definite object in front of me. If *"Angst"* is fear without a definite object, fear of "nothing in particular," that is fear of existence itself, then boredom is interest without a definite object; and this may, on the analogy with *"Angst,"* be our reaction to an interest in existence undivided, in and by itself. Now, it will be readily agreed that literature is incapable of conveying anything so abstruse as existence in and by itself. Literature is committed, through language, to evocations of specific and discrete objects; it is committed to particulars. Ludwig Wittgenstein speaks ironically of our vain hope

"that we could have pure beauty, unadulterated by anything beautiful." A literary undertaking that is concerned with the evocation of pure existence, or pure beauty, aims at an impossibility. In a great many of his stories this is, as I hope to show, Stifter's aim. Yet even though he undertakes the impossible and can never fully achieve it, his aim colors and determines his narrative means, and it is with these means that I am here concerned.

Stifter's writings belong to the German literature of the mid-nineteenth century. Like a great many of his contemporaries, especially the lyrical poets of the age, chief among them Mörike, he confines his work to the private sphere of experience. The settings these writers choose are rural and natural; the values they praise are those inherent in intimate human relations and in the soul of the solitary man. Their writings are characterized by a unique mixture of two preoccupations: the parochial and the existential. The notion of man as a political animal is largely alien to them (to Stifter after 1848 it is increasingly distasteful); it is certainly never a positive inspiration of their muse. In lyrical poetry such a limitation of themes can remain uncontentious and intuitive. Stifter wrote almost exclusively narrative prose—a form, or rather a variety of forms, which is less easily accommodated to such a limited range of themes.

Narrative prose no less than expository is the social and democratic form *par excellence*. It is uniquely involved in the historical and social circumstances, the living customs and moral standards of its readers who are also its speakers; and nineteenth-century realistic prose, as we know it from French or English fiction, is a singularly direct expression of this involvement. Therefore, the less compatible the preoccupations and standards of a writer's public are with the demands of his conscience, the more problematic will be his attitude towards the whole enterprise of conveying "to his readers also," "in *their* language," *his* vision of what the world is and what it ought to be. Stifter is among the first of that long line of German writers who have experienced and been unsettled by this quandary well before it disturbed English or even French writers. Where the social condition of man and the common everyday world are seen as provisional, the prose-writer will be faced with problems of composition quite different from those of the realistic tradition of nineteenth-century Europe.

In the lyrical poetry of Stifter's contemporaries—in Mörike and C. F. Meyer, but also in Heine—we notice a remarkable shift from story to image. It might be said that this increasing predominance of image over story makes these poets direct forebears of modern European poetry. We find much the same shift in Stifter's writings, only it occurs in a genre in which we do not expect it, and it is more radical. Stifter wrote two long novels and some thirty *Novellen*. Are these then stories without a story? Not quite. Certainly his early work, into the early 1840s, is full of palpable events and adventures, sometimes of a weird and wonderful kind, often inspired by Jean Paul. But even these early *Novellen* have not much by way of a plot, the chief carrier of story in narrative prose. "You can only create if you care," George Orwell wrote about Dickens.

Care—what about? Dickens cared about Mr. Dombey in his counting house; Stifter about the wanderer in the green forest. To invest creative energy in plot and story is to accept as meaningful, to care for, the social sphere in which alone the convolutions and proliferations of a plot are enacted. It is to accept the actual world, which is the world of men's social experience first and foremost, as a reality, hard or otherwise. It is to see "the world" as capable of yielding the profoundest interests, spiritual and moral as well as aesthetic. It is to acknowledge it as a creation not wholly alienated from its Creator. These are the unchallenged certainties, the *données* of realistic prose. Stifter seems to have had few of these certainties when he began writing, and none when, thirty years later, he ended his labors and his life.

It is not my suggestion that what is valuable in mid-nineteenth-century lyrical poetry becomes invalid in Stifter's prose; or that Stifter was a *poète manqué*. To say that he writes "poetic prose" is to beg many questions and answer none. The comparison should merely make clear something of the nature of the task Stifter set himself, and to suggest that he needed narrative means of a very special kind to accomplish it. To understand and appreciate his work we must abandon as far as possible the expectations with which we approach the realistic novelists of his age. He is at the opposite pole from a writer like Tolstoy, who has often been praised for having something to say to every kind of reader, and to each reader in almost every one of his moods. The reader to whom Stifter speaks is one who is willing to bypass the complexities of the actual world in order to gain a view of the bare lineaments of existence. Like Sartre's Roquentin [in *La Nausée*], Stifter writes as one who is engulfed by existence "in and by itself." Like Roquentin he senses its presence "just behind him," behind the things and people of the surrounding world. Like Roquentin he finds the actual social world bereft of a positive meaning. In this situation Roquentin tries deliberately, "gratuitously," to wipe out the film of existence on things and people. Stifter, motivated not by a deliberate search but an intuitive compulsion, seeks to penetrate to the grounds of existence. Sartre's prose is the prose of almost any naturalistic *monologue intérieur;* it speaks of the metaphysical undertaking explicitly, in philosophical terms; furthermore, the monologue is placed in a fully realized social world. The fact that Bouville, the scene of Sartre's action, is a dreary provincial backwater is neither here nor there: its reality is never challenged. What matters is that this firm rooting in everyday reality is a necessary part of Sartre's fiction, and thus also of his philosophical quest. The two—Bouville and interior monologue; realistic fiction and philosophy—are not one, but they belong together. Stifter's prose contains neither monologue nor anything like a fully realized social setting. He employs neither naturalistic incoherences nor the vocabulary of philosophy. Instead, he fashions a language that intimates the compulsion that moves him: the compulsion to bypass quotidian reality in a search for Being itself.

Are the grounds of man's existence propitious or malevolent? Can our reason span the meaning of our fate? Some of Stifter's stories suggest that it cannot. He then does his narrative utmost to build a protective wall between his characters and existence, yet it will not be walled in. The very things and landscapes, glaciers and rocks and trees, of which the wall is built belong to existence and let it through. Its encroachment on man is not (as in Sartre) nauseous and absurd, but tragic and absurd. There are other stories where the tragic and absurd is almost entirely avoided, where existence shows its propitious aspect. Or again, by joining the same bare lineaments of existence into a different pattern, he creates a utopian idyll. One is left with the impression that there is something fortuitous about which aspect of existence will prevail, that the grounds of man's being are indifferent to his fate. No one who has read a single page of Stifter's mature work could say that he indulges in the irrational. He does as much as is in his creative power to string the "golden chain of reasons" from causes to effects. But the chain does not reach all the way.

To what extent was Stifter, the *déraciné* son of a smallholder from the Bohemian forest, conscious of the nature of his undertaking? In his letters and in the famous preambles to some of his stories he speaks mainly of his didactic intention, of the moral uplift he wishes to inculcate through his fiction. And there is certainly a good deal of highmindedness in most of what he writes. The moral suasion, like the Christian piety that often accompanies it, belongs to the style. What he arrives at, finally, is a unique mixture of the disarmingly simple and the strangely (sometimes pedantically) contrived, which becomes second nature to him. But moral suasion is only one aspect of his art. Sometimes we notice that the moral tone becomes anxious, propitiatory, and that the propitiations fail to avert calamity, fail to reach the grounds of existence. The narrative movement characteristic of his stories begins with an elaborate description of natural setting. Wide-ranging, enumerative, and circumstantial, sometimes repetitious like a litany, the elements of the structure rise up and up, to the point where (so we feel) the very weight and size of the edifice will surely keep calamity out. And when all and more than all has been done towards that one end—what then? "One must show everything, in all its detail, without in the least sparing oneself. . . . But when that too has been done, Mr. Landsurveyor, then indeed everything necessary has been accomplished, one must content oneself, and wait" [Franz Kafka, *Das Schloss*, chapter 18], for now nemesis will strike.

Introducing one of the two main characters of *Der Waldgänger* (*The Forest Wanderer*, 1847), Stifter writes:

> Far back in the region of memories stands an old man whom the author once knew, who spoke in a somewhat foreign manner, to whose sayings he [the author] often listened, and to whose fate he, absorbed in his own feelings which seemed to him the center of the world, paid little attention. Because of their inconspicuousness this man's circumstances had not interested anybody, but after many years they became better known, and we wish to set them down for the sake of our recollection, if indeed a thing so little articulated, which produces its effects through its simple existence rather than through [being in a state of] excitation, can be represented at all.

The meaning of this passage seems clear enough. The "simple existence" together with its "inconspicuous circumstances" amounts to "the simple life"; this we readily equate with "the good life"; and to such a life, we agree, a "state of excitation," the discord of passions and of human strife, is at best irrelevant. As a matter of fact, in the light of the story that follows, our reading, in the course of which we equated "simple existence" with "the good life," turns out to be quite wrong. The life the story describes is tragic, flawed by a single wrong decision and its irredeemable consequences. ("Once you have answered the false alarm of the night bell," writes not Stifter but Kafka, "—and all, all is lost.") All, all the accoutrements of the good life have been accumulated and enumerated, to no avail. But when nemesis strikes it is, even at the climax, not in the form of an excitation but of calm desolation. The tragedy lies at the very core of that "simple existence" which is *not*, in this story at all events, "the good life." The solitary wanderer's fate is desolate (as it is in the Anglo-Saxon poem of that name), but as such it too belongs to the order of existence. *"Aber auch das ist im Recht"* ("that too is the law"), Rilke writes in the sonnet on the treacherous hunt of the doves—another tragic image relieved (or deprived) of the tension of drama. Tragedy without the tension of drama is like the evocation of "pure beauty unadulterated by anything that is beautiful."

If, then, the life recalled in that casually placed passage is less idyllic than it seemed, what is this "articulation" [*"etwas so wenig Gegliedertes"*], the absence of which is said to make the storyteller's task so difficult? It is contrasted with, and preceded by, "simple existence." For Schopenhauer, Stifter's contemporary, this "articulation" is the process of individuation; a Christian theologian sees it as the fall of man. The detailed consequences of that fall are most appropriately described in narrative prose. Indeed, what else do the great European realists of Stifter's age do except retrace the discrete shapes of the worldly obstacles that God has put into the path of men? But "the hardly individuated thing," *existence in and by itself*—how can narrative prose ever communicate that? A poet may try—

> The inner freedom from the practical desire,
> The release from action and suffering, release
>   from the inner
> And the outer compulsion, yet surrounded
> By a grace of sense, a white light still and mov-
>   ing,
> Erhebung without motion, concentration
> Without elimination. . . .
>   [T. S. Eliot, *Four Quartets,* "Burnt Norton"]

—mainly by enumerating what it is not. But a storyteller? How is he to begin? "Once upon a time there was no man who had no house in which he *was,* all alone"? He can hardly tell us more than that saddest of all fairytales which a grandmother tells the children at the end of Georg Büchner's *Woyzeck* (1837):

> Come, you shrimps. Once upon a time there was a poor child that had no father and no mother, they were all dead, and there was no one left in the world. They were all dead, and so it set off and searched night and day. And as there was

no one left on the earth it wanted to go up in the sky, and the moon seemed to have a friendly face. But when it came to the moon, it found it was a piece of rotten wood. So then it went to the sun, and when it came to the sun it was only a withered sunflower. And when it came to the stars they were little golden gnats, stuck on pins just as the shrike sticks them on the blackthorn. And when it wanted to go back to earth, the earth was just a pot that had been turned upside down. And it was all alone. So it sat down and cried, and it is still sitting there all alone.

For the Christian, the fall of man is preceded by a state of being he calls Paradise. This, something like this, is the setting of Stifter's greatest novel, *Der Nachsommer* (1857). But how to explain the sad isolation of Paradise? And what if that simple, undivided being which precedes individuation is itself not positive but negative? What if the Ancients were right who saw in Fate "the terrible ultimate stark ground of events . . . the last ultimate unreason of existence?"

These darker questions may be answered by *Der beschriebene Tännling* (*The Inscribed Firtree,* published 1845, revised 1850), a representative *Novelle* of Stifter's mature phase which leads toward and helps to explain *Der Nachsommer.* For all its dark implications, the story and overt message of this *Novelle* have the naïveté of a tale found in a village almanac. The bare retelling of it makes a modern reader blush with embarrassment. The tale, set in the early eighteenth century, concerns chiefly a poor and beautiful girl, Hanna, who lives with her old mother in a solitary mountain cottage near a well consecrated to the Holy Virgin; and a hot-tempered lumberman, Hanns, who is in love with the girl and uses his hard-earned wages to buy her precious gifts. An elaborate deer hunt is arranged in the region for the entertainment of the feudal prince (who owns the lands in which the tale is set) and of his numerous entourage of lords and ladies, among them Guido, who falls in love with Hanna. Hanns is determined to take his revenge on Guido, but in a dream a vision of the Virgin Mary saves him from committing the murder he had planned. The two men never meet; Hanna leaves with Guido for the great city and marries him; and the story closes with Hanna's visit to her native region a great many years later:

> A dark velvet cloak was draped about her body as she sat leaning back in the carriage. Her face was finely drawn and pale, her lips too were pale, her body had become rounder and heavier. Hanns, whose face was full of wrinkles, stood by the wayside.

She does not recognize him. The final paragraph underlines the message of the tale. Both had prayed to the Virgin of the Well; Hanna (according to ancient custom) on the day of her first confession had asked for a fine silken dress embroidered with gold and silver; what Hanns prayed for while contemplating the murder of Guido we do not know. When, after hearing of Hanna's wedding, the village girls recall that her wish was granted, an old smith replies: "She received the Virgin's curse, not her grace—the Virgin's wisdom, grace and miracle were granted to quite another person."

This tale could be told (and in a sense *is* told) in a very few pages. If we add up the passages in which the action is described, the very few lines of terse dialogue, the few paragraphs containing simple and unprobing character-descriptions, we shall find that most of the story's fifty-odd closely printed pages are devoted to its natural setting, to recitals of the various customs associated with the places of the action and other places nearby, and to a description of the hunt. Thus the girl, Hanna, is introduced only after more than six pages have been devoted to a detailed account of the mountainous landscape not far from the southwestern border of Bohemia and Upper Austria, an account which ranges widely over the whole area. The narrator begins as one who is finding his place on a detailed map of the region. He pinpoints the firtree of the title, its trunk covered with mementoes carved once in the sapling, but now scarred and gnarled throughout many decades of the tree's vigorous growth. He moves to a hill—but it is not yet the one on which stands the bare little house where Hanna will live with her mother; he moves on, to another neighboring forest and meadow; contemplates the effect of clouds and morning air on the color of the distant Alps; pauses near two solitary houses; moves to the little church nearby, dedicated to the Virgin of the Blessed Well in which Hanns will bathe his eyes and face; moves on, to the village of Oberplan (Stifter's native village), to tell the full story of the first miracle that happened at the well, and finally describes the house near the church in which Hanna is brought up.

Why does he linger so? We feel that he would much rather not tell the story at all, not disrupt the natural setting—which is no longer merely a "setting" but the center of his attention, the very substance and core of his tale. It is as if he were unwilling to turn to the tale of passion, betrayal and desolation. We notice that the story is divided into four sections, entitled "The Gray Bush," "The Clearing of Many Colors" (Hanns's place of work), "The Green Forest" (containing the description of the hunt), and "The Dark Tree" (in which Hanns, waiting for Guido, has the saving vision). But again, this division is more meaningful in terms of the changing landscapes than of the stages of action to which it roughly corresponds. The greyish-green hill; the clearing in the forest gleaming with the brilliant scarlet of wild strawberries and the mauve of raspberries, with the golden brown of singed bracken and the heavy black of bare earth; the sharply bounded lethal area of the dark-green forest ("*Jagdraum*") into which the wild animals are driven for massacre; the skyscapes—pristine blue, watery grey, dappled with baroque Bohemian cloud, hidden behind whitish mists—are not all these more important than the figures in the landscape? Certainly it is they rather than the figures that are the bearers of existence; they *are*. And what (the bewildered reader will ask) does *that* mean, what could it possibly mean?

A good part of the story of Stifter's later prose could be told by examining the ways he uses the verb "to be." As an exercise in "stylistics" such an examination sounds dull enough. Yet we would readily find a great many passages where the verb is used not as an inconspicuous link between subject and predicate nor yet as an auxiliary. We would find that in some peculiar and quite idiosyncratic

way it becomes "ontic," it sets out to intimate bare existence. English renderings of such passages are not illuminating, they fail to convey an effect which in German is unique and strange. Here are some examples from the first three pages of our story:

> *Die Säulen der Milchbäuerin sind durch feine aber deutlich unterscheidbare Spalten geschieden. Einige sind höher, andere niederer. Sie sind alle von oben so glatt und eben abgeschnitten, dass . . .*

The Pillars of rock are separated from each other by thin but distinct crevices. Some are higher, some lower. All are smoothly and evenly sliced off at the top, so that . . .

> *Ausser den drei Dingen, der Milchbäuerin, den Brunnenhäuschen und dem Kirchlein, ist noch ein viertes, das die Aufmerksamkeit auf sich zieht. Es ist ein alter Weg, der ein wenig unterhalb des Kirchleins ein Stück durch den Rasen dahingeht und dann aufhört, ohne zu etwas zu führen. Er ist von alten gehauenen Steinen gebaut, und an seinen Seiten stehen alte Linden; aber die Steine sind schon eingesunken . . .*

> *Die obenerwähnten Bäumesind die einzigen, die der Berg hat, sowie der Felsen der Milchbäurein der einzige bedeutende ist.*

Apart from the three things—the rock pillars, the little well house and the chapel, [there] is yet a fourth that attracts the attention. It is an old path, which for a while goes through the lawn [that lies] a little below the chapel, and then stops without leading anywhere. It is built of old hewn stone and lined on both sides with linden trees; but the stones are sunk in . . .

The trees mentioned above are the only ones the mountain has, likewise the rock is the only important one.

Such bare constructions are not in themselves unusual. But when they are repeated in sentence after sentence we may wonder whether what shapes this prose are peasant simplicities or high ontological aims. The natural tendency of German syntax to separate the auxiliary from the main verb is so intensified that the auxiliary *almost* ceases to communicate with the main verb or predicate. It thus ceases to be "auxiliary" and assumes an expressive gravity all its own; and this is done, not crudely, by multiplying intervening constructions and phrases, but through short, bare sentences. At this point, too, the spell of boredom this prose weaves may yield to a curious spell of fascination. We may sense uneasily that the simplest of means—and language yields no simpler statement than "the forest is green" or "the child was . . . beautiful"—are employed in the service of an intention both complex and unrealizable. For, of course, what Stifter seems to attempt cannot ultimately be done. No verb can stand without its predicate. Existence in and by itself, uncontaminated by anything existing, cannot be expressed. Individuation is inescapable. Yet if this "ontological" style fails to achieve its ultimate object, what it does achieve is remarkable enough.

The things of nature participate in an order of existence, this prose tells us, which men can do little more than disrupt. Some—a few villagers, barely mentioned—live close to that order. Hanna and Hanns too initially belong to it—she through her beauty, he through his vigor and energy. This order is presented as propitious and benign, but it is not the only order of being. Men—at least to the extent that they live in "the world"—belong to another order. The prince and his courtiers bring havoc to the countryside, slaughtering the animals of the forest, throwing the villagers into a state of "excitation and wildness" (*"Erregung und Übermut"*). At the climax of their bacchic abandon following the first part of the hunt, the crowd of villagers singles out Guido and Hanna and, with the repeated shout of "This is the most beautiful couple!" seals their fate. But this other order too, in all its violence and destructiveness, has a strangely impersonal, "ontic" quality about it.

The hunt, not the personal fate it changes, is the story's true climax. We recognize it as the symbol of Hanna's abrupt movement from the pastoral setting to the worldliness of the Prince's court, from one order to the other. This movement has been prepared for—even as a girl Hanna was shown to be susceptible to the fine clothes and jewels that Guido's world promises. Yet the change comes suddenly and silently; only a single brief, wholly impersonal comment from the author describes her feelings. As for Guido's feelings, they are conveyed by static images: a confusion, a deep blush, the picture, seen from afar, of him kneeling before Hanna—that is all. While two pages are given to the festive meal after the first meet, Hanna and Guido exchange not a single word. Hanns, we read, "knew nothing of all this"; then "he learned all"; and his night of agony, prayer and deliverance is conveyed, not through his emotions, but solely through the simple things he does, the places he goes to. These characterizations could not be more bare or more effective, nor could the contrast between them and their "settings" be more marked. Just as the descriptions of the countryside were more than symbols of human peace, so the description of the hunt is more than a symbol of human fate. For the hunt, though elaborately planned by the prince's servants and organized with the help of some of the villagers, does not give the impression of a human action at all. Its extremely powerful description begins with a piece of music (*"eine rauschende Waldmusik"*) played on wind instruments, echoing back from the forest in "notes of terror and sudden calls of fear [since] the forest knew only the sounds of thunder and storm, not the terrible sounds of music." There follows the call of a single hunting horn. Dogs are let loose into an area of the forest which has been roped off all round by impenetrable nets. A shot is heard. An anguished stag throws itself against the canvas, a wildcat shoots up a tree. Guns discharge their loads, bullets hit, explosions flash, white smoke fills the lethal area. But there are no people. The narrative voice is mainly passive, once or twice "one saw . . . one heard . . . ," for the rest it is the objects and animals themselves that seem to perform this rite of death; only when the hunt is over do the servants move in, to gather the corpses.

There are no elaborate verbal simplicities in this passage;

it is full of strife where the earlier scenes were full of peace. But once more we have the impression that something other than a human agency is at work, something other than the wills of individual men. It is again existence in and by itself, this time bearing death and destruction, that is invoked. It becomes clear that even the conflict between a countryside at peace and "the world" bearing terror and discord and desolation, is not the fullest statement of the story's theme. What the story intimates is this almost unutterable conflict between two modes of existence, one positive the other negative, in which men are involved but which extend beyond, behind them.

But may not all this be taken as an example of the pathetic fallacy, an age-old device for bodying forth human emotions? Stifter himself, in an earlier story [**Der Hochwald**], tells us so:

> there lies a propriety, I might almost say an expression of virtue, in the countenance of Nature before it has ever been touched by the hand of man, to which the soul must bow as to something virginal, pure and divine,—and yet it is after all man's soul alone which carries all its own inward greatness into the image of Nature.

It seems that, just as with his verbs of Being Stifter is attempting the impossible, so here he is merely stating the obvious. Yet if, returning to our story, we look at the way "the human soul" speaks to us we shall find that most of the human feelings and reactions too are rendered impersonally:

> *Die Liebe, die Zuneigung und die Anhänglichkeit wuchs immer mehr und mehr.*

> The love [between Hanna and Hanns], the sympathy and the attachment grew ever more.

And later, after the great hunt:

> *Das zufällige Nebeneinanderstehen Hannas und des schönen jungen Herrn war nicht ohne weitere Folgen geblieben.*

> The accidental encounter of Hanna and the handsome young nobleman did not remain without further consequences.

> *Weil die andern Herren, welche zur Besichtigung mancher Werke der Gegend fortgeritten waren, viele Tage ausblieben, konnte die Sache in Gang kommen und Hanna von Empfindungen ergriffen werden.*

> Because the other lords had ridden away to inspect several work-places in the region, staying away a number of days, the affair could start on its course and Hanna be gripped by emotions.

> *Endlich bemächtigte sich der Ruf dieser Sache und trug seine Gerüchte in der Gegend herum.*

> At last rumor took hold of the affair, and carried its gossip into the region.

Finally, there is the remarkable scene of the roll call (relentlessly repeated over and over again in **Witiko**). In preparation for the second meet the prince reads out the places of ambush, to make sure that each hunter knows where he has been posted. He begins: *"Herr Andreas bei der roten Lake."* ("Lord Andreas, by the Red Pool.") The reply is simple enough—*"Weiss sie nicht"*—and quite untranslatable. For one thing, English has no means of conveying Stifter's majestic use of *"wissen"* instead of the common *"kennen."* Moreover, should we heighten "I do not know the place" or rather "He does not know it" into the terse and impersonal "not known," then the effect of the whole passage is more like that of an Anglo-Saxon saga than a mid-nineteenth-century *Novelle:*

> *"Herr Andreas bei der roten Lake."*
> *"Weiss sie nicht."*
> *"Gidi wird dich hinführen."*
> *"Herr Gunibald bei der Kreixe."*
> *"Weiss sie."*
> *"Herr Friedrich vom Eschberg am gebrannten Steine."*
> *"Weiss ihn nicht."*
> *"Der Schmied Fierer wird Euch begleiten."*
> *"Herr Guido am beschriebenen Tännling."*
> *"Weiss ihn."*

> "Lord Andreas by the Red Pool."
> "Not known."
> "Gideon will lead you."
> "Lord Gunibald near the [old hut?]."
> "Known."
> "Lord Friedrich von Eschberg near the Burnt Rock."
> "Not known."
> "Fierer the blacksmith will accompany you."
> "Lord Guido near the Inscribed Firtree."
> "Known."

Yet this archaic bareness is no mock-heroic tableau; it is, we now see, only one more way in which Stifter attempts to go beyond the limits of individuation. More recent attempts of this kind—Ernst Jünger's coldly inhuman language of "the storm of steel," Michel Butor's *"chosisme"*—are not strictly relevant parallels. Stifter's characteristic mode is not that inhuman. Existence, he implies, has some measure of *order* and personal meaning. Both Hanna's and Hann's prayers are in some way answered by a just and merciful divinity. And yet, even this story leaves us with the impression that the search for existence is also a flight from the human—or rather, not a flight but a gentle and relentless moving away.

In Stifter's stories, and in his great novel too, a most delicate balance is struck between the barest of actions, the simplest psychology, and a high ontological aim. He does not suggest that man, the issue of individuation, is (as Roquentin puts it) *in the way*—not quite. Whenever he has occasion for an explicit statement, he affirms that man is able to participate in natural existence, and live in harmony with its order. *To be* in that region, however, to melt into its dark-green forests and bare grey rocks and blueish-white glaciers, is no longer to be quite recognizable in ours.

It may well be that my earlier comparison with Sartre's Roquentin seems unconvincing and adventitious, a mere fashionable anachronism. Certainly the difference in narrative tenors—in the means of the quest for Being—could hardly be greater. Yet the fundamental metaphysical in-

tention, it seems to me, remains the same. At the end of his fruitless search for being Roquentin is leaving Bouville. At the station he resolves to write a book. A novel? We do not know:

> "I don't quite know what kind of a book—but you would have to guess, behind the printed words, behind the pages, at something which would not exist, which would be above existence. A story, for example, something that could never happen, an adventure. It would have to be beautiful, and hard as steel, and make people ashamed of their existence."

Here Sartre's book closes and Stifter's **Der Nachsommer** begins. Beyond and behind its utopian construction, its didactic intention, its Goethean nature worship; beyond the moral and aesthetic lesson it teaches and behind the endless array of implements and things and *objets d'art*, **Der Nachsommer** is an attempt to evoke undivided, beautiful being, that which "could never happen," that which by implication and by its inherent perfection would "make people ashamed of their existence." The structure of **Der Nachsommer** is a good deal more complex and its compositional elements a good deal richer than those of our story. The novel addresses itself to the positive, propitious order of Being only; purposefully, relentlessly it excludes the negative, destructive order. Yet the ontological quest remains the same, and chief among the narrative means employed in that quest are those that I have mentioned in the course of examining the more modest *Novelle*. A country estate whose exquisite and prudent husbandry is rewarded by plentiful harvests and perfect harmony vouchsafes that "inner freedom from practical desire" of which the poet speaks. "The release from action and suffering" is attained by placing all action and all suffering far back, in the distant past. Instead of "the inner and outer compulsion," the hero is guided by gentle precept and a free inward development. "A sense of grace, a white light still and moving" illuminates every scene, every carefully wrought meeting and every gentle, undramatic parting. "Concentration without elimination" is attained by means of enumerations of objects and a circumstantiality without parallel in German, perhaps European, fiction. The novel reaches towards a quietus beyond individuation, it seeks to attain the unattainable. If indeed there were such a thing as *"Erhebung* without motion," then **Der Nachsommer** would be the work in which it is achieved. (pp. 239-50)

> *J. P. Stern, "Stifter's Fiction: 'Erhebung' without Motion," in* Novel: A Forum on Fiction, *Vol. 1, No. 3, Spring, 1968, pp. 239-50.*

David Luke (essay date 1968)

[*In the following excerpt, Luke discusses three of Stifter's short stories and their relationship to idyllic literature, pointing out that in these works Stifter purports to represent reality as harmonious perfection.*]

[**Limestone, Tourmaline,** and **The Recluse**] were all written toward the end of what is now often called the "Biedermeier" period of Austrian culture, which Stifter pre-eminently represents and yet transfigures. The last of them was first published in 1848. The Biedermeier "period," if it is possible to give it a chronological definition, corresponds roughly to that of Metternich's political ascendancy between 1815 and 1848 not only in Austria but effectively in the whole of Central Europe. Its outlook and values were the cultural accompaniment of a carefully sterilized autocratic anti-revolutionary regime. As in the eighteenth century, the development of German literature was still, or again, closely associated with the political powerlessness of the cultivated middle classes; and in the Biedermeier phase perhaps the most characteristic creative response to this situation was literature in the idyllic mode. Idyll had been a leading element in the German literary tradition since some of Goethe's finest work and since before Goethe. This is especially true if we use "idyll" in the wider and deeper sense given to this term by Schiller in his aesthetic theory, where an "idyll" is any work representing reality as the harmonious perfection which it should be but empirically is not, and where moreover the term is used to denote a *mode* of literature which can be realized in different forms or kinds (thus, among Goethe's works for instance, we might classify not only *Hermann and Dorothea* but also *Iphigenia in Tauris,* as well as perhaps Act 3 of Part II of *Faust* and even the *Roman Elegies,* as idyllic in Schiller's sense, although traditionally an overt erotic content is not associated with idyll). The obverse of idyll is what Schiller, by a rather more violent terminological extension, called satire: that is, any work whether tragic or comic that represents reality as the disharmonious imperfection which it is but should not be. Thus these two modes are closely involved with each other. In Biedermeier literature the idyllic mode was the more prominent, and its most characteristic realization was in the novel and the *Novelle.* The *Novelle* or long short story ("short novel" would in many cases be the more appropriate translation) had increased in importance in the nineteenth century and continued to do so: many of the finest works of German literature in both that century and ours are written in this form. (There are comparatively few examples in English: Melville's *Billy Budd* is one.) The *Novelle* can be tragic, comic, or idyllic, and at its most typical it is realistic and symbolic—"realistic" in the sense of excluding the Romantic conventions of fantasy and allegory, though there are some interesting hybrids between the *Novelle* and the *Märchen* or fairy story. It is as a writer of *Novellen* that Stifter began and was, and still is, best known; but development toward full artistic maturity seemed to involve for him a movement toward the major form of prose fiction, and he ended by creating two of the longest and finest novels in German literature, **The Late Summer (Der Nachsommer)** and **Witiko,** as well as expanding one of his already expanded stories into virtually an unfinished novel, **My Great-Grandfather's Papers (Die Mappe meines Urgrossvaters)**. When Stifter began writing stories in 1840 or thereabouts he was under the influence of some of the lesser German Romantics, particularly the sentimental and whimsical Jean-Paul Richter; but his development also tended away from this style. The German Romantic schools had in any case been a less important influence in Austria than the Classicism of Schiller and Goethe, which affected the leading Austri-

an writers profoundly. It is Stifter's work above all that suggests an affinity between Biedermeier, within its narrower scope, and the culture of Goethe's Weimar. He moves away from Romanticism not so much toward "modern" realism as cyclically or spirally back toward the kind of classicism that fuses reality with ideality. The constantly reiterated comparison of Stifter to Goethe is one that with all due reservations one simply cannot help making. In 1919 the Austrian critic Hermann Bahr wrote: "It is as if Nature had been so in love with the incomparable phenomenon Goethe that she tried to repeat it again, a subtle variant of it to be sure, a quieter version, on a smaller scale and with a change of emphasis . . . " There are of course very important differences, such as the absence or minimization of the erotic element in Stifter (he could never have written the *Roman Elegies*) and his total avoidance of irony and cynicism (he could never have created Mephistopheles). His talent is altogether more narrow and, in the best sense, provincial than Goethe's. But like Goethe he was passionately interested in the natural sciences and in the visual arts (they both tried to be painters as well as writers), and like Goethe he held himself aloof from contemporary political and social issues. Stifter was quite out of sympathy with the *littérature engagée* of the outlawed revolutionary "Young Germany" movement. He was by instinct a mildly liberal conservative, and remained unpolitical, sheltered, in general more or less untouched by influences alien to his artistic and moral vision. Neither French nor English literature of the period seems to have meant anything to him. Unlike his later Swiss contemporary Gottfried Keller (though they too can be interestingly compared), he was unaffected by positivistic thought and retained the Catholicism of his upbringing. He was poles apart from Heine and from the other great vulgarian of the period, Hebbel. Although capable of psychological realism he does not exploit it for its own sake. His realism is above all that of the devoted, reverent observer of the visible world, the Goethean student of nature, the landscape painter, the geologist and meteorologist. His great cumulative descriptions of forests and other scenery, which for all their haunting imaginative power are scientifically accurate, reflecting detailed specific knowledge and life-long experience, give a perennial Antaeus-like strength to Stifter's work: here he is literally close to the ground, "inspired by classical soil" as Goethe had felt in the streets of Rome—if that is also possible in the Austrian countryside. One might say that Stifter's essential achievement, in the post-Romantic epoch to which he belonged, was to develop his idyllic talent in such a way as to re-create, in his best and maturest work, the true monumental classical idyll, while at the same time giving it a different and more mysterious flavor—something perhaps of the flavor that distinguishes Mörike's finest poems from Goethe's. And at his best he succeeds, like Goethe in *Hermann and Dorothea,* in avoiding both the tediousness which is the pitfall of monumental classicity and the sentimentality which is the besetting vice of idyllicism.

His progress toward this artistic adulthood was slow and painful, as was his own personal development. To readers who do not confuse art with life or oversimplify the relationship between them, it comes as no surprise to learn that Stifter's life was anything but idyllically happy and that he ended it by committing suicide. It began in 1805 in humble circumstances in the unimportant Bohemian village of Oberplan near the border of Upper Austria. He was relatively fortunate in his education, being admitted at the age of twelve, after the early death of his father, to the Benedictine college of Kremsmünster, near Linz—a splendid Baroque abbey where it was easy for art and religion to become for Stifter, as they thereafter always remained, very closely associated with each other. The Catholicism which he learned here was humane, cultivated, and not unworldly. It incorporated something of the optimistic liberal Enlightenment of the eighteenth century which Joseph II had transplanted to Baroque Austria, thus making "Josephinism" respectable in wide circles and enabling it to act as a bridge for the influence of the Weimar classics. Kremsmünster seems to have laid the foundations of the optimistic attitudes which Stifter continued, like Goethe, to reassert—at least in his work—despite all his later difficulties and disillusionments and despite a basically melancholic temperament. In 1826 he proceeded to the University in Vienna, where he rather fecklessly failed to qualify himself even formally for any of the professions; it was in these student years that Stifter became a problem to himself and his friends. This was also the period of his unhappy love for Fanny Greipl, a girl with rich parents and many admirers who seems to have returned Stifter's affection, but the relationship foundered on his strangely neurotic irresolution, not wholly attributable to family and financial difficulties. He continued to refer pathetically to her as the eternal "bride of his imagination," while having already taken as his mistress the quite uneducated Amalie Mohaupt. Fanny married a civil servant and died not long after; Stifter married Amalie in 1837. The loss of Fanny remained with him as a tragic experience, which recurs in various disguises throughout his work. Amalie could not even spell, much less interest herself in literature: even in his marriage Stifter seems to have followed in Goethe's footsteps, though Amalie was by all accounts a less agreeable and more calculating person than Christiane Vulpius. She made, however, an efficient housewife, providing her husband with a well-ordered domesticity and the bourgeois comforts which they both enjoyed but could ill afford. Stifter was still living hand-to-mouth as a private tutor employed by aristocratic families with whom he became acquainted in Vienna (for a time he even taught Metternich's son, after the Chancellor's police spies had cleared him as politically sound). He painted assiduously, though achieving little success in this subvocation; in the 1840s, however, he began to acquire a little income, and some reputation, as a writer. His stories nearly always appeared first in almanacs and yearbooks and were later considerably revised for publication in his two main collections, the books which he called **Studies** (*Studien*) and **Stones of Many Colors** (*Bunte Steine*). The latter title reflects his interest in mineralogy which led him to rename these six stories after some of the stones which, like Goethe, he was given to collecting; the appropriateness of the new titles is variable and they do not really succeed in giving artistic unity to the book, which he rather misleadingly described as a book of stories for children, although this applies at most to three of them.

His marriage with Amalie remained childless (although some recent research suggests the possibility that before marrying him Amalie may have given birth to a child of which he may have been the father, and which died almost at once). This was one of Stifter's deepest sources of unhappiness and obscure self-reproach. His longing for children, for the self-that-one-might-have-been, was bound up with a strong educative impulse (both are reflected in . . . **The Recluse**, where the idealized younger generation is taught in good time to avoid the failures of the older; a similar situation recurs in the novel **The Late Summer**). Amalie's young niece Juliane was adopted in place of a daughter; she ran away from home twelve years later and drowned herself in the Danube. At one time Stifter felt he had found the ideal son-substitute in Gustav Scheibert, the son of a friend and colleague in Linz, but the young man also died prematurely; **Stones of Many Colors** is dedicated to his memory. Stifter remained passionately interested in education, and was apparently an excellent teacher, but he had tried in vain to secure a regular school-teaching appointment. In 1848, shortly after the March riots in Vienna to which he reacted at first with the enthusiasm of an idealistic liberal but very soon with increasing disillusionment and dismay, he moved to Linz where he was to spend the rest of his life. In 1850, at long last, the Vienna authorities appointed him as an inspector of schools for Upper Austria, though not until after he had been driven by financial embarrassment into a once-for-all sale of all the rights in his first and most popular book, the **Studies.** He began by seeing his new official position idealistically, as an opportunity to exercise a reforming influence on the whole of society, but disillusionment again rapidly set in, and in the ensuing years his letters to his publisher constantly lament his enslavement to trivial professional activities. He managed nevertheless to continue to write. **The Late Summer** appeared in 1857, and **Witiko** in 1865-7; and in addition to the finished **Studies** (published in 1844-50) and **Stones of Many Colors** (1853), he wrote some further *Novellen,* bringing the total of these to about thirty. Yet from about 1855 onwards his life was overshadowed by increasingly serious nervous and organic illnesses. He suffered from acute depressions and neurotic fears, and traveled restlessly in search of peace and relief. Eventually an incurable disease of the liver was diagnosed. In 1865, after it had been reported to Vienna that he could not live long, he was retired on full salary. The Emperor Francis Joseph granted him the title of *Hofrat,* and in 1867, with a certain symbolic appropriateness, he was also awarded a decoration by Grand Duke Karl Alexander of Saxe-Weimar, the grandson of Goethe's Karl August. In December of the same year he became hopelessly ill and bedridden, and one night in January 1868 he suddenly seized his razor and cut open his throat, dying two days later without regaining consciousness.

This action has seemed to some critics and biographers hard to reconcile with the idealistic character of Stifter's work; some have even refused to accept the facts, which were hushed up at the time. But (as we may learn from Nietzsche and others) even the most life-affirming gesture in art tells us nothing about the happiness or despair or otherwise of the artist's life. Knowledge of the tragic is inseparable from the true vision of goodness and beauty, just as an awareness of goodness and beauty is inseparable from true tragedy. At the end of a despairing letter to his publisher and friend Heckenast, Stifter nevertheless wrote: " . . . I do not want to have my suffering taken from me, for that would be to take God [*das Göttliche*] from me as well." These often-quoted words may also be taken to mean that he obscurely sensed that his art was rooted in suffering. He did not always write about himself with such mystic insight, perhaps not even with such truthfulness. The official, possibly the only *conscious* program for his art was that it was to be (to revert again to Schiller's categories) in the idyllic mode. But idyll is next door to tragedy, in the sense that it has pushed tragedy back to just beyond its boundaries; it is in fact the *anti-tragic* mode of art. Stifter's preferred gesture as a writer (again, like Goethe's) was anti-tragic. His intention, as he said, was "to portray the beauty of God and the world"; but this does not make his art superficial. And the fact that (as he added) he had no wish to combine this portrayal with an expression of his views on the German Customs Union does not mean that he had no message for his own time or for ours: for idyll, the obverse of "satire," is also by implication a criticism of life—this is, indeed, its indirect sadness. After 1848 especially, Stifter tried more than ever to build what he called "a divine bulwark [*ein Damm des Göttlichen*]"—to achieve in his writing a monumental simplicity, purity, harmony, and stillness, to create something which could be held up before his turbulent and vulgar age as an unspoken message, a reminder, a judgment. If *Hermann and Dorothea* was Goethe's response to the French Revolution and the 1790s, **Limestone, The Late Summer,** and *Witiko* were Stifter's to the mid-nineteenth century. Although he once wrote that "beauty has no purpose at all but to be beautiful," we must describe him as fundamentally a moralist and not an aesthete: indeed, he would not have understood the difference, for to him beauty and goodness were the same. Their portrayal is his characteristic art: the anti-tragic idyll. (pp. 3-11)

[Three of his short stories, **Tourmaline, The Recluse,** and **Limestone**] are studies in isolation, the response of the isolated person to his situation being significantly different in each case. The stories are, in fact, three variations on a theme which has a considerable history in German fiction (extending from well before Stifter's to at least Thomas Mann's time), namely, that of the *Sonderling,* the comic and/or tragic lonely eccentric or crank. A common treatment of this theme in the post-Romantic period was to make the eccentric see the error of his ways and achieve after all, usually through marriage, a "natural," normal life and a proper relatedness to society. This variant—the cured or converted eccentric—occurs in several of Stifter's most important stories and was later to be especially characteristic of Gottfried Keller; it reflects the development away from Romanticism in both these writers. [In **The Recluse,** the title character] is an eccentric who has been converted or disillusioned too late to retrieve his own life, and can only warn and educate his young nephew and heir, impressing upon him particularly the dangers of remaining unmarried; in **Tourmaline** the eccentric is married but marriage fails to save him; in **Limestone** he does not marry but finds, by renunciation, a solution on a different plane.

The Recluse was printed in its first form in 1844, having probably been written in the previous year; the revised and expanded version appeared in the fifth volume of **Studies** in 1850. To some extent even this final version represents the not yet mature period of Stifter's work, when he had not yet freed himself from the influence of Romantic sentimentalism. The idyll is here artistically impaired by overemphasis and overidealization. The whole account of the young hero's preparation for departure is disproportionately diffuse, and the first chapter in particular is a mere quasi-lyrical preface most of which might well be dispensed with. These are blemishes on what is nevertheless in many ways one of the most powerful and profound of Stifter's stories. The opening chapters are in fact structurally related to and balanced against the sections describing the "recluse" himself, who emerges all the more forcefully against the background of this world of simplehearted normal happiness and affectionate family ties—this sentimentalized version of the world of *Hermann and Dorothea.* (The scene between the two young people who discover their mutual love at the moment of separation even more strongly recalls Goethe's other short idyll, *Alexis and Dora.*) The Victor-Hanna-Ludmilla household is presented, both expressly and implicitly, as in various ways antithetical to that of Victor's uncle. Innocent youth is contrasted with cynical and decrepit age, neatness and care with slovenliness and dirt, love and trust with morbidly apprehensive self-insulation (rather like that of Tiberius on Capri), naïve Christian faith with a kind of sophisticated proto-Nietzschean individualism, the little house and village and church in the valley with the gloomy Hermitage and its ruined monastery where no bells ever ring—a place symbolizing, so to speak, the death or absence of God. There are also subtler linkages and parallels. Victor's "resolution never to marry," his description of himself as "the loneliest person in the world," and his general callow *Weltschmerz* gain significance by juxtaposition with his uncle's real failure and loneliness. There is a similar thematic relationship between the pathos of the boy's imminent departure from home (on which Stifter insists with such strange unrealism—after all, he is only leaving to take up a job in a different part of Austria) and the old man's dread of imminent death, his poignant clinging to what remains of his life as to the dregs of wine which he pours back into their bottles: in both cases the irretrievable preciousness of passing time is symbolically emphasized. Then again, there are certain latent affinities between the two ways of life which call for redifferentiation on another level. For example, both the uncle and Ludmilla carefully dust hoarded and useless objects, and both have long-established fixed mealtimes. Thus both households are what might now be called obsessionalistic; but one would not call Ludmilla or Victor neurotic. The descriptive affinity on one psychological plane is less significant than the qualitative difference. To Ludmilla and Hanna and Victor the meal is a ceremony of their life together, and they reverence the past in the things that symbolize it; whereas the old man's rituals are largely compulsive and dictated by hypochondria and fear (although his dusting of the stuffed birds is a kind of decayed or self-caricaturing remnant of a capacity to love and care for things, which shows itself more positively in his care of flowers and his strangely disguised love for Victor). These are the two poles of the Biedermeier world: the tragicomic eccentric on the one hand, on the other the apotheosis of normality and regularity and tradition, equated with the Good Life. The confrontation of the two, culminating in the mutually educative relationship between Victor and the old man, is what gives the story its structure and its fascination. But Stifter, whose insight into the "obsessional" character has the profundity of instinctive self-knowledge, perhaps put into the figure of the uncle more of himself than he realized. Victor, when he is released from the island and hears the church bells again, feels that the whole thing has been like a bad dream. In fact, to the reader, it is Victor who seems dreamlike and the uncle terribly real, almost the only "real" person in the story: the others are ideal contrast-figures, projected like a mirage out of the pain of embittered isolation. Victor is in certain ways a fairy-tale hero: the disadvantaged youth who turns out to be of aristocratic lineage and (a turn of events not uncommon in Stifter) inherits a fortune, after undergoing certain trials and ordeals (imprisonment by an at first apparently wicked magician, etc.), and then lives happily ever after. The story of course contains no overtly fantastic element, but perhaps its special flavor derives from this combination of the idyllic-*märchenhaft* with the realistic-tragic. Artistically it reaches its true level in the fourth chapter, "The Journey," of which the dramatic climax (and Stifter's fiction is rarely dramatic) is the first encounter between the boy and the old man. This has been prepared by the long account of Victor's gradual fateful approach to the lake-bound Hermitage, through an increasingly magnificent and wild landscape which seems to move with him and draw him on. The effect here is not static but dynamic, almost cinematographic: the painter Stifter has transcended painting. (It has been suggested that the topography of the uncle's strange retreat was based on certain features of the Traunsee area, which Stifter is known to have visited; but he rarely if ever transcribes a real landscape exactly or from one locality only.)

The first version of **Tourmaline,** under the title of (literally) *The Doorkeeper at the Mansion* (*Der Pförtner im Herrenhause*), was written not later than the summer of 1848 and possibly earlier, though it was not actually printed until 1852. The facts on which the story was based (though with much adaptation) were narrated to Stifter by the acress Antonie von Arneth, a cultured Viennese lady who had once been engaged to the poet Theodor Körner. The events had taken place "long ago," and the model for the famous actor was in all probability Josef Lange of the Burgtheater: his wife had been Aloisia Weber, the singer with whom Mozart was at one time in love and whose sister he later married (it was Lange, too, who painted what is probably the best-known portrait of the composer). In 1794, fourteen years after marrying Lange, Aloisia deserted her husband and children to go on concert tours, and never returned to Vienna. Stifter shifted the roles: in his story the actor is an unmarried philanderer, and the person deserted by his wife is the mysterious "*Rentherr*" [In a footnote, the critic adds "I can find no practicable English equivalent for this word, which simply means a man living on a private income (French *rentier*)."] (It is

characteristic, and in fact a "classical" feature, that in none of these three stories is the principal figure named: they are simply "the uncle," "the *Rentherr*," "the priest.") He retained certain details—the "Petersplatz" exists in Vienna and contains a house where Lange probably often visited Aloisia; the Arneths in fact lived in a suburb near the Army School of Pharmacy, etc. (at that time the fortified city wall had of course not yet been removed and the suburbs all lay beyond the encircling open area known as the *glacis*). The "Perron house" and the apparently hydrocephalic child have not been identified. The urban setting is untypical of Stifter's fiction. It is interesting however to compare the principal figure of **Tourmaline** both with Victor's uncle and with the hero of another "converted eccentric" story, **The Path through the Wood** (**Der Waldsteig**), a tale in the comic vein into which Stifter occasionally ventured, though perhaps with less success than Keller. In **The Path through the Wood,** which was written between **The Recluse** and **Tourmaline,** the eccentric Herr Tiburius (*sic*) has a number of traits in common with Victor's uncle and with the *Rentherr;* he lives on his private means and does no work, fills his rooms with innumerable portraits of celebrities and with luxurious adjustable furniture (for example, a desk which can be raised or lowered; cf. the movable sofas of different heights in **Tourmaline**) as well as pipe collections and other paraphernalia. The story of Tiburius anticipates Keller in its humorous treatment and conciliatory outcome: the obsessional hypochondriac encounters Nature, takes up painting, and ends up happily married to a good, simple, country girl. In **Tourmaline** as in **The Recluse** the theme is again treated tragically: as Stifter well knew, even marriage is no guarantee against the powers of darkness. By comparison with the style of **The Recluse** that of **Tourmaline** is uneffusive, even laconic. Much is left unsaid: this "dark" tale has the obscurity of reality, the same gaps of information. In the much inferior first version, Stifter's conception of the characters and motives is less equivocal: a moralizing paragraph at the end invites us to see the *Rentherr* as a wholly innocent victim of the brilliant but unscrupulous Dall—as an example of "deep love and purity of heart," forgiving his guilty wife with such kindness and generosity that she leaves him because she cannot bear his forgiveness. In the later version the moralizing reflections are placed at the beginning (as so often) and are much more reticent and ambiguous. The words ". . . when [man] surrenders utterly to the intensity of his joys and sorrows," in the context of the rest of this sentence, evidently refer to the husband; in which case Stifter's conception of him seems to have changed. He sensed, perhaps, the essential affinity between the uncommitted Romantic aestheticism of Dall—it is no accident that Dall is an *actor,* a man of many roles and no self—and the idle dilettantism of the *Rentherr* with his innumerable trivial occupations, his obsessive collection of pinned-up celebrities with whom he has no serious relationship. Has the *Rentherr*, fascinated by his hobbies and by Dall, neglected his wife and brought his misfortune on himself? Is his jealousy offended pride at his friend's betrayal of him rather than love for the woman? We can only guess. The *Rentherr*, who has not the analytical intellect of Victor's uncle, never explains himself, and soon passes into a pathetic limbo beyond the reach of explanation. It was characteristic of Stifter in general to refrain from probing into psychological depths: he merely hints at them. This was partly a matter of taste and delicacy—a sense of reverence for the mystery of the human mind which is in the last resort unfathomable, a disinclination to indulge or cater to mere curiosity. Moreover it is noticeable that in those few stories which raise psychological questions the characters concerned are generally tragic: to be psychologically *intéressant* is to have fallen from grace. Stifter preferred to write about innocence, about nature near to grace, rather than about dramatic destructive passions. This of course is why many readers find his work dull. A shift of perspective is needed. The drama is there in any case, but it is the subtler drama of the tension between Stifter's art and his life, felt as implicit in the art: of the constant dread which he seems to have felt, dread of chaotic forces within him and within humanity generally—forces which must be bound by idyllic beauty as by a spell. Order is to be constructed over the ever-present threat of disorder. Here again he is akin to Goethe; and in this connection it is interesting to note that one of his friends, discussing Stifter's reactions to 1848, adds the general comment that "this shrinking from the manifestations of the imperfection of our nature was perhaps the chief defect of his talent." In *Tourmaline,* as not often in Stifter, we have an approach to the phenomenon of "imperfection," indeed of evil, in human nature. He seems uneasy with the material, reflects that these matters are "shrouded in mystery," reaffirms the "inner law which is man's steadfast guide along the right path," and devotes nearly the whole latter half of the story to the account of the afflicted child's restoration to something like normality. Stifter was in fact dissatisfied even with the second version of this story, and told Heckenast that he would have liked to write a third which would be "a simple, clear, and heartfelt masterpiece."

The first version of *Limestone,* called *The Poor Benefactor* (*Der arme Wohltäter*), appeared in an almanac in December 1848 and may or may not have been written in the previous year; there is no reference to it in Stifter's correspondence. The revised and renamed version was included, like *Tourmaline,* in *Stones of Many Colors.* This story too has the more restrained style of Stifter's best later work, and more is suggested or implied than is actually said. There is again a generalizing preamble, the briefer equivalent of which in the original version amounts to the observation that "it is very touching to encounter someone in whom the moral law of reason [*die Vernunft als sittliches Gesetz*] is present in a very high degree, but who has insufficient intelligence [*Verstand*] to ascertain the means appropriate to his intentions." The peculiar German usage of the word "reason" here obscures the point that the principal figure in *Limestone* is half a simpleton and half a saint, and that the events of this story touch a sphere beyond that of human reason and morality. The qualitative difference between the isolation of Victor's embittered uncle or the crazed *Rentherr* on the one hand, and that of the priestly "eccentric" on the other, is that the priest's isolation is sacrificial. He does not cling to happiness or life or money or the cultivation of "the intensity of his joys and sorrows," for their own sake, but devotes himself entirely to what he considers to be the will of God and his objective duties, including the special enterprise of mercy and charity which he has secretly undertaken. The story is a specifically Christian one, though not specifically Catholic—in the first version the priest was a Protestant pastor; in making the change Stifter may have wished to give further religious significance to the theme of celibacy. In both versions the religious theme is central, though handled in this story with much greater subtlety than in *The Recluse* because its treatment here is symbolic and paradoxical. The very title of the original version—*The Poor Benefactor*—is a deliberate paradox. It has been pointed out that in the famous descriptions of the Steinkar landscape (which does not seem to be identifiable with any existing part of Austria) and of the thunderstorm and its aftermath, the numinous quality of these natural phenomena is heightened by an implied mysterious affinity or "correspondence" between them and the priest himself. The narrator notices at first the harsh, uninviting barrenness and monotony of this remote region of bare rock and sand, and the almost grotesque poverty and austerity of the priest: there is nothing here of the immediate outward attractiveness of Victor and his environment. But gradually his eyes are opened to the latent beauty of the Kar, just as he comes to understand and love the priest whose inner goodness he has instinctively sensed. The narrator is a surveyor, who has been sent to study and map out the district scientifically: but the priest, who has lived in this place, identified himself with it, and observed it for so many years, knows its meteorological and geological characteristics better than the scientist. The divine disguise takes time to penetrate. The priest's character is misjudged by many people and not fully revealed until after his death. His methods in the enterprise to which his will refers have in human terms been ludicrously inadequate; but the hidden, paradoxical, and incalculable workings of goodness (or, if one prefers, of divine grace and providence) crown it with success when he himself has been removed from any further part in it. There is thus a double transformation: not only is the priest's life retrospectively raised into a meaningfulness which both belongs to him and transcends him, but the arid Steinkar region itself is raised toward the level of humanity: in the building of the new school, raw nature takes on a further imprint of civilization—a process symbolized also by the completed activity of the surveyor, who is himself changed by his contact with the priest. Stifter holds a balance between a mystic sense of the numinous nonhuman or superhuman character of wild nature and the concept of cultivation or humanization. Man is not thought of as vanishing into insignificance before the grandeur of nature, but his relationship to nature must be one of humility and right understanding. Stifter's imagination was stirred and impressed by natural phenomena, whether they were large, exceptional, and cataclysmic or the tiny, normal, perpetually repeated events of growth and other cyclic processes; and he was also stirred and impressed by the unobtrusive normal everyday goodness of ordinary people in ordinary circumstances. His purpose, as he once defined it, was to mirror "the simplicity, greatness, and goodness of the human soul in merely ordinary events and situations." What did not appeal to him were the vast upheavals and extreme passions of the heroic and tragic literary tradition. His dispute with Hebbel arose out of this question of perspective, the question of what was "great" and what was "small." Hebbel, a dramatist in the grandiose tradition who specialized in larger-than-life, *intéressant* characters animated by monstrous passions and perverse motives generally, in 1849 dismissed Stifter in a satirical epigram as a mere miniaturist. Stifter replied with a much-quoted essay which he added to **Stones of Many Colors** as a preface and which is particularly relevant to **Limestone.** In it he gropingly attempts to formulate his radically different values.

> . . . The gentle breeze, the murmur of water, the growth of corn, the waves of the sea, the earth turning green, the radiance of the sky, the gleam of the stars, are things which I consider great: the majestic approach of a thunderstorm, the flash of lightning that cleaves houses, the tempest that lashes the breakers, the fire-belching mountain, the earthquake that lays waste whole lands, are phenomena which I do not consider greater than those others, in fact I consider them smaller, because they are merely the consequences of much higher laws. They occur in isolation and are the effects of unilateral causes. The force that makes the milk in a poor woman's saucepan boil over is the very same force that makes lava seethe up inside the volcanic mountain and pour down its slopes. These phenomena are merely more conspicuous and more easily attract the attention of the ignorant and unobservant; whereas the mind of the true inquirer tends especially toward the general totality of things, and only that can he acknowledge to be grand and imposing, because that alone is what preserves the world. Particularities pass and their effects can soon scarcely be seen . . . When humanity was in its childhood and its intellectual vision not yet touched by science, men were impressed by things that were conspicuous and obvious, and these moved them to fear and admiration: but when their minds were opened and they began to turn their attention to the interconnection of things, then particular phenomena sank lower in esteem, and the general law rose ever higher: wonders came to an end, and the wonder itself increased.

> And as it is with external nature, so it is also with the internal nature of mankind. A whole lifetime of just dealing, simplicity, self-mastery, understanding, effective activity within an allotted sphere, reverence for beauty: such a life, with a calm and peaceful death to end it, is what I consider great. Mighty emotions of the soul, terrible outbursts of anger, the thirst for revenge, the fiery spirit that hurls itself into action, the man who demolishes, changes, destroys, and in his passion often throws away his own life: all this I consider not greater, but smaller; for these things too are the products of particular and unilateral forces, just as are storms, volcanoes, and earthquakes.

Stifter here goes on to discuss what he calls "the gentle law . . . by which the human race is guided," that is, the moral law which tends toward the preservation of mankind in general against the particular egoism of individuals, and he concludes:

> . . . Yet it is above all in the normal, everyday, endlessly recurring acts of human beings that this law is most surely centered, for these are the lasting acts, they are the foundation, they are as it were the million root-fibers of the tree of life. Just as in nature the general laws operate quietly and ceaselessly, and the conspicuous phenomenon is only a particular expression of these laws, so too the moral law operates quietly and refreshingly, through the infinite relationships of man with man. And though some deeds that are done may be the marvels of the moment, these are only small evidences of this general power. So this law is what preserves mankind, just as the world is preserved by the law of nature.

If we interpret all this in the light of a story like **Limestone,** and vice versa, then the central point seems to be Stifter's insistence that particular events and acts should be placed and seen in a total context, in the almost cosmic nexus to which they belong. On a larger view, even on the purely scientific level, a thunderstorm is only the climax of a cyclic series of small, scarcely perceptible, atmospheric and electrical changes; and a long succession of daily acts of kindness or self-denial, small in themselves, must be seen in the light of their cumulative effect and ultimate consequences. In the last resort, the shift of perspective is a religious one. The fact that in the Preface, for the sake of polemical emphasis, he declares thunderstorms and similar cataclysms to be relatively insignificant does not mean that in his stories he does not sometimes make them his subject matter and write about them with great impressiveness: but they are seen by him, with the eye of affirmative faith, as manifestations within a whole, that is, within an infinite providential system in which even destructive forces and events are creatively absorbed and turned to good. This is the religious paradox. So too is the fact that the seemingly insignificant life and inadequate "benefaction" of the priest in the Kar can have effects far-reaching enough to defeat those of the storms and floods; or the possibility, even, of seeing the priest and the storm-flood as symbolically analogous to each other, since both belong and contribute to a total restorative, refreshing process which is both natural and supernatural. Even the practical outcome—a limited social improvement in a minor provincial district—takes on its full significance only when seen symbolically and *sub specie aeternitatis.* This is the dimension in which the "idyll" of this story operates, a dimension in which tragedy is also transcended. The priest's earlier personal love and suffering have taken their place in the totality, adding their special flavor to his life of renunciation and dedication. This is symbolized by the store of beautiful linen of which he feels so ashamed but which softens and humanizes his rigid asceticism: the "fine white silver" associated with the object of his shy youthful passion and which he could never bring himself to part with. Symbolically, too, the priest's linen and crucifix pass into the possession of the surveyor-narrator, who has occupied the typical pupil or disciple role, listening (like Victor, or like Heinrich Drendorf in **The Late Summer**) to the older man's life story, and who becomes the executor of his will and the communicator of his unspoken message.

It is partly in terms of the religious shift of perspective, as expressed in **Limestone** and in the Preface, that we must account for the strange disproportion of description to event, the swallowing up of "human interest" in an endless background of detail, which is a general feature of Stifter's work and a stumbling block to so many readers. This apparent disproportion is also a matter of artistic method, an application of the principle of cumulative effect, to which he refers in one letter where he speaks of his desire to lead his reader on "among familiar beloved things, until gradually he becomes spellbound and encircled, as one walks in springtime through the warm air, with everything in bud and the sun shining, and grows happy without knowing how." But the "happiness" which he thus seeks imperceptibly to induce is essentially, in a quite simple and primitive sense, a "religious" state of mind: an attitude of reverence and wonder toward ordinary natural things, in which even minutiae can seem important and the smallest human gestures momentous. To this frame of mind belongs inseparably a sense of the place of ceremony in ordinary life. Without such a feeling for ceremony, Stifter cannot be understood or appreciated. In *Limestone,* for instance, the frugal supper which the priest serves to his guest after they have sat through the thunderstorm is not only preceded by a blessing: the whole meal itself, like the lighting of the storm candle before it, is a ritual, a kind of prayer. Why else are we told not only that the priest brought in milk, bread, and strawberries, with glasses, knives, and spoons, but also—quite superfluously—that they drank the milk "from the glasses," cut the bread "with the knives," and ate the strawberries "with the spoons"? The actions are ceremonious, and repetition is a technique of ceremony: the unceremonious reader will find Stifter merely repetitious, laborious, and pedantic. A contemporary reviewer of *Witiko* wrote that its almost liturgical style was "enough to drive to despair a man of the nineteenth century *for whom time is money.*" It is hard to imagine a critical starting point more perfectly antithetical to the values of the author than this equation. For Stifter, time was something to which reverence is pre-eminently due. It is very noticeable that the magic of the past, the age of things, the way they have remained unchanged through time, or the way they have been affected by time, are themes which seem to move him to lyricism, to turn his prose into a kind of incantation. This happens in scenes in which some once familiar place is revisited:

> In the schoolroom everything was just as it had been. The big oak table still stood in the middle of the room, it still bore the marks we had made in its wooden surface . . . , it still showed the dried meandering inkstains . . . I opened the drawers. There, in those that had been mine, my schoolbooks still lay . . . the exercise books in which we had written our lessons were still there . . . and the drawers still contained our old dusty pens and pencils . . . I sat now studying my lessons at this same table where I had sat over them so many years ago. I slept in the same bed . . . , etc. (*Limestone*)

Or, in *The Recluse,* when Victor returns home, a familiar sequence of actions recurs yet again: "He crossed the first bridge and crossed the second, he walked past the great elder bush and in through the old garden gate . . . " A variant of this effect is the powerful elegiac sadness of pas-

sages describing places which are old but have fallen into disuse and decay: in *The Recluse* the deserted monastery, in *Tourmaline* the courtyard of the neglected old house, and in *Tourmaline* again—most compelling of all, for we have been here before and the spell of repetition can be woven—the empty but still fully furnished apartment when it is forcibly opened years after the mysterious disappearance of its occupants. On a psychological level, we may wonder whether decay itself did not fascinate Stifter, as it does the professor who lives in Herr Perron's house in order to watch the damp encroaching and the weeds growing through the stones; whether its appeal is not perhaps obscurely connected with his overmastering interest in the themes of orderly arrangement and maintenance, preservation and restoration. Yet on the aesthetic level we accept his treatment of these themes as the expression of something like a religious impulse of reverence, as a ceremony, a celebration of the rite of continuity. (pp. 12-27)

> *David Luke, in an introduction to* Limestone and Other Stories *by Adalbert Stifter, translated by David Luke, Harcourt Brace Jovanovich, 1968, pp. 3-34.*

Keith Spalding   (essay date 1969)

[*Spalding is a British scholar and an emeritus professor of German who is also the editor of* The Historical Dictionary of German Figurative Usage. *In this essay, Spalding traces Stifter's development as a moralist, identifying him as one of the most significant writers of the German Realist movement.*]

We owe it to Friedrich Hebbel whose ideas Adalbert Stifter rejected with every fibre of his being that we possess a clear credo in which Stifter sets out the aims of his writings. I am referring to the Preface to *Bunte Steine* (1853), in which he answered Hebbel and all his detractors. There he set up the signposts which mark the road he followed. (p. 183)

The Preface has been reprinted so often—indeed no commentator on Stifter has ever felt able to circumvent it— that it need not be quoted in its entirety here. Its importance, however, is tremendous. When one holds it against Stifter's numerous essays which deal with general subjects in a manner that is—on the whole—far from challenging, one is struck at once by the combination of passionate feeling and restrained formulation that characterizes every part of it.

Passion and restraint were indeed at war within Stifter. He was not by nature the Biedermeier type of bourgeois whom we meet in Spitzweg's paintings. On the surface he might appear solid, integrated, contented and secure. He looked sedate and stolid enough, performed his official duties with utter conscientiousness, conducted himself as an exemplary husband and staunch friend, enjoyed good food and choice wines and collected cacti. With his abhorrence of violence, of excesses in thought or deed, of heterodoxy and anarchical sentiment he certainly lived what he depicted in his works as the good life and what he preached in the Preface to *Bunte Steine.*

Yet this seemingly calm outward appearance hid a restless inner life beset by anxieties, revolts and profound dissatisfaction. One cannot explain this dissatisfaction by pointing to his poor background, the political climate of Metternich's Austria or the hostility of contemporary writers who adhered to the liberal, emancipating, iconoclastic views of Young Germany. Such adverse factors merely added to dissatisfactions, inadequacies and despairs which lay much deeper. Hermann Bahr was the first literary critic to point to them:

> Wer sich ausgestoßen fühlt, wen das Leben ängstigt, wer keine Macht hat, es unmittelbar zu gestalten, der flieht in die Kunst wie in eine tiefe Höhle und gräbt sich ein.
>
> Whoever feels exiled, terrified by life, impotent to shape it directly, flees to art as into a deep cave and buries itself in it.

Over the last forty years different terms have been used by literary commentators to describe Stifter's feelings of isolation and inadequacy, and psychologists have dissected his mental make-up, calling him sometimes a "late developer", sometimes "permanently immature". Such labels do not help; but many episodes lend substance to the view that Stifter never really mastered life.

The move from the simple village community in the Bohemian Forest where his father had earned a very moderate living as a small trader in flax and linen to one of the finest monastery schools in Austria, Kremsmünster, was the second shock to Stifter's sensitive nature—following closely on the first, his father's death in an accident, which had occurred when the boy was twelve. From a home in which simple affectionate women had taken care of him and a countryside little touched by Josephinian Enlightenment and cultural concerns Stifter was suddenly plunged into the rarified atmosphere of a school run by erudite monks, where he was taught by minds of great intellect and sophistication, swamped by knowledge and culture. Hardly had he found his feet in this new world and come to terms (of a kind) with the leaders of thought—both Classical and Romantic—who dominated cultured minds around 1820-30, when the next uprooting took place: the move from the rural cloistered Kremsmünster to the cosmopolitan and easy-going life of Vienna University. He appeared happy in the new surroundings, buoyed up by the writings of Jean Paul whom he adored, poor, but easily satisfied and earning enough through private lessons to suffer no real want, yet true enjoyment of life eluded him. The visits to his home between the University terms made him feel the widening gulf separating the village community he had sprung from and the ideal society of men that he dreamed of. There seemed to be no bridge between life as lived by the superstitiously religious, narrowly utilitarian, unimaginative folk at home and the life he believed in, which was patterned on ideas taken from Herder and Jean Paul. That he loved the people who led such dull and limited existences only increased his sense of isolation.

His studies, officially in the Faculty of Law, but in fact predominantly in the Faculty of Science, absorbed him intellectually, but real solace came only through art. Landscape painting attracted him most, but increasingly he turned to writing—exuberant, romantic prose which owed much to Jean Paul, and poetry revealing an abundance of feeling, but little merit, immediacy or originality. Neither the prose writings nor the poems of those years rank as literature, and Stifter left them unfinished. Indeed, everything in his life at that stage was halfhearted, undefined, incomplete—juvenile in fact, and the constant urge to be with younger people (which never left him throughout his life) suited this indeterminate existence for the next ten years. During that time he fell in love with Fanny Greipl but could never convince her that he was willing to settle down to an orderly existence, he painted but could not decide to gain his livelihood through painting, he wrote but did not publish anything. He applied for posts but somehow managed to miss the vital interview or avoided taking the qualifying examination or fell ill at a critical moment. He was himself aware of his instability and confessed his inner loneliness in a letter (to Sigmund Freiherr von Handel, June 17, 1836):

> O theurer, lieber Sigmund, ich fühle oft eine Einsamkeit, daß ich weinen möchte wie ein Kind, wenn ich nicht nebstbei doch ein so närrischer Teufel wäre, der flucht, wenn er weich wird, und kläglich schlechte Wize macht, wenn er gerne seiner Rührung Herr werden möchte . . .

The recipient of the letter might share and understand such emotionalism, but Fanny Greipl did not. When she learned that Stifter was also unfaithful, she broke off her engagement and Stifter felt once more tossed by an unkindly fate, baffled and insecure. Not that he yielded to pessimism—not yet. For the time being he lived a bohemian existence, disorganised rather than disorderly, teaching, painting, writing, willing to become a teacher of mathematics and physics should a suitable vacancy arise, finding happiness in the company of friends and pupils, but at the same time indulging in violent bouts of exuberance and dejection.

In this mood he fell in love with Amalie Mohaupt, partly out of spite because Fanny had rejected him. His statement to Fanny: "zeigen wollt ich eurem Hause, daß ich doch ein schönes, wohlhabendes und edles Weib zu finden wußte" indicates how much his disappointment, his frantic attempts to assert himself against an indifferent world and his romantic lack of realism had impaired his judgment. Amalie was not *wohlhabend* but penniless; not *edel* but totally mundane, uneducated and unimaginative; besides, she was not his *Weib* in the sense in which the average reader would take the word. They lived together and there appears to have been a child which died after a few weeks, but with typical undecidedness and fear of committing himself Stifter did not marry Amalie until 1837, two years after the letter to Fanny had been written.

It was in these years of drifting that Stifter started to grope for clarity by writing his first completed prose works. It is significant that they were short—he was clearly quite unable at this stage to handle material that required extensive treatment—and equally significant that they were not primarily intended for publication. When the manuscript of his first Novelle was discovered by a pupil who saw it sticking out of Stifter's jacket pocket, he allowed himself to be prevailed upon to have it published, and when an acquaintance a little later needed some material in a hurry, Stifter gave him another work of his; but these publications of **Der Condor** and **Feldblumen** were the work of chance. It is ironic that they brought him immediate acclaim and thus settled the pattern of his entire life from then onward. The would-be painter without a firm purpose was turned into a determined writer who wrestled with language with a thoroughness and dedication which had been entirely alien to him until then.

Stifter himself, ever intent on nobly putting a fine gloss on his entirely prosaic and disappointing marriage, maintained in the years to come that his new life had really begun when he married Amalie. This is totally untrue. His new life started when he fled to literature and in creating his own kind of prose disciplined his own existence.

Naturally he did not shake off his romantic enthusiasm and his tendency towards extremes in feeling at once. **Der Condor** and **Feldblumen** had been written under the influence of his erotic failures, of his inability to win Fanny and his realisation that in Amalie he had found an attractive body without a mind. In these stories he had tried to justify himself, to salvage his self-esteem. Significantly enough he never retouched these two works. He must have seen that artistically they were inferior to what he could do and that they reflected a state of mind which in calm recollection he could not approve of. All the other stories created in the early 'forties were changed when he had come to realize that restraint is better than extravagance, economy of words better than scintillating verbosity, intimation better than direct expression. It did not take him long to discover the need to prune, tone-down and polish. Within a few years his stylistic self-education was complete. To name but one example: his **Abdias** of 1842 is essentially a Romantic book, the version of 1845 by comparison is restrained, controlled, terse and economical, a work of early Realism.

As a creative artist Stifter underwent tremendous changes in those years. The "late developer" had become a man. It had taken him a long time to shake off his immaturity, his consciousness of professional ineffectualness and personal inadequacy. Now, with Fanny dismissed from his mind and Amalie established as an unrecognizably idealized figure, he saw his work as an author as his undoubted mission. He came to view the writer as a moral force, himself as an instrument of the Spirit charged with the task of spreading appreciation for moral values through his prose. It was this conviction which drove him to labour more conscientiously—re-writing the same passage again and again, chiselling, above all reducing every sentence to its absolute essentials. (pp. 184-88)

. . . He approached the content of stories as a teacher might—indeed, some critics have maintained (and in some parts of Stifter's works can demonstrate convincingly) that the pedagogue was stronger than the imaginative writer. He certainly limited his range by insisting that a moral purpose be reflected in all his writings. Hence the apparently unsophisticated story-content of his Novellen:

> A man gives up the woman he loves for the sake of his mission as a writer. He achieves true happiness through resignation and through acceptance of the gifts bestowed on him by God (**Das Haidedorf**). An egotist striving for distinction and, considering himself superior to others, merely succeeds in becoming peculiar, indeed foolish. Hunting for the particular, he misses the essentials of life and ends in madness (**Die Narrenburg**). A man panders to his whims and loses all sense of values. He is rescued by contact with nature and a simple girl who between them open his eyes to the futility of his existence and guide him step by step towards understanding and happiness (**Der Waldsteig**). In such a summary fashion one could, if one wanted to, survey all six volumes of Stifter's **Studien.** The essentials in Stifter's world do not change. Circumstances and incidents provide variety. Yet even though one story may lead us to Africa and deal with non-Christian characters (**Abdias**), another may take us to the plains of Hungary among owners of vast estates (**Brigitta**) and a third may return to the problem of the artist's place in the world (**Zwei Schwestern**), the same fundamentals are preached: Man's moral task is to fit into God's creation. If he has the wisdom to accept the eternal values, to search for what is permanent, to live the good life, he will find happiness. Resignation will be required as an essential part of self-fulfilment, since he is not granted what he wants. Through willing acceptance of his duties as a moral being he realises himself. If, on the other hand, he makes demands on life which leave the needs of those around him out of account, he will end tragically.

However "simple" the story-content may be, Stifter's **Studien** as works of art are not simple. The events in the stories may be few and unsensational, but the conception of the personalities in them is subtle, marked by profound psychological insight, and their behaviour is far from conventional and predictable. He does not shirk complications in motivation, nor does he shrink from a frank examination of sexual desire. He does not avoid embarrassing situations out of prudery—the unexpected arrival of a sleepwalking girl in a man's bed (in **Drei Schmiede ihres Schicksals**) is treated in a delicate way, and where an inferior artist might have introduced a salacious note, Stifter resorts to very skilfully contrived humorous treatment. Indeed, it must be stressed that his desire to write as a responsible moralist does not make him consider the comic and the humorous as unworthy of his purpose. The gallery of Stifter's heroes and heroines thus contains a delightful collection of oddities, queer originals and foolish specimens whose foibles are very subtly and very humorously analyzed. It would also be wrong to dwell on the "simple" story and the plain message without stressing the skill with which simple events and insignificant objects in every story are invested with symbolic significance. Sentences which on the surface read like unassuming descriptions without any undertones or hints of a deeper significance, turn out to be the bearers of a symbolic load when pondered in the context of the whole tale. It is surprising when one considers Stifter's clear desire to write a moral tale and his magisterial approach to writing, how unobtrusive his art can be. As in the case of all the best prose writers one can enjoy each Novelle as a story *per se*, then peel off its outer layer of surface actions and discover underneath not only one further possible interpretation of the story but a variety of intimated routes towards the exploration of the seemingly simple narrative. A story such as *Abdias,* Stifter's first excursion into an exotic world, has been read with enjoyment for over a century as the thoughtful and interesting life-story of a Jew from his beginnings amid the rubble of a ruined town in the African desert through an era of adventures, wealth and power to his withdrawal into a remote corner of Austria. Yet even to-day a number of distinguished critics are putting forward new suggestions on how to interpret this story, and the differences in their readings are such that we must marvel at the skill with which Stifter has suggested possible answers to the riddle of Abdias.

Simplicity in story-content and paucity of events go hand in hand with stylistic elaboration. Minute treatment of every element in his tales was dictated to him by his conviction that the important things of life are the unspectacular ones. If they were to be shown in their regular recurrence, their unchanging significance, then the writer had to take pains to go into every detail, make the regularity apparent by describing every phase and every aspect until the tangible object or the habitual activity has been made to take on an inner significance for the reader. Hence Stifter's long passages of unhurried descriptions of states, conditions, routine activities which tantalise the impatient reader. Stifter's prose, which wants to come to terms with reality and consciously avoids the rhetorical, the grand manner and the clever formulation, can only be appreciated fully by the reader who is content with each sentence as it comes, accepting it for its own sake and not looking upon it as a stepping-stone leading towards a climax or an unexpected turn of events. Indeed, Stifter would have considered himself a failure if the reader did experience surprise at the development of his characters. Life has its laws, and the incomprehensibly perverse in life is not fit subject-matter for the moralist writer. Stifter therefore described what stays within the law, the consistent flow of life, the meaningful routine, and since he confined himself to this unexciting side of life, he used every means at his disposal to give it literary significance.

He planned each sentence, weighed its parts and then arranged them in a balanced order. There might be two groups of two nouns each followed by an identical grouping furnished with an adjective each; the whole might then end in three verbs arranged in such a way as to produce a rhythmic ending, e.g. a dactyl followed by a spondee. The paragraph might then continue with a simple sentence (one noun with one weighty adjective and a simple verb), and this could be followed by a long period with three clauses—either of increasing weightiness and length or constructed in a descending order, terminating again with a rhythmic pattern. Every page, if subjected to minute analysis, shows results which are always equally striking: skilful numerical distribution of the parts of speech, measured cadences, subtle choice of epithets, intricate patterns of growing significance and increasing tension alternating with drawn-out periods suggesting hesitation of deliberation, leisurely sentences giving an impression of the passage of time, clipped staccato statements which with incisive terms throw sharp flashes on the screen of the reader's imagination—they all appear in an array of amazing variety on every page of the *Studien.*

This artistry was not imparted to him by some divine afflatus which made him write unconsciously in such a structurally perfect style. It was achieved by hard work, writing, re-writing, listening to the periods, judging whether they were adequate, searching patiently for the right word. This search for the really adequate entailed also the removal of every simile that did not add to the significance of the thing described, the deletion of every comparison or hyperbole that detracted from the proper appreciation of the object. Foreign words were unnecessary, indeed a hindrance to immediate perception of true meaning, so they had to go; simple words—often homely terms with a regional flavour and therefore certainly not the "best" words in a work of literature—took their place.

Things had to speak for themselves. *"Die Dinge"* and *"was die Dinge fordern"* occur again and again in Stifter's writings. This is what distinguishes him from the later Realists who tended to see things as symbols and therefore deprived them of part of their reality as objects. Stifter does not want the things he describes to "stand for", "to mirror", "to symbolize" or "to represent" anything which lies beyond the things themselves. What is, is real, significant, intended. Every detail matters because it reveals Nature's purpose. We must penetrate to its essence, appreciate its value, see the reason why it has the form we have before our eyes. It may not have any special interesting features and may seem dull because it belongs to the daily routine of our existence. All the more reason then, Stifter maintains, to look closely at it. There is to him nothing repulsive or unworthy in the regular, the periodically returning, the seemingly monotonous. The really important facets of life are composed of regular and monotonous activities and events: sunrise and sunset, sowing and reaping, work and rest. We must learn to look closely at them, penetrate to their essence through loving appreciation—indeed, worship and love are the keys to understanding as well as to the right way to live.

In this strain Stifter continued throughout the 'forties until the moderate optimism underlying the faith he had cherished up till then was destroyed by the Revolution of 1848. He had supported moves towards the establishment of a constitutionally limited monarchy and had hoped that a better world would arise through the granting of a more generous amount of freedom. The Revolution, when it came with violence, fanaticism and indeed civil war in some areas, disillusioned him completely. It became clear to him that an uneducated electorate was worse than a population without votes. Infuriated with the turn which things had taken, angry at his own optimism which now struck him as facile, he took the step he was to regret for the remainder of his life and accepted an appointment under the Ministry of Education. Based on Linz which now became his permanent home he inspected schools, supervised educational administration, rescued neglected works of art, wrote a text-book even, but the disappointments of office were greater than its joys. Worst of all, it limited the time he could devote to writing. Writing, however, mattered more to him now than ever before, because his urge to find solace in artistic creation was now reinforced by his almost missionary zeal to help in the education of mankind by depicting the right way to live.

That in this connection he should consider writing for and about children is not surprising. Schiller in a memorable passage near the beginning of his essay *Über naive und sentimentalische Dichtung* has made it plain why an idealist will always be attracted by the subject of children. (pp. 188-92)

Stifter can be assumed to have known the passage, and certainly the idea expressed by Schiller fitted his views, however unlikely Stifter himself was to formulate concepts with the clarity and penetration of which Schiller was capable. He certainly cared for children, understood them and could penetrate the world of their thoughts and emotions with uncanny insight.

All his spare moments now came to be devoted to what he called his **Kindergeschichten;** yet very soon it became obvious to him that the message he wanted to convey was not really comprehensible to children, because it was the same message which he had passed on in **Studien** (at least in their re-cast form as published between 1844 and 1850), except that it had acquired sterner undertones and reflected a deeper pessimism. Man had become more insecure, his destiny less predictable. His duties remained the same, but rewards and punishments were no longer so clearly recognizable as deserved or unavoidable as they had appeared before. By the time the collection was completed and furnished with the famous Preface, it presented a view of life which was beyond the understanding of children. **Kindergeschichten** became **Bunte Steine** (1853), Stifter's best-known creation, soon translated into other languages and seen by his contemporaries as the most mature product of the artist.

Apart from the sterner tone, **Bunte Steine** differs from **Studien** in several ways. The writer himself, who had been present as the narrator, occasionally offering a comment in **Studien,** has virtually disappeared in **Bunte Steine.** Besides, one new facet is added: stylization. Perhaps in an effort to be simple (which often strikes the reader as naive rather than simple), and with the totally undisguised intention of presenting the permanent, the recurring and the essential, Stifter stylised his statements, repeated simple formulae, introduced leitmotifs, pruned statements and conversations until they appeared primitive and trite. The effect of this is all the more striking because the reader soon discovers that all the stories move on two planes: the harmless, innocent, simple surface or foreground which contrasts with the dark, demonic, inscrutable forces whose presence in the background the reader cannot fail to perceive. Man lives his life as though he could control it, but the reader is made aware of the fact that we merely exist by God's grace.

Much has been written about Stifter's faith. Attempts to claim him as a true Catholic or as an undoubted Humanist remain equally unconvincing. They treat Stifter as though he had arrived at profoundly intellectual, logically consistent articles of faith; yet if one thing is clear, it is this:

Stifter's ratiocinative faculties were limited. He never constructed a logical system of thought. On the subject of religion his pronouncements verge on the platitudinous: Religion and Art become identical when Art reaches its most advanced stage, Art, Morality and Religion exist for their own sakes, Religion is the supreme flowering of the human soul. The power through which God expresses Himself in earthly phenomena is *das Göttliche;* hence Religion and Art are *göttlich. "Wir heißen das Göttliche, in so ferne es sinnlich wahrnehmbar wird, auch das Schöne".* The ideas behind a work of art, nature, the human form, the majesty of the moral law, the pre-destined path which the human race follows are all "divine".

There is a vagueness about these statements, as about his remarks on evil and sin which inclines one to the belief that his convictions, however strongly held, were not based on careful reasoning and that the views he expressed merely reflected in most general terms what Kremsmünster had taught him on the basis of the prescribed handbooks. There is no sign of a personal faith, of individual revelation or a direct relationship. There is never any mention of Christ by name; Christ appears only in allusions often as vague as those which refer to angels and to good spirits. Confessionalism is avoided in all his works, but this does not seem to betoken that he examined different approaches to religion and found them all wanting or all equally good. The tolerance advocated may be mere acceptance of the humanistic, enlightened teaching received at school, reinforced because it happened to coincide with his abhorrence of fanaticism and violence in any area of human existence. There is no coherent philosophy behind it.

The same results can be obtained if one examines Stifter's political views. Conservative in essence but shot through with some liberal aspirations, patriotic but tempered with a pacifist cosmopolitanism, moderate in temper, humanitarian and enlightened with echoes from Herder and Humboldt—such are the general features, and appropriate quotations could be adduced for all of them. When examined closely, they turn out to be as vague, oversimplified, unoriginal and undistinguished as his religious pronouncements. It was not in his nature to arrive at subtle distinctions, to set up logically unassailable systems, to reason brilliantly. Even in his scientific studies one does not come across original results or unusual insights but is struck by the collector's eagerness to string together facts and figures. There is no indication of a synoptic vision or the discovery of a unifying idea which characterized Goethe's scientific pursuits.

If Stifter can be seen as far from perceptive, original or strikingly independent in religious and political matters, it is not surprising that he should also fare badly when closely examined on the purely intellectual-linguistic level. Odd as it may seem, Stifter did not command a wide, varied or choice vocabulary. His grammatical knowledge was patchy, his syntax often far from faultless and his handling of different speech levels was poor to indifferent. The dialectal occasionally intrudes, colloquialisms stand out awkwardly and bookish words, often archaic even in Stifter's days, mar the simplicity of some sentences. In the last fifteen years of his life in particular he allowed ponderous compounds which belonged to civil service jargon (or reflect it in general structure) to intrude, and many of his own creations made up to avoid foreign terms are cumbersome inelegant failures. If his prose were to be judged simply from the technical-linguistic angle, Stifter would undoubtedly have to be called an uneven stylist. Some critics have seized upon this eagerly and have drawn from it quite erroneous conclusions regarding the quality of Stifter's writings.

An introductory essay on an author cannot stray from its principal subject and therefore the question cannot be entered into whether a man can write unevenly and still be a great writer. Suffice it to say that Stifter profoundly impressed such superb stylists as Nietzsche, Hofmannsthal and Thomas Mann, to name but three, as belonging to the greatest writers in the German language.

Stylistically, however, it was a mistake on Stifter's part when, in the last fifteen years of his life, he modelled himself increasingly on Goethe's style of the later decades, the *Altersstil.* Various factors pushed him in that direction: his growing aversion from the spirit of his era, the desire to turn to more comprehensive works in which he could paint a detailed ideal picture of the world, his turning away from both Schiller and from Romanticism towards Classical concepts in life and art. A *Bildungsroman* in the manner of *Wilhelm Meister* appeared to him as the most suitable genre, and so his all-too-rare moments of leisure were devoted to **Der Nachsommer,** the novel which was to alienate him from the general reading public for the next fifty years.

Der Nachsommer (1857) was bound to enrage the followers of Young Germany, but it was also certain to disappoint those readers who approved of the newly emerged Realist movement, for here Stifter depicted a world which one could not recognise as true; nor did it appear to delineate in minute realistic detail any society past or present. It was conceived as a novel, yet we gain no insight into psychological problems, are not introduced to fascinating characters, witness no important events. It is not even a "novel of development" in which the hero grows gropingly through trial and error into a personality. There is development, but only of a special kind, since the young characters Heinrich and Natalie will eventually be exactly like their old guides and teachers Risach and Mathilde: the experience leading them to the full realisation of their personalities will be based on living under the same code of laws as the older characters. Indeed the novel is an illustrated code of law setting out the guide-lines towards the perfect life. With infinite detail we are taken through the stages in which, in essence, the same territory is covered over which the reader had been taken in **Studien** and **Bunte Steine:** Man in his apprenticeship must begin with a study of nature in all its purposefulness, its interrelations, its unending variety and its beauty. Only when he has grasped all these aspects and stands in awed worship before this manifestation of the divine, determined to fit into the plan that nature has mapped out for mankind, can the seeker proceed to the next stage of self-realisation. He must learn to recognise the divine as manifested in art.

Advancing through craftsmanship and technical competence, followed by scientific or scholarly exploration, he will reach the highest stage which is Art—the divine in the garb of the beautiful. Creativity will follow, because true perception grants us insight. At that stage we are vouchsafed revelation and thus we approach the divine. Love will open our eyes, resignation will preserve our integrity. In this state of grace we appreciate the ordinary things of life and learn to cherish what is eternal. Routine is changed from something tedious into something sacred, it becomes a ritual. By filling our ordinary activities with meaning we make our lives meaningful, become personalities. Such attaining of meaningfulness can be expected to encompass wider and wider sections of humanity; gradually mankind will improve, rejecting violence, curbing passion, seeking harmony with nature, cherishing the beautiful. Thus by a utopian route Stifter returned to a kind of optimism, far removed from the lighthearted expectation of happiness for all mankind which had brightened the stages of his earlier career, but an optimistic affirmation all the same. (pp. 193-96)

Science as the new determinant of life, communication as the peacemaker, eventual victory of mind over matter—such were the items salvaged from the debacle of 1848. Mankind took little notice of them, and Hebbel offered the vacant crown of Poland to any person capable of reading **Der Nachsommer** to the end.

Stifter remained undeterred and started work on the next project. This was to encompass a considerable period of Bohemian history, and its first volume, *Witiko* (1865-67), dealt with events which fall into the twelfth century. If it had been conceived as straightforward history, it might well have been received more kindly by a generation fond of the works of Sir Walter Scott and Willibald Alexis. Events in the twelfth-century Bohemia were turbulent enough and their story did not lack elements of grandeur. Stifter, however, wanted to be "Homeric", totally unaware of how unsuitable Homer's style was to the work he had in mind. Goethe could be "Homeric" in *Hermann und Dorothea,* where he could use epic breadth and detailed description within an idyll; by writing in verse he could raise the presentation of intrinsically prosaic objects and situations to a level at which they become acceptable to the modern reader. Stifter, writing in prose and deciding on an historical novel robbed himself of the advantages Goethe had enjoyed. The adoption of an Homeric style combined with his pedagogical impulse to preach the gospel of the rule of law and of the victory of self-control over passion made him create a quasi-idyllic historical novel of the Middle Ages—a contradiction in terms. Whereas in **Der Nachsommer** the struggle for individual perfection had been presented convincingly because it concerned four people living fairly secluded lives, a similar striving in **Witiko** runs counter to the requirements of an epic story purporting to deal with armies, pressure groups and popular movements.

Some of the articles of Stifter's faith, such as respect for the individual, reverence for the private conscience, loving acceptance of the positive sides of tradition and its expression through ceremonial could find a legitimate place in

Witiko (and benevolent critics have fastened on to them, forgetting the fact that Stifter had had ample opportunity to present these articles of faith in stories more suitable for them), but his attempt at distinguishing between *Tat* and *Tätigkeit,* the former rejected as impulse-directed and often harmful, the latter praised as the positive contribution by men of worth towards the achievement of the good life, is entirely out of place here, indeed his genius for the ordinary things of life totally disqualified him as an historical novelist. The impression conveyed in the novel that a simple upright man need only persevere in his goodness, competence, piety and righteousness to achieve a position of power in the land contradicts what the reader knows of mediaeval history, leaves the existence of evil and the vulnerability of the good and the righteous out of account and therefore falsifies history.

Even Stifter enthusiasts have to admit that his writings had by that time reached a dangerous degree of stylisation. There is constant repetition of formulae, heavy accentuation of the ritualistic aspect of mediaeval life, pruning of the narrative of all ornament, hammering home of the ethical message in terms so simple as to border on the banal. No writer in German of any significance attempted anything like Stifter's style in *Witiko* until, some fifty years later, the Expressionists hurled forth their convictions in similarly contrived language.

Perhaps Stifter was reaching breaking-point. His health had certainly deteriorated to such an extent that he was allowed to retire from his official post. The adoption of two girls had not brought happiness, indeed the reverse—one had died of typhus, the other committed suicide. Financial worries seemed to be eternally with him, not because he had really insufficient means but because he always lived beyond his income. Pathological fear could assail him, and an outbreak of cholera in Linz made him flee to the country for safety and at the same time put him on the rack with shame for running away. He longed to be able to undertake journeys to distant parts, but plans to find inspiration in this way always miscarried either because there was no time or no money or because he could not face a protracted separation from his wife and his pets. Politically, Europe was moving in the wrong direction and Bismarck, whom he detested, appeared to be gaining all his objectives. The gap between reality and the world he believed in and depicted in his works had widened so much that the stylisation in *Witiko* (and remarks in some of his letters) can be seen as the utterance of an obsessed man who shouts because nobody wants to listen.

In 1868 illness gained the upper hand. Much of it may have been a psychic malaise, the tortured mind attacking the body, but in physical terms he suffered from chronic atrophy (some say cancer) of the liver; the pain was excruciating, and his periods of suffering became increasingly protracted. In the night of January 25/26, probably driven temporarily out of his mind by pain, he cut his throat with a razor. The idea of suicide had always been abhorrent to him, so much so that his strong denunciation of it strikes the observer as significant. He hated it and he feared death in a way that does not bear striking testimony to his Christian faith. Yet it would be unprofitable to join the large group of writers who have tried to "explain" his end. His achievements as a superb prose writer endure. His end merely illumines the ferocity of the struggle in which he was involved throughout his life.

It has become fashionable since the 'twenties to overpraise Stifter, and books calling him Goethe's equal and studies placing him on a par with Dante and Goethe surely overstep the mark. On the other hand, even so perceptive a critic as Friedrich Gundolf totally underestimated and misjudged Stifter. His reputation is not furthered by evaluations which deal in superlatives, and Stifter himself, a man of moderation, as he called himself, would have felt uneasy when shown some of the panegyrics now in vogue. It is fairer to say that he was one of the great moralists of the nineteenth century and one of its best and most dedicated writers among the Realist group. As regards style, he was undoubtedly "das Genie des Gewöhnlichen" and *"der deutsche Dichter der Nüance"*. (pp. 197-200)

> *Keith Spalding, "Adalbert Stifter," in* German Men of Letters: Twelve Literary Essays, Vol. V, *edited by Alex Natan, Dufour Editions, 1969, pp. 183-206.*

From a Nazi prison Dietrich Bonhoeffer praises *Witiko* in a letter to his parents:

My overriding interest for the last ten days has been *Witiko* which, after my giving you so much trouble to hunt for it, was discovered in the library here—a place where I shouldn't really have expected it. Most people would find its thousand pages, which can't be skipped but have to be taken steadily, too much for them, so I'm not sure whether to recommend it to you. For me it's one of the finest books I know. The purity of its style and character-drawing gives one a quite rare and peculiar feeling of happiness. One really ought to read it for the first time at the age of fourteen, instead of the *Kampf um Rom,* and then grow up with it. Even today's good historical novels, e.g. those by Gertrud Bäumer, can't compare with it—it's *sui generis.* I should very much like to have it, but it would hardly be possible to get hold of it. So far, the only historical novels that have made a comparable impression on me are *Don Quixote* and Gotthelf's *Berner Geist.*

> *Dietrich Bonhoeffer, in his* Letters and Papers from Prison, *edited by Eberhard Bethage, 1967.*

Margaret Gump (essay date 1974)

[*In this excerpt, Gump presents an overview of* Witiko, *pointing to various problems a modern reader may encounter in Stifter's difficult historical novel and briefly discussing its stylistic attributes.*]

[Stifter's second novel, *Witiko,*] appeared in 1867, twenty years after its conception. Lunding calls it "without doubt the strangest prose fiction in the 19th century," and Albrecht Schaeffer does not know of any work in European literature whose form has anything in common with *Witiko.* It is, therefore, not surprising that evaluations of the novel range from wholesale condemnations to exaggerated panegyrics—it has even been called a sacred book! When it first appeared, only a few close friends and the Grand Duke Carl Alexander of Sachsen-Weimar, grandson of Goethe's patron and friend Karl August, were much impressed by the work. The Grand Duke bestowed the Order of the White Falcon on Stifter, together with a letter of appreciation. Stifter was especially pleased that Goethe was supposed to have contributed the motto "Be alert" (*Seid wachsam*) to the order. The contemporary reviews were overwhelmingly negative. Stifter was accused of having chosen subject matter of no interest to his time; of superabundance of detail; of lack of suspense, warmth, psychological insight; of using an archaic, wooden, artificial style. He was compared with Walter Scott—a comparison which necessarily told against him. He knew and liked Walter Scott, but *Witiko* was never intended to be an imitation of Scott's kind of novel. *Ivanhoe,* Scott's most popular novel, which, like *Witiko,* deals with twelfth-century history, illuminates the uniqueness of Stifter's narrative. *Witiko* possesses none of the elements which might, even today, thrill the readers of *Ivanhoe:* chivalric romance, magnanimous superheroes and heroines, cruel villains, and noble robbers. It lacks *Ivanhoe*'s generally fast-moving, melodramatic action, its suspense, mysterious disguises, its horrors and last-minute rescues.

The negative attitude toward *Witiko* persisted for a long time. R. M. Meyer, a leading German literary historian at the turn of the century, saw in *Witiko* nothing but extreme mannerism, and this is how the novel strikes many a superficial reader today. Alfred Biese's much-used *Deutsche Literaturgeschichte* (1910) labeled it utterly unpalatable because of its prolixity. Even such a pioneer in Stifter research as Alois Raimund Hein could not appreciate *Witiko* as a whole. It was Hermann Bahr in his *Adalbert Stifter: Eine Entdeckung* (1919) who first gave this novel undivided praise. But a decade later, Friedrich Gundolf called it a wretched (*unseliges*) book, which showed the decline of the aging writer, and which we had better forget if we want to honor Stifter's memory. Hermann Hesse, on the other hand, giving Bahr full credit for his rediscovery of this completely forgotten work by Stifter, speaks of *Witiko* as a unique and movingly beautiful book. It is the only modern novel which gave him the feeling of an epic. From Thomas Mann, we have a paradoxical statement about the special charm its monotony (*Langweiligkeit*) holds for him. He sees in *Witiko* one of the greatest and most encouraging vindications of "*Langeweile.*" He says that "the bold purity, daring pedantry, spiritual uniqueness of this masterpiece" brought him "much solace and joy" at the beginning of his odyssey after Hitler came to power. The German theologian Bonhoeffer, awaiting trial in a Nazi prison, had a similar experience: "My overriding experience for the last ten days has been *Witiko.* . . . For me it is one of the finest books I know. The purity of its style and character drawing gives one a quite rare and peculiar feeling of happiness." No other praise could have given Stifter greater satisfaction. Except for *Witiko,* I know only of some verse by Goethe to which such moving testimony was given by victims of Nazi persecution. (pp. 118-19)

Political and military actions alternate with domestic scenes [in the novel], where Witiko, especially during his first stay in the valley of Plana, takes an active part in the life of the community and shares its frugal way of life. Among other things, this novel is a nostalgic return to the scenes of Stifter's childhood and youth, a hymn to his native woods, to the strength, simplicity, loyalty, and goodness of their inhabitants. The agility, toughness, and endurance acquired through their hard life in the forest enable these men to turn the tide in every battle under the leadership of Witiko. Because of their difficult life they are very practical people. They take along big sacks in which to put their booty, and they look upon war as a perfectly legitimate means of adding to their meager livelihood. One of the minor nobles of the woods says, "I went to war in order that right should prevail, that the oppressor be punished, and that a small landowner might perhaps expand a little."

All the wars in which Witiko and his men participate are "just" wars. This is hammered into the reader's mind at every opportunity. History, for Stifter, is nothing but a final triumph of the moral law: the good will be rewarded; the bad, punished. Whether the moral balance was in reality as neat as Stifter wants us to believe in *Witiko* is highly questionable. In his article, "Stifter's 'Witiko' und die geschichtliche Welt," [*Zeit-Schaigt für deutsche Philologie,* LXI (1936)] Hermann Blumenthal shows in a few concrete examples how Stifter occasionally retouched history by suppressing egotistic or strictly political motives in his heroes. Blumenthal also points out that, for Stifter, the cities of northern Italy which resisted the Holy Roman Empire of Barbarossa were nothing but breakers of the law, whereas for his source, Raumer, they had a political right of their own. Lunding remarks that, although Stifter could not come to terms with the "sneering amorality of history," he was determined to maintain the appearance of serene optimism and to awaken belief in an ordered universe, ruled by his gentle law. Rychner speaks of the optimism that Stifter as a moralist deliberately read into history.

The philosophical issue of the morality of history must necessarily become clouded in a novel about the Middle Ages, where the religious and the secular are completely fused. "Justice must triumph, because it is valid in heaven and on earth," is the leitmotif of Dimut, a "Bohemian Joan of Arc" [Erik Lunding, *Adalbert Stifter,* 1946]. Battle cries include in one breath "God, the Holy Trinity, the Empire and the King." Before the Italian campaign, relics are placed in a church "for the glory of God and the sake of the enterprise." The naïve woodlanders, Witiko's men, think nothing of offering a part of their booty to the Church. God and the saints are always on the side of right and justice; the Duke and his warriors never forget to pray to them before battle and to thank them after victory. Only once in the novel is there a hint that the other side might make the same claim. The very old Bolemil, who has seen many civil wars in his lifetime, says that the national saint, Saint Wenceslaus, may be of no avail to them in this present war, since both sides can ask for his help.

A war of defense, a war for right and justice is a "holy"

war, and those slain in it will find their reward in heaven. This is in keeping with the spirit of the Middle Ages, but modern man is wary of "just" and "holy" wars and rewards in heaven, all the more as this way of thinking is by no means a thing of the past. Modern man shudders to read of war sent by God as a means of purification and atonement for wrongdoing, even though we do not have to identify the speaker, the Bishop of Prague, with Stifter. We feel uneasy about a father who would rather see his three very young sons die than suffer the arrogance of the enemy, or about a husband who wants to console his wife with the fact that their son died a "heroic" death. The pacifist Stifter is hard put to deal with a century where personal feuds, wars of succession, and rebellions were the order of the day. Stifter takes infinite pains to prove that the "good" ruler resorts to war only after all negotiations have failed. In order to justify war to his woodmen, Witiko speaks of the enemy as being worse than wolves, since the enemy acts from greed and not from hunger. This is a far cry from the earlier war story *Bergmilch.* There only the chauvinistic lord of the castle compares the enemies to wolves which one has to kill, whereas his wife still sees the human beings in them. The constant need which Stifter feels to justify fighting in *Witiko* seems like an anachronism in the twelfth century. Even more of an anachronism is Duke Wladislaw's enlightened vision of a time when nations will act like individual beings, helping each other like friends and neighbors. Later on in the novel, he even wishes for a federation of all European nations.

Actual fighting, although vividly and convincingly depicted, occupies only about a twentieth part of the novel. Much more space is given to the description of councils, negotiations, preparations for battles and their aftermaths. War on Wladislaw's side is conducted in a more humane fashion than it was in the Middle Ages, or, for that matter, at any time. The idea of humane warfare is one of the greatest human fallacies. The burning pitch thrown from the battlements of Prague foreshadows napalm. Senseless devastation is strictly, but vainly, forbidden by Wladislaw: "And thus the warriors descended like a cloud on the land." All the Duke can do is punish the perpetrators of the crime afterward. After battles, a list of the dead is compiled (if possible) before they are buried, and great, loving care is given to the wounded. Once, even an emergency hospital is erected, and a physician from the Duke's camp is sent to the wounded! When, at the end of a campaign, rewards are distributed, the wounded receive special consideration. The families of the dead are compensated, and Witiko comforts the mothers.

Men are wounded or die in battle, villages are burned, cattle are taken away, crops are destroyed, but nowhere are suffering and deprivation described in naturalistic detail. It is very easy to overlook the torture of Bishop Zdik's men or the order to cut off the hands of those who tried to smuggle food into beleaguered Milan, because Stifter mentions both facts so casually. The very young fighters, Urban's nephew and Osel's three sons, are spared serious injury or death. Wounds heal, and Tom the Fiddler, whose right hand was injured, is capable of playing at Witiko's wedding, by means of an ingenious, although highly improbable, device. Had Stifter ever experienced the hor-

rors of war himself, he could not have maintained this optimistic outlook. The strongest pacifist plea in the novel is Witiko's laconic reply to the troubadour von Kürenberg's praise of war as glorious. "To us," Witiko says, "it brought destruction and sorrow."

In contrast to Stifter's other works, *Witiko,* because of its very subject matter, contains a good deal of hero worship and praise of bodily strength and courage, manliness, honor, and fame. Only once does Stifter's skepticism toward this customary way of thinking find its expression in *Witiko*—in the remarkable figure of Agnes, the daughter of the German Emperor Henry IV. When Witiko speaks to her of knightly deeds he wants to accomplish in order to win glory and fame for himself, Agnes answers, "This young knight again speaks of deeds . . . do we know, after all, what deeds are?" A little later, after giving a moving account of her own life and the woeful end of her father, she says

> I have seen enough deeds which have been praised and have caused evil. He who loves his wife, educates his children in the love of God, increases his possessions honestly, protects and improves the life of his subjects, has performed the right kind of deeds. And who knows whether it is not a better pursuit to embroider this piece of cloth to serve the Church or to soften the footsteps of an old man than to conquer and destroy duchies.

Agnes's words are more in accord with Stifter's general views on what is truly great, than a cliché like Bertha's parting words to Witiko before he goes to war: "Witiko, you are a man. Be a man, and think of those at home." Although on the "just"—that is, Duke Wladislaw's—side, the war is conducted as humanely as possible, there is still more violence to be found in *Witiko* than in any other work of Stifter. Abuse is heaped on the enemy, and vulgar words, found nowhere else in Stifter's work, are employed. Violent emotions—anger, desire for revenge, fury in the heat of battle—are depicted. There is nothing "gentle" in the battle scenes; to see, with Steffen, the gentle law still at work in the death-dealing weapon of the smith of Plan, is to deprive the word "gentle" of its meaning. Neither Steffen nor, for that matter, Stifter himself, wants to face the deep conflict which man encounters when he tries to punish violations of the gentle law, and then no longer can act in accordance with the law itself that demands "that every human being be protected as a jewel, inasmuch as every man is a jewel for all other men."

Witiko has been hailed by several modern critics as a model for political conduct. They base their claim on the high humanity, the sense of right and justice which animate the political leaders in the novel. We do not for one moment want to deny that such high ethics should prevail in politics. But it is hard for modern man to make the necessary analogies between the Middle Ages and our own time. In *Witiko,* we do not deal with a "timeless humanity," as Hüller [in *Adalbert Stifters "Witiko": Eime Pectung,* 1953] wants us to believe. Witiko is a Christian knight and not a "classical antique figure" (*Gestalt*). Life and politics in *Witiko* are God- and Church-centered; in our times they are not. The ideas of a Holy Empire and a divinely appointed ruler, which play such an important part toward the end of the novel, are alien to us, or idolatrous, if they appear in secular form, as in Hitler's case.

Our social structure also differs in every respect from that of the twelfth century. At that time, man's station in life was thought to be ordered by God; for the true Christian any rebellion against authority was sin. Man's first allegiance was to God; his second, almost equally strong allegiance, to his lord. Feudal society was held together by highly personal, mutual bonds of loyalty, trust, and gratitude. Witiko's relationship to Soběslaw and Wladislaw as their vassal, his relationship to his woodlanders as their leader and then their lord, are examples of such bonds. But such personal relationships, though beautiful and admirable, unfortunately, no longer suffice in modern mass society. We tend to forget that toward the end of the novel, Witiko becomes a feudal lord like his ancestors, because he is such an ideal feudal lord in his kindness, justice, and concern for his subjects, who love him and look upon him as one of themselves. But their claim that they chose him as their lord (*"Heil dem guten Witiko, den wir zu unserem Herrn erkoren haben"*), is invalid, for it was the Duke who gave Witiko the land. Witiko generously absolves his new subjects of one-tenth of the tribute they formerly owed the Duke; this means, of course, that nine-tenths remain. Witiko wants to remain humble, but the chivalric code of honor sets him apart from, and above, his men. It is easy to understand that criticism in Stifter's own time found glorification of feudalism inappropriate at a moment when attempts were being made to get rid of the last vestiges of feudalism.

One might, however, try to abstract a generally valid core of political wisdom from this medieval novel and take as ethical guidelines for political conduct the often quoted dialogue between Witiko and Cardinal Guido, the papal legate. After being praised by the Cardinal, Witiko modestly replies, "I tried to do what the nature of things requires. . . ." Whereupon the Cardinal answers, "If you strive to do what the nature of things requires, it would be good if all men knew what the nature of things requires and acted in accordance with it, because then they would fulfill the will of God." But Witiko is still not satisfied and says, "Often I do not know what the nature of things requires." The Cardinal concludes the discussion with the laconic remark, *"Dann folge dem Gewissen, und du folgst den Dingen"* (Then follow your conscience and you will fulfill what the nature of things demands). These words sound at first like a magic formula, an infallible guide in the most difficult situations. But our conscience can guide us only after we have a clear insight into the nature of things, into a given situation, and Witiko had just acknowledged that he is often lacking this insight.

In his book on **Witiko** [*Stifters Witiko: Vom Wesen des Politischen,* 1967], Weippert sees the problem, but tries to resolve it by making a rather unconvincing distinction between complete, scientific knowledge of the nature of things and that which is needed for action at a given moment without violating the nature of things. Two incidents in the novel itself show that the question is more complicated than the hypnotic words, *"Folge dem Gewissen, und*

du folgst den Dingen," would indicate. The first occurs at the assembly on the Wišehrad. To Bishop Silvester it is absolutely clear that conscience requires keeping one's oath and letting Soběslaw's son ascend the throne, even though the nephew is the better man. God, he argues, can save the country through the boy Wladislaw. Bishop Zdik, a thoroughly honest and unselfish man, acts in good conscience when he advises the assembly to elect the nephew—as do many good men along with him. There is no comment by Stifter, and the reader must draw his own conclusions. Are we to believe that Zdik did not probe his conscience deeply enough? His later repentance favors such an interpretation. But in the reader's mind the question remains, what would have happened if the absolute dictates of conscience had been followed and young Wladislaw, who turns out to be an extremely weak character, had ascended the throne. Would he have been able to prevent civil war? Would he not have been a helpless tool in the hands of such selfish men as Načerat and his followers?

The other case where Silvester represents an ethical standard differing from that of the actively engaged person is the much-discussed incident at Holobkau near Pilsen. In a chance encounter, Witiko lets three of the rebellious princes escape so that they can tell Konrad of Znaim of the superior strength of the Duke's army and the hopelessness of their fighting him. Witiko wants to prevent further bloodshed and also—this we learn much later—to keep the Duke from having to punish the rebellious princes immediately and thus perhaps too harshly. Witiko is not sure, however, whether acting on his own could be called "good" in the opinion of the highest ethical arbiter he knows—Bishop Silvester. When he asks him, the answer, somewhat to our surprise, is negative. Witiko, the Bishop says, had overstepped his duty as a soldier. Yet he, as well as Bishop Zdik, had acted in good faith (*"nach meinem guten Sinne"*).

The mild, almost mock, punishment which Witiko receives at the hands of the Duke for his arbitrary action as a soldier is a good example of how Stifter avoided the tragic in his later work. How differently the same conflict is treated by Kleist in his drama *Prinz Friedrich von Homburg!* Silvester is the purest incarnation of the ethical ideal in the novel; the others can only approximate it. He is, on another level, the spiritual brother of the priest in **Kalkstein,** equally humble and lovable. Does Stifter mean to intimate . . . that only the man of God, renouncing all earthly goods and his high office, withdrawing to the solitude of the monastery, is able to express the ethical ideal consistently, whereas the worldly knight Witiko cannot withdraw into solitude, but after a period of deliberation must take the risk of choice? The conflict between an absolute ethical ideal and any involvement in action, a conflict, at which Stifter only hints in **Witiko,** brings to mind Goethe's profound remark: *"Der Handelnde ist immer gewissenlos; es hat niemand Gewissen als der Betrachtende"* (The man of action is always without conscience, it is only the observer who has a conscience).

Even if we assume that the modern reader finds interest in a subject so remote from him as the internecine wars of twelfth century Bohemia, there still remains the hurdle of a highly stylized form with its lack of individualization and psychological depth. Stifter wanted to write a novel showing the triumph of moral law, not so much in the fate of individuals, as in that of entire nations. As he wrote to Heckenast on June 8, 1861, he wanted to write a novel with history as its main subject and individual characters as a matter of secondary importance. They are carried, he said, by the broad current of history which, at the same time, they help to form. The so-called historical novel is, for him, an "epic in prose." Thus he unfolds before us an immense canvas of people, shown at times in violent action, but more often in slow motion. He purposely avoids any psychological probing and any personal comment. Objectivity is his goal, and what cannot be shown outwardly is not shown at all.

Witiko is even less of an individual than Heinrich Drendorf in **Der Nachsommer.** He shows no real growth; there is no Risach, no *Rosenhaus* to open up new horizons for him. He has to observe the political developments in order to take sides. But, from the very beginning, he is reserved, prudent, self-controlled, loyal, and grateful. Wherever he goes, he takes care of his horse himself. Stifter never forgets to mention this trait as a symbol of Witiko's equal concern for matters small or big. How "good" he is we learn from testimonies by people close to him—a device Stifter often uses in his works. Witiko shares Heinrich's deadly seriousness, his complete lack of any sense of humor. He never displays any characteristics of youth, such as abandon, exuberance or imprudence. He rarely shows any emotion. He weeps over Soběslaw's death and has tears in his eyes when he sees his mother after an absence of four years. But he later tells his future father-in-law that he stayed with her as long as propriety (*die Gebühr*) demanded. He remains cool even in the heat of battle, as the Holobkau episode demonstrates. We may admire him, but we feel no true empathy with this knight "without fear and without reproach." Witiko's leather clothes, which he wears most of the time in "joy and sorrow", are symbols of the value he attaches to reliability rather than brilliant appearance. The Scarlet Rider and other splendidly clad knights good-naturedly nickname him "Leatherman."

The other characters have even less individuality than Witiko: they are prototypes. Wladislaw is the ideal ruler, *"ein schattenlos edler Schöner"* (a beautiful noble figure without blemish), Odolen a daredevil youth, Bolemil a wise old man, Načerat a demagogue and archtraitor, Silvester a man of almost Christlike kindness and simplicity. To the great number of individuals who take part in the action is added an even greater number of persons of whom we learn only the names and sometimes the offices. There is frequently a long listing of names in order to produce the impression of large crowds. But used too often, this device becomes fatiguing. Many of these persons we meet more than once, and we cannot help marveling that Stifter never loses sight of them, even after long intervals. Yet, we get somehow lost in this maze of names—at least when we read the novel for the first time. Max Stefl even found it necessary to add an index of persons to his Insel edition.

In order to appreciate **Witiko,** one has to study its struc-

ture as one would study a musical composition or an intricately woven tapestry. There is a rhythmic, orderly pattern in **Witiko,** as there is in nature with its constant change of seasons. War and peace, destroying and building, alternate in the novel. The same people reappear at well-spaced intervals. Certain patterns of action and behavior are repeated throughout. Perhaps the most typical example is the conduct of war with its identical sequence of events: the preparations for the campaign, the blessing of the departing warriors, the council, the futile, last-minute negotiations with the enemy, the prayer before battle, the actual fighting, the prayer of thanks after victory, the expression of gratitude and the distribution of rewards by the leaders. Other frequently used patterns are the paying and returning of visits, and the giving or exchanging of gifts. There are, of course, nuances, according to the wealth of host or giver. A sign of Witiko's having "arrived," for example, is the elaborate ritual with which he welcomes into his home Boreš, the castellan of the late Soběslaw, to whom Duke Wladislaw and his wife have entrusted their wedding gifts for Witiko and Bertha. The presentation of these exquisite gifts necessitates an even more elaborate ritual.

The basic principle of a highly stylized form, repetition, shows up strikingly in the spoken word. The readers of **Witiko** are startled or appalled, as the case may be, by its excessive use in the novel. Repetition of the same words or sentences is warranted, as Lunding has pointed out, when legal questions arise in council, and is thus quite frequently and effectively used by Stifter. Repetition is also appropriate on other solemn occasions, for example, when Witiko asks for Bertha's hand in marriage or at the above-mentioned presentation of wedding gifts. (The strictly regulated code of chivalric behavior met halfway Stifter's own tendency toward ceremonious speech.) Repetition, however, is unrealistic in the dialogue between Witiko and Bertha when, after six years, they revisit the clearing in the woods where they had first met. One lover picks up the words of the other six times in succession. At such a moment of strong emotion we expect a more artless expression, maybe even silence. Yet it should be emphasized that the terms "realistic" or "unrealistic" are not used to determine the esthetic value of the novel. This "strange" dialogue has a charm of its own and is entirely in keeping with the style of the work.

In order to be just to Stifter, one has to acknowledge, as Lunding has noted, that he also masters other, less stylized, and less abstract, modes of expression. There are, for instance, the dramatic battle scenes, the elaborate, greatly varied speeches in the elective assembly on the Wyšehrad, and Načerat's clever speech at the unofficial meeting of the Bohemian and Moravian nobles, a model of demagoguery, which strongly reminds us of Mark Antony's famous funeral oration in Shakespeare's *Julius Caesar*.

A detailed analysis of **Witiko**'s style is beyond the scope of this study. The main characteristics other than repetition are the prodigious epic breadth (where everything—great or small—is of equal significance), the simple syntax with its preference for coordination, the extreme scarcity of embellishing adjectives, of images and metaphors, the rare show of emotion, and the complete absence of any comment by the author. This factual style, which often verges on the dry, affects readers in different ways. Some will find it boring, whereas others will find that it conveys great peace and quiet. Most readers, however, will agree that this sober, restrained style reaches great heights in some passages, among the finest Stifter has written, the most moving being perhaps the short description of Soběslaw's death.

One aspect of the style which, to my knowledge, has been neglected by the critics, is the wide use of color for design and vivid visual impressions. Thus, the color of banners differentiates various groups in battles. The speakers in the elective assembly on the Wyšehrad are first identified only by what Witiko sees—the color of their hair, their beards, their eyes, their tunics, their caps and the feathers on them—before they identify themselves by name. This principle of identifying a person by his clothing is used throughout the novel. Stifter's desire to present only what can be seen immediately merges with the painter's delight in the colorful clothing of the Middle Ages. He always carefully harmonizes the color of hair, beard, and eyes with that of the clothing, as well as the colors of horses and riders. If there are crowds, brilliant *tableaux vivants* appear. It would be an interesting experiment to try to reproduce some of these with the brush.

Colors are used as leitmotifs and symbols. As with Risach, the greater the man, the simpler the clothing. Weak, young Wladislaw (Soběslaw's son) and the traitor Načerat wear splendid clothes in rich colors. Wladislaw is compared to a blue butterfly glittering in the sun. The Duke, on the other hand, after he has ascended the throne, wears a simple brown tunic, and his wife chooses the same color. As a carefree youth the Duke wore bright scarlet, and Stifter called him the Scarlet Rider. Very effective color contrasts are used to show the transitoriness of all earthly glory. Red blood soils the coat of horses and the shining clothes of men dying in battle. Their rosy faces turn ash-gray. No further comment by the author is needed.

All that has been said in this short analysis of *Witiko* is intended to show, among other things, that only patient rereading will open up the work to the reader. If I were to speculate on future critical evaluations of *Witiko*, I should be inclined to agree with Lunding that categorical value judgments are out of place and that the evaluation will fluctuate with the tastes of individuals and epochs. The number of people able to enjoy *Witiko* will be even smaller than in the case of *Der Nachsommer*. Like *Der Nachsommer*, the work has not yet found an English translator. (pp. 121-31)

> *Margaret Gump, in her* Adalbert Stifter, *Twayne Publishers, Inc., 1974, 172 p.*

Alexander Stillmark   (essay date 1975)

[*In the following essay, Stillmark discusses the interdependence of moral and aesthetic values in Stifter's early works.*]

Von meiner Kindheit an war immer etwas in

mir, wie eine schwermütig schöne Dichtung, dunkel und halbbewusst, in Schönheitsträumen sich abmühend—oder soll ich es anders nennen, ein ungebórner Engel, ein unhebbarer Schatz, den selber die Musik nicht hob.

These words with their warm confessional tone are attributed to the narrator of *Feldblumen,* a young painter who writes to his friend of his first encounter with the love of his life. They might equally have found a place in one of Stifter's private letters or in that searching biographical sketch *Mein Leben* in which he feels out the earliest stirrings of artistic perception and of the aesthetic sense. Each allusive image points to that deep-rooted impulse to seek out and to fathom beauty which, though present in most artists, is especially alive in the young Stifter. In him it is a conscious, dedicated quest, a blend of presentiment and assurance of an ideal, of definite yearning for and vague recollection of archetypal perfection. One is forcibly reminded of those "first affections, those shadowy recollections" which Wordsworth evokes in "Intimations of Immortality". They are, indeed, kindred spirits. The affinity between Stifter and Wordsworth seems never so close as in their most sensitive evocations of those primal experiences which survive for the artistic sensibility as continuing illuminations and imperishable truths. Both become mystics when they speak of beauty.

The fervent search for aesthetic truth characterizes Stifter's literary endeavours from the beginning. Devotion to beauty constitutes not merely a motif but the main motivation behind the early *Studien.* Indeed, it survives into maturity. The narrator of *Der Waldbrunnen,* for instance, finds himself enthralled by two manifestations of perfect beauty in women and the pursuit of these paragons of beauty determines the very structure of the tale. The quixotic figure of the painter Roderer in *Nachkommenschaften* offers an ironical variant on such pursuit of the ideal in that he doggedly persists in seeking beauty within a desolate moor—the bleakest and least likely of subjects. Finally, in the mature heart of Stifter's *œuvre,* amidst the speculative dialogues of *Der Nachsommer,* Risach pronounces with the authority of his author on the lure of beauty: "So hat Gott es auch manchen gegeben, dass sie dem Schönen nachgehen müssen und sich zu ihm wie zu einer Sonne wenden, von der sie nicht lassen können."

Few sentences could more happily convey the almost magnetic compulsion Stifter experienced in relation to beauty. He views beauty not as static, fixed and clearly determinable but rather as a force active and activating; a guiding light which draws the mind on to ever deeper contemplation and fuller illumination. It is in essence mysterious and elusive, as we learn from the narrator's preamble in *Brigitta,* and its secret nature may long remain hidden from the uncomprehending eye. It is significant that decisive revelations of beauty which Stifter often depicts at climactic moments of his narrative—Deborah on her deathbed seeing Abdias with loving eyes; Brigitta at the moment of reconciliation with Murai; Augustinus seeing the cornfield at sunset after his contemplated suicide; the narrator in *Kalkstein* looking back for the last time on the stony valley of the Kar; Heinrich Drendorf recognizing the splendour of the Greek muse during a storm—all follow periods of searching and trial entailing certain kinds of inner blindness. Beauty in Stifter waits upon discovery and often carries the force of revelation. What will emerge from subsequent analysis is that for Stifter the pursuit of beauty is most intimately linked with the crucial problem of self-fulfilment and the attainment of happiness. The quest for beauty is essentially a quest for human perfectibility.

Scant attention has been paid to the problem of determining what Stifter understood by the beautiful and this despite the central importance of the idea within his work. The assertive presence of the idea of beauty as a constituent of the early prose seems to me to demand particular evaluation and comment. What is striking about the early prose is a pronounced introspective quality; Stifter works in a highly expressive, self-conscious style with a strong tendency towards abstraction. The young writer is seen to develop those areas of thought and sensibility which are most important to him. He is feeling his way towards his own aesthetic in these exploratory works and the seeds of his mature conception of beauty are beginning to germinate. As Stifter matures, the abstract idea of beauty becomes increasingly transformed and assimilated into the formal features of his art. For this reason, the more rudimentary, experimental early prose can yield clearer insights, surprising anticipations of later developments and those sudden glimpses of focal aesthetic issues which impress by their pure ingenuousness.

The consistency with which Stifter portrays the young artist in his first works, though by no means an unusual feature in German letters, does draw attention to itself. The firm tradition of the "Künstlerroman" must certainly be counted as an important contributory factor. We have only to recall the landmarks Werther, Sternbald, Ofterdingen, *Maler Nolten, Der grüne Heinrich, Malte Laurids Brigge,* and the early Thomas Mann, to appreciate how constant is the line of succession which Stifter enters immediately after the Romantic generation. It is also remarkable that these are without exception "Jugendwerke", written before their authors had reached their mid-thirties. The evident compulsion felt by the young writer to mirror his own situation, his tendency to indulge in a narcissist exploration of the creative process, to feel the assurance of the inner world which he knows more intimately than the world at large, is understandable as a feature of immaturity; yet it is also a peculiar characteristic of German authors. The fact that Stifter's literary beginnings are steeped in the world of art is, in addition, attributable to his deep and prolonged indecision whether to continue as painter or writer. A young painter is made the hero of three of the works to be considered (*Julius, Der Condor, Feldblumen*) while *Das Haidedorf* is concerned with the awakening of the poet's gift. *Der Condor* in fact marks a decisive point in Stifter's career, not just because it brought him recognition but because in the writing he works out certain of his inmost concerns as a writer. The full and intricate treatment he gives there to the relationship between the moral and the aesthetic gives the work a crucial status within his *œuvre*. It will be considered last, both because it warrants more detailed interpretation and for the purposes of summary.

The figure of the youthful artist as a recurrent feature of Stifter's first literary efforts is not a random choice but a necessary device for self-exploration as well as for creative self-expression. In assuming the artist persona he is refining his own developing aesthetic, not merely in abstract terms—for his was not a theoretical cast of mind—but through the creative imagination. The basic pattern to which he works in these early *Studien* (the generic title appropriately hints at the tentative and provisional character of this art) embraces the artist's pursuit of beauty, a test of his dedication and finally some aesthetic insight which carries abiding conviction and acts as a sustaining force in his life.

The fragmentary form of Stifter's first literary effort *Julius,* written in the late 1820's, affords valuable insight into his deliberations about basic aesthetic notions. The narrative framework used itself introduces some critical distance and also gives scope for reflection and comment. It contains a few considered pronouncements on excellence in prose style which help to establish Stifter's priorities in poetics. The narrator describes the original model for his story as one which lacked all poetic embellishment and yet could make a profound impression:

> Der Inhalt dieses Manuscriptes mit seinem so eigenthümlichen, so anziehenden, präzisen, höchst einfachen, und doch so unnachahmlichen Stile, und Periodenbau begeitet von den betreffenden Bemerkungen des lebenserfahrenen Greises grub sich mit solcher Gewalt in mein Gemüth, dass ich fortwährend die Bilder jenes Ortes, und jener Personen nicht los werden konnte.

This deliberate, almost analytical manner of describing language points to a highly developed sense of craftsmanship in the writer. More especially, it shows us a mind decided upon a manner and a quality of writing which fulfil an envisaged ideal. It also comes close to describing Stifter's own prose as it later develops; an appealing originality of invention, hard precision and a clear simplicity of statement which combines with the distinctive accents of a personal style. These classicist principles come increasingly to the fore in Stifter's maturity as is attested by his frequent insistence on "Klarheit", "Natürlichkeit" and "Einfachheit."

The impulse towards perfection, the need for a model, for examplariness in form and ethical content are already distinguishing marks of Stifter's earliest phase of writing. The narrator in *Julius* laments the loss of the manuscript after repeated attempts to persuade its author to publish it for the benefit of humanity: "er möge doch eine so schöne Schrift nicht ungenützet liegen lassen, sondern dieselbe der Menschheit als einen Spiegel vorlegen." The mirror image acquires an unusual meaning here, and one which is wholly characteristic of Stifter's mode of thought. It is not to be understood as an image of uncompromising realism, of a total, unvarnished reflection of the world in the sense of a Stendhal. Stifter informs the image with a personal significance—for him the mirror is the instrument of revelation, the agent of enlightenment and improvement. He believed, with a simplistic faith quite untypical of his age, in the moral efficacy of art and literature and spoke of his own works as "sittliche Offenbarungen".

If one looks to the portrayal of character in *Julius,* one discovers a vocabulary of inwardness, an accentuation of spiritual endowments and a romantic emotionalism of tone. These are the terms in which the young artist, who stands on the threshold of manhood, is described:

> Die Ideen der Vernunft werden tiefer und heiliger—die Begriffe des Verstandes werden klarer und bestimmter—das Gemüth thut sich auf für jeden Eindruck des Sanften und Lieblichen, des Hohen und Grossartigen—das schuldlose Herz umschliesst mit Liebe die ganze Welt—vor allem aber eröffnet die Fantasie ihren unbegränzten Wirkungskreis: sie weilt mit Vergnügen in den Gebilden der schönen Künste, und entzückt und belebt die junge Seele mit Bildern einer poetischen glücklichen Zukunft.

The whole passage moves within the most general abstract concepts which no more than sketch an idealized portrait of the artist. The romantic and religiose overtones deny the description all colour, sensuous vitality and individuality. The only significant purpose of such portrayal lies in the evocation of moral aspirations and values in the creative artist.

This is a purpose Stifter faithfully pursues throughout the early works. The description of Maria, with whom Julius falls in love, shows a like concern for aesthetic and idea considerations in its accentuation of notional values:

> ein Engel des Himmels!—So missbraucht der Ausdruck seyn mag: er liegt der Fantasie zu nahe, als dass sie ihn nicht so gleich ergreifen sollte, wenn sie von einem Bilde der grössten irdischen Schönheit überrascht wird, und um so mehr, wenn diese Schönheit eine Ahnung sittlicher Reinheit anreget. Ein Engel! dachte Raphael und vergass fast seiner Botschaft. Die schwarzen Haare waren über der Stirne in zwey fast gleiche Theile reinlich getheilt, und fielen in zwey einfache Locken auf die Schultern nieder. Die freundliche Stirne, dunkelblaue Augen, ein edles Oval des Gesichtes bildete allerdings ein schönes Ganze, aber es giebt tausend solcher Köpfe, die wohl noch schöner sind, und doch bey weitem nicht so schön, denn der eigenthümliche Ausdruck, der in diesen Zügen wohnt, soll man ihn Verstand oder Ernst, Verstand oder Seele, Tugend oder Gottheit nennen, giebt dieser Gestalt eine tief ergreifende Bedeutung, dass man eher versucht würde, vor ihr andächtig niederzuknieen, als sie zu küssen.

The discussion of the conventionality of the angel as an image of beauty is a telling instance of Stifter's critical and self-aware approach to the problem of depicting beauty. The consciousness that he is dealing in a common coinage does not deter him but prompts him instead to add a reflective note which arrests the mind and challenges it to assess the pertinence of the image. By braving convention in this way, Stifter deftly surmounts it. The attempt to depict the sensuous charms of Maria's face ends, however, in a sense of futility since nothing distinctive of beauty has been captured by language. And so Stifter, the artist of

language, gropes for something beyond the commonplace physical detail and reaches for the inward expressiveness of personality. Each of the notions "Verstand, Ernst, Seele, Tugend, Gottheit", is considered in turn and is superseded in an effort to grasp that essential quality which appears to lie beyond these notional stepping-stones. This "Steigerung" of terms shows Stifter's aspiration to find words which can express that "unsichtbare Schönheit" of which he writes in one of his most revealing, though rarely quoted literary reviews: *Ernst Ritter's "Mohnkröner".* The neglect of the visual element implied by this concept places the entire accent on the moral connotations of beauty. Such a view of the spirituality and mystery of the beautiful derives from the Neoplatonic tradition with its roots in Plotinus. It was perpetuated in Thomist philosophy by the monastic orders and was taught to the young Stifter at Kremsmünster. The idea of beauty as an inner virtue, contained within and often concealed by the shell of outer appearances, became the unchanging canon of his aesthetics. His favourite formulation of the idea is often reiterated: "das Schöne ist das Göttliche im Kleide des Reizes."

The artist's quest for beauty and his need to discover an objective criterion for its existence are the motivating factors and the main connective within the loose structure of *Feldblumen,* formally the least characteristic of Stifter's *Studien.* Although a rambling, disjointed work which takes Stifter too far into romantic philosophizing and effusions of the heart, it is a mine of aesthetic ideas—though these too exist only as unrefined ores. Within the work, Stifter confronts us with a view of art which posits the discovery of beauty as the highest goal for the practising artist. Yet at the same time, as we shall see, he places doubt on the value of pursuing beauty for its own sake and this makes for a nice ambivalence.

The epistolary form of *Feldblumen* ensures a personal, confessional tone which mirrors the mind of the young painter whose thirst for manifestations of beauty is insatiable. The private enjoyment of beauty is his favourite pursuit in life, indeed, an obsession, so that he styles himself "ein Schönheitsgeizhals". He contrasts his own innocent pursuit with the material avarice of the "Metallgeizhals", for the artist wishes only to enjoy beauty selflessly: "nur die reine Form anbeten und den stofflichen Besitz endlich jemand anderem lassen." Yet when he falls in love with the "Paradiesgartenschönheit" Angela, he is not content merely to worship her beauty from afar but actually succumbs to jealousy and finally does possess her as his bride. This is a touch of playful irony of a kind only met with in the later stories such as *Der Waldsteig* or *Nachkommenschaften;* a rarer side of the writer which contrasts with his wonted solemnity.

Since Albrecht's inner world, his feelings and thoughts, make up the body of the work, each insight into the nature of beauty can only be understood and evaluated in relation to the artist's personality. By this means Stifter achieves closest interplay of aesthetic and moral notions; a device which reflects his inmost convictions on the nature of art. To appreciate the distinctive quality of the young artist's vision of beauty, some critical appraisal of the self-portrait he provides is necessary.

Albrecht's introspective, self-analytical cast of mind affords ample insight into those recesses of his soul where his artistic sensibilities and the yearning for beauty reside. He traces the origins of his devotion to art back to early youth when he secretly read exciting romances "aus einem schönen Ritterbuche" in a dovecote. (The book's power to inspire and to kindle aesthetic awareness, both as an object of beauty and as a stimulus to the imagination, is suggested by the ambiguity of the adjective "schön"). These indelible boyhood impressions have determined his idea of beauty. They have, above all, informed the idea with a sense of the extraordinary, have raised it above the common level of experience and provided an aura of mystery and wonder which survives into maturity: "immer suche ich noch, bildlich gesprochen, solche Taubenschläge, spanne mich aus der Gewerkswelt los und buhle um die Braut des Schönen." The words carry a familiar message. One catches in them something of that intense yearning for the exalted which breaks through the letters of the mature Stifter, the disillusioned inspector of schools burdened by debts and the petty cares of a narrow provincial existence. The beauty he seeks throughout life is the solace of loneliness, a sacred ransom for the barrenness of life; it is a beauty born of renunciation and pain. During work on *Der Nachsommer* Stifter writes to his publisher of the unequal struggle between daily drudgery and artistic calling:

> es zerreisst mir fast das Herz, wenn ich eben dieses Herz zu den lieben schönen hohen Dingen, die sich nach und nach in dasselbe finden, das Heu Stroh und den Häckerling des Amtes laden, und die Götter dadurch beschmutzen muss.

The creative writer in his priest-like calling could not, in Stifter's view, compromise or debase the high aesthetic criteria which serious art demanded. *Der Nachsommer* is the most imposing testimony to this will to create a beautiful artifact in defiance of personal circumstances and prevalent literary tastes. It was Stifter's determination to preserve the clarity of his vision, to sustain a purity of language and tone and to avoid the trivial and transitory which abounded in his age. His treatment of the beautiful throughout retains the characteristics of elevation, rareness and mystery.

Through the figure of Albrecht Stifter explores, and at the same time surmounts, that transcendent romantic yearning for a perfection that has no place in reality and is ultimately void. It finds expression in Albrecht's avid search for ideal human models, prototypes of beauty, to sketch. Above all it is alive in a utopian vision entertained by the young painter; a vision of the perfect life, strikingly vivid and complete in its details. Albrecht's "Tuskulum" consisting of "zwei, drei Landhäuser fast altgriechisch einfach", a lake-side setting, flower gardens and marble statues to delight the eye, is an illusory world of flawless beauty which is both artificial and sterile. Only superficial similarities link it with the serene detail of *Der Nachsommer;* more significant are the distinctions to be drawn.

The purpose of living in this dream-like setting, faintly evocative of a Claude Lorrain landscape, is seemingly none other than to be in continual contact with beauty: "In diesem Tuskulum nun wird gelebt und eine Schönheitswelt gebaut." An existence is conceived for a select circle of highminded friends which is free from all social and political obligations, all practical cares are tacitly excluded and no unruly passions are tolerated. In this earthly Elysium no one need care for what tomorrow may bring, since no change is foreseen: "jeder weiht seine Tätigkeit nur dem Allerschönsten." The vagueness of the implications of this expression prompts one to question both the sense and the conceivable aim of such an existence. It remains a selfish and immature day-dream, despite what is said of selfless enjoyment, being conjured up merely to satisfy the whim of an aesthete who has divorced beauty from life. It is Albrecht's principal flaw (and here the negative influence of Romanticism is evident) to live in a world of make-believe which feeds the imagination and the emotions but which provides no sure contact with real experience.

Herein lies the essential difference to the world created by Stifter in *Der Nachsommer.* "Das Rosenhaus" and "der Asperhof" are presented as authentic parts of the reality in the novel, not as the playful fantasies of a romantic dreamer. However much the novel may reflect Stifter's own cherished vision of a better life, his treatment of the young hero's growth in knowledge and awareness shows a clear purposiveness, a practical thoroughness and a concern for the physical world which renders the fiction whole and credible. This balanced relationship between the creative imagination and the real, tangible requirements of his chosen subject has not yet been established in the early Stifter. There is also a marked difference in the degree of seriousness inherent in his treatment. The elevation and solemnity of the language of the novel leaves no room for irony nor for that fanciful exuberance of the intellect at play which one finds in *Feldblumen.* Albrecht's whimsical, ebullient style à la Jean Paul has the effect of rendering ideas weightless and insubstantial. Stifter's personal attitude towards the chimerical temple of beauty in which an ideal existence is envisaged "unter lauter, grossen sanften Menschen" may best be deduced from the concluding passage of the work. Idle dalliance with aesthetic pleasure is there denounced by means of irony. The sceptical narrator holds out little hope of success for castle-building fantasts ("so überirdischen Köpfen") such as Albrecht.

The relationship of Albrecht to Angela forms what may be called the serious core of the work; it is crucial both to the question of how the artist views beauty and to an understanding of the development of Stifter's aesthetic ideal. Under guise of this relationship he depicts the artist's experience of beauty as the manifestation of something with transcendental, archetypal meaning. Prior to this revelatory experience Albrecht had already shown intuitive knowledge of it:

> Da dachte ich so, wie denn Gott mit den Linien und Formen des Menschenangesichts so eigen und am wunderbarsten den Geist der Schönheit verband, dass wir so mit Liebe hineinsehen und von Rührung getroffen werden;—aber kein

Mensch, dachte ich, kann eigentlich dieses
wundervolle Titelblatt der Seele so verstehen als
ein Künstler.

The phrases "Geist der Schönheit" and "Titelblatt der
Seele" are wholly typical of Stifter in alluding to that mysterious spiritual essence which, to his mind, underlies the
phenomenal. The artist with his gift of deeper, intuitive
perception is best fitted to discern the mystery; "die
wunderbare Magie des Schönen, die Gott den Dingen mit-
gab" as Stifter has called it.

Human beauty is generally depicted by Stifter as a quality
which emanates from an inner source, a form of radiance
which shines through the features with transfiguring
power. This is most clearly apparent during the moving
reconciliation scene at the end of ***Brigitta*** when the heroine appears transfigured by forgiveness and joy:

> Nun hob sie, noch in Tränen schimmernd, die
> Augen—und so herrlich ist das Schönste, was
> der arme, fehlende Mensch hienieden vermag,
> das Verzeihen—dass mir ihre Züge wie in un-
> nachahmlicher Schönheit strahlten und mein
> Gemüt in tiefer Rührung schwamm.

The links between the moral and the aesthetic are nowhere
so close as in ***Brigitta;*** the power of beauty to transform
and astound never so clearly dependent on moral virtues
and insights. Astonishment and awe in face of great beauty forms a striking motif in Stifter's works which has not,
to my knowledge, received the attention it deserves. Yet
it appears frequently and marks significant moments of
the narrative. Extraordinary human beauty is depicted as
a quality of great radiance and intensity which astonishes
the mind with the force of a revelation. This may be seen
in the violent reaction depicted in ***Der Hochwald*** at the
fateful moment when the two sisters first set eyes on Ronald: "Johanna hätte fast einen Schrei getan—so schön war
er—auch Clarissa wankte einen Augenblick." The motif
recurs in ***Die Narrenburg*** when Jodokus observes his
brother's response on first seeing Chelion: "Das sah ich
gleich, dass er vor der Schönheit meines Weibes erschrak
und zurückfuhr." It is present in the first version of ***Das
alte Siegel*** when Cöleste first sees Gustav: "Sie blieb betre-
ten stehen, nicht anders als sei sie sehr erschrocken—." It
also occurs in the late work ***Der Waldbrunnen*** when the
narrator sees the beautiful gypsy girl:

> und ich, der ich doch bereits in die reifenden
> Jahre trat, prallte fast zurück, als ich das Mäd-
> chen sah. Das war die schönste Menschenges-
> talt, die ich je in meinen Augen gemalt hatte.

The marked similarity, evident even in the verbal echoes,
within these recurring instances of the motif, suggests an
abiding conviction about the revelatory power of beauty.
It is a visionary experience which Stifter repeatedly tries
to capture; a kind of anamnesis which points to obscure,
ineffable origins (again "those shadowy recollections")
that have occupied great writing from Plato to Dostoevsky.

Albrecht's startled recognition of Angela's beauty in fact
forms the nucleus of the motif in Stifter. On that first encounter she stands, appropriately enough, in the "Para-
diesgarten" with her back towards him. Anxious to look
upon her face, he tries to attract her attention. When she
turns he is profoundly struck by her beauty: "Sie sah auch
um—und ich prallte fast zurück." The introspective
thoughts which ensue are quoted as the opening key-note
to this essay. It is Stifter's first attempt to depict archetypal beauty. Images which lie deep and half-forgotten in the
treasure-house of memory are resurrected in a visionary
moment. The significance of these images which arise in
the artist's mind should now appear more meaningful; all
of them are evocations of something pristine and precious
which was lost and has unexpectedly been regained:

> War sie so unermesslich schön?

> Ich weiss es nicht, aber es war mir wie einem
> Menschen, der in dunkler Nacht wandert in ver-
> meintlich unbekannter Gegend—auf einmal ges-
> chieht ein Blitz—und siehe, wunderbar vergol-
> det steht sein Vaterhaus und seine Kindesfluren
> vor den Augen.

This vision of beauty comes as an illumination in the sense
that it calls to mind an unremembered possession. It is the
experience of paradise regained. The astonishment lies in
the act of recognition, in the sense of encountering the familiar. The images used are noteworthy. The lightning signifies sudden revelation, whilst "Vaterhaus" and "Kindes-
fluren" suggest contact with those ineradicable, primal experiences which determine the artist's deepest convictions
about beauty. There are, without doubt, echoes of the Romantic motif of regression and homeward-journeying (as
in Ofterdingen's "immer nach Hause") and this, in turn,
may be said to hearken back to Neoplatonic anamnesis.
What is more pertinent to the present context and to
Stifter's situation as a modern writer is the peculiar intensity and conviction vested in the motif: Stifter's work reju-
venates and vitalizes an ancient tradition. It acquires a
freshness and unconstrained sincerity at the moment
when Albrecht gazes on Angela's perfection: "Ob ich in
sie verliebt wurde?—Nein, in diese war ich es seit meinem
ganzen Leben schon gewesen." The idea of encountering
an absolute, the certainty of truth which Stifter is communicating, lies in this awareness of timeless being. Angela
is incarnate beauty, the mediator of a perfection that is not
of this world. She is loved not as a woman but for the sake
of the beauty she manifests.

As a human figure Angela carries little conviction. Her
significance lies mainly on the level of ideas. Like Maria
in ***Julius*** she is an "angelic" invention; less a person than
the embodiment of an abstract conception: Stifter has
brought together in her intellectual accomplishments and
domestic virtues which are, doubtless, intended to blend
into a living portrait. Yet the attempts to individualize her
are contrived and she remains an improbably ethereal figure. The tendency to emphasize timeless and universal
qualities in human portrayal is always latent in Stifter and
most pronounced in ***Feldblumen.*** Angela is an artist's
study in the perfections of womanhood, an early sketch for
that ideal wholeness and purity which he only achieves in
the portraits of maturity. Albrecht refers to her as "die re-
chte, ernste Jungfrau, auf deren Stirne das Vollendungs-
siegel leuchtet" and his terms convey the contours of the

Madonna figure which remains a constant part of Stifter's conception of feminine beauty. This ideal is later to find fuller expression in the portrayal of Mathilde (**Der Nachsommer**) as well as in the female figures of **Die Mappe.**

Feldblumen is something of an oddity among Stifter's works; the speculative treatment of the subject-matter, the ruminations on aesthetic ideas, the digressive, ostentatious style are in marked contrast to the stricter narrative form and texture of **Der Condor** and **Das Haidedorf,** though all appeared in the same year, 1840. The latter two are succinct in style, show a delicate sense of composition, a subtle use of motifs and possess a stylistic unity which **Feldblumen** lacks. The common ground they share lies in the striking persistence of an interest in the artist's mind and imagination, in the aesthetic sensibility and in the mystery of beauty.

The charismatic nature of the poet's calling is an idea to which Stifter remains faithful in his writings and **Das Haidedorf** is his most explicit representation of the idea. The work, which has evident autobiographical accents, pictures the born poet marked out from other men by the special charism of his vocation. The boy Felix, reared among simple rural folk, emerges prophet-like from obscurity as the bearer of a special gift. The work explores those influences which stimulate the poet's native genius and which go to shape the creative imagination. Unlike Stifter's other early artist figures, Felix is a son of the soil, "ein herrlicher Sohn der Haide", raised in solitude, a stranger to the ways of society, a contemplative in a timeless natural setting. The lone heath in which this sensitive, impressionable mind develops is the first source and inspiration of his poetic gift. For the first time in Stifter nature attains that cosmic meaning which serves both as a substitute for the social world and as the mainspring of high moral and aesthetic values.

The increase of a sense of beauty and wonder in the boy poet is the first unconscious sign of his calling. He discovers the hues of the sunset on the wings of butterflies, hears strains of church music in the lark's singing and imagines himself sovreign ruler over the teeming wild life of the heath. He peoples his solitude with imaginary figures, exercising his gift of words by addressing speeches to them. Experience of nature acquires that absorbing intensity which is a key-note of Stifter's writing. Yet one also discerns in the artist a need to reach beyond this solitude, to enter new modes of experience:

> So lebte er nun manchen Tag und manches Jahr auf der Haide, und wurde grösser und stärker, und in das Herz kamen tiefere, dunklere und stillere Gewalten, und es ward ihm wehe und sehnsüchtig—und er wusste nicht, wie ihm geschah.

The vague longing which accompanies the poet's awakening powers again hints at that recurrent anamnesis which haunts the early Stifter. The poet is, as it were, carried along the path of self-fulfilment by a compelling impulse which Stifter acknowledges as godlike. The narrative voice is raised to confident exhortation: "Überlass den kleinen Engel nur seinem eigenen inneren Gotte." The poet's calling here assumes the dignity and inner surety of

a religious vocation: the gift of poetry appears as a kind of grace.

The other great formative influence in Felix's life is the ancient grandmother of whom it is said that she possesses "eine Dichtungsfülle ganz ungewöhnlicher Art". She appears an almost mythical figure who evokes the very spirit of poetry in Herder's sense. She is a repository of poetic truth, the unconscious mouthpiece of oracular wisdom and dark prophecy drawn from biblical sources and folklore, the bearer of a content too powerful for "dem schlechten Gefässe eines Haidebauerweibes". In this remarkable figure Stifter intimates something of the origins of poetry:

> wenn sie sanft lächelte, oder betete, oder mit sich selbst redete, wundersam spielend in Blödsinn und Dichtung, in Unverstand und Geistesfülle: so zeigte sie gleichsam, wie eine mächtige Ruine, rückwärts auf ein denkwürdiges Dasein.

The grandmother's use of language is unschooled, naive yet creative; though not herself an artist, she implants in the young poet a sense of the poetic. She is described as "spielend"; the notion of "play" as an essentially aesthetic activity is likely to have been influenced by Schiller. This idea is in strange combination with a fascination for the affinity of madness with genius which Stifter derives from the Romantics. This mythical personage who activates the creative imagination is shrouded by Stifter in an aura of mystery and grandeur. The sources of poetic inspiration appear in her as a fusion of startling opposites, of reason and unreason, simple-mindedness and sublimity, of harmony and dissonance. Nowhere else has Stifter treated the irrational element as the prime mover of poetry so finely. The peculiar blend of eloquence and obscurity, of illumination and mystery in the grandmother's speech instils in Felix an intuition about the grandeur of language. He does not attempt to order or reason out what he hears but merely opens his mind to a flood of stirring influences:

> da grauete er sich innerlich entsetzlich ab, und um so mehr, wenn er sie gar nicht mehr verstand—allein er schloss alle Tore seiner Seele weit auf und liess den phantastischen Zug eingehen, und nahm des andern Tags das ganze Getümmel mit auf die Haide, wo er alles wieder nachspielte.

This strange schooling, given and received in a "natural", unconscious way, is the making of the poet. When Felix decides to leave his sequestered life out of a need for knowledge of the world his path has been determined; he is about to fulfil the promise of his gift. At this point Stifter again affords us an insight through one of those deliberative touches of his early style. The narrative voice turns aside from the story and addresses the hero: "So ziehe mit Gott, du unschuldiger Mensch, und bringe nur das Kleinod wieder, was du so leichtsinnig fortträgst!" Such pointed asides have an almost didactic effect and betray something of the author's point of view. The poet's gift, repeatedly alluded to by the narrative voice, is the central motif of the story. The unique, charismatic value Stifter attaches to it is made clear by this emphatic address. The moral virtue implied by the attribute "unschuldig" equally forms a permanent part of Stifter's view of the artist; an aspect which finds further elaboration in **Der Condor,** as we shall see.

The distribution of accents and motifs within the narrative is highly significant. Stifter passes over in silence the poet's travels to the Orient and to those desert places which draw him by a secret affinity with his homeland. When asked by his mother where he has come from, he replies: "von der Haide Jordans", and questioned why he could not be found at a certain time, he explains: "denn ich war in der Wüste." The recurrent image of the heath or desert suggests, in symbolic terms, an unchanging and inviolate condition of being: the poet remains true to himself and retains his purity of heart. His inner virtue—inseparable from his artistic gift—remains unaltered wherever he travels like the desert landscapes which always lure him. It is notable that Stifter does not dwell upon the world beyond the heath—it exists merely to test the poet's integrity—but on the poet's precious gift which has been preserved whole and incorruptible.

The language used by Stifter to describe Felix on his return home is continually associated with the moral notions of goodness and purity. There is even a hint of transfiguration in the terms chosen: "es war ein solcher Glanz keuscher Reinheit um den Mann." The style increasingly yields to a tendency to explore and explain the moral groundwork of his nature:

> Was lebte denn in ihm, das ihn unangerührt durch die Welt getragen, dass er seine Körper als einen Tempel wiederbrachte, wie er ihn einst aus der Einsamkeit fortgenommen?

Stifter leaves the question in abeyance for the moment but is to return to it again. The image of the body as a temple with its definite biblical associations conveys that sense of inviolate purity, of dedication for a sacred office, which is crucial to Stifter's image of the artist. One is reminded of those stern, uncompromising terms with which Stifter the pedagogue and moral essayist characterizes the poet's status and role in society:

> Er ist der Lehrer, Führer, Freund seiner Mitbrüder, er kann ihnen ein Dolmetsch und Priester des Höchsten werden, wenn er in ihre Seelen als Dichter das Ideal des Schönen bringt.

The figure of Felix represents Stifter's single attempt to portray this exalted ideal of the moral leader and mediator of beauty. The beguiling simplicity of that ideal is reflected in the naive, spiritualized features of this early portrait.

Felix returns not as a prophet without honour but as one whose singular gift, though still unfulfilled, sets him morally above his fellowmen. His rootlessness, his failure in terms of worldly achievement, even his painful rejection by the parents of the girl he had hoped to marry, are treated incidentally, distantly; they appear almost immaterial in the light of his vocation. The deliberations of the narrative voice insistently draw us back to the focal point of interest—the poet's gift and the irresistible power of beauty:

> Was war es denn aber, was den Eltern und Nachbarn an ihm zurückgebracht worden ist?

Sie wussten es nicht.

> Ich aber weiss es. Ein Geschenk ist ihm geworden, das den Menschen hoch stellt, und ihn doch verkannt macht unter seinen Brüdern—das einzige Geschenk auf dieser Erde, das kein Mensch von sich weisen kann. Auf der Haide hatte es begonnen, auf die Haide musste er es zurücktragen. Bei wem eine Göttin eingekehrt ist, lächelnden Antlitzes, schöner als alles Irdische, der kann nicht anders thun, als ihr in Demuth dienen.

The question previously left open is now emphatically answered, and Stifter's personal dedication may be felt to give added weight to these words. That experience and knowledge of beauty gained by Felix since boyhood is summarily alluded to as the motive power in his life. The gift of poetry is represented by the traditional figure of the Muse, an allegory used by Stifter to communicate his idea of the transcendent quality in beauty. Like the Romantics before him, Stifter links the sources of poetry to those of religious experience. The aesthetic ideal transcends the world of appearances, the radiant Muse is "schöner als alles Irdische", and thus allegiance to the ideal has the compulsion of an act of faith.

There is a further significant feature in Stifter's portrayal of the artist which emerges briefly at the end of **Das Haidedorf:** it is the regenerative power of pain. At the moment of greatest personal desolation Felix experiences an uplifting form of bliss: "im tiefen, tiefen Schmerze war es, wie eine zuckende Seligkeit, die ihn lohnte." The strength which derives from renunciation, the joy which grows out of triumph over grief, are important characteristics of the young artist figure as they also form key motifs in Stifter's work. If such fusion of pain and pleasure is submerged in the diffuse and voluble style of **Feldblumen,** it emerges quite clearly in **Das Haidedorf** and figures prominently in **Der Condor.** Stifter is wont to depict this moment of strength in which the artist is vindicated, through the pregnant medium of a symbolic event. The instant in which suffering is converted to joy for Felix is marked by a parallel event in nature; the terrible drought which had threatened the life of the community is resolved in a gentle fall of rain.

Das Haidedorf traces the development of an artistic temperament, the growth of the imagination and sense of beauty, but does not show us the artist in his creative role. Felix leaves nothing to posterity but the future promise of his gift. **Der Condor,** by contrast, fixes attention on the practice and the products of art. Stifter is here concerned to illumine that most complex relationship of the artist to his creation and also to show something of the moral influence which enters into the process of making. This he achieves primarily through his sensitive depiction of personality and the love relationship. Within this context beauty derives its principal meaning from the notion of moral goodness. Stifter brings the ideas of moral and aesthetic content as criteria for artistic achievement into closest association with the love theme.

The artist's nature, both in its ethical potential and in its capacity to create beauty through art, remains the focal interest of the narrative. The extract from Gustav's diary which forms the opening section of the work is a narrative device which permits Stifter to eavesdrop on the inner thoughts and aspirations of the young painter. What we find recorded is a most significant experience in his life. Out of it the thematic threads of the ensuing narrative are spun. Gustav describes this episode in minute detail and this is a measure of its importance both for a reading of his state of mind and for subsequent interpretation of his art. It is for him a time of restive tension and expectancy, a time when the creative mind is stimulated and made receptive. The sensuous impressions of the night scene which his mind receives are later to be transformed into art; into two canvases depicting moonlit landscapes. Gustav faithfully records both the outward, physical and the inner, psychical impressions registered by his mind as he assimilates a living picture seen from his attic window:

> Der Mond natte sich endlich von den Dächern gelöset, und stand hoch im Blau—ein Glänzen und ein Flimmern und ein Leuchten durch den ganzen Himmel begann, durch alle Wolken schoss Silber, von allen Blechdächern rannen breite Ströme desselben nieder, und an die Blitzableiter, Dachspitzen und Thurmkreuze waren Funken geschleudert. Ein feiner Silberrauch ging über die Dächer der weiten Stadt, wie ein Schleier, der auf den hunderttausend schlummernden Herzen liegt.

The picture painted here in words is to return later in the story in the tangible form of the two paintings, acclaimed as masterpieces at an exhibition in Paris several years later. The narrator in turn describes the two canvases with unreserved admiration: "Es waren zwei Mondbilder—nein, keine Mondbilder, sondern wirkliche Mondnächte, aber so dichterisch, so gehaucht, so trunken, wie ich nie solche gesehen." The narrator's words point to a quality in this art evocative of intense experience; an emotive response not immediately apparent in the painter when he looked out upon the moonlit scene. The paintings are, in some mysterious way, distillations of that experience.

The narrative avoids explicitness and proceeds suggestively through a use of motifs and evocative images, allowing the reader to form connections. If a connective is sought between that vivid description of the moonlit night and the experiential intensity which seems to inform the two paintings, one is arrested by the description of Gustav at his easel in the full fervour of inspiration:

> Wie Einer, der heisshungrig nach Thaten ist, arbeitete er an dem Bilde, und wer ihn so gesehen hätte, wie er in Selbstvergessenheit die Augen über die gemalte Landschaft strömen liess, der hätte gemeint, aus ihnen müsse die Wärme und Zärtlichkeit in das Bild geflossen sein, die so unverkennbar und reizend aus demselben traten.

The artist's depth of feeling is apparent but the complex relationship of his emotion to the product of his skill is only intimated by a guarded use of the subjunctive ("der hätte gemeint"). And yet an essential part of Gustav's self has found release in art. His is a love chastened by suffering which has found strength in sublimating what it could not change; Cornelia's womanly pride and folly. When we

learn of Cornelia's response to his paintings at the exhibition, her role in the creation of this art becomes clearer. She responds not just to outward loveliness of form nor to the intoxicating atmosphere so delicately captured by the artist; she recognizes the beauty of soul manifested by this art. It is this inner quality of man's ethical nature informing these works which constitutes their beauty. The pure image of the moonlit night which reflects the chaste beauty of the artist's nature is resurrected as a tormenting rebuke to Cornelia:

> Wie zuckte in ihrem Gehirne all das leise Flimmern und Leuchten dieser unschuldigen, keuschen Bilder, gleichsam leise, leise Vorwürfe einer Seele, die da schweigt, aber mit Lichtstrahlen redet, die tiefer dringen, die immer da sind, immer leuchten, und nie verklingen, wie der Ton!

The words are strongly reminiscent of the earlier description of the moonlit night contained in Gustav's diary. In that first description Gustav had recorded in words an image of immaculate beauty which had appealed to his artistic sensibility. But the paintings which later recapture this experience are much more than reproductions of the artist's recollected impressions. They are the objective correlatives of Gustav's moral strength, a moral strength that has been sustained by sublimating an unworthy love. The ethical content of Gustav's art is made quite explicit in the expression "dieser unschuldigen, keuschen Bilder". But for the artist's ethical nature, which transfigures what it creates, such art would have been impossible. And the significant thing is that this ethical quality shines through and is apparent to the beholder. Here is the first instance of Stifter's conviction that the true artist must express, and be felt to express, a moral quality through the medium of his art.

Throughout this work Stifter gives accent to the moral connotations of the beautiful. His depiction of personality as the carrier of the idea of beauty is subtle and differentiated. Beauty is shown to be not merely a physical attribute but a mark of the soul. If one examines different connotations of the word "schön" when applied to Gustav and Cornelia one finds evidence of contrasting meanings. At times "schön" is used as a human attribute to reflect only superficial aspects of beauty; the surface appeal of features or expression. In other instances the term serves to express something of a spiritual nature. Gustav's passion for Cornelia is early described as "trotzigschön", indicating a resolute fervour kindled by the emotion, a manliness which lends charm to his childlike features. When Stifter speaks of "sein schönes Antliz" while teaching Cornelia to paint, the phrase draws meaning from his expression of that calm which cannot wholly contain "den leisen heissen Schmerz"; Gustav's bitter foreboding of discord. Again, at the moment of their supreme joy when Cornelia says to him, "bewahren Sie mir in Liebe und Wahrheit Ihr grosses, schönes Herz", her words clearly indicate his moral stature in her eyes, no less than when she prays that she may be worthy of his "schönes Künstlerherz". Both examples show the word "schön" used with moral emphasis and "Herz" is also a favoured figure of speech in Stifter which stands for man's moral essence. This, then, is the dominant aspect of his portraiture as with the other early artist figures.

If beauty in Gustav signifies what is primarily a moral endowment, in Cornelia it is weighted on the side of sensuous appeal. But the motif of beauty undergoes a significant change in its application to her. At first she is referred to by Gustav as "das schönste, grossherzigste, leichtsinnigste Weib", in that mixture of infatuation and sense of grievance which distinguishes this youthful love. Initially we receive only a fleeting impression of "die sanften Umrisse eines schönen, blassen Frauenantlizes", and the text refers simply to "die schöne Jungfrau" impatient to begin her adventurous balloon flight to prove her the equal of man. The term "schön" does little else here than flatter her physical charms. Her outward beauty is similarly alluded to during the scene in which love is declared, when we are told of "die schönen Finger, die sich gegen die Blüte des Antlizes drückten". All these references to Cornelia reveal something about her sensuous beauty, her seductiveness, but have virtually no ethical import.

Only when the love between Cornelia and Gustav is shown to break forth and establish a new bond between them does the idea of beauty acquire moral overtones in its application to Cornelia. For a brief moment the lovers coalesce in a single emotion which is depicted as good and pure. They experience a form of moral elevation that makes them exult. The fervent exchange between them is a solemn celebration of this moment:

> "Cornelia, was soll nun dieser Augenblick bedeuten?"
>
> "Das Höchste, was er kann," erwiederte sie stolz und leise.
>
> "Wohl, er ist das Schönste, was mir Gott in meinem Leben vorgezeichnet," sagte er, "aber hinter der grossen Seligkeit ist mir jetzt, als stände ein grosser langer Schmerz—Cornelia— wie werde ich diesen Augenblick vergessen lernen?!"

This foreboding sense of prolonged anguish even in the ecstasy of the moment lies at the heart of Stifter's art. For him there is no beauty without pain. It is the only point in the story which shows the lovers briefly united on the same level of moral aspiration. Cornelia's expression "das Höchste" and Gustav's response "das Schönste" are emotive abstractions which synthesize what Stifter is presenting as the high-point of aesthetic self-fulfilment in man. However, it lies within the nature of such an experience to be short-lived. The sufferings which result from the breach of faith are already prefigured in Gustav's doubts. Yet he, as an artist, withstands the test and is inspired to create something permanent. Cornelia seeks the beauty of transient pleasures and degenerates into a courtesan.

The work shows how art is able to capture and immortalize the fleeting perfection of a moment. When Gustav speaks of "die Frucht der heutigen Blume", it is a prophetic reference to his paintings. For now he feels within himself the capacity to create art in which something of the poignant beauty of this experience will live on:

> "O Cornelia, hilf mir's sagen, welch' ein

wundervoller Sternenhimmel in meinem Herzen ist, so selig, leuchtend, glänzend, als sollt' ich ihn in Schöpfungen ausströmen, so gross, als das Universum selbst".

Gustav's words sound a motif which at once recalls his description of the night sky; that recurring image of beauty which reflects his own nature. The image is now transferred from the external to the internal, from nature to the artist. Through such poetic allusion Stifter draws together features within the work which combine to elucidate his conception of beauty. The power of nature and of love to inspire, the moral sense and the creative impulse are features which merge into this portrait of the artist. Not only does Gustav feel the capacity to create something beautiful, at this supreme moment of his life he appears himself to embody the beautiful:

> er wurde vor ihren Augen immer schöner, wie Seele und Liebe in sein Gesicht trat, und die sah ihn mit Entzücken an, wie er vor ihr stand, so schön, so kräftig, schimmernd schon von künftigem Geistesleben und künftiger Geistesgrösse, und doch unschuldig, wie ein Knabe, und unbewusst der göttlichen Flamme, Genie, die um seine Scheitel spielte.

This transfigured description of the artist is, in fact, a portrait of his soul. There is the merest suggestion only of physical presence—all is light and radiance just as in the description of the starry firmament. Stifter uses a vocabulary which minimizes all outward features and draws in notions of a high morality and of religion. Beauty, realized in the artist at the height of inspiration, is represented as a supernatural, godlike quality. Here, in artistic terms, is the nucleus of Stifter's abiding view of the total interdependence of the aesthetic and the moral.

In complete contrast to the inner radiance descried in Gustav's nature the word "Schönheit" is devalued to a hollow term of flattery in its final application to Cornelia: "Paris wusste es nicht, als jenes Tages seine gefeiertste Schönheit in keinem Zirkel erschien, die Schönheit, welche tausend Herzen entzündete, und mit tausenden spielte—." Not only does the possessive adjective "seine" suggest forfeiture of freedom and a consequent denigration of personality, but "Schönheit" too has been deprived of all moral dignity. It has become an empty social cliché reflecting the superficiality of a world that judges only externals. If we recall an early impression of Cornelia seated "mitten in einem Walde fremder Blumen" (incidentally, this motif of the camelias, suggestive of the exotic and the dissolute, anticipates Dumas' *La Dame aux Camélias* by some six years) Stifter pointedly tempers his description of her with the moral idea. She then appears "voll jener Grazie der Vornehmen, aber auch voll jener höheren der Sitte, die den Menschen so schön macht". Cornelia's beauty is primarily external; the moral qualification seems appended almost as an afterthought. Her good breeding and gracious bearing are social accomplishments rather than an expression of her moral nature. Stifter's reflection in fact pronounces judgment on her in view of what she later becomes.

The figure of Cornelia is in no way raised to an ideal or

universal level. In this she differs fundamentally from the other female figures considered who inspire the artist as paragons of beauty. Her fallible humanity is drawn with an impressionistic deftness which places her among Stifter's subtler individual creations. Her part is to illumine the moral idea not through what she herself is but through what the artist, in loving her, perceives and creates. Although suffering must be endured, the artist's creative gain is fullest reward. For Stifter art remains the ultimate compensation.

The idea of beauty finds expression in this work in a two-fold sense. It is embodied in humanity—as portrayed in the lover relationship; and it is made manifest in art—as seen in Gustav's paintings. The two manners of representation are intimately connected; and a strikingly similar image is used by Stifter of both. Of love, it is said:

> Die Liebe ist ein schöner Engel, aber oft ein schöner Todesengel für das gläubige, betrogene Herz!

This pronouncement on the uncertain and fallible nature of the closest human relationship is set apart in the text for emphasis. The comment on Gustav's art—again a reflective interpolation by the narrator—has a striking resemblance:

> Es ist ein schöner Anblick, wenn der Engel der Kunst in ein unbewusstes, reizendes Jünglingsantlitz tritt, dassebe verklärt und es ohne Ahnung des Besitzers so schön und so weit über den Ausdruck des Tages emporhebt.

The connection between the artist's experience of love and of beauty is again intimated through an image: the angel. Stifter often uses it in conveying something of the mystery of beauty. In both instances it draws attention to a human condition finer and more intense than common experience. The purest love and truly inspired art both share in this heightened form of being. Yet art, which is not subject to change, can hold fast and communicate the beauty of a moment; and in Gustav's paintings we see how it can become the transfigured expression of a transitory passion. In this work Stifter reveals the power given to the artist to sublimate what is imperfect.

Seen together, Stifter's preoccupations with the artist figure in these first **Studien** move towards a common end: the discovery and refinement of an aesthetic. The tendency of his early style to introduce abstract notions (a feature too often overlooked by criticism) is directed particularly to this end. His somewhat simplistic belief in the moral efficacy of art and literature lies at the root of all his aesthetic ideas. The desire he expresses in his preface to the **Studien** (1843) "irgend ein sittlich Schönes fördern" (the point is made by this close coupling of adjective to noun, creating a single concept) is to remain the keynote of his life's work. The interdependence of moral and aesthetic values is, as we saw, a central feature of these works; the figure of the artist also represents the reconciliation of both ideas, for in him both are equally made manifest. The quest for a beauty that is also unblemished perfection is a feature which permeates not just Stifter's early prose but his mature writing also. His aesthetic develops to an ideal of high excellence which assumes a rarified, numinous quality. The paradigm of perfection which remains his life-long aspiration comes closest to being realized in the sequestered world of **Der Nachsommer.** That haunting anamnesis which is alive in the artist figures, and with which this essay opened, is but a yearning for another Eden. (pp. 142-60)

> *Alexander Stillmark, "Stifter's Early Portraits of the Artist: Stages in the Growth of an Aesthetic," in* Forum for Modern Language Studies, *Vol. XI, No. 2, April, 1975, pp. 142-64.*

Walter Horace Bruford   (essay date 1975)

[*A scholar known for his innovative social interpretations of literature, Bruford wrote on German history, language, and literature. In the following excerpt, he discusses Stifter's* Indian Summer *as a bildungsroman, analyzing what it reveals about its author's philosophy and his relation to his times.*]

Born as he was more than half a century later than Goethe (in 1805), in an environment different not only through the political and social changes brought by the early nineteenth century but by the fact of being an Austrian, surrounded by the scenery and immersed in the traditions of the Catholic south, Stifter cannot be expected to resemble Goethe at all closely in his work, for all his admiration of him as a writer. There is often something homely and slightly provincial about it, as there was, according to contemporaries, about his person and his conversation. He continued all his life to speak his native upper Austrian dialect and to look, as Clara Schumann wrote in 1847, 'by no means poetic'. 'His dialect too', she continued, 'does not sound very poetic, but in a conversation of any length his intellectual distinction is unmistakable.' In his writing however he always aims at the highest he knows. The High German literary language which he wrote was for him . . . 'an almost ceremonial abstraction' which does not flow naturally, but has to be consciously constructed, sentence by sentence, following as principal model the style of the older Goethe. In the same spirit he seems to delight in the punctilious politeness of his characters in **Der Nachsommer,** in the formal visits they pay to each other, in suitable costume, while staying in the same house. The severe restraint which marks every phase of the love story in the novel is clearly a product of the same attitude of mind in the author. He does not want to be merely natural, but to improve on nature with the help of freely accepted conventions, the value of which he has proved in his own experience. 'Bildung' has made him what he is, and he feels himself to be a missionary of true 'Bildung'. In his letters, when at the height of his powers, to friends and especially to his publisher, Heckenast, Stifter frequently speaks about his aims and achievements with a perhaps rather excessive self-confidence, though some of his writing, particularly his early contributions to *Wien und die Wiener* (1844), show that he was not quite so humourless as he sometimes sounds. (pp. 129-30)

Stifter speaks of the 'gentle' law which guides man and nature, not only because moral cultivation makes 'gentlemen' of the uncouth, but because he thinks of goodness as intrinsically attractive, as had always been the contention of the Enlightenment. He stresses the essentially peaceful and reasonable nature of man, the 'sociability' achieved by man, as Pufendorf had claimed in the late seventeenth century, with the help of his fellows and his social inheritance, his culture. What still interests Stifter particularly is man's humanity as opposed to his animality, his capacity to control his passions and develop his mind and sensibility, a capacity he finds present, as Tolstoy did in Russia, not only in the privileged and educated, but in simple country people unconsciously moulded by a civilizing Christian tradition. He presents the characters in his 'Novellen' as individuals who, for all their uniqueness, seem to grow out of their environment as its natural product. Johannes Aprent, a master at the Linz *Realschule* who knew Stifter particularly well and collaborated with him when he was a school inspector, says:

> What gives these stories their beautifully harmonious effect, which calms and satisfies the reader so completely, is that his characters are never set down arbitrarily like lay figures in some set of natural conditions, but that they themselves grow up naturally out of those conditions, so that the sisters in *Der Hochwald* are only the fairest flowers of the woods, and the boy in *Das Haidedorf* is the moorland's noblest product. That is why Stifter was firmly opposed to all those petty regulations, by which officials try to keep their hands on everything. [Quoted in Karl Privat, *A. Stifter,* 1946]

There is no other German novelist in whose work description is so prominent a feature, description not so much of the appearance or character of people—Stifter has no liking for analysis—as of their natural or man-made surroundings, particularly any evidence of the skill and taste of earlier generations revealing itself in concrete form. In wild nature there is always for Stifter the suggestion of a divine presence, and similarly in houses and gardens, villages and estates there is what Hegel would have called 'mind objectified', the reflection of human choice and effort in the past. Like Balzac, Stifter liked to describe a room, for instance, which has become a symbol of the character of the person who lives in it, and to leave it to us, as Staiger says [in *Stifter als Dichter der Ehrfurcht*, 1952], 'to guess at the workings of the mind'. 'He is chary of revealing, still more of explaining, the movements of the soul, because no mortal eye can see into its depths.' It is largely for this reason that three-quarters of the text of *Der Nachsommer* is description and only one quarter concerned with human actions, Staiger points out.

In spite of Stifter's obvious preoccupation with the idea of culture, Staiger would have us compare *Der Nachsommer* with *Wilhelm Meisters Wanderjahre* or Plato's *Republic* rather than with *Wilhelm Meisters Lehrjahre* and the 'Bildung' novels descended from it, like Mörike's *Maler Nolten* or Keller's *Der grüne Heinrich,* true novels with romantic plots, full of interest above all for the impressions they convey of clearly distinguished social classes in the actual world of their time. *Der Nachsommer* is much more of a utopia, 'an ideal world that never was and never will be'. In its construction it breaks away entirely from the pi-

caresque tradition and is more like a nineteenth-century Austrian version of *Hermann und Dorothea* than of the *Lehrjahre.* The idealization practised by Goethe throughout his short epic poem is based on his conception of something quintessential in human character and behaviour, what Viktor Hehn later called 'the natural forms of human life', which can be exemplified from any age. The theory of a modern classicism worked out by Goethe and Schiller in the 1790s had of course been based on this conception, which reflects their ambition to rival Homer and Sophocles in the handling of eternally human themes.

In reading *Der Nachsommer* one is frequently reminded of these Weimar theories, not only by Stifter's treatment of the central characters, but also by the views on art put into the mouth of Risach. Speaking to Heinrich about his library, for instance, in the chapter 'Die Erweiterung', Risach is made to say about the poets:

> They are the priests of the beautiful and as such, amidst the constant changes in prevailing views about the world, the human lot and even the divine, they keep us in touch with that in us which is everlasting. They present it to us in the garment of grace, which never ages, appears just as it is and neither judges or condemns.

Never losing sight of Goethe as his model, Stifter continually suggests that for Heinrich, who is made the narrator of the story, its heroine Natalie (the name comes of course from the *Lehrjahre*) shares something which he divines in the marble statue on Risach's stairway—a genuine Greek work found by him in Italy—and finds again in Nausicaea as he reads the *Odyssey*. All three seem to be fused for him into one ideal of beauty, with close affinities to the style in which women's heads are carved in his father's Greek gems. It is still among modern 'Bürger' that Stifter, like Goethe in *Hermann und Dorothea,* sees at least hints of 'noble humanity', but they are not simple, healthy citizens of a small market town or farmers' daughters, but peasants' sons who have through their own efforts, in trade or in the public service, raised themselves to a way of life in retirement resembling that of a country gentleman. To bring to us 'in the garment of grace' that which lasts for ever, to fulfil, that is, his highly abstract ideal of beauty, Stifter has to imagine a group of people quite as carefully chosen and as remote from normal reality in his day as the handful of characters in Goethe's poem. Almost all that Staiger says about Goethe's selection of detail applies equally here:

> The number of figures he introduces is limited. He has to refrain from mentioning by name [. . .] great personages of German history in the past or present. Even the family names of his citizens would be incompatible with the style in which he is writing. That they are Christian in their way of life may only be unobtrusively indicated, without any reference to dogmatic beliefs . . . The real must be discreetly arranged into the beautiful. Whatever resists this arrangement is dropped.

The effect in *Der Nachsommer,* as in *Hermann und Dorothea,* is to concentrate attention on family life, but the monotony is relieved here by far-ranging discussions between

Risach and Heinrich about cultural matters. They are the readiest means of doing what German novelists since Goethe or even Wieland have always desired, to convey ideas while telling a story, but the reflective passages do not arise so naturally from the narrative as in the *Lehrjahre,* where the author provides his hero with a wide experience of life in contrasted social circles. In spite of the difficulties always presented by a story overloaded with thought, serious German novelists down to Stifter's time and far beyond it continued to feel that as artists, and not merely entertainers, it was part of their business, in Jakob Burckhardt's words, 'to make the things of the mind attractive to a large and varied public'.

One effect of Stifter's preoccupation with general ideas is to make the love story, around which any action the novel may be said to have turns, extremely slow-moving. It seems as if the 'retardation' which Goethe and Schiller, in their theorizing about epic and dramatic style, found essential to the epic, is made doubly important here because of Stifter's wish to illustrate again the working of 'the gentle law'. Passion, even in the sense of a normal feeling for the opposite sex, has to be subjected in this utopia to deliberate rational restraint. Risach and Mathilde, frustrated in the natural fulfilment of their deep love because of the woman's intense resentment of the man's refusal, out of consideration for her parents' feelings, to defy the world and win her, find an autumnal happiness mingled with regrets in their 'Indian summer without a real summer first'. Reunited in friendship, their chief desire is that Natalie, Mathilde's daughter in her loveless marriage with a husband now dead, may by a happy marriage 'find the happiness which eluded her mother and her fatherly friend [. . .] When I first saw you standing at the garden fence of my house', Risach says to Heinrich, 'I thought, that is perhaps a husband for Natalie. Why I thought so I do not know. Later I thought the same again, but I knew why.'

That is almost the whole of the plot. The first two chapters of the novel are devoted to the development of Heinrich in childhood and youth, watched over and guided at every step by his father and surrounded by the loving care of mother, sister and devoted servants. It is soon evident that in this 'Bildung'-novel, unlike most, the hero is not to learn through his mistakes. It is a singularly harmonious family, no member of which ever seems tempted to take any step without the most unselfish and affectionate regard for all the others. The father, whose name is hardly ever mentioned, is a merchant in comfortable circumstances, whose way of life is typically that of a good 'Bürger' in a capital city, here evidently Vienna, though it is never named, at a period, also not stated, when his class still enjoys general respect and can think of its activity as wholly beneficial to society in general. Public and private interests work so well together in this novel that one is reminded rather of the ideal merchant in the *Spectator* and the German Moral Weeklies than of any individuals known to history. The traditional virtues of the middle class in the age of reason are much in evidence, a high regard for law and order and a good name among one's fellows, for economy of time and money, with due provision for the future and for accidents, a liking for well-ordered, clean and uncluttered surroundings at home and outside,

a willing observance of accepted decorum in every feature of social life, and so on. As in the *Lehrjahre,* the type of merchant the author has in mind is . . . the cautious merchant of the inland towns, rather than . . . the adventurous merchant of the ports, and amongst these cautious ones it is the older generation, like Wilhelm's father and Werner's, and not the younger Werner, obsessed by the aim of making his money productive, of *having* the cake, as Keynes used to say, and not eating it. But Heinrich's father has not only, from small beginnings, made a considerable fortune in trade, but at the same time, as we learn in the late chapter, 'Der Einblick', used every opportunity on his travels to extend his knowledge of old pictures, and denied himself many pleasures in order to lay the foundations of a collection of his own. He was well aware that there was no better way than this of insuring oneself against future losses. Almost the first things he tells his children about his old pictures is that they are very valuable. 'He said that he had only old ones, which have a stable value, always available if one is ever forced to sell them.' ('Die Häuslichkeit.') The same was true about his Greek gems, his antique furniture, old weapons and armour, and so on. All these possessions were a delight for him to behold, but genuine aesthetic appreciation was indissolubly combined in him with the true Bürger's feeling for economy, order, cleanliness etc. as sacrosanct. One is reminded of Goethe's father, who did not approve of spending money on things to be immediately consumed, but 'was not mean about acquiring things which combined intrinsic value with a good outward appearance', like the golden box with figures in relief, studded with jewels, which he promised his wife to mark the end of the Seven Years War.

One feature of which Heinrich seems to speak with admiration in the first chapter, his father's strict observation of fixed rules in handling his treasures, which is carried still further at Risach's home, the Rose House, with its richer collections, would seem to most modern readers to be pedantic fussiness. A room must never look as if it had been lived in, but rather as if it were a place for display, where nothing in use is left lying about. Herr Drendorf (as we finally hear he is called) had a good library and was fond of reading, but he would only read sitting at a special old carved table in his library, and made it a rule to put the book back in its place after use, in one of the glass-fronted cases with green silk curtains which concealed the books from visitors—and no doubt also protected their bindings from sunlight. In the Rose House too books are put back immediately after use, and there is a further rule that they must be read in an adjoining reading-room, not in the library itself: 'The books acquired importance and dignity, the room is their temple, and you do not work in a temple.' ('Der Besuch'.) This arrangement is also praised as 'an act of homage to intellect', one expression, one might say, of the reverence for intellectual creativeness which is one of Stifter's deepest feelings. With the formal speeches and ritual changes of clothes which are obligatory even on family visits, humour and informal talk are incompatible in this far from permissive society, where all take themselves and their friends and relations very seriously, and seldom question inherited customs and attitudes.

The type of formal education planned for Heinrich by his father and the views on education put into the mouth of Risach later remind us in general of the later Enlightenment period, with few modifications dating from later than Goethe. The discovery and development of the pupil's innate aptitudes in the manner of *Émile* is the basic theory implied, clarified here by the thought of the age of Goethe. 'A man is not here in the first place for the sake of society, but for his own sake. And if everyone is here for his own sake in a proper way, society benefits too.' ('Die Häuslichkeit'.) That is of course pure Goethe or Humboldt doctrine. . . . But both Goethe and Stifter, while declining to put society first, accepted consciously or unconsciously certain social assumptions of their time, for example that the right to exist for one's own sake does not belong to women in the same measure as to men, and not to all social classes alike, but mainly to the aristocracy, at least to that of intellect. The French Revolution might never have taken place for all the effect it seems to have had on the society of *Der Nachsommer,* and Romantic ideas about the emancipation of women have also left no trace. Even when Heinrich's family no longer lives in the old-fashioned way in a town house which served also as warehouse and office, but had moved out to a spacious villa in the suburbs, his mother 'devoted herself more busily than ever to domestic matters', and his sister, after sharing with him the same teachers for her elementary education, carried only one or two subjects further and 'had to be gradually introduced to domestic duties, so that she would some day be able to follow worthily in her mother's footsteps'. The point is emphasized later ('Die Erweiterung') when Klotilde, the sister, wishes to take up landscape-painting and Spanish with her brother, and her mother insists that she must not spend too much time on these diversions, 'for a woman's first duty is her home'. Mathilde, in spite of her higher social standing and very independent character, takes essentially the same view, that the role of women is a secondary one. Her promising son, Gustav, must be given every opportunity to prepare himself for the highest that life can offer, she tells Heinrich, but 'as for herself and Natalie, the life of women is always a dependent and supplementary one, and it feels in that fact reassurance and support'. She implies that as a widow, she is not entirely happy to have to decide so much for herself on her large estate. ('Der Bund'.)

The pronounced paternalism which is evident in all the chapters about Heinrich and his family, the entire neglect of the political element in life, the unquestioning acceptance by all alike of the existing social order and the absence of any expression of concern about the lot of the peasantry and the working class, all these features make on us now the impression not, as so many German critics have said, of a timeless utopia, but rather of an idealized recollection of an earlier, simpler stage in Germany's own history, a vision to which Stifter turns with relief after his experiences in Vienna in 1848. It is interesting to note how many of the central features of Stifter's ideal society correspond to those singled out by Ralf Dahrendorf as characteristic of the solidly based opposition to a modern parliamentary democracy which persisted, according to him, well into the twentieth century:

> German society remained illiberal in its structure and authoritarian in its constitution throughout the decades of industrialization. Although the absurd but effective combinations of old and new in the politics and society of Imperial Germany had lost their foundations in 1918, the Weimar Republic diverged seldom and timidly from the old models. Especially in times of crisis the longing for them grew strong. [*Gesellschaft und Demokratie in Duetschland,* 1965]

If this is true, it is a consideration of some importance when one tries to explain the rapidly growing popularity of *Der Nachsommer,* after long neglect, precisely in the difficult years which followed the First World War. Staiger sees this renewal of interest in Stifter as connected with the new understanding of the works of Goethe's old age, of Hölderlin and also, in music, of Johann Sebastian Bach (as well as of Bruckner as opposed to Wagner). This all represents a reaction, he thinks, against what had grown out of the older liberal humanism (Humanität), namely the belief in unrestricted self-assertion, a devil-take-the-hindmost struggle for money and power; and a new understanding for the element of reverence in the *old* Weimar humanism, which was a central feature still of Stifter's philosophy. Sociologists like Dahrendorf understandably find it difficult to divorce such attempts as this at a purely intellectual explanation from the conservatism in political, economic and social matters which was typical of most of the academic literary historians and critics who were behind the Stifter revival in the 1920s. J. P. Stern has illustrated from Stifter studies 'the peculiar paradox typical of much of German criticism. By and large, Stifter is regarded as the non-political writer *par excellence,* while at the same time many of the criticisms of his work follow more or less closely the course of German political history.'

It was natural enough that Stifter, shocked by the chaos he witnessed in Vienna in 1848, and fearful for the future of his country if the irresponsible demand for freedom were to spread unchecked, should give his utopia a setting recalling what seemed to him best in the fast disappearing old Austria where, as he persuaded himself, everyone had known his place and been content with it. Stifter makes it easier for himself to produce this illusion by choosing as his principal characters men who have either retired from the active pursuits of their maturity, like Herr von Risach, or are approaching retirement like Heinrich's father, never seen at work but only in moments of leisure with his family, or again young people still preparing themselves for active life, like Heinrich, and Mathilde's children, and not restricted through any lack of means by vocational requirements. It is important that they all happen to be by nature very likeable people, equable in temperament and carefully brought up to be full of consideration, especially for their own families. The merchant families in *Wilhelm Meisters Lehrjahre,* for instance, were far less shining examples of the domestic virtues. Stifter accepts the risk of dullness, which even in his day threatened the novelist who would not, in Chekhov's words, 'soil his imagination with the dirt of life'. Heinrich is shown to us therefore leading a completely happy boyhood and adolescence with a father, mother and sister who seem to have no problems which father cannot solve, and to be almost completely unaware of any problems in contemporary society. There is just a hint that in the more sophisticated household of Herr von Risach at the Rose House they are aware of social changes going on around them. Heinrich notices that there the family are not joined at meals by the servants, whereas at home his father's shop assistants still live with him in the old-fashioned way of the guilds and share family meals, except in the evening. Risach would have preferred, he says, to follow the old country custom, which tended to make faithful servants into 'good men and women, who are closely attached to the house in simple piety, as if to an immutable church, and to whom the master is a reliable friend', but the ever widening gulf between 'the so-called cultivated and uncultivated' has broken up what was formerly thought of as one family. Goethe, it will be remembered, had hoped for a 'piety to the world' to take the place of this 'piety to the home'. In *Der Nachsommer,* the brief mention of this problem is a sign of humane consideration on the part of the Drendorfs and Risach for their social inferiors, but it is almost the only expression in the novel of anything approaching the crisis of conscience about their social privileges which troubled so many of the gentry in Russia at that time. The social problems of Stifter's day in Germany already acute, receive no more mention in the novel than the political ones. As Hein pointed out already in the first full life of Stifter [*Adalbert Stifter,* 1904], the main characters of the novel live 'for their own sake' in a kind of 'opalescent world of magic' while 'obliging gnomes' apparently do the hard work. Towards his social superiors like the Princess ('Die Erweiterung') and her brilliant circle, Heinrich's attitude is very respectful, like Stifter's to Fürstin Schwarzenberg, but free from snobbery. Following Risach's advice 'to acquaint himself with life around him' and acquire general impressions of the world outside his actual studies, he joins a club frequented by educated people interested in the arts, and we learn in one short paragraph that he visits places of popular resort, to see 'the real populace' at its pleasures, and learn something of its varied customers and manners, but these seem to remain only an object of curiosity to him. These rather superficial contacts with people unlike himself are evidently made in response to Risach's criticism of his too early specialization in one branch of science, and the ideal suggested is, as at the end of the *Lehrjahre,* the man who becomes a master in some particular field of activity after sampling a great many. As Risach puts it: 'In youth we should try out our powers in an all-round way in order, as men, to be competent in one particular field.' This advice is given to Heinrich on his fifth visit to the Rose House ('Die Erweiterung') when he must be about twenty-two years old.

Up to this point Heinrich's education has been highly systematic, though in the later stages he has freely followed his interests. He has been privately educated and not been sent to any university. This again is a striking reversion on the author's part to much earlier times, before the great improvement of the German universities and before the radicalization of a considerable number of students in the reactionary decades after the Carlsbad Decrees. Taught by good tutors, at first along with his sister, he has become eager to devote his life to scholarship from pure interest in natural science. As an inspector of schools, Stifter of course had his own well-informed views on higher education as it should be in mid-century. After a thorough grounding in Latin and Greek Heinrich occupies himself intensively, by his own choice, with mathematics, while his sister turns, as we have said, to domestic subjects and the usual accomplishments, but both continue their physical education through gymnastics and riding. This is all perfectly normal, but a novel feature is that from the age of eighteen, Heinrich is given limited control of his share of the money left to the children earlier by a relative, and this freedom is gradually increased until, when he is twenty-four, it is complete. He is encouraged to learn the value of money, even without taking up an independent profession, by being asked to pay rent for the rooms he occupies at home—he prefers this to seeking other quarters—and to re-invest some of his income. All these details make Stifter's ideal young man appear as a prudent *rentier* rather like Schopenhauer, glad to enjoy his inherited privileges but careful with his resources and quite unlike the cultivated and generous, but so often feckless and extravagant young noblemen who abound in Russian literature, the best of whom are 'conscience-stricken gentry'.

In Stifter's account of his young hero's efforts to educate himself, when he feels that tutors can no longer help him, there are still traces of the universalistic tradition of 'Bildung' in Humboldt's time, but the aim is one that would have been approved of by Goethe's Abbé, to make sure that he samples a whole range of studies before deciding which shall finally claim him. The order in which they are taken is not then so important—it is different for Heinrich from that followed by Risach in educating Gustav ('Der Besuch'). From the age of eighteen, after what corresponds to school studies of classics and mathematics, he is sent away by his father each summer to learn something at first hand about the world outside. At first he stays with a friend of the family in a country house not far out of town, to get used to being separated from his family, who visit him often. Next year he goes to a farmhouse much further away and learns about farming and primary production, as well as something about the various ways in which wood and other raw materials are manufactured into useful articles, in factories run by water power for instance, close by. These are of course object lessons ('Anschauungsunterricht') on a grand scale. It is only after this that he takes up natural history, which becomes a subject of inexhaustible interest to him. Botany and geology, the collection of specimens on long walks in the woods and hills, and close study of the subject in books, lead on next summer to zoology and the exploration of more mountainous country, and these interests again to attempts to record what he sees in line and colour, and to understand the geology of the landscape. It is an entirely concrete study of nature, rising from the particular to the general, very much in the manner of Goethe himself in actual life and to some extent of Stifter, with scarcely a hint, in this particular work, of the mystical 'nature philosophy' or the meticulous painting in words which we find in so many of Stifter's stories. Heinrich describes himself to Risach, when he takes shelter in his mansion with its rose-covered main wall, as 'an ordinary rambler' of independent means, but Risach does not take him at his word. He sees that geology understood genetically, as the history of the earth, Heinrich's central interest, is an extremely wide field, and that collecting material is only the first stage of a genuinely scientific inquiry, such as he shows himself to have begun in many subjects, meteorology for instance, by keeping his eyes open on his estate.

It is only through Risach that Heinrich comes in full maturity to some knowledge and appreciation of painting, sculpture, literature and drama. He is not a poet or artist by nature, like the young Wilhelm Meister, and though surrounded by good pictures at home, he has not been moved by them or by the Greek gems in his father's collection, nor has he shown any sign of going beyond a purely scholarly knowledge of the classics. History, ancient or modern, does not seem to have been allowed any place in his curriculum at all. In an age so obsessed by history as that in which Stifter had lived, this omission is striking, and must mark his desire to emphasize the timeless, the idea that in spite of what everyone was saying around him, the clock could indeed be put back and the simplicities of an earlier age recaptured. So although Heinrich's boundless curiosity has made him eager to know at first hand and to understand his external physical environment and the material culture created by human labour and ingenuity on this basis, he has shown no particular interest in his country's history or legends, or in the development, still less the present problems, of its society. Risach, though he has played a great part in his country's recent history, never speaks of it, but he does develop Heinrich's aesthetic sense. His drawing and painting have only been used to record things observed, as one now uses a camera. It is only when he has begun to paint landscapes and not just objects that, on his fifth visit to the Rose House, he learns from a long conversation with Risach and the designer Eustach something about atmosphere and the use of the imagination in painting. 'The eye should be exercized and taught', he hears, 'but the soul must create, helped by the eye.' ('Die Erweiterung'.) A little later Risach discourses too on the poets as among the greatest benefactors of mankind, 'priests of the beautiful', expressing, as we have seen, Stifter's own view of literature. It is at this point that he advises Heinrich to take a holiday from science and see more of ordinary life in town and country. When he next goes home, Heinrich discovers that his father has always had a deep love of the arts, and now that his own understanding of them is beginning to ripen, much later than his interest in science, they have long talks about books and pictures, and the son realizes at last what unnoticed treasures have always surrounded him. Through Risach he learns to see revelations of the mind of departed artists and craftsmen in his antique furniture and the church monuments he, like Stifter, delights in restoring.

There is no suggestion in all this of any possible conflict between science and the humanities, for culture is one and indivisible, and as model for Heinrich, Stifter must have had someone like Alexander von Humboldt, explorer and author of *Kosmos*, in mind, a widely cultivated man if ever there was one, rather than the great scientific specialists, like Liebig, Wöhler, Bunsen, Helmholz, who with their exact laboratory methods were the real leaders in science in mid-century, and stimulating technology and industry

as never before. Another touch which reminds us how closely Stifter's ideals were associated with the past is Herr Drendorf's insistence on a kind of Grand Tour for his son as the final stage of his education. We think of such tours as belonging essentially to the aristocratic world of the eighteenth century, but merchant apprentices travelled too and as we have seen, Herr Drendorf's deepest interests had been awakened by foreign travel. Of course it is not considered necessary for Natalie to travel too, though the couple are engaged by this time, and their marriage has to be put off for no less than two years. Unlike Tolstoy's Natasha Rostov, Natalie takes this postponement without a murmur, but then, she never really comes to life at all. There will be no Marianne or Philine in Heinrich's life abroad. Sex is something that is never mentioned, so that Victorian English critics could not have found anything offensive in this novel, if they had known it, as they did in *Wilhelm Meister*. Marriage, at the age of twenty-five or so, marks the point at which Heinrich becomes fully adult and 'cultivated' ('Ausgebildet'), ready to take charge of a household of his own.

For Wilhelm, it will be remembered, it is the realization that he is a father—of an illegitimate son—that is said to be the beginning of wisdom, but not by any means the end of his 'Bildung'.

The discussion of the ideas about 'Bildung' expressed directly or indirectly in **Der Nachsommer** has thrown some light on Stifter's general philosophy and his relation to his times. There was no serious obstacle in the fact of his upbringing in a monastery school to his admiration for Weimar humanism . . . because his teachers were broadminded Benedictines strongly influenced by the enlightenment. As Karl Viëtor says:

> In the end a more positive view of the nature of man and of his role in the process of sanctification [than the Augustinian doctrine of grace] had prevailed and maintained itself in Catholic Christianity. Goethe was certainly inclined towards this [Pelagian] view, and the rigorous doctrine of orthodox Protestantism was clearly distasteful to him, but the belief in the essential and fundamental goodness of man was something he shared with all humanistic minds in the eighteenth century. That a man should think worthily of himself and feel reverence towards himself was the main principle of the new humanism. That did not make anyone into a disciple of Pelagius or a fellow-traveller of Catholicism, even if it is true that such views stand closer to the Catholic than to the Protestant tradition and practice [*Goethe*, 1949].

We are told that Stifter was a practising Catholic, one no doubt who regarded his religious duties as a matter of course, like his loyalty to the Emperor, and made no parade of either, but to judge by the way his characters behave in **Der Nachsommer**, this ideal world, the external practices of religion were not considered important by him, and his real faith was quite undogmatic. At any rate, although so many of the characters in the novel are fascinated by churches and by medieval religious art, we never hear of them attending a church service, except for the wedding of Heinrich and Natalie, priests play no part in their lives, silent grace before meals is mentioned but no other kind of prayer, and the nearest approach to the direct expression of religious feeling comes at such moments as when Heinrich contemplates the night sky at the Sternenhof on the day when he and Natalie have exchanged vows ('Die Entfaltung'), or when both, not yet acquainted, are moved to tears at a performance of *King Lear* ('Der Besuch'). The wedding service is described in two lines: 'At the church the parish priest of Rohrbach was waiting for us, we stepped in front of the altar and the wedding service was held.'

It is not surprising that people like these never speak of a future life or of any of the familiar Christian beliefs. The idea of redemption has no meaning in the absence of a sense of sin.

> In the ideas of revelation, creation, providence and original sin in the church creed this doctrine [of Stifter's Benedictine teachers] saw the symbolic representation of purely rational ideals. Our duties towards God are a refinement of rational duties and man himself becomes the highest aim, the crown of being [. . .] Stifter is Catholic only so far as enlightened idealism allowed. [Curt Hohoff, *Adalbert Stifter*, 1949]

Luise von Eichendorff, in spite of her deep admiration for Stifter's work, could not help remarking about *Der Nachsommer:*

> There is a suggestion of heathen, anti-Christian feeling about it all, and in none of your earlier works did the contrast with those of my poor brother seem to me so marked. Yet both of you are champions of the good and beautiful, each praises God in his own way, and the songs of the nightingale and the lark, though different, both delight us equally.

Instead of the hope of salvation, the inhabitants of the world of *Der Nachsommer* have before them the ideal of a truly civilized life on earth, a life fashioned to match their disciplined human desires. A spiritualized life of this kind, it seems to be conceded, is not natural but a triumph of culture, only possible in 'a few chosen circles' like those mentioned in the last paragraph of Schiller's *On the aesthetic education of man*. Stifter imagines a little enclave of harmony, untouched by the national and international, economic and social problems which beset the real world of his time. The leading figures in it have all come to despise the passions and the coarser pleasures of life, and to find lasting satisfaction only in personal relations inspired by unselfish love and a shared delight in all those forms of activity into which 'Geist' enters in some measure, so that they afford scope in varying degrees for intelligence, taste, knowledge and wisdom. Risach, thought of as a kind of Wilhelm von Humboldt, can indeed devote himself completely to the intellectual life only in old age, after many years spent in the capital in the service of the state, and Herr Drendorf only when he follows Risach into country retirement. Both have had to work like others for the freedom of their leisure hours, and only unceasing effort given to self-cultivation has opened up for them the cultural inheritance which is there for all. That both come from simple village homes is no doubt meant to suggest

that the good life is not an aristocratic privilege, but they do belong to an intellectual aristocracy, and that only through their exceptional endowment and the favour of fortune. Stifter's *Der Nachsommer* is a swan-song of liberal individualism of the eighteenth century type. Stifter can still be for many a 'missionary of true culture', a 'priest of the beautiful', who continues 'to make the things of the mind attractive to a large public', yet this novel has for most of us now a strong suggestion of that 'dull gleam, that mysterious milky-way brightness', as of a distant celestial world, that Nietzsche . . . was to find in classical German literature. It is an indication of the continuing hold of that culture over him, for all his iconoclasm, and a reminder of the centrality of the idea of 'Bildung' in German thought for well over a century, that we find *Der Nachsommer* included by Nietzsche, one of its earliest admirers, along with only four other books, in what he calls 'The treasure of German prose':

> If we leave aside Goethe's writings and especially *Goethe's Conversations with Eckermann,* the best German book there is, what is left of German prose literature that deserves to be read over and over again? Lichtenberg's *Aphorisms,* the first book of *Jung-Stilling's Life Story,* Adalbert Stifter's *Nachsommer* and Gottfried Keller's *Leute von Seldwyla*—and at present that is about all. [*Menschliches Allzumenschliches*]
>
> (pp. 131-46)

> *Walter Horace Bruford, "Adalbert Stifter: Der Nachsommer (1857)," in his* The German Tradition of Self-Cultivation: 'Bildung' from Humboldt to Thomas Mann, *Cambridge University Press, 1975, pp. 128-46.*

Russell A. Berman (essay date 1986)

> [*Berman is a professor of German literature who has published numerous articles. In the following excerpt, he proposes that Stifter has a largely ossified world view.*]

Although Stifter sets [*Der Nachsommer*] in the Biedermeier world of the 1820s, he does not reminisce nostalgically of Metternich's ancient régime. He is not a reactionary, for despite his denunciation of the revolution of 1848, he does not give up his own prerevolutionary liberalism. Instead he transforms it into the utopia of *Der Nachsommer,* where his own never particularly radical version of the Austrian Enlightenment tradition, the Josephinist belief in progress and reason, could be played out far from the democratic zealots of Vienna. Shielded from the real social pressures of the 1850s, these elements of the bourgeois world-view could be pushed to an extreme, which allows Stifter to examine their consequences in vitro. *Der Nachsommer* considers [capitalism's] potentialities, the probable results of bourgeois culture. As Uwe-Karsten Ketelsen remarks: "*Der Nachsommer* is not at all a dreamy pre-1848 idyll; it actually presumes the victory of the bourgeois revolution." Stifter's utopia is simultaneously inspired by the moderate ideology of that revolution and by the desire to respond to its consequences. Unlike the sanguine Freytag, Stifter constructs a utopia on the basis of a pessimistic world-view. Both the immanent chaos of natural history and the destructive trajectory of

---

Thomas Mann on Stifter's "magic" tedium (1945):

I was reading Stifter every night before going to sleep. I am among those who have read even *Witiko* conscientiously through to the end, and ever since I have regarded the work of that remarkable inspector of schools as one of the greatest and most encouraging vindications of tedium in literature. His tedium is after all something different from the well-known *noble ennui*: it is a tranquil, pale, pedantic magic that takes a firmer hold than most "interesting" work, and is living proof of what degree of tediousness can be made possible in some circumstances. For the storyteller this is an important, and in fact truly exciting discovery. But aside from that and in spite of that, what an extraordinary storyteller the man is, every so often plunging ahead into extremes, even into pathological byways. As I reread (or, in the case of some stories, read for the first time) the *Studien* and the *Bunte Steine,* and such feuilletonistic abnormalities as the description of the snowfall in the Bavarian forest and the frightening visit to the catacombs, I have become aware of his narrative genius with astonishment, with admiration that grows nightly. I keep talking about it to everyone. What a terrific thing *Abdias* is! And the children in the ice! and *Katzensilber,* in which such exquisite descriptions as those of the hailstorm and the fire are heaped one upon the other. And the absolutely unique milieu of *The Recluse.* There is something a little uncanny about the pedantic uncle with his "At breakfast." Moreover, the sensations that emerge from tedium are uncanny in the finest sense.

Thomas Mann, in his Letters, *selected and translated by Richard and Clara Winston, 1971.*

---

modern society unleash a process that threatens the possibility of meaning and the functioning of exchange. The postliberal novel he constructs and the utopia it describes are intended as alternatives, bastions of order against an impending social and semiotic entropy.

The construction of order in *Der Nachsommer* is mediated through the experience of the first-person narrator, Heinrich Drendorf, the son of a Viennese merchant. Financially independent at the age of eighteen, he spends extended summers hiking in the mountains of Upper Austria. During one such journey, he seeks shelter from an impending storm in the rose-covered house at the Asperhof, the estate of Freiherr von Risach, whose name, like Heinrich's, is not disclosed until much later. The Asperhof is a model farm, and Risach a cultured gentleman who engages his young guest in lengthy discussions of art, nature, education, and society, which all testify to Stifter's urgent search for security.

Risach eventually recounts how he had once fallen in love with the daughter of a wealthy family, Mathilde Makloden. Their relationship had come to a premature end because of misunderstandings and untempered passion. After a successful career in government service, Risach settled at the Asperhof. Later, the widowed Mathilde acquired the Sternenhof estate nearby, where she resides with her children, Gustav and Nathalie. At the conclusion of the novel, Nathalie and Heinrich marry. The young

couple's love complements the Indian summer of their elders.

Stifter constructed this image of idyllic harmony in opposition to the historic experience of extreme social unrest. Appalled by the progressive radicalization of the Viennese revolution, he echoed conservative interpretations of the French Revolution a half-century earlier by describing the uprising as a revolt of passion and unreason against sensible order. In a letter of September 4, 1859, he wrote to his publisher, Gustav Heckanst: "When unreason, hollow enthusiasm, then the meanness of emptiness and finally even crime spread and took possession of the world: my heart nearly literally broke." The frantic affirmation of order in *Der Nachsommer* is ultimately a response to the disorders of the revolution. The novel, full of so many reformist plans, is not hostile to change in general but only to revolutionary change, associated solely with the ominously passionate figure of Roland, an artist patronized by Risach. Yet the same Roland whose revolutionism is rejected has the potential to become a great painter because of precisely that fiery temperament which otherwise leads him to idiosyncratic political positions. In any case, Roland, the only figure linked to radical politics, does not play a major role in the novel, and his political disqualification is not a crucial issue. Although *Der Nachsommer* insists on order and denounces revolution, the emphasis on order structures the bulk of the text, while the opposition to revolution is no more than a peripheral concern. This peripheralization is itself a political practice, but the novel cannot be explained away by the hypothesis of a simple causality between Stifter's antiradicalism and the aesthetic form of the work.

The concern with order in *Der Nachsommer* is in fact less a response to the upheaval of the revolution than an integral element of Stifter's own liberalism: the necessary corrective to his vision of human progress. For Stifter, civilization, never a stable structure, is perpetually involved in change. Risach turns down Heinrich's promise never to change anything at the Asperhof since, as he insists to his young guest, change is inevitable. What holds for the individual applies all the more to the species, for which change is also the rule. At stake, however, is the precise character of change. Stifter's liberal hopes are mixed with a profound despair concerning the character of social development. He watches a process of progress unfold that threatens the substance of culture and the possibility of meaning, and he constructs his rigorous schemes of order as a strategic effort to counteract the erosion caused by this historical decline initiated by bourgeois society.

This historical process is thematized most generally as cultural decline; castles have crumbled and churches fallen into disrepair because the authentic values of an earlier medieval age have disappeared. Art works of the distant past, deemed superior, are contrasted with those of the present in order to trace a trajectory of decay. Thus Heinrich's father, the elder Drendorf, comments on his own preference for the painting of the sixteenth century: "It was a strong and powerful race that acted then. Then came a weakly and degenerate time. It was considered an improvement to make the forms richer and paler, to accentuate the color and deemphasize the shadow. The new age gradually came to disdain the old, which is why it let the latter decay. Indeed the coarseness accompanying this ignorance destroyed much, especially during wild and confusing periods." The decay and even destruction of the art works of the former high civilization are indicative of a loss of a sense of quality that is integral to cultural production. The path of historical progress since the Renaissance is marked by a loss of cultural meaning, which might, Drendorf explains, be overcome in the future in the context of profound changes. At this point Drendorf's utopian prediction is still less important than his fundamental denunciation of the present as a period in which cultural quality, unattainable by most, is preserved only in enclaves like Risach's Asperhof.

The various digressions on historical decline reiterate this pattern, but they remain abstract. Elsewhere Stifter suggests the specific causes of this process, foremost among which is the commodification of the object in capitalism, in regard to both its production and possession. While describing the history of his efforts to establish a shop to restore old furniture and works of art, Risach intimates how his own artisanal plans were instituted only against the class resistance of the workers:

> Building this house was not at all the most difficult task; it was much more difficult to find the workers. I had several cabinet-makers and had to fire them. Gradually I learned myself, and then the obstinacy of willfulness and station blocked my way. In the end, I took people who were not carpenters in order to train them here first. Yet these too, like the earlier group, had a sin often found in the working classes and probably others as well, the sin of complacency or carelessness which always says, "This way will do," and considers any further precautions unnecessary.

Risach's complaint that good help is hard to find corresponds to the overall cultural criticism: in an age of declining values and aesthetic barbarism, the erosion of the work ethic contributes, at least from the standpoint of the entrepreneur, to the lowering of production standards. Only the force of the rational carrier of culture who, overriding all artisanal self-understanding of the craftsman, fully determines the labor process can reestablish standards of quality. The Josephinist Enlightenment does not supplant the entropy of decay, which proceeds always on its own accord, but merely holds it off temporarily: progress is an opportunity, but decline is fate. Thus, for all Risach's efforts to obscure the antagonism of class difference—his clothing is egalitarian, and he rejects the artificial codes of hierarchy that prevail elsewhere in Austrian society— these differences reappear with ineluctable necessity in the forced harmony of the Rosenhaus. The gardener's bucolic imbecility and Roland's smoldering passion both reflect their social inferiority vis-à-vis the *grand seigneur*. Risach is modest enough to dine with his more skilled laborers, a patronizing gesture symptomatic of Stifter's liberalism. Unfortunately, however, the economic plans to which he devotes so much attention make this sort of culinary camaraderie difficult. Because the workers rise so much earlier in the morning, they prefer to eat at hours different from those of their employer. Therefore Eustach, Risach's draftsman, "himself requested that he choose the time and nature of his meals." The everyday ramifications of class structure, specifying who must work when and who need not, are thereby attributed to the free choice of the workers. Stifter proclaims the desideratum of a natural fraternity in which the artificiality of hierarchical etiquette has disappeared, but his own utopian schemes reproduce the signs of status in terms of the exigencies of the division of labor. No matter how nicely he treats his employees, Risach still occupies a privileged position from which he can observe the labor process as an aesthetic spectacle.

The class struggle behind the rose-covered facade is one aspect of the novel's seismographic registering of the process of capitalist expansion, which the book nevertheless excludes from explicit thematization. The mechanism of commodity production, with all its related labor conflicts, leads, furthermore, to a certain type of product: poorly made, poorly conceived, and lacking any essential tie to its purported purpose. This critique of modern commodities, which are contrasted with the superior artisanal products of medieval craftsmen, recurs throughout **Der Nachsommer** and represents an additional aspect of Stifter's indirect analysis of the consequences of the developing bourgeois society. (pp. 105-10)

Two further social sources of the nascent semiotic crisis of capitalism are located in **Der Nachsommer.** Nineteenth-century capitalism still depended strongly on an ideology of individualism in order to emancipate society from the restrictive legacies of premodern institutions. While the realist theoreticians in *Die Grenzboten* took issue with subjectivity as a form of romantic escapism in the name of a worldly realism, Stifter denounces excessive subjectivity as the cause of chaotic desires which threaten social permanence. Thus, not only capitalism but the corollary form of an individuality removed from a universal order is perceived as a danger. Risach instructs Heinrich:

> Because men are always desiring and praising something, because they leap into one-sidedness in order to satisfy themselves, they make themselves unhappy. If we only maintained order in ourselves, then we would have much more pleasure with the things of this earth. However if there are excessive wishes and desires in us, then we constantly heed them and are no longer able to grasp the innocence of things outside ourselves. Unfortunately we call them important when they are objects of our passion, and unimportant, when they have no relationship to us, although the reverse may often be the case.

This explicit denunciation of anthropocentrism and the related cult of interiority, Stifter's version of the end of man, parallels the two major narrative lines of the novel: the interpolated account of Risach's failed passion for Mathilde and the lengthy chronicle of the successful love between Heinrich and Natalie. The former relationship presents a negative, the latter a positive formulation of the overt message: the necessity of reconciling individuality with an overarching order. For the neo-humanist Stifter, this sort of reconciliation is possible only if the individual does not engage in an excessive specialization but rather mirrors the external order in his own universal education. That cultural strategy presupposes, however, a society without the division of labor that Stifter is unable to exclude from his own utopia. For Stifter, specialization is not like the Lutheran acceptance of worldly station as an expression of brotherly love; it is only the concretization of a putative self-interest and is linked therefore to individuality, interiority, emotionalism, and all the potential disorder of romanticism. The cipher of this threat is Roland with his sullen anger and his subjectivist painting.

The antinomic complement of romantic individualism, the logic of bureaucratization, also contributes to the crisis of meaning to which Stifter responds with his constructions of order. Paradoxically, the bureaucracy can claim to be the ultimate guarantor of order both in the fictional time-frame of the Metternich era and in the post-1848 context in which **Der Nachsommer** was written. Nevertheless Risach's account of his own experiences in the civil service constitutes a cogent essayistic interlude in which Stifter analyzes the assumptions and cultural consequences of an expanding state administration, which is as much a part of the Josephinist heritage as the more specifically bourgeois aspects of capitalism and individualism.

Near the conclusion of the novel, Risach finally reveals his identity and his past. He had pursued a career in government during the Napoleonic wars and had been more than modestly successful. Yet despite the predictions of a grand career, his insistence on personal independence was incompatible with the exigencies of an administrative bureaucracy. He retired prematurely in order to devote himself to his various horticultural and antiquarian interests in the countryside. He explains his basic incongruity in the civil service in terms of the nature of his own personality:

> You see, I lack two things necessary to be a servant of the state: the skill to obey, which is a basic condition of any organization of persons and things, and the skill of productive integration in a whole in active pursuit of goals beyond the immediately visible, which is also a basic condition of any organization. I always wanted to change the principles and improve the foundations instead of doing my best under the circumstances; I wanted to set the goals myself and to do each task in the manner most appropriate to it without regard for the whole and without considering whether my action might cause a gap somewhere else with consequences perhaps worse than my immediate success.

Stifter is here speaking as the pedagogic reformer and neo-humanist liberal who came into conflict with conservative powers in the immobile governmental bureaucracy. Yet it is also Risach who claims for himself the individual autonomy antithetical to the same sort of obedience that he demands of his own workers. The point is not Risach's escape from the bureaucratic Leviathan—he is after all Stifter's fictional cipher of a utopian exception—but rather the central role of bureaucratization itself in the crisis of modernity. Although bureaucracy demands obedience in the name of order, its substantive approach to any problem entails a radical dissection: the whole perpetually disappears from sight as it is divided up into an infinite num-

ber of disjointed parts, misperceived, like the atomistic individuals, as fundamentally separate units. Bureaucratic logic, therefore, erodes an initial totality and replaces it with a mosaic of fragments in which only the elite few are capable of recognizing patterns.

The crisis of meaning that ensues from this process of fragmentation is compounded by another of its features, the inability to recognize specific qualities. The state bureaucracy must function like a machine, and it therefore trains its agents in a manner which guarantees a smooth operation; neither individual growth nor individual characteristics can be taken into account. Here Stifter anticipates elements of the grand Weberian theme:

> The substance of this service must have a form that ensures that activities necessary to the state's goals continue without interruption or significant weakening when greater or lesser individual talents variously occupy the individual offices in which they operate. I could use an example and say that the most excellent clock would be one which was so built that it would run correctly even if all its parts were changed, replacing the good ones with bad ones, and the bad ones with good. Yet such a clock is hardly possible. State service, however, must form itself in this manner or renounce the development in which it finds itself today. It is understandable that the order of state service must be strict and that it is not permissible for individuals to attempt to give the regulations a significance different from the prescribed one: indeed it is understandable that for the sake of the preservation of the whole, an individual task must be performed less well than it might when considered in isolation.

Specificity and particularity disappear in the name of the untroubled functioning of the machine. Furthermore, this disappearance of individual qualities in the homogeneous temporality of the operation corresponds to a disappearance of quality as such. Because bureaucratization ignores quality, it necessarily privileges mediocrity, and those tasks that independent individuals would carry out well are carried out with only mechanical perfunctoriness by the bureaucrat. The order that this bureaucracy institutes is the emptiness of an entropy in which differences and complicated structures are simultaneously ignored and destroyed.

Stifter's analysis of bureaucracy continues implicitly in Risach's account of himself as the epitome of the nonbureaucratic personality. Just as Risach insists on bringing his own individual qualities into play in any activity, he shows particular interest in the individual attributes of every object before him. He directs his attention to concrete features, not generalizing formulas: "Since my childhood I have had a drive to produce things which are perceived with the senses. Mere connections and relationships as well as the deduction of concepts had little value for me, I could not place them in the assembly of matters in my mind." In contrast to Risach, with his sensuous perception and his "pleasure in everything produced that can be perceived," the bureaucracy is abstract and theoretical. Whereas Risach provides names and labels, the bureaucracy offers empty concepts. At this point, Stifter's anti-theoretical stance converges with key positions of the contemporary realists. Their differences, however, are more interesting. Dissatisfied with the idealist predilections of Weimar classicism and the pre-1848 radicalism of the young German authors, the realists transpose the generalizing function of the Hegelian spirit into the matter of the real world. This secularization permits them to claim that meaning is immanent in their world, and their project is the celebration of that meaning and its worldliness. In contrast, the metaphysical presupposition of **Der Nachsommer** is the disappearance of meaning. Modernity in the guise of capitalism, subjectivism, and bureaucracy has initiated a crisis: order is threatened, quality disappears, and the objects of the world, which Stifter so copiously describes, constantly escape the grasp of the subject and fall into the senselessness of disorganized mass. Precisely this recognition of the crisis is the key to the pedantic descriptions: the literary strategems of order constitute a resistance to the imminent entropy—not a reproduction of the capitalist world but, extrapolating its consequences, an effort to deny it. Thus Stifter maintains, "In the work I have wanted to sketch a life deeper and richer than usually appears."

The realist secularization of meaning generates a literary strategy in which detail can plausibly function as the carrier of sense in a perpetual and unregulated exchange between text and recipient. The world is filled with discrete units and specific traits, referring simultaneously to a fictional individuality and a general social type. . . . The realist novel presupposes and, by structuring the communicative relationship, produces the readership able to undertake the hermeneutic penetration of the aesthetic object, with only minimal help from the narrator. Because meaning is supposed to be stable and the readership capable of recognizing it, the process of reception needs no interventionist regulation, no direct commentary or disruptive interjection.

Stifter does not participate in this realist optimism regarding the accessibility of meaning or the fluidity of a laissez-faire exchange between text and reader unregulated by narrational effort. On the contrary, modernity plunges culture, the social structure of meaning, into a profound crisis. For Stifter, the act of writing as an act of address constitutes an effort to resist this crisis by imposing order where it is otherwise eroding. This problematic emerges most clearly as content in a series of key thematic concerns: the preservation of art works against decay, the conservation of the past in terms of local history, and the protection of domesticated nature against destruction. In an era of decline, order is not a replenishable natural resource, an attribute of being, but rather the achievement of those few who can resist the collapse: "They impede the pace of the calamity when the service of art begins to decay, and when the darkness should again become bright, they carry the torch forward". The dictum indicates the strategic intent of Stifter's narrational politics.

In all three major domestic scenes in **Der Nachsommer**—the Asperhof, the Sternenhof, and the Drendorf home—an unbreachable order of things prevails. Nothing is ever

out of place, and no object or room is ever used for a purpose other than its authentic one. Works of art and nature are catalogued, measured, and stored. Order must be preserved with such frantic rigor because disorder is always so close, as in the case of the thunderstorm that leads to the initial encounter between Heinrich and Risach. The same principle of order determines Stifter's style, his treatment of details as well as the structure of his sentences. The novel includes lengthy descriptions of the rooms in the various houses and all their furnishings. An object once introduced into the course of the narrative is never forgotten, no matter how inconsequential it seems. Stifter makes a point of describing how the basket Risach holds while feeding the birds is given to a servant in order to return it to its place: "When we had arrived there, he gave that which I had initially thought to be the cover of a basket but which was a specially woven, very flat and long feeding basket to a maid to put in its place, and we went into the dining room". The concern with the basket serves no other purpose than to demonstrate the rule of order, but Stifter is not yet done with it. After a tour of the house and its collections, Heinrich and Risach pass through the kitchen and the servants' quarters, where cleanliness, organization, and industry prevail. Pages later, the basket reappears in this idyll of diligence and order: "The long, fine basket, out of which my host had fed the birds, leaned in its own niche in the wall beside the door, which appeared to be its designated place."

In addition to this precise description of minutiae, Stifter uses other devices to impose order on a linguistic world that he considers constantly threatened by fragmentation. These devices are all the more necessary since, unlike Freytag, Stifter does not presume a communicative exchange with a hermeneutically capable recipient. His voice is that of a didact, leaving nothing open to question and no places of indeterminacy in the text. Precision is underscored by his excessive predilection for demonstrative forms, such as "oneself." After the novel's first sentence introduces the father, and the second sentence his house, the third one cannot simply assume the location but must pinpoint it as "in the same house." The desire for order also determines Stifter's use of punctuation, especially his omission of commas in serial listings: "Together with the father she took care of the fruit the flowers and the vegetables". "There were drawings of altars choral balustrades chairs individual figures painted windows and other objects that are found in churches". The separation that the commas would introduce among these discrete units is avoided, and the world takes on the appearance of a seamless totality. The same principle—establishment of unity through a punctuational device—explains the many series of sentences linked only by commas with no periodic breaks. Temporal and locational adverbs, such as "then" and "there," are used to link statements that might otherwise suggest separation. The length of a sentence is determined ultimately by the purported internal cohesiveness of an experience, no matter how many individual clauses must be strung together, as in the extended account of Heinrich's panoramic view from the mountaintop.

Stifter's exclusion of disruptive moments from the course of the text and his pedantic attention to the order of things and activities represent his literary response to the crisis of meaning inherent in *Der Nachsommer.* Not only is meaning as a resource in danger of exhaustion, but meaningful exchange with the reader can take place only with the aid of this absolutely closed speech. The epic breadth of Stifter's world is ultimately very narrow, since the horizons are always close. The report of Heinrich's journey after his engagement to Natalie is merely a list of the cities he visited, for to treat them concretely would have exploded the framework of the novel, and explosion is precisely what Stifter wants to avoid. He flees it, escaping into the safety of his periodic structures, just as Heinrich first enters Risach's home in order to avoid a summer storm that never happens.

Of the various sanctuaries of order in *Der Nachsommer,* the libraries are not the least important. As collections of books, they parallel the many other collections of gems, stones, paintings, prints, and roses. Yet in a novel in which the literary act is appropriated as a mechanism to establish order, these architectural centers of literature display a character that is particularly revealing in comparison to the model proposed in "Planning a Home Library" in *Die Grenzboten* in 1852, five years before the publication of *Der Nachsommer.* There, literature represented a place of sociability and exchange, not only in the reception process between author and reader but also among the readers themselves. Literature was a crystallizing center of a public sphere. Stifter's libraries are very different: the display of books, which the realist critic expressly advocated, is now proscribed. Heinrich's father has placed green silk behind the window panes of his bookshelves: "because he could not stand it if the titles of the books, usually printed in golden letters on their backs, could be read through the glass by everyone, as if he wanted to show off the books he owned." This explanation is not fully credible, since only a few lines later the reader is informed that Drendorf insisted that each room serve only one purpose; thus the library is only for private reading and not for public socializing, so the possibility of even being suspected of showing off his books could not arise.

A more likely interpretation of the curtains is suggested by the image itself and the piety with which the room is treated. The curtains before the texts lend them an aura of holiness and autonomous self-enclosure. Social concerns, indeed the human presence, are out of place in this literary world: "One was not allowed to disturb him there, and no one was permitted to walk through the library . . . He always replaced the book, in which he had read, in its exact spot in the shelf from which he had taken it, and if one went into the library just after he left it, one could see nothing at all which might indicate that someone had just been reading." The library not only has nothing to do with public sociability but also has very little to do with reading at all; the traces of the reading subject are constantly obliterated. No longer a communicative process, literature transforms itself into the contemplative adulation of the cultural object: the cult of art.

The separation of reading and contemplation finds its architectural concretization in the more spacious premises of the Asperhof. Risach's library is ultimately only an extrapolation of the elder Drendorf's on the grander dimensions afforded by greater wealth, just as Risach functions as an ersatz father for Heinrich with more possessions, in a substitutional process indicative of the repressed project of capitalist accumulation. In both libraries the rule holds that every book must be returned immediately to its place. In addition to this external similarity, each room serves only a single purpose. Yet while Drendorf combines the storage of books and their reading, Risach provides two separate spaces: the library itself, where the books are enshrined, and a separate reading room. This expansion clarifies the sacred character of Stifter's concept of literature: "Because nothing happened in the library except that only the books were there, it became sanctified in a certain sense, the books took on an importance and dignity, the room is their temple, and no one works in a temple. This order is also an homage to the spirit which is preserved in so many ways in these printed and written papers and parchments." The library is a sanctuary in which to keep the holy texts whose importance rests on their own autonomy and not on any interaction with their recipient. This denigration of the reception process is thematized repeatedly in the aesthetic excursions in *Der Nachsommer,* where the value of a work of art is treated as separate from and often antagonistic to the nature of its empirical reception.

The recognition that literature is presented not as a subjective experience but as the contemplative acceptance and adulation of hermetic works helps explain the peculiar path of Heinrich's own literary development. Initially he is simply unconcerned with literary matters. His first response to the collection of books at Asperhof is a disappointed. "It was almost only all poets," for whom he has little interest. In the course of his maturation process, however, he is gradually introduced to literature and learns to treasure the great authors of Stifter's neohumanist canon: Cervantes, Shakespeare, and above all Homer. Yet unlike Wilhelm Meister, the paradigmatic Bildungsroman hero with whom he begs to be compared, Heinrich merely meets this literature and loves it immediately. There are no interpretive difficulties, no fruitful misreadings, and no important literary critical passages associated with these textual encounters. The *King Lear* episode in *Der Nachsommer* has none of the weighty significance of the Hamlet problem for Goethe's novel. The canon is merely established as such, cultural material arbitrarily declared worthy of preservation. Therefore the literary gifts, a Goethe edition and the *Nibelungenlied,* are presented only as statements with no consequences for the subsequent development of the recipients or for the unfolding of the novel.

By separating the act of reading from social communication and transforming it into the adulation of a cult object beyond rational comprehension, Stifter sets up a social relation that can easily be transferred out of the world of letters and into a realm beyond social meaning: physical nature. Indeed the literary experiences in *Der Nachsommer* are rather scanty when compared with the abundant descriptions of nature, and this nature, which Stifter imbues with a sacred character, is presented as an object of scrutiny, a macrotext, deserving the same reverence accorded to the volumes in both the Drendorf and Risach libraries. Thus Heinrich reports:

> If any history is worthy of thought and research, it is the history of the earth, the most presentimental and appealing one that there is, a narrative in which humans are only a small insertion, and who knows how small, since they may be replaced by the histories of perhaps greater beings. The sources for the history of the earth are preserved deep inside it, as if in a document vault, sources set down perhaps in millions of documents, and it is only a matter of our learning how to read them without letting our eagerness and obstinacy falsify them. Who will ever have this history clear before his eyes? Will such a time come, or will only he know them fully who has known them from eternity?

At first, Stifter here sets up a general category of history, large enough to encompass both natural history, especially the history of the earth—a particular interest of the dilettante geologist Heinrich—and human history. Yet human history quickly loses any particularity: not only is it merely a chapter of natural history, but it is an insignificant one. Stifter transforms the Enlightenment belief in progress into speculation on greater future beings, and the vision of that magnificent future induces a denigration of the present, the domain of social humanity. This implicit antihumanism of the neohumanist converges with the antisubjectivism arising from both the contemporary critique of romanticism and Stifter's own distrust of capitalist individualism. The antisubjectivism in turn undergoes a misanthropic turn as an antianthropocentrism. Like the world of the realist Freytag, Stifter's world is constructed around a hidden text, but with a radically different intent. In Freytag's case, the textualized world becomes legible for the reader with the appropriate bourgeois vision, and the realist novel serves as the corollary primer. In Stifter's case, the text is as hidden as the books in Drendorf's library. The young geologist can collect minerals and measure lakes, just as Stifter does not expressly deny access to the "millions of documents" preserved in the inner sanctum of the earth. Yet the liberal Stifter, while not prepared to embrace unquestioned agnosticism, is not hopeful. The likelihood of human penetration of the mysteries of the world is small, and that holy knowledge is in the end reserved for a divine and eternal intelligence.

The reader in Stifter's libraries approaches a book in the same manner as the geologist approaches the earth. Both textual encounters take place in an atmosphere of cult. In both cases the preserved texts are vessels of knowledge, the authenticity of which depends in no way on the recipient's ratiocinative appropriation. Knowledge has nothing to do with social intersubjectivity, but rather with the subordination of the passive subject—whose passivity already implies a loss of authentic subjectivity—to the petrified canon. The matter at hand, be it the book or the mountain, the universalized structures of order, has a distant past and a distant future, but the present is dehistoricized and thereby moved beyond the realm of rational comprehension. Given his fear of social instability, Stifter can defend order only as absolute and impervious to the sublunary tamperings by human agency.

This dehumanization of the world transformed into a cult object provoked a sharp attack from the critic Walter Benjamin in 1918. Conceding Stifter's success in his "wonderful descriptions of nature," Benjamin nevertheless complains that they are intimately linked to "false metaphysical basic convictions . . . about that which man needs in his relationship to nature." Stifter's refusal to differentiate between greatness and smallness, thematized in the foreword to his *Bunte Steine* (*Stones of Many Colors,* 1853), leads to a privileging of the small, not only of the apparently irrelevant detail in descriptive treatments of nature but also of those aspects of human life closest to nature. The exclusion of greatness, however, leads to a truncation and distortion of human life, robbed of its adult maturity whereby it endeavors to overcome the mere givenness of the natural order by establishing a human one: "He indeed lacks the sense for the elementary relations of man to the world in their purified justification; in other words, the sense for justice in the highest sense of the word." For Benjamin, Stifter's cult of nature leads to a denigration of the proper activity of society, the search for justice, which in this context is both eschatological and political. Justice demands human subjectivity and historical change, both of which Stifter denies. Instead of a reordering of social affairs as specifically human, "in Stifter there was a convulsive impulse to link the ethical world and destiny with nature in another way, which seemed simpler but was in truth subhumanly demonic and ghostly." In truth it is a clandestine bastardization" [Hermann Kinder, *Poesie als Synthese,* 1973]. The utopia in *Der Nachsommer* pretends to be based on nature-as-harmony but in fact depends on nature-as-order, as the immovable and demonic idol of veneration. This act of veneration, in which social obligations are forgotten and the individual bows without resistance to the sheer force of structured power, is universalized as acceptance without will and directed toward nature, culture, and order. The wordly text is fully comprehensible, but no longer in the realistic sense. Gone is the notion that there are fundamental laws which individuals might appropriate in order to act; gone is the assumption that a reciprocal exchange of meaning is possible in communication. In Stifter's frozen world, the sole meaning of the various semiotic systems—clothes and weather in addition to mountains and books—is the exigency of subordination and the command to submit.

In *Der Nachsommer,* the reception structures of nature and literature are homologous. In both types of reception a passivity vis-à-vis the auratic object displaces the hermeneutic maturity of the implied reader in earlier bourgeois literature. Despite this parallel, the novel turns its attention overwhelmingly, in terms of sheer length of description, toward nature rather than literature. With regard to his relative devaluation of cultural objects and the heightened significance of material objects specifically located outside the dimension of intellectual comprehension and social communication, *Der Nachsommer* occupies a crucial position in the historical trivialization of the German Bildungsroman. In the course of the nineteenth century the framing narrative of social integration, which remains the defining feature of the genre, grows increasingly external to the immanent process of the hero's development. For Wilhelm Meister, integration into human society depends on the maturity of the human personality, mediated by the experiential integration of largely aesthetic products of culture. A century later the hero of Gustav Frenssen's *Jörn Uhl* (1901) establishes himself solely on the basis of a technical education: the mastery of nature qualifies the individual to enter a society in which technical logic prevails over human concerns. **Der Nachsommer** stands halfway between the two, still committed to the project of culture but prepared to reduce that culture to the facticity of nature. The cipher of this naturalization of human culture is Risach's mechanism for predicting weather, the extension of his own powers of observation through the nerve systems of animals. This extreme sensitivity to the environment is no ecological utopia but a capitulation to the power of nature in the province of Circe. An autonomous realm of culture falls apart in two directions: the subjectivity of the individual is denounced, while cultural objects, beyond rational appropriation, are integrated into the same cultic contemplation directed at nature.

The priority of nature over literature indicates a similar priority of observation over communication. The aesthetic corollary is the novel's descriptive rather than teleological narrative structure; the perceptual corollary is the preference for visual over verbal elements. Repeatedly Stifter underscores the privileged character of optical perception. Risach himself invokes his preference for concrete designations rather than abstract concepts as an explanation for his inability to carry on in the bureaucracy. Early in the novel the still unnamed narrator underscores his own descriptive nature: "Father used to say that I had to become a describer of things, or an artist who makes objects out of materials . . . or at least a scholar who investigates the traits and composition of things." This gift of description is transformed into Heinrich's extended efforts in drawing and painting. Not only does he insist that the picture reproduces the object with greater success than does verbal discourse, but he treats the pictorial image as in fact superior to the unmediated observation of the observed object itself:

> I read somewhere once that one comes to understand and to love objects more quickly and clearly if one sees drawings and paintings of them than if one sees them directly, because the limits of the drawing make everything smaller and more particular than in reality, where it may be large and mixed with other matters. In my case, this claim turned out to be valid. When I saw the architectural drawings in the rose-covered house, I understood the constructions more easily, judged them more easily, and I could not understand how I could have been less attentive in the past.

A social order that maintains itself as spectacle rather than substance necessarily grants the image priority over the experience.

The preference for the pictorial representation of an object refers not only, as in this case, to treatments of buildings and art objects but to those of nature as well. When Heinrich begins to paint, he recognizes the limits of his earlier verbal and cerebral appropriation of geological phenomena:

> The mountains stood before me in their beauty and fullness, as I had never seen them before. My research had always treated them as parts. Previously they had been merely objects; now they were images. One could sink oneself into the images because they had depth, and the objects were always spread out for contemplation. Just as in the past I had drawn objects of nature for scientific purposes . . . now I tried to draw and paint with oils on paper and canvas the full view, in which a series of figures, one behind another, floated in the scented air, in front of the heavens.

Stifter has Heinrich present two alternative modes of perception. Painting is associated with an image that renders beauty or charm and totality, in contrast with drawing which is appropriate only for objects of scientific research and teleological instrumentalization. Painting guarantees depth and fullness; drawing is rigid and flat. The antinomies of picture and object and, implicitly, of art and scientific rationality reproduce the same problematic of nature and culture. Stifter denigrates conceptual, rational, and communicative modes in which individuals can function as autonomous beings in the social activity of culture. He privileges structures in which individuals sink away in contemplation, surrender their rational facilities, and subordinate themselves to the object of cultic perception in its brute naturalness. . . . [Stifter's] descriptivism leads to an authoritarian positivism in which power structures are accepted because they are recognized and the subject, ashamed of his powerlessness, assists in his own eradication.

Stifter's cult of the visual is the apotheosis of the given. He does not suggest the presence of laws beneath the confusion of an empirical surface, since the surface, scrutinized by the seeing eye, is itself the law. The empirical is not subject to investigation or rational questioning, and there is no room for communication, for words, or for concepts. The only difference of opinion in the course of Heinrich's discourse, omitting Risach's autobiographical narrative of his past, is the initial debate over the weather. Otherwise every dialogue is marked by reciprocal agreement. Opinions are perhaps reinforced in this reciprocity, but neither of the interlocutors ever shows the need for reinforcement, and it is not negotiated through the subtle mechanisms of exchange that operated in Schröter's office. No new word is ever spoken, and the exclusion of the catalyst of communicative language from the static world represents a corollary to the visual priority, as Benjamin recognizes: "He can work only on the basis of the visual . . . this basic characteristic is linked to his total lack of a sense of revelation, which must be *heard*, i.e. it lies in a metaphysical acoustic dimension. Furthermore, the basic feature of his writings can be explained along these lines: quiet. Quiet is namely the absence of any acoustic sensation."

Stifter's nearly exclusive attention to the visually perceivable world doubtless emerges from the same historical experience implicit in the realists' credo, the rejection of theory and speculation in the wake of the defeat of the 1848 revolution. However, this intellectual historical parallel ignores the functioning mechanism of Stifter's text. The descriptivism fuels his frantic effort to hold onto the concrete details that he felt were rapidly escaping his grasp because of the entropy unleashed by capitalism. In addition, the priority of the image over the word guarantees the passive contemplation of an epic cosmos in which subjectivity withers because it is never called upon to speak. The close link between epic structure and submissive silence is at the center of the aesthetics of *Der Nachsommer,* and it anticipates similar problems of vision and spectacle inherent in the trivial realism of the commercial literature which the culture industry provided for the new mass reading public of the twentieth century.

In the explicit aesthetic discussions, Stifter advocates the classicist preferences of his own neo-humanism. Greek art, he argues, displays the moderation absent in modern pomp. Whereas Greek art presents order, wholeness, and truth, modern products are fragmented and false. Each type of art evokes a corresponding pattern of reception: "This is the high value of the artistic monuments of the ancient, serene Greek world . . . that they fill the spirit in their simplicity and purity . . . In contrast, in the modern world there is often a restless search for effect which cannot hold the soul but which is rejected by it as something untrue." Classical art, whole in itself, engenders order and calm; the contradictions of modern art generate commotion and conflict. The ancients' privileged access to simplicity and purity further indicates a greater proximity to nature: "It seemed to me as if they were more natural true simple and great than the men of the modern world, as if the seriousness of their being and their respect for themselves disallowed the excesses that later ages considered attractive." Not distorted by the subjective independence of modernity, a source of chaos and social entropy, Stifter's Greeks avoid conflict and uphold order because they are natural, which is to say, silent. Their universe is devoid of communication, since the linguistic autonomy of discursive subjects has not broken the social totality. The disparagement of communication and the cultic veneration of the given is appropriated by Risach himself, who collects books in languages he cannot read simply because of their greatness. Private reception is irrelevant, the symptom of an age of excessive individualism and unfettered subjectivity.

Stifter undertakes a strategic effort to counter that subjectivity by recasting the nineteenth century in the image of the epic totality of Homeric Greece. Conflict is excluded from the narrative by the avoidance of dissonant tones, with the exception of the deer-slaying and Roland's painting, and their significance is as peripheral to the central utopia as their peripheralization is characteristic. Conflict is further avoided by syntactic and punctuational devices: the omission of commas suggests an unbroken cosmos, and the order of the periodic structures echoes the regularity of the daily schedule at the Asperhof. Finally, Stifter explicitly imposes Greek forms onto contemporary experience during Heinrich's winter visit to Risach. The hero, immersed in the *Odyssey,* loses himself in contemplative reverie, "until Nausica finally stood at the pillars of the gate, simple and with profound emotion: then the smiling

beautiful image of Natalie appeared to me; she was the Nausica of today, so true so simple not flaunting her emotions nor falsifying them. The two figures melted into each other." Stifter had prepared the reader for this double exposure by earlier describing Natalie's physiognomy as similar to the image on one of Drendorf's Greek stones. She is the allegoric cipher for the renewal of the epic totality implicit in the propagation of classical aesthetics. This aesthetic position, however, reveals Stifter's specific political project: it is not Attic democracy that he attempts to revive, but the total order and nonconflictuality characterizing his understanding of the Greeks. Silence prevails, and activity recedes in both the art work and the envisioned society. Stifter endeavors to impede the ubiquity of real conflict and change in society with his literary strategy and his message of silent submission. His writing is a mechanism to impose epic terms onto fragmented life by denying contradictions and by aestheticizing politics through the imitation of Homeric models. (pp. 111-27)

The original sin in *Der Nachsommer* is the premature exchange of declarations of love between Risach and Mathilde. This transgression caused each to lead an unhappy life and is ultimately atoned for only in the union of Heinrich and Natalie. This second exchange of vows is, in a sense, inevitable after Heinrich first enters Risach's home, since there is no subsequent break in the chain of visits that eventually leads to his marriage. Nevertheless the approach to Natalie is tediously slow and time-consuming, and this contrast with the excessive speed of the older couple provides the key to Stifter's treatment of the exchange problematic. Exchange must take place, even within the epic stability of his world, but its destructive potential is defused by the impeding mechanism of convention. Certain speech is disallowed for years in order to avoid the harm caused by a too rapidly achieved intimacy. This lesson of the errors of Risach and Mathilde is carried into the novel in another way: the names of the central figures are not disclosed, either to the reader or to each other, until very late in the course of the narrative. Because Risach does not introduce himself by name to Heinrich, Heinrich, out of politeness, refuses to inquire, just as he refuses to pose many questions that might be deemed out of place.

The postponement of the intimacy of an act of exchange guards against the isolation that might follow from a too egregious failure. After the turmoil of romanticism and revolution, Stifter endeavors to introduce conventional regulation into the social sphere. This regulation takes on the character of a ritual. Nowhere are the rules expressed, let alone scrutinized. They are nevertheless always implicit in the constantly recurring patterns of order. The ritual is most evident in the exchange of gifts: the specific character of the gift is often ignored, since the point is rather the establishment of a social bond through the act. Neither the object that changes hands nor the dynamic process of change is significant, but only the establishment of order through the ritualized intercourse: When Heinrich visits distant relatives with his father, he discovers that the latter has brought gifts for everyone, although he did not even know whom he would encounter. Regardless of the specificity of the recipients, the objects are distributed as signs of gratitude for hospitality. This distribution, Stifter emphasizes, does not take place prematurely: "He had not wanted to bring the gifts at his initial arrival, for, although the people were only the normal valley inhabitants of this region, he considered it impolite to arrive loaded with presents, as if he wanted to say to them: 'I think that this is what you consider important.' Now, however, he had become indebted to them and could demonstrate his gratitude for the hospitable reception."

Like his son and Natalie but unlike Risach and Mathilde, Drendorf knows how to wait and how to respect the silently codified tropes of exchange. Excessive emotionality can only weaken the cohesiveness of social bonds, just as excessive individuality leads to isolation. The postponed exchange of names signals Stifter's radical denunciation of romantic subjectivism but also his answer to the social crisis. Convention, caution, and ritualized interaction may not guarantee eternal stability for the social order, but they can retard the processes which plunged the older generation into catastrophe. Heinrich shows how well he has learned the novel's lesson with his exclamation at his wedding: "Caution itself has led me to my fortune."

All exchange processes depend on rules, but ritualized exchanges grant greater importance to those rules than to the substance of the specific process. In *Der Nachsommer* ritualization is evident in the lack of concern with the exchanged material, in contrast to the underscored importance of the hidden goal of the process itself. The prolonged omission of names in a novel in which so little takes place indirectly and inadvertently creates a minimal suspense. The resolution occurs, however, not with the revelation of the names, which is a rather parenthetical event, but with the recognition that respect for the rules of communicative exchange—Heinrich's not asking the question—was the point all along. Thus Risach assures Natalie of Heinrich's goodness with the explanation: "He was always very modest, never pushed or inquired in a forward manner, and will certainly become a gentle husband."

This dynamic of ritualization determines not only the exchange of names and gifts but verbal exchange in general. Speech is robbed of its communicative substance, becoming instead a mechanism to establish formal social bonds. Heinrich first meets Risach when, believing a storm is imminent, he asks for shelter. Risach responds with the correct prediction that it will not rain but, more important, explicitly splits Heinrich's concern with the weather from the request for hospitality: "Those are actually two questions." By discounting Heinrich's concrete fear but nevertheless inviting him in, Risach establishes a social bond which culminates, hundreds of pages later, with the marriage. In the interim, the nameless figures are designated repeatedly by reference to this initial social institution as guest and host. Verbal exchange therefore does not function at all as a medium to exchange particular information; the use value of communication is eclipsed by the exchange process itself, designed to hold society together. Language is not externally referential; it is not about anything. It is rather the droning ritual chant with with which the community cements its internal cohesion. Risach admits at the end of the bonding process that he first enmeshed Heinrich in linguistic exchange not out of selfless altruism (for there was, after all, no threat from the weather) but out of selfish interest in Heinrich as a potential suitor for Natalie. Risach even boasts to her that it was he who found her a groom. Therefore Risach's extended discourse with Heinrich does not constitute instruction addressed to a Bildungsroman hero; it is rather a seduction, carried on by the ersatz father, acting for the unmarried daughter.

No difficulties trouble the speech in *Der Nachsommer.* No disputes or differences arise between speakers, and no speaker ever stumbles over his own words. No voice is ever raised, no whisper overheard. The long discussions, never interrupted, about flowers or art or history are devices to establish and display social stability. Benjamin identifies the perfunctory character of this talk: "Language, as spoken by Stifter's figures, is ostentatious. It is a display of feelings and thoughts in a deaf space. He absolutely lacks the capability of presenting any emotion the expression of which is what man primarily searches for in language." This speech is neither communicative nor authentically expressive, and both failures indicate the absence of full personalities. Stifter's figures interact solely in terms of the instrumentality of social stability. The accounts of Heinrich's speech are concerned neither with his personal interiority nor with the communicative accumulation of information necessary for growth, but solely with the establishment of his position in the silent world of epic order. Instrumental bonds are cemented through the perpetual speech acts, and the character of these bonds allows no room for deviation or motion.

Not only does the ritualization of speech among Stifter's characters ensure the immobility of the utopian order, but the speech directed at the reader represents an attempt to impose that order on the real world. Freytag tries to establish an exchange between equals, between the omniscient narrator and the hermeneutically mature readership that he presumes. Stifter presents a first-person narration characterized by an authoritarian mode of address. The narrator establishes the bourgeois context in the first sentence of the novel—"My father was a businessman"—but he does not introduce himself nor give the reader any hint of his own particular perspective. There is no anticipation of later events, and no interpretive openings are made via commentary. Rather, the reader is expected to submit to the course of the narration with no hint as to its probable direction. The objectivity of the account suggests a speaker without subjectivity and induces a similarly structured interlocutor: the implied reader of *Der Nachsommer* is expected to ask as few questions as did Heinrich in his sojourn at Risach's estate.

This suppression of the recipient's curiosity and the denial of individual subjectivity in general constitute the political act of the novel. Stifter responds to the perceived social crisis with a linguistic machine designed to produce order by denying individuality. Since Heinrich is satisfied not to know the name of his host, the reader ought not to expect to learn about the narrator. The fact that meaning is denied, and critical inquiry blocked, explains the conservative reception of the novel in the twentieth century. The limitation of exchange by convention and its counterpart, the ritualization of speech, determine the inner workings of the novel and the structure of its reading as well. The silence imposed on the reader testifies to the immanent ossification of realist prose. Despite Risach's diatribe against bureaucratization, the disappearance of individuality and the restrictions on freedom of which he complains reappear in the reader invoked by Stifter's discourse. **Der Nachsommer** is remarkable because it indicates this immanent tendency toward the trivialization of capitalist culture as early as the 1850s. A half-century later, when this reified form of communication had become all but universal, the rebellion of modernist writing would attempt to establish a radically new literary community emancipated from the strictures of established discursive practices. (pp. 129-33)

> *Russell A. Berman, "The Authority of Address: Adalbert Stifter," in his* The Rise of the Modern German Novel: Crisis and Charisma, *Cambridge, Mass.: Harvard University Press, 1986, pp. 105-33.*

FURTHER READING

Adler, Bruno. "New Light on Stifter." *German Life and Letters* XVIII (1964-65): 47-49.
>   Reviews briefly several works about Stifter's ideas on educational reform.

Barnes, H. G. "The Function of Conversations and Speeches in *Witiko*." In *German Studies Presented to H.G. Fiedler*, pp. 1-25. Oxford: The Clarendon Press, 1968.
>   Examines the speeches in *Witiko* as a means of characterization.

Blackall, Eric A. *Adalbert Stifter*. Cambridge: Cambridge University Press, 1948, 432 p.
>   Biographical and critical study.

Braun, Felix. "Reflections on Stifter's *Nachsommer*." *German Life and Letters* IV (October 1939): 25-32.
>   Discusses autobiographical elements in *Indian Summer*, particularly as they relate to Stifter's love life.

Browning, Barton W. "Cooper's Influence on Stifter: Fact or Scholarly Myth?" *Modern Language Notes* 89, No. 5 (October 1974): 821-28.
>   Shows that Cooper's *The Deerslayer* could not have influenced Stifter's *The Hochland*.

Fuerst, Norbert. "Three German Novels of Education: Stifter's *Nachsommer*." *Monatshefte* XXXVIII, No. 7 (November 1946): 413-25.
>   Compares Stifter's *Indian Summer* to Holderlin's *Hyperion* and Rilke's *Malte*, noting that all three novels "set out, not to please, but to reform."

George, E. F. "The Place of *Abdias* in Stifter's Thought and Work." *Forum for Modern Language Studies* III, No. 2 (April 1967): 148-56.
>   Discusses problems of solitude and divine order in Stifter's novella.

Gillespie, Gerald. "Space and Time Seen through Stifter's Telescope." *The German Quarterly* XXXVII, No. 2 (March 1964): 120-30.
>   Explains how Stifter uses perspective, both temporal and spatial, to illuminate the meaning of places and events in his works.

Gooden, Christian. "Two Quests for Surety—A Comparative Interpretation of Stifter's *Abdias* and Kafka's *Der Bau*." *Journal of European Studies* 5, No. 4 (December 1975): 341-61.
>   Maintains that Stifter's *Abdias* is a nineteenth-century prototype for Kafka's *Der Bau*, and that both stories involve a quest for absolute security.

Hallamore, G. Joyce. "The Symbolism of the Marble Muse in Stifter's *Nachsommer*." *Publications of the Modern Language Association of America* LXXIV, No. 4 (September 1959): 398-405.
>   Discusses the moral and humanizing effect of art in *Indian Summer*.

Klieneberger, H. R. "A New Approach to Stifter?" *German Life and Letters* XXV, No. 3 (April 1972): 231-36.
>   Argues that Stifter is not a major novelist, but rather an important writer who was driven by a deeply personal anxiety.

Lenel, Luise A. "Symbolism and Style in Flaubert and Stifter: A Comparative Study of *La Légende de St. Julien l 'Hospitalier* and *Der beschriebene Tännling*." In *Vistas and Vectors: Essays Honoring the Memory of Helmut Rehder*, edited by Lee B. Jennings and George Schulz-Behrend, pp. 142-51. Austin: University of Texas, Department of Germanic Languages, 1979.
>   Finds "remarkable parallels" between Stifter and Flaubert in their psychological development and sense of form.

———. "The Allure of Beauty in Stifter's *Brigitta*." *Journal of English and Germanic Philology* LXXXI, No. 1 (January 1982): 47-54.
>   Suggests that in *Brigitta* Stifter seeks to place the attraction of beauty under the control of discipline.

Rogan, Richard G. "Stifter's *Brigitta*: The Eye to the Soul." *German Studies Review* XII, No. 2 (May 1990): 243-51.
>   Discusses the relationship between inner and outer beauty in Stifter's *Brigitta*.

Silz, Walter. "Stifter's *Abdias*." In his *Realism and Reality: Studies in the German Novelle of Poetic Realism*, pp. 52-66. Chapel Hill: The University of North Carolina Press, 1954.
>   Views the protagonist of Stifter's *Abdias* as a hero with an unconquerable spirit.

Sjögren, Christine Oertel, ed. *The Marble Statue as Idea*. The University of North Carolina Studies in Germanic Languages and Literature, No. 72. Chapel Hill: The University of North Carolina Press, 1972, 119 p.
>   A collection of essays that use the concept of gestalt as the key analytical device for interpreting *Indian Summer*.

Stern, J. P. "Antecedents and Comparisons." In his *Re-Interpretations: Seven Studies in Nineteenth-Century German Literature*, pp. 7-41. New York: Basic Books, 1964.
>   Presents an overview of Stifter criticism in the twentieth century.

Swales, Martin, and Swales, Erika. *Adalbert Stifter: A Critical Study.* Anglica Germanica, Series 2. Cambridge: Cambridge University Press, 1984, 251 p.

    Discusses underlying frictions in Stifter's life and works.

Wassermann, F. M. "Adalbert Stifter in the Twentieth Century." *Books Abroad* 34, No. 2 (Spring 1960): 109-11.

    Surveys commentary on Stifter in the twentieth century and comments on the renewed interest in him.

Nineteenth-Century Literature Criticism

Cumulative Indexes
Volumes 1-41

How to Use This Index

The main references

Calvino, Italo
1923-1985.....CLC **5, 8, 11, 22, 33, 39,**
73; SSC 3

list all author entries in the following Gale Literary Criticism series:

CLC = *Contemporary Literary Criticism*
CLR = *Children's Literature Review*
CMLC = *Classical and Medieval Literature Criticism*
DC = *Drama Criticism*
LC = *Literature Criticism from 1400 to 1800*
NCLC = *Nineteenth-Century Literature Criticism*
PC = *Poetry Criticism*
SSC = *Short Story Criticism*
TCLC = *Twentieth-Century Literary Criticism*

The cross-references

See also CANR 23; CA 85-88;
obituary CA 116

list all author entries in the following Gale biographical and literary sources:

AAYA = *Authors & Artists for Young Adults*
AITN = *Authors in the News*
BLC = *Black Literature Criticism*
BW = *Black Writers*
CA = *Contemporary Authors*
CAAS = *Contemporary Authors Autobiography Series*
CABS = *Contemporary Authors Bibliographical Series*
CANR = *Contemporary Authors New Revision Series*
CAP = *Contemporary Authors Permanent Series*
CDALB = *Concise Dictionary of American Literary Biography*
CDBLB = *Concise Dictionary of British Literary Biography*
DLB = *Dictionary of Literary Biography*
DLBD = *Dictionary of Literary Biography Documentary Series*
DLBY = *Dictionary of Literary Biography Yearbook*
HW = *Hispanic Writers*
MAICYA = *Major Authors and Illustrators for Children and Young Adults*
MTCW = *Major 20th-Century Writers*
SAAS = *Something about the Author Autobiography Series*
SATA = *Something about the Author*
WLC = *World Literature Criticism, 1500 to the Present*
YABC = *Yesterday's Authors of Books for Children*

Aldanov, Mark (Alexandrovich)
 1886(?)-1957 .... **TCLC 23**
 See also CA 118

Aldington, Richard 1892-1962 ...... **CLC 49**
 See also CA 85-88; DLB 20, 36, 100

Aldiss, Brian W(ilson)
 1925- .... **CLC 5, 14, 40**
 See also CA 5-8R; CAAS 2; CANR 5, 28;
 DLB 14; MTCW; SATA 34

Alegria, Claribel 1924- .... **CLC 75**
 See also CA 131; CAAS 15; HW

Alegria, Fernando 1918- .... **CLC 57**
 See also CA 9-12R; CANR 5, 32; HW

Aleichem, Sholom .... **TCLC 1, 35**
 See also Rabinovitch, Sholem

Aleixandre, Vicente 1898-1984 ... **CLC 9, 36**
 See also CA 85-88; 114; CANR 26;
 DLB 108; HW; MTCW

Alepoudelis, Odysseus
 See Elytis, Odysseus

Aleshkovsky, Joseph 1929-
 See Aleshkovsky, Yuz
 See also CA 121; 128

Aleshkovsky, Yuz .... **CLC 44**
 See also Aleshkovsky, Joseph

Alexander, Lloyd (Chudley) 1924- .. **CLC 35**
 See also AAYA 1; CA 1-4R; CANR 1, 24,
 38; CLR 1, 5; DLB 52; MAICYA;
 MTCW; SATA 3, 49

Alfau, Felipe 1902- .... **CLC 66**
 See also CA 137

Alger, Horatio, Jr. 1832-1899 ..... **NCLC 8**
 See also DLB 42; SATA 16

Algren, Nelson 1909-1981 .... **CLC 4, 10, 33**
 See also CA 13-16R; 103; CANR 20;
 CDALB 1941-1968; DLB 9; DLBY 81,
 82; MTCW

Ali, Ahmed 1910- .... **CLC 69**
 See also CA 25-28R; CANR 15, 34

Alighieri, Dante 1265-1321 .... **CMLC 3**

Allan, John B.
 See Westlake, Donald E(dwin)

Allen, Edward 1948- .... **CLC 59**

Allen, Roland
 See Ayckbourn, Alan

Allen, Woody 1935- .... **CLC 16, 52**
 See also AAYA 10; CA 33-36R; CANR 27,
 38; DLB 44; MTCW

Allende, Isabel 1942- .... **CLC 39, 57**
 See also CA 125; 130; HW; MTCW

Alleyn, Ellen
 See Rossetti, Christina (Georgina)

Allingham, Margery (Louise)
 1904-1966 .... **CLC 19**
 See also CA 5-8R; 25-28R; CANR 4;
 DLB 77; MTCW

Allingham, William 1824-1889 .. **NCLC 25**
 See also DLB 35

Allison, Dorothy 1948- .... **CLC 78**

Allston, Washington 1779-1843 .... **NCLC 2**
 See also DLB 1

Almedingen, E. M. .... **CLC 12**
 See also Almedingen, Martha Edith von
 See also SATA 3

Almedingen, Martha Edith von 1898-1971
 See Almedingen, E. M.
 See also CA 1-4R; CANR 1

Alonso, Damaso 1898-1990 .... **CLC 14**
 See also CA 110; 131; 130; DLB 108; HW

Alov
 See Gogol, Nikolai (Vasilyevich)

Alta 1942- .... **CLC 19**
 See also CA 57-60

Alter, Robert B(ernard) 1935- ...... **CLC 34**
 See also CA 49-52; CANR 1

Alther, Lisa 1944- .... **CLC 7, 41**
 See also CA 65-68; CANR 12, 30; MTCW

Altman, Robert 1925- .... **CLC 16**
 See also CA 73-76

Alvarez, A(lfred) 1929- .... **CLC 5, 13**
 See also CA 1-4R; CANR 3, 33; DLB 14,
 40

Alvarez, Alejandro Rodriguez 1903-1965
 See Casona, Alejandro
 See also CA 131; 93-96; HW

Amado, Jorge 1912- .... **CLC 13, 40**
 See also CA 77-80; CANR 35; DLB 113;
 MTCW

Ambler, Eric 1909- .... **CLC 4, 6, 9**
 See also CA 9-12R; CANR 7, 38; DLB 77;
 MTCW

Amichai, Yehuda 1924- ...... **CLC 9, 22, 57**
 See also CA 85-88; MTCW

Amiel, Henri Frederic 1821-1881 .. **NCLC 4**

Amis, Kingsley (William)
 1922- ...... **CLC 1, 2, 3, 5, 8, 13, 40, 44**
 See also AITN 2; CA 9-12R; CANR 8, 28;
 CDBLB 1945-1960; DA; DLB 15, 27,
 100; MTCW

Amis, Martin (Louis)
 1949- .... **CLC 4, 9, 38, 62**
 See also BEST 90:3; CA 65-68; CANR 8,
 27; DLB 14

Ammons, A(rchie) R(andolph)
 1926- .... **CLC 2, 3, 5, 8, 9, 25, 57**
 See also AITN 1; CA 9-12R; CANR 6, 36;
 DLB 5; MTCW

Amo, Tauraatua i
 See Adams, Henry (Brooks)

Anand, Mulk Raj 1905- .... **CLC 23**
 See also CA 65-68; CANR 32; MTCW

Anatol
 See Schnitzler, Arthur

Anaya, Rudolfo A(lfonso) 1937- .... **CLC 23**
 See also CA 45-48; CAAS 4; CANR 1, 32;
 DLB 82; HW; MTCW

Andersen, Hans Christian
 1805-1875 .... **NCLC 7; SSC 6**
 See also CLR 6; DA; MAICYA; WLC;
 YABC 1

Anderson, C. Farley
 See Mencken, H(enry) L(ouis); Nathan,
 George Jean

Anderson, Jessica (Margaret) Queale
 .... **CLC 37**
 See also CA 9-12R; CANR 4

Anderson, Jon (Victor) 1940- .... **CLC 9**
 See also CA 25-28R; CANR 20

Anderson, Lindsay (Gordon)
 1923- .... **CLC 20**
 See also CA 125; 128

Anderson, Maxwell 1888-1959 ..... **TCLC 2**
 See also CA 105; DLB 7

Anderson, Poul (William) 1926- .... **CLC 15**
 See also AAYA 5; CA 1-4R; CAAS 2;
 CANR 2, 15, 34; DLB 8; MTCW;
 SATA 39

Anderson, Robert (Woodruff)
 1917- .... **CLC 23**
 See also AITN 1; CA 21-24R; CANR 32;
 DLB 7

Anderson, Sherwood
 1876-1941 ...... **TCLC 1, 10, 24; SSC 1**
 See also CA 104; 121; CDALB 1917-1929;
 DA; DLB 4, 9, 86; DLBD 1; MTCW;
 WLC

Andouard
 See Giraudoux, (Hippolyte) Jean

Andrade, Carlos Drummond de ...... **CLC 18**
 See also Drummond de Andrade, Carlos

Andrade, Mario de 1893-1945 ..... **TCLC 43**

Andrewes, Lancelot 1555-1626 .... **LC 5**

Andrews, Cicily Fairfield
 See West, Rebecca

Andrews, Elton V.
 See Pohl, Frederik

Andreyev, Leonid (Nikolaevich)
 1871-1919 .... **TCLC 3**
 See also CA 104

Andric, Ivo 1892-1975 .... **CLC 8**
 See also CA 81-84; 57-60; MTCW

Angelique, Pierre
 See Bataille, Georges

Angell, Roger 1920- .... **CLC 26**
 See also CA 57-60; CANR 13

Angelou, Maya 1928- .... **CLC 12, 35, 64, 77**
 See also AAYA 7; BLC 1; BW; CA 65-68;
 CANR 19; DA; DLB 38; MTCW;
 SATA 49

Annensky, Innokenty Fyodorovich
 1856-1909 .... **TCLC 14**
 See also CA 110

Anon, Charles Robert
 See Pessoa, Fernando (Antonio Nogueira)

Anouilh, Jean (Marie Lucien Pierre)
 1910-1987 ...... **CLC 1, 3, 8, 13, 40, 50**
 See also CA 17-20R; 123; CANR 32;
 MTCW

Anthony, Florence
 See Ai

Anthony, John
 See Ciardi, John (Anthony)

Anthony, Peter
 See Shaffer, Anthony (Joshua); Shaffer,
 Peter (Levin)

Anthony, Piers 1934- .... **CLC 35**
 See also CA 21-24R; CANR 28; DLB 8;
 MTCW

Antoine, Marc
 See Proust, (Valentin-Louis-George-Eugene-)
 Marcel

Antoninus, Brother
See Everson, William (Oliver)

Antonioni, Michelangelo 1912- ..... **CLC 20**
See also CA 73-76

Antschel, Paul 1920-1970...... **CLC 10, 19**
See Celan, Paul
See also CA 85-88; CANR 33; MTCW

Anwar, Chairil 1922-1949 .... **TCLC 22**
See also CA 121

Apollinaire, Guillaume .. **TCLC 3, 8, 51; PC 7**
See also Kostrowitzki, Wilhelm Apollinaris
de

Appelfeld, Aharon 1932- .... **CLC 23, 47**
See also CA 112; 133

Apple, Max (Isaac) 1941-........ **CLC 9, 33**
See also CA 81-84; CANR 19; DLB 130

Appleman, Philip (Dean) 1926- ..... **CLC 51**
See also CA 13-16R; CANR 6, 29

Appleton, Lawrence
See Lovecraft, H(oward) P(hillips)

Apteryx
See Eliot, T(homas) S(tearns)

Apuleius, (Lucius Madaurensis)
125(?)-175(?) .... **CMLC 1**

Aquin, Hubert 1929-1977........ **CLC 15**
See also CA 105; DLB 53

Aragon, Louis 1897-1982....... **CLC 3, 22**
See also CA 69-72; 108; CANR 28;
DLB 72; MTCW

Arany, Janos 1817-1882........ **NCLC 34**

Arbuthnot, John 1667-1735......... **LC 1**
See also DLB 101

Archer, Herbert Winslow
See Mencken, H(enry) L(ouis)

Archer, Jeffrey (Howard) 1940- .... **CLC 28**
See also BEST 89:3; CA 77-80; CANR 22

Archer, Jules 1915- .... **CLC 12**
See also CA 9-12R; CANR 6; SAAS 5;
SATA 4

Archer, Lee
See Ellison, Harlan

Arden, John 1930- .... **CLC 6, 13, 15**
See also CA 13-16R; CAAS 4; CANR 31;
DLB 13; MTCW

Arenas, Reinaldo 1943-1990 .... **CLC 41**
See also CA 124; 128; 133; HW

Arendt, Hannah 1906-1975 .... **CLC 66**
See also CA 17-20R; 61-64; CANR 26;
MTCW

Aretino, Pietro 1492-1556 .... **LC 12**

Arguedas, Jose Maria
1911-1969 .... **CLC 10, 18**
See also CA 89-92; DLB 113; HW

Argueta, Manlio 1936-............ **CLC 31**
See also CA 131; HW

Ariosto, Ludovico 1474-1533........ **LC 6**

Aristides
See Epstein, Joseph

Aristophanes
450B.C.-385B.C........ **CMLC 4; DC 2**
See also DA

Arlt, Roberto (Godofredo Christophersen)
1900-1942 .... **TCLC 29**
See also CA 123; 131; HW

Armah, Ayi Kwei 1939-......... **CLC 5, 33**
See also BLC 1; BW; CA 61-64; CANR 21;
DLB 117; MTCW

Armatrading, Joan 1950-......... **CLC 17**
See also CA 114

Arnette, Robert
See Silverberg, Robert

Arnim, Achim von (Ludwig Joachim von
Arnim) 1781-1831 .... **NCLC 5**
See also DLB 90

Arnim, Bettina von 1785-1859.... **NCLC 38**
See also DLB 90

Arnold, Matthew
1822-1888 .... **NCLC 6, 29; PC 5**
See also CDBLB 1832-1890; DA; DLB 32,
57; WLC

Arnold, Thomas 1795-1842 ...... **NCLC 18**
See also DLB 55

Arnow, Harriette (Louisa) Simpson
1908-1986 .... **CLC 2, 7, 18**
See also CA 9-12R; 118; CANR 14; DLB 6;
MTCW; SATA 42, 47

Arp, Hans
See Arp, Jean

Arp, Jean 1887-1966.............. **CLC 5**
See also CA 81-84; 25-28R

Arrabal
See Arrabal, Fernando

Arrabal, Fernando 1932- ... **CLC 2, 9, 18, 58**
See also CA 9-12R; CANR 15

Arrick, Fran..................... **CLC 30**

Artaud, Antonin 1896-1948 ..... **TCLC 3, 36**
See also CA 104

Arthur, Ruth M(abel) 1905-1979.... **CLC 12**
See also CA 9-12R; 85-88; CANR 4;
SATA 7, 26

Artsybashev, Mikhail (Petrovich)
1878-1927 .... **TCLC 31**

Arundel, Honor (Morfydd)
1919-1973 .... **CLC 17**
See also CA 21-22; 41-44R; CAP 2;
SATA 4, 24

Asch, Sholem 1880-1957 .... **TCLC 3**
See also CA 105

Ash, Shalom
See Asch, Sholem

Ashbery, John (Lawrence)
1927- ..... **CLC 2, 3, 4, 6, 9, 13, 15, 25,**
41, 77
See also CA 5-8R; CANR 9, 37; DLB 5;
DLBY 81; MTCW

Ashdown, Clifford
See Freeman, R(ichard) Austin

Ashe, Gordon
See Creasey, John

Ashton-Warner, Sylvia (Constance)
1908-1984 .... **CLC 19**
See also CA 69-72; 112; CANR 29; MTCW

Asimov, Isaac
1920-1992 ...... **CLC 1, 3, 9, 19, 26, 76**
See also BEST 90:2; CA 1-4R; 137;
CANR 2, 19, 36; CLR 12; DLB 8;
DLBY 92; MAICYA; MTCW; SATA 1,
26, 74

Astley, Thea (Beatrice May)
1925- .... **CLC 41**
See also CA 65-68; CANR 11

Aston, James
See White, T(erence) H(anbury)

Asturias, Miguel Angel
1899-1974 .... **CLC 3, 8, 13**
See also CA 25-28; 49-52; CANR 32;
CAP 2; DLB 113; HW; MTCW

Atares, Carlos Saura
See Saura (Atares), Carlos

Atheling, William
See Pound, Ezra (Weston Loomis)

Atheling, William, Jr.
See Blish, James (Benjamin)

Atherton, Gertrude (Franklin Horn)
1857-1948 .... **TCLC 2**
See also CA 104; DLB 9, 78

Atherton, Lucius
See Masters, Edgar Lee

Atkins, Jack
See Harris, Mark

Atticus
See Fleming, Ian (Lancaster)

Atwood, Margaret (Eleanor)
1939- .... **CLC 2, 3, 4, 8, 13, 15, 25, 44;**
SSC 2
See also BEST 89:2; CA 49-52; CANR 3,
24, 33; DA; DLB 53; MTCW; SATA 50;
WLC

Aubigny, Pierre d'
See Mencken, H(enry) L(ouis)

Aubin, Penelope 1685-1731(?)........ **LC 9**
See also DLB 39

Auchincloss, Louis (Stanton)
1917- .... **CLC 4, 6, 9, 18, 45**
See also CA 1-4R; CANR 6, 29; DLB 2;
DLBY 80; MTCW

Auden, W(ystan) H(ugh)
1907-1973 ..... **CLC 1, 2, 3, 4, 6, 9, 11,**
14, 43; PC 1
See also CA 9-12R; 45-48; CANR 5;
CDBLB 1914-1945; DA; DLB 10, 20;
MTCW; WLC

Audiberti, Jacques 1900-1965 ...... **CLC 38**
See also CA 25-28R

Auel, Jean M(arie) 1936-.......... **CLC 31**
See also AAYA 7; BEST 90:4; CA 103;
CANR 21

Auerbach, Erich 1892-1957 .... **TCLC 43**
See also CA 118

Augier, Emile 1820-1889 .... **NCLC 31**

August, John
See De Voto, Bernard (Augustine)

Augustine, St. 354-430 .... **CMLC 6**

Aurelius
See Bourne, Randolph S(illiman)

Baron Corvo
See Rolfe, Frederick (William Serafino
  Austin Lewis Mary)

Barondess, Sue K(aufman)
  1926-1977 . . . . **CLC 8**
See also Kaufman, Sue
See also CA 1-4R; 69-72; CANR 1

Baron de Teive
See Pessoa, Fernando (Antonio Nogueira)

Barres, Maurice 1862-1923 . . . . . . **TCLC 47**
See also DLB 123

Barreto, Afonso Henrique de Lima
See Lima Barreto, Afonso Henrique de

Barrett, (Roger) Syd 1946- . . . . **CLC 35**
See also Pink Floyd

Barrett, William (Christopher)
  1913-1992 . . . . **CLC 27**
See also CA 13-16R; 139; CANR 11

Barrie, J(ames) M(atthew)
  1860-1937 . . . . **TCLC 2**
See also CA 104; 136; CDBLB 1890-1914;
  CLR 16; DLB 10; MAICYA; YABC 1

Barrington, Michael
See Moorcock, Michael (John)

Barrol, Grady
See Bograd, Larry

Barry, Mike
See Malzberg, Barry N(athaniel)

Barry, Philip 1896-1949 . . . . **TCLC 11**
See also CA 109; DLB 7

Bart, Andre Schwarz
See Schwarz-Bart, Andre

Barth, John (Simmons)
  1930- . . . . . . **CLC 1, 2, 3, 5, 7, 9, 10, 14,**
                       27, 51; SSC 10
See also AITN 1, 2; CA 1-4R; CABS 1;
  CANR 5, 23; DLB 2; MTCW

Barthelme, Donald
  1931-1989 . . . . . **CLC 1, 2, 3, 5, 6, 8, 13,**
                          23, 46, 59; SSC 2
See also CA 21-24R; 129; CANR 20;
  DLB 2; DLBY 80, 89; MTCW; SATA 7,
  62

Barthelme, Frederick 1943- . . . . **CLC 36**
See also CA 114; 122; DLBY 85

Barthes, Roland (Gerard)
  1915-1980 . . . . **CLC 24**
See also CA 130; 97-100; MTCW

Barzun, Jacques (Martin) 1907- . . . . **CLC 51**
See also CA 61-64; CANR 22

Bashevis, Isaac
See Singer, Isaac Bashevis

Bashkirtseff, Marie 1859-1884 . . . **NCLC 27**

Basho
See Matsuo Basho

Bass, Kingsley B., Jr.
See Bullins, Ed

Bassani, Giorgio 1916- . . . . **CLC 9**
See also CA 65-68; CANR 33; DLB 128;
  MTCW

Bastos, Augusto (Antonio) Roa
See Roa Bastos, Augusto (Antonio)

Bataille, Georges 1897-1962 . . . . **CLC 29**
See also CA 101; 89-92

Bates, H(erbert) E(rnest)
  1905-1974 . . . . **CLC 46; SSC 10**
See also CA 93-96; 45-48; CANR 34;
  MTCW

Bauchart
See Camus, Albert

Baudelaire, Charles
  1821-1867 . . . . **NCLC 6, 29; PC 1**
See also DA; WLC

Baudrillard, Jean 1929- . . . . **CLC 60**

Baum, L(yman) Frank 1856-1919 . . . **TCLC 7**
See also CA 108; 133; CLR 15; DLB 22;
  MAICYA; MTCW; SATA 18

Baum, Louis F.
See Baum, L(yman) Frank

Baumbach, Jonathan 1933- . . . . . . **CLC 6, 23**
See also CA 13-16R; CAAS 5; CANR 12;
  DLBY 80; MTCW

Bausch, Richard (Carl) 1945- . . . . . . **CLC 51**
See also CA 101; CAAS 14; DLB 130

Baxter, Charles 1947- . . . . **CLC 45, 78**
See also CA 57-60; CANR 40; DLB 130

Baxter, George Owen
See Faust, Frederick (Schiller)

Baxter, James K(eir) 1926-1972 . . . . **CLC 14**
See also CA 77-80

Baxter, John
See Hunt, E(verette) Howard, Jr.

Bayer, Sylvia
See Glassco, John

Beagle, Peter S(oyer) 1939- . . . . **CLC 7**
See also CA 9-12R; CANR 4; DLBY 80;
  SATA 60

Bean, Normal
See Burroughs, Edgar Rice

Beard, Charles A(ustin)
  1874-1948 . . . . **TCLC 15**
See also CA 115; DLB 17; SATA 18

Beardsley, Aubrey 1872-1898 . . . . . **NCLC 6**

Beattie, Ann
  1947- . . . . **CLC 8, 13, 18, 40, 63; SSC 11**
See also BEST 90:2; CA 81-84; DLBY 82;
  MTCW

Beattie, James 1735-1803 . . . . **NCLC 25**
See also DLB 109

Beauchamp, Kathleen Mansfield 1888-1923
See Mansfield, Katherine
See also CA 104; 134; DA

**Beauvoir, Simone (Lucie Ernestine Marie
  Bertrand) de**
  1908-1986 . . . **CLC 1, 2, 4, 8, 14, 31, 44,**
                        50, 71
See also CA 9-12R; 118; CANR 28; DA;
  DLB 72; DLBY 86; MTCW; WLC

Becker, Jurek 1937- . . . . **CLC 7, 19**
See also CA 85-88; DLB 75

Becker, Walter 1950- . . . . **CLC 26**

Beckett, Samuel (Barclay)
  1906-1989 . . . . . **CLC 1, 2, 3, 4, 6, 9, 10,**
                          11, 14, 18, 29, 57, 59
See also CA 5-8R; 130; CANR 33;
  CDBLB 1945-1960; DA; DLB 13, 15;
  DLBY 90; MTCW; WLC

Beckford, William 1760-1844 . . . . **NCLC 16**
See also DLB 39

Beckman, Gunnel 1910- . . . . **CLC 26**
See also CA 33-36R; CANR 15; CLR 25;
  MAICYA; SAAS 9; SATA 6

Becque, Henri 1837-1899 . . . . **NCLC 3**

Beddoes, Thomas Lovell
  1803-1849 . . . . **NCLC 3**
See also DLB 96

Bedford, Donald F.
See Fearing, Kenneth (Flexner)

Beecher, Catharine Esther
  1800-1878 . . . . **NCLC 30**
See also DLB 1

Beecher, John 1904-1980 . . . . **CLC 6**
See also AITN 1; CA 5-8R; 105; CANR 8

Beer, Johann 1655-1700 . . . . **LC 5**

Beer, Patricia 1924- . . . . **CLC 58**
See also CA 61-64; CANR 13; DLB 40

Beerbohm, Henry Maximilian
  1872-1956 . . . . **TCLC 1, 24**
See also CA 104; DLB 34, 100

Begiebing, Robert J(ohn) 1946- . . . . . **CLC 70**
See also CA 122; CANR 40

Behan, Brendan
  1923-1964 . . . . **CLC 1, 8, 11, 15**
See also CA 73-76; CANR 33;
  CDBLB 1945-1960; DLB 13; MTCW

Behn, Aphra 1640(?)-1689 . . . . **LC 1**
See also DA; DLB 39, 80, 131; WLC

Behrman, S(amuel) N(athaniel)
  1893-1973 . . . . **CLC 40**
See also CA 13-16; 45-48; CAP 1; DLB 7,
  44

Belasco, David 1853-1931 . . . . **TCLC 3**
See also CA 104; DLB 7

Belcheva, Elisaveta 1893- . . . . **CLC 10**

Beldone, Phil "Cheech"
See Ellison, Harlan

Beleno
See Azuela, Mariano

Belinski, Vissarion Grigoryevich
  1811-1848 . . . . **NCLC 5**

Belitt, Ben 1911- . . . . **CLC 22**
See also CA 13-16R; CAAS 4; CANR 7;
  DLB 5

Bell, James Madison 1826-1902 . . . **TCLC 43**
See also BLC 1; BW; CA 122; 124; DLB 50

Bell, Madison (Smartt) 1957- . . . . . . **CLC 41**
See also CA 111; CANR 28

Bell, Marvin (Hartley) 1937- . . . . . **CLC 8, 31**
See also CA 21-24R; CAAS 14; DLB 5;
  MTCW

Bell, W. L. D.
See Mencken, H(enry) L(ouis)

Bellamy, Atwood C.
See Mencken, H(enry) L(ouis)

Bellamy, Edward 1850-1898 . . . . . . **NCLC 4**
See also DLB 12

Bellin, Edward J.
See Kuttner, Henry

Bontemps, Arna(ud Wendell)
1902-1973 . . . . **CLC 1, 18**
See also BLC 1; BW; CA 1-4R; 41-44R;
CANR 4, 35; CLR 6; DLB 48, 51;
MAICYA; MTCW; SATA 2, 24, 44

Booth, Martin 1944- . . . . **CLC 13**
See also CA 93-96; CAAS 2

Booth, Philip 1925- . . . . **CLC 23**
See also CA 5-8R; CANR 5; DLBY 82

Booth, Wayne C(layson) 1921- . . . . . **CLC 24**
See also CA 1-4R; CAAS 5; CANR 3;
DLB 67

Borchert, Wolfgang 1921-1947 . . . . . **TCLC 5**
See also CA 104; DLB 69, 124

Borel, Petrus 1809-1859 . . . . **NCLC 41**

Borges, Jorge Luis
1899-1986 . . . **CLC 1, 2, 3, 4, 6, 8, 9, 10,
13, 19, 44, 48; SSC 4**
See also CA 21-24R; CANR 19, 33; DA;
DLB 113; DLBY 86; HW; MTCW; WLC

Borowski, Tadeusz 1922-1951 . . . . . . **TCLC 9**
See also CA 106

Borrow, George (Henry)
1803-1881 . . . . **NCLC 9**
See also DLB 21, 55

Bosman, Herman Charles
1905-1951 . . . . **TCLC 49**

Bosschere, Jean de 1878(?)-1953 . . . **TCLC 19**
See also CA 115

Boswell, James 1740-1795 . . . . **LC 4**
See also CDBLB 1660-1789; DA; DLB 104;
WLC

Bottoms, David 1949- . . . . **CLC 53**
See also CA 105; CANR 22; DLB 120;
DLBY 83

Boucicault, Dion 1820-1890 . . . . . . **NCLC 41**

Boucolon, Maryse 1937-
See Conde, Maryse
See also CA 110; CANR 30

Bourget, Paul (Charles Joseph)
1852-1935 . . . . **TCLC 12**
See also CA 107; DLB 123

Bourjaily, Vance (Nye) 1922- . . . . **CLC 8, 62**
See also CA 1-4R; CAAS 1; CANR 2;
DLB 2

Bourne, Randolph S(illiman)
1886-1918 . . . . **TCLC 16**
See also CA 117; DLB 63

Bova, Ben(jamin William) 1932- . . . . **CLC 45**
See also CA 5-8R; CANR 11; CLR 3;
DLBY 81; MAICYA; MTCW; SATA 6,
68

Bowen, Elizabeth (Dorothea Cole)
1899-1973 . . . . . **CLC 1, 3, 6, 11, 15, 22;
SSC 3**
See also CA 17-18; 41-44R; CANR 35;
CAP 2; CDBLB 1945-1960; DLB 15;
MTCW

Bowering, George 1935- . . . . **CLC 15, 47**
See also CA 21-24R; CAAS 16; CANR 10;
DLB 53

Bowering, Marilyn R(uthe) 1949- . . . **CLC 32**
See also CA 101

Bowers, Edgar 1924- . . . . **CLC 9**
See also CA 5-8R; CANR 24; DLB 5

Bowie, David . . . . **CLC 17**
See also Jones, David Robert

Bowles, Jane (Sydney)
1917-1973 . . . . **CLC 3, 68**
See also CA 19-20; 41-44R; CAP 2

Bowles, Paul (Frederick)
1910- . . . . **CLC 1, 2, 19, 53; SSC 3**
See also CA 1-4R; CAAS 1; CANR 1, 19;
DLB 5, 6; MTCW

Box, Edgar
See Vidal, Gore

Boyd, Nancy
See Millay, Edna St. Vincent

Boyd, William 1952- . . . . **CLC 28, 53, 70**
See also CA 114; 120

Boyle, Kay
1902-1992 . . . . . **CLC 1, 5, 19, 58; SSC 5**
See also CA 13-16R; 140; CAAS 1;
CANR 29; DLB 4, 9, 48, 86; MTCW

Boyle, Mark
See Kienzle, William X(avier)

Boyle, Patrick 1905-1982 . . . . **CLC 19**
See also CA 127

Boyle, T. Coraghessan 1948- . . . . **CLC 36, 55**
See also BEST 90:4; CA 120; DLBY 86

Boz
See Dickens, Charles (John Huffam)

Brackenridge, Hugh Henry
1748-1816 . . . . **NCLC 7**
See also DLB 11, 37

Bradbury, Edward P.
See Moorcock, Michael (John)

Bradbury, Malcolm (Stanley)
1932- . . . . **CLC 32, 61**
See also CA 1-4R; CANR 1, 33; DLB 14;
MTCW

Bradbury, Ray (Douglas)
1920- . . . . **CLC 1, 3, 10, 15, 42**
See also AITN 1, 2; CA 1-4R; CANR 2, 30;
CDALB 1968-1988; DA; DLB 2, 8;
MTCW; SATA 11, 64; WLC

Bradford, Gamaliel 1863-1932 . . . . . **TCLC 36**
See also DLB 17

Bradley, David (Henry, Jr.) 1950- . . **CLC 23**
See also BLC 1; BW; CA 104; CANR 26;
DLB 33

Bradley, John Ed 1959- . . . . **CLC 55**

Bradley, Marion Zimmer 1930- . . . . . **CLC 30**
See also AAYA 9; CA 57-60; CAAS 10;
CANR 7, 31; DLB 8; MTCW

Bradstreet, Anne 1612(?)-1672 . . . . **LC 4**
See also CDALB 1640-1865; DA; DLB 24

Bragg, Melvyn 1939- . . . . **CLC 10**
See also BEST 89:3; CA 57-60; CANR 10;
DLB 14

Braine, John (Gerard)
1922-1986 . . . . **CLC 1, 3, 41**
See also CA 1-4R; 120; CANR 1, 33;
CDBLB 1945-1960; DLB 15; DLBY 86;
MTCW

Brammer, William 1930(?)-1978 . . . . **CLC 31**
See also CA 77-80

Brancati, Vitaliano 1907-1954 . . . . . **TCLC 12**
See also CA 109

Brancato, Robin F(idler) 1936- . . . . . **CLC 35**
See also AAYA 9; CA 69-72; CANR 11;
SAAS 9; SATA 23

Brand, Max
See Faust, Frederick (Schiller)

Brand, Millen 1906-1980 . . . . **CLC 7**
See also CA 21-24R; 97-100

Branden, Barbara . . . . **CLC 44**

Brandes, Georg (Morris Cohen)
1842-1927 . . . . **TCLC 10**
See also CA 105

Brandys, Kazimierz 1916- . . . . **CLC 62**

Branley, Franklyn M(ansfield)
1915- . . . . **CLC 21**
See also CA 33-36R; CANR 14, 39;
CLR 13; MAICYA; SAAS 16; SATA 4,
68

Brathwaite, Edward (Kamau)
1930- . . . . **CLC 11**
See also BW; CA 25-28R; CANR 11, 26;
DLB 125

Brautigan, Richard (Gary)
1935-1984 . . . . **CLC 1, 3, 5, 9, 12, 34, 42**
See also CA 53-56; 113; CANR 34; DLB 2,
5; DLBY 80, 84; MTCW; SATA 56

Braverman, Kate 1950- . . . . **CLC 67**
See also CA 89-92

Brecht, Bertolt
1898-1956 . . . . . **TCLC 1, 6, 13, 35; DC 3**
See also CA 104; 133; DA; DLB 56, 124;
MTCW; WLC

Brecht, Eugen Berthold Friedrich
See Brecht, Bertolt

Bremer, Fredrika 1801-1865 . . . . . **NCLC 11**

Brennan, Christopher John
1870-1932 . . . . **TCLC 17**
See also CA 117

Brennan, Maeve 1917- . . . . **CLC 5**
See also CA 81-84

Brentano, Clemens (Maria)
1778-1842 . . . . **NCLC 1**

Brent of Bin Bin
See Franklin, (Stella Maraia Sarah) Miles

Brenton, Howard 1942- . . . . **CLC 31**
See also CA 69-72; CANR 33; DLB 13;
MTCW

Breslin, James 1930-
See Breslin, Jimmy
See also CA 73-76; CANR 31; MTCW

Breslin, Jimmy . . . . **CLC 4, 43**
See also Breslin, James
See also AITN 1

Bresson, Robert 1907- . . . . **CLC 16**
See also CA 110

Breton, Andre 1896-1966 . . . **CLC 2, 9, 15, 54**
See also CA 19-20; 25-28R; CANR 40;
CAP 2; DLB 65; MTCW

Breytenbach, Breyten 1939(?)- . . **CLC 23, 37**
See also CA 113; 129

Bridgers, Sue Ellen 1942- . . . . **CLC 26**
See also AAYA 8; CA 65-68; CANR 11,
36; CLR 18; DLB 52; MAICYA;
SAAS 1; SATA 22

Bridges, Robert (Seymour)
1844-1930 . . . . **TCLC 1**
See also CA 104; CDBLB 1890-1914;
DLB 19, 98

Bridie, James . . . . **TCLC 3**
See also Mavor, Osborne Henry
See also DLB 10

Brin, David 1950- . . . . **CLC 34**
See also CA 102; CANR 24; SATA 65

Brink, Andre (Philippus)
1935- . . . . **CLC 18, 36**
See also CA 104; CANR 39; MTCW

Brinsmead, H(esba) F(ay) 1922- . . . . **CLC 21**
See also CA 21-24R; CANR 10; MAICYA;
SAAS 5; SATA 18

Brittain, Vera (Mary)
1893(?)-1970 . . . . **CLC 23**
See also CA 13-16; 25-28R; CAP 1; MTCW

Broch, Hermann 1886-1951 . . . . **TCLC 20**
See also CA 117; DLB 85, 124

Brock, Rose
See Hansen, Joseph

Brodkey, Harold 1930- . . . . **CLC 56**
See also CA 111; DLB 130

Brodsky, Iosif Alexandrovich 1940-
See Brodsky, Joseph
See also AITN 1; CA 41-44R; CANR 37;
MTCW

Brodsky, Joseph . . . . **CLC 4, 6, 13, 36, 50**
See also Brodsky, Iosif Alexandrovich

Brodsky, Michael Mark 1948- . . . . . **CLC 19**
See also CA 102; CANR 18, 41

Bromell, Henry 1947- . . . . **CLC 5**
See also CA 53-56; CANR 9

Bromfield, Louis (Brucker)
1896-1956 . . . . **TCLC 11**
See also CA 107; DLB 4, 9, 86

Broner, E(sther) M(asserman)
1930- . . . . **CLC 19**
See also CA 17-20R; CANR 8, 25; DLB 28

Bronk, William 1918- . . . . **CLC 10**
See also CA 89-92; CANR 23

Bronstein, Lev Davidovich
See Trotsky, Leon

Bronte, Anne 1820-1849 . . . . **NCLC 4**
See also DLB 21

Bronte, Charlotte
1816-1855 . . . . **NCLC 3, 8, 33**
See also CDBLB 1832-1890; DA; DLB 21;
WLC

Bronte, (Jane) Emily
1818-1848 . . . . **NCLC 16, 35**
See also CDBLB 1832-1890; DA; DLB 21,
32; WLC

Brooke, Frances 1724-1789 . . . . **LC 6**
See also DLB 39, 99

Brooke, Henry 1703(?)-1783 . . . . **LC 1**
See also DLB 39

Brooke, Rupert (Chawner)
1887-1915 . . . . **TCLC 2, 7**
See also CA 104; 132; CDBLB 1914-1945;
DA; DLB 19; MTCW; WLC

Brooke-Haven, P.
See Wodehouse, P(elham) G(renville)

Brooke-Rose, Christine 1926- . . . . . . **CLC 40**
See also CA 13-16R; DLB 14

Brookner, Anita 1928- . . . . . . **CLC 32, 34, 51**
See also CA 114; 120; CANR 37; DLBY 87;
MTCW

Brooks, Cleanth 1906- . . . . **CLC 24**
See also CA 17-20R; CANR 33, 35;
DLB 63; MTCW

Brooks, George
See Baum, L(yman) Frank

Brooks, Gwendolyn
1917- . . . . . . **CLC 1, 2, 4, 5, 15, 49; PC 7**
See also AITN 1; BLC 1; BW; CA 1-4R;
CANR 1, 27; CDALB 1941-1968;
CLR 27; DA; DLB 5, 76; MTCW;
SATA 6; WLC

Brooks, Mel . . . . **CLC 12**
See also Kaminsky, Melvin
See also DLB 26

Brooks, Peter 1938- . . . . **CLC 34**
See also CA 45-48; CANR 1

Brooks, Van Wyck 1886-1963 . . . . . . **CLC 29**
See also CA 1-4R; CANR 6; DLB 45, 63,
103

Brophy, Brigid (Antonia)
1929- . . . . **CLC 6, 11, 29**
See also CA 5-8R; CAAS 4; CANR 25;
DLB 14; MTCW

Brosman, Catharine Savage 1934- . . . . **CLC 9**
See also CA 61-64; CANR 21

Brother Antoninus
See Everson, William (Oliver)

Broughton, T(homas) Alan 1936- . . . **CLC 19**
See also CA 45-48; CANR 2, 23

Broumas, Olga 1949- . . . . **CLC 10, 73**
See also CA 85-88; CANR 20

Brown, Charles Brockden
1771-1810 . . . . **NCLC 22**
See also CDALB 1640-1865; DLB 37, 59,
73

Brown, Christy 1932-1981 . . . . **CLC 63**
See also CA 105; 104; DLB 14

Brown, Claude 1937- . . . . **CLC 30**
See also AAYA 7; BLC 1; BW; CA 73-76

Brown, Dee (Alexander) 1908- . . **CLC 18, 47**
See also CA 13-16R; CAAS 6; CANR 11;
DLBY 80; MTCW; SATA 5

Brown, George
See Wertmueller, Lina

Brown, George Douglas
1869-1902 . . . . **TCLC 28**

Brown, George Mackay 1921- . . . . **CLC 5, 48**
See also CA 21-24R; CAAS 6; CANR 12,
37; DLB 14, 27; MTCW; SATA 35

Brown, (William) Larry 1951- . . . . . . **CLC 73**
See also CA 130; 134

Brown, Moses
See Barrett, William (Christopher)

Brown, Rita Mae 1944- . . . . **CLC 18, 43**
See also CA 45-48; CANR 2, 11, 35;
MTCW

Brown, Roderick (Langmere) Haig-
See Haig-Brown, Roderick (Langmere)

Brown, Rosellen 1939- . . . . **CLC 32**
See also CA 77-80; CAAS 10; CANR 14

Brown, Sterling Allen
1901-1989 . . . . **CLC 1, 23, 59**
See also BLC 1; BW; CA 85-88; 127;
CANR 26; DLB 48, 51, 63; MTCW

Brown, Will
See Ainsworth, William Harrison

Brown, William Wells
1813-1884 . . . . **NCLC 2; DC 1**
See also BLC 1; DLB 3, 50

Browne, (Clyde) Jackson 1948(?)- . . . **CLC 21**
See also CA 120

Browning, Elizabeth Barrett
1806-1861 . . . . **NCLC 1, 16; PC 6**
See also CDBLB 1832-1890; DA; DLB 32;
WLC

Browning, Robert
1812-1889 . . . . **NCLC 19; PC 2**
See also CDBLB 1832-1890; DA; DLB 32;
YABC 1

Browning, Tod 1882-1962 . . . . **CLC 16**
See also CA 117

Bruccoli, Matthew J(oseph) 1931- . . **CLC 34**
See also CA 9-12R; CANR 7; DLB 103

Bruce, Lenny . . . . **CLC 21**
See also Schneider, Leonard Alfred

Bruin, John
See Brutus, Dennis

Brulls, Christian
See Simenon, Georges (Jacques Christian)

Brunner, John (Kilian Houston)
1934- . . . . **CLC 8, 10**
See also CA 1-4R; CAAS 8; CANR 2, 37;
MTCW

Brutus, Dennis 1924- . . . . **CLC 43**
See also BLC 1; BW; CA 49-52; CAAS 14;
CANR 2, 27; DLB 117

Bryan, C(ourtlandt) D(ixon) B(arnes)
1936- . . . . **CLC 29**
See also CA 73-76; CANR 13

Bryan, Michael
See Moore, Brian

Bryant, William Cullen
1794-1878 . . . . **NCLC 6**
See also CDALB 1640-1865; DA; DLB 3,
43, 59

Bryusov, Valery Yakovlevich
1873-1924 . . . . **TCLC 10**
See also CA 107

Buchan, John 1875-1940 . . . . **TCLC 41**
See also CA 108; DLB 34, 70; YABC 2

Buchanan, George 1506-1582 . . . . **LC 4**

Buchheim, Lothar-Guenther 1918- . . . **CLC 6**
See also CA 85-88

Buchner, (Karl) Georg
1813-1837 . . . . **NCLC 26**

Buchwald, Art(hur) 1925- . . . . **CLC 33**
See also AITN 1; CA 5-8R; CANR 21;
MTCW; SATA 10

Buck, Pearl S(ydenstricker)
1892-1973 . . . . **CLC 7, 11, 18**
See also AITN 1; CA 1-4R; 41-44R;
CANR 1, 34; DA; DLB 9, 102; MTCW;
SATA 1, 25

Campbell, Joseph 1904-1987 . . . . **CLC 69**
See also AAYA 3; BEST 89:2; CA 1-4R;
124; CANR 3, 28; MTCW

Campbell, (John) Ramsey 1946- . . . . **CLC 42**
See also CA 57-60; CANR 7

Campbell, (Ignatius) Roy (Dunnachie)
1901-1957 . . . . **TCLC 5**
See also CA 104; DLB 20

Campbell, Thomas 1777-1844 . . . . **NCLC 19**
See also DLB 93

Campbell, Wilfred . . . . **TCLC 9**
See Campbell, William

Campbell, William 1858(?)-1918
See Campbell, Wilfred
See also CA 106; DLB 92

Campos, Alvaro de
See Pessoa, Fernando (Antonio Nogueira)

Camus, Albert
1913-1960 . . . **CLC 1, 2, 4, 9, 11, 14, 32,**
63, 69; DC 2; SSC 9
See also CA 89-92; DA; DLB 72; MTCW;
WLC

Canby, Vincent 1924- . . . . **CLC 13**
See also CA 81-84

Cancale
See Desnos, Robert

Canetti, Elias 1905- . . . . . . **CLC 3, 14, 25, 75**
See also CA 21-24R; CANR 23; DLB 85,
124; MTCW

Canin, Ethan 1960- . . . . **CLC 55**
See also CA 131; 135

Cannon, Curt
See Hunter, Evan

Cape, Judith
See Page, P(atricia) K(athleen)

Capek, Karel
1890-1938 . . . . **TCLC 6, 37; DC 1**
See also CA 104; 140; DA; WLC

Capote, Truman
1924-1984 . . . . . **CLC 1, 3, 8, 13, 19, 34,**
38, 58; SSC 2
See also CA 5-8R; 113; CANR 18;
CDALB 1941-1968; DA; DLB 2;
DLBY 80, 84; MTCW; WLC

Capra, Frank 1897-1991 . . . . **CLC 16**
See also CA 61-64; 135

Caputo, Philip 1941- . . . . **CLC 32**
See also CA 73-76; CANR 40

Card, Orson Scott 1951- . . . . **CLC 44, 47, 50**
See also CA 102; CANR 27; MTCW

Cardenal (Martinez), Ernesto
1925- . . . . **CLC 31**
See also CA 49-52; CANR 2, 32; HW;
MTCW

Carducci, Giosue 1835-1907 . . . . . . **TCLC 32**

Carew, Thomas 1595(?)-1640 . . . . **LC 13**
See also DLB 126

Carey, Ernestine Gilbreth 1908- . . . . **CLC 17**
See also CA 5-8R; SATA 2

Carey, Peter 1943- . . . . **CLC 40, 55**
See also CA 123; 127; MTCW

Carleton, William 1794-1869 . . . . . . **NCLC 3**

Carlisle, Henry (Coffin) 1926- . . . . . . **CLC 33**
See also CA 13-16R; CANR 15

Carlsen, Chris
See Holdstock, Robert P.

Carlson, Ron(ald F.) 1947- . . . . **CLC 54**
See also CA 105; CANR 27

Carlyle, Thomas 1795-1881 . . . . . **NCLC 22**
See also CDBLB 1789-1832; DA; DLB 55

Carman, (William) Bliss
1861-1929 . . . . **TCLC 7**
See also CA 104; DLB 92

Carossa, Hans 1878-1956 . . . . **TCLC 48**
See also DLB 66

Carpenter, Don(ald Richard)
1931- . . . . **CLC 41**
See also CA 45-48; CANR 1

Carpentier (y Valmont), Alejo
1904-1980 . . . . **CLC 8, 11, 38**
See also CA 65-68; 97-100; CANR 11;
DLB 113; HW

Carr, Emily 1871-1945 . . . . **TCLC 32**
See also DLB 68

Carr, John Dickson 1906-1977 . . . . . . **CLC 3**
See also CA 49-52; 69-72; CANR 3, 33;
MTCW

Carr, Philippa
See Hibbert, Eleanor Alice Burford

Carr, Virginia Spencer 1929- . . . . . . **CLC 34**
See also CA 61-64; DLB 111

Carrier, Roch 1937- . . . . **CLC 13, 78**
See also CA 130; DLB 53

Carroll, James P. 1943(?)- . . . . **CLC 38**
See also CA 81-84

Carroll, Jim 1951- . . . . **CLC 35**
See also CA 45-48

Carroll, Lewis . . . . **NCLC 2**
See also Dodgson, Charles Lutwidge
See also CDBLB 1832-1890; CLR 2, 18;
DLB 18; WLC

Carroll, Paul Vincent 1900-1968 . . . . **CLC 10**
See also CA 9-12R; 25-28R; DLB 10

Carruth, Hayden 1921- . . . . **CLC 4, 7, 10, 18**
See also CA 9-12R; CANR 4, 38; DLB 5;
MTCW; SATA 47

Carson, Rachel Louise 1907-1964 . . . **CLC 71**
See also CA 77-80; CANR 35; MTCW;
SATA 23

Carter, Angela (Olive)
1940-1992 . . . . **CLC 5, 41, 76**
See also CA 53-56; 136; CANR 12, 36;
DLB 14; MTCW; SATA 66;
SATA-Obit 70

Carter, Nick
See Smith, Martin Cruz

Carver, Raymond
1938-1988 . . . **CLC 22, 36, 53, 55; SSC 8**
See also CA 33-36R; 126; CANR 17, 34;
DLB 130; DLBY 84, 88; MTCW

Cary, (Arthur) Joyce (Lunel)
1888-1957 . . . . **TCLC 1, 29**
See also CA 104; CDBLB 1914-1945;
DLB 15, 100

Casanova de Seingalt, Giovanni Jacopo
1725-1798 . . . . **LC 13**

Casares, Adolfo Bioy
See Bioy Casares, Adolfo

Casely-Hayford, J(oseph) E(phraim)
1866-1930 . . . . **TCLC 24**
See also BLC 1; CA 123

Casey, John (Dudley) 1939- . . . . **CLC 59**
See also BEST 90:2; CA 69-72; CANR 23

Casey, Michael 1947- . . . . **CLC 2**
See also CA 65-68; DLB 5

Casey, Patrick
See Thurman, Wallace (Henry)

Casey, Warren (Peter) 1935-1988 . . . **CLC 12**
See also CA 101; 127

Casona, Alejandro . . . . **CLC 49**
See also Alvarez, Alejandro Rodriguez

Cassavetes, John 1929-1989 . . . . **CLC 20**
See also CA 85-88; 127

Cassill, R(onald) V(erlin) 1919- . . . **CLC 4, 23**
See also CA 9-12R; CAAS 1; CANR 7;
DLB 6

Cassity, (Allen) Turner 1929- . . . . **CLC 6, 42**
See also CA 17-20R; CAAS 8; CANR 11;
DLB 105

Castaneda, Carlos 1931(?)- . . . . **CLC 12**
See also CA 25-28R; CANR 32; HW;
MTCW

Castedo, Elena 1937- . . . . **CLC 65**
See also CA 132

Castedo-Ellerman, Elena
See Castedo, Elena

Castellanos, Rosario 1925-1974 . . . . . **CLC 66**
See also CA 131; 53-56; DLB 113; HW

Castelvetro, Lodovico 1505-1571 . . . . . **LC 12**

Castiglione, Baldassare 1478-1529 . . . **LC 12**

Castle, Robert
See Hamilton, Edmond

Castro, Guillen de 1569-1631 . . . . **LC 19**

Castro, Rosalia de 1837-1885 . . . . . **NCLC 3**

Cather, Willa
See Cather, Willa Sibert

Cather, Willa Sibert
1873-1947 . . . . . . **TCLC 1, 11, 31; SSC 2**
See also CA 104; 128; CDALB 1865-1917;
DA; DLB 9, 54, 78; DLBD 1; MTCW;
SATA 30; WLC

Catton, (Charles) Bruce
1899-1978 . . . . **CLC 35**
See also AITN 1; CA 5-8R; 81-84;
CANR 7; DLB 17; SATA 2, 24

Cauldwell, Frank
See King, Francis (Henry)

Caunitz, William J. 1933- . . . . **CLC 34**
See also BEST 89:3; CA 125; 130

Causley, Charles (Stanley) 1917- . . . . . **CLC 7**
See also CA 9-12R; CANR 5, 35; CLR 30;
DLB 27; MTCW; SATA 3, 66

Caute, David 1936- . . . . **CLC 29**
See also CA 1-4R; CAAS 4; CANR 1, 33;
DLB 14

Cavafy, C(onstantine) P(eter) . . . . . . **TCLC 2, 7**
See also Kavafis, Konstantinos Petrou

Cavallo, Evelyn
See Spark, Muriel (Sarah)

Cavanna, Betty .... CLC 12
See also Harrison, Elizabeth Cavanna
See also MAICYA; SAAS 4; SATA 1, 30

Caxton, William 1421(?)-1491(?)..... LC 17

Cayrol, Jean 1911-............... CLC 11
See also CA 89-92; DLB 83

Cela, Camilo Jose 1916-...... CLC 4, 13, 59
See also BEST 90:2; CA 21-24R; CAAS 10;
CANR 21, 32; DLBY 89; HW; MTCW

Celan, Paul .... CLC 53
See also Antschel, Paul
See also DLB 69

Celine, Louis-Ferdinand
.... CLC 1, 3, 4, 7, 9, 15, 47
See also Destouches, Louis-Ferdinand
See also DLB 72

Cellini, Benvenuto 1500-1571 .... LC 7

Cendrars, Blaise
See Sauser-Hall, Frederic

Cernuda (y Bidon), Luis
1902-1963 .... CLC 54
See also CA 131; 89-92; HW

Cervantes (Saavedra), Miguel de
1547-1616 .... LC 6, 23; SSC 12
See also DA; WLC

Cesaire, Aime (Fernand) 1913- .. CLC 19, 32
See also BLC 1; BW; CA 65-68; CANR 24;
MTCW

Chabon, Michael 1965(?)- .... CLC 55
See also CA 139

Chabrol, Claude 1930- .... CLC 16
See also CA 110

Challans, Mary 1905-1983
See Renault, Mary
See also CA 81-84; 111; SATA 23, 36

Challis, George
See Faust, Frederick (Schiller)

Chambers, Aidan 1934- .... CLC 35
See also CA 25-28R; CANR 12, 31;
MAICYA; SAAS 12; SATA 1, 69

Chambers, James 1948-
See Cliff, Jimmy
See also CA 124

Chambers, Jessie
See Lawrence, D(avid) H(erbert Richards)

Chambers, Robert W. 1865-1933... TCLC 41

Chandler, Raymond (Thornton)
1888-1959 .... TCLC 1, 7
See also CA 104; 129; CDALB 1929-1941;
DLBD 6; MTCW

Chang, Jung 1952- .... CLC 71

Channing, William Ellery
1780-1842 .... NCLC 17
See also DLB 1, 59

Chaplin, Charles Spencer
1889-1977 .... CLC 16
See also Chaplin, Charlie
See also CA 81-84; 73-76

Chaplin, Charlie
See Chaplin, Charles Spencer
See also DLB 44

Chapman, George 1559(?)-1634...... LC 22
See also DLB 62, 121

Chapman, Graham 1941-1989 ...... CLC 21
See also Monty Python
See also CA 116; 129; CANR 35

Chapman, John Jay 1862-1933 ..... TCLC 7
See also CA 104

Chapman, Walker
See Silverberg, Robert

Chappell, Fred (Davis) 1936-.... CLC 40, 78
See also CA 5-8R; CAAS 4; CANR 8, 33;
DLB 6, 105

Char, Rene(-Emile)
1907-1988 .... CLC 9, 11, 14, 55
See also CA 13-16R; 124; CANR 32;
MTCW

Charby, Jay
See Ellison, Harlan

Chardin, Pierre Teilhard de
See Teilhard de Chardin, (Marie Joseph)
Pierre

Charles I 1600-1649 .... LC 13

Charyn, Jerome 1937- .... CLC 5, 8, 18
See also CA 5-8R; CAAS 1; CANR 7;
DLBY 83; MTCW

Chase, Mary (Coyle) 1907-1981 ...... DC 1
See also CA 77-80; 105; SATA 17, 29

Chase, Mary Ellen 1887-1973....... CLC 2
See also CA 13-16; 41-44R; CAP 1;
SATA 10

Chase, Nicholas
See Hyde, Anthony

Chateaubriand, Francois Rene de
1768-1848 .... NCLC 3
See also DLB 119

Chatterje, Sarat Chandra 1876-1936(?)
See Chatterji, Saratchandra
See also CA 109

Chatterji, Bankim Chandra
1838-1894 .... NCLC 19

Chatterji, Saratchandra .... TCLC 13
See also Chatterje, Sarat Chandra

Chatterton, Thomas 1752-1770 .... LC 3
See also DLB 109

Chatwin, (Charles) Bruce
1940-1989 .... CLC 28, 57, 59
See also AAYA 4; BEST 90:1; CA 85-88;
127

Chaucer, Daniel
See Ford, Ford Madox

Chaucer, Geoffrey 1340(?)-1400 ..... LC 17
See also CDBLB Before 1660; DA

Chaviaras, Strates 1935-
See Haviaras, Stratis
See also CA 105

Chayefsky, Paddy .... CLC 23
See also Chayefsky, Sidney
See also DLB 7, 44; DLBY 81

Chayefsky, Sidney 1923-1981
See Chayefsky, Paddy
See also CA 9-12R; 104; CANR 18

Chedid, Andree 1920-............ CLC 47

Cheever, John
1912-1982 ..... CLC 3, 7, 8, 11, 15, 25,
64; SSC 1
See also CA 5-8R; 106; CABS 1; CANR 5,
27; CDALB 1941-1968; DA; DLB 2, 102;
DLBY 80, 82; MTCW; WLC

Cheever, Susan 1943-......... CLC 18, 48
See also CA 103; CANR 27; DLBY 82

Chekhonte, Antosha
See Chekhov, Anton (Pavlovich)

Chekhov, Anton (Pavlovich)
1860-1904 ...... TCLC 3, 10, 31; SSC 2
See also CA 104; 124; DA; WLC

Chernyshevsky, Nikolay Gavrilovich
1828-1889 .... NCLC 1

Cherry, Carolyn Janice 1942-
See Cherryh, C. J.
See also CA 65-68; CANR 10

Cherryh, C. J. .... CLC 35
See also Cherry, Carolyn Janice
See also DLBY 80

Chesnutt, Charles W(addell)
1858-1932 .... TCLC 5, 39; SSC 7
See also BLC 1; BW; CA 106; 125; DLB 12,
50, 78; MTCW

Chester, Alfred 1929(?)-1971 .... CLC 49
See also CA 33-36R; DLB 130

Chesterton, G(ilbert) K(eith)
1874-1936 .... TCLC 1, 6; SSC 1
See also CA 104; 132; CDBLB 1914-1945;
DLB 10, 19, 34, 70, 98; MTCW;
SATA 27

Chiang Pin-chin 1904-1986
See Ding Ling
See also CA 118

Ch'ien Chung-shu 1910-.......... CLC 22
See also CA 130; MTCW

Child, L. Maria
See Child, Lydia Maria

Child, Lydia Maria 1802-1880 .... NCLC 6
See also DLB 1, 74; SATA 67

Child, Mrs.
See Child, Lydia Maria

Child, Philip 1898-1978 .... CLC 19, 68
See also CA 13-14; CAP 1; SATA 47

Childress, Alice 1920-.......... CLC 12, 15
See also AAYA 8; BLC 1; BW; CA 45-48;
CANR 3, 27; CLR 14; DLB 7, 38;
MAICYA; MTCW; SATA 7, 48

Chislett, (Margaret) Anne 1943-.... CLC 34

Chitty, Thomas Willes 1926-....... CLC 11
See also Hinde, Thomas
See also CA 5-8R

Chomette, Rene Lucien 1898-1981 .. CLC 20
See also Clair, Rene
See also CA 103

Chopin, Kate .... TCLC 5, 14; SSC 8
See also Chopin, Katherine
See also CDALB 1865-1917; DA; DLB 12,
78

Chopin, Katherine 1851-1904
See Chopin, Kate
See also CA 104; 122

Chretien de Troyes
c. 12th cent. - .... CMLC 10

Christie
  See Ichikawa, Kon

Christie, Agatha (Mary Clarissa)
    1890-1976 ...... **CLC 1, 6, 8, 12, 39, 48**
  See also AAYA 9; AITN 1, 2; CA 17-20R;
    61-64; CANR 10, 37; CDBLB 1914-1945;
    DLB 13, 77; MTCW; SATA 36

Christie, (Ann) Philippa
  See Pearce, Philippa
  See also CA 5-8R; CANR 4

Christine de Pizan   1365(?)-1431(?) .... **LC 9**

Chubb, Elmer
  See Masters, Edgar Lee

Chulkov, Mikhail Dmitrievich
    1743-1792 .... **LC 2**

Churchill, Caryl   1938- .... **CLC 31, 55**
  See also CA 102; CANR 22; DLB 13;
    MTCW

Churchill, Charles   1731-1764 .... **LC 3**
  See also DLB 109

Chute, Carolyn   1947- .... **CLC 39**
  See also CA 123

Ciardi, John (Anthony)
    1916-1986 .... **CLC 10, 40, 44**
  See also CA 5-8R; 118; CAAS 2; CANR 5,
    33; CLR 19; DLB 5; DLBY 86;
    MAICYA; MTCW; SATA 1, 46, 65

Cicero, Marcus Tullius
    106B.C.-43B.C. .... **CMLC 3**

Cimino, Michael   1943- .... **CLC 16**
  See also CA 105

Cioran, E(mil) M.   1911- .... **CLC 64**
  See also CA 25-28R

Cisneros, Sandra   1954- .... **CLC 69**
  See also AAYA 9; CA 131; DLB 122; HW

Clair, Rene .... **CLC 20**
  See also Chomette, Rene Lucien

Clampitt, Amy   1920- .... **CLC 32**
  See also CA 110; CANR 29; DLB 105

Clancy, Thomas L., Jr.   1947-
  See Clancy, Tom
  See also CA 125; 131; MTCW

Clancy, Tom .... **CLC 45**
  See also Clancy, Thomas L., Jr.
  See also AAYA 9; BEST 89:1, 90:1

Clare, John   1793-1864 .... **NCLC 9**
  See also DLB 55, 96

Clarin
  See Alas (y Urena), Leopoldo (Enrique
    Garcia)

Clark, (Robert) Brian   1932- .... **CLC 29**
  See also CA 41-44R

Clark, Eleanor   1913- .... **CLC 5, 19**
  See also CA 9-12R; CANR 41; DLB 6

Clark, J. P.
  See Clark, John Pepper
  See also DLB 117

Clark, John Pepper   1935- .... **CLC 38**
  See also Clark, J. P.
  See also BLC 1; BW; CA 65-68; CANR 16

Clark, M. R.
  See Clark, Mavis Thorpe

Clark, Mavis Thorpe   1909- .... **CLC 12**
  See also CA 57-60; CANR 8, 37; CLR 30;
    MAICYA; SAAS 5; SATA 8, 74

Clark, Walter Van Tilburg
    1909-1971 .... **CLC 28**
  See also CA 9-12R; 33-36R; DLB 9;
    SATA 8

Clarke, Arthur C(harles)
    1917- ...... **CLC 1, 4, 13, 18, 35; SSC 3**
  See also AAYA 4; CA 1-4R; CANR 2, 28;
    MAICYA; MTCW; SATA 13, 70

Clarke, Austin   1896-1974 .... **CLC 6, 9**
  See also CA 29-32; 49-52; CAP 2; DLB 10,
    20

Clarke, Austin C(hesterfield)
    1934- .... **CLC 8, 53**
  See also BLC 1; BW; CA 25-28R;
    CAAS 16; CANR 14, 32; DLB 53, 125

Clarke, Gillian   1937- .... **CLC 61**
  See also CA 106; DLB 40

Clarke, Marcus (Andrew Hislop)
    1846-1881 .... **NCLC 19**

Clarke, Shirley   1925- .... **CLC 16**

Clash, The .... **CLC 30**
  See also Headon, (Nicky) Topper; Jones,
    Mick; Simonon, Paul; Strummer, Joe

Claudel, Paul (Louis Charles Marie)
    1868-1955 .... **TCLC 2, 10**
  See also CA 104

Clavell, James (duMaresq)
    1925- .... **CLC 6, 25**
  See also CA 25-28R; CANR 26; MTCW

Cleaver, (Leroy) Eldridge   1935- .... **CLC 30**
  See also BLC 1; BW; CA 21-24R;
    CANR 16

Cleese, John (Marwood)   1939- ..... **CLC 21**
  See also Monty Python
  See also CA 112; 116; CANR 35; MTCW

Cleishbotham, Jebediah
  See Scott, Walter

Cleland, John   1710-1789 .... **LC 2**
  See also DLB 39

Clemens, Samuel Langhorne   1835-1910
  See Twain, Mark
  See also CA 104; 135; CDALB 1865-1917;
    DA; DLB 11, 12, 23, 64, 74; MAICYA;
    YABC 2

Cleophil
  See Congreve, William

Clerihew, E.
  See Bentley, E(dmund) C(lerihew)

Clerk, N. W.
  See Lewis, C(live) S(taples)

Cliff, Jimmy .... **CLC 21**
  See also Chambers, James

Clifton, (Thelma) Lucille
    1936- .... **CLC 19, 66**
  See also BLC 1; BW; CA 49-52; CANR 2,
    24; CLR 5; DLB 5, 41; MAICYA;
    MTCW; SATA 20, 69

Clinton, Dirk
  See Silverberg, Robert

Clough, Arthur Hugh   1819-1861 .. **NCLC 27**
  See also DLB 32

Clutha, Janet Paterson Frame   1924-
  See Frame, Janet
  See also CA 1-4R; CANR 2, 36; MTCW

Clyne, Terence
  See Blatty, William Peter

Cobalt, Martin
  See Mayne, William (James Carter)

Coburn, D(onald) L(ee)   1938- ...... **CLC 10**
  See also CA 89-92

Cocteau, Jean (Maurice Eugene Clement)
    1889-1963 .... **CLC 1, 8, 15, 16, 43**
  See also CA 25-28; CANR 40; CAP 2; DA;
    DLB 65; MTCW; WLC

Codrescu, Andrei   1946- .... **CLC 46**
  See also CA 33-36R; CANR 13, 34

Coe, Max
  See Bourne, Randolph S(illiman)

Coe, Tucker
  See Westlake, Donald E(dwin)

Coetzee, J(ohn) M(ichael)
    1940- .... **CLC 23, 33, 66**
  See also CA 77-80; CANR 41; MTCW

Coffey, Brian
  See Koontz, Dean R(ay)

Cohen, Arthur A(llen)
    1928-1986 .... **CLC 7, 31**
  See also CA 1-4R; 120; CANR 1, 17;
    DLB 28

Cohen, Leonard (Norman)
    1934- .... **CLC 3, 38**
  See also CA 21-24R; CANR 14; DLB 53;
    MTCW

Cohen, Matt   1942- .... **CLC 19**
  See also CA 61-64; CANR 40; DLB 53

Cohen-Solal, Annie   19(?)- .... **CLC 50**

Colegate, Isabel   1931- .... **CLC 36**
  See also CA 17-20R; CANR 8, 22; DLB 14;
    MTCW

Coleman, Emmett
  See Reed, Ishmael

Coleridge, Samuel Taylor
    1772-1834 .... **NCLC 9**
  See also CDBLB 1789-1832; DA; DLB 93,
    107; WLC

Coleridge, Sara   1802-1852 .... **NCLC 31**

Coles, Don   1928- .... **CLC 46**
  See also CA 115; CANR 38

Colette, (Sidonie-Gabrielle)
    1873-1954 ...... **TCLC 1, 5, 16; SSC 10**
  See also CA 104; 131; DLB 65; MTCW

Collett, (Jacobine) Camilla (Wergeland)
    1813-1895 .... **NCLC 22**

Collier, Christopher   1930- .... **CLC 30**
  See also CA 33-36R; CANR 13, 33;
    MAICYA; SATA 16, 70

Collier, James L(incoln)   1928- ..... **CLC 30**
  See also CA 9-12R; CANR 4, 33;
    MAICYA; SATA 8, 70

Collier, Jeremy   1650-1726 .... **LC 6**

Collins, Hunt
  See Hunter, Evan

Collins, Linda   1931- .... **CLC 44**
  See also CA 125

Demijohn, Thom
See Disch, Thomas M(ichael)

de Montherlant, Henry (Milon)
See Montherlant, Henry (Milon) de

de Natale, Francine
See Malzberg, Barry N(athaniel)

Denby, Edwin (Orr) 1903-1983 . . . . . **CLC 48**
See also CA 138; 110

Denis, Julio
See Cortazar, Julio

Denmark, Harrison
See Zelazny, Roger (Joseph)

Dennis, John 1658-1734 . . . . **LC 11**
See also DLB 101

Dennis, Nigel (Forbes) 1912-1989 . . . . **CLC 8**
See also CA 25-28R; 129; DLB 13, 15;
MTCW

De Palma, Brian (Russell) 1940- . . . . **CLC 20**
See also CA 109

De Quincey, Thomas 1785-1859 . . . **NCLC 4**
See also CDBLB 1789-1832; DLB 110

Deren, Eleanora 1908(?)-1961
See Deren, Maya
See also CA 111

Deren, Maya . . . . **CLC 16**
See also Deren, Eleanora

Derleth, August (William)
1909-1971 . . . . **CLC 31**
See also CA 1-4R; 29-32R; CANR 4;
DLB 9; SATA 5

de Routisie, Albert
See Aragon, Louis

Derrida, Jacques 1930- . . . . **CLC 24**
See also CA 124; 127

Derry Down Derry
See Lear, Edward

Dersonnes, Jacques
See Simenon, Georges (Jacques Christian)

Desai, Anita 1937- . . . . **CLC 19, 37**
See also CA 81-84; CANR 33; MTCW;
SATA 63

de Saint-Luc, Jean
See Glassco, John

de Saint Roman, Arnaud
See Aragon, Louis

Descartes, Rene 1596-1650 . . . . **LC 20**

De Sica, Vittorio 1901(?)-1974 . . . . . **CLC 20**
See also CA 117

Desnos, Robert 1900-1945 . . . . **TCLC 22**
See also CA 121

Destouches, Louis-Ferdinand
1894-1961 . . . . **CLC 9, 15**
See also Celine, Louis-Ferdinand
See also CA 85-88; CANR 28; MTCW

Deutsch, Babette 1895-1982 . . . . **CLC 18**
See also CA 1-4R; 108; CANR 4; DLB 45;
SATA 1, 33

Devenant, William 1606-1649 . . . . . . **LC 13**

Devkota, Laxmiprasad
1909-1959 . . . . **TCLC 23**
See also CA 123

De Voto, Bernard (Augustine)
1897-1955 . . . . **TCLC 29**
See also CA 113; DLB 9

De Vries, Peter
1910- . . . . **CLC 1, 2, 3, 7, 10, 28, 46**
See also CA 17-20R; CANR 41; DLB 6;
DLBY 82; MTCW

Dexter, Martin
See Faust, Frederick (Schiller)

Dexter, Pete 1943- . . . . **CLC 34, 55**
See also BEST 89:2; CA 127; 131; MTCW

Diamano, Silmang
See Senghor, Leopold Sedar

Diamond, Neil 1941- . . . . **CLC 30**
See also CA 108

di Bassetto, Corno
See Shaw, George Bernard

Dick, Philip K(indred)
1928-1982 . . . . **CLC 10, 30, 72**
See also CA 49-52; 106; CANR 2, 16;
DLB 8; MTCW

Dickens, Charles (John Huffam)
1812-1870 . . . . **NCLC 3, 8, 18, 26**
See also CDBLB 1832-1890; DA; DLB 21,
55, 70; MAICYA; SATA 15

Dickey, James (Lafayette)
1923- . . . . **CLC 1, 2, 4, 7, 10, 15, 47**
See also AITN 1, 2; CA 9-12R; CABS 2;
CANR 10; CDALB 1968-1988; DLB 5;
DLBD 7; DLBY 82; MTCW

Dickey, William 1928- . . . . **CLC 3, 28**
See also CA 9-12R; CANR 24; DLB 5

Dickinson, Charles 1951- . . . . **CLC 49**
See also CA 128

Dickinson, Emily (Elizabeth)
1830-1886 . . . . **NCLC 21; PC 1**
See also CDALB 1865-1917; DA; DLB 1;
SATA 29; WLC

Dickinson, Peter (Malcolm)
1927- . . . . **CLC 12, 35**
See also AAYA 9; CA 41-44R; CANR 31;
CLR 29; DLB 87; MAICYA; SATA 5, 62

Dickson, Carr
See Carr, John Dickson

Dickson, Carter
See Carr, John Dickson

Didion, Joan 1934- . . . . . **CLC 1, 3, 8, 14, 32**
See also AITN 1; CA 5-8R; CANR 14;
CDALB 1968-1988; DLB 2; DLBY 81,
86; MTCW

Dietrich, Robert
See Hunt, E(verette) Howard, Jr.

Dillard, Annie 1945- . . . . **CLC 9, 60**
See also AAYA 6; CA 49-52; CANR 3;
DLBY 80; MTCW; SATA 10

Dillard, R(ichard) H(enry) W(ilde)
1937- . . . . **CLC 5**
See also CA 21-24R; CAAS 7; CANR 10;
DLB 5

Dillon, Eilis 1920- . . . . **CLC 17**
See also CA 9-12R; CAAS 3; CANR 4, 38;
CLR 26; MAICYA; SATA 2, 74

Dimont, Penelope
See Mortimer, Penelope (Ruth)

Dinesen, Isak . . . . **CLC 10, 29; SSC 7**
See also Blixen, Karen (Christentze
Dinesen)

Ding Ling . . . . **CLC 68**
See also Chiang Pin-chin

Disch, Thomas M(ichael) 1940- . . . **CLC 7, 36**
See also CA 21-24R; CAAS 4; CANR 17,
36; CLR 18; DLB 8; MAICYA; MTCW;
SAAS 15; SATA 54

Disch, Tom
See Disch, Thomas M(ichael)

d'Isly, Georges
See Simenon, Georges (Jacques Christian)

Disraeli, Benjamin 1804-1881 . . **NCLC 2, 39**
See also DLB 21, 55

Ditcum, Steve
See Crumb, R(obert)

Dixon, Paige
See Corcoran, Barbara

Dixon, Stephen 1936- . . . . **CLC 52**
See also CA 89-92; CANR 17, 40; DLB 130

Doblin, Alfred . . . . **TCLC 13**
See also Doeblin, Alfred

Dobrolyubov, Nikolai Alexandrovich
1836-1861 . . . . **NCLC 5**

Dobyns, Stephen 1941- . . . . **CLC 37**
See also CA 45-48; CANR 2, 18

Doctorow, E(dgar) L(aurence)
1931- . . . . . **CLC 6, 11, 15, 18, 37, 44, 65**
See also AITN 2; BEST 89:3; CA 45-48;
CANR 2, 33; CDALB 1968-1988; DLB 2,
28; DLBY 80; MTCW

Dodgson, Charles Lutwidge 1832-1898
See Carroll, Lewis
See also CLR 2; DA; MAICYA; YABC 2

Doeblin, Alfred 1878-1957 . . . . **TCLC 13**
See Doblin, Alfred
See also CA 110; DLB 66

Doerr, Harriet 1910- . . . . **CLC 34**
See also CA 117; 122

Domecq, H(onorio) Bustos
See Bioy Casares, Adolfo; Borges, Jorge
Luis

Domini, Rey
See Lorde, Audre (Geraldine)

Dominique
See Proust, (Valentin-Louis-George-Eugene-)
Marcel

Don, A
See Stephen, Leslie

Donaldson, Stephen R. 1947- . . . . **CLC 46**
See also CA 89-92; CANR 13

Donleavy, J(ames) P(atrick)
1926- . . . . **CLC 1, 4, 6, 10, 45**
See also AITN 2; CA 9-12R; CANR 24;
DLB 6; MTCW

Donne, John 1572-1631 . . . . **LC 10; PC 1**
See also CDBLB Before 1660; DA;
DLB 121; WLC

Donnell, David 1939(?)- . . . . **CLC 34**

Donoso (Yanez), Jose
1924- . . . . **CLC 4, 8, 11, 32**
See also CA 81-84; CANR 32; DLB 113;
HW; MTCW

Dunne, Finley Peter   1867-1936.... **TCLC 28**
See also CA 108; DLB 11, 23

Dunne, John Gregory   1932-....... **CLC 28**
See also CA 25-28R; CANR 14; DLBY 80

Dunsany, Edward John Moreton Drax
    Plunkett   1878-1957
See Dunsany, Lord; Lord Dunsany
See also CA 104; DLB 10

Dunsany, Lord................... **TCLC 2**
See also Dunsany, Edward John Moreton
    Drax Plunkett
See also DLB 77

du Perry, Jean
See Simenon, Georges (Jacques Christian)

Durang, Christopher (Ferdinand)
    1949-.................... **CLC 27, 38**
See also CA 105

Duras, Marguerite
    1914-...... **CLC 3, 6, 11, 20, 34, 40, 68**
See also CA 25-28R; DLB 83; MTCW

Durban, (Rosa) Pam   1947-........ **CLC 39**
See also CA 123

Durcan, Paul   1944-........... **CLC 43, 70**
See also CA 134

Durrell, Lawrence (George)
    1912-1990 .... **CLC 1, 4, 6, 8, 13, 27, 41**
See also CA 9-12R; 132; CANR 40;
    CDBLB 1945-1960; DLB 15, 27;
    DLBY 90; MTCW

Durrenmatt, Friedrich
    .... **CLC 1, 4, 8, 11, 15, 43**
See also Duerrenmatt, Friedrich
See also DLB 69, 124

Dutt, Toru   1856-1877.......... **NCLC 29**

Dwight, Timothy   1752-1817...... **NCLC 13**
See also DLB 37

Dworkin, Andrea   1946-........... **CLC 43**
See also CA 77-80; CANR 16, 39; MTCW

Dwyer, Deanna
See Koontz, Dean R(ay)

Dwyer, K. R.
See Koontz, Dean R(ay)

Dylan, Bob   1941-...... **CLC 3, 4, 6, 12, 77**
See also CA 41-44R; DLB 16

Eagleton, Terence (Francis)   1943-
See Eagleton, Terry
See also CA 57-60; CANR 7, 23; MTCW

Eagleton, Terry................... **CLC 63**
See also Eagleton, Terence (Francis)

Early, Jack
See Scoppettone, Sandra

East, Michael
See West, Morris L(anglo)

Eastaway, Edward
See Thomas, (Philip) Edward

Eastlake, William (Derry)   1917-..... **CLC 8**
See also CA 5-8R; CAAS 1; CANR 5;
    DLB 6

Eberhart, Richard (Ghormley)
    1904-.............**CLC 3, 11, 19, 56**
See also CA 1-4R; CANR 2;
    CDALB 1941-1968; DLB 48; MTCW

Eberstadt, Fernanda   1960-........ **CLC 39**
See also CA 136

Echegaray (y Eizaguirre), Jose (Maria Waldo)
    1832-1916 .... **TCLC 4**
See also CA 104; CANR 32; HW; MTCW

Echeverria, (Jose) Esteban (Antonino)
    1805-1851 .... **NCLC 18**

Echo
See Proust, (Valentin-Louis-George-Eugene-)
    Marcel

Eckert, Allan W.   1931-.......... **CLC 17**
See also CA 13-16R; CANR 14; SATA 27,
    29

Eckhart, Meister   1260(?)-1328(?) .. **CMLC 9**
See also DLB 115

Eckmar, F. R.
See de Hartog, Jan

Eco, Umberto   1932-.......... **CLC 28, 60**
See also BEST 90:1; CA 77-80; CANR 12,
    33; MTCW

Eddison, E(ric) R(ucker)
    1882-1945 .... **TCLC 15**
See also CA 109

Edel, (Joseph) Leon   1907-...... **CLC 29, 34**
See also CA 1-4R; CANR 1, 22; DLB 103

Eden, Emily   1797-1869 .... **NCLC 10**

Edgar, David   1948-............. **CLC 42**
See also CA 57-60; CANR 12; DLB 13;
    MTCW

Edgerton, Clyde (Carlyle)   1944- .... **CLC 39**
See also CA 118; 134

Edgeworth, Maria   1767-1849...... **NCLC 1**
See also DLB 116; SATA 21

Edmonds, Paul
See Kuttner, Henry

Edmonds, Walter D(umaux)   1903-.. **CLC 35**
See also CA 5-8R; CANR 2; DLB 9;
    MAICYA; SAAS 4; SATA 1, 27

Edmondson, Wallace
See Ellison, Harlan

Edson, Russell................... **CLC 13**
See also CA 33-36R

Edwards, G(erald) B(asil)
    1899-1976 .... **CLC 25**
See also CA 110

Edwards, Gus   1939-............. **CLC 43**
See also CA 108

Edwards, Jonathan   1703-1758....... **LC 7**
See also DA; DLB 24

Efron, Marina Ivanovna Tsvetaeva
See Tsvetaeva (Efron), Marina (Ivanovna)

Ehle, John (Marsden, Jr.)   1925-.... **CLC 27**
See also CA 9-12R

Ehrenbourg, Ilya (Grigoryevich)
See Ehrenburg, Ilya (Grigoryevich)

Ehrenburg, Ilya (Grigoryevich)
    1891-1967 .... **CLC 18, 34, 62**
See also CA 102; 25-28R

Ehrenburg, Ilyo (Grigoryevich)
See Ehrenburg, Ilya (Grigoryevich)

Eich, Guenter   1907-1972 .... **CLC 15**
See also CA 111; 93-96; DLB 69, 124

Eichendorff, Joseph Freiherr von
    1788-1857 .... **NCLC 8**
See also DLB 90

Eigner, Larry..................... **CLC 9**
See also Eigner, Laurence (Joel)
See also DLB 5

Eigner, Laurence (Joel)   1927-
See Eigner, Larry
See also CA 9-12R; CANR 6

Eiseley, Loren Corey   1907-1977..... **CLC 7**
See also AAYA 5; CA 1-4R; 73-76;
    CANR 6

Eisenstadt, Jill   1963-............. **CLC 50**
See also CA 140

Eisner, Simon
See Kornbluth, C(yril) M.

Ekeloef, (Bengt) Gunnar
    1907-1968 .... **CLC 27**
See also Ekelof, (Bengt) Gunnar
See also CA 123; 25-28R

Ekelof, (Bengt) Gunnar............. **CLC 27**
See also Ekeloef, (Bengt) Gunnar

Ekwensi, C. O. D.
See Ekwensi, Cyprian (Odiatu Duaka)

Ekwensi, Cyprian (Odiatu Duaka)
    1921-........................ **CLC 4**
See also BLC 1; BW; CA 29-32R;
    CANR 18; DLB 117; MTCW; SATA 66

Elaine......................... **TCLC 18**
See also Leverson, Ada

El Crummo
See Crumb, R(obert)

Elia
See Lamb, Charles

Eliade, Mircea   1907-1986 .... **CLC 19**
See also CA 65-68; 119; CANR 30; MTCW

Eliot, A. D.
See Jewett, (Theodora) Sarah Orne

Eliot, Alice
See Jewett, (Theodora) Sarah Orne

Eliot, Dan
See Silverberg, Robert

Eliot, George
    1819-1880 .... **NCLC 4, 13, 23, 41**
See also CDBLB 1832-1890; DA; DLB 21,
    35, 55; WLC

Eliot, John   1604-1690 .... **LC 5**
See also DLB 24

Eliot, T(homas) S(tearns)
    1888-1965 .... **CLC 1, 2, 3, 6, 9, 10, 13,
        15, 24, 34, 41, 55, 57; PC 5**
See also CA 5-8R; 25-28R; CANR 41;
    CDALB 1929-1941; DA; DLB 7, 10, 45,
    63; DLBY 88; MTCW; WLC 2

Elizabeth   1866-1941............. **TCLC 41**

Elkin, Stanley L(awrence)
    1930- ... **CLC 4, 6, 9, 14, 27, 51; SSC 12**
See also CA 9-12R; CANR 8; DLB 2, 28;
    DLBY 80; MTCW

Elledge, Scott.................... **CLC 34**

Elliott, Don
See Silverberg, Robert

Elliott, George P(aul)   1918-1980..... **CLC 2**
See also CA 1-4R; 97-100; CANR 2

Elliott, Janice   1931-............. **CLC 47**
See also CA 13-16R; CANR 8, 29; DLB 14

Elliott, Sumner Locke 1917-1991 . . . **CLC 38**
See also CA 5-8R; 134; CANR 2, 21

Elliott, William
See Bradbury, Ray (Douglas)

Ellis, A. E. . . . . **CLC 7**

Ellis, Alice Thomas . . . . **CLC 40**
See also Haycraft, Anna

Ellis, Bret Easton 1964- . . . . **CLC 39, 71**
See also AAYA 2; CA 118; 123

Ellis, (Henry) Havelock
1859-1939 . . . . **TCLC 14**
See also CA 109

Ellis, Landon
See Ellison, Harlan

Ellis, Trey 1962- . . . . **CLC 55**

Ellison, Harlan 1934- . . . . **CLC 1, 13, 42**
See also CA 5-8R; CANR 5; DLB 8;
MTCW

Ellison, Ralph (Waldo)
1914- . . . . **CLC 1, 3, 11, 54**
See also BLC 1; BW; CA 9-12R; CANR 24;
CDALB 1941-1968; DA; DLB 2, 76;
MTCW; WLC

Ellmann, Lucy (Elizabeth) 1956- . . . . **CLC 61**
See also CA 128

Ellmann, Richard (David)
1918-1987 . . . . **CLC 50**
See also BEST 89:2; CA 1-4R; 122;
CANR 2, 28; DLB 103; DLBY 87;
MTCW

Elman, Richard 1934- . . . . **CLC 19**
See also CA 17-20R; CAAS 3

Elron
See Hubbard, L(afayette) Ron(ald)

Eluard, Paul . . . . **TCLC 7, 41**
See also Grindel, Eugene

Elyot, Sir Thomas 1490(?)-1546 . . . . . **LC 11**

Elytis, Odysseus 1911- . . . . **CLC 15, 49**
See also CA 102; MTCW

Emecheta, (Florence Onye) Buchi
1944- . . . . **CLC 14, 48**
See also BLC 2; BW; CA 81-84; CANR 27;
DLB 117; MTCW; SATA 66

Emerson, Ralph Waldo
1803-1882 . . . . **NCLC 1, 38**
See also CDALB 1640-1865; DA; DLB 1,
59, 73; WLC

Eminescu, Mihail 1850-1889 . . . . . **NCLC 33**

Empson, William
1906-1984 . . . . **CLC 3, 8, 19, 33, 34**
See also CA 17-20R; 112; CANR 31;
DLB 20; MTCW

Enchi Fumiko (Ueda) 1905-1986 . . . . **CLC 31**
See also CA 129; 121

Ende, Michael (Andreas Helmuth)
1929- . . . . **CLC 31**
See also CA 118; 124; CANR 36; CLR 14;
DLB 75; MAICYA; SATA 42, 61

Endo, Shusaku 1923- . . . . . **CLC 7, 14, 19, 54**
See also CA 29-32R; CANR 21; MTCW

Engel, Marian 1933-1985 . . . . **CLC 36**
See also CA 25-28R; CANR 12; DLB 53

Engelhardt, Frederick
See Hubbard, L(afayette) Ron(ald)

Enright, D(ennis) J(oseph)
1920- . . . . **CLC 4, 8, 31**
See also CA 1-4R; CANR 1; DLB 27;
SATA 25

Enzensberger, Hans Magnus
1929- . . . . **CLC 43**
See also CA 116; 119

Ephron, Nora 1941- . . . . **CLC 17, 31**
See also AITN 2; CA 65-68; CANR 12, 39

Epsilon
See Betjeman, John

Epstein, Daniel Mark 1948- . . . . **CLC 7**
See also CA 49-52; CANR 2

Epstein, Jacob 1956- . . . . **CLC 19**
See also CA 114

Epstein, Joseph 1937- . . . . **CLC 39**
See also CA 112; 119

Epstein, Leslie 1938- . . . . **CLC 27**
See also CA 73-76; CAAS 12; CANR 23

Equiano, Olaudah 1745(?)-1797 . . . . . . **LC 16**
See also BLC 2; DLB 37, 50

Erasmus, Desiderius 1469(?)-1536 . . . . **LC 16**

Erdman, Paul E(mil) 1932- . . . . **CLC 25**
See also AITN 1; CA 61-64; CANR 13

Erdrich, Louise 1954- . . . . **CLC 39, 54**
See also AAYA 10; BEST 89:1; CA 114;
CANR 41; MTCW

Erenburg, Ilya (Grigoryevich)
See Ehrenburg, Ilya (Grigoryevich)

Erickson, Stephen Michael 1950-
See Erickson, Steve
See also CA 129

Erickson, Steve . . . . **CLC 64**
See also Erickson, Stephen Michael

Ericson, Walter
See Fast, Howard (Melvin)

Eriksson, Buntel
See Bergman, (Ernst) Ingmar

Eschenbach, Wolfram von
See Wolfram von Eschenbach

Eseki, Bruno
See Mphahlele, Ezekiel

Esenin, Sergei (Alexandrovich)
1895-1925 . . . . **TCLC 4**
See also CA 104

Eshleman, Clayton 1935- . . . . **CLC 7**
See also CA 33-36R; CAAS 6; DLB 5

Espriella, Don Manuel Alvarez
See Southey, Robert

Espriu, Salvador 1913-1985 . . . . **CLC 9**
See also CA 115

Espronceda, Jose de 1808-1842 . . . **NCLC 39**

Esse, James
See Stephens, James

Esterbrook, Tom
See Hubbard, L(afayette) Ron(ald)

Estleman, Loren D. 1952- . . . . **CLC 48**
See also CA 85-88; CANR 27; MTCW

Evan, Evin
See Faust, Frederick (Schiller)

Evans, Evan
See Faust, Frederick (Schiller)

Evans, Marian
See Eliot, George

Evans, Mary Ann
See Eliot, George

Evarts, Esther
See Benson, Sally

Everett, Percival
See Everett, Percival L.

Everett, Percival L. 1956- . . . . **CLC 57**
See also CA 129

Everson, R(onald) G(ilmour)
1903- . . . . **CLC 27**
See also CA 17-20R; DLB 88

Everson, William (Oliver)
1912- . . . . **CLC 1, 5, 14**
See also CA 9-12R; CANR 20; DLB 5, 16;
MTCW

Evtushenko, Evgenii Aleksandrovich
See Yevtushenko, Yevgeny (Alexandrovich)

Ewart, Gavin (Buchanan)
1916- . . . . **CLC 13, 46**
See also CA 89-92; CANR 17; DLB 40;
MTCW

Ewers, Hanns Heinz 1871-1943 . . . **TCLC 12**
See also CA 109

Ewing, Frederick R.
See Sturgeon, Theodore (Hamilton)

Exley, Frederick (Earl)
1929-1992 . . . . **CLC 6, 11**
See also AITN 2; CA 81-84; 138; DLBY 81

Eynhardt, Guillermo
See Quiroga, Horacio (Sylvestre)

Ezekiel, Nissim 1924- . . . . **CLC 61**
See also CA 61-64

Ezekiel, Tish O'Dowd 1943- . . . . **CLC 34**
See also CA 129

Fagen, Donald 1948- . . . . **CLC 26**

Fainzilberg, Ilya Arnoldovich 1897-1937
See Ilf, Ilya
See also CA 120

Fair, Ronald L. 1932- . . . . **CLC 18**
See also BW; CA 69-72; CANR 25; DLB 33

Fairbairns, Zoe (Ann) 1948- . . . . **CLC 32**
See also CA 103; CANR 21

Falco, Gian
See Papini, Giovanni

Falconer, James
See Kirkup, James

Falconer, Kenneth
See Kornbluth, C(yril) M.

Falkland, Samuel
See Heijermans, Herman

Fallaci, Oriana 1930- . . . . **CLC 11**
See also CA 77-80; CANR 15; MTCW

Faludy, George 1913- . . . . **CLC 42**
See also CA 21-24R

Faludy, Gyoergy
See Faludy, George

Fanon, Frantz 1925-1961 . . . . **CLC 74**
See also BLC 2; BW; CA 116; 89-92

Fanshawe, Ann . . . . **LC 11**

Fante, John (Thomas) 1911-1983 ... **CLC 60**
See also CA 69-72; 109; CANR 23;
DLB 130; DLBY 83

Farah, Nuruddin 1945- .... **CLC 53**
See also BLC 2; CA 106; DLB 125

Fargue, Leon-Paul 1876(?)-1947 ... **TCLC 11**
See also CA 109

Farigoule, Louis
See Romains, Jules

Farina, Richard 1936(?)-1966 .... **CLC 9**
See also CA 81-84; 25-28R

Farley, Walter (Lorimer)
1915-1989 .... **CLC 17**
See also CA 17-20R; CANR 8, 29; DLB 22;
MAICYA; SATA 2, 43

Farmer, Philip Jose 1918- .... **CLC 1, 19**
See also CA 1-4R; CANR 4, 35; DLB 8;
MTCW

Farquhar, George 1677-1707 .... **LC 21**
See also DLB 84

Farrell, J(ames) G(ordon)
1935-1979 .... **CLC 6**
See also CA 73-76; 89-92; CANR 36;
DLB 14; MTCW

Farrell, James T(homas)
1904-1979 .... **CLC 1, 4, 8, 11, 66**
See also CA 5-8R; 89-92; CANR 9; DLB 4,
9, 86; DLBD 2; MTCW

Farren, Richard J.
See Betjeman, John

Farren, Richard M.
See Betjeman, John

Fassbinder, Rainer Werner
1946-1982 .... **CLC 20**
See also CA 93-96; 106; CANR 31

Fast, Howard (Melvin) 1914- ...... **CLC 23**
See also CA 1-4R; CANR 1, 33; DLB 9;
SATA 7

Faulcon, Robert
See Holdstock, Robert P.

Faulkner, William (Cuthbert)
1897-1962 .... **CLC 1, 3, 6, 8, 9, 11, 14,
18, 28, 52, 68; SSC 1**
See also AAYA 7; CA 81-84; CANR 33;
CDALB 1929-1941; DA; DLB 9, 11, 44,
102; DLBD 2; DLBY 86; MTCW; WLC

Fauset, Jessie Redmon
1884(?)-1961 .... **CLC 19, 54**
See also BLC 2; BW; CA 109; DLB 51

Faust, Frederick (Schiller)
1892-1944(?) .... **TCLC 49**
See also CA 108

Faust, Irvin 1924- .... **CLC 8**
See also CA 33-36R; CANR 28; DLB 2, 28;
DLBY 80

Fawkes, Guy
See Benchley, Robert (Charles)

Fearing, Kenneth (Flexner)
1902-1961 .... **CLC 51**
See also CA 93-96; DLB 9

Fecamps, Elise
See Creasey, John

Federman, Raymond 1928- ...... **CLC 6, 47**
See also CA 17-20R; CAAS 8; CANR 10;
DLBY 80

Federspiel, J(uerg) F. 1931- .... **CLC 42**

Feiffer, Jules (Ralph) 1929- .... **CLC 2, 8, 64**
See also AAYA 3; CA 17-20R; CANR 30;
DLB 7, 44; MTCW; SATA 8, 61

Feige, Hermann Albert Otto Maximilian
See Traven, B.

Fei-Kan, Li
See Li Fei-kan

Feinberg, David B. 1956- .... **CLC 59**
See also CA 135

Feinstein, Elaine 1930- .... **CLC 36**
See also CA 69-72; CAAS 1; CANR 31;
DLB 14, 40; MTCW

Feldman, Irving (Mordecai) 1928- .... **CLC 7**
See also CA 1-4R; CANR 1

Fellini, Federico 1920- .... **CLC 16**
See also CA 65-68; CANR 33

Felsen, Henry Gregor 1916- .... **CLC 17**
See also CA 1-4R; CANR 1; SAAS 2;
SATA 1

Fenton, James Martin 1949- .... **CLC 32**
See also CA 102; DLB 40

Ferber, Edna 1887-1968 .... **CLC 18**
See also AITN 1; CA 5-8R; 25-28R; DLB 9,
28, 86; MTCW; SATA 7

Ferguson, Helen
See Kavan, Anna

Ferguson, Samuel 1810-1886 ..... **NCLC 33**
See also DLB 32

Ferling, Lawrence
See Ferlinghetti, Lawrence (Monsanto)

Ferlinghetti, Lawrence (Monsanto)
1919(?)- .... **CLC 2, 6, 10, 27; PC 1**
See also CA 5-8R; CANR 3, 41;
CDALB 1941-1968; DLB 5, 16; MTCW

Fernandez, Vicente Garcia Huidobro
See Huidobro Fernandez, Vicente Garcia

Ferrer, Gabriel (Francisco Victor) Miro
See Miro (Ferrer), Gabriel (Francisco
Victor)

Ferrier, Susan (Edmonstone)
1782-1854 .... **NCLC 8**
See also DLB 116

Ferrigno, Robert 1948(?)- .... **CLC 65**
See also CA 140

Feuchtwanger, Lion 1884-1958 ..... **TCLC 3**
See also CA 104; DLB 66

Feydeau, Georges (Leon Jules Marie)
1862-1921 .... **TCLC 22**
See also CA 113

Ficino, Marsilio 1433-1499 .... **LC 12**

Fiedler, Leslie A(aron)
1917- .... **CLC 4, 13, 24**
See also CA 9-12R; CANR 7; DLB 28, 67;
MTCW

Field, Andrew 1938- .... **CLC 44**
See also CA 97-100; CANR 25

Field, Eugene 1850-1895 .... **NCLC 3**
See also DLB 23, 42; MAICYA; SATA 16

Field, Gans T.
See Wellman, Manly Wade

Field, Michael .... **TCLC 43**

Field, Peter
See Hobson, Laura Z(ametkin)

Fielding, Henry 1707-1754 .... **LC 1**
See also CDBLB 1660-1789; DA; DLB 39,
84, 101; WLC

Fielding, Sarah 1710-1768 .... **LC 1**
See also DLB 39

Fierstein, Harvey (Forbes) 1954- ... **CLC 33**
See also CA 123; 129

Figes, Eva 1932- .... **CLC 31**
See also CA 53-56; CANR 4; DLB 14

Finch, Robert (Duer Claydon)
1900- .... **CLC 18**
See also CA 57-60; CANR 9, 24; DLB 88

Findley, Timothy 1930- .... **CLC 27**
See also CA 25-28R; CANR 12; DLB 53

Fink, William
See Mencken, H(enry) L(ouis)

Firbank, Louis 1942-
See Reed, Lou
See also CA 117

Firbank, (Arthur Annesley) Ronald
1886-1926 .... **TCLC 1**
See also CA 104; DLB 36

Fisher, M(ary) F(rances) K(ennedy)
1908-1992 .... **CLC 76**
See also CA 77-80; 138

Fisher, Roy 1930- .... **CLC 25**
See also CA 81-84; CAAS 10; CANR 16;
DLB 40

Fisher, Rudolph 1897-1934 .... **TCLC 11**
See also BLC 2; BW; CA 107; 124; DLB 51,
102

Fisher, Vardis (Alvero) 1895-1968.... **CLC 7**
See also CA 5-8R; 25-28R; DLB 9

Fiske, Tarleton
See Bloch, Robert (Albert)

Fitch, Clarke
See Sinclair, Upton (Beall)

Fitch, John IV
See Cormier, Robert (Edmund)

Fitgerald, Penelope 1916- .... **CLC 61**

Fitzgerald, Captain Hugh
See Baum, L(yman) Frank

FitzGerald, Edward 1809-1883 .... **NCLC 9**
See also DLB 32

Fitzgerald, F(rancis) Scott (Key)
1896-1940 .... **TCLC 1, 6, 14, 28; SSC 6**
See also AITN 1; CA 110; 123;
CDALB 1917-1929; DA; DLB 4, 9, 86;
DLBD 1; DLBY 81; MTCW; WLC

Fitzgerald, Penelope 1916-...... **CLC 19, 51**
See also CA 85-88; CAAS 10; DLB 14

Fitzgerald, Robert (Stuart)
1910-1985 .... **CLC 39**
See also CA 1-4R; 114; CANR 1; DLBY 80

FitzGerald, Robert D(avid)
1902-1987 .... **CLC 19**
See also CA 17-20R

Flanagan, Thomas (James Bonner)
1923- .... **CLC 25, 52**
See also CA 108; DLBY 80; MTCW

Flaubert, Gustave
      1821-1880 ..... **NCLC 2, 10, 19; SSC 11**
      See also DA; DLB 119; WLC

Flecker, (Herman) James Elroy
      1884-1915 .... **TCLC 43**
      See also CA 109; DLB 10, 19

Fleming, Ian (Lancaster)
      1908-1964 .... **CLC 3, 30**
      See also CA 5-8R; CDBLB 1945-1960;
      DLB 87; MTCW; SATA 9

Fleming, Thomas (James) 1927- .... **CLC 37**
      See also CA 5-8R; CANR 10; SATA 8

Fletcher, John Gould 1886-1950 ... **TCLC 35**
      See also CA 107; DLB 4, 45

Fleur, Paul
      See Pohl, Frederik

Flooglebuckle, Al
      See Spiegelman, Art

Flying Officer X
      See Bates, H(erbert) E(rnest)

Fo, Dario 1926- .... **CLC 32**
      See also CA 116; 128; MTCW

Fogarty, Jonathan Titulescu Esq.
      See Farrell, James T(homas)

Folke, Will
      See Bloch, Robert (Albert)

Follett, Ken(neth Martin) 1949- .... **CLC 18**
      See also AAYA 6; BEST 89:4; CA 81-84;
      CANR 13, 33; DLB 87; DLBY 81;
      MTCW

Fontane, Theodor 1819-1898 ..... **NCLC 26**
      See also DLB 129

Foote, Horton 1916- .... **CLC 51**
      See also CA 73-76; CANR 34; DLB 26

Foote, Shelby 1916- .... **CLC 75**
      See also CA 5-8R; CANR 3; DLB 2, 17

Forbes, Esther 1891-1967 .... **CLC 12**
      See also CA 13-14; 25-28R; CAP 1;
      CLR 27; DLB 22; MAICYA; SATA 2

Forche, Carolyn (Louise) 1950- ..... **CLC 25**
      See also CA 109; 117; DLB 5

Ford, Elbur
      See Hibbert, Eleanor Alice Burford

Ford, Ford Madox
      1873-1939 .... **TCLC 1, 15, 39**
      See also CA 104; 132; CDBLB 1914-1945;
      DLB 34, 98; MTCW

Ford, John 1895-1973 .... **CLC 16**
      See also CA 45-48

Ford, Richard 1944- .... **CLC 46**
      See also CA 69-72; CANR 11

Ford, Webster
      See Masters, Edgar Lee

Foreman, Richard 1937- .... **CLC 50**
      See also CA 65-68; CANR 32

Forester, C(ecil) S(cott)
      1899-1966 .... **CLC 35**
      See also CA 73-76; 25-28R; SATA 13

Forez
      See Mauriac, Francois (Charles)

Forman, James Douglas 1932- ...... **CLC 21**
      See also CA 9-12R; CANR 4, 19;
      MAICYA; SATA 8, 70

Fornes, Maria Irene 1930- ...... **CLC 39, 61**
      See also CA 25-28R; CANR 28; DLB 7;
      HW; MTCW

Forrest, Leon 1937- .... **CLC 4**
      See also BW; CA 89-92; CAAS 7;
      CANR 25; DLB 33

Forster, E(dward) M(organ)
      1879-1970 .... **CLC 1, 2, 3, 4, 9, 10, 13,
            15, 22, 45, 77**
      See also AAYA 2; CA 13-14; 25-28R;
      CAP 1; CDBLB 1914-1945; DA; DLB 34,
      98; DLBD 10; MTCW; SATA 57; WLC

Forster, John 1812-1876 .... **NCLC 11**

Forsyth, Frederick 1938- ...... **CLC 2, 5, 36**
      See also BEST 89:4; CA 85-88; CANR 38;
      DLB 87; MTCW

Forten, Charlotte L. .... **TCLC 16**
      See also Grimke, Charlotte L(ottie) Forten
      See also BLC 2; DLB 50

Foscolo, Ugo 1778-1827 .... **NCLC 8**

Fosse, Bob .... **CLC 20**
      See also Fosse, Robert Louis

Fosse, Robert Louis 1927-1987
      See Fosse, Bob
      See also CA 110; 123

Foster, Stephen Collins
      1826-1864 .... **NCLC 26**

Foucault, Michel
      1926-1984 .... **CLC 31, 34, 69**
      See also CA 105; 113; CANR 34; MTCW

Fouque, Friedrich (Heinrich Karl) de la Motte
      1777-1843 .... **NCLC 2**
      See also DLB 90

Fournier, Henri Alban 1886-1914
      See Alain-Fournier
      See also CA 104

Fournier, Pierre 1916- .... **CLC 11**
      See also Gascar, Pierre
      See also CA 89-92; CANR 16, 40

Fowles, John
      1926- .... **CLC 1, 2, 3, 4, 6, 9, 10, 15, 33**
      See also CA 5-8R; CANR 25; CDBLB 1960
      to Present; DLB 14; MTCW; SATA 22

Fox, Paula 1923- .... **CLC 2, 8**
      See also AAYA 3; CA 73-76; CANR 20,
      36; CLR 1; DLB 52; MAICYA; MTCW;
      SATA 17, 60

Fox, William Price (Jr.) 1926- ..... **CLC 22**
      See also CA 17-20R; CANR 11; DLB 2;
      DLBY 81

Foxe, John 1516(?)-1587 .... **LC 14**

Frame, Janet .... **CLC 2, 3, 6, 22, 66**
      See also Clutha, Janet Paterson Frame

France, Anatole .... **TCLC 9**
      See also Thibault, Jacques Anatole Francois
      See also DLB 123

Francis, Claude 19(?)- .... **CLC 50**

Francis, Dick 1920- .... **CLC 2, 22, 42**
      See also AAYA 5; BEST 89:3; CA 5-8R;
      CANR 9; CDBLB 1960 to Present;
      DLB 87; MTCW

Francis, Robert (Churchill)
      1901-1987 .... **CLC 15**
      See also CA 1-4R; 123; CANR 1

Frank, Anne(lies Marie)
      1929-1945 .... **TCLC 17**
      See also CA 113; 133; DA; MTCW;
      SATA 42; WLC

Frank, Elizabeth 1945- .... **CLC 39**
      See also CA 121; 126

Franklin, Benjamin
      See Hasek, Jaroslav (Matej Frantisek)

Franklin, (Stella Maraia Sarah) Miles
      1879-1954 .... **TCLC 7**
      See also CA 104

Fraser, Antonia (Pakenham)
      1932- .... **CLC 32**
      See also CA 85-88; MTCW; SATA 32

Fraser, George MacDonald 1925- .... **CLC 7**
      See also CA 45-48; CANR 2

Fraser, Sylvia 1935- .... **CLC 64**
      See also CA 45-48; CANR 1, 16

Frayn, Michael 1933- ...... **CLC 3, 7, 31, 47**
      See also CA 5-8R; CANR 30; DLB 13, 14;
      MTCW

Fraze, Candida (Merrill) 1945- ..... **CLC 50**
      See also CA 126

Frazer, J(ames) G(eorge)
      1854-1941 .... **TCLC 32**
      See also CA 118

Frazer, Robert Caine
      See Creasey, John

Frazer, Sir James George
      See Frazer, J(ames) G(eorge)

Frazier, Ian 1951- .... **CLC 46**
      See also CA 130

Frederic, Harold 1856-1898 ...... **NCLC 10**
      See also DLB 12, 23

Frederick, John
      See Faust, Frederick (Schiller)

Frederick the Great 1712-1786 ...... **LC 14**

Fredro, Aleksander 1793-1876 ..... **NCLC 8**

Freeling, Nicolas 1927- .... **CLC 38**
      See also CA 49-52; CAAS 12; CANR 1, 17;
      DLB 87

Freeman, Douglas Southall
      1886-1953 .... **TCLC 11**
      See also CA 109; DLB 17

Freeman, Judith 1946- .... **CLC 55**

Freeman, Mary Eleanor Wilkins
      1852-1930 .... **TCLC 9; SSC 1**
      See also CA 106; DLB 12, 78

Freeman, R(ichard) Austin
      1862-1943 .... **TCLC 21**
      See also CA 113; DLB 70

French, Marilyn 1929- ...... **CLC 10, 18, 60**
      See also CA 69-72; CANR 3, 31; MTCW

French, Paul
      See Asimov, Isaac

Freneau, Philip Morin 1752-1832 .. **NCLC 1**
      See also DLB 37, 43

Friedan, Betty (Naomi) 1921- ...... **CLC 74**
      See also CA 65-68; CANR 18; MTCW

Friedman, B(ernard) H(arper)
      1926- .... **CLC 7**
      See also CA 1-4R; CANR 3

Friedman, Bruce Jay 1930-.... **CLC 3, 5, 56**
See also CA 9-12R; CANR 25; DLB 2, 28

Friel, Brian 1929-.......... **CLC 5, 42, 59**
See also CA 21-24R; CANR 33; DLB 13;
MTCW

Friis-Baastad, Babbis Ellinor
1921-1970 .... **CLC 12**
See also CA 17-20R; 134; SATA 7

Frisch, Max (Rudolf)
1911-1991 ..... **CLC 3, 9, 14, 18, 32, 44**
See also CA 85-88; 134; CANR 32;
DLB 69, 124; MTCW

Fromentin, Eugene (Samuel Auguste)
1820-1876 .... **NCLC 10**
See also DLB 123

Frost, Frederick
See Faust, Frederick (Schiller)

Frost, Robert (Lee)
1874-1963 ... **CLC 1, 3, 4, 9, 10, 13, 15,**
26, 34, 44; PC 1
See also CA 89-92; CANR 33;
CDALB 1917-1929; DA; DLB 54;
DLBD 7; MTCW; SATA 14; WLC

Froy, Herald
See Waterhouse, Keith (Spencer)

Fry, Christopher 1907-....... **CLC 2, 10, 14**
See also CA 17-20R; CANR 9, 30; DLB 13;
MTCW; SATA 66

Frye, (Herman) Northrop
1912-1991 .... **CLC 24, 70**
See also CA 5-8R; 133; CANR 8, 37;
DLB 67, 68; MTCW

Fuchs, Daniel 1909-........... **CLC 8, 22**
See also CA 81-84; CAAS 5; CANR 40;
DLB 9, 26, 28

Fuchs, Daniel 1934-............. **CLC 34**
See also CA 37-40R; CANR 14

Fuentes, Carlos
1928-...... **CLC 3, 8, 10, 13, 22, 41, 60**
See also AAYA 4; AITN 2; CA 69-72;
CANR 10, 32; DA; DLB 113; HW;
MTCW; WLC

Fuentes, Gregorio Lopez y
See Lopez y Fuentes, Gregorio

Fugard, (Harold) Athol
1932-....... **CLC 5, 9, 14, 25, 40; DC 3**
See also CA 85-88; CANR 32; MTCW

Fugard, Sheila 1932-............. **CLC 48**
See also CA 125

Fuller, Charles (H., Jr.)
1939-................. **CLC 25; DC 1**
See also BLC 2; BW; CA 108; 112; DLB 38;
MTCW

Fuller, John (Leopold) 1937-....... **CLC 62**
See also CA 21-24R; CANR 9; DLB 40

Fuller, Margaret .... **NCLC 5**
See also Ossoli, Sarah Margaret (Fuller
marchesa d')

Fuller, Roy (Broadbent)
1912-1991 .... **CLC 4, 28**
See also CA 5-8R; 135; CAAS 10; DLB 15,
20

Fulton, Alice 1952-............. **CLC 52**
See also CA 116

Furphy, Joseph 1843-1912........ **TCLC 25**

Fussell, Paul 1924-............... **CLC 74**
See also BEST 90:1; CA 17-20R; CANR 8,
21, 35; MTCW

Futabatei, Shimei 1864-1909...... **TCLC 44**

Futrelle, Jacques 1875-1912 ..... **TCLC 19**
See also CA 113

G. B. S.
See Shaw, George Bernard

Gaboriau, Emile 1835-1873...... **NCLC 14**

Gadda, Carlo Emilio 1893-1973 .... **CLC 11**
See also CA 89-92

Gaddis, William
1922-........ **CLC 1, 3, 6, 8, 10, 19, 43**
See also CA 17-20R; CANR 21; DLB 2;
MTCW

Gaines, Ernest J(ames)
1933-................. **CLC 3, 11, 18**
See also AITN 1; BLC 2; BW; CA 9-12R;
CANR 6, 24; CDALB 1968-1988; DLB 2,
33; DLBY 80; MTCW

Gaitskill, Mary 1954-............ **CLC 69**
See also CA 128

Galdos, Benito Perez
See Perez Galdos, Benito

Gale, Zona 1874-1938 .... **TCLC 7**
See also CA 105; DLB 9, 78

Galeano, Eduardo (Hughes) 1940-... **CLC 72**
See also CA 29-32R; CANR 13, 32; HW

Galiano, Juan Valera y Alcala
See Valera y Alcala-Galiano, Juan

Gallagher, Tess 1943-.......... **CLC 18, 63**
See also CA 106; DLB 120

Gallant, Mavis
1922-............ **CLC 7, 18, 38; SSC 5**
See also CA 69-72; CANR 29; DLB 53;
MTCW

Gallant, Roy A(rthur) 1924-........ **CLC 17**
See also CA 5-8R; CANR 4, 29; CLR 30;
MAICYA; SATA 4, 68

Gallico, Paul (William) 1897-1976 ... **CLC 2**
See also AITN 1; CA 5-8R; 69-72;
CANR 23; DLB 9; MAICYA; SATA 13

Gallup, Ralph
See Whitemore, Hugh (John)

Galsworthy, John 1867-1933.... **TCLC 1, 45**
See also CA 104; CDBLB 1890-1914; DA;
DLB 10, 34, 98; WLC 2

Galt, John 1779-1839........... **NCLC 1**
See also DLB 99, 116

Galvin, James 1951-............. **CLC 38**
See also CA 108; CANR 26

Gamboa, Federico 1864-1939...... **TCLC 36**

Gann, Ernest Kellogg 1910-1991.... **CLC 23**
See also AITN 1; CA 1-4R; 136; CANR 1

Garcia, Christina 1959-.......... **CLC 76**

Garcia Lorca, Federico
1898-1936 .. **TCLC 1, 7, 49; DC 2; PC 3**
See also CA 104; 131; DA; DLB 108; HW;
MTCW; WLC

Garcia Marquez, Gabriel (Jose)
1928-... **CLC 2, 3, 8, 10, 15, 27, 47, 55;**
SSC 8
See also Marquez, Gabriel (Jose) Garcia
See also AAYA 3; BEST 89:1, 90:4;
CA 33-36R; CANR 10, 28; DA;
DLB 113; HW; MTCW; WLC

Gard, Janice
See Latham, Jean Lee

Gard, Roger Martin du
See Martin du Gard, Roger

Gardam, Jane 1928-.............. **CLC 43**
See also CA 49-52; CANR 2, 18, 33;
CLR 12; DLB 14; MAICYA; MTCW;
SAAS 9; SATA 28, 39

Gardner, Herb.................... **CLC 44**

Gardner, John (Champlin), Jr.
1933-1982 .... **CLC 2, 3, 5, 7, 8, 10, 18,**
28, 34; SSC 7
See also AITN 1; CA 65-68; 107;
CANR 33; DLB 2; DLBY 82; MTCW;
SATA 31, 40

Gardner, John (Edmund) 1926-..... **CLC 30**
See also CA 103; CANR 15; MTCW

Gardner, Noel
See Kuttner, Henry

Gardons, S. S.
See Snodgrass, W(illiam) D(e Witt)

Garfield, Leon 1921-............. **CLC 12**
See also AAYA 8; CA 17-20R; CANR 38,
41; CLR 21; MAICYA; SATA 1, 32

Garland, (Hannibal) Hamlin
1860-1940 .... **TCLC 3**
See also CA 104; DLB 12, 71, 78

Garneau, (Hector de) Saint-Denys
1912-1943 .... **TCLC 13**
See also CA 111; DLB 88

Garner, Alan 1934-............... **CLC 17**
See also CA 73-76; CANR 15; CLR 20;
MAICYA; MTCW; SATA 18, 69

Garner, Hugh 1913-1979.......... **CLC 13**
See also CA 69-72; CANR 31; DLB 68

Garnett, David 1892-1981.......... **CLC 3**
See also CA 5-8R; 103; CANR 17; DLB 34

Garos, Stephanie
See Katz, Steve

Garrett, George (Palmer)
1929-.................. **CLC 3, 11, 51**
See also CA 1-4R; CAAS 5; CANR 1;
DLB 2, 5, 130; DLBY 83

Garrick, David 1717-1779.......... **LC 15**
See also DLB 84

Garrigue, Jean 1914-1972 .... **CLC 2, 8**
See also CA 5-8R; 37-40R; CANR 20

Garrison, Frederick
See Sinclair, Upton (Beall)

Garth, Will
See Hamilton, Edmond; Kuttner, Henry

Garvey, Marcus (Moziah, Jr.)
1887-1940 .... **TCLC 41**
See also BLC 2; BW; CA 120; 124

Gary, Romain .... **CLC 25**
See also Kacew, Romain
See also DLB 83

Godwin, William 1756-1836..... **NCLC 14**
See also CDBLB 1789-1832; DLB 39, 104

Goethe, Johann Wolfgang von
1749-1832 ...... **NCLC 4, 22, 34; PC 5**
See also DA; DLB 94; WLC 3

Gogarty, Oliver St. John
1878-1957 .... **TCLC 15**
See also CA 109; DLB 15, 19

Gogol, Nikolai (Vasilyevich)
1809-1852 ..... **NCLC 5, 15, 31; DC 1;
SSC 4**
See also DA; WLC

Gold, Herbert 1924-....... **CLC 4, 7, 14, 42**
See also CA 9-12R; CANR 17; DLB 2;
DLBY 81

Goldbarth, Albert 1948-........ **CLC 5, 38**
See also CA 53-56; CANR 6, 40; DLB 120

Goldberg, Anatol 1910-1982 .... **CLC 34**
See also CA 131; 117

Goldemberg, Isaac 1945- .... **CLC 52**
See also CA 69-72; CAAS 12; CANR 11,
32; HW

Golden Silver
See Storm, Hyemeyohsts

Golding, William (Gerald)
1911- ..... **CLC 1, 2, 3, 8, 10, 17, 27, 58**
See also AAYA 5; CA 5-8R; CANR 13, 33;
CDBLB 1945-1960; DA; DLB 15, 100;
MTCW; WLC

Goldman, Emma 1869-1940....... **TCLC 13**
See also CA 110

Goldman, Francisco 1955-......... **CLC 76**

Goldman, William (W.) 1931-.... **CLC 1, 48**
See also CA 9-12R; CANR 29; DLB 44

Goldmann, Lucien 1913-1970 ..... **CLC 24**
See also CA 25-28; CAP 2

Goldoni, Carlo 1707-1793 .... **LC 4**

Goldsberry, Steven 1949-......... **CLC 34**
See also CA 131

Goldsmith, Oliver 1728-1774........ **LC 2**
See also CDBLB 1660-1789; DA; DLB 39,
89, 104, 109; SATA 26; WLC

Goldsmith, Peter
See Priestley, J(ohn) B(oynton)

Gombrowicz, Witold
1904-1969 .... **CLC 4, 7, 11, 49**
See also CA 19-20; 25-28R; CAP 2

Gomez de la Serna, Ramon
1888-1963 .... **CLC 9**
See also CA 116; HW

Goncharov, Ivan Alexandrovich
1812-1891 .... **NCLC 1**

Goncourt, Edmond (Louis Antoine Huot) de
1822-1896 .... **NCLC 7**
See also DLB 123

Goncourt, Jules (Alfred Huot) de
1830-1870 .... **NCLC 7**
See also DLB 123

Gontier, Fernande 19(?)- .... **CLC 50**

Goodman, Paul 1911-1972.... **CLC 1, 2, 4, 7**
See also CA 19-20; 37-40R; CANR 34;
CAP 2; DLB 130; MTCW

Gordimer, Nadine
1923- .... **CLC 3, 5, 7, 10, 18, 33, 51, 70**
See also CA 5-8R; CANR 3, 28; DA;
MTCW

Gordon, Adam Lindsay
1833-1870 .... **NCLC 21**

Gordon, Caroline
1895-1981 .... **CLC 6, 13, 29**
See also CA 11-12; 103; CANR 36; CAP 1;
DLB 4, 9, 102; DLBY 81; MTCW

Gordon, Charles William 1860-1937
See Connor, Ralph
See also CA 109

Gordon, Mary (Catherine)
1949- .... **CLC 13, 22**
See also CA 102; DLB 6; DLBY 81;
MTCW

Gordon, Sol 1923-................. **CLC 26**
See also CA 53-56; CANR 4; SATA 11

Gordone, Charles 1925-.......... **CLC 1, 4**
See also BW; CA 93-96; DLB 7; MTCW

Gorenko, Anna Andreevna
See Akhmatova, Anna

Gorky, Maxim.................... **TCLC 8**
See also Peshkov, Alexei Maximovich
See also WLC

Goryan, Sirak
See Saroyan, William

Gosse, Edmund (William)
1849-1928 .... **TCLC 28**
See also CA 117; DLB 57

Gotlieb, Phyllis Fay (Bloom)
1926- .... **CLC 18**
See also CA 13-16R; CANR 7; DLB 88

Gottesman, S. D.
See Kornbluth, C(yril) M.; Pohl, Frederik

Gottfried von Strassburg
fl. c. 1210- .... **CMLC 10**

Gottschalk, Laura Riding
See Jackson, Laura (Riding)

Gould, Lois .... **CLC 4, 10**
See also CA 77-80; CANR 29; MTCW

Gourmont, Remy de 1858-1915.... **TCLC 17**
See also CA 109

Govier, Katherine 1948-.......... **CLC 51**
See also CA 101; CANR 18, 40

Goyen, (Charles) William
1915-1983 .... **CLC 5, 8, 14, 40**
See also AITN 2; CA 5-8R; 110; CANR 6;
DLB 2; DLBY 83

Goytisolo, Juan 1931- .... **CLC 5, 10, 23**
See also CA 85-88; CANR 32; HW; MTCW

Gozzi, (Conte) Carlo 1720-1806 .. **NCLC 23**

Grabbe, Christian Dietrich
1801-1836 .... **NCLC 2**

Grace, Patricia 1937-............. **CLC 56**

Gracian y Morales, Baltasar
1601-1658 .... **LC 15**

Gracq, Julien................. **CLC 11, 48**
See also Poirier, Louis
See also DLB 83

Grade, Chaim 1910-1982 .... **CLC 10**
See also CA 93-96; 107

Graduate of Oxford, A
See Ruskin, John

Graham, John
See Phillips, David Graham

Graham, Jorie 1951-............... **CLC 48**
See also CA 111; DLB 120

Graham, R(obert) B(ontine) Cunninghame
See Cunninghame Graham, R(obert)
B(ontine)
See also DLB 98

Graham, Robert
See Haldeman, Joe (William)

Graham, Tom
See Lewis, (Harry) Sinclair

Graham, W(illiam) S(ydney)
1918-1986 .... **CLC 29**
See also CA 73-76; 118; DLB 20

Graham, Winston (Mawdsley)
1910- .... **CLC 23**
See also CA 49-52; CANR 2, 22; DLB 77

Grant, Skeeter
See Spiegelman, Art

Granville-Barker, Harley
1877-1946 .... **TCLC 2**
See also Barker, Harley Granville
See also CA 104

Grass, Guenter (Wilhelm)
1927- .. **CLC 1, 2, 4, 6, 11, 15, 22, 32, 49**
See also CA 13-16R; CANR 20; DA;
DLB 75, 124; MTCW; WLC

Gratton, Thomas
See Hulme, T(homas) E(rnest)

Grau, Shirley Ann 1929- .... **CLC 4, 9**
See also CA 89-92; CANR 22; DLB 2;
MTCW

Gravel, Fern
See Hall, James Norman

Graver, Elizabeth 1964-........... **CLC 70**
See also CA 135

Graves, Richard Perceval 1945- .... **CLC 44**
See also CA 65-68; CANR 9, 26

Graves, Robert (von Ranke)
1895-1985 ..... **CLC 1, 2, 6, 11, 39, 44,
45; PC 6**
See also CA 5-8R; 117; CANR 5, 36;
CDBLB 1914-1945; DLB 20, 100;
DLBY 85; MTCW; SATA 45

Gray, Alasdair 1934- .... **CLC 41**
See also CA 126; MTCW

Gray, Amlin 1946- .... **CLC 29**
See also CA 138

Gray, Francine du Plessix 1930-.... **CLC 22**
See also BEST 90:3; CA 61-64; CAAS 2;
CANR 11, 33; MTCW

Gray, John (Henry) 1866-1934 .... **TCLC 19**
See also CA 119

Gray, Simon (James Holliday)
1936- .... **CLC 9, 14, 36**
See also AITN 1; CA 21-24R; CAAS 3;
CANR 32; DLB 13; MTCW

Gray, Spalding 1941- .... **CLC 49**
See also CA 128

Gray, Thomas 1716-1771....... **LC 4; PC 2**
See also CDBLB 1660-1789; DA; DLB 109;
WLC

Author Index

Guthrie, Isobel
See Grieve, C(hristopher) M(urray)

Guthrie, Woodrow Wilson 1912-1967
See Guthrie, Woody
See also CA 113; 93-96

Guthrie, Woody . . . . **CLC 35**
See also Guthrie, Woodrow Wilson

Guy, Rosa (Cuthbert) 1928- . . . . **CLC 26**
See also AAYA 4; BW; CA 17-20R;
CANR 14, 34; CLR 13; DLB 33;
MAICYA; SATA 14, 62

Gwendolyn
See Bennett, (Enoch) Arnold

H. D. . . . . **CLC 3, 8, 14, 31, 34, 73; PC 5**
See also Doolittle, Hilda

Haavikko, Paavo Juhani
1931- . . . . **CLC 18, 34**
See also CA 106

Habbema, Koos
See Heijermans, Herman

Hacker, Marilyn 1942- . . . . **CLC 5, 9, 23, 72**
See also CA 77-80; DLB 120

Haggard, H(enry) Rider
1856-1925 . . . . **TCLC 11**
See also CA 108; DLB 70; SATA 16

Haig, Fenil
See Ford, Ford Madox

Haig-Brown, Roderick (Langmere)
1908-1976 . . . . **CLC 21**
See also CA 5-8R; 69-72; CANR 4, 38;
CLR 31; DLB 88; MAICYA; SATA 12

Hailey, Arthur 1920- . . . . **CLC 5**
See also AITN 2; BEST 90:3; CA 1-4R;
CANR 2, 36; DLB 88; DLBY 82; MTCW

Hailey, Elizabeth Forsythe 1938- . . . **CLC 40**
See also CA 93-96; CAAS 1; CANR 15

Haines, John (Meade) 1924- . . . . **CLC 58**
See also CA 17-20R; CANR 13, 34; DLB 5

Haldeman, Joe (William) 1943- . . . . . **CLC 61**
See also CA 53-56; CANR 6; DLB 8

Haley, Alex(ander Murray Palmer)
1921-1992 . . . . **CLC 8, 12, 76**
See also BLC 2; BW; CA 77-80; 136; DA;
DLB 38; MTCW

Haliburton, Thomas Chandler
1796-1865 . . . . **NCLC 15**
See also DLB 11, 99

Hall, Donald (Andrew, Jr.)
1928- . . . . **CLC 1, 13, 37, 59**
See also CA 5-8R; CAAS 7; CANR 2;
DLB 5; SATA 23

Hall, Frederic Sauser
See Sauser-Hall, Frederic

Hall, James
See Kuttner, Henry

Hall, James Norman 1887-1951 . . . **TCLC 23**
See also CA 123; SATA 21

Hall, (Marguerite) Radclyffe
1886(?)-1943 . . . . **TCLC 12**
See also CA 110

Hall, Rodney 1935- . . . . **CLC 51**
See also CA 109

Halliday, Michael
See Creasey, John

Halpern, Daniel 1945- . . . . **CLC 14**
See also CA 33-36R

Hamburger, Michael (Peter Leopold)
1924- . . . . **CLC 5, 14**
See also CA 5-8R; CAAS 4; CANR 2;
DLB 27

Hamill, Pete 1935- . . . . **CLC 10**
See also CA 25-28R; CANR 18

Hamilton, Clive
See Lewis, C(live) S(taples)

Hamilton, Edmond 1904-1977 . . . . . . **CLC 1**
See also CA 1-4R; CANR 3; DLB 8

Hamilton, Eugene (Jacob) Lee
See Lee-Hamilton, Eugene (Jacob)

Hamilton, Franklin
See Silverberg, Robert

Hamilton, Gail
See Corcoran, Barbara

Hamilton, Mollie
See Kaye, M(ary) M(argaret)

Hamilton, (Anthony Walter) Patrick
1904-1962 . . . . **CLC 51**
See also CA 113; DLB 10

Hamilton, Virginia 1936- . . . . **CLC 26**
See also AAYA 2; BW; CA 25-28R;
CANR 20, 37; CLR 1, 11; DLB 33, 52;
MAICYA; MTCW; SATA 4, 56

Hammett, (Samuel) Dashiell
1894-1961 . . . . **CLC 3, 5, 10, 19, 47**
See also AITN 1; CA 81-84;
CDALB 1929-1941; DLBD 6; MTCW

Hammon, Jupiter 1711(?)-1800(?) . . **NCLC 5**
See also BLC 2; DLB 31, 50

Hammond, Keith
See Kuttner, Henry

Hamner, Earl (Henry), Jr. 1923- . . . **CLC 12**
See also AITN 2; CA 73-76; DLB 6

Hampton, Christopher (James)
1946- . . . . **CLC 4**
See also CA 25-28R; DLB 13; MTCW

Hamsun, Knut . . . . **TCLC 2, 14, 49**
See also Pedersen, Knut

Handke, Peter 1942- . . **CLC 5, 8, 10, 15, 38**
See also CA 77-80; CANR 33; DLB 85,
124; MTCW

Hanley, James 1901-1985 . . . **CLC 3, 5, 8, 13**
See also CA 73-76; 117; CANR 36; MTCW

Hannah, Barry 1942- . . . . **CLC 23, 38**
See also CA 108; 110; DLB 6; MTCW

Hannon, Ezra
See Hunter, Evan

Hansberry, Lorraine (Vivian)
1930-1965 . . . . **CLC 17, 62; DC 2**
See also BLC 2; BW; CA 109; 25-28R;
CABS 3; CDALB 1941-1968; DA;
DLB 7, 38; MTCW

Hansen, Joseph 1923- . . . . **CLC 38**
See also CA 29-32R; CAAS 17; CANR 16

Hansen, Martin A. 1909-1955 . . . . . **TCLC 32**

Hanson, Kenneth O(stlin) 1922- . . . . **CLC 13**
See also CA 53-56; CANR 7

Hardwick, Elizabeth 1916- . . . . **CLC 13**
See also CA 5-8R; CANR 3, 32; DLB 6;
MTCW

Hardy, Thomas
1840-1928 . . . . . **TCLC 4, 10, 18, 32, 48;
SSC 2**
See also CA 104; 123; CDBLB 1890-1914;
DA; DLB 18, 19; MTCW; WLC

Hare, David 1947- . . . . **CLC 29, 58**
See also CA 97-100; CANR 39; DLB 13;
MTCW

Harford, Henry
See Hudson, W(illiam) H(enry)

Hargrave, Leonie
See Disch, Thomas M(ichael)

Harlan, Louis R(udolph) 1922- . . . . . **CLC 34**
See also CA 21-24R; CANR 25

Harling, Robert 1951(?)- . . . . **CLC 53**

Harmon, William (Ruth) 1938- . . . . . **CLC 38**
See also CA 33-36R; CANR 14, 32, 35;
SATA 65

Harper, F. E. W.
See Harper, Frances Ellen Watkins

Harper, Frances E. W.
See Harper, Frances Ellen Watkins

Harper, Frances E. Watkins
See Harper, Frances Ellen Watkins

Harper, Frances Ellen
See Harper, Frances Ellen Watkins

Harper, Frances Ellen Watkins
1825-1911 . . . . **TCLC 14**
See also BLC 2; BW; CA 111; 125; DLB 50

Harper, Michael S(teven) 1938- . . **CLC 7, 22**
See also BW; CA 33-36R; CANR 24;
DLB 41

Harper, Mrs. F. E. W.
See Harper, Frances Ellen Watkins

Harris, Christie (Lucy) Irwin
1907- . . . . **CLC 12**
See also CA 5-8R; CANR 6; DLB 88;
MAICYA; SAAS 10; SATA 6, 74

Harris, Frank 1856(?)-1931 . . . . **TCLC 24**
See also CA 109

Harris, George Washington
1814-1869 . . . . **NCLC 23**
See also DLB 3, 11

Harris, Joel Chandler 1848-1908 . . . **TCLC 2**
See also CA 104; 137; DLB 11, 23, 42, 78,
91; MAICYA; YABC 1

Harris, John (Wyndham Parkes Lucas)
Beynon 1903-1969 . . . . **CLC 19**
See also CA 102; 89-92

Harris, MacDonald
See Heiney, Donald (William)

Harris, Mark 1922- . . . . **CLC 19**
See also CA 5-8R; CAAS 3; CANR 2;
DLB 2; DLBY 80

Harris, (Theodore) Wilson 1921- . . . . **CLC 25**
See also BW; CA 65-68; CAAS 16;
CANR 11, 27; DLB 117; MTCW

Harrison, Elizabeth Cavanna 1909-
See Cavanna, Betty
See also CA 9-12R; CANR 6, 27

Harrison, Harry (Max) 1925- . . . . **CLC 42**
See also CA 1-4R; CANR 5, 21; DLB 8;
SATA 4

Harrison, James (Thomas) 1937-
See Harrison, Jim
See also CA 13-16R; CANR 8

Harrison, Jim .... **CLC 6, 14, 33, 66**
See also Harrison, James (Thomas)
See also DLBY 82

Harrison, Kathryn 1961- .... **CLC 70**

Harrison, Tony 1937-............. **CLC 43**
See also CA 65-68; DLB 40; MTCW

Harriss, Will(ard Irvin) 1922-...... **CLC 34**
See also CA 111

Harson, Sley
See Ellison, Harlan

Hart, Ellis
See Ellison, Harlan

Hart, Josephine 1942(?)-.......... **CLC 70**
See also CA 138

Hart, Moss 1904-1961 .... **CLC 66**
See also CA 109; 89-92; DLB 7

Harte, (Francis) Bret(t)
1836(?)-1902 ...... **TCLC 1, 25; SSC 8**
See also CA 104; 140; CDALB 1865-1917;
DA; DLB 12, 64, 74, 79; SATA 26; WLC

Hartley, L(eslie) P(oles)
1895-1972 .... **CLC 2, 22**
See also CA 45-48; 37-40R; CANR 33;
DLB 15; MTCW

Hartman, Geoffrey H. 1929-....... **CLC 27**
See also CA 117; 125; DLB 67

Haruf, Kent 19(?)- .... **CLC 34**

Harwood, Ronald 1934-........... **CLC 32**
See also CA 1-4R; CANR 4; DLB 13

Hasek, Jaroslav (Matej Frantisek)
1883-1923 .... **TCLC 4**
See also CA 104; 129; MTCW

Hass, Robert 1941-............. **CLC 18, 39**
See also CA 111; CANR 30; DLB 105

Hastings, Hudson
See Kuttner, Henry

Hastings, Selina................... **CLC 44**

Hatteras, Amelia
See Mencken, H(enry) L(ouis)

Hatteras, Owen................ **TCLC 18**
See also Mencken, H(enry) L(ouis); Nathan,
George Jean

Hauptmann, Gerhart (Johann Robert)
1862-1946 .... **TCLC 4**
See also CA 104; DLB 66, 118

Havel, Vaclav 1936-........ **CLC 25, 58, 65**
See also CA 104; CANR 36; MTCW

Haviaras, Stratis .... **CLC 33**
See also Chaviaras, Strates

Hawes, Stephen 1475(?)-1523(?) ..... **LC 17**

Hawkes, John (Clendennin Burne, Jr.)
1925- ...... **CLC 1, 2, 3, 4, 7, 9, 14, 15,
27, 49**
See also CA 1-4R; CANR 2; DLB 2, 7;
DLBY 80; MTCW

Hawking, S. W.
See Hawking, Stephen W(illiam)

Hawking, Stephen W(illiam)
1942-...................... **CLC 63**
See also BEST 89:1; CA 126; 129

Hawthorne, Julian 1846-1934 ..... **TCLC 25**

Hawthorne, Nathaniel
1804-1864 .... **NCLC 39; SSC 3**
See also CDALB 1640-1865; DA; DLB 1,
74; WLC; YABC 2

Haxton, Josephine Ayres 1921- .... **CLC 73**
See also CA 115; CANR 41

Hayaseca y Eizaguirre, Jorge
See Echegaray (y Eizaguirre), Jose (Maria
Waldo)

Hayashi Fumiko 1904-1951...... **TCLC 27**

Haycraft, Anna
See Ellis, Alice Thomas
See also CA 122

Hayden, Robert E(arl)
1913-1980 ...... **CLC 5, 9, 14, 37; PC 6**
See also BLC 2; BW; CA 69-72; 97-100;
CABS 2; CANR 24; CDALB 1941-1968;
DA; DLB 5, 76; MTCW; SATA 19, 26

Hayford, J(oseph) E(phraim) Casely
See Casely-Hayford, J(oseph) E(phraim)

Hayman, Ronald 1932-............ **CLC 44**
See also CA 25-28R; CANR 18

Haywood, Eliza (Fowler)
1693(?)-1756 .... **LC 1**

Hazlitt, William 1778-1830...... **NCLC 29**
See also DLB 110

Hazzard, Shirley 1931- .... **CLC 18**
See also CA 9-12R; CANR 4; DLBY 82;
MTCW

Head, Bessie 1937-1986........ **CLC 25, 67**
See also BLC 2; BW; CA 29-32R; 119;
CANR 25; DLB 117; MTCW

Headon, (Nicky) Topper 1956(?)-... **CLC 30**
See also Clash, The

Heaney, Seamus (Justin)
1939- .... **CLC 5, 7, 14, 25, 37, 74**
See also CA 85-88; CANR 25;
CDBLB 1960 to Present; DLB 40;
MTCW

Hearn, (Patricio) Lafcadio (Tessima Carlos)
1850-1904 .... **TCLC 9**
See also CA 105; DLB 12, 78

Hearne, Vicki 1946-.............. **CLC 56**
See also CA 139

Hearon, Shelby 1931-............. **CLC 63**
See also AITN 2; CA 25-28R; CANR 18

Heat-Moon, William Least......... **CLC 29**
See also Trogdon, William (Lewis)
See also AAYA 9

Hebert, Anne 1916- .... **CLC 4, 13, 29**
See also CA 85-88; DLB 68; MTCW

Hecht, Anthony (Evan)
1923- .... **CLC 8, 13, 19**
See also CA 9-12R; CANR 6; DLB 5

Hecht, Ben 1894-1964 .... **CLC 8**
See also CA 85-88; DLB 7, 9, 25, 26, 28, 86

Hedayat, Sadeq 1903-1951........ **TCLC 21**
See also CA 120

Heidegger, Martin 1889-1976 ...... **CLC 24**
See also CA 81-84; 65-68; CANR 34;
MTCW

Heidenstam, (Carl Gustaf) Verner von
1859-1940 .... **TCLC 5**
See also CA 104

Heifner, Jack 1946-.............. **CLC 11**
See also CA 105

Heijermans, Herman 1864-1924 ... **TCLC 24**
See also CA 123

Heilbrun, Carolyn G(old) 1926-..... **CLC 25**
See also CA 45-48; CANR 1, 28

Heine, Heinrich 1797-1856 .... **NCLC 4**
See also DLB 90

Heinemann, Larry (Curtiss) 1944- .. **CLC 50**
See also CA 110; CANR 31; DLBD 9

Heiney, Donald (William) 1921-..... **CLC 9**
See also CA 1-4R; CANR 3

Heinlein, Robert A(nson)
1907-1988 ...... **CLC 1, 3, 8, 14, 26, 55**
See also CA 1-4R; 125; CANR 1, 20;
DLB 8; MAICYA; MTCW; SATA 9, 56,
69

Helforth, John
See Doolittle, Hilda

Hellenhofferu, Vojtech Kapristian z
See Hasek, Jaroslav (Matej Frantisek)

Heller, Joseph
1923- .... **CLC 1, 3, 5, 8, 11, 36, 63**
See also AITN 1; CA 5-8R; CABS 1;
CANR 8; DA; DLB 2, 28; DLBY 80;
MTCW; WLC

Hellman, Lillian (Florence)
1906-1984 ..... **CLC 2, 4, 8, 14, 18, 34,
44, 52; DC 1**
See also AITN 1, 2; CA 13-16R; 112;
CANR 33; DLB 7; DLBY 84; MTCW

Helprin, Mark 1947- ..... **CLC 7, 10, 22, 32**
See also CA 81-84; DLBY 85; MTCW

Helyar, Jane Penelope Josephine 1933-
See Poole, Josephine
See also CA 21-24R; CANR 10, 26

Hemans, Felicia 1793-1835 ...... **NCLC 29**
See also DLB 96

Hemingway, Ernest (Miller)
1899-1961 ... **CLC 1, 3, 6, 8, 10, 13, 19,
30, 34, 39, 41, 44, 50, 61; SSC 1**
See also CA 77-80; CANR 34;
CDALB 1917-1929; DA; DLB 4, 9, 102;
DLBD 1; DLBY 81, 87; MTCW; WLC

Hempel, Amy 1951-.............. **CLC 39**
See also CA 118; 137

Henderson, F. C.
See Mencken, H(enry) L(ouis)

Henderson, Sylvia
See Ashton-Warner, Sylvia (Constance)

Henley, Beth .... **CLC 23**
See also Henley, Elizabeth Becker
See also CABS 3; DLBY 86

Henley, Elizabeth Becker 1952-
See Henley, Beth
See also CA 107; CANR 32; MTCW

Henley, William Ernest
1849-1903 .... **TCLC 8**
See also CA 105; DLB 19

Hennissart, Martha
See Lathen, Emma
See also CA 85-88

Henry, O............... **TCLC 1, 19; SSC 5**
See also Porter, William Sydney
See also WLC

Henryson, Robert 1430(?)-1506(?).... **LC 20**

Henry VIII 1491-1547............. **LC 10**

Henschke, Alfred
See Klabund

Hentoff, Nat(han Irving) 1925- ..... **CLC 26**
See also AAYA 4; CA 1-4R; CAAS 6;
CANR 5, 25; CLR 1; MAICYA;
SATA 27, 42, 69

Heppenstall, (John) Rayner
1911-1981 .... **CLC 10**
See also CA 1-4R; 103; CANR 29

Herbert, Frank (Patrick)
1920-1986 .... **CLC 12, 23, 35, 44**
See also CA 53-56; 118; CANR 5; DLB 8;
MTCW; SATA 9, 37, 47

Herbert, George 1593-1633......... **PC 4**
See also CDBLB Before 1660; DLB 126

Herbert, Zbigniew 1924- .... **CLC 9, 43**
See also CA 89-92; CANR 36; MTCW

Herbst, Josephine (Frey)
1897-1969 .... **CLC 34**
See also CA 5-8R; 25-28R; DLB 9

Hergesheimer, Joseph
1880-1954 .... **TCLC 11**
See also CA 109; DLB 102, 9

Herlihy, James Leo 1927- .... **CLC 6**
See also CA 1-4R; CANR 2

Hermogenes fl. c. 175- .... **CMLC 6**

Hernandez, Jose 1834-1886...... **NCLC 17**

Herrick, Robert 1591-1674 .... **LC 13**
See also DA; DLB 126

Herring, Guilles
See Somerville, Edith

Herriot, James 1916- .... **CLC 12**
See also Wight, James Alfred
See also AAYA 1; CANR 40

Herrmann, Dorothy 1941-........ **CLC 44**
See also CA 107

Herrmann, Taffy
See Herrmann, Dorothy

Hersey, John (Richard)
1914-1993 .... **CLC 1, 2, 7, 9, 40**
See also CA 17-20R; 140; CANR 33;
DLB 6; MTCW; SATA 25

Herzen, Aleksandr Ivanovich
1812-1870 .... **NCLC 10**

Herzl, Theodor 1860-1904....... **TCLC 36**

Herzog, Werner 1942- .... **CLC 16**
See also CA 89-92

Hesiod c. 8th cent. B.C.- .... **CMLC 5**

Hesse, Hermann
1877-1962 ... **CLC 1, 2, 3, 6, 11, 17, 25,**
69; SSC 9
See also CA 17-18; CAP 2; DA; DLB 66;
MTCW; SATA 50; WLC

Hewes, Cady
See De Voto, Bernard (Augustine)

Heyen, William 1940- .... **CLC 13, 18**
See also CA 33-36R; CAAS 9; DLB 5

Heyerdahl, Thor 1914-............ **CLC 26**
See also CA 5-8R; CANR 5, 22; MTCW;
SATA 2, 52

Heym, Georg (Theodor Franz Arthur)
1887-1912 .... **TCLC 9**
See also CA 106

Heym, Stefan 1913-............. **CLC 41**
See also CA 9-12R; CANR 4; DLB 69

Heyse, Paul (Johann Ludwig von)
1830-1914 .... **TCLC 8**
See also CA 104; DLB 129

Hibbert, Eleanor Alice Burford
1906-1993 .... **CLC 7**
See also BEST 90:4; CA 17-20R; CANR 9,
28; SATA 2; SATA-Obit 74

Higgins, George V(incent)
1939- ....**CLC 4, 7, 10, 18**
See also CA 77-80; CAAS 5; CANR 17;
DLB 2; DLBY 81; MTCW

Higginson, Thomas Wentworth
1823-1911 .... **TCLC 36**
See also DLB 1, 64

Highet, Helen
See MacInnes, Helen (Clark)

Highsmith, (Mary) Patricia
1921- ....**CLC 2, 4, 14, 42**
See also CA 1-4R; CANR 1, 20; MTCW

Highwater, Jamake (Mamake)
1942(?)- .... **CLC 12**
See also AAYA 7; CA 65-68; CAAS 7;
CANR 10, 34; CLR 17; DLB 52;
DLBY 85; MAICYA; SATA 30, 32, 69

Hijuelos, Oscar 1951- .... **CLC 65**
See also BEST 90:1; CA 123; HW

Hikmet, Nazim 1902-1963........ **CLC 40**
See also CA 93-96

Hildesheimer, Wolfgang
1916-1991 .... **CLC 49**
See also CA 101; 135; DLB 69, 124

Hill, Geoffrey (William)
1932- ....**CLC 5, 8, 18, 45**
See also CA 81-84; CANR 21;
CDBLB 1960 to Present; DLB 40;
MTCW

Hill, George Roy 1921- .... **CLC 26**
See also CA 110; 122

Hill, John
See Koontz, Dean R(ay)

Hill, Susan (Elizabeth) 1942- .... **CLC 4**
See also CA 33-36R; CANR 29; DLB 14;
MTCW

Hillerman, Tony 1925-............ **CLC 62**
See also AAYA 6; BEST 89:1; CA 29-32R;
CANR 21; SATA 6

Hillesum, Etty 1914-1943 .... **TCLC 49**
See also CA 137

Hilliard, Noel (Harvey) 1929-...... **CLC 15**
See also CA 9-12R; CANR 7

Hillis, Rick 1956-................ **CLC 66**
See also CA 134

Hilton, James 1900-1954........ **TCLC 21**
See also CA 108; DLB 34, 77; SATA 34

Himes, Chester (Bomar)
1909-1984 .... **CLC 2, 4, 7, 18, 58**
See also BLC 2; BW; CA 25-28R; 114;
CANR 22; DLB 2, 76; MTCW

Hinde, Thomas .... **CLC 6, 11**
See also Chitty, Thomas Willes

Hindin, Nathan
See Bloch, Robert (Albert)

Hine, (William) Daryl 1936- .... **CLC 15**
See also CA 1-4R; CAAS 15; CANR 1, 20;
DLB 60

Hinkson, Katharine Tynan
See Tynan, Katharine

Hinton, S(usan) E(loise) 1950- ..... **CLC 30**
See also AAYA 2; CA 81-84; CANR 32;
CLR 3, 23; DA; MAICYA; MTCW;
SATA 19, 58

Hippius, Zinaida .... **TCLC 9**
See also Gippius, Zinaida (Nikolayevna)

Hiraoka, Kimitake 1925-1970
See Mishima, Yukio
See also CA 97-100; 29-32R; MTCW

Hirsch, Edward 1950- .... **CLC 31, 50**
See also CA 104; CANR 20; DLB 120

Hitchcock, Alfred (Joseph)
1899-1980 .... **CLC 16**
See also CA 97-100; SATA 24, 27

Hoagland, Edward 1932-......... **CLC 28**
See also CA 1-4R; CANR 2, 31; DLB 6;
SATA 51

Hoban, Russell (Conwell) 1925- .. **CLC 7, 25**
See also CA 5-8R; CANR 23, 37; CLR 3;
DLB 52; MAICYA; MTCW; SATA 1, 40

Hobbs, Perry
See Blackmur, R(ichard) P(almer)

Hobson, Laura Z(ametkin)
1900-1986 .... **CLC 7, 25**
See also CA 17-20R; 118; DLB 28;
SATA 52

Hochhuth, Rolf 1931-........ **CLC 4, 11, 18**
See also CA 5-8R; CANR 33; DLB 124;
MTCW

Hochman, Sandra 1936-.......... **CLC 3, 8**
See also CA 5-8R; DLB 5

Hochwaelder, Fritz 1911-1986...... **CLC 36**
See also Hochwalder, Fritz
See also CA 29-32R; 120; MTCW

Hochwalder, Fritz................. **CLC 36**
See also Hochwaelder, Fritz

Hocking, Mary (Eunice) 1921-..... **CLC 13**
See also CA 101; CANR 18, 40

Hodgins, Jack 1938-............. **CLC 23**
See also CA 93-96; DLB 60

Hodgson, William Hope
1877(?)-1918 .... **TCLC 13**
See also CA 111; DLB 70

Hoffman, Alice 1952-............. **CLC 51**
See also CA 77-80; CANR 34; MTCW

Hoffman, Daniel (Gerard)
1923- .... **CLC 6, 13, 23**
See also CA 1-4R; CANR 4; DLB 5

Hoffman, Stanley 1944-............ **CLC 5**
See also CA 77-80

Hoffman, William M(oses) 1939- . . . **CLC 40**
See also CA 57-60; CANR 11

Hoffmann, E(rnst) T(heodor) A(madeus)
1776-1822 . . . . **NCLC 2**
See also DLB 90; SATA 27

Hofmann, Gert 1931- . . . . **CLC 54**
See also CA 128

Hofmannsthal, Hugo von
1874-1929 . . . . **TCLC 11**
See also CA 106; DLB 81, 118

Hogan, Linda 1947- . . . . **CLC 73**
See also CA 120

Hogarth, Charles
See Creasey, John

Hogg, James 1770-1835 . . . . **NCLC 4**
See also DLB 93, 116

Holbach, Paul Henri Thiry Baron
1723-1789 . . . . **LC 14**

Holberg, Ludvig 1684-1754 . . . . **LC 6**

Holden, Ursula 1921- . . . . **CLC 18**
See also CA 101; CAAS 8; CANR 22

Holderlin, (Johann Christian) Friedrich
1770-1843 . . . . **NCLC 16; PC 4**

Holdstock, Robert
See Holdstock, Robert P.

Holdstock, Robert P. 1948- . . . . **CLC 39**
See also CA 131

Holland, Isabelle 1920- . . . . **CLC 21**
See also CA 21-24R; CANR 10, 25;
MAICYA; SATA 8, 70

Holland, Marcus
See Caldwell, (Janet Miriam) Taylor
(Holland)

Hollander, John 1929- . . . . . . **CLC 2, 5, 8, 14**
See also CA 1-4R; CANR 1; DLB 5;
SATA 13

Hollander, Paul
See Silverberg, Robert

Holleran, Andrew 1943(?)- . . . . **CLC 38**

Hollinghurst, Alan 1954- . . . . **CLC 55**
See also CA 114

Hollis, Jim
See Summers, Hollis (Spurgeon, Jr.)

Holmes, John
See Souster, (Holmes) Raymond

Holmes, John Clellon 1926-1988 . . . . **CLC 56**
See also CA 9-12R; 125; CANR 4; DLB 16

Holmes, Oliver Wendell
1809-1894 . . . . **NCLC 14**
See also CDALB 1640-1865; DLB 1;
SATA 34

Holmes, Raymond
See Souster, (Holmes) Raymond

Holt, Victoria
See Hibbert, Eleanor Alice Burford

Holub, Miroslav 1923- . . . . **CLC 4**
See also CA 21-24R; CANR 10

Homer c. 8th cent. B.C.- . . . . **CMLC 1**
See also DA

Honig, Edwin 1919- . . . . **CLC 33**
See also CA 5-8R; CAAS 8; CANR 4;
DLB 5

Hood, Hugh (John Blagdon)
1928- . . . . **CLC 15, 28**
See also CA 49-52; CAAS 17; CANR 1, 33;
DLB 53

Hood, Thomas 1799-1845 . . . . **NCLC 16**
See also DLB 96

Hooker, (Peter) Jeremy 1941- . . . . . . **CLC 43**
See also CA 77-80; CANR 22; DLB 40

Hope, A(lec) D(erwent) 1907- . . . . **CLC 3, 51**
See also CA 21-24R; CANR 33; MTCW

Hope, Brian
See Creasey, John

Hope, Christopher (David Tully)
1944- . . . . **CLC 52**
See also CA 106; SATA 62

Hopkins, Gerard Manley
1844-1889 . . . . **NCLC 17**
See also CDBLB 1890-1914; DA; DLB 35,
57; WLC

Hopkins, John (Richard) 1931- . . . . . . **CLC 4**
See also CA 85-88

Hopkins, Pauline Elizabeth
1859-1930 . . . . **TCLC 28**
See also BLC 2; DLB 50

Hopley-Woolrich, Cornell George 1903-1968
See Woolrich, Cornell
See also CA 13-14; CAP 1

Horatio
See Proust, (Valentin-Louis-George-Eugene-)
Marcel

Horgan, Paul 1903- . . . . **CLC 9, 53**
See also CA 13-16R; CANR 9, 35;
DLB 102; DLBY 85; MTCW; SATA 13

Horn, Peter
See Kuttner, Henry

Hornem, Horace Esq.
See Byron, George Gordon (Noel)

Horovitz, Israel 1939- . . . . **CLC 56**
See also CA 33-36R; DLB 7

Horvath, Odon von
See Horvath, Oedoen von
See also DLB 85, 124

Horvath, Oedoen von 1901-1938 . . . **TCLC 45**
See also Horvath, Odon von
See also CA 118

Horwitz, Julius 1920-1986 . . . . **CLC 14**
See also CA 9-12R; 119; CANR 12

Hospital, Janette Turner 1942- . . . . . **CLC 42**
See also CA 108

Hostos, E. M. de
See Hostos (y Bonilla), Eugenio Maria de

Hostos, Eugenio M. de
See Hostos (y Bonilla), Eugenio Maria de

Hostos, Eugenio Maria
See Hostos (y Bonilla), Eugenio Maria de

Hostos (y Bonilla), Eugenio Maria de
1839-1903 . . . . **TCLC 24**
See also CA 123; 131; HW

Houdini
See Lovecraft, H(oward) P(hillips)

Hougan, Carolyn 1943- . . . . **CLC 34**
See also CA 139

Household, Geoffrey (Edward West)
1900-1988 . . . . **CLC 11**
See also CA 77-80; 126; DLB 87; SATA 14,
59

Housman, A(lfred) E(dward)
1859-1936 . . . . **TCLC 1, 10; PC 2**
See also CA 104; 125; DA; DLB 19;
MTCW

Housman, Laurence 1865-1959 . . . . . **TCLC 7**
See also CA 106; DLB 10; SATA 25

Howard, Elizabeth Jane 1923- . . . **CLC 7, 29**
See also CA 5-8R; CANR 8

Howard, Maureen 1930- . . . . . **CLC 5, 14, 46**
See also CA 53-56; CANR 31; DLBY 83;
MTCW

Howard, Richard 1929- . . . . . . **CLC 7, 10, 47**
See also AITN 1; CA 85-88; CANR 25;
DLB 5

Howard, Robert Ervin 1906-1936 . . . **TCLC 8**
See also CA 105

Howard, Warren F.
See Pohl, Frederik

Howe, Fanny 1940- . . . . **CLC 47**
See also CA 117; SATA 52

Howe, Julia Ward 1819-1910 . . . . . **TCLC 21**
See also CA 117; DLB 1

Howe, Susan 1937- . . . . **CLC 72**
See also DLB 120

Howe, Tina 1937- . . . . **CLC 48**
See also CA 109

Howell, James 1594(?)-1666 . . . . **LC 13**

Howells, W. D.
See Howells, William Dean

Howells, William D.
See Howells, William Dean

Howells, William Dean
1837-1920 . . . . **TCLC 41, 7, 17**
See also CA 104; 134; CDALB 1865-1917;
DLB 12, 64, 74, 79

Howes, Barbara 1914- . . . . **CLC 15**
See also CA 9-12R; CAAS 3; SATA 5

Hrabal, Bohumil 1914- . . . . **CLC 13, 67**
See also CA 106; CAAS 12

Hsun, Lu . . . . **TCLC 3**
See also Shu-Jen, Chou

Hubbard, L(afayette) Ron(ald)
1911-1986 . . . . **CLC 43**
See also CA 77-80; 118; CANR 22

Huch, Ricarda (Octavia)
1864-1947 . . . . **TCLC 13**
See also CA 111; DLB 66

Huddle, David 1942- . . . . **CLC 49**
See also CA 57-60; DLB 130

Hudson, Jeffrey
See Crichton, (John) Michael

Hudson, W(illiam) H(enry)
1841-1922 . . . . **TCLC 29**
See also CA 115; DLB 98; SATA 35

Hueffer, Ford Madox
See Ford, Ford Madox

Hughart, Barry 1934- . . . . **CLC 39**
See also CA 137

Hughes, Colin
See Creasey, John

Hughes, David (John) 1930- .... **CLC 48**
See also CA 116; 129; DLB 14

Hughes, (James) Langston
1902-1967 .... **CLC 1, 5, 10, 15, 35, 44;**
DC 3; PC 1; SSC 6
See also BLC 2; BW; CA 25-28R;
CANR 1, 34; CDALB 1929-1941;
CLR 17; DA; DLB 4, 7, 48, 51, 86;
MAICYA; MTCW; SATA 4, 33; WLC

Hughes, Richard (Arthur Warren)
1900-1976 .... **CLC 1, 11**
See also CA 5-8R; 65-68; CANR 4;
DLB 15; MTCW; SATA 8, 25

Hughes, Ted
1930- .... **CLC 2, 4, 9, 14, 37; PC 7**
See also CA 1-4R; CANR 1, 33; CLR 3;
DLB 40; MAICYA; MTCW; SATA 27,
49

Hugo, Richard F(ranklin)
1923-1982 .... **CLC 6, 18, 32**
See also CA 49-52; 108; CANR 3; DLB 5

Hugo, Victor (Marie)
1802-1885 .... **NCLC 3, 10, 21**
See also DA; DLB 119; SATA 47; WLC

Huidobro, Vicente
See Huidobro Fernandez, Vicente Garcia

Huidobro Fernandez, Vicente Garcia
1893-1948 .... **TCLC 31**
See also CA 131; HW

Hulme, Keri 1947- .... **CLC 39**
See also CA 125

Hulme, T(homas) E(rnest)
1883-1917 .... **TCLC 21**
See also CA 117; DLB 19

Hume, David 1711-1776 .... **LC 7**
See also DLB 104

Humphrey, William 1924- .... **CLC 45**
See also CA 77-80; DLB 6

Humphreys, Emyr Owen 1919- ..... **CLC 47**
See also CA 5-8R; CANR 3, 24; DLB 15

Humphreys, Josephine 1945- .... **CLC 34, 57**
See also CA 121; 127

Hungerford, Pixie
See Brinsmead, H(esba) F(ay)

Hunt, E(verette) Howard, Jr.
1918- .... **CLC 3**
See also AITN 1; CA 45-48; CANR 2

Hunt, Kyle
See Creasey, John

Hunt, (James Henry) Leigh
1784-1859 .... **NCLC 1**

Hunt, Marsha 1946- .... **CLC 70**

Hunter, E. Waldo
See Sturgeon, Theodore (Hamilton)

Hunter, Evan 1926- .... **CLC 11, 31**
See also CA 5-8R; CANR 5, 38; DLBY 82;
MTCW; SATA 25

Hunter, Kristin (Eggleston) 1931-... **CLC 35**
See also AITN 1; BW; CA 13-16R;
CANR 13; CLR 3; DLB 33; MAICYA;
SAAS 10; SATA 12

Hunter, Mollie 1922- .... **CLC 21**
See also McIlwraith, Maureen Mollie
Hunter
See also CANR 37; CLR 25; MAICYA;
SAAS 7; SATA 54

Hunter, Robert (?)-1734............. **LC 7**

Hurston, Zora Neale
1903-1960 .... **CLC 7, 30, 61; SSC 4**
See also BLC 2; BW; CA 85-88; DA;
DLB 51, 86; MTCW

Huston, John (Marcellus)
1906-1987 .... **CLC 20**
See also CA 73-76; 123; CANR 34; DLB 26

Hustvedt, Siri 1955-............... **CLC 76**
See also CA 137

Hutten, Ulrich von 1488-1523...... **LC 16**

Huxley, Aldous (Leonard)
1894-1963 .. **CLC 1, 3, 4, 5, 8, 11, 18, 35**
See also CA 85-88; CDBLB 1914-1945; DA;
DLB 36, 100; MTCW; SATA 63; WLC

Huysmans, Charles Marie Georges
1848-1907
See Huysmans, Joris-Karl
See also CA 104

Huysmans, Joris-Karl.............. **TCLC 7**
See also Huysmans, Charles Marie Georges
See also DLB 123

Hwang, David Henry 1957-........ **CLC 55**
See also CA 127; 132

Hyde, Anthony 1946- .... **CLC 42**
See also CA 136

Hyde, Margaret O(ldroyd) 1917- ... **CLC 21**
See also CA 1-4R; CANR 1, 36; CLR 23;
MAICYA; SAAS 8; SATA 1, 42

Hynes, James 1956(?)-............ **CLC 65**

Ian, Janis 1951- .... **CLC 21**
See also CA 105

Ibanez, Vicente Blasco
See Blasco Ibanez, Vicente

Ibarguengoitia, Jorge 1928-1983.... **CLC 37**
See also CA 124; 113; HW

Ibsen, Henrik (Johan)
1828-1906 ..... **TCLC 2, 8, 16, 37; DC 2**
See also CA 104; DA; WLC

Ibuse Masuji 1898-............... **CLC 22**
See also CA 127

Ichikawa, Kon 1915-.............. **CLC 20**
See also CA 121

Idle, Eric 1943-.................. **CLC 21**
See also Monty Python
See also CA 116; CANR 35

Ignatow, David 1914-...... **CLC 4, 7, 14, 40**
See also CA 9-12R; CAAS 3; CANR 31;
DLB 5

Ihimaera, Witi 1944- .... **CLC 46**
See also CA 77-80

Ilf, Ilya...................... **TCLC 21**
See also Fainzilberg, Ilya Arnoldovich

Immermann, Karl (Lebrecht)
1796-1840 .... **NCLC 4**

Inclan, Ramon (Maria) del Valle
See Valle-Inclan, Ramon (Maria) del

Infante, G(uillermo) Cabrera
See Cabrera Infante, G(uillermo)

Ingalls, Rachel (Holmes) 1940-..... **CLC 42**
See also CA 123; 127

Ingamells, Rex 1913-1955 .... **TCLC 35**

Inge, William Motter
1913-1973 .... **CLC 1, 8, 19**
See also CA 9-12R; CDALB 1941-1968;
DLB 7; MTCW

Ingelow, Jean 1820-1897 .... **NCLC 39**
See also DLB 35; SATA 33

Ingram, Willis J.
See Harris, Mark

Innaurato, Albert (F.) 1948(?)- .. **CLC 21, 60**
See also CA 115; 122

Innes, Michael
See Stewart, J(ohn) I(nnes) M(ackintosh)

Ionesco, Eugene
1912- .... **CLC 1, 4, 6, 9, 11, 15, 41**
See also CA 9-12R; DA; MTCW; SATA 7;
WLC

Iqbal, Muhammad 1873-1938 ..... **TCLC 28**

Ireland, Patrick
See O'Doherty, Brian

Irland, David
See Green, Julian (Hartridge)

Iron, Ralph
See Schreiner, Olive (Emilie Albertina)

Irving, John (Winslow)
1942- .... **CLC 13, 23, 38**
See also AAYA 8; BEST 89:3; CA 25-28R;
CANR 28; DLB 6; DLBY 82; MTCW

Irving, Washington
1783-1859 .... **NCLC 2, 19; SSC 2**
See also CDALB 1640-1865; DA; DLB 3,
11, 30, 59, 73, 74; WLC; YABC 2

Irwin, P. K.
See Page, P(atricia) K(athleen)

Isaacs, Susan 1943- .... **CLC 32**
See also BEST 89:1; CA 89-92; CANR 20,
41; MTCW

Isherwood, Christopher (William Bradshaw)
1904-1986 .... **CLC 1, 9, 11, 14, 44**
See also CA 13-16R; 117; CANR 35;
DLB 15; DLBY 86; MTCW

Ishiguro, Kazuo 1954- ...... **CLC 27, 56, 59**
See also BEST 90:2; CA 120; MTCW

Ishikawa Takuboku
1886(?)-1912 .... **TCLC 15**
See also CA 113

Iskander, Fazil 1929- .... **CLC 47**
See also CA 102

Ivan IV 1530-1584 .... **LC 17**

Ivanov, Vyacheslav Ivanovich
1866-1949 .... **TCLC 33**
See also CA 122

Ivask, Ivar Vidrik 1927-1992....... **CLC 14**
See also CA 37-40R; 139; CANR 24

Jackson, Daniel
See Wingrove, David (John)

Jackson, Jesse 1908-1983 .... **CLC 12**
See also BW; CA 25-28R; 109; CANR 27;
CLR 28; MAICYA; SATA 2, 29, 48

Jackson, Laura (Riding) 1901-1991 .. **CLC 7**
See also Riding, Laura
See also CA 65-68; 135; CANR 28; DLB 48

Jones, D(ouglas) G(ordon) 1929-.... **CLC 10**
See also CA 29-32R; CANR 13; DLB 53

Jones, David (Michael)
1895-1974 .... **CLC 2, 4, 7, 13, 42**
See also CA 9-12R; 53-56; CANR 28;
CDBLB 1945-1960; DLB 20, 100; MTCW

Jones, David Robert 1947-
See Bowie, David
See also CA 103

Jones, Diana Wynne 1934- .... **CLC 26**
See also CA 49-52; CANR 4, 26; CLR 23;
MAICYA; SAAS 7; SATA 9, 70

Jones, Edward P. 1951-.......... **CLC 76**

Jones, Gayl 1949-.............. **CLC 6, 9**
See also BLC 2; BW; CA 77-80; CANR 27;
DLB 33; MTCW

Jones, James 1921-1977.... **CLC 1, 3, 10, 39**
See also AITN 1, 2; CA 1-4R; 69-72;
CANR 6; DLB 2; MTCW

Jones, John J.
See Lovecraft, H(oward) P(hillips)

Jones, LeRoi .... **CLC 1, 2, 3, 5, 10, 14**
See also Baraka, Amiri

Jones, Louis B. .... **CLC 65**

Jones, Madison (Percy, Jr.) 1925- ... **CLC 4**
See also CA 13-16R; CAAS 11; CANR 7

Jones, Mervyn 1922- .... **CLC 10, 52**
See also CA 45-48; CAAS 5; CANR 1;
MTCW

Jones, Mick 1956(?)- .... **CLC 30**
See also Clash, The

Jones, Nettie (Pearl) 1941- .... **CLC 34**
See also CA 137

Jones, Preston 1936-1979 .... **CLC 10**
See also CA 73-76; 89-92; DLB 7

Jones, Robert F(rancis) 1934-....... **CLC 7**
See also CA 49-52; CANR 2

Jones, Rod 1953- .... **CLC 50**
See also CA 128

Jones, Terence Graham Parry
1942- .... **CLC 21**
See also Jones, Terry; Monty Python
See also CA 112; 116; CANR 35; SATA 51

Jones, Terry
See Jones, Terence Graham Parry
See also SATA 67

Jong, Erica 1942-.......... **CLC 4, 6, 8, 18**
See also AITN 1; BEST 90:2; CA 73-76;
CANR 26; DLB 2, 5, 28; MTCW

Jonson, Ben(jamin) 1572(?)-1637...... **LC 6**
See also CDBLB Before 1660; DA; DLB 62,
121; WLC

Jordan, June 1936-.......... **CLC 5, 11, 23**
See also AAYA 2; BW; CA 33-36R;
CANR 25; CLR 10; DLB 38; MAICYA;
MTCW; SATA 4

Jordan, Pat(rick M.) 1941- .... **CLC 37**
See also CA 33-36R

Jorgensen, Ivar
See Ellison, Harlan

Jorgenson, Ivar
See Silverberg, Robert

Josipovici, Gabriel 1940-........ **CLC 6, 43**
See also CA 37-40R; CAAS 8; DLB 14

Joubert, Joseph 1754-1824 .... **NCLC 9**

Jouve, Pierre Jean 1887-1976...... **CLC 47**
See also CA 65-68

Joyce, James (Augustine Aloysius)
1882-1941 .... **TCLC 3, 8, 16, 35; SSC 3**
See also CA 104; 126; CDBLB 1914-1945;
DA; DLB 10, 19, 36; MTCW; WLC

Jozsef, Attila 1905-1937......... **TCLC 22**
See also CA 116

Juana Ines de la Cruz 1651(?)-1695 ... **LC 5**

Judd, Cyril
See Kornbluth, C(yril) M.; Pohl, Frederik

Julian of Norwich 1342(?)-1416(?) .... **LC 6**

Just, Ward (Swift) 1935-........ **CLC 4, 27**
See also CA 25-28R; CANR 32

Justice, Donald (Rodney) 1925- .. **CLC 6, 19**
See also CA 5-8R; CANR 26; DLBY 83

Juvenal c. 55-c. 127 .... **CMLC 8**

Juvenis
See Bourne, Randolph S(illiman)

Kacew, Romain 1914-1980
See Gary, Romain
See also CA 108; 102

Kadare, Ismail 1936- .... **CLC 52**

Kadohata, Cynthia................. **CLC 59**
See also CA 140

Kafka, Franz
1883-1924 ...... **TCLC 2, 6, 13, 29, 47;
SSC 5**
See also CA 105; 126; DA; DLB 81;
MTCW; WLC

Kahn, Roger 1927-............... **CLC 30**
See also CA 25-28R; SATA 37

Kain, Saul
See Sassoon, Siegfried (Lorraine)

Kaiser, Georg 1878-1945 .... **TCLC 9**
See also CA 106; DLB 124

Kaletski, Alexander 1946-......... **CLC 39**
See also CA 118

Kalidasa fl. c. 400- .... **CMLC 9**

Kallman, Chester (Simon)
1921-1975 .... **CLC 2**
See also CA 45-48; 53-56; CANR 3

Kaminsky, Melvin 1926-
See Brooks, Mel
See also CA 65-68; CANR 16

Kaminsky, Stuart M(elvin) 1934- ... **CLC 59**
See also CA 73-76; CANR 29

Kane, Paul
See Simon, Paul

Kane, Wilson
See Bloch, Robert (Albert)

Kanin, Garson 1912-.............. **CLC 22**
See also AITN 1; CA 5-8R; CANR 7;
DLB 7

Kaniuk, Yoram 1930-............. **CLC 19**
See also CA 134

Kant, Immanuel 1724-1804 ...... **NCLC 27**
See also DLB 94

Kantor, MacKinlay 1904-1977 ...... **CLC 7**
See also CA 61-64; 73-76; DLB 9, 102

Kaplan, David Michael 1946- ...... **CLC 50**

Kaplan, James 1951- .... **CLC 59**
See also CA 135

Karageorge, Michael
See Anderson, Poul (William)

Karamzin, Nikolai Mikhailovich
1766-1826 .... **NCLC 3**

Karapanou, Margarita 1946-....... **CLC 13**
See also CA 101

Karinthy, Frigyes 1887-1938...... **TCLC 47**

Karl, Frederick R(obert) 1927- ..... **CLC 34**
See also CA 5-8R; CANR 3

Kastel, Warren
See Silverberg, Robert

Kataev, Evgeny Petrovich 1903-1942
See Petrov, Evgeny
See also CA 120

Kataphusin
See Ruskin, John

Katz, Steve 1935-............... **CLC 47**
See also CA 25-28R; CAAS 14; CANR 12;
DLBY 83

Kauffman, Janet 1945-........... **CLC 42**
See also CA 117; DLBY 86

Kaufman, Bob (Garnell)
1925-1986 .... **CLC 49**
See also BW; CA 41-44R; 118; CANR 22;
DLB 16, 41

Kaufman, George S. 1889-1961..... **CLC 38**
See also CA 108; 93-96; DLB 7

Kaufman, Sue .... **CLC 3, 8**
See also Barondess, Sue K(aufman)

Kavafis, Konstantinos Petrou 1863-1933
See Cavafy, C(onstantine) P(eter)
See also CA 104

Kavan, Anna 1901-1968......... **CLC 5, 13**
See also CA 5-8R; CANR 6; MTCW

Kavanagh, Dan
See Barnes, Julian

Kavanagh, Patrick (Joseph)
1904-1967 .... **CLC 22**
See also CA 123; 25-28R; DLB 15, 20;
MTCW

Kawabata, Yasunari
1899-1972 .... **CLC 2, 5, 9, 18**
See also CA 93-96; 33-36R

Kaye, M(ary) M(argaret) 1909-..... **CLC 28**
See also CA 89-92; CANR 24; MTCW;
SATA 62

Kaye, Mollie
See Kaye, M(ary) M(argaret)

Kaye-Smith, Sheila 1887-1956..... **TCLC 20**
See also CA 118; DLB 36

Kaymor, Patrice Maguilene
See Senghor, Leopold Sedar

Kazan, Elia 1909-.......... **CLC 6, 16, 63**
See also CA 21-24R; CANR 32

Kazantzakis, Nikos
1883(?)-1957 .... **TCLC 2, 5, 33**
See also CA 105; 132; MTCW

Kazin, Alfred 1915- .... **CLC 34, 38**
See also CA 1-4R; CAAS 7; CANR 1;
DLB 67

Keane, Mary Nesta (Skrine) 1904-
See Keane, Molly
See also CA 108; 114

Keane, Molly..................... CLC 31
See also Keane, Mary Nesta (Skrine)

Keates, Jonathan 19(?)-.......... CLC 34

Keaton, Buster 1895-1966........ CLC 20

Keats, John 1795-1821..... NCLC 8; PC 1
See also CDBLB 1789-1832; DA; DLB 96,
110; WLC

Keene, Donald 1922-............. CLC 34
See also CA 1-4R; CANR 5

Keillor, Garrison................ CLC 40
See also Keillor, Gary (Edward)
See also AAYA 2; BEST 89:3; DLBY 87;
SATA 58

Keillor, Gary (Edward) 1942-
See Keillor, Garrison
See also CA 111; 117; CANR 36; MTCW

Keith, Michael
See Hubbard, L(afayette) Ron(ald)

Kell, Joseph
See Wilson, John (Anthony) Burgess

Keller, Gottfried 1819-1890...... NCLC 2
See also DLB 129

Kellerman, Jonathan 1949-........ CLC 44
See also BEST 90:1; CA 106; CANR 29

Kelley, William Melvin 1937-...... CLC 22
See also BW; CA 77-80; CANR 27; DLB 33

Kellogg, Marjorie 1922-........... CLC 2
See also CA 81-84

Kellow, Kathleen
See Hibbert, Eleanor Alice Burford

Kelly, M(ilton) T(erry) 1947-...... CLC 55
See also CA 97-100; CANR 19

Kelman, James 1946-............. CLC 58

Kemal, Yashar 1923-.......... CLC 14, 29
See also CA 89-92

Kemble, Fanny 1809-1893....... NCLC 18
See also DLB 32

Kemelman, Harry 1908-........... CLC 2
See also AITN 1; CA 9-12R; CANR 6;
DLB 28

Kempe, Margery 1373(?)-1440(?) ..... LC 6

Kempis, Thomas a 1380-1471 .... LC 11

Kendall, Henry 1839-1882....... NCLC 12

Keneally, Thomas (Michael)
1935-...... CLC 5, 8, 10, 14, 19, 27, 43
See also CA 85-88; CANR 10; MTCW

Kennedy, Adrienne (Lita) 1931-.... CLC 66
See also BLC 2; BW; CA 103; CABS 3;
CANR 26; DLB 38

Kennedy, John Pendleton
1795-1870 .... NCLC 2
See also DLB 3

Kennedy, Joseph Charles 1929-...... CLC 8
See Kennedy, X. J.
See also CA 1-4R; CANR 4, 30, 40;
SATA 14

Kennedy, William 1928-... CLC 6, 28, 34, 53
See also AAYA 1; CA 85-88; CANR 14,
31; DLBY 85; MTCW; SATA 57

Kennedy, X. J..................... CLC 42
See also Kennedy, Joseph Charles
See also CAAS 9; CLR 27; DLB 5

Kent, Kelvin
See Kuttner, Henry

Kenton, Maxwell
See Southern, Terry

Kenyon, Robert O.
See Kuttner, Henry

Kerouac, Jack ..... CLC 1, 2, 3, 5, 14, 29, 61
See also Kerouac, Jean-Louis Lebris de
See also CDALB 1941-1968; DLB 2, 16;
DLBD 3

Kerouac, Jean-Louis Lebris de 1922-1969
See Kerouac, Jack
See also AITN 1; CA 5-8R; 25-28R;
CANR 26; DA; MTCW; WLC

Kerr, Jean 1923-................. CLC 22
See also CA 5-8R; CANR 7

Kerr, M. E. .... CLC 12, 35
See also Meaker, Marijane (Agnes)
See also AAYA 2; CLR 29; SAAS 1

Kerr, Robert .... CLC 55

Kerrigan, (Thomas) Anthony
1918-..................... CLC 4, 6
See also CA 49-52; CAAS 11; CANR 4

Kerry, Lois
See Duncan, Lois

Kesey, Ken (Elton)
1935-.......... CLC 1, 3, 6, 11, 46, 64
See also CA 1-4R; CANR 22, 38;
CDALB 1968-1988; DA; DLB 2, 16;
MTCW; SATA 66; WLC

Kesselring, Joseph (Otto)
1902-1967 .... CLC 45

Kessler, Jascha (Frederick) 1929-.... CLC 4
See also CA 17-20R; CANR 8

Kettelkamp, Larry (Dale) 1933-.... CLC 12
See also CA 29-32R; CANR 16; SAAS 3;
SATA 2

Keyber, Conny
See Fielding, Henry

Khayyam, Omar 1048-1131...... CMLC 11

Kherdian, David 1931-........... CLC 6, 9
See also CA 21-24R; CAAS 2; CANR 39;
CLR 24; MAICYA; SATA 16, 74

Khlebnikov, Velimir .... TCLC 20
See also Khlebnikov, Viktor Vladimirovich

Khlebnikov, Viktor Vladimirovich 1885-1922
See Khlebnikov, Velimir
See also CA 117

Khodasevich, Vladislav (Felitsianovich)
1886-1939 .... TCLC 15
See also CA 115

Kielland, Alexander Lange
1849-1906 .... TCLC 5
See also CA 104

Kiely, Benedict 1919-.......... CLC 23, 43
See also CA 1-4R; CANR 2; DLB 15

Kienzle, William X(avier) 1928-.... CLC 25
See also CA 93-96; CAAS 1; CANR 9, 31;
MTCW

Kierkegaard, Soeren 1813-1855... NCLC 34

Kierkegaard, Soren 1813-1855.... NCLC 34

Killens, John Oliver 1916-1987..... CLC 10
See also BW; CA 77-80; 123; CAAS 2;
CANR 26; DLB 33

Killigrew, Anne 1660-1685.......... LC 4
See also DLB 131

Kim
See Simenon, Georges (Jacques Christian)

Kincaid, Jamaica 1949-........ CLC 43, 68
See also BLC 2; BW; CA 125

King, Francis (Henry) 1923-..... CLC 8, 53
See also CA 1-4R; CANR 1, 33; DLB 15;
MTCW

King, Stephen (Edwin)
1947-.............. CLC 12, 26, 37, 61
See also AAYA 1; BEST 90:1; CA 61-64;
CANR 1, 30; DLBY 80; MTCW;
SATA 9, 55

King, Steve
See King, Stephen (Edwin)

Kingman, Lee.................... CLC 17
See also Natti, (Mary) Lee
See also SAAS 3; SATA 1, 67

Kingsley, Charles 1819-1875..... NCLC 35
See also DLB 21, 32; YABC 2

Kingsley, Sidney 1906-........... CLC 44
See also CA 85-88; DLB 7

Kingsolver, Barbara 1955-........ CLC 55
See also CA 129; 134

Kingston, Maxine (Ting Ting) Hong
1940-................. CLC 12, 19, 58
See also AAYA 8; CA 69-72; CANR 13,
38; DLBY 80; MTCW; SATA 53

Kinnell, Galway
1927-.......... CLC 1, 2, 3, 5, 13, 29
See also CA 9-12R; CANR 10, 34; DLB 5;
DLBY 87; MTCW

Kinsella, Thomas 1928-......... CLC 4, 19
See also CA 17-20R; CANR 15; DLB 27;
MTCW

Kinsella, W(illiam) P(atrick)
1935-.................... CLC 27, 43
See also AAYA 7; CA 97-100; CAAS 7;
CANR 21, 35; MTCW

Kipling, (Joseph) Rudyard
1865-1936 .... TCLC 8, 17; PC 3; SSC 5
See also CA 105; 120; CANR 33;
CDBLB 1890-1914; DA; DLB 19, 34;
MAICYA; MTCW; WLC; YABC 2

Kirkup, James 1918- .... CLC 1
See also CA 1-4R; CAAS 4; CANR 2;
DLB 27; SATA 12

Kirkwood, James 1930(?)-1989 ...... CLC 9
See also AITN 2; CA 1-4R; 128; CANR 6,
40

Kis, Danilo 1935-1989 .... CLC 57
See also CA 109; 118; 129; MTCW

Kivi, Aleksis 1834-1872 .... NCLC 30

Kizer, Carolyn (Ashley) 1925-... CLC 15, 39
See also CA 65-68; CAAS 5; CANR 24;
DLB 5

Klabund 1890-1928.............. TCLC 44
See also DLB 66

Klappert, Peter 1942-............ CLC 57
See also CA 33-36R; DLB 5

Klein, A(braham) M(oses)
1909-1972 . . . . **CLC 19**
See also CA 101; 37-40R; DLB 68

Klein, Norma 1938-1989 . . . . **CLC 30**
See also AAYA 2; CA 41-44R; 128;
CANR 15, 37; CLR 2, 19; MAICYA;
SAAS 1; SATA 7, 57

Klein, T(heodore) E(ibon) D(onald)
1947- . . . . **CLC 34**
See also CA 119

Kleist, Heinrich von 1777-1811 . . . . **NCLC 2**
See also DLB 90

Klima, Ivan 1931- . . . . **CLC 56**
See also CA 25-28R; CANR 17

Klimentov, Andrei Platonovich 1899-1951
See Platonov, Andrei
See also CA 108

Klinger, Friedrich Maximilian von
1752-1831 . . . . **NCLC 1**
See also DLB 94

Klopstock, Friedrich Gottlieb
1724-1803 . . . . **NCLC 11**
See also DLB 97

Knebel, Fletcher 1911-1993 . . . . **CLC 14**
See also AITN 1; CA 1-4R; 140; CAAS 3;
CANR 1, 36; SATA 36

Knickerbocker, Diedrich
See Irving, Washington

Knight, Etheridge 1931-1991 . . . . . . **CLC 40**
See also BLC 2; BW; CA 21-24R; 133;
CANR 23; DLB 41

Knight, Sarah Kemble 1666-1727 . . . . . **LC 7**
See also DLB 24

Knowles, John 1926- . . . . . . **CLC 1, 4, 10, 26**
See also AAYA 10; CA 17-20R; CANR 40;
CDALB 1968-1988; DA; DLB 6; MTCW;
SATA 8

Knox, Calvin M.
See Silverberg, Robert

Knye, Cassandra
See Disch, Thomas M(ichael)

Koch, C(hristopher) J(ohn) 1932- . . . **CLC 42**
See also CA 127

Koch, Christopher
See Koch, C(hristopher) J(ohn)

Koch, Kenneth 1925- . . . . **CLC 5, 8, 44**
See also CA 1-4R; CANR 6, 36; DLB 5;
SATA 65

Kochanowski, Jan 1530-1584 . . . . **LC 10**

Kock, Charles Paul de
1794-1871 . . . . **NCLC 16**

Koda Shigeyuki 1867-1947
See Rohan, Koda
See also CA 121

Koestler, Arthur
1905-1983 . . . . **CLC 1, 3, 6, 8, 15, 33**
See also CA 1-4R; 109; CANR 1, 33;
CDBLB 1945-1960; DLBY 83; MTCW

Kogawa, Joy Nozomi 1935- . . . . **CLC 78**
See also CA 101; CANR 19

Kohout, Pavel 1928- . . . . **CLC 13**
See also CA 45-48; CANR 3

Koizumi, Yakumo
See Hearn, (Patricio) Lafcadio (Tessima
Carlos)

Kolmar, Gertrud 1894-1943 . . . . . . **TCLC 40**

Konrad, George
See Konrad, Gyoergy

Konrad, Gyoergy 1933- . . . . . . **CLC 4, 10, 73**
See also CA 85-88

Konwicki, Tadeusz 1926- . . . . . **CLC 8, 28, 54**
See also CA 101; CAAS 9; CANR 39;
MTCW

Koontz, Dean R(ay) 1945- . . . . **CLC 78**
See also AAYA 9; BEST 89:3, 90:2;
CA 108; CANR 19, 36; MTCW

Kopit, Arthur (Lee) 1937- . . . . **CLC 1, 18, 33**
See also AITN 1; CA 81-84; CABS 3;
DLB 7; MTCW

Kops, Bernard 1926- . . . . **CLC 4**
See also CA 5-8R; DLB 13

Kornbluth, C(yril) M. 1923-1958 . . . . **TCLC 8**
See also CA 105; DLB 8

Korolenko, V. G.
See Korolenko, Vladimir Galaktionovich

Korolenko, Vladimir
See Korolenko, Vladimir Galaktionovich

Korolenko, Vladimir G.
See Korolenko, Vladimir Galaktionovich

Korolenko, Vladimir Galaktionovich
1853-1921 . . . . **TCLC 22**
See also CA 121

Kosinski, Jerzy (Nikodem)
1933-1991 . . . **CLC 1, 2, 3, 6, 10, 15, 53, 70**
See also CA 17-20R; 134; CANR 9; DLB 2;
DLBY 82; MTCW

Kostelanetz, Richard (Cory) 1940- . . **CLC 28**
See also CA 13-16R; CAAS 8; CANR 38

Kostrowitzki, Wilhelm Apollinaris de
1880-1918
See Apollinaire, Guillaume
See also CA 104

Kotlowitz, Robert 1924- . . . . **CLC 4**
See also CA 33-36R; CANR 36

Kotzebue, August (Friedrich Ferdinand) von
1761-1819 . . . . **NCLC 25**
See also DLB 94

Kotzwinkle, William 1938- . . **CLC 5, 14, 35**
See also CA 45-48; CANR 3; CLR 6;
MAICYA; SATA 24, 70

Kozol, Jonathan 1936- . . . . **CLC 17**
See also CA 61-64; CANR 16

Kozoll, Michael 1940(?)- . . . . **CLC 35**

Kramer, Kathryn 19(?)- . . . . **CLC 34**

Kramer, Larry 1935- . . . . **CLC 42**
See also CA 124; 126

Krasicki, Ignacy 1735-1801 . . . . **NCLC 8**

Krasinski, Zygmunt 1812-1859 . . . . **NCLC 4**

Kraus, Karl 1874-1936 . . . . **TCLC 5**
See also CA 104; DLB 118

Kreve (Mickevicius), Vincas
1882-1954 . . . . **TCLC 27**

Kristeva, Julia 1941- . . . . **CLC 77**

Kristofferson, Kris 1936- . . . . **CLC 26**
See also CA 104

Krizanc, John 1956- . . . . **CLC 57**

Krleza, Miroslav 1893-1981 . . . . **CLC 8**
See also CA 97-100; 105

Kroetsch, Robert 1927- . . . . . . **CLC 5, 23, 57**
See also CA 17-20R; CANR 8, 38; DLB 53;
MTCW

Kroetz, Franz
See Kroetz, Franz Xaver

Kroetz, Franz Xaver 1946- . . . . **CLC 41**
See also CA 130

Kroker, Arthur 1945- . . . . **CLC 77**

Kropotkin, Peter (Aleksieevich)
1842-1921 . . . . **TCLC 36**
See also CA 119

Krotkov, Yuri 1917- . . . . **CLC 19**
See also CA 102

Krumb
See Crumb, R(obert)

Krumgold, Joseph (Quincy)
1908-1980 . . . . **CLC 12**
See also CA 9-12R; 101; CANR 7;
MAICYA; SATA 1, 23, 48

Krumwitz
See Crumb, R(obert)

Krutch, Joseph Wood 1893-1970 . . . . **CLC 24**
See also CA 1-4R; 25-28R; CANR 4;
DLB 63

Krutzch, Gus
See Eliot, T(homas) S(tearns)

Krylov, Ivan Andreevich
1768(?)-1844 . . . . **NCLC 1**

Kubin, Alfred 1877-1959 . . . . **TCLC 23**
See also CA 112; DLB 81

Kubrick, Stanley 1928- . . . . **CLC 16**
See also CA 81-84; CANR 33; DLB 26

Kumin, Maxine (Winokur)
1925- . . . . **CLC 5, 13, 28**
See also AITN 2; CA 1-4R; CAAS 8;
CANR 1, 21; DLB 5; MTCW; SATA 12

Kundera, Milan
1929- . . . . **CLC 4, 9, 19, 32, 68**
See also AAYA 2; CA 85-88; CANR 19;
MTCW

Kunitz, Stanley (Jasspon)
1905- . . . . **CLC 6, 11, 14**
See also CA 41-44R; CANR 26; DLB 48;
MTCW

Kunze, Reiner 1933- . . . . **CLC 10**
See also CA 93-96; DLB 75

Kuprin, Aleksandr Ivanovich
1870-1938 . . . . **TCLC 5**
See also CA 104

Kureishi, Hanif 1954(?)- . . . . **CLC 64**
See also CA 139

Kurosawa, Akira 1910- . . . . **CLC 16**
See also CA 101

Kuttner, Henry 1915-1958 . . . . **TCLC 10**
See also CA 107; DLB 8

Kuzma, Greg 1944- . . . . **CLC 7**
See also CA 33-36R

Kuzmin, Mikhail 1872(?)-1936 . . . . **TCLC 40**

Lawton, Dennis
  See Faust, Frederick (Schiller)

Laxness, Halldor.................. **CLC 25**
  See also Gudjonsson, Halldor Kiljan

Layamon fl. c. 1200-........... **CMLC 10**

Laye, Camara 1928-1980....... **CLC 4, 38**
  See also BLC 2; BW; CA 85-88; 97-100;
  CANR 25; MTCW

Layton, Irving (Peter) 1912-..... **CLC 2, 15**
  See also CA 1-4R; CANR 2, 33; DLB 88;
  MTCW

Lazarus, Emma 1849-1887........ **NCLC 8**

Lazarus, Felix
  See Cable, George Washington

Lazarus, Henry
  See Slavitt, David R(ytman)

Lea, Joan
  See Neufeld, John (Arthur)

Leacock, Stephen (Butler)
  1869-1944.................. **TCLC 2**
  See also CA 104; DLB 92

Lear, Edward 1812-1888......... **NCLC 3**
  See also CLR 1; DLB 32; MAICYA;
  SATA 18

Lear, Norman (Milton) 1922-...... **CLC 12**
  See also CA 73-76

Leavis, F(rank) R(aymond)
  1895-1978.................. **CLC 24**
  See also CA 21-24R; 77-80; MTCW

Leavitt, David 1961-............ **CLC 34**
  See also CA 116; 122; DLB 130

Leblanc, Maurice (Marie Emile)
  1864-1941.................. **TCLC 49**
  See also CA 110

Lebowitz, Fran(ces Ann)
  1951(?)-................... **CLC 11, 36**
  See also CA 81-84; CANR 14; MTCW

le Carre, John......... **CLC 3, 5, 9, 15, 28**
  See also Cornwell, David (John Moore)
  See also BEST 89:4; CDBLB 1960 to
  Present; DLB 87

Le Clezio, J(ean) M(arie) G(ustave)
  1940-..................... **CLC 31**
  See also CA 116; 128; DLB 83

Leconte de Lisle, Charles-Marie-Rene
  1818-1894................. **NCLC 29**

Le Coq, Monsieur
  See Simenon, Georges (Jacques Christian)

Leduc, Violette 1907-1972........ **CLC 22**
  See also CA 13-14; 33-36R; CAP 1

Ledwidge, Francis 1887(?)-1917... **TCLC 23**
  See also CA 123; DLB 20

Lee, Andrea 1953-.............. **CLC 36**
  See also BLC 2; BW; CA 125

Lee, Andrew
  See Auchincloss, Louis (Stanton)

Lee, Don L........................ **CLC 2**
  See also Madhubuti, Haki R.

Lee, George W(ashington)
  1894-1976.................. **CLC 52**
  See also BLC 2; BW; CA 125; DLB 51

Lee, (Nelle) Harper 1926-...... **CLC 12, 60**
  See also CA 13-16R; CDALB 1941-1968;
  DA; DLB 6; MTCW; SATA 11; WLC

Lee, Julian
  See Latham, Jean Lee

Lee, Lawrence 1903-............. **CLC 34**
  See also CA 25-28R

Lee, Manfred B(ennington)
  1905-1971................... **CLC 11**
  See also Queen, Ellery
  See also CA 1-4R; 29-32R; CANR 2

Lee, Stan 1922-................. **CLC 17**
  See also AAYA 5; CA 108; 111

Lee, Tanith 1947-.............. **CLC 46**
  See also CA 37-40R; SATA 8

Lee, Vernon...................... **TCLC 5**
  See also Paget, Violet
  See also DLB 57

Lee, William
  See Burroughs, William S(eward)

Lee, Willy
  See Burroughs, William S(eward)

Lee-Hamilton, Eugene (Jacob)
  1845-1907................. **TCLC 22**
  See also CA 117

Leet, Judith 1935-............. **CLC 11**

Le Fanu, Joseph Sheridan
  1814-1873.................. **NCLC 9**
  See also DLB 21, 70

Leffland, Ella 1931-............. **CLC 19**
  See also CA 29-32R; CANR 35; DLBY 84;
  SATA 65

Leger, (Marie-Rene) Alexis Saint-Leger
  1887-1975................... **CLC 11**
  See also Perse, St.-John
  See also CA 13-16R; 61-64; MTCW

Leger, Saintleger
  See Leger, (Marie-Rene) Alexis Saint-Leger

Le Guin, Ursula K(roeber)
  1929-.... **CLC 8, 13, 22, 45, 71; SSC 12**
  See also AAYA 9; AITN 1; CA 21-24R;
  CANR 9, 32; CDALB 1968-1988; CLR 3,
  28; DLB 8, 52; MAICYA; MTCW;
  SATA 4, 52

Lehmann, Rosamond (Nina)
  1901-1990.................. **CLC 5**
  See also CA 77-80; 131; CANR 8; DLB 15

Leiber, Fritz (Reuter, Jr.)
  1910-1992.................. **CLC 25**
  See also CA 45-48; 139; CANR 2, 40;
  DLB 8; MTCW; SATA 45;
  SATA-Obit 73

Leimbach, Martha 1963-
  See Leimbach, Marti
  See also CA 130

Leimbach, Marti................. **CLC 65**
  See also Leimbach, Martha

Leino, Eino..................... **TCLC 24**
  See also Loennbohm, Armas Eino Leopold

Leiris, Michel (Julien) 1901-1990... **CLC 61**
  See also CA 119; 128; 132

Leithauser, Brad 1953-........... **CLC 27**
  See also CA 107; CANR 27; DLB 120

Lelchuk, Alan 1938-............. **CLC 5**
  See also CA 45-48; CANR 1

Lem, Stanislaw 1921-....... **CLC 8, 15, 40**
  See also CA 105; CAAS 1; CANR 32;
  MTCW

Lemann, Nancy 1956-.......... **CLC 39**
  See also CA 118; 136

Lemonnier, (Antoine Louis) Camille
  1844-1913................. **TCLC 22**
  See also CA 121

Lenau, Nikolaus 1802-1850...... **NCLC 16**

L'Engle, Madeleine (Camp Franklin)
  1918-..................... **CLC 12**
  See also AAYA 1; AITN 2; CA 1-4R;
  CANR 3, 21, 39; CLR 1, 14; DLB 52;
  MAICYA; MTCW; SAAS 15; SATA 1,
  27

Lengyel, Jozsef 1896-1975......... **CLC 7**
  See also CA 85-88; 57-60

Lennon, John (Ono)
  1940-1980................. **CLC 12, 35**
  See also CA 102

Lennox, Charlotte Ramsay
  1729(?)-1804.............. **NCLC 23**
  See also DLB 39

Lentricchia, Frank (Jr.) 1940-...... **CLC 34**
  See also CA 25-28R; CANR 19

Lenz, Siegfried 1926-........... **CLC 27**
  See also CA 89-92; DLB 75

Leonard, Elmore (John, Jr.)
  1925-............. **CLC 28, 34, 71**
  See also AITN 1; BEST 89:1, 90:4;
  CA 81-84; CANR 12, 28; MTCW

Leonard, Hugh
  See Byrne, John Keyes
  See also DLB 13

Leopardi, (Conte) Giacomo (Talegardo
  Francesco di Sales Save
  1798-1837................. **NCLC 22**

Le Reveler
  See Artaud, Antonin

Lerman, Eleanor 1952-............ **CLC 9**
  See also CA 85-88

Lerman, Rhoda 1936-............ **CLC 56**
  See also CA 49-52

Lermontov, Mikhail Yuryevich
  1814-1841................. **NCLC 5**

Leroux, Gaston 1868-1927....... **TCLC 25**
  See also CA 108; 136; SATA 65

Lesage, Alain-Rene 1668-1747....... **LC 2**

Leskov, Nikolai (Semyonovich)
  1831-1895................. **NCLC 25**

Lessing, Doris (May)
  1919-.... **CLC 1, 2, 3, 6, 10, 15, 22, 40;
  SSC 6**
  See also CA 9-12R; CAAS 14; CANR 33;
  CDBLB 1960 to Present; DA; DLB 15;
  DLBY 85; MTCW

Lessing, Gotthold Ephraim
  1729-1781................... **LC 8**
  See also DLB 97

Lester, Richard 1932-............ **CLC 20**

Lever, Charles (James)
  1806-1872................. **NCLC 23**
  See also DLB 21

Leverson, Ada 1865(?)-1936(?).... **TCLC 18**
  See also Elaine
  See also CA 117

Long, Emmett
See Leonard, Elmore (John, Jr.)

Longbaugh, Harry
See Goldman, William (W.)

Longfellow, Henry Wadsworth
1807-1882 . . . . **NCLC 2**
See also CDALB 1640-1865; DA; DLB 1, 59; SATA 19

Longley, Michael 1939- . . . . **CLC 29**
See also CA 102; DLB 40

Longus fl. c. 2nd cent. - . . . . **CMLC 7**

Longway, A. Hugh
See Lang, Andrew

Lopate, Phillip 1943- . . . . **CLC 29**
See also CA 97-100; DLBY 80

Lopez Portillo (y Pacheco), Jose
1920- . . . . **CLC 46**
See also CA 129; HW

Lopez y Fuentes, Gregorio
1897(?)-1966 . . . . **CLC 32**
See also CA 131; HW

Lorca, Federico Garcia
See Garcia Lorca, Federico

Lord, Bette Bao 1938- . . . . **CLC 23**
See also BEST 90:3; CA 107; CANR 41; SATA 58

Lord Auch
See Bataille, Georges

Lord Byron
See Byron, George Gordon (Noel)

Lord Dunsany . . . . **TCLC 2**
See also Dunsany, Edward John Moreton Drax Plunkett

Lorde, Audre (Geraldine)
1934- . . . . **CLC 18, 71**
See also BLC 2; BW; CA 25-28R; CANR 16, 26; DLB 41; MTCW

Lord Jeffrey
See Jeffrey, Francis

Lorenzo, Heberto Padilla
See Padilla (Lorenzo), Heberto

Loris
See Hofmannsthal, Hugo von

Loti, Pierre . . . . **TCLC 11**
See also Viaud, (Louis Marie) Julien
See also DLB 123

Louie, David Wong 1954- . . . . **CLC 70**
See also CA 139

Louis, Father M.
See Merton, Thomas

Lovecraft, H(oward) P(hillips)
1890-1937 . . . . **TCLC 4, 22; SSC 3**
See also CA 104; 133; MTCW

Lovelace, Earl 1935- . . . . **CLC 51**
See also CA 77-80; CANR 41; DLB 125; MTCW

Lowell, Amy 1874-1925 . . . . **TCLC 1, 8**
See also CA 104; DLB 54

Lowell, James Russell 1819-1891 . . **NCLC 2**
See also CDALB 1640-1865; DLB 1, 11, 64, 79

Lowell, Robert (Traill Spence, Jr.)
1917-1977 . . . **CLC 1, 2, 3, 4, 5, 8, 9, 11, 15, 37; PC 3**
See also CA 9-12R; 73-76; CABS 2; CANR 26; DA; DLB 5; MTCW; WLC

Lowndes, Marie Adelaide (Belloc)
1868-1947 . . . . **TCLC 12**
See also CA 107; DLB 70

Lowry, (Clarence) Malcolm
1909-1957 . . . . **TCLC 6, 40**
See also CA 105; 131; CDBLB 1945-1960; DLB 15; MTCW

Lowry, Mina Gertrude 1882-1966
See Loy, Mina
See also CA 113

Loxsmith, John
See Brunner, John (Kilian Houston)

Loy, Mina . . . . **CLC 28**
See also Lowry, Mina Gertrude
See also DLB 4, 54

Loyson-Bridet
See Schwob, (Mayer Andre) Marcel

Lucas, Craig 1951- . . . . **CLC 64**
See also CA 137

Lucas, George 1944- . . . . **CLC 16**
See also AAYA 1; CA 77-80; CANR 30; SATA 56

Lucas, Hans
See Godard, Jean-Luc

Lucas, Victoria
See Plath, Sylvia

Ludlam, Charles 1943-1987 . . . . . **CLC 46, 50**
See also CA 85-88; 122

Ludlum, Robert 1927- . . . . **CLC 22, 43**
See also AAYA 10; BEST 89:1, 90:3; CA 33-36R; CANR 25, 41; DLBY 82; MTCW

Ludwig, Ken . . . . **CLC 60**

Ludwig, Otto 1813-1865 . . . . **NCLC 4**
See also DLB 129

Lugones, Leopoldo 1874-1938 . . . . . **TCLC 15**
See also CA 116; 131; HW

Lu Hsun 1881-1936 . . . . **TCLC 3**

Lukacs, George . . . . **CLC 24**
See also Lukacs, Gyorgy (Szegeny von)

Lukacs, Gyorgy (Szegeny von) 1885-1971
See Lukacs, George
See also CA 101; 29-32R

Luke, Peter (Ambrose Cyprian)
1919- . . . . **CLC 38**
See also CA 81-84; DLB 13

Lunar, Dennis
See Mungo, Raymond

Lurie, Alison 1926- . . . . **CLC 4, 5, 18, 39**
See also CA 1-4R; CANR 2, 17; DLB 2; MTCW; SATA 46

Lustig, Arnost 1926- . . . . **CLC 56**
See also AAYA 3; CA 69-72; SATA 56

Luther, Martin 1483-1546 . . . . **LC 9**

Luzi, Mario 1914- . . . . **CLC 13**
See also CA 61-64; CANR 9; DLB 128

Lynch, B. Suarez
See Bioy Casares, Adolfo; Borges, Jorge Luis

Lynch, David (K.) 1946- . . . . **CLC 66**
See also CA 124; 129

Lynch, James
See Andreyev, Leonid (Nikolaevich)

Lynch Davis, B.
See Bioy Casares, Adolfo; Borges, Jorge Luis

Lyndsay, Sir David 1490-1555 . . . . **LC 20**

Lynn, Kenneth S(chuyler) 1923- . . . . **CLC 50**
See also CA 1-4R; CANR 3, 27

Lynx
See West, Rebecca

Lyons, Marcus
See Blish, James (Benjamin)

Lyre, Pinchbeck
See Sassoon, Siegfried (Lorraine)

Lytle, Andrew (Nelson) 1902- . . . . . . **CLC 22**
See also CA 9-12R; DLB 6

Lyttelton, George 1709-1773 . . . . **LC 10**

Maas, Peter 1929- . . . . **CLC 29**
See also CA 93-96

Macaulay, Rose 1881-1958 . . . . . **TCLC 7, 44**
See also CA 104; DLB 36

MacBeth, George (Mann)
1932-1992 . . . . **CLC 2, 5, 9**
See also CA 25-28R; 136; DLB 40; MTCW; SATA 4; SATA-Obit 70

MacCaig, Norman (Alexander)
1910- . . . . **CLC 36**
See also CA 9-12R; CANR 3, 34; DLB 27

MacCarthy, (Sir Charles Otto) Desmond
1877-1952 . . . . **TCLC 36**

MacDiarmid, Hugh . . . . . **CLC 2, 4, 11, 19, 63**
See also Grieve, C(hristopher) M(urray)
See also CDBLB 1945-1960; DLB 20

MacDonald, Anson
See Heinlein, Robert A(nson)

Macdonald, Cynthia 1928- . . . . . . **CLC 13, 19**
See also CA 49-52; CANR 4; DLB 105

MacDonald, George 1824-1905 . . . . . **TCLC 9**
See also CA 106; 137; DLB 18; MAICYA; SATA 33

Macdonald, John
See Millar, Kenneth

MacDonald, John D(ann)
1916-1986 . . . . **CLC 3, 27, 44**
See also CA 1-4R; 121; CANR 1, 19; DLB 8; DLBY 86; MTCW

Macdonald, John Ross
See Millar, Kenneth

Macdonald, Ross . . . . . **CLC 1, 2, 3, 14, 34, 41**
See also Millar, Kenneth
See also DLBD 6

MacDougal, John
See Blish, James (Benjamin)

MacEwen, Gwendolyn (Margaret)
1941-1987 . . . . **CLC 13, 55**
See also CA 9-12R; 124; CANR 7, 22; DLB 53; SATA 50, 55

Machado (y Ruiz), Antonio
1875-1939 . . . . **TCLC 3**
See also CA 104; DLB 108

Mano, D. Keith 1942- .... **CLC 2, 10**
See also CA 25-28R; CAAS 6; CANR 26;
DLB 6

Mansfield, Katherine ... **TCLC 2, 8, 39; SSC 9**
See also Beauchamp, Kathleen Mansfield
See also WLC

Manso, Peter 1940- .... **CLC 39**
See also CA 29-32R

Mantecon, Juan Jimenez
See Jimenez (Mantecon), Juan Ramon

Manton, Peter
See Creasey, John

Man Without a Spleen, A
See Chekhov, Anton (Pavlovich)

Manzoni, Alessandro 1785-1873 .. **NCLC 29**

Mapu, Abraham (ben Jekutiel)
1808-1867 .... **NCLC 18**

Mara, Sally
See Queneau, Raymond

Marat, Jean Paul 1743-1793 .... **LC 10**

Marcel, Gabriel Honore
1889-1973 .... **CLC 15**
See also CA 102; 45-48; MTCW

Marchbanks, Samuel
See Davies, (William) Robertson

Marchi, Giacomo
See Bassani, Giorgio

Margulies, Donald .... **CLC 76**

Marie de France c. 12th cent. -.... **CMLC 8**

Marie de l'Incarnation 1599-1672.... **LC 10**

Mariner, Scott
See Pohl, Frederik

Marinetti, Filippo Tommaso
1876-1944 .... **TCLC 10**
See also CA 107; DLB 114

Marivaux, Pierre Carlet de Chamblain de
1688-1763 .... **LC 4**

Markandaya, Kamala ...... **CLC 8, 38**
See also Taylor, Kamala (Purnaiya)

Markfield, Wallace 1926- .... **CLC 8**
See also CA 69-72; CAAS 3; DLB 2, 28

Markham, Edwin 1852-1940 ...... **TCLC 47**
See also DLB 54

Markham, Robert
See Amis, Kingsley (William)

Marks, J
See Highwater, Jamake (Mamake)

Marks-Highwater, J
See Highwater, Jamake (Mamake)

Markson, David M(errill) 1927- .... **CLC 67**
See also CA 49-52; CANR 1

Marley, Bob .... **CLC 17**
See also Marley, Robert Nesta

Marley, Robert Nesta 1945-1981
See Marley, Bob
See also CA 107; 103

Marlowe, Christopher
1564-1593 .... **LC 22; DC 1**
See also CDBLB Before 1660; DA; DLB 62;
WLC

Marmontel, Jean-Francois
1723-1799 .... **LC 2**

Marquand, John P(hillips)
1893-1960 .... **CLC 2, 10**
See also CA 85-88; DLB 9, 102

Marquez, Gabriel (Jose) Garcia...... **CLC 68**
See also Garcia Marquez, Gabriel (Jose)

Marquis, Don(ald Robert Perry)
1878-1937 .... **TCLC 7**
See also CA 104; DLB 11, 25

Marric, J. J.
See Creasey, John

Marrow, Bernard
See Moore, Brian

Marryat, Frederick 1792-1848 .... **NCLC 3**
See also DLB 21

Marsden, James
See Creasey, John

Marsh, (Edith) Ngaio
1899-1982 .... **CLC 7, 53**
See also CA 9-12R; CANR 6; DLB 77;
MTCW

Marshall, Garry 1934- .... **CLC 17**
See also AAYA 3; CA 111; SATA 60

Marshall, Paule 1929- .. **CLC 27, 72; SSC 3**
See also BLC 3; BW; CA 77-80; CANR 25;
DLB 33; MTCW

Marsten, Richard
See Hunter, Evan

Martha, Henry
See Harris, Mark

Martin, Ken
See Hubbard, L(afayette) Ron(ald)

Martin, Richard
See Creasey, John

Martin, Steve 1945- .... **CLC 30**
See also CA 97-100; CANR 30; MTCW

Martin, Violet Florence
1862-1915 .... **TCLC 51**

Martin, Webber
See Silverberg, Robert

Martin du Gard, Roger
1881-1958 .... **TCLC 24**
See also CA 118; DLB 65

Martineau, Harriet 1802-1876.... **NCLC 26**
See also DLB 21, 55; YABC 2

Martines, Julia
See O'Faolain, Julia

Martinez, Jacinto Benavente y
See Benavente (y Martinez), Jacinto

Martinez Ruiz, Jose 1873-1967
See Azorin; Ruiz, Jose Martinez
See also CA 93-96; HW

Martinez Sierra, Gregorio
1881-1947 .... **TCLC 6**
See also CA 115

Martinez Sierra, Maria (de la O'LeJarraga)
1874-1974 .... **TCLC 6**
See also CA 115

Martinsen, Martin
See Follett, Ken(neth Martin)

Martinson, Harry (Edmund)
1904-1978 .... **CLC 14**
See also CA 77-80; CANR 34

Marut, Ret
See Traven, B.

Marut, Robert
See Traven, B.

Marvell, Andrew 1621-1678......... **LC 4**
See also CDBLB 1660-1789; DA; DLB 131;
WLC

Marx, Karl (Heinrich)
1818-1883 .... **NCLC 17**
See also DLB 129

Masaoka Shiki. .... **TCLC 18**
See also Masaoka Tsunenori

Masaoka Tsunenori 1867-1902
See Masaoka Shiki
See also CA 117

Masefield, John (Edward)
1878-1967 .... **CLC 11, 47**
See also CA 19-20; 25-28R; CANR 33;
CAP 2; CDBLB 1890-1914; DLB 10;
MTCW; SATA 19

Maso, Carole 19(?)- .... **CLC 44**

Mason, Bobbie Ann
1940- .... **CLC 28, 43; SSC 4**
See also AAYA 5; CA 53-56; CANR 11,
31; DLBY 87; MTCW

Mason, Ernst
See Pohl, Frederik

Mason, Lee W.
See Malzberg, Barry N(athaniel)

Mason, Nick 1945- .... **CLC 35**
See also Pink Floyd

Mason, Tally
See Derleth, August (William)

Mass, William
See Gibson, William

Masters, Edgar Lee
1868-1950 .... **TCLC 2, 25; PC 1**
See also CA 104; 133; CDALB 1865-1917;
DA; DLB 54; MTCW

Masters, Hilary 1928- .... **CLC 48**
See also CA 25-28R; CANR 13

Mastrosimone, William 19(?)- ...... **CLC 36**

Mathe, Albert
See Camus, Albert

Matheson, Richard Burton 1926- ... **CLC 37**
See also CA 97-100; DLB 8, 44

Mathews, Harry 1930-......... **CLC 6, 52**
See also CA 21-24R; CAAS 6; CANR 18,
40

Mathias, Roland (Glyn) 1915-...... **CLC 45**
See also CA 97-100; CANR 19, 41; DLB 27

Matsuo Basho 1644-1694........... **PC 3**

Mattheson, Rodney
See Creasey, John

Matthews, Greg 1949- .... **CLC 45**
See also CA 135

Matthews, William 1942-......... **CLC 40**
See also CA 29-32R; CANR 12; DLB 5

Matthias, John (Edward) 1941-...... **CLC 9**
See also CA 33-36R

Matthiessen, Peter
1927- .... **CLC 5, 7, 11, 32, 64**
See also AAYA 6; BEST 90:4; CA 9-12R;
CANR 21; DLB 6; MTCW; SATA 27

Maturin, Charles Robert
1780(?)-1824 .... **NCLC 6**

Morrison, James Douglas 1943-1971
  See Morrison, Jim
  See also CA 73-76; CANR 40

Morrison, Jim .... **CLC 17**
  See also Morrison, James Douglas

Morrison, Toni 1931-..... **CLC 4, 10, 22, 55**
  See also AAYA 1; BLC 3; BW; CA 29-32R;
    CANR 27; CDALB 1968-1988; DA;
    DLB 6, 33; DLBY 81; MTCW; SATA 57

Morrison, Van 1945- .... **CLC 21**
  See also CA 116

Mortimer, John (Clifford)
  1923- .... **CLC 28, 43**
  See also CA 13-16R; CANR 21;
    CDBLB 1960 to Present; DLB 13;
    MTCW

Mortimer, Penelope (Ruth) 1918-.... **CLC 5**
  See also CA 57-60

Morton, Anthony
  See Creasey, John

Mosher, Howard Frank 1943-..... **CLC 62**
  See also CA 139

Mosley, Nicholas 1923-........ **CLC 43, 70**
  See also CA 69-72; CANR 41; DLB 14

Moss, Howard
  1922-1987 .... **CLC 7, 14, 45, 50**
  See also CA 1-4R; 123; CANR 1; DLB 5

Mossgiel, Rab
  See Burns, Robert

Motion, Andrew 1952-........... **CLC 47**
  See also DLB 40

Motley, Willard (Francis)
  1912-1965 .... **CLC 18**
  See also BW; CA 117; 106; DLB 76

Mott, Michael (Charles Alston)
  1930-.................... **CLC 15, 34**
  See also CA 5-8R; CAAS 7; CANR 7, 29

Mowat, Farley (McGill) 1921- ..... **CLC 26**
  See also AAYA 1; CA 1-4R; CANR 4, 24;
    CLR 20; DLB 68; MAICYA; MTCW;
    SATA 3, 55

Moyers, Bill 1934-.............. **CLC 74**
  See also AITN 2; CA 61-64; CANR 31

Mphahlele, Es'kia
  See Mphahlele, Ezekiel
  See also DLB 125

Mphahlele, Ezekiel 1919-......... **CLC 25**
  See also Mphahlele, Es'kia
  See also BLC 3; BW; CA 81-84; CANR 26

Mqhayi, S(amuel) E(dward) K(rune Loliwe)
  1875-1945 .... **TCLC 25**
  See also BLC 3

Mr. Martin
  See Burroughs, William S(eward)

Mrozek, Slawomir 1930-........ **CLC 3, 13**
  See also CA 13-16R; CAAS 10; CANR 29;
    MTCW

Mrs. Belloc-Lowndes
  See Lowndes, Marie Adelaide (Belloc)

Mtwa, Percy (?)-................ **CLC 47**

Mueller, Lisel 1924-........... **CLC 13, 51**
  See also CA 93-96; DLB 105

Muir, Edwin 1887-1959 .... **TCLC 2**
  See also CA 104; DLB 20, 100

Muir, John 1838-1914 .... **TCLC 28**

Mujica Lainez, Manuel
  1910-1984 .... **CLC 31**
  See also Lainez, Manuel Mujica
  See also CA 81-84; 112; CANR 32; HW

Mukherjee, Bharati 1940-......... **CLC 53**
  See also BEST 89:2; CA 107; DLB 60;
    MTCW

Muldoon, Paul 1951-.......... **CLC 32, 72**
  See also CA 113; 129; DLB 40

Mulisch, Harry 1927-............ **CLC 42**
  See also CA 9-12R; CANR 6, 26

Mull, Martin 1943-.............. **CLC 17**
  See also CA 105

Mulock, Dinah Maria
  See Craik, Dinah Maria (Mulock)

Munford, Robert 1737(?)-1783 .... **LC 5**
  See also DLB 31

Mungo, Raymond 1946-.......... **CLC 72**
  See also CA 49-52; CANR 2

Munro, Alice
  1931- .... **CLC 6, 10, 19, 50; SSC 3**
  See also AITN 2; CA 33-36R; CANR 33;
    DLB 53; MTCW; SATA 29

Munro, H(ector) H(ugh) 1870-1916
  See Saki
  See also CA 104; 130; CDBLB 1890-1914;
    DA; DLB 34; MTCW; WLC

Murasaki, Lady................. **CMLC 1**

Murdoch, (Jean) Iris
  1919- ...... **CLC 1, 2, 3, 4, 6, 8, 11, 15,
    22, 31, 51**
  See also CA 13-16R; CANR 8;
    CDBLB 1960 to Present; DLB 14;
    MTCW

Murphy, Richard 1927-........... **CLC 41**
  See also CA 29-32R; DLB 40

Murphy, Sylvia 1937-............. **CLC 34**
  See also CA 121

Murphy, Thomas (Bernard) 1935-... **CLC 51**
  See also CA 101

Murray, Albert L. 1916- .... **CLC 73**
  See also BW; CA 49-52; CANR 26; DLB 38

Murray, Les(lie) A(llan) 1938- ..... **CLC 40**
  See also CA 21-24R; CANR 11, 27

Murry, J. Middleton
  See Murry, John Middleton

Murry, John Middleton
  1889-1957 .... **TCLC 16**
  See also CA 118

Musgrave, Susan 1951- .... **CLC 13, 54**
  See also CA 69-72

Musil, Robert (Edler von)
  1880-1942 .... **TCLC 12**
  See also CA 109; DLB 81, 124

Musset, (Louis Charles) Alfred de
  1810-1857 .... **NCLC 7**

My Brother's Brother
  See Chekhov, Anton (Pavlovich)

Myers, Walter Dean 1937- .... **CLC 35**
  See also AAYA 4; BLC 3; BW; CA 33-36R;
    CANR 20; CLR 4, 16; DLB 33;
    MAICYA; SAAS 2; SATA 27, 41, 70, 71

Myers, Walter M.
  See Myers, Walter Dean

Myles, Symon
  See Follett, Ken(neth Martin)

Nabokov, Vladimir (Vladimirovich)
  1899-1977 .... **CLC 1, 2, 3, 6, 8, 11, 15,
    23, 44, 46, 64; SSC 11**
  See also CA 5-8R; 69-72; CANR 20;
    CDALB 1941-1968; DA; DLB 2;
    DLBD 3; DLBY 80, 91; MTCW; WLC

Nagai Kafu...................... **TCLC 51**
  See also Nagai Sokichi

Nagai Sokichi 1879-1959
  See Nagai Kafu
  See also CA 117

Nagy, Laszlo 1925-1978........... **CLC 7**
  See also CA 129; 112

Naipaul, Shiva(dhar Srinivasa)
  1945-1985 .... **CLC 32, 39**
  See also CA 110; 112; 116; CANR 33;
    DLBY 85; MTCW

Naipaul, V(idiadhar) S(urajprasad)
  1932- .... **CLC 4, 7, 9, 13, 18, 37**
  See also CA 1-4R; CANR 1, 33;
    CDBLB 1960 to Present; DLB 125;
    DLBY 85; MTCW

Nakos, Lilika 1899(?)-........... **CLC 29**

Narayan, R(asipuram) K(rishnaswami)
  1906- .... **CLC 7, 28, 47**
  See also CA 81-84; CANR 33; MTCW;
    SATA 62

Nash, (Frediric) Ogden 1902-1971 .. **CLC 23**
  See also CA 13-14; 29-32R; CANR 34;
    CAP 1; DLB 11; MAICYA; MTCW;
    SATA 2, 46

Nathan, Daniel
  See Dannay, Frederic

Nathan, George Jean 1882-1958... **TCLC 18**
  See also Hatteras, Owen
  See also CA 114

Natsume, Kinnosuke 1867-1916
  See Natsume, Soseki
  See also CA 104

Natsume, Soseki .... **TCLC 2, 10**
  See also Natsume, Kinnosuke

Natti, (Mary) Lee 1919-
  See Kingman, Lee
  See also CA 5-8R; CANR 2

Naylor, Gloria 1950- .... **CLC 28, 52**
  See also AAYA 6; BLC 3; BW; CA 107;
    CANR 27; DA; MTCW

Neihardt, John Gneisenau
  1881-1973 .... **CLC 32**
  See also CA 13-14; CAP 1; DLB 9, 54

Nekrasov, Nikolai Alekseevich
  1821-1878 .... **NCLC 11**

Nelligan, Emile 1879-1941....... **TCLC 14**
  See also CA 114; DLB 92

Nelson, Willie 1933-............. **CLC 17**
  See also CA 107

Nemerov, Howard (Stanley)
  1920-1991 .... **CLC 2, 6, 9, 36**
  See also CA 1-4R; 134; CABS 2; CANR 1,
    27; DLB 6; DLBY 83; MTCW

Neruda, Pablo
1904-1973 .... **CLC 1, 2, 5, 7, 9, 28, 62; PC 4**
See also CA 19-20; 45-48; CAP 2; DA; HW; MTCW; WLC

Nerval, Gerard de 1808-1855...... **NCLC 1**

Nervo, (Jose) Amado (Ruiz de)
1870-1919 .... **TCLC 11**
See also CA 109; 131; HW

Nessi, Pio Baroja y
See Baroja (y Nessi), Pio

Neufeld, John (Arthur) 1938- ...... **CLC 17**
See also CA 25-28R; CANR 11, 37; MAICYA; SAAS 3; SATA 6

Neville, Emily Cheney 1919-....... **CLC 12**
See also CA 5-8R; CANR 3, 37; MAICYA; SAAS 2; SATA 1

Newbound, Bernard Slade 1930-
See Slade, Bernard
See also CA 81-84

Newby, P(ercy) H(oward)
1918- .... **CLC 2, 13**
See also CA 5-8R; CANR 32; DLB 15; MTCW

Newlove, Donald 1928- .... **CLC 6**
See also CA 29-32R; CANR 25

Newlove, John (Herbert) 1938-..... **CLC 14**
See also CA 21-24R; CANR 9, 25

Newman, Charles 1938-.......... **CLC 2, 8**
See also CA 21-24R

Newman, Edwin (Harold) 1919- .... **CLC 14**
See also AITN 1; CA 69-72; CANR 5

Newman, John Henry
1801-1890 .... **NCLC 38**
See also DLB 18, 32, 55

Newton, Suzanne 1936-........... **CLC 35**
See also CA 41-44R; CANR 14; SATA 5

Nexo, Martin Andersen
1869-1954 .... **TCLC 43**

Nezval, Vitezslav 1900-1958 ...... **TCLC 44**
See also CA 123

Ngema, Mbongeni 1955- .... **CLC 57**

Ngugi, James T(hiong'o)........ **CLC 3, 7, 13**
See also Ngugi wa Thiong'o

Ngugi wa Thiong'o 1938-.......... **CLC 36**
See also Ngugi, James T(hiong'o)
See also BLC 3; BW; CA 81-84; CANR 27; DLB 125; MTCW

Nichol, B(arrie) P(hillip)
1944-1988 .... **CLC 18**
See also CA 53-56; DLB 53; SATA 66

Nichols, John (Treadwell) 1940- .... **CLC 38**
See also CA 9-12R; CAAS 2; CANR 6; DLBY 82

Nichols, Leigh
See Koontz, Dean R(ay)

Nichols, Peter (Richard)
1927- .... **CLC 5, 36, 65**
See also CA 104; CANR 33; DLB 13; MTCW

Nicolas, F. R. E.
See Freeling, Nicolas

Niedecker, Lorine 1903-1970.... **CLC 10, 42**
See also CA 25-28; CAP 2; DLB 48

Nietzsche, Friedrich (Wilhelm)
1844-1900 .... **TCLC 10, 18**
See also CA 107; 121; DLB 129

Nievo, Ippolito 1831-1861 .... **NCLC 22**

Nightingale, Anne Redmon 1943-
See Redmon, Anne
See also CA 103

Nik.T.O.
See Annensky, Innokenty Fyodorovich

Nin, Anais
1903-1977 ..... **CLC 1, 4, 8, 11, 14, 60; SSC 10**
See also AITN 2; CA 13-16R; 69-72; CANR 22; DLB 2, 4; MTCW

Nissenson, Hugh 1933-........... **CLC 4, 9**
See also CA 17-20R; CANR 27; DLB 28

Niven, Larry .... **CLC 8**
See also Niven, Laurence Van Cott
See also DLB 8

Niven, Laurence Van Cott 1938-
See Niven, Larry
See also CA 21-24R; CAAS 12; CANR 14; MTCW

Nixon, Agnes Eckhardt 1927-...... **CLC 21**
See also CA 110

Nizan, Paul 1905-1940.......... **TCLC 40**
See also DLB 72

Nkosi, Lewis 1936-.............. **CLC 45**
See also BLC 3; BW; CA 65-68; CANR 27

Nodier, (Jean) Charles (Emmanuel)
1780-1844 .... **NCLC 19**
See also DLB 119

Nolan, Christopher 1965-......... **CLC 58**
See also CA 111

Norden, Charles
See Durrell, Lawrence (George)

Nordhoff, Charles (Bernard)
1887-1947 .... **TCLC 23**
See also CA 108; DLB 9; SATA 23

Norfolk, Lawrence 1963-......... **CLC 76**

Norman, Marsha 1947-........... **CLC 28**
See also CA 105; CABS 3; CANR 41; DLBY 84

Norris, Benjamin Franklin, Jr.
1870-1902 .... **TCLC 24**
See also Norris, Frank
See also CA 110

Norris, Frank
See Norris, Benjamin Franklin, Jr.
See also CDALB 1865-1917; DLB 12, 71

Norris, Leslie 1921-.............. **CLC 14**
See also CA 11-12; CANR 14; CAP 1; DLB 27

North, Andrew
See Norton, Andre

North, Anthony
See Koontz, Dean R(ay)

North, Captain George
See Stevenson, Robert Louis (Balfour)

North, Milou
See Erdrich, Louise

Northrup, B. A.
See Hubbard, L(afayette) Ron(ald)

North Staffs
See Hulme, T(homas) E(rnest)

Norton, Alice Mary
See Norton, Andre
See also MAICYA; SATA 1, 43

Norton, Andre 1912- .... **CLC 12**
See also Norton, Alice Mary
See also CA 1-4R; CANR 2, 31; DLB 8, 52; MTCW

Norway, Nevil Shute 1899-1960
See Shute, Nevil
See also CA 102; 93-96

Norwid, Cyprian Kamil
1821-1883 .... **NCLC 17**

Nosille, Nabrah
See Ellison, Harlan

Nossack, Hans Erich 1901-1978..... **CLC 6**
See also CA 93-96; 85-88; DLB 69

Nosu, Chuji
See Ozu, Yasujiro

Nova, Craig 1945-.............. **CLC 7, 31**
See also CA 45-48; CANR 2

Novak, Joseph
See Kosinski, Jerzy (Nikodem)

Novalis 1772-1801 .... **NCLC 13**
See also DLB 90

Nowlan, Alden (Albert) 1933-1983 .. **CLC 15**
See also CA 9-12R; CANR 5; DLB 53

Noyes, Alfred 1880-1958 .... **TCLC 7**
See also CA 104; DLB 20

Nunn, Kem 19(?)-............... **CLC 34**

Nye, Robert 1939-............. **CLC 13, 42**
See also CA 33-36R; CANR 29; DLB 14; MTCW; SATA 6

Nyro, Laura 1947-.............. **CLC 17**

Oates, Joyce Carol
1938-..... **CLC 1, 2, 3, 6, 9, 11, 15, 19, 33, 52; SSC 6**
See also AITN 1; BEST 89:2; CA 5-8R; CANR 25; CDALB 1968-1988; DA; DLB 2, 5, 130; DLBY 81; MTCW; WLC

O'Brien, E. G.
See Clarke, Arthur C(harles)

O'Brien, Edna
1936- ... **CLC 3, 5, 8, 13, 36, 65; SSC 10**
See also CA 1-4R; CANR 6, 41; CDBLB 1960 to Present; DLB 14; MTCW

O'Brien, Fitz-James 1828-1862... **NCLC 21**
See also DLB 74

O'Brien, Flann........ **CLC 1, 4, 5, 7, 10, 47**
See also O Nuallain, Brian

O'Brien, Richard 1942- .... **CLC 17**
See also CA 124

O'Brien, Tim 1946-.......... **CLC 7, 19, 40**
See also CA 85-88; CANR 40; DLBD 9; DLBY 80

Obstfelder, Sigbjoern 1866-1900... **TCLC 23**
See also CA 123

O'Casey, Sean
1880-1964 .... **CLC 1, 5, 9, 11, 15**
See also CA 89-92; CDBLB 1914-1945; DLB 10; MTCW

O'Cathasaigh, Sean
  See O'Casey, Sean

Ochs, Phil 1940-1976 . . . . CLC 17
  See also CA 65-68

O'Connor, Edwin (Greene)
  1918-1968 . . . . CLC 14
  See also CA 93-96; 25-28R

O'Connor, (Mary) Flannery
  1925-1964 . . . CLC 1, 2, 3, 6, 10, 13, 15,
                          21, 66; SSC 1
  See also AAYA 7; CA 1-4R; CANR 3, 41;
    CDALB 1941-1968; DA; DLB 2;
    DLBY 80; MTCW; WLC

O'Connor, Frank . . . . CLC 23; SSC 5
  See also O'Donovan, Michael John

O'Dell, Scott 1898-1989 . . . . CLC 30
  See also AAYA 3; CA 61-64; 129;
    CANR 12, 30; CLR 1, 16; DLB 52;
    MAICYA; SATA 12, 60

Odets, Clifford 1906-1963 . . . . CLC 2, 28
  See also CA 85-88; DLB 7, 26; MTCW

O'Doherty, Brian 1934- . . . . CLC 76
  See also CA 105

O'Donnell, K. M.
  See Malzberg, Barry N(athaniel)

O'Donnell, Lawrence
  See Kuttner, Henry

O'Donovan, Michael John
  1903-1966 . . . . CLC 14
  See also O'Connor, Frank
  See also CA 93-96

Oe, Kenzaburo 1935- . . . . CLC 10, 36
  See also CA 97-100; CANR 36; MTCW

O'Faolain, Julia 1932- . . . . CLC 6, 19, 47
  See also CA 81-84; CAAS 2; CANR 12;
    DLB 14; MTCW

O'Faolain, Sean
  1900-1991 . . . . CLC 1, 7, 14, 32, 70
  See also CA 61-64; 134; CANR 12;
    DLB 15; MTCW

O'Flaherty, Liam
  1896-1984 . . . . CLC 5, 34; SSC 6
  See also CA 101; 113; CANR 35; DLB 36;
    DLBY 84; MTCW

Ogilvy, Gavin
  See Barrie, J(ames) M(atthew)

O'Grady, Standish James
  1846-1928 . . . . TCLC 5
  See also CA 104

O'Grady, Timothy 1951- . . . . CLC 59
  See also CA 138

O'Hara, Frank
  1926-1966 . . . . CLC 2, 5, 13, 78
  See also CA 9-12R; 25-28R; CANR 33;
    DLB 5, 16; MTCW

O'Hara, John (Henry)
  1905-1970 . . . . . . CLC 1, 2, 3, 6, 11, 42
  See also CA 5-8R; 25-28R; CANR 31;
    CDALB 1929-1941; DLB 9, 86; DLBD 2;
    MTCW

O Hehir, Diana 1922- . . . . CLC 41
  See also CA 93-96

Okigbo, Christopher (Ifeanyichukwu)
  1932-1967 . . . . CLC 25; PC 7
  See also BLC 3; BW; CA 77-80; DLB 125;
    MTCW

Olds, Sharon 1942- . . . . CLC 32, 39
  See also CA 101; CANR 18, 41; DLB 120

Oldstyle, Jonathan
  See Irving, Washington

Olesha, Yuri (Karlovich)
  1899-1960 . . . . CLC 8
  See also CA 85-88

Oliphant, Margaret (Oliphant Wilson)
  1828-1897 . . . . NCLC 11
  See also DLB 18

Oliver, Mary 1935- . . . . CLC 19, 34
  See also CA 21-24R; CANR 9; DLB 5

Olivier, Laurence (Kerr)
  1907-1989 . . . . CLC 20
  See also CA 111; 129

Olsen, Tillie 1913- . . . . . CLC 4, 13; SSC 11
  See also CA 1-4R; CANR 1; DA; DLB 28;
    DLBY 80; MTCW

Olson, Charles (John)
  1910-1970 . . . . . CLC 1, 2, 5, 6, 9, 11, 29
  See also CA 13-16; 25-28R; CABS 2;
    CANR 35; CAP 1; DLB 5, 16; MTCW

Olson, Toby 1937- . . . . CLC 28
  See also CA 65-68; CANR 9, 31

Olyesha, Yuri
  See Olesha, Yuri (Karlovich)

Ondaatje, Michael
  1943- . . . . CLC 14, 29, 51, 76
  See also CA 77-80; DLB 60

Oneal, Elizabeth 1934-
  See Oneal, Zibby
  See also CA 106; CANR 28; MAICYA;
    SATA 30

Oneal, Zibby . . . . CLC 30
  See also Oneal, Elizabeth
  See also AAYA 5; CLR 13

O'Neill, Eugene (Gladstone)
  1888-1953 . . . . TCLC 1, 6, 27, 49
  See also AITN 1; CA 110; 132;
    CDALB 1929-1941; DA; DLB 7; MTCW;
    WLC

Onetti, Juan Carlos 1909- . . . . CLC 7, 10
  See also CA 85-88; CANR 32; DLB 113;
    HW; MTCW

O Nuallain, Brian 1911-1966
  See O'Brien, Flann
  See also CA 21-22; 25-28R; CAP 2

Oppen, George 1908-1984 . . . . CLC 7, 13, 34
  See also CA 13-16R; 113; CANR 8; DLB 5

Oppenheim, E(dward) Phillips
  1866-1946 . . . . TCLC 45
  See also CA 111; DLB 70

Orlovitz, Gil 1918-1973 . . . . CLC 22
  See also CA 77-80; 45-48; DLB 2, 5

Orris
  See Ingelow, Jean

Ortega y Gasset, Jose 1883-1955 . . . TCLC 9
  See also CA 106; 130; HW; MTCW

Ortiz, Simon J(oseph) 1941- . . . . CLC 45
  See also CA 134; DLB 120

Orton, Joe . . . . CLC 4, 13, 43; DC 3
  See also Orton, John Kingsley
  See also CDBLB 1960 to Present; DLB 13

Orton, John Kingsley 1933-1967
  See Orton, Joe
  See also CA 85-88; CANR 35; MTCW

Orwell, George . . . . TCLC 2, 6, 15, 31, 51
  See also Blair, Eric (Arthur)
  See also CDBLB 1945-1960; DLB 15, 98;
    WLC

Osborne, David
  See Silverberg, Robert

Osborne, George
  See Silverberg, Robert

Osborne, John (James)
  1929- . . . . CLC 1, 2, 5, 11, 45
  See also CA 13-16R; CANR 21;
    CDBLB 1945-1960; DA; DLB 13;
    MTCW; WLC

Osborne, Lawrence 1958- . . . . CLC 50

Oshima, Nagisa 1932- . . . . CLC 20
  See also CA 116; 121

Oskison, John M(ilton)
  1874-1947 . . . . TCLC 35

Ossoli, Sarah Margaret (Fuller marchesa d')
  1810-1850
  See Fuller, Margaret
  See also SATA 25

Ostrovsky, Alexander
  1823-1886 . . . . NCLC 30

Otero, Blas de 1916- . . . . CLC 11
  See also CA 89-92

Otto, Whitney 1955- . . . . CLC 70
  See also CA 140

Ouida . . . . TCLC 43
  See also De La Ramee, (Marie) Louise
  See also DLB 18

Ousmane, Sembene 1923- . . . . CLC 66
  See also BLC 3; BW; CA 117; 125; MTCW

Ovid 43B.C.-18th cent. (?) . . . CMLC 7; PC 2

Owen, Hugh
  See Faust, Frederick (Schiller)

Owen, Wilfred 1893-1918 . . . . . . TCLC 5, 27
  See also CA 104; CDBLB 1914-1945; DA;
    DLB 20; WLC

Owens, Rochelle 1936- . . . . CLC 8
  See also CA 17-20R; CAAS 2; CANR 39

Oz, Amos 1939- . . . CLC 5, 8, 11, 27, 33, 54
  See also CA 53-56; CANR 27; MTCW

Ozick, Cynthia 1928- . . . . . . CLC 3, 7, 28, 62
  See also BEST 90:1; CA 17-20R; CANR 23;
    DLB 28; DLBY 82; MTCW

Ozu, Yasujiro 1903-1963 . . . . CLC 16
  See also CA 112

Pacheco, C.
  See Pessoa, Fernando (Antonio Nogueira)

Pa Chin
  See Li Fei-kan

Pack, Robert 1929- . . . . CLC 13
  See also CA 1-4R; CANR 3; DLB 5

Padgett, Lewis
  See Kuttner, Henry

Padilla (Lorenzo), Heberto 1932- . . . CLC 38
  See also AITN 1; CA 123; 131; HW

Percy, Walker
1916-1990 . . . **CLC 2, 3, 6, 8, 14, 18, 47, 65**
See also CA 1-4R; 131; CANR 1, 23;
DLB 2; DLBY 80, 90; MTCW

Perec, Georges 1936-1982 . . . . **CLC 56**
See also DLB 83

Pereda (y Sanchez de Porrua), Jose Maria de
1833-1906 . . . . **TCLC 16**
See also CA 117

Pereda y Porrua, Jose Maria de
See Pereda (y Sanchez de Porrua), Jose
Maria de

Peregoy, George Weems
See Mencken, H(enry) L(ouis)

Perelman, S(idney) J(oseph)
1904-1979 . . . **CLC 3, 5, 9, 15, 23, 44, 49**
See also AITN 1, 2; CA 73-76; 89-92;
CANR 18; DLB 11, 44; MTCW

Peret, Benjamin 1899-1959 . . . . **TCLC 20**
See also CA 117

Peretz, Isaac Loeb 1851(?)-1915 . . . **TCLC 16**
See also CA 109

Peretz, Yitzkhok Leibush
See Peretz, Isaac Loeb

Perez Galdos, Benito 1843-1920 . . . **TCLC 27**
See also CA 125; HW

Perrault, Charles 1628-1703 . . . . **LC 2**
See also MAICYA; SATA 25

Perry, Brighton
See Sherwood, Robert E(mmet)

Perse, St.-John . . . . **CLC 4, 11, 46**
See also Leger, (Marie-Rene) Alexis
Saint-Leger

Perse, Saint-John
See Leger, (Marie-Rene) Alexis Saint-Leger

Peseenz, Tulio F.
See Lopez y Fuentes, Gregorio

Pesetsky, Bette 1932- . . . . **CLC 28**
See also CA 133; DLB 130

Peshkov, Alexei Maximovich 1868-1936
See Gorky, Maxim
See also CA 105; DA

Pessoa, Fernando (Antonio Nogueira)
1888-1935 . . . . **TCLC 27**
See also CA 125

Peterkin, Julia Mood 1880-1961 . . . . **CLC 31**
See also CA 102; DLB 9

Peters, Joan K. 1945- . . . . **CLC 39**

Peters, Robert L(ouis) 1924- . . . . **CLC 7**
See also CA 13-16R; CAAS 8; DLB 105

Petofi, Sandor 1823-1849 . . . . **NCLC 21**

Petrakis, Harry Mark 1923- . . . . **CLC 3**
See also CA 9-12R; CANR 4, 30

Petrov, Evgeny . . . . **TCLC 21**
See also Kataev, Evgeny Petrovich

Petry, Ann (Lane) 1908- . . . . . . **CLC 1, 7, 18**
See also BW; CA 5-8R; CAAS 6; CANR 4;
CLR 12; DLB 76; MAICYA; MTCW;
SATA 5

Petursson, Halligrimur 1614-1674 . . . . **LC 8**

Philipson, Morris H. 1926- . . . . **CLC 53**
See also CA 1-4R; CANR 4

Phillips, David Graham
1867-1911 . . . . **TCLC 44**
See also CA 108; DLB 9, 12

Phillips, Jack
See Sandburg, Carl (August)

Phillips, Jayne Anne 1952- . . . . . **CLC 15, 33**
See also CA 101; CANR 24; DLBY 80;
MTCW

Phillips, Richard
See Dick, Philip K(indred)

Phillips, Robert (Schaeffer) 1938- . . . **CLC 28**
See also CA 17-20R; CAAS 13; CANR 8;
DLB 105

Phillips, Ward
See Lovecraft, H(oward) P(hillips)

Piccolo, Lucio 1901-1969 . . . . **CLC 13**
See also CA 97-100; DLB 114

Pickthall, Marjorie L(owry) C(hristie)
1883-1922 . . . . **TCLC 21**
See also CA 107; DLB 92

Pico della Mirandola, Giovanni
1463-1494 . . . . **LC 15**

Piercy, Marge
1936- . . . . **CLC 3, 6, 14, 18, 27, 62**
See also CA 21-24R; CAAS 1; CANR 13;
DLB 120; MTCW

Piers, Robert
See Anthony, Piers

Pieyre de Mandiargues, Andre 1909-1991
See Mandiargues, Andre Pieyre de
See also CA 103; 136; CANR 22

Pilnyak, Boris . . . . **TCLC 23**
See also Vogau, Boris Andreyevich

Pincherle, Alberto 1907-1990 . . . **CLC 11, 18**
See also Moravia, Alberto
See also CA 25-28R; 132; CANR 33;
MTCW

Pinckney, Darryl 1953- . . . . **CLC 76**

Pineda, Cecile 1942- . . . . **CLC 39**
See also CA 118

Pinero, Arthur Wing 1855-1934 . . . **TCLC 32**
See also CA 110; DLB 10

Pinero, Miguel (Antonio Gomez)
1946-1988 . . . . **CLC 4, 55**
See also CA 61-64; 125; CANR 29; HW

Pinget, Robert 1919- . . . . **CLC 7, 13, 37**
See also CA 85-88; DLB 83

Pink Floyd . . . . **CLC 35**
See also Barrett, (Roger) Syd; Gilmour,
David; Mason, Nick; Waters, Roger;
Wright, Rick

Pinkney, Edward 1802-1828 . . . . . **NCLC 31**

Pinkwater, Daniel Manus 1941- . . . . **CLC 35**
See also Pinkwater, Manus
See also AAYA 1; CA 29-32R; CANR 12,
38; CLR 4; MAICYA; SAAS 3; SATA 46

Pinkwater, Manus
See Pinkwater, Daniel Manus
See also SATA 8

Pinsky, Robert 1940- . . . . **CLC 9, 19, 38**
See also CA 29-32R; CAAS 4; DLBY 82

Pinta, Harold
See Pinter, Harold

Pinter, Harold
1930- . . **CLC 1, 3, 6, 9, 11, 15, 27, 58, 73**
See also CA 5-8R; CANR 33; CDBLB 1960
to Present; DA; DLB 13; MTCW; WLC

Pirandello, Luigi 1867-1936 . . . . . **TCLC 4, 29**
See also CA 104; DA; WLC

Pirsig, Robert M(aynard)
1928- . . . . **CLC 4, 6, 73**
See also CA 53-56; MTCW; SATA 39

Pisarev, Dmitry Ivanovich
1840-1868 . . . . **NCLC 25**

Pix, Mary (Griffith) 1666-1709 . . . . **LC 8**
See also DLB 80

Pixerecourt, Guilbert de
1773-1844 . . . . **NCLC 39**

Plaidy, Jean
See Hibbert, Eleanor Alice Burford

Plant, Robert 1948- . . . . **CLC 12**

Plante, David (Robert)
1940- . . . . **CLC 7, 23, 38**
See also CA 37-40R; CANR 12, 36;
DLBY 83; MTCW

Plath, Sylvia
1932-1963 . . . . **CLC 1, 2, 3, 5, 9, 11, 14,
17, 50, 51, 62; PC 1**
See also CA 19-20; CANR 34; CAP 2;
CDALB 1941-1968; DA; DLB 5, 6;
MTCW; WLC

Plato 428(?)B.C.-348(?)B.C. . . . . **CMLC 8**
See also DA

Platonov, Andrei . . . . **TCLC 14**
See also Klimentov, Andrei Platonovich

Platt, Kin 1911- . . . . **CLC 26**
See also CA 17-20R; CANR 11; SATA 21

Plick et Plock
See Simenon, Georges (Jacques Christian)

Plimpton, George (Ames) 1927- . . . . . **CLC 36**
See also AITN 1; CA 21-24R; CANR 32;
MTCW; SATA 10

Plomer, William Charles Franklin
1903-1973 . . . . **CLC 4, 8**
See also CA 21-22; CANR 34; CAP 2;
DLB 20; MTCW; SATA 24

Plowman, Piers
See Kavanagh, Patrick (Joseph)

Plum, J.
See Wodehouse, P(elham) G(renville)

Plumly, Stanley (Ross) 1939- . . . . . . **CLC 33**
See also CA 108; 110; DLB 5

Poe, Edgar Allan
1809-1849 . . . **NCLC 1, 16; PC 1; SSC 1**
See also CDALB 1640-1865; DA; DLB 3,
59, 73, 74; SATA 23; WLC

Poet of Titchfield Street, The
See Pound, Ezra (Weston Loomis)

Pohl, Frederik 1919- . . . . **CLC 18**
See also CA 61-64; CAAS 1; CANR 11, 37;
DLB 8; MTCW; SATA 24

Poirier, Louis 1910-
See Gracq, Julien
See also CA 122; 126

Poitier, Sidney 1927- . . . . **CLC 26**
See also BW; CA 117

Robinson, Jill 1936- . . . . CLC 10
See also CA 102

Robinson, Kim Stanley 1952- . . . . . . CLC 34
See also CA 126

Robinson, Lloyd
See Silverberg, Robert

Robinson, Marilynne 1944- . . . . CLC 25
See also CA 116

Robinson, Smokey. . . . . CLC 21
See also Robinson, William, Jr.

Robinson, William, Jr. 1940-
See Robinson, Smokey
See also CA 116

Robison, Mary 1949- . . . . CLC 42
See also CA 113; 116; DLB 130

Roddenberry, Eugene Wesley 1921-1991
See Roddenberry, Gene
See also CA 110; 135; CANR 37; SATA 45

Roddenberry, Gene . . . . CLC 17
See also Roddenberry, Eugene Wesley
See also AAYA 5; SATA-Obit 69

Rodgers, Mary 1931- . . . . CLC 12
See also CA 49-52; CANR 8; CLR 20;
MAICYA; SATA 8

Rodgers, W(illiam) R(obert)
1909-1969 . . . . CLC 7
See also CA 85-88; DLB 20

Rodman, Eric
See Silverberg, Robert

Rodman, Howard 1920(?)-1985 . . . . . CLC 65
See also CA 118

Rodman, Maia
See Wojciechowska, Maia (Teresa)

Rodriguez, Claudio 1934- . . . . CLC 10

Roelvaag, O(le) E(dvart)
1876-1931 . . . . TCLC 17
See also CA 117; DLB 9

Roethke, Theodore (Huebner)
1908-1963 . . . . . . CLC 1, 3, 8, 11, 19, 46
See also CA 81-84; CABS 2;
CDALB 1941-1968; DLB 5; MTCW

Rogers, Thomas Hunton 1927- . . . . . CLC 57
See also CA 89-92

Rogers, Will(iam Penn Adair)
1879-1935 . . . . TCLC 8
See also CA 105; DLB 11

Rogin, Gilbert 1929- . . . . CLC 18
See also CA 65-68; CANR 15

Rohan, Koda . . . . TCLC 22
See also Koda Shigeyuki

Rohmer, Eric. . . . . CLC 16
See also Scherer, Jean-Marie Maurice

Rohmer, Sax . . . . TCLC 28
See also Ward, Arthur Henry Sarsfield
See also DLB 70

Roiphe, Anne Richardson 1935- . . . CLC 3, 9
See also CA 89-92; DLBY 80

Rojas, Fernando de 1465-1541 . . . . . . LC 23

Rolfe, Frederick (William Serafino Austin
Lewis Mary) 1860-1913 . . . . . . TCLC 12
See also CA 107; DLB 34

Rolland, Romain 1866-1944 . . . . TCLC 23
See also CA 118; DLB 65

Rolvaag, O(le) E(dvart)
See Roelvaag, O(le) E(dvart)

Romain Arnaud, Saint
See Aragon, Louis

Romains, Jules 1885-1972 . . . . CLC 7
See also CA 85-88; CANR 34; DLB 65;
MTCW

Romero, Jose Ruben 1890-1952 . . . TCLC 14
See also CA 114; 131; HW

Ronsard, Pierre de 1524-1585 . . . . LC 6

Rooke, Leon 1934- . . . . CLC 25, 34
See also CA 25-28R; CANR 23

Roper, William 1498-1578 . . . . LC 10

Roquelaure, A. N.
See Rice, Anne

Rosa, Joao Guimaraes 1908-1967 . . . CLC 23
See also CA 89-92; DLB 113

Rosen, Richard (Dean) 1949- . . . . . . CLC 39
See also CA 77-80

Rosenberg, Isaac 1890-1918 . . . . . . TCLC 12
See also CA 107; DLB 20

Rosenblatt, Joe . . . . CLC 15
See also Rosenblatt, Joseph

Rosenblatt, Joseph 1933-
See Rosenblatt, Joe
See also CA 89-92

Rosenfeld, Samuel 1896-1963
See Tzara, Tristan
See also CA 89-92

Rosenthal, M(acha) L(ouis) 1917- . . . CLC 28
See also CA 1-4R; CAAS 6; CANR 4;
DLB 5; SATA 59

Ross, Barnaby
See Dannay, Frederic

Ross, Bernard L.
See Follett, Ken(neth Martin)

Ross, J. H.
See Lawrence, T(homas) E(dward)

Ross, Martin
See Martin, Violet Florence

Ross, (James) Sinclair 1908- . . . . CLC 13
See also CA 73-76; DLB 88

Rossetti, Christina (Georgina)
1830-1894 . . . . NCLC 2; PC 7
See also DA; DLB 35; MAICYA;
SATA 20; WLC

Rossetti, Dante Gabriel
1828-1882 . . . . NCLC 4
See also CDBLB 1832-1890; DA; DLB 35;
WLC

Rossner, Judith (Perelman)
1935- . . . . CLC 6, 9, 29
See also AITN 2; BEST 90:3; CA 17-20R;
CANR 18; DLB 6; MTCW

Rostand, Edmond (Eugene Alexis)
1868-1918 . . . . TCLC 6, 37
See also CA 104; 126; DA; MTCW

Roth, Henry 1906- . . . . CLC 2, 6, 11
See also CA 11-12; CANR 38; CAP 1;
DLB 28; MTCW

Roth, Joseph 1894-1939 . . . . TCLC 33
See also DLB 85

Roth, Philip (Milton)
1933- . . . . . . CLC 1, 2, 3, 4, 6, 9, 15, 22,
                                        31, 47, 66
See also BEST 90:3; CA 1-4R; CANR 1, 22,
36; CDALB 1968-1988; DA; DLB 2, 28;
DLBY 82; MTCW; WLC

Rothenberg, Jerome 1931- . . . . CLC 6, 57
See also CA 45-48; CANR 1; DLB 5

Roumain, Jacques (Jean Baptiste)
1907-1944 . . . . TCLC 19
See also BLC 3; BW; CA 117; 125

Rourke, Constance (Mayfield)
1885-1941 . . . . TCLC 12
See also CA 107; YABC 1

Rousseau, Jean-Baptiste 1671-1741 . . . LC 9

Rousseau, Jean-Jacques 1712-1778. . . LC 14
See also DA; WLC

Roussel, Raymond 1877-1933 . . . . . TCLC 20
See also CA 117

Rovit, Earl (Herbert) 1927- . . . . CLC 7
See also CA 5-8R; CANR 12

Rowe, Nicholas 1674-1718 . . . . LC 8
See also DLB 84

Rowley, Ames Dorrance
See Lovecraft, H(oward) P(hillips)

Rowson, Susanna Haswell
1762(?)-1824 . . . . NCLC 5
See also DLB 37

Roy, Gabrielle 1909-1983 . . . . CLC 10, 14
See also CA 53-56; 110; CANR 5; DLB 68;
MTCW

Rozewicz, Tadeusz 1921- . . . . CLC 9, 23
See also CA 108; CANR 36; MTCW

Ruark, Gibbons 1941- . . . . CLC 3
See also CA 33-36R; CANR 14, 31;
DLB 120

Rubens, Bernice (Ruth) 1923- . . . CLC 19, 31
See also CA 25-28R; CANR 33; DLB 14;
MTCW

Rudkin, (James) David 1936- . . . . . . CLC 14
See also CA 89-92; DLB 13

Rudnik, Raphael 1933- . . . . CLC 7
See also CA 29-32R

Ruffian, M.
See Hasek, Jaroslav (Matej Frantisek)

Ruiz, Jose Martinez . . . . CLC 11
See also Martinez Ruiz, Jose

Rukeyser, Muriel
1913-1980 . . . . CLC 6, 10, 15, 27
See also CA 5-8R; 93-96; CANR 26;
DLB 48; MTCW; SATA 22

Rule, Jane (Vance) 1931- . . . . CLC 27
See also CA 25-28R; CANR 12; DLB 60

Rulfo, Juan 1918-1986 . . . . CLC 8
See also CA 85-88; 118; CANR 26;
DLB 113; HW; MTCW

Runeberg, Johan 1804-1877 . . . . . . NCLC 41

Runyon, (Alfred) Damon
1884(?)-1946 . . . . TCLC 10
See also CA 107; DLB 11, 86

Rush, Norman 1933- . . . . CLC 44
See also CA 121; 126

Sarton, (Eleanor) May
1912- . . . . **CLC 4, 14, 49**
See also CA 1-4R; CANR 1, 34; DLB 48;
DLBY 81; MTCW; SATA 36

Sartre, Jean-Paul
1905-1980 . . . **CLC 1, 4, 7, 9, 13, 18, 24,**
44, 50, 52; DC 3
See also CA 9-12R; 97-100; CANR 21; DA;
DLB 72; MTCW; WLC

Sassoon, Siegfried (Lorraine)
1886-1967 . . . . **CLC 36**
See also CA 104; 25-28R; CANR 36;
DLB 20; MTCW

Satterfield, Charles
See Pohl, Frederik

Saul, John (W. III) 1942- . . . . **CLC 46**
See also AAYA 10; BEST 90:4; CA 81-84;
CANR 16, 40

Saunders, Caleb
See Heinlein, Robert A(nson)

Saura (Atares), Carlos 1932- . . . . **CLC 20**
See also CA 114; 131; HW

Sauser-Hall, Frederic 1887-1961. . . . **CLC 18**
See also CA 102; 93-96; CANR 36; MTCW

Saussure, Ferdinand de
1857-1913 . . . . **TCLC 49**

Savage, Catharine
See Brosman, Catharine Savage

Savage, Thomas 1915- . . . . **CLC 40**
See also CA 126; 132; CAAS 15

Savan, Glenn . . . . **CLC 50**

Saven, Glenn 19(?)- . . . . **CLC 50**

Sayers, Dorothy L(eigh)
1893-1957 . . . . **TCLC 2, 15**
See also CA 104; 119; CDBLB 1914-1945;
DLB 10, 36, 77, 100; MTCW

Sayers, Valerie 1952- . . . . **CLC 50**
See also CA 134

Sayles, John (Thomas)
1950- . . . . **CLC 7, 10, 14**
See also CA 57-60; CANR 41; DLB 44

Scammell, Michael . . . . **CLC 34**

Scannell, Vernon 1922- . . . . **CLC 49**
See also CA 5-8R; CANR 8, 24; DLB 27;
SATA 59

Scarlett, Susan
See Streatfeild, (Mary) Noel

Schaeffer, Susan Fromberg
1941- . . . . **CLC 6, 11, 22**
See also CA 49-52; CANR 18; DLB 28;
MTCW; SATA 22

Schary, Jill
See Robinson, Jill

Schell, Jonathan 1943- . . . . **CLC 35**
See also CA 73-76; CANR 12

Schelling, Friedrich Wilhelm Joseph von
1775-1854 . . . . **NCLC 30**
See also DLB 90

Scherer, Jean-Marie Maurice 1920-
See Rohmer, Eric
See also CA 110

Schevill, James (Erwin) 1920- . . . . . . **CLC 7**
See also CA 5-8R; CAAS 12

Schiller, Friedrich 1759-1805 . . . . **NCLC 39**
See also DLB 94

Schisgal, Murray (Joseph) 1926- . . . . . **CLC 6**
See also CA 21-24R

Schlee, Ann 1934- . . . . **CLC 35**
See also CA 101; CANR 29; SATA 36, 44

Schlegel, August Wilhelm von
1767-1845 . . . . **NCLC 15**
See also DLB 94

Schlegel, Johann Elias (von)
1719(?)-1749 . . . . **LC 5**

Schmidt, Arno (Otto) 1914-1979. . . . **CLC 56**
See also CA 128; 109; DLB 69

Schmitz, Aron Hector 1861-1928
See Svevo, Italo
See also CA 104; 122; MTCW

Schnackenberg, Gjertrud 1953- . . . . . **CLC 40**
See also CA 116; DLB 120

Schneider, Leonard Alfred 1925-1966
See Bruce, Lenny
See also CA 89-92

Schnitzler, Arthur 1862-1931 . . . . . . **TCLC 4**
See also CA 104; DLB 81, 118

Schor, Sandra (M.) 1932(?)-1990 . . . **CLC 65**
See also CA 132

Schorer, Mark 1908-1977 . . . . **CLC 9**
See also CA 5-8R; 73-76; CANR 7;
DLB 103

Schrader, Paul (Joseph) 1946- . . . . . . **CLC 26**
See also CA 37-40R; CANR 41; DLB 44

Schreiner, Olive (Emilie Albertina)
1855-1920 . . . . **TCLC 9**
See also CA 105; DLB 18

Schulberg, Budd (Wilson)
1914- . . . . **CLC 7, 48**
See also CA 25-28R; CANR 19; DLB 6, 26,
28; DLBY 81

Schulz, Bruno 1892-1942 . . . . . . **TCLC 5, 51**
See also CA 115; 123

Schulz, Charles M(onroe) 1922- . . . . **CLC 12**
See also CA 9-12R; CANR 6; SATA 10

Schuyler, James Marcus
1923-1991 . . . . **CLC 5, 23**
See also CA 101; 134; DLB 5

Schwartz, Delmore (David)
1913-1966 . . . . **CLC 2, 4, 10, 45**
See also CA 17-18; 25-28R; CANR 35;
CAP 2; DLB 28, 48; MTCW

Schwartz, Ernst
See Ozu, Yasujiro

Schwartz, John Burnham 1965- . . . . **CLC 59**
See also CA 132

Schwartz, Lynne Sharon 1939- . . . . . **CLC 31**
See also CA 103

Schwartz, Muriel A.
See Eliot, T(homas) S(tearns)

Schwarz-Bart, Andre 1928- . . . . **CLC 2, 4**
See also CA 89-92

Schwarz-Bart, Simone 1938- . . . . **CLC 7**
See also CA 97-100

Schwob, (Mayer Andre) Marcel
1867-1905 . . . . **TCLC 20**
See also CA 117; DLB 123

Sciascia, Leonardo
1921-1989 . . . . **CLC 8, 9, 41**
See also CA 85-88; 130; CANR 35; MTCW

Scoppettone, Sandra 1936- . . . . **CLC 26**
See also CA 5-8R; CANR 41; SATA 9

Scorsese, Martin 1942- . . . . **CLC 20**
See also CA 110; 114

Scotland, Jay
See Jakes, John (William)

Scott, Duncan Campbell
1862-1947 . . . . **TCLC 6**
See also CA 104; DLB 92

Scott, Evelyn 1893-1963. . . . . **CLC 43**
See also CA 104; 112; DLB 9, 48

Scott, F(rancis) R(eginald)
1899-1985 . . . . **CLC 22**
See also CA 101; 114; DLB 88

Scott, Frank
See Scott, F(rancis) R(eginald)

Scott, Joanna 1960- . . . . **CLC 50**
See also CA 126

Scott, Paul (Mark) 1920-1978. . . . **CLC 9, 60**
See also CA 81-84; 77-80; CANR 33;
DLB 14; MTCW

Scott, Walter 1771-1832. . . . . **NCLC 15**
See also CDBLB 1789-1832; DA; DLB 93,
107, 116; WLC; YABC 2

Scribe, (Augustin) Eugene
1791-1861 . . . . **NCLC 16**

Scrum, R.
See Crumb, R(obert)

Scudery, Madeleine de 1607-1701 . . . . . **LC 2**

Scum
See Crumb, R(obert)

Scumbag, Little Bobby
See Crumb, R(obert)

Seabrook, John
See Hubbard, L(afayette) Ron(ald)

Sealy, I. Allan 1951- . . . . **CLC 55**

Search, Alexander
See Pessoa, Fernando (Antonio Nogueira)

Sebastian, Lee
See Silverberg, Robert

Sebastian Owl
See Thompson, Hunter S(tockton)

Sebestyen, Ouida 1924- . . . . **CLC 30**
See also AAYA 8; CA 107; CANR 40;
CLR 17; MAICYA; SAAS 10; SATA 39

Secundus, H. Scriblerus
See Fielding, Henry

Sedges, John
See Buck, Pearl S(ydenstricker)

Sedgwick, Catharine Maria
1789-1867 . . . . **NCLC 19**
See also DLB 1, 74

Seelye, John 1931- . . . . **CLC 7**

Seferiades, Giorgos Stylianou 1900-1971
See Seferis, George
See also CA 5-8R; 33-36R; CANR 5, 36;
MTCW

Seferis, George . . . . **CLC 5, 11**
See also Seferiades, Giorgos Stylianou

Spiegelman, Art 1948- . . . . CLC 76
See also AAYA 10; CA 125; CANR 41

Spielberg, Peter 1929- . . . . CLC 6
See also CA 5-8R; CANR 4; DLBY 81

Spielberg, Steven 1947- . . . . CLC 20
See also AAYA 8; CA 77-80; CANR 32;
SATA 32

Spillane, Frank Morrison 1918-
See Spillane, Mickey
See also CA 25-28R; CANR 28; MTCW;
SATA 66

Spillane, Mickey . . . . CLC 3, 13
See also Spillane, Frank Morrison

Spinoza, Benedictus de 1632-1677 . . . . LC 9

Spinrad, Norman (Richard) 1940- . . . CLC 46
See also CA 37-40R; CANR 20; DLB 8

Spitteler, Carl (Friedrich Georg)
1845-1924 . . . . TCLC 12
See also CA 109; DLB 129

Spivack, Kathleen (Romola Drucker)
1938- . . . . CLC 6
See also CA 49-52

Spoto, Donald 1941- . . . . CLC 39
See also CA 65-68; CANR 11

Springsteen, Bruce (F.) 1949- . . . . . . CLC 17
See also CA 111

Spurling, Hilary 1940- . . . . CLC 34
See also CA 104; CANR 25

Squires, (James) Radcliffe
1917-1993 . . . . CLC 51
See also CA 1-4R; 140; CANR 6, 21

Srivastava, Dhanpat Rai 1880(?)-1936
See Premchand
See also CA 118

Stacy, Donald
See Pohl, Frederik

Stael, Germaine de
See Stael-Holstein, Anne Louise Germaine
Necker Baronn
See also DLB 119

Stael-Holstein, Anne Louise Germaine Necker
Baronn 1766-1817 . . . . NCLC 3
See also Stael, Germaine de

Stafford, Jean 1915-1979 . . . CLC 4, 7, 19, 68
See also CA 1-4R; 85-88; CANR 3; DLB 2;
MTCW; SATA 22

Stafford, William (Edgar)
1914- . . . . CLC 4, 7, 29
See also CA 5-8R; CAAS 3; CANR 5, 22;
DLB 5

Staines, Trevor
See Brunner, John (Kilian Houston)

Stairs, Gordon
See Austin, Mary (Hunter)

Stannard, Martin . . . . CLC 44

Stanton, Maura 1946- . . . . CLC 9
See also CA 89-92; CANR 15; DLB 120

Stanton, Schuyler
See Baum, L(yman) Frank

Stapledon, (William) Olaf
1886-1950 . . . . TCLC 22
See also CA 111; DLB 15

Starbuck, George (Edwin) 1931- . . . . CLC 53
See also CA 21-24R; CANR 23

Stark, Richard
See Westlake, Donald E(dwin)

Staunton, Schuyler
See Baum, L(yman) Frank

Stead, Christina (Ellen)
1902-1983 . . . . CLC 2, 5, 8, 32
See also CA 13-16R; 109; CANR 33, 40;
MTCW

Stead, William Thomas
1849-1912 . . . . TCLC 48

Steele, Richard 1672-1729 . . . . LC 18
See also CDBLB 1660-1789; DLB 84, 101

Steele, Timothy (Reid) 1948- . . . . CLC 45
See also CA 93-96; CANR 16; DLB 120

Steffens, (Joseph) Lincoln
1866-1936 . . . . TCLC 20
See also CA 117

Stegner, Wallace (Earle) 1909- . . . CLC 9, 49
See also AITN 1; BEST 90:3; CA 1-4R;
CAAS 9; CANR 1, 21; DLB 9; MTCW

Stein, Gertrude
1874-1946 . . . . TCLC 1, 6, 28, 48
See also CA 104; 132; CDALB 1917-1929;
DA; DLB 4, 54, 86; MTCW; WLC

Steinbeck, John (Ernst)
1902-1968 . . . . . CLC 1, 5, 9, 13, 21, 34,
45, 75; SSC 11
See also CA 1-4R; 25-28R; CANR 1, 35;
CDALB 1929-1941; DA; DLB 7, 9;
DLBD 2; MTCW; SATA 9; WLC

Steinem, Gloria 1934- . . . . CLC 63
See also CA 53-56; CANR 28; MTCW

Steiner, George 1929- . . . . CLC 24
See also CA 73-76; CANR 31; DLB 67;
MTCW; SATA 62

Steiner, Rudolf 1861-1925 . . . . TCLC 13
See also CA 107

Stendhal 1783-1842 . . . . NCLC 23
See also DA; DLB 119; WLC

Stephen, Leslie 1832-1904 . . . . TCLC 23
See also CA 123; DLB 57

Stephen, Sir Leslie
See Stephen, Leslie

Stephen, Virginia
See Woolf, (Adeline) Virginia

Stephens, James 1882(?)-1950 . . . . . . TCLC 4
See also CA 104; DLB 19

Stephens, Reed
See Donaldson, Stephen R.

Steptoe, Lydia
See Barnes, Djuna

Sterchi, Beat 1949- . . . . CLC 65

Sterling, Brett
See Bradbury, Ray (Douglas); Hamilton,
Edmond

Sterling, Bruce 1954- . . . . CLC 72
See also CA 119

Sterling, George 1869-1926 . . . . TCLC 20
See also CA 117; DLB 54

Stern, Gerald 1925- . . . . CLC 40
See also CA 81-84; CANR 28; DLB 105

Stern, Richard (Gustave) 1928- . . . CLC 4, 39
See also CA 1-4R; CANR 1, 25; DLBY 87

Sternberg, Josef von 1894-1969 . . . . . CLC 20
See also CA 81-84

Sterne, Laurence 1713-1768 . . . . LC 2
See also CDBLB 1660-1789; DA; DLB 39;
WLC

Sternheim, (William Adolf) Carl
1878-1942 . . . . TCLC 8
See also CA 105; DLB 56, 118

Stevens, Mark 1951- . . . . CLC 34
See also CA 122

Stevens, Wallace
1879-1955 . . . . TCLC 3, 12, 45; PC 6
See also CA 104; 124; CDALB 1929-1941;
DA; DLB 54; MTCW; WLC

Stevenson, Anne (Katharine)
1933- . . . . CLC 7, 33
See also CA 17-20R; CAAS 9; CANR 9, 33;
DLB 40; MTCW

Stevenson, Robert Louis (Balfour)
1850-1894 . . . . NCLC 5, 14; SSC 11
See also CDBLB 1890-1914; CLR 10, 11;
DA; DLB 18, 57; MAICYA; WLC;
YABC 2

Stewart, J(ohn) I(nnes) M(ackintosh)
1906- . . . . CLC 7, 14, 32
See also CA 85-88; CAAS 3; MTCW

Stewart, Mary (Florence Elinor)
1916- . . . . CLC 7, 35
See also CA 1-4R; CANR 1; SATA 12

Stewart, Mary Rainbow
See Stewart, Mary (Florence Elinor)

Stifter, Adalbert 1805-1868 . . . . . . NCLC 41

Still, James 1906- . . . . CLC 49
See also CA 65-68; CAAS 17; CANR 10,
26; DLB 9; SATA 29

Sting
See Sumner, Gordon Matthew

Stirling, Arthur
See Sinclair, Upton (Beall)

Stitt, Milan 1941- . . . . CLC 29
See also CA 69-72

Stockton, Francis Richard 1834-1902
See Stockton, Frank R.
See also CA 108; 137; MAICYA; SATA 44

Stockton, Frank R. . . . . TCLC 47
See also Stockton, Francis Richard
See also DLB 42, 74; SATA 32

Stoddard, Charles
See Kuttner, Henry

Stoker, Abraham 1847-1912
See Stoker, Bram
See also CA 105; DA; SATA 29

Stoker, Bram . . . . TCLC 8
See also Stoker, Abraham
See also CDBLB 1890-1914; DLB 36, 70;
WLC

Stolz, Mary (Slattery) 1920- . . . . CLC 12
See also AAYA 8; AITN 1; CA 5-8R;
CANR 13, 41; MAICYA; SAAS 3;
SATA 10, 70, 71

Stone, Irving 1903-1989 . . . . CLC 7
See also AITN 1; CA 1-4R; 129; CAAS 3;
CANR 1, 23; MTCW; SATA 3;
SATA-Obit 64

Wiesel, Elie(zer) 1928-..... **CLC 3, 5, 11, 37**
See also AAYA 7; AITN 1; CA 5-8R;
CAAS 4; CANR 8, 40; DA; DLB 83;
DLBY 87; MTCW; SATA 56

Wiggins, Marianne 1947-......... **CLC 57**
See also BEST 89:3; CA 130

Wight, James Alfred 1916-
See Herriot, James
See also CA 77-80; SATA 44, 55

Wilbur, Richard (Purdy)
1921- .... **CLC 3, 6, 9, 14, 53**
See also CA 1-4R; CABS 2; CANR 2, 29;
DA; DLB 5; MTCW; SATA 9

Wild, Peter 1940-................ **CLC 14**
See also CA 37-40R; DLB 5

Wilde, Oscar (Fingal O'Flahertie Wills)
1854(?)-1900 ...... **TCLC 1, 8, 23, 41;**
SSC 11
See also CA 104; 119; CDBLB 1890-1914;
DA; DLB 10, 19, 34, 57; SATA 24; WLC

Wilder, Billy .... **CLC 20**
See also Wilder, Samuel
See also DLB 26

Wilder, Samuel 1906-
See Wilder, Billy
See also CA 89-92

Wilder, Thornton (Niven)
1897-1975 ..... **CLC 1, 5, 6, 10, 15, 35;**
DC 1
See also AITN 2; CA 13-16R; 61-64;
CANR 40; DA; DLB 4, 7, 9; MTCW;
WLC

Wilding, Michael 1942-........... **CLC 73**
See also CA 104; CANR 24

Wiley, Richard 1944-............. **CLC 44**
See also CA 121; 129

Wilhelm, Kate .... **CLC 7**
See also Wilhelm, Katie Gertrude
See also CAAS 5; DLB 8

Wilhelm, Katie Gertrude 1928-
See Wilhelm, Kate
See also CA 37-40R; CANR 17, 36; MTCW

Wilkins, Mary
See Freeman, Mary Eleanor Wilkins

Willard, Nancy 1936-........... **CLC 7, 37**
See also CA 89-92; CANR 10, 39; CLR 5;
DLB 5, 52; MAICYA; MTCW;
SATA 30, 37, 71

Williams, C(harles) K(enneth)
1936- .... **CLC 33, 56**
See also CA 37-40R; DLB 5

Williams, Charles
See Collier, James L(incoln)

Williams, Charles (Walter Stansby)
1886-1945 .... **TCLC 1, 11**
See also CA 104; DLB 100

Williams, (George) Emlyn
1905-1987 .... **CLC 15**
See also CA 104; 123; CANR 36; DLB 10,
77; MTCW

Williams, Hugo 1942-............. **CLC 42**
See also CA 17-20R; DLB 40

Williams, J. Walker
See Wodehouse, P(elham) G(renville)

Williams, John A(lfred) 1925-.... **CLC 5, 13**
See also BLC 3; BW; CA 53-56; CAAS 3;
CANR 6, 26; DLB 2, 33

Williams, Jonathan (Chamberlain)
1929- .... **CLC 13**
See also CA 9-12R; CAAS 12; CANR 8;
DLB 5

Williams, Joy 1944-............. **CLC 31**
See also CA 41-44R; CANR 22

Williams, Norman 1952- .... **CLC 39**
See also CA 118

Williams, Tennessee
1911-1983 .... **CLC 1, 2, 5, 7, 8, 11, 15,**
19, 30, 39, 45, 71
See also AITN 1, 2; CA 5-8R; 108;
CABS 3; CANR 31; CDALB 1941-1968;
DA; DLB 7; DLBD 4; DLBY 83;
MTCW; WLC

Williams, Thomas (Alonzo)
1926-1990 .... **CLC 14**
See also CA 1-4R; 132; CANR 2

Williams, William C.
See Williams, William Carlos

Williams, William Carlos
1883-1963 ... **CLC 1, 2, 5, 9, 13, 22, 42,**
67; PC 7
See also CA 89-92; CANR 34;
CDALB 1917-1929; DA; DLB 4, 16, 54,
86; MTCW

Williamson, David (Keith) 1942-.... **CLC 56**
See also CA 103; CANR 41

Williamson, Jack.................. **CLC 29**
See also Williamson, John Stewart
See also CAAS 8; DLB 8

Williamson, John Stewart 1908-
See Williamson, Jack
See also CA 17-20R; CANR 23

Willie, Frederick
See Lovecraft, H(oward) P(hillips)

Willingham, Calder (Baynard, Jr.)
1922- .... **CLC 5, 51**
See also CA 5-8R; CANR 3; DLB 2, 44;
MTCW

Willis, Charles
See Clarke, Arthur C(harles)

Willy
See Colette, (Sidonie-Gabrielle)

Willy, Colette
See Colette, (Sidonie-Gabrielle)

Wilson, A(ndrew) N(orman) 1950- .. **CLC 33**
See also CA 112; 122; DLB 14

Wilson, Angus (Frank Johnstone)
1913-1991 .... **CLC 2, 3, 5, 25, 34**
See also CA 5-8R; 134; CANR 21; DLB 15;
MTCW

Wilson, August
1945- .... **CLC 39, 50, 63; DC 2**
See also BLC 3; BW; CA 115; 122; DA;
MTCW

Wilson, Brian 1942-............. **CLC 12**

Wilson, Colin 1931- .... **CLC 3, 14**
See also CA 1-4R; CAAS 5; CANR 1, 22,
33; DLB 14; MTCW

Wilson, Dirk
See Pohl, Frederik

Wilson, Edmund
1895-1972 .... **CLC 1, 2, 3, 8, 24**
See also CA 1-4R; 37-40R; CANR 1;
DLB 63; MTCW

Wilson, Ethel Davis (Bryant)
1888(?)-1980 .... **CLC 13**
See also CA 102; DLB 68; MTCW

Wilson, John 1785-1854.......... **NCLC 5**

Wilson, John (Anthony) Burgess
1917- .... **CLC 8, 10, 13**
See also Burgess, Anthony
See also CA 1-4R; CANR 2; MTCW

Wilson, Lanford 1937-....... **CLC 7, 14, 36**
See also CA 17-20R; CABS 3; DLB 7

Wilson, Robert M. 1944-......... **CLC 7, 9**
See also CA 49-52; CANR 2, 41; MTCW

Wilson, Robert McLiam 1964- ..... **CLC 59**
See also CA 132

Wilson, Sloan 1920-............. **CLC 32**
See also CA 1-4R; CANR 1

Wilson, Snoo 1948-............. **CLC 33**
See also CA 69-72

Wilson, William S(mith) 1932- ..... **CLC 49**
See also CA 81-84

Winchilsea, Anne (Kingsmill) Finch Counte
1661-1720 .... **LC 3**

Windham, Basil
See Wodehouse, P(elham) G(renville)

Wingrove, David (John) 1954-...... **CLC 68**
See also CA 133

Winters, Janet Lewis .... **CLC 41**
See also Lewis, Janet
See also DLBY 87

Winters, (Arthur) Yvor
1900-1968 .... **CLC 4, 8, 32**
See also CA 11-12; 25-28R; CAP 1;
DLB 48; MTCW

Winterson, Jeanette 1959-......... **CLC 64**
See also CA 136

Wiseman, Frederick 1930-......... **CLC 20**

Wister, Owen 1860-1938 .... **TCLC 21**
See also CA 108; DLB 9, 78; SATA 62

Witkacy
See Witkiewicz, Stanislaw Ignacy

Witkiewicz, Stanislaw Ignacy
1885-1939 .... **TCLC 8**
See also CA 105

Wittig, Monique 1935(?)-.......... **CLC 22**
See also CA 116; 135; DLB 83

Wittlin, Jozef 1896-1976 .... **CLC 25**
See also CA 49-52; 65-68; CANR 3

Wodehouse, P(elham) G(renville)
1881-1975 ... **CLC 1, 2, 5, 10, 22; SSC 2**
See also AITN 2; CA 45-48; 57-60;
CANR 3, 33; CDBLB 1914-1945;
DLB 34; MTCW; SATA 22

Woiwode, L.
See Woiwode, Larry (Alfred)

Woiwode, Larry (Alfred) 1941-... **CLC 6, 10**
See also CA 73-76; CANR 16; DLB 6

Wojciechowska, Maia (Teresa)
1927- .... **CLC 26**
See also AAYA 8; CA 9-12R; CANR 4, 41;
CLR 1; MAICYA; SAAS 1; SATA 1, 28

Zaturenska, Marya 1902-1982.... **CLC 6, 11**
See also CA 13-16R; 105; CANR 22

Zelazny, Roger (Joseph) 1937- ..... **CLC 21**
See also AAYA 7; CA 21-24R; CANR 26;
DLB 8; MTCW; SATA 39, 57

Zhdanov, Andrei A(lexandrovich)
1896-1948 .... **TCLC 18**
See also CA 117

Zhukovsky, Vasily 1783-1852 .... **NCLC 35**

Ziegenhagen, Eric .... **CLC 55**

Zimmer, Jill Schary
See Robinson, Jill

Zimmerman, Robert
See Dylan, Bob

Zindel, Paul 1936- .... **CLC 6, 26**
See also AAYA 2; CA 73-76; CANR 31;
CLR 3; DA; DLB 7, 52; MAICYA;
MTCW; SATA 16, 58

Zinov'Ev, A. A.
See Zinoviev, Alexander (Aleksandrovich)

Zinoviev, Alexander (Aleksandrovich)
1922- .... **CLC 19**
See also CA 116; 133; CAAS 10

Zoilus
See Lovecraft, H(oward) P(hillips)

Zola, Emile (Edouard Charles Antoine)
1840-1902 .... **TCLC 1, 6, 21, 41**
See also CA 104; 138; DA; DLB 123; WLC

Zoline, Pamela 1941- .... **CLC 62**

Zorrilla y Moral, Jose 1817-1893.. **NCLC 6**

Zoshchenko, Mikhail (Mikhailovich)
1895-1958 .... **TCLC 15**
See also CA 115

Zuckmayer, Carl 1896-1977....... **CLC 18**
See also CA 69-72; DLB 56, 124

Zuk, Georges
See Skelton, Robin

Zukofsky, Louis
1904-1978 .... **CLC 1, 2, 4, 7, 11, 18**
See also CA 9-12R; 77-80; CANR 39;
DLB 5; MTCW

Zweig, Paul 1935-1984........ **CLC 34, 42**
See also CA 85-88; 113

Zweig, Stefan 1881-1942 .... **TCLC 17**
See also CA 112; DLB 81, 118

Literary Criticism Series
Cumulative Topic Index

This index lists all topic entries in the Gale Literary Criticism Series *Contemporary Literary Criticism, Literature Criticism from 1400 to 1800, Nineteenth-Century Literature Criticism,* and *Twentieth-Century Literary Criticism.*

American Literary Criticism CLC 65: 361-405

Gay and Lesbian Literature CLC 76: 416-39

German Exile Literature TCLC 30: 1-58
   the writer and the Nazi state, 1-10
   definition of, 10-14
   life in exile, 14-32
   surveys, 32-50
   Austrian literature in exile, 50-2
   German publishing in the United States, 52-7

German Expressionism TCLC 34: 74-160
   history and major figures, 76-85
   aesthetic theories, 85-109
   drama, 109-26
   poetry, 126-38
   film, 138-42
   painting, 142-47
   music, 147-53
   and politics, 153-58

Glasnost and Contemporary Soviet Literature CLC 59: 355-97

Gothic Novel NCLC 28: 328-402
   development and major works, 328-34
   definitions, 334-50
   themes and techniques, 350-78
   in America, 378-85
   in Scotland, 385-91
   influence and legacy, 391-400

Harlem Renaissance TCLC 26: 49-125
   principal issues and figures, 50-67
   the literature and its audience, 67-74
   theme and technique in poetry, fiction, and drama, 74-115
   and American society, 115-21
   achievement and influence, 121-22

Havel, Václav, Playwright and President CLC 65: 406-63

Holocaust, Literature of the TCLC 42: 355-450
   historical overview, 357-61
   critical overview, 361-70
   diaries and memoirs, 370-95
   novels and short stories, 395-425
   poetry, 425-41

drama, 441-48

Hungarian Literature of the Twentieth Century TCLC 26: 126-88
   surveys of, 126-47
   Nyugat and early twentieth-century literature, 147-56
   mid-century literature, 156-68
   and politics, 168-78
   since the 1956 revolt, 178-87

Irish Literary Renaissance TCLC 46: 172-287
   overview, 173-83
   development and major figures, 184-202
   influence of Irish folklore and mythology, 202-22
   Irish poetry, 222-34
   Irish drama and the Abbey Theatre, 234-56
   Irish fiction, 256-86

Italian Futurism
   See Futurism, Italian

Italian Humanism LC 12: 205-77
   origins and early development, 206-18
   revival of classical letters, 218-23
   humanism and other philosophies, 224-39
   humanisms and humanists, 239-46
   the plastic arts, 246-57
   achievement and significance, 258-76

Madness in Twentieth-Century Literature TCLC-50: 160-225
   overviews, 161-71
   madness and the creative process, 171-86
   suicide, 186-91
   madness in American literature, 191-207
   madness in German literature, 207-13
   madness and feminist artists, 213-24

Muckraking Movement in American Journalism TCLC 34: 161-242
   development, principles, and major figures, 162-70
   publications, 170-79
   social and political ideas, 179-86
   targets, 186-208
   fiction, 208-19
   decline, 219-29
   impact and accomplishments, 229-40

Multiculturalism in Literature and Education CLC 70: 361-413

Native American Literature CLC 76: 440-76

Naturalism NCLC 36: 285-382
   definitions and theories, 286-305
   critical debates on Naturalism, 305-16
   Naturalism in theater, 316-32
   European Naturalism, 332-61
   American Naturalism, 361-72
   the legacy of Naturalism, 372-81

Natural School, Russian NCLC 24: 205-40
   history and characteristics, 205-25
   contemporary criticism, 225-40

Negritude TCLC 50: 226-361
   origins and evolution, 227-56
   definitions, 256-91
   Negritude in literature, 291-343
   Negritude reconsidered, 343-58

New Criticism TCLC 34: 243-318
   development and ideas, 244-70
   debate and defense, 270-99
   influence and legacy, 299-315

Newgate Novel NCLC 24: 166-204
   development of Newgate literature, 166-73
   Newgate Calendar, 173-77
   Newgate fiction, 177-95
   Newgate drama, 195-204

New York Intellectuals and *Partisan Review* TCLC 30: 117-98
   development and major figures, 118-28
   influence of Judaism, 128-39
   Partisan Review, 139-57
   literary philosophy and practice, 157-75
   political philosophy, 175-87
   achievement and significance, 187-97

Nigerian Literature of the Twentieth Century TCLC 30: 199-265
   surveys of, 199-227
   English language and African life, 227-45
   politics and the Nigerian writer, 245-54
   Nigerian writers and society, 255-62

poetry and poetics 238-58
drama 258-75

Supernatural Fiction in the Nineteenth Century NCLC 32: 207-87
major figures and influences, 208-35
the Victorian ghost story, 236-54
the influence of science and occultism, 254-66
supernatural fiction and society, 266-86

Supernatural Fiction, Modern
TCLC 30: 59-116
evolution and varieties, 60-74
"decline" of the ghost story, 74-86
as a literary genre, 86-92
technique, 92-101
nature and appeal, 101-15

Surrealism TCLC 30: 334-406
history and formative influences, 335-43
manifestos, 343-54
philosophic, aesthetic, and political principles, 354-75
poetry, 375-81
novel, 381-86
drama, 386-92
film, 392-98
painting and sculpture, 398-403
achievement, 403-05

Symbolism, Russian TCLC 30: 266-333
doctrines and major figures, 267-92
theories, 293-98
and French Symbolism, 298-310
themes in poetry, 310-14
theater, 314-20
and the fine arts, 320-32

Symbolist Movement, French
NCLC 20: 169-249
background and characteristics, 170-86
principles, 186-91
attacked and defended, 191-97
influences and predecessors, 197-211
and Decadence, 211-16
theater, 216-26
prose, 226-33
decline and influence, 233-47

Theater of the Absurd TCLC 38: 339-415
"The Theater of the Absurd," 340-47
major plays and playwrights, 347-58
and the concept of the absurd, 358-86
theatrical techniques, 386-94
predecessors of, 394-402
influence of, 402-13

Tin Pan Alley
See **American Popular Song, Golden Age of**

Transcendentalism, American
NCLC 24: 1-99
overviews, 3-23
contemporary documents, 23-41
theological aspects of, 42-52
and social issues, 52-74
literature of, 74-96

Travel Writing in the Twentieth Century TCLC 30: 407-56
conventions and traditions, 407-27
and fiction writing, 427-43
comparative essays on travel writers, 443-54

***Ulysses* and the Process of Textual Reconstruction** TCLC 26: 386-416
evaluations of the new *Ulysses,* 386-94
editorial principles and procedures, 394-401
theoretical issues, 401-16

Utopian Literature, Nineteenth-Century
NCLC 24: 353-473
definitions, 354-74
overviews, 374-88
theory, 388-408
communities, 409-26
fiction, 426-53
women and fiction, 454-71

Vampire in Literature TCLC 46: 391-454
origins and evolution, 392-412
social and psychological perspectives, 413-44
vampire fiction and science fiction, 445-53

Victorian Autobiography NCLC 40: 277-363
development and major characteristics 278-88
themes and techniques 289-313
the autobiographical tendency in Victorian prose and poetry 313-47
Victorian women's autobiographies 347-62

Victorian Novel NCLC 32: 288-454
development and major characteristics, 290-310
themes and techniques, 310-58
social criticism in the Victorian novel, 359-97
urban and rural life in the Victorian

novel, 397-406
women in the Victorian novel, 406-25
Mudie's Circulating Library, 425-34
the late-Victorian novel, 434-51

World War I Literature TCLC 34: 392-486
overview, 393-403
English, 403-27
German, 427-50
American, 450-66
French, 466-74
and modern history, 474-82

Yellow Journalism NCLC 36: 383-456
overviews, 384-96
major figures, 396-413
the role of reporters, 413-28
the Spanish-American War, 428-48
Yellow Journalism and society, 448-54

Young Playwrights Festival
1988—CLC 55: 376-81
1989—CLC 59: 398-403
1990—CLC 65: 444-48

NCLC Cumulative Nationality Index

Nationality Index